The **Rough Guide** to the

# Pyrenees

written and researched by

## Marc Dubin

NEW YORK • LONDON • DELHI

www.roughguides.com

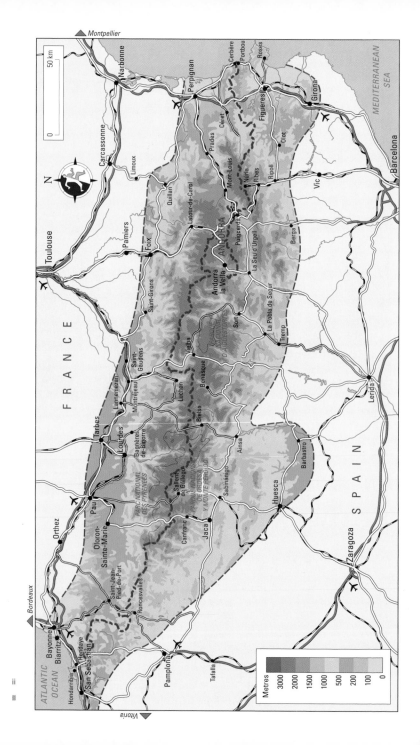

Introduction to the

# Pyrenees

**Anyone could find their perfect retreat in the Pyrenees, a range encompassing a diversity of landscapes rarely equalled in Europe. Between balmy Mediterranean beaches and the more turbulent Atlantic coast lie lush meadowland, snow-clad peaks, canyons of sinuously sculpted rock, dense broadleaf forest, weirdly eroded limestone pinnacles and sheer, overgrown valleys that get perhaps two hours of sun daily.**

These mountains challenge and invite rather than intimidate. Generally rounded and crumbling, their peaks – including 3404-metre **Aneto**, the highest Pyrenean summit, plus the next-ranking peaks of **Posets**, **Monte Perdido** and **Vignemale** – are attainable by any determined and properly equipped walker, even with little experience of such terrain. Other natural wonders beckon to the averagely fit: the **Valle de Ordesa**, most spectacular of many canyons, can be traversed on gentle footpaths, as can the great glaciated amphitheatre of the **Cirque de Gavarnie** just north. The stalactite-draped cavern of **Lombrives** is the largest cave in Western Europe open to the public, while the **Sala de la Verna** in one of the world's deepest cave systems – the Gouffre Pierre-Saint-Martin – requires no great physical effort. You can raft down various foaming rivers on both sides of the range, including the **Noguera Pallaresa** in Catalunya and the **Gállego** in Aragón, as well as several tamer ones on the French side. **Canyoners** of all ability levels are well catered to in the "pre-Pyrenean" **Sierra de Guara**, also in Spanish Aragón.

**Walking** the Pyrenees from end to end has become a classic endeavour. Thousands have followed the **Haute Randonnée Pyrénéenne** (HRP) to either side of the watershed; the more circuitous but less demanding **Grande Randonnée 10** (GR10) entirely within France; or the equally spectacular Spanish **Gran Recorrido 11** (GR11). Detailed maps for the entire range show numerous other, briefer itineraries, suitable for hikers at all levels.

Pyrenean **wildlife** is exceptionally rich, despite the devastating impact of human activity on many species. Deer and wild boar hide in the forests, and in certain dense woodlands a dwindling number of **brown bear** still manage to survive. In contrast, the ubiquitous **isard** (Pyrenean chamois) abounds, as do shy **wildcats**; **marmots** are plentiful (and audible); while majestic **birds of prey** patrol the skies. The **capercaillie**, a bird now extinct in the French Alps, still (just) survives in the Pyrenees, while the tiny **desman**, an aquatic mole, is unknown elsewhere in Western Europe, except the Picos de Europa.

Traces of **human habitation** in the Pyrenees predate recorded history by millennia, with artefacts found (and displayed) at various caves in the Ariège, the Couserans and the Comminges regions. Among the prehistoric **caves** around **Tarascon-sur-Ariège**, the **paintings** in the **Grotte de Niaux** rank as the best open to public view worldwide.

## Marmots

Throughout the high Pyrenees you will hear, though probably not see, the **marmot** (*marmotte* in French; *marmota* in Castilian), a now-common dweller above the tree line that once disappeared from these mountains after centuries of hunting for its fur. This robust rodent – reaching a length of 75cm – was reintroduced to the French Central Pyrenees from 1948 onwards, and has now spread to both sides of the range. The rather indiscriminate manner of this restocking, and its few natural enemies, has led to an explosion in marmot populations, with control measures – especially after gnawing damage was discovered to hydroelectric pipes – now being considered.

The shrill alarm shriek emitted by "sentry" individuals sends the colony scurrying down its extensive tunnel system, generally dug on warm, south-facing scree slopes at around 2000m – a habitat where its fawn-grey fur makes the marmot almost invisible. Since their rapid increase in numbers, however, colonies are now found below the 2000-metre contour. Despite their cuddly appearance and anthropomorphic habit of standing on two legs, marmots can be fierce, fighting to the death over territorial disputes.

## Fact file

- The Pyrenees, approximately 435km **long** as the crow flies and 50km **broad** at the widest points exceeding 1000m elevation, spans two national states – **France** and **Spain** – while entirely incorporating a third, **Andorra**. On the Spanish flank, Pyrenean territory makes up significant parts of the **autonomías** (autonomous regions) of Catalunya, Aragón, Navarra and País Vasco (Euskadi), which are further subdivided into the provinces of (from east to west) Girona, Lleida, Huesca, Pamplona and Gipuzkoa. In France, the **départements** of (from west to east) Pyrénées-Atlantiques, Hautes-Pyrénées, Ariège, Aude and Pyrénées-Orientales incorporate substantial tracts of high mountain.

- **Population** density averages fewer than ten individuals per square kilometre, and the total number of year-round inhabitants on both sides of the Pyrenees does not exceed 1.5 million – the vast majority living in the largest towns or conurbations of Pau, Perpignan, Bayonne-Anglet-Biarritz, Girona, San Sebastián, Tarbes, Huesca, Jaca, Figueres and Olot.

- The main Pyrenean employers are tourism, pastoralism and local government. Otherwise, hydroelectric power generation, coastal fishing, light industry in the towns and timber are the only other significant **economic activities**. Mining and farming are no longer practised on any significant scale.

Hundreds of extraordinary **Romanesque churches and monasteries** constitute the Pyrenees' architectural highlights, including such renowned examples as Saint-Martin-de-Canigou, Serrabone, Santa Maria de Ripoll, Sant Climent de Taüll and a host of others in the Vall de Boí, Saint-Bertrand-de-Comminges, San Juan de la Peña, and Saint-Engrâce in the Haute-Soule. So-called "Roman" **bridges** still linking isolated villages are even older, though not always pre-Christian. In the west of the range, numerous monuments attest to the thousands during the Middle Ages who followed the **pilgrimage trail** to Santiago de Compostela in Galicia via the fabled Puerto de Ibañeta near Roncesvalles, or the nearby Col du Somport. From the Mediterranean to the Ariège, the strength of the **Cathar** heresy is reflected in many immensely evocative ruined **castles**, notably the crag-top citadel of Montségur, site of this faith's effective extinction.

The **people** of the Pyrenees are as disparate as the landscape. The Eastern and Western Pyrenees are the respective homelands of Catalans and Basques, each with a tenaciously preserved cultural vitality embodied in the sombre *sardana*, the Catalan communal dance, or the lightning-quick Basque game of *pelota/pelote*. As you traverse the Pyrenees you'll hear Catalan, Aranese, Aragonese and Euskera (the Basque tongue), plus others – notably the Gascon dialect of Occitan – not officially accorded the status of a distinct language. For centuries before the final unifications of France and Spain, every valley effectively constituted a mini-republic with its own argot, jealously guarding customary privileges against encroachment from distant central governments, further defying them with a thriving trade in **smuggling**. Remoteness and neglect always made the mountains a refuge for political as well as religious dissidents, most recently during the Spanish Civil War and World War II when thousands of **refugees** took advantage of shepherds' and smugglers' knowledge to evade capture. After 1968, many disillusioned French protesters and "alternative" types again took up residence in the back country, swelling the traditional local vote for the political Left – and adopting the enduring local habit of self-sufficiency. Indeed the Pyreneans' historical disregard for the often-altered boundaries between France and Spain has been vindicated and accentuated by the post-1993 European single market, as old border posts lie abandoned and a strong regional identity bridging the watershed has reasserted itself.

After decades of being eclipsed by the Alps, the Pyrenees have come into their own as a **travellers' destination**. Infrastructure and amenities improve each year, exemplified by increasing numbers of quality lodgings, ever-multiplying adventure-sport outfitters and a plethora of no-frills airlines offering service into previously sleepy regional airports. It has never been easier to visit these mountains.

# Where to go

f you've only got two weeks in hand, the Pyrenees are too vast to tour entirely, but **public transport** is good enough to explore a region roughly corresponding to one of this book's chapters. Rail networks will get you within striking distance of the premier areas, and buses are often available to take you deeper into the mountains. A circuit of the Eastern Pyrenees could begin at Perpignan, continue south by train along the

## Regional languages

Since the 1980s, regional languages have made a dramatic comeback across the Pyrenees. The process is more advanced on the Spanish side, whose 1978 constitution devolves considerable discretion to the country's autonomous regions. In Catalunya, Catalan has officially displaced Castilian on everything from road signs to transport schedules to museum labelling – not to mention in the considerable map publication programme undertaken by the local government, or *Generalitat*. In Aragón, the process is confined largely to the occasional village-outskirts sign, though mountaineering maps often show all features in Aragonese, and local nationalists suitably "edit" Castilian road-signs with spray paint. In Navarra, there's been a backlash by Castilian-speakers against the Euskera village nomenclature imposed by the Basque-speaking minority in the north, but in neighbouring Gipuzkoa Euskera reigns supreme. In traditionally centralized France, minority languages have little official status, being restricted mostly to "folkloric" manifestations, but even here bilingual road signage is becoming common in the Basque counties (see photo) and Catalan-speaking areas of Roussillon. Catalan place-names are even beginning to appear on those paragons of Gallic rectitude, the IGN-based Cartes des Randonnées.

Mediterranean coast, move west by road through the verdant Garrotxa to the Ripollès, then north by rail to the sunny plain of the Cerdanya/Cerdagne, and finally return to Perpignan by another train through the dramatic Têt valley. Circular itineraries can be constructed in other parts of the range – around Andorra or in the Basque country, for example – and even isolated, underpopulated zones such as the Maladeta and Posets massifs lend themselves to loops on foot from trailhead villages served by buses. With a **car** or **bicycle**, you could see the best of two consecutive chapters in two to three weeks.

If you want to concentrate on one area, the **Ariège** suits most tastes with fabulous scenery, cave art, ruined castles and almost every form of outdoor activity. Over the border in Catalunya, the **Parc Nacional de Aigüestortes i Sant Maurici**, easily accessible from the Val d'Aran, Vall de Boí or the Noguera Pallaresa, makes a fine introduction to the glacially sculpted high peaks. Gavarnie, Barèges or Cauterets in France, and Torla or Bielsa in Spain, are comfortable, respective gateways for the French **Parc National des Pyrénées** and the Spanish **Parque Nacional de Ordesa y Monte Perdido**, contiguous national parks in the heart of the range. For walks and climbs on the highest summits further east, make the all-purpose resorts of **Benasque** or **Luchon** your bases, while the westernmost high peaks can also be easily explored from villages such as **Lescun** or **Sallent de Gállego**. During winter, these settlements are conveniently close to many of the best **ski resorts**, including Astún,

Candanchú, Gourette, Barèges-La Mongie, Espiaube, Cerler, Baqueira-Beret and Boí-Taüll, on a par with the better-known winter sports centres in more commercialized **Andorra**.

Towards the west, **Pau** is the largest, most cosmopolitan Pyrenean city, on a main route to **Jaca**, historic county town of the Aragonese mountains. They're the most logical and congenial gateways to the surreal karst country extending between the French **Vallée d'Aspe** and the Spanish valleys of **Echo** and **Ansó**. Southeast of Jaca, the **Sierra de Guara** is available for visits most of the year owing to lower altitude. Inland from the surf-pounded Atlantic coast, with its elegant resorts of **San Sebastián** and **Biarritz**, the seductively green horizons and sumptuous domestic architecture of the **Basque country** await, with graceful **Bayonne** and atmospheric **Saint-Jean-Pied-de-Port** as focuses. Mediterranean beaches are more varied – at least at the picturesque port-resorts of **Collioure** or **Cadaqués** – and the climate reliably sunny. From here you can make forays inland to Catalunya's volcanic **Garrotxa basin** or the gorge-slashed foothills of Roussillon's **Canigou massif**. Whichever part of the range you visit, sample both sides of the border if possible – the north-to-south change of landscape, climate and culture is one of the delights of the Pyrenees.

# When to go

The best time to visit obviously depends on what you want to do. Snowfall permitting, the **downhill/cross-country ski season** gets under way in January, lasting until mid-April. With the spring thaw, **rafting** and **canoeing** become practicable, while the summer **walking** season begins in early June – also a good time for riding, cycling and the more extreme pursuits of **canyoning** and **parapente**. In autumn the crowds depart and the mountain trails are left to solitary walkers not afraid of the odd snow flurry.

Try to **avoid the French and Spanish national summer holidays** from mid-July to the end of August. It's better to come after this stampede rather than before: spring and autumn offer equal solitude, but high passes may still be blocked until July, and in September you'll have complete freedom of the mountains. **Thunderstorms** also cause problems in summer: the Pyrenees are beset by them, with several storms a week guaranteed during July and August. During **winter**, the **February half-term break** is pretty frantic in or near any ski resort, while March at the same spots can be comatose, as many proprietors close down for all or part of the week until the **Easter rush**.

**Weather** in the Pyrenees resists generalization, as microclimates abound. The Barèges valley, for example, has particularly idiosyncratic weather, where a warm May can be followed by heavy June snowfall. In summer, marine cooling action gives each coastal strip a temperature several degrees lower than a few miles inland, while for every 100–200m of ascent, temperature falls by as much as one degree Celsius. The French slopes are especially prone to the converse phenomenon of temperature inversion, when valleys become colder than the peaks, which protrude like islands from a sea of cloud.

## Average temperatures (°C)

| | Jan | Mar | May | July | Sept | Nov |
|---|---|---|---|---|---|---|
| **Mediterranean coast** | | | | | | |
| Perpignan | 12.4 | 12.5 | 20.1 | 28.4 | 26.1 | 15.8 |
| **Andorra** | | | | | | |
| Ransol | -2.1 | 1.4 | 7.3 | 13.6 | 10.9 | 2 |
| **Alto Aragón** | | | | | | |
| Panticosa | 0.1 | 2.6 | 8.2 | 15.5 | 12.3 | 4.1 |
| **Atlantic coast** | | | | | | |
| Bayonne | 10 | 12,2 | 18 | 27.2 | 24.2 | 15.4 |

## things not to miss

*It's not possible to see everything that the Pyrenees has to offer in one trip – and we don't suggest you try. What follows is a selective and subjective taste of the region's highlights, listed in no particular order: spectacular hikes, outstanding natural features, exquisite Romanesque churches and alluring resorts.*

**01** **Grand Bayonne** Page **521** • Half-timbered housefronts engagingly sythesize Basque and Gascon domestic architecture.

## 02 Cadaqués Page 134 • One of the most attractive and congenial Mediterranean resorts, and a welcome goal at the end of a GR11 traverse.

## 04 La Concha beach, San Sebastián Page 544 • This blonde-tan sweep of sand ranks among the most popular – and sheltered – beaches on the Basque coast.

## 06 Cremallera de Núria Page 175 • This narrow-gauge railway line is one of two in the Catalan Pyrenees providing an unforgettable ride up a steep river valley.

## 03 High-altitude spas Page 329 • The Pyrenees are well sown with elegant thermal pools, such as the one here at Luchon, ideal for soaking away post-trek or -ski aches.

## 05 Spanish turismo rural Page 39 • Restored rural properties usually offer the most characterful and best-value accommodation across the Spanish Pyrenees.

## 07 Skiing Page 365 • Barèges-La Mongie is the largest and (usually) most reliably snowy ski domaine in the underrated Pyrenees, where facilities (and prices) are beginning to rival the Alps.

## 08

### Cirque de Gavarnie

Page **388** • Overhyped it may be, but one of the largest glacial formations in Europe still impresses mightily.

## 09

### Château de Puilaurens

Page **92** • Among the many magnificent "Cathar" castles in the Eastern Pyrenees, though the Cathar sect didn't originally build every one of them.

## 10

### Cirque de Lescun

Page **418** • The old stone village of Lescun perfectly offsets the eponymous karstic cirque topped by jagged summits.

## 11

### Valle de Ordesa

Page **435** • Banded limestone walls don't get deeper or more dramatic than at Spain's first national park.

# 12

**High-altitude lakes** Page **428**
• The Pyrenees have several hundred of these beauties, left behind by the last ice age, on both sides of the frontier; pictured here is lower Lago de la Munia.

**14 Wildflowers** Page **588** • Few European ranges can match the Pyrenees in their variety of summer flora at all altitudes.

**13 Tramezaygues, Audressein** Page **323** • The fourteenth-century frescoes at this riverside Couserans church are some of the most charming – and most easily visible – on the French side.

**16 Canyoning in the Sierra de Guara** Page **464** • Plumb the water-polished depths of Europe's mecca for this family sport.

**15 High-mountain trekking** Page **389** • This glacier at the Brèche de Roland looks intimidating, but most of the Pyrenean summits and passes are accessible to the averagely fit and non-technically equipped.

# Contents

# Using this Rough Guide

We've tried to make this Rough Guide a good read and easy to use. The book is divided into six main sections, and you should be able to find whatever you want in one of them.

## Front section

The front colour section offers a quick tour of the Pyrenees. The **introduction** aims to give you a feel for the region, with suggestions on where to go. We also tell you what the weather is like and include a basic regional fact file. Next, our author rounds up his favourite aspects of the region in the **things not to miss** section – whether it's stunning scenery, great hikes or an attractive resort. Right after this comes the Rough Guide's full **contents** list.

## Basics

You've decided to go and the basics section covers all the pre-departure nitty-gritty to help you plan your trip. This is where to find out which airlines fly to your destination, what to do about money and insurance, about Internet access, food, security, public transport, car rental – in fact just about every piece of **general practical information** you might need.

## Guide

This is the heart of the Rough Guide, divided into user-friendly chapters, each of which covers a specific region. Each chapter starts with a list of

**highlights** and an **introduction** that helps you to decide where to go. Likewise, introductions to the various towns and smaller regions within each chapter should help you plan your itinerary. We start most town accounts with information on arrival and accommodation, followed by a tour of the sights, and finally reviews of places to eat and drink. Longer accounts also have a directory of practical listings. Each chapter concludes with **public transport** details for that region.

## Contexts

Read Contexts to get a deeper understanding of the Pyrenees. We include a brief **history**, articles about wildlife and the environment and a detailed further reading section that reviews dozens of **books** relating to the Pyrenees.

## Index + small print

Apart from a **full index**, which includes maps as well as places, this section covers publishing information, credits and acknowledgements, and also has our contact details in case you want to send in updates and corrections to the book – or suggestions as to how we might improve it.

# Map and chapter list

- Colour section
- Contents
- **B** Basics

- **1** The Eastern Pyrenees
- **2** Andorra and around
- **3** The Val d'Aran region
- **4** Around the National Parks
- **5** The Western Pyrenees

- **C** Contexts
- **L** Language
- **I** Index + small print

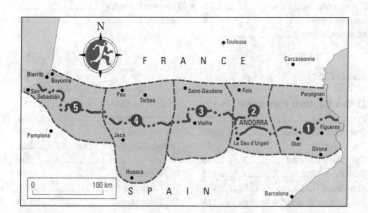

# Contents

**17 Camino de Santiago/Chemin de Saint-Jacques** Page **508** • Saint-Jean-Pied-de-Port and its Nive River bridge mark the start for the Pyrenean stage of this millennial, still-popular pilgrimage route.

**19 Tour de France** Page **366** • Almost every year, the world's most famous bicycle race visits the central Pyrenees in several days of gruelling stages.

**18 Pont de Llierca** Page **166** • This graceful bridge in Alta Garrotxa is one of a number of "Roman" bridges in the range – some indeed pre-Christian, some much later.

**20 Summer festivals** Page **259** • You'd be exceptionally unlucky not to coincide with at least one saint's-day bash, such as this one at Taüll, during your stay.

**21**
**Gliding and para-penting** Page **68** • Thermal conditions over much of the range are perfect for realizing your dreams of non-motorized flight.

# Contexts

## 551–604

# Language

## 605–632

# Index and small print

## 640–656

5

# Basics

# Basics

# Getting there

From the UK and Ireland the most convenient, economical way of getting to the Pyrenees is to fly – flights from London take just under two hours to Girona, less to Biarritz, Pau, Toulouse, Carcassonne and Perpignan. Reaching the Pyrenees overland has been simplified since the opening of the Channel Tunnel for Eurostar and Eurotunnel services, with onward TGV trains from Paris, though plane fares will still generally cost less than rail tickets. There are also two ferry services direct to northern Spain, bypassing France. From North America, choice of arrival airports will be limited to Barcelona, Bilbao and Toulouse, usually via busier European hubs. From Australia or New Zealand, it's possible to fly direct to Paris, though indirect routeings via Asia will be cheaper, and arriving in Toulouse or Barcelona via European hubs is no more costly.

Airfares to the Pyrenees depend on the **season**. From Europe and North America the highest fares are in effect from June to early September (plus Easter week), when the weather is best; fares drop during the "shoulder" seasons – April/May and late September/October – and you'll get the best prices during the low season, November to March (excluding Christmas and New Year weeks, plus – from Europe – February half-term when prices are hiked up for eager skiers and seats are at a premium). Australian and New Zealand fares have their low season from mid-January to the end of February and October/November; high season is mid-May to August, plus December to mid-January; and shoulder season the rest of the year. **Airport taxes** typically add on an extra £20–30/$35–55 per return fare; on the following pages all air fares quoted include tax.

You can often cut costs by going through a **specialist flight agent** – either a consolidator, who buys up blocks of tickets from the airlines and sells them at a discount, or a **discount agent**, who in addition to dealing with discounted flights may also offer special student and youth fares and a range of other travel-related services such as travel insurance, rail passes and car rental.

Finally, don't overlook the possibility of getting to the Pyrenees on accumulated **frequent-flyer** miles. These days there are numerous ways to build up the required

amount, and such tickets have powerful advantages over purchased tickets: they are usually valid for up to a year, and most (though not all) programmes allow you to change the return date for a reasonable fee, typically in the region of £35/$50. Routeings may be indirect (eg London–Frankfurt –Toulouse), and you will still be liable for all taxes (typically around £50 within Europe). From the UK or Ireland, programmes which include Pyrenean airports on a round-trip basis require a balance of 17,000–20,000 miles; from North America, expect to have 60,000–70,000 deducted.

## Booking flights online

Many airlines and discount travel **websites** allow you to book your tickets online; the airlines will reward you with a slight discount for an **e-ticket**, as it's called, though general discount travel sites usually charge a small booking fee for both paper and e-tickets. Even if you don't end up actually buying your ticket online, websites are worth a visit to clue you up on what the prevailing published economy fares are. Some general travel sites like Expedia or Travelocity (see overleaf) offer substantially discounted "mystery" or "bargain" fares, where you don't get to see the scheduling (often uncivilized), or the airlines used, until after you've bought the ticket. The major airlines' own sites tend to give you a choice of only non-changeable/non-refundable and full economy fares; for the numerous options in between you'll have to ring them, and forgo any web discount. The cheapest of the airlines' published fares, designated by a bewildering "alphabet soup" of capital letters, require a minimum stay of three days away, over a Saturday night, with a typical maximum period of thirty or sixty days, and make you liable to penalties (including total loss of ticket value) if you miss your outbound departure or change your return date. When exploring a quoted fare on a website, always click the link to conditions spelled out in small print – airlines may require you to tick a box saying you've read them.

### Online booking agents and general travel sites

Ⓦ**www.cheapflights.co.uk** (UK & Ireland),
Ⓦ**www.cheapflights.com** (US),
Ⓦ**www.cheapflights.ca** (Canada) or
Ⓦ**www.cheapflights.com.au** (Australia & New Zealand). The most comprehensive source of flight deals: not a booking site itself, but maintains links to the travel agents offering the deals.
Ⓦ**www.cheaptickets.com** Discount flight specialists (US only).
Ⓦ**www.etn.nl/discount.htm** A hub of consolidator and discount agent web links, maintained by the nonprofit European Travel Network.
Ⓦ**www.expedia.co.uk** (UK & Ireland),
**www.expedia.com** (US) or Ⓦ**www.expedia.ca** (Canada). Discount airfares, all-airline search engine and daily deals.
Ⓦ**www.geocities.com/thavery2000** An extensive list of airline websites and US toll-free numbers.
Ⓦ**www.kelkoo.co.uk** Useful UK-only price-comparison site, checking several sources of low-cost flights (and other goods and services) according to specific criteria.
Ⓦ**www.lastminute.com** (UK & Ireland),
**www.lastminute.com.au** (Australia) or
**www.lastminute.co.nz** (New Zealand). Good holiday-package and flight-only deals available at very short notice.
Ⓦ**www.opodo.co.uk** Popular and reliable source of cheap UK airfares. Owned by, and run in conjunction with, nine major European airlines.
Ⓦ**www.priceline.co.uk** or **www.priceline.com** Bookings from the UK/US only. Name-your-own-price auction website that can knock around forty percent off standard website fares. You can't choose the airline or flight times (although you do specify dates)

and the tickets are non-refundable, non-transferable and non-changeable.
Ⓦ**www.skyauction.com** Bookings from the US only. Flight-only and travel packages up for auction. Best strategy is to bid the maximum you're willing to pay, since if you win you'll pay just enough to beat the runner-up regardless of your maximum bid.
Ⓦ**www.travel.com.au** and
Ⓦ**www.travel.co.nz** Australia ☎1300 130 482 or 02/9249 5444, New Zealand ☎0800 468 332. Comprehensive online travel companies, with discounted fares.
Ⓦ**www.travelocity.co.uk** (UK & Ireland),
Ⓦ**www.travelocity.com** (US) or **www.travelocity.ca** (Canada). Destination guides, hot web fares and deals for car rental, accommodation and lodging as well as fares.
Ⓦ**www.travelselect.com** A subsidiary of lastminute.com (see above) that's useful and fairly easy to use, but without most of the guff and banner adverts of the better-known sites.
Ⓦ**www.travelshop.com.au** Australian website offering discounted flights, packages, insurance and online bookings.
Ⓦ**www.zuji.com.au** Another Aussie site with destination guides, hot fares and great deals for car rental, accommodation and lodging.

## Flights from the UK and Ireland

Air travel to Pyrenean foothill airports has been revolutionized since the late 1990s with the provision of year-round direct flights by both no-frills, point-to-point airlines and the major national carriers. It's no longer necessary to tolerate the severe limitations of ski-season charters – which have effectively disappeared – or resign yourself to flying into much remoter Bilbao or Barcelona; you can even purchase advantageous one-way tickets with all the no-frills carriers and get the train back (or vice versa). No-frills airlines usually fly from remote, minor airports, charge for rudimentary food and drink on board, and often have baggage restrictions. They rely strictly on e-tickets, faxing or emailing you a booking reference number which you must retain. The earlier you book, the better the result – fares are "load sensitive", ie the cheapest seats fill first; you can easily pay as much as with a major airline (or more) if you leave it to the last minute. Most of the no-frills airlines do let you change the date of each travel leg for a fee of £15–25 – plus any difference in the prevailing fare since the time of original booking.

With no fewer than six airlines piling in from Britain (plus Aer Lingus from Ireland), **Toulouse** is shaping up to be the major gateway airport for the region. Even Air France offers low-season fares of about £80 and £177 from London Heathrow (2–3 daily) and Birmingham (1 daily) respectively, rising to just over £110 and £200 respectively in summer. British Airways also provides three daily flights from London Gatwick, starting at about £90 and working up to £140 in summer; through fares from Manchester, with an obligatory stop at Gatwick, begin at about £150. Also from Manchester, bmi provides one daily through service year-round – expect to pay about £130 on average; they also have a seasonal service from Aberdeen, Edinburgh and Glasgow. Subsidiary bmibaby does year-round Saturday services from Cardiff for as low as £30 return, or three weekly all year from East Midlands for similar prices. British European fares out of Southampton (1 daily) start at £80 in low season, from Bristol (1 daily) slightly more, and from Birmingham (1 daily) about £130 at the peak Easter skiing season; with prior notice, skis are carried for £15 each way. Air France also offers daily flights from Birmingham in winter only, but these are much pricier. EasyJet, with two daily services from London Gatwick, can be the cheapest at £30–50 round trip at slow seasons, but has famously uncivilized departure times. From Dublin, Aerlingus offers three weekly services, starting at €114 and rising to almost €300 at peak times.

**Biarritz**, **Pau**, **Carcassonne** and **Perpignan** are all served once daily year-round by Ryanair from London Stansted (with feeder flights from Scotland and Ireland, though Ryanair as a "point-to-point" airline takes no responsibility for missed connections). Low-season winter fares begin at £15 one way – but £40–50 is more typical in summer, rising to over £100 each way during peak skiing times. This airline also has a nasty habit of charging for luggage in excess of 15 kilos, thus potentially wiping out any savings – ring them for their current policy, especially if you're taking skis. British European also flies into Perpignan (1 daily,

most of the year) from Birmingham and Southampton; expect to pay £90–105 round trip, though "seat sales" at £80 are common.

**Girona** is the only really convenient airport on Spanish side with direct flights from the UK or Ireland. Ryanair currently offers the sole year-round service, from Stansted (4 daily), Glasgow (1 daily), Bournemouth (1 daily), Liverpool (1 daily), and Dublin (Sat/Sun all year, possibly extra days in summer). Fares from the UK are rarely much under £100, and can rise to well over £200 in peak skiing or summer season. From Ireland, budget a minimum of €250, climbing to €400 at prime times.

**Bilbao** is a good two-hours-plus by train from San Sebastián and the edge of the Pyrenees, but is well served by year-round flights: one daily each from Heathrow on British Airways and Iberia, common-rated at £100 minimum round-trip, plus one daily on easyJet from Gatwick and Stansted for roughly the same; easyJet's daily flight from Bristol is a relative bargain at £60–90 return. From Dublin, Aerlingus lays on four weekly flights between late March and late October; reckon on €196 during Easter week.

Given this plethora of flights from regional UK airports pinpointing Pyrenean foothill airports, frequent flights into distant **Barcelona** from the largest UK airports (on easyJet, Iberia, BA and bmi) are merely noted for the record, though high passenger volume produces some economies of scale, with fares in the region of £80–140 return even in peak season. From Dublin, twice-daily flights on Aerlingus start at about €150, though more realistically you'll pay €230 at Easter, over €300 at peak season on short notice.

## Airlines

**Aer Lingus** UK ☎ 0845/084 4444, Ireland ☎ 0818/365 000, ⓦ www.aerlingus.ie.
**Air France** UK ☎ 0845/0845 111, Ireland ☎ 01/605 0383, ⓦ www.airfrance.fr.
**bmi** (British Midland) UK ☎ 0870/607 0555, Ireland ☎ 01/407 3036, ⓦ www.flybmi.com.
**bmibaby** UK ☎ 0870/264 2229, Ireland ☎ 01/407 3036, ⓦ www.bmibaby.com.
**British Airways** UK ☎ 0845/722 2111, ⓦ www.britishairways.com.
**British European** UK ☎ 0870/5676 676, Ireland

☎1890/925 532, ⓦwww.flybe.com.
**easyJet** ☎0870/600 0000, ⓦwww.easyjet.com.
**Iberia** ☎0990/341341, ⓦwww.iberia.com.
**Ryanair** UK ☎0871/246 0000, Ireland ☎01/609
7800, ⓦwww.ryanair.com.

## Flight agents

**Aran Travel International** Galway
☎091/562595. Good-value flights to all parts of the
world.
**Joe Walsh Tours** Dublin ☎01/676 0991, ⓦwww
.joewalshtours.ie. General budget fares agent.
**McCarthys Travel** Republic of Ireland ☎021/427
0127, ⓦwww.mccarthystravel.ie. General flight
agent.
**North South Travel** ☎01245/608291,
ⓦwww.northsouthtravel.co.uk. Friendly, competi-
tive flight agency, offering discounted fares worldwide – profits are used to support projects in the
developing world, especially the promotion of sustainable tourism.
**Rosetta Travel** Belfast ☎028/9064 4996,
ⓦwww.rosettatravel.com. Flight and holiday agent,
specializing in deals from Belfast.
**Spanish Travel Services** London ☎020/7387
5337. Spanish flight-only specialists.
**STA Travel** ☎0870 160 0599,
ⓦwww.statravel.co.uk. Worldwide specialists in
low-cost flights and tours for students and under-
26s. A dozen branches across England, especially on
or near university campuses.
**Trailfinders** UK ☎020/7938 3939, ⓦwww
.trailfinders.com, Republic of Ireland ☎01/677 7888,
ⓦwww.trailfinders.ie. One of the best-informed and
most efficient agents for independent travellers;
branches in all the UK's largest cities, plus Dublin.

## Packages and specialist operators

**Package holiday** deals can be worth considering, especially if you book early, at the last
minute, or outside of peak season. There are
an increasing number of high-quality, specialist hiking, skiing or rural-accommodation-
based packages available on both sides of
the range. Fly-drive deals are well worth considering, too, as a combined air ticket and car
rental arrangement can be excellent value.
**Alto Aragón** ☎01869/337339,
ⓦwww.altoaragon.co.uk. The best and most varied
offerings for the Spanish Pyrenees: horse-riding in
the Sierra de Guara, cross-country skiing near
Benasque, and well-planned 8- or 15-day treks,
including supported traverses of selected sections of
the GR11 and HRP. Also self-guiding holidays from
selected quality hotels. Prices from £595 for 8 days,
land only.
**La Balaguère** ☎0033/5.62.97.20.21,
ⓦwww.balaguere.com. Well-respected adventure
travel outfit based at a *gîte* in Arrens-Marsous,
France; they offer a wide variety of treks and expeditions in the Pyrenees, though English-language guiding cannot be guaranteed.
**Borderline Holidays** ☎0033/5.62.92.68.95,
ⓦwww.borderlinehols.com. Friendly and small
British-run, Barèges-based company offering guided
walking and wildlife holidays in summer (late May to
late Sept) and affordable, quality skiing packages in
winter (late Dec to Easter) for £475–535 half-board
per person for one week, based in a small village
*pensión*. Flights Stansted–Pau included in winter; in
summer, budget £305–315 a week half-board per
person, land only.
**Exodus Expeditions** ☎020/8675 5550,
ⓦwww.exodus.co.uk. Broad array of year-round, 8-
day holidays, most beginning at their own lodge near
Luchon but taking in the Spanish side too. Winter offerings in small groups include snowshoeing trips (£480),
cross-country skiing out of Ax-les-Thermes (£455) and
ski mountaineering (£540). Summer outings include a
variety of walks on both sides of the border from day-
strolls to tough HRP traverses (£370–420), a multi-
activity holiday based near Luchon, and mountain-biking (£395). All prices land only.
**Iglu** ☎020/8542 6658, ⓦwww.iglu.com. General
marketers of skiing holidays; all the Andorran resorts
represented, from £350 per person per week including flights.
**Inntravel** ☎01653/629000,
ⓦwww.inntravel.co.uk. Upmarket summer programme includes supported 7-to-10-day hikes in the
French Basque foothills, the Garrotxa and the Catalan
Pyrenees (including the French Cerdagne). Also
cycling tours, Girona city-breaks, horse-riding at *Can
Jou* (see p.165), and cross-country skiing holidays
based at Valcebollère in the Cerdagne.
**Naturetrek** ⓦwww.naturetrek.co.uk. Wide range
of 8-day butterfly, botanical and birding trips on both
sides of the border, based either in Gèdre (France) or
Berdún (Spain); fairly pricey at £895–985 land only.
**Pyrenean Mountain Tours** ☎01635/297209,
ⓦwww.pyrenees.co.uk. Extensive summer hiking
programme, using Luz-Saint-Sauveur as a focus:
includes 8- or 15- day outings around Mont
Perdu/Monte Perdido, the HRP between Pic du Midi
and Vignemale, the GR10 and GR11, and the "Seven
Valleys of Lavedan," priced at £495–524 per person.
Also winter/spring 8-day ski-tours along the HRP in
the French Parc National, and around
Posets/Maladeta.

**Sherpa Expeditions** ☎020/8577 2717, ⓦwww.sherpa-walking-holidays.co.uk. Self-guiding, 8-day inn-to-inn walk in the southwestern Ordesa country (June–Sept); also an escorted, 15-day high-level traverse from Lescun to the Gavarnie area (July–Aug). Both are pricey, either side of the £800 mark, land only.

**Ski Miquel Holidays** ☎01457/821200, ⓦwww.miquelhols.co.uk. One- or two-week packages, with English-speaking instructor, at Baqueira-Beret in the Val d'Aran.

## Flights from the US and Canada

The only Pyrenean gateway airports that feature advantageously on North American travel websites and the transatlantic airlines' own routes are Toulouse (France), Bilbao (Spain) and Barcelona (Spain). Whether you fly into one of these, or to Paris or Madrid and travel overland from there, will depend on your budget and your schedule.

If you don't mind spending a few days in a big city first, or if you were planning to visit other parts of Europe anyway, it might not be worth flying all the way to the Pyrenees. Discounted flights to **London**, Paris and (to a lesser extent) Madrid are easy to find, and from London you can explore the various no-frills or overland options outlined on p.10 and pp.16–18.

Of the airports cited above, **Barcelona** is by far the biggest, and usually the most economical choice – Delta has direct flights from Atlanta and New York JFK, while a dozen other airlines fly there via Madrid or other European capitals. But through fares to **Toulouse** and **Bilbao** can be surprisingly attractive, and shouldn't be overlooked – though Bilbao is well over two hours' land journey from the mountains.

Fares to **Barcelona from the US** are much the same as those for Madrid, which is served non-stop by Iberia from Chicago, Miami and New York; Delta's direct service from JFK and Atlanta can be surprisingly pricey, though much less costly as part of a stopping itinerary. Figure on $430 from New York in the low season, $820 in the high season, perhaps via Madrid on Iberia or via London Heathrow on British Airways. From Miami, budget $570/870, the latter with a feeder flight to Delta's direct service from

Atlanta. From San Francisco, allow $630/1080, either a two-stop itinerary via New York and Madrid, or one-stop on Delta via Atlanta. From Chicago, the range is $590–$850, again on American plus Iberia, or via Atlanta on Delta. To Bilbao, fares can be pricier at $580/$940 from Chicago (via Madrid or London), $680/$1250 from San Francisco (via Paris or London), $500/$900 from New York (via Barcelona or London), and $530/$970 (via Madrid or London). Canadian fares are broadly similar; count on CDN$1060/CDN$1400 from Toronto or Montréal to Barcelona via London, Paris or Amsterdam, CDN$1060/CDN$1500 to Bilbao hubbing through Paris or London.

On the French side of the Pyrenees, there's a fair selection of direct flights **into Paris** from most points in the US, and the strong links between France and Canada's Francophone community keep Canadian fares reasonable too. Air France offers the most frequent, though typically expensive, service; indirect flights will yield the minimum fares quoted here. Figure on $430 in low season, $670 in high season from New York; from LA or San Francisco, $500/$1050; and from Chicago, $470/$950. From Montréal or Toronto, expect to pay CDN$900/CDN $1600 direct to Paris on Air France or Air Canada, while multi-stop flights from Vancouver clock in at CDN$1400/CDN $2000.

Closer to the mountains, **Toulouse** may prove a worthwhile target for a through fare: $420/980 from New York via Munich or Madrid, $600/$1350 via Paris or London from San Francisco, $380/$1200 from Chicago via Amsterdam or Paris. Flights from Canada to Toulouse are unlikely to be competitive.

### Airlines

**Air Canada** ☎1-888 247–2262, ⓦwww.aircanada .com.
**Air France** ☎1-800 237-2747, Canada ☎1-800/667-2747, ⓦwww.airfrance.com.
**American Airlines** ☎1-800 433-7300, ⓦwww.aa.com.
**British Airways** ☎1-800 AIRWAYS, ⓦwww.ba.com.
**Continental Airlines** domestic ☎1-800/523-3273, international ☎1-800/231-0856, ⓦwww.continental.com.
**Delta Air Lines** domestic ☎1-800 221-1212,

international ☎1-800 241-4141,
🌐www.delta.com.
**Iberia** ☎1-800 772-4642, 🌐www.iberia.com.
**KLM/Northwest** US domestic ☎1-800 225-2525, international ☎1-800 447-4747,
🌐www.klm.com.
**Lufthansa** US ☎1-800 645-3880, Canada ☎1-800/563-5954, 🌐www.lufthansa.com.
**Swiss** ☎1-877 FLY-SWISS, 🌐www.swiss.com.
**TAP Air Portugal**    ☎1-800/221-7370,
🌐www.tap-airportugal.pt.
**United Airlines** domestic ☎1-800 241-6522,
international ☎1-800 538-2929,
🌐www.united.com.
**Virgin Atlantic Airways** ☎1-800 862-8621,
🌐www.virgin-atlantic.com.

## Travel companies

**Air Brokers International** ☎1-800/883-3273 or
415/397-1383, 🌐www.airbrokers.com.
Consolidator and specialist in RTW tickets.
**Airtech** ☎212/219-7000, 🌐www.airtech.com.
Standby seat broker; also deals in consolidator fares
and courier flights.
**Educational Travel Center** ☎1-800/747-5551 or
608/256-5551, 🌐www.edtrav.com. Low-cost fares
worldwide, student/youth discount offers, rail passes.
**Flightcentre** US ☎1-866 WORLD-51, 🌐www
.flightcentre.us, Canada ☎1-888/WORLD-55,
🌐www.flightcentre.ca. Rock-bottom fares worldwide.
**New Frontiers** US ☎1-800/677-0720 or
212/986-6006, 🌐www.newfrontiers.com. Discount
firm, specializing in travel from the US to Europe.
**STA Travel** US ☎1-800/329-9537, Canada ☎1-888/427-5639, 🌐www.statravel.com. Worldwide
specialists in independent travel; also student IDs,
travel insurance, car rental, rail passes, etc.
**Student Flights** ☎1-800/255-8000 or 480/951-1177, 🌐www.isecard.com/studentflights.
Student/youth fares, plus student IDs and European
rail and bus passes.
**TFI Tours** ☎1-800/745-8000 or 212/736-1140,
🌐www.lowestairprice.com. Consolidator with global fares.
**Travel Avenue** ☎1-800/333-3335, 🌐www
.travelavenue.com. Full-service travel agent that
offers discounts in the form of rebates.
**Travel Cuts** US ☎1-800/592-CUTS, Canada ☎1-888/246-9762, 🌐www.travelcuts.com. Popular,
long-established student-travel organization, with
worldwide offers.
**Travelers Advantage** ☎1-877/259-2691,
🌐www.travelersadvantage.com. Discount travel
club, with cashback deals and discounted car rental.
Membership required ($1 for 3 months' trial).

**Travelosophy** ☎1-800/332-2687, 🌐www
.itravelosophy.com. Good range of discounted and
student fares worldwide.

## Package tours

Package tours may not sound like your kind
of travel, but don't dismiss the idea out of
hand. If time is limited and you want to get
straight up into the Pyrenees, it might be
worthwhile to have a company make the
arrangements. An organized trip can also
ensure a worry-free first week as you find
your feet on a longer tour.

That said, not many North American companies feature the Pyrenees. Most of those
that do specialize in vehicle-supported **hiking trips**, which – given the dollar's current
woes – cost a hefty $2800–3800 per week.

## Specialist operators

**BCT Scenic Walking** ☎1-800/473-1210,
🌐www.bctwalk.com. Offers an 8-day jaunt through
the Spanish Basque foothills, with light walking.
**Mountain Travel/Sobek** ☎1-888/MTSOBEK,
🌐www.mtsobek.com. 8-day trans-border trek in
the central Pyrenees.
**Saranjan Tours** ☎1-800/858-9594, 🌐www
.saranjan.com. Spain specialists offering an ambitious, 9-day tour from La Seu to San Sebastián, with
moderate walking; also 8-day tour divided between
the upper Costa Brava and the Catalan Pyrenees.
**Travel Square One** ☎1-800/468 6562. North
American agents for Agama Taller de Viatges, an
enthusiastic Catalan agency running Aragonese,
Catalan and trans-border Pyrenean treks; also tailor-
made itineraries.
**Wilderness Travel** ☎1-800/368-2794,
🌐www.wildernesstravel.com. Somewhat rushed
12-day whistle-stop tour of highlights from Bilbao to
Barcelona.

## Flights from Australia and New Zealand

There are no direct flights to the Pyrenees from
Australia or New Zealand, and you'll probably
aim initially for **Paris**, **Barcelona** or **Madrid**.
Reckon on a minimum 24 hours' flying time
via Asia, or 30 hours via North America – not
counting time spent on stopovers – with flights
via Asia typically cheaper. Air France's services to Paris from several points in Australia,
plus Auckland, are the most direct, though
fares are not the cheapest.

Most regular return **economy fares** to Madrid, Barcelona, Paris or Toulouse cost between A$2100 in the low season and A$3300 in the high season from eastern Australian gateways; from Perth or Darwin expect to pay A$100–200 less if travelling via Asia, A$400 more if routeing via the USA. Fares from Auckland cost between NZ$2500–3100 depending on season.

Alternatively, you can find a rock-bottom return fare to a **European hub city** with Garuda or Sri Lanka Airlines for around A$1600/NZ$1850 low season, and then either pick up a cheap flight (see pp.10–11) or travel overland to the Pyrenees. However, with the high living and transport costs in northwestern Europe, this rarely works out any cheaper in practice, unless you specifically intend to see the intervening territory.

**From Australia** several airlines fly via Asia into Barcelona or Madrid. The lowest fares are usually offered by Japan Airlines (to Madrid, with an overnight stop in either Tokyo or Osaka included in the fare) – from A$1800 in the low season to A$2900 in the high season. Mid-range fares to Madrid with Thai Airways and Lauda Air via their respective gateway cities of Bangkok and Vienna run at A$2000–3000; Air France offers direct service to Paris for about the same. Toulouse is an attractive destination, with low-season fares from Sydney of about A$2000, rising to A$2500 in high season.

Travelling **from New Zealand** via Asia, Thai Airways (via Sydney) has through fares from Auckland to Barcelona, and Japan Airlines has flights to Madrid – all with either a transfer or overnight stop in their carrier's home city – for NZ$2500/3100 (low/high season).

If you're planning to visit the Pyrenees as part of a wider world trip, then **Round-the-World** tickets (valid for a year) offer greater flexibility and are better value than a straightforward return flight. The most comprehensive and flexible routes are put together by airline marketing groups Star Alliance and Oneworld; starting at around A$2300/NZ$3500, they're priced according to mileage flown or how many continents you stop in.

## Airlines

**Air France** Australia ☏ 1300/361 400, New Zealand ☏ 09/308 3352, ⓦ www.airfrance.com.
**Air New Zealand** Australia ☏ 13 2476, ⓦ www.airnz.com.au; New Zealand ☏ 0800/737 000, ⓦ www.airnz.co.nz.
**Alitalia** Australia ☏ 02/9244 2445, New Zealand ☏ 09/308 3357, ⓦ www.alitalia.com.
**British Airways** Australia ☏ 1300/767 177, New Zealand ☏ 0800/274 847, ⓦ www.ba.com.
**Garuda Indonesia** Australia ☏ 02/9334 9970, New Zealand ☏ 09/366 1862, ⓦ www.garuda-indonesia.com.
**Japan Airlines** Australia ☏ 02/9272 1111, New Zealand ☏ 09/379 9906, ⓦ www.japanair.com.
**KLM** Australia ☏ 1300/303 747, New Zealand ☏ 09/309 1782, ⓦ www.klm.com.
**Lauda Air** Australia ☏ 1800/642 438 or 02/9251 6155, New Zealand ☏ 09/522 5948, ⓦ www.aua.com.
**Lufthansa** Australia ☏ 1300/655 727, New Zealand ☏ 0800/945 220, ⓦ www.lufthansa.com.
**Qantas** Australia ☏ 13 13 13, New Zealand ☏ 0800/808 767 or 09/357 8900, ⓦ www.qantas.com.
**Singapore Airlines** Australia ☏ 13 10 11, New Zealand ☏ 0800/808 909, ⓦ www.singaporeair.com.
**SriLankan Airlines** Australia ☏ 02/9244 2234, New Zealand ☏ 09/308 3353, ⓦ www.srilankan.lk.
**Swiss** Australia ☏ 1800/883 199, New Zealand ☏ 09/977 2238, ⓦ www.swiss.com.
**Thai Airways** Australia ☏ 1300/651 960, New Zealand ☏ 09/377 3886, ⓦ www.thaiair.com.

## Travel agents

**Flight Centre** Australia ☏ 13 31 33, ⓦ www.flightcentre.com.au. New Zealand ☏ 0800 243 544, ⓦ www.flightcentre.co.nz.
**Holiday Shoppe** New Zealand ☏ 0800/808 480, ⓦ www.holidayshoppe.co.nz.
**New Zealand Destinations Unlimited** New Zealand ☏ 09/414 1685 ⓦ www.holiday.co.nz.
**Northern Gateway** Australia ☏ 1800/174 800, ⓦ www.northerngateway.com.au.
**STA Travel** Australia ☏ 1300/733 035, New Zealand ☏ 0508/782 872, ⓦ www.statravel.com.
**Student Uni Travel** Australia ☏ 02/9232 8444, ⓦ www.sut.com.au; New Zealand ☏ 09/379 4224, ⓦ www.sut.co.nz.
**Trailfinders** Australia ☏ 02/9247 7666, ⓦ www.trailfinders.com.au.
**travel.com.au** and **travel.co.nz** Australia

☎ 1300/130 482 or 02/9249 5444; New Zealand ☎ 0800/468 332. Comprehensive online travel company, with discounted fares.

## Specialist operators

**Peregrine Adventures** Australia ☎ 03/9663 8611, ⓦ www.peregrine.net.au. Offers at least one annual itinerary in the Pyrenees, eg "Pyrenees and Val d'Auzun", a week's worth of day-hikes including the cirques of Gavarnie and Estaubé. A$1895 land only.

**Walkabout Gourmet Adventures** Australia ☎ 03/5159 6556, France ☎ 04.92.75.15.60, ⓦ www.walkaboutgourmet.com. Nicely routed 14-day, early-summer walking trip through the Pyrenees from Collioure to Biarritz; day-walks on both sides of the range, bracketed by vehicle transfers and gourmet meals. A$3625 land only.

## By rail

From London to the French side of the Pyrenees takes just ten to eleven hours using **Eurostar** from London to Paris, and then a TGV (*train à grande vitesse*) on from there; you'll change stations in Paris, from Nord to Montparnasse or Austerlitz, but it's an otherwise congenial itinerary, leaving London Waterloo between 9 and 10am, arriving in the foothills the same eveing. The useful **Rail Europe** website only allows booking through to the major TGV termini of Biarritz, Lourdes, Tarbes, Toulouse and Perpignan; for anywhere else, eg Girona in Spain, you'll need to ring them. **Tickets** can be bought anywhere from 7 to 60 days in advance; off-season fares to all French destinations are pretty standard at about £110 for a non-changeable, non-refundable Leisure ticket, or £170 for a partly changeable Leisure Flexi fare. In summer or peak skiing season you'll need to add £30 to each of these figures, but provided you buy at least a month in advance, prices compare quite well with no-frills fares when you consider that you're not paying £20–30 to reach a remote airport.

Booking by phone, you can get a couple of **add-ons** to bring you that little bit closer to the hills. Alighting the Lourdes-bound TGV at Pau, you could change to the service up the Aspe valley via Oloron-Sainte-Marie, with rail-bus service beyond Oloron to Canfranc in the Aragonese Pyrenees. Rail Europe can

also get you an add-on ticket continuing past Toulouse (where the TGV service stops) up to Latour-de-Carol in the French Cerdagne; here you must change trains and buy another ticket for the Spanish network, entering Spain at Puigcerdà. This route gives handy access to the Ariège and the Carlit massif, as well as Andorra.

## Rail passes

If you plan to use the rail network to visit other regions of France and Spain or other European countries, you might consider buying a **rail pass**.

### Eurail pass

The **Eurailpass**, which must be purchased before arrival in Europe (and cannot be purchased by European residents), allows unlimited free first-class train travel in France, Spain and 16 other countries, and is available in increments of 15 days, 21 days, 1 month, 2 months and 3 months. If you're under 26, you can save money with a **Eurailpass Youth**, which is valid for second-class travel, or, if you're travelling with 1 to 5 other companions, a joint **Eurailpass Saver**, both of which are available in the same increments as the Eurailpass. You stand a better chance of getting your money's worth out of a **Eurailpass Flexi**, which is good for 10 or 15 days' first-class travel within a 2-month period. This, too, comes in under-26/second-class (**Eurailpass Youth Flexi**) and group (**Eurailpass Saver Flexi**) versions.

In addition, a scaled-down version of the Eurailpass Flexi, the **Eurail Selectpass**, is available which allows travel in your choice of 3, 4 or 5 of the 17 countries Eurail covers (they must be adjoining, by either rail or ship) for any 5 days, 6 days, 8 days, 10 days or 15 days (5-country option only) within a 2-month period. In this plan, Belgium, the Netherlands and Luxembourg are taken as one "country." Like the Eurailpass, the Selectpass is also available in first-class, second-class youth, or first-class saver options.

Details of prices for all these passes can be found on ⓦ www.eurail.com, and the passes can be purchased from one of the agents listed below.

### Euro Domino pass

The **Euro Domino pass**, only open to European residents and available from Rail Europe (SNCF) or STA, offers unlimited rail travel through any one of 28 European and North African countries for between three (£127) and eight (£239) days within a calendar month; passengers under 26 pay £91 and £179 respectively. You can buy as many separate country passes as you want.

### InterRail

**InterRail** passes cover eight European "zones" and are available for either 12- or 22-day or one-month periods; you must have been resident in Europe for at least six months before you can buy the pass. Two types of passes are available – one for people under 26 and a more expensive one for the over-26s. France is in the zone including Belgium, the Netherlands and Luxembourg. A 12-day pass to travel in this area is £125/182 (under/over 26), a 22-day pass £149/219; a two-zone pass valid for a month is £195/275; a three-zone £225/320, and an all-zones £265/379. The pass is available from the same outlets as the Eurodomino (see above). InterRail passes do not include travel between Britain and the Continent, although InterRail pass holders are eligible for discounts on rail travel in Britain and Northern Ireland. The InterRail pass and the Eurodomino Freedom pass both give a discount on the London–Paris Eurostar service.

---

### Rail contacts

### In the UK and Ireland

**Eurostar** ☎ 0870/160 6600, ⓦ www.eurostar.com.
**Iarnród Éireann** Republic of Ireland ☎ 01/703 1885, ⓦ www.irishrail.ie.
**International Rail** UK ☎ 0870/751 5000, ⓦ www.international-rail.com.
**The Man in Seat 61** ⓦ www.seat61.com. Named after British rail buff Mark Smith's favourite seat on the Eurostar, this non-commercial site helps you plan a train journey from the UK to just about anywhere in Eurasia. You can't buy tickets here, but all the necessary links are provided.
**Rail Europe** ☎ 0870/584 8848, ⓦ www.raileu-

rope .co.uk. Good web-booking facility for major, TGV-served Pyrenean stations.

### In North America

**DER Travel** ☎ 1-888/337-7350, ⓦ www.dertravel .com/rail.
**European Rail Services** Canada ☎ 1-800/205-5800 or 416/695-1211, ⓦ www.europeanrailser-vices .com.
**Europrail International Inc** Canada ☎ 1-888/667-9734, ⓦ www.europrail.net.
**Rail Europe** US ☎ 1-877/257-2887, Canada ☎ 1-800/361-RAIL, ⓦ www.raileurope.com.

### In Australia and New Zealand

**CIT World Travel** Australia ☎ 02/9267 1255 or 03/9650 5510, ⓦ www.cittravel.com.au.
**Rail Plus** Australia ☎ 1300/555 003 or 03/9642 8644, ⓦ www.railplus.com.au.
**Trailfinders** Australia ☎ 02/9247 7666, ⓦ www.trailfinder.com.au.

## By car: Channel Tunnel or ferry

The fastest way for **drivers** to get across **to the continent** is the **Eurotunnel** service via the Channel Tunnel; the alternative is one of the time-honoured **ferry** crossings (see below). Eurotunnel operates shuttle trains 24 hours a day, for cars, motorcycles, buses and their passengers. The service runs continuously between Folkestone and Coquelles, near Calais, with up to four departures per hour (only one per hour midnight–6am) and takes 35min (45min for some night departure times), though you must arrive at least 30min before departure. It is possible to turn up and buy your ticket at the toll booths (after exiting the M20 at junction 11a), though in busy seasons booking is advisable. **Rates** depend on the time of year, time of day and length of stay; it's cheaper to travel between 10pm and 6am, while the highest fares are reserved for weekend departures and returns in July and August. For current information, contact the **Eurotunnel Customer Services Centre** at ☎ 0870/535 3535, ⓦ www.eurotunnel.com.

Traditional cross-Channel options are the **ferry** links between Dover and Calais (quickest and cheapest) and Newhaven and Dieppe, or, if you're headed for the Western Pyrenees you could consider crossing to Le

Havre (from Portsmouth), Cherbourg (from Portsmouth and Poole), St Malo (from Portsmouth and Poole) or even Roscoff (from Plymouth). Any of these latter routes cuts out the long detour around Paris, and opens up some interesting drives through Brittany and along the French Atlantic coast. Irish drivers may prefer lines bypassing Britain, direct to Roscoff or Cherbourg.

Ferry **prices** vary according to the time of year and, for motorists, the size of your car. The Dover–Calais runs, for example, start at about £120 one-way for a car and two adults; from Ireland (eg Cork–Roscoff), allow €200. Return fares are always better value, even more so if you're able to book well in advance. It's well worth playing around with dates and times to find the best deals; mid-week, midday sailings are usually cheapest. Two good cut-price fare outlets are Ferry Savers (℡0870/990 8492, ⓦwww.fer-rysavers.com) and EuroDrive (℡020/8324 4009, ⓦwww.eurodrive.co.uk).

### Ferries to Santander and Bilbao

Direct car and passenger ferry services from England to Spain are convenient but expensive, and seem designed primarily for individuals hauling chattel to Spanish second homes.

The ferry from **Plymouth to Santander** (four hours' drive from the west end of the Pyrenees) is operated by Brittany Ferries, takes 18 hours and runs on Wednesdays and Sundays from March to November. Ticket prices vary enormously according to the season, the number of passengers carried and the length of your stay; for example, a return ticket for a car and two adults for two weeks over Easter will cost about £500, while a high-summer open ticket can approach £700. Foot passengers pay around £45–95 one-way (depending on season), and everyone has to book some form of accommodation; a Pullman seat is cheap-est at £5, and two-berth cabins are available for £70–90.

P&O provides a twice-weekly ferry service from **Portsmouth to Bilbao**, ninety minutes closer to the mountains than Santander. The journey takes approximately 35 hours and leaves Portsmouth on Saturdays and Tuesdays. Return fares for a car and two people work out at between £540 and £935, according to season, with foot passengers paying £200–325 (cabins included). This sailing is significantly cheaper for motorcyclists than for cars, especially if you can find one of the frequent discounts offered by motorcycling publications. The route is often inoperative for ship maintenance during a few weeks in January.

### Ferry companies

**Brittany Ferries** UK ℡0870/536 0360, ⓦwww.brittanyferries.com; Ireland ℡021/4277 801, ⓦwww.brittanyferries.ie. Portsmouth to Santander; Portsmouth to St Malo; Plymouth to Roscoff; Poole to Cherbourg; Cork to Roscoff.
**Condor Ferries** UK ℡0845/345 2000, ⓦwww.condorferries.co.uk. Poole to St Malo via Guernsey or Jersey; Weymouth to St Malo via Guernsey & Jersey; Poole to Cherbourg; Portsmouth to Cherbourg.
**Hoverspeed** UK ℡0870/240 8070, ⓦwww .hoverspeed.co.uk. Dover to Calais; Newhaven to Dieppe.
**Irish Ferries** UK ℡0870/517 1717, Northern Ireland ℡0800/0182 211, Ireland ℡1890/313 131, ⓦwww.irishferries.com. Rosslare to Cherbourg and Roscoff (March to late Sept).
**P&O Irish Sea** Ireland ℡1800/409 049, ⓦwww.poirishsea.com. Dublin to Cherbourg, Rosslare to Cherbourg.
**P&O Ferries** UK ℡0870/520 2020, ⓦwww .poferries.com. Dover to Calais; Portsmouth to Cherbourg; Portsmouth to Le Havre; Portsmouth to Bilbao.
**SeaFrance** ℡0870/571 1711, ⓦwww.seafrance.com. Dover to Calais.

# Red tape and visas

EU citizens, plus nationals of Norway and Iceland, have no problems moving around the Pyrenees, since the range straddles two member nations, France and Spain (whilst Andorra also has no visa requirements). For most other nationals life has been made easier by the relaxation of various tourism restrictions. If you make a brief excursion across the border in the mountains, it is still advisable to carry a passport or other ID, since hotels and refuges often demand identification – especially in Spain, where non-EU citizens must fill out a registration card at every lodging.

Citizens of Canada, the USA, New Zealand and Australia do not need visas beforehand to enter France, Spain or Andorra. Both France and Spain are members of the **Schengen Group** (essentially the entire EU as it was before May 2004, minus Britain and Eire, plus Norway and Iceland), which has coordinated visa policy among its members. This means that you are allowed **ninety days' cumulative stay in any period of 180 days**, and must leave the Schengen Zone entirely for three months once you've used up your ninety-day allotment. There are no longer any border-control posts between France and Spain in the mountains, and non-EU/EEA arrivals will only be stamped in at the region's various airports. But you could be swept up in periodic ID checks mounted against illegal immigrants in both countries, and be required to account

for yourself. These regulations are unlikely to change, but just to be sure – or if you want something more involved such as a residence permit – contact the embassies/consulates listed below.

## French embassies in non-EU countries

**Australia** ☎02/6216 0100.
**Canada** ☎613/789 1795.
**New Zealand** ☎04/802 7787.
**USA** ☎202/944-6000.

## Spanish embassies in non-EU countries

**Australia** ☎02/6273 3555.
**Canada** ☎613/747-2252.
**USA** ☎202/452-0100.

# Information and maps

The national tourist organizations of both France and Spain have numerous overseas outlets, well stocked with literature, and are also conspicuously represented in towns at home. Both sides of the Pyrenean range itself are also meticulously mapped, though so far French products often have a slight edge over Spanish in terms of quality.

## French information offices

Overseas branches of the **French Government Tourist Office** (⊛www

.franceguide.com) give away large quantities of maps and glossy brochures for every region of France, including useful lists of hotels and campsites and festival programmes.

In the French Pyrenees you'll find a tourist information centre – **Office du Tourisme**, as it's usually called – in practically every town and many villages. From these you can get specific local information – including, most importantly, the **météo** or daily weather report, posted in the window – and you should always ask for the free town plan. Many bureaux also publish hotel and restaurant listings, bus and train timetables and local car and walking itineraries. In mountain regions they are often right next door to local trekking and climbing organizers.

### French Government Tourist Offices abroad

**Australia** Level 20, 25 Bligh St, Sydney ☏ 02/9231 5244, ✉ france@bigpond.net.au.
**Britain** 178 Piccadilly, London ☏ 09068/244 123, 60p/min, ✉ info@mdlf.co.uk.
**Canada** 1981 Avenue McGill College, Suite 490, Montréal ☏ 514/876 9881, ✉ mfrance@attcanada .net.
**Ireland** 10 Suffolk St, Dublin ☏ 1560/235 235, ✉ frenchtouristoffice@eircom.net.
**New Zealand** contact the office in Australia.
**USA** 9454 Wilshire Blvd, Suite 715, Beverly Hills ☏ 310/271 6665, ✉ fgto@gte.net; 1 Biscayne Tower, Suite 1750, 2 South Biscayne Building, Miami ☏ 305/373 8177; 676 North Michigan Ave, Suite 3360, Chicago ☏ 312/751 7800; 444 Madison Ave, 16th Floor, New York ☏ 212/838 7800, ✉ info@francetourism.com.

## Spanish information offices

The **Spanish National Tourist Office** (SNTO; ⊛ www.tourspain.es) similarly produces and gives away an impressive variety of maps, pamphlets and special interest leaflets. Visit one of their offices before you leave home and stock up, especially on city plans, as well as province-by-province lists of hotels, hostales and campsites. However, be aware that most overseas staff can be less than helpful, palming you off with obsolete pamphlets only vaguely connected with your query.

In the **Spanish Pyrenees** itself you'll find instead separately administered provincial or municipal **Turismos** (Turismes in Catalan). These vary enormously in quality – those of

the Basque country and Catalunya are usually excellent – but while they are generally extremely useful for regional information and local maps, they cannot be relied on to know anything about what goes on outside their patch. Like their French counterparts, they post **weather reports**, often for three days at a time, on their windows.

### SNTO offices abroad

**Australia** The Spanish National Tourist Office (SNTO), 1st Floor, 178 Collins St, Melbourne, VIC ☏ 03/9650 7377 or 1/800 817 855.
**Britain** 22–23 Manchester Square, London W1U 3PX ☏ 020/7486 8077, ⊛ www.tourspain.co.uk.
**Canada** 2 Bloor St West, 34th Floor, Toronto, Ontario M4W 3E2 ☏ 416/961-3131, ⊛ www .tourspain.toronto.on.ca.
**New Zealand** contact the office in Australia.
**USA** 666 Fifth Ave, 35th Floor, New York, NY 10103 ☏ 212/265-8822; San Vincente Plaza Bldg, 8383 Wilshire Blvd, Suite 956, Beverly Hills, CA 90211 ☏ 323/658-7188; 845 North Michigan Ave, Suite 915-E, Chicago, IL 60611 ☏ 312/642-1992; 1221 Brickell Ave, Suite 1850, Miami, FL 33131 ☏ 305/358-1992, ⊛ www.okspain.org.

## Pyrenean trekking maps

Maps specifically dedicated to the Pyrenees are a problem if you want to trek through the entire range. A scale of at least 1:50,000 is essential, and the **1:25,000 TOP 25** series published by the French **Institut Géographique National** (IGN) would be better for the northern slopes. Apart from the enormous expense of thirty-odd sheets at that scale, they're tedious to carry. In principle, it would be better to buy maps as you go, because of the stiff mark-up overseas; in practice, however, you would be wise to buy the most indispensable maps before arrival, as they're often sold out in their area of use.

A compromise for the GR10/HRP traverse on the **French side** would be the **1:50,000 Cartes de Randonnées** published jointly by the IGN and Randonnées Pyrénéennes (Rando Éditions), numbered from 1 to 11 going from west to east. They cover the entire range from coast to coast, with gîtes d'étape, refuges and recommended GR and Tour routes highlighted. Note that no. 9, "Montségur", is currently out of print, with no plans to reissue it. These maps are generally

When using a compass in the Pyrenees, note that the magnetic declination from true north is a maximum of 3° west.

excellent, though not perfect – a number of paths are shown incorrectly, partly owing to last revision dates for some of 1990–93, though most were revised in the period 1998–2001. At about €9 apiece (£8.95 in the UK) though, the complete set of 1:50,000 sheets still represents a substantial investment in money and pack weight. For both IGN and Cartes de Randonnées maps, relevant titles are quoted throughout the text.

The most widely available Spanish productions for the **Spanish** side of the range are the maps of Catalunya-based **Editorial Alpina** – mostly 1:25,000 and 1:40,000, one at 1:30,000 – covering the most popular walking areas between the Catalan coast and Navarra (relevant titles are quoted throughout the text; ⓦ www.editorialalpina .com). The accompanying booklets (Castilian or Catalan, rarely in English) supply useful information about accommodation, walking routes, winter mountaineering and caves, but the maps themselves don't cover the Basque country, and trail tracings are often woefully inaccurate, scarcely changed since the maps first appeared in the late 1940s. It's better to buy Editorial Alpina titles in Spain: not only are they much cheaper there (€5–6 versus £8–9), but you'll want the most current cartography, which does improve over time, albeit at a painfully slow pace – overseas stocks are often out of date. New editions since 1998 have predominantly green jackets (older ones are red or orange), with a booklet format of 21cm x 11.5cm, waterproof maps (with ten-metre contour intervals, since 2002) and improved detail on the French side of the border (where applicable).

The only serious alternative to Editorial Alpina, now preferred by many, are the 1:50,000 **Mapas Excursionistas**, produced jointly by the Institut Cartogràfic de Catalunya (ⓦ www.icc.es) and Rando Éditions, and modelled exactly on the French 1:50,000 *Cartes des Randonnées*. They're numbered 20 to 24 from east to west – from the Garrotxa region to Ansó/Echo – and

retail for €8–9 in Spain (£8.95 in the UK). What you lose in terms of scale compared to the Alpinas, you more than gain in accuracy and clarity. The ICC also produces two of its own series of maps: the **Mapa comarcal de Catalunya**, large 1:50,000 folding sheets for each county (*comarca*), and the **Mapa topogràfic de Catalunya** at 1:25,000.

Where necessary, the above series can be supplemented by the full range of **topographical maps** issued by the Spanish government's Instituto Geográfico Nacional (IGN), the Mapa Topográfico Nacional de España. These are available at scales of 1:100,000, 1:50,000 and occasionally 1:25,000. Though not quite up to the standard of French products, the maps have taken a quantum leap in quality since the late 1990s, replacing Castilian with local place names, indicating magnetic declination from true north and including useful regional language vocabularies in the margins. Moreover, a plain-blue-jacketed folding series, analogous to the French Série Bleue and produced together by IGN and MOPU (the ministry of public works), has recently appeared for many areas at scales of 1:50,000 and occasionally 1:25,000. Many bookshops in Spain, and a few specialist overseas stores, stock these maps, though as with the Editorial Alpina products, you'll find them much cheaper on arrival – typically €2.50 – and again less accurate than their French equivalents.

## Pyrenean road maps

In terms of **road maps**, the Spanish-produced Firestone "Pireneos" 1:200,000 map is the best one **covering the entire range**, showing both sides of the border at the same level of detail and even indicating parts of the French GR10 and Spanish GR11. Although two-sided, it's very easy to unfold and use, but available only in Spain (€5) – look for the blue-fringed red cover. Despite not having been updated since the mid-1990s, it remains remarkably accurate – nothing else sold overseas is anywhere near as useful – but beware of some defective recent printings where coverage is incomplete (the "eastern" and "western" halves of coverage may not meet up). If you want to try and special-order it from a map retailer abroad, the product number is T-33, and the ISBN is 84-86907-16-7. Failing that, Reise Know-How's "Pyrenäen mit Andorra" at 1:250,000 (€7.90) is a harder-wearing, waterproof fallback, including the Sierra de Guara – as well as a multitude of decidely minor churches.

For the **French side** only, two one-sided IGN "TOP 250" *Série Rouge* 1:250,000 maps document the entire range: no. 113, "Pyrénées Languedoc Roussillon", and no. 114, "Pyrénées Occidentales". A better French production, and perhaps a good compromise – especially for **cyclists** – between such a vague road map and a bulky stack of *randonnée* maps is the IGN 1:100,000 Série Verte. This shows contours and the GR10, covering the whole French side (and some of Spain) in four one-sided sheets: no. 69 "Pau Bayonne", no. 70 "Tarbes Bagnères-de-Luchon", no. 71 "Saint-Gaudens Andorre" and no. 72 "Perpignan Béziers".

Road maps for the **Spanish side** of the range are best bought in bookshops (*librerías*), street kiosks or service stations in Spain itself. Among the best are those published by Editorial Almax, which also produces reliable indexed street plans for the main cities.

## Map outlets

### In the UK and Ireland

**Stanfords** 12–14 Long Acre, London WC2 ☎020/7836 1321, ⊛www.stanfords.co.uk. Also at 39 Spring Gardens, Manchester ☎0161/831 0250, and 29 Corn St, Bristol ☎0117/929 9966.
**Blackwell's Map Centre** 50 Broad St, Oxford ☎01865/793 550, ⊛maps.blackwell.co.uk. Branches in Bristol, Cambridge, Cardiff, Leeds, Liverpool, Newcastle, Reading & Sheffield.
**The Map Shop** 30a Belvoir St, Leicester ☎0116/247 1400, ⊛www.mapshopleicester.co.uk.

**National Map Centre** 22–24 Caxton St, London SW1 ☎020/7222 2466, ⊛www.mapsnmc.co.uk.
**National Map Centre Ireland** 34 Aungier St, Dublin ☎01/476 0471, ⊛www.mapcentre.ie.
**The Travel Bookshop** 13–15 Blenheim Crescent, London W11 ☎020/7229 5260, ⊛www .thetravelbookshop.co.uk.
**Traveller** 55 Grey St, Newcastle upon Tyne ☎0191/261 5622, ⊛www.newtraveller.com.

### In the US and Canada

**110 North Latitude** US ☎336/369-4171, ⊛www.110nlatitude.com.
**Book Passage** 51 Tamal Vista Blvd, Corte Madera, CA 94925 ☎1-800/999-7909, ⊛www.bookpassage .com.
**Distant Lands** 56 S Raymond Ave, Pasadena, CA 91105 ☎1-800/310-3220, ⊛www.distantlands.com.
**Globe Corner Bookstore** 28 Church St, Cambridge, MA 02138 ☎1-800/358-6013, ⊛www.globecorner.com.
**Longitude Books** 115 W 30th St #1206, New York, NY 10001 ☎1-800/342-2164, ⊛www .longitudebooks.com.
**Map Town** 400 5 Ave SW #100, Calgary, AB, T2P 0L6 ☎1-877/921-6277, ⊛www.maptown.com.
**Travel Bug Bookstore** 3065 W Broadway, Vancouver, BC, V6K 2G9 ☎604/737-1122, ⊛www.travelbugbooks.ca.
**World of Maps** 1235 Wellington St, Ottawa, ON, K1Y 3A3 ☎1-800/214-8524, ⊛www.worldofmaps .com.

### In Australia and New Zealand

**Map Centre** ⊛www.mapcentre.co.nz.
**Mapland** 372 Little Bourke St, Melbourne ☎03/9670 4383, ⊛www.mapland.com.au.
**Map Shop** 6–10 Peel St, Adelaide ☎08/8231 2033, ⊛www.mapshop.net.au.
**Map World** 371 Pitt St, Sydney ☎02/9261 3601, ⊛www.mapworld.net.au. Also at 900 Hay St, Perth ☎08/9322 5733.
**Map World** 173 Gloucester St, Christchurch ☎0800/627 967, ⊛www.mapworld.co.nz.

# Insurance

**Even though EU reciprocal health care privileges apply across the Pyrenees (except Andorra), you'd do well to take out an insurance policy before travelling to cover against theft, loss and illness or injury. Before paying for a new policy, however, it's worth checking whether you are already covered: some all-risks home insurance policies may cover your possessions when overseas, and many private medical schemes offer supplemental cover for abroad. In Canada, provincial health plans usually provide partial cover for medical mishaps overseas, while holders of official student/teacher/youth cards in Canada and the US are entitled to meagre accident coverage and hospital in-patient benefits. Students will often find that their student health coverage extends during the vacations and for one term beyond the date of last enrolment.**

After exhausting the possibilities above, you might want to contact a specialist travel insurance company, or consider the travel insurance deal we offer (see box). A typical travel insurance policy usually provides cover for the loss of baggage, tickets and – up to a certain limit – cash or cheques, as well as cancellation or curtailment of your journey. Many policies can be chopped and changed to exclude coverage you don't need – for example, sickness and accident benefits can often be excluded or included at will. If you do take medical coverage, ascertain whether benefits will be paid as treatment proceeds or only after return home, and whether there is a 24-hour medical emergency number. When securing baggage cover, make sure that the per-article limit – typically under £500 – will cover your most valuable possession. If you need to make a claim, you should keep receipts for medicines and medical treatment, and in the event you have anything stolen, you must obtain an official statement from the police.

## Extra cover

Ordinary travel insurance policies are rarely valid for sporting activities such as skiing, trekking, whitewater rafting, climbing or horse-riding, and certainly not for parapenting, canyoning or caving. For these you'll have to take out extra cover such as that supplied by the French Carte Neige, which can be obtained in sports centres, equipment

### Rough Guides Travel Insurance

Rough Guides offers its own low-cost travel insurance, especially customized for our statistically low-risk readers by a leading British broker, provided by the American International Group (AIG) and registered with the British regulatory body, GISC (the General Insurance Standards Council). There are five main Rough Guides insurance plans: No Frills for the bare minimum for secure travel; Essential, which provides decent all-round cover; Premier for comprehensive cover with a wide range of benefits; Extended Stay for cover lasting four months to a year; and Annual multi-trip, a cost-effective way of getting Premier cover if you travel more than once a year. Premier, Annual Multi-Trip and Extended Stay policies can be supplemented by a "Hazardous Pursuits Extension" if you plan to indulge in sports considered dangerous, such as scuba-diving or trekking. For a policy quote, call the Rough Guide Insurance Line: toll-free in the UK ⓣ0800/015 09 06 or ⓣ+44 1392 314 665 from elsewhere. Alternatively, get an online quote at ⓦwww.roughguides.com/insurance.

shops and clubs. It's inexpensive, valid Europe-wide and lasts a year, but basically meets just the cost of recovery, offering only limited medical expenses and no property protection. Spanish ski resorts tend to offer recovery insurance as a top-up to lift-pass prices. In Britain, Snowcard Insurance Services (☎01327/262805) specializes in mountaineering and activity holiday travel insurance.

# Health

Properly documented citizens of all EU countries are entitled to take advantage of each other's health services under the same terms as the residents of the country. In summer 2004, traditional form E111 – obtained from post offices in the UK – and most other E-forms are set to be replaced by a Europe-wide benefits "Smart card".

Only citizens of EU member states are covered under this scheme; anyone else is strongly advised to take out travel insurance with medical cover (see above), and supplementary health insurance for EU nationals is advisable in any case.

## France

General health care in France is of the highest standard, and no vaccinations are required when entering the country. Under the French health system every hospital visit, doctor's consultation and prescribed medicine incurs a **charge** (though not up front in an emergency). Documented EU citizens are entitled to a refund (usually between 70 and 100 percent) of any medical and dental expenses they incur, providing the doctor is government registered (a *médecin conventionné*). This can still leave a hefty shortfall, especially after a stay in hospital (accident victims even have to pay for the ambulance that takes them there).

To find a **doctor** stop at any *pharmacie* and ask for an address. Consultation fees for a visit should be €23–27 and in any case you'll be given a **Feuille de Soins** (Statement of Treatment) for later documentation of private or social insurance claims. Prescriptions should be taken to a *pharmacie* which is also equipped – and obliged –

to give first aid (for a fee). For minor illnesses pharmacists will dispense free advice and a wide range of medication. The medicines you buy will have little stickers (*vignettes*) attached to them, which you must remove and stick to your *Feuille de Soins* together with the prescription itself. In serious emergencies in France you will always be admitted to the nearest **hospital** (*hôpital*) – an ambulance can be summoned by dialling ☎18. Another useful phone number is ☎15, the national medical emergency service.

Since complicated bureaucracy is involved in getting a refund through your social security department back home, it's better to have ordinary travel insurance, which usually allows almost full reimbursement (less the first few pounds or dollars of the excess), and covers the cost of repatriation. If you're travelling in your own vehicle, you may want to have breakdown cover which includes return of the vehicle if you're incapacitated.

## Spain

No inoculations are required for Spain; the worst that's likely to happen to you is that you might fall victim to an upset stomach. Wash fruit and avoid *tapas* that look like they were cooked last week.

For minor complaints, go to a farmacia – you'll find one in all but the smallest villages.

Pharmacists are highly trained, willing to give advice (often in English) and able to dispense many drugs that would be available only on prescription in most other countries. They keep usual shop hours (Mon–Fri 9am–1.30pm & 5.30–8pm), but some open late and at weekends, while a rota system keeps at least one open 24 hours. The rota is displayed in the window of every pharmacy, or check in one of the local newspapers under *Farmacias de guardia*.

In more serious cases you can get the address of an English-speaking **doctor** from the nearest relevant consulate, or with luck from a *farmacia*, the local police or tourist office. In emergencies dial ☎091 for the *Servicios de Urgencia*, or look up the *Cruz Roja Española* (Red Cross) which runs a national ambulance service. Treatment at (often excellent) public hospitals for EU citizens is free; otherwise you'll be charged at private hospital rates, which can be expensive. Accordingly, it's essential to have some kind of comprehensive travel insurance.

### Spas

On both sides of the Pyrenees, but especially in France, you'll come across thermal spas. They were the original, eighteenth- or nineteenth-century impetus for tourism in these parts, and while many have been remodelled in Brutalist style, a few others retain their Belle Époque decor. They used to be the exclusive preserve of the elderly and/or the unwell – the *curistes*, in French – who would stay for weeks on end, with the French social security system footing the bill. Since the millennium, however, the authorities have made it clear that they will no longer subsidize indefinite stays at the waters, and in order to survive economically the spas have had to reinvent themselves. *Remis en Forme* (Get in Shape) programmes, with gyms, yoga classes and similar trappings, are now the rule, designed to attract a younger, more active clientele. Spas are typically open only during summer, with morning hours reserved for the dwindling numbers of *curistes*, and late afternoons for casual trade. But increasing numbers of thermal stations near ski resorts – Barèges, Luchon, St-Lary-Soulan, Eaux-Bonnes, Cauterets, for example – have a late-afternoon session in winter, aimed at chilled and muscle-sore skiers. Take advantage, when available.

# Costs, money and banking

Prices in the Pyrenees don't differ greatly from those in towns away from the mountains. If you do spend less than you anticipate on a Pyrenean holiday, it will be because there isn't much scope to go financially wild once you're off the beaten track. If you're travelling alone you'll end up spending much more than you would in a group of two or more – sharing rooms (and wine) saves considerably.

### French costs

Because of the relatively low cost of accommodation and eating out, at least by northern European standards, the French Pyrenees are not outrageously expensive to visit. **On average**, staying exclusively at *gîtes* or refuges, or camping, and being strong-willed about denying yourself cups of coffee and culture, you could just about survive on £25/US$40 per person per day, including one inexpensive restaurant meal. For a more comfortable existence, including a basic, shared hotel room and restaurant or café stops, you need to budget about £37–40/$62–67 per person per day. If you're planning to stay in fancier lodgings, and eat and drink to your heart's content, £55/$90 per day per head wouldn't be an unreasonable estimate.

Two or more people will find that sharing **hotel accommodation** can occasionally be as cheap as staying at refuges or at a *gîte d'étape* – certainly the case with relatively basic hotels in our category ❶ (see p.37) – though a more usual minimum estimate for a double room would be £20–25/$33–42), corresponding to category ❷ .There are large numbers of decent **restaurants** with three- or even four-course menus for £9–13/$15–22). **Picnic** or **overnight-trek fare**, obviously, is much less costly. Note that **museums and monuments**, at an average of €2.50–3 per entrance, can make substantial inroads into a daily budget.

**Transport** will inevitably be a large item of expenditure if you're not strictly on a walking tour. Buses are less expensive than trains, though prices vary enormously from one operator to another. Rental bikes cost about £10/$17 per day. For fuel prices, see "Getting Around", pp.31 and 34.

## Spanish costs

The Spanish Pyrenees, like northern Spain generally, are no longer a budget destination. Food and lodging prices have both increased considerably since the late 1980s, and especially in the more popular parts of the Catalan Pyrenees, you can easily spend more than on the French side.

**On average**, if you're prepared to buy your own picnic lunch, stay in inexpensive *pensiones* or *casas rurales*, and stick to the most basic eating places, you could get by on £27/US$45 per person per day. If you intend to upgrade your accommodation, experience town nightlife and eat fancier meals then you'll need more like £45/$75 a day. At £60/$100 a day and upwards you'll only be limited by your energy reserves – though of course if you're planning to stay in the best hotels, this figure won't even cover your room.

**Room prices** vary according to season and locale, but on the Spanish side you'll find little below e14 (£10/$16.50) single, €25 (£17.50/$29.50) double (non-en-suite), €20 single (£14/$23.50), €35 double (£24.50 /$41) for en-suite facilities. Refuges or *albergues* tend to cost €8–12 per head.

The cost of **eating** can vary wildly, but in most towns or villages there'll be at least one restaurant offering a basic three-course meal for somewhere between €9 and €16 (£6.30–11.20/$10.50–18.80). Alternatively, your accommodation may offer advantageous half-board rates for roughly the same. Drink, wine in particular, costs little: £3/$5 will see you through a substantial intake of house wine in bulk, or a small bottle of very good stuff.

Long-distance **transport**, if used extensively, may prove a major expense. Although per-kilometre prices compare well with the rest of Europe, rural Pyrenean journeys between nearby places tend to be long because of tortuous routeings. Urban transport in the handful of large towns almost always operates on a flat fare of about €1.

Most of the above costs are affected by **where you are and when**. Big towns and popular resorts are invariably more expensive than remoter areas, and certain regions – notably the industrialized lowlands of Euskadi and Catalunya – are pricier across the board.

One thing to look out for on prices generally is the addition of value added tax – IVA – which may come as an unexpected extra when you pay the bill for food or accommodation. The magic words, often in small print at the bottom of the menu, are *IVA (no) incluido* in Castilian or *IVA (no) inclós* in Catalan. Even fairly modest restaurants and hotels often add seven percent IVA to the total after the fact.

## Currency

Spain and France are two of twelve European Union countries that changed over to a single currency, the **euro** (€), in February 2002. The fixed conversion rate of the French franc against the euro was €=6.5597, of the Spanish peseta €=166.386ptas; many till receipts in each country continue to show the value in both new and old currencies. For the most up-to-date **exchange rates** of the US dollar or the pound sterling against the euro, consult the very useful currency speculators' website, Ⓦwww.oanda.com.

All local prices in this book are given in euros. "Rounding up" of odd euro equivalents of franc or peseta prices has prevailed since February 2002, effectively making the two countries about two percent more expensive in 2003 than in early 2002, even before inflation was taken into account.

Euro notes exist in denominations of 5, 10, 20, 50, 100, 200 and 500 euros, and coins in denominations of 1, 2, 5, 10, 20 and 50 cents and 1 and 2 euros. Each country in the euro-zone strikes its own coins (just one face is distinctive), but the other face – and all notes – are uniform throughout Europe. Any euro coins or notes can be used in any of the countries of the euro zone.

## Banks and exchange

**French** banking hours are Monday to Friday 9am–4.30pm, many closing at midday (noon–2pm or 12.30–2.30pm). A few are open Saturday 9am–noon, but all close on Sundays and holidays. Rates of exchange for dollars, sterling or Swiss francs, and commissions, vary. The Crédit Mutuel usually offers the best rates and takes the least commission; it also keeps Saturday-morning hours.

There are **money-exchange counters (bureaux de change)** at airports and big-city train stations. You'll also find **automatic bill-changer machines** in such places, accepting notes in dollar, sterling and major non-euro currencies such as Swiss francs. However, rates for both these facilities tend to be poor and commissions high.

**Spanish bancos** (banks) and **cajas de ahorro** (savings banks) have branches in all but the smallest towns, and some are prepared to change traveller's cheques – though stick to major brands like Amex, Visa and Thomas Cook to avoid refusal. In Catalunya (and some way beyond into Aragón) La Caixa is a ubiquitous savings bank.

Banking hours are Mon–Fri 8.30am–2pm, Sat 8.30am–1pm (except June–Sept when banks close on Sat). In heavily touristed areas, such as the Catalan or Basque coasts, you may find **casas de cambio** (exchange booths), with more convenient hours (though "no commission charged" often means a poor exchange rate).

## Credit and debit cards

**Credit/debit** cards are widely accepted in **France**; always ask beforehand, however, in smaller hotels and restaurants. Transactions are debited with immediate effect, the waiter or desk clerk running your card through an online swipe reader without use of the PIN number. Some machines may reject cards without a "smart chip" (*pouce* in French) – it's best to bring at least one card with an embedded chip. Visa – known as **Carte Bleue** in France – is almost universally recognized; American Express and Mastercard rank considerably lower, with only Crédit Agricole and the Crédit Mutuel providing facilities for the latter. Very few French retailers are likely to accept American Express.

Cash advances on credit cards can be obtained at most bank counters, but with a PIN number you can take advantage of the numerous electronic autotellers (**ATMs**) dotted across the Pyrenean foothills. The words for "ATM" in French are *guichet automatique*, or *distributeur de billets*. Many of these – in particular ATMs attached to post offices (**La Poste**) – also accept debit cards of the Cirrus and/or Plus systems, but the machines have been known to eat or refuse incompatible cards. Debit cards are considerably cheaper to use in this manner, with commissions of two percent versus nearly four percent for credit cards, but your home bank will levy a minimum charge of about £1.50/$2, so you might not want to be constantly withdrawing small sums. Lost or stolen cards should be reported either to your own-country emergency number, or one of the following French hotlines: Carte Bleue (Visa) ☏08.00.90.11.79; American Express ☏01.47.77.72.00; Mastercard ☏08.00.90.13.87.

Any Visa or Mastercard credit card, as well as any **debit card** that is part of the Cirrus or Plus systems, can be used for **withdrawing cash** from the numerous ATMs in the Pyrenean foothills and resorts in **Spain**. The Castilian for "ATM" is *cajero automatico*. As in France, Spanish "holes in the wall" are highly sophisticated and will give instructions in a variety of languages. Surcharges are as for use on the French side.

Leading **credit cards** are also recognized by major retailers, car rental firms, petrol stations and expensive hotels or restaurants. American Express and Visa are the most useful; Mastercard is less widely accepted. In case of loss or theft, the in-Spain numbers to dial are: American Express, ☎915 720 303; Visa, ☎900 974 445; Mastercard, ☎900 971 231.

## Traveller's cheques and visa "travel money"

**Traveller's cheques** are one of the safest ways of carrying your money, available from major banks (whether you have an account there or not), usually for a service charge of one to two percent of the amount purchased. Your own bank or travel agent may offer cheques free of charge provided you meet certain conditions – it's always worth asking first. The overriding problem in the Pyrenees is that, even if euro-denominated, only banks – and almost no merchants – will accept them, with the former levying heavy commissions. UK-based travellers may have

better luck with International Postal **Giro Cheques**, which work like ordinary bank cheques except that you cash them at post offices, more common and with longer opening hours than banks.

A possible compromise between travellers' cheques and ordinary credit/debit cards is **Visa TravelMoney**, a disposable pre-paid debit card linked to a PIN, which works in all ATMs accepting Visa cards. You load up your account with funds before leaving home, and when they run out, simply dispose of the card. You can buy up to nine cards to access the same funds – useful for couples or familes – and it's wise to buy at least one extra as a back-up in case of loss or theft. For information on the closest sales outlets for the cards, check the Visa TravelMoney page at wusa.vis.com/personal/cards/visa_travel_money.html, though Thomas Cook or Citicorp are the most likely ones.

# Getting around

If you're not driving, cycling or walking, getting around the Pyrenees takes a bit of organization and attention to detail. There are surprisingly good bus services (and sometimes trains) along the main valley floors and between major centres, but timings are often geared to school and work hours. Approximate journey times and frequencies can be found in the "Travel Details" at the end of each chapter, and local peculiarities are also pointed out in the text.

If you intend to hitch in the Pyrenees, it's always safest to try and arrange a lift in advance by asking at your hotel, *gîte* or refuge. However, this guide **does not recommend hitching** as a reliable means of transport; in peak season you can wait for hours for a ride, as scores of crammed-full vehicles pass you by. The same risks apply as for hitching anywhere else.

## France

France has the most **extensive rail network** in Western Europe, although rural services have been severely cut back since the 1980s. Trains are an excellent way of travelling parallel to the line of the mountains and along the coasts, but lines tend to give out as the gradients increase and the populations dwindle. However, where the train stops an **SNCF** (the French rail company) bus often continues the route. Private **bus** services are confusing, uncoordinated and often poorly publicized – where possible, it is much simpler to use SNCF. If you have the time and the vehicle, **driving** or **cycling** are both excellent ways of seeing the Pyrenean foothills.

## Trains

SNCF trains are by and large clean, fast and frequent, and their staff usually courteous and helpful; all but the smallest stations have an information desk/ticket window. Many rent out bicycles, sometimes of rather doubtful reliability, and slower trains, stopping at most stations, are often marked on timetables with a bicycle symbol – meaning you can travel with a bike as free accompanied luggage (see below for details). "Car" at the top of a timetable column means it's an SNCF bus service, for which train tickets and passes are valid.

Regional **rail maps** and complete timetables are on sale at tobacconist shops, though you will find them for free at the biggest tourist offices. Leaflet **timetables** for a particular line are available free at stations, and again many tourist offices. Complete timetables and fare quotes are also available at ⓦwww.sncf.fr.

All **tickets** – though not passes – must be **date-stamped** in the orange machines at station platform entrances or foyers. It is an offence if you don't "*compostez votre billet*", and people caught riding without tickets are liable to a heavy spot fine. Train journeys may be broken any time, anywhere, but after a break of 24 hours you must date-stamp your ticket again upon resuming your journey.

While **InterRail** (p.17) and **Eurail** (p.16) passes are valid on all trains, and worth investigating before you leave home, the SNCF itself offers a range of **discount fares** on *Période Bleue* (blue period) days – off-peak travel days; you can pick up a leaflet showing when blue period applies at SNCF stations. **Couples** or **groups** of up to four are entitled to a 25 percent discount on return fares if they travel together and start their journey on a blue-period day.

One of the most useful passes is the **Euro**

**Domino pass** (see p.17). **Other SNCF discount passes** are available only in France from major stations, or online (ⓦwww.voyages-sncf.com). If you're **over 60**, a *Carte Senior*, valid for a year (€46), will give you up to half off most journeys starting in a blue period, including TGVs, a 25 percent reduction on white-period (normal period) fares, and 30 percent off most international journeys from Western Europe – for example, Britain to the Pyrenees. Identical reductions are available for under-26s with the one-year **Carte 12–25** (€44), and to **families** of up to five using an **Enfant Plus Carte** (€58), for which one child under 12 is the designated holder.

## Buses

With the exception of SNCF services, **buses** play a generally minor role in the Pyrenees. Their most frustrating characteristic is that they rarely serve regions outside the SNCF network – which is precisely where you need them. Where they do exist (mostly in the foothills), timetables are constructed to suit working, school and market hours – it will be a real stroke of luck if one is going where and when you want. Buses are, generally speaking, cheaper and slower than trains.

Larger towns usually have a **gare routière** (bus station), often next to the train station. However, private bus companies tend to leave from an array of different points around town. Their locations and schedules are usually available from tourist offices, or at the very least there will be a timetable posted at the stop.

## Driving and vehicle rental

**Using a car** gives you enormous advantages of access to remote areas. If you're camping or trekking, the ability to carry extra equipment can make driving an attractive proposition, but you will only save money – especially with a rented vehicle – if there are several of you to share the cost. Breakdown liability and the complication of point-to-point treks are other minuses.

**Car rental** arranged on the spot costs upwards of €300 per week; you need to be at least 21. It's normal to leave an indemnity of €300–450 against any damage to the car not covered by the CDW premium; this is usually done on a credit-card slip which should be destroyed upon safe return of the vehicle. We recommend that you pay any top-up premium requested (sometimes called a Franchise Waiver or Super Collision Damage Waver) to eliminate this liability.

Cars are delivered with a full tank of fuel and must be returned full; there's usually an extra fee if you pick the car up on arrival at one airport and leave it at another. Among the British rental agencies listed opposite, Transhire usually has the best rates for the French Pyrenees – typically £125–150 per week. Renault Clio diesel saloons are often available as a roomy Group B car, and their fuel economy easily offsets the slightly higher rental price – you'll need at least B standard for mountain gradients.

Any EU (including British) **drivers' licence** is valid in France, but North Americans and antipodeans require an International Driving Permit (available from the AAA for a small fee). The vehicle registration document and the insurance papers must be carried; if it's a rental car, agency staff should point them out to you. If you bring your own car with right-hand drive, have your headlight dip adjusted to the right before you go – it's a legal requirement, as is a GB sticker – and, as a courtesy, paint them yellow or stick on black glare deflectors. All major car manufacturers have service stations in France, and if you need a tow, look under *Dépannages* (Breakdowns) in the *Pages Jaunes* (Yellow Pages). If you have an accident or break-in, make a report to the local police (and keep a copy) in order to make an insurance claim.

The main **rule of the road** to remember in France is the law of *priorité à droite*, which means that you must often give way to traffic coming from your right, even from a minor road. Having been a major cause of accidents, it is being phased out, and so only applies in built-up areas, where you have to be vigilant – watch the roadside for signs with a **yellow diamond** on a white background, which means that you have the right of way; the same diamond with an oblique black line through it means you must yield to right-hand traffic. Signs saying *STOP* or

*CEDEZ LE PASSAGE* also mean you must give way. Roundabouts (*ROND-POINTS*), of which there are many in Pyrenean towns, work just like those in Britain, except in the opposite direction: signs always warn you *VOUS N'AVEZ PAS LA PRIORITÉ*. Other common warning signs are *BOUE* (mud), *CHAUSSÉE DÉFORMÉE* (uneven surface), *DÉVIATION* (diversion), *ÉBOULEMENT* (landslide debris), *GRAVILLONS* (loose chippings), *NIDS DE POULES* (potholes), *SAUF RIVERAINS* (residents only), and *VERGLAS FRÉQUENT* (frequent ice slicks). For **information on road conditions** call the multilingual Autoroutel (☎08.92.68.10.77; €0.34/min) or consult their website at ⓦwww.autoroutes.fr

The main N-numbered highways swarm with *gendarmes* (see p.57) manning drunk-driver checkpoints and speed traps; failure to wear a seatbelt nets you a spot **fine** of €25. The minimum fine for speeding is €90 if you pay within three days; over 40kph over the limit and you'll have a court appearance as well as a fine. **Speed limits** are as follows: 130kph/80mph on toll autoroutes; 110kph/68mph on dual carriageways; 90kph/56mph on other roads; and 50kph/37mph in towns. For all drivers in bad weather, and those with less than two years' experience, the out-of-town limits are 110kph, 100kph and 80kph respectively. All this notwithstanding, driving in France remains a stressful experience. The country has the dubious honour of being tied with Spain for third place amongst EU states for level of **unsafe driving** and accident fatalities (Portugal and Greece are first and second, respectively). If you're not doing at least 20kph over the applicable speed limit, you can be guaranteed of having someone crawling up to your rear bumper, except on the remotest and narrowest roads.

Motorway – **autoroute** – driving, though fast, is very boring when it's not hair-raising, and the **tolls** are expensive: Paris to Perpignan, for example, costs around €60. On the whole, don't waste your money on the toll routes, of which there are few in the Pyrenees anyway; a French N (*nationale*) or RN (*route nationale*) **road** is the equal of a good UK "A" road, or a well-maintained state highway in the US. In the Pyrenees, you will become acquainted of necessity with the D (*départementale*) roads: many quite good, with two lanes (but no verge), others one-lane and barely paved. Some have been constructed over high passes or along cor-niches with spectacular views in mind; minor roads over the passes are typically **snowed up** between November and May, though giant signboards may advise you of opened, snowploughed corridors and chain require-ments, especially near ski resorts.

**Fuel** (*essence*) prices are fairly standard for continental Europe at just under €1.20 a litre for lead-replacement "super", just over €1.10 for 95–98 octane "normal", and under €1 a litre for diesel (*gas-oil*) – though it's cheaper if you buy it at out-of-town super-market chains like Leclerc or Champion.

**Scooters** are relatively easy to rent and although they're not built for any kind of long-distance touring, they're ideal for exploring the environs of foothill towns. Places which rent out bicycles (see below) usually have scooters, too; expect to pay €30 per day for a 50cc Suzuki, or €40 per day for an 80cc scooter. **Crash helmets** are now compulsory when using any motorized two-wheelers; you must also keep the head-light on at all times.

### Car-rental agencies

#### In Britain
Avis ☎0870/606 0100, ⓦwww.avis.com.
Budget ☎0800/181 181, ⓦwww.budget.com.
National ☎0870/536 5365,
ⓦwww.nationalcar.co.uk.
Hertz ☎0870/844 8844, ⓦwww.hertz.com.
Sixt ⓦwww.e-sixt.com
Suncars ☎0870/500 5566, ⓦwww.suncars.com.
Thrifty ☎01494/751 600, ⓦwww.thrifty.com.
Transhire ☎0870/789 8000,
ⓦwww.transhire.com.

#### In Ireland
Avis Northern Ireland ☎028/9024 0404, Republic of Ireland ☎01/605 7500, ⓦwww.avis.ie.
Budget Republic of Ireland ☎0903/277 11,
ⓦwww.budget.ie.
Cosmo Thrifty Northern Ireland ☎028/9445 2565, ⓦwww.thrifty.com.
Hertz Republic of Ireland ☎01/676 7476,
ⓦwww.hertz.ie.
Sixt Republic of Ireland ☎1850/206 088,
ⓦwww.irishcarrentals.ie.

Thrifty Republic of Ireland ☎1800/515 800,
ⓦwww.thrifty.ie.

#### In North America
Alamo ☎1-800/522-9696, ⓦwww.alamo.com.
Auto Europe US ☎1-800/223-5555, Canada
☎1-888/223-5555, ⓦwww.autoeurope.com.
Avis US ☎1-800/331-1084, Canada ☎1-800/272-5871, ⓦwww.avis.com.
Budget ☎1-800/527-0700, ⓦwww.bud-getrentacar .com.
Dollar US ☎1-800/800-4000, ⓦwww.dollar.com.
Europe by Car ☎1-800/223-1516,
ⓦwww.europebycar.com.
Hertz US ☎1-800/654-3001, Canada ☎1-800/263-0600, ⓦwww.hertz.com.
National ☎1-800/227-7368, ⓦwww.national-car.com.
Thrifty ☎1-800/367-2277, ⓦwww.thrifty.com.

#### In Australia
Avis ☎13 63 33 or 02/9353 9000,
ⓦwww.avis.com.au
Budget ☎1300/362 848, ⓦwww.budget.com.au
Dollar ☎02/9223 1444, ⓦwww.dollarcar.com.au.
Hertz ☎13 30 39 or 03/9698 2555,
ⓦwww.hertz.com.au.
National ☎13 10 45, ⓦwww.nationalcar.com.au.
Thrifty ☎1300/367 227, ⓦwww.thrifty.com.au.

#### In New Zealand
Apex ☎0800/93 95 97 or 03/379 6897,
ⓦwww.apexrentals.co.nz.
Avis ☎09/526 2847 or 0800/655 111,
ⓦwww.avis.co.nz.
Budget ☎09/976 2222, ⓦwww.budget.co.nz.
Hertz ☎0800/654 321, ⓦwww.hertz.co.nz.
National ☎0800/800 115,
ⓦwww.nationalcar.co.nz.
Thrifty ☎09/309 0111, ⓦwww.thrifty.co.nz.

## Cycling

**Bicycles** (*vélos*) have high status in France. All the car ferries from Britain carry them for little or nothing; SNCF makes minimal charges; and individual French people respect cyclists, as both traffic and potential customers. Restaurants and hotels along the way are nearly always obliging about looking after your bike, even to the point of allowing it into your quarters. Local motorists normally give you plenty of room – it's the lumbering foreign camper van you have to watch out for.

You can normally load your bike straight onto the train at your **ferry port of disembarkation**, though you must first go to the ticket office of the station – don't just try to climb on the train with it. Eurostar allows you to take your bicycle within your normal baggage allowance, provided it's dismantled and stored in a special bike bag, whose flat dimensions don't exceed 120cm x 90cm. However, Eurostar can be awkward about this, insisting that it be brought to the station 24 hours beforehand. More likely, it will be sent on unaccompanied, with guaranteed arrival within 24 hours (register it up to 10 days in advance – book through Esprit Europe on ✆0870/850850); the fee is £20 each way. British Airways and Air France both take bikes free within the normal baggage weight allowance; Ryanair and other no-frills carriers are notoriously stingy in this respect. You may have to box them, you should definitely deflate the tyres, and arrange everything in writing beforehand with the airline – otherwise ground crew at check-in desks may try to charge you up to £60/$100.

The SNCF runs various schemes for cyclists, all detailed in the free leaflet *Guide du Train et du Vélo*, available from most train stations. Trains marked with a bicycle in the timetable are usually the only ones on which you can travel with an intact bike as free accompanied luggage in the luggage van. Otherwise, you have to send your bike bundled up as registered luggage for a fee of €34: two-day delivery is promised, though this service doesn't operate at weekends.

At most French train stations, **rental bikes** are also available. For around €11 per day, you can expect to get an averagely well-maintained Peugeot, and this can be returned to any other station (as long as you specify which when renting). The SNCF does not ask for a deposit, but does require a guarantee such as a credit-card number. For a bit more (up to €15/day), you can rent better bikes from campsites and *gîtes d'étape*, as well as from some tourist offices and specialist bike shops (which are more likely to have mountain bikes; see below). Most rental bikes are **not insured**, however, and you will be billed for replacement or repair if it's stolen or damaged; check whether your travel insurance policy covers this.

Lately more and more cyclists are using **mountain bikes** (VTT or *Vélos Touts Terrains* in French) for touring holidays. However, it's actually less strenuous, and much quicker, to cycle long distances on asphalt and carry luggage on a traditional touring or racing model.

Most sizeable foothill towns have well-stocked **retail** and **repair shops**, where parts are normally cheaper than in Britain or the US. However, with a foreign-made bike it's wise to carry spare tyres, as French sizes differ. It's still not that easy, either, to find parts for mountain bikes, with French enthusiasm mainly directed towards highly geared road-racers. Inner tubes are not a problem, as they adapt to either tyre size, though make sure you have the right valves.

## Spain

On the Spanish side, there are few trains into the central Pyrenees; rail services mainly connect the towns of the Atlantic and Mediterranean coasts. On shorter or less obvious routes buses tend to be quicker, and will also take you closer to your destination; some train stations are several kilometres from the town or village they serve, with no guarantee of a connecting bus. Car rental may also be worth considering, with costs among the lowest in Europe (if prearranged).

### Trains

RENFE, the Spanish rail company, operates a horrendously complicated variety of train services. Of the three main categories, the cheapest are *regionales*, equivalent to buses in speed and cost; *regional exprés* and *Delta trens* tend to cover longer distances. Most of the services in this guide are *regional exprés* or *Delta*, though *exprés* doesn't always mean speed, with the 150km from Barcelona to Puigcerdà taking three hours to cover. Slightly faster is the largo recorrido (long-distance) express, such as the Barcelona–Huesca line. On a few lines, buses are susbstituted for trains, as on the French side. To sort out conflicting or missing schedules, ring the centralized RENFE information and reservation number on ✆902 240 202 – though you'll need to speak Spanish – or look at ⓦwww.renfe.es (English version available).

RENFE offers a range of **fares**, discounted by 25–40 percent for those over 60, the disabled, children aged 4 to 11 years and groups of more than ten. Return fares are also discounted by ten percent on *regionales* (valid 15 days) and twenty percent on *largo recorridos* (valid 60 days) – you can buy a single, and so long as you show it when you buy the return, you'll still get the discount.

**Tickets** can be bought at stations between sixty days and fifteen minutes before the train leaves, from the *venta anticipada* window, or in the final two hours from the *venta inmediata* window. If you board the train without a ticket the conductor may charge you up to double the normal fare. Many of the stations on the three surviving mountain lines (Barcelona–Puigcerdà, Lleida–La Pobla de Segur, and Huesca–Canfranc) are no longer staffed or keep very limited hours; if you do get on these trains without a ticket it's always best to find the conductor first and explain, rather than wait to have them find you. Avoid such situations entirely by buying tickets beforehand at **travel agents** displaying the RENFE logo – they have a sophisticated computer system which can also make seat reservations, obligatory on *largo recorrido* trains; the cost is the same as at the station. You can **change** the departure date of an electronically issued, reserved-seat, *largo recorrido* ticket up to one hour before your originally scheduled departure, for a token charge. A full **cancellation** of the same type of ticket entails losing fifteen percent of the purchase price, provided it's done at least half an hour before scheduled departure.

**InterRail** (see p.17) and **Eurail** (p.16) passes are valid on all RENFE trains (though not on the Núria *cremallera*), but there's a supplement for travelling on the fastest trains. The apparently random nature of these **surcharges** – which seem to depend on the individual train guard – can be a source of considerable irritation. It's better to know what you're letting yourself in for by reserving a seat in advance, something you'll be obliged to do in any case on some trains. For a few euros you'll get a large, computer-printed ticket which will satisfy even the most unreasonable of guards.

European residents might alternatively consider purchasing a Spanish **Euro Domino pass** before setting out (see p.17), though you won't get much value from them travelling, say, between your arrival airport and a trek trailhead.

## Buses

**Buses** will probably meet most of your public transport needs; most small Pyrenean villages are accessible by services originating in the provincial or *comarcal* (county) capital. Service, especially in Catalunya, is generally reliable, with prices pretty standard at around €6 per 100 kilometres. All Pyrenean towns have a single main bus station; newer terminals are often on the fringes of town.

All buses are drastically reduced **on Sundays and holidays** – it's best not even to consider travelling to out-of-the-way places on these days. The Castilian words to look out for on timetables are *diario* (daily), *laborables* (workdays, including Saturday) and *domingos y festivos* (Sundays and holidays). On Catalan timetables, the equivalent expressions are *diari* (daily), *feiners* (workdays), *festius* (holidays), *dissabtes* (Saturdays) and *diumenges* (Sundays).

## Driving

The advantages and disadvantages of having a car on the Spanish side are as for France, though fuel prices are cheaper than in Britain or France, and vehicle crime is rampant – never leave anything of value visible in the car. Major river-valley roads are generally good, the mountain corniches more than serviceable, and traffic, while a little hectic in the cities, is moderately well behaved – though see the note on p.30 on Spanish and French accident rates.

All **EU driving licences** are honoured in Spain – but North American or Australasian drivers should get hold of an International Driving Permit (available in North America from the AAA or CAA), now an EU-required backup for non-European licences. Away from main roads you yield to vehicles approaching from the right, but at roundabouts (*rondadores*) you yield to those approaching from the left. **Speed limits** are posted – the maximum on urban roads is 50kph, other roads 90kph, motorways 120kph – and (on the main highways at least) speed traps are common, especially in the morning. If you're stopped for any violation, the Spanish police can and usually will levy a stiff **on-the-spot fine** before letting you go on your way, especially since as a foreigner you're unlikely to want, or be able, to appear in court. Motorcycle-borne *policía* or *Guardia Civil Tráfica* are also on the lookout for non-belt-wearers, though unlike in France you may get off with just a warning to buckle up. Parking laws are rigorously enforced in large towns, and any illegally parked vehicle will be removed promptly – with a sticker left on the road telling you where to pay the hefty fine (€90 and up) to retrieve it.

Spanish mechanics are most familiar with what the locals drive – small Fords, Renaults, Opels, Citroëns, Peugeots, Fiats/Seats – so with a larger or more unusual model you may have some problems should you **break down**.

**Fuel** currently costs about €0.87 per litre for Súper Sín Plomo 98, €0.88 for lead-replacement Súper 97, €0.80 for *Sin Plomo* (Lead-Free) 95, and €0.72 for diesel (*gasoleo*). In **Andorra**, the respective figures are €0.77, €0.80, €0.73 and €0.56 per litre. In villages off the main routes, you may not get the full range of choice. **Credit cards** are accepted at almost all stations on main highways. They are also taken at the motorway **toll** gates either side of Girona, though the amount is often trivial; stick the card in the reader and the bar opens. Otherwise you must have exact change for the coin slots, or go to the few attended gates. The **tolls** themselves add up – about €7 from Figueres to Barcelona airport – so these motorways are best avoided unless you're in a hurry.

## Vehicle rental

You'll find a limited choice of car rental companies in large towns, with the biggest ones like Hertz and Avis represented at Girona and Barcelona airports. You'll need to be 21 (and have been driving for at least a year), and you're looking at from €30 per day for a small car (much less by the week). As in France, Transhire (see p.31) is among the best of the British agencies, substantially undercutting the large companies – rates from Girona work out at £100–130 a week. Alternatively, check out the companies listed on p.31 for special discounts and promotions. If you have any choice in the matter, avoid the Seat Arosa – though easy to park, it has a dinky 800cc engine, a top speed of about 85km/hr, and scarcely room for two adults with luggage.

Renting **scooters and motorcycles** (from €18–24 per day, cheaper by the week) is also possible. You have to be 14 to ride a machine under 75cc, 18 for one over 75cc. Crash helmets are obligatory, though they're often of the "derby" type usually worn by cyclists in Britain. Scooters and motorcycles are often rented out with agency insurance that doesn't include theft – make sure your travel policy does.

## Cycling

Touring the Spanish Pyrenees by **bicycle** is a rewarding experience, though paradoxically the often superior state of the roads compared to the French side means nerve-wracking, higher-speed traffic. Cars tend to toot horns before they pass, which can be alarming at first but is useful once you're used to it. Always ride single file in any case – roads, while well surfaced, rarely have verges or multiple lanes. Remember also that even the foothills of the Pyrenees are horrifically steep – and torrid in summer, with none of the moderating mist of the French slopes.

That said, in the wake of Miguel Indurain's multiple Tour de France triumphs, the Spanish are keen cycling fans – which means that you'll be well received and find reasonable facilities. There are bike shops in the larger towns and parts can often be found at auto repair shops or garages – look for Michelin signs. Cycle-touring guides to most of the Pyrenees can be found in good bookshops – written in Spanish, Catalan or Euskera, of course.

Getting your bike there should present few problems. For transport by air, see pp.10,13 and 14. Spanish **trains** are also reasonably accessible, though bikes can only go on a train with a guard's van (*furgón*) and must be registered – go to the *Equipajes* or *Paquexpres* desk at the station. Most *hostales* can find somewhere safe for overnight storage.

# Accommodation

Finding a place to stay in the Pyrenees presents few problems, as long as you avoid the peak seasons. On both sides of the range, these are: Christmas and New Year, the February half-term week, Easter week, and mid-July to mid-August. Campsites are less of a problem in peak season, though drivers of caravans and camper-vans should book ahead.

## France

Almost every French Pyrenean town (excepting the notoriously pricey Basque coast) has at least one budget hotel, and a handful of more comfortable ones. Even during low season, reserving a room a couple of nights in advance can be reassuring; it saves trudging around and ensures that you know what you'll be paying. Full **accommodation lists** for each province are available from any French Government Tourist Office (see p.20) or from local tourist offices. It's worth getting hold of these, together with **Logis de France**'s (ⓦwww.logis-de-france.fr) handbook, which lists hotels, renowned for their consistently salubrious – if not always innovative – food and good-value rooms (each one is surveyed annually); they're recognizable on the spot by a green-and-yellow logo of a hearth.

### Hotels and chambres d'hôte

All French Pyrenean **hotels** are graded from zero to four stars. Prices more or less correspond to the number of stars, though the system is a little haphazard, having more to do with ratios of bathrooms-per-guest, and the presence or absence of lobbies, than with genuine quality; renovated single-star hotels are often very good. However, unless you patronize fairly expensive, modernized

hotels, you will have to contend with traditional French **pillows**, best described as sausages or long sacks of cement, often inextricably worked into the bedding; consider bringing your own small inflatable or orthopedic pillow. At the budget level, rooms with a shower cost more, though for those without, an extra charge of about €2–3 is often made each time you use the shower down the hall. A **taxe de séjour** of €0.20–0.60 per person per day, according to the star rating, may be added to the final bill.

**Breakfast**, too, can add €4–6 per person to a bill – though there is no obligation to take it and you will nearly always do better at a café. Officially it is illegal for hotels to insist on your taking **meals** – but they often do, and in busy resorts you may not find a room unless you agree to *demi-pension* (half-board). This can work in your favour, however, as *demi-pension* rates will often save you twenty percent of the cost of room and board taken separately. **Single rooms** (usually just smaller, and often less comfortable, doubles) are only marginally less expensive than more generously proportioned quarters, so sharing always slashes costs. Most hotels willingly provide rooms with extra beds, for three or more people, at good discounts.

Many Pyrenean hotels take a **month or so off** per year – usually sometime between

November and May, unless they're in a major skiing area. You may also find that their restaurant and reception close one night, plus one day, a week. We've given days and months of closure where known, but it's always best to phone ahead to check.

In country areas, in addition to standard hotels, you will come across **chambres d'hôte**, bed-and-breakfast accommodation in someone's house or farm. These vary in standard but are certainly affordable, falling mostly into the ❸ category; in some instances they are good sources of traditional home-cooking. Leaflets available in tourist offices list most of them.

## Hostels, gîtes d'étape and refuges

Bona fide *Auberges de Jeunesse* (**youth hostels**) are confined to the towns of Biarritz, Bayonne, Pau and Tarbes, and for groups of two or more won't be cheaper than a basic hotel. For single travellers, however, they are invaluable (at €9–15 per night for a dormitory bunk), and allow you to cut costs by preparing your own food in their kitchens, or eating in inexpensive canteens. Stays are usually limited to three consecutive nights, though you may be able to negotiate longer stays in off-peak times. To use them, you are supposed to be a member of the International Youth Hostel Federation, but you can often join on the spot.

Far more useful for budget travellers in the countryside is the **gîte d'étape**, especially popular in trekking or cycling areas. In the Pyrenees, *gîtes* are administered under the umbrella of the publishing and outdoors activities organization Randonnées Pyrénéennes, which was originally established to create a chain of medium-category hostelries for trekkers, cyclists and horse-riders. All *gîtes* must have self-catering kitchen facilities, some form of heating, a minimum of fifteen bunks in dormitories or private rooms (bedding provided only for the latter), laundry, shower and toilet facilities; they may or may not be open year-round. Hot evening meals are often provided, and basic re-provisioning might be possible. A bunk will be €8–13, a meal will rarely cost more than €12.50, and doubles where available gener-

ally fall in category ❶ or the lower half of ❷. Description of a *gîte* as a **Rando'Plume** means either that rooms are of extraordinarily high standard – typically with some en-suite facilities, and a low number of bunks per dorm, with proper linen – and/or that the *gîte* is affiliated to some upmarket activity centre in the area (a trekking or winter sports outfitter, horse-riding, parapente, etc), whose devotees make up the main clientele.

Although *gîtes* must give priority to long-distance travellers on a traverse, it is sometimes possible to use one as a base for several nights; if you do this, the manager will almost certainly be able to share an intimate knowledge of the region. Rando Éditions walkers' maps show the location of gîtes, and they are noted in the individual GR *topo-guides*.

Most **mountain refuge huts** are open only in summer (June–Sept), though in winter there is nearly always at least a simple annexe with sleeping platforms and perhaps a fireplace or stove. A few refuges are still extremely basic and antiquated, while most others are passably comfortable and modern – with hot showers in some cases. Almost all of them have cooking facilities and offer meals, though these are often not the best value (€9–14 with the emphasis on wine and carbohydrates), the price reflecting the fact that foodstuffs usually have to be brought in by mule or helicopter. Especially in or around the Parc National des Pyrénées, refuges are often packed to the seams in summer, and there have been reports of trekkers having to sleep on and under tables – for the normal fee. Costs range from €10 to €13 per night, half-price if you're a member of a climbing organization affiliated to the Club Alpin Français; either a membership card or your passport will be held as security against payment. A few refuges are affiliated not with the CAF but with CIMES (Centre d'information Montagne et Sentiers; ⓦwww.cimes-pyrenees.net).

Rando Éditions publishes a complete guide, *Gîtes d'étape et Refuges*, available in French bookshops for €18.30 or online at ⓦwww.gites-refuges.com. Failing this, look for the free folding pamphlet, available in many Pyrenean tourist offices, detailing the 150-odd certified *gîtes d'étape* and CIMES refuges in the Pyrenees and foothills.

## Accommodation price codes

All the accommodation establishments listed in this book, on both sides of the Pyrenees, have been price-graded according to the following scale. Spanish prices include seven-percent IVA (VAT) where applied. Youth hostels, mountain refuges, *albergues* and *gîtes d'étape*, all in the range of €7–15 per person, fall outside this scheme. Categories indicate the cheapest available double room in each hotel during high season. Remember, though, that many of the budget places will also have more expensive rooms including en-suite facilities, and that in France the cheaper rooms are often the first to fill. B&B and HB denote, respectively, when the price includes breakfast, and when it includes half-board. Mountain refuges and the bare handful of hostels have exact per-person prices given where known; otherwise they rarely exceed €13. In the case of apartments intended for 4–6 persons, the actual prices are given.

In Spain, rooms in the ❶ band correspond to the most basic pensiones without private bath, as well as the older non-en-suite *turismos rurales*; there will, however, often be a washbasin in the room, along with the minimum of furniture besides a decently firm bed. In France, ❶ means the most basic hotel rooms, which may be unmodernized: exposed wiring, saggy beds, interwar wallpaper, musty carpets, and – enthroned in one corner – a so-called *cabinet de toilette*, a sink side by side with a bidet. In Spain, ❷ rooms, whether in a *hostal* or a better class of *turismo rural*, will be bigger and probably have a private bathroom, with a so-called *medio baño* or very short bathtub meant to be used primarily as a shower; there will also be a modicum of extra furniture, possibly a balcony, maybe a telephone. In France, ❷ will almost certainly have a partitioned area – possibly even a proper separate room – with a sink, shower and bidet, but the toilet may still be down the hall. Spanish ❸ and ❹ rooms will be impeccably furnished, with telephones, full bathtubs, TV, built-in closets, and heating plus double glazing; at ❹, on-site restaurants (as opposed to just breakfast provision) are pretty certain, while sizeable common areas and swimming pools make their appearance. Spanish ❺ will get you all these goodies, plus swish accoutrements like spot lighting, parquet floors, original artwork, designer fixtures and maybe key-cards to work the electric switch. At French ❸, full en-suite facilities with a toilet are just about guaranteed, as are sizeable gardens and common areas, but you won't see bathtubs – or proper pillows, as opposed to the dreaded "cement sacks" (see p.35) – until ❹, which should also give such benefits as swimming pools and off-street parking, and sometimes a building of outstanding architectural interest. In category ❺, French facilities will be completely modernized – possibly a bit bland and sterile – while ❻ in both countries, away from the coast at least, guarantees most creature comforts and distractions. You don't get much extra for your money once beyond ❼'s lower limits, and except for a few unusual spots in the Central Pyrenees, or famously pricey San Sebastián, this book does not include many such.

❶ Up to €25
❷ €26–40
❸ €41–55
❹ €56–70
❺ €71–85
❻ €86–100
❼ Over €100

### Camping

Practically every village and town in the Pyrenees has at least one **campsite** to cater for the thousands of French people who spend their holiday under canvas – or in a caravan. The cheapest – at €4–6 per person per night – is usually the **camping municipal**, run by the local municipality. When officially open, they are always clean, and often situated in prime locations, though hot water can be unreliable. Out of season, many managers don't even bother to collect the overnight charge.

On the coast especially, there are **superior categories** of campsite, where you'll pay prices similar to those of a *gîte d'étape* or hostel for the facilities: bars, restaurants, sometimes swimming pools. These have rather more status than the *campings municipals*, with people often spending a whole holiday in one place. If you plan to do the same, and particularly if you have a caravan or camper, or a substantial tent, it's wise to reserve in advance. Count on €7 a head all-in with a tent, €9 with a camper van.

Inland, **camping à la ferme** – on somebody's farm – is another possibility, though facilities often leave much to be desired. Lists of sites are available from local tourist boards.

Throughout the guide we've given exact **opening months** for campsites (often May to September); where no opening months are shown, the campsite is (theoretically) open all year round.

Lastly, a **word of caution**: never camp rough (*camping sauvage*, as the French call it) on anyone's land without first asking permission. If the dogs don't get you, guns might – farmers have been known to shoot before asking any questions. In many parts of the Pyrenees *camping sauvage* on public land – including the beaches – is not tolerated, or is subject (as in the Parc National des Pyrénées) to severe restrictions.

## Spain

*Do you remember an Inn, Miranda?*
*Do you remember an Inn?*
*And the tedding and the bedding*
*Of the straw for a bedding,*
*And the fleas that tease in the High Pyrenees,*
*And the wine that tasted of tar?*

The quality of Spanish Pyrenean lodging (and wine, see p.47) has improved immeasurably since Hilaire Belloc penned this ditty in the early 1900s. Salubrious, reasonably priced rooms are the norm in the Spanish Pyrenees, and in almost any inland town you'll be able to find a double in the ❷ category. Only in major coastal resorts, particularly in San Sebastián or some of the Costa Brava ports, will you have to pay more. Festivals tend to result more in accommodation filling quickly rather than outrageous rate hikes.

In Spain you don't tend to pay a premium for a central location, though you do get a comparatively bad deal if travelling on your own. There are relatively few bona fide **single rooms**, and you will often get charged sixty to seventy percent of the double rate. In Catalunya particularly, **half-board** is often encouraged or obligatory, and usually very good value.

There's little scope for **bargaining** in high season, when peak prices are adhered to; during the rest of the year, official rates (always posted in the entry hall) may be half to two-thirds as much. Most places have triples or quads at not much more than the double-room price – a good deal, especially if you are travelling with children. Remember always to establish whether quoted rates include seven-percent **IVA** (Value Added Tax) or not; usually they don't, but proprietors may waive it as a small concession.

### Fondas, pensiones, hostales and hoteles

The least expensive category of place to stay, just about extinct in the Pyrenees, is a **fonda** (identifiable by a square blue sign with a white "F" on it, and often above a bar or restaurant), closely followed up the price scale by **pensiones** (*pensió* in Catalan singular; "P"). Since the 1990s, most surviving *fondas*, even if they keep the name, have been reclassified as one- or two-star pensiones; the original meaning of *fonda* (from the Arabic *funduq*), now being reverted to, is a roadside taverna in an isolated area (not offering beds). *Pensiones* usually serve food, and an increasing number may offer rooms only on a half-board basis.

Slightly more expensive are **hostales** (*hostals* in Catalan; marked "Hs") and **hostal-residencias** ("HsR"). These are categorized from one to three stars, but prices vary enormously according to location and facilities – a place in a slightly down-at-heel medieval quarter with no car-parking facilities is bound to cost less than new premises on a suburban street or the town's access road. Most *hostales* offer good, if functional rooms, often with private shower, and, for doubles at least, can be excellent value. The *residencia* designation means that no meals other than perhaps breakfast are served. Faced, however, with competition from *turismo rural* (see below), many town-centre *hostales* in the budget range, perceived as poor value in comparison, have folded since the 1990s.

Moving up the scale you finally reach fully-fledged **hoteles** ("H"), again star-graded (from one to five) by the authorities. One-star hotels cost no more than three-star *hostales* – sometimes they're actually less expensive, and remain officially graded as *hostales* – but at three stars you pay a lot more, and at four or five you're in luxury facilities with prices to match. Near the top end of this scale there are also state-run **paradores**: occasionally beautiful places converted from castles, monasteries and other minor Spanish monuments (though the few purpose-built ones are hideous). Even if you can't afford to stay, the older buildings are often worth a look, and usually have pleasant bars. People over 65 may find that they can in fact afford them; most *paradores* are discounted thirty percent to OAPs except on peak days.

Outside all these categories you will sometimes find **habitaciones** (rooms; *habitacions* in Catalan) advertised in private houses or above bars. If you're on a very tight budget these can be worth seeking out – particularly if you're offered one at a bus station and the owner is prepared to bargain. In Catalunya, look for signs reading *dormir i esmorzar* (bed and breakfast) or *dormir i menjar* (beds and meals).

The approximate equivalent of the Logis de France scheme in Spain is the Catalunya-based **Casa Fonda** (Ⓦwww.casafonda .com), a fifty-strong chain of *fondas*, *hostals* and hotels. At these you're guaranteed certain standards, specifically hands-on management, up-to-date lodging and an often excellent *menjador*.

## Turismo rural

Each of the autonomous communities featured in this book – Catalunya, Aragón,

Navarra and Gipuzkoa – give official support to "**agroturismo**" programmes, akin to French *chambres d'hôte*, but by no means equivalent. *Turismos rurales*, as they're better known, are either a private residence where extra rooms are rented out; self-contained, self-catering flats or cottages; or, at their best, a bed-and-breakfast or half-board-basis inn occupying a medieval farmhouse. They have gone from strength to strength in Spain since the early 1990s, booked months in advance for peak times. The fad for them – especially among big-city yuppies – shows no sign of abating, and deservedly so: top-drawer *turismos rurales* comprise some of the best accommodation the Spanish Pyrenees have to offer. A few are still working cattle- or pig-farms, with all the barnyard smell and noise that entails.

In Catalunya they are termed *cases de pagès*, or belong to the Girona province *turisme rural* scheme. In Aragón and Navarra they're variously called *casas de payés*, *casas rurales*, *viviendas de turismo rural*, or *landa etxeak*, while in Gipuzkoa they are identified by a rectangular green sign with white lettering, or a sun-and-sea-scape in a circular plaque with the word *nekazalturismoa*. Each autonomous region publishes comprehensive guide-booklets or lists to all their *agroturismo* outfits, available from the better-stocked tourist offices. To have been included in this guide, they satisfy certain criteria: they are attended most of the year (too many proprietors just throw up an unstaffed modern villa, call it an *agroturismo*, and post the keys to advert-answerers); possess some architectural merit; are near points of interest or along a major trail; welcome walk-in, short-term trade; and offer breakfast if not half-board, providing regional and/or vegetarian specialities.

## Albergues, refuges and pilgrim accommodation

Spanish **albergues juveniles** (youth hostels) are only really useful to solo, short-term travellers who may not find any other kind of vacancy during the Pyrenean summer; local ones are detailed in the guide. Most hostels have curfews, are often block-reserved by school groups for weeks on end, and demand production of a YHF membership card. At €8–11 per bunk, you can easily pay nearly as much as for sharing an inexpensive double room in a *casa rural* or one-star *pensión*.

There are, however, a number of privately run, similarly priced but less institutional **albergues** conforming to the notion of a French *gîte d'étape*, strategically sited in select mountain villages. These are often aimed more specifically at trekkers or those pursuing a particular local activity (skiing, canyoning, etc).

Additionally, in the high Pyrenees the **Federación Aragonesa de Montañismo**, the Federación Navarra de Montaña, plus three Catalunyan clubs – the FEEC, the CEC and the UEC – and a handful of private individuals all run a number of **refugios** (refuges; *refugis* in Catalan). Like their French counterparts, these are simple, inexpensive dormitory huts for climbers and trekkers, generally equipped with bunk-beds, a common room and cooking space (except in the CEC huts where self-catering is forbidden). Toilets are sometimes outside, and (hot) showers are occasionally available. As in France, some sort of emergency adjacent shelter is occasionally open all year, and the most popular refuges are generally staffed from mid-June to late September, plus selected weekends and holiday weeks (Christmas, Easter) during the snowy months.

As on the French side, quite a number of older Spanish *refugios* have been renovated and/or enlarged since 1990, often with little regard for the immediate environment. Critics of the trend note that many such new facilities resemble roadhouses rather than alpine huts, and just encourage what's disparagingly called **dominguismo** in Castilian – "Sunday-tripping" by those with little true knowledge of, or affection for, the mountains. At the same time, many smaller, unstaffed huts in strategic high-altitude locales go to rack and ruin for lack of maintenance.

The cost of **accommodation** in the staffed refuges is €8–11.15, unless you're a member of a reciprocally recognized alpine club, in which case you'll get half off at club-affiliated refuges. At a typical cost of €12–14, **meals** have improved in quality since the

early 1990s, and now always consist of at least three courses – soup and/or salad, a meat dish, dessert or fruit, and wine.

Pilgrims following the **Camino de Santiago** can take advantage of basic, dorm-style accommodation specifically reserved for pilgrims along the route; the best places, often attached to medieval churches, are detailed in the text.

*Albergues* aside, if you have any **problems** with Spanish rooms – overcharging, most obviously – you can usually encourage an immediate resolution by asking for an *hoja de reclamaciones* (complaints sheet). By law all establishments must stock these in a prominent place and provide them on demand to an unhappy customer. Once it's filled out (neatly, in English, is acceptable), you send it off to the government of the province or autonomous region.

## Camping

There are scores of authorized **campsites** in the Spanish Pyrenees, including coastal areas. If you plan to camp extensively, the *Guía de Campings* (€6.50), listing full prices, facilities and exact locations, is available at most Spanish bookshops. In peak season, sites charge €4–5 per person on the coast, €2.50–3.50 up in the hills, plus as much again for a tent and a similar amount for car or caravan.

However, mountain trekkers will find the majority of Pyrenean sites biased towards use by **caravans**, and equipped with amenities (electric power hookup, sewage purge tanks, etc) that they don't really need or want. Many sites, even some newer ones, are squalid, shadeless and packed out at peak times. Tent-friendly and attractive deviations from this norm are singled out in the text. Also of potential interest for trekkers are the various **áreas de acampada libre** or "free camping zones" dotted about the Catalan and Aragonese Pyrenees. Some of them are not "free", levying a token charge, but all are fairly basic, at or below the level of the most modest *camping à la ferme* or *camping municipal* in France. But you do always get toilets and cold running water, possibly picnic furniture and a tiny drinks bar. Throughout the guide we've given exact opening months for campsites (often May to September); where no **opening months** are shown, the campsite is (theoretically) open all year round.

**Camping outside campsites** is legal – with certain restrictions. There must be fewer than ten in your group, and you're not allowed to camp in urban areas, areas prohibited for military or touristic reasons, or within 1km of an official campsite. In practice this means that you can't camp on developed beaches (though you can, discreetly, nearby), but with a little sensitivity you can set up a tent for a short period almost anywhere in the mountains. (Notable exceptions are the Ordesa/Monte Perdido, Posets-Maladeta and Aigüestortes national/natural parks, where camping is prohibited outside designated areas.) Whenever possible ask locally first.

# Eating and drinking

Not surprisingly, the best Pyrenean restaurant food is based on what's available locally, which means a preponderance of river (sometimes farmed) trout, salmon, fresh chestnuts, wild mushrooms or berries, goat meat, and game such as wild boar, rabbit and pigeon. In the mountains, ordinary restaurants often rely on a small fixed menu, with little in the way of à la carte dishes, though special requests for vegetarian meals should produce some response. French and Spanish menu readers are given in "Language" on pp.611 and 623.

## France

Mountain restaurants within easy reach of major centres are often popular and consequently expensive, but elsewhere most restaurants are low-key, informal and reasonably priced. Go wherever the largest numbers of locals go – the favourites will be particularly easy to locate on a Sunday lunchtime, when whole families turn out for the weekly get-together. Except in the foothill towns, which often have at least one Chinese/Vietnamese and Moroccan eatery apiece, you'll find little in the way of non-European food.

### Breakfast, snacks and picnics

A croissant, *pain au chocolat* or a sandwich in a bar or café, with a hot chocolate or coffee, is generally the best way to eat **breakfast** – at a fraction of the price charged by most hotels, where for €4.50 and up you'll usually just get a pile of stale if toasted bread and foil-sealed jam, plus a pot of tea or coffee. *Brasseries* (see below) are also possibilities for coffee and a quick bite. If you're standing at the counter (cheaper than sitting down), you may see a basket of croissants or some hard-boiled eggs (usually gone by 9.30 or 10am). Help yourself – the waiter will keep an eye on how many you've eaten and bill you accordingly.

At **midday** you may find cafés offering a *plat du jour* (chef's daily special) for €5–12, or *formules*, a limited or no-choice menu. *Croque-Monsieurs* or *Croque-Madames* (variations on the grilled-cheese sandwich) are on sale at cafés, brasseries and street stalls, along with *frites*, *crêpes*, *gaufres* (waffles), *glaces* (ice creams) and assorted sandwiches.

**Crêpes** or filled pancakes are particularly

popular for light meals, but at €2.50–6.50 each aren't the best value as you need two (or three) to fill up. The more expensive savoury buckwheat variety (*galettes*) are served as a main course, the sweet light-flour ones for dessert. Pizzerias, often *au feu du bois* (wood-fired oven), are also common and somewhat better value at €8.50–12.50, though quality varies.

For **picnics**, the local *halle* (covered produce market) or supermarket will provide anything you want in the way of cheese, pâté and salad ingredients. For more elaborate **takeaway food**, there's nothing to beat the *charcuteries* (delicatessens) which you'll find everywhere, even in small villages. Such shops sell meat dishes (mostly pork-based), salads and fully prepared main courses; these are also available less expensively at supermarket *charcuterie* counters. You buy by weight, or ask for *une tranche* (a slice), *une barquette* (a carton), or *une part* (a portion). *Boulangeries* or **bakeries** often sell not just bread but an array of baked snacks with meat or cheese in them, such as quiche, eminently suitable for a lunch on the hoof.

## Full meals and restaurants

In the Pyrenees, the main eateries are restaurants, also known as *auberges* or *relais*, with **brasseries** being comparatively rare. The few brasseries there are will serve quicker meals at most hours of the day, while **restaurants** tend to stick to the traditional meal times of noon–2pm (or 2.30pm in the larger towns) and 7–9pm (10pm in towns). After 9pm or so, restaurants may serve only à la carte meals – invariably more expensive than the set menu (*menu* in French). **Serving hours** can be extremely inflexible, to the sorrow of many unsuspecting visitors; even if a place is still packed at its 10pm closing time, you won't be seated or served if you arrive at 10.01, or at 9.50 for that matter. Even if you're staying in a particular hotel-restaurant, they will be loath to reopen their kitchen, and will demand to know from 6pm onwards whether you're planning to dine there that night. To be on the safe side, assume that you're guaranteed a meal only between 12.15–1.30pm and 8.15–9pm, though we make a point of

highlighting establishments whose kitchen functions later than usual. In small towns it will be impossible to get anything other than a bar sandwich after 9.30pm; in major cities or busy resorts like Biarritz, town-centre brasseries will serve until 11pm or midnight and one or two may stay open all night.

For the more upmarket places it's wise to make reservations – easily done on the same day. Don't forget that hotel restaurants are open to non-residents, and often very good value; in many small Pyrenean villages, the sole hotel may also have the only restaurant. As noted under "Accommodation" (p.35), Logis de France establishments are always safe and salubrious, if somewhat bland in the menu. Otherwise, avoid places that are half-full at peak time and be suspicious of overlong menus (whose ingredients will rarely be fresh); asking locals will usually elicit strong views and sound advice.

**Prices** and menus are almost always posted outside. Normally there is a choice between one to four **menus** – with a set number of courses and limited choices within those. At the bottom of the price range, *menus* revolve around standard dishes such as steak (*steak*) and chicken (*poulet*) served with fried potatoes (*frites*), or various concoctions involving innards. Look for the *plat du jour*, which may be a regional dish and more appealing. Increasingly, however, restaurants are offering a range of menus, the more expensive of which allow wider choice, and run to four or five courses. For €19 and up, you should expect an array of regional dishes, or *haute cuisine* dining. Weekend or evening menus are always pricier than mid-week lunch ones.

Going **à la carte** is always more expensive, but does offer greater flexibility and, in the better restaurants, unlimited access to the chef's specialities. A perfectly legitimate tactic is to have just two courses instead of the expected three or four. You can share dishes or just have several starters – a useful strategy for vegetarians; there's rarely a minimum charge.

In the French **sequence of courses**, any salad – sometimes vegetables, too – arrives separately from the main dish, and cheese precedes – or is the alternative to – dessert. You will be offered coffee, which always costs extra, to finish off the meal. The waiter/waitress will approach with the words *Ça-y-était*? to take finished plates away, which inevitably throws some people as the expression isn't in most phrasebooks. Incidentally, you address staff as *monsieur* or *madame* (or *mademoiselle* if a young woman), never by the school-French *garçon*.

On menus or bills, *TTC* means that all local taxes and sales tax (IVA) are included; *service compris* or *s.c.* means the service charge is included (less common). *Service non compris*, *s.n.c.* or *servis en sus* means that it isn't and you need to allow for an additional fifteen percent. Wine (*vin* – see below for more) or a drink (*boisson*) may be included, though rarely on menus under €23.

The French are well-disposed towards **children** in restaurants, not just in the ubiquitous offering of cut-price *menu enfants*, but by fostering an atmosphere – even in otherwise fairly snooty establishments – that positively welcomes kids. It is regarded as self-evident that large family groups should be able to eat together. More difficult to accept may be the idea of **dogs** in the dining room, considered quite normal (though more and more places have signs up forbidding the practice). The French are absolutely besotted with their pooches, and it may come as a shock to realize that a significant number of your fellow diners are concealing pets under the table.

## Vegetarians and vegans

Vegetarians should expect a somewhat lean time in the French Pyrenees. The magic words are *je suis végétarien(ne)*; *est-ce qu'il y a des plats sans viande ou poisson?* (I'm a vegetarian; are there any dishes without meat or fish?). *Crêperies* and pizzerias can be good standbys; elsewhere you'll have to hope for a sympathetic proprietor willing to replace a meat dish on a *menu* with an omelette. Vegans should probably forget altogether about eating in French restaurants and resort to self-catering.

## Alcoholic drinks

Where you can eat you can invariably drink, and to some extent the reverse applies. **Drinking** is done at a leisurely pace whether as a prelude to food (*apéritif*), a sequel (*digestif*), or accompanying a meal, and **cafés** are the standard places to do it. Every bar or café has to display its full price list (usually without a fifteen-percent service charge added), with the cheapest drinks at the bar (*au comptoir*), increasing progressively for sitting at a table inside (*la salle*), or on the terrace (*la terrasse*). You pay when you leave, and it's quite acceptable to sit for an hour over one cup of a coffee.

**Wine** (*vin*) is drunk at just about every meal or social occasion. Red is *rouge*, white *blanc*, or there's *rosé*. *Vin de pays* or *vin ordinaire* – house wine – is generally drinkable and always cheap; it may be disguised, bottled and marked up as the house *cuvée*. In wine-producing areas the local *vin de pays* can be very good indeed. In bars you normally buy wine by the glass – just ask for *un rouge* or *un blanc* – though in restaurants you generally order *un quart* or *un pichet* (250ml), *un demi-litre* (half a litre) or *une carafe* (a litre jug). The basic terms are *brut*, very dry; *sec*, dry; *demi-sec*, sweet; *doux*, very sweet; *mousseux* or *pétillant*, sparkling; *méthode champenoise*, mature and sparkling.

A.O.C. (*Appellation d'Origine Contrôlée*) wines are another matter. They can be excellent value at the lower end of the quality scale, where lenient French taxes keep prices down to €3–5 a bottle, but move up and you're soon paying serious prices; restaurant mark-ups of A.O.C. wines can be well over 100 percent. Popular Pyrenean A.O.C. wines include red, white and rosé Côtes-de-Saint-Mont from north of Tarbes; the ubiquitous but palatable Buzet (red and rosé); and Bi Dou Rey, an excellent sparkling rosé from Béarn. From the central Pyrenees is the more specialist Madiran, a high-tannin, full-bodied red used also in cooking; from the environs of Pau comes Jurançon, a dry, almost vinegary white, also used at the stove. Irouléguy, from the *domaine* of the namesake village in the Pays Basque, is excellent, and available as rosé, a rather tannin-y red and white. At the opposite end of the range, Banyuls is found in both Spain and France near the namesake town, as either a dry or sweet dessert wine.

Alsatian brands such as Kanterbrau, Karlsbrau, Kronenbourg and Gold (small bottles, strongest at 6.1 percent) account for virtually all of the **beer** served in the Pyrenees; there's also the refreshing, tequila-flavoured Desperados (5.9 percent). Draught (*à la pression*) is the cheapest drink you can have next to coffee and wine – although the smallest glass, *un demi* (330ml) rarely costs less than €2. **Cider** (*cidre*) is fairly common in the Pyrenees, as *brut* or *doux* – six percent is the usual strength.

Stronger alcohol is consumed from as early as 5am as a pre-work fortifier, and right through the day according to inclination. *Pastis*, the generic term for aniseed-flavoured drink such as Pernod or Ricard, is served diluted with water and ice (*glaçons*) – very refreshing and not expensive. **Cognac** or **Armagnac** brandies and the dozens of *eaux de vie* (brandies distilled from fruit) are **digestifs**. **Liqueurs**, heavily flavoured with *ginepi*, assorted wild berries or chataigne, are popular aperitifs, as are *pineau*, cognac and grape juice, and *kir*, dry white wine with a dash of blackcurrant syrup, or with champagne for a *kir royal*. In the centre and west of the Pyrenees, **sweet dessert** wines such as Murançon are popular. A Pay Basque speciality is the green or yellow **Izarra** liqueurs, strong and bitterly herbal. Measures are generous, but they don't come cheap; the same applies for imported **spirits** like whisky.

### Water, soft drinks and hot drinks

In cafés bottled (sweetened) nectars such as apricot (*jus d'abricot*) and blackcurrant (*cassis*) still prevail, but you can buy unsweetened **fruit juice** in supermarkets; the best, heavily promoted brand, with 30–40 percent fruit pulp in assorted flavours, is Pago. You can also get fresh orange and lemon juice (*orange/citron pressé*) at a price; otherwise it's just the standard fizzy canned stuff, such as Rio (based on blood-orange juice), or Fun Tea, essentially Lipton's peach- or lemon-flavoured iced tea. Rather better are **sirops** – concentrated pure-fruit essences dissolved in **water**, served at many mountain

refuges and cafés. Bottles of mineral water (*eau minérale*) and spring water (*eau de source*) – either sparkling (*gazeuse*) or still (*plate*) – abound, but there's usually nothing wrong with tap water (*l'eau du robinet*).

**Coffee** is usually espresso in small cups, very strong. *Un café* or *un express* is black; *un crème* is with milk; *un grand café crème* or *un grand crème* is a large cup of milky coffee. In the morning you can also ask for *un café au lait* – espresso in a large cup or bowl filled up with hot milk. *Un déca* is decaf, widely available but only as powdered in a sachet. Ordinary tea (*thé*) is Lipton's ninety percent of the time; to have it served with milk, ask for *un peu de lait frais* (some fresh milk).

The most common varieties of **herbal teas** (infusions or tisanes) are *verveine* (verbena), *tilleul* (linden blossom), *menthe* (mint) and *camomille* (camomile). Unlike tea, *chocolat chaud* – hot chocolate – lives up to the high standards of French food and drink and can be had in any café.

## Spain

There are two ways to eat out in Spain: you can go to a *restaurante* or *comedor* (dining room; *menjador* in Catalunya) and have a full meal, or you can have a succession of *tapas* (small snacks) or *raciones* (larger ones) at one or more bars. Bars tend to work out pricier but are sometimes more interesting, allowing you to do the rounds and sample different local or house specialities.

### Breakfast, snacks and sandwiches

For **breakfast** you're best off in a bar or café, though *hostales* and *pensiones* will serve the "Continental" basics. Especially at hotels in Catalunya, you may be offered the choice of a heartier **savoury breakfast** (*esmorzar de forquilla* in Catalan, *desayuno salado* in Castilian) – instead of coffee and pastry, you'll be given a spread of ham, salami, cheese and wine, sometimes with omelettes and sausages too, at roughly the same price.

Another typical Catalan snack or breakfast dish is **pa amb tomaquet**, "bread with tomato" – the ingredients, including garlic cloves, are supplied for you to make it yourself. Cut the garlic cloves crossways (not lengthwise) and rub the exposed surface furiously into the bread slices; then halve the preferably mushy tomatoes, and mash this next onto the surface. You're not expected to eat the bruised remains of the vegetables.

The traditional Spanish breakfast is *chocolate con churros* – greasy, tubular doughnuts (not for the weak of stomach) dunked in thick drinking chocolate. But most places also serve *tostadas* (toast) with oil (*con aceite*) or butter and jam (*con mantequilla y mermelada*), or more substantial dishes such as fried eggs (*huevos fritos*). *Tortilla* (potato omelette) also makes an excellent breakfast, perhaps along with *magdalenas* (little cupcakes).

Coffee and pastries or rolls (*pasteles* or *bollos*) are available at most cafés, too, though for a wider selection of cakes you should head for one of the many excellent *pastelerías*. In larger towns, especially in Catalunya, there will often be *a panadería* or *croissantería* serving quite an array of appetizing (and healthier, whole-grain) baked goods besides the obvious bread, croissants and pizza.

Most bars offer **sandwiches** (*bocadillos*), usually outsize affairs in French bread which will do for breakfast or a light lunch. If you want them wrapped to take away, ask for them *para llevar*. Incidentally, don't ask for a sandwich – in Spain this means a toasted cheese and ham *sandwich*, usually on rather limp processed bread slathered with mayonnaise.

## Tapas

One advantage of eating in **bars** is that you can experiment. Many places have food laid out on the counter, so you can see what's available and order by pointing without necessarily knowing the names; others have blackboards (see the lists in "Language" on p.624). **Tapas** (**pinchos** or **pintxos** in the Basque Country) are small platters – three or four small chunks of fish or meat, or a dollop of salad – that traditionally used to be served free with a drink. These days you have to pay for anything more than a few olives, but a single helping rarely costs more than €3.50 unless you're somewhere very flash.

In much of the Pyrenees, alas, *tapas* more often than not consist of just a cube of cheese or some tinned shellfish – there simply isn't the same choice as further south, or on the coast.

**Raciones**, literally "portions" (€5–8), are simply bigger plates of the same, intended for sharing among a few people, and can be enough in themselves for a light meal. The bigger the group you are the better; half a dozen *tapas* or *pinchos* and three *raciones* can make a varied and quite filling meal for three or four diners.

**Tascas**, **bodegas**, and **cervecerías** are all types of bar where you'll find *tapas* and *raciones*. Most of them have different sets of prices depending on whether you stand at the bar to eat (the basic charge) or sit at tables (up to fifty percent more expensive – and even more if you sit out on a terrace).

Wherever you have *tapas*, it is important to find out what the local "**special**" is. Spaniards will commonly move from bar to bar, having just the one dish that they consider each bar does best. A bar's "non-standard" dishes can all too often be microwaved – not a good way to reheat fried squid.

## Full meals and restaurants

For a full meal, **comedores** (or **menjadors** in Catalunya) are the places to seek out if your main criteria are price and quantity. In the Pyrenees you will see them attached to a bar (often in a room behind), or more likely as the dining room of a *pensión* or *hostal*. You'll pay €8–13 for a **menú del día**, a complete meal of several courses, usually with house wine; many *pensiones* and *hostales* offer only this, and no **a la carta**. At the upper end of this price range, you should expect four courses – a salad, then usually a soup, a main course and a dessert, and unlimited access to a soup tureen and wine bottle. You'll be gently pushed to take coffee after the *postre* or dessert, and it will almost always be charged extra.

Incidentally, the *comedores* of the **fancier hostales** share only the name with their humbler cousins; they can be very upmarket indeed, with table linen, uniformed waiting staff and fare – and bills – to match.

Incidentally, off the beaten tourist track, menus **in Catalunya** are often in Catalan only – thus the translation list on p.626.

Only in the largest Pyrenean towns such as San Sebastián (Donostia), Huesca or Olot will you find **cafeterías** or snack bars. These can be good value, especially the self-service places, but their emphasis is more on rather dull northern European fare. Food here often comes as a **plato combinado** – literally "combined plate", *plats combinats* in Catalan – which will be something like egg and chips or calamares and salad (or maybe a weird combination like steak and a piece of fish), often with bread and a drink included. This will cost in the region of €4.50–7 per plato; *cafeterías* often serve some kind of *menú del día* as well. You may prefer to get your *plato combinado* at a bar, which in small towns with no *comedores* may be the only way to eat inexpensively.

Moving up the scale, there are **restaurantes** and (in San Sebastián) **marisquerías**, the latter specializing in fish and seafood. The humbler *restaurantes* are often not much different in price and style to *comedores*, and may also have *platos combinados* available. A *menú del día* or *menú de la casa* (which means the same thing) is often better value, though: three courses plus wine and bread for €9–18. Patronize a flash restaurant, or one of the fancier *marisquerías* (as opposed to a basic seafront fish-fry place), and prices escalate rapidly.

To avoid confusion, always ask for **la carta** when you want a menu; *menú* is short for the fixed-priced *menú del día*. In all but the most rock-bottom establishments it is customary to leave a small **tip** if service merits it; the amount is up to you, though ten percent of the bill is quite sufficient. Service is normally included in a *menú del día*. The other thing to take account of in mid-range and top-end restaurants is the addition of IVA, a seven-percent sales tax on your bill. It should say on the menu (thus, *IVA no incluido*; in Catalan, *IVA no inclòs*) if you have to pay this. *Menús* sometimes include this; *a la carta* meals never do.

Spaniards **eat very late** by Anglo-Saxon or French standards, so many places serve food from around 1 until 4pm and from 8 to 11.30pm. However, stricter labour laws and the phasing out of exclusively family-staffed businesses mean that 1–3.15pm and 8.30–10.30pm are now more realistic schedules, with 3pm and 10pm last orders not uncommon. **Andorra** is more French in its dining habits than Spanish; you'll have trouble finding lunch after 2.30pm or supper after 9.30pm, and hotel breakfast is served at 8am, not 9am as in Spain. Many restaurants close on Sunday evening and Monday all day.

## What to eat

If you like **fish and seafood**, you'll be in heaven in Spain, since this forms the basis of a vast variety of *tapas* and proves fresh and excellent even hundreds of kilometres from the sea. It's not cheap, though, so rarely forms part of the lowest priced *menús* (though you may get the most common fish: cod, hake or squid) but do make the most of what's on offer. Fish stews (*zarzuelas*) and rice-based *paellas* (which also contain meat, usually rabbit or chicken) are often memorable. Paella comes originally from Valencia, but you'll find versions of it all over the Pyrenees – regrettably much of it prepackaged and microwaved.

**Meat** is typically grilled and served with a few fried potatoes and a couple of salad leaves, or cured/dried, served as a starter or in sandwiches. *Jamón serrano*, the Spanish version of Parma ham, is superb, though the best varieties from Extremadura and Andalucía are extremely expensive. **Game** is quite common in the hills – typically venison, rabbit or boar – and almost always freshly hunted.

**Vegetables** seldom amount to more than a token garnish to the main dish, though at the better restaurants there will often be a few more elaborate vegetable-based recipes offered. It's more usual to start your meal with a **salad**, hearty vegetable soups or a plate of boiled potatoes. **Dessert** in the less expensive places is nearly always fresh fruit or flan, the Spanish *crème caramel*. There are also assorted kinds of *pudín* – rice pudding or various blancmange mixtures. Even in fancy restaurants you'll seldom find much better – stick to fruit and cheese, or make a separate foray to a *pastelería* (cake-shop). Worth a mention, if only for their grotesqueness, are certain dessert **oddities**: frozen citrus fruit (*limon and naranja*) stuffed with sorbet of the corresponding flavour; *músic* (nuts in muscatel); *trufes* (frozen "truffles"); and various other decadent ice cream concoctions, mostly made by Camy and Menorquina, the principal nationwide factories. Indeed, if offered ice cream it's best to go up to the glass-front chiller and point to your choice; descriptions and ingredients are complicated, and the trade names not too informative. If you encounter a genuine *heladería* (ice cream parlour) that whips up its own, count your blessings. *Gelats casolans* is Catalan for ice cream (or sorbets) made in-house; Jinonenca is a Pyrenees-wide brand of decent gelato.

## Vegetarians and vegans

**Vegetarians** have a fairly hard time of it in Spain: there's always something to eat, but you may get weary of eggs and omelettes (*tortilla francesa* is a plain omelette, *con champiñones* with mushrooms). The phrase to learn is *Soy vegetariano. Hay algo sin carne?* (I'm a vegetarian. Is there anything without meat?); you may have to add *y sin mariscos* (and without seafood) *y sin jamón* (and without ham) to be really safe.

In the larger Pyrenean foothill towns you'll find a bare handful of vegetarian and non-European restaurants that serve vegetable dishes. Otherwise, superb fresh produce is always available in the markets and shops, while cheese, fruit and eggs are found everywhere. In restaurants you're faced with the extra problem that pieces of meat – especially ham, which the Spanish don't seem to regard as real meat – are often added to vegetable dishes to "spice them up". For example, *ensalada ilustrada* consists of lettuce, eggs, olives, asparagus spears, tomato wedges – plus a few chunks of ham that you'll have to flick aside.

If you're a **vegan**, you're either going to have to be not too fussy or accept weight loss if you're away for any length of time. Some salads and vegetable dishes are strictly vegan; fruit and nuts are widely available.

## Alcoholic drinks

**Vino** (wine), either *tinto* (red) – *ví negre* in Catalunya – *blanco* (white, *ví blanc* in Catalan) or *rosado/clarete* or *rosat* (rosé), invariably accompanies every meal and is, as a rule, inexpensive. *Jóven* means new or unaged, while *con crianza* means a minimum of two years' aging before sale. Reds are more notable; from Navarra try Viña Orvalaiz (also as white and rosé), while from the Rioja region, around Logroño near the Basque country, Marqués de Caceres is a good mid-range label. There are also dozens of Pyrenean wines, from Catalunya (Bach, Sangre de Toro) and the Somontano domaine of Aragón (Viñas del Vero, and Bodega Pirineos Montesierra red/rosé), which you will often find as the house wine.

Bulk wine from the barrel is rare nowadays – most establishments serve a full, sealed container of the house-bottled or special-ordered vintage (*caserío or de la casa*). This can be great – especially the very light rosé or red wines from around Tremp – or lousy, but at least it will be distinctive. In a bar, a small glass of wine will generally cost around €0.75–1; in a restaurant, if wine is not included in the *menú*, prices start at around €5 a large bottle. If it is included, you'll usually get a whole bottle for two people, a *media botella* (a third to a half of a litre) of red or rose – never white – for one. Often wine will appear in a *porrón* (porró in Catalan), a glass vessel which looks like a melted salad-dressing cruet. Uncork the larger opening on top, brandish it aloft, and potentially make a mess by aiming a stream of wine from the narrow jet into your waiting mouth. Or take the easy way out by filling glasses through the top hole. In Catalunya, **cava** is the generic term for sparkling wine, and champagnes (*champaña*) that dare not speak their name lest they attract the wrath of the French. Freixenet will be familiar to Britons, Reimat Brut, Codorniu and Castillo de Perelada less so, but the latter three equally worthy. *Marc de cava* is the distilled spirit made from the spent pressings of the cava process.

Probably the most famous Spanish wine is **sherry** or *vino de jerez*, made exclusively in Andalucía in a triangular region west of Jerez de la Frontera. Served chilled or at room temperature, it's perfect for washing down *tapas*; the main distinctions are *fino* or *seco* (dry sherry), *amontillado* (medium dry) and *oloroso* or *dulce* (sweet).

**Cerveza**, lager-type beer, is generally pretty good, though more expensive than wine. It comes in 300- to 330-ml bottles (*botellines*) or, for about the same price, on tap – a *caña* of draught beer is a small, 125-ml glass, a *caña doble* 250 ml. Many bartenders will assume you want a doble, so if you don't, say so. You get a *tubo* (tall narrow glass) or a *jarra media* (squat stein); 500-ml measures – a full *jarra* – are available as well. Locally brewed brands, such as Ambar in Aragón, or Estrella Damm and Vell Damm (strongest at 7.2 percent) in Catalunya, tend to be more exciting than nationally available ones like Águila, Mahou or Cruz Campo. **Cider** (*sidra*) is common in the western Pyrenees; the best commercial brand is Zapiain.

In mid-afternoon – or even at breakfast – many Spaniards take a *copa* of liqueur with their **coffee**. The best are *orujo*, distilled from grape pressings like Italian *grappa*, and 45 percent alcohol; or *coñac*, excellent local brandy with a distinct vanilla flavour (try Magno, Soberano, or Carlos III ("Tercero") to get an idea of the variety). Most brandies are produced in Jerez, but an equally good Catalan one is Mascaró, resembling armagnac. In the Western Pyrenees, *pacharan* (often spelled *patxaran*) is a brandy made from rowanberries, not to be confused with the French wine Pacherenc. If you're in the Garrotxa, try *ratafia*, a nut-and-spice-based apéritif.

Most **spirits** are ordered by brand name, since there are generally less expensive Spanish equivalents for standard imports. Larios Gin from Málaga, for instance, is about half the price of Gordon's Gin. Specify *nacional* to avoid getting an expensive foreign brand. Spirits can be very expensive at the trendier bars, though measures tend to be generous. Mixed drinks are universally known as *copas* or Cubata, though strictly speaking the latter is rum and Coke.

## Water, soft drinks and hot drinks

In the Pyrenees you can drink the **water** almost everywhere, and a *jarrón* or carafe of tap water (*agua de grifa*) will be provided in restaurants and cafés – unless there is something wrong with the local spring, in which case bottled water will be offered, often on the house. Such *agua mineral* comes either as sparkling (*con gas*) or still (*sin gas*). Of the soft drinks, try *granizado* (fruit-syrup-flavoured slush), the ubiquitous *Bitter Kas* (like a nonalcoholic Campari, very refreshing) or *horchata* (a milky drink made from chufa or tiger nuts). You can get such drinks from *horchaterías* and *heladerías* (ice cream parlours), or in Catalunya from the wonderful milk bars known as *granjas*. Fruit juices, typically orange, are called *zumos*.

**Café** (coffee) – served in cafés, *heladerías* and bars – is invariably espresso, slightly bitter and, unless you specify otherwise, served black (*café solo*). If you want it white ask for *café cortado* (*café tallat* in Catalan), a small cup with a drop of milk, or *café con leche* (made with lots of hot milk). For a large cup ask for a *doble* or *grande*; decaff is *descafeinado*. Coffee is also frequently mixed with brandy or cognac, known as a *carajillo*. Iced coffee is *café con hielo*, a good high-summer refresher. Spanish **hot chocolate** (*chocolate caliente*) can be very good indeed as long as you avoid Cola Cao brand – an insipid formula aimed at small children.

**Té** (tea) is also available at most bars, although Spaniards usually drink it black. If you want milk it's safest to ask afterwards, since ordering *té con leche* might well get you a glass of warm milk with a teabag floating on top. Most bars keep herbal teas such as *manzanilla* (camomile), *hierba luisa* (lemon verbena) and *menta poleo* (spearmint).

# Communications and media

Both the French and Spanish postal and telecommunications systems work reasonably well, and with a smattering of secondary-school or university language study, you can derive enjoyment – or at least information – from the respective French and Spanish newspapers and magazines.

## France

French **post offices** are signed as *La Poste* in bright yellow and blue (ⓦwww.laposte.fr). Pyrenean post offices are generally open 9am to noon and 2pm to 5pm, Monday to Friday and Saturday 9am to noon, though in the smaller villages lunch hours and closing times can vary. You can have letters sent to any post office; they should be addressed (preferably with the surname underlined and in capitals) **Poste Restante**, Poste Centrale, followed by the name of the town and its postcode. To collect your mail you need a passport and there'll be a charge of €0.46 per item. Ask for all your names to be checked, as filing systems tend to be idiosyncratic; letters may only be held for fifteen days.

**Stamps** (*timbres*) can be bought from tobacconists (*tabacs*), as well as from post offices, while large letters or small packets are best sent at a main *poste*, where they'll probably be more conversant with overseas rates. Standard postcards and letters (under 20gm) within the EU cost €0.46, to North America €70 and to the Antipodes €0.80. If you need to send something quickly within the EU, a self-seal cardboard "express" envelope – €1.55 postage included – is sold which can hold several documents or a very small object, with a two-day delivery guarantee. The postal service in the mountains is extremely efficient, though a little more relaxed than elsewhere in France. If there's snow blocking the road the post might not get collected, for instance, but delays are on the whole no more common than down in the lowlands.

### Telephones and Internet

You can make **domestic and international phone calls** from any phone box (*cabine*) and can receive calls where there's a blue logo of a ringing bell – the number is usually on a metal plaque overhead. Phone cards (*télécartes*), obtainable from PTT branches, train stations and some tabacs, are issued as 50 units (€7.40) and 120 units (€14.75). Coin boxes are being phased out, though a few still exist in cafés, bar basements and rural districts; they take coins of 10, 20, and 50 cents and €1. You can also use credit cards in many call boxes, subject to a minimum charge.

For all calls within France, dial all ten digits of **the number**. Numbers beginning with ☏08.00 are toll-free; those beginning with ☏08.36 are premium rate (typically €0.34/minute), while those beginning with ☏06 are mobiles and also expensive to ring.

**Cheap rates** are from 7pm to 8am Monday to Friday, from midnight to 8am and noon to midnight on Saturday, and all day Sunday. Calls from a public phone to the UK or North America will cost €0.22 per minute at peak rate, to Australia or New Zealand €0.48 per minute; it's cheaper to call from a private phone, and obviously much more from a hotel. You can avoid payment altogether with a **reverse-charge** or **collect call** – known in French as *téléphoner en PCV* – by contacting the international operator (see box).

Coverage for roaming dual-band **mobile phones** (*portables* in French) can be poor in the higher Pyrenees – especially in the depopulated Ariège – but is adequate in the foothills. There are three local networks which your UK-based handset will automatically select, all of which cost around the same: a whopping £0.70 per minute, whether you call across the valley or back home. Vodaphone, T-Mobile and O2 do, however, offer discount plans which lower the price of receiving calls to about £0.30/min. North Americans need a triband rig to enjoy any service in Europe.

Partly owing to a low rate of personal computer ownership, and partly to the lingering presence of France's own, 1980s-vintage, clunky Minitel system, **Internet** use was slow to catch on in France, though this has been remedied with a vengeance in the last few years. However, the low population density of the Pyrenees means that there are almost no Internet cafés, though a few post offices and tourist offices are beginning to offer access. If you can't live without your email, one possible strategy is to carry a laptop with you, plugging in whenever you find a hotel with a suitable wall socket, and dialling your ISP long distance if need be. French phone sockets are wired differently from the RJ-11 standard plug (Spain, US) or the UK's flat plug, so come prepared with the necessary adaptor.

### Useful telephone numbers

**Speaking clock** ☎ 36.99
**Directory enquires** ☎ 12 (€0.44 for two requests)
**International operator** ☎ 31.23
**Mountain weather** Météo France – the national meteorological service – operates a 24-hour weather forecast hotline, with special extensions for snow conditions, avalanche risk, etc. For the basic forecast, dial ☎08.36.68.02.xx (€0.46/min) – the last two variable digits are uniquely assigned to each *département*. For example ☎08.36.68.02.65 for Midi-Pyrénées (basically the central Pyrenees), ☎08.36.68.02.64 for Pyrénées-Atlantiques (the west of the range, including the Pays-Basques), ☎08.36.68.02.66 for Pyrénées-Orientales (the east around Perpignan) and ☎08.36.68.02.09 for the Ariège.

### Phoning abroad from France

**Australia** dial ☎ 00 + 61 + area code minus first 0 + number.
**Britain** dial ☎ 00 + 44 + area code minus first 0 + number.
**Ireland** dial ☎ 00 + 353 + area code minus first 0 + number.
**New Zealand** dial ☎ 00 + 64 + area code minus first 0 + number.
**North America** dial ☎00 + 1 + area code + number.

### Phoning France from abroad

France no longer has area codes per se; the first two digits of the ten-digit number indicate the region of the country (eg "04" covers the southeast, "05" means the southwest) or the type of service.
**From Australia** dial ☎ 011 + 33 + number minus first 0.
**From Britain, Spain & Ireland** dial ☎ 00 + 33 + number minus first 0.
**From New Zealand** dial ☎ 0044 + 33 + number minus first 0.
**From North America** dial ☎ 011 + 33 + number minus first 0.

## The media

A reasonable selection of **foreign newspapers** is on sale in selected resorts and larger towns such as Pau or Perpignan. Among **French national dailies**, *Le Monde* is the most intellectual and somewhat austere, though a recent makeover introduced colour photos. *Libération* (*Libé* for short) is moderately left-wing, pro-European, independent and more colloquial, with good, selective, feature coverage and a colour format; it tends to sell out quickly. *L'Humanité* is the far-left, Communist-affiliated paper, struggling to survive. Among various right-of-centre papers, *Le Figaro* is the most respected and readable.

**Weeklies** include the left-leaning *Le Nouvel Observateur*, its conservative counterweight *L'Express*, and the centrist *Marianne*. The best investigative journalism can be found in the satirical weekly *Canard Enchaîné*, while *Charlie-Hebdo* fits the mould of the UK's *Private Eye* or *Spy* in the US.

Nationwide **monthlies** include the young and trendy *Nova*, with excellent listings for cultural events. The bimonthly **Pyrénées** (widely available, €6.90) is well worth a browse for destination features, news snippets and suggestions for obscure trekking or touring routes; twice a year, there are *hors série* special issues devoted to distinct topics (eg the Basque country, Cathar castles, family day-walks).

French **TV** has six terrestrial channels, three public – F2, F5/Arte and F3 – one subscription – Canal Plus, with some unencrypted programmes – and two commercial open broadcasts – TF1 and M6. F5/Arte is devoted to high-brow fare including opera, films and critics' panels. Canal Plus is the main movie channel (and funder of the French film industry), though F3 screens a fair selection of serious films, especially (undubbed) late Sunday after midnight. The main news broadcasts are at 8pm on F2 and TF1, the most watched channels. **Cable/satellite** networks, available in better hotels, include BBC World, BBC Prime, CNN, MTV, Eurosport, Planète (strictly documentaries), Ciné Premier and Canal Jimmy.

With the appropriate portable **radio**, you can tune into the BBC (local frequencies from ⓦwww.bbc.co.uk/worldservice), Radio Canada (ⓦwww.rcinet.ca) and Voice of America (ⓦwww.voa.gov).

## Spain

**Post offices** in Spain – marked *Correos* in Castilian, *Correus* in Catalan – are generally open Monday to Friday from 8am to noon and again from 5 to 7.30pm, though you will encounter variable schedules in the Pyrenees. Main branches in the largest towns may have considerably longer hours, without midday closure; there's usually only one post office in each town.

"You can have letters sent **poste restante** (*Lista de Correos*) to any Spanish post office: they should be addressed (preferably with the surname underlined and in capitals) to *Lista de Correos* followed by the name of the town and province. To collect, take along your passport and, if you're expecting mail, ask the clerk to check under all of your names – letters are often found filed under first or middle names.

**Outbound mail** is reasonably reliable, with letters or cards taking around five days to a week to the rest of Europe, a week to ten days to North America or Australia.

## Telephones and Internet

Spanish public **phone boxes** work well, though you can't phone them back. If you can't find one, many bars also have pay phones you can use. The phone boxes have been adapted to take euro-coins, but it's less hassle to buy a **phone card** (€6 or €12 from a *kiosko* or *tabac*), or use the most common **credit cards** (€1.20 minimum). With credit cards, the swipe readers are rather temperamental; you'll know you've succeeded when the LCD display says "pro-

cessing" in the local language. Spanish provincial (and some overseas) dialling codes are displayed in most cabins, as well as dialling – and credit card – instructions in English. The local **ringing tone** is long, **engaged** is shorter and rapid; the standard Castilian response is *dígame* (speak to me).

For **international calls**, you can use any phone box, or go to a shopfront *locutorio*, where you pay afterwards. International and domestic rates are slightly cheaper on Saturday and Sunday, and after 6pm (within Spain) or midnight (international) on weekdays. If you're using a phone box to call abroad without a phone card or a credit card, insert at least €2 initially to ensure a connection.

Dual-band **mobile phones** (*moviles* in Castilian) from the UK work better in Spain than in France: the Spanish are obsessed with them and coverage, especially in Catalunya, is respectable. There are three local networks, but as in France it matters not which one you use – it's the same extortionate rate of £0.70/min. Also as in France, North Americans will require triband handsets.

As for the **Internet**, *cibercafés* are as lacking in the Spanish Pyrenees as on the French side, but for different reasons: personal computer ownership is very high, especially in the wealthier parts of Catalunya and the Basque country. If you're addicted to your email, see the advice under France, opposite; RJ11 phone sockets are standard in Spain, with hard-wiring of phones into walls less common.

### Useful telephone numbers

**Directory Enquiries** ☎1003
**International Operator** (Europe) ☎1008
**International Operator** (rest of world) ☎1005
**Time** ☎093
**Mountain weather**: Catalan Pyrenees (general) ☎933 256 391; Girona province ☎906 365 317; Lleida province ☎906 365 325; Huesca province (Aragón) ☎906 365 322; Navarra province (western Pyrenees) ☎906 365 331. You can also check snow and weather conditions online at ⓦwww.inm.es (Spain) and ⓦwww.icc.es/allausb (Catalunya).

### Phoning abroad from Spain

**Australia** dial ☎00 + 61 + area code minus first 0 + number.

**Britain** dial ☎ 00 + 44 + area code minus first 0 + number.
**Eire** dial ☎ 00 +353 + area code minus first 0 + number.
**New Zealand** dial ☎ 00 + 64 + area code minus first 0 + number.
**North America** dial ☎ 00 + 1 + area code + number.

### Phoning Spain

Like France, Spain no longer has area codes per se, but nine-digit unitary numbers. The first three digits are particular to each province or type of service (eg, ☎ 901 is akin to the UK's 0845 lo-call prefix, ☎ 906 is equivalent to UK 0870).
**From Australia** dial ☎ 011 + 34 + nine-digit number.
**From Britain, France & Ireland** dial ☎ 00 + 34 + nine-digit number.
**From New Zealand** dial ☎ 0044 + 34 + nine-digit number.
**From North America** dial ☎ 011 + 34 + nine-digit number.

### Andorra

Andorra has its own **phone code**, ☎ 376, prefixing six-digit subscriber numbers. UK-based mobiles enjoy good reception in the principality, despite its extreme topography. For more details, see p.209.

## The media

**British newspapers** and the *International Herald Tribune* are on sale during the summer season in most large foothill towns, particularly Girona and San Sebastián.

Among **Spanish newspapers** the best are currently Madrid's *El Mundo* and Barcelona's *La Vanguardia*, both of which are fairly liberal in outlook and have good arts and foreign news coverage, including comprehensive regional "what's on" listings and supplements each weekend. Madrid's *El País*, long

the top-ranked quality daily, has become a somewhat boring read, though it still employs exceptional (and independent) columnists. The regional press is generally run by local magnates and is predominantly right-wing, though often supporting local autonomy movements. Nationalist dailies include *Avui* in Catalunya, printed largely in Catalan, and the Basque papers *El Diario Vasco* and *Deia*.

If you can read Spanish, glossy bimonthly **El Mundo de los Pireneos** (ⓦ www .elmundodelospirineos.com; €5) should be your first stop for excellent news analyses, hiking or skiing tips and features on Pyrenean personalities, festivals and impending ecological /development crises on both sides of the border. Issued by outdoor publishers SUA Edizoak in Bilbao, it's currently more vital and less repetitive than its opposite number in France; back issues are available for €4.50 each plus shipping costs (☎ 902 181 471, ecliente@elmundode-lospirineos.com).

Even up in the mountains, you'll inadvertently catch more **TV** than you expect (or want to) sitting in bars and restaurants; older Spaniards are reckoned to be the continent's champion tube-heads in terms of annual hours per person spent in front of the box. Soaps – known as *culebrones* in Castilian – are a particular speciality, either South American *telenovas*, which take up most of the daytime programming, or British or American exports. Sports fans are well catered for, with regular live coverage of football/soccer and basketball matches. In Catalunya, channels 3 and 4 broadcast exclusively in Catalan.

The FM dial is often rewarding, particularly *Catalunya Músic* (88.6 or 103FM), a mix of classical and world-music programming, which can even be picked up in the high-altitude wilds of the Cerdanya or Aigüestortes.

# Opening hours and public holidays

Almost everything on either side of the Pyrenees – shops, museums, churches, tourist offices, most banks – closes for a siesta of at least two hours in the hottest part of the day. There's a lot of variation but basic summer working hours are 9.30am to 1.30pm and 4.30 to 8pm in Spain, and 9am to noon or 1pm and 2 or 3pm to 6.30 or 7.30pm in France. In both countries certain shops do now stay open all day, and with the advent of the French 35-hour week there has been a move towards shorter, "normal" working hours. Nevertheless, you'll get far less aggravated if you accept that the early afternoon is best spent asleep, or in a restaurant, or both.

## France

**Food shops** in France often don't reopen until halfway through the afternoon, closing between 7.30 and 8pm or just before the evening meal. Sunday and Monday are the standard French **closing days**, though you'll always find at least one *boulangerie* (baker's) open. Street markets tend to operate in the mornings only.

**Museums** open between 9 and 10am, close for lunch at noon until 2pm or 3pm, with an afternoon shift only until 5pm or 6pm. Summer times may differ from winter times; if so, both are indicated in the listings. Summer hours usually extend from early June to mid-September, occasionally even from Palm Sunday to All Saints' Day, but sometimes they apply only during July and August. Don't forget closing days – usually Monday or Tuesday, sometimes both.

**Cathedrals** are almost always open all day, with charges only for the crypt, treasuries or cloister, and little fuss about how you're dressed. Small village **churches**, however, can often be closed, so you may have to go during Mass to take a look, on Sunday morning or at other times which you'll see posted up on the door. In small towns and villages, however, getting the key is not difficult – ask anyone nearby or hunt out the priest, whose house is known as the *presbytère*.

### French national holidays

There are thirteen **French national holidays** (jours fériés), when most shops and businesses, some museums, though not (usually) restaurants, are closed. They are:

**January 1** New Year's Day
**Easter Sunday**
**Easter Monday**
**Ascension Day** (forty days after Easter)
**Pentecost/Whitsun** (seventh Sunday after Easter, plus the Monday)
**May 1** May Day/Labour Day
**May 8** Victory in Europe Day
**July 14** Bastille Day
**August 15** Assumption of the Virgin Mary
**November 1** All Saints' Day
**November 11** 1918 Armistice Day
**December 25** Christmas Day

## Spain

Most **museums** observe the siesta with a break between 1 and 4 in the afternoon, and close on Sunday afternoons and all-day Monday. Summer hours usually run from May until September. Anywhere run by the Patrimonio Nacional, the national organization that preserves monuments, is free to EU citizens on Wednesday – take your passport to prove your nationality.

Getting into **churches** can present more of a problem. The really important ones, including most cathedrals, operate in much the same way as museums and almost always have some entry charge to see their most valued treasures and paintings, or their cloisters. Other churches, though, are usually kept locked, opening only for worship in the early morning and/or the evening (between around 6 and 9pm). So you'll either have to try at these times, or find someone with a key. The sacristan or custodian almost always lives nearby and most people will know where to direct you. You're expected to give a small tip, or donation. For all churches "decorous" dress is required, ie no shorts, bare shoulders, etc.

**Public holidays** can (and will) disrupt your plans at some stage. Besides the Spanish national holidays listed below, there are scores of **local festivals** (different in every town and village, usually marking the local saint's day); any of them will mean that everything except bars (and *hostales*, etc) locks its doors.

In addition, **August** is Spain's own holiday month, when the big cities are semi-deserted, and many of the shops and restaurants, even museums, close. In contrast, it can prove nearly impossible to find a room in the more popular coastal and mountain resorts at these times; similarly, seats on planes, trains and buses at this time should be booked well in advance. **Easter**, incidentally, is worse; whereas people's summer breaks are slightly staggered – and indeed July is becoming nearly as busy as August – at Eastertime the entire population is on the move, and every desirable (and most undesirable) accommodation is booked literally months ahead.

## Spanish national holidays

**January 1** *Año Nuevo* (New Year's Day)
**January 6** *Tres Reyes* (Three Kings; Epiphany)
**Maundy Thursday** *Jueves Santo* (not in Catalunya)
**Good Friday** *Viernes Santo*
**Easter Sunday** *Pascua, Domingo de la Resurrección*
**Easter Monday** *Lunes de Pascua*
**May 1** *Fiesta de Trabajo* (May Day/Labour Day)
**Corpus Christi** (early or mid-June)
**June 24** *Día de San Juan* (St John's Day), the king's name-saint
**July 25** *Día de Santiago* (St James of Compostella)
**August 15** *Assunción de la Virgen* (Assumption of the Virgin)
**October 12** *Virgen del Pilar* (National Day)
**November 1** *Todos Santos* (All Saints' Day)
**December 6** *Día de la Constitución* (Constitution Day)
**December 8** *Día de la Concepción Inmaculada* (Immaculate Conception)
**December 25** *Navidad* (Christmas Day)

 # Festivals

Especially in July and August, it's practically impossible not to stumble on some sort of festival during your stay: either a tourist-board-organized concert series, often in a wonderful medieval venue, or a brass band and drinks in a pennant-hung village square. On both sides of the Pyrenees religion and folk history are the main launching platforms for a party, but apart from the occasional Mass to ensure everybody is spiritually insured, the festivities rarely dwell on solemn matters. Even pilgrimages are often celebrated with great gusto and, like many of the town and village celebrations, involve a colourful and photogenic procession. Festivals in major resorts tend to be more visitor-oriented, though, featuring music, art and theatre programmes.

The list of festivals is potentially endless, and although you'll find the major events detailed in boxes at the beginning of each chapter, we don't pretend that it's exhaustive. Note that **saints'-day** festivals can vary in date, often being observed over the weekend closest to the dates given in our listings. In many cases the fun occurs on the evening before the date given, with only a Mass taking place on the morning concerned. Local tourist offices should have more information about what's going on in their area at any given time. Outsiders are always welcome at festivals, the main problem being that during any of the most popular ones you'll find it difficult to find a bed. If you're planning to coincide with a major festival, try to reserve your accommodation well in advance.

## France

Catholicism is still deeply ingrained in the culture of the French Pyrenees; thus saints' days still bring people out in all their finery, ready to indulge before or after Mass has been said. Such occasions, along with the celebrations focused on wine and food production, are usually very genuine affairs intended for a local audience. Other festivals, based on historical events, folklore or literature, are more obviously money-spinners and forums for municipal prestige. Finally, there are the cultural seasons of the larger towns and resorts, centred on film, music or drama, which while enjoyable enough have few pretensions to religious significance.

Some **harvest** celebrations are public,

with charges levied for sampling; others – in the smaller vineyards and cooperatives – are a private celebration for the pickers and packers, though here again there are often open days for public tastings of previous years' produce. From early September the **Roussillon** wine region is particularly active, and later in the month there are *Fêtes des Pommes* all over the place (especially the **Têt valley**), with plenty of opportunity to sample and buy local produce from apple jelly to potent cider. An unusual variation on the harvest *fête* is the late October celebration of the pepper crop at Ezpeleta, in the Western Pyrenees.

**Easter Week** is normally marked by special church services, processions and associated parties. One of the most striking is the *Procession de la Sanch* at **Perpignan**, where penitents parade in red robes, tall pointed hats and masks reminiscent of Ku Klux Klan garb. Many small towns and villages have their own processions, often venerating an image from the parish church – a popular example is the *Procession de la Vierge* at **Font-Romeu** in September. A good example of the often more boisterous folklore festivals is the *Fête de l'Ours* at **Arles-sur-Tech** in February, which involves a lot of men chasing another lot of men dressed in bear costumes.

Most local carnivals are held in midsummer, and usually involve several days of eating, drinking and merrymaking; as a rule, they do not prompt the increased hotel prices of some better-known events.

Throughout the French Pyrenees, **Bastille Day** (July 14) is commemorated by marvellous firework displays. Innumerable other **historical events**, of varying degrees of importance, are celebrated all over the region.

**Sports** events are great crowd-pullers, none more so than the **Tour de France** bike race, which visits the Pyrenees in July – even the police relax and enjoy themselves, loosening collars and accepting cool drinks. *Boules* tournaments and – in Basque areas – *pelote* championships are also guaranteed to stop normal business.

## Spain

It's hard to beat the experience of arriving in some Spanish Pyrenean village, expecting no more than a bed for the night, to discover the streets festooned with flags and streamers, a band playing in the plaza and the entire population out celebrating the local *fiesta*. Everywhere in the range, from the tiniest hamlet to the great cities, will take at least one day off a year to devote to partying. Usually it's the local saint's day, but there are celebrations, too, of harvests, of deliverance from the Moors, of safe return from the sea – any excuse will do. It's often the obscure and unexpected event which proves to be most fun; there is always music, dancing, traditional costume and an immense spirit of enjoyment. The main event of most fiestas is a parade, either a solemn one behind a revered holy image, or a more light-hearted affair with fancy costumes and *gigantones* (*gegants* in Catalan), grotesque giant figures which trundle down the streets terrorizing children.

**Easter**, perhaps the major national religious feast, is observed in a particularly poignant manner in Catalunya, where several municipalities have elaborate and vivid Good Friday eve processions. In particular, several towns enact Passion plays, involving a *Via Crucis* (Stations of the Cross), culminating in a mock Crucifixion with local volunteers as Christ and the Two Thieves.

As in France, **harvest** time is also a big excuse for boozy celebrations, especially in the **Alt Empordà** region. Many of the festivals in the Spanish Pyrenees are more conspicuously **religious** than on the French side, with more weight given to the procession of the revered holy image before the partying begins. Better-known Catalan events include *Carnival* at various villages along the Noguera Pallaresa, the festival of *Sant Marc* at the shrine of Queralt on April 25 and – all over Catalunya – bonfires as the centrepiece of *Dia de Sant Joan* (June 21–24, variable) observances. The Corpus Christi **Festa de Patum** at **Berga** is the biggest late-spring bash in Catalunya, renowned for its high spirits and outrageous *gigantones*.

**Folkloric** and **rural** festivals are celebrated enthusiastically, often including demonstrations of dwindling skills in addition to the normal shenanigans: examples are Rialp's sheep-shearing contest in June and the traditional log-rafting at La Pobla de Segur on the first Sunday in July. An unusual **historical** event is the battle of the women, fought on the first Friday in May at Jaca, celebrating the role played by townswomen in a defeat of the Muslim enemy in 795.

Spain also has a succession of **local cultural programmes** in July and August, particularly at **San Sebastián**, and near **Sallent de Gállego** in Aragón, where the *Pirineos Sur* world music festival is now an established fixture on the tours of top performers.

## Bullfights

**Bullfights** (*corridas*) are an integral part of many Pyrenean festivals, on both sides of the frontier, with the larger foothill towns often staging a three- or four-day season in summer. Followers of *Los Toros*, as Spaniards refer to bullfighting, are increasing in number as Franco's patronage of the practice is forgotten, with the elaborate argot of the *corrida* attaining cult status among the young.

In France, the resurgence of *Les Taureaux*, as it's called there, has been attended by fierce debate over whether *corridas* are really a traditional folkloric manifestation of the regions concerned – Languedoc-Roussillon and the Basque country – precisely those areas with a large population descended from Spanish immigrants settled there since the beginning of the twentieth century. Thus advocates have been at pains to demonstrate evidence of bullfighting in France from before 1900; it appears that the first *corrida* north of the border was staged in Bayonne in 1853, and spectacles still take place south of a line approximately joining Bayonne, Toulouse and Nîmes.

If you spend any time at all in the Pyrenees during the season (which runs March–Oct), you will encounter bullfights, at least on a bar TV, and that will probably make up your mind whether you wish to attend a *corrida*. If you decide to go, try to see the biggest and most prestigious event available (tickets €18 and up), where star performers are likely to despatch the bulls with "art" and a successful, "clean" kill. There are few sights worse than a matador making a prolonged and messy kill, while the audience whistles and hurls cushions into the ring – unfortunately more likely in France, where there's not as yet significant homegrown talent in man or beast, and often second-rate bullfighters (and bulls) have to be imported.

# Crime, police and personal safety

In general both sides of the Pyrenees are remarkably safe, with weather and terrain often posing the greatest threats. In the foothill towns and busy ski resorts, take normal precautions: keep your wallet in your front pocket and your handbag under your elbow, and you won't have much to worry about. If you get confronted – only likely in the region's largest cities – hand over the goods and start dialling the cancellation numbers for your travellers' cheques and credit cards.

## France

All the comments about leaving cars unattended under "Spain", overleaf, apply to France as well, with an extra need for vigilance in such larger towns as Perpignan, Pau and Bayonne. Foreign cars with their distinctive number plates are easy to spot, rental vehicles much less so. Good insurance is the only answer, but even so do not tempt fate by leaving vehicles unlocked or valuables in plain sight, either lapse probably invalidating the best of policies.

### Police and possible offences

There are two main types of French police: the **Police Nationale**, covering large and mid-sized towns, and the **Gendarmerie Nationale**, covering everywhere else. If you need to report a theft, or other incident, you can go to either to fill out a *constat du vol* (required by most insurance companies). Although the police are not always as cooperative as they might be, it is their duty to assist you if you've lost your passport or all your money. You can be stopped anywhere and asked to produce ID but under new crime-prevention measures, the police also have powers to search you and your car without a warrant. Specifically in the Pyrenees, **game wardens** patrol on the lookout for folk fishing/hunting out of season or without a licence, and you can be asked to open backpacks or large camera cases to prove you've no contraband on you.

A different proposition are the **CRS** (*Compagnies Républicaines de Sécurité*), sporadically dressed in green combat gear and armed with riot equipment, whose brutality in the May 1968 battles turned public opinion to the side of the students. But in the Pyrenees you may come across specialized **mountaineering sections** of the CRS; unlike their urban brethren, these are unfailingly helpful, friendly and approachable, providing rescue services and guidance.

If you have an **accident** while driving, you are required to fill in and sign a *constat à l'aimable* (jointly agreed statement); car insurers are supposed to give you this with a policy, as are car rental agencies, though in practice few seem to have heard of it.

For non-criminal **driving violations** such as speeding or not wearing seat belts, the police used to levy on-the-spot fines, but are now more likely to issue citations which must be paid at the applicable municipality within a certain number of days.

Should you be arrested on any charge, you have the right to contact your consulate or embassy. People caught smuggling or possessing **drugs**, even a few grams of marijuana, are liable to find themselves in jail, and consulates will not be sympathetic.

### Personal safety and racial issues

Lone women travellers may be warned about *"les Arabes"*: routine French **racism**, which even the French themselves admit to. If you are Arab, Asian or black your chances of completely avoiding unpleasantness are slim. Empty hotels claiming to be full, police demanding your papers and abusive treatment from immigration officials are distinctly possible.

In the Pyrenees specifically, locals are slowly getting used to seeing school outings including members of racial minorities, or the odd person of colour out on the trail or the ski slopes, but French nationals of Arab or black African descent are still a rarity in the region.

### Spain

While you're unlikely to encounter any trouble during the course of a normal visit to the Spanish Pyrenees, there are a few habitual problem areas.

If you have a **car**, and especially if you're doing loop treks with the vehicle left at a trailhead, leave as little as possible in view, or indeed in the car at all. At the very least take the tape deck with you, or hide it. In the lonelier valleys organized gangs rifle parked cars, and they're not too picky about what they steal: tools, clothing, and registration papers in particular. Glass shards all over the ground where you intend to park are a good indication that there's a problem; the vehicles themselves are rarely stolen, if that's any consolation. **Cars with French number-plates** are more likely to be vandalized in the Spanish Basque country – this is usually ascribed to retaliation by ETA sympathizers for the French crackdown on them. Rental vehicles, fortunately, are not conspicuously labelled as such.

**Looking for hotel rooms**, don't leave any bags unattended anywhere. This applies especially to buildings where the *pensió(n)* or *hostal* is on a higher floor – don't br tempted to leave baggage in the hallway or ground-floor lobby.

If your car or room is burgled, you need to **go to the police** to report it, not least because your insurance company will require a police report. Don't expect a great deal of concern if your loss is relatively small – and expect the process of completing forms and formalities to take ages. In the unlikely event that you're **mugged**, or otherwise threatened, never resist; hand over what's wanted and go straight to the police, who on these occasions will be more sympathetic.

### Police and possible offences

There are three basic types of Spanish **police** – the *Guardia Civil*, the *Policía Municipal* and the *Policía Nacional* – and it's worth remembering that, though polite enough in the usual course of events, they can be extremely unpleasant if you get on the wrong side of them.

The **Guardia Civil**, in green uniforms, are the most officious and the ones to avoid. Though their role has been drastically cut back since they operated as Franco's right hand – you'll see many of their barracks abandoned in the Pyrenees – they remain a reactionary and distrusted force.

If you do need the police – and above all if you're reporting a serious crime such as rape – always go to the more sympathetic **Policía Municipal**, who wear blue-and-white uniforms with red trim. In the countryside there may be only the *Guardia Civil*; though they're usually helpful, they are inclined to resent the suggestion that any crime exists on their turf and you may end up feeling as if you are the one who stands accused.

The brown-uniformed **Policía Nacional** are mainly seen in cities, armed with submachine guns and guarding key installations such as transport stations, post offices and their own barracks. They are also the force used to control crowds and demonstrations. In Euskadi there exists an additional autonomous Basque police force, the *ertzaintza*, distinguished by their red berets.

As in France, you're supposed to carry some kind of **identification** at all times, and the police can stop you in the streets and demand it. In practice they're rarely bothered if you're clearly a (white) foreigner routinely trekking back and forth across the border ridge, but it's still wise to have passport or other ID handy, since mountain refuges require them as security against payment.

**Nude bathing** or **unauthorized camping** are activities more likely to bring you into contact with officialdom, though a warning to cover up or move on is more likely than any real confrontation. In the Pyrenees, pitching a tent in any suitable place – except right in view of a *refugio* or in a protected national park – is the norm. **Topless** (and often bottomless) tanning is commonplace at all the trendier coastal resorts, but by Pyrenean streams and lakes, where attitudes are rather more traditional, you should take care not to upset local sensibilities.

If you have an **accident while driving**, try not to make a statement to anyone who doesn't speak English. Car rental agencies will provide you, in the glove box, with a bilingual statement to be filled in by both drivers if another car is involved.

Spanish **drug laws** are somewhat ambiguous at present. After the PSOE came to power in 1982, cannabis use (possession of up to 8gm of hashish, *chocolate* in Castilian) was decriminalized. Subsequent pressures, and an influx of harder drugs, have changed that policy and – in theory at least – any drug use is now forbidden. You'll see signs in bars reading "*porros no*" (no joints/spliffs), which you should heed. However, the police are in practice little worried about personal use. Larger quantities (and any other drugs) are a very different matter.

Should you be **arrested** you have the right to contact your **consulate**, and although they're notoriously reluctant to get involved they are required to assist you to some degree if you have your passport stolen or lose all your money. If you've been detained for a drugs offence, don't expect any sympathy or help from your consulate.

## Personal safety and racial issues

Spain's macho image has faded dramatically in the post-Franco years and there are now relatively few parts of the country where foreign women, travelling alone, are likely to feel threatened or attract unwanted attention.

As elsewhere in Europe, the **largest towns** have their no-go areas, where street crime and especially drug-related hassles are prevalent, but there is little of the pestering and propositions that you have to contend with in, say, the larger Italian cities. The culture of outdoor *terrazas* (terrace bars) and the tendency of Spaniards to move around in large, mixed crowds, filling central bars and streets late into the night, help to make you feel less exposed.

It is in **more isolated regions**, separated by less than a generation from desperate poverty (or still starkly poor), that most serious problems can occur. In some areas you can walk for hours without reaching an inhabited farm or house, or meeting anyone. It's rare that this poses a threat – help and hospitality are much more the norm – but you are certainly more vulnerable. That said, **back-country trekking** is all the rage in the Pyrenees, and many women happily tramp the range from end to end without incident.

Despite – or more likely because of – having been at the receiving end of prejudice during their several decades of emigration to northern Europe, Spaniards are beginning to display some of the same **racist attitudes** long espoused by their French neighbours. These have been aggravated by continual, large-scale illegal immigration of African "boat people" across the Strait of Gibraltar. Anyone darker than expected for "tourists" should perhaps expect some raised eyebrows in the Pyrenees, where most people of colour seen thus far tend to be Arab or black African immigrants in menial jobs across the foothills of Catalunya.

# The great outdoors

Although high-rise resort apartments and wide pistes make skiing the most conspicuous outdoor pursuit of the Pyrenees, walking is a more widely practised Pyrenean recreation, and much of the range is crossed with well-maintained footpaths. In addition to these, the mountains and their coastal fringes offer a range of variously energetic diversions, whether gentle cross-country rides on horseback, scuba plunges in the Mediterranean, or the pulse-racing thrills of parapente.

## Walking

The Pyrenees rank among the top half-dozen walking areas in Europe. Unlike the Alps, where the high peaks are beyond the skills of the average person, any fit walker with a little determination can reach most of the major summits. Throughout the Pyrenees, paths and trails of varying length are marked and (variably) maintained, some by activity clubs and mountaineering federations, others by local government. Many tourist offices will have details of shorter itineraries, and at least some information on the major walking routes.

### Long-distance routes

The principal **long-distance routes** are listed below; summaries are given where applicable throughout the Guide.

•**Haute Randonnée Pyrénéenne** (HRP) is the shortest and toughest traverse from Atlantic to Mediterranean, sticking close to the frontier, mainly in France but crossing into Spain when the terrain dictates, with many variants entirely in Spain. It's planned as a 45-day hike covering nearly 500km, staying in mountain refuges and unstaffed shelters. Not all of it is difficult but some sections do call for map-reading skills, a head for heights and the use of crampons and ice-axe for much of the season. Often the HRP is not waymarked, but in places it merges with the well-marked GR10 – which can also make a good alternative to the hardest parts of the HRP. Georges Véron has written a detailed if slightly dated description – see "Books", in *Contexts*.

•**Grande Randonnée 10** (GR10) is a lower-level traverse, entirely in France, about 300km longer than the HRP. Most nights can be spent in *gîtes d'étape*, huts, or village accommodation, but there are sections where a tent or bivouac is necessary. The GR10 is marked in its entirety with red-and-white paint bars, and described in detail by the French Topoguide series; the best English-language guide is Douglas Streatfeild-James' *Trekking in the Pyrenees* (Trailblazer, UK) – see "Books" in *Contexts*.

•**Gran Recorrido 11** (GR11) is the Spanish equivalent of the GR10, a well-marked itinerary – again with red-and-white bars – which mostly uses well-established footpaths. Much of this route – which includes some of the wildest, most spectacular scenery in the Pyrenees, and a good compromise between the HRP and GR10 – is served by a mix of attended refuges and unstaffed huts, though again a tent or the willingness to bivouac is occasionally required. The Basque-country section of the trail west of Isaba is, alas, less than brilliantly marked and maintained.

Thorough documentation of this *Senda Pirenaica*, as it's often called in Castilian, exists mainly in Spanish or Catalan, with the Catalunyan, Aragonese and Navarran alpine clubs each publishing a convenient paperback *topoguía* detailing the portion of the GR11 falling within their autonomous region. Alternatively, there's the mammoth, non-portable ring-binder edition combining all three regions, published jointly by PRAMES, FEDME and the Federación Aragonesa de Montaña – the loose pages, which include 1:50,000 mapping, are meant to be replaced periodically with updates. In English, there's a single summary pocket guide, Paul Lucia's *Through the Spanish Pyrenees*: GR11 (see "Books" in Contexts), though *Trekking in the Pyrenees* (as above) covers the meatiest portion of the GR11, from the vicinity of Otsagabia to the Vall Ferrera, with extra coverage of the Ordesa park.

•**GR15**, the *Sendero Prepirenaico*, runs parallel to the GR11 at a much lower altitude, and can thus be followed when the higher elevations are inaccessible due to snow; in this guide it is described only at the southern fringes of the Ordesa region, and in the Valle de Chistau.

•**GR19** is a short trail confined to Alto Aragón, which crosses the GR15 and is most useful as a pleasant way between Biadós, the Valle de Gistau and Ordesa.

•**GR36/GR4** is one of several major north–south traverses of the Pyrenees, in this case from Albi in France to Montserrat in Spain, via Canigou and the Cerdagne /Cerdanya. GR36 is the French designation, GR4 the Spanish.

•**GR7** is the second major north–south traverse, reaching the Pyrenees in the Pays de Sault, curving through Andorra and into Spain as far as Barcelona. It is described in both a French *topo-guide* and a Catalan-produced *topoguía*.

•**GR107**, from Montségur (France) to Berga (Spain), claims to follow the route of fleeing Cathars. A *topo-guide/topoguía* should now be available; some of its variants share the GR7.

•**GR65**, the modern version of the medieval Camino de Santiago/Chemin de Saint Jacques pilgrimage route, crosses the Pyrenees from Saint-Jean-Pied-de-Port in the French Basque Country, via the Ibañeta pass and Roncesvalles to Pamplona and then across northern Spain to Santiago de Compostela. The entire route is covered in detail by various guides, published by Cicerone Press or the confraternity of St James. The traditional Aragonese spur of the main route is now marked as the GR65.3, which enters Spain from the Vallée d'Aspe at the Somport pass, then descends to Jaca where it turns ninety degrees west, joining the GR65 southwest of Pamplona at Puenta la Reina. The Aragonese mountain club (FAM) describes this route in a *topoguía* available in English.

Mention must be made of **variants** (*variantes* in both French and Castilian), which are exactly what they sound like: alternative routings diverging briefly from the main GR, often of greater difficulty or providing necessary side links to villages just off the principal trail. Both the GR11 and GR10 have been substantially rerouted in spots during recent years, in response to requests from both walkers and farmers, the latter no longer wanting people traipsing through or past their land. Old sectors, if not altogether abandoned, tend to be demoted to *variante* status. One problem arising from the re-marking, or fresh plotting of **new trails**, is that the marking committee volunteers tend to do their work with little fanfare, leaving villagers none the wiser; when asked, locals will thus often deny that any path has been (re-) marked in their neighbourhood.

On both sides of the frontier there exist PR trails (**pequeño recorrido** in Castilian, **petit randonnée** in French), usually marked in yellow and white (in Spain), in yellow and red (France), or sometimes blue and yellow or even green and blue; these are itineraries designed to be completed within a day by persons with limited experience of high-mountain walking. Nonetheless, they are also of use to long-haul trekkers, often sparing you some fairly miserable road-tramping, and frequently sharing, or running parallel to, the course of a GR route. They are found in greatest numbers around Benasque and Ansó/Hecho in Spain, and Ax-les-Thermes,

Luchon or Cauterets in France, though any tourist board worth its salt seems to be devising these for their resort or valley. Locally produced guidelets describe most of them.

In the French Pyrenees, there are also more than twenty **local circuits** called Tours, lasting from three to seven days. These are all indicated with varying precision on the 1:50,000 maps published by Rando Éditions (Randonnées Pyrénéennes) and some of the IGN ones, and most are also described in guidebooks from the same publisher. The best of these loops are summarized in the relevant chapters of this guide. On the Spanish side, you'll have to devise your own itineraries, using the Editorial Alpina maps and booklets, plus the other publications listed in *Contexts*.

## Walking skills and equipment

Gauging the **distance** that can be covered in a day obviously depends on many variables, the most significant being level of fitness, type of terrain and load being carried. As rough estimates, most people can walk at about 4.5km per hour over flat country with a fairly light load, and climb at most 500m/1550ft per hour off-road; with a full (15- to 20-kilo) pack, they rarely exceed a rate of 350m/1150ft per hour's climb off-road. You should knock off 50m per hour from these figures for bad trail surface or heavy loads, and always assume that going downhill is no quicker than ascending – if you love your knees, it won't be. If you're not used to it, 1000m of ascent in a single day, with a full pack, is pretty exhausting. You should reckon on **10km horizontally and 1000m of ascent as a sustainable daily average** at first. If you are reasonably fit you could doubtless manage 20km and/or 2000m of climb, but you probably won't feel much like walking the next day. As an idea of what really experienced individuals can achieve, the participants of the Cauterets-to-Vignemale race, involving 52km horizontally and 2700m of ascent, take between four and a half and eight hours. **Trailhead signs** on the Spanish side of the range often predict wildly optimistic times for the hikes ahead – take them with a grain of salt; by

contrast, French estimates are often rather slower than reality.

Plenty of people attempt a Pyrenean traverse without having done any serious walking before. There's no reason why you shouldn't, but you must follow a few basic guidelines. As a rule of thumb you can carry a quarter of your own body weight comfortably in a **backpack**. A frame pack takes its load more easily but one of the hi-tech soft packs with internal struts is more versatile, closer fitting and with nothing to get caught on rocks when scrambling.

You shouldn't skimp on **boots**. Although serious mountain footwear weighs 800–1100 grammes each foot, you don't notice it when they're being worn. High-tech, synthetic boots not only tend to be hotter than old-fashioned leather ones, but often fail to provide vital ankle support – as do trainers, which should never be worn on anything more than an hour-long, level stroll, without a full pack. As a compromise between flimsy trainers and rigid, expensive monsters designed to accommodate crampons, there are numerous all- or part-leather designs with knobbly tread, moisture-wicking liner and some degree of stiffening around the ankle. **Socks** should be mixed-composition: cotton plus synthetic fibres for warmer conditions, wool plus polypro for colder ones.

If you love your knees, you'll also need a **walking stick** or some other self-arrest device. If you're following the GR10 or GR11 from west to east, simple sticks or the more elaborate pilgrim's *makila* are easy to buy in the Basque country. In the central part of the range, hi-tech telescoping poles with snow tips are widely sold in the busier trailhead resorts. Alternatively, find some deadfall or abandoned cuttings in a beech grove, and fashion your own stick with the saw attachment of a pocket knife. It will take about fifteen minutes to strip the bark and sharp nubbins down to the pale yellow wood, but the result is superbly strong, even though tiny cracks develop as the stick dries out. Judge the length as you would a ski pole – the grip should be comfortable with your forearm extended at a right angle.

Unless you're going up above 2500m or are camping in winter, there's no need for a specialist **tent**, though you should always pick one that's self-supporting. The most up-to-date two-person tents can weigh less than four kilos, if optimistically rated in terms of capacity: two people will fit snugly, with no room for gear inside. Six or seven kilos is a more realistic allowance. You can manage most traverses with a good poncho or cagoule and the use of caves, huts, refuges and *gîtes d'étape*. A big poncho keeps you and your pack dry when you're on the trail, while at night you can roll it around your sleeping bag, or rig it as a canopy. It's not too comfortable, but many consider the saving on weight and bulk worthwhile.

As far as **clothing** is concerned, follow the **layer** principle. Ascending on a hot day, you'll want only shorts and a T-shirt (plus a dry spare for after lunch). Silk ski tops are also excellent in middling temperature conditions, as they wick sweat out and dry quickly, but in colder conditions you'll also need a long-sleeved shirt. There are all kinds of part-synthetic **pile/fleece** garments nowadays, warm and easy to wash. A fleece vest over a wool shirt, with long underwear as the lowest layer, should be as much warmth as you'll ever need.

For the HRP or **winter** walking you're going to need gaiters to stop snow going down your boots, crampons (which fit only stiff mountaineering boots) and an ice-axe – plus the skill to use it effectively.

A good **sleeping bag** is essential. Down gives the best insulation relative to weight and bulk, but its efficiency falls drastically when it gets damp, which it's bound to do unless you have a proper tent, and a poncho to protect your pack by day. Artificial filling is better, though much heavier and less compressible. Underneath either sort of bag you'll need a foam **mat** to protect it. Also get a sleeping-bag **liner** – cotton or thermal – which you can wash and dry easily en route.

Complete your personal gear with a brimmed **sun hat**, a warmer ski-type **cap** for higher altitudes, **gloves**, **sunglasses**, **sunscreen**, including **lip-balm** with a sun-protection factor, and some sort of **insect repellant** – Pyrenean biting flies can be fierce. For navigation a **compass** and **pocket altimeter** are both vital, together with the appropriate maps; a GPS device is optional.

## Water and food

On a non-strenuous day the average person needs two litres of **water** from liquids and from food. Hiking you need at least **twice** that, and ski touring **three times** as much. In the mountains you can usually get fresh water along the way. Check your map for habitation upstream, as plenty of mountain villages still discharge untreated sewage into rivers; if there's nothing upstream a vigorous flow will be safe. If in doubt – ie if there are signs of livestock – add water purification tablets (available from all outdoor shops) or boil for four minutes.

On an easy walk you'll need forty calories minimum per day per kilo of body weight – fifty for a tough hike and as much as sixty for ski touring. Fats provide the most energy for their weight, at around 7500 calories per kilo; dehydrated main-meal foods can give you 5000 calories per kilo; nuts and chocolate work out at around 4500 calories per kilo. Picking up **supplies** on the GR10, GR7 or GR65 is easy, as they're designed to pass through plenty of villages. On the HRP or the GR11 you'll probably have to make diversions. It is possible to pick wild food along the way – in season you'll find edible mushrooms plus things like wild spinach, wild strawberries, wild raspberries, hazelnuts and herbs – but these have low caloric value and should be regarded only as supplements to the trekking diet.

For isolated treks you will need a **stove**. The best is the multi-fuel or MSR type, which is light, powerful – and expensive. Next best are French-made Bleuet 206 or English-made Coleman 3001 HPX butane-cartridge stoves, as their fuel is clean, light and almost universally available – the Coleman cartridges somewhat less so, though they are self-sealing and can thus be safely removed if necessary. However, butane stoves don't burn well at low temperatures or when the cartridge is running out. For supper, packet soups, dried potatoes, couscous or thin pasta, supplemented with dry cheese or cured meat, are high-calorie, lightweight and fuel-efficient. Although there's often little else to buy in high villages, avoid canned goods, as they're not only heavy but aggravate Pyrenean litter problems no matter where you dispose of them. For short excursions, a vacuum flask of hot water rehydrates dried foods.

## Climbing

Although the principal summits of the Pyrenees can be reached with only rudimentary climbing skills, the range has technical routes as demanding as any elsewhere. There are few places in the Pyrenees where you can't climb, but particularly good areas include Aigüestortes, Maladeta and the entire Ordesa country in Spain, and the Haute-Garonne, Vallée d'Aure, Cirque de Gavarnie and the tops of the Aspe and Ossau valleys in France.

The traditional climbing grades 1 to 6 were long ago surpassed with the arrival of new techniques and equipment – routes at level 8 and 9 are now routinely tackled. Some climbers find artificial walls worthwhile, with Tarbes having one of the biggest climbing walls, but plenty of mountain villages have now installed them, including Luz-Saint-Sauveur. Spain has a climbing wall at its mountaineering school at Benasque, though it's intended for Spanish or select overseas guides. There's a public wall in Sallent de Gallego, plus a few other Spanish villages.

There are plenty of climbing courses on offer to summer visitors throughout the Pyrenees, most of them charging in the region of € 70 for four to six hours' tuition.

### Mountain rescue phone numbers

There's an ongoing debate about the true utility of **mobile phones** as a mountain safety device. They do have reception in surprisingly remote places, particularly on the top of ridges. But you cannot count on them to be working exactly when and where you need them – especially if they've been damaged in an accident – and they should never encourage you to take chances that you otherwise wouldn't. Do take them along by all means, but they are only an aid to safety, not a guarantee of it.

**SPAIN**
**Navarra** ☎ 112
**Aragón** ☎ 112
**Catalunya** ☎ 085 (also for forest fires)
**Roncal** ☎ 948 893 248

**Jaca** ☎ 974 311 350
**Snowpack and avalanche risk (Dec–April; Navarra)** ☎ 906 365 331
**Snowpack and avalanche risk (Dec–April; Huesca)** ☎ 906 365 322
**Snowpack and avalanche risk (Dec–April; west Catalunya)** ☎ 935 671 577
**Snowpack and avalanche risk (Dec–April; east Catalunya)** ☎ 935 671 576

**ANDORRA** ☎ 112

**FRANCE**
**Pyrenees (general)** ☎ 17
**Oloron-Sainte-Marie** ☎ 05.59.39.86.22
**Pierrefitte-Nestalas** ☎ 05.62.92.75.07
**Gavarnie valley** ☎ 05.62.92.48.24
**Luchon** ☎ 05.61.79.28.36 or 05.61.79.83.79
**Perpignan** ☎ 04.68.61.79.20
**General alpine conditions (Dec–April)** ☎ 08.36.68.04.04
**Snowpack and avalanche risk (Dec–April)** ☎ 08.36.68.10.20

## Caving

The northern and southern foothills of the Pyrenees are largely Cretaceous or Jurassic **limestone**, and some of the high peaks are too, for example Monte Perdido, Europe's highest limestone mountain. Although limestone is soluble, it's also nonporous, which means it dissolves only at tiny cracks where water can penetrate. Over millennia, this dissolving action produces vertical potholes and vast caverns. Thus, below the bizarrely eroded limestone around Pic d'Anie lurks the deepest cave system yet discovered in the Pyrenees, and one of the deepest in the world: the **Gouffre Pierre-Saint-Martin**. The Pyrenees also boasts the world's highest **ice caves** (caves hung with frozen waterfalls), at the top of the Cirque de Gavarnie.

If you've never done any caving, are not in the least athletic, but would still like to experience it, there are several managed caves open to the public, such as **Grandes Canalettes** near Villefranche-de-Conflent (see p.98) or the **prehistoric** painted caves like **Niaux** (see p.238) and **Bédeilhac** in the Ariège (see p.238). The next stage of difficulty would be a cave like **L'Aguzou** in the Aude, where small pre-booked, fully equipped parties are guided around an unilluminated system (see p.92).

If you're intent on caving as a sport, you need to make arrangements through your own caving club or by signing up with a commercial school. It is possible to head off with your own gear if you know what you're doing, but many of the best caverns are locked, and only approved people can get the key. Rewarding areas include the karst country around **Pic d'Anie**, the entire **Cirque de Gavarnie/Monte Perdido** region, the **Comminges** and northern **Couserans**, the **Pays de Sault**, the **Ariège**, the **Aude**, the **Serra del Cadí**, the **Alta Garrotxa** region and the **Têt valley** around Villefranche-de-Conflent.

## Skiing

The comparatively gentle slopes of the Pyrenees are the perfect place to savour the delights of **ski mountaineering** and **cross-country** skiing for the first time. Compared with the Alps, the risk of avalanche is less, and the chance of falling into a crevasse or having a similar accident is minimal. There is no better way of getting real solitude than ski-traversing in the Pyrenees in winter. To learn, sign on with a guide in a resort like Barèges or Gavarnie, both spots giving access to marvellous itineraries ranging from one day to several. If you're already a mountain walker and a competent downhill skier, you're well on the way.

In terms of **downhill skiing**, snow quality on prepared runs seldom approaches the powder standard more often found in the Alps or North America – late in the season things get downright mushy and/or thin near the bottom. As a general rule, resorts in the eastern half of the range have these problems compounded by low precipitation and strong sun (also a problem on much of the Spanish side of the border), and by wind, which either packs the snow hard or scours it away. In the west there is a tendency to mist – also a great snow-eater – and rain, brought in by the Atlantic weather systems. Don't set out specially for a week's holiday without checking conditions at your chosen resort first. Always worth a look is the Ski Club of Great Britain's website, ⓦwww.ski-club.co.uk; they feature about ten of the top Pyrenean resorts (including all those in Andorra), with current snow reports, amaz-ingly frank resort profiles, customer comments and links to package operators.

**Snowboarding** – *surfismo* in Castilian, *surfisme* in French/Catalan – is now a Big Thing in the Pyrenees, and boarders – *surfistas/surfistes* respectively – are well catered to in virtually every resort. Snow-blading is somewhat less widespread.

### Eastern resorts

Proximity to the Mediterranean means that snow can be unreliable at the eastern resorts of **Vallter 2000, Núria and Massella/La Molina in Spain, and Cambre d'Aze or Puigmal 2600** in France. For ski mountaineering and cross-country skiing, on the other hand, the higher reaches of this region are a delight, with little risk of avalanche.

**Pas de la Casa** offers the most reliable snow immediately around **Andorra**, but the development itself is a monstrosity. Best all-rounders within Andorra are **Ordino-Arcalis**, set amongst magnificent high-mountain wilderness, or **Soldeu El Tarter**. Andorra in general is trying to reinvent itself as a family skiing destination, and shed its enduring reputation as a downmarket, wintertime Club 18–30.

Back in France, **Ax-Bonascre** is another blot on the landscape – but when you get up the lifts the scenery is sublime. Just south, in the contiguous Capcir and Cerdagne regions, the most famous resort is **Font-Romeu**, though **Porté-Puymorens, Les Angles, Formiguères** and **Puyvalador** are all superior. For **cross-country skiing** (*ski de fondo* in Castilian, *ski de fond* in French and Catalan), the whole of the Cerdagne /Cerdanya and much of the Serra del Cadí are a playground of trails, bathed in sunshine during spring.

### Central and western resorts

Spain has several serious resorts near the **Val d'Aran**; the best of these are **Port-Ainé**, in the Noguera Pallaresa valley, **Boí-Taüll**, beside the Aigüestortes park, and **Baqueira-Beret**, at the head of the valley and the only one with an international reputation. Ski resorts in **Aragón**'s stretch of the

Pyrenees – following massive investment and an unsuccessful bid to host the 2010 Winter Olympics – are well equipped, particularly **Cerler**, **Formigal**, **Candanchú** and **Astún**. Usually, however, the **north slope** of the **central French Pyrenees** provides the most reliable conditions; **Barèges-La Mongie** comes first for its size and recent infrastructure improvements. Other normally dependable destinations in this area include **Piau-Engaly**, **Saint-Lary Soulan**, **Cauterets** and **Gavarnie-Gèdre**. In the far west, both **Gourette** and **Arette-la-Pierre-Saint-Martin** have a reasonable snow record owing to their Atlantic exposure.

Every significant resort in the Pyrenees is described in the Guide, with details of top-point elevation and the number and type of pistes. The system for **grading pistes** is based on a universal **colour code**: green for beginners, blue for easy, red for intermediate and black for advanced skiers. It's not a completely dependable system – a red run in one resort might rate only as blue in another – but it should give a fair idea of what to expect. Unlike in the Alps, **beginners** are usually well looked after – Gavarnie, Soldeu and Port-Ainé, for example, all have long green runs from their top lifts.

## Costs and packages

Pyrenean skiing, especially on the French side, **costs marginally less** than in the Alps because the range lacks international cachet (though Biarritz, Pau, Perpignan and Toulouse airports allow convenient, year-round access), and the **clientele** is almost totally local and family-oriented. There's little of the snootiness or nocturnal excess occasionally met with in the Alps, and as a foreigner (particularly in Spain) you'll be the object of benign curiosity or outright friendliness – though again in Spain you may have trouble finding English-speaking **instruction**. In France, the local *École du Ski Français* will have at least one multilingual instructor per resort; rates hover around €30 for one or two persons per lesson at a less popular spot. On the Spanish side, rates charged by the *Escuela Española de Esquí* are comparable. **Infrastructure** is adequate to quite good, best wherever sums have been spent on snow cannons, new lifts

or piste extension. But especially in eastern Spain and Andorra, *pistes/pistas* are often **poorly marked** by Alps standards; the margin lollipops (*espiolettes/espiolets*) may not be colour-keyed, so it's fairly easy to stray onto the wrong run.

**Package holidays** are often the cheapest way of skiing – you may well find a UK-based deal offering tuition, equipment rental, accommodation and insurance at under £700 for two weeks. In such cases be sure to check the piste diagram in the resort brochure carefully – if a run ends below 1800m it's unlikely that you'll get snow, whether natural or artificial, all the way down. The main destination promoted in Britain is Andorra, though some agents (and ski websites, see p.65) offer Baqueira-Beret, Barèges-La Mongie and Piau-Engaly as well. Whether you arrive on a package or under your own steam (see below), you should take advantage of the slower midweek periods and thus avoid the weekends and major holiday breaks when all accommodation is booked months in advance.

Arranging matters **on the spot**, expect to pay (in Spain) €20–28 for a peak-season day **lift pass**; in Andorra €23–32; and in France €19–25 depending on the complexity and quality of the lift and piste scheme – some of the Mickey-Mouse French resorts can be very cheap indeed (under €17). Skis, boots and poles typically **rent** at €15 daily for anything medium-perfomance and above, including **"carving"** – adapted skis some 10cm shorter than conventional ones, which are much more manoeuvrable, confidence-building and forgiving of minor mistakes. Slope evacuation **insurance** tends to be pushed in Spain; at €1–2 per day it's probably a good idea. Obviously multi-day passes or long-term rental are more advantageous; you'll need to present a passport-sized photo for three days or over. In Spain at least, an increasing number of resorts are offering the possibility of arranging on-the-spot **"mini-packages"**. Local tourist offices keep literature detailing valley hotels which offer all-in deals of half-board and lift pass which save a good 25 percent compared to doing it *"a la carta"*, even more if you restrict yourself to weekdays.

**Cross-country** skiing is altogether less costly – reckon on €5.50–7 per day for access; gear rental is also about a third cheaper than downhill.

## Cycling

Cyclists shouldn't be daunted by the Pyrenees. You can find plenty of rolling hills and even some almost flat terrain – the Cerdanya/Cerdagne, for example. There are numerous recognized circuits on the French side and recommended mountain-biking routes are marked in red on the Randonnées Éditions maps. On the Spanish side there aren't as many planned routes – though more and more Spanish guides to bike-touring are being published – and the hotter weather discourages all but the hardiest from cycling inland, though you should find company as you approach the sea, particularly on the Santiago de Compostela route. For more information on cycling see p.31 and p.34.

## Horse-riding

Horse-riding is available throughout the Pyrenees, mostly in the foothills. The classic mount of the high mountains is the native Mérenguais breed – the Ariège is the place to ride these stocky horses, especially the village of **Mérens-les-Vals** south of Ax-les-Thermes or at **Aulus-les-Bains** in the Couserans. There's also a prominent stable at **L'Estanguet** in the Vallée d'Aspe. On the Spanish side, there are renowned stables at **La Miana** in the Garrotxa, as well as two near **Puigcerdà** in the Cerdanya. If you're only looking for a day or two's riding, you'll have plenty of opportunities as you tour around. A full day in the saddle should cost around €70, while part-day rates of €13 per hour are standard.

## River sports

The Pyrenees have plenty of rivers suitable for canyoning, **hydrospeed**, **kayaking** and **rafting**, especially in the east of the range and in Aragón around the Ordesa park and the Sierra de Guara.

**Canyoning** involves jumping into a suitably smooth watercourse and letting it take you along, sometimes whooshing down waterfalls, occasionally abseiling down vertical drops, usually merely wading through near-freezing water. For the easier rivers you don't need any special abilities or equipment other than a wet suit and knowing how to swim, but tougher sections require helmets, inflatables, ropes and abseiling skills. Obviously it can be dangerous, so unless you know what you're doing, it's best to go in an escorted group, with gear and guidance included (see the box on p.264 for more on this). The undisputed canyoning centre for the Pyrenees, if not all of Europe, is the **Sierra de Guara** though it's also practised in the **Garganta de Escuaín** (both in Spain).

**Hydrospeed** is the same principle applied to really violent water: you cling to a sort of floating toboggan, wearing a wet suit, padding, helmet and Day-Glo coloured buoyancy jacket. You look stupid, but once you've launched yourself into the waterfalls and whirlpools you don't really care. It's great fun, but can be dangerous, despite the armour. Sample prices in Spain are €42 for a seven-kilometre beginner's session of hydrospeed.

The Spanish **Noguera Pallaresa** is the most celebrated **rafting** and **kayaking** river of the whole range, but there are plenty of others, just as good and less crowded, where tuition and equipment are also available. These include the drainages of the **Têt**, **Aude**, **Ariège**, **Salat**, **Adour**, **Aure**, **Louron**, **Gave d'Oloron**, **Gave de Pau**, **Ossau**, **Aspe**, and **Nive** in France, and the **Veral**, **Aragón**, **Ara**, **Gállego**, **Ésera**, **Noguera Ribagorçana** and **Segre** in Spain. To help you find every stretch of worthwhile white water, look no further than Patrick Santal's specialist guide *White Water Pyrénées* (see p.603).

## Scuba diving

While there is a centre or two in Biarritz on the French Atlantic, most Pyrenean **scuba facilities** line the Catalan coast, between Collioure and Roses. These take advantage of the clearer Mediterranean, and in particular the marine reserve off Cap de Creus. The thermocline here is about 12m deep, where the temperature dips to 12°C all year (versus 22°C at the surface in summer), so you'll want a 7mm wetsuit.

There are several centres on the Spanish side between Roses and Llança, most of them both CMAS and PADI certified and many (in theory) operating year-round on demand. Although many centres only quote rates as part of an all-inclusive package with an affiliated hotel, where available per-dive prices for qualified divers cost €21–25 (equipment not included), while a full PADI or CMAS Open Water Diver course will typically set you back just over €300. Under-16s are not allowed to dive in Spain, though this archaic law is set to change as we go to press.

## Airborne sports

**Hot-air ballooning** is practised in the Cerdanya and the Garrotxa, with standard rates of €120–135 for 75 minutes, champagne breakfast in mid-air included. Airfields at Cerdanya and Luchon are the main venues for **light aviation** and **glider flights**.

The relatively new sport of **parapente** is a blend of hang-gliding and parachuting,

the arc-shaped parapente steering something like a hang-glider but having no rigid parts. You take off by running or skiing down a slope until you get enough lift; in 1000m of descent you might cover a distance of 4–6km. In the early days there were frequent accidents but improvements in design and teaching now make it relatively safe, if a bit expensive. You can take a single-flight for €40–65, but a full two-week course, taking you to a stage where you should be able to go off on your own, costs well over €700.

Major venues in the central Pyrenees include **Accous**, **Barèges**, **Saint-Lary-Soulan**, **Val Louron**, **Luchon** and **Guzet-Neige** in France, and **Ager** and **Castejón de Sos** in Spain. Areas near the coast tend to be unsuitable because of the unpredictability of the winds, but **Baigura**, near Saint-Jean-Pied-du-Port in the French Pays-Basques, is beginnning to make a name for itself.

# Directory

**Addresses** French ones are written as: 18 bis rue Henri-Foucault 1er, which means an annexe or sub-premises of no.18 Henri-Foucault Street, on the first floor. Common abbreviations – used in this book – are pl for *place*, rte for *route*, av for *avenue* and bd for *boulevard*. Spanish addresses are written as: c/Picasso 2, 4° izda. – which means Carrer or Calle Picasso no. 2, 4th floor, left-(*izquierda*) hand flat or office (dcha. – *derecha* – is right; cto. *centro* or centre). Other confusions in Spanish addresses result from the different spellings, and sometimes words, used in Catalan, Aragonese and Euskera – all of which are steadily replacing their Castilian counterparts – and from the removal of Franco and other

Falangist heroes from the main *avenidas* and plazas. A dwindling number of maps – including some official ones – haven't yet caught up with either local-language or post-Falangist renaming. In some towns dual numbering systems are also in effect, and looking at the house plates it's difficult to tell which is the old and which the new scheme. **Children/babies** don't pose great travel problems in either country. Local tourist offices do a good job of detailing attractions or activities for kids. Both rail systems charge nothing for under-fours, and offer heavily discounted fares for under 11s/under 12s. All Pyrenean accommodation welcomes them: French hotels charge by the room, with small supplements for extra beds, while Spanish lodgings offer triples and quads. The more old-fashioned family-run places in both countries may offer baby-sitting services, or least keep an ear cocked while you go out briefly. Disposable nappies (*couches à jeter* in French) and feeding materials are widely available, though baby foods and milk powders tend to be heavily sweetened or very rich. In both countries, kids are allowed in all bars and restaurants, and on the French side there's usually a *menu enfants* (basically steak, chips and ice cream). Spanish *hostales* and *pensiones* may prepare food specially on request – or even provide self-catering facilities to do so.

**Cinema** There are just a few cinemas in the French Pyrenees – notably in Luchon – with most others in the foothill or gateway towns. Students get discounts and foreign films are sometimes shown in their original language with subtitles (look for *version originale* or *v.o.* in the listings). On the Spanish side; there are again cinemas in larger foothill and coastal towns, like San Sebastián and Girona; admission is reasonable at €5. The majority of what's screened is Hollywood mainstream poorly dubbed into Spanish; you'll sometimes find films in their original language with subtitles. Look for *voz original* or *versión original* (*subtitulada*), abbreviated "*v.o.*", in the listings; "*v.e.*" means *versión español*.

**Consulates** Closest UK consulates to the Pyrenees are in Bilbao, Toulouse and Barcelona; the US is represented in Barcelona and Toulouse.

**Electricity** in both France and Spain is 220V out of double, round-pin wall sockets. Travellers from Britain and Australasia will need the appropriate three-to-two adaptors for appliances, and North Americans will additionally require a step-down transformer.

**Equipment** for skiing, climbing and other mountain activities is slightly more expensive in France or Spain than in the USA, but usually much less than in the UK – and you'll find some bargains in Andorran mega-stores. The range and profusion of products is also striking; addresses of the better shops are given in the Guide.

**Fishing** In France, you need to become a member of a fishing club to get rights – this is not difficult, any tourist office will give you a local address. In Spain, fortnightly permits are easily and cheaply obtained from any ICONA office – there's one in every big town (addresses from the local tourist office).

**Laundries** are not that common outside the bigger towns of the French Pyrenees– look in the Yellow Pages under "*Laveries Automatiques*" or "*Laveries en libre-service*". If you want to wash your own, carry laundry hand-wash powder or cold-water washing liquid, and keep quantities small and incon-spicuously dried in hotels, as it's often expressly forbidden to wash clothes in rooms. On the Spanish side, you'll find a few self-service *lavanderías automáticas* in towns like Jaca, Benasque or Olot, but oth-erwise they're absent – you normally have to leave your clothes for the full (and somewhat expensive) works. You're not allowed official-ly to leave laundry hanging out of windows over a street, though this law is increasingly ignored. A dry cleaner is a *tintorería*.

**Swimming pools** The *piscine municipale* (French), or *piscina municipal* (Castilian) is a feature of most Pyrenean towns, even quite small places, and reasonably priced (€2.50–3 for a swim). They're a lifesaver in high summer and an excellent way to get the kinks out of muscles fatigued from trekking, though the water is almost never heated.

**Time** Both France and Spain are always one hour ahead of Britain since the institution of uniform EU Daylight Savings. Except for a few weeks in April, both countries are six hours ahead of US Eastern Standard Time, nine ahead of US Pacific Standard Time.

**Toilets** are called *les toilettes* or *WC* (pro-nounced "*vay say*") in France, but variously *los servicios* (*servei* in Catalan), *baños*, *aseos*, *retretes*, or *sanitarios* in Spain. On both sides of the range they're apt to be averagely clean, with paper not guaranteed and the hole-in-the-ground, squat-type not unknown. Incidentally, *lavabo* means wash basin in both Castilian and French. In France, toilets are usually found downstairs or upstairs in bars or restaurants, along with the phone; in Spain they tend to be on the same floor as the *comedor/menjador*. Bar-restaurant and museum toilets are usually free, though keep a few coins handy for ones in train/bus stations.

# Guide

# Guide

# The Eastern
# Pyrenees

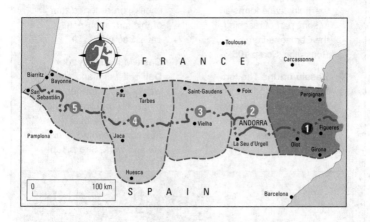

CHAPTER ONE # Highlights

✳ **Château de Puilaurens**
The largest and most
intricate of the so-called
Cathar castles overlooks
piney foothills. **See p.92**

✳ **Scuba near Cala
Jóncols** Some of the
Costa Brava's most pro-
tected and sea-life-rich
dive sites lie off this
remote bay. **See p.137**

✳ **Train Jaune** Part serious
transport, part funfair ride,
the Train Jaune forms an
integral part of reaching
the Cerdagne from
Roussillon. **See p.105**

✳ **Besalú bridge** The fortified medieval bridge at
the entrance to Besalú is
perhaps the grandest in
all the Pyrenees.
**See p.155**

✳ **Canigou summit** Climb
the spiritual mecca of
Catalonians both sides
of the border, and maybe
coincide with the
Midsummer's Eve festivi-
ties. **See p.103**

✳ **Girona** Girona is the
most atmospheric of the
Catalan provincial capi-
tals. **See p.146**

✳ **Grotte de l'Aguzou** Take
a real hands- (and
knees-) on escorted tour
of this formation-rich
cave. **See p.92**

✳ **Casa-Museu Salvador
Dalí** The weird and
wacky artist's former
home at Port Lligat is the
best of several local
museums devoted to his
life and work. **See p.136**

# The Eastern Pyrenees

The **Eastern Pyrenees**, despite their comparatively modest height, are among the best-loved and most visited areas of the range. This is partly due to convenient airports at Perpignan and Carcassonne in France, and Girona in Spain, though the ocean-tempered climate and sparkling scenery certainly helps. The nearby Mediterranean intensifies the light, while landscapes alternate between coastal wetlands and arid scrub, or low-altitude orchards and alpine forests. There's a correspondingly wide variety of wildlife: waterfowl and upland birds of prey stipple the skies, while the terrain supports a surprising number of mammals, small and large, not yet eradicated by avid local hunters.

Running along the crest of the easternmost Albères/Albera section of the Pyrenees, the **border** is breached by just three road passes: the coastal **Col dels Balistres**, the **Col du Perthus** in the middle of the chain – supposedly used by Hannibal, and today the route of the main highway – and the **Col d'Ares** in the west. However, off-road vehicles and hikers can cross east of the Col du Perthus at the **Col de Banyuls**, rather isolated despite its close proximity to the resort-speckled Mediterranean. There are, of course, numerous other footpaths and tracks across the mountains, used by smugglers for centuries and by refugees escaping north during the Spanish Civil War, and south in World War II.

For the **Catalan people** in both Spain and France, the national border is a fiction – even more so since the European Union did away with Customs controls in 1995. Locals regularly cross back and forth on foot or by vehicle, as they always have done with their flocks and contraband. But while Catalan (*Català*) is the official language of Spanish Catalonia (*Catalunya*), it's no more than an option in the schools of Roussillon or French Catalonia; there is scarcely any interest in a politically unified, cross-border Catalan state, the universal presence of *els quatre barres* (the red-and-yellow Catalan pennant) and the increasing citation of Catalan place-names in France notwithstanding. The whole of Catalonia was last under one ruler in the mid-seventeenth century, and the glories of the early medieval Catalan-Aragonese kingdoms are an even more distant memory.

Artificial though the border may be, it's useful to consider the Eastern Pyrenees as three distinct parts: the **French valleys**, draining predominantly northeast from the main Pyrenean crest between the Cerdagne and the sea; the **Mediterranean coast**, shared between the two parts of Catalonia; and the more uniformly south-facing **Spanish valleys**.

**Perpignan** is the only substantial town on the French side and the inevitable transport hub for the French valleys; most visitors head southwest up the parallel valleys of the **Tech** and **Têt**, where congenial towns like **Céret**, **Arles-sur-Tech**, **Prats-de-Molló** and **Prades** serve as handy forward bases.

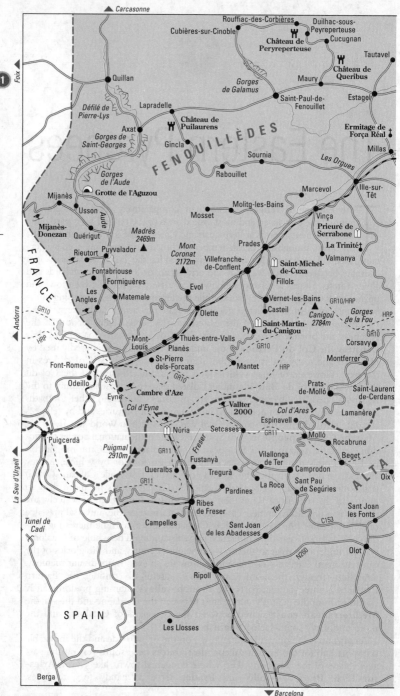

▲ Carcasonne

Rouffiac-des-Corbières
Cubières-sur-Cinoble
Duilhac-sous-Peyreperteuse
Château de Peyreperteuse
Cucugnan
Tautavel
Château de Queribus
Maury
Estagel
Ermitage de Força Réal
Millas

Quillan
Gorges de Galamus
Saint-Paul-de-Fenouillet

Défilé de Pierre-Lys
Lapradelle
Château de Puilaurens
FENOUILLÈDES
Les Orgues

Axat
Gincla
Sournia
Ille-sur-Têt

Gorges de Saint-Georges
Rabouillet
Marcevol

Gorges de l'Aude
Mijanès
Grotte de l'Aguzou
Molitg-les-Bains
Vinça
Prieuré de Serrabone

Usson
Mosset
La Trinité

Mijanès-Donezan
Quérigut
Madrès 2469m
Prades
Saint-Michel-de-Cuxa
Valmanya

Rieutort
Puyvalador
Mont Coronat 2172m
Villefranche-de-Conflent
Fillols

Fontabriouse
Evol
Vernet-les-Bains
Canigou 2784m
GR10/HRP
Gorges de la Fou
HRP

Formiguères
Casteil

Les Angles
Matemale
Olette
Saint-Martin-du-Canigou
Py
GR10
Corsavy

GR10
Mont-Louis
Thuès-entre-Valls
Planès
Mantet
HRP
Montferrer

Font-Romeu
St-Pierre dels-Forcats
GR10
Prats-de-Molló
Saint-Laurent-de-Cerdans

Odeillo
HRP
Cambre d'Aze
Lamanère

Eyne
Col d'Eyne
Vallter 2000
Col d'Arès
Espinavell

Puigcerdà
Núria
Setcases
Molló
GR11
Rocabruna

Puigmal 2910m
Freser
Vilallonga de Ter
Camprodon
Beget
Oix

Queralbs
GR11
Fustanyà
Tregurà
La Roca
Sant Pau de Segúries
ALTA

Pardines
Ribes de Freser
Ter
Sant Joan les Fonts

Tunel de Cadí
Campelles
Sant Joan de les Abadesses
C153
Olot

Ripoll
N260

SPAIN

Les Llosses

Berga

▼ Barcelona

◀ Andorra
GR10
HRP

◀ La Seu d'Urgell

FRANCE

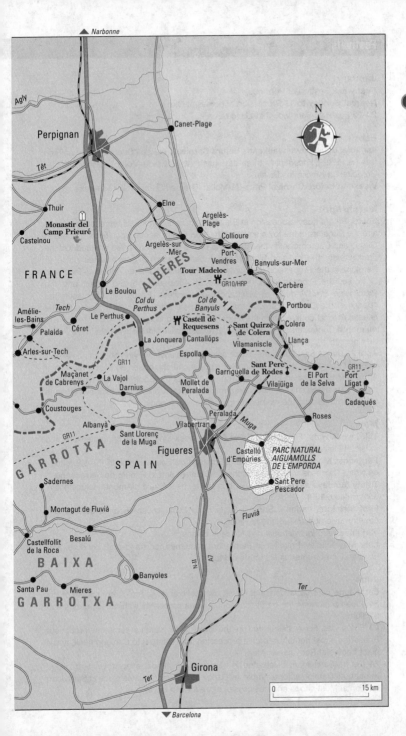

## January
**First week** Festival at Portbou.
**Nearest Sunday to 17** Procession of horses at Olot.
**20–22** *Festa de Sant Vicent* at Llança.

## February
**Variable, usually two weekends before Carnival** *Fête de l'Ours* at Arles-sur-Tech (see p.117); *L'Encadanat*, three-day bash at Prats-de-Molló; *Mascarade des Grégoires* at Amélie-les Bains.
**Weekend before Carnival** Prats-de-Mollo: *Fête de l'Ours*, similar to Arles's.

## March/April
**Easter** Palm Friday procession at Besalú, culminating in locals representing Jesus and the Apostles in the town square. On Good Friday, hooded penitents process in Girona and Camprodon; in the latter a *Via Crucis* or Passion is also enacted. On the French side, the red-and-black-robed *Procession de la Sanch* takes place at Perpignan; the *Procession Nocturne des Pénitents Noirs* at Arles-sur-Tech and Collioure; the *Procession du Ressuscité* at Arles-sur-Tech and Céret; and the *Procession de l'Angelet* at Villefranche-de-Conflent. Easter Monday sees the "Dance of the Cuckold" at Cornellà de Terri, near Banyoles, which celebrates the release of local couples from the feudal *droit de seigneur*.
**All month** *Confrontation* at Perpignan, a retrospective film festival held in the Palais du Congrès.
**April 23** *Dia de Sant Jordi*, the patron saint of Catalunya. Varying observance everywhere (if only a procession to the nearest rural church); observed Easter Monday if April 23 is before or on Easter. It's also the "Day of the Book" (as well as the birthday of Cervantes and Shakespeare), marked by men presenting their sweethearts with a red rose, and the women reciprocating with a book.

## May
**Third week** *Fires i Festes de la Santa Creu*, a week-long festival of processions and music at Figueres.
**Pentecost Monday** Processions at L'Ermitage de Saint-Antoine in the L'Ermitage de Nôtre-Dame-de-Vie at Villefranche-de-Conflent and at Prieuré de Serrabonne.
**Trinity Sunday** *Fête de l'Ermitage de la Trinité*, near Boule d'Amont, including *sardanes*, see p.139).
**First fortnight, variable Sunday** *Festa de la Lana*, sheep-shearing contest and country-style public wedding at Ripoll.
**Variable** *Curso International de Música* at Girona.
**Late May** Medieval market at Perpignan: costumed food-and-craft vendors, jugglers and street-entertainers in the old town.

## June
**Early June** *Fête de la Cerise at Céret*, over several days; the cherry capital of the Pyrenees celebrates the traditional source of its prosperity with music, dance and bullfights.
**23** *Fêtes des Feux*, celebrated in the evening on various summits throughout Roussillon, most notably a torchlit procession from Castillet to Canigou peak, and a giant bonfire at Banyuls-sur-Mer.
**24** *Dia de Sant Joan*, celebrated in some way in almost every town and village throughout Catalonia; for example, a "Dance of the Giants" takes place at Sant Joan les Fonts. Most shops and businesses close for two days.

**End month** Three-day *fête de Sant Eloi*, with blessing of traditionally indispensable mules at Amélie-les-Bains on the Sunday.

*29* **Dia de Sant Pere** is another excuse for festivities all over Catalonia.

### July

**All month** Estivales (Ⓦwww.estivales.com) at Perpignan. Music and dance festival with international acts.

**Sunday closest to 10** *Sant Cristobal in Olot*, with traditional dances and processions.

**Nearest weekend to 14** Food stalls, flamenco, street bands, taurine sports in Céret.

**Mid-month** *Ciné-Recontres at Prades*; week-long retrospective film festival.

*25* *Festa de Sant Jaume* at Portbou.

**Variable** *Sardanes* (see p.139) at Ripoll and Camprodon; *Salon des Arts* at Quillan.

**End month** International Sardana Festival at Céret, extending over three days.

**End month** Tuïr la Catalana at Thuir: a celebration of *Roussillonais* culture and cuisine.

**July 28–30** *Festa Major* at Arles-sur-Tech, featuring boisterous processions.

### July/August

Music festivals at Besalú, Cadaqués, Camprodon, Castellfollit de la Roca, Girona, Llançà, El Port de la Selva, Ripoll and Sant Pere de Rodes.

**Early July to mid-Aug** *Festival Castell de Peralada*. World-ranking names stage jazz, classical, opera and dance events in the gardens of the castell. Current info at Ⓦwww.festivalperalada.com.

**Mid-July to late Aug** *Les Jeudis de Perpignan*: Thursday evening festival featuring street performers and live music in many bars and squares.

*Festival Isaac Albeniz* at Camprodon; classical concerts at Sant Pere church.

**End July to mid-Aug** *Festival Pau Casals* at Prades. Over 25 classical musical concerts with world-class soloists and groups, in a programme ranging from Bach to Ravel. Venues include Saint-Michel-de-Cuxa and other regional churches. Information on ℡04.68.96.33.07, Ⓦwww.prades-festival-casals.com.

Regattas of *llaguts* (six-man catboats) and lateen-riggers at Cadaqués.

### August

**First fortnight** Amateur village violinists and accordionists play strictly by ear at Camprodon.

**1–10** *Festa Major*, including the Chasse à l'Ours, at Saint-Laurent-de-Cerdans.

**6** Annual festival at El Port de la Selva.

**10–12** Annual festival at Castelló d'Empuries.

**14–15** Festivals at Santa Pau, Darnius, Ribes de Freser.

**Mid-month** *Festa Lyric* at Argelès-sur-Mer: celebration of Catalan song and verse.

**Mid-month** *Festival International de la Sardane* at Céret, in the arena north of town.

**Aug 16** *Festa Major* at Collioure. Vincent the patron saint is feted with merrymaking, fireworks over the water, dancing and a corrida (book in advance through the Turisme).

**23–25** *Fête de Saint-Louis* at Le Perthus.

**29** *Fête Folklorique* at Banyuls-sur-Mer.

**Late Aug–early Sept** *Schubertiada* festival at Vilabertran.

### September

**All month** Commemorative *trobador* (troubadour) events at Castelló d'Empuries.

**1** Shepherds' *Festa de Sant Gil,* at the Núria meadows.

**First week, especially 5–6** General festivites at Cadaqués.

*continued overleaf*

**First week** *Festival de Musique en Catalogne Romane* at Elne: classical music events in the cathedral.

**First weekend** *Fête Médiévale* at Arles-sur-Tech: a rollicking festival complete with fire-eaters.

**First Sunday** Sheepdog trials at Ribes de Freser.

**7–8** Celebrations at Olot, in particular a "Dance of the Giants", and also at Núria.

**10** Dance of the *Pabordes* at Sant Joan de les Abadesses.

**11** *La Diada*, National day celebrations with *sardanes* all over Catalunya (Spain).

**24** Annual festival at Besalú.

**29** Annual festival at Colera.

**Late Sept** *Méditerranéennes de Céret* (℡01.44.79.00.36, ℮azimuthprod @wanadoo.fr): three-day Latin/Mediterranean music festival, drawing huge crowds.

**October**

**7** *Grande Fête Patronale* in Thuir and Amélie-les-Bains.

**Second fortnight** *Tria de Mulats*, selection of mares and foals by livestock dealers, at Espinavell.

**Last week** *Fires de Sant Narcis* in Girona; also *Festa de Sant Martiriano* in Banyoles.

**Penultimate weekend** Grape harvest and wine festival at Banyuls-sur-Mer.

**Last two weekends** *Jazzebre* at Perpignan: eclectic programme ranging from mainstream jazz to klezmer, performed by world-ranking musicians and groups.

**November**

**11** *Foire de la Saint-Martin* in Perpignan.

**December**

**Last two weeks** Christmas activities in Perpignan include a Christmas market, *pessebres* (manger scenes), a Christmas market, a public *cagatió* (see p.86) and concerts.

Monumental interest is lent by medieval fortifications at **Mont-Louis** and **Villefranche-de-Conflent**, defending the Têt approaches to Perpignan, and by compelling Romanesque foothill monasteries like the **Prieuré de Serrabone**, **Saint-Michel-de-Cuxa** and **Saint-Martin-du-Canigou**. The peak of **Canigou** itself, beacon and effective logo of the region, offers several approaches and a variety of walking routes.

Because of the precipitous descent of the Pyrenean foothills, the Mediterranean coast is predominantly rocky, the shore road and rail line forging along as corniche routes. Only at northerly **Argelès-sur-Mer** and **Roses** in the south do the hills recede, permitting sandy beaches – and extensive holiday development. In between, the French **Côte Vermeille** boasts several small port-resorts like **Collioure**, whose setting first attracted summer patronage from artists over a century ago. The Spanish **Costa Brava**, or rather the northern fraction of it abutting the Pyrenees, has its own artistic associations, most tangibly at **Cadaqués** and, just inland, at **Figueres**, respectively the backdrop for Salvador Dalí's later years and childhood. Natural attractions along this bit of coast include relatively uncrowded coves around low-key holiday centres like **Portbou** and **Llançà**, and the bird-haunted marshes of the **Parc Natural dels Aiguamolls de l'Empordà**.

Poised just below the Spanish foothills, **Girona** – like Perpignan on the other side of the border – is the staging-post for nearby valleys; unlike with Perpignan, you may well stay longer than planned in this charming, manageable city. Following the Fluvià River inland from here – first north, then west – takes you past medieval **Besalú** and **Santa Pau** through the volcanic **Garrotxa** country, en route to the lively county town of **Olot**. Higher up, superb medieval monasteries dominate the heart of such small towns as **Ripoll** and **Sant Joan de les Abadesses**. However, the heads of the valleys seem less densely settled than in France, with only **Camprodon** and **Núria** conspicuous as (pre-) alpine hill stations.

Most of the Eastern Pyrenees is well served by **public transport**. The international **train** line links Perpignan and Barcelona, running along the Côte Vermeille and the northern Costa Brava before turning inland to Figueres and Girona. There are also trains along the Têt valley, and from Barcelona to Ripoll and Ribes de Freser – with an extension from the latter to Núria along the incredible *cremallera* rack-and-pinion rail line (see p.175). **Buses** serve the Têt and Tech valleys, the resorts of the Côte Vermeille, parts of the Costa Brava and much of the Albères/Albera and Garrotxa, though – as ever – services tend to dwindle near the tops of the valleys on either side of the watershed.

# The French valleys

Good international and local transport connections make **Perpignan**, 30km north of the border, the main gateway for the **French valleys** of the Eastern Pyrenees. Once the seat of a medieval kingdom that straddled the mountains, modern Perpignan is one of the most vital and multicultural cities of the Pyrenees, thanks to the influence of substantial immigrant communities from Spain and North Africa and a growing university population.

The favourite routes inland from Perpignan lie along the **Têt** and **Tech** valleys, respectively northwest and southeast of the Canigou massif. **Prades**, famous for its summer music festival held in the medieval monastery of Saint-Michel-de-Cuxa, serves effectively as the "capital" of the Têt, whose other principal attractions are the fortified towns of **Villefranche-de-Conflent** and **Mont-Louis**, linked by the touristic **Train Jaune** – a narrow-gauge, electrically powered train service which spectacularly negotiates the river valley. **Céret**, with its modern art collection, forms an attractive introduction to the Tech watershed, while the spa town of **Amélie-les-Bains** and medieval **Arles-sur-Tech** beckon up-valley.

Higher up, an ascent of **Canigou** is essential to any exploration of the Eastern Pyrenees. It's essentially the sacred mountain of Catalonia, and though it's far from the highest, the beauty of the approaches to the peak is impeccable, as are the views towards Marseille and Andorra from the top.

# Perpignan

**PERPIGNAN** (Perpinyà in Catalan), the capital of Roussillon or French Catalonia, is the most ethnically diverse city in the Pyrenees. A substantial fraction of its population is descended from Spanish Catalans who poured across the border in the final days of the Spanish Civil War, desperate to avoid reprisals at the hands of Franco's Castilian and Moroccan troops. There's also a sizeable Romany contingent, and some of the suburbs were settled by French colonists fleeing the upheavals associated with the Maghrebi independence movements of the 1950s and 1960s. More recently, immigrants from Morocco and Algeria, escaping unstable, repressive regimes or simply in search of a brighter economic future, have moved into a run-down district in the centre of town.

The melting-pot atmosphere of the city makes it difficult for a distinctly Catalan atmosphere to coalesce, though townspeople are happy to set themselves apart from the rest of France by promoting this identity – even if their own spoken Catalan is limited to a few Gallic-inflected phrases. Unfortunately, Perpignan is far from a model of tolerance – Le Pen's racist Front National party and its derivatives have historically done well here at the polls.

The city has had a surprisingly quiet history. Too far from the sea to serve as a port, Perpignan was a sizeable if unremarkable town until the thirteenth century, when it began to boom as a textile centre. Jaume II of Mallorca and Roussillon enhanced this prosperity in 1276, when he made Perpignan his alternative mainland capital (Montpellier being the other). That kingdom evaporated in 1349, however, absorbed by the Catalan-Aragonese Crown, whose own nearby capital, Barcelona, eclipsed Perpignan. In subsequent centuries it was the object of repeated sieges by France, finally becoming French territory with the 1659 Treaty of the Pyrenees.

## Arrival, information and local transport

The small **airport**, Perpignan-Rivesaltes, 6km north of town, handles daily flights to and from several French cities, as well as London Stansted (operated by Ryanair); meagre facilities include shops, a bar and restaurant and a half-dozen car-rental booths. The airport **shuttle bus** (€4.50) makes the twenty-minute trip up to six times daily – rather tightly timed to meet the flights – stopping at the bus station (see below), the train station, and the Place de Catalogne; a taxi into the centre will cost around three times the bus fare.

Perpignan's **train station**, at the west end of avenue Général-de-Gaulle, was once dubbed "the centre of the world" by Salvador Dalí; the milestone which once read "Centre du Monde: 0.0km" has been removed, and the station is now topped by a large statue of the artist, apparently falling over onto his backside or reaching out to embrace the heavens, depending on your interpretation. To get into the heart of the city from here, walk along the avenue, through place de Catalogne, and cross the River Basse at **place Arago**, close by the *quartier de piétonnes* (pedestrian zone) – a twenty-minute hike – or take one of the frequent #2 city buses buses from avenue Général-de-Gaulle to the "Castillet" stop. If you arrive by long-distance bus or airport shuttle, you'll be dropped at the **gare routière**, just off avenue du Général-Leclerc near Pont Arago, a short distance northwest of place de la Résistance.

**Driving** in or around Perpignan is a nuisance, the bypass involving a maddening series of roundabouts. For the old town, drive straight in along the "Route National" and follow signs for the "Centre". There are some enclosed fee-garages, but also free and metered street **parking** on most roads outside of

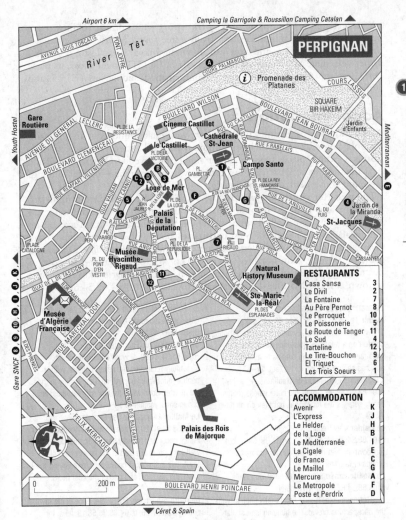

**PERPIGNAN**

Airport 6 km ▲    Camping la Garrigole & Roussillon Camping Catalan ▲

Mediterranean ▲

Youth Hostel ◄

Gare SNCF ◄  8, 9, 10, H, J, K ◄

**RESTAURANTS**

| Casa Sansa | 3 |
| Le Divil | 2 |
| La Fontaine | 7 |
| Au Père Pernot | 8 |
| Le Perroquet | 10 |
| Le Poissonerie | 5 |
| Le Route de Tanger | 11 |
| Le Sud | 4 |
| Tarteline | 12 |
| Le Tire-Bouchon | 9 |
| El Triquet | 6 |
| Les Trois Soeurs | 1 |

**ACCOMMODATION**

| Avenir | K |
| L'Express | J |
| Le Helder | H |
| de la Loge | B |
| Le Mediterranée | I |
| La Cigale | E |
| de France | C |
| Le Maillol | G |
| Mercure | A |
| Le Metropole | F |
| Poste et Perdrix | D |

0 ——— 200 m

N

▼ Céret & Spain

the pedestrian area. The car park of the Palais des Rois is a good option; avoid leaving your car in the seedier areas of the old town.

The **municipal tourist office** (mid-June to mid-Sept Mon–Sat 9am–7pm, Sun 10am–4pm; mid-Sept to mid-June Mon–Sat 9am–6pm, Sun 9am–noon; ☎04.68.66.30.30, ⊛www.perpignantourisme.com) is in the Palais des Congrès, the white building at the eastern end of the leafy Promenade des Platanes which runs parallel to boulevard Wilson; they can supply you with the free *Perpignan Mag* (monthly in summer, otherwise quarterly), which will keep you abreast of cultural events in the city. There's also a less useful **departmental tourist office** (Mon–Fri 9am–12.30pm & 1.30–6pm; ☎04.68.51.52.53, ⊛www.cg66.fr) at 1 avenue des Palmiers, just off boulevard Georges-Clemenceau.

Your feet are the best option for city **transport** – the compact old town can be crossed in twenty minutes. Alternatively, a free *navette* (shuttle bus) circulates through the old town, and you can also rent **bikes** (see "Listings", p.89). Otherwise, there are plenty of **city buses** run by CTP; their kiosk in place Peri, near the *Palmarium* café, supplies information and tickets (€1.05, also available from drivers).

## Accommodation

Accommodation is plentiful in Perpignan, with establishments in all price and comfort ranges, although the most common are small and serviceable, few-frills **hotels**. Cheaper places tend to cluster along noisy avenue Général-de-Gaulle near the train station, but they're a long way from the sights – central lodgings are more convenient and comfortable.

The well-run **youth hostel** (☎04.68.34.63.32; closed mid-Dec to mid-Jan; curfews 11am–4pm & 11pm) abuts a noisy main road between the train and bus stations in Parc de la Pépinière, behind the police station on avenue de Grande-Bretagne. The two closest **campsites**, both with a swimming pool, are clearly signposted from the city centre: well-equipped *Roussillon Catalan* on route de Bompas 8km north of town (☎04.68.63.16.92; March–Oct), out of bus range, and the smaller, more basic but shady *La Garrigole*, 5km northwest of town at 2 rue Maurice-Lévy, reachable by bus #19 (☎04.68.54.66.10).

### Near the station

**Avenir** 11 rue de l'Avenir ☎04.68.34.20.30, ⓦwww.avenirhotel.com. Unprepossessing, simple comfort on a relatively quiet side street, with a wide range of rooms from singles to a family quad; also has secure parking (extra fee). ❶–❸

**L'Express** 3 av Général-de-Gaulle ☎04.68.34.89.96. Small, old hotel whose rooms barely surpass the functional, but they do all have TV. ❷

**Le Helder** 4 av Général-de-Gaulle ☎04.68.34.38.05, ⑤04.68.34.31.09. Clean but run-down budget hotel, with larger rooms for groups or families. ❷

**Le Méditerranée** 62bis av Général-de-Gaulle ☎04.68.34.87.48, ⓦwww.hotel-mediterranee.com. Trendy hotel that's popular with the backpacking crowd. The building isn't stellar and service is rather lax, but a bar, cybercafé and laid-back atmosphere compensate. ❸

### In the centre

**La Cigale** 78 bd Jean-Bourrat ☎04.68.50.20.14, Ⓔhotelcigaleperpignan@wanadoo.fr. Modernized, comfortable hotel at the far end of the Promenade des Platanes, near the church of St-Jacques. Good facilities and service. ❸

**de France** 16 Quai Sadi Carnot ☎04.68.34.92.81, Ⓔfrancehotel@wanadoo.fr. Beautifully appointed nineteenth-century hotel perfectly located on the edge of the old town, overlooking the canalized Basse River. ❹

**De la Loge** 1 rue Fabriques-Nabot ☎04.68.34.41.02, ⓦwww.hoteldelaloge.gr. Beautifully renovated medieval mansion with a central fountain-courtyard, on a quiet alley in the old quarter. Good value for two-star facilities; air con in some rooms. ❸

**Le Maillol** 14 impasse des Cardeurs ☎04.68.51.10.20, Ⓔhotellemaillol@worldonline.fr. Funky decor and friendly service in this clean, well-kept hotel. Located in the heart of the old town, this is the most convenient for enjoying the town and nightlife, and one of the best deals going. ❸

**Mercure** 5-bis cours Palmarole, edge of old town ☎04.68.35.67.66, ⑤04.68.35.58.13. Ideal for families, this has five suites in addition to well-equipped doubles. ❺

**Le Metropole** 3 rue des Cardeurs ☎04.68.34.43.34, ⓦwww.hotelmet.com. Basic, backpackers' favourite in a narrow, bistro-lined street not far from the Loge. ❷

**Poste et Perdrix** 6 rue Fabriques-Nabot ☎04.68.34.42.53, ⑤04.68.34.58.20. Nineteenth-century hotel with gorgeous period details and balconies. Excellent value for rooms en-suite and not. Closed late Feb to early March. ❷–❸

# The City

Perpignan's medieval walls were demolished in the early 1900s to allow expansion. They were replaced by wide boulevards, which in fact maintain the separation of the city's older districts – where most monuments and museums are – from the new ones. Overriding impressions are favourable: the Mediterranean is perceptible to the east, the River Têt skirts the town to the north, while the narrow River Basse threads through the centre, dispensing welcome greenery along its banks. Between place de la Loge and place Rigaud, the old streets are now a maze of upscale boutiques.

## The place de la Loge and around

The marble-paved **place de la Loge** has been the city's forum for eight centuries, and now lies at the heart of the pedestrianized zone. However, the square itself is so small and narrow that you may not realize you've reached it until you spot the voluptuous statue of Venus by Aristide Maillol (see box on p.127). The *place*'s principal landmark, the 1397-built Gothic **Loge de Mer**, was once the city's stock exchange and headquarters for maritime trade (symbolized by the weathervane in the shape of a medieval sailing ship); the fast-food restaurant which for years defaced the ground floor has, after public outcry, been replaced with a café-restaurant more in keeping with the lacy balustrades and gargoyles adorning the upper storeys. The adjoining building is the sixteenth-century **Hôtel de Ville** (with a second Maillol bronze, *La Méditerranée*, in the courtyard) and next door again stands the fifteenth-century **Palais de la Députation**, once home to the Roussillon parliament. The square long served as the scene of grisly executions, notably during the seventeenth-century Catalan revolt against newly imposed French rule. During World War II, place de la Loge's busy pavement cafés were the place to meet *passeurs*, the men – and sometimes women – who guided refugees across the Pyrenees into Spain.

To the north of place de la Loge rises the fourteenth-century, red-brick **Le Castillet**, the emblem of the city, a surviving fragment of the medieval walls later used as a prison. The adjoining **Porte Notre-Dame** was added in 1478 by Louis XI as the main entrance to the town through its now mostly vanished walls. The whole building, with its massive nail-studded doors and spiral stone staircase, is now home to the **Casa Païral** (daily except Tues: May–Sept 10am–7pm; Oct–April 11am–5.30pm; €4), a beautifully designed museum celebrating Roussillonaise rural culture and the anti-French rebellions of 1661–74, when the tower held captured Catalan insurgents. The place de Verdun, on the south side of Le Castillet, is the setting for summer evening

---

## Discounted museum admission

For €6 you can purchase a **Passeport Musées** for Perpignan, which gives you access to four of the city's fee-entry museums – not including the Palais des Rois. The Palais is included, however, in the "**Inter-site**" discount card, which entitles you to reductions of fifteen to fifty percent on the entrance fees to 38 museums and monuments in the *département* of Pyrénées-Orientales, including the most important fortresses and churches of the Tech and Conflent valleys. The Inter-site card is free and valid for one year, and the reductions take effect after you have visited your first monument. Both passes are available at participating museums and monuments, and you can get the Inter-site card at tourist offices throughout the *département*.

performances of the *sardana*, the solemn Catalan folk dance (see p.139). Nearby, at 1 boulevard Wilson, stands the battered but splendidly ornate **Cinéma Castillet**, the oldest cinema in France, now converted into an eight-screen complex.

A couple of minutes' walk to the southwest of place de la Loge at 16 rue de l'Ange is the **Musée Hyacinthe-Rigaud** (daily except Tues: May–Sept noon–7pm; Oct–April 11am–5.30pm; €4), housed in a seventeenth-century palace, originally the workshop of local artist Hyacinthe Rigaud (born 1659), a favourite of Louis XIV. Later it served as a studio and living space for Picasso, Dufy and Cocteau; today it holds a good collection of modern art, including works by Maillol, Alechinsky and the aforementioned artists. From here, you can continue southwest along adjoining rue Maréchal Foch to no. 52, where a small **Musée d'Algérie Française** (Wed 3–6pm; free) commemorates France's domination of North Africa with bitter nostalgia.

### The cathedral and medieval Perpignan

East of place de la Loge and place Gambetta – the latter scene of the town's open-air market for centuries – stands the **Cathédrale Saint-Jean** (Mon & Wed–Sat 10am–noon & 2–5pm, Tues & Sun 2–5pm; free). It was commissioned in 1324 by Sancho, king of Mallorca, and elevated to cathedral status in 1602 when the diocese was transferred here from Elne. Adjacent stands the Romanesque St-Jean-le-Vieux (closed for renovations), the two churches joined by mammoth buttresses. The cathedral's striking exterior sports bands of polished river stones sandwiched by brick, while inside there's a majestic, columned nave, whose side chapels, though badly damaged, retain some elaborate sixteenth- and seventeenth-century retables. Leaving through the south transept, poke your head in the **chapel** on the left, which is presided over by an excellent fourteenth-century polychrome crucifixion, known as the *Dévot Christ*, and most likely the work of a Rhineland sculptor. Past the chapel, on the left, is the entrance to the **Campo Santo** (April, May & Sept Tues–Sun noon–7pm; Oct–March Tues–Sun 11am–5pm; closed July & Aug), one of France's oldest cemeteries, going back six centuries – it is now used for concerts in summer.

### The caganer and cagatió

Among the Catalan folkloric customs that have survived centuries of French domination are two rather strange ones associated with **Christmas**. The Catalans are known for their elaborate Nativity scenes (*pessebres*), populated by hordes of figurines. However, looking carefully at the local version, among the various shepherds, angels and wise men you'll notice a small figure, usually dressed in peasant garb and a traditional Catalan red cap. This is the **caganer** or "shitter": a crouching man, poised with pants around his ankles, in the act of defecation. Similarly, although Catalan children customarily receive presents on the day of the Three Kings (Jan 6), the **cagatió** (the "shitting log") ensures that they don't go completely empty-handed at Christmas. This consists of a log with a painted-on face, draped with a red cloth at its posterior end. As children gather round the *cagatió*, beating it with sticks and singing a song invoking bowel movements, the blanket is withdrawn to reveal the sweets that it has apparently "excreted". You can purchase your own *caganers* (which now come in various guises including policemen, football referees and political figures) and *cagatiós* at Perpignan's Christmas market, held in front of the cathedral during the four weeks of Advent.

On the far side of Campo Santo, the lively rue de la Révolution Française, with its cafés and bars, intersects a major thoroughfare running into the slums of old Perpignan, which spread southeast to **place Cassanyes**, at the former limits of the city walls. Inhabited almost exclusively by recent arrivals from North Africa, with a Roma enclave centred on **place du Puig** (pronounced "pooch"), this can seem an intimidating district, its refuse piles and hung-out washing stereotypical images of immigrant poverty, though it has improved in recent years. Between the **place Fontaine-Neuve** – its "new" water-source some 700 years old – and place du Puig stands the fourteenth-century **church of St-Jacques** (daily: July & Aug 3–7pm; Sept–June 2.30–5.30pm), the nucleus of Perpignan's oldest parish, originally founded by Jaume I (see below) in honour of his patron saint a hundred years earlier. Since then it has been the seat of the Confraternitat de la Sanch ("blood" in old Catalan), dedicated to the Holy Blood of Christ; each Maundy Thursday, its members process as penitents from the church through town, barefoot and hooded in red or black (so as not to take pride in their piety), carrying heavy candles or crosses. Behind the church the secluded, quiet **Jardin de la Miranda** (daily: July & Aug 3–7pm; Sept–June 2.30–5.30pm) occupies a section of the city's old fortifications and provides an airy respite for the inhabitants of this quarter.

## The Palais des Rois de Majorque

Perpignan's most famous sight, and the kernel around which it grew, is the massive **Palais des Rois de Majorque** (daily: June–Sept 10am–6pm; Oct–May 9am–5pm; €3) on the southern fringes of the old city; the entrance is on the west side of the complex in rue des Archers, around fifteen minutes' walk from place de la Loge, or slightly longer from the church of St-Jacques.

The history of Perpignan is more or less synonymous with that of the palace, originally built in the late thirteenth century as a residence for Jaume I of Mallorca, son of Jaume I of Aragón and Valencia ("The Conqueror"), who captured Muslim Mallorca. At his death the king divided his kingdom between his two sons: to the elder, Pere II, went the titles of Count of Barcelona and King of Aragón and Valencia, along with the greater portion of the realm; the remainder, including Roussillon and Mallorca, went to the younger Jaume. The two branches of the family were immediately at each other's throats, and stayed that way until Roussillon was reunited with Aragón and Catalonia during the fourteenth century by the powerful Pere III. Having passed to the French in 1475, then back to the Catalans in 1493, Perpignan changed hands for the last time in 1642, a couple of years after France had occupied Roussillon in the wake of the revolt of the Catalans against the Habsburg rulers of Madrid. In September of that year, after a siege that was at times commanded personally by Louis XIII and Cardinal Richelieu, Perpignan fell. Vauban, military engineer to Louis XIV, constructed the imposing outer walls in the fit of over-enthusiastic fortification that followed the confirmation of French sovereignty by the 1659 Treaty of the Pyrenees.

After ascending a broad zigzagging ramp designed to accommodate cavalry, you enter a grassy park, with the square thirteenth-century **castle** ahead of you. Passing into the splendid two-storey **courtyard**, with its two storeys of dissimilar, part-Gothic, part-Moorish arches, you ascend the stairs to the former kings' apartments, now a wine boutique. Opposite you'll find the unsullied but sparsely furnished queen's apartments, which have delicately vaulted period ceilings and windows. Between the two sets of royal quarters are the so-called king's and queen's **chapels**, one on the upper floor and one on the lower, both retaining interesting Gothic details including carved corbels and fading frescoes. The palace frequently holds temporary exhibitions on local history and culture (included in admission).

## Eating, drinking and nightlife

Don't dally when pondering **dinner**: most of Perpignan's restaurant shutters seem to roll down at 10pm sharp, though you can get served later at several brasseries which stay open till midnight, including the popular *Arago* and *Café Vienne* in the palm-shaded place Arago, or the Art Deco *Brasserie le Vauban* at 29 Quai Vauban. For a fix of Asian or North African food, head for the eastern side of the old town, particularly rue Llucia, where modest establishments serve up stir-fries and couscous/tajine dishes – you'll find food like this in very few other places along the Pyrenees.

**Café** life is centred on place de la Loge – call in at *Brasserie de la Loge* or *Grande Café de la Bourse* – and place de Verdun, where the *Grande Café de la Poste*, shaded by huge plane trees, is the best. *Café de la Paix* in place Arago is another popular choice, but best of all is the huge, airy *Palmarium*, on the opposite side overlooking the River Basse, a self-service place very popular with the locals, where you can linger for hours over a coffee. All of these serve reasonably priced menus at mealtimes.

Perpignan is not a great city for **nightlife**, but in July and August the town comes alive on Thursday nights with a **street festival** featuring markets and music. Otherwise there are **bars** scattered throughout town: *Casa Nova*, at 8 rue de la Fusterie, features Afro-Cuban sounds; there's the Spanish *bar musical*, *La Movida*, 45 avenue Général-Leclerc; while *O'Shannon* at 3 rue de l'Incindie is the local headquarters for stout. Most of Perpignan's **discos** are on the fringes of town, but in the centre you can dance at *Napoli*, 3 place Catalogne (Wed–Sat 11pm–3am), and *L'Uba*, 5 boulevard Mercader (Wed–Sat 11pm–3am; closed mid-July to mid-Aug; €10). *La Baratina* is a large disco in 5-bis place de la Sardane (Thurs–Sun; up to €10), catering to crowds aged from 18 to 70, depending on the night. Besides the Castillet **cinema**, there's the Rive Gauche four-plex at 29 quai Vauban, with some VO screenings.

### Restaurants

**Casa Sansa** 3 rue Fabriques-Nadal ☎04.68.34.21.84. Catalan cuisine served up in this comfortable establishment, founded in 1846 in one of the old town's most beautiful streets. Wheelchair-accessible. *Menus* €24–38 (children's *menu* available). Closed Sun.

**Le Divil** 9 rue Fabriques-Nebot ☎04.68.34.57.73. Swish, designer restaurant tucked away in a little alley near the *loge*. The speciality is wood-grilled meats, including succulent shoulder of lamb. *Menus* €12–29. Closed Sun & Mon.

**La Fontaine** 12 rue du Théâtre ☎04.68.51.09.39. Quaint and homey little place deep in the old town. Home-cooked Franco-Catalan *menus* with a range of salalds, and tempting desserts. Open until 1am. Closed Mon eve, all Sun.

**Au Père Pernot** 16 av Général-de-Gaulle ☎04.68.51.33.25. Locally respected Catalan cooking featuring a variety of meat and fish dishes, as well as an array of homemade soups. *Menus*

€12–30. All-you-can-eat pancake brunch Sat noon–4pm. Closed Sun.

**Le Perroquet** 1 av Général-de-Gaulle ☎04.68.34.34.36. By the station on the north side of the street, with a good choice of Catalan specialities. *Menus* from €20. Closed Wed Sept–April.

**La Poissonerie** 12 rue Lazare-Escarguel ☎04.68.34.02.01. Cheery seafood place not far from the *loge*. Snack on a plate of a dozen oysters (€12.50) or splurge on the Super Neptune platter which feeds 4 or 5 people for €120.

**La Route de Tanger** 1 rue du Four St-Jean ☎04.68.51.07.57. Welcoming Moroccan restaurant with the usual *tajines* and couscous as well as more adventurous fusion recipes. *Menu* €12. Closed Sun & Mon lunch.

**Le Sud** 12 rue Louis-Bausil ☎04.68.34.55.71. Eclectic and delicious Mediterranean cuisine served up in the heart of Perpignan's Roma quarter. No *menu*, allow €30 for à la carte. Closed Jan–March.

Tarteline 10 rue Petite la Monnaie. Good stop for delicious homemade quiches and tarts, to eat in or take away. *Menu* at €8 (also children's *menu*). Open lunchtime only Mon–Fri (except hols).

Le Tire-Bouchon 20 av Général-de-Gaulle ☏04.68.34.31.91. A small family-run brasserie, the best of those in the vicinity of the station. *Menu* at €13, although an à la carte meal for two can easily run over €50. Closed Wed eve, all Sun & Mon.

El Triquet 9 rue Lazare ☏04.68.35.19.18.

Friendly Spanish-run eatery specializing in Catalan cuisine as well as *tapas. Plats* from €8. Closed Sun & Mon.

Les Trois Soeurs 2 rue Fontfroide, off place Gambetta ☏04.68.51.22.33. Camp, Spanish-flavoured place featuring free jazz (Wed 7.30pm Oct–June) and a (for women only) male revue and dinner theatre (Sat 7.30pm Oct–June). In addition to the *carte*, strong on seafood, there are *tapas* and set lunch menus from €15. Closed Sun & Mon.

## Listings

Airlines Ryanair ☏08.92.55.56.66, ⓦwww.ryanair.com.

Airport Aéroport de Perpignan Rivesaltes ☏04.68.52.60.70, ⓔaeroport@perpignan.cci.fr.

Bicycle rental Véloland, 95 av Mal Juin ☏04.68.08.19.99; Cycles Mercier, 20 av Gilbert Brutus ☏04.68.85.02.71.

Car rental Avis, 13 bd du Conflent ☏04.68.34.26.71; Budget, 9 av Général-de-Gaulle ☏04.68.56.95.95; Europcar, 28 av Général-de-Gaulle ☏04.68.52.95.29; Leclerc, 27 av Général-de-Gaulle ☏04.68.34.77.74; Sixt, 48 av Général de Gaulle ☏04.68.35.62.84.

Hospital Centre Hospitalier, av du Languedoc (☏04.68.61.66.33), on the north side of the city, reached via avenue Maréchal-Joffre.

Internet access La G@re, 62bis av Général-de-Gaulle, or Arena Games, 9 rue de Docteur Pous (daily 3pm–midnight).

Laundry Laverie Foch, 23 rue Maréchal Foch (daily 9am–7pm); Laverie St-Jean, 3 rue Cité E.

Bartisol, near Campo Santo (daily 7.30am–7pm).

Markets General market in place de la République (Mon 7am–1pm, Tues–Sat 7am–12.30pm & 4.30–7.30pm); antiques in Allées Maillol (Sat 8am–6pm); organic food in place Rigaud (Sat 8am–noon). The most colourful market takes place on Saturday and Sunday mornings in the tree-shaded place Cassanyes, where French, Arab and African traders sell cheap clothes, crafts and all sorts of local produce.

Police avenue de Grande Bretagne ☏04.68.35.70.00, and allée Marc Pierre ☏04.68.66.30.70.

Swimming pool Champs de Mars, rue Paul Valéry (Mon & Sat 12.15–1.30pm, Tues, Thurs & Fri 6.30–8pm; €3).

Taxis ☏04.68.35.15.15 or 046.09.36.96.86. There are also taxi stands at place de Verdun, at the train station and on place Arago.

Travel agency Nouvelles Frontières, 40 bd Clemenceau ☏04.68.35.50.55.

# The upper Aude valley

The dramatic, short-lived **Aude** is one of the great rivers of the French Pyrenees, matched in the east of the range only by the Ariège. Rising on the east side of the Carlit Massif, it is restrained for a time by the dams of Matemale and Puyvalador, then let loose to hurtle through gorges to **Quillan**. Just upstream from the gorges, around **Quérigut**, sprawl vast forests of beech and pine interspersed with lush meadows. This is the **Donezan**, a scenic – but poor and neglected – corner of the Ariège. From Quillan, the Aude flows north to Carcassonne, then east to the sea between Narbonne and Béziers.

## Quillan

Clustered on the west bank of the Aude about halfway between its sources and Carcassonne, **QUILLAN** makes a handy stopover on the way to the high

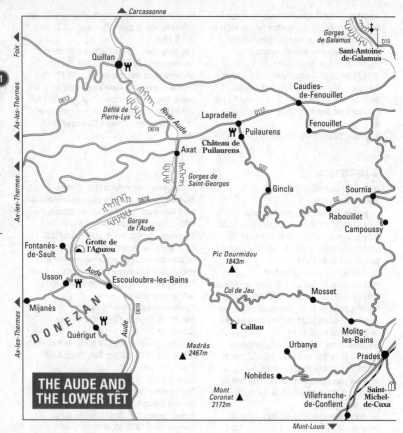

Carcassonne

Gorges
de Galamus

D10

Sant-Antoine-
de-Galamus

Foix

Quillan

Caudies-
de-Fenouillet

Ax-les-Thermes

D613

Défilé de
Pierre-Lys

River Aude

D618

Lapradelle

D117

Fenouillet

Ax-les-Thermes

Puilaurens

Château de
Puilaurens

Axat

D22

Gorges de
Saint-Georges

Gincla

Sournia

Ax-les-Thermes

D618

Gorges
de l'Aude

Grotte de
l'Aguzou

Rabouillet

D2

Campoussy

Fontanès-
de-Sault

Aude

Pic Dourmidou
1843m

Usson

Escouloubre-les-Bains

Col de Jau

Mosset

Mijanès

Caillau

D O N E Z A N

D618

Aude

Quérigut

Molitg-
les-Bains

Madrès
2467m

Urbanya

Prades

Ax-les-Thermes

Mont
Coronat
2172m

Nohèdes

Villefranche-
de-Conflent

Saint-
Michel-
de-Cuxa

**THE AUDE AND
THE LOWER TÊT**

Mont-Louis ▼

Pyrenees. The main attraction of this semi-industrialized place is the river itself,
running right past the town and furnishing ample opportunity for canoeing
and rafting. The only monument of interest is the ruined **castle** on the east
bank of the Aude just across the Pont Vieux. Built on the site of a Visigothic
fortress, it was burned by Huguenots in 1575 and partly dismantled in the
eighteenth century, but the remnants are still worth a scramble.

Train and bus **terminals** are central, opposite the least expensive **hotel** in
town – *Le Terminus*, at 45 boulevard Charles-de-Gaulle (℡04.68.20.94.67,
℻04.68.20.93.33; ❷). All other accommodation is on this same, noisy street,
which doubles as the D117. You won't get any peace and quiet, but will get
more comfort for much the same money at the *Cartier*, no. 31
(℡04.68.20.05.14, @hotel.cartier@wanadoo.fr; closed mid-Dec to mid-
March; ❷) or the *Canal* at no. 36 (℡04.68.20.08.62; ❷). All have attached
**restaurants** (*menus* €11–14), though the *Canal* closes Sunday evening and
Monday.

The **tourist office** occupies a prominent kiosk beside the train station (summer Mon–Sat 8am–noon & 2–7pm, Sun 9am–noon; ℡04.68.20.07.78,

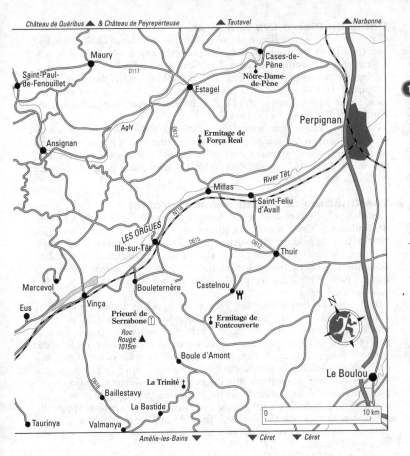

Maury

Saint-Paul-
de-Fenouillet

D117

Cases-de-
Pène

Nôtre-Dame-
de-Pène

Estagel

Agly

Ansignan

D612

Perpignan

Ermitage de
Força Real

River Têt

Millas

Saint-Feliu
d'Avall

N116

LES ORGUES

Ille-sur-Têt

D615

D612

Thuir

Marcevol

Vinça

Bouleternère

Castelnou

Eus

Prieuré de
Serrabone

Ermitage de
Fontcouverte

Roc
Rouge
1015m

Boule d'Amont

N

Le Boulou

D618

La Trinité

Baillestavy

La Bastide

0                    10 km

Taurinya

Valmanya

Ⓦwww.ville-quillan.com), and can help with Grotte de l'Aguzou reservations (see overleaf) among other things.

The Centre International de Séjour Sports et Nature, at the southern edge of town en route to Axat, has a **gîte d'étape** (☏04.68.20.33.69), and organizes **canoeing** and **rafting**, as well as climbing and canyoning trips. *La Sapinette* (☏04.68.20.13.52; March–Oct) at 21 rue René-Delpech, off boulevard Jean Bourrel, is the closest and better equipped of two **campsites**. You can rent **bikes** from Cycles Benassis (☏04.68.20.18.91).

## South from Quillan: gorges and caves

The road **south from Quillan** is a fabulous approach to the eastern peaks of the Pyrenees. Coursing down from the Capcir plateau, the Aude has cut successively through granite, gneiss and schist, and finally soft limestone, carving spectacular caves (*grottes*) and ever-deeper gorges. Public transport is limited to a Monday, Wednesday and Friday afternoon summer **bus** service to Quérigut, 44km south of Quillan, provided by Petit Charles and returning the same day.

## Défilé de Pierre-Lys and Axat

Gorge country begins almost immediately after you leave Quillan heading south, with rock overhangs blasted where necessary to allow passage. The narrowest bit is the **Défilé de Pierre-Lys**, 8km south, where climbers can usually be seen swinging above the road. Four kilometres beyond the defile, there's a campsite, *Le Moulin du Pont d'Aliès* (☎04.68.20.53.27; April–Nov), plus canteen, at the junction where the D117 peels east towards Lapradelle and the Château de Puilaurens (see below).

Continuing south 1km beyond the junction on the D618 brings you to **AXAT**, where an old bridge – under which rafters often put in – links the through-road district with the east-bank quarter. There's just one **hotel** here, the *Auberge La Petite Ourse* (☎04.68.20.59.20; closed part Sept; ❹), at 16 route Nationale, the main street.

## The Château de Puilaurens and around

Lapradelle, 6km east of Axat, is the closest point on the D117 to the **Château de Puilaurens** (daily: July & Aug 9am–8pm; April–June & Sept 10am–7pm; Nov–March 10am–6pm; €4), perched majestically on a 700-metre-high ridge. Without wheeled transport, the castle is just under an hour's walk distant: 2km along the D22 to Puilaurens hamlet, then about a thirty-minute climb up a marked path. With a car, there's a 1500-metre access road beginning 300m south of the hamlet.

Built originally by the Visigoths, Puilaurens was enlarged not long before its indirect conquest by the anti-Cathar crusade (see p.246) in 1255 or 1256, which captured the Cathar champion Chabert de Barbaira and made the cession of all his local strongholds the condition of his release. You enter from the west, via a stepped maze of chicanes or staggered low walls; much of the interior is dilapidated, but be sure to catch the view east over piney hills from outside the southeast postern gate, and the point on the **western donjon** complex where you're allowed briefly on the curtain wall for an eyeful in the opposite direction. Nearby, on the parapet, are machicolations which apparently doubled as latrines, and the so-called **Tour de la Dame Blanche**, with rib vaulting and a *porte-voix* wormhole for communication between different storeys of the tower.

Back at **LAPRADELLE**, the *Hôtel Viaduc* – named after the disused rail viaduct opposite – has better food than its appearance suggests (*menus* from €11) and will do for an overnight stay (☎04.58.20.53.01; ❷). The next closest facility to the castle is 6km southeast at tiny **GINCLA**, where Logis de France member *Hostellerie du Grand Duc* (☎04.68.20.55.02, ✉host-du-grand-duc@ataraxie.fr; closed Nov–March & Wed low season; ❹) also has a well-regarded restaurant.

## Grotte de l'Aguzou

If you have time, try to visit the **Grotte de l'Aguzou**, 15km southwest of Axat towards the upstream end of the Gorges de l'Aude. The guided tour of this magnificent complex is as close as a non-specialist can get to real speleology, and is thus very popular, so it's best to book well in advance (contact Philippe Moreno, ☎04.68.20.45.38, ✉grotte.aguzou@wanadoo.fr). Equipped with overalls, helmet and lamp, groups of four to ten (€50 full day, €30 half-day) are taken into the unlit cave system at 9am, and through the *grandes salles* of stalactites, stalagmites, columns and draperies, some of which are 20m high. Lunch (bring your own) is taken 600m underground – then it's on to the "gardens of crystals": some grow in long needles from the rock, some like pine cones dusted by hoarfrost, and others clear and convoluted like the accidents of a Venetian glass-blower.

If you're on foot, the best place to **stay** for an early start is the designated *camping sauvage* area by the river, 300m from the cave entrance. With a car or bike, head for **ESCOULOUBRE-LES-BAINS**, about 8km up the valley, where *Maison Roquelaire* (☎04.68.20.47.29, ✉maison.roquelaire@free.fr; ❷ B&B) makes evening meals available to hikers and cyclists, and has a hot spring on site.

## The Donezan

In the twelfth century the **Donezan** region (⊛www.donezan.com) and its then-capital **USSON** – in the southern neck of the Gorges de l'Aude – became a sort of forerunner to Andorra: separated from the rest of the Ariège by the **Col de Pailhères** (2001m), it was granted financial privileges on account of its inaccessibility. Today Usson, like the rest of this remote region of seven villages, houses barely enough people to function as a *canton*. The spa of Usson-les-Bains 1km downstream is boarded up and for sale, while the dry-stone walls around the fields are as dilapidated as the **château** (Feb–April & Nov–Dec hols 2–6pm; May & June Sat, Sun & hols 1–6pm; July & Aug daily 10am–1pm & 3–7pm; most Sept daily 10am–1pm & 2–6pm; late Sept to mid-Oct Sat & Sun 2–6pm; closed Christmas hols; €4.70), the first place of safety for the four Cathars who escaped the massacre at Montségur (see p.249). Dating back at least to the eleventh century, the castle was mostly in the hands of the counts of Foix from the thirteenth to the sixteenth century.

Just above Usson, 3km along the D25 to Ax-les-Thermes, **MIJANÈS** is an immensely attractive stone-built village, where you may **stay** and **eat** year-round at the simple but perfectly adequate *Relais de Pailhères* (☎04.68.20.46.97; ❷), with good-sized, wood-floored rooms. Except for *Maison Roquelaire* (see above), this is the only facility of such a standard between Quillan and Quérigut, with people coming from some distance away to patronize it, so reservations are advisable at weekends.

Some 13km west, on north-facing slopes near the Col de Pailherès, the tiny, nine-run **Mijanès-Donezan** downhill ski station (just four drag lifts) is only usable during snowy winters (the top point is just 2000m). Cross-country skiers are probably better served by the 36km of prepared trails in the area.

These days, **QUÉRIGUT**, 7km south of Usson, is the capital of the region. It stands at the head of a slope of neglected terraces, notable only for the stump of the **Château de Donezan**, the last stronghold of the Cathar leaders, who held out here eleven years after the fall of Montségur. **Accommodation** is either at the ageing *Hôtel du Donezan* (☎04.68.20.42.40, ⊛www.hotel-donezan.com; closed mid-Nov to mid-Dec; ❷), uphill from the church opposite the fountain (it also has the town's only **restaurant**), or at the *Auberge du Cabanas* **gîte** (☎04.68.20.47.03; 17 dorm bunks) out at the Col des Hares. There's also a **campsite**, *Le Bousquet*, down by the stream below the village.

# The lower Têt

From Perpignan the Têt valley (also known as the Conflent) provides a fast if initially not very scenic route southwest into the Pyrenees. The **lower Têt valley** skims the base of Canigou peak, and its most interesting parts are found some 30km southwest of Perpignan, where **Ille-sur-Têt** provides a jumping-off point for the spectacular rock formations of **Les Orgues** to the north and, just west, the narrow Boulès gorge climbs south to the region of **Les Aspres**, within whose wooded isolation you'll find the magnificent Romanesque **priory of Serrabone**.

Further upstream along the Têt valley, you'll come to **Prades**, an attractive town and classic access point for the Canigou massif and, skirting the north side of the the famous massif, you reach **Villefranche-de-Conflent**, which marks the transition to the upper Têt, covered on p.105.

## Upstream towards Prades

From Saint Feliu d'Avall on the N116, a six-kilometre detour southeast (or 13km directly southwest from Perpignan on the D612a) brings you to **THUIR** (Tuïr), known chiefly as the main producer of the red aperitif wine called Byrrh (pronounced "beer"). You can visit the winery at 6 boulevard Violet (mid-Jan to March, Nov & Dec Mon, Wed & Thurs 3pm; April & Oct Mon–Sat 9–11.45am & 2.30–5.45pm & Sun 5.45pm; May, June & Sept daily 9–11.45am & 2.30–5.45pm, July & Aug daily 10–11.45am & 2–6.45pm; €1.60) and taste the sweet ferment, which is aged in a cathedral-like gallery of enormous oak vats.

From Thuir you can head directly to Ille-sur-Têt (13km) along the D615, or detour via **CASTELNOU**, an atmospheric, fortified stone village capping a hilltop 5km west from Thuir. Besides a gate and perimeter walls, you'll find a proper tenth-century **castle** (Jan Sat & Sun 11am–5pm; Feb, March & Dec daily 11am–5pm; April–June daily 10am–7pm; July & Aug daily 10am–8pm; Sept–Nov daily 11am–6pm; €4.50), with good views. The best day to come is Tuesday when a local **market** (June–Sept) breathes extra life into the place. You can **eat** very well at *Le Patio* (closed part Oct & part Jan; ☎04.68.53.23.30), offering Catalan cuisine in a relaxed, intimate atmosphere from €20; it's just up the street from Castelnou's old gate. The route beyond the village curves through the exquisite low hills of the eastern Aspres, past the picturesque **Ermitage de Fontcouverte**, before dropping down to Ille-sur-Têt. The whole detour is 25km from Thuir.

### Ille-Sur-Têt and around

Ille-Sur-Têt (Illa) has an attractive medieval quarter of narrow alleys, within which the **Centre d'Art Sacré** (mid-June to Sept daily 10am–noon & 2–7pm; Oct to mid-June Mon & Wed–Fri 10am–noon & 3–6pm, Sat & Sun 3–6pm; €3.20) occupies the seventeenth-century Hospice d'Illà – the local headquarters of the medieval Hospitaller Knights – and hosts temporary exhibitions of local religious art. More remarkable are the clay cliffs just across the River Têt, 1km or so on the road north towards Bélesta, which the elements have eroded into extraordinary figures known as **Les Orgues** ("the Organs"), so called because of their resemblance to the pipes of the church instrument. Rising dramatically up from a deep tributary of the Têt, they can be explored by a series of footpaths laid out within the gorge (July & Aug daily 9.30am–8pm; April–June & Sept daily 10am–6.30pm; Oct–March Mon–Fri 10am–12.30pm & 2–5pm, Sat & Sun 10am–5pm; €3.20).

### Practicalities

Ille's **train station** is a five-minute walk south of the town centre, which is where you'll find the town's **tourist office** (July & Aug Mon–Fri 9am–noon & 2–7pm, Sat & Sun 9am–noon & 2–6pm; Sept–June Mon–Fri 9am–noon &

2–6pm, Sat 9am–noon; ℡04.68.84.02.62, ⓦwww.ille-sur-tet.com). Accommodation options are either noisy or overpriced; it's better to continue 8km upstream, beyond the fortified village of Bouleternère, to **VINÇA**, where you can stay (simply) and eat (well) – *menus* €11–29 – at *La Petite Auberge* (℡04.68.05.81.47; closed Sun eve, Wed, 25 Dec–4 Jan; ❶–❷), 74 avenue Général-de-Gaulle (the N116 on the Prades side of town). The nearby reservoir provides good swimming, windsurfing and canoeing.

## Les Aspres: La Prieuré de Serrabone

The gentle hills of **Les Aspres** are best entered by turning south at Bouleternère and continuing through the gorge of the River Boulès. About 8km along, the steeply winding D84 leads 4km west up to the most celebrated Romanesque monument in Roussillon, the **Prieuré de Serrabone** (mid-Jan to Oct daily except public hols 10am–6pm; €3), whose exterior blends with the surrounding rocky landscape. The hilltop setting with a sheer drop behind is impressive, and the surrounding flora so lush and diverse that a botanical garden has been created around the priory.

Small slabs of local schist cover most of the plain exterior, and only the stubby paired columns of the cloister gallery – topped by ornate, well-preserved capitals – anticipate the richness inside. Halfway along the almost windowless nave, against the bare walls, stands a fastidiously decorated tribune of rose marble, in effect an interior cloister reminiscent of some Spanish Mozarabic churches. Excavated columns found here suggest that much of the original priory – founded in the twelfth century – was as elaborate as the tribune.

Continuing south for 14km along the twisty D618, through the village of Boule d'Amont, brings you to the chapel of **La Trinité**, just before the Col Xatard (752m). Superb ironwork adorns the outside of the door, and inside there's a *Christ en Majesté*, a figure of the same type as the *Majestat* at Beget (see p.167).

From Col Xatard, the D618 drops south into the Tech valley at Amélie-les-Bains, 22.5km away. Another attractive option for drivers is to complete a loop back to the Têt valley at Vinça. This road goes via the tiny village of La Bastide, 8km from Col Xatard, then takes in Valmanya and Baillestavy (see "The Canigou Massif", p.98).

## Prades and Saint-Michel-de-Cuxa

Halfway up the Têt valley, **PRADES** (Prada in Catalan), with its distinctively pink marble masonry and pavements, is by far the area's largest town. It is also the birthplace (in 1915) of Thomas Merton, the American Catholic mystic and author of *The Seven Storey Mountain*, who eventually settled in a Trappist monastery in Kentucky. But Prades is best known for its summer **music festival**, first staged in 1950 by the Catalan cellist **Pablo Casals** (Pau Casals in Catalan; 1876–1973). In exile here from Franco's Spain, Casals composed such works as the oratorio *The Crib* and the popular *Song of the Birds*, after which he named his house. A one-room **Musée Pablo Casals** (July & Aug Mon–Fri 9am–noon & 2–6pm; rest of year Mon–Fri 9am–noon & 2–5pm; free), housed in the same building as the municipal tourist office (see below), commemorates the virtuoso. The church of **Saint-Pierre**, in the main place de la République, contains a huge and sumptuous seventeenth-century retable by the Catalan sculptor Josep Sunyer. Prades is in fact conspicuously Catalan in feel, hosting a summertime Catalan course (10 days in Aug; ℡04.68.96.10.84) and having established the first Catalan-language primary school in France. On Tuesdays and Saturdays an excellent market fills the square and surrounding streets.

Much of the music festival takes place at the restored ninth-century monastery of **Saint-Michel-de-Cuxa** (May–Sept Mon–Sat 9.30–11.50am & 2–6pm, Sun 2–6pm; Oct–April Mon–Sat 9.30–11.50am & 2–5pm, Sun 2–5pm; €3.80), whose single square tower suddenly appears above a copse of poplars 3km south of town, on the orchard-lined road to Taurinya (Torinyà). Saint-Michel reached its peak as a Benedictine community in the eleventh century, then went into slow decline: closed and abandoned in 1790, much of its stone was pillaged during the Revolution, some of it eventually finding its way – like many other Romanesque fragments from the region – to the Cloisters Museum in New York. Since 1937, the premises have been restored in stages, replacing where possible original masonry retrieved from surrounding villages, and re-tenanted by a small community of Benedictines. Highlights of a visit include a subterranean crypt consisting of a circular chapel dating back to the monastery's foundation, and the remains of the broad cloister, with carved twelfth-century column capitals.

### Practicalities

The **train station** is at the southern edge of Prades, about ten minutes' walk from the centre; **buses** set you down on the N116 (avenue Général-de-Gaulle), the main road through the centre. The **tourist office** (July & Aug Mon–Sat 9am–12.30pm & 2–7pm, Sun 9am–noon; Sept–June Mon–Fri 9am–noon & 2–5pm; ☎04.68.05.41.02, ℱ04.68.05.21.79, ⬤www.prades-tourisme.com), at 4 rue Victor-Hugo, is a mine of information about everything from *chambres d'hôtes* to walking or biking trails and climbing Canigou. The **music festival office** is next door (☎04.68.96.33.07, ⬤www.prades-festival-casals.com). You can rent touring and mountain **bikes** at Cycles Cerda on chemin de las Bouchères (near the "Super U" supermarket), or Cycles Flament, 8 rue Arago.

For cheap but salubrious **accommodation**, you can't beat the faded elegance of the white-painted, simply furnished *Hostalrich*, at 156 avenue Général de Gaulle (☎04.68.96.05.38, ℱ04.68.96.00.73; ❶), still run by a family who were friends of Casals. The best alternative is *Les Glycines* at 129 avenue Général-de-Gaulle (☎04.68.96.51.65, ⬤www.glycines.com; ❷), spotlessly clean and friendly. The beautifully sited municipal **campsite** (☎04.68.96.29.83; April–Sept), in the valley just east of the town centre off chemin du Gaz, also has chalets (for 5) for rent by the week or weekend, and a great view of Canigou.

Otherwise, for more accommodation try **MOLITG-LES-BAINS**, the spa which lies 7km away on the north bank of the river. Molitg has two surviving one-star hotels, as well as the two-star *Col de Jau* (☎04.68.05.03.20, ℱ04.68.05.04.38; ❸). If money's no object, burn it on the *Grand Hotel Thermal* (☎04.68.00.00.50; ❻), with marble cladding everywhere, an on-site spa and a good restaurant.

Apart from the stodgy but sustaining *Hostalrich* (*menu* at €12), Prades **restaurants** include the more exciting *El Patio*, at 19 place de la République (closed Wed), serving both traditional and Andalusian-style food at about €20 per head; *Le Jardin d'Aymeric* at 3 avenue du Général-de-Gaulle, with a regularly changing regional *menu* (€19–29; closed Sun eve & Mon); and *L'Hostal de Nougarols* at Codalet on the road to Saint-Michel-de-Cuxa (closed Tues evening & Wed), serving wood-oven pizzas and Catalan specialities for a bit more.

## West from Prades

The D14, through Molitg and beyond, is a quiet and beautiful way of travelling **west to the Aude valley**. The road climbs 5km from Molitg to **MOSSET**, an atmospheric, partly fortified old village whose life and times are engagingly described by Rosemary Bailey (see p.597 in "Books"). Here you'll find the *Ferme-Auberge Mas Lluganas* (℡04.68.05.00.37, Ⓕ04.68.05.04.08; ❷ B&B) with rustic accommodation in the farmhouse, or *chambres d'hôtes* in nearby *La Forge* (❷ B&B); they also do home-cooked meals using their own produce. The road then goes over the **Col de Jau** (1504m) where a track leads 5km south to the **Refuge Caillau** (1537m; ℡04.68.05.00.06), close to the route of the **Tour du Coronat**, a very easy four-day walking circuit in the forests and open hillsides around Mont Coronat. Northwest of the Col de Jau, the road drops 19km through fir forests to join the Aude 4km above Axat.

## Villefranche-de-Conflent

Some 6km beyond Prades the Têt valley narrows dramatically into a gorge, where the high walls of **VILLEFRANCHE-DE-CONFLENT** almost block the way. As there's almost no construction outside the walls, the town looks much as it did three hundred years ago: an elongated, two-street place squeezed between the palisade just to the south and the river. Within the ramparts, the atmosphere of the past is strongest on the bank of the Têt, by the thirteenth-century **Saint-Pierre**; the best view is from the far side, where the weathered red-tiled roofs and the tower of the twelfth-century church of **Saint-Jacques** peer over the ramparts. But more satisfying, perhaps, than any man-made constructions are the vast cave complexes (see below) that riddle the strata below and around the town.

Villefranche (Vilafranca in Catalan) dates from 1092, when Guillaume Raymond, count of Cerdagne, granted the charter for the foundation of Villa Libéra, soon called Villafranca and finally Villefranche, as strategic counter to the counts of Roussillon. His seat was at Corneilla, just up the valley of the Cady, and the logical site for a stronghold was here, at the confluence of the Cady and the Têt. Some remnants from that period still stand, notably the **Tour d'en Solenell** on the little square known as the **Placette**. In 1654 Villefranche – then controlled by Spain – was besieged by Louis XIV's troops, and fell after eight days' fighting. After the Treaty of the Pyrenees annexed Roussillon, the French rebuilt the Spanish fortifications according to plans drawn up by Vauban.

As you walk the maze-like **ramparts** (daily: Feb–May & Oct–Dec 10am–12.30 & 2–6pm; July & Aug 10am–8pm; June & Sept 10am–7pm; €3.50), their vulnerability to attack from the surrounding heights is obvious – a defensive weakness that Vauban remedied by adding various bastions and building the upper château now known as **Fort Libéria** (daily: June–Sept 9am–8pm; Oct–May 10am–6pm; €5.50), high above the main town on the steep northern bank of the Têt. This castle has seen extensive use as a prison: interns have included a group of seventeenth-century Versailles noblewomen, confined in isolation and silence for over thirty years, on charges of witchcraft and poisoning, as well as German POWs during World War I. You reach the fort by hiking up a winding dirt road which starts just outside Villefranche's eastern gates, or on the complimentary minibus departing from outside the Porte de France.

## The caves

The most celebrated incident in Villefranche's history was the 1674 revolt against French rule, which culminated in the betrayal of **Charles de Llar** and his co-conspirators by Llar's daughter Inès. The tale was melodramatized by Louis Bertrand in his novel *L'Infante*, published in 1930. Llar's hiding place was the Cova Bastéra, now known as the **Grottes de la Préhistoire** (daily: July & Aug 10am–8pm; Sept–June 10am–noon & 2–6pm; €5), a cave that he could enter and exit from within the walls of the town; today's entrance is just west of the walls. Consider buying a combined ticket, also good for the limestone **Grottes des Canalettes** (April–Sept 10am–6.30pm; off-season call ☎04.68.05.20.76; 45min guided tour; €6), 1km along the road south towards Vernet-les-Bains. The most spectacular caves, however, are the adjoining **Grottes des Grandes Canalettes**, which demand a separate ticket (April to mid-June & mid-Sept to Oct daily 10am–6pm; mid-June to mid-Sept daily 10am–6.30pm; Nov–March Sun & school hols 2–5pm; by appointment ☎04.68.96.23.11, ⊛www.grottes-grandes-canalettes.com; 1hr guided tour; €7; €10 for entry and *son et lumière*). Entry is via a 160-metre passageway, hollowed out by water over 400 million years; the water dripping down the sides is now directed over moulds to create limestone images for sale at the shop. Beyond a door you enter a succession of huge, fancifully named chambers crammed with stalactites, stalagmites, pillars and tiny, feathery formations. Beyond the *Dôme Rouge* lies the *Gouffre sans Fond* (The Bottomless Pit), stretching for several kilometres and the domain of speleologists only.

## Practicalities

Main-line **trains** from Perpignan terminate in Villefranche, at the **station** 400m north of the town; for *Train Jaune* services further up the Têt (see p.105) simply change platforms. Buses to Vernet-les-Bains stop at the train station and just outside the Porte de France. The **tourist office** (Feb–Dec daily 10am–12.30pm & 2–5.30pm; ☎04.68.96.22.96) runs a booth at the entrance to the ramparts, where they sell local hiking and biking guides (€5–9). **Jeep excursions** up Canigou depart from outside the train station (contact M. Bouzan on ☎04.68.05.62.28).

The only **hotel** here is the magnificent old *Auberge du Cèdre* (☎ & ⓕ04.68.96.05.05; closed Nov–April; ❷), situated just east of the old walls, near the *gare*, though there are welcoming **chambres d'hôtes** with a swimming pool, *Mireille Pena* (☎04.68.96.52.35, ⓔmpebafain@aol.com; ❹), located off the same lane. The most interesting of the **restaurants** are the pricey, innovative *Auberge Saint-Paul* on place de l'Eglise (allow €45; closed Mon; Sun eve & Tues low season), and *Le Menestrel* (some vegetarian dishes) in rue St-Pierre, the alley leading down to the Pont St-Pierre (and on to Fort Libéria).

# The Canigou Massif

Rising in splendid isolation to 2784m between the Tech and Têt valleys, the **Pic du Canigou** (Canigó in Catalan) is the great landmark of Catalonia, visible across the coastal plains from both the French and Spanish Mediterranean coast. Though well inside French territory, the mountain became a symbol for lost Catalan independence and enduring cultural unity during the nineteenth-century literary renaissance, endorsed today by the small Catalan flags and other patriotic paraphernalia festooned from its summit cross. Before modern topographic surveys had covered the entire Pyrenees, Canigou was thought erroneously to be the range's highest peak – a curious conceit, given the handful of 2800-metre-plus frontier peaks visible just southwest between Mantet and Núria.

There are essentially only two ways of reaching the top of Canigou – via the **Chalet des Cortalets** (2150m) on the northern slopes, or via the **Refuge Grand Mariailles** (1718m) to the southwest. The various approaches to these shelters are detailed below. Routes from the Tech valley on the south are longer and therefore not specifically recommended for climbing Canigou – although you might use them to move from the Tech to the Têt, taking in Canigou along the way. When not clouded over, the peak affords breathtaking views – check conditions before setting out. Autumn is generally the best time to bag the **summit**, when it's snow-free (unlike in late spring); conditions are not optimal in summer, owing to the heat and reduced visibility.

If you're serious about exploring the massif – which is a partly protected natural reserve, good for several days' trekking – either Rando Éditions' 1:50,000 "Canigou/Vallespir/Fenouillèdes" *carte de randonnées*, or the TOP 25 1:25,000 **map** no. 2349ET "Massif du Canigou", is a mandatory investment, available at shops and souvenir stalls in all surrounding villages. Editorial Alpina's 1:40,000 "Massís del Canigó" may also be of interest, not least for giving all place names in Catalan.

## Northern approaches to Canigou

The northeasterly route up Canigou is the quiet and impressively steep (but not difficult) approach from **Valmanya**. To its northwest, a 4WD track from near **Prades** is the scenic but busy alternative.

### The Valmanya route

From Vinça in the Têt valley, the D13 follows the River Lentilla south along the eastern flanks of Canigou, past Finestret (4km). From here the **GR36** cuts through the wooded western slopes and fields of the valley, rejoining the road at Baillestavy (12km from Vinça). As the russet streaks on nearby rocks suggest, the Canigou massif is rich in iron ore; there's a mine above the village and traces of a first-century forge by the river.

The Resistance stronghold of **VALMANYA** (Vallmanya), another 5km by road or GR trail, was destroyed by the Germans in 1944 – some of the houses were reduced to rubble, others set ablaze. Despite rebuilding and the magnificent setting at 874m, there's a lingering sadness to the place; on the plus side, it now has a 22-bunk *gîte d'étape*, Le Roc de l'Ours (℡04.68.05.93.99, ℮ valmanya@wanadoo.fr; mostly triples and quads), well placed to end a day's march from Vinça.

From Valmanya, the **GR36** climbs sharply west through woods to **Ras del Prat Cabrera** (1739m), where it meets a track from Villerach, near Prades, and more attractively the **GR10**, which traverses a bit higher via la Tartère to the *Chalet des Cortalets*. Alternatively, minor trails head south from Valmanya to intersect the GR10 at the forestry hut at **Estanyol** or the **Abri du Pinatell**. You could just about make the return trip from Valmanya to Canigou's summit in a day, but it's more manageable with a night at or near *Chalet des Cortalets*.

### The Prades route

The gentlest ascent to *Chalet des Cortalets* is the one used by the 4WD taxis (roughly €25 per person) from Prades; booking offices in Prades include Ria (℡04.68.05.27.08) and Corbières Grand Riad (℡04.68.05.24.24). If you're driving, take the D35 out the south side of Prades to Villerach (8km; signposted as "Clara-Villerach"), where a dirt track rises to the chalet 20km away – an hour's drive. (If you're on foot, there are much better hiking approaches – read on.) This is a superb route, often shadowing the River Llech, each turn revealing a new arrangement of rock, water, sky and forest. An ordinary car can easily get as far as the ruined hut at Prat Cabrera (1650m), an hour's walk from the *Chalet des Cortalets*, and – with extra care and ideal conditions – all the way to Cortalets.

## Northwestern approaches: Vernet-les-Bains and around

More direct footpaths from the northwestern side begin from Fillols and Casteil, both above Vernet-les-Bains, the closest proper town to the massif. The D116 leads 6.5km south from Villefranche to **VERNET-LES-BAINS**, the pleasantest of the spas around Canigou, though it's still somewhat stuffy. English visitors like Rudyard Kipling made the place fashionable during the nineteenth century, and a waterfall, 3km out of town on a well-marked track, is even called the **Cascade des Anglaises**. Along with the thermal plunge-pools and adjoining therapy wings – first installed in 1377 – a range of more contemporary pastimes is now offered (mountain biking, canyoning, hydrospeed and caving), though the baths are still the focus of activity. The often-overlooked old quarter is capped by the ninth-century but much-restored double church of **Nôtre-Dame-del-Puig/Saint-Saturnin**, which incorporates remaining bits of a castle. You can also visit the town's **geological museum** (daily 9.30am–noon & 2–6pm; €3), with its collection of local fossils.

Vernet has a *gîte d'étape* (℡04.68.05.51.30; 32 bunks; closed Nov) in chemin St-Saturnin, on the left bank of the Cady next to the municipal pool. The town's best accommodation is a pair of Logis-de-France-affiliated, two-star **hotels**, each offering a range of amenities and reasonable value: the *Eden*, 2 promenade du Cady (℡04.68.05.54.09, ℻04.68.05.60.50; closed Nov–March; ❷), and the *Princess*, rue de Lavandiers (℡04.68.05.56.22, ☜www.hotel-princess.com; closed Dec–March 15; ❸). Nearest **campsites** are *Les Cerisiers* (℡04.68.05.60.38; mid-May to Sept), on the same side of the river as the *gîte*, and *Dels Bosc*, 1km north on the Villefranche road (℡04.68.05.51.62; April–Sept). **Eating out**, you can dine on wood-roasted meats and tasty homemade desserts in the elegant surroundings of pricey *Le Cortal* (closed Mon and Oct & Nov), up in the old quarter behind the church at rue de Château. The **tourist office** is on place de la Mairie (Mon–Fri 9am–noon & 2–6pm; ℡04.68.05.55.35, ☜www.ot-vernet-les-bains.fr). **Jeep-taxis** up Canigou (same price as from Prades) and to the monastery can be arranged through Garage Villaceque (℡04.68.05.66.58).

### The Fillols routes

The standard **walking ascent** from Vernet is by a footpath that begins 1km northeast along the D27, towards the tiny village of **FILLOLS**. This climbs within three hours to the derelict **Refuge de Bonneaigue** (Bonaigua; 1741m) and the **GR10**, along which the *Chalet des Cortalets* is another ninety minutes' walk.

For those with a 4WD or a very sturdy car, a track begins some 5km from Vernet, just past Fillols; this route is also used by taxis from the two villages –

you can book one at the *Café de l'Union* in Fillols (☎04.68.05.63.06), as well as arrange a meal. The track rises gradually at first, past *Les Sauterelles* **campsite** (☎04.68.05.63.72; June–Sept), then with dramatic steepness in a series of tight hairpins to the large **Refuge de Balatg** (1610m), the derelict *Cabane des Cortalets* (1975m), and finally the chalet itself. This isn't as pretty a route as that from Prades – and the poorer surface makes it inadvisable for conventional cars – but a more open topography produces awesome views.

## Casteil – and Saint-Martin-du-Canigou

From Vernet-les-Bains the paved road (covered by 4 daily buses, Mon–Sat) leads 2500m south to **CASTEIL** (Castell), where you can eat and stay at either *Relais St-Martin* (☎04.68.05.56.76; ❶), or more picturesque two-star *Le Molière* (☎04.68.05.50.97, ✉hotelrest@lemoliere.com; ❷), with garden-view front rooms and a friendly summer restaurant under the mulberries (great country cuisine from €17). There's also a campsite, *Camping St-Martin* (☎04.98.05.52.09; April–Sept), with a swimming pool. Casteil is an appealing, quiet hamlet, well placed for Canigou and the GR10, the latter less than an hour away on the **Col de Jou**, accessible by a delightful short trail designated "Itinéraire 1" that shortcuts the road. On the ridge just east stands the restored twelfth-century **Tour de Goa**, reached by another path from the *col* which eventually drops to the spa at Vernet.

### Saint-Martin-du-Canigou

You're most likely to visit Casteil for the nearby monastery of **Saint-Martin-du-Canigou**, whose image is ubiquitous, celebrated on local book covers, postcards and posters. Access is only by a thirty-minute climb up the path, or 4WD from Casteil on a steep, narrow road, which helps protect the place from the worst tour-bus excesses – as does its continued use by an active religious community.

Built from tan stone and roofed with grey slates, the monastery ranks as one of the most gorgeous monuments in the Eastern Pyrenees, and the surrounding woods of sweet chestnut, beech and aspen form a perfect backdrop to the pinnacle of rock on which it stands. The foundation stone of the building was laid in 1001 by Count Guifred de Cerdagne, who retired with his second wife Elisabeth to the monastery in 1035; you can see their purported **sarcophagi** at the base of the tower. Severely damaged by an earthquake in the fifteenth century – the tower lost a storey – and thoroughly pillaged after abandonment in 1782, Saint-Martin (Sant Martí in Catalan) was restored in two phases (1902–32 and 1952–82), initially through the efforts of the bishop of Perpignan. The glory of the place resides in its **cloister capitals**, retrieved by the good cleric from a particularly wide dispersal.

The monastery is now occupied by an unusual mixed order of monks and nuns, called the "Beatitudes", with a sprinkling of lay workers. Ordinarily, visitors are allowed only on **guided tours** (hourly: Feb to Easter Mon & Wed–Sat 10am, noon & 2.30–4.30pm, Sun 10am, 12.30pm & 2.30–4.30pm; Easter to mid-June & late Sept Mon–Sat 10am, noon & 2.30–4.30pm, Sun 10am, 12.30pm & 2.30–4.30pm; mid-June to mid-Sept Mon–Sat 10am, noon & 2–5pm, Sun 10am, 12.30pm & 2–5pm; €3.85). The "Beatitudes" sponsor extended retreats by individuals (write to the abbey at 66820 Casteil, or phone ☎04.68.05.50.03).

Descending from the rear of the complex, you can take an alternative marked footpath for half an hour back to Casteil via the entrance to the **Gorges du Cady**, where the river falls 500m over a distance of 3km, making this a popular spot for canyoning.

Abbey of Saint-Martin-du-Canigou △

## Saint-Martin to Mariailles or Cortalets

At the rear of the monastery grounds another path leads up to a signposted viewpoint. You can continue on the path, an excruciatingly steep but shady, beautiful and well-marked route, for just under three hours to the **Col de Segalès** (2040m, spring 5min away) on the GR10. Despite the grade, this provides the most direct all-trail access from the Vernet area to the staffed *Refuge Grand Mariailles* (see p.104), another ninety minutes of up-and-down trekking, south of the *col* by a roundabout route. The three-hour traverse north to *Cortalets* is quite scenic and a bit more direct, but again there is a fair bit of roller-coastering and a short stretch of track-walking. Many people do the Saint-Martin-to-Cortalets leg in reverse, as part of an east–west traverse of the massif, beginning from Valmanya or Batère (for which see pp.99 & 118).

## Cortalets to the summit

A *maquisard* hideout in the last war, and consequently heavily shelled by occupation forces, the restored **Chalet des Cortalets** (2150m; ☎04.68.05.63.57 or 04.68.96.36.19; 111 places; mid-May to late Oct) is now run by the Club Alpin Français. There are double rooms as well as made-up beds in the **dormitories**; **meals** in the bar-restaurant cost about €12. Be warned that despite its capacity the refuge can fill, and the tracks bring up cars full of revellers – as opposed to walkers – at weekends to picnic at the tables around the little lake, ten minutes' walk west of the refuge. **Tents** are tolerated on the lake shore, and next to another smaller pond closer to *Cortalets*.

### The summit

The normal, well-marked approach **to the summit** goes past the larger lake, with its fine view up into the summit cirque, then climbs south along the ridge leading from **Pic Joffre**, which often teems with isards at sunset. It takes a little over ninety minutes and provides only a slight sense of exposure as you reach the wrought-iron summit cross and *table d'orientation*. In clear weather, the views taking in everything from Andorra to the sea are as hoped for.

At midsummer (observed in Catalonia on the eve of June 23–24, the *Festa de Sant Joan*), the refuge and the peak are spots to avoid or gravitate towards depending on your temperament: seemingly half the population of Barcelona descends for merrymaking and the lighting of the traditional bonfire, torches from which are then relayed to ignite numerous others in Catalan villages on both sides of the frontier. Even at other times, a patriotic Catalan or two is prepared to bivouac the night beside the peak's highest cairn.

There is an alternative, less frequented and even more dramatic route, climbing south from *Chalet des Cortalets* along the **Crête de Barbet** to the **Porteille de Valmanya** (2591m), a beautiful ridge-walk. Beyond the *porteille*, follow the ridge a bit below it to the left – the sharp drop northeast is alarming – before clambering up a boulder-gully to the summit (2hr 30min). The Pic Joffre and Barbet routes can, of course, be combined to make a circuit.

## Southwestern approaches: the Rotja valley

To tackle ascents of Canigou **from the southwest**, take a bus from Prades or Villefranche (Mon–Sat 1–2 daily) along the **Rotja valley** to **SAHORRE** (Saorra). This has an ancient church plus an excellent, admirably set **hotel**, *La Chataigneraie* (☎04.68.05.51.04; ✉chataignotel@aol.com; ❸), with a pool and good **restaurant**.

**PY** (Pi del Conflent), 6km upstream, remains a traditional mountain village

– certainly compared to more-visited Casteil or Mantet (see below) – but even here there are plenty of houses for sale and signs of seasonal occupation. So far the only concessions to tourism are a horse-riding stable, one *gîte d'étape* (☎04.68.05.58.38; 13 dorm bunks; June to mid-Sept) and a combination café-restaurant-*épicerie*.

The usual approach to Canigou from Py is to follow the **GR10** northeast to the **Col de Jou** (1125m), then descend into the ravine upstream from Casteil, shortcutting the dirt road most of the way to the large, comfortable **Refuge Grand Mariailles** (1718m; ☎04.68.05.57.99, ✉mjordronneau@wanadoo.fr; 55 bunks; closes Jan), three hours on foot from Py. After a night at *Mariailles*, take the GR10 east into the forest via the **Col Vert**, then into Cady valley. From Jasse de Cady the footpath heads west to the Col de Segalès and continues to the *Chalet des Cortalets* (route described overleaf).

The direct way to the **summit** from Jasse de Cady, though, is to continue east-northeast along the Cady valley, past the basic, unstaffed Refuge Arago, to the **Porteille de Valmanya** (2591m), then up to the summit as described on p.103.

## Mantet

From Py the paved road climbs steeply southwest through countless hairpins, many of which can be bypassed on the GR10, though generally it's a dull, steep hike. When you reach the **Col de Mantet** (1761m), two-plus hours' walking from Py, a glorious wilderness unfolds before you: the village of Mantet is invisible, clinging to the slope 200m below the *col*, while further south spreads the beautiful Alemany valley, its eastern flank covered in pines. The far end of the valley, where the **Porteille/Portella de Mantet** (2412m) leads into Spain, is a *réserve naturelle* home to isards.

The inhabitants of **MANTET** (Mentet) were expelled by the Nazis towards the end of World War II, and the village was resettled only in the 1960s. It's since been expensively restored for holiday homes, and despite having only twenty or so permanent inhabitants, Mantet supports a 22-place *gîte* attached to the local horse-riding centre, *La Cavale* (☎04.68.05.57.59, ✉info@la-cavale .fr), including some triples (**②**) and quads, and on the road below an *auberge* (☎04.68.05.51.76; **❹** HB only), its good **restaurant** open to others with advance notice.

### Walks from Mantet

From Mantet a spectacular **route up Canigou** involves climbing through the woods southeast from the Col de Mantet to the **Pla Ségala**, and then along the ridge to **Roc Colom** (2507m). Here, pick up the **HRP** and follow it along the line of rock teeth known as Les Esquerdes de Rotja to **Collade des Roques Blanches** (2252m) and then **Pla Guillem** (2277m), where there is a simple, unstaffed refuge. It's already a long day but if you still have daylight and strength, the *Refuge Grand Mariailles* – an hour-plus descent further – is much more congenial.

Canigou aside, this is a great walking and horse-riding area. Especially worthwhile treks are south along the **Ressec valley** (east of the main Alemany valley) to the source of the Mantet stream (4hr), and along the **Caret valley** (west of the Alemany), with its groups of ruined stone cottages and shady riverside path. The **GR10** climbs from the Alemany valley west over the **Col del Pal** (2294m) into the **Carança valley** and the *Refuge Ras de Carança* (4hr 30min from Mantet; see p.108). From here, you can stick with the GR10 until Mont-Louis; head north down the valley for Thuès (see p.107) or south into Spain at Núria (see p.176).

# The upper Têt

The lower Têt finishes at Villefranche-de-Conflent, above which the shaggy flanks of the **upper Têt** close dramatically around the *Train Jaune* line and the N116; these forge separately along the river to Mont-Louis, at the top of the Têt. En route there are a number of small villages, on the valley floor or perched just above, which make serviceable bases for excursions into the hills. Of these, the hot springs and no-nonsense **Carança gorge** near **Thuès**, and the **Mont Coronat** area north of **Olette**, are the most rewarding.

Many **abandoned villages and farmsteads** on the Têt valley slopes have become home to colonies of ageing hippies and more punkified "travellers". The presence of these mainly non-French interlopers in an isolated and conservative mountain society still causes tension, but most locals have grown accustomed to their flamboyant appearance and accepted them in a quiet spirit of rural *convivencia*. At any rate, these settlers, frequently seen operating market stalls in lower-altitude centres, are here to stay – after more than twenty years of continuous habitation they have acquired legally binding "squatter's rights" to their properties and cannot be evicted from the hamlets, many of which still lack utilities or any other municipal services.

## Excursions north of the Têt

Most of the villages along the Têt valley aren't really worth leaving the train for, but some give access to marvellous hikes just north. At **OLETTE**

---

### The Train Jaune

The best way to move up the Têt valley towards the Cerdagne is on the **Train Jaune** (*Tren Groc* in Catalan), once an essential local service, but now more of a fun ride – during summer some carriages are open-air. Built early in the twentieth century, the railway climbs 63km from Villefranche (427m) to Latour-de-Carol (1231m), where it connects with the trans-Pyrenean railway between Toulouse and Barcelona. Tourism saved the scenic narrow-gauge line from closure in the early 1970s, but a repertory melodrama still features threats of funding cutbacks, counter-protests and a general future uncertainty. As it is, return tickets are valid for only 24 hours, with **fares** double those of French main-line services; as an example, Villefranche to Mont-Louis and back (the most popular stretch) will cost at least €16.

From late May to September there are four to six daily **departures** in each direction; the first leaves Latour-de-Carol soon after 8am, and takes two and a half hours to reach Villefranche. During the rest of the year, service is cut to two round-trips. Since most of the line is single track, there are often delays caused by long halts at Mont-Louis or Font-Romeu to allow the uphill train to pass, the first of these leaving Villefranche well before 8am. The train is scheduled to stop only at certain stations, designated in capital letters on the timetables and train maps; if you want to alight at one of the smaller, unstaffed stations (designated *arrêts facultatifs* on carriage placards) you have to notify the driver in advance. Similarly, to get on at such stations, you have to flag the train down. When walking near the line, beware the electrified "third rail", an exposed potential safety hazard.

For information on timetables and prices, contact the following stations: Villefranche-Vernet-Fuilla (☎04.68.96.56.62); Mont-Louis (☎04.68.04.23.27); Font-Romeu (☎04.68.30.03.12); Bourg-Madame (☎04.68.04.53.29); or Latour-de-Carol (☎04.68.04.80.62). You might also consult ⊛www.ter-sncf.com/trains_touristiques /train_jaune.htm.

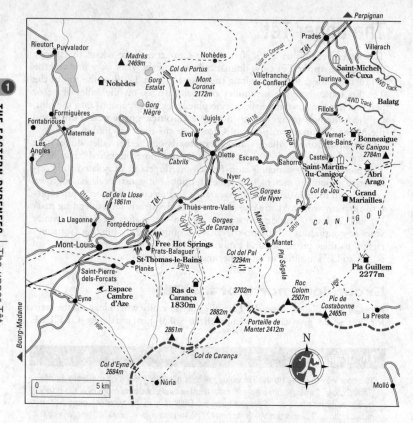

(Oleta), much the biggest place between Villefranche and Mont-Louis (with the only grocery shop en route), you can **stay** and **eat** comfortably at *La Fontaine* (℡04.68.97.03.67, 🖷04.68.97.09.18; closed Jan, Tues eve & Wed low season; **②–③**), on the main street. From Olette, a path and road lead 2.5km north to **EVOL**, where the church of **Saint André** contains a splendid painted retable by the so-called Maître du Roussillon, dating from 1428. The massive ruined **château**, just above the village on the onward road to the Col de Portus, was built in 1260. Between Olette and Evol the D4 peels off into the tranquil **Cabrils valley**, a longer, steeper (1861m at the Col de la Llose/Coll de la Llosa) but more attractive road to Mont-Louis than the Têt route.

### The Tour du Coronat

From Olette it's also 3km by road northeast to **JUJOLS**, usual start of the four-stage, waymarked **Tour du Coronat** around the **Mont Coronat** massif. There's a good *gîte d'étape* in Jujols, *Les Cardabeilles* (℡04.68.97.02.40; 25 places as doubles, quads, dorm), and another in **NOHÈDES** (℡04.68.96.38.15), but you'll still need to camp out one night. The highlight of the tour is actually

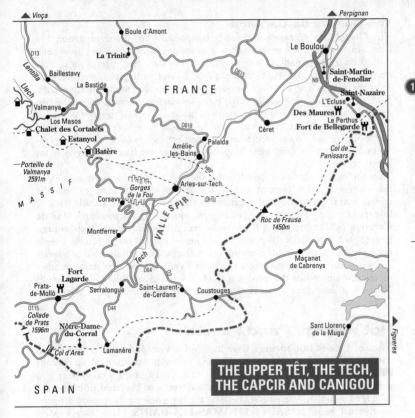

THE UPPER TÊT, THE TECH,
THE CAPCIR AND CANIGOU

slightly off its western extension, the **Col de Pertus/Coll de Portos** (1736m), from where you climb 300m to the lakes of **Gorg Estelat** and **Gorg Nègre**, situated at the foot of the gentle **Pic Madrès** (2469m).

## The Carança gorge area

A few minutes past Olette on the *Train Jaune* at **NYER** (*Camping La Catalane*; ☎04.68.97.07.63), the road south from the station through the village climbs into the impressive **Gorges de Nyer**. However, you're probably better off staying on the train until Thuès-Carança station, four minutes above the small spa of Thuès-les-Bains and gateway to the even more spectacular Gorges de Carança. The nearby village of **THUÈS-ENTRE-VALLS** is home to a delightful **gîte-campsite**, *Mas de Bordes* (☎04.68.97.05.00, ☏04.68.97.11.51), next to the church, also with self-catering suites; follow signs up the path from the train stop or the main road (N116). This restored farm is part of a 300-hectare property that includes its own outdoor hot springs, a remote log cabin and a meadow for pitching tents. The place is always mobbed during July and August, when you must ring ahead; good *table d'hôte* dinners are provided for about €14, a blessing since the village itself is not up to much.

### The Gorges de Carança

The **Gorges de Carança** are clearly signposted from the train station and from Thuès village, and more notices at its mouth (over which the *Train Jaune* clatters on a bridge) advise you to enter at your own risk. After a short walk from the car park, the path divides: the left-hand path (signposted for Roc Madrieu) climbs steeply up the wooded side of the valley, while the right-hand path (over a small bridge) follows the more spectacular corniche route; the two converge at the *pont des singes* (suspension bridge). The first ninety minutes of corniche walkway are the most amazing, poised over sheer four-hundred-metre drops – not for the vertigo-prone. Next are a series of nerve-racking cat-walks, ladders and wobbly metal suspension bridges, the latter not advisable for heavily laden walkers.

Yet the overall elevation gain towards the border is the gentlest around, so the canyon makes a popular outing: it's best to start off early to beat the crowds and the heat. Beyond the narrows, the route becomes a shady, stream-side trail on the west bank; the countryside opens out, and you reach **Ras de Carança** (1831m) in about three-and-a-half hours. The rather basic **refuge** here (℡04.68.04.13.18; 19 places; staffed June–Sept 15) offers equally simple meals, and there's plenty of camping space nearby. To reach the first of a series of lakes – the easternmost along the main Pyrenees crest – requires another ninety minutes, while the border at Coll de Carança, and the GR11 towards Núria, is at least three hours distant and thus beyond the scope of a day-trip from Thuès.

## Hot springs – and Planès

If you're a fan of **hot springs**, leave the train at **Fontpédrouse** (Fontpedrosa) station, the stop above Thuès-Carança, and follow the twisty road up towards **PRATS-BALAGUER** village on the south slope. From the second hairpin, a path leads east down to a trio of open and undeveloped **thermal pools** on the far side of the valley. Alternatively, head for the large, beautifully renovated, open-air thermal baths at **SAINT-THOMAS-LES-BAINS** (daily except Mon 10am–8pm, July & Aug until 9pm; €3.50), 3km from Fontpédrouse station, open all year round for an open-air hot dip or hamam after skiing or hiking.

Just before Planès, the *Train Jaune* passes over the 150-metre-long **Pont Gisclard** suspension bridge, which carries the track 80m above the river. It was designed by mathematician and engineer Albert Gisclard, who was tragically killed by a runaway train on the very day of the official bridge trial in 1909. The peculiar triangular church at **PLANÈS** was once thought to be an adapt-ed Muslim structure, but the bell-tower is typically Cerdagnois, and the dome surrounded by three semicircular half-domed apses has close parallels through-out the region. Near Planès, there's a 24-place *gîte d'étape*, Le Malaza (℡ & ⑮04.68.04.83.79), with two dorms, a handful of doubles (❷), and evening meals (€12).

## Mont-Louis and around

The next *Train Jaune* station – **La Cabanasse** – serves the garrison town of **MONT-LOUIS**, at 1600m the highest on the Têt, lying 14km southeast of the river's source, the Lac des Bouillouses. Known as the gateway to the Cerdagne, Mont-Louis (10min walk northeast of the station) is the masterpiece of **Vauban**, Louis XIV's military engineer, built quickly but solidly between 1679 and 1682. In contrast to the high, fragile walls of Villefranche, the moated **ram-parts** (Tues–Sat 10am–noon & 2–6pm; €2) of Mont-Louis are massive and

A footbridge over the Gorges de Carança △

low to maximize resistance to artillery fire. Even Vauban admitted that the fortifications might fail in their intended function; indeed, throughout the eighteenth century hostile armies entered France through the Cerdagne, bypassing
the citadel.

Though promoted as a resort, Mont-Louis is still essentially a military town,
with French commandos occupying its citadel and training on surrounding
slopes. Apart from the ramparts, Mont-Louis' only other attraction is the
world's first **solar oven** (*four solaire*), built in 1949 and now open for guided
tours (year round except Dec 1–15 at 10am, 11am, 2pm, 3pm, 4pm; €5); the
huge mirror for the oven stands in the moat, just left of the main gate (Porte
de France). There's another *four solaire* in nearby Odeillo (see p.225).

There is a **tourist office** in rue du Marché (July & Aug 9.30am–noon &
2–7pm; Sept–June Tues–Sat 10am–noon & 2–6pm; ☎04.68.04.21.97,
☜www.mont-louis.net). The most comfortable **accommodation** is to be
found at *La Volute* (☎ & ℱ04.68.04.27.21; ❸), a B&B set in the seventeenth-
century former governor's mansion; and the attractively furnished *Hotel La
Taverne*, 10 rue Victor Hugo (☎04.68.04.23.67, ☜www.bernagie.fr; closed for
some of March and part of Nov & Dec; ❸–❹), with excellent Catalan *menus*
from €15. But the best value is offered by *Hôtel Lou Rouballou*
(☎04.68.04.23.26, ℱ04.68.04.14.09; closed May & Oct/Nov; ❷), near the
barracks in rue des Ecoles-Laïques, whose celebrated **restaurant** (closed
lunch, and Wed low season) offers mushrooms, boar, duck and *ollada* (stew)
among other local delicacies (set menus €20–30). The closest **campsite**, *Pla*

*de Barres* (☏04.68.04.21.18; mid-June to mid-Sept), lies 3km west along the road towards Lac des Bouillouses, beautifully set under the pines by a stream.

### The Eyne area: skiing and walking

The road from Mont-Louis to Planès passes through **SAINT-PIERRE-DELS-FORCATS**, one of the base villages for the amalgamated ski zones known as the **ESPACE CAMBRE D'AZE** (Cambra d'Ase), after the eponymous peak overhead (2711m), cloven by a quarry-like cirque. Heading right at the fork above Saint-Pierre takes you to **EYNE** (Eina), the other base village (the *Train Jaune* stop is Bolquère-Eyne); a joint ski pass covers both zones. The 25 runs, served almost entirely by drag lifts, are biased towards beginners and intermediates, though some are quite long and end scenically amidst the pines. Espace Cambre d'Aze is north-facing, with respectable top points of 2400m/2300m for the two sectors (where the few advanced pistes start), but snow can be unreliable this close to the Mediterranean – 257 snow canons help combat any deficit.

Saint-Pierre has no short-term accommodation, but at Eyne you can stay at the two-star *Le Roc Blanc* (☏04.68.04.72.72; ❸), or at the **gîte/chambres d'hôtes** *Cai Pai* (☏04.68.04.06.96; 30 places), each of which serve up excellent country-style meals for under €17. Half- or full-day horse-riding and botanical outings are available through *Le Licol Vert* (☏04.68.04.72.48).

Southeast of Eyne lies the **Col d'Eyne** (or **Coll de Núria**; 2684m), the second most important bird migration corridor in the Pyrenees, after the Col Organbidexka (see p.495) in the Basque country; autumn migrations produce the greatest variety, including honey buzzards, kites and falcons, as well as bee-eaters and other rarities. A signposted path about 300m west of Eyne village, part of the HRP, runs up to the *col* through a forested valley, which is blessed with a peculiar microclimate and thus supports a wealth of flowers and herbs in its meadows. After three-plus hours the HRP attains the *col*, then follows the ridge east (soon in tandem with the GR11) until the head of the Carança valley.

# The Capcir

Between the upper Têt valley and the gorges of the upper Aude spreads the sedimentary plateau called the **Capcir** (✆www.capcir-pyrenees.com). Bare and extremely flat – traits accentuated by the large artificial lakes of Matemale and Puyvalador – it's cradled by densely wooded slopes that sweep up to Pic Madrès and the Carlit Massif, with only the **ski-resort** pistes interrupting the trees. One of the harshest winter climates in southern France makes this excellent cross-country ski terrain, while summer promises wonderful, easy walking, with several refuges or *gîtes d'étape*, plus hotels in a number of villages.

## Capcir ski resorts

All of the Capcir **ski resorts** lie on, or just off, the D118 road served by the taxi-bus. Nearest to Mont-Louis, northeast-facing **LES ANGLES** is also the area's largest and most advanced centre, with 32 pistes, more than half of them red-rated, totalling over 40km. Two *télécabines* and a chair-lift get you up from the base station and village (1650m) to a plateau at 1900–2000m, where there's another chair-lift to the secondary top station, 2325-metre **Roc d'Aude**; from here two drag lifts give access to the true summit at **Mont Llaret** (2377m).

Numerous drag lifts and 255 snow canons fill any gaps in coverage. Chalets rather than high-rises predominate, but the old village has still been almost completely swamped. **Accommodation** is in five hotels, best value being *Le Coq d'Or*, place du Coq d'Or (℡04.68.04.42.17, ℻04.68.04.44.84; ❹), and *Llaret*, 12 avenue de Balcère (℡04.68.30.90.90, ℻04.68.30.91.66; closed May–June & mid-Sept to Nov; ❹).There are also two local **gîtes d'étape**: *Les Cimes*, at 1-bis rue des Pics-Verts (℡04.68.30.93.03, ✉monique.escoubet @libertysurf.fr; 30 places), and *Equisud* on Route de la Forêt (℡04.68.04.43.62, ⊕www.equisud.com; 24 places).

## Formiguères and Matemale
**FORMIGUÈRES**, 6km further north, is far more attractive with its shops (some selling outdoor gear), cafés and crêperies giving it the feel of a county town. Its **church of Sainte-Marie** features an unusual triangular facade culminating in the belfry; inside is a masterful, seventeenth-century Majestat, typical of the Catalan region.The seventeen downhill runs (total 20km), through the conifers between 2350m and 1700m, are pitched at strong intermediates, but more interesting perhaps are the over 100km of local **cross-country skiing trails**.

On the southeast corner of the church square there's a helpful **tourist office** (July & Aug 8.30am–12.30pm & 2.30–6.30pm; Sept–June 9am–noon & 3–6pm ℡04.68.04.47.35, ⊕www.formigueres.net) which, among other things, rents keys for the municipal tennis courts. Formiguères has two **hotels**: the one-star *Picheyre* behind the church (℡04.68.04.40.07, ✉hotel-picheyre@wanadoo.fr; ❷; closed late April to early June & Nov) and the fancier *Auberge de la Tutte*, on the road out of town by the junction for Les Angles (℡04.68.04.40.21; ❸).There's a 20-place *gîte d'étape* in an old barn, with a few doubles and meals offered, at Espousouille (℡ & ℻04.68.04.45.37), a kilometre or two up through the trees by footpath – but 6km by road. The **restaurant** in the *Picheyre* is resolutely old-fashioned, good value at €15 (no à la carte), but dull of menu, like lunching at your gran's and with a clientele to match.

If that doesn't suit, the *Auberge de la Belle Aude* (℡04.68.04.40.11, ℻04.68.04.39.89; ❷) in **MATEMALE**, a deceptively large village tucked in a hollow by the Aude 4km south, has more comfortable accommodation and traditional Catalan *menus*, which include typical dishes such as *boules de picoulat,* as well as roast meats and fish, starting at €17; they've even managed to squeeze in a tiny pool under a conservatory for rare *capcinoise* hot days.

## Puyvalador and Rieutort
The ski station at **PUYVALADOR**, at the north end of the Capcir plateau, is 5km west of its namesake reservoir and village (which has no amenities). It's the smallest of the Cerdagne ski resorts, with just sixteen east- or north-facing runs between 2382m (the **Pic du Ginèvre**) and 1700m, with more here for beginners or weak intermediates than at Formiguères. The only tourist facilities at this end of the plateau, outside the ski station, are at **RIEUTORT**, 2km west of Puyvalador village. Here Vagabond'ane (℡04.68.04.41.22) on the main square rents mules and organizes donkey safaris; in winter snowshoeing is offered instead. Some fifty paces above the square you can feast on trout and crayfish straight from a tank at the excellent *Al Cortal* (℡04.68.04.45.00; open supper only during ski season; lunch and dinner in summer; weekends only otherwise), with slightly pricey four-course *menus* from €28.

## Hiking: the Tour du Capcir

The Capcir woodlands are eminently suitable hiking territory, well within the capabilities of a novice walker. Randonnées Pyrénéennes issues maps and booklets describing the **Tour du Capcir**, a four-day circuit (easy to pick up at Espousouille, Puyvalador or Matemale) that runs along both sides of the valley as well as taking in **Pic Madrès** (2469m) to the east. You can make use of the *gîte d'étape* at Espousouille, the hotel at Matemale plus the staffed refuges at Bouillouses (see p.231) and Camporells, with one night either camping out or staying in the unstaffed *Refuge de Nohèdes*, a little to the southeast of Madrès summit. The *Refuge de Camporells* (2240m; ☎04.68.04.49.86; open mid-June to mid-Sept), by the cluster of eponymous lakes on the western leg of the *tour*, is wonderfully set in an area rich in wildlife, also partly accessible by the chair lift that operates even in summer at Formiguères (45min walk from the top of the lift to the refuge).

The Tour du Capcir grazes the Tour du Carlit on the west and the Tour du Coronat on the east, allowing the possibility of adding portions of either of these to your itinerary.

# The Tech valley and the Albères

The **Tech valley** (or Vallespir) is the southernmost in France, and its exceptional sunshine (300 days a year) and relatively low rainfall nurture a flora that includes oranges, cacti and bougainvillea – as well as dense forest on the higher slopes. Proximity to the border made the Tech a major escape route from occupied France during World War II. The easiest mid-elevation pass into Spain, the Col d'Ares, was so heavily patrolled that *passeurs* had to use more remote routes along the main **Albères** ridge, whose enduring loneliness still appeals to casual walkers. Fugitives assembled at **Céret** or **Le Boulou** would be led out over one of two *cols*, either Lly or Llosa; from **Amélie-les-Bains** there was a tough ascent over the 1450-metre Roc de Frausa. From **Arles-sur-Tech**, further up the valley, the route led to **Saint-Laurent-de-Cerdans** and the Col des Massanes into Alto Garrotxa, or **Coustouges** and along the Riou Majou into Alt Empordà. From the tiny spa of **La Preste** and the small walled town of **Prats-de-Molló**, escapees fled along the ancient paths of the *contrabandiers*, through the Col del Pal or the Collade de Prats. The solitude of the **Albères** ridge – extending from Saint-Laurent-de-Cerdans in the west to the Mediterranean at Banyuls-sur-Mer – is intruded on east of the Tech only at **Le Perthus**, little better than a border shopping town and truck-stop. Besides the crossing at Le Perthus, the D115 road up the Tech valley slips into Spain at the **Col d'Ares**, a scenic and almost equally popular route.

## Le Boulou

**LE BOULOU**, a traffic-clogged little spa town situated just off the autoroute 20km south of Perpignan, is the **cork** capital of France. At the beginning of the 1900s there were 140 square kilometres of cork oaks locally, planted as a substitute for grapevines destroyed by phylloxera. Cultivated primarily to produce stoppers for the champagne industry, the plantations shrank to around 50 square kilometres in the face of competition from less expensive Portuguese

Like much of the central and eastern Pyrenees on either slope, the **Albères** are well sown with **Romanesque churches and monasteries**, erected between the eleventh and thirteenth centuries. Though much more populated than it is now, the region was never especially wealthy, and the isolation and subsquent neglect of these monuments meant that many of their original features, which would have been remodelled beyond recognition elsewhere, have survived intact. Romanesque churches are typically compact and squat, with few windows and a single nave overarched by simple barrel-vaulting. Scupltors of the period excelled at relief work, especially biblical scenes populated by bulbous-featured characters adorning column capitals, corbels and the tympanum above the main door. Less commonly, striking frescoes once covered the interiors of many Romanesque churches; boldly coloured, surprisingly modern-looking designs served, as elsewhere around the Mediterranean, to illustrate biblical scenes and sacred personages for contemporary illiterate parishioners.

These churches can be visited on a circuit by bicycle, scooter or car in a day – a stimulating break from the beach-side hedonism of Argelès and Collioure. Buses serve the D618 between Argelès and Le Boulou only sporadically; non-suicidal cyclists can avoid the first stretch of this busy road by using older, quieter, parallel routes. Some 4km west out of Argelès, your first stop will be **SAINT-ANDRÉ**, where an old abbey-church in allée de la Liberté houses the **Musée Transfrontalier d'Art Roman** (June–Sept Mon–Sat 9am–noon & 2–6.30pm; Oct–May Wed–Sat 10am–noon & 2–5.30pm; €2), which is visited on an hour-long guided tour. Outside these hours, content yourself with a look at the lintel over the entrance, showing Christ surrounded by angels and apostles. A further 4.5km takes you to **SAINT-GÉNIS-DES-FONTAINES**, once home to an ancient **Benedictine abbey**. Most of this has disappeared (the cloister in particular to Philadelphia), but the two-metre lintel over the church doorway is one of the earliest (1020) examples of Romanesque sculpture in France – an engagingly primitive array of apostles and angels. Inside (June–Sept Mon–Fri 10am–noon & 3–7pm, Sat & Sun 9am–noon & 3–7pm; Oct–May daily 9.30am–noon & 2–5pm; €2), the single row of short columns in the fine thirteenth-century cloister supports semicircular arches of multicoloured local marble, as well as capitals carved with fantastic creatures and a crucified Christ.

From here a minor road leads 3km south to Laroque-des-Albères, from where the D11 goes west to Villelongue-dels-Monts. From here a steep and winding road, intermittently signposted for the "Église", leads up to the former Augustine convent and pilgrims' hostel of **Santa Maria Vilar** (daily 3–6pm; 1hr guided tour €4). Originally founded in 1089, the present church dates to 1149, although sections, like the impressive Carolingian hall, are older. The main attraction here are the beautiful eleventh- and twelfth-century frescoes, featuring both geometric and human motifs. Santa Maria is home to a well-reputed *Festival Lyrique*, featuring Gregorian chant and troubadours (July & Aug Sat 9pm; €16), an event worth planning for. From Laroque you can follow the D2 east back to Argelès, or from Santa Maria continue on the D11 to Montesquieu-des-Albères (3km) before descending to the D618.

cork, but a recent revival has been spurred by chronic brush fires, as cork oak is very flame-resistant and therefore a better bet than more combustible crops.

In town, it's worth pausing at the **Église Sainte-Marie**, whose portal features a fine Romanesque marble tympanum frieze; more works by the same anonymous artist can be found at a small **history museum**, the *Espace des Arts*

(Mon–Fri 9am–noon & 2–6pm, Sun 9am–noon; free), and at the **Monastir del Camp Prieuré** (tours on the hour Fri–Wed 10am July–Sept 10am–noon & 3–6pm; €4), some 11km north, beyond Passa.

South of Le Boulou, just beyond the River Tech and the local spa, stands the remarkable **chapel of Saint-Martin-de-Fenollar** (mid-June to mid-Sept daily 10.30am–noon & 3.30–7pm; rest of year daily except Tues 2–5pm; €3). Its twelfth-century frescoes – including a rare image of the Virgin reclining in a bed after the Nativity – are the best Romanesque wall paintings in Roussillon, and their clarity and simplicity of line may well have influenced Picasso, who sometimes stayed in nearby Céret.

A stretch of the non-toll N9 follows the line of the Roman Via Domitia, and there's evidence of the antiquity of the route 4km south of Saint-Martin, where a pair of ruined Roman forts cap the steep outcrops flanking the road. The one to the west, known as the **Château des Maures**, can be reached only by fording a stream. The nearby **church of Saint-Nazaire** contains frescoes reminiscent of those at Saint-Martin, and possibly by the same painter (key available from the *mairie* in L'Écluse village).

### Practicalities

Le Boulou's **tourist office** (Mon–Fri 9am–noon & 2–6pm, Sun 9am–noon; ℡04.68.87.50.95, ✆www.ot-leboulou.fr) is on the central place de la Mairie. Some **accommodation** here might come in handy during high season: try *Hôtel Le Grillon d'Or* (℡04.68.83.03.60, ✉le-grillon@wanadoo.fr, ❸) in 40 rue de la République (*menus* €15–35), or elegantly rustic *Le Relais des Chartreuses* (℡04.68.83.15.88; mid-March to Oct; ❺–❼), occupying an old Catalan *masia* (farmhouse) at 106 avenue d'En Carbonner. Both have swimming pools.

## Le Perthus and the frontier zone

On the night of February 5, 1939, a column of twenty thousand Spanish Republicans arrived at the border post of **LE PERTHUS** (El Portús, Castilian; or Els Límits, Catalan), 4km beyond L'Écluse, to seek sanctuary in France. More recently it was armies of consumers who came here in search of foodstuffs, booze and perfume, until EU price convergence stemmed the flow. Filling up with cheaper petrol on the Spanish side is still popular though. In fact, nipping into Spain by car, less than a euro's toll on the autoroute, will likely save you an hour's delay in frequently bottle-necked Le Perthus. If you're on a GR10 traverse and looking for a place to stay, your only choice is *Chez Grand-Mère* at the summit of the main road (℡04.68.83.60.96, ℻04.68.83.63.72; closed Christmas to mid-Feb; ❷ or ❹ HB).

In Roman times the Via Domitia crossed the Albères 2km west at the **Col de Panissars**, which is probably the way Hannibal came in 218 BC. When Pompey returned victorious from Spain a century and a half later, he ordered a triumphal monument to be built at the *col*, and the excavated base of this edifice is now visible through barbed wire. On a nearby hill on the French side rises the **Fort de Bellegarde** (July–Sept daily 10.30am–6.30pm; €3). Constructed in the sixteenth century and later reinforced by Vauban, it contains two rows of dilapidated buildings and the deepest well in Europe (63m) within an enclosure of mighty walls, giving superb views south into Spain and north across Roussillon. Both fort and monumental base are reached by a narrow dirt road doubling as a section of the GR10 (20min walk from Le Perthus).

The **GR10** and the **HRP**, here combined, pass through Le Perthus/Panissars on their east–west route along the summits of the Albères. Banyuls-sur-Mer, on the Côte Vermeille (see p.126), lies nine hours east of Le Perthus along the GR10. There's just one facility en route, not well placed for lunch: the *Chalet de l'Albère* (☎04.68.83.62.20), two-and-a-half hours distant at the **Col de l'Ouillat**, a twenty-place *gîte d'étape* with **restaurant** aimed also at those arriving by car on the D71. Heading west on the GR10/HRP, the nearest amenities are at **LAS ILLAS**, just under half a day away but the only spot to divide the twelve-hour stage to Arles-sur-Tech. Choose between the well-run *gîte d'étape* (☎04.68.83.23.93; April–Sept; 19 places, dorm & doubles), or the *Hostal de Trabucayres* (☎04.68.83.07.56; ❷) just up the road, with a decent restaurant.

## Céret

The cherry orchards of **CÉRET**, 8km upstream from Le Boulou, are the basis of its prosperity, yielding around 4000 tonnes of fruit in late spring. It's a friendly, bustling town – the Catalan feel reinforced by bilingual street nomenclature – with a shady old quarter of narrow and winding streets that open onto small squares like **plaça dels Nou Raigs** (Nine Spouts), named after the central fountain. Only parts of the two medieval gates remain obvious, though many houses are incorporated into the fortification walls themselves. According to legend the single-arched **Pont du Diable** – one of three bridges that span the Tech at Céret – was built with diabolic assistance in 1321 in return for the soul of the first *Céretian* to cross. The engineer who made the bargain duly sent a cat over first, but the trick backfired as none of the locals would then risk the Devil's vengeance by using the bridge themselves.

The best time to visit is during any of the town's famous summer **festivals** (see pp.78–79), which have a markedly Catalan and Spanish flavour, but you'll have to plan ahead, as accommodation sells out well in advance. Like Prades on the Têt, Céret was a sanctuary for refugees from Franco's regime, with many artists passing through or staying here. Long before the Spanish Civil War, the town had been a temporary home to such luminaries as Pablo Picasso, Marc Chagall and lesser-known Catalan and French artists, including Pierre Brune, who in 1950 opened the **Musée d'Art Moderne** at 8 boulevard Maréchal Joffre (mid-June to mid-Sept daily 10am–7pm; rest of year Wed–Mon 10am–6pm; ❻www.musee-ceret.com; €5.50). A small but varied collection does justice to Fauvists, Cubists and Surrealists; highlights include a series of painted ceramic bowls with bull motifs by Picasso, masterpieces by Juan Gris and nudes from Pignon.

Other town sights include a small **archeological museum** (daily 10am–noon & 2–6pm; €1.50) tucked behind one of the old gates, the **war memorial** by Aristide Maillol in the old town and the **monument** to the composer Déodat de Sévérac by the Catalan sculptor Manolo in avenue Clemenceau, just around the corner from boulevard Maréchal Joffre. If you head north 100m from the town centre on avenue d'Espagne, you'll find **Le Capelleta** (Sat 10.30am–12.30pm & 3.30–7pm; free), a tiny church with a well-executed Romanesque lintel over the entrance, and temporary art exhibits inside.

### Practicalities

Buses from Perpignan stop 250m north of the old quarter at the bottom of avenue Clemenceau. The **tourist office** (July & Aug Mon–Sat 9am–12.30pm & 2–7pm; Sept–May Mon–Fri 10am–noon & 2–5pm, Sat 10am–noon;

①04.68.87.00.53, ⓦwww.ot-ceret.fr) is at the top of avenue Clemenceau, on the corner of boulevard Maréchal-Joffre. The most central **accommodation** is provided by the cheerfully decorated one-star *Vidal*, atmospherically housed in the old bishop's palace at 4 place Soutine (①04.68.87.00.85, ⓦwww.hotelvidalceret.com; closed Feb & Nov; ❷). Opposite stands the balconied, modern two-star *Les Arcades* (①04.68.87.12.30, ⓕ04.68.87.49.44; ❸), and you might also try the two-star *Pyrénées*, at 7 rue de la République (①04.68.87.11.02, ⓔericlegentil@wanadoo.fr; March–Dec; ❸). All these places have a variety of rooms available, with and without bath. The most comfortable option, however, is *Le Mas Trilles* (①04.68.87.38.37, ⓕ04.68.87.42.62; ❺) at Le Pont de Reynes, a small hotel (meals for residents only) set in a seventeenth-century *mas* overlooking the Tech. There are several local **campsites**, two of them on route de Maureillas: *Les Cerisiers* (①04.68.87.00.08; March–Oct) and *Saint-Georges* (①04.68.87.03.73).

The hotels all have **restaurants**, of which the best value is the parquet-floored one (closed Wed) attached to the *Vidal*, with *menus* at €21–27, and a snack outlet too (€2–3 per dish). Otherwise, try bistro-creperie *Le Pied dans le Plat* (closed Sun; from €11.50), with outdoor seating on plaça dels Nou Raigs. Social life at the *Grand Café* in boulevard Maréchal Joffre is perhaps not what it was when the "*bande* Picasso" hung out there, but it's still a good place to sit outside with a glass of wine and a plate of *frites*; there are more **cafés** around the corner by the Porte de France. Finer dining can be found at *Les Feuillants* (①04.68.87.37.88; closed Sun eve & Mon), set in a grand old house at 1 boulevard La Fayette (*menus* €30 & 46). Saturdays see a morning farmers' **market** along the old walls, the street stalls groaning with local produce.

## Amélie-les-Bains

The spa of **AMÉLIE-LES-BAINS**, 8km up the valley, tends to attract the elderly and unwell, and unless you're taking a cure, there's not much to do here. Nor is it worth pausing to see the Gorges du Mondony, poor relation of the nearby Gorges de la Fou (see below), while Fort les Bains (part of Vauban's defences), perched high above the town, is not open to visit. From Amélie you can cut through Les Aspres on the D618 road to the lower Têt (see p.93).

The **tourist office** (July & Aug Mon–Sat 9am–7pm; Sept–June Mon–Fri 9am–noon & 2–6pm Sat 9am–noon; ①04.68.39.01.38, ⓦwww.amelie-les-bains.com) is near the bus stop on quai du Huit. Unless you're on an HRP traverse, it's unlikely you'll want to stay, though there's a glut of **accommodation**. Easily the most characterful is *Le Castel-Émeraude*, a converted folly on the riverbank Route de la Corniche (①04.68.39.02.83, ⓦwww.lecastelemeraude.com; closed Dec–Feb; ❸–❹), with a restaurant (*menus* €15–30).

## Arles-sur-Tech

**ARLES-SUR-TECH**, 4km further along the valley, is quieter and more atmospheric than Amélie, its medieval quarter focused on the **abbey of Sainte-Marie**. The first abbey, built late in the eighth century, was soon destroyed by Viking raiders and the present church (Mon–Sat 9am–noon & 2–6pm; €3.50) was consecrated in 1046. Before passing through the main door built into its impressive facade, check out the grilled-off marble block just to the left. This is **La Sainte-Tomb**, formerly a reliquary for the bones of two obscure early saints, and now focus of a phenomenon that has resisted scientific explanation: since the bones were removed, this sacrophagus has produced over 500 litres of water annually, drawn off and distributed to the faithful on July 30. The church itself has some interesting side chapels and a tranquil, thirteenth-century **cloister**, with pointed double-columned arches surrounding an attractive garden of box and cypress. The cloister leads to the **Musée du Fer**, which re-creates the town's medieval iron-smelting and mining industries (April–June & Sept–Oct Mon–Fri 2–7pm; July & Aug Mon–Fri 10am–noon & 3–7pm, Sat 3–7pm; €2).

Arles is most famous, however, for its February **Fête de l'Ours**, a pagan holdover claimed to be among the oldest observances in Europe. Traditionally, bears were said to interrupt their hibernation at the February new moon, terrorizing the villagers, who devised the ploy of luring the boldest animal with a local girl, before chaining the bear and then shaving it. There being a contemporary shortage of bears, these days a young man is dressed in a bear skin and blackface, hunted down by the crowds, captured and stripped, after which a communal meal is served.

### Practicalities

The **tourist office** (Mon–Sat 9am–noon & 2–6pm; ☎ & ℻ 04.68.39.11.99, ⊛ www.villes-arles-sur-tech.fr), in rue Barjou at the top of the town, has suggestions for walks and trails around Arles, plus a local map (the GR10, which passes through the town, is not well signposted locally); it also keeps a list of *chambres d'hôtes*. The only **hotel** is the comfortable two-star *Les Glycines*, 7 rue du Jeu-de-Paume (☎ 04.68.39.10.09, ℮ hotelglycines@wanadoo.fr; closed Nov 15–Feb; ❸), which also has the best **restaurant** in town, with a shaded terrace and Catalan specialities (*menus* from €18). The alternatives for eating out are *La Treille* (☎ 04.68.39.89.59; Sept–May closed Mon) at the beginning of boulevard Riuferrer, with a pleasant vine-shaded terrace (€12 *menu*), or the grill-bar at the Musée Jean Cordomi (March–Dec 10am–10pm), opposite the *mairie*. There are several **campsites**, including the scenic *Riuferrer* (☎ 04.68.39.11.06), on the west side of town, near the mouth of the Freixe stream; *Le Vallespir* (closed Nov–March; ☎ 04.68.39.90.00) on the road to Amélie-les-Bains; and the naturist *Le Ventous* (☎ 04.68.87.83.38, ⊛ www.perso.club-internet.fr/le vento; June–Sept), on the road to Prats-de-Molló.

### The Gorges de la Fou

A couple of kilometres up the main valley road from Arles are the **Gorges de la Fou** (April–Nov daily 10am–6pm, weather permitting – phone ☎ 04.68.39.16.21 if in doubt; €5), one of the great – if touristy – spectacles of the Eastern Pyrenees. You need at least an hour to cover the 1500m of metal walkway to the end and back, squeezing between 200-metre-high walls, so close together that they have trapped falling rocks. In places, water erosion has made the walls as smooth as plaster, and on occasion the storm-swollen torrent has swept part of the walk away. If you can't make it to the Gorges de Kakouetta in the French Basque country (see p.492), these are a respectable consolation prize.

### Walking out of Arles: to the Albères or Canigou

The GR10 climbs **southeast** from town through the Arles forest to Montalba d'Amélie (no facilities), at the head of the Mondony gorge, and onto the summit ridge of the Albères, just below Roc de Frausa (1450m). There's little habitation between Arles and the *gîte* at Las Illas (see p.115), a long (8.5hr) day's trek away.

Heading **northwest**, you could do the **Arles-to-Cortalets** approach in a single day, given an early enough start, but it's an arduous trek of over nine hours, beyond the capabilities of most walkers. From Arles, it's wisest to forgo the first, unsightly section of the GR10 in favour of the blue-dot-marked "Dolmen 1hr 30min" path, which leaves the road towards the campsite, just above the town swimming pool. You can break the trek four hours along at the *Auberge de Batère* (T04.68.39.12.01; April–Oct; 39 places, dorms and doubles ❷) installed in the old miners' hostel at **BATÈRE**, which has a good bistro. The ironworks are evident as an ugly scar resulting from open-cast extraction between the twelfth and seventeenth centuries. If you're in a group, you can save yourself some rather tedious trekking by taking a **taxi** up to this *gîte*, along the paved D43 side-road, which begins from the west end of Arles. After 7km you'll pass the stone-built village of **CORSAVY**, with its Romanesque chapel of Saint-Martin-de-Corsavy and a restaurant or two.

Alpine Canigou truly begins just west of the *gîte* at the **Col de le Cirère** (1731m), beyond which unfurls the section of corniche trail dubbed the **Balcon du Canigou** for its sweeping views northeast. Two hours beyond Batère, the forestry hut at Estanyol (potable spring) fits eight at a pinch, or you can camp adjacent; the *Chalet des Cortalets* (p.103) is still almost three hours away along the GR10.

## Minor upper Tech villages

Accessible both along the D44 from Corsavy and the D54 from the main valley floor, **MONTFERRER**, 6km from Arles by the shortest route, is – with its ruined castle and Romanesque church – one of the most attractive settlements in the upper Tech. Set amongst dense forest and crags, with sweeping views east to the opposite side of the valley, it enjoys its status as the truffle capital of Roussillon; the village can also muster a good campsite with a swimming pool.

Some 7km beyond Arles-sur-Tech, the D3 side-road ascends south from the main D115 through chestnut forests to the village of **SAINT-LAURENT-DE-CERDANS** (9km from the junction). During World War II the local clergy oversaw the passage of refugees southwest towards Mont Nègre, crossing the frontier by the Col des Massanes (1126m), or up to Coustouges for the Riou Majou trail. Nowadays, marked variants of the HRP run east and west along the border.

*Passeurs* normally asked their clients to wear espadrilles, quieter than ordinary shoes and giving good traction on rocky surfaces. Saint-Laurent was once a major producer of *bigatanes*, the special Catalan espadrille with a double rope sole and ankle-laces. You can see how espadrilles were made from esparto in the **Musée d'Arts et Traditions Populaires** (May, June & Sept daily 10am–noon & 3–6pm; July & Aug 10am–noon & 2–7pm; Oct–April Mon–Fri 10am–noon & 3–6pm; €2). Beside the Laurent stream are a pair of **campsites**, while the nearest **hotel** is the very comfortable but pricey *Domaine de Falgos*, converted from an old barn off the road to Coustouges (T04.68.39.51.42, Wwww.silencehotel.com; closed Jan & Feb; ❼).

From Saint-Laurent the road climbs 5km further east to the tiny hamlet of **COUSTOUGES** (Costojas), from where the spine of the Albères rises northeast to the highest point of the chain at **Roc de Frausa** (1450m). The large church, built in unusual pink sandstone and granite, and with a richly carved portal, would have also served the villages over the present frontier at the time of its construction in the twelfth century.

You can vary the road return to the Tech valley by detouring along the D64 to **SERRALONGUE**, which offers a fine eleventh-century **church** with an elevated pavillion used by priests of old to ward off destructive storms (another such structure is found at Son, p.271). The D44 from the Tech valley floor continues up to delightfully secluded **LAMANÈRE**, the southernmost village in France, also reachable by path west from Coustouges. The closest facility to Lamanère is a 45-place *gîte d'étape* an hour's walk west, at Ermitage Nôtre-Dame-du-Coral (℡04.68.39.75.00).

## Prats-de-Molló

From Arles, the D115 climbs 19km to the medieval town of **PRATS-DE-MOLLÓ**. The present road follows the path of a former railway (the old station houses can be seen en route), since the old road, with houses and bridges, was washed away by disastrous floods during October 1940. During the seventeenth century, when the Treaty of the Pyrenees subjected this area to the outrageous tax policies of Louis XIV, Prats-de-Molló and a number of other towns and villages revolted. Living at the far end of what was then a densely wooded valley, the rebels probably thought they could act with impunity when they murdered the king's tax collectors. Indeed, they held off two battalions before the forces of Maréchal de Noailles made a surprise attack over the western flanks of Canigou to put down the insurrection. **Fort Lagarde** (daily: April–June 2–6pm; July & Aug 10am–6pm; Sept–March 2–5pm; €3.50), which dominates the town from above, was built in 1680 under the direction of Vauban, as much to subdue the local population as to keep the Spanish at bay; the town walls, raised on fourteenth-century foundations, are another Vauban relic from this period. To climb up to the fort (about 25min), head for Porte de la Fabrique, then either follow the footpath that winds up the hill from behind the church or take the covered walk that starts in a ruined building to the right of the cemetery entrance. The fort itself has been beautifully restored, and there are superb views all round from the ramparts. An extra attraction here is the **Visite-Spectacle** on summer afternoons, when horsemen dressed as cavaliers re-create eighteenth-century cavalry exercises, with trick riding, sword fights and the firing of muskets and cannons (daily except Sat: June 3.30pm; July & Aug 2.30pm & 4pm; €7).

With Canigou at its back and the River Tech in front, picturesque Prats-de-Molló has become a tourist attraction, but is still surprisingly unspoilt – particularly the old *ville haute* within the city wall, with its steep, cobbled streets and ancient fortified church. In summer, the pedestrianized streets buzz with activity; at other seasons most hotels are locked up, and locals pass the time playing *boules* under the plane trees of Le Foiral, the huge square outside the walls, where markets and fairs have been held since 1308.

### Practicalities

The **tourist office** in place du Foiral (July & Aug daily 9am–12.30pm & 1.30–6.30pm; April–June, Sept & Oct Mon–Sat 9am–noon & 2–6pm; Jan–March, Nov & Dec Mon–Fri 9am–noon & 2–6pm; ℡04.68.39.70.83, ⊛www.pratsdemollolapreste.com) has a wealth of information, including maps and advice for walking in the Haut-Vallespir. The best **place to stay** is stone-built, Logis de France-affiliate *Hôtel des Touristes* (℡04.68.39.72.12, Ⓔrestauranthoteltouriste@minitel.net; closed Nov–March; ❸) at 3 avenue Haut-Vallespir, decorated with original antique furniture. Otherwise the family-orientated *Le Relais*, 3 place Joseph Trinxeria (℡04.68.39.71.30, ⊛www.lerelaishotel.com; ❷), and friendly *Le Bellevue* overlooking place du

Foiral (☎04.68.39.72.48, ⊕www.lebellevue.fr.st; closed Dec to mid-Feb; ❸) are good and also serve reasonable meals. A better choice for **eating**, however, is *Costabonne* (☎04.68.39.70.24) at 6 place du Foiral, renowned for its homemade *foie gras* (*menus* from €12.50). Among local **campsites**, those with the longest seasons are *St Martin* (☎04.68.39.77.40; closed Dec) and *Can Nadal* (☎04.68.39.77.89; April–Nov), about 1km along the road towards La Preste.

### Onward routes above Arles-sur-Tech

From Prats the road (no public transport) climbs 14km to the **Spanish border** at **Col d'Ares**, dropping on the other side to Camprodon (see p.171). Roughly halfway to the border, just beyond the Col de la Seille on the left, you'll find the *Ferme-Auberge La Coste d'Adalt* (☎04.68.39.74.40; ❸), a working farm with spotless rooms and good food, near the terminus of the path and track coming west from Lamanère.

The easiest of the former escape trails is the one west to the **Collade de Prats** (1596m) from the south bank of the Tech, just south of Arles. The route passes the ruined **Tour de Mir**, one of the signal towers built by Jaume of Mallorca in the late thirteenth century, like the Tour Madeloc above the Côte Vermeille (see p.125); allow two-and-a-half hours to the pass and the HRP.

Prats-de-Molló can also be used as a base for ascending Canigou from the south. Take the road to the **La Preste** spa (1130m, 8km west), then the track up north to the Collade des Roques Blanches and the Pla Guillem area (see p.104 for these, and onward directions to the peak). The only facility, about halfway along, is the *Chalet de Conques* (1600m; ☎04.68.39.23.49), a twelve-place *gîte*.

# The Mediterranean coast

The Pyrenees meet the sea with magnificent abruptness. Approaching from the north, the flat strands of the Côte Radieuse end at **Argelès–Plage**, succeeded by the rocky coves and low foothills of the **Côte Vermeille**. This colourful clash of land and water has long attracted artists, especially the group of early twentieth-century French painters known as the **Fauves** (Wild Beasts) for their vividly emotional use of colour and form, and who spent their summers at **Collioure**, immediately southeast of Argelès.

Continuing along the coast, the N114 traces an ever more tortuous course as a corniche road to the easternmost point of the French Pyrenees, where the mountains plummet into the Mediterranean at **Cap Cerbère**. Here the sea floor drops precipitously to a depth of 40m, a habitat protected since 1974 by the *réserve marine* between **Banyuls-sur-Mer** and **Cerbère**. Once the most elegant resort of the Côte Vermeille, Banyuls was the home of sculptor Aristide Maillol (see box p.127); it also marks one end of the **GR10** and the **HRP** trails, which both cross to the Atlantic coast, 400km away.

Beyond the border at **Portbou**, the orderly vineyards of France give way to more dishevelled ones behind the Spanish **Costa Brava**, ravaged during the nineteenth century by phylloxera. The **Serra de l'Albera** – as the Albères are called on this side – is once again a major wine producer, and at harbours like **Llança** and **El Port de la Selva**, fishing is still important and the coastline remains relatively unknown to non-Catalans. The major – if grossly overrated – local sight is the pre-Romanesque monastery of **Sant Pere de Rodes**, in the hills above El Port de la Selva.

At **Cap de. Creus** the Spanish Pyrenees reach the sea, as does Spain's trans-Pyrenean footpath, the **GR11**. The rugged landscape continues around the cape to **Cadaqués** and **Portlligat**, both pregnant with the memory of Surrealist artist Salvador Dalí, who lived here for decades. Beyond atmospheric **Castelló d'Empuriés** and the **Aiguamolls de l'Empordà** sanctuary, you're back to broad sandy beaches and mass-market resorts; just inland, the county town of **Figueres** is most remarkable for its Teatre-Museu Dalí.

**Public transport** is generally adequate, with frequent buses and trains between Perpignan and every resort of the Côte Vermeille. On the Spanish side trains and buses are nearly as good as long as you stick to the main N260 between Figueres and the frontier and the C260 linking Figueres to Cadaqués, but connections into the Serra de l'Albera can be problematic.

# The Côte Vermeille

When the Fauves discovered the **Côte Vermeille**, which extends southeast from Argelès-sur-Mer to the Spanish border, they took natural inspiration for their revolutionary use of colour: the sunsets (from which the coast earned its name) are a gentle red, the sea is turquoise and, as Matisse wrote, "no sky is more blue than that at Collioure". The beauty of this stretch of coastline has inevitably been exploited, but in the hills behind you'll often be on your own.

## Elne

Standing on a hill just 6km from the sea, on the main train and bus lines between Perpignan and Argelès, the ancient fortified town of **ELNE** (Elna in Catalan) was once the capital of Roussillon. Despite heavy beach-bound traffic whizzing past on the main road bypassing the town to the east, the old quarter inside its sixteenth-century ramparts is eerily quiet after dark. Elne's one great attraction is the former **cathedral of Sainte-Eulalie** (daily: April & May 9.30am–6pm; June–Sept 9.30am–7pm; Oct 9.30am–12.30pm & 2–6pm; Nov–March 9.30am–12.30pm & 2–5pm; €5), the seat of Roussillon's bishops until their transfer to Perpignan in 1602. The **cloister**, built from Céret marble, is the highlight: one intact side of twelfth-century Romanesque pillars and capitals, immaculately carved with motifs such as foliage, lions, goats and biblical figures, is complemented on the other three sides by fourteenth-century Gothic work that has been made to harmonize perfectly. A small museum in the twelfth-century Saint-Laurent chapel, reached via the cloister, is mainly devoted to exhibits found in the excavations of Roman villas around Elne. Opposite the cathedral, at 3 rue Balaguer, is the **Musée Terrus** (same times and ticket as the cathedral), dedicated to the landscape painter Etienne Terrus (1857–1922), a contemporary of the Fauves and friend of Maillol (whose bust of Terrus stands on the Plateau des Garaffes, nearby); the *salon de thé*, on the first floor, has a panoramic view.

### Practicalities

The **train station** lies about ten minutes' walk west of the old town; **buses** stop

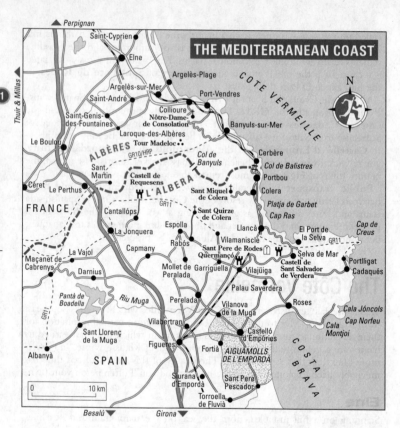

THE MEDITERRANEAN COAST

at the parking place in the centre of the old town, near the cathedral. The **tourist office** is at 2 rue du Docteur-Bolte (July & Aug Mon–Fri 9.30am–noon & 2–6pm, Sat 9.30am–noon; June & Sept Mon–Fri 9.30am–noon & 2–5pm, Sat 9.30am–noon; Oct–May Mon–Fri 9.30am–noon & 2–5pm; ☎04.68.22.05.07, ⒲www.ot-elne.fr), between the **post office** and the Hôtel de Ville. Of the three **hotels**, the modest *Cara Sol* (☎04.68.22.10.42, ⒲www.hotelcarasol.com; ❷), on boulevard Illibéris at the edge of the old town, offers the best value and location, with great views from the front rooms over the Tech valley, the Albères and Canigou. More upmarket is the farmhouse cosily renovated as the two-star *Le Weekend*, 29 avenue Paul Reig (☎04.68.22.06.68, Ⓔhotel.weekend@libertysurf.fr; closed mid-Oct to Jan; ❸), just off the Argelès road, with a celebrated garden **restaurant** (*menus* from €16). There are two municipal, summer-only **campsites**: *Les Padraguets* (☎04.68.22.21.59) on the Argelès road and *Al Mouly* (☎04.68.22.08.46) on boulevard d'Archimède.

## Argelès-sur-Mer

Poised at the northern edge of the Côte Vermeille, **ARGELÈS-SUR-MER** (Argelers) has the last wide, sandy beach until Roses, in Spain. At the end of the Spanish Civil War thousands of refugees lived in detention camps here, many of whom succumbed to the harsh conditions. When World War II began in autumn 1939, the desperation of camp life, civic and monetary incentives from the French government and a further opportunity to combat fascism impelled nearly ten thousand refugees to volunteer to serve in the French army. Nowadays, Argelès is a mass-tourism mecca, wooing visitors with holiday essentials like mini-golf, gambling and beauty contests.

The town itself is divided into old **Argelès-Ville**, a little inland, and new **Argelès-Plage**, which annually receives up to three hundred thousand French, Belgian, Dutch and English visitors. Plage Nord and Plage des Pins are smooth, sandy and potentially windblown **beaches**, whereas **Le Racou** – the first bay of the Côte Vermeille – is more intimate and offers a taste of mountain coastline. The only cultural attraction is the old town's **Casa de les Albères** (June–Sept Mon–Fri 9am–noon & 3–6pm, Sat 9am–noon; €2), in place des Castellans, a small museum of local art and traditions, mostly agricultural tools and implements.

### Practicalities

The **train station** is a few minutes' walk west of the centre of the old town, while **buses** stop opposite the Hôtel de Ville. An hourly bus service (€2) runs in summer between the station, the old town and the beach (Plage Nord). A summer-only **tourist office** in the old town (July & Aug Mon–Sat 9.30am–12.30pm & 2.30–6.30pm; ☎04.68.95.81.55) sits by the Hôtel de Ville on allée Ferdinand-Buisson; Argelès-Plage has its own office (summer daily 8.30am–8pm; winter Mon–Fri 9am–noon & 2–6pm, Sat 9am–noon; ☎04.68.81.15.85, @www.argeles-sur-mer.com), in place de l'Europe.

**Accommodation** can be difficult to find in midsummer, especially for a short stay. Of the hotels in Argelès-Ville the plushest is *La Belle Demeure* (☎04.68.95.85.85, @belle.demeure@little-france.com; ❹–❼), a renovated Catalan farmhouse on Chemin du Roua. If you're on a budget the two-star *Clair Logis*, 78 route de Collioure (☎04.68.81.03.27, ☎04.68.95.93.01; ❷), is a good choice. There are more than fifty **campsites** in the neighbourhood: *Calanque de l'Ouille* (☎04.68.81.12.79; April–Sept) and *Mini Camping* (☎04.68.81.08.72; April–Sept) are two desirable seafront establishments in the direction of Collioure. Among dozens of hotels in Argelès-Plage, the two-star *Les Mimosas*, 51 avenue des Mimosas (☎04.68.81.14.77, @hotel-lesmimosas@wanadoo.fr; ❸), and *Al Pescadou*, rue des Aloès (☎04.68.81.13.21, @alpescadou@9online.fr; ❸), are small, basic and nondescript, but well situated. For more character, try *Les Charmettes* at 30 avenue du Tech (☎04.68.81.09.84, @hotel.chaumiere@infonie.fr; ❹), a converted villa with air-conditioned rooms and a decent seafood restaurant (*menus* €13–18; closed lunch in high season, all Thurs in low season). Otherwise, the **restaurant** situation is bleak, rarely surpassing mediocre beach-town fare. One of the few places that stands out is *Amadeus* (closed Mon April–Nov & Jan; ☎04.68.81.12.38) on avenue des Platanes (near Argelès-Plage's tourist office), which offers reasonable Catalan *menus* from €20.

## Collioure

About 11km east of Argelès-sur-Mer, **COLLIOURE** (Cotlliure) – a true Côte Vermeille town – to a certain extent still banks on its maritime and artistic past. Established as a trading port by the Phoenicians and ancient Greeks, Collioure was later occupied by the Romans, Visigoths and Arabs. Altogether, the place has been the focus of nearly a dozen territorial squabbles, including four invasions by the French and two by the Spanish. The sixteenth-century **Fort Sainte-Elme** (now privately owned), overlooking the town from the south, and the seventeenth-century **Fort Miradou** to the north (still used by the military), are reminders of this turbulent past.

In the early 1900s, invaders of a different sort appeared: the group of painters – including Matisse and Derain – known as **Les Fauves** made Collioure their summer base. Some of their original work adorns the bar at *Hostellerie des Templiers* (see below); you can also follow the *Chemin du Fauvisme* around the town, a trail of twenty reproductions of paintings by Matisse and Derain placed on the sites where they were painted (map available from the tourist office). The refugee Republican poet Antonio Machado arrived at the camps in nearby Argelès with his family in January 1939, but died of pneumonia fifteen days later; after an appeal initiated by Pablo Casals, André Malraux and Albert Camus, he was reburied in Collioure's cemetery in 1956. A Picasso poster, *Hommage à Antonio Machado*, forms part of the small permanent collection at Collioure's **Musée d'Art Moderne** (daily 10am–noon & 2–6pm; closed Tues Sept–June; €3), housed in the beautiful Villa Pams on the edge of the town in route de Port-Vendres, also with temporary exhibitions by artists associated with the region. The historical novelist Patrick O'Brian, whose *Master and Commander* was lavishly filmed in 2003, lived as a recluse just outside of town from 1949 almost until his death in 2000.

The artistic tradition of Collioure survives today, albeit with less distinction: none of the art is avant-garde and the forest of easels that occupies the promenade in summer produces mainly tame souvenirs, but there are also a few serious commercial galleries. Many of these are in the old quarter of the town, the **Mouré**, its steep, narrow streets lined by pastel-tinted houses and assorted shops and cafés. Lateen-rigged fishing boats might be moored in the **harbour** itself, or drawn up on the palm-lined beach; those no longer used by fishermen are now beautifully restored and sailed as pleasure vessels by their new owners. The working fleet – distinguished by bow-lamps – brings in the famous local catch of *boquerones* (salt-cured anchovies, an important component in local cookery) and sardines (grilled fresh).

The **Château-Royal** (daily: June–Sept 10am–6pm; Oct–May 9am–5pm; €4), the imposing fortress which dominates the harbour, was founded by the Templars in the twelfth century, rebuilt for use as a part-time residence by the kings of Mallorca and Aragón two hundred years later, and modernized by Vauban after the Treaty of the Pyrenees. Impressive as it may seem from afar, the castle scarcely merits a visit except to attend a concert hosted in the ramshackle courtyard. Inside, bare rooms have a few mediocre, unlabelled exhibitions (a skimpy, French-only "explanatory" pamphlet is available for €2). However, the two **beaches** – one sandy, one pebbly – which bookend the castle are worth some time, though they're hopelessly crowded in summer.

At the opposite end of the harbour, the **Église Nôtre-Dame-des-Anges** was erected in the seventeenth century, replacing the ancient Sainte-Marie, razed on the orders of Vauban. The distinctive round bell-tower – once doubling as the lighthouse – onto which it was grafted has been damaged many times by storm and war: the base dates from the thirteenth century, the middle from the fourteenth to seventeenth centuries, and the bell-chamber from the nineteenth. It's worth taking a look inside the church (daily 8am–noon & 2–5.30pm) to see the magnificent gilt retable, carved and painted in three tiers, by seventeenth-century Catalan sculptor Joseph Sunyer. Beyond the church, the tiny **Chapelle-Saint-Vincent** stands above the sea on a rocky peninsula, with the south-facing Saint Vincent beach on one side and the nudist Plage Nord on the other.

## Practicalities

Collioure's **train station** is less than ten minutes' walk west of the centre, along avenue Aristide-Maillol; **buses** stop at the central car park, off avenue Général-de-Gaulle. *Collioure Location* (☏04.68.82.24.59) at 7 avenue Général-de-Gaulle rents **bikes** and **scooters** by the day or week. **Parking** on the street is usually a nightmare; you'll probably have to head for the large and reasonably priced car park on the hill overlooking the sea behind the castle. The helpful **tourist office** is just behind the harbour in place du 18 Juin (July & Aug daily 9am–8pm; Sept–June Mon–Sat 9am–noon & 2–6.30pm; ☏04.68.82.15.47, ⓦwww.collioure.com); there's also an information kiosk (July–Sept Mon–Sat 9am–5pm) in the small tower by the beach on the other side of the castle.

Southeast of the harbour are some desirable sea-view **hotels**, the best of which are *Triton*, 1 rue Jean-Bart (☏04.68.98.39.39, ⓔhoteltriton@wanadoo.fr; closed Nov & Feb; ❸), and *Les Caranques* (☏04.68.82.06.68, ⓔlescaranques@little-france.com; closed Oct 15–March; ❸–❹). The most unusual accommodation is *Hostellerie des Templiers*, 12 quai de l'Amirauté (☏04.68.98.31.10, ⓦwww.hotel-templiers.com; closed Jan; ❸–❹), in which the individually decorated rooms, staircases and dining rooms are filled with original artworks. Parking nearby isn't possible, and reservations are essential: try to book for the main building, not one of the less attractive annexes. For something quieter and plusher, check into attractive, courtyarded *La Casa Païral*, in impasse des Palmiers (☏04.68.82.05.81, ⓔcontact@hotel-casa-pairal.com; closed Nov–March; ❻). There are two summer-only **campsites** to the north of the town, near the coast: *Les Amandiers* (☏04.68.81.14.69), in the sheltered bay known as L'Ouille; and, better, *La Girelle*, plage d'Ouille (☏04.68.81.25.56).

For **eating out**, there's a range of reasonable *crêperies* and pizza-pasta places around the old Mouré quarter, but it's worth the premium to sit on fashionable rue Camille Pelletan, by the harbour, and watch the world go by – the most atmospheric café-bar being that of *Hostellerie des Templiers*, now filled with drawings and paintings donated by Matisse, Maillol, Picasso and Dufy, among others, in exchange for bed and board. You can also sit outside and eat more substantially at *Le Trémail* at 1 rue Arago (☏04.68.82.16.10; closed Jan, Mon, & Tues low season), with seafood-heavy *menus* from €20. **Markets** (Wed & Sun morning) are held in place du Maréchal-Leclerc.

## Walks south from Collioure

For an easy walk out of Collioure, take rue de la République from the harbour, cross the main road and follow signs for **Nôtre-Dame-de-Consolation**, reached by track within ninety minutes. This old, ruined hermitage is much loved locally for its barbecue and *boules* area. To fill a half-day's hiking, continue, mostly on path, to **Tour Madeloc** on the crest of a ridge (360m), descending on Banyuls-sur-Mer (4hr 30min from Collioure), the final distance on the GR10 and HRP footpaths. The tower, also accessible by paved road from Banyuls, was built by Jaume I of Mallorca at the end of the thirteenth century as one of a chain of such signal stations.

# Port-Vendres

**PORT-VENDRES**, 4km east of Collioure, is marred by the busy main road, but for a genuine, unsophisticated fishing port, this is your best (indeed only) choice on the Côte Vermeille. You probably won't want to stay longer than it takes to look around the port and tuck into a fish lunch at one of the numerous quayside **restaurants**, or to watch the fish auctions held at the far end of the port every weekday evening (usually 5–7pm). A huge fish-processing factory dominates one side of the harbour, while sardine- and tuna-fishing boats are moored under the Maillol-designed war memorial opposite, with nets and other paraphernalia piled along the harbour wall. Salt has taken its toll on Maillol's work, and the uncharacteristically draped figures have lost limbs, noses and various other features.

To the Romans the town was *Portus Veneris* (Port of Venus), a place of strategic trading importance. During the Middle Ages its significance diminished in direct relation to the rising star of neighbouring Collioure, but by the eighteenth century it had recovered somewhat through the business of shipping Roussillon wines. In 1830 it became the primary port for dispatching soldiers and supplies to the French colony in Algeria, a link that lasted for more than a century.

## Banyuls-sur-Mer to the frontier

As the road crosses the Col du Père Carnère and drops towards the Plage des Elmes, the once-elegant wine town of **BANYULS-SUR-MER** comes into view, with dry-stone walls and orderly rows of vines stretching into hills behind it. Banyuls is famous for its eponymous dessert wine, which the French tend to drink as an aperitif (but the Spanish Catalans after meals). If you fancy a tipple, try a 45-minute **guided tour** of one of the larger cellars, such as the Cellier des Templiers en route du Mas-Reig (April–Oct daily 10am–7.30pm; Nov–March Mon–Sat 10am–1pm & 2.30–6.30pm; free).

Less fashionable than Collioure, Banyuls is still a lively, popular seaside resort, albeit marred by a busy road running along the seafront. The wide, stony main beach is less attractive than some smaller bays to the north and south, but the whole town comes alive in the evenings when everyone gets together to promenade along the seafront, play *boules* or eat at one of the many beach cafés and seafood restaurants.

Don't leave Banyuls without visiting the **Laboratoire Arago**, the large white building overlooking the port. Run by the marine biology and land ecology department of the Sorbonne, its **aquarium** (daily: July & Aug 9am–noon & 2–10pm; rest of year 9am–noon & 2–6.30pm; €4) comprises over forty tanks of fascinating local specimens, including seahorses, bright red starfish and wicked-looking eels, along with a comprehensive display of local birds. The coastal waters of this area, rich in marine life due to the Pyrenees' steep underwater descent, were the first *réserve marine* declared in France, indeed across the Mediterranean. Those with requisite qualifications can **dive** within the reserve area by contacting Plongez Rederis Club, operating from the port (℡04.68.88.31.66 or 04.68.92.02.01).

### Practicalities

The **train station** lies at the western edge of town, while **buses** stop on the coastal boulevard. The **tourist office** is on the seafront, opposite the *mairie* (July & Aug daily 9.30am–12.30pm & 2.30–7pm; Sept–June Tues–Sat 9.30am–12.30pm & 2–6.30pm; ℡04.68.88.31.58, ⊛www.banyuls-sur-mer.com). Recommended one-star **hotels** in the quieter back streets include *Le Manoir*, 20 rue de Maréchal-Joffre (℡04.68.88.32.98; closed Nov & Dec;

## Aristide Maillol (1861–1944)

Sculptor **Aristide Maillol**, the local Banyuls boy made good, began his profession-al life as a painter and tapestry designer; recognition came only in his forties, after he had devoted himself to sculpture and returned to Banyuls-sur-Mer from Paris.

In 1904, his Parisian admirers brought him to the attention of **Count Harry Kessler**, who became Maillol's patron and confidant over the next three decades. The two men could hardly have been more different: Kessler, son of a wealthy Prussian indus-trialist, known as the "Red Count" for his political leanings, the passion of his repressed homosexuality directed towards art collecting and generous sponsorship; Maillol, a Catalan peasant through and through, never picking up the tab for anything, apolitical at best, accused of pro-Falange or pro-Nazi sympathies at the worst of times. Yet the collaboration between them endured almost until 1937, when Kessler, driven into exile from Germany four years previously, died impoverished in Paris.

Unlike Rodin, Maillol initially had no taste for the **male nude**, and later found it dif-ficult to find local peasants willing to pose; Kessler, with his contacts among hand-some athletes, dancers and labourers, solved the problem. In 1922, Kessler attempted to complete Maillol's "classical" education – classicism in embryo was how many saw his work – by taking him on a surprisingly productive trip to Greece. There was not, after all, that great a distance between Maillol's vision and the ancient masterpieces, nor between Kessler's tastes and the Greek youths.

In the best tradition of bohemian artisits, Maillol's long and unhappy marriage to the suitably jealous Clotilde Maillol was punctuated by dalliances with female models in his old age; Clotilde nearly wrecked his studio when she caught him *in flagrante* with Lucile Passavant, in 1930. But it was his next and last model-mistress, **Dina Vierny**, who really eclipsed Clotilde. Maillol was introduced to Vierny in 1935, and by 1938, aged just 19, she was living next door to him in Banyuls, and spending most days with the sculptor up in the hills at his retreat. After the Nazi occupation of northern France, Vierny – of Russian-Jewish background, and a Communist sympathizer – joined the Comité de Secours Américain pour Intellectuels Antifascistes, and helped to smuggle a number of Jews, dissidents and other anti-Nazis over the border. Apparently Maillol, whatever his political views, taught her the best route into Spain.

When the Vichy regime got wind of her activities, Vierny was confined to house arrest in Banyuls, and then picked up by the Gestapo when she escaped to Paris in early 1943. Maillol appealed to his old acquaintance **Arno Breker**, the official Third Reich sculptor then resident in Paris, to help secure her release. A little flattery of Breker and the Nazi elite's reciprocal artistic admiration of Maillol – thus the accu-sations of collaboration – did the trick. Vierny was saved from deportation to a con-centration camp in October 1943, and warned to stay out of trouble, but after a brief period at Banyuls, she drifted back to Paris and never saw Maillol again. The latter died of injuries sustained in a car crash in September 1944 – but not before he had made Vierny, and his son Lucien by Clotilde, his joint heirs and executors.

Upon Clotilde's death in 1952, Lucien – never much of a businessman – made Vierny sole executor, and between 1964 and 1996 she honoured Maillol's memory by founding three French **museums** dedicated to his work: two in Paris, and one at Maillol's country retreat, **La Métairie** (for directions, see "Walks from Banyuls"), where he is buried in a tomb topped by his *La Pensée*. The farmhouse museum (daily: May–Sept 10am–noon & 4–7pm; Oct–April 10am–noon & 2–5pm; ⓦwww.museemaillol.com; €3.50), installed in the rooms where he lived and worked, displays more than thirty bronze statues, with supporting photographs.

Elsewhere nearby, major works by the sculptor include, in Banyuls proper, a half-relief war memorial on the **Ile Grosse**, the islet at the end of the jetty; a sculpture in the garden of the *mairie* (access via the back gate from av Général-de-Gaulle); and another, *La Jeune Fille*, on the raised promenade above the harbour. Maillol's birth-place, now a Catalan crafts shop, is at 6 rue du Puig del Mas.

●), and its near neighbour the *Sant Sebastian* (℡04.68.88.34.90; ●). For a reasonably priced hotel on the seafront, try *El Llagut*, 18 avenue du Fontaulé (℡04.68.88.00.81, @www.al-fanal.com; ●–●), near the port, where many rooms have a sea-view balcony. Another good option is comfortable, well-appointed *Les Elmes* (℡04.68.88.03.12, @www.hotel-des-elmes.com; closed mid-Nov to mid-Dec; ●) perched on the cliffs at the north end of town, with a private beach. **Camping** is at the *Camping du Stade*, rue Jean Boin (℡04.68.88.31.70; mid-June to early Sept), or the cheaper *Camping Municipal La Pinède* nearby, on route du Mas-Reig (℡04.68.88.32.13; March–Nov).

Banyuls has a good choice of **restaurants** specializing in fresh seafood. The priciest, with starched tablecloths and live lobster tanks, cluster opposite the sea front; the most reliable of these is *Le Sardinal*, 4-bis place Paul-Reig. Of the less expensive choices top-ranked is *Les Canadells*, just off the main boulevard at 4 avenue du Général-de-Gaulle, with excellent *menus* (from €10 at lunch, €16 at dinner; closed Sun eve, & Mon Oct–March) and specializing in *zarzuela*. Nearby rue Saint-Pierre is home to more, including *El Celler* at no. 15, with a reasonable set menu and a shaded summer patio; and *Casa Miguel*, at no. 3, with Spanish and Catalan specialities. The best value, however, is *La Littorine* (℡04.68.88.03.12), Plage les Elmes, where you can savour roast lobster, fire-grilled bass, or squid in its own ink (from €26). The local morning **market** is held year-round on Sundays and Thursdays.

### West of Banyuls: Maillol's tomb and Col de Banyuls

The four-kilometre trip from Banyuls to **Maillol's tomb** and country house makes a pleasant excursion up into the vine-clad Albères. Walk, cycle or drive the length of avenue Général-de-Gaulle, past the PTT, and under a bridge. Shortly afterwards, where the road curves to the right, take the left-hand road, following the line of a river: signs from here point to the "Musée et Tombeau de Maillol".

Keen hikers could continue to the **Col de Banyuls** (357m) and into Spain (consult Rando Éditions' *Carte de Randonnées* 1:50,000 "Roussillon" map, or the Editorial Alpina 1:80,000 "Cadaqués" map). Once over the pass – used by many refugees from the Spanish Civil War and from Nazism – you can continue to Espolla via Sant Quirze de Colera, or follow the GR11 to Llança; either of these options requires a fairly long day.

### Cerbère

The Côte Vermeille comes to an end at **CERBÈRE**. The harbour is quite pretty and the mountain backdrop impressive, but the beach negligible. Depending on the service, train passengers change either here or on the Spanish side at Portbou (see below), where the rail line changes track size: a deliberate manoeuvre by the Spaniards during the late nineteenth century to hamper any possible invasion from Europe. In Cerbère, you can **stay** and **eat** at *La Dorade* on the harbour (℡04.68.88.41.93; ●) or tent down at the municipal *Camping Cap Peyrefite* (℡04.68.88.41.17).

# The Costa Brava

The **Costa Brava**, synonymous with the first – and worst – stirrings of post-war package tourism, extends from the border to just north of Barcelona. Yet despite rampant commercialization, it's still possible to encounter quiet stretches of shoreline, graced by the dramatic cliffs, pine-fringed coves and pebble beaches that prompted all the development in the first place. This is more likely in the northern portion of the Costa Brava, near the Mediterranean terminus of the GR11 trail at Cap de Creus; accordingly coverage is restricted to smaller, more human-scale resorts north of the Golf de Roses, where tired hill-walkers will appreciate a few days by the sea.

Upon crossing the border at the **Col dels Balistres** (Col des Balitres in French), you'll notice an abrupt change from the tidy viniculture of the French hillsides to the shaggier Spanish slopes. The effects of the phylloxera plague during the late nineteenth century were compounded by a killing frost in 1956 which finished off commercial olive production. There have been continual brush- and forest-fires in the region ever since, which have left the Cap de Creus in particular 85 percent deforested; pockets of pines survive only at southerly coves, around villages or in folds of hillsides where the flames have skipped over them.

This deterioration of the agricultural economy has been accelerated through migration to Barcelona and beyond, and by the exponential growth of tourism. The northernmost resorts – **Portbou**, **Colera**, **Llançà** and **El Port de la Selva** – are still very much for Catalans and passing French motorists, with little of the internationally pitched development that has blighted the *costa* further down. In season, **Cadaqués** is more cosmopolitan and, thanks to Dalí, has a palpably arty feel. You'll never find complete tranquillity nearby in summer, but if you're willing to walk a bit there are some nearly empty beaches on the **Cap de Creus** peninsula, as well as worthwhile inland sites, like the clumsily restored Benedictine monastery of **Sant Pere de Rodes** or the wildlife reserve at **Aiguamolls de l'Empordà**. As a base for the latter, medieval **Castelló d'Empuries** is far preferable to tatty Roses.

## Portbou

**PORTBOU**, just 3km below the border, is the northernmost settlement of the Costa Brava, its isolation and good anchorage formerly making it a smugglers' haven. The village is arrayed around a superbly protected bay in the green foothills of the Albera, amidst the sort of scenery that moved Catalan poet Fernando Agulló to bestow the epithet *brava* (rugged) on what had previously been merely the *Costa de Llevant* (East Coast). Besides the main, stony harbour-beach, small, clean coves flank the harbour on either side, accessible by paths threading over the rocks – **Tres Platgetes** and **Platja del Pi** (part nudist) to the north are the most popular. The road in from the south climbs vertiginously up to the 202-metre **Col de Frere**, allowing tremendous views before dropping into town.

Portbou's main claim to fame is as the terminus of the Barcelona rail line: the **massive station**, built in 1872, is – with its shunting sidings – nearly as large as the town. For more than a century, Portbou lived from border traffic and the disparity in luxury-goods prices between France and Spain; since the advent of the European single market, and the closure of eighty-plus customs agencies, the place is struggling to reinvent itself as a holiday destination.

Historically, the most illustrious – and ill-fated – visitor was German-Jewish Marxist philosopher **Walter Benjamin**, who arrived here on September 27, 1940, as a refugee from the Nazis. When it appeared that the Spanish would deny him entry and deport him back to certain death – he was near the top of the Gestapo's "wanted" list – he committed suicide by ingesting an overdose of morphine. Today he is honoured locally up at the *mirador* by a plaque on the wall of the cemetery, where he was interred for five years, and by Israeli sculptor Dani Karavan's 3D art installation *Passagem*, a claustrophobic metal tunnel leading down towards the sea, open to the sky only for the last few steps before a glass barrier above the roiling surf, and a five-language inscription quoting Benjamin.

### Practicalities

There's a small **Turisme** booth (May–Sept daily 9am–8pm; ☎972 125 161) on harbourfront Passeig Lluis Companys. Among a limited range of overpriced **accommodation**, *Hostal Costa Blava* at c/Alcalde Benjamí Cervera 20 (☎972 390 386; June–Sept; ❸) has some sea views and en-suite rooms, while the cheerful rooms of *La Masia* at Passeig Lluis Companys 1 (☎972 390 372; ❹) have balconies overlooking the beach.

Most **restaurants** on the seafront *passeig* are poor value; best bet is *L'Ancora*, offering excellent seafood paella and beer in large steins. The *Art in Café*, c/Mercat 11 (daily 8am–1am), serves tasty crêpes, salads and juices while you surf the **Internet**. The little nearby **market** hall itself trades in the mornings.

## Colera and Platja de Garbet

Some 10km from the border, **COLERA** – signposted as "Sant Miquel", its official name – is a shabby, down-at-heel place, with high-rise blocks crammed into the narrow gulch draining to the coarse-pebble bay, and marred further by the giant rail viaduct that splits Colera in two. Not surprisingly, Colera is frequented mainly by Spanish holidaymakers, who splash about in water rather cleaner than the town's off-putting name implies. **Accommodation** is limited to the two-star *Hotel La Gambina* on the harbour front (☎972 389 172; ❹), with the best **restaurant**, and *Hostal Mont-Mercé* at Passeig del Mar 107 (☎972 389 126; ❸).

For a better beach and cheaper lodging head south 2km to **Platja de Garbet**, where the eponymous campsite (☎972 389 001; April–Oct) is poor, but the affiliated *Pensió Garbet* (❷) with en-suite rooms is perfectly adequate. Two adjacent **restaurants** face the scenic, gravel-and-sand bay: one reasonable and attached to the *pensió*, the other with table nappery and bow-tied waiters, offering expensive seafood or more affordable *tapas*.

## Llançà

The rail line leaves the coast at **LLANÇÀ**, set back from its port to preclude the attentions of pirates. The place historically bred rugged fishermen, on account of its relatively exposed, north-facing harbour, but has been opened up to tourism by the road and rail route to France – and, especially at the port, is brazen in its attempts to cash in.

Llança-Port lies 2.5km from the **train station** (buses stop outside), but the (not very) old town is much closer, just off to the right as you emerge. Once prosperous thanks to its marble industry, Llançà-Vila does not have a great deal to commend it, except for an attractive, café-ringed **Plaça Major** with the **Arbe de la Llibertat**, a huge tree planted in 1870. This is flanked by an outsize fifteenth-century episcopal palace attached to an eighteenth-century parish church, as well as the renovated fourteenth-century **Torre de la Plaça** (Mon–Fri 5.30–9pm, Sat 6.30–9pm). Nearby, the **Museu de l'Aquarella Martínez Lozano** (June–Sept Mon–Sat 7–9pm, Sun 11am–1pm & 7–9pm; rest of year Sat & Sun 11am–1pm & 6–8pm; €2) showcases varied works collected by Martínez Lozano himself, as well as his own watercolours.

At first glance the **port** seems to be dominated by its yacht marina, a coarse-sand beach backed by the concreted Passeig Maritim and a **car park**; the fish depot and commercial anchorage lie around the corner, under the landmark headland of **Es Castellar** which everyone climbs to get sweeping views.

For better, more secluded **beaches**, you'll need to head 2–3km north to **Cap Ras**, a promontory covered by a forested nature reserve criss-crossed by trails. First you'll pass the strand of **Grifeu**, but it's best to continue to the cape itself, where north-facing **Borró** is the main sandy bay near the parking area. Beyond Borró, accessible by path only, lie more protected coves popular with nudists.

### Practicalities

The **Turisme** lies halfway along Avinguda d'Europa (July & Aug Mon–Sat 9.30am–9pm; rest of year Mon–Fri 9.30am–2pm & 4.30–8pm, Sat 10am–1pm & 5–7pm; ☎972 380 855, ⊛www.llanca.net), the road linking Vila with Port. The most durable local **scuba outfit** is Centre d'Immersió Cap de Creus (☎972 120 000, ⊛www.cicapcreus.com), c/Martínez Lozano 9.

For **accommodation**, there are a few choices in Vila: *Pensió Can Pau*, c/Puig d'Esquer 4 (☎972 380 270; ❷); *Hostal Florida*, c/Floridablanca 17 (☎972 120 161; July & Aug only; ❸), with its own car park; *Hotel Carbonell* around the corner on c/Major 19 (☎972 380 209; ❸), or *Hostal Maria Teresa*, on the slope above town at c/Colomer 18 (☎972 380 004, ⊛www.hmteresa.com; May–Oct; ❸), a 1970s compound with 1990s-redone, balconied rooms, offering "alternative" courses such as yoga and reiki, as well as Internet access and ample parking. Alternatively, stay down in Port at renovated *Hostal Miramar*, Passeig Maritim 7 (☎972 380 132; March–Sept; ❹), overlooking the quieter side of the pedestrianized beach esplanade; its near-neighbour *Hotel Berna* at no. 13 (☎972 380 150; May–Sept; ❹); *Hotel La Goleta*, two blocks inland at the corner of c/Pintor Torroella and c/Roger de Flor (☎972 380 125, ☏972 120 686; ❹), with antique-furnished, air-con rooms; or out at the pink, slightly kitsch *Hotel Grifeu* (☎972 380 050; April–Sept; ❺), behind Grifeu beach.

Reliable, affordable **restaurants** amongst a somewhat tacky bunch include *La Brasa*, two blocks inland at Plaça de Catalunya 6 (*menú* €18, *carta* €34 and up), specializing in grilled meat and fish, and the nearby *Celler de Llança* at c/Lepanto 5, a tavern-bar with a short but sweet *carta* (allow €15–20) of omelettes, salads, tuna, anchovies and snails.

# El Port de la Selva and inland

From Llançà, it's 8km along the coastal road (regular buses in summer) to El Port de la Selva; you can **walk** part-way, via **Platja de la Gola** and **Cau del Llop**, as far as the Punta de S'Arenella promontory and its lighthouse, on the **Camí de Ronda**, a not entirely continuous shoreline trail designated as the GR92.

Occupying the eastern side of a large bay formed by the promontory of Cap de Creus, whitewashed **EL PORT DE LA SELVA** is primarily a locals' family resort, but also the first place, heading south, that you'll see other foreigners in any numbers. It's not extravagantly picturesque (though rather more so than Llançà), but makes a good base for the Cap de Creus *parc natural* just northeast. Though the pleasure-craft marina is now larger, the **fishing fleet** still plays a major role: unless the *tramontana* is blowing, boats venture forth most days to set their nets.

**Buses** stop on the seafront, near the giant, free municipal **car park**. A

**Turisme** operates in the town hall near the fishing port (June–Sept daily 8am–10pm; Oct–May Mon–Fri 8am–3pm, Sat 9am–1pm; ☎972 387 025). Weekend flats and villas for Catalans – especially on the western shore of the bay – predominate, so short-term **accommodation** choices are somewhat limited. Top-end quarters are *Hotel Porto Cristo*, c/Major 59 (☎972 387 062, ⓦwww.hotelportocristo.com; closed Nov–Feb; ❼), a converted mansion with luxuriously appointed units in four grades. *Pensió Sol y Sombra*, one quiet block inland from the water at c/Nou 8 (☎972 387 060, ⓔsolisombra@oem.es; ❷–❸), is by a hair the cheapest option, also with pricier en-suite/balconied rooms; nearest alternative is the large-roomed *Hostal La Tina* at c/Major 15 (☎972 387 149, ⓦwww.hostalllatina.com; ❷–❸), which also offers studios. You might take up their offers of half-board – *La Tina's menjador* is good and popular, if pricey at €27–30 *a la carta* – as there are few recommendable independent **restaurants** here, other than expensive *Ca L'Herminda*, seafood specialists operating out of basement premises at c/Illa 7.

**Nightlife**, while hardly cutting-edge, is more varied: *Cal Sereno* (7pm–3am), at c/Cantó dels Pescadors 4 near *Sol I Sombra*, is another subterranean premises with a nautical past, *Café Espanya* at c/Illa 1 functions 17 hours a day, with a waterside terrace and mixed clientele, while *Gus* at the north end of the esplanade doubles as an **Internet** café. The town's **scuba centre** is French-run *Centre d'Immersió Port de la Selva*, at c/Platja 9 (☎972 126 584, ⓦwww.cips-dive.com). The preferable of two licensed local **campsites** is gigantic *Port de la Vall* at the far western edge of town (☎972 387 186; April–Oct), sloping down to its own patch of beach.

## Beaches

**Platja Gran**, at the southwestern edge of town, is popular despite exposure to the wind and steep shelving. The shore road heading north ends after a couple of kilometres at **Cala Tamariua**, a sheltered, part-nudist pebble cove. An obvious path leads 25 minutes further to the narrow pebble inlet of **Cala Fornells**, guarded by an ancient lime kiln. Beyond this point, the trail becomes faint, and sea-going excursions are more rewarding.

## Selva de Mar

Medieval parent of El Port de la Selva, the tranquil oasis-village of **SELVA DE MAR**, 2km inland, is an atmospheric, semi-fortified place right under the Castell de Sant Salvador de Verdera. Little round towers pop up here and there along the lanes that converge on the stepped Plaça Camp de l'Obra. Walkers' signposts point up the stream valley to a **watermill** (El Molí del Salt del Aigua), assorted fountains, and up to the twelfth-century **church** of San Sebastià, now the cemetery chapel.

You can **stay** at *Fonda Felip* on the *plaça* (☎972 387 271; Easter–Sept; ❷), which, being good value, generally requires pre-booking. They also do **meals**, as does *Ca L'Elvira* on the lower perimeter road (several *menús*). Opposite *Fonda Felip*, **bar** *El Celler de la Selva*, a former haunt of Dalí, has occasional live music sessions in summer.

## Sant Pere de Rodes

Just below the summit of the Serra de Roda, with views of a magnificent stretch of coastline, stands the Benedictine monastery of **Sant Pere de Rodes** (daily except Mon: June–Sept 10am–8pm; Oct–May 10am–2pm & 3–5.30pm; free on Tues, otherwise €3.60, plus €1.50 per car). It's 8km up the paved **road** from El Port; if you're approaching **by foot**, rather than follow the GR11 –

which is forced repeatedly onto the access road – it's better to use the marked trail through the Vall de Santa Creu, beginning at Molí de la Vall, just past the *Port de la Vall* campsite. Count on ninety minutes from Port de la Selva, emerging just below the monastery at the spring which possibly prompted founding of the monastery in the first place.

According to legend, when Rome was threatened by barbarians, seventh-century Pope Boniface IV ordered the Church's most valuable relics – including **Saint Peter's head** – to be hidden, and dispatched three monks to find a safe refuge. The monks eventually dropped anchor at Armen Rodes (now El Port de la Selva), where they hid their treasures in a cave on the remote cape. Subsequently unable to relocate the hiding place, the trio founded Sant Pere rather than return to face the pope's wrath. In any case, the monastery was probably built over a pagan temple dedicated to the Pyrenean Venus, Afrodita Pyrene – a theory bolstered by the discovery of fragments of pagan sculptures and Corinthian capitals in the area.

The first reference to Sant Pere dates from 879; by the late tenth century it was the wealthiest and most powerful foundation in the region. Inevitably the monastery aroused local jealousy, and fortified itself against attacks by nearby feudal lords. After 300 years of splendour, physical and moral decline set in, and by 1789 the last discredited monks had departed and the buildings abandoned to the elements and to plunderers.

Sant Pere *used* to be one of the most romantic ruins in Catalonia, but following a brutal 1990s restoration with abundant civil engineering and concrete (and not much sensitivity) in evidence, the monastery now ranks as a textbook-case tourist-trap. No original columns or capitals remain in the cloister; only the lofty **church** retains its mystery and original stonework from the tenth to fourteenth centuries, including column capitals carved with wolves' and dogs' heads. The crypt also remains as it was, while a steep spiral staircase leads up to tiny Sant Miquel chapel, then to the *girola* (ambulatory) above the apse, which retains a few Romanesque fresco fragments. It's most worthwhile showing up for the annual series of July piano concerts (8pm each Sun, some Wed).

## Castell de Sant Salvador de Verdera

From the monastery a steep, narrow path climbs 25 minutes more to the mountaintop and the severely ruined **Castell de Sant Salvador de Verdera**, contemporary of Sant Pere and another possible site of the temple of Venus. Its views south across the bay of Roses and the now-drained marshlands of the Empordà plain made it the perfect watchpoint for frequent invasions (French or Moorish), normally from the sea. Take extreme care once atop the walls – there are no barriers between you and many sheer drops.

## Dolmens – and Vilajuïga

A road snakes between Sant Pere and Vilajuïga, 9km west, on the Barcelona–Portbou train line and served by bus to Cadaqués, Roses and Figueres. Small signs along the way indicate paths to **dolmens** at **Vinyes Mortes**, dating from 4000 BC. Particularly impressive is a pair of tombs left of the road, under 3km from the monastery car park (near where there are more signposted dolmens). The marked **path** down to Vilajuïga shortcuts a considerable amount of the curvy road.

**VILAJUÏGA** can offer the ruined Visigothic **Castell de Quermançó** just north, guarding a pass in the N-II highway (a minor, signposted road goes right by), and an eleventh/twelfth-century **synagogue** in the centre. Cool, damp and barrel-vaulted, this now serves as the antechamber to the hideous late-medieval

**Església de Sant Feliu**.Vilajuïga has a single, rather drab *hostal* and a few restaurants; you'll find much better facilities 3.5km west in Garriguella (see p.143).

## Cadaqués and Portlligat

CADAQUÉS is the most pleasant base on the Pyrenean Costa Brava, reached only by a single, winding road over the bare hills behind Port de la Selva or Roses, and thus retaining an air of isolation. Bougainvillea-draped, white-washed houses lining narrow, cobbled streets, a tree-lined promenade and craggy headlands to either side of a picturesque harbour make it irresistible.

Already by the 1920s and 1930s the place had begun to attract the likes of Utrillo, Picasso, Chagall, Man Ray, García Lorca, Buñuel, Thomas Mann and Einstein. But Cadaqués really "arrived" as an **artistic-literary colony** after World War II when Surrealist painter Salvador Dalí and his wife Gala settled at nearby Portlligat, attracting for some years a floating bohemian community. The impecunious hippie crowd that flocked here during the 1960s and 1970s has been largely succeeded by a relatively well-heeled trendy set, albeit (especially in bars after 11pm) a youthful and unpretentious one. Outside peak season Cadaqués can be great and even in midsummer – despite the crowds and high prices – you'll probably have fun.

The extravagantly large landmark **Església de Santa Maria** – conspicuous whether you approach by sea or land – has guided generations of seafarers past the rocks and reefs at the harbour entrance. It might have been better to site it less conspicuously: the village suffered numerous pirate raids, the worst in 1543 at the hands of the Ottoman "admiral" Barbarossa, who sacked the town and burned the original church. The present edifice was built in the seventeenth century and has a remarkable Baroque altarpiece carved by Pedro Costa – including a gilded relief of Atlas supporting the world – and a side chapel on the left decorated by Dalí. Every summer, the church hosts a **classical music festival** (late July to late Aug) – rather tamer, perhaps, than the traditional saint's day rites where local fishermen used to tether live lobsters to the altar.

Close to the church, the **Museu de Cadaqués** on c/Narcís Monturiol (variable hours and price) features changing exhibits of local artists, or displays relating to unusual aspects of Dalí's work.

Local **beaches** are all tiny and pebbly, but lie within walking distance along either shore of the southeast-facing harbour. The best, on the southwest shore, are **Platja Sa Conca**, and – 45 minutes from centre quay, partly on the Camí de Ronda – isolated **Cala Nans**.

### Practicalities

**Buses** (several daily from Figueres, two a day from El Port de la Selva) arrive at the little SARFA bus office on c/Sant Vicenç, on the edge of town, from where it's less than ten minutes' walk, following c/Unió and c/des Vigilants, to the central beachside Plaça Frederic Rahola. Having a **car** is a distinct liability here – you're usually forced to use the large fee car **park** near the bus stop, though there are free spaces on the coast road south and at the Rec de Palau lot (follow signs to hotels *Rocamar* and *Llané Petit*). The **Turisme** is one block in from the beachside square at c/des Cotxes 2 (July–Sept Mon–Sat 9am–9pm, Sun 10.30am–1pm; Oct–June Mon–Sat 10.30am–1pm & 5–7pm; ☎972 258 315).

### Accommodation

The least expensive, non-en-suite **accommodation** is at either *Pensió Cala d'Or* at c/Tórtora 2, left and then 100m inland as you face the water (☎972

258 149; ❷), with just four rooms, or *Pensió Vehí* (☎972 258 470; March–Oct; ❷), better situated, below the church at c/Església 6. Moving one notch up in comfort, the *Hostal Cristina*, with limited parking (☎972 258 138; ❸), and the slightly plusher, balconied *Hostal Marina* (☎972 258 199; April–Dec; ❸) are both just behind the waterfront on c/Riera, offering small, en-suite rooms; rooms at *La Fonda*, well inland at c/Tórtora 64 (☎972 258 019; ❸), overlook a vegetable patch, with parking just conceivable nearby. The area's dozen hotels predictably trade on the arty reputation, charging well over the odds; relatively good-value exceptions include *Misty* on Carretera Portlligat (☎972 258 962; closed Jan & Feb; ❹), a low-rise garden hotel grouped around a small pool (limited parking); the two-storey *Aparthotel Calina*, on the scrappy beach at Portlligat (☎972 258 851, ⊛www.hotelcalina.com; closed early Jan to late March), with a large pool, parking, and a variety of units ranging from simple doubles (❺) to spacious studios (❻); or, for even more luxury, *Llané Petit* on the shore road 1km south of town (☎972 258 050, ✉llanepetit@ctv.es; ❼), again with a mix of large, balconied rooms by a small beach. For those finishing a GR11 traverse, the noisy *Camping Cadaqués* (☎972 258 126; April–Sept) beckons, 1km along the road to Portlligat.

## Eating, drinking and nightlife

The seafront drive Riba Nemsi Llorens, between the Portitxó pebble beach behind the Dalí statue and Es Baluard headland, is lined with fairly indistinguishable seafood restaurants and some more memorable bars. It's worth poking around the backstreets for a **meal**; the only real budget spots are the *menjador* of *Fonda Cala d'Or* (closed Sun low season), a smoky, kitsch-decor holdover from the hippie days, where the service is friendly, the food basic (*paella, gambas, arròs negre*), and prices (€9–14 for three courses) equally so, and *Celeste* at c/Nou 1, just inland from Port d'Alguer cove, where €15 will see you to several kinds of pasta dishes – it becomes a bar after 11pm. For affordable seafood, try either the sea-view *menjador* of *Pensió Vehí*, with specialties like tuna mousse in red-pepper sauce and *menús* from €13.50, or *La Sirena* just downhill on c/Es Call, with pebble-court seating, a sensibly limited fish list, creative desserts and an *a la carta* bill of €27–30. Last but not least, *Casa Anita* at c/Miquel Rosset 16 is a long-running, obligatorily sociable institution where diners are seated together at long tables, the hearty Catalan country fare's excellent and queues form early in the evening.

Miquel Rosset, one block inland from port and perpendicular to main artery Avinguda Caritat Serinyana, is also home to much of Cadaqués' **nightlife** – eg *Tropical* at no. 19, where a candlelit garden leads to an appropriately surreal interior with marine decor and Antillean soundtrack. But other worthy candidates are scattered along the waterfront. *L'Hostal/Jazz Rock Club*, behind Portitxó beach and the Dalí statue, opened in 1901, became a favourite haunt of the great man plus other luminaries, and is still the place to be seen, with live music many nights. There may be more live acoustic sounds after 11pm at Cuban-decor *Café de la Habana*, towards the south end of town at Porta d'en Pampà, while *Si Té 7* just past Port d'Alguer is excellent for a late nightcap, with patrons spilling out from the tiny bar onto the seawall. For less strictly alcoholic indulgence, *Rosa Azul* on a tiny shaded *plaça* at Port d'Alguer does ice cream as well as drinks, while the enduringly popular, municipally run *Casino Societat de l'Amistat* on Es Portal beachfront operates long hours and is one of three **Internet** cafés in town.

## Portlligat and Cap de Creus

From Cadaqués a paved road serpentines 1.5km north over the ridge to **PORTLLIGAT**, with views over a striking seascape as you descend. For five decades Salvador Dalí lived here with his wife and muse, Gala, having from 1930 onwards gradually converted a series of waterside fishermen's cottages into a labyrinthine home that has all the quirks you would expect. It now operates as the **Casa-Museu Salvador Dalí** (mid-March to mid-June & mid–Sept to 6 Jan Tues–Sun 10.30am–6pm; mid-June to mid-Sept daily 10.30am–9pm; closed early Jan to mid-March; reservations mandatory on ☎972 251 015; €8) and, despite the strictly controlled access (maximum 8 people per group), it's worth the advance planning to see first-hand how the bizarre couple lived until Gala's death in 1982. The wall-art is reproduction – the originals are in the museum at Figureres (see p.139) – but all the furnishings actually belonged to Dalí and Gala.

Tours begin at the **Hall of the Bear**, the first hut acquired and named after its stuffed beast; next you take in the master's **studio**, the exotically draped **model's room**, and the so-called **Yellow Room** with its large windows and giant snail clock. Above this are the couple's **bedroom**, a **Photo Room** with a gallery of celebrity visitors, and last and best the domed **Oval Room**, Gala's sitting room which boasts stunning acoustics. Then it's upstairs to see the **garden**, topped by egg forms, and a phallic **swimming pool** where the couple entertained guests.

From Portlligat, a spectacular road goes 6km through a desolate landscape to **Cap de Creus**, the easternmost point on the Iberian peninsula and site of some wild New Year's Eve parties. Without your own **transport**, you can take a minibus run by Passarella, Avinguda Caritat Serinyana 23, use the seasonal fake train from Portitxó cove (10am–6pm), or **walk** from Portlligat along a particularly demanding section of the Camí de Ronda. Following this path gets you, after twenty minutes, to partly **nudist Platja de San Lluís**, best of the **beaches** en route; just before the headland there's a pair of wilder coves, **L'Infern** and **Cala Jugadora**. At Cap de Creus proper, you'll find the terminus of the GR11, a real **lighthouse** (vintage 1853), a fake one built closer to the edge for the 1971 film *The Light at the End of the World*, and a ramshackle, popular and surprisingly decent **bar-restaurant** (Mon–Thurs noon–8pm, Fri–Sun 11am–midnight) with an eclectic menu, unimprovably perched terrace-tables and appropriate taped sounds.

# Roses

**ROSES**, 17km from Cadaqués on the south flank of the peninsula, was founded by Greek colonists in the eighth century BC, who named it Rhodes after their original home. By the eleventh century AD the town's fine natural harbour had effectively supplanted that of nearby Castelló d'Empúries, by then silting up. After Barbarossa's 1543 raid, Carlos I of Spain built the now-derelict, star-shaped fortress of **La Ciutadella**, dismantled by the French during the Peninsular War.

The fortress and four kilometres of fringing beach on the wide **Golfo de Roses** are the extent of interest; Roses is principally engaged in flogging cheap, high-rise flats to Spaniards and foreigners, now that package tourism in the area has levelled off. Some sources make much of its palm-fringed esplanade, but overall the town is extremely grim.

## Practicalities

**Buses** stop near the corner of c/Gran Via Pau Casals, the inland ring road, and c/Riera Ginjolas. On the seafront promenade there's a **Turisme** (daily:

June–Sept 9am–9pm; Oct–May 9am–1pm & 4–8pm; ☎972 257 331). The only characterful **accommodation** in the immediate area is just outside the satellite resort of Santa Margarida, right off the road linking it with Palau-Saverdera: *Mas la Torre* (☎972 255 453; open all year by arrangement; ❹), an isolated cattle ranch that's part of the local *turisme rural* scheme. The en-suite rooms – some balconied, those in the medieval tower of the name with vaulted ceilings – are comfortable, the common areas pleasant. Near the aforementioned roundabout, in Canals de Santa Margarida, is a **bar-restaurant**, *El Rancho*, most remarkable for its extended hours (7pm–3am) in a country where constrained meal times are increasingly the rule. The rodeo-kitsch interior is popular with locals and foreigners, plus there's an outdoor terrace; aside from assorted coffee cocktails, the fare is limited to grills and salads, and portions are small, but so are prices (€17–19 for 3 courses), and quality is decent.

## The coast to Cala Jóncols

From the eastern edge of Roses, signs direct you towards the paved road for Cala Montjoi and Cala Jóncols, 13km distant. **Walkers** (in spring or autumn only) will take a full day to cover the distance to Cadaqués on the Camí de Ronda/GR92. En route, you pass a succession of unshaded sand-and-pebble coves, or at least the side roads to them: the lovely horseshoe-shaped **Cala Murtra** and the pine-fringed **Cala Rostella**, both part-naturist, are the first you'd want to stop for. **Cala Montjoi**, 6km along, is the home of *El Bullí* **restaurant**, one of the most famous in Spain, sporting three Michelin stars (☎972 150 457, ⊛www.elbulli.com; closed Oct–March, & Mon & Tues April–June); you don't always have to book, but you will part with a minimum of €100 per person. Just beyond, the pavement gives out in the vicinity of scenic **Cala Calitja** and **Cala Pelosa**, after which the track skirts the base of the Cap de Norfeu headland before dropping bumpily to **Cala Jóncols** (even jeeps should not attempt to proceed further to Cadaqués).

Here there's an excellent if pricey seafood **restaurant**, *El Chiringuito*, just behind the beach, and further inland in lovely poolside grounds, the rustic *Hotel Cala Jóncols* (☎972 253 970, ⊛www.calajoncols.com; Easter–Oct; ❹ HB only). This, with both doubles and top-floor family suites, is currently more or less the exclusive province of the Euro Divers **scuba school** (⊜calajoncols @euro-divers.com), which does two escorted dives daily (at 10am and 4pm), plus a weekly night dive. The protected bay between Cabo Figueres and Cabo Norfeu is among the best on the Costa Brava for red corals, invertebrates and walls, with nearly a score of sites visited in repertory, according to conditions.

## Castelló d'Empúries

The delightful medieval town of **CASTELLÓ D'EMPÚRIES**, halfway between Roses and Figueres on the Riu Muga, is intrinsically worthwhile in itself, and as a base for exploring the nearby wildlife sanctuary at Aiguamolls de l'Emporda. A five-minute walk from the outskirts takes you into a medieval precinct that's lost little charm despite being so close to the beach-bound hordes. Formerly the capital of the Counts of Empúries, the town's narrow streets are lined with well-preserved Gothic buildings, including the thirteenth-century **Església de Santa Maria** on terraced Plaça Mossèn Cinto Verdaguer. It was intended to be the seat of a bishopric, but opposition from rival Girona meant this never happened, and Castelló was left with a church vastly surplus to requirements. The elaborate portal features carved figures of the apostles, including (on the far right) Judas Thaddeus, a copy of the original image (now in the museum inside the church; €2) which was defaced by medieval townspeople in the mistaken belief it was Judas Iscariot. Beyond the pair of **belfries** flanking the facade (the right one unfinished), there's an earlier one on the north side, overlooking the **Lonja del Mar**, still used as a covered market.

### Practicalities

**Buses** halt at the south edge of town; **cars** should also be parked nearby unless you're patronizing the recommended hotels, which have private space. A **Turisme** (Easter–Sept daily 9am–9pm; ☏972 250 426) is housed in the Casa Communal (Llotja) on arcaded **Plaça dels Homes**, the de facto hub of life with its cafés. The best of several places to **stay**, in the heart of the old quarter, is the two-star *Hotel Canet* (☏972 250 340, ⊛www.hotelcanet.com; ❸), at Plaça Joc de la Pilota 2; they've a luxury annexe in a restored palace around the corner, *Hotel de la Moneda*, with three grades of rooms (❺–❼) and a pool/gym/spa used by both hotels.

Connoisseurs of **cases rurals** will want to consider three nearby offerings. The first is *La Caputxeta*, just across the river and C260 from Castelló and accessed via the "Castelló Nou" exit from the roundabout (☏972 250 310, ⊛www.caputxeta.com; ❸ B&B), with spotless, tiled-floor rooms (shared baths), a self-catering kitchen and a choice of continental or traditional Catalan breakfast; despite being sited by a commercial park and golf course, it's not at all claustrophobic, with a garden and parking. In **FORTIÀ** village, 4km south from the next junction west on the C260, *Can Bayre* on Plaça de l'Església (☏972 534 324, ⊛www.canbayre.com; ❹) is a state-of-the-art *turisme rural*, occupying a sensitively converted sixteenth-century manor house. **SIURANA D'EMPORDÀ**, 18km away beyond the C31, can offer *El Molí* (☏972 525 139, ⊛www.girsoft.com/elmoli; ❸ B&B), mostly comprising family quads (❻), with half-board available; though it's a working cattle ranch, and more Scandinavian than Iberian in feel, *El Molí* remains popular and must be reserved two months in advance.

Local **restaurant** options are similarly varied. Top honours go to the everpopular *menjador* of the *Canet*, where a Baroque church façade, lit up at night, overlooks the dining terrace; the €16 *menú* is, unusually for this price, interesting, while *a la carta* (endives, sole, dessert, drinks) won't go much over €26. Behind Santa Maria church and the Lonja del Mar, *Portal de la Gallarda* is a tad cheaper for simple fare, stressing grilled game and meat. At the southern outskirts, on the corner of Avinguda Generalitat and c/Santa Clara, *Hostal Ca L'Anton* – while not brilliant lodgings – has a popular, traditional *menjador*; and 3km northwest in Vilanova de la Muga, affordable *La Resclosa* (☏972 507 526; closed Mon) is celebrated for its cod and duck recipes.

## Parc Natural dels Aiguamolls de l'Empordà

Southeast of Castelló lies the **Parc Natural dels Aiguamolls de l'Empordà** (daily; free), an important wetland reserve created by the Catalan government in 1983 to save what remained of the Empordà marshlands, much reduced from their original extent by decades of agricultural and tourist enterprise. The marshes and local rice paddies attract a wonderful selection of birds, as well as less promoted small mammals like water voles, otters and red foxes; avian sightings, including the rare garganey duck and purple gallinule, are most frequent in the morning and evening during migration periods (March–May & Aug–Oct).

To reach the heart of the park from Castelló d'Empúries, take the road south towards Sant Pere Pescador. After about 4km, you'll see a sign on the left for the **visitors' centre** at El Cortalet (daily: April–Sept 9.30am–2pm & 4.30–7pm; Oct–March 9.30am–2pm & 3.30–6pm; ⊕972 454 222, ⊛www.aiguamolls.org), where there's ample parking, a free map of walking routes, binoculars for rent and (arranged in advance) guided tours by staff ornithologists. The more popular of two principal **marked paths** is shaded **La Massona** (2hr round trip to the beach and back), with a series of **hides** along the way; nos. 5 and 7 will be most rewarding in summer, as the adjacent water-holes rarely dry up. A converted rice silo nearby functions as an aerial **observatory** – you'll need a good head for heights.

# Figueres

**FIGUERES** is the capital of Alt Empordà county – the upper part of the massive alluvial plain formed by the rivers Muga and Fluvià. For most visitors its chief appeal lies in the fact that **Salvador Dalí** (1904–89) was born, began his career and died here, yet if you linger after touring the museum devoted to his work, you'll discover a pleasant provincial town with a busy, café-lined *rambla*, browsable shops and adequate food and lodging.

## The Teatre-Museu Dalí

Figueres' **Teatre-Museu Dalí** (July–Sept daily 9am–7.15pm; Oct–June Tues–Sun 10.30am–5.15pm; €7.50; ⊛www.dali-estate.org) is the most visited museum in Spain after Madrid's Prado, but it's as much a theatrical fantasy, appealing to a universal love of absurdity and participation, as it is a conventional art collection. Appropriately enough, before destruction at the end of

---

### The sardana

The main difference between the **sardana** – the national dance of Catalonia – and other folk dances is that it's the inheritance of the entire community, rather than the realm of specialists. However, this doesn't mean that you can simply barge in and have a go. It's a very complex dance, and etiquette requires that you join a circle of dancers of your own standard. Following the arm movements isn't too challenging, as every dancer holds hands with his or her neighbours in the circle – consequently, your limbs will be hauled up and down at the appropriate moments. But the footwork is fiendishly difficult, with the step changing mid-bar and the beat changing mid-step. Musical accompaniment is provided by a band known as a **cobla**, comprising five wind instruments, five brass horns, a double bass and percussion. The rite-like intensity, the linking of the hands and the upright posture suggest that the *sardana* may have originated with the ancient Greek settlers who established the port of Roses (though cynics claim it was artificially resuscitated during the nineteenth century as part of the resurgence in Catalan national feeling).

On summer Sundays and festival days the *sardana* is danced all along the Costa Brava (and on the Côte Vermeille too), as well as at plenty of inland towns and villages – particularly on *La Diada* (National Day), September 11. Dates for other major *sardanes* are given in the "Festivals" feature on pp.78–79.

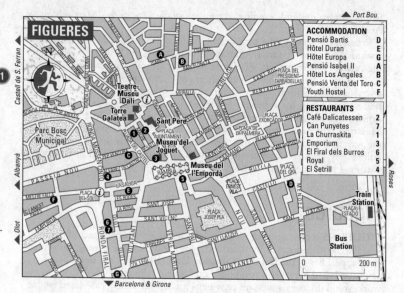

▲ Port Bou

**FIGUERES**

| ACCOMMODATION | |
|---|---|
| Pensió Bartis | D |
| Hôtel Duran | E |
| Hôtel Europa | G |
| Pensió Isabel II | A |
| Hôtel Los Ángeles | B |
| Pensió Venta del Toro | C |
| Youth Hostel | F |

| RESTAURANTS | |
|---|---|
| Café Dalicatessen | 2 |
| Can Punyetes | 7 |
| La Churraskita | 1 |
| Emporium | 3 |
| El Firal dels Burros | 6 |
| Royal | 5 |
| El Setrill | 4 |

▼ Barcelona & Girona

the Spanish Civil War, the building *was* the municipal theatre, and venue for Dalí's first exhibition of paintings in 1918 (when he was 14). Upon reconstruction in 1974, the artist set about fashioning it into an inspired repository for some of his most bizarre works. Having moved to the adjacent Torre Galatea in 1984, Dalí died there on January 23, 1989; his body now lies behind a simple granite slab in a basement gallery of the museum.

The **building**, on Plaça Gala i Salvador Dalí, was designed as an exhibit itself. Three-cornered imitation bread rolls speckle the exterior walls, one of which is painted terra-cotta pink; topped by a huge metallic-glass dome, the roof line is studded with giant eggs and faceless bronze mannequins preparing to dive from the heights. In the courtyard, the **Rainy Cadillac** contains three vine-and snail-infested mannequins, with a statue of a buxom Biblical queen on the bonnet, while overhead a totem pole of tyres supports Gala's rowboat, from which hang pendulous blobs of resin, made using condoms as moulds. Inside, steps from the stage area under the dome lead to the **Mae West Room**, where a carefully manipulated viewing of some draperies and a labial red sofa converge into a portrait of the actress. The **Palau de Vent** on the first floor is dominated by the ceiling painting of Gala and Dalí ascending to heaven, their grubby feet dangling in the viewer's face.

All the pranks and optical illusions can distract from the reality that there's far more "serious" art here than generally credited, both by Dalí and other artists of his choosing. Lesser-known "conventional" canvases from the 1920s (*Portrait of His Sister*) are juxtaposed with more stereotypically surreal later material like *Soft Self-Portrait with Bacon* and *Portrait of Picasso*, while *The Spectre of Sex Appeal* seems the epitome of Dalí's shame-ridden pathology. Gala as *Atomic Leda* and *Galatea of the Spheres* are two of many portraits of his muse, culminating in the Portlligat-set *Dalí from the Back Painting Gala from the Back* (1972–73), though there are some of friends too, such as *Laurence Olivier as Richard III*.

# The rest of town

The oft-overlooked **Museu de l'Empordà** at Rambla 1 (July–Sept Tues–Sat 11am–9pm, Sun & public holidays 11am–2pm; Oct–June Tues–Sat 11am–7pm, Sun & public holidays 11am–2pm; €2 or same ticket as Teatre-Museu Dalí), hosts a serious collection, albeit labelled in Catalan only, bolstered by donations from the Prado and wealthy Figuerans. The first floor combines Greek and Roman ceramics with medieval polychrome wood Virgins, while upstairs there's a gallery of Empordan sculptors and painters, of which the "modern" division of local landscapes and portraits is best. The third floor, devoted to abstract and figurative depiction of the region, is enlivened with works by Dalí, Joan Miró, Ramon Reig and Antoni Tàpies among others, though these holdings are occasionally removed for temporary exhibits. Figueres also has a toy museum with over four thousand items from all over Catalunya, the **Museu del Joguet** (June–Sept Mon–Sat 10am–1pm & 4–7pm, Sun 11am–1.30pm & 5–7.30pm; Oct–May same hours but closed Sun pm & Mon; €4.50), housed in a beautiful old hotel in the *rambla*, above *Café Emporium*. The statue at the bottom of the *rambla* honours Narcís Monturiol, a local who distinguished himself by inventing the submarine.

The only other sight is the huge **Castell de Sant Ferran** (daily: June–Sept 10.30am–8pm; Oct–May 10.30am–2pm; €4.50), 1km northwest of town – follow Pujada del Castell from just beyond the Dalí museum. Built in 1753 to defend against French invasion – and failing signally in that role twice during the Napoleonic Wars – it remains one of the vastest citadels in Europe. Sant Ferran served as the last bastion of the Republicans in the Civil War, when Figueres became their capital for a week in February 1939 after the fall of Barcelona. Earlier in the war, it had been used as a barracks for newly arrived members of the International Brigades before they moved on to the front; Chelsea sculptor Jason Gurney, writing in *Crusade in Spain*, described his quarters as the "most beautiful barracks in Spain ... the building, and its setting in the Pyrenean foothills ... exquisite". The outer circuit of star-shaped **walls** exceeds 3km, so you might consider shelling out another €6 for a three-hour tour which includes a jeep ride around the perimeter, and then a dinghy trip through the cathedral-like **water cisterns** under the parade ground, engineering marvels sufficient to outlast a year's siege, and the highlight of any visit.

# Practicalities

The **train station** lies 600m directly east of the centre, in Plaça Estació; the **bus station**, across the same *plaça*, issues tickets for both local (mostly SARFA and TEISA) and international buses. The focal point of Figueres – the *rambla* – is reached from the stations by walking west along c/Sant Llàtzer and then turning right at c/Nou. **Parking** a car is nearly impossible in the centre; either pay to use designated car parks or resign yourself to walking in from the outskirts.

There's a small, seasonal **tourist information booth** in the train station (June–Sept only Mon–Sat 9.30am–1pm & 4–7pm); the helpful central **Turisme** is at Plaça del Sol (July & Aug daily 9am–9pm; rest of year Mon–Sat 9.30am–1pm & 4–7pm, Sun 9.30am–1pm; ☎972 503 155, ⊛www.figueres.net). Both can provide a town map, handy accommodation lists, and timetables for onward transport.

## Accommodation

**Accommodation** options range from basic to upmarket, with several adequate central choices, though many of the better hotels (with ample parking) lie on main roads out of town. Acceptable budget options include *Pensió Bartis*, c/Mendez Nunyez 2 (☎972 501 473; ❷), near the bus and train stations; the friendly *Pensió Venta del Toro* on c/Pep Ventura 5 (☎972 510 510; ❷), with a *menjador* downstairs; and *Pensió Isabel II*, c/Isabel II 16 (enquire at Muralla 12; ☎972 504 735; ❷), where airy bathrooms compensate for small, air-con rooms. For two-star comfort, there's the quiet but slightly overpriced *Hotel Los Ángeles* at c/Barceloneta 10 (☎972 510 661, ☜www.hotelangeles.com; ❸), where bathrooms are the same size as the smallish bedrooms, done up in vulgar-Spanish-Modern (off-street parking costs extra), or the better-value *Hotel Europa* at Ronda Firal 18 (☎972 500 744, ℱ972 671 117; ❸). Top standard downtown is at the three-star *Duran* on c/Lasauca 5 (☎972 501 250, ☜www.hotelduran.com; ❻), originally a carters' inn dating from 1855, with comfortable if slightly dark rooms.

There's a good **youth hostel** (☎972 501 213; closed Sept), at c/Anicet Pagès 2, off Plaça del Sol; Figueres also has a **campsite** about 3km out on the N-II northwest towards France: smallish, shady *Pous* (☎972 675 496; April–Oct).

## Eating and drinking

The gaggle of touristy **restaurants** flanking the narrow streets around the Dalí museum are generally worth avoiding in favour of less obvious prospects. An exception here is *La Churraskita* at c/Magre 5 (closed Mon), purveying Argentine-style grills, pizzas and pasta. The pub-like facade of *El Setrill* at Tortellà 10 conceals a full-on eatery doing big portions of hearty food (weekday *menú* €7). Ronda Firal has more late-serving, budget choices: *El Firal dels Burros* at no. 15, a *bodega* where cheese and paté accompanies wine, or *Can Punyetes* at no. 25, doing more carnivorous fare in a rustic environment. For a bit more outlay, head for the *menjador* of *Hotel Duran* where generously proportioned regional dishes like duck with pears come with a modern flair (€12 *menú*, €20-plus *a la carta*).

Classic **cafés** on the *rambla*, which unusually doubles as a busy traffic circle, include *Emporium* at no. 10, with snacks and tables inside or out, and the *Royal* opposite at no. 28, with *modernista* tiled walls, a slightly alternative clientele, and *orxata* served as it should be. Among the more tourist-pitched places on Plaça Ajuntament near the Dalí museum, *Café Dalicatessen* at c/Sant Pere 17–19 offers good juices, pots of Earl Grey tea and fresh croissants. Figueres has traditionally been fairly comatose **late at night**, with most local youth making a beeline for Roses or L'Escala, but lately there are always at least two clubs trying their luck on the north side of Plaça del Sol.

# North and west of Figueres

During World War II, the region **north of Figueres** was so deserted that there were no Guardia Civil stationed between the **Castell de Requesens** and Portbou, which made the **Serra de l'Albera** ridge a favoured escape route from France. The stretch between **Garriguella** in the east and **Cantallóps** in the west remains fairly low-key, with semi-abandoned villages tucked between vineyards, olive groves and cork-oak plantations. Since the 1980s, many foreigners – mainly Dutch and German – have moved in to convert crumbling local farms, and Catalan day-trippers scour the countryside at weekends, replenishing their cellars at the many wineries that dot the area, especially around Capmany. Below the foothills, places like **Peralada**, **Mollet de Peralada** and **Vilabertran** have always been more going concerns than the isolated Alberan hamlets.

The most interesting outings **west from Figueres** visit the large villages of **Maçanet de Cabrenys**, **Darnius** and **Sant Llorenç de la Muga**, either side of the forest-fringed **Pantà (Reservoir) de Boadella**, less impressive than it seems on the map, especially after dry winters, but still attracting watersports enthusiasts.

## Vilabertran, Peralada and Mollet de Peralada

Easily overlooked, quiet **VILABERTRAN**, 2km northeast of Figueres, has two claims on your attention: a former Augustinian monastery, and an excellent restaurant. The **Canònica de Santa Maria de Vilabertran** (June–Sept Tues–Sat 10am–1.30pm & 3–6.30pm, Sun 10am–1.30pm; Oct–May Tues–Sat 10am–1.30pm & 3–5.30pm; €2.40, free on Tues), with its fine Lombard belfry pierced by three tiers of arcaded windows, dominates the village. The late eleventh-century monastic **church**, now the venue of a prestigious late-summer Schubert festival, was carefully chosen for the Christmas Day 1322 marriage of Jaume II of Aragón and Catalan queen Elisenda de Montcada. Hosting a royal wedding bestowed tax-free status on Vilabertran, but as it was (and is) a tiny place, this hardly affected the royal coffers. Pride of the church is an ornate **silver crucifix** in the northerly Capella dels Dolors; the cloister for once is disappointing, its column capitals bare of relief art. Try and schedule a **meal** at late-serving *L'Hostalet d'en Lons* (closed Mon), a vaulted former wine warehouse at the northwest edge of town; there's no *menú*, but a huge *panaché de verduras*, savoury *xipirones* with parsley and garlic and a *flan de coca*, washed down by the light house rosé, will just leave change from a €20 note.

Some 5km further northeast, you reach fortified **PERALADA**, a medieval town centred on its arcaded *plaça*. The main sight is the moated **castle**, which contains a casino, a wine factory, the stage and seating for the prestigious annual **summer festival** and a museum (July–Sept daily 10am–8pm; Oct–June Tues–Sun 10am–6.30pm; €4.50) featuring glassware, ceramics and antiquarian books. Local **restaurants** are generally expensive, but *Cal Sagristà* at c/Rodona 2 (closed Mon) does moderately priced home-style dishes. Even better, head 6.5km further north to eat hearty country fare at *Ca La Maria* (closed Sun night, Mon night, Tues all day), another cavernous former wine warehouse in the very centre of **MOLLET DE PERALADA**. Under €27 nets you generous starters of salami and olives, *bacalla amb xamfaina* (cod in tomato sauce), stir-fried artichoke hearts and pear tart washed down with a *porró* of *Banyuls* dessert wine. Despite overstretched service, it's an Alt Empordà institution and highly recommended.

## The Serra de l'Albera

The **Serra de l'Albera** is perhaps better for car-touring and cycling than walking; narrow but paved country roads link well-spaced hamlets and wine-tasting bodegas, while wide dirt tracks lead to remote dolmens and churches. Gateway to the region is **GARRIGUELLA**, reached by a different seven-kilometre road from Peralada and itself distributed to either side of the GI603 road.

Most of the village lies north of the highway, but most facilities are in a little neighbourhood to the south, including some prime **accommodation** in the *turisme rural* scheme: *Can Coll* at no. 3 on the Peralada road (T 972 530 116; ❸ B&B) and the more sumptuous *Can Garriga* a little further south at c/Figueres 1–3 (T 972 530 184, w www.cangarriga.net; ❺ B&B), a lovely walled compound with a grassy front garden and vaulted ground-floor rooms that fill quickly. On Plaça de Baix, near both of these, you can **eat** well at *Can Battle*.

**ESPOLLA**, 9km northwest of Garriguella on the GI603, is home, at the east edge of town, to the **Centre d'Informació** (May–Oct daily; Nov–April weekends only; T 972 545 039) for the **Parc Natural de l'Albera**, created all around here in 1986 to help protect the local environment and its distinctive fauna, which includes tortoises and a dwarf wild cow. Otherwise this is a typical Alt Empordà wine village, its shuttered houses crammed into a labyrinth of streets that come to life each year during the grape harvest. Currently the only **accommodation** is *Can Giro*, a seventeeth-century *casa de pagès* on Plaça San Jaume 1 (no phone; ❷). Prehistorians will delight in two local Neolithic **dolmens**, lying either side of Espolla. Take the GI602 southwest towards Sant Climent Sescebes; at a rising bend 1km along, turn right onto a dirt track for another 700m to the eerie **Cabana Arqueta**, standing alone in the shade of oaks. Harder to find is **Dolmen del Barranc**, the only carved tomb in the area: it lies 3km from the village off the track leading north towards the frontier Col de Banyuls.

Sleepy **RABÓS D'EMPORDÀ**, 4km southeast of Espolla, is crowned by a superb fortified church – the apse is the tower – and can muster a good local **restaurant** at the village entrance, *Can Tomas* (closed Wed). But Rabós is most known as the start-point of the six-plus-kilometre dirt track up to the fortified Benedictine monastery of **Sant Quirze de Colera**, off-limits for interminable restoration, though the three-aisled, tenth-century church appears startlingly impressive in its wild setting. Adjacent is a handy, reasonable **restaurant**, *Corral de Sant Quirze* (lunch daily except Wed, supper also in summer), occupying the former monastic stables. The **GR11** passes through, and camping is possible if the monastery's spring hasn't dried up, but you're well advised to avoid summer walking in the often shadeless Albera, where water can be unreliable.

From Espolla, 23km of roundabout driving leads to appealing **CANTALLÓPS**, though there's also a sporadic bus service from Figueres. Cantallóps has a single **pensió** at the outskirts if you get stuck, *Can Pau* (T 972 554 881; ❷), and a **restaurant** in the village, but you're really here to continue for 7km of wide, well-signposted dirt track to the **Castell de Requesens** (Recasens; July 15–Sept 15 daily 11am–7pm; rest of year 11am–5pm Sat/Sun/hols only; €2), set amidst a marvellous countryside of cork oaks (their harvested bark duly stacked for collection) and a few cedars. Originally founded in the ninth century, the castle might best remain admired from afar by purists; after a chequered history, it spent two decades from 1942 as a Guardia Civil barracks, whose tenants graffitoed and vandalized the place to a deplorable extent, their contemporary alterations wrecking its fabric. The masonry gets older and less spoiled as you climb the various levels of labyrinthine cisterns, vaulted halls, kitchens, latrines and parapets; though you're denied access to the highest towers, the views are superb.

## Sant Llorenç de la Muga and Albanyà

There are three weekly **buses** from Figueres to these settlements; **driving** yourself, follow signs out of town for the N-II to La Jonquera, and keep an eye peeled for the poorly marked turning for Llers, and then to **SANT LLORENÇ DE LA MUGA**, about 17km west of the town. Without there being much specific to see, this large, fortified village, nestled in pines along the upper Riu Muga, makes an excellent destination; it's linked to Maçanet de Cabrenys (see below) by a marked but rough track (hikes, bikes or jeeps only; 9.5km) skirting wetlands on the reservoir's west shore. The medieval stone houses form much of the defensive perimeter, but there are two portcullised thirteenth-century gates – one on the west, the other opening onto an old *camí* to Girona – and stout towers at scattered points, for example behind the twelfth-century parish church. Entering Sant Llorenç from the north, you pass a lovely, massive fourteenth-century **bridge** – like Besalú's (see p.155) in miniature – and a millrace leading down to a dilapidated **mill**; the only **place to eat** is *Sa Muga* on the central Rambla, and you can **drink** at either *El Lluro* on Plaça Baixa, or the municipally run *Societat La Fraternitat* on the Rambla. Thus far the only **accommodation** is *Hostal Can Toni*, a modern place on the outskirts (☎972 569 225; ❸), though you'll also find a small-scale, tent-friendly **campsite**, *La Fradera* (☎972 542 054; Easter–Oct), 1.5km west.

By contrast, **ALBANYÀ**, 7km upstream from Sant Llorenç, is nothing special, though it too has a minuscule medieval core with an arched gate giving onto the old *camí* to Sant Llorenç. If you're on a **GR11** traverse you'll necessarily pass through, as Albanyà lies between the **Col de Bassegoda** – 11km west and the boundary of Alta Garrotxa *comarca* – and Maçanet de Cabrenys (20km or four walking hours north). The asphalt gives out 1.5km west of Albanyà at the caravan-dominated, off-putting *Camping Bassegoda*; since Albanyà's single hotel-restaurant has closed, trekkers might prefer to continue east towards *Camping La Fradera* after perhaps replenishing supplies at the single **shop**. The closest indoor **accommodation**, 1.5km beyond Albanyà, is *Can Carreras* (☎972 569 199; ❸ B&B), off by itself near the river, though it's a working hog-farm, with all the attendant noise and aromas.

## Darnius, Maçanet de Cabrenys and La Vajol

North of the Pantà de Boadella – accessible from the Muga valley by a link road below the dam, or directly off the N-II – lies **DARNIUS**, with a weekday bus service to Figueres with the company David i Manel. It's not exactly a thriving place, though it does have two good **accommodation** options nearby. Closest is a *casa de pagès* at the south edge of town, near the stop-lights: massive, vaulted *Can Massot* (☎972 535 193; ❸ B&B), with extensive common areas including a lovely breakfast room and self-catering kitchens. More luxurious and unusual is *Hotel La Central* (☎972 535 053 or 661 807 008, ⊛www.hlacentral.com; ❺–❼), 6km southwest along a well-marked and graded dirt track. This *modernista* chalet in idyllic streamside surroundings bills itself as a "Centre de Salut i Esport", with a full spa and activity programme; the rooms, in three grades, are irreproachable – the tower suites the most distinctive. The in-house **restaurant** with its waterfall-wall out the rear window excels at seafood; monkfish, *escalivada*, lemon mousse and drinks will run to €27 *a la carta*, though you can dine for under €20.

You may prefer to carry on from Darnius through dense cork-oak groves to livelier and more atmospheric **MAÇANET DE CABRENYS**, 26km from Figueres. The **bus** stops just south of this densely built, oval-shaped medieval ensemble, next to a summer-only **Turisme** (Mon–Sat except Wed pm 10.30am–1.30pm & 5–7pm, Sun 10am–2pm; ☎972 544 297). Of the two places to **stay** and **eat**, go for welcoming Casa Fonda affiliate *Hostal La Quadra* on the northwest edge of town (☎ 972 544 032, ⓦ www.laquadra.com; closed 2 weeks in June; ❸ B&B), with a variety of rooms thoroughly redone in 2003, private parking and a sustaining basement **restaurant** where *a la carta* won't top €16; the front **bar** is popular with villagers, though you might also frequent cavernous *La Pau* on the main square. The only specific local "sight" is **O Pedra Dreta**, a menhir dating from around 3000 BC and standing 2m high on the western fringe of the village, just beyond Mas Pitxo. There's also a useful **cross-border road** (paved but narrow) to Coustouges in France, via the hamlet of Tapis.

Under your own steam, you can vary a return to Figueres or the N-II by looping north (7km from Maçanet) via the compact knolltop village of **LA VAJOL**, famous for its sweeping views of the Alt Empordà. Plaça Major is a popular venue for **eating**, at either the superior *Hostal La Vajol* or *Casa Comaulis* (closed Mon). Though the GR11 skims by, there's currently **no short-term accommodation**.

# The Spanish valleys

The higher valleys of the Spanish Eastern Pyrenees begin well away from the Mediterranean coast. Easiest access to the mountains is via **Girona**, 40km south of Figueres, an ancient capital with ample cultural appeal; it also has Catalunya's largest airport outside Barcelona, handling year-round flights from Britain. From Girona, the usual route involves heading northwest through lakeside **Banyoles** to the exquisite medieval town of **Besalú**, then west into the heart of the volcanic **Garrotxa** region, centred on the town of **Olot**. Continuing in the same direction brings you to **Ripoll** and its famous monastery, or to **Sant Joan de les Abadesses**, with another monastic cathedral. Just northeast of here, **Camprodon** is the first town truly enclosed by foothills, but for a more dramatic introduction to the Spanish Catalan Pyrenees, the upper **Freser valley** awaits just north of Ripoll, with its popular narrow-gauge train and grandiose Marian shrine at **Núria**.

**Public transport** connections from Girona towards the hills are initially excellent, with numerous daily bus departures as far as Olot, via Banyoles and Besalú, from where onward links to Camprodon and Ripoll are spotty. Frequent train and bus departures serve Figueres and the coastal resorts northeast of Girona.

## Girona

The obvious gateway to any eastern approach to the Spanish Pyrenees, **GIRONA** spills down a fortified hill above the occasionally stagnant but carp-clogged Riu Onyar, just before it joins the Ter. Like Perpignan – the equivalent gateway city on the French side – it has a distinctly Arab flavour, but here

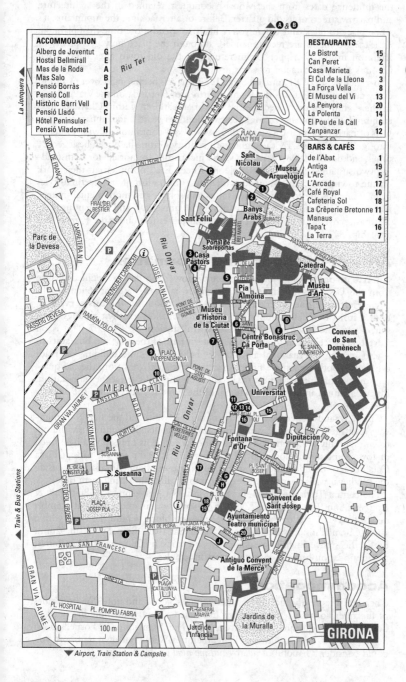

**ACCOMMODATION**

Alberg de Joventut                 G
Hostal Bellmirall                      E
Mas de la Roda                        A
Mas Salo                                  B
Pensió Borràs                          J
Pensió Coll                                F
Històric Barri Vell                     D
Pensió Lladó                             C
Hôtel Peninsular                        I
Pensió Viladomat                      H

**RESTAURANTS**

Le Bistrot                    15
Can Peret                     2
Casa Marieta                9
El Cul de la Lleona        3
La Força Vella               8
El Museu del Vi            13
La Penyora                  20
La Polenta                   14
El Pou de la Call            6
Zanpanzar                  12

**BARS & CAFÉS**

de l'Abat                          1
Antiga                            19
L'Arc                                5
L'Arcada                         17
Café Royal                      10
Cafeteria Sol                   18
La Crêperie Bretonne    11
Manaus                           4
Tapa't                            16
La Terra                          7

**GIRONA**

0        100 m

the influence dates from the Moorish conquest, retained in the architecture and narrow streets of its old quarter. Before or after tackling the mountains, it's a fine place to relax, and where you're likely to spend more time than planned. At least two nights are recommended: although the place now gets plenty of attention from day-trippers, calm returns to the old town after dark, when Girona's abiding character reasserts itself.

So-called "City of a Thousand Sieges", Girona has been fought over in almost every century since it was the Roman fortress of Gerunda on the Via Augusta. In the eighth century it became the seat of an earldom within Charlemagne's empire; the Muslims stayed for over two hundred years, a fact apparent in the web of narrow central lanes, and there was also a continuous Jewish presence through six centuries. By the eighteenth century Girona had been besieged 21 times, and during 1808–09 it earned the nickname "Immortal" for withstanding two sustained assaults by Napoleon's forces. Each occupier left their mark on the town, and connoisseurs can identify a succession of architectural styles from Romanesque to *modernisme*. But as palpable as any monumental interest is the feel of a confident, young (thanks to the university) and prosperous place that has recovered from years of neglect and repression under the Franco dictatorship.

## Arrival, transport and information

Girona's **airport**, 13km south of the city, now has a daily scheduled service from the UK year-round. The small arrivals hall has three car rental booths (Avis, Hertz and one other), as well as a ticket booth for the **bus service** to both Girona train/bus stations (€1.65) and Barcelona; if their timings don't suit, a taxi into town costs €16. The **train station** (☎972 207 093) is off Carretera Barcelona in the modern, western part of the city; the **bus station** – also serving international arrivals – is behind the same building on Plaça d'Espanya. Both are a mere fifteen-minute walk southwest from the old quarter. You're more likely to use a **taxi** – the handiest ranks are at the train station, Plaça Catalunya and the old-town end of the Pont de Pedra – than the city bus lines.

Girona is sandwiched by the toll autopista A7 (west) and the free N-II highway (east). If you **drive** in, you'll find **parking** generally nightmarish: the old town especially is a controlled-access zone for residents only, so you'll be fined or towed unless your lodgings provide parking. Use the fee car park at Plaça Catalunya, or compete for free spaces up on Passeig Fora Muralla, just outside the medieval walls near the university campus (difficult during term time).

The central **Turisme** (Mon–Fri 8am–8pm, Sat 8am–2pm & 4–8pm; July & Aug also Sun 9am–2pm; ☎972 226 575, ⊛www.ajuntament.gi) is at Rambla de la Llibertat 1, the tree-lined promenade one block behind the river, with a satellite branch inside the train station (Mon–Sat 10am–8pm, Sun 10am–2pm); both offices have English-speaking staff and stock useful maps and brochures, accommodation lists and local transport timetables.

## Accommodation

There are a score of officially classified *pensions*, *hostals* and hotels on both sides of the river, so with few exceptions (indicated below) you shouldn't need to book ahead. The nearest **campsite** is *Can Toni*, 8km south at Fornells de la Selva (☎972 476 117), with excellent amenities. With your own transport, you could consider a handful of nearby *turisme rural* establishments.

**Alberg de Joventut** c/dels Ciutadans 9, near Plaça del Vi ☎972 218 003. Girona's youth hostel has a central old-town location and smart modern facilities. However, it's exclusively a student residence in term time, and if you're over 30 it's actually more expensive than a cheap *pensió*. Curfew 11pm.
**Hostal Bellmirall** c/Bellmirall 3 ☎972 204 009. Prime location near the cathedral, in a refurbished fifteenth-century building with artily exposed pointing in the stone walls. Now under the friendly ownership of two young ladies, who have furnished it with antique décor throughout and made five of the seven rooms en suite, while maintaining famously good breakfasts, served in the courtyard in summer. Reservations required; parking permit provided for nearby Plaça Sant Domènec; closed Jan–Feb. ❹ B&B
**Pensió Borràs** Travesia Auriga 6, but enquiries Plaça Bell-lloc 4 ☎972 224 008. Friendly, salubrious cheapie redolent of the 1980s; three of the six rooms have both en-suite bath and balcony. ❶
**Pensió Coll** c/Hortes 24 ☎972 203 086. Modern building with just eight simple rooms, in a central location near the Plaça de la Constitució. ❷
**Històric Barri Vell** c/Bellmirall 4/A ☎972 223 583, ✆ http://historic.go.to. In a restored building, superb two-, four- or six-person flats (❹) with fully equipped kitchens represent the best value in Girona. The same friendly management has opened a luxury hotel adjacent (❺ B&B), its eight state-of-the-art units (including two suites) boast-

ing double glazing, designer baths, satellite TV, air con and Internet access. Private parking for both.
**Pensió Lladó** c/de la Barca 31 ☎972 210 998. Thoroughly unprepossessing exterior, but en-suite rooms here are clean and cheap (like the restaurant of the *Bar Girona* downstairs), uncontrolled street parking is conceivable nearby, and you're close to many monuments and museums. ❶
**Hotel Peninsular** c/Nou 3 ☎972 203 800, ✆ peninsular@novarahotels.com. Well-located, if bland, hotel on a pedestrian street just across the Pont de Pedra from the old town, with large, air-con rooms. ❹
**Pensió Viladomat** c/de Ciutadans 5, 2º ☎972 203 176. Vast warren of variable rooms in this central building, ranging from old-fashioned family suites through bathless single cells to modern doubles which fill quickly in summer. ❷–❸

### Turisme rural in the area
**Mas de la Roda** c/Creu 31, Bordils, 10km northeast on the C255 ☎972 490 052, ✆www.masdelaroda.com. Four sizeable, en-suite, non-smoking rooms offered individually at this well-restored stone house; organic suppers prepared by French-speaking proprietor. ❹ B&B
**Mas Saló** Barri Vilosa, Sant Martí Vell, 10km northeast on opposite side of C255 from preceding ☎972 490 201, ✆www.ruralplus.com/massalo. Rambling old house, sleeping up to 8 in wood-furnished rooms, set in gardens with a pool. A good solution for families at €300 per night flat rate.

## The City
Although most of the modern city, including the attractive nineteenth-century **Mercadal** district, sprawls west of the Riu Onyar, all points of interest are concentrated in the compact medieval quarter, or **barri vell**, spilling down the eastern hillside to a row of multi-storeyed pastel houses leaning over the riverbank. As it only takes twenty minutes to walk from end to end, this fascinating zone of parapeted walls, stepped streets and secluded courtyards is easy to explore thoroughly. Recent restoration and inevitable gentrification have not yet managed to completely banish the everyday life of local shops and bars. Girona's student contingent provides a healthy balance to chi-chi galleries and high-end outlets for designer clothing and furniture, reflecting the fact that Girona and its province have the highest per-capita income in Spain.

### The Catedral and the Museu d'Art
Balanced on a steep slope scaled by a majestic Baroque staircase, the **Catedral** (July–Sept Tues–Sat 10am–8pm, Sun 10am–2pm; March–June Tues–Sat 10am–2pm & 4–7pm; Oct–Feb 10am–2pm & 4–6pm), is the focus of the *barri vell* and an outstanding example of "Catalan Gothic". There has been a place of worship here since a temple was built in Roman times, and a mosque stood on the site before the foundation of the cathedral in 1038. Most of the building

dates from the fifteenth century, though parts are 400 years older, notably the five-storey **Torre de Carlemany** and the Romanesque **cloisters**.

The main Rococo **facade**, remodelled in the eighteenth century, writhes with exuberant ornamentation: floral motifs, coats-of-arms, and niche statues (most of them 1960s copies) in three tiers. Inside, the aisle-less cathedral overwhelms you with its single **nave** spanning 22.5m, the second widest Gothic vault in the world after St Peter's in Rome. Contemporary sceptics deemed the proposed design unsafe, and the vault was raised in 1417 only after an appeal by the architect, Guillermo Bofill, to an independent panel of architects. The walls rise to stained-glass windows portraying St George and the Ascension, the single object interrupting the sweep of space being an enormous organ installed late in the nineteenth century.

Admission to the cloisters is by the same ticket that gets you into the **Museu Capitular** (same hours as cathedral; €3), a small if overstuffed collection of religious art whose highlights are Beatus's *Commentary on the Apocalypse*, made in 975 by Mozarabic miniaturists, and (in the last room) a magnificent eleventh-century, Italian-made *Tapestry of the Creation*, the finest surviving specimen of Romanesque textile, depicting in strong colours the forces of light and darkness, the creation itself, and seasonal rural activities. The irregularly shaped cloisters themselves (1180–1210) feature minutely carved figures and scenes on double columns.

Girona's **Museu d'Art** (March–Sept Tues–Sat 10am–7pm, Sun 10am–2pm; Oct–Feb Tues–Sat 10am–6pm, Sun 10am–2pm; €2), in the well-restored episcopal palace next door, has galleries arranged chronologically as you climb through five floors. Early wings highlight Romanesque art, particularly rare manuscripts, such as an eleventh-century copy of Bede and an amazing martyrology from the monastery of Poblet, and impressive *Majestats* (wooden images of Christ garbed in a tunic). The top two floors progress through Renaissance works to the collection of nineteenth- and twentieth-century Catalan art, including a selection of pieces by the "Olot School" (see p.159), depictions of the French siege and some entertaining pieces of *modernista* sculpture.

### Sant Feliu

One of Girona's best-known landmarks is the blunt tower of the **Església de Sant Feliu**, nicely framed as you descend the cathedral steps. Shortened by a lightning strike in 1581 and never repaired, the belfry tops a hemmed-in church that happily combines Romanesque, Gothic and Baroque styles. The north transept contains the **tomb of Sant Narcís**, patron of the city, while some elegantly sculpted Roman and early Christian **sarcophagi** are embedded in the wall either side of the high altar. At the foot of the western steps there used to stand **El Cul de la Lleona** (The Lioness's Arse), a copy of a twelfth-century statue of a lioness climbing a pillar; amidst all the urban renewal hereabouts it's gone missing, though should it reappear you can kiss its backside – legend has it that act guarantees your return to the city.

### The Banys Arabs

Very near the cathedral, reached by going through the **Portal de Sobreportas** (fourteenth century but built on visible Roman foundations), and then turning right, stand the so-called **Banys Arabs** or "Arab Baths" (April–June & Sept Mon–Sat 10am–7pm; July & Aug Mon–Sat 10am–8pm; Oct–March Mon–Sat 10am–2pm; Sun & hols all year 10am–2pm; €1.50), probably built by Moorish craftsmen during the twelfth century after the

Islamic occupation of Girona had ended. The finest of their type in Spain outside of Granada, they have the usual under-floor heating system in the *caldarium* (steam room) and the Roman-derived layout of four principal rooms. The *apodyterium* (changing room) is the most interesting; there are niches for one's clothes and a stone bench for relaxation after bathing, while the room is unusually lit by a central vaulted skylight supported by an octagon of columns.

## The Museu Arqueològic and the city walls

From the Banys Arabs it's a short downhill stroll, over the usually dry Riu Galligants, to the **Museu Arqueològic** (summer Tues–Sat 10.30am–1.30pm & 4–7pm, Sun 10am–2pm; winter Tues–Sat 10am–2pm & 4–6pm, Sun 10am–2pm; €1.80), housed in the former Benedictine monastery of **Sant Pere Galligants**. The twelfth-century **church** itself contains Roman artefacts, including a vivid mosaic showing a chariot race, unearthed in 1876 at a nearby Roman villa. Extensive galleries above the cloisters methodically outline the region's history from Paleolithic to Roman times, but unless you read Catalan or Spanish, or pay €1.50 for the English-language guidebook, you'll get little out of these exhibits.

Near the museum you can gain access to the nearby Passeig Arqueològic, with steps through landscaped grounds beside the Banys Arabs leading up onto the **city walls**, from where there are fine views over Girona and the Ter valley. Once onto the ramparts (daily 8am–10pm; free), you can walk right round their perimeter, with intermediate exits behind the Sant Domènec convent and at the gate of the university, before the final descent to Plaça Catalunya, at the south end of the old town.

## The Call or Aljama

Heading south instead of north from the Portal de Sobreportas, c/de la Força leads past the **Call**, reached via the intersecting c/Sant Llorenç and considered the best-preserved Jewish quarter in Western Europe. A **Jewish community** of 25 families was well established in Girona by the late ninth century, with an initial settlement near the cathedral shifting up to **Carrer de la Força**, which follows the course of the Roman Via Augusta. With a population of over three hundred at its peak, the new quarter became known as the *Call* or the **Aljama**, forming an autonomous municipality within Girona, under royal protection in exchange for payment of a tribute. Cabbalistic scholarship thrived here under the leadership of **Rabbi Moisés Ben Nahman** (born 1194; Nahmánides or Bonastruc ça Porta in Catalan), and members of the community excelled in the professions – commerce, property speculation and banking – reserved for them by custom. But from the thirteenth century onwards, Gironan Jews suffered systematic and escalating physical persecution; in 1391 a mob stormed the *Call* and killed forty of its residents, after which the neighbourhood became a restrictive ghetto like those of northern Europe, until the expulsion of the Jews from Spain in 1492.

The Jewish ghetto wasn't allowed to open windows, or more than one door, onto c/de la Força, so the inmates created a maze-like, multi-level complex of rooms, stairways and all-important courtyards, which in the final century of Jewish life here contained the synagogue, kosher slaughterhouse and communal baths. The **Centre Bonastruc Ça Porta** (May–Oct Mon–Sat 10am–8pm; Nov–April Mon–Sat 10am–6pm; all year Sun 10am–3pm; €2) at c/de la Força 8 comprises much of this, plus a café, small bookshop and the **Museu d'Història dels Jueus**. This, opened in 2001, is unfortunately still experiencing some teething pains, and the only reliable exhibit is a room full of enormous

**grave steles** inscribed in Hebrew, recovered after being pillaged from the Bou d'Or cemetery on Montjuïc hill northeast of town. In contrast to much of the speculative archeology of the Call, their fervent inscriptions are the most definitive legacy of Jewish medieval life here.

### The Museu d'Història de la Ciutat

Housed in the eighteenth-century Capuchin monastery of Sant Antoni at c/de la Força 27, the **Museu d'Historia de la Ciutat** (Tues–Sat 10am–2pm & 5–7pm, Sun 10am–2pm; €2) completes the *barri vell*'s complement of museums, and despite Catalan-only labelling, is likely to prove the most rewarding one – and certainly the most eclectic. A portion of the monastic catacombs is on the right as you enter, with niches for the (vanished) deceased. The entire ground floor is devoted to the development of local industry and technology, with an antique dealer's bonanza (salvaged from around the province) of ancient phones, printing presses, dynamos and even an arc-lamp cine projector. The first floor covers the history of broadcasting in Catalunya – complete with some magnificent old radio sets – and Roman Gerunda, featuring a rather crude mosaic from a villa on the surrounding plain. On the top floor you'll find a modern art exhibition, plus material on the evolution of the *sardana*.

## Eating, drinking and nightlife

Most of Girona's more adventurous **restaurants** and **bars** (along with some obvious tourist-traps) are grouped along and just off c/de la Força, or on c/Ballesteries, while outdoor daytime **cafés** cluster on or around the Rambla de la Llibertat, and on the parallel Plaça del Vi. Formal **nightlife** is varied, with venues scattered across the *barri vell*, Mercadal and the former tradesmen's quarter of **Pedret**, about 700m north of the old quarter between the rail line and the riverbank.

### Restaurants

**Le Bistrot** Pujada de Sant Domènec 4. Despite the name, a full-on restaurant-bar packed at meal times with the *beau monde* of Girona, for good reason: excellent gourmet-*minceur* lunch-only *menú* (eggplant terrine, cod in sauce, homemade chocolate cake, bottled house wine) for the amazing sum of €11. Stylish, Belle-Époque tile-floor surroundings inside, with jazz soundtrack, or occasional live classical music. At suppertime in summer, massively popular tables on the steps outside.

**Can Peret** c/Sacsimort 4–6. In summer the roof terrace fills with locals by 10pm for the sake of no-nonsense *a la carta* (allow €17 plus drink), with plenty of vegetarian starters like goat's cheese and squash *gratinat*, plus grills, *embutits* and some seafood as mains. Winter *menjador* operates inside.

**Casa Marieta** Plaça Independència 5. One of Girona's oldest restaurants, with a high-ceiling *menjador* and home-style meat, fish and stews. Allow €22 *a la carta*. Closed Sun pm and Mon.

**El Cul de la Lleona** c/Calderers 8. Cosy if potentially pricey bistro specializing in Moroccan dishes;

three courses (including house wine and lovely Catalan or North African sweets) will run to €25. Also a much cheaper "local" *menú* (€11) at lunchtime, plus summer tables on the nearby fountain-*plaça*. Closed Sun & Mon.

**La Força Vella** c/de la Força 4. *Menús* (€9) served in the stone-clad area in front of the bar; fare encompasses snails, sausage, rabbit and squid. Open 1–4pm & 7–11pm.

**El Museu del Vi** c/Cort Reial 8. Slightly touristy bar-restaurant serving up typical dishes in its rough-plastered *menjador*. Plenty of filling *plats combinats* and a *menú* (€9), plus excellent *torradas* (toasts). Closed Mon.

**La Penyora** c/Nou del Teatre 3. Catalan *nouvelle cuisine* in suitably minimalist surroundings; slow service and *a la carta* bills in excess of €25, though there's a much cheaper lunch *menú*. Closed Tues.

**La Polenta** c/Cort Reial 6. Tiny, generally busy vegetarian restaurant serving delicious organic fare (*menú* €9). Closed Thurs eve, Sun & Aug.

**El Pou de la Call** c/de la Força 14. More elaborate than usual recipes and ingredients in exceptionally pleasant surroundings right next to the

*Call*; the €12 *menú* (drink extra) comprises three courses such as vegetarian *terrina*, squid rings with parsley and garlic, plus baked apple with custard, but *a la carta* (allow €27) is more varied. No outdoor seating, but air-con premises.

**Zanpanzar** c/Cort Reial 10–12. Started life in 2000 to great acclaim as a *tapas* bar doing Basque-style *pintxos*; has now graduated to being a full-on restaurant, with well-executed meat and fish dishes (*a la carta* only; allow €20–25). Closed Sun & Mon.

## Bars and cafés

**Antiga** Plaça del Vi 8. A nice line in cakes, puddings and other sweet delights at this *xocalateria* under the arches. To wash it down, *orxata* (in summer), *sucs* (juices) and *batuts* (shakes).

**L'Arc** Plaça de la Catedral 9. The only café in Girona with a cathedral on the terrace. During the day it's a pleasant spot for coffee or *orxata*, while at night it becomes a secluded hideaway.

**L'Arcada** Rambla de la Llibertat 38. Bar-café tucked under the arcades, with designer-minimalist interior and sought-after outdoor tables, serving good breakfast pastries and pizzas. Also *tapas* and an Italian-flavoured lunch *menú* (€10)

**Café Royal** Plaça Independència 1. Pleasant corner spot that's equally good for breakfast, juices or a tipple from late afternoon onwards.

**Cafeteria Sol** Plaça del Vi. No-nonsense bar, right by *Antiga*, that's good for breakfast under the arcade.

**La Crêperie Bretonne** c/Cort Reial 14. Savoury and sweet crêpes (€3–6), prepared by a French ex-pat, plus salads and Breton cider. Vast interior belies narrow street frontage, which is dominated by a converted minibus (part of the pantry). Summer tables in the street. Closed Sun, & Wed lunchtime in winter.

**Manaus** c/Calderers 6. Tropical fruit juices and nothing but, served in summer on the nearby fountain-*plaça*.

**Tapa't** c/Cort Reial 1. A decent *tapas* bar with generous portions, where you can assemble a small meal for €10–11.

**La Terra** c/Ballesteries 23 (tiny sign on door). Popular student hangout, open from 6pm until late: a wonderfully cavernous space, with glazed tiles everywhere and river-view windows. Juices, foreign beers, coffees.

## Clubs

**Nummulit** c/Nord 7, Mercadal. Gay-friendly bar playing mainly 1980s music to a mixed crowd and wide age range.

**Particular** c/Pedret 76. Friendly music bar in a 600-year-old lime kiln, with a mixture of hip-hop and ethnic/modern beats. Thurs–Sat 10pm–2am.

**La Sala del Cel** c/Pedret 118. Vast, multi-level club (including chill-out rooms and terraces) whose visiting and resident DJs draw crowds from across the province. Daily 11pm–6am.

**La Taverna de l'Abat** c/Galligants, opposite Museu Arqueològic. Occupying a sixteenth-century episcopal manor, this combines the functions of snack bar and venue for live music (world, tango, jazz). Daily except Mon 11am–4pm and 8pm–2am.

# Listings

**Banks and exchange** You'll find several banks with ATMs on Rambla de la Llibertat and at the east end of the Pont de Pedra.

**Books and maps** Ulyssus, c/Ballesteries 29, is an excellent travel-book specialist with lots of Spanish- and Catalan-language guides to Catalunya, plus all Editorial Alpina and Catalan government ICC maps.

**Buses** The most important companies are TEISA (ⓦ www.teisa-bus.com), handling all services northeast through the Garrotxa to Olot, with connections from there into the comarques of Ripoll and Cerdanya; and SARFA (ⓦ www.sarfa.com), which handles most departures northeast towards Figueres and the northern Costa Brava.

**Car rental** Most agencies are in or near the train station – for example, Avis (ⓣ 972 206 933) and Hertz (ⓣ 972 210 108). Otherwise, pick cars up at the airport.

**Hospital** Dr Josep Trueta, Avgda França 60 (ⓣ 972 202 700), at the northern outskirts of town, is best for emergencies; urban bus #2 gets you there.

**Internet access** El Magatzem d'Internet, c/Ballesteries 20, operates normal shop hours Mon–Fri, noon–8pm Sat; €2.60/hr.

**Laundry** Bugaderia El Sol, c/Ballesteries 4.

**Newspapers** English-language papers are available at the kiosks on Plaça de Independencia and along Rambla de la Llibertat.

**Police** Policia Municipal are in the Ajuntament (ⓣ 092).

# The Fluvià valley and the Garrotxa

Northwest of Girona lies the lush, humid Garrotxa region, watered by the Riu Fluvià and its various tributaries. South of the Fluvià extends the volcanic **Baixa Garrotxa**, where eleven millennia of erosion have moulded dormant cinder cones into rounded and fertile hills. The more northerly **Alta Garrotxa** is an area of deserted farms set amidst low chunky limestone mountains, the highest of which – the 1558-metre Puig de Comanegra – straddles the frontier.

The easiest route through the area – served by buses – involves following the C150 from just north of Girona, through lakeside **Banyoles**, to the junction of the N260 at resolutely medieval **Besalú**. West of there, a patch of new divided highway past **Castellfollit de la Roca**, whose houses peer over a sheer basalt cliff, comes as a shock. For a glimpse of back-country Garrotxa, especially with your own vehicle, use the narrower C524 from **Banyoles** to **Olot**, capital of the Garrotxa region, via atmospheric **Santa Pau**. Near Santa Pau, there's easy, scenic walking in the **Parc Natural de la Zona Volcanica**, set aside to protect the best of the Garrotxa, including the surviving beech wood known as **La Fageda d'en Jordà**.

## Banyoles

The Pyrenees are only on the horizon at **BANYOLES**, 21km from Girona, but it's a moderately pleasant place to pass a few hours, or the night, on the way to Besalú or Santa Pau. What makes Banyoles special is the **Estany** (lake), fed by underground springs and 75m at its deepest point just offshore from the swimming club. Cruises, rowing boats and pedaloes are on offer, while private waterside *pesqueres* (private fishing gazebos), hotels and restaurants further domesticate the *estany*, a process completed by its hosting of the 1992 Olympic rowing events. An eight-kilometre walking or cycling circuit of the lake passes through tiny **Porqueres** hamlet, whose barrel-vaulted, twelfth-century church of **Santa Maria** has unusual column capitals flanking the entrance.

Back in the somewhat drab town, the arcaded **Plaça Major**, studded with plane trees, has hosted a Wednesday market since the thirteenth century. From here, it's 200m northeast to the **Museu Arqueològic Comarcal** (July & Aug Tues–Sat 10.30am–1.30pm & 4–7.30pm, Sun 10.30am–2pm; Sept–June Tues–Sat 10.30am–1.30pm & 4–6.30pm, Sun 10.30am–2pm; €1.80; Catalan labelling only but English crib sheet provided). Installed in a thirteenth-century almshouse on Plaça de la Font, the collection used to contain the famous jawbone of a pre-Neanderthal woman found in the nearby Serinyà caves, but nowadays a replica is displayed; authentic specimens include Paleolithic tools and Pleiocene/Pleistocene bison, rhino and elephant bones, all found in local quarry works. Galleries of historical eras feature three bronze figures of the Roman deities Lar, Fortuna and Mercury, remounted in a *lararium* or household shrine that would have graced local villas from the first to seventh centuries, as well as medieval painted plates, found in a dry well in the almshouse.

### Practicalities

All **buses** stop on Passeig de la Indústria, with the ticket office nearby at the intersection with c/Àlvarez de Castro, the road in from Girona. The Plaça Major lies 200m northeast of here, while the **Turisme**, which gives out a town plan, is at Passeig de la Indústria 25 (Mon–Fri 9am–2pm & 4.30–7pm, Sat 10am–1.30pm; ☎972 575 573); there's also a summer-only wooden annexe on lakeside Passeig Darder. A little **fake train** shuttles in summer between the town and Porqueres along the lake-shore.

## Accommodation

With Girona and Besalú so near, few will choose to stay in Banyoles, though there's plenty of **accommodation** in all price ranges. For backpackers, the *Alberg de Joventut* at c/del Migdia 10 (☎972 570 432) has smart dorms and, if full, will refer you to the affiliated *Alberg de l'Estany* in the lakeside Club Natació 41 (☎972 516 747). Two pleasant, modern budget *pensions* sit just a couple of blocks back from the water: *Fonda La Paz* (☎972 570 432; ❷) at c/Ponent 18, and *Can Xabanet* (☎972 570 375, ☏972 570 252; ❷) around the corner on Plaça del Carmé 24–27. Of two lakeside establishments, pleasant *Hotel l'Ast* (☎ & ☏972 570 414; ❺) on Passeig Dalmau 63, with a pool, is more affordable, though room views are of trees rather than the water. The best campsite is lakeshore *El Llac* (☎972 570 305), on the way to Porqueres, just below and before the church.

With your own transport, three local **turismes rurals** may appeal. *Can Ribes* (☎972 573 211, ⊛www.canribes.com; ❹ B&B), 6km south of Banyoles beyond the hamlet of Camós (also reached from Girona via the Palol de Revardit exit from the N-II) is geared for resident Spanish-language courses in the attic, but welcomes all-comers with a grassy garden and superb views east, a fridge full of cold drinks and savoury Catalan breakfast. The downsides are somewhat primitive furnishings (it was one of the first *casas rurales* established; not all rooms are en suite) and less than brilliant suppers. More universally popular, 14km east of Banyoles just off the N-II, is *Mas Alba* in Terradelles village (☎972 560 488, ⊛www.masalba.com; ❸ B&B), with riding stables and organic-produce dinners. About halfway to Besalú on the C150, just off the highway in Serinyà, *Can Solanas* (☎972 593 199, ✉cansolanas@terra.es; ❺ B&B) is somewhat pricey, but well-kept, with a pool and multilingual management.

### Eating and drinking

Stopping in for lunch or supper at one of the town's many **restaurants** makes more sense. There's a worthy cluster of designer-interior ones on, or just off the Plaça Major: *Brasseria El Capitell*, at no. 14 (closed Mon), specializing in cod and meat; *El Rebost d'en Pere* at c/Ángel Guimerà 14, 100m southwest of the *plaça*, a tiny spot run by a young couple, with cutting-edge cuisine; and *La Cisterna* at c/Àlvarez de Castro 36 (closed Mon), which takes minimalist decor to the point of clinical sterility, but is always packed at lunch thanks to a good-value €11 *menú*. More traditional but salubrious *menjadors* are those of *Fonda La Paz* (€7 lunch *menú*, €10 dinner, €21 *a la carta*) and equally popular *Can Xabanet*, where the €7 *menú* is a bit limited, but €21 is well spent *a la carta* on such dishes as shellfish-stuffed peppers or duck with prunes, served in leisurely fashion by bow-tied waiters. Finally, pushing the boat out in all senses, there's *Gil's Marisqueria* on c/de la Sardana near the Club Natació, though it too has an affordable €12 seafood lunch *menú*. After dark, a few low-key **bars** get going under the arcades of Plaça Major.

## Besalú

From the road, the imposing eleventh-century **fortified bridge** by the confluence of the Fluvià and Capellada rivers is the only sign of anything remarkable about **BESALÚ**, 16km from Banyoles. But pass under the portcullis in the bridge's central toll-house and you'll enter a medieval settlement that's been a preserved historical monument since 1966. Steep narrow streets, sunbaked squares and cave-like arcaded shops bear silent witness to an illustrious history out of proportion to its current humble status. Besalú was an important town before the medieval period – Roman, Visigothic, Frankish and Muslim despots came and went – but all the surviving monuments date from the tenth to twelfth centuries, when it briefly became the seat of a small, independent principality under the dynasty of Guillem el Pilós.

As at Girona, Christian intolerance drove the Jews from Besalú, and their **Miqvé** (ritual bathhouse) was later turned into a dyeworks. Originally attached to a synagogue, now excavated above, the Miqvé (5 daily visits, €1; enquire at the Turisme) hides inconspicuously down by the river, at the end of signposted Baixada de Mikwè, underneath the bridge-viewing platform. It proves to be a high, single-vaulted chamber, with steps leading down into the former plunge pool.

Continuing in the same direction, you'll reach the porticoed **Plaça de la Llibertat**, enveloped by medieval buildings such as the thirteenth-century Casa de la Vila, now home to the *Ajuntament*, the weekly Tuesday market and the tourist office. Majestically arcaded c/Tallaferro leads uphill to the ruined shell of **Santa Maria** (no admission), which for just two years was the cathedral of the bishopric of Besalú; political union with Barcelona ended this short-lived episcopal independence.

Further west, you emerge onto a vast, fan-shaped square, the Prat de Sant Pere, dominated by the Benedictine monastic **Església de Sant Pere**. The barrel-vaulted interior is impressive enough, with a fine colonnaded ambulatory preserving some carved column capitals, but the church's most distinctive feature is the arched Gothic window of the west facade, flanked by a pair of grotesque stone lions; it's best admired from a pair of cafés immediately opposite.

Working your way up c/Ganganell brings you to extensively rebuilt **Sant Vicenç**, whose side entrance arches bear intricately carved mythical monsters; this church, too, has a Gothic rose window, high up on its southwest facade, while the little landscaped square around it, Plaça Sant Vicenç, is far more intimate than Prat de Sant Pere.

### Practicalities

**Buses** stop on the main road, from where it's a short walk south to the central Plaça de la Llibertat. The **Turisme** here (daily 10am–2pm & 4–7pm; ☎972 591 240) keeps the usual stock of brochures, as well as keys to locked monuments. **Parking** is best on the far side of the old bridge, near where the *turistic* **fake train** commences its to-ings and fro-ings.

**Staying** at one of the five lodgings is highly recommended, since Besalú's character changes completely once the daily quota of trippers has departed. The pin-neat, en-suite *Fonda Venència* at c/Major 6 (☎972 591 257; ❷) represents excellent value; *Habitacions-Residència Marià*, Plaça de la Llibertat 7 (☎972 590 106; ❷), is a more atmospheric, rambling old building, also with heated en-suite rooms; while Casa Fonda affiliate *Fonda Siqués* (☎972 590 110, ✉siques@grupcalparent.com; ❸), just east of the bus stop on the main through highway, will prove the noisiest of the three, but is actually a comfortable one-star hotel with air-con and a plunge-pool, used by self-guided walking tours. The same management has opened a better-value annexe, three-star *Hotel Comte Tallaferro* (☎972 59 336, ✉tallaferro@grupcalparent.com; ❸–❹) at c/Ganganell 2, with a small roof terrace and rear patio. The rooms themselves, four of them facing Prat de Sant Pere, range from "standard" doubles to galleried family quads to skylit top-floor suites, with some disabled facilities. The most unusual accommodation in town, however, has to be *Hotel Els Jardins de la Martana*, occupying a three-storey mansion from 1910 at the far end of the bridge on c/Pont 2 (☎972 590 009, ◉www.lamartana.com; ❼ B&B). The large rooms all have balconies, antique-tile floors, fridges and state-of-the-art bathrooms; common areas include a panelled library with fireplace and gardens dropping in two levels to the river.

There's also an excellent **casa rural** about 10km northeast. Take the minor road 5km north to Beuda village, then swing east to continue a similar distance to **Segueró**, where *Can Felicià* (☎972 590 523; ◉www.canfelicia.com; ❻ HB) occupies the old schoolhouse next to the church. Homey rooms transcend the former institutional status, there's a plunge-pool on the lawn, and the village-based chef has earned a reputation for excellent cooking. The closest recommended **campsite** to Besalú lies just off the N260, about 5km towards Figueres: *Masia Can Coromines* (☎972 591 108, ◉coromines@grn.es; March–Oct), centred on an ancient farmhouse doubling as a well regarded pizzeria, plus a few rooms (❸) and apartments upstairs. This is Spanish camping as it should be: 52 spaces predominantly for tents, a nice big pool with a grassy verge and a lively bar.

The best-value food in Besalú is probably at *Cal Parent*, the Cuina Volcànica-affiliated (see p.161) **restaurant** of *Fonda Siqués* (€27 gastro-*menú* or pricier *a la carta*; closed Sun pm & Mon). *Curia Reial* at Plaça de la Llibertat 14 (closed Mon pm & Tues) is popular for its lovely river-and-bridge-view terrace and vaulted bar with pool table; the food is decent (allow €25 *a la carta*), though service can lag. The relatively posh option is *Pont Vell*, c/Pont Vell 28, which has tables more or less under the bridge and gives you the run of its *carta* for about €30.

## Castellfollit de la Roca

**CASTELLFOLLIT DE LA ROCA**, 14km west of Besalú, promises great things, as its church and houses perch atop a sixty-metre precipice overlooking the Riu Fluvià. Arrival is most impressive by night, when spotlights play on the natural basalt columns underpinning the village. But as the road curls around and up, Castellfollit proves disappointing, its main street lined by tightly packed rows of grubby buildings giving no hint of the extraordinary palisade. Despite the 2003 opening of a four-lane bypass tunnelling around the village, Castellfollit still hasn't recovered from being threaded by the main road for so long.

You might leave your vehicle, however, to sample the view from the cliff: head south from the prominent clocktower to the church and the banistered viewing platform behind. On the main street, 100m downhill from the clocktower, Castellfollit's **Museum of Sausages** (Mon–Sat 9.30am–1.30pm & 4–8pm, Sun 9.30am–2pm & 4.30–8pm), run by the Sala family to celebrate a century and a half in the skin-stuffing business, is almost certainly unique, as claimed. Pungent with the aroma of sausages, it's mainly an excuse to sell them (counter on the premises); the exhibits consist mostly of antique production machinery.

The only **accommodation** is the two-star *Pensió Cala Paula*, next to the clocktower at Plaça de Sant Roc 3 (☎972 294 032; ❷), surprisingly comfortable, with a decent, popular ground-floor **bar-restaurant**.

## Olot

Capital of the Garrotxa *comarca*, **OLOT** is more rewarding than its sprawling, anonymous outskirts suggest. Follow any of the narrow lanes north into the

▲ **C**, **D**, **1** & **2**　　▲ Besalú & Girona　　　　　　　　　　　　　　▲ Batet de la Serra

**OLOT**

◀ Volcà Montsacopa

◀ Ripoll & Sant Joan

▲ Volcà Montolivet

C524 Santa Pau & La Fageda ▶

▶ Pont & Parc de les Mores

**13** ▲ Casal dels Volcans (600m)

ORTA DE LES FEXES ▲ B (50m)

C. SANT CRISTOFOR

C. SANT BERNAT

CARRER SANT BERNAT

PLAÇA DE LES RODES

PARE ANTONI SOLER

PONT NOU

PLAÇA PALAU

CONZE DE SEPTEMBRE

PLAÇA DEL CARME

C. DEL TURA

C. MAJOR

C. CLAVARIA

CELS SASTRES

C DELS SASTRES

PLAÇA MAJOR

C. BELLAIRE

C. SERRA I GINESTA

CARRER BISBE LORENZANA

**Bus Station**

Riu Fluvià

PLAÇA SANT ROC

PLAÇA MORA

C. HOSPICI

**Museu Comarcal** ⓘ

C. ANTONI LLOPS

C. MANA VAYREDA

PONT DE CAL RUSSET

CTRA SANTA PAU ▶

**Casa Solà Morales**

PASSEIG D'EN BLAY

**Sant Esteve**

PLAÇA DEL MIG

**Bullring**

PLAÇA DE BRAUS

**Teatre Principal**

C. SANT RAFEL

CARRER MULLERAS

CARRER SABINA SUREDA

CARRER JOAQUIM VAYREDA

PASSEIG BISBE GUILLAMET

CARRER SANT PERE MÀRTIR

SANT FERRIOL

CARRER PARE ROCA

PLAÇA CLARA

CARRER DE PANYO

CARRER BISBE VILANOVA

AVDA CLAVÉ

DR JOAQUIM DANÉS

CARRER PERE LLOSES

REIS CATÒLICS

PASSEIG DE BARCELONA

PLAÇA ESPANYA

AVDA CATALUNYA

N

0　　200 m

**RESTAURANTS/BARS**

| | |
|---|---|
| Bar 617 | 3 |
| Bar del Carmé | 9 |
| Bar Malem | 8 |
| Bruixes e Maduixes | 5 |
| Café 1900 | 6 |
| Cocodrilo | 4 |
| Les Cols | 1 |
| La Dolce Vita | 12 |
| La Garrotxa | 11 |
| L'Hostalet | 13 |
| Ca la Nàsia | 2 |
| Ramón | 10 |
| La Terra | 7 |

**ACCOMMODATION**

| | |
|---|---|
| Alberg Torre Malagrida | F |
| Mas La Garganta | A |
| Mas El Guitart | C |
| Hostal Sant Bernat | B |
| Pensió Vila | E |
| La Torra de Santa Margarida | D |

*barri vell* from the through road, and the scene changes to one of intimate squares, elegant shops, a pleasant *rambla* and convivial bars. It's also one of the most cosmopolitan towns in the Pyrenees, with noticeable Chinese, Senegalese and Sikh communities. Most of the centre consists of eighteenth- and nineteenth-century buildings, a consequence of two devastating 1427–1428 earthquakes which levelled the medieval town. Olot lies between three (dormant) volcanic cones easily accessible without long treks or drives; the bare-topped **Volcà de Montsacopa** in particular is worth the walk up on local "Itinerari 17", with its picturesque summit chapel of Sant Francesc affording good views. Frequent bus connections and a fair choice in food and lodging (some of this just out of town) make Olot a likely base for touring the Garrotxa.

The town's enduring prosperity is based on its crafts tradition. A religious-images business began here in 1880, remaining a major industry until the 1950s. Cotton-milling also flourished during the late eighteenth century, alongside workshops printing textiles with coloured patterns; the latter were instrumental in the formation of the Escola Pública de Dibuix (Public School of Drawing) in 1783. Joaquim Vayreda i Vila (1843–94), a founder of the Olot School of painters, which included Josep Berga i Boix and Modest Urgell, was a pupil at the drawing school, but an 1871 trip to Paris brought him under the spell of Millet's rural painting and exposed him to the Impressionists. From these influences, and the earth-coloured Garrotxa scenery, sprang the distinctive style of the Olot artists.

## The Town

Some of the best work produced by the Olot School can be seen in the **Museu Comarcal de la Garrotxa** (Mon & Wed–Sat 11am–2pm & 4–7pm; Sun 11am–2pm; €1.50), installed in a converted eighteenth-century hospital at c/Hospici 8. The galleries were being refurbished in 2003, with temporary exhibits on the ground floor, but the permanent collection upstairs should still include Joaquim Vayreda's *Les Falgueres*, typical in its rendering of the Garrotxa light, and Ramon Casas' famous *La Càrrega*, long thought to depict the violent suppression of a 1902 Barcelona demonstration, but actually painted in 1899; the "Paris Cigarettes" poster series consists of local entries for a contest sponsored by an Argentine manufacturer. Sculpture is also strongly represented, notably the work of Miquel Blay i Fabrega and Josep Clarà i Ayals; other pieces by this pair can be seen around town in the eponymous Plaça Clarà, and Passeig d'en Blay. Extensive exhibits also document rural and town crafts. Besides the saints' images from religious workshops, the secular figures of Ramon Amadeu are outstandingly vivid and, on occasion, humorous. Olot's specialization in textiles nurtured numerous late-nineteenth-century workshops for the production of *barretinas* or *gores* – the typical Catalan men's cap.

A well-signposted half-hour walk from the centre brings you to the landscaped **Parc Nou** (April–Sept 9am–9pm; Oct–March 9am–7pm), where – especially if you read Catalan or Castilian – you'll learn about the Garrotxa volcanic region from the displays, photographs, diagrams and rock samples in the **Casal dels Volcans** (daily except Tues, & Sun pm: July–Sept 10am–2pm & 5–7pm; Oct–June 10am–2pm & 4–6pm; €1.80), occupying a mansion in the park, along with an information centre for activities throughout the Garrotxa.

## Practicalities

All bus services use the central **bus station** at the east end of c/Bisbe Lorenzana. Arriving by **car**, you can usually find **parking** spaces, both fee-paying and free, near the post office; otherwise it's best to use the two central enclosed car parks shown on the map. There are **taxi** ranks at Plaça Clarà and the bus station.

The county **Turisme** (Mon–Sat 10am–2pm & 5–8pm, Sun 11am–2pm; ☎972 260 141) is housed just inside the entrance of the Museu Comarcal, stocking the all-important schematic map (inside the "Parc Natural de la Zona Volcànica" folding brochure) of the designated walking routes through the Garrotxa. At the southeast end of Passeig d'en Blay, with its whimsical Teatre Principal, the Drac **bookstore** on the ground floor of another *modernista* building keeps commercial maps and guides (in Spanish or Catalan) for the area.

## Accommodation

Since the closure of some marginal *hostals*, in-town lodgings are limited; if you've got your own transport you're well advised to cast your net a bit wider to include *turismes rurals* in neighbouring hamlets. The nearest **campsite** is *La Fageda* (☎972 271 239), 4km distant on the minor road to Santa Pau, well laid out and with its own pool. Olot's **youth hostel**, the *Alberg Torre Malagrida*, Passeig de Barcelona 15 (☎972 264 200; closed Sept, midnight curfew), lies well southwest of the centre, in an adapted 1920s villa overlooking the river, about halfway to the Casal dels Volcans.

The pick of the surviving conventional **accommodation** is *Hostal Sant Bernat*, Carretera de les Feixes 29–31 (☎972 261 919, ⊕www.bernat.com; ❷), whose secure garage makes it the best urban choice if you have a car or bike. It's slightly remote at the northeastern end of the town, but quiet, excellent value and very friendly, offering singles, doubles and triples with bath, heating and TV. The clean, modern rooms at *Pensió Vila*, c/Sant Roc 1, on the corner of Plaça Major (☎972 269 807; ❷), including a few cheaper non-en-suite singles, aren't as good value and can get noisy at weekends.

With transport, you may as well continue to one of three excellent **cases de pagès**, within 5km or so of Olot. First choice, with booking mandatory, has to be Inès Puigdevall's *Mas La Garganta*, at the edge of La Pinya hamlet (☎972 271 289; ⊕www.masgarganta.com; ❹ B&B, ❻ HB). To get there, follow signs west out of Olot's Plaça Clarà towards Riudaura. This rambling hillside farmhouse looks southwest over the very flat, fertile Vall d'en Bas – headwaters of the Fluvià – towards Puigsacalm volcano; there's a pool, and bikes to rent by the hour or day (ideal for exploring the valley). The seven minimally restored en-suite rooms are tasteful, with double beds or quads suitable for families, and central heating guaranteeing year-round operation. The food's excellent, served on a balcony with arguably the best view in the Garrotxa; supper might be mussels *marinière*, wild sea bass and profiteroles, washed down with Galician *vinho verde*. Vegetarian options are available on request, plus there's a kitchen with a fireplace for self-catering.

Over the next ridge, in the **Vall de Bianya** traced by the C153 road to Camprodon, is another pair of establishments. On the hillside south of Hostalnou de Bianya village, *Mas El Guitart* (☎972 292 140, ⊕guitart@agtat.es; minimum stay 2 days; ❸) perches just above the Romanesque *ermita* of Santa Margarida, with mock-antique-furnished woodfloor rooms. There are also self-catering apartments for four, a duck-pond and a plunge-pool. More old-fashioned and homey, but still en suite, is *La Torre de Santa Margarida* about 1.5km east, closer to Llocalou (☎972 291 321; ❸), a working cattle farm where at least two roaring fires heat common areas during colder months (vital on this north-facing slope).

## Eating and drinking

Olot in particular and the Garrotxa generally is the focus of the **Cuina Volcànica** group, whose restaurateur members undertake to use eleven core local ingredients – including beans, boar and truffles – in their recipes. That said, outstanding city-centre choices are few, and with transport and a fuller wallet, you'll do better exploring worthy possibilities on the outskirts, or just out of town.

**Ca la Nàsia** 1km west of La Canya suburb in Llocalou hamlet ☎972 290 200. Fancy spot specializing in *faisà a la terra* (pheasant cooked with raisins in a clay pot), game and wild mushrooms. Reservations advised. Closed Mon & late July.

**Les Cols** at the northern outskirts of town on Crta de la Canya, towards the C153 ☎972 269 209. The typical *masia* exterior belies the ultra-modern interior where excellent *cuina de mercat* (seasonal ingredients as found in the market) prevails. Reservations suggested. Lunch till 3.30pm, supper to 11pm. Closed Sun, Mon, Tues eve & mid-July to mid-Aug.

**La Dolce Vita** Passeig de Barcelona 1. Smart and trendy *trattoria* serving the best pizza-based meals in town for around €16; also meat and pasta dishes.

**La Garrotxa** c/Serra i Ginesta 14. Don't be put off by the institutional decor of this self-service Cuina Volcànica restaurant near the museum. A changing list of specials (€8 *menú* or *a la carta*) – fish soup,

pork cheek, grilled quails, potatoes stuffed with sardines – represents excellent value, if not always flawless execution. Open daily except Sun & hol eves.

**L'Hostalet** in Les Hostalets d'en Bas, 10km from Olot on the C152, less from La Pinya ☎972 690 006. The best of three restaurants in the very attractive village of Les Hostalets d'en Bas, this Cuina Volcànica affiliate offers three courses for around €18 *a la carta*, including own-made desserts. Reserve in advance. Closed Sun pm, Tues & a random month in summer.

**Ramón** Plaça Clarà 11. Bar serving mid-priced Catalan *tapas* plus an economical *menú*; its under-arcade seating also makes a good vantage point if you just want a drink.

**La Terra** c/Bonaire 22. One of a number of "hippie bars" in the neighbourhood (see below), this one actually does a decent vegetarian *menú* for under €10. Meal service Mon–Fri 1–4pm only.

## Nightlife and entertainment

More than a dozen **bars** and **cafés** between the bullring and Plaça Verge del Carmé at the eastern end of the *barri vell* cater to all tastes. Aside from a few on Passeig d'en Blay (the only places for an outdoor drink), two to pick out are arty, genteel *Cocodrilo* on c/Sant Roc and *Café 1900* at c/San Rafel 18–20, offering herb teas or stronger stuff on two-level premises. More youthful, alternative choices include *Bar 6T7* at c/dels Sastres 35; *Bruixes e Maduixes* at c/Bonaire 11; Senegalese-run *Bar Malem*, c/Pare Antoni Soler 6, a spacious, converted clothing factory decorated with original artwork; and the raucous *Bar del Carmé*, Plaça del Carmé 3, which plays all sorts of music.

Two **cinemas** screen first-run fare: the Colom on Passeig d'en Blay and the Núria at Verge del Carmé 8, off the *plaça*. Most concerts and other events in the **summer festival** take place in Plaça del Mig, just downhill from Sant Esteve church.

# The Baixa Garrotxa volcanic zone

In 1985 the Catalan parliament designated much of the **Baixa Garrotxa** (⊛www.garrotxa.com), a 120-square-kilometre area extending southeast of Olot, as the **Parc Natural de la Zona Volcànica de la Garrotxa**. Since most of it is private property, with 40,000 inhabitants nearby, this means less than one might think. The volcanic cones, and the **Fageda d'en Jordà** beech wood between the cones and Olot, gained some necessary protection, but cinder-quarrying (for building materials) had already spoiled some of the proposed park.

## Flora and fauna of the Garrotxa region

The lower slopes of the Garrotxa region's distinctive hills nurture **forests** of ever-green oak (*Quercus mediterraneo-montanum*), yielding higher up to deciduous oak and beech woods, with subalpine meadows and pastures at higher altitudes. More than 1500 species of **vascular plant** have been recorded within the park, ranging from typical forest-floor dwellers like snowdrops, yellow wood anemones and rue-leaved isopyrum, to high-altitude specialities like ramonda and Pyrenean saxifrage. In addition, the Garrotxa contains a number of Iberian rarities, several of which are found nowhere else: the white-flowered *Allium pyrenaicum*, typical of rocky lime-stone cliffs; Pyrenean milkwort (*Polygala vayredae*), a woody species with large pinkish-purple flowers; and shrubby gromwell (*Aithodora oleifolia*), a climbing plant with pale pink flowers that turn blue with age.

A phenomenal 143 species of **bird** have been observed in the region. Since three-quarters of the park is covered with forest, goshawks, tawny owls, short-toed treecreepers, great spotted woodpeckers and nuthatches are common. Flocks of bramblings and hawfinches take refuge in the beech woods during winter, while the more barren volcanic summits support alpine choughs and alpine accentors. Summer visitors include short-toed eagles, hobbies, wrynecks, red-backed shrikes and Bonelli's warblers, along with Mediterranean species such as subalpine war-blers, golden orioles and bee-eaters.

Forest-dwelling **mammals** include beech martens, wildcats, genets, badgers and acorn-loving wild boar, as well as a number of small insectivores – common, pygmy and Etruscan shrews – and the noctural oak dormouse, characterized by its "Lone Ranger" mask and long, black-tufted tail. Otters are also occasionally sighted along the rivers.

The Baixa Garrotxa is not a zone of belching steam and molten lava. It's been nearly twelve thousand years since the last eruption, during which time the ash and lava have weathered into a fertile soil whose luxuriant vegetation – includ-ing extensive fields of corn, beans (the tiny local white *fegolets* are especially esteemed) and various grains – masks the contours of the dormant volcanoes. There are thirty cones in all, the largest of them around 160m higher than their surroundings and 1500m wide at the base.

### Santa Pau

The central village of the volcanic zone, medieval **SANTA PAU**, 9km south-east of Olot, presents to the outside world a defensive perimeter of continuous and almost windowless house walls. Slightly less discovered than Besalú, it's even more atmospheric, though verging on the twee. At the very least, it's a mandatory meal stop, and would make a good base for exploring the park's network of signposted paths and tracks.

**Buses** on the minor Olot-Mieres-Banyoles route call daily (often at uncivil hours). With a **car**, you're obliged to park on the outskirts; a pair of well-engi-neered paths take you into the old quarter from the west. Santa Pau's outer archways open onto dark, ancient buildings, many sympathetically converted into business premises and homes. The core of the village is the engagingly sloping thirteenth-century **Firal dels Bous** (Cattle Market; also known as Plaça Major), with arcaded shops, the **Turisme** (summer Mon & Wed–Sat noon–6pm, Sun noon–3pm; ☎972 680 349), and the restored Gothic church of **Santa Maria** with its fine interior rib vaulting. At no. 6 of the adjacent Plaçeta dels Balls, overlooked by the three-storeyed tower of the Balls family, you'll find pricey but tasty **meals** at Cuina Volcànica member *Cal Sastre* (closed Sun night & Mon, open Fri & Sat only in winter), though several other restaurants – notably normal-priced *Can Rafelic* on Plaçeta San Roc – have sprung up on the approaches to the old quarter.

In terms of **accommodation**, best value is *Can Menció* at Plaça Major 14 (T972 680 014, Eenricjoub@bsab.com; closed 15–30 Sept; ❷), with seven very sweet en-suite wood-trimmed rooms, some with balcony and all with designer baths; there's a rear-facing lounge with self-service bar, and up front the village's liveliest proper bar, with ringside seats of the *plaça*. By contrast, *Cal Sastre*'s hotel at c/de les Cases Noves 1 (T972 680 049, F 972 680 481, Wwww.calsastre.com; ❻) on the village outskirts is, despite its antique decor and lawn garden, overpriced, with stuffy, non-air-con rooms and equally stuffy management. In the modern part of town, across the highway, there's the *Alberg de Joventut Bella Vista* (T972 680 512), with gardens and a pool, also providing basic meals. Some 3km back towards Olot, *Lava* (T972 680 358) is a large, well-positioned campsite in the shadow of two cones; *Masia Can Patxet*, 2km east (T972 680 066), is smaller, calmer and more tent-friendly.

## Loop walks long and short

One way to get acquainted with the Baixa Garrotxa is to take a **loop walk** out of Olot (or Santa Pau), largely avoiding paved roads and easily completable in a single day. Various numbered and signposted itineraries prepared by the park authorities are often just out-and-back or forked; this route combines the virtues of several.

From the Pont and Parc de les Mores at the southern edge of Olot, follow the signposts for "Itinerari 3" across the Riu Fluvià, from where it's an hour south along surfaced country lanes – equally suited to mountain-biking (as is most of this circuit) – to the **Fageda d'en Jordà**. Although much reduced, this beech forest is still a treat in the autumn when the leaves are turning; within half an hour more you emerge on the far side of the spooky, maze-like groves, deserted except for the tourist *carruatges* (horsecarts) visiting from Santa Pau.

Turn left when you meet the **GR2** long-distance trail, then right when you encounter the track ("Itinerari 1") to Sa Cot. Stay on the GR2, which soon becomes a proper path as it heads east for thirty minutes to the medieval chapel of **Sant Miquel de Sa Cot**, a popular picnic spot.

The **Volcà Santa Margarida** is visible just behind the chapel, and within forty minutes you should be up on its rim and down in its grassy caldera, where another tiny *ermita* (country chapel) sits at the bottom; allow at least an extra hour for this side trip. From the turn-off to Santa Margarida – just fifteen minutes from Sant Miquel – you resume progress on part of "Itinerari 4", and descend to the **Font de Can Roure**, source of the only water en route, before skirting Roca Negra with its disused quarry and entering Santa Pau: 45 minutes from the shoulder of Santa Margarida, and some three hours from Olot (not counting the detour to the caldera).

Rather than follow the onward GR2 east, bear west at **Can Mascou** and approach Volcà Croscat via the *Lava* campsite. You skirt the northeast flank of Croscat, badly scarred by quarrying; from the campsite it's another hour, along a progressively narrowing track to the high (720m) plateau of **Batet de la Serra**, scattered with handsome farms.

Here you meet a marked path-and-track coming west from the Serra de Sant Julià del Mont, turning west yourself to follow this route briefly before taking

**THE GARROTXA & EL RIPOLLÈS**

Llançà

Perpignan

Figueres

N-II

Terradelles

Girona

Sant Llorenç
de la Muga

S P A I N

Banyoles

Macavet de Cabrenys

Albanyà

GR11

Sant Lloreç
de la Muga

Seguró

Maià de Montcal

Beuda

Serinyà

Camós

Estany
de Banyoles

Porqueres

C150

C524

Amélie-les-Bains

El Pont d'en Valentí

Sadernes

ALTA GARROTXA

Sant Aniol d'Aguja

Col des
Massanes
1126m

R.Llierca

Oix

Pont de Llierca

Tortellà

Argelaguer

Besalú

Sant Jaume
de Llierca

Montagut
de Fluvià

N260

La Miana

GR2

El Torn

Santa Margarida

Mieres

BAIXA GARROTXA

Castellfollit
de la Roca

Sant Julià
905m

Batet
de la Serra

Sant Julià

Volcà
Croscat

Santa Pau

Volcà
Santa Margarida

Sant
Miquel
de Sa
Cot

GR2

Prats-de-
Molló

Col d'Ares 1513m

Rocabruna

Riu Beget

Beget

El Tallò
1288m

Sant Joan
les Fonts

Olot

FAGEDA
D'EN JORDA

Les Preses

F R A N C E

La Preste

R.Ritort

Molló

Bolós

Camprodon

Puig Ou
1306m

Vall de Bianya

Hostalnou

Riudara

La Pinya

Vall d'en Bas

Els Hostalets
d'en Bas

Espinavell

Setcases

GR11

Vilallonga
de Ter

La Roca

Riu Ter

Sant Pau
de Seguries

Coll de
Caubet

C26

Vallfogona

N260

Vallter
2000

Ulldeter

Abella

Tregurà

Surroca

Sant Joan de
les Abadesses

Riu Ter

Coma de Vaca

Gorges
del Freser

Pardines

Ogassa

Ripoll

Col de Caranca
2727m

Núria

GR11.7

Queralbs

Fustanyà

Ribes de Freser

R.Núria

Campelles

Riu Freser

Sant Quirze
de Besora

Barcelona

N

0    10 km

the beautiful, well-marked *camí*, partly cobbled in basalt, which passes the hamlet of **Santa Maria de Batet** on its way down to Olot at "Itinerari 8". It takes just under another hour of downhill progress, or a total of something less than seven hours on the day, to emerge at the top of c/Sant Cristòfor, which crosses the river into central Olot at the Pont de Santa Magdalena.

If you're not committed to such a long day, you can drive or ride a bus to the parking area for Volcà de Santa Margarida; here you're directly on the circular "Itinerari 1", which takes in the Fageda d'en Jordà, Sant Miguel de Sacot and the cones of Santa Margarida and Croscat in a **two-to-three-hour tour**. There are *centres d'informació* en route at Can Serra (Fageda d'en Jordà) and Can Passavent (Croscat) where you can find all the information you might need.

### La Miana

**From Santa Pau** the GR2 continues briefly north towards the scenic Serra de Sant Julià del Mont, then veers east away from "Itinerari 6" down a valley to Besalú. East of the summit and accessible by a 45-minute spur trail from the streamside hamlet of El Torn are a group of excellent *turismes rurals* at **La Miana**, which can also be reached by a signposted, 6.5-kilometre dirt track from Sant Jaume de Llierca on the Besalú–Olot road. The proprietors have indicated the side path in from El Torn, as well as down from the summit of Sant Julià, itself reachable by using itineraries 6 and 8. They have also signposted onward, non-GR trails to Sant Ferriol and Besalú (3hr).

Can Jou (☎972 190 263 or 660 656 633, ⊛www.canjou.com; ❺ B&B, ❼ HB), co-managed by the helpful Michael Peters, has capacity for fifteen in modernized, en-suite rooms and sits right on the Coll de Jou with views south and west, especially from the idyllic pool just above the *masia*. Michael, his wife Rosina and assistants also run the area's best **horse-riding** programme, with half-day rides around the mountain, full-day excursions to Santa Pau, and longer trips to the coast on request. That said, there's a good mix of nationalities, and horsey, hiking and sedentary dispositions among the clientele. Just 300m east is the amazing *Rectoria de la Miana* (☎972 190 190; ❺ HB, vegetarian on request), a medieval manor house complete with crumbling twelfth-century Romanesque chapel used for musical workshops. Every room – most with their own bath – is unique and antique-furnished, meals being served in the arcaded ground-floor hall. Both places enjoy incredible tranquillity in the middle of forested nowhere and are thus massively popular; reserve rather than showing up on spec.

If you come up empty at La Miana, there's one more *casa rural* in the immediate vicinity: *El Turrós* (☎972 687 350, ⊜turros@agtat.es; ❹ HB), just under 4km north down the dirt track towards Sant Jaume de Llierca, and then another very rough kilometre down a steep drive. Though falling within the municipality of Argelaguer, the nearest village on the main highway, this is the *only* road access in. This rambling country manor has a maximum capacity of twelve in four rooms and is particularly good for families, though not so convenient for walkers as *Can Jou* or *Rectoria de la Miana*.

## The Alta Garrotxa

The Alta Garrotxa stretches north from the main Besalú–Olot road as far as the frontier summits. Unlike the lower Garrotxa, the rock strata here are mostly limestone, riddled with more than a hundred catalogued caves. For walkers or mountain-bikers it's a rewarding area as well, especially in spring or late autumn when the highest Pyrenees are inaccessible. Editorial Alpina's 1:40,000 "Garrotxa" map is a useful – though as ever far from infallible – aid; the ICC's 1:50,000 Mapa Comarcal is better.

## North to France: the Llierca valley

From a point 2km east of Castellfollit de la Roca, a paved but one-lane road past Montagut de Fluvià traces the Llierca up to Sadernes. Continuing on the main Llierca valley route brings you after 5km to the wonderfully photogenic **Pont de Llierca**, a medieval bridge with one of the greatest drops to the water in the Pyrenees. You can swim in the river-pools below, but resist the temptation to imitate the local youth diving from the span – one was knocked unconscious and drowned in 2003.

The asphalt gives out just below **SADERNES**, which notwithstanding its depiction on maps, is barely a hamlet, let alone a village. This has as a focus the sparely handsome tenth-century church of **Santa Cecília**, sacked by the Republicans in 1936, subsequently restored and now usually locked; surviving interior treasures, including a carved Crucifixion, apsidal frescoes and an image of the saint, have been whisked away to museums in Girona and Barcelona. One of the few other buildings here is the popular *Hostal de Sadernes*, which despite its name offers **meals** only, served to a limited schedule (Oct–June Fri pm to Sun pm, plus hols; July–Sept daily, but drink only Wed); the food is hearty country fare – *mongetes amb ventresca*, mixed grill, sweet (€17 for 3 courses, drink extra) – served on the arcaded ground floor of an old farmhouse. There's a convenient if basic adjacent **campsite**, *Sadernes* (☎972 687 526, ⓦwww.sadernes.com), staked out by semi-permanent caravans but with some tent space.

Just past the church, the road is seasonally barred (July–Sept 15 10am–5pm), with parking space provided. Upstream from Sadernes, the dirt track steadily worsens as you begin to thread the scenic gorge of the Llierca; after 2.5km you reach the short side path to **El Pont d'en Valentí**, a medieval bridge much used by smugglers of old, with a ruined mill on the far side. Beyond this point vehicles are banned all year – there's another barrier, and parking proves nearly impossible anyway along this stretch. From the bridge it's ninety minutes on foot, first on the track and then by trail veering off to the ninth-century **Ermita de Sant Aniol d'Aguja**, a landmark, rather squat chapel astride the GR11. Dedicated to an obscure third-century local saint, this has a charming legend attached to it; Aniol, fleeing Roman persecutions in Gaul, slept on this spot but was roused by two persistent oxen. Taking this as a sign from God (the ox being the Evangelist Matthew's symbol for the self-sacrifice of Christ), Aniol returned to his homeland and was promptly martyred in 208 AD. Yearly on Ascension Day there occurs here the **Aplec dels Francesas**, a pilgrimage festival attended by various Alta Garrotxa folk and the inhabitants of Sant Llorenç (Saint Laurent) de Cerdans, the closest large village on the French side of the border (see "The upper Tech", p.118). This, or higher, smaller Coustouges can be reached by continuing northeast on the footpath from the refuge towards the much-used **Col des Massanes** (1126m) on the frontier.

## Northwest to El Ripollès: Oix, Beget and Rocabruna

Staying in Spain, a more populated route heads **northwest** into the Ripoll region, covered in the next section. From just below Castellfollit de la Roca, take the paved but one-lane road 10km northwest to **OIX**, which dominates a bowl-shaped, intensely cultivated valley. The attractive village, surrounded by huge modern barns, features the Romanesque **church** of Sant Llorenç and a small but graceful medieval **bridge** just 1km east. Right opposite the church on Plaça Major, you can **stay** at the *Hostal de la Rovira* (T & F 972 294 347; ❹ B&B), a restored mansion, whose rooms – all different – have tubs in the bathrooms and pastel decor, plus a ground-floor **restaurant**; you can eat independently a few steps away at *Ca la Cristina* (closed Mon; €10 *menú*). The most reliable local **campsite**, 1km west, is *Els Alous*, in a plantation of trees (T 972 294 173; April–Oct), with a pool.

## Beget

The easiest-to-find onward road passes the old bridge. Paved as well as wide, it leads northwest 18km, passing little other than the high hamlet of Sant Miquel de Pera and ambling cattle, to the showcase village of **BEGET**, done up by lowlanders as a weekend retreat verging on the embalmed. Two slender bridges link three neighbourhoods separated by the confluence of two streams, and the graceful twelfth-century church of **Sant Cristòfor**, standing at the entrance to the village, is celebrated for its particularly solemn and serene *Majestat*. All but a dozen or so of these Catalan wooden images of a fully dressed Christ were destroyed in 1936; this example, perhaps as old as the church itself, is one of the very few that can be seen in its intended context (keys available at house no. 7 when the church is closed). Beget has three **restaurants**, two with **accommodation**: *Can Joanic*, by the church (T 972 741 241; ❷), which has rooms (including singles) sharing bathrooms above a fair-value *menjador* with a riverside terrace, and the pricier *El Forn* (T 972 741 230; ❺ HB) near the top of the village, where en-suite, heated rooms and the outdoor terrace have commanding views. The food here is slightly more ambitious – rabbit with figs and such, though still affordable, and sustaining rather than elegant. The GR11 passes through Beget, and these are the only places to stay on the stretch of trail between Rocabruna and Albanyà.

## Rocabruna

Some 7km west on either the GR11 or the now-much-narrower road, **ROCABRUNA**, with its ruined castle and stubby but handsome Romanesque church, stands just below the watershed traditionally dividing the Garrotxa from El Ripollès, the county of Ripoll (though the modern administrative boundary is between Beget and Oix). The onward road remains unnervingly narrow along the 7km more to the Camprodon–Molló highway. The only **accommodation**, 2km west on the main road and then 1km down a dirt track, but almost astride the GR11, is the friendly, English-speaking *turisme rural Casa Etxalde* (T 972 130 317, W www.geocities.com/etxaldeberri). This offers three en-suite doubles (❸) plus a pair of two-bedroom apartments, as well as a tiny self-catering kitchen. Half-board is available, but perhaps surprisingly for such a tiny place, Rocabruna has two independent **restaurants** good enough to draw crowds on weekend nights from far off. *Can Pluja* (T 972 741 064) has tables on two levels and honest, straightforward mountain food like goat chops and blackberry sorbet; allow €24 *a la carta* with drink. At *Can Po* (T 972 741 045), reckoned one of the best eateries in the region, a meal of cold lentil-and-smoked-fish salad, duck *confit*, prunes in armagnac and house wine runs to €21, but you can easily drop €35 a head by sampling the premium wine list.

# El Ripollès

Moving towards Cerdanya and Andorra along the main roads from the Costa Brava, you really begin to feel among high mountains in the *comarca* (county) of **El Ripollès**. The N260 climbs west from Olot through densely tree-clad foothills to the Coll de Caubet, then drops to the county town of **Ripoll** along the scenic Vallfogona valley. You can also approach less directly along the C153 from Olot to Sant Pau de Seguries, a route made much easier by tunnels under the Coll de Capsacosta.

From Ripoll the C26 heads northeast via **Sant Joan de les Abadesses** and **Camprodon**, both – like Ripoll – graced with fine Romanesque monuments – until the frontier and road crossing at the Col d'Ares/Aras (1513m); winter sport enthusiasts patronize the ski station of **Vallter 2000**.

Due north of Ripoll, road and rail climb gently to **Ribes de Freser** and then more sharply west out of the *comarca* via the Collada de Toses. At Ribes, there's the option of riding the dramatic, narrow-gauge *cremallera* railway up the gorge to **Queralbs** and **Núria**, the combined pilgrimage shrine and all-year resort below the summit of 2910-metre **Puigmal**. Walkers can link the valleys of Ter and Núria by hiking between Setcases and Queralbs, via two staffed refuges and the marvellous Riu Freser.

Ripoll is the **public transport** hub, with trains heading north to Puigcerdà and the French border, while the most regular bus lines head east to Olot and northeast to Sant Joan and Camprodon.

## Ripoll

**RIPOLL** occupies so prominent a place in Catalunya's history that it's impossible not to be initially disappointed by this rather shabby place, buzzed by traffic and divided by the manifestly polluted Riu Ter. The inhabitants seem to agree, resigned to working here but deserting it in droves on Saturday afternoon when Ripoll assumes the air of a ghost town. But just ten minutes' walk from the southeast corner of town – where trains and buses stop – stands one of the most remarkable monuments in the Catalan Pyrenees, the Monestir de Santa Maria, founded in 888 by **Guifré el Pilós** (Wilfred the Hairy) to spur Christian resettlement of the surrounding valleys following their wresting from Muslim rule. This archetypal "fighting Christian" was killed in 898, struck by a Muslim chief's lance during a raid.

### The Town

Following an 1835 fire, the Benedictine **Monestir de Santa Maria** lay in ruins; today's barrel-vaulted nave (daily 8am–1pm & 3–7pm) is a copy of the original structure erected over Guifré's tomb by Abbot Oliba in the early eleventh century. (Oliba and his immediate successors created an important library here, instrumental in the preservation of Islamic scholarship.) The magnificent Romanesque **west portal**, however, survived the fire, and is now protected against the elements by a glass conservatory. Erected in the twelfth century, and now the main entrance, this portal squirms with carvings of religious and astrological subjects: the Apocalypse (across the top), the Book of Kings (to the left), Exodus (to the right), scenes from the lives of David, St Peter and St Paul (at the bottom), and the months of the year (around the inner side of the pillars).

The double-columned **cloisters** (daily 10am–1pm & 3–7pm; €1), far less damaged in the succession of earthquakes, sackings and fires visited on the monastery, are particularly beautiful. The column **capitals**, dating from the twelfth-century Romanesque "Golden Age", portray monks and nuns, beasts mundane and mythical, plus secular characters of the period. They completely overshadow the nominal **Museu Lapidari** here, which displays assorted stonework, sarcophagi and funerary art along the walls. Next door to Santa Maria, but entered from it, the **Museu Etnogràfic** (hours in flux; €2.50) has supplanted the Museu dels Pireneus which used to occupy the fourteenth-century church of **Sant Pere** across the same Plaça Abat Oliba. You're now only able to get into this church when it serves as a venue for Ripoll's **music festival**, staged on successive weekends during July and August.

Besides the monastery and museum there's little to detain you, though it's worth climbing around the back of Sant Pere to a **terrace** from where you can overlook Santa Maria. A nearby bar has tables here, too, certainly the nicest seats in town. Down in the modern district, two *modernista* buildings may claim your attention: the spouting stone flourishes of **Can Bonada**, c/del Progés 14, on the way to the bus and train stations, and the tiny church of **Sant Miquel de la Roqueta** (1912), a couple of blocks up the hill, looking like a pixie's house with a witch's cap on top – and designed by Antoni Gaudí's contemporary Joan Rubió.

### Practicalities

The **train and bus stations** stand within sight of each other, just a ten-minute walk from the heart of town, over the Pont d'Olot to the Plaça de l'Ajuntament. Under the sundial on Plaça d'Abat Oliba, the **Turisme** (Aug daily 10am–2pm & 4–8pm; Easter, June, July & Sept daily 9.30am–1.30pm & 4–7pm; Oct–May Mon–Sat 9.30am–1.30pm & 4–7pm, Sun 10am–2pm; ☏972 702 351) dispenses plenty of maps, pamphlets and local transport timetables.

Aside from this helpful spot, conventional tourism in Ripoll marches resolutely backwards: **accommodation** tends to be overpriced and uninspiring, making it highly advisable to base yourself somewhere nearby and make a flying visit. If you do decide to stay, the least expensive option is the 2001-refurbished, en-suite *Habitacions Paula*, Plaça de l'Abat Arnulf 6 (☏972 700 011; ❷), 70m west of the tourist office. Next niche up is the *Hostal del Ripollès* on Plaça Nova (☏972 700 215; ❸), entered through its ground-floor pizzeria; overpriced *Pensió La Trobada*, across the river at Passeig Honorat Vilamanyà 4 (☏972 714 353; ❹), is your final option.

**Eating** and **drinking** venues are hardly plentiful. *Pizzeria Piazetta* on the ground floor of the *Hostal del Ripollès* is relatively reasonable and appetizing, as is *Canaules* next door; these are the only notable full-service restaurants in the centre. For *tapas* and crêpes, *Bar El Punt* at Plaça de l'Ajuntament 10 has tables both outside and in the air-conditioned premises.

If you have transport, it's worth forgoing all of the preceding in favour of two **cases de pagès** adhering to the *turisme rural* programme, 18–23km distant on the road to Berga, near the hamlet of **Les Llosses**. Some 6km north of the road stands isolated *La Riba* (☏972 198 092; ❸ B&B, ❺ HB), a huge sixteenth-century *mas* with individually let rooms, a pool and ample common areas. A bit west, in equally remote **Palmerola** hamlet, *Mas Moreta* (☏972 198 095; ❹ B&B, ❼ HB) opened in 2003 to a high standard and is worth considering.

## Sant Joan de les Abadesses

The small town of **SANT JOAN DE LES ABADESSES**, 11km northeast of Ripoll, owes its existence to the eponymous **monastery** (daily: July & Aug 10am–7pm; May, June & Sept 10am–2pm & 4–7pm; March–April & Oct

10am–2pm & 4–6pm; Nov–Feb 10am–2pm, also 4–6pm weekends; €2) founded in 887 by Guifré el Pilós, apparently for the benefit of his daughter Emma, the first abbess. The institution was closed temporarily in 1017 by Pope Benedict III as a result of politically motivated accusations of immorality (see box below) by Comte (Count) Bernat Tallaferro, to whom devolved – not coincidentally – all the prior feudal privileges of the convent. The present church, consecrated in 1150, is a single-nave structure of impressive austerity, built to a Latin-cross plan with five apses, and housing a curious thirteenth-century wooden sculpture depicting Christ's deposition, the *Santíssim Misteri*, in its main chapel. According to the printed handouts, the figure of Christ retains on his forehead "a piece of Holy Bread . . . preserved untouched for seven hundred years". Admission to the monastery also includes entry to the Gothic **cloisters** and the **Museu del Monestir**, whose well-presented exhibits include ornate chalices, curiosities such as a crucifix in rock crystal and a fine series of late medieval altarpieces.

Other than the monastery, there are few specific sights in Sant Joan, but the old quarter boasts a fair-sized grid of ancient houses lining streets almost short-er than their names, all leading to a small but appealingly arcaded **Plaça Major**. The slender twelfth-century bridge down in the well-tilled valley was only restored in the 1970s, after being destroyed in fierce fighting of February 1939, during the final Republican retreat of the Civil War. Having strolled around and scared the pigeons from the abandoned shell of **Sant Pol** church in the centre, you've pretty much exhausted the potential of the town.

## The legend of Comte Arnau

The monastery at Sant Joan de les Abadesses is inextricably linked with numerous legends concerning one **Comte (Count) Arnau**, a quasi-historical feudal lord of the eleventh century, notorious for his parsimony towards his serfs. More sensationally, he is immortalized in local folk-song and poetry as a Ripollès Don-Juan equivalent, renowned for his lust and fecklessness in various amorous adventures. Arnau even managed to secure the affections of Sant Joan's incumbent abbess, Engelberga, whom he visited at night on horseback by means of an enormous, long tunnel from his lands between Gombrèn and Campdevànol, some 15km west. Her death hard-ly curtailed his ardour or his appearances, as in the meantime he had managed to seduce a fair number of the lower-ranking nuns; the new abbess attempted to secure all the orifices of the convent, so to speak, but Arnau had concluded a pact with the Devil and used his new-found satanic powers to filter through the very walls.

However, unlike Don Juan, the count eventually fell genuinely and abjectly in love with a young local lass, who understandably failed to return such sentiments given his rather chequered history. To escape his continued advances, she enrolled as a novice at the nunnery; after a humbling vigil at the gates, Arnau managed to gain entrance by conventional methods, only to find the object of his affections recently dead. As he approached the bier, she returned to life just long enough to denounce his various misdemeanours in an other-worldly voice. Filled with terror and remorse, Comte Arnau fled back to his feudal estates, condemned both before and after death to eternally wander the hills above. On stormy nights he has also been seen as a mournful ghost in the cloister of the monastery itself, but the favoured venue for his hauntings remains the vicinity of Gombrèn, where the count supposedly appears as a baleful apparition on horseback, accompanied by spectral packs of hunting dogs in full howl.

**Practicalities**

**Buses** arrive at a shelter behind the monastery church apse; the well-stocked **Turisme** (Mon–Sat 10am–2pm & 4–7pm, Sun 10am–2pm; ☎972 720 599) occupies the cloistered, fifteenth-century **Palau de Abadia** (Episcopal Palace), just fifty paces left of the Museu del Monestir's entrance.

In theory Sant Joan would make a far pleasanter base than Ripoll, with frequent bus links in each direction; in practice this may prove difficult, given the same process of attrition in lodging. Sole surviving **accommodation** consists, in the new district near the bus stop, of *Pensió Ca la Nati* at c/Pere Rovira 3 (☎972 720 114; ❷), with shared baths, and *Pensió Fonda Can Janpere*, around the corner at c/del Mestre Josep Andreu 3 (☎972 720 077; ❸), offering comfortable en-suite rooms with heating and TV. Preferable to either, if you have a car, is the **turisme rural** *Mas Mitjavila*, 10.5km northwest of Sant Joan at the hamlet of **OGASSA** (☎972 722 020, ✉masmitjavila@tiscali.es; ❹ B&B). From the north side of the new bridge, follow the asphalt road 4.2km to the old iron-miners' village of **Surroca**, and then continue the remaining distance on a concrete driveway. With the adjacent tenth-century church of Sant Martí d'Ogassa, *Mas Mitjavila* was once a dependency of the monastery of Sant Joan, and enjoys a superb eyrie-like setting 1350m up, overlooking the valleys of Ripoll. Non-identical rooms are rustic but with all mod cons, including kitchens; some are more like suites, sleeping up to six. Supper (served in the former, converted sheep barn) and own-farm produce are both available.

Back in town, far and away the best **restaurant** is *Can Janpere*, with a €13.50 *menú* and a more adventurous *carta* featuring mushrooms in various guises, roast goat and duck in orange sauce (allow €24, drink included). Otherwise you can sit outside at the pleasant cafés on the main *rambla*, Passeig Comte Guifré.

# Camprodon

Following the lively Riu Ter upstream from Sant Joan, the first place that feels like a real mountain town is **CAMPRODON** (950m; ⊛www.valldecamprodon.org), a fact exploited during the late nineteenth century by the Catalan bourgeoisie who arrived by a (now defunct) rail line from Ripoll to spend summer in the hills. The tracks' former course is now a marked cycling route, **La Ruta del Ferro**, opened as far as Sant Pau de Seguries. Camprodon, 14km from Sant Joan, still retains the prosperous air of former times, with shops full of leather goods, outdoor gear, cheese and sausages. Ornate villas front a *rambla* (Passeig de la Font Nova) clogged with towering trees, and other town houses are occasionally embellished with *modernista* flourishes.

Like Ripoll, Camprodon straddles the confluence of two rivers, here the Ter and the Ritort, and is knit together by little bridges. The principal one, the sixteenth-century **Pont Nou**, still has a defensive tower. From here you can follow the narrow main commercial street east to the restored Romanesque monastic church of **Sant Pere** (consecrated in 904, not to be confused with the larger church of Santa Maria adjacent), near the northeast end of town. There is also a small castle overhead, easiest reached by crossing the Pont Nou and then climbing the narrow lanes on the far side.

Camprodon was the birthplace of the composer **Isaac Albéniz** (1860–1909), a fact which neither the town nor the region made much of until recently – probably because there is little distinctively Catalan in the music he produced during wanderings which took him to London (1890–93), Paris, Nice and finally Cambo-les-Bains in the Basque country. (His most celebrated work, for piano or guitar, is entitled *Iberia*.) However, the great man now has a street, and a **café** on c/València (recommended for croissants and coffee), named after him, a bust near Sant Pere, a July/August **music festival** in his honour, and a less worthwhile **museum** near Pont Nou commemorating his life and times (daily 11am–2pm & 4–7pm; €2.50).

### Practicalities

**Buses** from Ripoll stop 300m south of the main Plaça d'Espanya, where you'll find the **Turisme** (all year round Tues–Sat 10am–2pm & 4–7pm, Sun 10am–2pm; ☎972 740 010) in the *Ajuntament* building.

**Accommodation** tends to be expensive, on account of the town's role as a minor ski resort, with advance reservations advisable summer and winter. On often noisy c/Josep Morer there's Casa Fonda member *Can Ganasi* at no. 9 (☎972 740 134; ❸) and *Hostal Sayola* at no. 4 (☎972 740 142; ❸), both with en-suite rooms. The better-value *Hostal La Placeta* (☎972 740 807; ❸) overlooks Plaça del Carmé, just east of c/Josep Morer and the first square you reach as you come into town from Sant Joan. For a splurge, try the *modernista* Hotel *de Camprodon* on Plaça del Dr. Robert 3 (☎972 740 013, ⊕972 740 716; ❺), with particularly elegant common areas. The nearest **campsite** is *Vall de Camprodon*, 2km or so down the road towards Ripoll (☎972 740 507).

*Can Ganasi's* **restaurant** offers at least two *menús* plus local dishes such as duck and trout, while *Hostal La Placeta* also has a salubrious attached *menjador* (dinner only). Otherwise *Bar-Restaurant Núria*, at Plaça d'Espanya 11, is a characterful place and features a good-value lunch *menú* (*a la carta* only at night, including such delights as "prog legs"). A relative newcomer worth trying is *El Pont 9*, with views to the river bridge and a *menú* priced similarly to *Núria's*. Local specialities, besides the ubiquitous *ànec amb peras* (duck with pears), include *pinyes*, extremely rich and dense pine-nut sweets, sold at bakeries throughout the town.

# Beyond Camprodon: the Ter and Ritort valleys

**Beyond Camprodon** you're increasingly dependent on your own transport and ultimately your own legs. The majority of people who venture this way are either hikers, or skiers driving northwest up the **Ter valley** to the runs of Vallter 2000, or moving northeast up the **Ritort** bound for France. The construction of holiday flats for lowlanders now reigns supreme, but you still catch a glimpse of the area's former agricultural economy in the herds of grazing horses, and cattle ambling home at dusk.

The first settlement that might prompt a stop is rather ordinary **VILA-LLONGA DE TER**, 5km from Camprodon. Opposite the standard-issue Romanesque church of **San Martí** on the main *plaça* are two **accommodation** possibilities: Casa Fonda affiliate *Hostal Pastoret* (☎ & ⊕972 740 319; ❸ B&B, ❺ HB) at c/Constitució 9, and the unstaffed *Hostal Cal Mestre* around the corner at c/del Pou 1 (info at c/Major 3; ☎972 740 407; ❸). There's a **campsite**, *Conca de Ter* (☎972 740 629), at the outskirts, devoted mainly to well-anchored caravanners. Just one **bus** daily from Camprodon passes through on its way to Setcases (see below).

Immediately south of Vilallonga, on the far side of the valley, the hamlet of **LA ROCA** huddles strikingly under its unmissable namesake monolith; there are two restaurants here and another at road's end 4km west in **ABELLA**. Despite tempting depictions on some maps, the track beyond to Pardines (see p.175) over the Coll de Pal is nearly impossible even for jeeps.

Alternatively, you can bear left 1km past Vilallonga for the steep detour to **TREGURÀ**, 5km from the main road; perched on a sunny hillside at 1400m, with sweeping views east over the valley, the upper part of this double village has a church dating from about 980. There are also two places to **stay**, the better being welcoming *Fonda Rigà* (☎972 136 000; ❸ B&B, ❺ HB), with its massively popular and reasonable **restaurant**.

### Setcases

Back in the Ter valley, **SETCASES**, 6km northwest of Vilallonga, has been completely gentrified since the 1980s. Once an important agricultural village, it was almost totally abandoned until the nearby ski station began to attract hoteliers, chalet developers and second-home owners. The ski trade ensures that some short-term beds and food are relatively pricey in winter; Setcases straddles the GR11, a half-day's march west from Molló or two hours east from the Refugi d'Ulldeter (see below). If you need to stay, the most affordable **accommodation** stands adjacent on the riverbank road: the *Hostal Ter* (☎972 136 096; ❸) or the *Nueva Can Tiranda* (☎972 136 052, ✉tiranda@intercom.es; ❷), though you may be required to take half–board – as you definitely are in the village centre at *Hostal El Molí* (☎972 136 049; ❻ HB). At those rates, the relative luxury of *Hotel La Coma* (☎972 136 073; ❺ B&B), at the village entrance, might work out good value. Local trippers flock here to **eat** at weekends, most notably at the independent restaurant *Can Jepet* (closed Thurs Oct–June; ☎972 136 104). Prices are slightly bumped up (no *menú* at weekends), but so are portion sizes, making the food – well-presented salads, grilled quail with artichoke and roast peppers, genuinely homemade *flan* – excellent value at under €22 a head.

### Vallter 2000

Situated at the head of the valley, below the frontier summits of Bastiments (2883m) and Pic de la Dona (2704m), compact **VALLTER 2000** is the easternmost downhill ski resort in the Pyrenees. Although south-facing, the glacial bowl here has a chilly microclimate that lets snow linger into April most years – though pistes remain heavily dependent on canons. Even beginners get bored with the two nursery runs, though weak intermediates will find plenty of challenge in the two-kilometre blue (Jordi Pujol) or easy red (El Clot) runs from the top station of 2535m (served by chair lift on busy days, otherwise drag lifts). Only strong intermediates should attempt the five-kilometre Riu-Xalet joint piste, nominally blue but ending in a narrow, strongly red drop to the low point at 1910m, from where another chair lift returns to the resort centre at 2200m. Here you'll find equipment rental and a better-than-average restaurant. In short, enough to keep you interested for the duration of a weekend, when Barcelonans flood the place; certain Camprodon and Ter valley hotels offer advantageous all-in packages of half-board and lift pass.

### Hiking west: the GR11 and GR11.7

From Setcases, you can follow the GR11 and then the GR11.7 to a pair of useful refuges, though you're obliged to road-walk towards Valleter 2000 for the first hour or so of the GR11. Some three hours along, you arrive at the **Refugi d'Ulldeter** (2235m elevation; ☎972 192 004, ◉www.ulldeter.net; 52 places; open daily Christmas/Easter weeks, late June to mid-Sept & weekends all year), just south of the Vallter ski resort. Its restaurant is open to all, and the three-storey stone chalet makes a particularly good halt coming east on the GR11/HRP from Núria. Otherwise, the GR11.7 diverges south from the Coll de la Marrana (2529m) overhead, threading the scenic Coma de Freser en route, to reach the 1999-built **Refugi Coma de Vaca** at the top of the Gorges del Freser within three hours – a popular snowshoeing or skiing route in winter. This FEEC refuge, run by the welcoming Xavier and Yolanda (2020m; 42 places; staffed Easter, mid-June to mid-Sept; ℡972 198 082, or off-season by arrangement on ℡936 824 237), offers above-average meals, hot showers and a full activities programme, including rock-climbing and winter mountaineering. Summer weekends the refuge is booked solid, but quiet otherwise except for the numerous bells on the grazing cows of the name. You can also get here from Núria (see p.176), or from Tregurà via the Coll dels Tres Pics (2396m) in about four hours, but that approach involves mostly track-trudging up to the pass.

### Along the Ritort

From Camprodon, the road up to the **Col d'Ares** (1513m) and down into France initially follows the relatively treeless **Ritort valley**. The main, slight attractions of **MOLLÓ**, 8km from Camprodon (bus on Sat only), are the Romanesque church of Santa Cecília, with its four-storey bell-tower, and *El Costabona* **restaurant** on the central *plaça*. The best place to **stay** in the village is *Hotel Restaurant Calitxó*, a modern structure on the outskirts (℡972 740 386, ℻972 740 746; ❺ B&B); the rooms are of good standard, with balconies, wood trim everywhere and tubs in the baths, but it's rather overpriced except in low season (❹). Especially if on a GR11 traverse, you may prefer a **casa de pagès** 3km north in Ginestosa district, *Can Illa* (℡972 740 512; ❷), accessible by road or a half-hour, yellow-and-white-marked spur path. A working cattle ranch with sweeping views, *Can Illa* has mostly en-suite rooms, double beds, self-catering kitchen, a lounge with wood stove, and a refuge-type dorm for groups. Your final chance of food and a place to stay before the border is the well-kept *Habitacions El Quintà* (℡972 741 374; ❸) with balconied rooms at the base of attractive hillside **ESPINAVELL**, 2.2km northeast of the main road (4.2km in total from Molló; turn off before Ginestosa); half-board is also available through the affiliated *Restaurant Les Planes* next door.

Another option, a little east of the Ritort valley, just off the start of the road up to Rocabruna, is a *casa de pagès* best suited for connoisseurs of the middle of nowhere: *Mas Tubert* (℡972 130 327, ✉tubert@abaforum.es; ❼ HB). It's 7km by rough track from the *urbanització* of Font Rubí, itself about 6km from either Camprodon or Molló. Rooms are medium-sized if rustic, evening meals *nouvelle* verging on the precious (miniature frozen-liver lollies, etc).

## The upper Freser valley

From Ripoll, the Freser valley rises to Ribes de Freser and then climbs more steeply to Queralbs, where it swings eastwards through a gorge of remarkable beauty. Just above Queralbs, to the north, the Riu Núria has scoured out a second gorge, beyond which lie the ski station and valley sanctuary of Núria itself (1967m), the usual point of access to Puigmal (2910m) and other frontier peaks.

### Ribes de Freser

Generally bypassed in the rush up to Núria, dull but unobjectionable **RIBES DE FRESER** offers little to the traveller except accommodation – better value than anything in Ripoll – and, out of season, its integrity as a real town. Local shops sell sacks of grain, seeds, oils and other agricultural and domestic

## The cremallera railway

The **cremallera** ("Zipper" in Catalan) railway, built in 1931, is the last rack-and-pinion line operating in Catalunya, a miniature – though rather more daring – version of the *Train Jaune* just over the border. After a leisurely start through the lower valley – and a usual change of trains at Queralbs – the blue-and-white, two-car conveyance lurches up into the mountains relying on its third rail, following the river between great crags before starting to climb high above both valley and forests.

Services **depart** Ribes-Enllaç daily year-round except during November. "Low season" (weekdays Dec–June except Christmas, New Year and Easter, plus Oct) sees 7 daily departures between 7.30am and 6.30pm; there's an additional, final departure around 8.30pm Fridays. "High season" (winter holidays, plus July–Sept) features a minimum of 12 daily trains from about 7.30am until 6.30pm, plus extra departures on holiday dates. Trains pass through Ribes-Vila – where there's a weather report posted – six minutes later, though the day's first train always starts at Ribes-Vila, *not* Ribes-Enllaç. The **journey time** up or down is theoretically 40 minutes; return adult **tickets** to Núria from Ribes cost around €14 (one-way is about forty percent less). Rail passes of any kind are not valid. For current information phone ☎972 732 020, or see ⊛www.valldenuria.com/valldenuria/crem.htm.

paraphernalia, all displayed in a wonderfully random manner, plus there's a lively weekly market. More organized diversions consist of a much-used *petanca* court in the centre, and an annual sheepdog contest every September.

Alight any regular **train** on the Barcelona–Puigcerdà line at "Ribes de Freser-RENFE" for the ten-minute walk into town, or just cross the platform to "Ribes-Enllaç" and take the *cremallera* (see box above), which makes another stop in the town centre (Ribes-Vila) before trundling off into the mountains.

If **staying** appeals, pick of the bunch is *Mas Ventaiola* (☎972 727 948), a *casa de pagès* 1km north of Ribes-Vila station, reached via the cemetery track taking off from the Pardines road. Perched on the hillside and refurbished in exemplary taste, this offers en-suite rooms (❷), a few quad apartments, plus fully equipped kitchens and common areas. Otherwise, in the town itself, near Ribes-Vila station, the quietest choices are *Hotel Caçadors,* c/Balandrau 24–26 (☎972 727 006, ℻972 728 001; ❹), offering a range of en-suites in two separate premises, or the plainer rooms at *Hostal Porta de Núria* just around the corner at c/Nostra Senyora de Gràcia 3 (☎972 727 137; ❸). If you're still stuck, there's a helpful **Turisme** on Plaça de l'Ajuntament (Tues–Sat 10am–2pm & 5–8pm, Sun 11am–1pm; ☎972 727 728) by the church of Santa Maria, mostly destroyed like so many in 1936 and rebuilt a decade later, or repair to the **campsite** *Vall de Ribes*, 800m from Ribes-Vila station on the Pardines road (☎972 728 820); it's basic but pleasant, with tents welcome on the lower terraces, and a few chalets to rent. For **eating** out, the restaurant at the *Caçadors* is decent if slightly overpriced; count on €23 for three courses *a la carta*, with a *menú* at weekday lunches.

### Pardines and Campelles

If you still come up empty – a possibility in midsummer, or during ski season – two outlying villages, each 6km from Ribes in opposite directions, have more **accommodation** and **eating** possibilities. **PARDINES** (1250m), reached via a two-lane road east, enjoys a wonderful hilltop setting only slightly marred by sprouting apartments; the medieval core, whose Romanesque church of **Sant**

**Esteve** sports a round, thirteenth-century fortified belfry, remains atmospheric and reassuringly livestock-patrolled. Flanking the main square with its vaulted fountain is *Hostal Can Serra* (☎972 728 078; ❷ B&B), also serving meals. **CAMPELLES**, to the southwest at a similar altitude, is less compact and more gentrified, and has the year-round *Pensió Costa* (☎972 727 274; ❺ HB), with a country-style *menjador*.

## Queralbs and Fustanyà

The only intermediate stop on the *cremallera*, **QUERALBS** (1220m) is an attractive, stone-built village, though now being dwarfed by apartment complexes on its outskirts, and suffering from the attentions of too many tourists at peak season. Near the highest point, close to where the GR11 passes through, stands the twelfth-century church of **Sant Jaume**, adorned with a fine colonnaded south portico. Reasonable en-suite **accommodation** is provided by *Hostal L'Avet*, on the main street 80m in from the car park (☎972 727 377; daily summer, weekends only Oct 15–June 20; ❺ HB). Rooms are small and wood-trimmed, with meals (available to all comers) at adjacent **restaurant** *Ca La Mary*, where €16 or so nets you very good *table d'hôte* fare.

For year-round board and lodging, head 3km out of Queralbs to well-signposted *Mas La Casanova* on the opposite side of the valley (☎972 198 077; ❸ B&B), in **FUSTANYÀ** hamlet, by its church of **Sant Sadurní**, the oldest in the region. This en-suite *casa de pagès* is a superbly restored farmhouse with a literary pedigree: the classic Catalan play *Terra Baixa* had as main characters the former inhabitants. The current, outgoing proprietress provides reasonable (€10) *table d'hôte* suppers, and there are also large family suites; the only drawback is that the predominantly wood construction amplifies sounds between floors.

## Núria

Beyond Queralbs, the *cremallera* railway hauls itself up the precipitous valley to **NÚRIA**, twenty minutes further on. Once the train passes the entrance to the Gorges del Freser, seen tantalizingly to the right, and enters the Gorges de Núria, the views are dramatic – when you're not passing through a sequence of tunnels.

Having cleared a final tunnel, you emerge into a south-facing bowl, with a small, dam-augmented lake at the bottom and – at the far end – the hideously monolithic, *café-au-lait*-coloured **Santuari de Nuestra Senyora de Núria** (1964m), founded in the eleventh century on the spot where an image of the Virgin was miraculously found. Local shepherds actually revere **Sant Gil**, an eighth-century Benedictine abbot who crossed over from France, set up shop in this valley, and attempted to proselytize the then-pagan herdsmen. The Virgin of Núria, of more general appeal, is believed to bestow fertility on female pilgrims, and many Catalan girls – presumably the result of successful supernatural intervention – are named after her.

The sanctuary building combines a dull church, tourist office (which posts weather reports), bar, restaurants, ski centre and **hotel** all in one. Rates at the *Hotel Vall de Núria* (☎972 732 000, ☏972 732 001; 2 nights min; ❻–❼ HB) vary according to season – winter is cheaper – and its **restaurant** is equally pricey. The only indoor budget lodging is the youth hostel *Pic de L'Àliga* (☎972 732 048), marvellously poised at the top of the ski centre's cable-car line (often not running in summer). **Camping** is permitted only at a designated area behind the sanctuary complex.

Besides the hotel, **eating** options include *La Cabana dels Pastors*, behind the complex, sporadically offering expensive bistro fare at midday only; the *Bar Finestrelles*, downstairs in the sanctuary building, with typical bar snacks; and, best value of all, the lunchtime-only *Autoservei* self-service restaurant in the west wing, where you can eat reasonably well for €12–16. Activities laid on in the valley include an archery range, pony-riding programme (high summer only) and boating on the lake.

## Winter activities

Downhill **skiing** at Núria is surprisingly popular, given that the lift system is very limited, the chair lift only reaches 2262m, and the maximum altitude difference is a paltry 288m. The longest, blue Les Creus run from the top station, is only 1750m, while red-rated Mulleres traces just over a kilometre down from Point 2262, so Núria is best for beginners and weak intermediates.

**Off-piste**, the summits of **Pic/Puig de Finestrelles** (2829m) and **Puigmal** (2910m) are fairly easy to conquer. Finestrelles looms due northwest of the sanctuary, reached by following the namesake valley and then bearing away a little to the west before curving back towards the top. The approach to Puigmal begins in the same way, but soon turns southwest along the **Coma de l'Embut**; at the precipitation gauge swing southeast for the Collada de l'Embut and, once through, make straight for the summit. Each ascent takes three to five hours, depending on conditions and skill; crampons may be required. It's possible to take in both peaks as a full day's outing, passing between them along the frontier ridge.

## Walking

Summer **walkers** can follow similar routes detailed on Editorial Alpina's 1:25,000 "Puigmal-Vall de Núria-Ulldeter" map and accompanying booklet, most notably east along the **GR11**, which attains its greatest altitude following the frontier ridge and the HRP for a few hours – a risky stretch in poor visibility – en route to the Refugi d'Ulldeter. At the Coll de Carança, you have the option of descending into France to Ras de Carança (see p.104); the area's three staffed refuges promote a figure-eight-shaped "**Three Refuges Traverse**", using well-defined paths and taking four to five days.

A **return to Queralbs** on foot along the river gorge is perhaps the most popular hike out of Núria. The GR11 threads the gorge on a high-quality, well-marked path, but you'll still want sturdy boots and a water bottle (there are a few drinkable torrents and springs en route). You'll need two to two and a half hours descending, depending on load and stops, three to three and a half hours going up. The trail generally adopts the opposite side of the gorge to the *cremallera* tracks, giving you the opportunity to watch the little train at work; the valley begins to open out below Sallent del Sastre, and after crossing back to the west bank for good at the Pont de Cremal, you'll see the Freser gorge yawning to the east.

### The two gorges walk

A more challenging, **five-hour descent**, traced correctly on the recommended Alpina map, gives you the best of **both local gorges**. This route starts alongside the cable car to the youth hostel, with an initial ten minutes up the Camí de les Creus to a Via Crucis, where the onward GR11.7 is signed as the **Camí dels Enginyers** (Engineer's Trail), named after the engineers who came after 1945 to make a feasibility study for a dam in the valleys here – luckily it wasn't profitable. As you proceed, past the first announcement for Coma de Vaca, spectacular views open south and the terrain becomes more rugged, the path more of a corniche. While there's little net altitude change between Núria and the refuge, roller-coaster progress means you need to be fit; there's occasional scrambling over boulder falls and little metal ladders, with a cable and pegs about two hours along to get you over some steep patches, hazardous if wet. The *camí* attains its high point a few minutes further at the **Coll dels Homes**, and the hut appears suddenly at the base of a slope two-and-a-half hours from Núria.

After lunch here (recommended), resume course on the **Camí de les Gorgues del Riu Freser**, marked only with red dots. Head initially southeast from the refuge, then bear right after ten minutes; once over the rocky promontory, descend on gentle, well-graded switchbacks. An hour below Coma de Vaca, you're in forest, with the river close by on the right. Next, cross the Freser on a plank bridge, and remain on the right bank thereafter: first in open meadow, then following a corniche path, with intermittent cobbling, high above the gorge. Pass the **Salt del Grill** stream, and just under two hours from the refuge, the wood bridge and signage for the Central Electric of Daió de Baix, where the Núria and Freser streams unite. The only boring bit involves following a cement drive out to the main road, and a final haul up the asphalt to the Queralbs *cremallera* car park (2hr 20min).

Truly hard cases can instead head from the refuge up the Coma de Vaca itself (red-dot markings) to the Coll de Carança, and thence down to Núria, for a five-hour trajectory; it's best to do this only with an early start during late June/July, and on a Friday or Saturday when there's a late train downhill.

# Travel details

## French trains

NB SNCF buses may substitute for trains on these lines; services are reduced Sun/hols. Frequencies on the *Train Jaune* (see p.105) are included here.
**Perpignan** to: Argelès (26 daily; 20min); Banyuls-sur-Mer (26 daily; 30min); Carcassonne (24 daily; 1hr 15min–2hr); Cerbère (26 daily; 40min); Collioure (24 daily; 25min); Elne (24 daily; 10min); Ille-sur-Têt (8 daily; 25–30min); Prades (9 daily; 45min); Villefranche-de-Conflent (12 daily; 50min).
**Quillan** to: Carcassonne (3–4 daily; 55min).
**Villefranche** to: Font-Romeu (6–8 daily; 1hr 15min); Ille-sur-Têt (18 daily; 30min); Latour-de-Carol (5 daily; 2hr 45min); Mont-Louis (6–8 daily; 1hr); Perpignan (12 daily; 50min); Prades (14 daily; 10min).

## Spanish trains

**Figueres** to: Barcelona (21 daily; 1hr 40min); Colera (8 daily; 25min); Girona (21 daily; 30min); Portbou (12 daily; 30min).
**Girona** to: Barcelona (21 daily; 1hr 25min); Llançà (12 daily; 1hr); Portbou (12 daily; 1hr 10min).
**Ripoll** to: Barcelona (10–11 daily; 1hr 50min–2hr 20min); Puigcerdà (6 daily; 1hr 10min; 2–3

continue 7min more to French station of Latour-de-Carol).

## French buses

**Argelès-sur-Mer** to: Céret (1–2 daily; 1hr); St-Génis (Tues & Thurs daily; 22min).
**Arles-sur-Tech** to: Coustouges (2–4 daily; 40min); Prats-de-Molló (6 daily; 15min); St-Laurent-de-Cerdans (2–4 daily; 30min).
**La Cabanasse/Mont-Louis** to: Puyvalador via Les Angles, Matemale and Formiguères (2 daily in summer and ski season at 10.35am and 6pm, returns mid-afternoon and dawn; 50min).
**Perpignan** to: Argelès (3 daily; 30min); Arles-sur-Tech (6–8 daily; 1hr 15min); Amélie-les-Bains (6–8 daily; 1hr); Axat (2 daily; 1hr 40min); Banyuls-sur-Mer (3 daily; 1hr 10min); Cerbère (3 daily; 1hr 15min); Céret (14 daily; 55min); Collioure (3 daily; 45min); Elne (3 daily; 35min); Font-Romeu (2–3 daily; 2hr 30min); Ille-sur-Têt (11 daily; 35min); Latour-de-Carol (2–3 daily; 3hr); Le Boulou (12 daily; 20min); Le Perthus (6 daily; 45min); Mont-Louis (4 daily; 2hr 15min); Port-Vendres (3–6 daily; 55min); Prades (7 daily; 1hr); Prats-de-Molló (7 daily; 1hr 40min); Quillan (2–5 daily, 1hr 30min); Saint-Génis (4 daily; 45min); Saint-Laurent-de-

Cerdans (3 daily Mon–Sat, 2 Sun; 1hr 45min);
Thuir (3–5 daily; 25min); Vernet-les-Bains (4 daily;
1hr 25min); Villefranche-de-Conflent (7 daily; 1hr
15min).

**Quillan** to: Axat (2 daily; 20min); Carcassonne (2
daily; 1hr 20min); Comus (1–2 daily; 1hr 5min);
Perpignan (2 daily; 1hr 30min); Quérigut (3 weekly
in summer; 1hr 30min).

**Villefranche-de-Conflent** to: Casteil (3–4 daily;
15min); Prades (14 daily Mon–Sat, 7 Sun; 10min);
Sahorre (1–2 daily Mon–Sat; 15min); Vernet-les-
Bains (12 daily Mon–Sat, 7 Sun; 10min).

## Spanish buses

**Figueres** to: Barcelona (3–8 daily; 1hr 30min);
Cadaqués (5 daily; 1hr 10min); Castelló
d'Empúries (hourly; 15min); Espolla (1 daily
Mon–Sat; 35min); Girona (4–8 daily Mon–Sat, 3
Sun; 1hr); Llançà (2 daily; 25min); Maçanet de
Cabrenys via Darnius (1–2 daily Mon–Sat;

45–55min); Roses (every 30min; 40min); Vilajuïga
(1 daily; 50min).

**Girona** to: Banyoles (15 daily Mon–Sat, 5 on Sun;
30min); Barcelona (6–9 daily Mon–Sat, 3 on Sun;
1hr); Figueres (6–10 daily Mon–Sat, 4 Sun;
50min); Olot (14 daily Mon–Sat, 5 Sun; 1hr
20min).

**Olot** to: Banyoles via Besalú (6–7 daily Mon–Sat, 4
Sun; 40min); Banyoles via Mieres (1 daily Mon–Sat
at 7.15am, returns 12.45pm; 1hr); Barcelona (7
daily Mon–Sat, 5 Sun; 2hr 15min); Besalú (9–10
daily Mon–Sat, 6 on Sun; 30min); Camprodon (1–2
daily; 45min); Figueres (4 daily; 1hr); Ripoll (1
daily; 45min); Santa Pau (Wed & Sat am, plus 2
Mon; 15min); Sant Joan de les Abadesses (1 daily;
30min); Vall d'en Bas (12 daily; 15min).

**Ripoll** to: Camprodon (6–8 daily; 45min);
Guardiola de Berguedà (1 daily Mon–Fri at
5.25pm; 2hr); La Pobla de Lillet (1 daily Mon–Fri at
5.25pm; 1hr 45min); Sant Joan de les Abadesses
(6–8 daily; 20min).

# Andorra and around

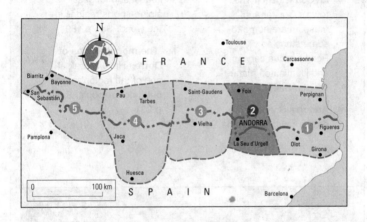

CHAPTER TWO # Highlights

✳ **Grotte de Niaux** Check out the cave art in the most impressive of Tarascon's painted prehistoric caves. See p.238

✳ **Montségur castle** Marvel at the heroism of the Cathars' last stand in this beautiful ruined castle. See p.249

✳ **La Seu d'Urgell** The town's cloister and museum are home to some stunning Romanesque carving and illuminated manuscripts. See p.202

✳ **Andorra** Shop till you drop for ski and mountain gear in the Pyrenees' biggest bargain-basement bazaar. See p.206

✳ **The Carlit massif** Hike through, around or over the easternmost high-mountain region of the range. See p.229

✳ **La Molina** Ski at the oldest, and one of the largest and longest alpine-sports regions in the world. See p.189

✳ **The mountain spa of Dorres** Have a soak at one of the region's rare outdoor hot-pools. See p.231

# Andorra and around

$A$ pproaching the principality of Andorra from the Mediterranean, you begin to encounter permanently snow-tipped mountains and almost every kind of Pyrenean landscape. On the Spanish side, the best appetizer for high peaks en route to Andorra is the **Parc Natural del Cadí-Moixeró**, featuring that most distinctive Spanish Catalan peak, the cloven **Pedraforca**. In 1906 Pablo Picasso came to Gòsol at the foot of this mountain in search of fresh inspiration, and much of what he found still exists: unspoilt, vividly coloured scenery, golden eagles soaring overhead and herds of isards. The Cadí remains largely free of ski development and is excellent for spring or autumn hiking and mountain-biking.

**La Seu d'Urgell**, capital of the Spanish *comarca* (county) of **Alt Urgell**, north and west of the Cadí, is one of the main gateways to Andorra, and pivotal to its history. La Seu's bishops controlled the principality with the nobility of Foix in a unique feudal power-sharing arrangement that endured, more or less peacefully, for over seven centuries, until Andorra voted for full independence in 1993. There are just two ways of entering **Andorra** by road: along the Valira valley from La Seu d'Urgell, or from the Ariège valley in France. At each frontier, and for a considerable distance beyond, duty-free megastores peddling cut-price consumer goods line streets congested with shoppers' cars. But some of Andorra does remain untrammelled by development, and on foot you can traverse the principality (almost) without touching asphalt or seeing a single shop.

Like Catalonia in general, the mountain-ringed plateau of **Cerdanya**, southeast of Andorra, was partitioned by the 1659 Treaty of the Pyrenees, a division that left **Llívia** as an island of Spanish territory surrounded by the **Cerdagne**, the French part of this formerly unified territory. **Puigcerdà** on the Spanish side, once capital of the entire district, is now a kilometre or so from the border at Bourg-Madame. To the north, behind the mega-resort of **Font-Romeu**, rises the **Carlit Massif**, the easternmost high-alpine region in the Pyrenees.

The **Ariège valley**, north of Andorra, makes an excellent choice if you have time for only one other region near the principality. The caves around **Tarascon** include the world's most stunning publicly accessible prehistoric paintings at **Niaux**, and a magnificent forest of stalactites and stalagmites at **Lombrives**, the largest cave open to the public in Europe. For walkers, **Ax-les-Thermes** is the most attractive place to stay, with the entire length of the Ariège accessible by train, and a trio of long-distance footpaths – the **HRP**, **GR10** and **GR7**– within easy reach.

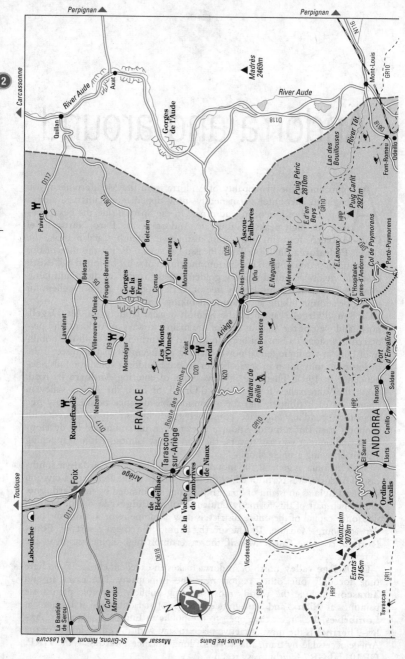

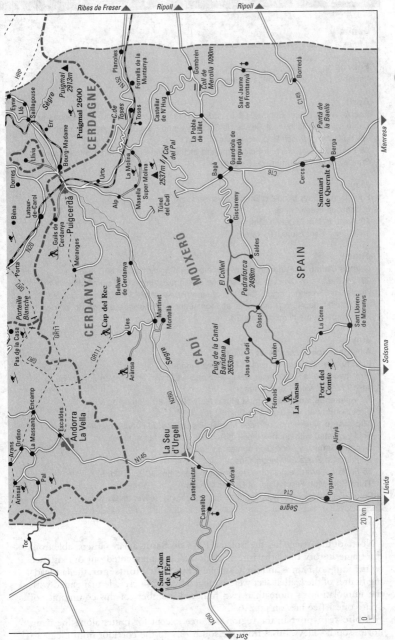

## Festivals

**January**
**17** *Festa de Sant Antoni* in Sant Llorenç de Morunys.

**February**
**Variable** Carnival week at La Molina.

**April**
**Easter week** Easter Sunday, *La Truitada* at Bagà; Easter Monday, processions to Santa Maria de Talló, near Bellver de Cerdanya, and Sant Jaume de Frontanyà; following Sunday, *Pascuilla* celebrations at Llívia.
**25** *Festa de Sant Marc* in Puigcerdà and at the shrine of Queralt; on the closest Sunday, *aplec* to Santuari de Falgars.

**May**
**8** Festival at Sant Miquel d'Engolasters (Andorra).
**8** Tarascon livestock fair.
**10** *Aplec a Sant Miquel*, Gisclareny.
**15** *Aplec a Sant Isidre*, Gisclareny.

**June**
**Corpus Christi** *La Patum* in Berga – one of the biggest bashes in Catalunya.
**23–24** The eve of *Día de Sant Joan*, one of the most important saint's days in the Cerdanya/Cerdagne, marks the start of summer. *Festa de Sant Joan de Cornudell* at Castellar de N'Hug; fireworks at Montségur, and solstice events on or near Pedraforca on the night of June 23.

**July**
**All month** *Son et Lumière* at Puivert.
**First two weeks** Jazz festival at Escaldes, Andorra.
**First two weeks** *Résistances*, festival of new wave film at Tarascon-sur-Ariège.
**11–19** *Mercat Medieval* at Bagà.
**All weekends, and into August** Music festival at Sant Llorenç de Morunys.
**First Sunday** Annual festival in Puigcerdà.
**Mid-month** Week-long *Journées Médiévales de Gaston Fébus*; medieval market at Foix (repeated with another week in August); country fair at Lavelanet.
**Second Saturday** Accordion contest at Saldes.
**20** *Festa de Santa Margarida*, Gòsol.
**25** *Festa Major* at Sant Jaume de Frontanyà, and Escaldes (Andorra).
**Third Sun–Mon** *Festa Major* at Canillo (Andorra).
**25–27** *Festa Major* at Sant Jaume de Frontanyà and Bellver de Cerdanya.

North of the Ariège lies the isolated **Pays de Sault**, an area inseparable from the tragic history of Catharism, a religion all but persecuted out of existence by the kings of France and the Catholic Church. At **Montségur**, the last leading figures of the Cathar sect were besieged by a 1244 crusade that ended with the immolation of more than two hundred members of this community of "pure ones" (see box on pp.246–247).

**Public transport** in the region is scarce except for routes along the main north–south valleys. Buses from the south run up the corridor from Lleida to La Seu d'Urgell and Andorra, and from Berga to Puigcerdà. The last surviving

**Last Sun–Tues** *Festa Major* at Sant Julià de Lòria (Andorra).
**Late in the month** Six-day *Festival du Folklore International* at Quillan, with groups from around the world.
**Last weekend** Latin American festival at Tarascon-sur-Ariège.

### August
**All month** *Son et Lumière* at Puivert.
**1–3** *Festa Major de Sant Esteve*, Bagà.
**First weekend** *Festa Major* at Andorra la Vella.
**14–15** Music festival at La Pobla de Lillet.
**14–17** *Festa Major* with dancing at Gòsol.
**15** *Fête* at Font-Romeu.
**15–17** *Festa Major* at Encamp and La Massana (Andorra).
**Penultimate Sunday** *Festa del Llac* at Puigcerdà, with fireworks, parade and closing ball; sheepdog (*gossos d'atura* in Catalan) trials at Castellar de N'Hug.
**Last Sunday** Annual fair at La Seu d'Urgell.
**Variable** Medieval fair at Ax-les-Thermes.

### September
**First two weeks** *Fête* at Foix, with markets, music and torchlit procession.
**First Sunday** *Sardana* competition at Berga.
**8** *Festa* at Meritxell (Andorra); *Procession de la Vierge* from Font-Romeu to Odeillo; *romería* from La Pobla de Lillet to Falgars.
**16–17** *Festa* at Ordino (Andorra).
**Third Sunday** Sheepdog trials at Fornells de la Muntanya.
**28–29** *Festa Major* at Castellar de N'Hug.
**30** Tarascon livestock fair.

### October
**First Sunday** *Festa Major* at Gisclareny; mushroom festival at Berga.
**Third Sunday** *Foire de La Guinguette* at Bourg-Madame.
**31** *Fira de Tots Sants*, Gòsol.

### November
**1** *Sant Ermengol* celebrations in La Seu d'Urgell.

### December
**4** *Festa de Santa Bàrbara*, Saldes.
**24** *La Fia-Faia* torchlit procession at Bagà.

trans-Pyrenean rail line links Ripoll, Puigcerdà, Ax-les-Thermes and Foix, with a change of trains at the border station of Latour-de-Carol. Exceptional east–west bus services include one between La Seu and Puigcerdà, and another between Quillan and Foix, crossing the Pays de Sault.

# The Cadí-Moixeró Park and around

Slightly west of Ripoll and Ribes de Freser begins the **Parc Natural del Cadí-Moixeró**, an area of more than four hundred square kilometres that extends north to Alt Urgell and the Cerdanya, and west almost as far as the Riu Segre. Too steep for modern agriculture and unsuitable for downhill skiing, the greater part of the Cadí-Moixeró massif – essentially a giant block of lime-stone – is perfect for hiking and climbing. The area's highest mountain, **Puig de la Canal Baridana**, and the whole **Serra del Cadí** range are complete-ly unexploited, and even the much-visited peak of **Pedraforca** bears only slight marks of development. The boundaries of the actual park are inconspic-uously posted with black-on-white "*parc natural*" signs, generally just outside most of the towns and villages described – there are no entrance booths or other means of controlling access.

Although the designation *parc natural* does not guarantee strict **wildlife** pro-tection, the Cadí-Moixeró now shelters Spain's largest herd of chamois (isard in Catalan); hunting controls have allowed their number to grow from around fifty to nearly a thousand. Red and roe deer had been hunted out, however, and were only reintroduced during the 1980s. Capercaillie breed here, as do the golden eagle and the black woodpecker, symbol of the park. Botanists will appreciate the green-petalled *Xatardia scabra*, endemic to the Eastern Pyrenees and common on local scree slopes. Also widespread are the deep-blue *Gentiana alpina*; the violet-flowered Ice Age survivor, *Ramonda myconi*; and *Rhododendron ferrugineum*. Lower slopes are heavily forested with dense stands of pine and silver fir.

The main C16 from the south – used by buses from Barcelona and Manresa to **Berga** – cuts the park into two unequal portions. The Cadí watershed and half the Moixeró lie west of the **Túnel del Cadí**, where the C16 disappears under the range to emerge near Puigcerdà; the rest of the Moixeró, including Castellar de N'Hug and the ski resorts of **La Molina** and **Masella**, lies to the east.

## Approaches from Ripoll

**From Ripoll** (p.168), two routes skirt the eastern fringes of the *parc natural*: the northerly N152, relatively well served by public transport, passing two popular ski resorts; and the southerly GI402 towards the C1411, skimming the edge of the Moixeró region and seeing just one bus a day (more regular serv-ices run from Berga).

### The Rigart valley and northerly ski resorts

The more **northerly** route west from Ripoll ascends the valley of the **Riu Rigart** from Ribes de Freser; the train line to Puigcerdà hugs the bottom of the valley, while the N152 takes a higher course, allowing a good look south over the Serra Montgrony. Beyond the Collada de Toses, technically in the

Cerdanya, the ski resort of **Alp 2500** is the easternmost really serious winter-sports area in the Catalan Pyrenees.

## Planoles, Fornells and Toses

**PLANOLES** village, 7km from Ribes on a south-facing slope, is nothing out of the ordinary, but it straddles the GR11 and makes a good base for the Freser valley and for ski slopes to the west. Most local **accommodation** is of the second-home variety, but there's an outstanding, well-kept *casa de pagès, Mas Cal Sadurní* (☏972 736 135; ❺ HB only), unimprovably set on a natural terrace just uphill from the train station. This offers doubles and family-size quads, mostly en suite, in a superbly restored farmhouse. It's packed out most weekends, but the in-house restaurant closes Tuesday and Wednesday, when your best local **eating** option is the widely acclaimed *Restaurant-Casino* behind the church (closed Mon; lunch only, all-inclusive *menú* €9).

The hamlet of **FORNELLS DE LA MUNTANYA**, 8.5km beyond Planoles, has another **casa de pagès**, the blandly modern, en-suite *Cal Pastor* (☏972 736 163, ✉ramongasso@logicontro.es; ❸). Fornells is really noteworthy for its single, friendly **restaurant**, *Can Casanova* (closed Mon eve & Tues), serving large portions of hearty mountain cuisine from a limited menu. It's good value at under €20 per person, including a strong, ruby house wine, and (unusually nowadays) serves lunch until 4.30pm, so reservations are suggested (☏972 736 075).

**TOSES**, 3.5km beyond Fornells, is the last village in the Rigart valley and, at 1450m, has good claim to being one of the highest permanently inhabited villages in Spain. It enjoys views east towards El Ripollès and 4km west to the **Collada de Toses** (1800m), which closes off the horizon. The only **accommodation** option, 100m from the leased-out train station with its bar and ski rental, is the good-value *Cal Santpare* (☏972 736 226, ❻www.calsantpare.com; ❹ B&B, ❺ HB). Food at the ground-floor restaurant (closed Wed) is basic but sustaining, the en-suite rooms heated and comfortable.

The glory of Toses is its tenth-to-twelfth-century church of **San Cristófol**, at the highest, east end of the village, with a simple barrel-vaulted nave and a rectangular, gable-roofed "Lombard" belfry. The ancient key (obtain 10am–1pm from *Cal Pep* on the square, your other eating possibility) allows you inside to study the apsidal **frescoes**, skilful copies of originals in the Museu d'Art de Catalunya in Barcelona. The main theme, Christ's Ascension, is half-destroyed, but well preserved around the lancet window is an image of a lad hefting a sheep – highly apt for this pastoral community.

Beyond Toses, road and train enter Cerdanya over and under the Collada de Toses – the railway by the amazing **Cargol tunnel**, where the line executes a full circle to gain altitude. The pass affords excellent views west, the bare rolling mountains of the Montgrony range relieved by swathes of deep-green forest.

## Skiing Alp 2500 – and Alp village

**LA MOLINA**, its lift-bases scattered 4–7km from the pass on the north flank of 2409-metre Puigllançada, ranks as the oldest ski resort in Spain, inaugurated in 1909. From as early as 1922 special Sunday return trains from Barcelona catered to enthusiasts, though for some years the line only ran to Toses, from where intrepid skiers had to proceed through an unfinished rail tunnel by torchlight, then trudge up the slopes to begin their runs – there were no lifts until 1942. Local villagers derived great amusement from these pioneer skiers with their clumsy wooden footwear – "Throw them on the fire and get some

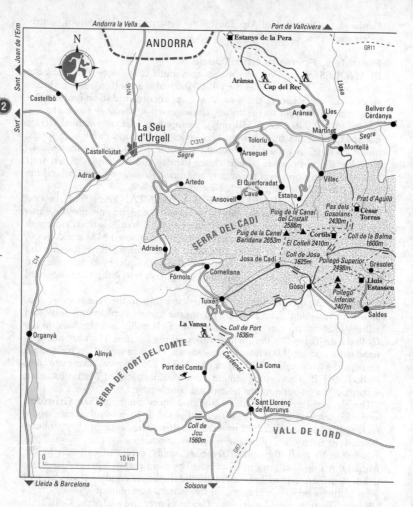

benefit from them!" was a typical comment, according to Ernest Mullor, Catalan ski champion of the era. Needless to say, the sport took off, and in 1967 another resort opened at **MASELLA**, 4.5km west of La Molina, on the slopes of 2536-metre Tosa d'Alp.

Both La Molina and Masella have their own websites (Ⓦ www.lamolina.com and Ⓦ www.masella.com), though they're marketed together as **ALP 2500**. By Spanish Pyrenean standards the skiing is impressive: the two resorts, sharing a lift pass, are linked via chair/bubble lifts and runs focused on Tosa d'Alp, forming (arguably) the largest ski area in the Pyrenees. La Molina is publicly owned by the Catalan government, and probably better suited for beginners; slightly larger Masella has passed into private hands, and is widely considered the better managed of the two. Certainly it has the edge in scenic appeal, provision of strategic chair lifts and length of runs, including five kilometres of consecutive

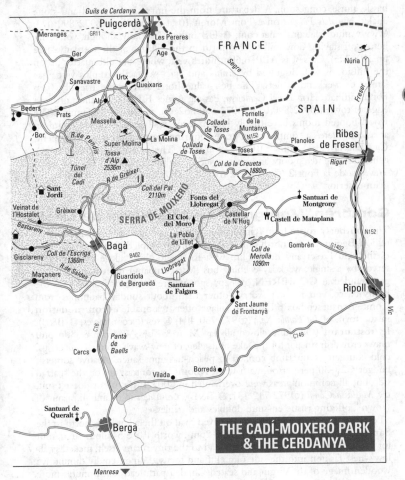

THE CADÍ-MOIXERÓ PARK
& THE CERDANYA

blue and red runs from Tosa d'Alp summit to Pla de Masella at 1650m, one of the greatest altitude drops in the range. Despite the northerly orientation and forest cover, both resorts rely heavily on snow canons and may close early in the day during spring.

**Getting to the slopes** is easiest with your own car, though during winter one "**Bus Blanc**" departs from the Cerdanya flatlands early morning, with two well-spaced returns in the afternoon. One route serves Ger, Bolvir, Llívia and Puigcerdà; the other begins at Martinet, plying Bellver, Prats, Alp and other villages. You can forget about local **trains** unless you're happy to shell out for a taxi or imitate the 1920s aficionados – both La Molina's and Alp's train stations are considerably remote from the action.

With few exceptions, **accommodation** at the foot of the slopes is overpriced, sterile and beset in high season by what Spaniards call *mucho follón* –

hassle, noise, congestion. A departure from the norm is the wood-and-stone chalet *Niu dels Falcons* on c/Font Moreu 10 at La Molina (☎972 892 073; ⓦwww.niudelsfalcons-xalet.com; ❼ HB only). Generally, though, you're far better off staying downhill to the north in the villages of the Cerdanya (see pp.219–225). Closest is **ALP**, 6.5km northwest, where the old quarter up on the hillside is well disguised by *avant-* and *après-*ski facilities, plus vast phalanxes of weekend chalets. The best-value hotel here is the friendly, Casa Fonda affiliate *Aero Hotel Cerdanya*, Passeig Agnès Fabra 4, on the northeast edge of town (☎972 890 033, ⓕ972 890 862; ❺), popular with families. The wood-floored rooms have mildly kitsch decor, wall art adorns the common areas, and there's a competitively priced gourmet **restaurant** in the basement, *Ca l'Eudald* (*menú* from €10, *a la carta* €25). The two other choices in the centre are slightly snooty and charge accordingly, for example *Hostal Roca* at Travessia de la Font 2 (☎ & ⓕ972 890 011; ❺), its updated decor belying its grim exterior.

## Gombrèn, Montgrony and La Pobla de Lillet

The **southerly route** from Ripoll aims right at the heart of the Cadí-Moixeró region. Beginning just north of Ripoll, at Campdevànol, this minor road crosses the Riu Freser and heads 8km west to the foothill village of Gombrèn, served by a single, weekday-evening bus (Mir company) from Ripoll. If you get stranded at **GOMBRÈN**, a sleepy spot where the church-clock tolls the hours twice, you needn't worry (other than about sundry hauntings from Comte Arnau; see box p.170): the village offers reasonable **accommodation** in the form of *La Fonda Xesc* (☎972 730 404, ⓔxesc@cconline.es; ❹ B&B). Its **restaurant** (Oct–June closed all day Mon & Tues, Wed pm & Sun pm) draws crowds from afar for the sake of its elegant new-wave cuisine (*yuca* crisps, cold courgette soup, lamb cooked in peach-hazelnut sauce, creative sorbets); budget €25–30 per person, with wine. Rooms by contrast are on the spartan side, but all common areas were overhauled in 2003. If it's full or doesn't suit, try *Masia la Canal* (☎972 712 131; ❸ B&B), a *casa de pagès* some 4km out of "town", offering rustic en-suite doubles and triples.

Less than 3km beyond Gombrèn, a paved road on the right leads north to the **Santuari de Montgrony** (daily 9am–8pm), worth the 5.5-kilometre detour for its spectacular setting. Steep steps lead to the tiny shrine itself, tucked swallow's-nest fashion into the side of a cliff and focused on an eqully diminutive wooden image of the Virgin and seated Child; a path leads ten minutes more over the hillside to the cruciform, Romanesque church of **Sant Pere**. Part of the shrine is now an agreeable old **inn** (☎972 198 022; ❹ HB only), with an attached, beamed-ceiling **restaurant** (closed Tues Oct–June). With your own transport you can continue another 13km from the *santuari* to Castellar de N'Hug (see below), an easier drive than the way up from La Pobla de Lillet, passing the tiny, ruined **Castell de Mataplana**.

The main GI402 road west continues 16km from Gombrèn to the **Coll de Merolla** (1090m) with its rather improbable **refuge** (☎972 731 291; 40 bunks), of more interest for its restaurant – with some weird rock formations to the southwest and excruciating curves each side of the watershed. On entering Barcelona province, the GI402 becomes the B402 and drops to **LA POBLA DE LILLET**, 28km from Ripoll. Here two ancient bridges arching over the infant Llobregat River and the old districts on either side make for a pleasant half-hour stroll, though there's little else to see besides a pair of minor Romanesque churches – ruined, monastic Santa Maria and the curious, circular

Sant Miquel – both 1500m east of town and both closed indefinitely for restoration. There's a **Turisme** (daily Easter & June–Sept 10am–2pm & 5–8pm) by the smaller of the bridges. **Accommodation** and **dining** are restricted to the central *Hostal Can Pericas*, c/Furrioles Altes 3 (☎938 236 162; ❸), its food only average and the service slow; and the slightly shabbier *Hostal Cerdanya* at Plaça del Fort 5 (☎938 236 083; ❷).

# Fonts del Llobregat and Castellar de N'Hug

From La Pobla there's a steady eleven-kilometre ascent northeast towards Castellar de N'Hug. Without transport you can try hitching – or waiting for the evening **bus** (Mon–Sat) from Berga via La Pobla. Three kilometres out of La Pobla on the left stands **El Clot de Moro**, a flamboyant *modernista* building designed by Rafael Guastavino in 1901 as a cement factory; today it functions as the **Museu del Ciment Asland** (daily July to mid-Sept 10am–2pm & 4–7pm; rest of year weekends only 10am–3pm), with exhibits on the industry.

Approaching Castellar, you'll pass the **Fonts del Llobregat**, source of the river that divides Spanish Catalunya in two, entering the sea at Barcelona. Numerous jets of water burst from the rock of a densely wooded ravine, the most powerful forming a broad, photogenic waterfall. Every year hundreds of Catalans come here as if on pilgrimage – summer droughts reduce many of Catalunya's rivers to nothing, so there's great pride in any durable water source, and this one has never stopped in living memory, even during the driest year. Coming uphill, the main access is by a signposted turning at about "Km8", leading past the giant *Hostal Les Fonts* to a car park and old water mill, a few minutes' walk from the cascades. You can also get here via a fifteen-minute stepped path from the bottom of Castellar de N'Hug.

Heaped up against the ridge of the Serra de Montgrony, **CASTELLAR DE N'HUG** (1400m) makes a good if slightly touristy base for the Moixeró section of the park, or (in winter) for Alp 2500 (see p.190); high seasons are September to October, when people hunt mushrooms in surrounding forests, and the ski season of January–February. There's a fair amount of inexpensive **accommodation**: top choices are the friendly *Hostal Fonda La Muntanya* (☎938 257 065; ❹ HB only; open all year) at Plaça Major 4, with excellent, copious dinners and rooms spread over two premises, or the *Pensió Fanxicó* (☎938 257 015; ❹ HB only) across the way. An airy fallback, at the southeast edge of the village on the road towards the Santuari de Montgrony and La Molina, is *Hostal Alt Llobregat* (☎938 257 074; ❸ B&B), with very plain though balconied rooms.

North from Castellar, the paved, bleakly scenic BI4031, sporadically snow-ploughed in winter, continues 15.5km over the range to La Molina and the Collada de Toses via the **Coll de la Creueta** (1880m).

# Sant Jaume de Frontanyà and beyond

The eleventh-century church at **SANT JAUME DE FRONTANYÀ**, unquestionably the finest Romanesque church in the region, lies just 12km southeast of La Pobla, accessible by a paved road, though older maps may not show it as such. The turning south from the B402, 2km east of La Pobla, is well marked.

Built in the shape of a Latin cross with three apses, this Augustinian foundation has an engaging setting at the foot of a naturally terraced cliff. The twelve-sided, squinch-supported lantern was unique in Catalunya until the restoration of the monastery at Ripoll. Inside, the church is chilly and bare, and evocative in its emptiness (both restaurants have keys – see below).

The surrounding hamlet, all of a dozen stone houses, offers two characterful **restaurants**, *Hostal Sant Jaume* and *Fonda Cal Marxandó*, the latter with inexpensive **rooms** (☎938 239 002; ❷) above its beam-ceilinged *menjador*. Despite its tag, *Sant Jaume* has no accommodation, but very decent *a la carta* food: Garrotxa beans with sausage, duck in *rattafia* sauce, sweet and drink for under €21, rather less than its rival.

From Sant Jaume the road continues 9km south to nondescript **BORREDÀ** on the C149, where small lumber mills on the outskirts slowly process the lush surrounding forest. If you get stuck here – possible, as just one weekly (Sat) bus goes to Berga – there's only the *Baix Pirineu* **restaurant** on the main street, with rooms suitable for emergencies. It's another 21km southwest to Berga past the **Pantà de la Baells**, a reservoir on the Llobregat, where at low water local boaters claim you can see the cupola and crumbled walls of a submerged monastic church.

# Berga and around

From the south, the major public-transport approach to the Cadí park is the twice-daily bus from Barcelona to **BERGA**, where the Pyrenees rear up with startling abruptness. The town itself is fairly dull, bearing ample traces of its long history as an industrial centre, but it does offer a ruined castle, a well-preserved medieval core and – as capital of Berguedà – onward connections to higher settlements in the county, provided by the ATSA bus company at the top of Passeig de la Pau.

Another reason to come to Berga is for the town's **Festa de la Patum** at Corpus Christi, one of Catalunya's most famous festivals. For three days in June, huge figures of giants and dwarves process to hornpipe music along streets packed with red-hatted Catalans intent on a good time. A dragon attacks onlookers in the course of a symbolic battle between good and evil, firecrackers blazing from its mouth, while the climax comes on the Saturday night, with a dance performed by masked men covered in grass.

Not surprisingly, **accommodation** is impossible to find during the festival unless you've booked weeks in advance; at other times you should have few problems. There are eight officially licensed places to stay, most of them reasonably priced: try the small but well-appointed *Hotel Passasserres*, c/La Valldan (☎938 210 645; ❸), with sauna, gym and off-street parking; *Pensió Passeig*, Passeig de la Pau 12 (☎938 210 415; ❷), run by the electrical appliance store below; or the very central two-star *Hotel Queralt*, Plaça de la Creu 4 (☎938 210 611; ❹), whose en-suite rooms have all mod cons. There's also a **campsite**, out of town on the C16 (☎938 211 250); if you need assistance, the **Turisme** is just behind it (June–Sept daily 9am–1pm & 4–8 pm; Oct–May reduced hours; ☎938 221 500). The best **restaurant** in town is the *Sala* at Passeig de la Pau 27 (closed Sun dinner & Mon), where, unusually, vegetables feature prominently – count on about €33 for an *a la carta* meal, less for the *menú*. If your budget won't stretch that far, the *menjador* of the *Hostal Guiu*, carretera de Queralt, offers regional specialities.

## West of Berga: Sant Llorenç de Morunys

Just one **bus** a day serves the magnificent, scenic road skirting the southern rim of the Pyrenean foothills for 32 winding kilometres to Sant Llorenç de Morunys. There's little to stop for along this route other than the panoramic, eighteenth-century **Santuari de Queralt** (4km west of Berga), which houses a far older image of the Virgin and marks one end of the GR107 trail (see p.196).

The chief appeal of **SANT LLORENÇ DE MORUNYS** lies in its setting near the head of the Vall de Lord, but the ancient city walls enclosing a defensive huddle of houses, and steep, narrow streets leading to several portals, will reward a half-hour stroll. The eleventh-century monastic **church** has a beguilingly odd interior, one of its two chapels being overwhelmed by Baroque gilt work, the altar by a huge fifteenth-century retable. The cloisters, with their plain-capitalled columns, are currently closed for restoration.

Sant Llorenç has an adequate amount of **accommodation** (except perhaps during the ski season), though none is in the old quarter, or particularly inexpensive. If travelling by public transport you should plan on spending the night, as the daily bus from Berga arrives in the evening. The best options are the *Hostal La Catalana*, Plaça del Dr Ferran 1 (☎973 492 272; ❸), or the *Hostal Piteus* (☎973 492 340; ❷), opposite on the through road, which also has pricier penthouse apartments. There's a **campsite**, too, *Morunys* (☎973 492 213; July–Sept), 2km north of town, just off the side road to La Pedra hamlet. In the old walled town, *Can Peratà*, on c/Santa Isabel, at the corner of c/San Nicolau, is a decent independent **restaurant**.

## Onwards from Sant Llorenç

The views are startling in whichever direction you strike off from Sant Llorenç, though it's best to have a car or bike as there's no public transport (except south to the county town of Solsona). If you hitch, it's best not to accept partial rides, as traffic to the west especially is sparse.

To the **west** the road climbs 8km to the **Coll de Jou** (1560m), then briefly along a corniche before dropping through a tunnelled gorge to join the C14, 44km further along, in the Segre river valley near Organyà. Along this paved one-lane road there's little but farming hamlets, each individual house signposted. The only substantial place en route is **ALINYÀ**, tucked into a Shangri-La valley with a trio of hamlets overhead: La Vall de Mig, L'Alzina (the highest), and Llobera (the lowest), with a single local *casa de pagès*, *Lluïsa del Peretó* (☎973 370 181; ❷), which also offers **meals**.

To the **north** of Sant Llorenç looms the ski resort of **PORT DEL COMTE**, reached via the village of La Coma, 5km from Sant Llorenç near the sources of the Cardener, or by a more direct road that climbs from the Coll de Jou. There's not much for beginners here – most runs are red-rated – and most lifts are drag-type; despite a respectable top point of almost 2400m, the south and east orientation of most slopes means thin snow cover and an early seasonal closure.

**Accommodation** at the slopes is restricted to a luxury hotel and some apartments. More reasonable options are in **LA COMA**, 11km east and downhill, at the simple *Hostal Casa Nin* (☎973 492 354; ❷), in the village centre by the church, or the fancier *Hotel Fonts del Cardener* (☎973 492 377; ❹), also offering apartments, 1km north of the village on the highway. The latter has an excellent **restaurant** with an emphasis on mushrooms (in season) and local sausages.

The **GR7** heads north from Sant Llorenç via La Coma to the 1636-metre **Coll de Port**, then on to Tuixèn – a day's march – but the marked route is so often track or asphalt rather than path that you'd be best advised to arrange a ride along the paved road. At Tuixèn (see p.198) you're at the very edge of the Cadí park.

## North of Berga: Guardiola de Berguedà and Bagà

The towns along the Llobregat and Grèixer valleys **north of Berga** were once centres of a flourishing smuggling trade with Andorra, protected from law-enforcing pursuers by the Serra del Cadí. Nowadays the Túnel del Cadí cuts under that mountainous screen, allowing passage for the C16, and neither **Guardiola de Berguedà** nor **Bagà** retains any suggestion of illicit activity. Of the two, Bagà is the more enticing, with better accommodation options.

Strung out grimly along the old course of the C16 (a new bypass avoids the town), **GUARDIOLA DE BERGUEDÀ** is on the bus route from Berga to La Pobla de Lillet and just 1500m north of the turning for Saldes and Gòsol (see below). Its sole **accommodation** option, *Pensió Guardiola* (☎938 227 048; ❶), on the main street at the south end of town, also does meals. There's just one daily early-evening bus to Saldes and Gòsol – it doesn't enter town, but turns at the junction 1500m south.

**BAGÀ**, 5km further north and the second largest town in the county after Berga, has considerably more going for it in a tiny old quarter with an arcaded *plaça* and several **accommodation** options. First choice is *Hotel Fonda Ca L'Amagat* (☎938 244 032; ❸), a member of the Casa Fonda chain, in a quiet location in the heart of the old town. Otherwise, try *Hotel La Pineda*, c/Raval 50 (☎938 244 515; ❸), at the eastern end of the main shopping street. On the southeast edge of town, *Hostal Cal Batista* (☎938 244 126; ❷) occupies two unexciting modern buildings, but staying here does solve parking problems, and it's also a well-regarded **restaurant** serving local trout and rabbit *all-i-olli*. A **campsite**, the *Bastareny* (☎938 244 420), 1km west of town, caters mostly to caravans. Back in the centre, the **park information office** at c/La Vinya 1 (☎938 244 151) can provide **certified guides** who offer a range of activities (trekking, snowshoeing, winter mountaineering) depending on the season.

Continuing north through the five-kilometre **Túnel del Cadí** (which charges an exorbitant €8.55 per saloon car; no pedestrians or bicycles) brings you into the Cerdanya, for which see p.219. To the west of Bagà runs the GR107, "El Camí dels bons homes", which begins in France and is allegedly the route used by fleeing Cathars (see pp.246–248); locally it links Bagà with Gòsol (see below) via Gisclareny.

# The Serra del Cadí

The western part of the Cadí-Moixeró park – the karstic **Serra del Cadí** – offers equipped and experienced hikers three or four days' trekking through wild, lonely areas. Numerous tracks and paths cross the range, though the favourite excursion for most visitors remains the ascent of **Pedraforca**. As in other limestone massifs, finding fresh **water** can be problematic, and that – combined with the intense summer heat at this relatively low altitude – means that peak (non-winter) visitor seasons are May to June and September. The Cadí supports several fairly well-placed, seasonally staffed **refuges**, accessible from a number of foothill villages, which are in turn served poorly or not at all by bus, so you may have to walk or use other means of transport from the larger towns down-valley. Extended explorations of this region require possession of the Editorial Alpina 1:25,000 "Serra del Cadí-Pedraforca" and "Moixeró" **maps** and guide booklets.

From the Llobregat valley north of Berga there are two main ways west into the Cadí. **From Bagà**, a partly paved track follows the Riu Bastareny to the hamlet of Gisclareny. A much busier paved road begins just south of **Guardiola de Berguedà** and leads to Gòsol, via Saldes.

## From Bagà: via the Bastareny valley

The fourteen-kilometre vehicle route up the **Bastareny valley** begins at the riverside campsite on the west side of Bagà: from there the road crosses the river, passes through a tunnel, turns to track, then climbs steeply through dense forest to naked white cliffs on the south side of the **Coll de l'Escriga** (1360m). The views over the Saldes valley are superb, the river glinting far below, with range upon range of mountain unfurling south.

**GISCLARENY**, 3km beyond the pass, is little more than a handful of spread-out farms (total population of 31) and two **campsites**, one of which – *Cal Tesconet* (☎608 493 317 or 937 441 016), 1500m west of the hamlet centre – also operates a **refuge** (24 places). Beyond Gisclareny, the track continues through **Coll de la Balma** (1600m), where it divides left (southwest) in a sharp down-and-up to the village of Saldes (see below) via the lushly forested Gresolet valley, and right (west) in a more level if less interesting trajectory via El Collel. The former route takes about three hours on foot, the latter at least five. If for any reason Gisclareny doesn't suit, the **Gresolet** area also has **accommodation** at *Casi-Refugi del Gresolet* (1280m; ☎600 605 530, Ⓦwww.refugidelgresolet.com; 43 places).

The twisty road up the Bastareny valley can be negotiated on mountain bike or by 4WD; if on foot, you might do better to skip it for the direct Bagà–Gisclareny **path**, shown on the Editorial Alpina "Moixeró" map. From the *Cal Tesconet* refuge (where you'll need to confirm directions), a path drops down into the beeches and silver firs of Gresolet en route to Saldes, two hours shorter – assuming you don't lose the way – than the roundabout track option.

### Traverses of the Moixeró

By staying with the Bastareny valley-bottom track rather than going through the Bastareny tunnel, you'll reach a cluster of farms at **VEINAT DE L'HOSTALET**, from where a good trail leads up via the Gorge dels Empredats to the staffed FEEC *Refugi de Sant Jordi* (1640m; ☎919 239 860 or 933 322 381; 48 places; daily Easter & late June to early Sept), four hours from Bagà. Once over the Coll de Pendis (1800m), just above the refuge, you have to dodge – and briefly use – an unsightly 4WD track, but mostly it's marked path (part of the GR107) for a further four hours to Bor in the Segre valley, linked by paved road to Bellver de la Cerdanya. From the refuge you can also ridge-walk east along the Moixeró watershed all the way to Massella, a popular route in winter for cross-country skiers.

## From Guardiola: via the Saldes valley

The minor road from just south of **Guardiola to Saldes** and Gòsol is quite spectacular, with steep drops into the Riera de Saldes giving way to brilliant views of Pedraforca beyond the hamlet of Maçaners (Massanés). **Campsites** and accommodation spaced at intervals along the road attract sufficient cars – mostly Catalan vacationers – in summer almost to guarantee a lift. The *El Bergueda* campsite (☎938 227 432), 3km from the turning off the main road, is farmhouse-based; *Cal Susen* (☎938 258 103), 10.5km along just outside Maçaners, is fairly basic; the *Repòs del Pedraforca* (☎938 258 044), 13.5km from the turning, offers a pool and bungalows; while at the "Km 15" marker, south of the road, the isolated *Pensió Cal General* (☎938 258 054; ❷) makes a feasible base if you have your own vehicle.

### Saldes

**SALDES**, a small village 18km from Guardiola, set dramatically at the foot of Pedraforca, is an ideal starting point for explorations of the peak. Here you'll find two stores with staple provisions suitable for trekking, plus two inexpensive **inns** where reservations are usually mandatory: the *Pensió Carinyena* (☎938 258 025; ❷) near the church, and *Cal Manuel* (☎938 258 041; ❸), on Plaça Pedraforca (where cars park), serving **meals**. Better value, however, is *Cal Xic* (☎938 258 081; ❹ HB), a **casa de pagès** 1500m west of the village in Cardina hamlet, at the start of the road up towards Pedraforca. Although it's a modern, somewhat sterile building, the simple, en-suite rooms are heated, clean and cheerful, and asking for a *desayuno salado* gets you ham, sausages, cheese and a *porrón* to wash it all down with.

Beyond Saldes the scenery changes abruptly, first to the black-stained rocks of a lignite mine, then into speckled, deeply eroded gold-and-red rock, then back to lush, extensive pasture and forest. Mining activities have destroyed the old trail between Saldes and Gòsol, leaving walkers no alternative but to hitch or trudge along the road.

### Gòsol

The old stone village of **GÒSOL** (1430m), 10km beyond Saldes, is a more substantial place, spilling invitingly from a castellated hill. Pablo Picasso came here during the summer of 1906 and stayed several weeks in fairly primitive conditions, inspired by the striking countryside; one of the streets off the Plaça Major is named after him. Well established by the ninth century, the original village now lies in ruins, a fifteen-minute walk above the present one; the twelfth-century castle commands sweeping views of the valley, and the less spectacular rear flank of Pedraforca.

Gòsol makes a good alternative base to Saldes for explorations of the entire Cadí; the GR107 goes through here, linking with the saddle of El Collell to the north (see p.201). There are two **hostals**, both with decent attached restaurants: *Cal Francescó* (☎ & ℻973 370 075; ❷, or ❹ HB), on the little roundabout as you come into town, or the smaller central *Triuet*, Plaça Major 4 (☎973 370 072; ❷). Should these be full, there are also three *casas de pagès* nearby, two nearly adjacent on the same street. There's also a **campsite**, *Cadí de Gòsol* (☎973 370 134), southwest of the village, reached by dirt road from beside *Cal Francisco*.

#### West of Gòsol: Josa de Cadí and Tuixèn

To skirt the Cadí by vehicle, keep on the sparsely travelled dirt track – just manageable in an ordinary car – west to Josa de Cadí. If it's closed for works, you'll need to follow another more direct track (17km), of similar rough standard, to Tuixèn. This is signed as the "Camí de Molí" and begins near Gòsol's campsite. The Josa-bound track climbs in two long hairpins to the **Coll de Josa** (1625m), 5km from Gosòl, where there are superb views north, with the summit of Cadí ahead; from here the track drops through Scots pine to the Riu Josa.

**JOSA DE CADÍ**, 6km beyond the pass on a church-capped hill with one slope plunging to a ravine, is one of the most picturesquely set villages in Catalunya. Despite its remoteness it has become another second-home venue for urban Catalans – the traditional dwellings with windows outlined in chalky blue paint and ancient wooden doors are fast disappearing, replaced by modern conversions. As there's no bar or accommodation here, you'll have to proceed another 8km southwest to **TUIXÈN** (**TUIXENT**), more geared towards tourists than some of the other Cadí villages. Dominated by the hilltop Romanesque church of Sant Esteve with its square tower, it's an attractive and relatively lively place set at the edge of a gently sloping valley. Tuixèn has a **park information office** (☎973 370 132), just off the main square that doubles as a car park, though its opening hours are unpredictable. All **accommodation** stands on or near c/Coll, the short street linking the parking area with the nominal Plaça Major down the hill. The best choices are *Can Farratgetes*, at no. 7 (☎973 370 034; ❹ HB only), its dining room available to all; and the English-speaking *Pensió Can Custodi*, c/de la Riba 1, on the corner with Plaça Major (☎973 370 033; ❸ B&B or ❹ HB), boasting en-suite rooms and the best local **restaurant**, featuring sustaining four-course *menús*. The closest thing to a youth hostel in the Cadí is the *Alberg de Muntanya Cal Cortina* (☎973 370 224), opposite *Can Farratgetes*, with a lively ground-floor bar and a *menjador* upstairs; it also does all-inclusive snow-shoeing and cross-country skiing packages at the excellent **LA VANSA** resort a few kilometres south, criss-crossed with 35km of marked trails between 1660m and 2135m.

South of Tuixèn, a paved road rises a steep 8km to the Coll de Port with its bar-restaurant and the side road for La Vansa, continuing to Sant Llorenç de Morunys (30km). In the opposite direction another road threads through the villages of Cornellana (9km), Fórnols de Cadí (12km) and Adraén (19km), their houses largely renovated as summer homes. **FÓRNOLS** has the best facilities, with a **restaurant** in the village centre and, in the valley below, a **campsite**, *Molí de Fórnols* (☎973 370 021), next to which is a limited-capacity *casa de pagès* of the same name (❷). This northern route is nominally the GR7, which reaches La Seu d'Urgell after a good seven hours' walking. The path, often track or sliced up by the road, is not brilliant and you're better off driving, cycling or hitching this stretch from Tuixèn.

## Walks and climbs on Pedraforca

**Pedraforca** is for Spanish Catalonia what Canigou is to Roussillon: the logo and mascot of the region, and accordingly much loved. The name means "stone pitchfork", supposedly the Devil's, and indeed from afar the mountain does look like an upended goat's hoof. The distinctive two-pronged summit – **Pollegó Superior** (2498m) and **Pollegó Inferior** (2407m) – is divided by a gentler saddle, **l'Enforcadura** (2348m). In medieval times, local witches' covens met here, and it's still a popular place to camp on the eve of 24 June, *El Dia de Sant Joan*, when some personality from the Catalan "alternative" world generally organizes an after-dark, summer-solstice event either here or down in Saldes.

From behind *Cal Xic*, some 1500m west of Saldes, a partly paved road winds just under 5km to within fifteen minutes' walk of the well-signed, FEEC-owned **Refugi Lluís Estassen** (1668m; ☎608 315 312; 100 places). It offers

Alpine refuge, Pedraforca △

hot showers and evening meals, and is open all year, though the peak seasons are spring and autumn, especially at weekends, when big-wall climbers come to tackle the sheer north face of Pedraforca. The refuge sits just above the car park and **Mirador de Gresolet**, which looks down into the Gresolet valley.

### The ascent

Despite appearances, a **walking ascent** of the peak is strenuous but not technically difficult, and it's well documented by the Alpina Serra del Cadí-Pedraforca map. From the refuge you have a choice of a relatively dull but easy out-and-back walk from the east, or a more challenging and exciting loop over the mountain, beginning north of the summit. In either case a dawn start is advisable, or you'll be baked by the summer sun against the bare rock.

For the **simpler approach**, head south forty minutes from the refuge fountain along a narrow but well-trodden path through pine and box, to the base of the giant scree gully leading up to l'Enforcadura. Turning sharply west up this gully, guided by a few red-and-yellow paint splodges, brings you to the saddle in just under two hours from the refuge, after a very slippery, mostly trailless climb. At l'Enforcadura, you'll glimpse Gòsol to the west – and a gentler, distinct trail slithering up the **Tartera de Gòsol** (*tartera* means scree-gully in Catalan). From l'Enforcadura it's another 25 minutes north up a reasonable, obvious trail to the top of Pollegó Superior, with its assorted Catalan flags, "mailbox" for dedications and the expected views. Return is by the same route, for a total outing of just under five hours.

The **more difficult** circuit starts west from the *Refugi Lluís Estassen* along a trail shaded in the morning, then climbs sharply up to the **Collada de Verdet** (2244m; 2hr), where you meet another path coming up from Gòsol. From this pass you turn south, then east, creeping along the spine of Pedraforca towards Pollegó Superior; a rope and a partner are suggested if you suffer from vertigo, and it will soon be obvious why you can't use this section going downhill. You descend to l'Enforcadura and return to the refuge as in the first itinerary, after a six-hour-plus day.

## A south–north traverse of the Cadí

From the south, the peaks of the Cadí appear as a chain of rounded summits separated by shallow saddles, but seen from the north they form a wall of sheer, bare rock, dropping 500m in places. A one-to-two-day **traverse from south to north** takes in all aspects of the Cadí, coming down into the Cerdanya to intercept the Puigcerdà–La Seu d'Urgell road.

For traverses, Gòsol is a slightly better starting point than Saldes; from its centre, take the GR107, which soon dwindles to a path heading northeast through jagged rock teeth to the strategic pass known as **El Collell** (1845m; 2hr 15min), with fine views east over Gresolet and west towards Josa de Cadí. El Collell is also accessible in about an hour from *Refugi Lluís Estassen*, a rather unexciting if shady track walk. No motorized vehicles are allowed on the mountain slopes north of the pass, though they may continue east.

Stay with the track coming up from the refuge as it curls east towards Gisclareny for another kilometre, then take the zigzagging, obvious path on your left (north), towards the watershed of the Cadí. The ascent to the **Pas dels Gosolans** (2430m; 3hr from El Collell) is not easy and takes longer than expected, owing to the up-and-down, limestone-dell topography and the necessity of clearing the minor Serra Pedragosa.

At the pass – essentially a slight notch in the watershed, well used by smugglers in years past – you're near the roof of the Cadí, with awesome views west along the crest and north across the Segre valley. Plainly visible below, the *Refugi Cèsar Torras* at **Prat d'Aguiló** (2037m; ☎639 714 087 or 973 250 135; 30 places; staffed daily in summer, weekends most of the year) is an hour's descent along a steep path negotiating a convenient spur. From the refuge and its spring you should arrange a ride along the 15km of track north via Montellà to Martinet, on the main Puigcerdà–La Seu d'Urgell road, roughly halfway between the two towns.

A more advanced **ridge-walking** option veers west just before the Pas dels Gosolans; two conspicuous paths head to the top of the Cortils canyon, where you'll find a rare spring and a former shepherds' cottage to shelter. You should overnight here before completing a long day west cross-country along most of the Cadí summits, taking in **Puig de Canal Baridana** (2653m), the highest of the range. The main problem, however, with this traverse is that both of the nearest *canals* ("ravines" in local dialect) draining from the peak line are trailless and savagely steep – rated F+ by alpinists and choked by snow or scree according to season – making a descent to the north highly problematic.

## West of the Cadí: routes to Alt Urgell

Daily buses from Barcelona and Lleida, bound for La Seu d'Urgell, head into the *comarca* of **Alt Urgell** along the C14 road, which threads through the impressive gorge of Tresponts as it follows the Riu Segre upstream. Exciting as the scenery is, only one spot – **ORGANYÀ** – calls for a brief stop en route. A small, round building on the main road contains both the local

**tourist office** (summer Mon–Sat 10am–2pm & 6–9pm, Sun 10am–2pm; winter Mon–Sat 11am–2pm & 5–7pm, Sun 11am–2pm; ☎973 382 002) and what is possibly the oldest document in the Catalan language. Written in the twelfth century, the **Homilies d'Organyà** are annotations to some Latin sermons, discovered in a local presbytery at the beginning of the twentieth century and now displayed in back-lit glass cases. If you get stranded here – and Organyà isn't the most attractive town – there's just one **hostal** on the bend of the through road almost opposite, *La Cabana* (☎973 383 000; ❷), with a **restaurant**.

# La Seu d'Urgell and around

Even though it's the capital of Alt Urgell, **LA SEU D'URGELL** (pronounced "*Sodurjell*"), beside the Riu Segre 23km upstream from Organyà, is a rather sleepy place, overshadowed by the excesses of nearby Andorra. Nevertheless its medieval core, two or three modern hotels and decent canoeing facilities on the Segre (a legacy of the 1992 Olympics), make for an attractive halt.

## The Town

Named after the imposing cathedral (La Seu) at the end of c/Major, the town has always had a dual function as episcopal seat and commercial centre; there's a street farmers' market each Tuesday and Saturday, attracting vendors from throughout the *comarca*. By 820 this was already the seat of a bishopric – there's still an episcopal palace and active seminary here – with all the parishes of Andorra belonging to the counts of Urgell. But in the wake of the Moorish retreat this nobility headed south, and by the early twelfth century La Seu's bishops had acquired these possessions. Ambiguities of jurisdiction eventually led to a conflict between the bishops and the French nobility of Foix, settled in the 1278 Act of Paréatge, which allowed for joint control of Andorra.

The original cathedral and city, on the hill where Castellciutat (see below) now stands, was destroyed in the eighth century by Muslim invaders. The present **Cathedral** (June–Sept Mon–Sat 10am–1pm & 4–7pm, Sun 10am–1pm; Oct–May Mon–Fri noon–1pm, Sat & Sun 11am–1pm) was consecrated in 839, but completely rebuilt in 1175 and restored several times since. Nonetheless, it retains some graceful interior decoration and fine cloisters with droll capitals; admission to the latter is around the back of the church. The ticket (€2.50) also gets you into the adjacent eleventh-century chapel of Sant Miquel and the Museu Diocesano; to see only the cloister and chapel costs €1. The **Museu Diocesano** (same hours as cathedral) merits a visit for a brilliantly coloured tenth-century Mozarabic manuscript with miniatures, the *Beatus*, a commentary on the Apocalypse of Saint John.

Other than these few sights, time is most agreeably spent strolling the dark, cobbled and arcaded streets west of the cathedral, where you'll find many of La Seu's best bars and restaurants. A strong medieval feel is accentuated by the fine buildings lining c/dels Canonges (parallel to c/Major); the town's fourteenth-century stone corn measures still stand under the arcade on c/Major.

### Castellciutat

Comprehensive panoramas of the Segre valley can be enjoyed from the village of **CASTELLCIUTAT**, just 1km southwest of town, and its nearby ruined castle (now a luxury hotel). Follow c/Sant Ermengol across the river and up to the

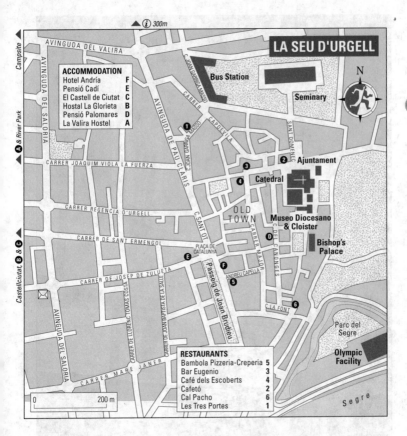

**ACCOMMODATION**

| | |
|---|---|
| Hotel Andría | F |
| Pensió Cadí | E |
| El Castell de Ciutat | C |
| Hostal La Glorieta | B |
| Pensió Palomares | D |
| La Valira Hostel | A |

**RESTAURANTS**

| | |
|---|---|
| Bambola Pizzeria-Creperia | 5 |
| Bar Eugenio | 3 |
| Café dels Escoberts | 4 |
| Cafetó | 2 |
| Cal Pacho | 6 |
| Les Tres Portes | 1 |

village, which glories in views that La Seu never gets. There's still some farming on the slopes below the tiny stone church and a couple of very comfortable accommodation options (see below), making the village a nice retreat from La Seu. You can vary your route to Castellciutat or back by following the walkways through the very pleasant, riverside **Valira** park, with its modern cloister made from pink stone. Salvador Dalí, Pablo Casals, Albert Einstein, Winston Churchill and Groucho Marx are among the famous twentieth-century characters (mainly men) whose heads decorate the capitals; one reproduces a fragment of Picasso's *Guernica* in 3D, alongside posturing Francoist figures.

## Practicalities

The **bus station** is on c/Joan Garriga Massó, just north of the old town; local services include the thrice-daily Alsina Graells buses to Puigcerdà and much more frequent La Hispano-Andorrana departures to Andorra (for details, see p.208). The **Turisme** (Mon–Sat 10am–2pm & 5–8pm; ☎973 351 511) is on avinguda de les Valls d'Andorra, the main road into town from the north. Drivers should use the handy free **parking** area signposted east of the cathedral.

Cathedral Cloister, La Seu d'Urgell △

## Accommodation

There's very little **budget accommodation** in La Seu, with *Pensió Palomares*, c/dels Canonges 38–40 (☎973 352 178; ❶), being about the only option: it's a warren of windowless chipboard closets rented out as rooms, tolerable only if you obtain one of the multi-bed front rooms with balcony. Otherwise there's *La Valira* **youth hostel** (☎973 353 897; closed Sept), at the western end of c/Joaquim Viola la Fuerza beyond the *petanca* court, by the Valira park. The colossal **campsite**, *En Valira* (☎973 351 035), is 300m northeast of the hostel, at avinguda del Valira 10. Of the mid-range **hotels**, the best placed is the *Andría*, Passeig Joan Brudieu 24 (☎973 350 300; ❺), an elegant if faded establishment, whose rooms offer all mod cons. Less attractive, but friendly and adequate, is the *Pensió Cadí* (☎973 350 150; ❹) at c/Josep de Zulueta, close to Plaça de Catalunya.

The only **luxury options** are in Castellciutat, with the exclusive spa-hotel *El Castell de Ciutat*, built into the castle walls (☎973 350 704; ❼), being top of the heap. The nearby *Hostal La Glorieta* is perched above the river on the road up to the village (☎973 351 045, ✆973 354 261, ✉glorietavalirasl@tiscali.es; ❻), with a pool and restaurant.

## Eating and drinking

Traditional **tapas bars** are dying out in La Seu's old town, with *Bar Eugenio* at c/Major 20 being the most reliable survivor, flanked by the sort of modern bar-cafés – *Café dels Escoberts* at no. 24, and *Cafetó* at no. 6 – that have displaced its rivals. For good-value **restaurant** meals, *Cal Pacho*, in a quiet corner on c/la Font (at the southern end of c/Major, then east), has a lunch *menú*, and *a la carta* dishes in the evening – cod-stuffed peppers and roast goat will set you back around €18, dessert and drink extra.

In the new town, *Les Tres Portes* at c/Joan Garriga Massó 7 (closed Tues & Wed) offers nouvelle *a la carta* fare (allow €28) in a chalet-style house with a patio. The *menjador* of the *Hotel Andria* also serves gourmet *a la carta* dishes at similar prices, featuring home-reared chicken and mushrooms in season. For snacks, there's the *Bambola Pizzeria-Creperia* at c/Andreu Capella 4, just east of the main *passeig*.

# West of La Seu: Castellbò and Sant Joan de l'Erm

Four kilometres southwest of La Seu a minor road climbs west along the River Solanell, between cornfields and then over successively more scrubby rises, to the village of **CASTELLBÒ**, 14km from La Seu. This was the seat of Arnau de Castellbó, whose marriage to Arnalda de Caboet was a key event in Andorran history (see overleaf). The only thing to see now is the thirteenth-century church of **Santa Maria**, an example of Romanesque-Gothic transitional style with pointed arches and Romanesque ironwork. The sole **accommodation** here is *Molí del Pau* (☎973 351 608), a four-room apartment (❹, or €150 Fri–Mon), though there's also a smallish **campsite**, *Buchaca* (☎973 352 155; May–Oct), with a shop, on the edge of the village.

Beyond Castellbò the road climbs to the *Refugi Pla de la Basseta* (☎973 298 015; 83 places; open all year) at **SANT JOAN DE L'ERM**, a superb **cross-country ski** resort with 150km of trails between 1600 and 2150m. Westward progress is by 4WD and mountain-bike tracks, which emerge just below the downhill ski centre of Port-Ainé (see p.266). Those without transport can hitch or take the twice-daily minibus along 45km of paved road west from

**ADRALL**, 7km south of La Seu, to Sort in the Noguera Pallaresa. Adrall itself has a clutch of **restaurants** on the through road, more country-style than anything in La Seu – *Can Pere* comes recommended for good food and an entertaining proprietor.

# Andorra

After seven hundred years of feudalism, modernity has finally forced itself upon the **PRINCIPALITY OF ANDORRA**, 450 square kilometres of mountainous land between France and Spain. A referendum held on March 14, 1993 (henceforth a big national holiday) produced an overwhelming vote in favour of a democratic constitution, replacing a system in effect since 1278, when the Spanish bishops of La Seu d'Urgell and the French counts of Foix settled a long-standing quarrel by granting Andorra semi-autonomous status under joint sovereignty. In 1185 the marriage of Arnalda d'Isarn de Caboet and Arnau de Castellbò united the Andorran possessions granted to the families by the bishops of La Seu. Their only daughter Ermensende later married Roger-Bernard II, count of Foix, who claimed sole rights to Andorra when Arnau died without male issue. The bishops of La Seu contested this, claiming that sovereignty reverted to them with the cessation of the male line of Castellbó. The consequent strife between the bishops and the house of Foix came to an end with the 1278 Act of Paréatge, through which La Seu d'Urgell and Foix became *co-seigneurs* of Andorra. (Incidentally, the Act also forbade the building of castles in Andorra, which explains their absence here.)

Despite a certain devolution of powers – the counts' sovereignty passed to the French king and later to the French president – the principality largely managed to maintain its independence over the centuries. The Spanish and French *co-seigneurs* appointed regents who took little interest in day-to-day life here. The country was instead run by the Consell General de les Valls (General Council of the Valleys), made up of representatives from Andorra's seven valley communes, who ensured that the principality remained well out of the European mainstream – it even managed to stay neutral during the Spanish Civil War and World War II.

During these conflicts, Andorra began its meteoric economic rise, as locals first smuggled goods from France into Spain during the Civil War and, a few years later, goods from Spain into German-occupied France. After World War II, this evolved into legitimate duty-free trade in alcohol, tobacco and electronics, coupled with the huge demand for winter skiing. Much of the principality became an unsightly drive-in megastore, with the main through-road clogged with French and Spanish visitors after cut-price hi-fi and electrical gear, mountain bikes, ski equipment, car parts and a tankful of discount petrol. Seasoned Spain-watcher John Hooper has called Andorra "a kind of cross between Shangri-La and Heathrow Duty-Free", while the Spanish daily broadsheet *El Pais* once dismissed it as a "high-altitude Kuwait".

Ironically, though, this tax-free status contained the seeds of Andorra's belated conversion to democracy. Although the inhabitants enjoyed one of Europe's

ANDORRA

highest standards of living, twelve million visitors a year began to put a strain on the country: infrastructure was sorely stretched, the valleys were increasingly blighted by speculators' building sites and the budget deficit grew alarmingly since little entrepreneurial wealth went into the public sector. Spanish entry to the EU in 1986 only exacerbated the situation, reducing the difference in price of imported goods between Spain and Andorra to the current twenty percent. However, the damage has long since been done; Andorra's commercial growth has pretty much killed off trade in the nearest French/Spanish towns.

The 1993 referendum was an attempt to come to terms with contemporary Europe's economic realities. Or rather, some of them, since none of the parties involved in the debate seriously proposed the introduction of direct taxation: there is still no income tax in Andorra, and barely any indirect tax either. Instead the strategy has been to transform Andorra into a kind of "offshore" banking centre, to rival the likes of Gibraltar, Liechtenstein and the Caymans, with the slight whiff of unsavouriness that attaches to such places.

Following the referendum, the state's first **constitutional election** was held in December 1993. Only the ten thousand native Andorrans were entitled to vote (out of a total population then of sixty thousand) and an eighty percent

## Andorra practicalities

### Getting there

**From Spain**, there are four daily direct buses from **Barcelona** (6am, 7am, 2.30pm & 7pm; 4hr 30min), and hourly (Mon–Sat 7am–8pm) services from **La Seu d'Urgell** on La Hispano Andorrana, taking forty minutes to reach the capital of Andorra la Vella, and a further five minutes to Escaldes. On Sundays, there are five departures between 7.45am and 6.30pm.

**From France**, daily buses co-run by Hispano Andorrana and Pujol Huguet leave **L'Hospitalet** at 7.35am and 7.45pm, arriving at Pas de la Casa 25 minutes later; from **Latour-de-Carol** there are departures at 10.45am and 1.15pm, taking 45 minutes to reach Pas de la Casa. During July and August, there is an additional service from **Ax-les-Thermes** at 4.20pm. From Pas de la Casa the onward bus journey to Andorra la Vella takes a further hour.

Even if you're **driving** you might consider leaving the car behind and taking the bus – in high season (summer or winter) the traffic is so bad that the bus isn't much slower, and parking in Andorra la Vella is an ordeal. Drivers are well advised to use the giant car parks provided in the largest towns, or kerbside meters – traffic police and tow-trucks are both very industrious. On the plus side, petrol is famously cheap – about twelve to fifteen percent less than in Spain, even greater savings compared to France – so fill up before leaving.

### Leaving Andorra

Buses back to La Seu d'Urgell leave from Plaça Guillemó in Andorra la Vella, parallel to the main road, though the service originates in Escaldes (Mon–Sat 14 daily between 8.05am and 9.05pm; Sun 5 daily between 8.20am and 7.20pm). To France, La Hispano-Andorrana and Pujol Huguet (☏376 821 372, ⓦwww.andorrabus.com) run two buses a day from Andorra la Vella to Pas de la Casa (1hr) at 5.45am and 5pm, with services at 7.30am and 10.30am to Latour-de-Carol. During July and August, there's an additional departure at 1.30pm to Ax-les-Thermes.

### Getting around

Internal **bus services** leave from Plaça Guillemó and are cheap and frequent on the

turnout gave Oscar Ribas Reig, outgoing head of the Consell General, the biggest share. His Agrupament Nacional Democratic took eight seats in the new 28-seat parliament – also dubbed the **Consell General** – and formed a coalition with other right-wing parties to usher in the new democratic era. Since then, Andorran citizens (those born here, or who have lived here over 20 years) can vote and join trade unions or political parties, while their government now has the right to run its own foreign policy and judicial system. The country has also been (since 1993) a full member of the United Nations and the Council of Europe.

Given all this, it's useful to remember that as recently as 1950 Andorra was all but cut off from the rest of the world – an archaic region which, romantically, happened also to be a separate country. There are still no planes or trains, but for many visitors that is the full extent of any attractive quaintness. For much of the year it can take an hour in bumper-to-bumper traffic to drive the few kilometres from La Seu d'Urgell to Andorra la Vella, the capital. Surprisingly, the main crop here, which you see on either side of the road and in every available space up to 1600m altitude, is tobacco. In the higher valleys, large-scale ski following routes (between about 7.30am and 9pm): Andorra la Vella–Sant Julià de Lòria; Andorra la Vella–Encamp–Canillo; and Andorra la Vella–La Massana–Ordino.

### Customs

French, Spanish and Andorran police may board buses looking for faces that don't fit, and ask luggage bays to be opened, as a check against illegal immigrants. Inspections of goods when entering are nonexistent, but on leaving, the Spanish police are very interested in just how many consumer durables all EU nationals have acquired – the French at Pas de la Casa seem much less active.

### Currency, mail and phones

Andorra never had its own money, and the euro is now its common **currency**. There's a shared **postal system**, with both a French and Spanish post office in Andorra la Vella and Canillo, for example. Andorra has its own phone system and **phone code** – ☏376 – applicable to the whole republic. A single **mobile** network, MobileAnd/STA, provides surprisingly good coverage even in the deepest valleys.

### Population and language

The **population** of Andorra is currently around sixty-five thousand, of which about twelve thousand are native Andorrans; the rest are mainly Portuguese, Spanish and French "guest workers" or permanent residents, with a smattering of other nationalities. Catalan is the official **language**, but Spanish and, to a slightly lesser extent, French are widely understood.

### Ski passes

**Skiing** is big business here. Since the late 1990s, about €80 million have been invested in state-of-the-art lift systems – something reflected in the **pass prices**, which now nearly equal those of the French Alps. You can reduce the dent in your wallet by purchasing a joint pass, valid for five out of six consecutive days at any of Andorra's resorts.

resorts have already monopolized the most attractive corners of the state, with further enlargements mooted.

But it's worth leaving the capital and main developments behind to see some of the scenery that attracted early visitors. Although the highest point (Alt de Coma Pedrosa on the western border) reaches just 2946m, there is still wilderness aplenty here. Scots pine is endemic, and the mountain pines *Pinus uncinata* or *Pinus mugo* thrive at altitudes up to 2200m, or even 2400m on south-facing slopes; moisture-craving silver fir grows on north-facing slopes between 1600 and 2000m. Wild boar, golden eagles and griffon vultures are native species, but bears aren't any longer – the last confirmed sighting was in 1978.

# Through Andorra by road

The main through road – jointly the CG1 from the Spanish frontier to

Andorra la Vella and the CG2 from the latter to the French border – runs 38km north, then east, through the main valley draining Andorra. The CG3 heads northwest to the dead-end, and therefore quieter, Valira del Nord.

# Andorra la Vella

With its stone church of **Sant Esteve**, fast-flowing river and appealing setting amidst crags and green slopes, the capital **ANDORRA LA VELLA** must have once been an attractive little town. The main street, avinguda Princep Benlloch/avinguda Meritxell, is now a seething mass of tourist restaurants (specializing in six-language menus), tacky bars and brightly lit shops crammed with everything from electricals, perfumes and watches to cars and kitchenware.

There's some respite in the narrow streets of the *barri antic* (old quarter), above the Riu Valira and south of the main street. Besides the church, its sole monument is the **Casa de la Vall** in c/de la Vall (free guided tours Mon–Sat 10am–1pm & 3–7pm, also Sun June–Oct 10am–2pm). Built in 1580 for the wealthy Busquet family, this solidly built stone house was purchased by the Consell General in 1702; it now houses the Sala de Sessions of Andorra's parliament and the chief courtroom (Tribunal de Corts). Between Sant Esteve and the town hall, Rambla Molines leads to the raised Plaça del Poble, laid out as a spacious pedestrian square with stone benches, sculptures, flower beds, fountains and a covered picnic place; there are cafés, toilets and telephones here too, and the tourist office (see below) is nearby. The church of **Santa Coloma**, over 1km west of the centre in the namesake suburb, merits a look for the oddity of its round tower – nearly all Romanesque churches have square ones.

## Practicalities

**Buses** leave passengers on avinguda Princep Benlloch, near the church of Sant Esteve. For drivers, there are about half a dozen open-air **car parks** scattered around town; the huge, covered Planta de la Creu car park, right under the Turisme, usually has space.

Andorra la Vella's **Turisme**, on c/Dr Vilanova (Mon–Sat 9am–1pm & 3–7pm, Sun 10am–1pm; ☎376 820 214), east of the old quarter, has lists of accommodation, restaurants and bus timetables, and also sells a good topographical map of Andorra. It's the main information post for the entire principality, though smaller booths keep similar hours in the more sizeable villages – in particular Ordino, Canillo, Escaldes-Engordanay and Encamp.

There are several reasonable places to **stay**: the friendly, basic *Hostal del Sol*, at Plaça Guillemó 3 (☎376 823 701; ❶); *Hotel Florida*, nearby at c/La Llacuna 15 (☎376 820 105; ❺), with comfortable, balconied rooms; and the *Hotel Racó d'en Joan*, in the old quarter at c/de la Vall 20 (☎376 820 811; ❷), which also has an attached restaurant.

You're probably better off, though, lingering just long enough for something to **eat**; intense competition fosters low prices. Best value in the *barri antic* is *Minim's* (*Casa Leon*), tucked away in the tiny Placeta de la Consorcia (closed Wed Oct–June), a small, stylish place with three French-cuisine *menús*. Another fairly central and characterful place is the basic and cheap *Restaurant Macary*, c/Mossèn Tremosa 6, just northeast of the Plaça Princep Benlloch, serving Spanish rather than Catalan dishes. The best place for a cake and a drink is the *Granja Pastisseria del Barri*, opposite the church of Sant Esteve.

The town has a fair bit of evening entertainment, including two **cinemas**

(Modern Triplex at avinguda Meritxell 26 and Principat at avinguda Meritxell 44) and *Àngel Blau*, a live jazz **club** in c/de la Borda.

## Escaldes-Engordany

Andorra la Vella merges seamlessly with **ESCALDES-ENGORDANY**, in effect a suburb, its pavements still choked with visitors keen to dunk themselves in the hot spa which gave the place its name. The ultramodern thermal baths of **Caldea**, with their landmark glass pyramid and indoor/oudoor lagoons, provide the latest in hydrotherapy and luxury beauty treatments (daily 10am–11pm, last admission 9pm); €26 for 3hr; ☎376 828 600, ⓦwww.caldea.ad). Cultural interest is provided by the work of Catalan sculptor Josep Viladomat i Maçanes (1899–1989), 250 of whose pieces are on display at the **Museu Viladomat** on c/Josep Viladomat (Mon–Fri 10am–1pm & 4–8pm, Sat 10am–1pm; €1.80); his stylistic affinities lie with Miquel Blay and Josep Clarà of Olot (see p.159).

The twelfth-century church of **Sant Miquel d'Engolasters**, one of the most attractive Romanesque churches in the area, stands on a plateau east of Escaldes. Its original frescoes, like those of many Andorran churches, have been appropriated by the Museu Nacional d'Art de Catalunya in Barcelona, and those inside the church are reproductions. The quickest way there is via the road climbing to the Engolasters reservoir, which passes the church after 4km. To make a day of it, follow the **GR7** from the main street in Escaldes for two hours to just beyond the hamlet of Ramio, where you take the marked footpath towards Encamp (see below) for another hour.

There's an abundance of **accommodation** in Escaldes, though most is aimed at the free-spending ski crowd. The few basic, budget options include *Residència Pont de la Tosca* at avinguda Miquel Mateu 6 (☎376 821 938; ❷); *Residència Astòria* at avinguda de les Escoles 16 (☎376 820 515; ❶); and the *Núria* at c/Santa Anna 11 (☎376 821 572; ❷). The most reasonable **eating** is found at *Restaurant Bon Profit*, avinguda Carlemany 53, with *a la carta* from €13, and *Pizzeria Roma*, on the same street at no. 95, offering Italian dishes from €22.

## The Valira del Nord

For a bit of peace and quiet you can head up the **Valira del Nord** (also known as Valira d'Ordino) from Escaldes, but you'll have to wait until you get past dreary La Massana, 7km northwest, for it to begin.

### Arinsal and Pal

The left-hand (northwesterly) CG4 road at La Massana climbs 4km to the popular, mushrooming and quite hideous ski-village of **ARINSAL**, served during winter by up to five daily buses from Andorra la Vella. Starting in Arinsal's centre, a bubble-lift gets you up to Point 1551 (as does the bus), where there's a chairlift to Point 1950m, base for most of the 23 runs. These tend to be short and sharp except for a number of wide blue pistes that can be taken in sequence for a long descent from near the resort's top point of 2560m, just this side of the Spanish border. Overall, in conjunction with Pal (see below), it's a good venue for beginners and weak intermediates.

Much of the **accommodation** is British-package-style, but you could always try one of the more modest establishments within a few paces of the telecabin: the basic *Hotel Poblado* (☎376 835 122, ⓔhospoblado@andornet.ad;

❷ ); *Hotel Comapedrosa* (☎ 376 737 950; ❸ ); and *Hotel Micolau* (☎ 376 835 052, Ⓔ hmicolau@arinsal.com; ❺ ). Owing to large numbers of self-catering apartments there are relatively few independent **restaurants** – *El Rusc* (pricey but tasty Basque cuisine in a pleasant environment) and *Jan* are about the size of it – but Arinsal is noted for its **nightlife**: *Rocky Mountain* (rock, jazz and blues), or *Surf* (rock and Irish) are both durable clubs going until 3am in ski season, while *Quo Vadis* is a popular video bar.

About 6km south of Arinsal, up yet another side valley, **PAL** is very attractive by Andorran standards, a stone-built village with its fine belfried Romanesque church of Sant Climent but unfortunately no short-term accommodation, though the single **restaurant**, *La Borda*, is excellent. Some 5km further you reach the **Pal ski centre**, 200m lower than Arinsal and thus heavily dependent on snow canons (Ⓦ www.palarinsal.com; joint lift pass and physical link with Arinsal). That said, the skiing is challenging enough with most runs red-rated, though several blue ones are found in the Setúria zone; the chairlift from Els Fontanells at 1810m gets you up to the 2358-metre summit of Pic de Cubil and the best pistes. The road carries on 24km out of Els Fontanells to the village of Alins in Spain (see p.267), via the 2300-metre Port de Cabús (passable only in summer) and the hamlet of Tor.

### Ordino to Llorts

Back at La Massana, the right-hand (northeasterly) CG3 road leads 3km on to **ORDINO** – a quiet, agreeable place where a handful of old stone edifices mingle with new chalets and apartment buildings. One of the seventeenth-century family mansions in the middle of the village, with splendid carved wood furniture and patterned pebble floors, is now open as the **Museu-Casa d'Areny-Plandolit** (guided tours July & Aug Tues–Sat 9am–9pm, Sun 10am–2pm; Sept–June Tues–Sat 9.30am–1.30pm & 3–6.30pm, Sun 10am–2pm; €2.40). The best place **to eat** is *Topic*, opposite the free central car park, a restaurant-café-pizzeria-bar which serves supper until 10.30pm, while *Hotel Santa Barbara* on the *plaça* (☎ 376 837 100, Ⓕ 376 837 092; ❹ ) is an agreeable place to **stay**. Just 2km beyond Ordino, there's a pleasant riverside campsite at **SORNÀS**, the *Borda d'Ansalonga* (☎ 376 850 374, Ⓕ 376 850 445; closed May & Oct). Just before the campsite is another late-serving **eatery**, *La Farga/Les Fargues*, a good-value grill where the *menú*, including grilled rabbit and house wine, costs under €20.

As you proceed up Valira del Nord proper, along the 8km or so north of Ordino, the landscape becomes more appealing, with fewer tower-cranes and high rises, though even here there are chalet developments and incongruously fancy restaurants overlooking disused pastures. Just over 2km north of Ordino at **LA CORTINADA**, you can visit the partly Romanesque church of **Sant Martí de la Cortinada** (July & Aug daily 10am–1pm & 3–7pm; free). In the original twelfth-century apse, frescoes uncovered in 1968 show scenes of hunting, harvesting, music-making and fantastic animals as well as the patron saint. During the sixteenth century, the church was curiously re-oriented northwards, with subsequent additions of a carillon, a women's gallery and convertible pews which could be inverted for social chats after services.

Reasonable **accommodation** en route includes the stone-clad *Hotel Cal Daina* in La Cortinada (☎ 376 850 988, Ⓦ www.hotelcaldaina.com; ❷–❸ ); well-worn but spacious rooms at *Hotel Arans* 500m beyond in **ARANS** hamlet, near the GR11 (☎ 376 850 111, hotelarans@andorra.ad; ❸ ); and the *Pensió Vilaró* (☎ 376 850 225; ❷ ), slightly isolated just below the village of **LLORTS**, some

5km from Ordino. Llorts also offers one of the better rural **restaurants** in Andorra, *L'Era del Jaume* (closed Sun pm; bookings recommended ☎376 850 667), by the church. It specializes in grills as well as vegetable-based dishes, such as mushroom *escalivada*; stick to the house wine and lunchtime *menú* if on a budget, otherwise you're looking at €27 a head *a la carta* for small portions.

### El Serrat and Ordino-Arcalis

At the head of the valley, 18km from Andorra la Vella (3 daily buses), stands **EL SERRAT**, astride the HRP and graced by tumbling waterfalls and horse-riding stables. This also has the last **accommodation** before the ski centre (see below): the *Hotel Bringué* (☎376 850 300, Ⓦwww.hotelbringue.com; ❹) and the good-value *Hotel Ahotels El Serrat* (☎376 735 735, Ⓔelserrat@ahotels.com; ❹ HB only), with a well-regarded restaurant.

From El Serrat the CG3 climbs steeply to the ski resort of **ORDINO-ARCALIS** (Ⓦwww.valordino.com), which, owing to high points of over 2600m and a chilly microclimate, retains the best-quality Andorran snow well into April. It's probably the most aesthetic place to ski in the principality, with a largely Spanish clientele, plus appealing views north over the Tristaina lakes (see below) and border ridge beyond. Ordino-Arcalis is good for intermediate-to-advanced skiers, with five well-placed chair-lifts to the top of mostly blue and red runs ranging from 1km to over 2km in length. The resort has two focuses: **La Coma** at road's end (2150m, 27km from Andorra la Vella), with a decent restaurant open for lunch year-round except May and November (allow €13 for self-service, €25 upstairs at the full-service), and **Les Hortells** at about 1940m. In summer, the base of the La Coma lift is the starting point for easy hikes north into the cirque containing the three attractive **Tristaina lakes**. Around and between them all, paths are waymarked in a variety of colour schemes; allow an hour and a half for a full circuit.

## The Valira del Orient

It's around 33km from Escaldes to the French border at Pas de la Casa along the **Valira del Orient**, a route served as far as Soldeu by hourly buses from the capital. You're unlikely to be tempted to get off anywhere for casual touring, although those with a car or with skiing in mind have several possibilities.

### Encamp and Meritxell

**ENCAMP**, 6km from Escaldes, is the first tolerable place to stay beyond Escaldes. In the centre, among old stone houses and concrete high-rises, the modern town hall stands out like a giant video screen. For a pleasant stroll, follow the riverside walkway north along the west bank to the unspoilt village of **Les Bons**, with its tiny twelfth-century Romanesque chapel of **Sant Romà** (daily July & Aug 10am–1pm & 3–7pm; free) with reproduction frescoes and a four-storey defensive tower standing nearby. There's a comfortable and quiet **hotel** in Encamp, *L'Orri de Rusca*, at avinguda Coprincep Episcopal 98 bis (☎376 832 320, Ⓕ376 832 678; ❸), though it has no restaurant; the only budget options are the balconied *Pensió Benito* at avinguda Coprincep Episcopal 51 (☎376 831 226; ❷) and the stone-clad *Residència Relax* at c/Bellavista 8–14 (☎376 834 777; ❷). An ambitious funicular, the **Funicamp**, transports skiers up to the runs of El Tarter (see below) from the centre.

Some 3km past Encamp, a small road climbs south to the **Santuari de Meritxell** (daily July & Aug 9am–9pm; rest of year daily except Tues 9.15am–1pm & 3–6pm), the ugly shrine designed by Barcelona Olympics architect Ricardo Bofill to replace a Romanesque building that burned down in 1972. The fire also destroyed the ancient carving of Our Lady of Meritxell, described by writer Nina Epton as having "the barbaric appeal of a recently converted Christian with her long astonished face and enormous black Byzantine eyes". A replica stands in her place. The local September 8 festival (Birth of the Virgin) is one of the four main national holidays, when most things in Andorra shut down.

## Canillo

**CANILLO** (1562m), beautifully situated 6km beyond Encamp, makes one of the best compromise bases in Andorra, lying along the main road (and bus route) between Andorra la Vella and the nearby ski resort of Soldeu–El Tarter, but far enough away to retain some dignity and character. On the eastern fringe of the town, the belfried Romanesque church of **Sant Joan de Caselles** (July & Aug daily 10am–1pm & 3–7pm; free) is largely eleventh-century, with a fifteenth-century porch; highlights include a 3D stucco *Crucifixion*, with personified Sun and Moon, plus lance-wielding Romans, and an exquisite sixteenth-century altarpiece, portraying the life and martyrdom of John the Evangelist. The big recreational attraction is the **Palau de Gel** (daily 10am–11pm, though some facilities close at 10pm), with an ice rink, indoor pool, gym, sauna and squash courts. Prices start at €5.50 for a gym-sauna session, up to €12.80 including skate rental for a session on the ice. When snow levels are sufficient, a bubble-lift rises to **El Forn**, an additional domain of the El Tarter ski centre (see below). Incidentally, the direct road to Ordino via the **Coll d'Ordino** is scenic but slow going – allow forty minutes by car for the 19km.

**Hotels** line the main through road, c/General, with two inexpensive choices: the rock-bottom, slightly shabby *Commerç* (☎376 851 020; ❷), which has excellent *table d'hôte* suppers; and an older, French-style, creaky-floored place just down the street, the *Canigó* (☎376 851 024; ❷), with big, en-suite rooms at the back, though their dinner is poor. Affordable comfort can be had at *Les Terres* on the uphill side of town (☎376 851 550, ℱ376 851 461; ❸). Among several local **campsites**, the tree-shaded *Camping Santa Creu* (☎376 851 462; mid-June to Sept) is recommended, near the centre on the south bank of the river. Of the few independent **restaurants** the best is *Molí del Peano* (closed mid-May to mid-June & mid-Oct to mid-Nov) where you can enjoy duck, goat's cheese salad, homemade mousse and a beer or two for about €24, or cheaper *menús* for €12.50–15.50.

### Soldeu-El Tarter

Development at **SOLDEU** village, at the head of the valley 19km from the capital, is surprisingly restrained, considering nearly half the ski pistes in Andorra are nearby. In fact Soldeu is the most attractive all-round ski resort in the principality, with English-speaking instruction widely available and plenty of nightlife for all ages.

Most of the **hotels** line the boulevard, and while the British package industry tends to get first crack at them, it's worth trying *Bruxelles* (☎376 851 010, ℱ376 852 099; closed Oct & Nov; ❷), or the chalet-like *Roc de Sant Miquel* (☎376 851 079, ℮hotelroc@andorra.ad; ❸). From **EL TARTER**, just below Soldeu, a narrow road heads north up the lovely **Vall d'Incles**. There's an inexpensive, beautifully set if basic **campsite**, *Camping Font de Ferosins* (☎376 851 341; mid-June to mid-Sept), at the far end of the valley, well placed for the HRP – allow an hour's walk from the main road.

**Restaurants** and **bars** not affiliated with Soldeu's hotels are limited and Brit-oriented. *Aspen* is the most popular pub, serving Tex-Mex food in season, while on the upper lane, *Fat Albert's Pub/Restaurant* and *Cort del Popaire* (closed May & Nov) are both good for local cuisine. It's worth noting that there have been persistent complaints about poor or even unhygienic food in some hotels and restaurants in the resort and all sources recommend that you stick to bottled water.

The joint **ski centre** of Soldeu-El Tarter (Ⓦwww.soldeu.ad) ranks as the most extensive in the principality, with ample skiing for all ability levels amongst its 52 runs – it's the best place in Andorra for beginners and is frequented mainly by British and Spanish families. Chair lifts are numerous, runs well planned and the views north to the French border ridge magnificent. You're pampered with an initial bubble-lift from the Soldeu rental centre to **Pla dels Espiolets** (2250m), the novice's area, focus of some very long green runs (Os, Duc, Gall de Bosc). Gall de Bosc in particular offers a tranquil descent – 8km if you take it all the way from 2560-metre Tossal de la Llosada – through the trees right back into the basement of the bubble-lift building. Intermediate and advanced skiers will find the **Pla Riba Excorxada** zone at 2100m (main restaurant) more suitable, with chair-lifts up to **Tosa dels Espiolets** (ca. 2400m) and **Cap de Clots** (2388m) giving access to more challenging red and blue runs. From Cap, two drag-lifts ascend **Tossal de la Llossada**, from where virtually all the runs are accessible, including the easterly Solana del Forn area, with its 2600-metre top point and blue/red runs served by two more chairlifts.

## Pas de la Casa

Over the **Port d'Envalira** (though a tunnel is under construction) the road descends steeply down bald hillsides draining towards France and the ghastly, high-rise border town of **PAS DE LA CASA** (Ⓦwww.pasgrau.com). A kind of Ibiza-on-Snow, Pas de la Casa attracts hordes of young Toulousains and Brits in search of "snow, sex and sangria", as the Ski Club of Great Britain puts it, plus duty-free goodies. After a hard night at the bars, the youth in question enjoy advanced skiing between points at 2600m and 2050m. Runs are linked to those of **Grau Roig** in the next valley: 29 lifts serve 53 runs (mostly red). There are also links to Soldeu-El Tarter, with which a centuries-old feud has finally been patched up to allow shuttling between the two using the Andorra-wide pass on the same day.

Among Pas de la Casa's predominantly pricey **hotels**, *Hotel Residència Casado*, close to the ski slopes at c/Catalunya 23 (☎376 855 219, Ⓔhotelcasado @andorra.ad; ❹), stands out as helpful, clean and good value. Cheaper options slightly further from the ski lifts include the faded but central *Hotel La Muntanya*, c/Catalunya 12 (☎376 855 318; ❷), and *Hotel El Chat*, c/La Solana (☎376 855 361; ❺ HB only), just uphill from the two main chairlifts.

# Through Andorra on foot

To cross Andorra on foot, the main routes are the **GR7**, which skirts the southeastern mountains; the **GR11**, which cuts more or less through the middle; and the **HRP**, which keeps to the northern fringes of the principality. Most of the alpine shelters en route are small, unattended and pretty basic. The best **maps** are the Catalan Mapa Excursionista no. 21 "Andorra-Cadí"; the Randonnées Pyrénéennes 1:50,000 no. 7 "Haute-Ariège-Andorre"; and the Editorial Alpina 1:40,000 "Andorra". The eastern half of Andorra is also shown on the French IGN 1:50,000 "Cerdagne-Capcir" sheet and the IGN 1:50,000 "Fontargente" map. The Andorran tourist authorities supply a useful, if schematic, free map showing the location and size of all the Andorran mountain refuges.

## Southwest from the Porteille Blanche: the GR7

Many walks into and around Andorra follow the old paths of the smugglers who carried heavy parcels of Andorran tobacco and other contraband across the border, often at night to avoid detection. Porta (see p.228 for access details), at the top of the Carol valley in France, was one of the great smuggling villages in the Pyrenees, on account of its link with Andorra along the Campcardos (Campquerdós) valley, now the route of the **GR7**.

A three-hour climb up the valley from Porta brings you to the **Porteille Blanche** (Portella Blanca; 2517m). The meeting of borders here allowed *paquetaires* in trouble to step quickly into France, Andorra or Spain according to who was pursuing them. From here, veer northwest towards **Pic Negre d'Envalira** (2825m), just south of the source of the Ariège; the summit has views into the valley of the Valira del Orient to the northwest. West of Pic Negre, the GR7 descends to the Grau Roig ski station, and finally to **BORDES D'EN VALIRA**, 3km north, where you'll find **accommodation** at the *Hotel Confort* (☎376 852 288; ❷) and the barracks-like *Hotel Peretol* (☎376 851 264; ⓔhotelperetolsoldeu@yahoo.com; ❷).

Next day you continue via the lake-spangled **Circ dels Pessons** to the **Clots (Ponds) de la Gargantillar**, where there is a large refuge at **Estany l'Illa**. The next one – a more logical choice for an overnight – is the tiny *Refugi del Riu dels Orris* at **Pla de l'Ingla**, at the head of the beautiful **Madriu** valley. Here you can continue on the GR7 ,along the valley to Escaldes, or cut through the **Coll de la Maïana** to the west, reaching the Andorra la Vella–La Seu d'Urgell road near Santa Coloma.

## West from the Ariège: the GR10/HRP

The routes **west** from the top of the Ariège into the Incles valley are beautiful approaches to the best Andorran landscape. From the train station at **Hospitalet-Près-l'Andorre**, the **HRP** variant initially climbs the Siscar valley, then switches to the Baldarques, going past the **Étang de Pedourrès** to the **Étang de Couart**, where it joins a path from Mérens-les-Vals.

Coming from **Mérens-les-Vals**, you can take the **GR10** southwest up the more inspiring **Mourgouillou valley**. After a little under two hours, the GR climbs west and to the right for a steepish climb of another ninety minutes to the modern, staffed *Refuge de Ruhle* (2185m; ☎05.61.65.65.01; 50 places; June–Sept). For Andorra, go straight on, past the **Étang de Comte**, through the defile and over the chaos of boulders to link up with the HRP at the Étang de Couart. From the lake, amid bleak, rocky terrain, the HRP cuts through the Port de Juclars between the double **Estanys de Juclar (Juclà)** – just inside Andorra, with an unstaffed *refugi* (2310m; 50 places) – and then down to the head of the **Vall d'Incles**, where you can stay overnight at the recommended campsite.

To avoid going down to Soldeu and the main road along the Valira del Orient, continue on the HRP to El Serrat, near the head of the Valira d'Ordino, and finally into France via the **Port de l'Abeille/Abella** or the **Port de Rat**. There are three ways to do this, more or less parallel to each other.

The easiest route is the most southerly, climbing west from the head of the Incles valley, dropping down into the head of the **Ransol valley** and up to the **Coll de la Mina**. A more difficult route passes the small *Refugi Cabana Sorda* (2295m; 20 places) on **Estany de Cabana Sorda**, then runs parallel to the base of the frontier peaks to Coll de la Mina. The hardest and wildest route goes north from Incles through the **Port de Fontargente** to the two Fontargente lakes, then curves west to re-enter Andorra through the **Port de Soulanet/Solaneta**.

Whichever one you choose, you can use the unstaffed **Refugi Sorteny** (1970m, 25 places) towards the end of the trek. From here it's a ten-minute walk to the top of the 4WD track 5km up from El Serrat. Fit walkers will manage the Incles–El Serrat hike in eight hours; the main caveat is to take plenty of water for this stretch, as springs are not always reliable.

## West from the Cerdanya: the GR11

From Spanish Cerdanya, the logical starting points are the villages of Meranges (see p.221) just south of the GR11, and Lles (see p.220), further west and well inside Lleida province. Either route occupies a fairly leisurely two days; the Meranges-based one is of better quality.

**From Meranges** a rough track leads up to the *Refugi de Malniu* (2200m; ☎938 257 104 or 616 855 535; 32 places; open sporadic weekends year-round, Easter break, late June to late Sept). The half-hour walk from the Malniu hut to its namesake lakes is the most popular family outing, but trekkers prefer the 2.5-hour jaunt northwest along the **GR11** to the FEEC-run *Refugi J Folch i Girona* (2400m; ☎934 120 777; same opening periods as Malniu hut), below the cluster of lakes in the Circ d'Engorgs. From the Engorgs area the route heads west into Lleida province, across the Llosa valley and past the crude **Cabana dels Esparvers**, entering Andorra and the Madriu valley via the **Port de Vallcivera** (2519m).

The less challenging route **from Lles** actually starts from the Cap del Rec cross-country ski area (see p.220), 6km north and above the village. From here, **GR11.10** heads west-northwest for 2hr 45min to the scenic lakes and FEEC-managed *Refugi Estanys de la Pera* (2333m; ☎973 293 108 or 679 410 492; 38 bunks, staffed late June to late Sept), though the surface en route is entirely 4WD track (closed to cars Nov–May).

From Aransa (see p.220) any car can reach the parking area and tarn at **Les Pollineres**, from where it's forty minutes on the poorly marked GR11.10 (now path) up to the refuge, a popular lunch stop for trippers doing this day hike. Beyond the lake the path slips north over the **Port de Perafita** (2587m), then down into the eponymous Andorran cirque, before rejoining the main GR11 near the bottom of the Madriu valley. The route then veers north-northeast, skimming above the Engolasters dam, to arrive at Encamp.

# West out of Andorra: the HRP and GR11

There are several trails **west out of Andorra** towards the Montcalm-Estats-massif on the Franco-Spanish border; the main ones are the HRP from near El Serrat, initially into France, and the easier GR11 from Encamp directly to Spain.

The classic option begins at the ski station of Ordino-Arcalis, from which a clear trail – part of the HRP – climbs the short distance to **Port de Rat** (2542m) on the French frontier. From there you drop sharply to the track running south from the Soulcem dam, then climb equally steeply on the far side to the **Port de Bouet** (2520m) on the Spanish border. Descend on the path west until you meet a track at the **Pla de Bouet/Boet** (camping possible); the *Refugi de Vall Ferrera* (see p.268) lies a few minutes' walk north. Even with a lift to the trailhead at Ordino-Arcalis, it's a challenging day of about seven walking hours; if you have to hoof it from El Serrat, add two hours more.

The **GR11** from Encamp passes through more developed areas and has its fair share of roller-coastering, but facilities en route mean you can do without a tent if you make arrangements in advance. Allow just under two hours from Encamp to reach the **Coll d'Ordino** (1979m) on the minor Canillo–Ordino road; a non-GR path about 1.5km south of Canillo also gives access to the pass. Descend west along the Segudet stream valley, then veer northwest away from Ordino through La Cortinada and Arans villages, nearly five hours into the day. You can use the recommended accommodation here (see p.212), or the *Mitxeu* **campsite** in nearby Llorts (☎376 324 557; July to mid-Sept) if you don't fancy the sharp ascent up to the **Coll de les Cases** (1964m) the same day, with a gentler drop to Arinsal – just over seven hours' walking from Encamp.

From Arinsal you climb west into the valley of **Aigües Juntes**, in the shadow of 2946-metre Alt de Coma Pedrosa, reaching after a couple of hours the *Refugi de Coma Pedrosa* (2265m; ☎376 327 955; June–Oct), Andorra's only staffed refuge, with sixty places, food and hot showers, five minutes' walk from the attractive Estany de les Truites. From the refuge you climb sharply northeast through the Circ de Coma Pedrosa, past Estany Negre, and then negotiate the **Port de Baiau** (2796m) where snow often remains until July. Once on the Spanish side, you face a steep, scree-laden descent to the lake and simple, unstaffed *Refugi Josep Maria Montfort* (approx. 2500m; 12 places) at the head of the **Baiau valley**, along which the GR11 bears northwest to intersect briefly with the HRP below the Port de Bouet, en route to the *Refugi de Vall Ferrera*.

# Cerdanya/Cerdagne

The fertile, gently rolling upland of the **Cerdanya** (Catalan) or **Cerdagne** (French) – about one-fifth of the way west along the Pyrenean watershed – has never quite been able to decide whether it is French or Spanish. Essentially the mountain-ringed basin of a prehistoric lake, once the largest in the Pyrenees, the region's lack of natural frontiers fostered an ambiguous identity. The 1659

Treaty of the Pyrenees imposed nominal allegiances, which arbitrarily divided a region that considered itself Catalan in language and culture. Yet development of overt French or Spanish national consciousness and a hardening of the notoriously porous frontier were a long time coming. The French and Spanish languages didn't acquire official status here until the early 1800s, following the French Revolution, a border war of 1793–95 and the Napoleonic campaigns. A formal boundary was marked for the first time only by the supplementary Treaty of Bayonne in 1866.

Given its former military significance, good **roads** have long converged on the region. Mont-Louis, on the eastern fringe of the French Cerdagne, had a road – now the **N116** – in from Villefranche-de-Conflent as early as the seventeenth century, while Napoleon ordered the construction of the original **N20** from the north, terminating at Bourg-Madame. Spanish development lagged behind, but during the 1950s the **N260** was sealed from La Seu d'Urgell, west of the Spanish Cerdanya, as was the **C16** from points south, both meeting at **Puigcerdà**, at the geographical centre of the region.

Because of its gentle terrain, the Cerdanya/Cerdagne hosted the first – and now last-surviving – trans-Pyrenean **rail line**, between Barcelona and Toulouse via Puigcerdà and Latour-de-Carol. Threatened abolition of service between Puigcerdà and Ripoll was only averted in 1985 by a massive Cerdan letter-writing campaign to Spanish Premier Felipe Gonzalez, coupled with half-serious threats by local authorities to request renegotiation of the Treaty of the Pyrenees and secession to France. Although still running, it has become the "misery line" of Catalunya, underfunded and poorly maintained, with journeys regularly taking nearer five hours than the scheduled three hours.

# The Cerdanya

The name **Cerdanya** refers to the Spanish portion of the upper Segre valley (a high plateau which continues on the French side as far as Mont-Louis). To its north mountains rise up to the Andorran frontier, their slopes dotted with tiny villages high above the Riu Segre, near the top of tributary streams. On the southern side, the Cadí mountains form an impressive barrier, with more sleepy settlements tucked away at the base of the range. The frontier at **Puigcerdà** is connected by 6km of road to anomalous **Llívia**, former capital of the region and now a Spanish enclave in French territory. The Cerdanya remains marginally more rural and traditional than the French side, though it was already a popular summer holiday area for wealthy Barcelonans in the nineteenth century. Since the early 1990s this trend has accelerated, with blocks of holiday flats mushrooming at the edge of, and dwarfing, nearly every village. Skiing, both downhill and cross-country, provides the main impetus for all this construction; but golf, horse-riding, and even gliding and hot-air ballooning are growing in popularity, the gently rolling countryside being ideal for such activities.

## Martinet – and cross-country skiing resorts

Climbing from La Seu along the N260, which follows the Riu Segre upstream, the first place of any significance is **MARTINET**. It is here that the track emerges from the refuge at Prat d'Aguilo, in the Cadí to the south, and whilst the Cadí's north face looks impregnable, it's not that difficult to reverse the hiking directions given on p.201. Martinet is mostly strung uninspiringly along the through road, c/El Segre, but if you need to **stay** choose between the *Hostal Miravet*, north of the highway at c/de les Arenes 2 (✆973 515 016; ❸), with views across a little stream, or *Cal Zet* (✆973 515 105; ❷), a *casa de pagès* in **MONTELLÀ** village, 3km south and uphill. Local **meal** options are limited – try the *Tupinet* in Montellà, on the central fountain-square.

## Lles and Cap del Rec

From the western edge of Martinet a narrow paved road climbs steeply north to two villages, each the gateway to their respective cross-country skiing centres. It's 9km, bearing right at the fork just below it, to the somewhat higgledy-piggledy village of **LLES** (often "Lles de Cerdanya"; 1471m), a good base for the popular ski centre 6km further on. The most reliable and comfortable **accommodation** and **eating** is at *Ca L'Abel* (✆973 515 048; ❸), with newish, tile-floored units – the upstairs ones are airy, with high ceilings – and a country-style restaurant adjacent. Otherwise, *Fonda Domingo*, near the top of the village (✆973 515 087; ❸), has good views and a pricey restaurant, while *Cal Rei* is the local *casa de pagès* (✆973 515 213, ✉cal.rei@lles.net; ❹).

Exposed to the full glare of the sun at 1942m, the **CAP DEL REC** cross-country ski resort at the road's end has 29km of marked runs. There's the *Refugi Eduard Jornet I Esteve* (✆973 293 049; 60 places) and a restaurant here, both of which remain open in summer, with a local horse-riding centre and rental mountain bikes providing the means for exploring the myriad local tracks.

## Aránsa

Returning to the fork 1.5km below Lles and then heading 4.5km northwest brings you to **ARÁNSA** (Aránser), much more of a piece architecturally than Lles, and set on a spur of land looking out at the Cadí's north wall. Near the village entrance you'll find the best **accommodation** and **eating** choices: *Hostal Restaurant Pas de la Pera* (✆973 515 001; ❸) and *Cal Sandic* (✆973 515 193, ⓦwww.agroturisme.org/sandic.htm; ❺ HB only), whose restaurant is open to all. The road continues to Les Pollineres trailhead for the Estanys de la Pera, via the Aránsa **cross-country ski station**, 6km along, with 32km of marked pistes between 1850m and 2150m. At the ski station *El Fornell* **restaurant** (lunch only in ski season, late July & Aug), run by a kind family, serves grill *menús* only – allow €15, plus drink.

# Bellver de Cerdanya

Eight kilometres east from Martinet, **BELLVER DE CERDANYA** sits on the bank of the trout-laden Segre, 18km west of Puigcerdà, and on the GR107. Its semi-fortified hilltop old town, with an arcaded Plaça Major and a massive church at the summit, merits a stop, despite the dominating telecom antenna. A short stroll south of town, the Romanesque church of **Santa María de Talló** is a plain twelfth-century building, with a few decorative touches in the nave and apse, and a wooden statue of the Virgin as old as the building itself.

The **Turisme** occupies an old chapel at Plaça Sant Roc 9 (Easter, Christmas, June 15–Sept 15 Mon–Sat 11am–1pm & 6–8pm, Sun 11am–1pm; ✆973 510 229), while the best **accommodation** by far is *Fonda Biayna*, c/Sant Roc 11 (✆973 510 475, ✉fondabiayna@ctv.es; ❹ B&B), an atmospheric, rambling old mansion serving as an inn since 1880, and now a Casa Fonda affiliate. The listing, wooden-floored double rooms all have small bathrooms and antique furnishings. The downstairs *menjador* with its swirling fans lays on an excellent supper for €14 (including house wine); specials such as wild mushrooms (May to early July) attract supplements. The adjacent lively bar has a summer terrace which hosts Saturday-night entertainment, such as films and live music. On the outskirts of Bellver, there's a riverside **campsite**, *Solana del Segre* (☎973 510 310), with pleasant plots for tents.

### Meranges and Guils Fontanera

From Ger, about halfway between Bellver and Puigcerdà, a narrow road leads 10km northwest past hayfields, hamlets and copses of silver birch and maple to **MERANGES** (1450m). Once a crucial outpost in the smuggling trade, the village is now too remote for the second-home complexes that ring neighbouring villages and remains an idyllic spot below a pair of lake-filled basins at the foot of **Pic Farinós** and **Puig Pedrós**. The only **accommodation** here is prestigious *Hotel Can Borrell* (☎972 880 033, ⦿www.canborrell.com; ❼), a converted farmhouse with rustic decor and a well-regarded restaurant. The alternative for **dining** is the basic, inexpensive *Can Joan* in the village centre.

Just before Puigcerdà, another minor road heads northwest to **GUILS DE CERDANYA**, a small village too close to the big town to have many tourist facilities of its own. It is, however, home to the newest and most ambitious **cross-country ski resort** in the Cerdanya, **Guils Fontanera**, with 45km of marked pistes.

## Puigcerdà

Although founded by King Alfonso I of Aragón in 1177 as a new capital for then-unified Cerdanya, **PUIGCERDÀ** (pronounced "Poocherda") retains no compelling medieval monuments, partly owing to heavy bombing during the Civil War. The church of Santa Maria was one of the casualties, but its fortymetre-high **bell-tower** still stands in the namesake *plaça*. The east end of town, down the pleasant, tree-lined Passeig Deu d'Abril, escaped more lightly; here, you can see medieval murals in the gloomy parish church of **Sant Domènec**. Dwelling morbidly on the saint's martyrdom, surviving fragments show Dominic's head being cloven in two by a sabre – he's already been run through by a sword.

The town's greatest attraction is its atmosphere: if you've just arrived from France, the streets and squares, with busy pavement cafés and well-stocked shops, present a marked contrast to moribund Bourg-Madame. Allow at least enough time for a meal or an evening in a bar, though Puigcerdà does not offer much value in budget accommodation. French day-trippers certainly approach it this way, crowding out the bars and eateries during summer. Enjoyable outdoor cafés line the merged *plaças* of Santa María and dels Herois; between drinks, you can explore the old quarter between Plaça de l'Ajuntament and Passeig Deu d'Abril, or amble up to a small recreational lake, five minutes' walk north.

### Arrival and information

Puigcerdà is on the rail line from Barcelona to Latour-de-Carol, a mere seven minutes away; from Latour, three trains daily have instant connections for Toulouse (4hr). From Puigcerdà's **train station** (outside which **buses** also stop) in Plaça de l'Estació, steep steps lead up to Plaça de l'Ajuntament in the

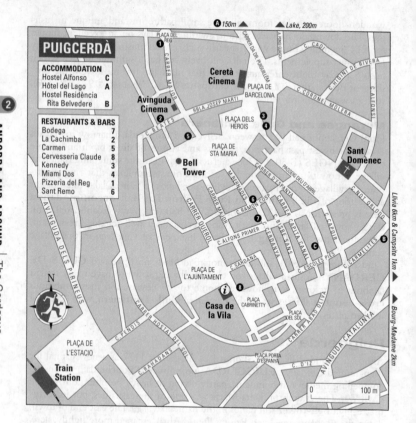

**PUIGCERDÀ**

**ACCOMMODATION**
| | |
|---|---|
| Hostel Alfonso | C |
| Hôtel del Lago | A |
| Hostel Residència | |
| Rita Belvedere | B |

**RESTAURANTS & BARS**
| | |
|---|---|
| Bodega | 7 |
| La Cachimba | 2 |
| Carmen | 5 |
| Cervesseria Claude | 8 |
| Kennedy | 3 |
| Miami Dos | 4 |
| Pizzeria del Reg | 1 |
| Sant Remo | 6 |

heart of town, with views west over the Cerdanya. At the top of the steps, to the right, stands the **Casa de la Vila**, a replacement for the Gothic original destroyed in the Civil War, with the central **Turisme** alongside at c/Querol 1 (June to mid-Sept daily 9am–2pm & 3–8pm; mid-Sept to May Mon 9am–1pm, Tues–Sat 10am–1pm & 4–7pm; ☎972 880 542). However, you're more or less expected to use the giant **regional branch** (June to mid-Sept daily 9am–2pm & 3–8pm; mid-Sept to May Mon–Sat 9am–1pm & 4–7pm, Sun 10am–2pm; ☎972 140 665), 1500m southwest of town near the *Puigcerdà Park Hotel*, stocked with leaflets and more convenient with your own transport. From the centre of Puigcerdà it's 2km to the adjacent small town of Bourg-Madame (see p.228) in France.

## Accommodation

There's not a great choice of **accommodation** in town, and you should consider various alternatives in the villages around Puigcerdà (see opposite). Of the less expensive options, the central, friendly *Hostal Alfonso*, c/d'Espanya 5 (☎972 880 246; ❸), with decent upper-storey rooms, is worth a try, as is the French-run *Hostal Residència Rita Belvedere* at c/Carmelites 6–8 (☎972 880 356), offering excellent views and a choice of old-style (❷) or more expensive modern rooms (❸), though it's only open daily from late July to late Sept and on holidays and weekends the rest of the year. For a splurge, there's none better than the popular *Hotel del Lago*, c/Dr Puiguillém 7 (☎972 881 000, ⓦwww.hotel-lago.com; ❻), with a breakfast gazebo in the garden, a fair-sized pool and parking.

None of the three local caravan-dominated **campsites** is really appropriate for tenters; the most convenient is the hedge-fringed *Stel* (☎972 882 361), with bungalows for rent, 2km out of Puigcerdà on the road to Llívia, just before you cross into France.

### Eating, drinking and entertainment

High prices and stodgy menus abound in Puigcerdà, but there are still a few reasonable places to **eat**. At the budget end, *Sant Remo* at c/Ramon Cosp 9 is a straightforward *menjador* above a bar with *menús* at €7.50–9.50; the *Carmen* on Plaça de Santa Maria, with an upstairs *menjador*, is similar. Slightly more upmarket is *La Cachimba* at c/Beates 12, which serves pizzas as well, though for the best wood-oven-baked pizzas head for *Pizzeria del Reg*, on Plaça del Reg, at the top end of c/Major – allow €12 per person.

The **bars** with outdoor seating on Plaça dels Herois and the adjoining Plaça de Santa Maria – in particular the adjacent *Kennedy* and *Miami Dos* – are usually busy and good for a drink and *tapas*, though not full meals. *Cervesseria Claude* on the arcaded Plaça Cabrinetty serves international beers, and you can sit indoors or out, tippling your way around the world's brews. The atmospheric *Bodega*, at c/Miguel Bernades 4, has a clientele of locals and French tourists, with wine served from the barrels that line the walls.

Finally, Puigcerdà has the only **cinemas** in the Cerdanya: the Avinguda at c/Major 53, and the Ceretà, in the old casino on Plaça Barcelona, also the venue for a late-July **music festival**.

## Villages around Puigcerdà

You'll find better-value accommodation, and often food, in the hamlets and villages south of Puigcerdà, home to some of the more distinguished members of Girona's *turisme rural* scheme. Top billing goes to the superb *Residència Sant Marc*, 1.5km south of town on the road to **Les Pereres** hamlet (☎972 880 007 or 936 322 260; ❻ HB only; advance booking recommended in summer). Accommodation at this 150-hectare stud farm is based in a 1913 belle époque mansion with huge, elegant common areas and old-fashioned but unmusty units (including an attic family suite). It's decorated with antique furniture, wood floors and artistic tiles in the large bathrooms. Equestrian holidays are also offered in the centre of **AGE**, 2km east of Les Pereres and 3km southeast of Puigcerdà, at *Cal Marrufès/Hipica Age* (☎972 141 174, ⓦwww.calmarrufes.com; ❹ B&B; also family quads), a tasteful restoration of an old stone-built farm.

Sleepy **URTX**, 5km south of Puigcerdà, has yet to be disfigured by too many new chalet-apartments and is home to *Cal Mateu* (☎972 890 495; ❸), a working dairy farm by the church, offering good-value en-suite rooms with full-sized bathtubs. Its decor is bland modern rather than rustic, but there are self-catering facilities next to the common-room-with-fireplace, and the managing couple are disarmingly friendly. Urtx proper hasn't any other facilities; the closest decent **food** is 1500m downhill inside the semi-converted Queixans RENFE station, where *L'Estació* (closed Wed) offers two lunch *menús* as well as *a la carta* at €15–19 per head. The portions of *escalibada* and *botifarra amb mongetes* aren't huge, but the ingredients are fresh and the presentation exemplary.

Finally, in resolutely rural **SANAVASTRE**, accessible *only* from the Alp–Prats road (not from the main highway to La Seu), *Can Simó* (☎972 890 240; all year; ❸) is an engagingly rustic dairy-farm with en-suite rooms, and meals provided on request: it's at the edge of the village, tucked in a hollow just beyond the airstrip runway. Nearby, in **PRATS** village, *Cal Furné* (☎972 890 565; ❸) sits at the narrowest point of the through road, with a wood-beamed *menjador* and secure parking.

## Llívia

The Spanish town of **LLÍVIA**, 6km from Puigcerdà but totally surrounded by French territory, is a curious place indeed. French history books claim that Llívia's anomalous status resulted from an oversight. According to the traditional version of events, in the exchanges that followed the Treaty of the Pyrenees, the French delegates insisted on possession of 33 Cerdan villages between the Ariège and newly acquired Roussillon. The Spanish agreed, then pointed out that Llívia was technically a town not a village, and thus excluded under the terms of the handover. Llívia had in fact been capital of the valley until the foundation of Puigcerdà, and Spain had every intention of retaining it at the negotiations, which were held in Llívia itself.

The Romans were perhaps the first to recognize the strategic value of their settlement here, named Julia Livia. Its castle was destroyed on the orders of Louis XI in 1479, but there's still a strong medieval feel to the town centre, not least in the fifteenth-century fortified **church** (June–Sept daily 10am–1pm & 3–7pm; Oct–May Tues–Sun 10am–1pm & 3–6pm), which features a curious, nail-reinforced door and carved stone floor. Inside is a beautiful gilt altarpiece, delicately carved and painted with cherubs and scenes from the Nativity, and (in the third side chapel on the north) a polychrome wood triptych showing Christ between John the Baptist and Saint Peter, a fine example of the Romanesque-Gothic transitional style. On August weekends, a popular music festival takes place in and around the church.

Opposite the church, the unusual **Museu Municipal** (April–June Tues–Sat 10am–6pm, Sun 10am–2pm; July & Aug daily 10am–7pm; Sept Tues–Sun 10am–7pm; Oct–March Tues–Sat 10am–4.30pm, Sun 10am–2pm; €2) contains the oldest pharmacy in Europe, functioning in Llívia from 1594 until 1918. Displays emphasize apothecarial pots and hand-painted boxes of herbs, as well as local Bronze Age relics, old maps and even the eighteenth-century bell mechanism from the church. The entry ticket may also get you into the fifteenth-century **Tour Bernat de So**, adjoining the church.

### Practicalities

There are several **buses** daily from Puigcerdà (the Alsina Graells coach stops in front of the train station and in Plaça Barcelona), but the ninety-minute walk isn't too strenuous: bear left at the junction 1km outside town, just before the border at Bourg-Madame, keeping to the main road. From French territory, the turn-off to Llívia is completely unmarked; your only clue is the highway overpass above the *Train Jaune* tracks.

Most visitors just stay long enough for a **meal** – not a bad idea given the limited choice of accommodation. In the main Plaça Major at no. 1, there's the attractive *Can* Ventura restaurant (closed Mon eve & Tues), with flower-filled balconies, serving Cerdanyan cuisine made from the freshest ingredients for an extravagant €30 (no *menú*). *Cal Cofa*, nearby at c/Frederic Bernades 1, is a cheaper (€24) alternative for country fare. Further up the slope near the church, the good-value *Can Francesc* at c/dels Forns 7–15 has courtyard dining in summer and a three-course €11 *menú* including such delights as *trinxat*, trout and dessert.

The few places to **stay** tend to fill quickly. Of the two hotels on the busy main road the better equipped is the *Llívia* (☎972 146 000, ✉llivia@grn.es; ⑤), with a pool, tennis courts and private parking

# The Cerdagne

The **Cerdagne** is the sunniest area in the French Pyrenees; the ripe colours of summer grain and hay on its treeless hills reinforce this impression. It is bracketed on the west by **Bourg-Madame**, opposite Spanish Puigcerdà, and on the east by Mont-Louis at the head of the Têt valley, the plateau's usual point of entry from the French side. To the southeast rises **Puigmal**, one source of the River Sègre, while it's flanked to the northwest by the mountains of the **Carlit Massif**, home to the overrated ski station of **Font-Romeu** as well as some excellent walks.

The *Train Jaune* (see p.105) continues from Mont-Louis as far as **Latour-de-Carol**, from where regular **train** services run north into the Ariège under the **Col de Puymorens**. The **road** that snaked over the pass until 1995 now runs through the Tunnel de Puymorens.

## Font-Romeu and around

Sprawling at the foot of Roc de la Calme, at the southeast corner of the Carlit Massif, **FONT-ROMEU** (*Train Jaune* station: Odeillo/Via) is one of the most famous ski resorts in the Pyrenees. Its reputation represents a triumph of marketing over reality, since the vaunted *Cité Préolympique* was just an altitude training centre for the 1968 Mexico City Olympics. Its high point is a mere 2213m, the maximum vertical descent only 500m. Adjacent and barely higher is the ugly, purpose-built resort of Superbolquère, better known as **PYRÉNÉES 2000**. The two linked resorts have forty pistes between them, but drag-lifts predominate; the vast majority of the runs are for beginners, and only a handful are north-facing, which is why it has 460 snow-canons (the most in Europe). It does, however, have 90km of marked cross-country skiing trails – the second biggest extent in the French Pyrenees. In summer Font-Romeu keeps its holidaymakers occupied with an Olympic swimming pool and the usual assortment of sporting facilities; year round there's plenty of nightlife.

### The Ermitage

*Font-Romeu* is Catalan for "pilgrim's spring", named after a legendary cowherd who uncovered a buried figure of the Virgin and a source of clear water, having been led to the spot by a bull. The image of the Virgin has been installed in the barracks-like **Ermitage**, off av Emmanuel Brousse (daily early July to early Sept 10am–noon & 3–6pm), a seventeenth-century enlargement of the original fourteenth-century shrine. The Catalan artist Josep Sunyer sculpted the retable in 1707, and five years later created a sumptuous "bedroom" for the Virgin, known as the *camaril*.

On September 8 the Virgin is taken down the hill to **ODEILLO**, returning on Trinity Sunday. Odeillo has the only other "sight" in the immediate area – the **Four Solaire**, or solar power station (daily 10am–12.30pm & 2–6pm, July

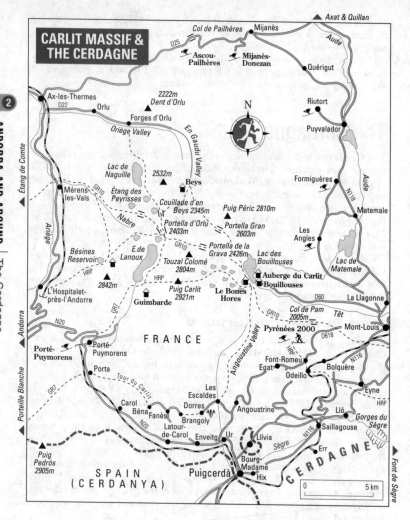

CARLIT MASSIF & THE CERDAGNE

& Aug 10am–7.30pm; €5). It no longer functions as a generator, but rather as a museum and PR exercise, with full-moon-powered demonstrations on summer evenings.

## Practicalities

From the **train station** it's a fairly steep two-kilometre walk north to Font-Romeu, passing Odeillo about halfway. **Accommodation** in Font-Romeu tends to be expensive, but with eighteen thousand beds you should find something. For a list of holiday apartments ask at the **tourist office**, near the top of avenue Emmanuel Brousse (daily 9am–12.30pm & 2–6.30pm; ☎04.68.30.68.30, ⊛www.font-romeu.fr). The best budget option is the **gîte**

*Les Cariolettes*, 1 rue de Fontanilles (☏04.68.30.25.48, ⓦwww.gite-cariolettes .com; ❶), a renovated old house offering doubles, triples and quads, as well as a common room and barbecue patio; staff will also prepare picnic lunches. The cheapest **hotel** is *L'Oustalet*, in rue des Viollettes (☏04.68.30.11.32, Ⓕ04.68.30.31.89; ❸), with an outdoor swimming pool, closely followed by *Le Regina*, on avenue Emmanuel Brousse (☏04.68.30.03.81, ehotel.regina@ laposte.net; ❸). West of town at 5 rue des Écureuils, *Hôtel Y Sem Bé* (☏04.68.30.00.54, ⓦwww.hotel-ysembe.com; ❹) enjoys views over much of the Cerdagne.

Up in **BOLQUÈRE** – a bit handier for those on a GR10 traverse, if characterless – there are a couple of good-value **hotels**, in particular *L'Ancienne Auberge* (☏04.68.30.09/51; ❸), and a *gîte d'étape* on avenue des Erables: *Les Ramiers* (☏04.68.30.37.48, Ⓔles.ramiers@wanadoo.fr; 37 places), with a range of doubles, triples and quads.

For **food**, *La Chaumière* at 96 avenue Emmanuel Brousse (☏04.68.30.04.40; closed Sun & Mon, plus June & July) is an excellent bet with regional-cuisine *menús* from €14.

## Southwest to Latour-de-Carol

Beyond Odeillo, the *Train Jaune* winds its way across the open plain to depopulated **SAILLAGOUSE** (1302m), where **accommodation** options include a youth hostel (☏04.68.04.71.69), the *Hôtel Planes*, place de Cerdagne (☏04.68.04.72.08, ⓦwww.planotel.fr; closed mid-Oct to mid–Dec; ❸), also with a fancier annexe on rue du Torrent (❹).

From Saillagouse you can drive or pedal southeast through the **Gorges du Sègre** to the picturesque village of **LLÓ**, home of the *Auberge Atalaya* (☏04.68.04.70.04, Ⓔatalaya@francimel.com; closed Nov–Easter except Christmas; ❼), which serves high-quality **meals**, plus a *gîte d'étape*, *Cal Miquel* (☏04.68.04.19.68; 20 places). Beyond Lló a dirt track climbs through the gorge to the well-placed but basic and unstaffed *Cabane de la Culasse*, after which the track becomes a path to the **Col de Finestrelles** (2604m), above Núria in Spanish Catalonia (see p.176). From the *col* there are three attractive choices: you can drop back southwest to the **Font de Sègre**, 400m below the 2795-metre summit of **Pic de Sègre** (it's a day from Lló to the *font* and back); carry on into Spain; or pick up the **HRP** along the crests.

### Err and Puigmal 2600

The next *Train Jaune* stop serves **ERR**, a tiny village at the foot of heavily wooded Puigmal – and another place with a "found Virgin" legend. The twelfth-century effigy is housed in the **Chapelle de la Vierge**, considerably enlarged in the eighteenth century. Separated from it by the cemetery is the church of **Saint-Genis**, which an almost indecipherable inscription says is the burial place of Bishop Radulf of Urgell, a close relative of Guifré el Pilos of Ripoll. The only accommodation at Err is its *gîte d'étape* (☏04.68.04.74.20; 17 places; dorms only).

Some 7km southeast of Err, on the north slopes of 2913-metre Puigmal, lies **PUIGMAL 2600**, one of the Cerdagne's smaller ski stations. There are 25 runs, the majority red and black, ending most of their descents scenically amongst the pines. There are few snow canons, so check conditions before setting out.

## Bourg-Madame and Hix

Skirting Llívia, the *Train Jaune* reaches the border at **BOURG-MADAME**, which in 1815 changed its name from Les Guinguettes d'Hix to honour the wife of the duc d'Angoulême, bearer of the title "Madame Royale". It became an important trading town over the course of the eighteenth century, as both a smuggler's entrepôt and legitimate competitor to Puigcerdà. But it hasn't amounted to much since then, and insofar as EU unification negates national borders, Bourg-Madame is visibly depressed and fading, its vitality sapped by its more favoured neighbour. The best **hotel** is the two-star *Celisol* (℡04.68.04.53.70; ❷), while there are two year-round **campsites**: *Le Sègre* on route de Toulouse (℡04.68.04.65.87) and the *Caravaneige Mas Piques* (℡04.68.04.62.11).

Just to the east, **HIX**, now virtually part of Bourg-Madame, was the summer home of the counts of Cerdagne; its eleventh-century chapel, considered one of the oldest Romanesque structures in the area, has a delicacy which only such early examples display.

## Latour-de-Carol/Enveitg

From Bourg-Madame, Puigcerdà is plainly visible on its hill; it's quicker (and cheaper) to get off the *Train Jaune* here and walk across the border. If you stay on board, the line ends fifteen minutes further at the Gare Internationale of **LATOUR-DE-CAROL/ENVEITG**, the interchange for trains south to Barcelona and north for Toulouse. Several trains a day cross the border **into Spain**.

The train station lies between the two villages, though it's actually much closer (700m) to larger Enveitg – though neither is much bigger than the vast railyards of the international exchange itself. Because this is the main road between Spain and the Ariège, there are some very tacky, overpriced **hotels** in Enveitg to avoid – your best bet is *L'Auberge Catalane* at 10 avenue de Puymorens in Latour-de-Carol (℡04.6894.80.66, ⓦwww.auberge-catalane.fr; closed May & mid-Nov to mid-Dec; ❸), with cheerful rooms above a terrace and a **restaurant** serving country fare (*menu* €14.50–27.50; closed Sun eve & Mon). The closest **campsite** is the riverside *Municipal de l'Oratory* in Latour-de-Carol (℡04.68.04.83.70).

# Northwest to the Col de Puymorens

After years of controversy, the tunnel beneath the **Col de Puymorens** (1920m; Pimorent in Catalan) northwest of Latour was completed in 1995 and the rapid toll road (cars €7.50) – like the railway – now disappears under the *col* to reappear in the Ariège.

## Porta

On the way up to the pass you'll see the much-photographed but seldom-visited towers at Carol, all that's left of a castle built to defend the Cerdagne from Foix. Near the top of the climb, 13km from Latour, the village of **PORTA** has a pretty old quarter slightly uphill, though all its amenities are on the main road, including a *gîte d'étape*, *La Pastorale* (℡04.68.04.83.92, ⓔenoff@wanadoo.fr; 28 places), serving the **GR7**, and the *Auberge du Campcardos* (℡04.68.04.82.26; ❷), whose **restaurant** is rather overpriced – you're better off heading to the *Auberge la Cajole*. Hikers should come supplied, as there's no shop.

## Porté-Puymorens

The nearby ski station above the village of **PORTÉ-PUYMORENS** (Ⓦ www.porte-puymorens.net) – locally referred to as Porté, and thus easily confused with Porta – is probably the best the French Catalan Pyrenees has to offer. While the Col de Puymorens marks the shift from the arid Cerdagne to the damp Ariège, lots of snow often falls on the Cerdan side and stays there, protected from the worst wind. The 17 runs here are fairly evenly distributed amongst all difficulties, with high points at a respectable 2400m and 2500m, and four well-placed chairlifts. There are also 25km of trails for *ski de fond* and a whole gamut of non-ski leisure facilities.

The village itself has a nice valley setting, off the main highway. The smartest hotel here is the *Hôtel Restaurant du Col* (℡ 04.68.04.82.06, 🖶 04.68.04.87.22; ❹) down in the village, and there's also a **gîte**, *Ferme d'en Garcie* (℡ 04.68.04.95.44, 🄴 nathalie.komaroff@wanadoo.fr; 31 places, including 6 doubles ❶), which also operates the local **horse-riding** centre. The valley-bottom **campsite** *La Rivière* (℡ 04.68.04.82.20) runs all year, but you're unlikely to want to stay in winter.

Overall, Porté has a bit more going for it than Porta; the **GR7** east into the Carlit Massif is easy to find at the far end of the village. The path provides the gentlest grade into the Carlit, but is also the most spoiled western approach, what with overhead cable-cars, various damworks and the generally dull topography. For an alternative trailhead for Carlit, consider L'Hospitalet (for the HRP) or Mérens-le-Vals (for the GR10), both slightly north on the Latour–Toulouse rail line.

# The Carlit Massif

The granite ridges of the lake-spangled **Carlit Massif** occupy a compact area just north of the Cerdanya/Cerdagne, the last truly alpine region of the Pyrenees – east of here, Canigou notwithstanding, only foothills undulate on the horizon. Being easy of access, these mountains are popular; the lakes – even when not dammed – can be a little overly manicured. The massif's upland marshes have been disrupted by EDF dams which manipulate water levels, most notably at Lac des Bouillouses and several other reservoirs. There are still some relatively unspoiled corners, however, and ample scope for several days of trekking or scrambling.

The ascent of **Puig Carlit** (2921m) lies within the capabilities of any reasonably fit person, especially from Lac des Bouillouses on its eastern slopes. Three major walking routes – the **HRP**, the north–south **GR7** and the trans-Pyrenean **GR10** – as well as marked secondary trails cross the massif, while segments of the GR7 and GR10 comprise sections of the less demanding **Tour du Carlit**. For all of these explorations you'll want the IGN 1:50,000 *Carte de Randonnées no. 8*, "Cerdagne-Capcir"; the IGN TOP 25 no. 2249 ET is also well worth having.

## Traverses and alpine loops

The three western **trailhead villages** are Mérens-les-Vals (p.234), L'Hospitalet-près-l'Andorre (p.232) and Porté (above). Each of the suggested routes converge near the centre of the range, close to the focal Porteille d'Orlu.

**From Porté**, the GR7 leaves the village at the first hairpin, climbing gradually east and then north towards the grey concrete wall of the **Lanoux** dam, four hours from Porté – not a particularly aesthetic trip. Just beyond, at the entrance to the Fourats valley, the decrepit, three-person *Abri de la Guimbarde* overlooking the reservoir is only useful in dire emergencies. Most people prefer to camp on the grass below, or get an early enough start from Porté to finish the day at a more exciting spot. The GR7 continues northeast for another ninety minutes above the lakeshore, initially quite steeply, before joining the GR10 which cuts roughly east-west across the top of the lake from the easy pass of Porteille de la Grave.

**From Mérens-les-Vals**, the GR10 climbs sharply up the **Nabre valley** to reach the staffed **Refuge des Bésines** (2104m; ☎05.61.05.22.44; 50 places) next to the Bésines reservoir in something over five hours; the HRP **from L'Hospitalet-près-l'Andorre** gets you there in roughly half the time. There are no more refuges east of Bésines towards the GR10/GR7 intersection, only a limited number of **campsites** at the north end of Lanoux.

From Lanoux, the climb up the south grade of the **Portella d'Orlu** (2403m) is deceptively easy, but once up top the Carlit reveals its other uncompromising nature in the view north: granite spires, giant boulder falls and drifting cloud. It's vital to keep west here for the grassy route skirting the **Étang de Feury**, avoiding the deadly rocks. At Feury a nameless variant heads west via the **Porteille de Madides** (2.5km) to shortcut the GR10, joining the latter at Courals de la Présasse and allowing rapid descent to Mérens-les-Vals.

Even if the mist doesn't close in, you'll still need about three hours to descend northeast from the Porteille d'Orlu along the often poorly marked GR7 to **Étang d'en Beys** (1980m), a natural lake surrounded by scree, pasture and clumps of rhododendron. Here the useful **refuge** managed by the Orlu municipality (☎05.61.64.24.24; 49 places; staffed late May–late Sept) is strategically located below the intersection of several traverse routes.

From the lake it's about two hours down to the end of the road tracing the **Oriège valley**, three hours coming uphill, but it's strongly suggested that you elect another way to finish a traverse or circuit. Particularly if you have left a vehicle at Lac des Bouillouses (see below), which lies one day's reasonable march via the Porteille de la Grave, you can return another way. Some twenty minutes below the lake, you part with the GR7 and adopt a cairned and paint-splodged (but unnamed) route which curls around through the **Portella Gran** (2603m), before descending through a lake-speckled valley enclosed by 2810-metre **Puig Péric** to Bouillouses, all within six hours.

If you're going to finish a traverse in the Oriège valley (see p.235), you might reduce the amount of road-tramping by following yet another anonymous but marked route up to the easy **Couillade d'en Beys** (2345m), then descend past the easterly **Peyrisses** lake to the **Naguille reservoir**, finally dropping by track to the Forges d'Orlu in about five hours.

## Climbing the peak

If you're merely intent on bagging the summit of Puig Carlit, a quick approach can be made from Mont-Louis **on the east** side, up the very narrow but paved D60 road. During peak season, private cars are banned from the 13km of access road up to **Lac des Bouillouses** – you must park near the bottom and take a *navette* most of the way. For purist hikers who don't mind a long slog, the **GR10** out of Bolquère climbs gently through woods to the **Col del Pam** (2000m), where it links with the HRP coming from Font-Romeu; both continue past ski lifts and pistes to Lac des Bouillouses (5hr from either town).

There's plenty of **accommodation** and **food** at the Bouillouses lake, actually a huge reservoir dating from the early 1900s. The CAF-run *Refuge des Bouillouses* (☎04.68.04.20.76; 40 places; dorms from €10; doubles ❹ HB only) is the cheapest option, east of the dam wall at just under 2000m. Tucked inconspicuously behind this is the smallish, privately managed *Auberge du Carlit* (☎04.68.04.22.23) with rooms (❷), as well as a *gîte*, and meals provided. As at nearly all the restaurants in this area, regional food dominates, including solid but simple meat dishes, with occasional flourishes, such as *poulet catalan*, served in a thick tomato and mushroom sauce. Just above the west end of the dam at 2050m looms the gigantic *Refuge Le Bones Hores* (☎04.68.04.24.22, ℱ04.68.04.13.63; ❺ HB only), popular with families.

Beside *Refuge Le Bones Hores*, where a placard informs fishermen which lakes are legally open, you adopt the **HRP**, whose course is scantily marked with faded paint splodges but deeply grooved into the terrain and sometimes cairned. You arc up gently through the woods, between **Étang Negre** and **Étang del Viver**, twenty minutes along; the next natural lake, **de les Dugues**, is just 45 minutes above the dam, and thus a hugely popular outing. The crowds will thin out as you press on past the necklace of smaller lakes – Castellá, Trebens and Sobira – under the shadow of **Touzal Colomé** (2804m), and finally up the ridge that leads to the summit from the east. This is a superb climb, the tarns glinting in the sun, the grass green in June but a faded ochre by August, and the scree-strewn pyramid of Carlit overhead. There and back from Lac des Bouillouses is at most six-and-a-half hours, an easy day's walk in good conditions – though rather ominously there are green sheds by most of the lakes to shelter from the foul weather that frequently appears without warning. If you just want to take in the lakes, it's only a three-hour round-trip from the dam to the highest one, Sobira, at 2310m.

**From the west**, the ascent of Carlit is a little more difficult, a good four hours one way starting in the vicinity of the *Abri de la Guimbarde*, close to the Lanoux dam (see p.229). Again using HRP cairns and blazes, follow the **Fourats valley** east to its tiny lake and then keep going straight to the summit, or if that looks too formidable, bear away towards the *col* on the south and approach the summit along the line of the ridge, dropping a little way down the eastern slope when the ridge gets too narrow.

## The Tour du Carlit

The **Tour du Carlit**, aimed at hikers of middling experience, is meant to take three days, much of it by track through lower altitude zones. If you're coming by regular train, the easiest places to pick up the circuit are Porta or Porté-Puymorens. If you're on the *Train Jaune*, get off at Béna-Fanès, the stop before Latour-de-Carol, and try to hitch the 6km up to Béna.

From Porta you begin with a short day's walk southeast over the grimly named Col de l'Home Mort (2300m) to **BÉNA**, a delightful hamlet with an equally wonderful *gîte d'étape* (☎04.68.04.81.64, ℰgiteauberge@bena.org; 40 places, mostly doubles and quads), housed in a restored *mas* or Catalan farmhouse. You could lengthen the day by pressing along the track east, via the hamlets of Fanès and Brangoli, to the attractive and well-positioned village of **DORRES**, which offers the characterful *Hotel-Restaurant Marty* (☎04.68.30.07.52; ❸) and a public outdoor **hot spring** for bathing (daily 8.30am–7.30pm, later closing in summer; €3). The second day is less enchanting as you skirt Les Escaldes spa to thread north through the Angoustrine valley on a dirt track, before linking with the GR10 at **Lac des Bouillouses**. The third day's walking follows the GR10 west over the gentle **Portella de la Grava** (2426m), alongside the infant River Têt, to intersect the GR7; you then reverse the directions given under "Traverses and alpine loops" (see pp.229–230) for a descent to Porté.

# The Ariège and the Pays de Sault

Draining north from the Col du Puymorens, the **Ariège valley** is one of the most depressed areas of France, with low income levels, high unemployment and an ageing population. Coming directly from the Cerdanya, where the disposable incomes of Barcelonans and Gironans have a striking impact on the landscape, a visitor could be mistaken for thinking Spain the wealthier country. Unsurprisingly, perhaps, the Ariège has long been a stronghold for nonconformists and antiroyalists, and, in more recent times, the political Left. This political affiliation is owed more to local perception of neglect by the national government than to any deeply held Marxist convictions.

The Ariège is a much-frequented corner of the Pyrenees, visitor patronage sustaining a tourist industry which is one of the region's few going concerns. Natural attractions such as the **Oriège** tributary valley and the bear-sheltering forests west of the river are enhanced by the prehistoric painted caves around **Tarascon**. On the main valley floor, **Mérens-les-Vals** and **Ax-les-Thermes** are serviceable bases for excursions into the surrounding mountains, including the severe fastness of the Carlit. Further downriver, the showcase town of **Foix** is almost in the flatlands, but allows access to the gorge-furrowed, Cathar-haunted **Pays de Sault**, an eerie tableland extending between the Ariège and the Aude valley to the east. Here, the Cathars began the local tradition of rebelling against Church and State almost eight centuries ago, antecedents which the modern *Ariègeois* acknowledge with pride.

## The upper Ariège

The train line from the Cerdagne emerges from the Col de Puymorens tunnel at **L'HOSPITALET-PRÈS-L'ANDORRE**, where several transport routes converge: the HRP goes through here, as do buses to and from Andorra, and trains south into the Cerdagne and north to Toulouse. There's a basic, unremarkable one-star **hotel** – *Puymorens* (☎05.61.64.23.03; ❷) – plus the preferable *Gîte Hospitalité* (☎ & ℻05.61.05.23.14, ✉gitedetape.lhospitalet@libertysurf.fr; closed Nov) and a municipal **campsite** (☎05.61.05.20.04; June–Oct). Heading into the Carlit Massif, the **HRP** gets you quickly to grips with the mountains, offering the shortest approach from the west as it climbs unusually gently to the dam and the refuge at Bésines, where you link up with the GR10.

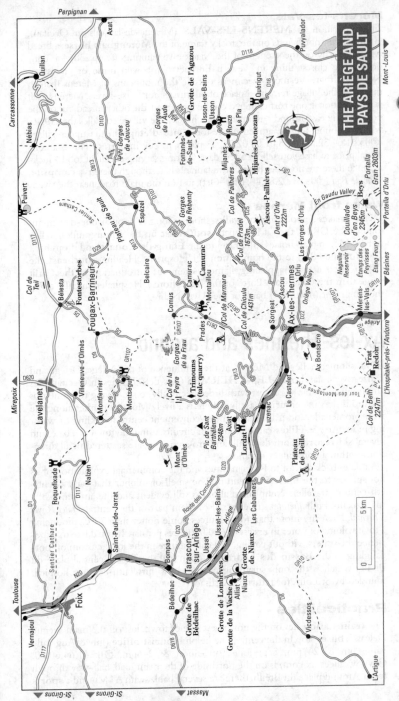

THE ARIÈGE AND
PAYS DE SAULT

Perpignan

Axat

Quillan

Carcassonne

Nébias

D118

Puyvalador

Mont-Louis

Grotte de l'Aguzou

Usson-les-Bains • Usson

Quérigut

Rouze • Le Pla

D16

Gorges de l'Aude

Gorges de Joucou

Fontanès-de-Sault

Mijanès

Mijanès-Donezan

En Gaudu Valley

Portella d'Orlu

Portella Gran 2603m

Puivert

Espézel

Gorges de Rebenty

Col de Pailhères

Ascou-Pailhères

Dent d'Orlu 2222m

Beys

Couillade d'en Beys 2345m

Portella d'Orlu

Bélesta

Fontestorbes

Fougax-Barrineuf

Plateau de Sault

Belcaire

Camurac

Camurac

Montaillou

Col de Marmare

Col de Pradel 1673m

Les Forges d'Orlu

Orlu

Naguille Reservoir

Étangs des Peyrisses

Étang Faury

Bésines

Lavelanet

Villeneuve-d'Olmès

Comus

Gorges de la Frau

Prades

Col de Chioula 1431m

Sorgeat

Ascou

Ax-les-Thermes

Orlu Valley

Mérens-les-Vals

Montferrier

Montségur

Col de la Peyre

Trimouns (talc quarry)

Col de Marmare

Ax Bonascre

Tour des Montagnes d'Ax

L'Hospitalet-près-l'Andorre

Roquefixade

Nalzen

Mont d'Olmès

Pic de Sant Barthélemy 2348m

Axiat

Lordat

Plateau de Beille

Le Castelet

Prat Redor

Col de Beïl 2247m

Saint-Paul-de-Jarrat

Bompas

Ussat-les-Bains

Luzenac

Les Cabannes

Tarascon-sur-Ariège

Ussat

Route des Corniches

Foix

Bédeilhac

Grotte de Bédeilhac

Grotte de Niaux

Grotte de Lombrives

Alliat

Niaux

Grotte de la Vache

Vicdessos

Vernajoul

L'Artigue

Toulouse

Massat

St-Girons

St-Girons

Sentier Cathare

5 km

0

233

## Mérens-les-Vals

The reputation of **MÉRENS-LES-VALS** (Merenç-de-las-Vals in Occitan), 10km further north, rests on the stocky frame of the **Mérenguais horse**, a breed which – partly on the strength of the Niaux cave paintings (see p.238) – is considered the closest thing in Western Europe to the wild horse of prehistory. Nowadays there are more specimens outside the mountains of Mérens than in them, but the village remains a place of pilgrimage for horse-lovers. Mérens itself is unexceptional: one part clustered on the main road, the other spread out on the slopes to the east around a Romanesque church. The village straddles the GR10, which accounts for the attractively restored **gîte d'étape** in the upper village (℡05.61.64.32.50, ℻05.61.04.02.75; 38 places, mostly in dorms). This is a congenial place to base yourself for a few days' walking, serving excellent food – luckily, since there are no other hotels or restaurants here, though there is a **campsite**, *Ville de Bau* (℡05.61.02.85.40; May–Oct), just off the main road, near the river.

### Walks from Mérens

Mérens makes a good base for **walks**, short or long. A popular one-day circuit follows the GR10, then a local path **southwest** up the Mourgouillou valley (where Mérenguais horses still graze) to the **Étang de Couart**, and drops back down on the HRP to the train station at L'Hospitalet. Heading **southeast**, the GR10 offers a more appealing, if more strenuous introduction to the Carlit range than the GR7 from Porté or the HRP from L'Hospitalet, initially along the true right (northeast) bank of the River Nabre.

# Ax-les-Thermes and around

Eight kilometres beyond Mérens, at the confluence of the Ariège, Oriège and Lauze rivers, stands **AX-LES-THERMES** (Acs-dels-Tèrmes in Occitan). It's an unobjectionable spa resort with little specifically to see owing to numerous disastrous fires in centuries past, but there is a lively Monday market along the river promenade, and it makes the most convenient centre for skiing or walking in the Ariège. **Hikes** can be routed in circuits, using the town as a base, and several **ski resorts**, both downhill and cross-country, are scattered in all directions within a convenient distance.

Ax dates back at least to Roman times and the commercial exploitation of its hot springs to the thirteenth century. The smell of sulphur that early twentieth-century travellers complained about is still evident and the ambience of a spa remains. Four *thermes* still exist, all of them part of the central *Hôtel Royal Thermal*. There are more than forty sources, some hotter than 70°C, producing a total volume of water in excess of 600,000 litres per day. If you'd like to experience the waters without paying, you can indulge in the local custom of foot-dangling in the **Bassin des Ladres**, an open bath beside the central place du Breilh, which is the only surviving portion of a thirteenth-century hospital, founded by St Louis for returning Crusaders.

## Practicalities

The **train station** lies on the northwest side of town, just off the main avenue Delcassé; **buses** stop in the centre. The helpful **tourist office** (July & Aug daily 9am–1pm & 2–7pm; Sept–June 9am–noon & 2–6pm; ℡05.61.64.60.60, ⓦwww.vallees-ax.com) is on the northside of the main road, half-way through town. Around place du Breilh, there are several banks with ATMs, and a **sports**

**shop** (Telemark) selling trekking and skiing gear, while **bikes** can be rented in nearby Saivgnac at L'Eskimo Sport (☎05.61.64.02.85).

Thanks to the baths and the local skiing there is a wide selection of **hotels** in and around town. *Le Bellevue* (☎05.61.64.20.78, ☎05.61.64.65.44; ❷) is the cheapest option, though *L'Auzeraie* at 7 avenue Delcassé (☎05.61.64.20.70, ✉auzeriae@free.fr; ❸) gives better value for money. More upmarket are *Le Grillon* on rue Saint Udaut, 300m from place du Breilh (☎05.61.64.31.64, ⓦwww.hotel-le-grillon.com; closed late Oct to early Dec; ❸, ❺ HB only in summer), with a particularly good restaurant (*menus* €16 & €26); and *Le Chalet* on avenue Turrel opposite Le Teich baths (☎05.61.64.24.31, ⓦwww.le-chalet.fr; closed Nov–Feb, Sun eve & Mon; ❸), with some river-view rooms and a decent restaurant (€16–38). The municipal **campsite**, *Malazéou* (☎05.61.64.69.14), is beside the Ariège, 500m from the train station.

Other than the hotel dining rooms and restaurants, **eating** prospects aren't brilliant in Ax, though *La Petit Fringale* on rue Piétonne is worth a stop for its *montagnard* cuisine (from €15) and shady terrace. For **snacks**, there are numerous cheap *boulangeries* and over-the-counter pizza places in rue de l'Horloge, leading off the place du Marché. More atmospheric venues for a **drink** are the *Grand Café* and *Brasserie Le Club* on place Roussel.

## The Oriège valley

Extending east from Ax, the damp, leafy **Oriège valley** allows access to both the Carlit peaks and the **Réserve Nationale d'Orlu**, created south of the road in 1975 to benefit a growing herd of isards as well as roe deer, golden eagles and lammergeiers. Under the shadow of the distinctive Dent d'Orlu, a favourite of technical climbers, the D22 road heads up the valley to **ORLU**, where there's camping at the *Municipal* (☎05.61.64.30.09) and a popular *gîte d'étape* aimed at walkers, the *Relais Montagnard* (☎05.61.64.61.88; 34 places). A path from **Les Forges d'Orlu** further up the valley permits a link-up with the Tour des Montagnes d'Ax (see below), via a climb from near the power station to the dam at **Naguille**.

At a popular picnic area some 12km from Ax, the asphalt ends and all private cars are banned from further progress along a track which climbs south into the *réserve* through the **En Gaudu valley**, meeting the GR7 below the Étang d'en Beys with its refuge. If you prefer to approach the Carlit via the Oriège, it's well worth splashing out for a taxi to the picnic grounds: the walk is tedious and steep, with little chance of a lift in either direction.

## Walks around Ax-les-Thermes

The Bureau des Guides et Accompagnateurs Montagne des Vallées d'Ax, next door to the tourist office (☎05.61.64.31.51), maintains a list of seventeen brief **walks** around the town, ranging from twenty minutes to seven hours; it also keeps information on all the mountain huts and refuges, climbing courses and weather forecasts. For a full day's hike, take the suggested itinerary to the attractive village of **Sorgeat** and link this hike with other sections.

Of the long-distance walks, the five-day, four-night **Tour des Montagnes d'Ax** is recommended, since it covers a variety of terrain, including parts of the Carlit already described. You can begin at **Le Castelet**, on the main road 5km northwest of Ax, climbing south for a day to hook up with the GR10 at the **Col de Belh** (2247m); nearby is the staffed *Refuge de Rulhe* (2185m; ☎05.61.65.65.01; 50 places). The route then heads east to cross the Ariège valley at Mérens-les-Vals, your second overnight stop. From there you stick with the GR10, and later the GR7, all the way to the *Refuge d'en Beys* (see p.230), which will be your third night out after a very long day, unless you take the Porteille de Madides shortcut (see p.230), or you could insert an extra overnight stay at the *Refuge des Bésines* (see p.230), at the junction of the two trails. From this refuge, you've a shorter day up to the gentle Couillade d'en Beys and then on to the Oriège valley floor as described on p.235.

## Skiing around Ax-les-Thermes

The nearest ski station to Ax is **AX-BONASCRE**, 8km south up the D820; in winter there are ski-bus services from the town. Bonascre is a hideous knot of black-clad high-rises at 1400m, but it's a different matter once you get into the *télécabine* (€9) and up to the **Plateau du Saquet** (2040m) with its beginners' area. The snow record is good, there are 70km of pistes (mostly red-rated, some over 3km long) and the top point is 2305m – with the beautiful Andorran frontier peaks as a backdrop.

Three valleys west of Bonascre, the **Plateau de Beille** rivals Font-Romeu in offering some of the best cross-country skiing on the French side. The 60km of pistes range in length from one to twenty kilometres, at just under 2000m – which should ensure adequate snow. The plateau is reached by a sixteen-kilometre *route forestière* from the village of Les Cabannes, 15km down the main N20 road.

North of Ax there's potentially good cross-country skiing to be had around the **Col de Chioula** (1431m), with 60km of trails; be wary of the low altitude, though, and check conditions before setting out. A pretty drive 13km east of Ax leads to tiny **ASCOU-PAILHÈRES**, which offers just sixteen downhill runs, totalling 20km, and a top point of 2030m. The longest two runs are blue-rated, though the station has a couple of shorter, challenging red and black pistes.

## The Route des Corniches

A scenic alternative to the N20 along the floor of the Ariège valley is the **Route des Corniches**, between Ascou and Bompas, which you can access from Ax by taking the serpentine D613 (the Belcaire road) up past Ascou. About halfway along you pass the village of **AXIAT**, which has an appealing Romanesque church and lies a short way south of the extremely unappealing **talc quarry** at **Trimouns**.

This huge, ghastly scar produces around 300,000 tons of talc per season, eight percent of the world's total; so far about thirteen million tons have gone, leaving eleven million to be scoured from the earth. The workers are mainly Spanish, Portuguese and Moroccan, who supplement their income by selling semiprecious stones to tourists (regular tours of the quarry June–Sept). It was by the trail over the Col de la Peyre, just above the quarry, that the four Cathars from Montségur made their escape (see p.247).

Just below Axiat stands the castle of **LORDAT**. Although it escaped dismantling during the sixteenth-century Wars of Religion, apparently because it was too big, the castle is now comprehensively ruined, but worth a look all the same. The church above has a distinctive squat, square bell-tower, with a double series of arches on each face. The corniche comes back to the base of the valley at Bompas, 3km north of Tarascon on the road to Foix.

# Tarascon-sur-Ariège and its caves

A small, utilitarian mining and metallurgy centre where traffic roars past on the highway, **TARASCON-SUR-ARIÈGE** has nothing to suggest that it's the heart of one of the most fascinating areas in Europe. Any account of the emergence of the human species must include the caves around Tarascon, which together constitute an unequalled display of **prehistoric painting and artefacts**. There are four main sites, all accessible in a single day if you have your own transport.

Yet the town itself is more rewarding than first impressions suggest, and worth an hour's stroll. From the east bank of the Ariège, where riverside cafés provide pleasant vantage points, a narrow pedestrian lane leads up past craft shops and even narrower alleys to the old quarter. Here the church of St-Michel presides over a partly arcaded square, with various surviving bits of the razed medieval walls here and there: the **Tour Saint-Michel**, and the **Porte d'Espagne** with a fountain inside. From the gate, a short hike past walled orchards up to the **Tour du Castella**, now a clocktower, is worthwhile for the views over the five valleys that converge here. Tarascon also hosts two lively livestock **fairs**, on May 8 and September 30, timed for the passing of the transhumant herds.

## Practicalities

Buses and trains call frequently from nearby Ax-les-Thermes and Foix; the **train station**, also serving as the **bus** stop, is on the left bank of the Ariège, in the northern half of town. The **tourist office** (July & Aug daily 9am–7pm; Sept–June Mon–Sat 9am–6pm; ℡05.61.05.94.94, Ⓔpays.de.tarascon @wanadoo.fr) is inside the multipurpose hall known as the Espace François Mitterrand, on avenue des Pyrénées in the centre.

The quietest and most attractive of the central **hotels** is the *Confort* on the riverside quai Armand-Sylvestre (℡ & Ⓕ05.61.05.61.90; ❸), with some rooms facing a courtyard where light snacks are served. For rooms facing the river and a cosy fireside lounge, try *Hostellerie de la Poste* (℡05.61.05.60.41, Ⓔhostellerieposte@aol.com; ❸), 200m north on the main through road. The best option, however, is 1km out of the town centre, on route Saurat, the eighteenth-century manor house *Domaine Fournie* (℡05.61.05.54.52, ⒺContact @domaine-fournie.com; *table d'hôte* meals at €15; ❸), set within impressive grounds. There are two **campsites**: *La Bernière* (℡05.61.05.78.01), near the junction of the road to Bédeilhac, and the municipal *Pré Lombard* (℡05.61.05.61.94), upstream from town on the right bank. All the hotels have **restaurants**, with the best food and service at *Hostellerie de la Poste,* which offers a reasonably priced *menu* featuring *auzinat*, a rich hotpot of cabbage, potato, sausage and game.

## The caves

The high concentration of caves in the Ariège is due mostly to the amount of limestone in the hillsides, a rock ideally suited to the millennial work of seeping water that creates caverns. What served as shelters and places of ritual for early humans later came in handy as hideouts for religious dissidents during the Christian era.

## Grotte de Niaux

Unquestionably the finest of the Pyrenean prehistoric caves is the **Grotte de Niaux**, 2km southwest of Tarascon, which can only be viewed on a twenty-person, 45-minute guided tour (daily: July & Aug 9.15am–5.30pm, English tours at 9.30am & 1pm; Sept 10am–5.30, English at 1pm; Oct–June Tues–Sun tours at 11am, 2.30pm & 4pm; €9; reservations mandatory; ☏05.61.05.88.37, ⓦwww.sesta.org).

The current entrance to Niaux is a tunnel created in 1968 near the low and narrow natural opening under an enormous rock overhang. Using flashlights for illumination, you penetrate 900m (from a total 4km of galleries) to see some of the famous black outlines of horse and bison, minimally shaded yet capturing every nuance. Studies have shown that these drawings and those of the ibex and stag in the recess further back were produced around 10,800 BC with a "crayon" made of bison fat and manganese oxide. A line of footprints left by the artists can be seen in a part of the cave that was opened up in 1970, while their primitive script is represented by dots and bunches of lines on the wall of the main cavity.

**NIAUX** village itself, between the cave and Tarascon, has a small, private **Musée Pyrénéen** (July & Aug daily 9am–8pm; Sept–June 10am–noon & 2–6pm; €6), which displays a splendid collection of tools, furnishings and archival photos illustrating the vanished traditions of the Ariège. Exhibits also explain local Pyrenean architecture, specifically its use of *lauzes* (stone slabs), *ardoise* (slate) and occasionally *chaume* (thatch) for roofing. About halfway between Niaux and Tarascon, keep your eyes peeled for the picturesque remains of a medieval smelting works by the riverside.

## Grotte de la Vache

The **Grotte de la Vache** at Alliat (July & Aug daily 10am–6pm; Easter–June & Sept Mon & Wed–Sun 2.30–4.15pm; other times by arrangement; ☏05.61.05.95.06; €7) is well worth the couple of kilometres' journey across the valley from Niaux; a path, beginning some 150m before the Niaux museum, slightly shortcuts the road. Excavations over three decades have revealed remains of ten thousand years of habitation from 15,000–12,500 BC to the Bronze Age. Around 30,000 fragments of flint tools were unearthed here and over 6000 complete tools, mainly for engraving in rock; some pieces are displayed in the cave.

## Grotte de Bédeilhac

To reach the **Grotte de Bédeilhac** (Easter–June & Sept to mid-Dec Mon–Sat 2.20–4.15pm; July & Aug daily 10am–6pm; mid-Dec to Easter Mon–Sat 2.30–4.15pm & Sun 3pm; ☏05.61.05.95.06, €8) above the eponymous village, you have to return to Tarascon and cover 5km along the D618 towards Saurat. This cave, a hollow in the ridge of Soudour, contains examples of every known technique of Paleolithic art, including polychrome painting (now faded to monochrome). The imposing entrance yawns 35m wide by 20m high, making it easy to understand how the Germans managed to adapt the cavern as an aircraft hangar during World War II. Although the art inside is not as immediately powerful as at Niaux, its diversity compensates: low reliefs in mud, paintings of bison, deer and ibex, and stalagmites used to model figures.

In the village below, you can **stay** at the *Relais d'Étape* (☏05.61.05.15.56; ❷) and **eat** at the adjacent *Auberge de la Grotte*, on the through road next to the *mairie* and the post office.

## Cave art

The **painted caves** of the Pyrenees were created by nomadic and semi-nomadic communities of Cro-Magnon man during the Late Paleolithic period, 10,000 to 35,000 years ago. Various theories, none yet definitive, have been put forward to explain the purpose of this cave art. According to the pioneering French paleo-anthropologist **Abbé Breuil** (1877–1961), known as the "Pope of Prehistory," cave art served a **magical function**, to ensure "that the game should be plentiful, that it should increase and that sufficient should be killed". The frequency with which ibex, wild boar, reindeer and bison appear on the walls makes this notion attractive, but there are objections to it, the most obvious being that the animal remains found in the caves show that the species depicted were not the main food supply. Moreover, although some of the animals are marked by symbols that might be arrows, over ninety percent of them are not. The Late Paleolithic period was also a time of plenty, when hunters would have needed no magical assistance.

Breuil's disciples **André Leroi-Gourhan** (1911–86) and **Annette Laming-Emperaire** (1917–1977) maintained that cave art was arranged in a **specific layout**, much like the decorative schemes of frescoed Christian churches. Their surveys of 62 caves revealed that hands were depicted only at the entrance to caves or in the centre, and that mammoths and bison were confined to the centre. They suggested that arrangement of images reflected a sexual polarity, with bison symbolizing the female element, and horses the male. Others have argued that the weak illumination available to the cave-dwellers – grease and a wick perhaps, or wooden torches – would not have allowed them to see the cave decorations as a unity. A problem is also posed by the way successive outlines overlaid each other to the extent that they became indecipherable, even though suitable areas of blank rock were available to either side. Nevertheless, most experts agree that there is some sort of pattern: bison and horses, for example, are thirty times more likely to occur in the central area than are deer.

The most cogent refutation of the above theories was published in 1996 by Jean Clottes, a French prehistorian and cave-art expert, and David Lewis-Williams, a South African archeologist specializing in the art and beliefs of the Kalahari Bushmen, one of the last surviving hunter-gatherer societies with strong parallels to European Paleolithic culture. Their work, *Les Chamanes de la Préhistoire* (Éditions Seuil), proposes that many of the images were created by **shamans** in a trance or other altered state, and that "the paintings and engravings do not represent real animals that are hunted for food in an actual landscape; rather they are visions drawn from the subterranean world of spirits because of their supernatural powers and ability to help the shamans".

Undoubtedly the caves will continue to stimulate speculation. The apparent stylistic development of the paintings, along with similarities between decorative work in caves hundreds of kilometres apart, suggests that there was some sort of coherent "school" of artistic development, as well as communication between widely dispersed groups. A great many decorated caves of the Pyrenees are closed to the general public to protect the paintings; application through a caving organization might gain access to some of these. The most spectacular examples, though, are open to all. After the Tarascon group, the next major Pyrenean cave is **Gargas**, with its vast array of hand prints in red and black, many with apparently mutilated fingers (see p.329). Whatever its purposes and origins, Pyrenean cave art offers an extraordinary aesthetic experience, marvellously conjuring shape and movement from the most basic natural materials, and even, in places, exploiting the very contours of the rock. Niaux itself contains an excellent example of such artistic opportunism: one of the bison carved on the clay floor is formed around holes caused by dripping water, which now function as an eye and wound marks.

### Grotte de Lombrives

The **Grotte de Lombrives** (Easter–May & Oct to early Nov Sat & Sun tours at 10am, 10.45am & 2.30pm, plus May Mon–Fri 2–5.30pm; June & Sept daily tours at 10am, 10.45am & 2–5.30pm; July & Aug daily 10am–7pm; or by appointment, ☎05.61.05.98.40; €6.60), 3km south of Tarascon along the N20, near Ussat-les-Bains, may disappoint if you've already seen Niaux, Vache and Bédeilhac. Access by underground train gives it the atmosphere of an amusement-park – as do the nocturnal *spectacles* regularly staged here in July and August – but the stalagmite formations are superb, and the sheer size of the complex is impressive. It is, in fact, the largest cavern in western Europe open to tourists, and would take five days' walking to see entirely. Groups of eight or more can arrange three- or five-hour walks around the cave by ringing the number above.

Lombrives was inhabited around 4000 BC, but all the material found here now rests in museums such as that at Foix. Its later history is embellished by legends of the last Cathars walled up inside in 1328, and of 250 soldiers subsequently disappearing without trace, the victims of cave-dwelling bandits. For a specialized visit, you can book on one of the *Visites longue durées caractère spéléologique*, which are run from June to September.

# Foix

**FOIX**, 16km downstream from Tarascon, is the smallest *départemental* capital in France, and the most agreeable base in the valley if you don't mind catching a train or bus to get into the mountains. A non-industrial livelihood based on bureaucracy and tourism has helped preserve its old town of narrow alleys in the triangle between the Ariège and the Arget rivers, where a few of the overhanging houses date from the fourteenth to sixteenth centuries; especially attractive are place Pyrène and place Saint-Vincent with their fountains, though many junctions in the old town sport some sort of water-quirk. All lanes seem to lead eventually to the conspicuously large church of **Saint-Volusien** in the north of the old town, originally Romanesque but almost completely reconstructed after being razed during the Wars of Religion. Its eponymous square, along with the Halles des Grains just off cours Gabriel-Fauré, hosts lively Wednesday and Friday **markets**: produce and plants are sold at place Saint-Volusien; and meat, cheese, savouries and pastries at the metal-roofed *halles*, which serves as a prime drinking venue other days.

Presiding over everything is the grey hilltop **castle** (daily: May, June & Sept 9.45am–noon & 2–6pm; July & Aug 9.30am–6.30pm; Oct–April Wed–Sun 10.30am–noon & 2–5.30pm; €4), not so much a single fortification as three magnificent, dissimilar towers from different eras, dramatic when viewed from any angle. From 1012, the castle on this site was the seat of the counts of Foix, whose association with the Cathar faith led to its being besieged four times by Simon de Montfort, who failed to break the fort's resistance. Count Roger-Bernard II – known as *Le Grand* – was a determined opponent of the anti-Cathar crusade, but perhaps made his most lasting contribution to history by marrying Ermensende of Castellbò early in the thirteenth century, thereby linking the fortunes of Foix and Andorra (see p.206). That dynasty ended illustriously with Henri III of Foix-Béarn and Navarre, who annexed what had

## Gaston Fébus

Throughout the central Pyrenees, you'll encounter the name of local hero **Gaston Fébus** (or Phébus), Count of Foix and Viscount of Béarn. Although ultimately frustrated in his plans, he is still celebrated for his struggle towards regional independence and his character, which epitomized the chivalric ideals of the Middle Ages – as well as for his invention of *hypocras*, a spiced-wine drink still enjoyed around Foix. Poet, soldier and provincial aristocrat, Gaston was born in 1331 and died sixty years later, but it is difficult to disentangle the events of the intervening years from the myths – many self-promoted – that sprung up around him. The troubadour poets acknowledged him as a friend and embellished his deeds in their lyrics, while Jean Froissart – chronicler of the Hundred Years' War – was invited by Fébus to write his biography. Gaston was a poet himself and the author of a book on hunting – an example of the genre of "self-help" books for image-conscious nobles of the era. His surname, Fébus, was his own invention, derived from the Occitan for sun and celebrating his long, golden hair. Although an autocratic ruler, who abolished the legislative councils of town-dwellers and set himself up as the highest judicial authority in his realms, he cultivated a reputation as a fair-minded and dauntless soldier, always leading his men into battle with the cry *Fébus avan* (Fébus at the front).

His great ambition was to create an autonomous kingdom of the Pyrenees, adding by conquest the regions of Bigorre and Soule to his inherited domains of Nébouzan (around Saint-Gaudens), Béarn (in the far west) and Foix. This goal was made impossible by the continuing Hundred Years' War, which divided the loyalties of his subjects; Gascony on the west was ruled by the English Crown – in particular the Black Prince (in direct control 1362–71), while to the east lay Languedoc, subject to France. In addition, feuding between the leading families of the area kept him occupied; one of his most significant victories came in 1362, when he crushed his Gascon arch-enemies, the English-allied Armagnacs. In time he lost the appetite to pursue his grand plan, by most accounts after 1380, when it seems Fébus killed his only son on discovering the son's role in a plot to assassinate him.

Thereafter, determined that his enemies should not succeed where he apparently had failed, Fébus dedicated himself to campaigning for a strong, united France, pledging his lands to the French Crown by inheritance. Yet this was not to happen until 1589, with the accession to the Parisian throne of Henri III of Foix-Béarn and Navarre, a descendant of Fébus's fierce rivals, the d'Albrets.

become a Pyrenean mini-state to the Crown when he became Henri IV of France. But the biggest name in Foix is that of the fair-haired knight whose features can be seen on postcards all over town – Gaston III, known as Gaston Fébus (see box above).

The best part of a castle visit is clambering up worn stairs in the southern and central towers for startling views across the valley. The interior houses the rather listless **Musée d'Ariège**, whose exhibits range from prehistoric to medieval times, plus some uninspiring interactive displays of local crafts and products.

## Practicalities

The **train station** sits on the right bank of the Ariège, a ten-minute walk east of the centre; most **buses** stop on the central cours Gabriel-Fauré, near the Resistance monument, although some will drop you off behind the post office. **Car rental** can be arranged through ADA, 59 avenue du Général Leclerc

(☎05.61.68.38.38); Europcar, Route d'Espagne (☎05.61.02.32.74); or Hertz, RN20 Peysales (☎05.61.65.15.99). The **tourist office** at 45 cours Gabriel-Fauré (July & Aug Mon–Sat 9am–7pm, Sun 10am–noon & 2–6pm; Sept–June Mon–Sat 9am–noon & 2–6pm; ☎05.61.65.12.12) can be reached from the train station by walking south along the east bank of the Ariège and then crossing the Pont-Neuf.

Most **accommodation** is in the old town, on the west bank of the Ariège, though little of it is inspiring. If you have the means, the quietest and most comfortable option is the three-star *Hôtel Audoye Lons*, on 6 place Duthil, near the Pont Vieux (☎05.61.65.52.44, ✉hotel-lons-foix@wanadoo.fr; closed late Dec to early Jan; ❸). *De La Barbacanne*, 1 avenue de Lérida (☎05.61.65.50.44, ℱ04.61.65.50.44; closed Nov–March; ❷), and *L'Echauguette*, 1 rue Paul Laffont (☎05.61.2.88.88, ℱ05.61.65.29.49; ❷–❸), are a notch down in price, though both suffer from traffic noise. The *Eychenne*, 9 rue Nöel-Peyrévidal (☎05.61.65.00.04, ℱ05.61.65.56.63; ❷), is the cheapest, with decent enough rooms, though the bar on the ground floor is very lively at night; across the street at no. 16 is the friendly **youth hos-**

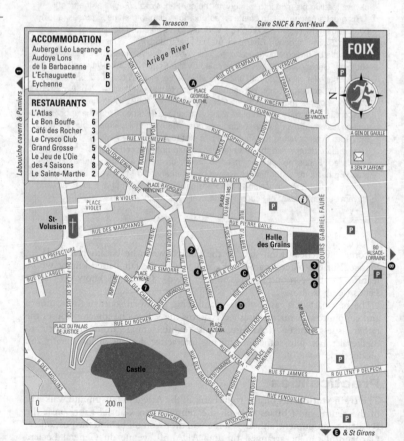

ACCOMMODATION
Auberge Léo Lagrange **C**
Audoye Lons **A**
de la Barbacanne **E**
L'Echauguette **B**
Eychenne **D**

RESTAURANTS
L'Atlas **7**
Le Bon Bouffe **6**
Café des Rocher **3**
Le Crysco Club **1**
Grand Grosse **5**
Le Jeu de L'Oie
des 4 Saisons **4**
Le Sainte-Marthe **2**

FOIX

▲ Tarascon    Gare SNCF & Pont-Neuf ▲

Ariège River

Castle

0    200 m

▼ ❶ & St Girons

**tel** *Auberge Léo Lagrange* (☎05.61.65.09.04, ✉leogagrange-foix@wanadoo.fr; 4-bunk dorms; €15).

The best area for **eating** is rue de la Faurie, the old blacksmiths' bazaar at the centre of the old town, where the best of several establishments is *Des 4 Saisons* at no. 11 (closed Sun–Thurs eve off-season; €13.50–16), whose interesting gimmick is to bring to your table a *pierrade* (hot ceramic square), on which you cook fish and meat yourself – they also do a wide range of crêpes. *Le Jeu de L'Oie* (closed Sat noon & Sun in winter) nearby at no. 17 is also worth trying for more traditional fare. A pricier but worthwhile option is *Le Sainte-Marthe*, at 21 rue Peyrevidal (☎05.61.02.87.87; closed Wed off-season, Tues & part of Feb), with a street-side terrace and a range of specialities, including *cassoulet* (*menus* €24–33). *L'Atlas*, on place Pyrène (closed Sat lunch & Mon), serves up authentic Moroccan cuisine (€14.50–22) beneath the shadow of the town's church.

There is a row of café-restaurants which occasionally double as night-time **music-bars** on the west side of the cours Gabriel Fauré, on either side of the old market hall. *Café des Rocher, Grand Grosse* and *Le Bon Bouffe* all have decent if unspectacular dinner menus for €10–15, and stay open for drinking. Later on, you can head to *Le Crysco Club*, at 3 cours Irénée Cros (Wed–Sat 10pm–3am), on the far side of the *pont vieux* over the Ariège.

# West of Foix: Labouiche and the road to Saint-Girons

Some 3km along the Vernajoul road northwest from the centre of Foix lies the subterranean **river-cavern of Labouiche** (April, May, Oct & Nov Mon–Sat 2–5.15pm, Sun 10–11.45am & 2–5.15pm; June & Sept Mon–Sat 10–11.15am & noon–5.15pm, Sun 10–11.45am & 2–5.15pm; July & Aug Mon–Sat 9.30am–5.30pm, Sun 10–11.45am & 2–5.15pm; €7.50), which claims to be the longest navigable cave in western Europe. It appears never to have been inhabited, and indeed high water levels in winter completely block access. The amusement-park atmosphere of Lombrives (see p.240) prevails here also: twelve-person boats give 75-minute rides along the 1500m of galleries open to the public. Highlights are the waterfall and a small chamber full of formations, both at the upstream end of the river. These and other curiosities are described by guides who do their best to keep up a witty patter, while hauling the crafts along using ceiling-mounted cables.

The D117 main road west from Foix climbs rapidly to the **Col de Bouich** (599m) before descending through the Aujole and Baup valleys to arrive at St-Girons and St-Lizier (see p.315). There's little to detain you en route, although you might stop at **La Bastide de Serou**, just under halfway, to have a drink in the square outside its old market building.

There are two unusual English-run **chambres d'hôte** along the D117, best suited for those with transport. At **RIMONT**, 34km from Foix, excellent accommodation is offered at *Le Guerrat*, Suzanne Morris and Trevor Warman's working organic farm (open mid-May to mid-Oct; ☎05.61.96.37.03, ✉leguerrat@aol.com; ❷), with strict vegan meals available. At **LESCURE**, 4km further on, Nicholas Goldsworthy's hilltop *La Baquette* (☎ & 🖷05.61.96.37.67; ❷) can arrange guided walks and tours of the local wildlife and flora. Heading south from La Bastide de Serou towards Massat (it's also accessible by a minor road 19km direct from Foix), you'll find one of the better hotels in this area at the **Col des Marrous**: *Auberge les Myrtilles* (☎05.61.65.16.46, ⊛perso.wanadoo.fr/auberge.les.myrtilles; ❸; closed

Nov–Jan & Mon & Tues in low season) a rustically decorated hotel with amenities such as an indoor pool and jacuzzi, as well as a fine country restaurant (*menus* €14–21).

# The Pays de Sault

If you haven't got a car or a bike, the magnificent **Pays de Sault** – the upland area bounded by the Aude, the Ariège and the main road from Quillan to Foix – can be crossed in a few days on foot, making occasional use of sporadic public transport. A network of **walking itineraries** – the Tour du Pays de Sault, the Tour du Massif de Tabe, the Piémont and the GR107, plus forestry tracks – provide ways of exploring. The most popular route is the **Sentier Cathare**, which begins at Foix and arrives at Montségur in two stages via **Roquefixade**, then continues to the Mediterranean; it's easy walking much of the year (avoid midwinter and midsummer), with strategically placed accommodation in *gîtes d'étape*.

Regular **bus services** cross the Pays de Sault: one links the train station in Quillan with the one in Foix, via **Puivert** and **Lavelanet**, 10km north of Montségur; the other runs from Quillan via Belcaire and Camurac to **Comus**, 12km southeast, from where Montségur can be reached through the Gorges de la Frau. Because departures are slightly more frequent from the east, the two routes described below approach the area from Quillan.

Much of the Pays de Sault is a spacious agricultural plateau, but it contains more vertiginous terrain, too. At the southeast edge, the dramatic D107 road from Axat to Ax-les-Thermes runs through the **Rebenty** and **Joucou** gorges and over the **Col du Pradel** (1673m), a tough but wonderful cycling route. Further west beyond the heart of the Sault looms the clifftop castle **Montségur**, the greatest stronghold of the Cathars.

The vast highlands are composed primarily of limestone, and thus riddled with caves and ravines such as the spectacular **Gorges de la Frau**. Above ground, its agriculture has changed little since Cathar times; pesticides have yet to infiltrate the region's ecosystem, so the silhouettes of birds of prey are fixtures in the sky.

Neither of the region's downhill **ski stations** is worth much effort. **Les Monts d'Olmes** resort, southwest of Montségur, is focused on a seedy apartment development at the base of twenty runs which, though north-facing, barely reach 2000m elevation. **Camurac**, due north of Ax-les-Thermes along the D613 near Camurac village, is even dinkier and lower (1800m), with the base station consisting of a "village" of decaying institutional chalets for assorted youth groups.

There is good **cross-country skiing** on the plateau, however, with a small rental and tuition operation at **Comus** and especially good terrain at the **Col de Marmare**.

## Puivert

Although it's just a twenty-minute drive out of Quillan, the countryside around **PUIVERT** feels quite different, a vast upland planted with corn and sunflowers, buzzed by amateur pilots using the small airport near the middle. The village itself offers all amenities, including the **gîte d'étape** *Le Relais des Marionnettes* (☎04.68.20.80.69, ✉michel.dubrunfaut@wanadoo.fr; 22 places;

❷), and the **restaurant** *Dame Blanche*, with hearty menus. Less than 1km south of the village is a small lake with a **campsite** (℡04.68.20.00.58; May–Sept) and swimming area (daily except Mon), a welcome sight whether you've been cycling, driving or hiking.

Puivert's **château** (daily: April–Sept 8am–8pm; Oct–March 10am–5pm; €4), standing alone like a cardboard cut-out atop a gently rounded hill 1km or so east of the village, fell to the anti-Cathar crusade in 1210. More a place of culture than of arms, it was closely associated with the **troubadour** poets, whose preoccupation with themes of romance and war was starkly at odds with the asceticism and (initial) pacifism of the Cathars. Indeed most troubadours were unsympathetic to Cathar belief; what united them was the Occitan language, then spoken across southern France. For the troubadours the *langue d'Oc* was simply the natural language of poetry and love; for the Cathars it expressed their defiance of the Norman North. Little remains of the pre-1210 structure; most of what's visible dates from the fourteenth century. Visits concentrate on the various floors of the *donjon*, with stairs all the way to the roof; the chapel features vigil seats at the north and south windows, a wall font and ceiling rib-vaulting culminating in a keystone embossed with images of the Virgin and St George. The highest chamber is dubbed the "musicians' room" after its eight *culs-de-lampes* or torch sockets at the termini of more rib-vaulting, each sculpted in the form of a figure playing a different period instrument.

## Northern approaches to Montségur

From Puivert the road heads west over the Col de Teil, the divide between the Aude and the Ariège, and the Pyrenean watershed: east of it, rivers flow to the Mediterranean, while on the west they empty into the Atlantic. You can walk from Puivert to Montségur along the **Sentier Cathare**, a long but not difficult day of some 25km, mostly through dense fir forests.

### Bélesta, Fougax-Barrineuf and Lavelanet

A better place to begin the walk, however, is 11km west at **BÉLESTA**, the next stop on the bus route and a far more manageable village than Lavelanet (see below). If you get stranded there's **accommodation** at the *Le Troubador* (℡05.61.01.60.57; ❷) on the through road, with a restaurant (lunch from €10.50; dinner from €15) and **camping** on the east side of the village at *Le Val d'Amour* (June–Sept). Attractions begin almost immediately on the way south: some 1500m out of Bélesta, the route to Montségur passes **Fontestorbes**, an artesian spring (*source intermittente*) under a rock overhang that in summer spurts water for six minutes evenly separated by 32-minute pauses (in winter the water flows continuously). From the spring you can continue directly to Montségur by walking along various marked GRs (3hr), or taking a longer detour via the Gorges de la Frau, 8km south (see below).

The most direct approaches pass through the double village of **FOUGAX-BARRINEUF**, 2km southwest, which has a fine **restaurant**, *Les Cinque Fours* (open May–Sept), occupying an old bone-comb factory (formerly an important local industry, established by Protestants between the sixteenth and eighteenth centuries). The portions aren't huge, but the €12.50 *menu* is quite adequate as a four-course lunch.

**LAVELANET**, 8km west of Bélesta on the D117, has little to offer other than onward bus connections, its **tourist office** on the central roundabout (July & Aug Mon–Sat 9am–noon & 2–7pm, Sun 9am–noon; Sept–June

The origins of Cathar belief seem to lie in **Manicheism**, a dualistic Middle Eastern doctrine expounding the concept of the material world as an invasion of the world of Light by the powers of Darkness. This first found practical expression in Europe among the Bogomils of the Balkan peninsula during the tenth century, who – following years of persecution – converted to Islam under the Ottomans. By the twelfth century a modified version of this belief system, probably introduced by returning Crusaders exposed to Bogomilism, had taken hold in the south of France, especially in the area of Albi where the first disputation between these dualists and the Church authorities took place in 1165 – hence the alternative name of **Albigeois** (or Albigenses) for the Cathars.

According to Cathar thinking, God reigned over the spiritual world, the Devil created the material world, and Christ was God's messenger, an apparently physical manifestation of the spiritual world, with whom souls could be united and so be released into immortality. In line with their disdain of the material realm, the most austere believers shunned milk and meat, and considered marriage or procreation evil. These and other Cathar beliefs posed a number of problems for the Church of Rome. Firstly, Cathars denied the doctrine of the Virgin Birth, the mystery of Christ's fully human and fully divine nature, and insisted that the Catholic faithful, in worshipping any Creator of matter, were in fact worshipping the Devil. They were **antimaterialists** by definition – asceticism was seen as the only route to redemption – and thus had no need for sumptuous buildings or trappings favoured by the Church. They were initially **pacifists**, and condemned the Crusades, one of the methods used to increase papal and aristocratic fortunes. Moreover, the austere spirituality of their leaders – the *parfaits* and *parfaites* (lay adherents were known simply as *bons hommes* and *bonnes femmes*) – was a constant rebuke to the dissolute clergy of the Church, while their close contact with the population met the needs of common folk habitually ignored by Catholic institutions. On top of all this, their conviction that they were exempt from feudal vows of allegiance made them politically attractive to independent-minded petty nobility – and exceedingly dangerous to distant, centralizing powers.

Following the election of **Pope Innocent III** in 1198, some years were spent trying to peacefully convince the heretical clergy of the error of their ways. But it was not until 1208 that Innocent, his patience exhausted, formally declared a crusade and succeeded in convincing the previously reluctant king of France, Philippe Auguste, to provide forces. Ranged against this formidable combination were the *seigneurs* of Languedoc, who had been in constant territorial competition with the bishops of the region, and many of whose subjects had become adherents of Catharism.

The first target was **Raymond VI of Toulouse**, excommunicated by the pope in 1207 for his tacit approval of Catharism (and, nearly as bad in the papal view, employment of Jews). Early the following year Raymond succeeded in persuading the papal legate Pierre de Castelnau to have the excommunication lifted, but on the day after agreement was reached the legate was murdered by a servant of Raymond, providing his enemies with a pretext for military action.

In July 1209 an army led by the archbishop of Narbonne and new legate, **Arnaud Amaury**, invaded Languedoc, with a heavy contingent of English mercenaries in its ranks. Béziers was besieged, taken suprisingly quickly and its entire population – a figure put by some authorities at twenty thousand – massacred for refusing to surrender a score or so Cathars in their midst. When asked how the Catholic citizens were to be distinguished from the heretics, Amaury supposedly replied: "Kill them all, God will recognize His own." Apocryphal utterance or not, this effectively became the motto of a campaign distinguished even by medieval standards for its brutality. After more protracted resistance, Carcassonne fell, eventually to be handed over – as Béziers had been – to the professional Norman crusader **Simon de Montfort**. For a few years Raymond VI played a double game to survive and to have his excommunication definitively revoked, even marching with the crusaders on occasion. But by 1213 the inexorable de Montfort, terrorizing the population with his atrocities, was in control of virtually all of Languedoc, forcing Raymond VI and his son to flee to the English court of King John, the elder Raymond's brother-in-law. When the two Raymonds returned from exile in 1216, they resumed battle with de Montfort at Toulouse, which their arch-foe was besieging – a campaign that cost him his life in June 1218.

Their success was fairly short-lived; although the younger Raymond, who formally succeeded his father in 1222, managed to regain lost territory and reorganize the Cathar communities therein, a new scorched-earth campaign was unleashed in summer 1226 by the fanatical Parisian king **Louis VIII**. After see-saw battles, Raymond VII sued for peace in 1229; though remaining count of Tolouse, by the terms of the peace treaty he had to submit to public humiliations, the razing of the walls of Toulouse, the loss of his possessions beyond the Rhône, heavy financial indemnities to the Catholic Church, and the marriage of his only daughter to the younger brother of the new Parisian king, the underage Louis IX. Raymond, who died in 1249, was never henceforth able to provide the Cathar community with anything resembling comprehensive protection, and indeed in order to prove his zeal as a "defender of the faith" and stave off repeated attempts at excommunicating him, Raymond denounced heretics and burnt them at the stake of his own accord.

Though the first wave of military crusades had finished, the Cathar heresy was still far from being eradicated, especially in the Pyrenean foothills. In 1233, the new pope Gregory IX authorized the creation of the infamous **Inquisition**, to be supervised by Dominican and Franciscan monks. The Dominican order itself had been founded in 1206 by Domingo de Guzmán, later known to the world as **Saint Dominic**, a proselytizer who came specially from Castille to the Cathar heartland to counter the growing heresy. Leaving violent coercion to others, his preferred strategies were strenuous disputations with Cathar theologians, imitation of their austere habits and the founding of a convent at Prouille to receive Cathar women who recanted their beliefs. But the inquisitors of the late 1230s who fanned out across Languedoc employed the harsher methods for which they became subsequently notorious, and aroused such resistance that at Raymond VII's request, the pope briefly suspended their activities in 1237.

Inquisitorial convictions, imprisonments, stake-burnings and confiscations of the property of aristocratic sympathizers with Catharism resumed in 1240, and the Cathars still at liberty reacted in a manner which sealed their fate. In May 1242, a group of 85 knights from Montségur, led by **Pierre-Roger de Mirepoix**, went to Avignonet and hacked the eleven chief inquisitors to death as they slept. The retaliatory assault on Montségur, by a force of almost ten thousand men, began in May 1243, and continued through the winter – the first time in the Cathar crusades that the fighting was not suspended when the weather turned. On March 2, 1244, de Mirepoix, despairing of relief, agreed terms: the two hundred-plus non-Cathar soldiers within the citadel would be allowed to go unmolested, but after two weeks' truce the Cathars themselves were to abjure their faith or submit to whatever fate their tormenters devised for them. On the night of March 15, in contravention of the terms, four Cathars climbed down the cliffs, escaped over the Col de la Peyre and recovered the Cathar "treasure" from a cave where it had been hidden at Christmas. What happened to it is a mystery, giving rise to legends – especially in German sources – identifying the treasure as the Holy Grail, and the Cathars themselves as the Knights of the Round Table. The next day Montségur surrendered, and the 225 surviving Cathar civilians who refused to abjure their beliefs were burned on a mass pyre, those who could not walk being thrown on with their stretchers.

*continued overleaf*

In effect, Catharism ceased to exist as a significant force in France after the holo-caust at Montségur, though two of the four escapees later appeared in Lombardy, where proceeds from the "treasure" would support a refugee Cathar community established there. Quéribus and Puilaurens – the final Cathar fortifications in Roussillon – came under royal control between 1255 and 1258. When Raymond VII's daughter died childless in 1271, all of Languedoc passed to the French Crown. From then on, Catharism persisted mainly as an underground network, with safe houses and escape routes extending across the mountains into Spanish Aragonese and Catalan villages, where it was more openly practised until the Inquisition got to work there during the fifteenth century. The last significant figure in Cathar history, Guilhem Bélibaste, was executed in 1321, having been caught returning from Spain to proselytize, and the last Lombard *bons hommes* were rooted out by the Inquisition in 1412, the same year they visited the village of Montaillou.

Mon–Sat 9am–noon & 2–7pm; ☎05.61.01.22.20, ⒺⓁ lavelanet.tourisme @wanadoo.fr), and the clean, modern *Camping de Lavelanet* southwest of the centre (☎05.61.01.55.54; April–Sept).

# The southern approach to Montségur via Comus

From Monday to Friday there are two late-afternoon buses from Quillan to Comus, some 40km southwest. The only **hotel** in the region is at **BEL-CAIRE**: the *Bayle* (☎04.68.20.31.05, Ⓔ hotel-bayle@ataraxie.fr; ❷), with a restaurant. If you've read Emmanuel Le Roy Ladurie's *Montaillou* you may want to get off at Camurac, 6km beyond Belcaire and 3km short of Comus, walk-ing the rest of the way via Montaillou village, subject of the book and a detour that takes about two hours. **CAMURAC** offers **accommodation** at the *Auberge du Pays de Sault* (☎04.68.20.32.09; ❷) and *Camping les Sapins* (☎04.68.20.38.11).

**MONTAILLOU** (Montelhó in Occitan) subscribed to the Cathar heresy long after the fall of Montségur, until the Inquisition, directed by the bishop of Pamiers, set to work here during the 1320s. The records compiled by the inquisitors were so precise that Le Roy Ladurie was able to re-create every aspect of the villagers' lives, from the minutiae of domestic economics to the details of their sexual habits. Fewer than twenty people live here permanently now, all of them descendants of the Cathars, as you can see by comparing their surnames with those on the headstones in the ancient graveyard.

**COMUS** isn't much bigger than Montaillou, but does have an excellent **gîte d'étape**, the *Gîtes et Loisirs de Montagne* (☎04.68.20.33.69, Ⓔ anne@gites-comus.com; 38 places), which specializes in **caving**, the limestone hereabouts being peppered with two hundred known caves. Montségur is 13km away, through the **Gorges de la Frau**. From Comus, take the GR107, formerly the GR7B, which drops down as a mule track between fields to a wide gorge that suddenly becomes a defile, where thousand-metre cliffs admit sun only in the early afternoon. The gorge widens again as you meet the dead-end of the D5 coming south from Bélesta and Fougax-Barrineuf. There are two ways of con-tinuing to Montségur: west along the Sentier Cathare, wrapped in tree-shade alongside a stream (turn off at the first farm, 45min along the D5), or on a bridle trail beginning about an hour along the road, offering higher, more open ground. Either way, walking time from Comus is four hours.

## Montségur

The ruined castle of **MONTSÉGUR** lives up to the promise of its distant view, its plain stone walls poised emphatically above the straggling, namesake village on a 1207-metre-high *pog* (from the Occitan *puèg*, or "peak"). The original fortifications were built by Guillaume "Short-Nose", duke of Aquitaine, but between 1204 and 1232 it was reconstructed as a bastion of the Cathars under the direction of Guilhabert de Castres, leader of the sect. Drastically eroded into naked vertical faces and gullies, the *pog* would have been a formidable defence. Only on the western side can you walk up to the summit (about 30min) through the *prat dels cremats* where the surviving Cathars were burned to death after the castle fell (a stone memorial pays tribute to them); see p.246–248.

The beauty of **the site** (daily: Feb 10.30am–4pm; March 10am–5pm; April, Sept & Oct 9.30am–6pm; May–Aug 9am–7.30pm; Nov 10am–5.30pm; Dec 10.30am–4.30pm, €3.50) impresses you first since the original walls were reduced by half after the siege, and all internal structures are gone except the simple keep, now open to the sky. Then you begin to wonder how that last Cathar community of five hundred could have held out so long in such a small area. Although some lived in now-vanished houses at the foot of the walls on the north and west faces, there was still a sizeable garrison here, together with the *faydits* – local aristocrats dispossessed by the crusade against Catharism. What's left of it takes no more than a few minutes to view – rather disappointingly, you're no longer allowed to climb up on the walls, merely to traverse the keep to visit the west *donjon*. But it's not so much what you see at Montségur that makes the trip unforgettable, as what your imagination can re-create from its remnants.

Down in the village, 1km below, a one-room **archeological museum** (daily: summer 10am–noon & 2–5.30pm; winter 2–4.30pm, free) displays artefacts excavated since the 1950s from the original village up beside the walls, from both pre- and post-Cathar periods – mostly food bones, personal effects, tools and surviving fragments of houses.

### Practicalities

Despite its small size, Montségur village has a seasonal **tourist office** (July–Sept daily 10am–1pm & 2–6pm; ☏ & ℻05.61.03.03.03, ⓦwww .citaenet.com/montsegur), of most use for information on the GR107; check also the local *topoguide*, which they occasionally stock. If you'd like to stay the night, the more reliable of the two **hotels** is the *Costes* (☏05.61.01.10.24, ⓔcontact@chez.costes.com; closed mid-Nov to April; ❷), with a rustic restaurant featuring game and *ariègeois* specialities for €16–27 (closed Sun eve, & Mon in low season). Otherwise, there's an excellent, welcoming *chambre d'hôte* in the village, *L'Oustal* (☏05.61.02.80.70, ⓔserge.goma@wanadoo.fr; ❸ B&B, ❺ HB), with simple but abundant food and modernized facilities. *L'Occitadelle* is the one – fortunately excellent – independent **restaurant** specializing in fire-cooked *foie* sausages and local trout (from €15; closed Fri). There's also a **gîte d'étape** (phone as for *Costes*; April to mid-Nov), while the closest **campsite** (tents only) is the *Point Acceuil Jeunes* (☏05.61.01.10.27) at the lower end of the village on the Bélesta side.

## Roquefixade

Approximately 8km west of Lavelanet, the village of Nalzen is the best point along the D117 for access to **ROQUEFIXADE**, the westernmost Cathar castle and last stop on the Sentier Cathare before Foix. A two-kilometre side road leads up to the village of Roquefixade, rebuilt after the Cathar crusades as a *bastide*. From the high end of the village it's a twenty-minute climb to the castle (free), which takes its name (originally *roca fissada*) from the vast natural fissures augmenting its defences. Perched at the west end of a long ridge, it's bigger than it appears from below but utterly ruined; your main reward is the view over the valley below with its clustered villages, and south (weather permitting) to the high Pyrenean ridge.

A **gîte d'étape** (℡05.61.03.01.36; 12 places) stands by the base of the path up to the castle, and their outdoor seating is good for a drink after the climb. Alternative **accommodation** is available at the *Relais des Pogs* (℡05.61.01.14.50, ⓦperso.wanadoo.fr/gite-relais-des-pogs), with doubles (❷) and dorm space.

# Travel details

## FRANCE

**Trains**

**Foix** to: Ax-les-Thermes (7 daily; 50min); L'Hospitalet-près-l'Andorre (7 daily; 1hr 15min); Tarascon-sur-Ariège (9 daily; 15min–20min); Toulouse (11 daily; 1hr 15min–1hr 30min).
**Latour-de-Carol** to: Ax-les-Thermes (7 daily; 55min); Bourg-Madame (5 daily; 15min); Foix (7 daily; 1hr 40min–2hr); L'Hospitalet-près-l'Andorre (9 daily; 25min); Mont-Louis (4 daily; 1hr 20min); Puigcerdà (4 daily; 7min); Tarascon-sur-Ariège (9 daily; 1hr 25min–1hr 45min); Toulouse (6 daily; 2hr 30min–2hr 45min); Villefranche-de-Conflent (4 daily; 2hr 25min–2hr 45min).

**Buses**

**Ax-les-Thermes** to: Foix (2 daily; 1hr); Pas de la Casa (July & Aug only 1daily; 1hr 10min); Tarascon-sur-Ariège (2 daily; 30min).
**Comus** to: Quillan (1–2 daily Mon–Fri; 1hr).
**Foix** to: Lavelanet (2–3 daily; 35min); Quillan (Mon–Sat 1 daily in afternoon; 2hr); St-Girons (4 daily; 45min).
**L'Hospitalet-près-l'Andorre** to: Andorra la Vella (2 daily; 1hr 15min–1hr 35min); Pas de la Casa (2 daily; 25–35min).
**Latour-de-Carol** to: Font-Romeu (4 daily; 50min); Perpignan (4 daily; 3hr).
**Lavelanet** to: Foix (1–3 daily; 30min); Quillan (Mon–Sat 2 daily in afternoon; 45min).

## SPAIN

**Trains**

**Puigcerdà** to: Barcelona (6 daily; 3hr 10min); Latour-de-Carol (4 daily; 7min); Ripoll (6 daily; 1hr 10min).

**Buses**

**Berga** to: Barcelona (4–5 daily; 2hr); Borredà (1 daily Mon–Sat afternoon, returns next morning; 30min); Castellar de N'Hug (1 daily Mon–Sat late afternoon, returns next morning; 1hr 20min); Gòsol via Saldes (1 daily late afternoon, returns next morning; 1hr); La Pobla de Lillet (2–4 daily; 1hr); Ripoll (1 daily; 1hr 20min); Sant Llorenç de Morunys (1 daily Mon–Fri late afternoon, returns next morning; 1hr).
**Puigcerdà** to: Alp (4 daily; 10min); Bagà (4 daily; 35min); Berga (4 daily; 1hr); Llívia (5 daily; 5min); La Molina (1 daily; 30min); La Seu d'Urgell (3 daily; 1hr).
**La Seu d'Urgell** to: Andorra la Vella (14 daily Mon–Sat, 5 Sun; 40min); Barcelona (4 daily; 3hr 30min); Lleida (2 daily with Alsina Graells; 2hr 20min); Puigcerdà (3 daily with Alsina Graells at 9.15am, 12.30pm & 7pm; 1hr).

## ANDORRA

**Domestic buses**

**Andorra la Vella** to: Arcalis (12 daily in ski season; 45min); Arinsal (5 daily; 30min); El Serrat (3 daily; 30min); Encamp (every 15min 7.20am–8.30pm, last bus 9.30pm; 15min); Escaldes-Engordany (every 15min 7am–9.30pm; 8min); Ordino (every 30min 8am–9pm; 20min); Pas de la Casa (4 daily summer, 6 winter; 1hr 30min); Soldeu (hourly 8am–8pm; 45min).

**International buses**

**Andorra la Vella** to: Ax-les-Thermes (July & Aug only; 2hr 15min); L'Hospitalet-près-l'Andorre (2 daily; 1hr 30min); Latour-de-Carol (2 daily; 2hr).

# The Val d'Aran region

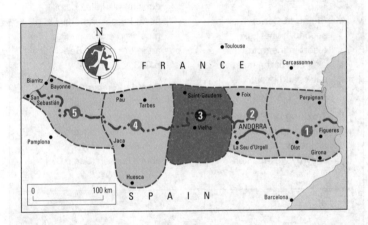

CHAPTER THREE Highlights

✳ **Rafting on the Noguera
Pallaresa** The most
boisterous river in the
Pyrenees attracts
novices and experts
alike. See p.264

✳ **The Vall de Boí** A
UNESCO-protected val-
ley, home to a remark-
able concentration of
eleventh-century
Romanesque churches.
See p.289

✳ **Skiing at Cerler** The
second-highest ski
resort in the range is
also one of the most ver-
satile, and beautifully
set. See p.302

✳ **Trekking on Posets**
Traversing this unspoilt
alpine massif is made
easy by well-marked

trails and strategically
sited refuges. See p.306

✳ **Saint-Bertrand-de-
Comminges** An ancient
cathedral, with ingen-
ious, carved choir stalls
and an atmospheric
cloister, is the centre-
piece of this fortified village. See p.327

✳ **Notre-Dame de
Tramezaygues** The fres-
coes in this little church
at Audressein are the
most impressive sacred
art in the region. See
p.323

✳ **Port de Vénasque**
Retrace the steps of the
pioneering nineteenth-
century mountaineers
with this easy day-walk
above Luchon. See p.333

# 3

# The Val d'Aran region

Isolated from Spain and draining towards France, the **Val d'Aran** is something of a curiosity: the frontier here is thrust so far north that both sources of the Garonne, one of southern France's major rivers, lie in Spanish territory. Owing to easy access from both Spain and France, the Val d'Aran makes an obvious starting point into the surrounding mountains. Although heavily developed for skiers and summer weekenders from Toulouse and Barcelona, the Aran region itself is not lacking in interest.

The popular image of the Pyrenees as two separate mountain chains, overlapping for some 70km at the Val d'Aran, is misleading. The definitive geomorphological map of the range, produced in 1973 by the French company Elf-Aquitaine, shows that the watershed is merely distorted here. A significant spur off the main ridge which would ordinarily point south–north is actually deflected east–west, giving the illusion of separate peak lines. In fact, only some low hills to the west in the Basque country are tectonically separate from the main Pyrenean chain.

Between Aran and Andorra, the easternmost of the Pyrenean "three-thousanders", **Montcalm** and **Estats**, loom over remote valleys on either side of the border. Their approaches see few visitors, except along the banks of the mighty **Noguera Pallaresa**, one of the great Pyrenean rivers which flows from just east of Aran south to Lleida. South of Aran, and also accessible from the Noguera Pallaresa valley, spreads the only national park in the Catalan Pyrenees, the **Parc Nacional d'Aigüestortes i Estany de Sant Maurici**, a 15,000-hectare wonderland of crags, tarns and dense forest, delighting hikers, alpine skiers and naturalists alike.

**Maladeta** – the great massif southwest of Aran, in Alto Aragón – was erroneously translated from the Aragonese *Mala Eta* ("The Highest Point") as "The Accursed" by early French climbers, thanks to the terrifying glaciers that once dominated this part of the range. Their fearful crevasses delayed the first successful ascent of **Aneto** – the 3404-metre roof of the Pyrenees – until 1842, using a long and convoluted route avoiding the ice. Owing to global warming, today's glaciers are scant vestiges of those that once covered the peaks, and modern maps and equipment further reduce this terrain's power to intimidate.

Immediately west of Maladeta looms the comparatively unsung massif of **Posets**, second highest in the Pyrenees and equally beloved by alpine aficionados. Together these two great mountains form a vast region far easier seen and crossed on foot or skis than by vehicle, so it comes as a welcome surprise to find the comfortable town of **Benasque**, mountaineering capital of eastern Aragón, at the bottom of the Ésera valley separating the two mountains. There's

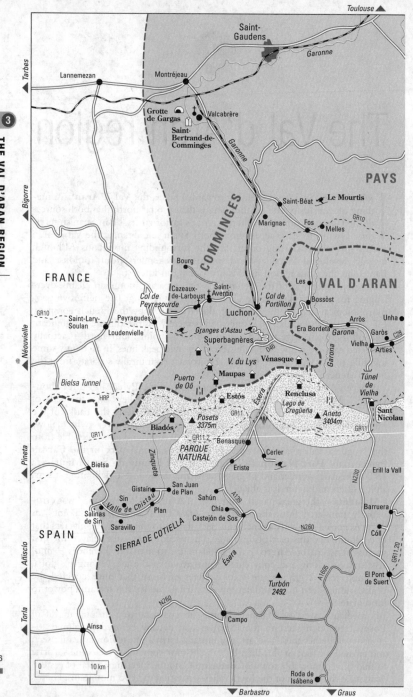

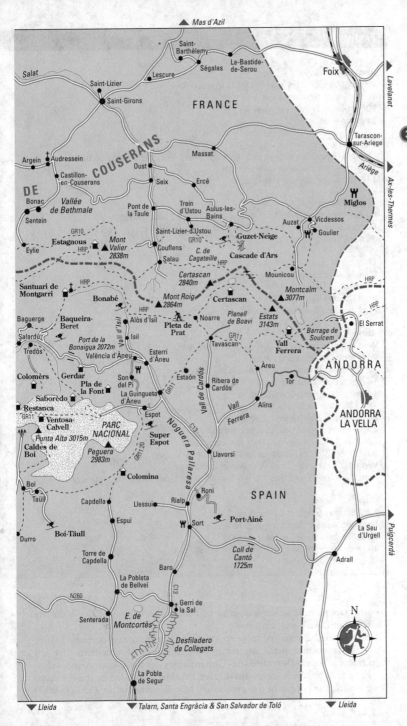

▲ Mas d'Azil

Saint-Barthélemy
Ségalas
La-Bastide-de-Serou
Lescure
Foix
Salat
Saint-Lizier
Saint-Girons
FRANCE
Massat
Tarascon-sur-Ariege
Argein
Audressein
Oust
COUSERANS
Castillon-en-Couserans
DE
Bonac
Vallée
de Bethmale
Sentein
Seix
Ercé
Trein
d'Ustou
Aulus-les-Bains
Pont de
la Taule
Auzat
Vicdessos
Miglos
GR10
Eylie
Estagnous
HRP
Mont
Valier
2838m
Saint-Lizier-d.Ustou
Couflens
GR10
Salau
C. de Cagateille
Guzet-Neige
Cascade d'Ars
HRP
Goulier
Mounicou
Santuari de
Montgarri
HRP
Certascan
2840m
Montcalm
3077m
HRP
Bonabé
Mont Roig
2864m
Certascan
Baguerge
Baqueira-Beret
HRP
Alòs d'Isil
Noarre
Planell
de Boavi
Estats
3143m
El Serrat
Salardú
Port de la
Bonaigua 2072m
Isil
Pleta de
Prat
Barrage de
Soulcem
HRP
Tredòs
València d'Àneu
GR11
Tavascan
Vall
Ferrera
Colomèrs
Gerdar
Esterri
d'Àneu
Àreu
ANDORRA
Pla de
la Font
Son
del Pi
Estaón
Ribera de
Cardós
Tor
Saborèdo
La Guingueta
d'Àneu
Vall de Cardós
Vall
Alins
ANDORRA
LA VELLA
Restanca
GR11
Ventosa-
Calvell
Espot
Ferrera
Punta Alta 3015m
PARC
NACIONAL
Super
Espot
GR11.20
Llavorsí
Caldes de
Boí
Peguera
2983m
Noguera Pallaresa
Boí
Colomina
Roní
Taüll
Capdella
Llessui
Rialp
SPAIN
Durro
Espui
Sort
Port-Ainé
Boí-Taüll
C13
La Seu
d'Urgell
Torre de
Capdella
Coll de
Cantó
1725m
Adrall
Baro
La Pobleta
de Bellveí
C13
N260
Gerri de
la Sal
Senterada
E. de
Montcortès
Desfiladero
de Collegats
N
La Pobla
de Segur

▼ Lleida          ▼ Talarn, Santa Engràcia & San Salvador de Toló          ▼ Lleida

## Festivals

### January
**7** *Festa Major de Sant Julià* at La Guingueta d'Àneu and Espui.
**16** Festival at Gerri de la Sal.
**20** Festival at El Pont de Suert.
**24** Leather fair at Sort.

### February
**Variable** Shrove Tuesday at Sort, Rialp, Esterri d'Àneu and Pobleta de Bellveí.
**12** *Festa Major de Santa Eulàlia* at Erill la Vall.
**14** *Festa Major de Sant Valentí* at Boí.

### March/April
**Easter** Particularly lively festivities at Alins and La Pobla de Segur.
**Sunday after Easter** *Fira de la Pasqüeta* at Esterri d'Àneu.
**28 April** Spring fair at Sort.

### May
**3** *Festa de la Santa Creu* at Salardú.
**6** Festival at Llavorsí.
**First Sunday** Festival at Arròs.
**First and last Sunday** Festival at Gerri de la Sal.

### June
**Whit Sunday** Festival at Mare de Déu de les Ares.
**Whit Monday** Festival at Arròs.
**12** Wool fair at Rialp; sheep-shearing at Llessuí.
**14** *Romeria de Sant Quirç* at Taüll.
**16** *Romeria de Sant Quirç* at Durro.
**Third Sunday** Festival at Es Bordes.
**23** *Feux de la Saint Jean* at Luchon.
**23–24** Festivals at Arties, Lés, Boí, Isil and Saint-Lizier.
**28–29** *Festa de Sants Pau i Pere* at Alins and Tor.
**30** *Ball de Benás* in honour of San Marcial at Benasque.
**Variable** *Festival du Chant Pyrénéen* at Luchon.
**Late June** *Raiers*, old-time log-raft festival, at Sort, continues into early July.

### July
**First Sunday** *Raiers* at La Pobla de Segur.
**First two weeks** Classical music festival at Saint-Lizier.
**2** Festival at Santuari de Montgarri.
**10** *Festa Major de Sant Cristòfol* at Erill la Vall.

no other appreciable settlement until you reach the villages of the **Valle de Chistau**, on Poset's western flank.

If Spain has the region's most spectacular high-mountain scenery, France boasts the finest man-made attractions. Two millennia of settlement have left their traces at **Saint-Bertrand-de-Comminges**, on the Garonne, and a similar air of antiquity pervades **Saint-Lizier**, originally founded by the Romans. Long before, the people of the prehistoric Magdalenian culture (15,000–8000

**19–20** *Festa Major* at La Guingueta d'Àneu.
**24** Festival at Llavorsí.
**24–25** *Festa de Sant Jaume* at La Pobla de Segur and Arties.
**31** Festival at Gerri de la Sal.
**Third weekend** *Festa Major dels Rosers* at Taüll; torchlight procession *(faies)* Fri pm, live bands Sat pm, folk dancing Sun noon.
**Mid-July to mid-August** Music festival at Saint-Lizier.
**End July to August** Music festival at Saint-Bertrand-de-Comminges.
**All month** International Canoe Rally on the Noguera Pallaresa.

### August

**Early part of the month** Music festival at Saint-Lizier.
**First Sunday** *La Pujada* Catalan-Occitan solidarity festival at the Port de Salau.
**1–3** *Festa Major de Sant Feliu* and canoe-racing at Sort; *Festa Major* at Barruera.
**2–3** *Festa de Sant Esteve* in Tredòs.
**15** Canoe-racing at Rialp.
**Second weekend** *Festa Major* at El Pont de Suert.
**10** *Festa Major de Sant Martí* at Torre de Capdella.
**15–16** Festivals at several Baixaran villages, including Bossòst.
**Third Sunday** Flower festival at Luchon.
**27** *Festa de Sant Llisser* at Alòs d'Isil.
**Fourth Sunday** *Festa Major* at Capdella.

### September

**7–9** Birth of the Virgin observances at Sort, Esterri d'Àneu, Ribera de Cardós, Barruera, Durro, Cóll, Vielha and Es Bòrdes.
**21** Traditional fair at Vicdessos.
**22** *Festa Major* at Ermita de Sant Maurici.
**Weekend closest to 26** *Festa Major de Sants Cosme i Damià* at Tredòs.
**Last Sunday** *Festa de Sant Miquel* at Llessuí.

### October

**8** Fair at Vielha.
**20** Annual festival at Bossòst.

### November

**7–9** Grand Autumn Fair at Sort.
**23** *Festa de Sant Climent* at Taüll.
**30** *Festa de Sant Andreu* at Salardú.

### December

**9** *Festa de Santa Llogaia* at Espot.
**24** Festival at La Guingueta d'Àneu.

BC) left drawings and sculptures in several caves, including mysterious, "mutilated" hand outlines at the **Grotte de Gargas** near Saint-Bertrand. Depopulation is severe across this French region, particularly in the Pays de Couserans extending south from Saint-Girons to the Val d'Aran; its isolation meant that traditional customs, costumes and occupations persisted into the early twentieth century.

The only major signs of development on either side of the frontier are unsightly **hydroelectric schemes** that occupy almost every canyon. Neither the sites – often still littered with construction debris – nor the pylons marching away from them were conceived with much consideration for aesthetics, wildlife preservation or the wishes of the admittedly dwindling number of local residents.

**Public transport** is fairly sketchy on the French side, though things improve during the ski season. In Spain, bus services are hardly more frequent, again a consequence of rural depopulation. **Trains** from the south stop at La Pobla de Segur, while in the north there is a foothill rail (or rail-bus) service only on the spur line from Montréjeau to Luchon. By contrast, the busy main highway between Montréjeau and La Pobla, threading the entire length of Aran and passing close to Aigüestortes, has a relative abundance of **buses**, as does the road which heads south from Vielha, capital of Aran, to Lleida. Away from this central hub, Benasque in the west has adequate bus services, as does much of the Couserans, with all connections through its regional capital of Saint-Girons.

# The Montcalm-Estats Massif and around

The joint massif of French **Montcalm** (3077m) and border-straddling **Estats** (3143m), the highest mountain in Catalonia, is so remote that until the late 1980s a few bears and lynx were still thought to be living somewhere below the summits. Tucked into a fold of land where the Spanish and French borders meet the westernmost corner of Andorra, this is one of the least-known areas of the Pyrenees – and one of the least accessible. Public transport on both the French and Spanish sides stops about 20km distant, from which point it's a good day's walk to the flanks of the mountain.

There are three usual ways into the massif or its foothills: by road from the **Vicdessos valley** in the Ariège; by track, then trail, from the Spanish valleys of Cardós and Ferrera, in turn reached from the larger **Noguera Pallaresa** downstream; or by footpath **from Andorra** (a route covered on p.218). The two **summits** are connected by a ridge walk that crosses the border; to the west a particularly beautiful but challenging section of the HRP zigzags along the frontier towards Aran.

## The Vicdessos valley

Steep-sided, damp and thick with deciduous forest, the **Vicdessos valley** is a sunless, uncomfortable place to live in winter. However, it does have intrinsic interest – specifically castles at **Miglos** and **Montréal de Sos** – aside from being the most convenient French corridor to Montcalm.

There are occasional (weekdays in term time, every Friday and alternate

Mondays otherwise) late afternoon buses from Foix and Tarascon-sur-Ariège up the valley as far as Auzat, which leaves you about 10km short of Mounicou, and the Pinet alpine hut just above it, the usual Montcalm base-camp.

## Miglos and around

Heading up-valley along the D8, you might stop briefly at the ruined fourteenth-century château of **Miglos**, perched atop a rocky outcrop a couple of kilometres upstream from Niaux. The medieval locals, resenting taxation by its owner Guillaume Arnaud d'Arnave, petitioned Gaston Fébus (see p.241), who obliged them by substituting his own taxes. The château was later razed by Cardinal Richelieu, though the towers – best seen from the northerly approach road – remain intact.

If you have your own transport you could detour down the dead-end D24 to **SIGUER**, where the three-storey, brick-and-timber **Maison des Comptes de Foix** just off the square (closed for restoration) is a splendid Renaissance hunting lodge used by Gaston Fébus, and another 3km to **LERCOUL**, a tiny hamlet clinging to the top of a near-vertical cliff. The GR10 passes through both villages as it comes west from Mérens-les-Vals, then continues over the Col de Lercoul to the village of **GOULIER**, above Vicdessos. Goulier has two **gîtes d'étape**: *Relais de L'Endron* (℡05.61.03.87.72, ℉05.61.03.80.66), on the outskirts, pitched as an outdoor-activity-coordinating centre with a few rooms (❶) as well as a dorm, and the central, welcoming and well-run *Al Cantou* (℡05.61.64.81.84). Both offer half-board rates, not a bad idea as Goulier village has no shop.

## Vicdessos and Auzat

**VICDESSOS**, 9km beyond Capoulet, and its close neighbour **AUZAT** are the southernmost outposts of civilization in the valley. Important foundry centres in decades past, neither has much to recommend it now, though Auzat is pleasant enough, with a little stream coursing through between rows of plane trees, and Vicdessos has a Thursday street market.

At the nearby Templar château of **Montréal de Sos**, a medieval mural of the Holy Lance and Grail was discovered in 1890 but has since faded almost to invisibility. The ruins stand on a mound above the tiny hamlet of Olbier, reached by a footpath from the east bank of the river just past Auzat, or by a track beginning halfway along the road connecting Vicdessos and Goulier. The Templars were responsible for many pilgrims' hospices in the Pyrenees, but became too rich for the liking of the Catholic Church and its allies, who in 1307 accused them of corruption, heresy and sexual depravity, tortured their leaders and finally burnt them to death. The view from the ruins is fabulous, marred only by the aluminium works at Auzat, the last significant source of local employment. During the Middle Ages locals who worked in a now-exhausted iron mine at nearby Rancié had the right to sell whatever they extracted to one of the numerous local forges.

### Practicalities

There's just one local hotel, the fair-value, one-star *Hotel Hivert* in Vicdessos (℡05.61.64.88.17; ❷), on the through road, with an attached **restaurant** (the only one hereabouts). Alternatively there are *chambres d'hôte* at *Les Marmousets* (℡05.61.64.81.62; ❸), between Vicdessos and Auzat, in the main house and in two chalets, plus *La Bonne Auberge* (℡ & ℉05.61.03.80.99; ❶) in Auzat proper, serving well-priced *menus* (from €11). Each village has a **campsite**: the large *La Bexanelle* at Vicdessos (℡05.61.64.82.22), with cabins, and *La Verniere* at Auzat (℡05.61.64.84.46).

The **Maison des Montagnes** in Auzat (July & Aug daily 8am–noon & 2–6pm; Sept–June Mon–Fri 8am–noon, Thurs also 2–6pm, Sat 9am–noon; ℡05.61.64.87.53) is quite helpful, with so few passing tourists to attend to. There's also a **tourist office** in Vicdessos (℡05.61.64.82.59). Organized local activities are limited, though you can ride horses at the Centre Equestre in Ournac, 2km south of Auzat (℡05.61.64.84.66), or soar like a bird with a parapente school, Les Aigles du Montcalm (℡05.61.64.87.53; early May to early Oct).

## The ascent of Montcalm

Around 10km south of Auzat and 1km past the village of **MARC** (just two *chambres d'hôte*; ℡05.61.64.83.86; ❷ B&B), you'll find an inexpensive, rather poorly maintained *gîte d'étape* (℡05.61.64.87.66) at the tiny hamlet of **MOUNICOU**, situated on both the GR10 and a northerly variant of the HRP. If you've arrived early enough in the day, you might prefer to walk uphill for three hours to the modern **Refuge de Pinet** (2246m; ℡05.61.64.80.81; 50 places; daily June–Sept, weekends May & Oct). Staying there makes the **ascent of Montcalm** a more manageable five-to-six-hour round-trip. Alternatively, in seven to eight hours you can just trek one-way from Pinet to the *Refugi de Vall Ferrera* (see p.268) in Spain – a beautiful and popular traverse, though you'll need crampons early in the season. The requisite IGN 1:25,000 **maps** are TOP 25 2148OT *Montcalm-Estats* or Editorial Alpina's *Pica d'Estats/Mont-roig*, though you could just about manage with Rando Éditions' Carte de Randonnées no. 7, *Haute-Ariège/Andorre*.

From Marc, follow the side road west towards L'Artigue for about thirty minutes to a car park at road's end, from where a path waymarked with yellow paint leads to the Pinet refuge. Montcalm looks formidable from here, its summit looming almost 1000m overhead, the bare rock sunless above the grass and trees. The easy going lies all behind you, and the only emergency campsite is beside the **Étang de Montcalm**. Next, you scramble over scree and rock – with one very steep section – to the **Tables de Montcalm**, a sort of gangway rising south, then clamber up rocks to the right, finally reaching a relatively easy shoulder of the summit. The walk along the ridge up to Estats takes another forty minutes. To descend, either retrace your steps or reverse the instructions from the Vall Ferrera (see p.267).

## Trekking west of Marc

At Marc, the **GR10** runs up onto the hillsides above the west bank of the River Vicdessos to the hamlet of Hérout. There it bears northwest, climbing very steeply to the dammed lakes of Escales and Bassiès and up again to Étang d'Alate, from where you descend to the **Port de Saleix** (1794m) and then west through forest to Aulus-les-Bains (p.321) – eight hours' walking in total. You can break this sector at the *Refuge des Étangs de Bassiès* (1660m; ℡05.61.61.89.98; staffed daily June–Aug, weekends only May, Sept & Oct; 50 places), above the higher and smaller natural lake.

Beyond Marc, the **HRP** leaves L'Artigue car park, then climbs west-south-west to the **Port de l'Artigue** (2481m; 4hr) on the Spanish frontier. From the pass you drop to a cluster of lakes in the Spanish **Guiló valley**, threading northwest among them to the **Port de Colatx/Port de Couillac** (2418m). The first day's goal, the **Étang de la Hillette** (1797m), lies two hours below, magnificently situated above the Cirque de Cagateille (total 8–9hr from Marc). There are plans to build a staffed refuge here, but for the time being you'll have to make do with the crude *Cabane de la Hillette*.

Instead of climbing to the Port de Colatx, you can follow the Spanish variant of the HRP, which next intersects the French route at the Port de Salau (see p.321); your first shelter is the *Refugi de Certascan* (see p.269). Staying on the French side, beyond La Hillette the HRP grazes the border just below the **Port de Marteret/Materet** (2217m) before veering northwest towards the Col de Crusous (2300m) on the shoulder of Cap de Ruhous, prelude to a steady descent to Salau (8hr from La Hillette).

If either you or the weather are not up to this, opt for the beautiful half-day ramble from La Hillette down the **Cirque de Cagateille** (see p.321 for more details), through the woods and along the Cors stream, reaching the D38 and the GR10 at Saint-Lizier-d'Ustou, with Trein-d'Ustou 3km further (see p.321 for their respective accounts).

# Up the Noguera Pallaresa

The **Noguera Pallaresa**, the most powerful river in the Spanish Pyrenees, was once used to float logs down to the sawmills at **La Pobla de Segur**, a job now done by truck. This is the Pyrenean river every rafter wants to tackle, but if you're not of that persuasion, the valley is primarily a way of reaching the mountains to either side, or arriving in the Val d'Aran. To ascend Estats or Montcalm, you leave the Noguera Pallaresa at Llavorsí, heading northeast along the valleys of **Cardós** and **Ferrera**; for Aran, the busier C13 road continues northwest, via the **Vall d'Àneu**, up to the seasonally open **Port de Bonaigua**.

### Access from the east

Access to the valley is easiest via La Pobla de Segur, which has public transport connections in three directions. Coming into the Noguera Pallaresa **from the east**, twice-daily minibuses are now available in either direction – book seats on the phone numbers in "Travel Details" at the end of the chapter. Otherwise, drive or hitch along the 46-kilometre road from Adrall (near La Seu d'Urgell) to Sort, or take one of a number of mountain-biking or walking routes. The four-wheel-drive track from Sant Joan de l'Erm, beyond Castellbó (west of La Seu), drops to the Noguera Pallaresa between Rialp and Llavorsí, near the Port-Ainé downhill ski resort. There's also a track from Ars, just outside Andorra's extreme southwest corner, coming down to Tirvia near Llavorsí. From inside Andorra there's another track – passable to most cars in summer – from Pal over the Port de Cabús, descending into Spain at Tor, at the head of the Tor valley; from there you move into the Vall Ferrera valley at Alins and finally into the Cardós valley, not far from Llavorsí. Yet another possibility is to use the **HRP variant** from El Serrat in the northwest corner of Andorra to Tavascan.

### La Pobla de Segur and around

**LA POBLA DE SEGUR** has intrinsically little to offer; you only come here for onward connections. Besides buses further north along the Noguera Pallaresa (and seasonally beyond to Vielha in the Val d'Aran), services journey west to El Pont de Suert, Boí and Capdella for entering the Aigüestortes region.

## Rafting on the Noguera Pallaresa

The main **rafting season** on the Noguera Pallaresa lasts from April until September, though some organizations offer programmes from March to October if snowmelt (and the power company) are amenable.

The original rafts for the journey to the sawmills of La Pobla de Segur were logs lashed together ten-wide, controlled by a long, stern-mounted oar. Today's water-sport versions are reinforced inflatables, up to 6.5m long and weighing around 100kg. If you sign up for a trip – which guarantees a soaking and as much excitement as any well-balanced person would want – you'll usually share a **boat** with seven others, including your guide/pilot, who sits in the rear. Standard **gear** includes crash helmet, buoyancy jacket (*chaleca*), wet suits (water temperature in April is a bracing 8°C), lightweight paddles, but *not* gloves. You need bare fingers to keep hold of the T-grip at the end of the oar (*remo*), of which you should never let go – even on the calmer stretches a sudden bump could catapult it from your hands and knock your neighbour's teeth out.

Everyone keeps one foot in stirrups, but it's certain that you'll **go overboard** – the more mischievous skippers make sure everyone takes a spill during the first moments of easy paddling, so that you lose your fear of the water. When you get pitched in, just "go with the flow", floating on your back feet first with your knees slightly bent to brace for impact against submerged rocks; crewed boats float faster downstream than you do, but you'll be thrown a fifteen-metre line if necessary.

Since groups are mostly local, it's worth knowing a few Spanish **commands**: *adelante* (row forward), *atrás* (paddle backward), *alto* (stop rowing), *contrapeso derecho/izquierda* (throw your weight to the right/left, when entering a rapid).

The fourteen-kilometre stretch of river between Llavorsí and Rialp is the easiest and most commonly rafted, while the 18km from Sort to Desfiladero de Collegats is advanced and even more scenic. Daily **departures** are typically at 11am and noon; in the former case you'll be in the water by 11.20am, and clambering into the return shuttle van at Rialp by 12.40pm. **Prices** in the valley for rafting start at about €29 for a two-hour trip, Llavorsí–Rialp or Sort–Collegats, or €50 for the entire 35-kilometre distance (a full afternoon's outing, packed lunch €13 extra).

La Pobla is served year-round by a twice-daily Alsina Graells **bus** from Barcelona (departs from Plaça de la Universitat) and by three daily **trains** from Lleida which terminate here. The bus from Barcelona continues up the Noguera Pallaresa through Sort and Llavorsí, passing the side road for the Cardós and Ferrera valleys, and within 7km of Espot, a major entry point to the Aigüestortes national park (see p.283). From June to mid-November, the morning service continues over the pass into the Val d'Aran. Morning train and bus services from Lleida should arrive before the first bus up the Noguera Pallaresa at 11.40am; another service goes at 2.20pm.

**Trains** arrive in the new town (station open Mon–Fri 6am–2pm only), from where you walk 200m north up the road and then over the bridge to a plexiglass shelter at the base of the old town. This is the bus terminal; current schedules are posted. You don't want to get stranded, as La Pobla no longer has accommodation, and the *Turisme* at the north end of town (Mon–Sat 9am–2pm) is not terribly helpful.

### Talarn, Santa Engràcia and San Salvador de Toló

The closest spots to **stay** and **eat** lie outside **Tremp**, 13km downriver from La Pobla, just beyond the giant **Sant Antoní reservoir**. The large, fortified hill town of **TALARN**, 2km northwest of Tremp, proves to be a gem, its houses (plus a few ad hoc towers) forming a defensive perimeter, with an old church at the low end of the maze of interior lanes. Just inside from the car-park plaza at c/Soldevila 2, *Casa Lola* shines as a beacon of country cuisine, attracting clientele from near and far; about €21 will net you wild mushroom salad, *girella* (tasty lamb-and-rice haggis) and a choice from the most extravagant dessert list in the region (eg violet-blossom sorbet), with excellent local red wine. Proprietress Florita is a character, giving free *pa amb tomaquet*-making lessons to the uninitiated; she also has ten spotless, air-con studio apartments upstairs, a few with terraces (☎973 650 814, ✉casalola@eresmas.com; ❸).

Just below Talarn a narrow but paved ten-kilometre road heads west to **SANTA ENGRÀCIA**, surely the most spectacularly set village in Catalunya, tumbling off the south flank of a rock monolith offering 270-degree views. This was the limit of the Cretaceous-era sea, and the entire region is a geologist's paradise of stacked sedimentary rock and exposed fossils. Here Richard and Sandra Loder manage *Casa Guilla* (☎973 252 080 or 659 901 413, ⓦwww.casaguilla.com; ❻ HB only; closed Dec–Feb), a restored, rambling farmhouse poised like the prow of a ship at the monolith's east end, with sweeping views. En-suite accommodation consists of just a family/group quad upstairs and two doubles downstairs, but there's a lovely mineral-water pool, basement bar, generous continental breakfast and group evening *table d'hôte* meals. The area is a mecca for birders, botanists and geologists alike, so reservations are mandatory. If they're full – a frequent occurrence – the closest comparable lodgings lie 31km southeast of Tremp, 6km outside **SAN SALVADOR DE TOLÓ**: *Casa Pete y Lou/Tros de la Font* (☎973 252 309, ⓦwww.casapeteylou.com; ❷ B&B). This is a completely isolated hilltop farmhouse, again with just three non-en-suite rooms; breakfast (and by arrangement, supper) relies largely on own-made/grown bread and produce.

## Gerri de la Sal and around

From La Pobla de Segur the C13 road threads through the red and steel-grey rocks of the **Desfiladero de Collegats**, an impressive gorge hewn by the Noguera Pallaresa through 300-metre-high cliffs. Unfortunately, since a series of tunnels was blasted through much of the defile, drivers see little of it, though the narrow, abandoned old road is still open to cyclists and pedestrians. The Catalan intelligentsia have been coming to admire the scenery here for well over a century, and the portion of the canyon labelled **L'Argenteria**, with its sculpted, papier-mâché-like rockface streaked with rivulets, supposedly inspired Antoní Gaudí's La Pedrera apartment building in Barcelona.

As the canyon opens out, you emerge at the rickety village of **GERRI DE LA SAL** – "de la Sal" because of the local salt-making industry. Salt pans are still in use by the riverside, but more obvious is the Benedictine monastery of **Santa Maria**, founded in 807. The present twelfth-century structure, with its huge and dilapidated bell-wall, faces the village on the far side of a beautiful old bridge. The church interior (Easter & June–Sept 11am–1pm & 4.30–7.30pm; €1.50; otherwise phone ☎973 662 068 for entry) is a three-aisled basilica, with soaring barrel vaulting upheld by four fluted columns. Even if you don't make it inside it's worth having a look at the unusual arched hay-loft running along the south side of the building's exterior.

Gerri has just a **restaurant** and bar; 4km north in tiny **BARO**, *Bar Restaurante Cal Mariano* (☎973 662 077; ❷) offers rooms and food and there's a large, riverbank **campsite**, the *Pallars Sobirà* (☎973 662 033).

### West to La Pobleta de Bellveí: the Estany de Montcortès

The minor road from Gerri de la Sal to La Pobleta de Bellveí, 17km west, makes a pristine, tranquil run through rolling uplands speckled with picturesque villages. It's ideal for mountain-biking or driving, but not good for hitching or walking: there's little traffic and the initial punishing climb up to Peramea is unshaded. This road, incidentally, is wrongly shown on both recommended touring maps (see p.21) – it's not a dead-end, and it's paved all the way. From Bretui, 10km along, you have fine views into the gorge of Cortscastells, a tributary of Collegats, but the high point of the route is the idyllic little **Estany de Montcortès** (1065m), just west of the eponymous village. Though warm and reed-fringed, this attractive karstic lake drops suddenly to thirty-metre depths, so there's no bottom muck to contend with. Several wooden jetties allow access to deep water, and a swim is just the thing if you're cycling or motoring by. Beyond lies a sharp, featureless descent to La Pobleta de Bellveí in the Vall Fosca (see p.288).

## Sort to Port-Ainé

**SORT**, 30km north of La Pobla, retains an old core of tall, narrow houses plus a tiny castle, now overwhelmed by ranks of apartment buildings. This development is due to the area's reputation as one of the premier river-running spots in Europe; after the spring thaw the river swarms with kayakers, canoeists and rafters, equipped with hi-tech gear. And every year, during late June/early July, valley communities stage the *Raiers* (Rafters) festival, re-enacting the exploits of the old-time timber pilots who could show the modern daredevils a thing or two.

Because of an upmarket clientele, Sort prices itself beyond passing trade, and in any case it's not a place to linger unless you're here for the action (which can be exhilarating; see box overleaf). Its main street is exclusively devoted to rafting and adventure shops; among these, Rubber River (☎973 620 220, ⓦwww.rubber-river.com) is reputable and recommended, with its own garden-set **hotel**, the two-star *Florido* (☎973 620 337; ❺). The **bus** stops at an obvious shelter on Plaça Catalina Albert, at the north end of town where the two through roads meet. **RIALP**, 3km north, is a marginally more appealing mix of old houses and new boutiques; its bus stop is at the bar under the *Hotel Victor*.

### Skiing: Port-Ainé

Though still shown on maps, the ski station at Llessuí, 16km west of Sort, closed long ago. **PORT-AINÉ**, 14km northeast of Rialp, has filled the breach, offering some of the best beginners' and intermediates' skiing in the Catalan Pyrenees on 28 longish runs. First impressions may not be good: the café and restaurant are a bit shabby, rental gear (only at Point 2080) is limited and better sought in Rialp (see above), and the resort layout is a Heath-Robinsonesque affair whereby you must often buy passes at Point 1650 and then go up the main chairlift to Point 2080 in street shoes unless you've shown up with gear. There's an intermediate stop, part-time ticket booth and car park at 1960m. Once logistics are sorted, the skiing and setting are glorious. From the beginners' runs around Point 2080 there's a short drop to a chair-lift mounting 2440-metre Pic de l'Orri, the start of most pistes. These include the aptly named 4300-metre Bella Vista green run along the ridge and through the pines, and the 2300-metre Les Pilones red run to the base of the Pic de l'Orri lift. Piste colour-coding is overrated – blues are rather greenish, reds blueish – but the north-facing valley generally enjoys powdery snow, even in spring. A large three-star **hotel** has been built at Point 1960 (☎973 627 627, ⓦwww.port-aine.com; ❻); otherwise the closest **accommodation** are two *cases de pagès*: *Casa Macià* (☎973 620 837; ❷) and *Casa Millet* (☎973 623 125; ❷) in the village of **RONÍ**, 9km downhill on the side road in.

## Llavorsí

The most attractive place to stay along this stretch of the valley is **LLAVORSÍ**, 10km above Rialp. Despite extensive modernization, a rash of bar/restaurants and rafting outfitters on the main road, plus a mammoth power substation across the way, this tight huddle of stone-built houses and slate roofs at the confluence of the Noguera Pallaresa and Cardós rivers still retains some character. There are two good riverside **campsites**, both with pools and bars: the *Aigües Braves*, 1km north of town (☎973 622 153; March–Sept), and the smaller, municipally run *Riberies* east of the centre, basic but tent-friendly (☎973 622 151; mid-June to mid-Sept). **Accommodation** catering for the river trade, while abundant, should be reserved in advance during the rafting season. Try the high-standard *Hotel Lamoga* (☎973 622 006, ⓔlamoga@muntanyes-delpirineu.com; ❹ B&B, ❺ HB); the simpler *Hostal de Rey*, adjacent on the riverfront (☎973 622 011, ⓔmcaste@mixmail.com; ❸ B&B); or the *Hostal Noguera* (☎973 622 012; ❷), on the opposite bank. Much the best **eating** in town is at *Lamoga's menjador*, where *a la carta* at €16.50 for three courses plus a beer is much better value than the dull *menú*.

Several **activities outfitters** offer rafting, canyoning, hydrospeed, mountain-biking and rock-climbing. Longest established are the bizarrely named Yeti Emotions (☎973 622 201, ⓦwww.yetiemotions.com), 500m south of Llavorsí, on the west bank of the river opposite a road tunnel, and the central and friendly Rafting Llavorsí (☎973 622 158, ⓦwww.raftingllavorsi.com).

## The Vall Ferrera

From Llavorsí, the initially paved road up to the *Refugi de Vall Ferrera* – base for the ascent of Estats and Montcalm – ambles through an underpopulated area of pastures and hayfields, the latter scythed in July; hitch or get a taxi (☎973 624 411 or 973 624 353) if you're without a vehicle. The first part of the route follows the Cardós valley (see below) from Llavorsí; after about 4km, you turn off east along the **Vall Ferrera**, which, as the name suggests, traditionally lived from iron-mining and -smelting. At **ALINS**, 13.5km from Llavorsí, there's a choice of en-suite **accommodation**: the plush *Hotel Salòria* (☎973 624 341; ❹ B&B), offering full savoury breakfasts and balconied rooms, and the *Hostal Muntanya* (☎973 624 358; ❸), with a respected, family-run restaurant on the ground floor. If Alins is full or too busy for your taste, *Casa Gabatxó* (☎973 624 322; ❸), in Araós 6km downstream back towards Llavorsí, is the most highly regarded of the valley's dozen-plus *cases de pagès*, offering half-board as well.

Another 5km beyond Alins along the main valley lies the tiny village of **ÀREU**, the last settlement before Estats, and on the GR11. The local iron industry required a huge amount of timber for charcoal; accordingly the local **Museu de la Fusta** (Lumber Museum) showcases a working hydro-powered *serradora* or sawmill (July–Sept only; ☎973 624 355 to summon custodians; €2). Àreu has a small shop and a pleasant, tent-oriented **campsite**, the *Pica d'Estats* (☎973 624 347; open Easter & June–Sept), with a pool and a bar. The most obvious indoor **accommodation** is the rambling *Hotel Vall Ferrera*

(☎973 624 343; ❺ HB only); they also have the main village **restaurant**. Àreu also offers ample, less expensive lodging in the *casa de pagès* scheme, for example *Casa Besoli* (☎973 624 415; ❷), in the upper quarter.

The route up the mountain continues, first via dirt track and then, 3.5km above Àreu, along the marked east-bank trail #17, "Camí Vell del Port de Boet/Pla de Boet", routed in common with the GR11, to just below the **Refugi de Vall Ferrera** (1940m; ☎973 624 378; 30 places; open and staffed June–Sept), nearly four hours from Àreu. Kayakers should note that the stretch of river here, though short (4km), presents some of the best, and least commercialized, white water in the Catalan Pyrenees.

Next day, allow four to five hours to climb **Estats**. Follow the marked path north through the Sottlo valley and past the photogenic lakes of Sottlo and Estats, then up into the Port de Sottlo (2893m); from here a short ridge walk east leads to the summit. You can then either retrace your steps, or continue to the Pinet refuge (see p.262).

## Other onward routes from Vall Ferrera

**Southeast** of the *Vall Ferrera* refuge, the HRP variant and GR11 lead into Andorra by different sets of passes – described on p.218; the GR11 is easier, not exceeding 2517m elevation en route, at the small unstaffed refuge of Baiau just before the frontier. Northwards, then **westwards**, you can make the traverse to Tavascan (9hr – see below) initially via the Sotllo lake, where you should bear west over the 2618-metre Coll de Barborte to the **Baborte** lake (3hr 30min from Refugi Vall Ferrera; unlocked 8-person refuge adjacent) and **Planell de Boavi** (7hr), a beautiful but occasionally over-subscribed wilderness camping area among birches and firs.

## The Vall de Cardós

If you keep to the road up the broader, more developed **Vall de Cardós** instead of taking a right into the Vall Ferrera, you'll pass through **RIBERA DE CARDÓS** (10km from Llavorsí), a sizeable and attractive village with a twelfth-century, squat-belfried church and a giant active sawmill, last vestige of the valley's wood-cutting industry. For **accommodation**, try the well-equipped *Hostal Sol i Neu* (☎973 623 137; open March–Oct; ❹), by the river at the south entry to the village, or the modest *Hostal Cal Quet*, also on the through road (☎973 623 124; ❸). There's **camping** at the caravan-oriented, riverside *La Borda del Pubill* (☎973 623 088), with a pool and tennis courts, and *Del Cardós* (☎973 623 112; April–Sept), with similar amenities, north of the village.

### Tavascan

The road continues past other steeple-crowned hamlets surrounded by hayfields and grazing sheep to **TAVASCAN** (often "Tabascan"), 20km from Llavorsí, where the single high street is a solid mass of accommodation. This recent gentrification is due largely to a **cross-country ski station** at **Pleta de Prat**, 11km northwest past Noarre hamlet, which has a couple of newish chairlifts and a few token downhill runs. Yet Tavascan is a larger, more traditional village than it appears from the through road, with an old bridge over the Riu Tavascan above the church; the **GR11** slips over this and through lanes of old houses on the west bank.

Of the three **hotels** on the high street the simplest is the friendly, low-key *Marxant* (☎973 623 151, ✉marxant@autovia.com; ❺ HB only), something of a trekkers' haven despite its plain, well-worn 1970s en-suite rooms. Evening meals – typically salad, omelette, rabbit or boar with mushrooms – are more than decent. For more comfort at similar prices, the adjacent *Hotel Llacs del Cardós* (☏973 623 178, ℻973 623 126; ❹, or ❻ HB) is arguably better value, all rooms having balconies; or for a real splurge, there's the co-managed three-star *Hotel Estanys Blaus* opposite (same phone; ❻), with rear rooms overlooking the river. The sole budget option is the rather ordinary *Pensió Feliu* (☏973 623 163; ❷, or ❹ HB), also with a restaurant. Also on the high street you'll find the last grocery store before the wilderness. The nearest **campsite**, *Bordes de Graus* (☏973 623 246; April–Oct), lies an inconvenient 5km up towards the ski centre, but it's pleasant, friendly and caravan-free. Another site, *Serra* (☏973 623 117; July–Sept), roughly the same distance south in Lladorre village, is closer to the valley's assorted attractions.

## Hikes out of the Vall de Cardós

If you're traversing along the **HRP** (see below), a case can be made for skipping Tavascan altogether, since you have to lose and regain a lot of altitude to get there. As noted, however, the **GR11** goes through Tavascan, and for the less committed hiker forms the partial basis of a six-hour **loop-walk**, dubbed the "Itinerari Panoràmic per l'Alt Cardós", which takes in several villages clinging to the side of the upper valley, using sections of the GR11 plus local PR paths for lateral links. The route, shown on a placard beside the *Hotel Marxant*, heads south from Tavascan to the villages of Aineto and Lleret on the GR11, crosses to the east bank of the valley at Lladorre, then climbs up to Boldís Jussà and Boldís Sobirà to rejoin the GR11 for a northerly descent to Tavascan.

Above Tavascan there's a choice of access to the high peaks: the more easterly dirt track, towards Planell de Boavi, is the direct route to Pic de Certascan (2853m); the paved road northwest, beyond the power station, connects at Noarre with the HRP towards the Val d'Aran. Both lead to delightful wildernesses of long valleys and tarn-spangled cirques up against the border.

For the **Certascan area**, take a turn-off at the Montalto dam 6km beyond Tavascan on the rough track towards Boavi, and climb steeply up the Sierra Marinera past the western shore of the superb **Estany de Naorte**, with the summit of Estats just visible above the low, rounded hills and sparse pines on the opposite bank. Some three and a half hours in total from Tavascan you reach the **Llac de Certascan**, star of many a postcard, and at over 100m deep and 1200m long, claimed to be the largest natural lake in the Pyrenees. (With a 4WD vehicle, you can drive to within 20min of the lake.) At the south end stands the *Refugi de Certascan* (2240m; ☏973 623 230, ⓦwww.certascan.com; 40 places; staffed mid-June to Sept), with hot showers, meals and cooking facilities; from here the **Pic de Certascan** is an easy half-day, round-trip ascent.

### The HRP and GR11

Since the refuge sits beside the **HRP** it's possible to follow this west for six hours to the hamlet of **Noarre** (no facilities), but it's a tough section with lots of cross-country route-finding, only feasible in good conditions. From Noarre, or from the next wilderness campsite another hour upstream at **Pleta de l'Arenal**, you can continue west to Salardú in Aran. This involves two or three days' walking on the HRP or one of its variants; the quickest heads due west for Alòs d'Isil, about ten hours away via a necklace of lakes at the base of 2864-metre **Mont Roig**. The only facility en route, under two hours west of Pleta de l'Arenal, is the unstaffed *Refugi Mont Roig-Enric Pujol* (2290m; 18 places), an ambitious target for a day's trek west from Certascan, but well placed for exploring the lakes, as well as the peak.

Alternatively, the Cardós valley is linked to both the Vall Ferrera and the Vall d'Àneu (see below) by the easier though less dramatic **GR11**. From just above Àreu in the Vall Ferrera, the route cuts over Montarenyo ridge via the Coll de Tudela to Boldís and Tavascan, then bears sharply southwest over another 2500-metre spur to La Guingueta d'Àneu via Estaon and Lleret. The Àreu–Tavascan sector makes for an easy day's walking of about six hours; Tavascan–La Guingueta is getting on for nine hours, with a *casa de pagès* in Lleret the only facility en route.

## The Vall d'Àneu

From Llavorsí the main C13 continues upstream along the Noguera Pallaresa, past the Espot turning (see p.283) and the placid Pantà de la Torrasa, to **LA GUINGUETA D'ÀNEU** at the head of the reservoir. This is the first of three villages incorporating the name of the local valley, **Vall d'Àneu**, and consists mostly of a small cluster of roadside **accommodation**. The best option is the one-star *Hotel Poldo* (☎973 626 080; ❹), with a pool and attached restaurant emphasizing spit-grilled meats; opposite stands the more economical *Hostal Ortau* (☎973 626 086; ❷).

### Esterri d'Àneu

**ESTERRI D'ÀNEU**, 4km further beyond the lake, was transformed in the early 1990s from sleepy farming community to chic resort. Parts of town still form as graceful an ensemble as you'll see in the Catalan Pyrenees – the few huddled houses between the road and the river, an arched bridge and slender-towered Sant Vicenç church – but the new apartment buildings and fancy hotels to the south are another matter.

Among **accommodation** choices, best value is the delightful *Fonda Agustí* (☎973 626 034; ❹ HB only), quietly set behind the church in Plaça de l'Església, serving enormous **meals** to all comers in its old-fashioned *menjador*. For more comfort, and some river-view rooms, try *Pensió La Creu* at c/Major 3 (☎973 626 437, ⓦwww.pensiolacreu.com; ❹). The closest **campsite**, *La Presalla* (☎973 626 031; April–Sept), renting out chalet-huts, is 1.5km south of the village. From late November to May, the village is usually also the end of the line for the bus from Barcelona.

### The Vall d'Isil

From the centre of Esterri d'Àneu, you can bear north along a narrow, paved road up the **Vall d'Isil**, its atmospheric villages little visited and effectively abandoned, some of them (like Arreu) squatted by "alternative" types from the big city. The highlight, 11km along just before **ISIL** (alias Gil), is the engaging Romanesque church of Sant Joan, with its fine south portal, two Gothic windows retaining some tracery, its apse just about in the river, and pairs of strange carved figures studding the roofline. Since the inn near the old bridge ceased operations, there's just a single *casa de pagès* on the west bank, *Casa Fuster* (☎973 626 196; ❷). **ALÒS D'ISIL**, 12km from Esterri at the end of the paved route and with another tiny medieval bridge, has **accommodation** outside the village, a welcome sight if you're trekking along the HRP: *Xalet-Refugi el Fornet* (☎973 626 520; 40 places, meals served), operating in winter also for users of the **Bonabé cross-country ski centre** 4km north along a dirt track.

## València d'Àneu

Three kilometres further up the main road (now the C28), **VALÈNCIA D'ÀNEU**, with its traditional stone houses and small Romanesque church of Sant Andreu, was always far less developed than Esterri d'Àneu, but with the Baqueira-Beret resort over the pass set to expand, chalet construction has begun in earnest. València was once much more important than its current sleepiness suggests. An archeological dig on the outskirts has brought to light the remains of a tenth-century **castle**, apparently the power base of local counts who ruled over many of the surrounding valleys.

An excellent choice for **accommodation** here is the good-value *Hotel La Morera* (☏973 626 124, ⓦwww.hotel-lamorera.com; ❺ B&B), with variable-sized balconied rooms, a valley-side pool and an excellent restaurant – as long as you go *a la carta* rather than half-board: for under €20 you can stuff yourself with hearty country fare. In the old quarter, at the top of c/Major, the cosier *Hotel La Paller* (☏973 626 129; ❸ B&B) features rustic decor and a rear lawn garden. On or just off the same street are two *cases de pagès*: *Casa Campaner* (☏973 626 251; ❷), near the *Felip* (see below), and *Casa Sala* facing the church (☏973 626 254; ❷). Currently the only independent **restaurant** in the village, again on c/Major, is *Felip*, with a €10 *menú* or an ample *carta*.

## Son del Pi and the Port de la Bonaigua

About 1km beyond València d'Aneu, then 4km south following signs for Estaís, is **SON (DEL PI)**, remarkable for its eleventh-to-twelfth-century fortified church of **Sants Just i Pastor** (daily: summer 10am–2pm & 5–8pm; out of season hours vary). The church has a four-storey Lombard-type belfry with a pyramidal roof, while a sixteenth-century *retable* and carved stone font (previously a Visigothic sarcophagus) grace the interior. Its most unusual feature is the round tower by the gate, the *Comunidor*, which the local priest used to climb and, sacred Host in hand, cast spells against destructive storms and avalanches. The village is a beauty as well, with the chalet-style *Restaurant-Refugi Casa Masover* opposite the church (☏973 626 383); if it's shut, the nearest comparable facility is the **Refugi Pla de la Font**, poised between here and Espot, and accessible by 9km of good dirt track (☏973 620 164; 20 places; open mid-June to late Sept plus Dec–May weekends/hols).

Beyond València and the turning for Son, the road quits the Noguera Pallaresa and climbs above the quilt of green and brown fields around Esterri. The Riu de la Bonaigua takes over as the roadside stream, lined by forests of silver birch, pine and fir. Views get ever more impressive as you approach the treeline, above which is perched the **restaurant-bar** of *Mare de Déu de les Ares*, next to the eponymous *ermita*. There's a good, varied lunch *menú* for about €15, but the place shuts at 6pm; the nearest accommodation is about 5km back down the valley, at the **Refugi del Gerdar** (1550m; ☏973 250 170, ⓦwww.refugigerdar .com), nestled in the fir forest of Gerdar, offering four-to-six-bed rooms and a full-service restaurant.

Two hairpins above the *ermita*, you'll notice the seasonally busy car park and trailhead for the path up into the Vall Gerber (see p.279 for this route). Near the top of the bleak **Port de la Bonaigua** (2072m; usually closed in winter owing to avalanche risk), half-wild horses graze and you get simultaneous panoramas of the valleys you've just left and the Val d'Aran to come.

# The Val d'Aran

Though undeniably on the French side of the Pyrenean watershed, the **Val d'Aran** has long been under Spanish sovereignty. This oddity seems even more pronounced when you consider that Andorra, while opening towards Spain, was long semi-autonomous (and opted for full independence in 1993), and that the Cerdanya/Cerdagne, despite a lack of pronounced natural demarcations, is divided between the two countries. However, in June 1990 a special law of the Catalan Generalitat restored a degree of self-rule to the valley.

Cut off from the outside world for centuries, the Val d'Aran evolved its own language – **Aranès** – which is only spoken in the valley. It's based largely on medieval Gascon, plus elements of Catalan and a generous sprinkling of Basque vocabulary. The valley's name, for example, is not Aranès but pure Basque, and "Val" is technically redundant – *aran* means "valley" in Euskera. (From here westwards, Basque place-names are commonly encountered, tide-markers of the former extent of a people now restricted to the west end of the range.) The Aranès **spelling of local place-names** is now exclusively used on local signs and tourist literature (if not yet on internationally published maps), so is given preference in the following account, with Castilian or Catalan in parentheses.

Aran has strong historical links to both France and Spain, and was a source of conflict as long ago as 1192, when it passed from the counts of Comminges to the kings of Aragón. In 1808 Napoleon announced its annexation, sending in 2500 French troops. Only a thousand reached the Val d'Aran – the rest deserted – but were enough to briefly expel the Spanish. The valley was a stronghold of Republicanism during the Spanish Civil War and a refuge for the defeated afterwards, safe behind passes snowed up half the year. It was invaded once again by Franco's Nationalists in 1944, in particular his greatly feared Moroccan auxiliaries who brutally suppressed opposition by massacring the population of several villages. The isolation of Aran was finally relieved by the boring of the **Túnel de Vielha** in 1948 (using the slave labour of Republican POWs), allowing the N230 road to directly link the valley with the provincial capital of Lleida.

Since Franco's passing, life in the valley has changed dramatically. Your first clues are the high-tension electricity pylons from Llavorsí over the Port de la

## The sources of the Garona/Garonne

The river draining the Val d'Aran begins life as the **Garona**, then in France becomes the **Garonne**, swinging northeast through Saint-Gaudens and Toulouse, and northwest to the Atlantic at Bordeaux. The river has two commonly accepted sources: the Ruda stream at the east end of the valley, fed by the Saborèdo lakes, and the Joeu, in the west beyond Vielha, up against the French frontier.

Contrary to what was believed until 1931, the **Joeu** doesn't rise in Aran at all, but in the Maladeta-Aneto Massif to the southwest, on the opposite side of the watershed from the Val d'Aran. In that year, French speleologist Norbert Casteret (see p.326) proved that the Joeu was a resurgence by emptying 55 kilos of dye into the **Forau dels Aigualluts**, the sinkhole for the Aneto glacier's meltwater. In Casteret's own words: "Next day, the Garonne revealed its secret. For twenty-seven hours a million cubic yards of bright green water poured down the Val d'Aran and for over fifty miles into France."

Bonaigua and heavy traffic through the tunnel to the valley capital of Vielha. At peak skiing times – two million visitors to Aran were recorded during February/March 2003 – the tunnel can simply no longer cope, and a second one is now being bored to double car capacity. Scythe-wielding hay-reapers of past summers have been replaced by Massey-Ferguson balers, the hayfields themselves overlooked by holiday chalets that have sprouted at the edge of every village. The increasing number of restaurants and sports shops and the constant year-round traffic on the C28 valley-floor road combine to make the Val d'Aran one of the most expensive, overdeveloped and (unless you're skiing) overrated corners of the Spanish Pyrenees. With the Spanish royal family setting its imprimatur on the Baqueira-Beret ski centre and members of the "commoner" government regularly holidaying here too, the sky's the limit for prices.

All that said, if you leave the main route in favour of side valleys like the Ruda or the Unhòla, you can recapture something of the region as it used to be. But don't expect superlative wilderness walking: Aran is best viewed as a comfortable rest stop on Pyrenean traverses, rather than a target in its own right.

# Nautaran

**Nautaran**, "High Valley" in Aranés, is the more scenic eastern part of the region and a good start- or end-point for walks in the Aigüestortes park. Salardú is the largest of a cluster of villages well set near the top of the valley, most within walking distance of each other. From almost any elevated point in Nautaran you'll be treated to full-on views of snowy Maladeta, hovering like a ghost to the west. The local architecture resembles very much that of French Gascony, utterly unlike that of the Spanish valleys to the east and south. Sturdy Nautaranese houses are traditionally stone with slate roofs, so there's surprisingly little to distinguish a 400-year-old home from a four-year-old one. Many display dates on the lintels – not of the same vintage as the local **Romanesque churches**, though some date back to the sixteenth century.

## Baqueira-Beret

The road descent west from Port de la Bonaigua invariably concentrates minds – and isn't for the acrophobic or those with dodgy brakes, given its hairpins and sharp drop into the Ruda valley. The first place below the pass is **BAQUE-IRA-BERET**, a huge skiing development frequented by French and Catalan tourists, and the primary engine of change in the region; the road linking the resort core at Baqueira to Point 1700 and the Beret sector was serpentined for maximum access to the ranks of chalet apartments.

The *urbanizació* itself is modern, posey and has little to offer other than four- or five-star hotels, but it's no trouble to stay nearby at Salardú or Tredòs (see below) and show up for some of the best **skiing** in these mountains – with one important qualification. All of the Beret and much of the Baqueira-Bonaigua zones face west or south, and the snow, especially after February, can get mushy early in the day, closing slopes by 3pm. The most reliable, north-facing runs descend to **Orri** (1850m), with its own car park and lifts, and also the link to **Beret** (1850–2516m), most suitable for beginners and weak intermediates, though you'll need your own transport to reach it by road. Beret's development is dwarfed by its grand setting, though you face long slogs from car park to facilities, and between lifts. More advanced skiers can use chairlifts from the hotels and apartments, at Points 1500 and 1700 in Baqueira centre, to get up to the 2500-metre **Cap de Baqueira**, start of numerous, mostly red-rated pistes in open bowls above the trees. The small, south-facing **Bonaigua** sector, immediately below the pass, has just a few intermediate runs and isn't worth any special detour at present, though it will form the springboard of future expansion onto the slopes towards the east.

Lift passes are among the stiffest priced in the Pyrenees, but gear rental is normal for Spain, and you are pampered with lots of chairlifts (15 out of 23) and an interlinked domain of 47 runs (further information at Ⓦ www.baqueira.es).

## Salardú

SALARDÚ, a few kilometres further west, is the notional capital of Nautaran and a logical base for explorations: large enough to offer a reasonable choice of accommodation and food, but small enough to feel pleasantly remote (except during August or peak ski season). Staying gives you the opportunity to visit surrounding villages, all centred on beautiful **Romanesque churches**. Salardú's is the large, thirteenth-century **Sant Andreu**, set in its own pleasant grounds and surrounded by a cluster of characterful houses with steeply pitched roofs. The church doors, usually open, are flanked by the most elaborate portal in the valley, its carved column capitals featuring birds feeding their young and four eerie little human faces. Once inside, you can enjoy some fine sixteenth-century fresco patches, restored in 1994, including *Christ Enthroned*, the *Assumption*, various saints and smudged panels of the Four Virtues. The only jarring note is sounded by the clock in the octagonal fifteenth-century belfry, which tolls with an electronic tone (programmed to fall silent between midnight and 7am) instead of a bell.

### Practicalities

There's a wooden **Turisme** hut (summer daily 10am–1.30pm & 4.30–8pm) just off the main road at the turning for Bagergue, near the bus stop. The single village **bank** has an ATM. There is also a **swimming pool** (mid-June to Aug daily 11am–7pm) if you fancy a dip.

Even at the height of the summer you should find a **bed** (though not necessarily a room) in Salardú. Dependable hostels aimed specifically at **hikers** include the *Refugi Rosti*, Plaça Major 1 (☎973 645 308, Ⓕ973 645 814; closed May–June & Oct–Nov; six-bunk dorms €17 B&B, non-en-suite doubles ❺ HB), in a rambling, 300-year-old building on the main square, and *Refugi Juli Soler i Santaló* (☎973 645 016; dorms €11, 4-to-6-bunk en-suite rooms €17), 200m east of the Turisme booth, next to the pool.

For conventional **accommodation**, try the *Pensió Casat* (☎973 645 056; ❸ B&B) at c/Major 6, whose front rooms have tiny balconies, or heated, en-suite ones at *Residència Aiguamòg* (☎973 645 996; ❹ B&B) on c/Sant Andreu 12, both pretty central. In addition to these, eight more expensive **hostals** and **hotels** advertise themselves conspicuously; one of the quieter and more reasonable is the *Hotel deth Pais* in cul-de-sac Plaça dera Pica, with parking (☎973 645 836, Ⓕ973 644 500; ❹ B&B), whose rather plain rooms have underfloor heating and balconies if south-facing. Top of the heap is the 2001-built *Hotel Colomèrs* near the bank on c/dera Mola 8 (☎973 644 556, Ⓕ973 644 170; ❹ B&B summer, ❺ B&B winter), with designer rooms and a few luxe suites (❼).

For **meals**, non-guests can enjoy excellent *menús* at the recommended *menjador* of the *Refugi Juli Soler i Santaló*, or spend about €24 *a la carta* across the river at *Prat Aloy*, linked to the *Hotel deth Pais*. Alternatives are scarce, since the handful of independent village restaurants are overpriced and suffer frequent management changes. While the restaurant at the *Refugi Rosti* is decent enough with a €15 four-course *menú*, its main appeal is the nicest **bar** in town: *Delicatesen*.

## Villages around Salardú

**UNHA** (Unya), 700m up the hill into the Unhòla valley, has a church of the same age as that in Salardú, though you're more likely to be interested in the half-dozen **restaurants**, particularly *Es de Don Joan (Casa Carmela)* and *Casa Restaurante Perez* – the latter the most economical and most consistently open, also offering **accommodation** at *Casa Benito* (☎973 645 752; ❸).

BAGERGUE, 2km higher up the road (or reached via the marked GR211 path from Unha and Garòs), remains the most countrified (and at 1419m, the highest) of the Nautaran settlements, and offers yet another handsome church – plus several **restaurants**. Most famous is *Casa Peru* (supper only; reserve on ☎973 645 437), which deserves the plaudits adorning its entrance. An *olha aranesa* (sausage, carrot and potato hotpot) to die for, venison meatballs in wild mushroom sauce, wild-fruit flan with *merengue* plus good house wine costs €27 – far less than the more pretentious places in Salardú or Arties, with courteous service to boot. You may **stay** at *Residencia Seixes* (☎973 645 406, Ⓦwww.aranweb.com/seixes; ❸ B&B) by the village entrance, with warm wood-decor rooms, fine views and off-street parking – weekend prebooking is necessary most of the year.

## Tredòs

Across the river from Salardú and about twenty minutes' walk upstream along the signposted *Camin Reiau* (King's Road), **TREDÒS** – once the prettiest of the Nautaran villages – has had its old core overlaid by a rash of new ski chalets. However it retains a massive twelfth-century church – one of whose murals was removed to the Cloisters Museum in New York – with freestanding belfry. And in the centre is a find: the *Restaurante Saburedo*, where the construction crews for all those apartments **eat**. The food's hearty rather than haute, with four courses (giant salad, onion soup, a meat dish, stewed pears) plus house wine for about €15. If you're taken with the village, they also have **rooms** (☎973 645 089; ❸), as does *Casa Micalot* (☎973 645 326; ❸) on the same lane. If money's no object, the palatial *Hotel De Tredòs*, just above the village on the road to Baquiera Beret (☎973 644 014, Ⓦwww.hoteldetredos.com; ❹ low, ❼ high season), can arrange one-week ski packages, and has a small lawn-pool for summer.

## Arties and Garòs

**ARTIES**, 3km west and downstream from Salardú, has the usual complement of recent holiday homes, with more under construction. However, if you're driving and/or Salardú is full, Arties has considerable appeal, particularly its high-quality food and lodging (see below), and the old village core straddling the Garona River. There are two **churches**: the central, ninth-to-fourteenth-century Santa María, with Templar fortifications, and the deconsecrated Sant Joan on the main road, now home to a small **museum** of changing exhibits (Tues–Fri 5–8pm, Sat 10am–1pm & 5–8pm, Sun 10am–1pm; €1.50). The village is otherwise known for its **hot springs**, long closed but set for renovation. The *camí* leading past them (marked as the GR211.1) cuts out 3km of the busy main highway, rejoining it at Casarilh village, a boon if you're cycling.

Budget **accommodation** includes, on the through highway, en-suite *Pensió*

Montarto above the *Bar Consul* (☎973 640 803; ❸), and the much better and quieter *Pensió Barrie,* alias *Casa Portolá* (☎973 640 828; ❷), at c/Mayor 21 in the old quarter, which has three floors of wood-and-tile decor en-suite rooms with bathtubs, the top two storeys very alpine with skylights and dormer windows. A considerable notch up in price is the *Hotel Besiberri* by the stream at c/Deth Fòrt 4 (☎973 640 829, ⓕ973 642 696; ❺ B&B; closed Nov). Rooms (except for the rambling attic suite, €120 for 4) are smallish but well-appointed; lovely common areas and savoury Catalan breakfasts really make the place. A **campsite**, *Era Yerla d'Arties* (☎973 641 602), just below the village on the Vielha side, is considered the best in the valley but, as so often, is crammed with caravans.

There are about half-a-dozen **restaurants** of a slightly higher standard and better value for money than in Salardú, though many engage in the common local trick of jacking up prices during ski season. Tried-and-tested options include *Montagut* (closed Wed lunch & all Tues) up on the highway, with attentive service and three *menús* at €10–23, the mid-priced one featuring French-sourced specialities such as duck pâté and duck confit. In the same building as *Montagut,* the friendly Zimbabwean-run *El Pollo Loco* (Dec–April) offers four *menús* (one vegie) at €9–20, with local pâtés, as well as duck, game and chicken, all washed down with natural cider. On the other side of the highway opposite the church, *Sidreria Iñaki* is a fairly genuine outlet for Basque-style meals and tapas such as *txistorra* and *alubias de Tolosa*. Hub of the old quarter is Plaça Urtau, where there's (by Aran standards) lively **nightlife**, with at least one of three clubs and music bars here open in any given season.

The village of **GARÒS**, 3km west, is the lowest-altitude community of Nautaran, completely ringed with new, stone-built holiday cottages. Yet its old core, focused on the twelfth-to-fourteenth-century church of San Julian, retains some charm, and offers quality **accommodation** at *Garòs Ostau* (☎973 642 378, ⓦwww.aran.org/ostaugaros; closed early July & early Sept) en route to the church at the (current) edge of the village. Choose between larger, woodsy rooms with views of the church and meadow (❻ B&B) or much smaller village-view units (❺ B&B). There's also a central **cake-and-pie** salon, *La Tarteria* (open 9am–1pm & 4.30–8pm), with all fare baked on the premises; they're a good option for breakfast, with fresh juices, scones, brownies and English teas, and they've also begun offering *table d'hôte* supper for €22 (8.30–9pm only).

# Mijaran and Baixaran

From Nautaran you continue west into **Mijaran** (Mid-Valley) and the major town of **Vielha**, capital of the entire region, served by two long-distance bus routes: one from Barcelona via La Pobla de Segur (during snow-free seasons only), the other from Lleida via El Pont de Suert, culminating in the 5300-metre **Túnel de Vielha**. You emerge from the tunnel mouth just above the town at the southwest corner of the valley, close to the old but still-used pilgrim's and drover's track descending from the 2442-metre Port de Vielha, which used to guarantee Vielha's isolation. The N230 road then heads north to the French border just 28km away, through **Baixaran**, the lower part of the valley.

# Vielha

The ride towards **VIELHA** (Viella) from either direction is more memorable than the town itself, and there's little reason to stay if you have your own transport or can make a bus connection. A sort of mini-Andorra-la-Vella (without the bargains), Vielha has been intensely developed since 1990, with numerous supermarkets, boutiques and restaurants. The demise of La Tuca ski centre just south hasn't slowed growth; urban density expands yearly, leaving little open space in the centre, except for a pedestrian walkway along the Garona. Amongst all this glitz, members of Spain's crack alpine warfare squad occupy barracks just east of the centre.

If you have time to kill, pop into the parish church of **Sant Miquèu**, right in the centre on the east bank of the Riu Nere. Its twelfth-century wooden bust, the *Cristo de Mijaran* – probably part of a *Descent from the Cross* – is one of the finest specimens of Romanesque art hereabouts. The **Museu dera Val d'Aran**, c/Major 26 (Tues–Sat 10am–1pm & 5–8pm, Sun 11am–2pm; €1.50), across the river, merits a look for its coverage of Aranese history and folklore. The only other diversion is the mammoth **Palai de Gèu** (Ice Palace) across the river, with a swimming pool, ice rink and gym (pool, gym, sauna Mon–Fri 8.30am–9.30pm, Sat & Sun 11am–9pm; ice rink Mon–Fri 5.30–9pm weekdays, Sat & Sun 4.30–9pm; €11.60 for all facilities including skate hire).

## Practicalities

**Buses** stop at two marquees opposite each other, just downhill from the major roundabout at the west end of town; schedules are posted, tickets are bought on the bus. The **Turisme** (daily 9am–9pm; ☎973 640 110), offering maps and accommodation lists, is opposite the **post office** at c/Sarriulera 6, by the church square.

There's no shortage of **accommodation** in Vielha, but most is aimed at ski clientele, with little of outstanding value. Heading north from the church, you'll find the best of the inexpensive places by turning left along the main street and then right down the lane across the bridge, towards the main car park. Just off to the left, and at Plaça Sant Orenç 3, there's the *Hotel El Ciervo* (☎973 640 165; ❹); the nearby one-star *Pensió Puig*, c/Camin Reiau 4 (☎973 640 031; ❷); and the tiny en-suite *Pension Casa Vicenta* across the way at no. 3 (☎973 640 819; ❸). For more comfort, try the *Hotel Turrull* at c/Camin Reiau 7 (☎973 640 058; ❹), which encourages half-board at its ground-floor restaurant (*menú* €11).

Vielha's best-value **restaurant** is *Basteret*, c/Major 6b, where ham-stuffed trout, cheese salad, blueberry cheesecake and house wine costs around €21. For slightly more outlay, try *a la carta* fare at *Eth Cornèr* on Passeig dera Llibertat 7, or head 2km east to the hamlet of Escunhau, where *Casa Turnay* (closed May, June, Oct & Nov; reserve on ☎973 640 292) features Aranese-style game, fish and ornate vegetable dishes.

# Baixaran

You can continue down the Garona through **ARRÒS** (6km) and **ERA BORDETA** (Es Bòrdes; 9km), both of which play a key role in Aranese architecture. Era Bordeta supplies the granite for the walls and Arròs the slates for the slightly concave roofs that planners require in Nautaran and Mijaran. Arròs itself, though, is almost in the **Baixaran** (Lower Valley) region; its balconied houses around an octagonal belfry have rendered white walls and red-tiled roofs. There are two big summer-only **campsites** at Arròs: the *Artigané* (☎973 640 189) and the *Verneda* (☎973 641 024), plus two smaller ones just past Era Bordeta. Short-term **accommodation** is limited to a single *casa de pagès*, *Casa Marion* (☎973 640 341; ❷).

Baixaran is "low" indeed at 800m and fully exposed to the mists that habitually drift up the Pyrenean north slope. Its focus is **BOSSÒST**, 16km from Vielha, where the houses are strung out along the main road and on both sides of the river, alternating with tacky shops. Its twelfth-century Romanesque church has a carved tympanum and three apses with raised Lombard brickwork. Apart from the church, there's no reason to stop (except for petrol, which is much cheaper than in France), and it's only 4km more to **LES**, with a spa (May–Sept) and some decent accommodation options, such as *Hotel Europa* (☎973 648 016; ❹), with a good restaurant. From here, it's a further 9km to the French border and bus terminus at Eth Pònt de Rei (Pont de Rei), and 20km to the first significant French town, Saint-Béat.

An alternative road out of Bossòst into France, from just south of the village, climbs through dense woods to the French border at **Coll deth Portilhon** (Col du Portillon in French), then descends sharply to Luchon.

# Walking and biking from the Val d'Aran

Numerous tracks and rather fewer footpaths allow you to walk or mountain-bike from the valley in every direction. Editorial Alpina publishes a 1:40,000 "Val d'Aran" map of the whole area, but if you stray outside its coverage you'll need adjacent 1:25,000 sheets as well – "Montgarri" if you're going east; either Alpina's or the official Catalan 1:25,000 map for the national park to the south; "La Ribagorça" together with "Maladeta/Aneto" if you're headed west. The French Cartes des Randonnées "Couserans-Cap d'Aran" (1:50,000 sheet no. 6) is the most useful for trans-border treks north from Aran.

## East to Montgarri and the Vall d'Isil

An easy excursion takes you **east** along the sources of the Noguera Pallaresa, which flows initially northeast before curling south. Make an early start **from Salardú or Bagergue** to join the asphalt road from Baqueira into the Noguera Pallaresa valley; keep on it, past the first trickle of the river, until the surface becomes dirt track just past the last ski lifts. You're now on the broad **Plan de Beret**, with grass and cows in the foreground, and a tangle of frontier peaks in the far distance. Four walking hours (15km) out of Salardú – half that time on a mountain bike – you reach the twelfth-century **Santuari de Montgarri**, next to which are two refuges, the more established being *Refugi Amics de Montgarri* (1657m; ☎639 494 546; 50 places), also open in winter for cross-country skiers. You can either overnight here or continue for the same distance again to Alòs d'Isil (see p.270), with its refuge. Although the track makes for dull walking, it's an attractive route with some sweeping views from the plateau, especially beyond Montgarri. From Alòs, you can reverse the itinerary described on p.269 to arrive in the Vall de Cardós, or descend 12km to Esterri d'Àneu.

## North towards France

To head **into France** from the upper Noguera Pallaresa, follow an HRP variant east from Montgarri or north from Alòs through the Port de Salau, or a less-used route over the Coll de la Pala/Col de la Pale (2522m) to the *Refuge des Estagnous* (see p.324), on the west side of **Mont Valier** (2838m); the Salau route is much lower and easier.

It's also possible to enter France at a more westerly point using the initially dreary, rutted track up the **Unhòla valley** from Bagergue, passable in its lower reaches by 4WD and mountain-bike. Beyond some abandoned mines, the landscape and the trail improve before reaching **Estany de Liat** (4–5hr). Here you can link with another section of the HRP, climbing due north from the lake through the **Portilhon d'Albi** (2457m) on the frontier, with the tiny Albi tarns scattered on both sides. Once through the pass you drop down over scree towards the French Albi tarn; from there, head north, contouring along the ridge behind, then northeast to the **Col de la Serre d'Araing**, where you pick up the GR10. After that, simply follow the GR down to the northeast corner of the **Étang d'Araing** reservoir, under the bare pyramid of **Pic de Crabère** (2630m), where there is a **refuge** (9–10hr from Salardú). The Étang d'Araing reservoir is about three hours west on foot from Eylie, the roadhead to Sentein and Saint-Girons, and lies on the Tour du Biros (see p.318 for details of refuge and *tour*).

## South to Aigüestortes

South of Nautaran, two lengths of part-paved road; a track-then-trail; and a narrow path run towards the beautiful Aigüestortes region. Only the latter two approaches make for enticing walking, and are described first.

### Via Saborèdo

The approach to Saborèdo begins on the south side of the river at Tredòs as a sparsely waymarked track, before curling past the edge of Baqueira and along the west bank of the Riu de Ruda. Although you can hear traffic descending from Bonaigua overhead, you'll see little other than wide green pasture until you sight the **Circ de Saborèdo** and the jumble of shattered granite peaks along the north edge of the Aigüestortes park. Some two-and-a-half hours from Salardú the track crosses the Ruda; then the grade stiffens, the surface underfoot becomes coarse pebbles, and a proper path begins some three-and-a-half hours along. After another hour's climb you reach the somewhat basic but friendly *Refugi de Saborèdo* (2310m; ☎973 253 015; 21 places; staffed Feb & March on request; Easter & mid-June to Sept). The next refuge is a further three hours' walking, through the easy Port de Ratèra (2530m), to the *Refugi d'Amitges* (2380m; ☎973 250 109; 66 places; staffed Feb & March on demand, Easter week, mid-June to Sept & hols), inside the park by Estany Gran.

### Via Gerber

A quicker if more challenging route to the Amitges refuge takes off from a popular car park and information placard 2.5km southeast of the Port de la Bonaigua. Take the obvious, green-and-orange-marked trail, initially next to ski-lift hardware, south along the **Vall Gerber** past the swimmable **Estanyola de Gerber** (2020m; 30min), the trout-stocked **Estany Petit** (2120m; 50min) and the magnificent **Estany Gerber** (2165m; 1hr). Now the crowds thin out as the trail worsens and steepens en route to **Estany de l'Illa** (1hr 45min with daypack, 2hr 30min with full pack) and its simple *Refugi de Mataró* (2460m; 8 places). Continue south into the park proper, negotiating the **Coll d'Amitges** (2740m), between Tuc de Saborèdo and Pic d'Amitges, before descending steeply to the Amitges refuge (see above). This could be problematic after a snowy winter, requiring crampons and ice-axe on the north flank – allow three hours from Mataró with a full pack.

The **Col de Gerber** (2587m), half-hour west of *Refugi de Mataró* on the route to Amitges, provides great views over Estany Glaçat towards Maladeta, and also allows access to the Circ de Saborèdo. The path becomes faint beyond the Estany de l'Illa, and almost nonexistent as you round Glaçat high above its north shore, with some tricky scrambling at one point before dropping to its outlet (2hr 30min from the car park). The going's easier to the dammed **Lac Major de Saborèdo** (2340m; 3hr); follow the outflow to the staffed hut (3hr 15min), which makes an excellent lunch stop.

You're now poised to complete a popular **one-day circuit** combining the two approaches detailed above. After 25 minutes further down the path from the refuge to the start of the rough track continue perhaps another forty minutes, clear of the forest, to a grassy hillside (1850m) studded with boulders, and cairns marking the way back to the car park (if you reach the bridge over the Riu Ruda, you've gone too far). After a thirty-minute zig-zag climb, hot work even in late afternoon, the grade slackens as you contour around the hillside to cross a service track to assorted hilltop antennae, some five hours into the day. The trail, now broad, was the major route down from the Bonaigua pass in pre-highway days; drop east, following the left-hand (northerly) set of high-tension cables to arrive at your starting-point. Though it's five-and-a-half hours' walking at a brisk pace, allow an eight-hour day out, with rests and lunch stop.

### Via Aiguamotx

From Tredòs, a partly paved road ascends steeply up the attractive **Vall d'Aiguamotx** (Aiguamoth) towards the exquisite **Circ de Colomèrs**; walking the steep road is neither attractive nor exquisite, so arrange a ride if possible. The potholed road finishes after about 8km at the luxury *Banys/Banhs de Tredòs* hotel, leaving another ninety minutes on dirt track, then path to the *Refugi de Colomèrs* (2125m; ☎973 253 008; 40 places; staffed weekends Feb & March, Easter week, mid-June to late-Sept, major holidays).

The refuge sits by a dam, but there are dozens of natural lakes and tarns in the cirque, set among stands of black pine. A sketch map of day-hikes – a two-hour circuit waymarked in red and yellow, and a four-hour loop blazed in red – is available from the warden. Full-pack treks from Colomèrs include the five-hour hike south, then west via the **Port de Colomèrs** (2604m) to the popular *Refugi Ventosa i Calvell* (see p.295). Alternatively, four hours' walk west along the joint HRP/GR11.18 takes you via the easier **Port de Caldes** (2567m) and the **Port d'Oelhacrestada** (2474m) to the *Refugi de la Restanca* (see below). En route you skirt the foot of **Montardo d'Aran** (sometimes Montarto; 2830m) – an easy ascent with fabulous views over Aran.

### Via Valarties

The friendly **Refugi de la Restanca** (2010m; ☎608 036 559; 80 places; staffed most weekends, Easter week & mid-June to late Sept) can be reached directly from Arties via a road threading up the **Valarties**. However, there's little chance of hitching it, and the way up on foot, dotted by day-trippers' parked cars and illicitly placed tents, is even less inspiring than the Aiguamotx slog, if shorter. After 5km, asphalt yields to dirt, ending 3km later at the bottom of a short, sharp climb to the *Restanca* refuge near the eastern end of the reservoir dam.

## West to Maladeta

The *Restanca* refuge permits the quickest access from the Aran to the **Maladeta** massif, via the refuges and camping spots near the south end of the Túnel de Vielha. You have the choice from **Lac dera Restanca** of the longer, more difficult HRP – around **Lac de Mar** and **Lac Tort de Rius** (7hr) – or the GR11, which makes an easy, direct and well-marked traverse past **Lac de Rius** (5hr). The HRP is recommended if you're an experienced, lightly laden trekker, since Mar is one of the area's most impressive lakes: a bare island hunkers in the middle, with a chaos of huge grey boulders on the shore, and Besiberri Nord peak looming to the south.

The HRP and GR11 rejoin briefly at the **Refugi Sant Nicolau** (aka *Er Ospitau de Vielha*), rebuilt on the site of a medieval pilgrims' hospice (1650m; ☎973 697 052; 49 places; open year-round except May, Nov & Dec 24–Jan 7). Though just above the main highway and paired tunnel mouths, it's the only amenity for miles around, and a welcome sight. Hosts Sebas and Juani provide reasonable meals to all comers (not Sun eve mid-Sept to June; not Sat lunch in summer), though there's no shop. Otherwise, there's the large but dilapidated and unstaffed **Refugi de Conangles**, 1500m south along the well-blazed GR11.

### Approaches from the Noguera Ribagorçana

The Noguera Ribagorçana has its source near the tunnel; crossing it you forsake Catalunya for Aragón and face three different approaches to Maladeta and beyond.

The **HRP** takes the classic route west via the Molières valley and the **Coret de Molières** (formerly Coll de Mulleres, 2935m, crampons/ice-axe often necessary) – a gruelling but spectacular traverse, which can be split by overnighting at the simple, metal-shed *Refugi Mulleres* (2360m; 8 places; unstaffed, always open), above a chain of tarns just below the pass. The **Cap deth Hòro/Cap de Tòro** (2969m), a fifteen-minute scramble up the north side of the saddle, gives a magnificent view over Maladeta's northeast glacier – where one branch of the Garona rises – and into the Joeu valley, where the infant river emerges after 4km underground.

The **GR11** continues south from the Conangles shelter to the head of the **Senet (Basserca) reservoir**, where it crosses the road at Pont de les Salenques and dips into the mouth of the **Salenques valley**, keeping to the south (true right) bank. Fairly well marked at first, the route (as well as the stream valley) divides about an hour along.

The inconspicuous right-hand option crosses the stream, then labours northwest through rhododendron-cloaked boulders prior to an exhausting slither up through scree and usually snow to the **Coll de les Salenques** (2807m); camping is possible two-thirds of the way in meadows at the base of the sharpest climb. There's an easier gradient down the other side to the **Plan dels Aigualluts**, one of the best wild campsites in the Pyrenees, also easily accessible from the Coret de Molières.

The waymarked, left-hand bearing is the **official GR11**, which threads through the lake-speckled **Vall d'Anglòs**, then over the easy **Coll de Ballibierna** (2728m), affording spectacular views of Maladeta's southwest face. Passing more lakes on the descent, the GR11 meets the track coming up the **Ball de Ballibierna**, and follows it down to Benasque – again a long day out of the Noguera Ribagorçana, best broken with a night out on either side of the pass. There's a tiny, wooden shepherds' shelter at 2220m, beside the easterly Ibón de Anglòs.

## Approach via the Joeu valley

The easiest, though nowadays least used, approach to the Maladeta region starts from Era Bordeta, 9km west of Vielha on the N230 road. From here you walk (or taxi) south down the **Joeu valley** as far as the **Pla de l'Artiga** (8km; 1465m; simple unstaffed refuge) and the resurgence of waters from the Forau dels Aigualluts. From here a path climbs west to the **Pòrt dera Picada/Port de la Picada** (2470m; 3hr from the Pla), through which you descend gently to either follow the Ésera valley in front of you downstream, or slip over the nearby Port de Venasque towards Luchon.

# The Aigüestortes-Sant Maurici region

Water is the salient feature of the **Parc Nacional d'Aigüestortes i Estany de Sant Maurici**, a region of flashing streams and waterfalls, nearly 400 lakes reflecting harsh granite peaks, and reed-fringed upland marshes. Rain or snow falls on these mountains – some reaching 3000 metres – almost half the days of the year. The name *Aigüestortes* ("Twisted Waters") has something of an unintentional subtext, as local streams have been diverted through enormous galleries into the mountainsides, and the lakes and reservoirs, thus tapped (Sant Maurici among them), intermittently become mud-bowls. The region has been exploited in this way since 1914, when Swiss- and German-designed hydroelectric works were undertaken to power the rapidly industrializing cities of lowland Catalunya.

The park bounded by the Val d'Aran, the Noguera Pallaresa and the Noguera Ribagorçana was established in 1955 during the hydroelectric schemes' expansion, no conflict being apparent to the Francoist government. Under rules laid down by the International Union for the Conservation of Nature, no hydro-electric exploitation is permitted in such a reserve, but as this is still Catalunya's only fully fledged national park, the authorities proudly brandish the title despite a continuing lack of international recognition. The arrogance of the bureaucrats of the era was epitomized in a 1970s pamphlet published by the Instituto Nacional Para la Conservación de la Naturaleza (ICONA): "Some changes have occurred recently with the construction of hydroelectrical installations which the country needs, and Nature has had to pay her tribute to man, The King."

But attitudes are slowly changing and park authorities wage constant battle with FECSA-ENHER (the power corporation) in an attempt to limit their depredations. The park's western area increased considerably during 1986 through the cession of lands by the Boí municipality, then again in 1996, when a huge area north of Caldes de Boí was incorporated. Some 140 square kilometres now enjoy full protection, though further expansion is unlikely given the spiralling costs of compensating FECSA-ENHER and other private landowners. It's easy to steer clear of the dams, and recommended **hiking routes** keep to the wilder corners as far as possible. There's something for walkers of all abilities here: from the simple mid-altitude track-jaunt across the park east to west, to gruelling climbs over jagged passes requiring snow equipment, by way of several popular trekkers' traverses using the GR11 or its variants. The **Sant Nicolau valley** and its tributaries (in the west) have many glacially formed lakes and cirques, as well as the water-meadows of Aigüestortes. Eastern sector highlights include the Peguera valley around the Josep María Blanc refuge, as well as the Estany de Sant Maurici itself, at the head of the Escrita valley. Just outside the park, in the 27,000-hectare so-called "peripheral zone of protection", are more lake-spangled cirques, particularly towards the Val d'Aran.

### Flora and fauna

The most common **trees** in Aigüestortes-Sant Maurici are fir and Scotch pine, plus silver birch and beech, especially on north-facing slopes. There's an abundance of **flowers** in spring and early summer, with blooms present until August above 2000m.

**Isards** are the most conspicuous **mammals**, easily seen in winter when harsh weather drives them downhill, but staying on the high summits in summer. Perhaps the most curious animal of this region is the long-nosed, mole-sized **desman**, which lives in holes along the stream banks, feeding on aquatic insects; its timidity and nocturnal habits make it almost invisible. The species suffers in polluted areas; its western European territory is now confined to the Pyrenees and the Picos d'Europa. The **otter** is also elusive, **wild boar, fox**, and **hare** less so. Outside its spring display-time, the **capercaillie** is glimpsed only when flushed out by chance; **ptarmigan** are similarly shy, and **black woodpeckers** are more likely to be heard than sighted. You will almost certainly see spectacular **birds of prey**: **golden eagles** soaring with open-V wings; **griffon vultures** floating high above like huge tasselled scarves; and **kestrels** hovering, tails fanned, wings pumping to maintain altitude.

# Approaches to Aigüestortes

There are four chief **bases** from which to explore the Aigüestortes park and environs. Access to the Sant Maurici and Monestero areas is from the village of **Espot**, just beyond the eastern fringe of the park and within 7km of the La Pobla de Segur–Val d'Aran bus route. Possible approaches from the Val d'Aran are covered on p.279–280. Quickest access to the high, remote peaks around the Circ de Saburó is via **Capdella**, at the head of the Vall Fosca, one valley west of the Noguera Pallaresa and served by occasional bus from La Pobla de Segur. Finally, for the western Aigüestortes zone, or the many lakes below Besiberri peak, the usual entry is from **Boí** or **Taüll**, the former served by bus from La Pobla via El Pont de Suert, which is also on a bus route from Vielha.

## Espot

The main disadvantage of an approach through **ESPOT** is the probability that you'll have to road-walk the very steep 7km from the turning on the main C13 highway where the Barcelona–Vielha bus drops you, and a similar distance beyond the village to the usual park entrance. Take a **4WD-taxi** if there's one

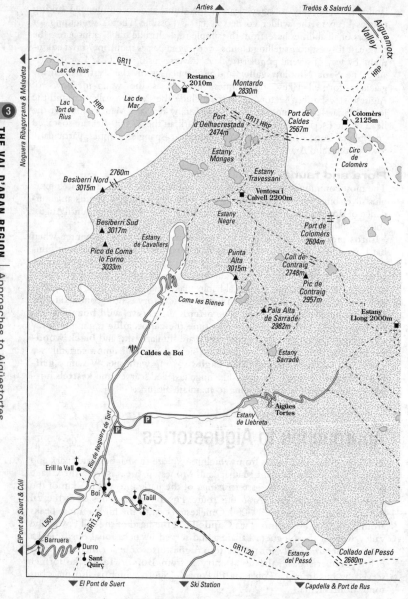

waiting at the turn-off; if not, one should appear within an hour (€4 per person for the trip up to the village).

Espot (1320m) is surprisingly unspoiled, despite decades of use as a tourist centre; in recent years a few marginal hotels have been converted into holiday flats. The village is split into two distinct sections: the less-visited area across the

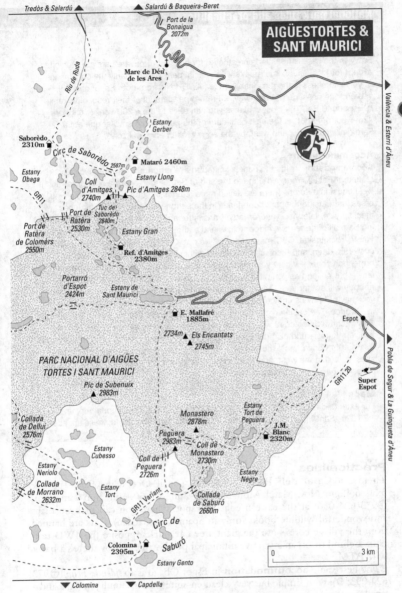

### AIGÜESTORTES & SANT MAURICI

▲ Tredòs & Salardú    ▲ Salardú & Baqueira-Beret

Port de la Bonaigua 2072m

Mare de Déu de les Ares

Riu de Ruda

Estany Gerber

Saborèdo 2310m

Circ de Saborèdo    2587m    ▲ Mataró 2460m

Estany Obaga

Estany Llong

Coll d'Amitges 2740m    ▲    Pic d'Amitges 2848m

GR11

Port de Ratèra 2530m    Tuc del Saborèdo 2840m

Port de Ratèra de Colomèrs 2550m

Estany Gran

■ ▲ Ref. d'Amitges 2380m

Portarró d'Espot 2424m    Estany de Sant Maurici

■ E. Mallafré 1885m

2734m ▲ Els Encantats 2745m

Espot ●

PARC NACIONAL D'AIGÜES TORTES I SANT MAURICI

Pic de Subenuix 2983m

Monastero 2878m    Estany Tort de Peguera

■ J.M. Blanc 2320m

Super Espot

GR11.20

Collada de Dellui 2576m

Peguera 2983m    ▲ Coll de Monastero 2730m

Estany Cubesso

Coll de Peguera 2726m

Estany Nèriolo    Collada de Morrano 2632m

Estany Tort    GR11 Variant    Collada de Saburó 2660m

Estany Negre

Circ de Saburó

Colomina 2395m ■

Estany Gento

0 —————— 3 km

▼ Colomina    ▼ Capdella

▶ València & Esterri d'Àneu

▶ Pobla de Segur & La Guingueta d'Àneu

ancient La Capella bridge and beyond the church (Espot Solau, south-facing Espot) – where goat droppings speckle the cobbled streets – and Espot Obago (north-facing), where hay still spills from barns tucked behind the various tourist facilities.

## National park rules and practicalities

### Park entry

**Entry** to the park is free, and unrestricted for hikers, but private cars are prohibited except for local shepherds' trucks with special permits. Ordinarily the only means of vehicle access is the reasonably priced 4WD-taxis from both Espot and Boí; you arrange passage (€4 one-way, €8 return per person) at their respective ranks in Espot and Boí. The closest places you can drive to are a 200-vehicle car park 4km west of Espot, at the east boundary of the park, and a smaller one at La Farga, north of Boí in the west, by the edge of the peripheral zone.

### Accommodation

**Accommodation** inside the park is limited to five **mountain refuges**, typically staffed at Easter, from mid-June to the end of September, and major *puentes* (long weekends) in autumn. There are seven more refuges in equally impressive alpine areas just outside the park boundaries in the peripheral zone. Each refuge has meal service, telephone and/or radio transmitter and bunks (€9–12) for your sleeping bag, all but one have indoor toilets and a shower; FEEC-managed places allow you to cook inside, CEC-managed ones do not. Camping wild in the park is officially forbidden, and technically restricted within the 27,000-hectare "peripheral protection zone" – where you're supposed to secure a permit from the nearest village – but as long as you pitch your tent well away from refuges and paths nobody will bother you. During July and August (plus weekends in June and Sept) you may not have a choice, as all the more popular park-centre refuges fill weeks in advance. The best way to reserve space is via the website ⊛www.carrosdefoc.com, which gives you booking access to nine of the region's twelve refuges – and also details the loop itinerary linking them all. (The record for this is 10hr 35min; most mortals take about a week.) There are managed campsites at Taüll in the west, and at Espot to the east. All the approach villages have *cases de pagès, hostals* and hotels.

### Maps

For extended explorations, you'll need current editions of the Editorial Alpina 1:25,000 "Sant Maurici" and "Montardo/Vall de Boí" **map-booklets**; these are easily

### Practicalities

There's a **Casa del Parc Nacional** (April–Oct daily 9am–1pm & 3.30–6.45pm; Nov–March Mon–Sat 9am–2pm & 3.30–6pm, Sun 9am–2pm; ☎973 624 036) at the eastern edge of Espot, where you can pick up maps and wonderful wildlife books (only in Spanish or Catalan). Cars are banned from the village core – use the giant, free **car park**, opposite the 4WD **taxi** rank. Behind this is an attractive municipal **pool**, while nearby there's a **bank** with ATM.

The best-value **accommodation** in Espot Obago is *Residència Felip* (☎973 624 093; ❷), with simple but very clean en-suite rooms, laundry service and a small garden. Also worth trying are the adjacent *Pensió La Palmira* (☎973 624 072; ❷) and the two-star *Hotel Roya* (☎973 624 040, ☞973 624 041; ❺). There are three **campsites** close by: the smallish *Sol i Neu* (☎973 624 001; June–Sept), just a few hundred metres from the village, has excellent facilities including a swimming pool; *De La Mola*, 2km further down the hill (☎973 624 024; July–Sept), also has a pool. At the far (upstream) edge of Espot beyond the available in all gateway villages except Capdella. If you're willing to forgo the included pamphlet (text only in Castilian or Catalan), you can buy a two-for-the-price-of-one map-only packet, entitled "Parc Nacional d'Aigüestortes i Estany de Sant Maurici". The Catalan Generalitat's Mapa Topogràfic de Catalunya 1:25,000 folding map no. 1 is much more accurate, with 20-metre contour intervals, but a bit difficult to read. If you intend to approach from the north, you'll also need the 1:40,000 "Val d'Aran" Alpina, and if you're moving west towards Maladeta, the 1:25,000 "La Ribagorça" makes a good investment. Sketched handouts at the various park information offices generally prove insufficient for route-finding – get a proper commercial map if you intend to leave the most popular paths.

### Weather and route conditions

Be aware of, and prepared for, bad **weather**, which as everywhere in the Pyrenees can arrive rapidly and without warning. In midsummer many rivers are passable which at other times are not, but temperature contrasts between day and night are still very marked. Local climatic patterns in recent years have alternated between daily rain showers throughout July and August, or prolonged drought, with a general trend towards warmer, drier summers. The best time to see the wonderful colour contrasts of the vegetation is autumn or early summer. Many passes, even those mapped with a bona fide trail, will be difficult or impossible after a harsh winter owing to snowpack. If you're doing an unusual traverse, tell the warden of the refuge you'll be leaving, who should be able to give current route pointers and, if there's any cause for concern, phone or radio ahead your estimated time of arrival.

### Skiing

In winter, the park is excellent for cross-country (nordic) and high-mountain **skiing**, though there are no marked routes. Many of the refuges open for a week or two around Christmas and Easter, and selected weekends and school holidays in between. There are currently two downhill ski resorts on the fringes of the park – Boí-Taüll in the west and Super Espot in the east – with another planned for the Pic de Llena above Capdella.

old bridge, the tiny *Solau* (☏973 624 068) also rents out apartments sleeping four at *Casa Peret de Peretó* (❸), a good fallback if the village centre is full.

Quality **eating** and economical *menús* are limited. The *menjador* of the *Pensió La Palmira* is decent, while the favourite lunch-time halt is the vine-shrouded *Ju Quim* in the centre (*menú* €14). Two well-stocked **supermarkets** and another shop sell maps, camping gas cartridges, and the like.

### Super Espot

Around Espot, you can see how development has encroached on the park. Two kilometres above the village, parts of the **SUPER ESPOT** ski centre (ⓦ www.espotesqui.com) edge into the peripheral protection zone. Its 31 runs are laid out with two chair lifts from Point 1500 (gear rental and lift tickets) to Point 2000, and further lifts to the tops of mostly intermediate pistes at 2300m, or more advanced runs from 2500m. Despite a northeasterly orientation, its snow record can't match most neighbouring resorts; by March many runs may be closed, and the whole place can shut for the day at 3pm.

### Into the park

The road divides in the middle of the village. The left side leads up to **Super Espot**; right takes you west into the park. It's 3.5km to its boundary and the designated car park at **Prat de Pierró**, and 7km to the end of the asphalt at **Estany de Sant Maurici**, where there's a seasonal information post beside the dam. The GR11 trail avoids most of the road, or local 4WD taxis provide an inexpensive way to avoid dull road-walking.

Once at the lake, there is a classic postcard view to the south, dominated by the 2700-metre spires of **Els Encantats** ("The Enchanted Ones"). In legend, these were once two hunters and their dog, who snuck off hunting instead of attending church on the day of the patron saint's festival. Lured heavenward by a spectral stag, the three were turned to stone by a divine lightning bolt.

Another enticing trail leads southwest from Espot Obago in just under four hours to the **Refugi Josep Maria Blanc** (☎973 250 108; 2320m; 40 places; open Easter & mid-June to late Sept), inside the park boundary on **Estany Tort de Peguera**. You can then continue another four hours to the Colomina shelter (see below), over the 2680-metre **Collada de Saburó**; the entire way from Espot is a well-travelled route, marked as the variant GR11.20.

## Capdella

The half-dozen villages of the narrow **Vall Fosca** are mostly tucked away, out of sight, up the slopes. There are few tourist facilities as yet along the valley floor, and the bus service from Pobla de Segur has dwindled to three a week (Mon, Wed, Fri at 5.15pm). Buses terminate in the lower of the two parts of **CAPDELLA** (30km from La Pobla), based around the Central (de Energia), the oldest hydroelectric generator in these mountains. For **accommodation** (both Easter to November), *Hostal Leo* (☎973 663 157; ❺ HB), originally catering to power company workers, is elegant if rather dour, while *Hotel Monseny*, 800m south and officially in Espui village (☎973 663 079; ❺ HB), is a modern structure with friendlier management. Both only offer half-board, since there's no shop or other restaurants in either part of the village. Just past the upper, residential quarter of Capdella, an excellent, 2001-built **hostel**, *Refugi Tacita* (1300m; ☎973 663 121; ⓦ www.tacitahostel.com), is run by a welcoming couple who offer excellent meals and pick-up service from the bus stop in La Pobla de Segur. The closest independent **restaurant**, *L'Era del Marxant*, is in LA POBLETA DE BELLVEÍ, 17km south and 3km up from Senterada, where the Vall Fosca and its Riu Flamisell join the main highway.

### Into the park

From Capdella, a half-day trek past the ugly Sallente dam takes you to the wonderful **Refugi Colomina** (2395m; ☎973 252 000; 40 places; staffed early Feb, mid-March to mid-April & mid-June to Sept), an old wooden chalet ceded to mountaineers by FECSA-ENHER and set among the alpine lakes of the **Circ de Saburó**, just south of the park boundary in the peripheral zone. You can skip the steepest hiking by taking the *teléferic* (July–Sept; €6 one-way, €9.60 same-day return) from the road's end at the back of the Sallente reservoir to within 45 minutes' walk of the refuge. The immediate surroundings of the refuge have a few two-to-three-hour walks, most notably the circuit of the Circ de Saburó.

## El Pont de Suert

The route into the southwestern area of Aigüestortes begins just past **EL PONT DE SUERT**, a small town 41km northwest of La Pobla de Segur; all

**buses** stop at a roadside terminal at the southeast edge of town. La Pobla's most remarkable, central sight is an unmissably hideous **modern church**. With a baptistry like a vertical egg and a brick belfry resembling the head of Spielberg's ET, it was designed by engineer Eduardo Torroja and architect J. Rodríguez Millares, and erected in 1955 as a bizarre homage to the Romanesque churches further up the valley (see below). The "egg" and the vaulting of the Nissen-hut-like nave are made entirely from curved, prestressed concrete panels, considered a daring technique back then but now looking rather dated.

El Pont de Suert is pleasant enough if you need to spend the night before catching the daily bus north to Boí (11.15am, June–Sept only), but you should-n't have to because the morning buses from Vielha, Lleida and La Pobla all connect with the Boí service. The old town, a small maze of arcaded streets, compensates for the grim buildings lining the highway, but it's not exactly a tourist hot spot, with only two **accommodation** options: *Hotel Mestre* at Plaça Major 8 (☏973 690 306; ❹), with a pleasant river-view **restaurant**, and *Hotal Cotori* (☏973 690 096; ❷), nearby on the post office plaza. Out on the main thoroughfare, modern *Pensió Canigó* (☏973 690 350; ❷) has helpful management and secure bicycle storage.

## North towards Boí

Some 2km northwest of El Pont de Suert, a good road threads north (right) along the **Vall de Boí**, following the Noguera de Tor towards Caldes de Boí, and passing the access for several villages on the way. It's an area crammed with **Romanesque churches** dating from the eleventh and twelfth centuries, when the valleys were more populous and wealthy than any time since, and could hire master masons from Lombardy. As a happy result, these churches have never been rebuilt, and rank as the finest in Catalunya. All were constructed with astonishing detail and elegance from hand-split chunks of local stone, roofed by slates and graced by literally over-the-top belfries. Unfortunately most of the frescoes on view today are reproductions, the originals having long since been whisked away to the Museu d'Art de Catalunya in Barcelona. The entire valley was declared a UNESCO heritage site in 2001, which should slow the growth of modern chalets at Boí and Taüll.

All the churches detailed following share the same **visiting hours and admission** (summer daily 10am–2pm & 4–8pm; winter Mon–Sat 10.30am–2pm & 4–7pm, Sun 10.30am–2pm; €1), except where otherwise stated.

### Cóll and Barruera

Some 8km upstream there's a turn-off left to the hillside village of **CÓLL**, with the twelfth-century church of **Santa María de l'Assumpció**; its west portal and masonry are particularly fine, but the grounds are usually locked. You're more likely to detour for *Hotel Casa Peyró* (☏973 297 002; ❹), whose en-suite rooms are bland Spanish-modern – wood floors, TV, pastel colours. But its restaurant is regarded as one of the best in the area – not cheap at €27–30 a head, but worth it, especially the *entrantes*.

**BARRUERA**, 5km further on and much larger, has several places to **stay**, best value being *Casa Coll* (☏973 694 005; ❷), an echoing old mansion near the top of c/Major in the old town. The salubrious rooms (some en-suite) are on the top floor, with a kitchen on the ground floor. For a more convention-al alternative, try the high-quality Casa Fonda member *Hotel Farre d'Avall*

(☎973 694 029, @farredavall@valldeboi.es; ❹) in the village centre, with limited parking and a restaurant. Opposite the petrol station stands the **Turisme** which serves the entire valley (Mon–Sat 10am–2pm & 5–7pm; ☎973 694 000). On main thoroughfare Passeig Sant Feliu a recommended guides' bureau, Cara Sur (☎973 694 132, @carasur@yahoo.es), organizes canyoning, caving and snowshoe expeditions. Just opposite the cramped campsite stands Barruera's Romanesque church, the riverside **Sant Feliu**, with its engaging thirteenth-century portal and creaking interior.

## Durro and Erill La Vall

Another fine Romanesque church graces **DURRO**, 3km away on the hillside to the east, reached by a steep road from Barruera's petrol station. The bell-tower of **La Nativitat de la Mare de Déu** is the tallest in the valley, its raised brickwork contrasting with crude masonry and a stark southern portal. Durro is situated on the variant GR11.20 linking El Pont de Suert with Boí, Taüll and the Colomina refuge (see above). Coming from Boí (see below), the well-signed path starts just over the little bridge behind the old district, climbs 45 minutes to a shrine on a saddle, then drops to Durro fifteen minutes later. Another fifteen minutes along the GR11.20 brings you to the twelfth-century *ermita* of **Sant Quirç**, prominent on the ridge opposite.

Further on, just before the turn-off for Boí, a one-kilometre side road leads west to **ERILL LA VALL**, also linked to Boí by a useful non-GR path (thirty minutes). Erill's twelfth-century church of **Santa Eulàlia** has an unusual arcaded porch and a climbable, six-storey belfry rivalling Sant Climent's in Taüll (see p.292); the interior holds a museum of religious folk art, dominated by a replica of a carved, seven-figure twelfth- or thirteenth-century *Deposition*, complete with the two Thieves. In high season Erill is more likely to have a vacancy than Boí or Taüll, with choice **accommodation** including the recently refurbished *Hostal La Plaça*, opposite the belfry (☎973 696 026, @hostalaplaza@eresmas.com; ❸), with comfortable rooms and galleried family suites. Alternatively, the nearby *Hostal L'Aüt* (☎973 696 048, ℻973 696 126; ❺ HB) has plain rooms but the village's best **restaurant**: its simple but abundant fare (€15 will buy mushroom sautée, grilled quail, dessert and a beer) attracts diners from the whole valley. Just before the entrance to the village, *Casa Pernallé* (☎973 696 049) has plentiful off-street parking, a choice of characterful old, non-en-suite rooms (❷) and modern, bland en-suites (❸; HB on request).

## Boí

**BOÍ** stands 1km above the main road, which continues up to Caldes de Boí (see opposite); buses usually take you into the centre. On arrival, the village proves something of an anticlimax: a tiny, gatewayed medieval core huddled around a crag, swamped by car parks, modern buildings, old houses defaced with new brick repairs, and overpriced accommodation. Even the twelfth-century church of **Sant Joan** has been extensively renovated, the only vestiges of the original building being the squat belfry and part of the apse; a cycle of reproduction frescoes in the spandrels of the north-aisle arcade features animals symbolic of the Christian virtues (eg the camel for submission).

## Practicalities

The **Casa del Parc Nacional** (daily: April–Oct 9am–1pm & 3.30–6.45pm; Nov–March 9am–2pm & 3.30–6pm; ☎973 696 189), under an arch in the old quarter, provides information and sells local maps at a slight mark-up. If you need to **stay** in Boí, a good budget choice is *Hostal Pascual*, down by the junction and bridge, halfway to Erill (℡973 696 014; ❷ B&B). Despite being a little out of the way and externally nondescript, it has helpful owners, private parking and pleasant conservatory seating for the *menjador*. For more comfort in the village itself, try the central *Hotel Pey* (℡973 696 036; ❹), with a popular terrace overlooking the main Plaça del Treio. There are also a couple of *cases de pagès* through the stone archway in the old quarter (eg, *Casa Tenda* (℡973 696 034; ❷) – look for the *habitacions* sign.

**Eating** out, you'll do no better than the *Casa Higinio*, 200m up the road to Taüll, above the village centre. Its wood-fired range produces excellent meat dishes, or try the fine *escudella* (minestrone soup) and trout. A big *menú* accompanied by local wine and coffee comes to around €13 – allow plenty of time for service. The 4WD **taxis** to the park gather on Plaça Treio, and there's an **ATM** at the bank behind the supermarket.

### Into the park – and Caldes de Boí

It's 3.5km from Boí to the national park entrance and another 3.5km to the scenic waterfalls of **Aigüestortes**, tumbling from water-meadows to feed the reedy **Estany de Llebreta**, where half-wild horses roam. One final kilometre above the falls – passed closely by both road and trail #5, the "Ruta de la Nutria/Llúdriga" (see below) – is a summer-only park information booth; an adjacent map placard suggests day-hikes, with corresponding time estimates. The most popular stroll, about an hour one-way, leads east from the information post to Estany Llong.

The 4WD taxis from Boí take you as far as the booth. Vehicles wait to depart until they're full; last return from Aigüestortes is at 7pm in midsummer. The closest you can get to the park boundary in your own vehicle is the car park at La Farga, or there's another smaller one 1.5km east, right at the boundary. If you leave your car at either and arrange to meet a taxi to take you further uphill, at day's end you can follow the trail signed for the "Aparcament" from the info booth which shortcuts the road by 45 minutes.

Alternatively, you can flag down the one midday bus from the junction of the Boí side road up to the large **spa** complex of **CALDES DE BOÍ** (June–Sept only), 6km upstream. The four-star *Hotel Manantial* here is beyond the financial reach of most travellers, but the adjacent two-star *Caldes* (℡973 696 230; ❼ HB), a renovated old building with plush, non-fusty rooms, is perhaps the best-value spa **accommodation** in the region, with every imaginable hydrotherapy.

From Caldes de Boí, it's 4km to the large car park below the high dam at the south end of Estany de Cavallers. The dam itself marks the trailhead for walks towards the beautiful natural lakes northwest of the park, just below the Besiberri and Montardo peaks.

## Taüll

**TAÜLL** – 3km above Boí by road or forty minutes on a fairly steep but well-marked section of the GR11.20 – had been a much larger medieval village before an avalanche divided it into two districts; ruined house foundations were found in the empty space between during the 1980s. More recently, it has been massively affected by the ski resort of Boí-Taüll (see below) on the mountainside a few kilometres southeast. There's an enormous holiday complex 1500m beyond the village at Pla de l'Ermita, en route to the ski station, and even in summer Taüll is targeted by tour coaches and family cars in search of panoramic picnic spots. Yet away from the peripheral ski chalets, the old core retains plenty of character, and is certainly preferable to Boí as a base.

Two of the best local Romanesque churches stand in the village, consecrated on successive days in 1123. Of the pair, **Sant Climent de Taüll** is more immediately impressive by virtue of its six-storey belfry and original triple apse. The stark interior, doubling now as a museum of religious artefacts, retains copies of vivid murals showing Christ, saints and apostles, plus scenes from the New Testament and the Apocalypse. These, however, are outshone by a sixteenth-century retable of St Anne, the Virgin and Christ as a seated group, and a fine thirteenth-century polychrome wood statue of Christ Enthroned. Climb the rickety wooden steps to the top of the bell-tower, and you're rewarded with sweeping views through delicately arched windows.

At the heart of the upper quarter, **Santa Maria** (daily 10am–8pm; free) is similar in design, though its belfry has only four storeys. After a millennium of subsidence, there's not one right angle remaining in the building, with the tower in particular at an engaging list. The mural (again a reproduction), soberly coloured in reddish brown, yellow and blue, depicts the Adoration of the Virgin and Child by the Three Kings.

## Practicalities

The best budget **accommodation** is the *Pensió Sant Climent* at the village entrance (☎973 696 052; ❷ B&B), with en-suite rooms and cosy attic apartments sleeping four (€72), while *Casa Plano Minguero* (☎973 696 117; ❷) is well located in the upper part of the village with its own parking. For more comfort, also in the upper quarter, the *Santa Maria* (☎973 696 170, ✉santamaria@taull.com) is a converted old house with rustic wood-decor rooms (❹) plus suites (❺) and garden studios (❸) facing a courtyard, while *El Xalet de Taüll* just uphill (☎973 696 095, ⓦwww.elxaletdetaull.com; ❺) has engaging management and a breakfast room/library with a plate-glass panoramic window, which justify the price as much as the wood-panelled rooms.

*Cases de pagès* include *Ca de Corral* (☎973 696 176 or 973 696 028; ❷), with rustic, en-suite rooms on the top floors of an old house well situated in the lower part of the village. Non-en-suite rooms are found at *Casa Llovet*, Plaça Franc 5 (☎973 696 032; ❶), or *Casa Xep* (☎973 696 054; ❷), just below Plaça Santa María. A **campsite** (☎973 696 082), also with bungalows, spreads attractively on the slope below Sant Climent.

When **dining** out, the *menjador* at *Sant Climent* is the popular, cheap-and-cheerful option (reserve in season), where sustaining if not haute cuisine meals will set you back €9–12, with drink. *El Caliu*, at the top of Taüll in a modern apartment building, is also well regarded (€13 *menú*; €21 *carta*), though its portions tend towards the *minceur*. Last but not least, just beside Sant Climent, David and Consell's *Mallador* is the most popular village **bar** with elaborate snacks (no food May–early June & mid Oct–Nov), garden seating in summer, a cutting-edge soundtrack, tasteful souvenir stall and **Internet** access.

## Day-hike to the Estanys del Pessó

The two **Estanys del Pessó**, just northwest of the eponymous pass, are a favourite day-hike destination from Taüll. The trailhead for the eastbound GR11.20 is 4km up from the village, at a bend in the road to the ski station (see below); you can drive another 600m to a disused quarry, but it's hardly worth it. Just over half an hour along, turn up and left onto a minor trail initially marked with yellow-topped stakes – the way is steep but fairly well defined. It's 1hr 15min from the road-bend to the lower lake, and another fifteen minutes to the upper lake (2492m), swimmable on a warm day. You're just outside the park, but the (likely) solitude and the line of often storm-lashed peaks to the northeast is as good as anything in it. Allow 1hr 20min for the return trip down to the road.

### Skiing: Boí-Taüll

The ski centre at **Boí-Taüll** (@ www.boitaullresort.es), some 11km southeast of Taüll, is the newest in the Catalan Pyrenees and the only rival to Baqueira-Beret for really serious skiing with 41 pistes, more than half red-rated, and 16 lifts, mostly drag-type. It's not the best resort for beginners or weak intermediates, as their runs tend to be short, but advanced skiers can tackle the six-kilometre off-piste descent of the Vall de Moró, typically an hour to drop the 1000m. Boí-Taüll has the highest lift-top in the range (2750m), start of a four-kilometre advanced run, and the snow quality is good in the glacial bowl facing north to Besiberri and other peaks beyond the Cavallers reservoir. With a 2020-metre bottom point at Pla de Vaques, the centre will probably survive global warming, unlike many other Pyrenean resorts, though early closures are common on spring days. Lift passes and on-site gear rental are pricey; Taüll or Barruera offer better rates.

# Walking in Aigüestortes

Initial stretches of trail or track into Aigüestortes are detailed in the preceding sections "Approaches to Aigüestortes" and "South to Aigüestortes". Moving deeper into the region, the clearly signposted **GR11** path skims the northern margins of the park, linking Espot with the Túnel de Vielha; variant **GR11.20** connects Espot and the Vall de Boí. There are also numerous waymarked (but unnumbered) lateral paths which permit any number of circuits and traverses in the best of the park and peripheral zone, including the so-called *Carros de Foc* (Chariots of Fire) itinerary linking most of the refuges. Less exciting, and sometimes overly subscribed because of its ease, is the east–west track crossing the park from Estany de Sant Maurici to the springs of Aigüestortes.

If you want solitude and wilderness, stick to the more difficult south–north trails, which run perpendicular to most hiker traffic. Map, altimeter and compass are essential when departing from more trammelled routes – it's easy to get lost amongst the hundreds of lakes and lookalike granite whalebacks dividing them, especially in cloudy conditions.

## Traverses

Three good traverses of the park start from the *Refugi Colomina* (see p.288), in addition to the one to/from Espot via the *Refugi Josep Maria Blanc* (see p.288).

### North to Refugi Ernest Mallafré via Monestero valley

Heading north through the often snow-clogged, steep **Coll de Peguera** (2726m) and down the beautiful **Monestero valley**, it's a six-hour hike to the **Refugi Ernest Mallafré**, near the dam and roadhead at Sant Maurici (1885m; @973 250 118; 24 places; mid-June to Sept). If it's full, you'll need to reserve enough energy and daylight to continue ninety minutes to the more comfortable **Refugi d'Amitges** (see p.279). Next day you could leave the park via the gentle **Port de Ratèra de Colomèrs**, finishing this less strenuous leg at the

Agulles d'Amitges, Aigüestortes region △

*Refugi de Colomèrs* (see p.280), where you're poised to continue along the routes described on p.279–280.

### Northwest to Refugis d'Estany Llong, Ventosa i Calvell and Restanca

A more adventurous route heads northwest from *Refugi Colomina* through the easy trekkers' passes **Collada de Dellui** (2576m) or **Collada de Morrano** (2632m) to the **Refugi d'Estany Llong** (2000m; ☎008 821 650 100 090; 36 places; open Easter week & June to mid-Oct) beside the lake of that name. If it's full, the nearby, unstaffed *Refugi de la Centraleta* (8 bunks, fireplace) will be your home for the night. The Dellui route descends through the valley of that name, speckled with natural lakes, additionally (with a slight detour) past the scenic tarns of Corticelles.

On the following day, you climb for three and a half hours to the cirque-bound Estany de Contraig, with two very sharp grades on route. This lies just below the **Coll de Contraix** (2748m) another hour along, with stunning views but requiring snow equipment after a heavy winter. From here you must drop along the nastily steep north side (self-arrest device always required) to the very popular **Refugi Ventosa i Calvell** (2200m; ☎973 297 090; 80 places; open select winter weekends & mid-June to Oct), 2hr 15min below the pass beside **Estany Negre**, where again you're near the heart of a lake-rich glacial basin. From here, you can walk an easy four hours to the *Refugi de la Restanca* (p.280) in the peripheral zone.

### West to Taüll

From *Colomina*, it's possible to head west through deserted country along the GR11.20 **to Taüll**, a long nine-hour day via one of two passes. The easy **Port de Rus** carries both the variant and the old spa patrons' *camí* from Capdella, but it's more exciting to maintain altitude by the park boundary, via a series of lakes and the inconspicuous **Collado del Pessó** (2760m), testing your cross-country skills.

### Sant Maurici to Aigüestortes

If you're not fully committed to alpine trekking, but are in reasonable physical condition, stick to the broad *camí* **between Sant Maurici and Aigüestortes**. Take a 4WD-taxi to/from one or both ends of the fifteen-kilometre traverse, which can be walked in six hours (allow another 4hr to Boí if you miss the last taxi). You definitely won't be alone, and will mostly look up at the peaks rather than down from them. The exceptional moments come either side of the **Portarró d'Espot** (2424m), where you can detour for moderate ridge-touring. The main track took its present form early in 1953, when in a typical pharaonic gesture General Franco commanded that it be widened with hand tools so that his private jeep could be driven through that summer. Much of the poor labourers' work has since reverted to nature – 4WD vehicles can no longer pass – though keen walkers regard the route as far too easy for serious consideration. Still, if you spread it over two days with an overnight at *Estany Llong* (see above), there are some excellent day-treks to be enjoyed from the refuge.

## Peak ascents

Featured on countless posters, postcards, window-stickers and T-shirts, the spikey profile of **Els Encantats** is the park's de facto logo. Like the Agulles d'Amitges near the *Refugi Amitges*, the pinnacles are a favourite of technical climbers, but experienced mountain walkers equipped with a rope can reach the top of **Encantat Gran** (2745m) in about five hours from the *Ernest Mallafré* refuge, via the gully separating the twin summits.

The second highest peak inside the park, **Pala Alta de Sarradé** (Serrader on some maps; 2982m), is a much easier goal, reached from Boí by the track to the park entrance, then via Estany Sarradé and a gully to the summit – a 4WD taxi cuts journeys from five to three and a half hours one-way. Its neighbour and highest park summit, **Punta Alta** (3015m), is usually climbed from the Cavallers dam, via a path up the vale and tarns of **Coma les Bienes** and then scrambling.

The third-highest summit, **Pic de Peguera** (2983m), is a nontechnical ascent if tackled from the Coll de Monestero, half an hour to the east; this pass is less than two hours from the *Josep Maria Blanc* hut and three from *Ernest Mallafré*. From the *coll* a cairned route leads southwest to the top in 45 minutes; however the final scramble up (or especially down) a steep, partially blocked couloir can be daunting.

# Maladeta and Posets

The trough-like **Ésera valley** drains the heart of the Pyrenees' high mountain wilderness, with Aneto peak (3404m) crowning the **Maladeta** massif to the east, and **Posets** (3375m) looming on the west. Since the creation of the **Parque Natural Posets–Maladeta** in 1994, both ranges have enjoyed some protection from development. **Benasque** is the pivotal point, a small valley-bottom town that lives for alpine tourism but has managed to retain some rural Aragonese character, not least in a vigorous campaign to promote renewed use of the **regional language**. Aragonese town names are noted below in parentheses following the Castillian, since you still see the latter on city-limits and road signs; the convention is reversed for place names in the mountains, since on most hiking maps – including Editorial Alpina's – Aragonese now takes precedence.

Accompanying the resurgence of regional feeling, efforts have been made throughout under-resourced Alto Aragón to improve the quality of tourist services and information – especially trail guides and maps – to match Catalan standards. Aragonese Pyreneans feel, with some justice, that the Catalans benefit disproportionately from tourism, and have misrepresented regional history and linguistics. Local advocates point out that Catalunya was long subsumed within the kingdom of Aragón, and that the yellow-and-red Catalan flag is based on the original, horizontal Aragonese version.

Not scaled until 1842, **Aneto** was long visited by mountaineers rather than walkers, not so much for any technical difficulty – though the climb does have vertiginous final moments – as for its inaccessibility. The former approach from France through the Portillón de Benasque was superseded in the 1970s with the extension of the C139 from Benasque to within a short walk of both the Portillón de Benasque, just northwest, and the *Refugio de la Renclusa* (south of the road's end), the standard base for the conquest of Aneto.

MALADETA, POSETS AND
THE PARQUE NATURAL

3

The most momentous day at the **Portillón de Benasque/Port de Vénasque** – the historic route across the watershed – was April 1, 1938, when thousands of Spanish Republicans fled from a Nationalist advance that had cut them off in the Ésera cul-de-sac. Many others didn't make it after being trapped in a snowstorm the next day. At the end of World War II, a large number of the surviving Republicans met their deaths when they returned to contest Franco's rule in Spain.

Though marginally lower than Aneto, and thus less known, the sculpted **Posets** massif with its paradisical valleys is popular with the Spanish, and has more staffed refuges than any other major Pyrenean peak. If you don't want to bag the 3375-metre summit, a westward traverse or half-circuit is the best and most scenic passage west – otherwise you have to detour way south on the bus to Barbastro before heading up the Cinca valley, a route poorly covered by public transport.

# The Ésera valley

The **Ésera valley** remains a dead end for cars, and since the area's inclusion in the local *parque natural* further restrictions on private traffic have come into effect (see below). Park status has ended long-mooted plans for a tunnel through the frontier ridge to Luchon in France, which many locals had campaigned for during the 1980s. It's an issue on the French side too, where people feel aggrieved that the Alps has had 300km of tunnel built since 1960, versus under 40km in the Pyrenees.

Coming from the **south** you can reach the Ésera valley by bus from Barbastro (in turn served by frequent buses from Huesca or Lleida), where twice-daily departures take two hours to reach Benasque. From El Pont de Suert and the Noguera Ribagorçana valley to the **east**, along a lonely 41-kilometre stretch of the N260 to Castejón de Sos, you're dependent on your own vehicle or bike; hitching this road can be very slow. En route, you'll notice road-signs "edited" by Catalan nationalists – this is part of **La Franja**, a transition zone between Aragón and Catalunya inhabited by Catalan-speakers. The only public transport towards Aragón from El Pont de Suert is the daily bus southwest to Graus, via the cathedral outpost of Roda de Isábena.

## Roda de Isábena

Attractive hill villages are ten-a-penny in Aragón, but **RODA DE ISÁBENA**, 32km south of the N260 in the middle of nowhere just above the A1605 road between El Pont de Suert and Graus, is unique for its superb Romanesque **cathedral** at the heart of town. Originally a tenth-to-eleventh-century monastic church, it has three aisles, Lombard apses and an eighteenth-century octagonal belfry visible from afar, but there ends any conformity to the norm. The ornate entrance portal, with six series of capitalled columns inside a Renaissance portico, breaches the south wall, since the west end of the nave is occupied by a carved choir and a fine organ, claimed one of the best in Europe. Mass is celebrated on the sarcophagus of San Ramón, squirming with twelfth-century carvings of the Annunciation, the Nativity and the Flight into Egypt. Immediately below the raised altar is a vast triple crypt, the central section with worn column capitals but the northerly one graced by brilliant Romanesque frescoes of the Baptism, Saint Michael weighing the souls of the dead, and Christ in Glory surrounded by the Tetramorph (the four symbols of the

Evangelists). Admission is only by guided visit (daily every 45min 11.15am–1.30pm & 4.30–7.15pm; €2), though you can see the twelfth-century cloister and its colonnade (eroded like the crypt's) by eating at the excellent restaurant (see below) in the former refectory. Apart from that, there's little to do but wander the attractive streets and take in 360-degree views from the *mirador* by the refectory, where it's easy to see why the medieval counts of Ribagorça chose Roda as their capital and citadel.

## Practicalities

Most visitors arrive in their own vehicle; besides the A1605 highway from the N260, a paved but narrow road runs 22km east from Campo in the Ésera valley, emerging on the A1605 7km north of Roda. Unless you're staying the night, you must use the **car park** on the outskirts of town. Roda is a popular Spanish weekend retreat, and booking **accommodation** is necessary all year. Top choices include the excellent-value *Hospedaría de Roda*, right on the multi-level central plaza (☎974 544 554, ℱ974 544 500; ❸), whose rooms have views and all mod cons, or the friendly, English-speaking *Casa Simón* (☎974 544 528 or enquire at *Bar Mesón de Roda*), with en-suite rooms (❷) and four-bed apartments (€40).

The *Mesón de Roda* on the plaza serves decent meals and breakfasts with a ringside seat for people-watching, but the best **restaurant** by far is the *Hospedería La Catedral* (reservations necessary on ☎974 544 545). Its *carta* has plenty of vegetable-based *entrantes*, meat and game for seconds, homemade desserts and a local wine list, and proves so reasonable (€15–17) that there's little point in having the *menú*.

## Castejón de Sos and Sahún

The N260 meets the Ésera at **CASTEJÓN DE SOS** (Castilló de Sos), 14km south of Benasque. If you've come up from Barbastro, it's the first place you'll see with much mountain character, at least in the tiny, fortified old quarter north of the highway. The unique local topography has made it a mecca for **parapentists**, with two international competitions here annually. If you want to stay, there's moderately priced **accommodation** on or just off the through road, c/El Real. Top choices include the well-kept, en-suite *Hostal Plaza*, central but quiet at Plaza El Pilar 2 (☎974 553 050, ⓦwww.aneto.com /hostalplaza; ❸); the *Hostal Sositana* towards the east end of town on the north side of c/El Real (☎974 553 094; ❷), with a bar and *comedor*; and the partly en-suite *Casa Miranda* opposite (☎974 553 222; ❶). There's also a central *albergue*, affiliated with a parapente school: *Pájaro Loco* at c/El Real 48 (☎974 553 516, ⓦwww.aneto.com/pajaroloco; six-bunk dorms).

### Sahún

If you have your own vehicle, the relatively unspoilt hillside village of **SAHÚN** (Saunc), 7km up the valley on the west slope, makes a more atmospheric base, especially in high season. There are several places to **stay**, including the *Hostal Casa Lacreu* on the Plaza Mayor (☎ & ℱ974 551 335; ❸), a restored manor house with spotless en-suite rooms, an arcaded bar and cheery, good-value *comedor*. Most accommodation in the village consists of *casas rurales*; of these, *Casa Alquesera*, at the north end of town next to the church belfry (☎974 551 396), offers a high standard for three- and four-place apartments (❹), while the single, centrally heated apartment at *Casa Colás* (no sign), 70m out the church door, downhill, then right (☎974 551 398) sleeps six at €70 per day and boasts a full kitchen with dishwasher. *Casa Falisia* (℡ 974 551 340; ➋) at the far south edge of Sahún is mostly without en-suite facilities, basic and a bit dated.

Prime outings from Sahún are the **all-day hikes** along locally marked *caminos* 9 and 10. Number 9 heads north past the deconsecrated Guayén (Guayente) monastery (now a private educational foundation), then west along the Aigüeta de la Ball to a series of lakes at about 2400m. Number 10 goes west, then north along the Aigüeta de Llisat stream to the scattered *ibones* of Barbarisa at 2360m. Both are designed for moderately fit walkers, and get a fraction of the patronage of the "classic" walks up-valley (see pp.300–306); these routes can be linked via the 2538-metre Collado de la Ribereta to form a loop.

# Benasque and Cerler

Surrounded by hayfields in a wide part of the Ésera valley, **BENASQUE** (Benás) strikes most people as an agreeable place, combining modern amenities with old stone houses, some built as summer homes for the Aragonese nobility in the seventeenth century. The town was once a seat of the counts of Ribagorça, who provided a castle and perimeter walls, both razed during the Napoleonic wars. The surviving old quarter, with its thirteenth-century church of **San Marcial** and fifteenth-century **Torre Juste**, is still homogeneous, atmospheric and large enough to get lost in.

Despite murmurings of despoliation, modern Benasque and its nearby ski annexe of Cerler aren't nearly as obtrusive as the new developments in the Val d'Aran – and, before or after the rigours of Aneto or Posets, you'll welcome the chance to indulge in a little luxury. Benasque seems to attract a younger, less staid clientele than Aran – mostly Barcelonans intent on a good time indoors or out – and so has plenty of nightlife as well.

### Arrival and information

**Buses** from Barbastro stop on the main Avda de los Tilos, a little south of the compact old quarter. The not terribly helpful **Turismo** (daily: summer 9am–2pm & 4–9pm; winter 10am–2pm & 5–9pm; ℡ 974 551 289) can be found at the southeast corner of the old town, dispensing pamphlets on local walks as well as publicity for local activities, and providing **Internet** access. Several **banks** have ATMs – the only ones you'll see for some distance, trekking east or west – plus there's a **laundry** on the bypass road, Carretera Francia, east of the Torre Juste.

### Accommodation

Budget **accommodation** in and around the old town is restricted to *Casa Pichuan*, on quiet c/El Castillo (℡ 974 551 275), offering both en-suite rooms (➋) and self-catering units; the somewhat shabby *Fonda Vescelia*, c/Mayor 3 (℡ 974 551 654, ℻ 974 552 802; ➋; good single rates), run essentially as a mountaineer's inn with a cheap *comedor*, a vast selection of teas, plus **Internet** access; and the non-en-suite *Hostal Salvaguardia* at c/San Marcial 5 (℡ 974 551 039; ➊), a last-resort cheapie despite its prime position by the church – and above a disco.

For more comfort, try the en-suite *Hotel Aragüells* (℡ 974 551 619, Ⓦ www.hotelaraguells.com; ➌) at Avenida de los Tilos 1, the main commercial street, or the *Hotel Avenida* next door at no. 3 (℡ 974 551 126, Ⓦ www.h-avenida .com; ➍), a long-standing mountaineers' hangout. Otherwise, the Valero Llanas family own much of the lodging in town, spread over five hotels and *hostales*;

consult ⓦwww.hoteles-valero.com, or call at the conspicuous *Hotel Aneto*, just south of the A139 skirting town on the Anciles road (☎974 551 061, 🖷973 551 509; ❸), which has a pool, tennis courts, gym, sauna and parking. Less institutional and homier is one of Benasque's three-star hotels, the *San Marsial* at the north end of town at Ctra. Francia 77 (☎ 974 551 616, ⓦwww .hotelsanmarsial.com; ❺).

The closest authorized **campsites** begin 4km upstream along the Ésera valley, conveniently near the GR11 junction: *Aneto* (☎974 551 141; year-round), *Chuise* (☎974 552 121; summer only) and *Ixeia* (☎974 552 129; June–Sept). Of the three, the *Chuise*, at the mouth of the Estós valley, is the most basic and tent-friendly. Rough camping is frowned upon anywhere near the valley floor.

## Eating and drinking

Competition means reasonable *menús* at several local **bars** and **restaurants**. Try the *comedores* of the *Bar Bardanca* at c/Las Plazas 6, with a hearty *menú* for €8 and a cheerful environment (if sullen service), or the *Bar Sayó* on c/Mayor 13, which includes quails or sardines on its three-course *menú* (€11.50). The best pizzas are at *Pirenáica*, out on Carretera Francia, while carnivores should head for *Asador Ixarso*, behind the *Turismo* (*a la carta* only at €21). For a splurge, *La Parilla* on Carretera Francia serves nouvelle Aragonese cooking – stuffed vegetables and creative puddings – as a *menú* (€14) or *a la carta* (from €28). Finally, you can cobble together breakfast at the popular *Pastellaria Flor de Nieve* at c/Major 17. In the shopping centre across the road from the *Hotel Avenida*, *Ñam Ñam* has zero atmosphere in its ground-floor bar but reasonably priced, tasty *tapas* and a more enticing *comedor* upstairs. Most of Benasque's other **bars** cluster around the lower reaches of c/Mayor and Plaza Mayor; there's even an Irish theme pub, *Molly Malone's*.

## Activities and equipment

Everything in Benasque revolves around the great outdoors, evident from the number of people strolling about in brightly coloured Gore-Tex. Three rival **guiding centres** – Casa de la Montaña, Avda. de Los Tilos (☎974 552 094), Equipo Barrabés (☎974 551 056, ⓦwww.barrabes.com) and Compañia de Guías Valle de Benasque (☎974 551 336, ⓦwww.guiasbenasque.com) near La Parilla, with a café open until 11pm – organize climbing, alpine skiing, canyoning, rafting and trekking expeditions, including both nearby summits in five days. The lower reaches of the rivers in the Estós and Ballibierna valleys offer some of the best **kayaking** in the Spanish Pyrenees, the latter watercourse for experts only. You can **horse-ride** with the Centro Ecuestre in Anciles (☎974 551 098), and go **boating** on the Linsoles reservoir with Grist Kayak in Eriste (☎974 551 692). Of the **mountaineering equipment shops**, one of the biggest in Spain, if not Europe, is Galleria Barrabés, near the corner of the A139 and Avda. de los Tilos: four floors of outdoor gear, with a café on the third floor and an annexe across the road. There's also Deportes Aigualluts/Casa de la Montaña, with three outlets on Avda de los Tilos.

Most useful of the local guidebooks on sale is *Senderos de Pequño Recorrido: Valle de Benasque*, issued by the Aragonese mountain club together with an invaluable map, worthwhile even if you don't read Spanish. If you're unsure about tackling high-mountain walks, then the various local yellow-and-white-or blue-and-white-blazed *pequeño recorrido* (PR) **short-haul paths** make an ideal introduction. The PR itineraries, routed to avoid roads as much as possible, lead to surrounding villages, lower altitude alpine attractions, and also to all three local refuges.

## Cerler: ski centre and village

**CERLER** (Sarllé), a small dependency of Benasque reached by a six-kilometre road or the one-hour PR-1 path, ranks as the highest (1540m) village in Aragón. It's an attractive enough if slightly twee place, worth considering as a base if you've a car, though the old quarter is now engulfed by straggly, low-density modern chalets which come to life in winter courtesy of the adjacent **ski centre** (ⓦwww.cerler.com). This narrowly avoided closure in the early 1990s through massive government investment in high-speed lifts and snow canons. A top point of 2630m, second only to Boí-Taüll in the range, and a well-linked system of lifts (half are chairs) has vastly improved this intermediate resort, with fifteen red and fifteen blue runs among its 45 pistes. There are two sectors, separated by conical Pic de Cerler: Ampriu to the northeast, reached by a potholed, eight-kilometre road, with more advanced runs from the top point down to 1900m (good restaurant), and Cerler proper, with longer, easier runs (including a lovely green through trees) north from 2372-metre Cogulla peak. The Coll d'Ampriu (2260m) is the main link between the two sectors, with most of action centred around Cota 2000 (where there's another good restaurant).

The best **accommodation** in the old village is at *Casa Cornel*, c/Obispo 11 (℡974 551 102, ⓦwww.casacornel.com), with good-standard *hostal* rooms in a stone building facing a courtyard (❸), and a newer wing opposite of large, well-heated parquet-floored rooms with solid-wood furniture (❺). Ample parking and frequent rate discounts are further attractions; the restaurant is adequate, best patronized *a la carta* rather than on a half-board basis. *Casas rurales* include the en-suite *Casa Llorgodo*, c/La Fuente, above the church plaza (℡974 551 067, ❶), or, abutting the church at the top of the path up from Benasque, *Casa La Abadia* (℡974 551 641, ❷), with good views. There are two independent **bar-restaurantes**: *La Picada*, the hub of village life, serving snails and mushrooms in season, and *La Borda del Mastín*, specializing in *carnes a la brasa*.

# Into the Parque Natural Posets-Maladeta from Benasque

Benasque offers the only road access to the **Parque Natural Posets-Maladeta**, which extends from the Noguera Ribagorçana in the east to the Valle de Chistau in the west. The lowest reaches of the Ésera valley are not included up to the Baños de Benasque, an old spa or *balneario* 10km from Benasque (see below). **Private vehicle traffic** into the park is restricted between June 1 and September 15. The track east into the Ballibierna (Vallhiverna) valley, 6km above Benasque, is closed for entry from 7am to 8pm, and the barrier is lifted for cars exiting only from 10 to 11am and again from 3 to 6pm. The A139 splits some 11.5km north of Benasque; the right-hand option leads after 1500m to a car park at **El Vado**, beyond which passage is generally forbidden. Guards tend the barriers; the only exceptions are for those continuing about 500m from El Vado to the car park of the Hospital de Benasque (see below). During the closed period, there's a **shuttle-bus service** (8am–8.45pm, plus two pre-dawn departures; €3 one-way or return) from here to La Besurta, road's end (16km from Benasque) and start of the paths to the *Refugio de la Renclusa* and the Forau dels Aigualluts. Other routes covered by the same company include Benasque to **La Besurta**, via Plan de Senarta and Baños de Benasque (6 daily 4.30am–6pm; €5 one way) and Benasque-Senarta-Refugio de Pescadores in the Valle de Ballibierna (3–4 daily; €9), which cuts out a considerable, dull track-section of the GR11. At other times of the year, those without cars wanting a jump-start to excursions might use the **alpine taxi** services of Angel Lledo (℡608 930 450), Daniel Villegas (℡609 448 894) or Manolo Mora (℡974 551 157).

**Camping** within the *parque natural* had been forbidden since the park opened; however a law passed in 2000 permits a one-night tent stay at all points above 2000m – legalizing this previously widespread practice.

### Baños de Benasque and Llanos del Hospital

The **Baños de Benasque** (Bañs de Benás), part of the Valero **hotel** empire (℡974 344 000, 𝔽974 344 249; mid-June to Sept; ❹), presents itself as a contemporary spa with full hydrothereapy and massage programmes. The premises however, remain resolutely old-fashioned, with a rather funky plunge-pool downstairs and a popular bar above it, where terrace tables are at a premium on fair days. There's also a smallish **campsite** just downhill at Plan de Bañs, the *Baños* (℡974 344 002; July to mid-Sept).

From the baths, the best **hike** heads east up the Ball d'Alba to its cluster of lakes. Start out along the old *camino* northeast towards the Hospital de Benasque; after about ten minutes veer east onto a much fainter side trail which climbs sharply along the bank of the Turonet gully to a saddle at 1975m (50min along). After a brief dip, the ascent continues east-southeast, and within another hour you should arrive at the largest of the three **Ibons d'Alba**, tucked away on the west flank of the Maladeta massif, just below 3107-metre Pico de Alba. Allow about three-and-a-half hours for the round-trip.

The derelict old pilgrims' hospice of **Hospital de Benasque** (13km from Benasque), a Templar foundation of the twelfth century, has been revamped and enlarged by an activities group as the *Llanos del Hospital* (℡974 552 012, 🆆www.llanosdelhospital.com; all year). It offers pricey **lodging** in various formats: *albergue* with five-to-seven-bunk dorms, en-suite bathrooms and linen provided (€18.50 per person), or *hostal* (double rooms ❸; suites ❼). It's also the focus of a popular **cross-country skiing** centre, whose routes extend up-valley to La Besurta; in winter you're virtually obliged to take half-board, multi-day "packages". On the ground floor are a convivial **bar** and a highly regarded **restaurant**, with *menús* at three price scales and lots of regional dishes (such as *recau*, a chickpea-and-greens hotpot) available *a la carta*.

The best and most popular summer excursion near *Llanos del Hospital* is an easy two-and-a-half-hour round-trip **hike** to two small tarns and one sizeable lake to the north, the largest bodies of water on the Spanish side of this frontier ridge. The least complicated trailhead, with parking available year-round, is at the abrupt end of the left-hand fork in the A139, west of El Vado. The path, shown pretty accurately on the Alpina "Maladeta/Aneto" map, climbs north to cross the Torrente de Gorgutes, then veers briefly east to skim above the two well-hidden **Ibones de la Solana de Gorgutes** (de la Montañeta), the smaller being shallow and warm enough to swim in. The route then curls west to the **Ibón de Gorgutes**, with the 2367-metre **Puerto de la Glera** just behind, an easy pedestrian route into France.

# Maladeta climbs and walks

Despite its forbidding appearance from a distance, the **Maladeta massif** offers scope for day-hikes, traverses and circuits of various levels of difficulty, as well as alpine ascents. The main drawback walking around Maladeta is that there's only one staffed refuge, better positioned for peak-climbers than long-distance trekkers. For any other extended forays you'd do well to have a **tent**. The relevant **maps** are either Editorial Alpina 1:25,000 "Maladeta/Aneto", or Rando Editions 1:50,000 Mapa Excursionista no. 23, "Aneto-Posets".

# The ascent of Aneto

The **ascent of Aneto** typically begins at the **Refugio de la Renclusa** (2140m; ☎974 552 106; 150 places; staffed Christmas, Easter, Sat & Sun Easter–June, daily July–Sept, emergency shelter in winter), located well north of the summit close to the border. The final stop of the summertime shuttle-bus from El Vado at the La Besurta parking area is 45 minutes' hike below *Renclusa*. If you need to walk the whole distance, a forestry track runs most of the way along the east bank of the Ésera, with more path short-cuts on the opposite bank once past *Llanos del Hospital* – the entire way marked as the four-and-a-half-hour **PR-4**.

Unless you're incredibly fit and experienced, plan for a full day to the summit and back with necessary stops, starting before sunrise. Walking equipment must include **crampons**, **ice-axe** and a **rope**. For less experienced climbers, the ascent is the most commonly offered guided excursion in Benasque.

### Routes – and their history

There are two basic routes on the northeast face, which can be combined as a circuit. The standard itinerary heads south from the refuge, climbing steeply towards the pass known as **Portillón Inferior** (2742m). Before the top, bear southwest to the next pass along, **Portillón Superior** (2870m), which you should reach in about three hours.

Now you have your first good view of Aneto, with the secondary peak of **Maladeta** (3308m) to your right. The guide Pierre Barrau – who had made the first recorded ascent of Maladeta with Frédéric Parrot on September 29, 1817 – was killed when he fell unroped into a crevasse on the Maladeta glacier in 1824. The death helped to postpone further conquest of Aneto for twenty years. Barrau's body was only recovered when it emerged from the ice over a century later.

A gully descends on the far side of Portillón Superior to a saddle, beyond which ice fields lead to the Aneto glacier. During summer months, a "path" will have been worn across it, a little whiter than the grit-stained glacier to either side. It should be perfectly safe but rope up if there is any doubt. You now traverse 2500m south-southeast to the **Collado de Coronas** (3196m; 4hr 30min from the refuge), just below which a summertime lake forms every several years, a brilliant blue on a sunny day.

Climb east beyond the *collado*, possibly with crampons and ice-axe, to the broad jumble of rocks known as the **Puente de Mahoma**. Negotiated on all fours, this represents 50m of sheer terror for the inexperienced, especially if iced up (its name refers to "Mohammed's rope", the Islamic bridge over Hell to Paradise). On the other side of the bridge the **Aneto summit** (3404m) is staked by a large cross and what looks like a small rocket, but turns out to be a Virgin and Child on a metal pedestal. Savour your triumph, but don't linger, especially if clouds close in – climbers have been killed by lightning in the mid-afternoon.

The first to stand here, on July 20, 1842, were the Russian Platon de Tchihatcheff, the French count Albert de Franqueville, and their guides, Bernard Ursule, Pierre Redonet, Jean Argarot and Pierre Sanio. However, they did not use the route described, avoiding the formidable northerly glacier by skirting anticlockwise and climbing the smaller Coronas glacier on the southwest side of the ridge. Today, these pioneers would take the classical modern route, since Aneto's glaciers – like most in the Pyrenees – are a third the size they were in the nineteenth century.

To make a **circuit**, descend to Collado de Coronas and then bear right on another path east across the glacier to the Plan dels Aigualluts (below) and the **Forau dels Aigualluts/Trou du Toro** – a pit of grey, splintered rock into which cascading waters of the Aneto glacier disappear before re-emerging in the Joeu valley. Beside a green shed-refuge, upstream from the sinkhole, an initially very faint path leads directly west back to the *Refugio de la Renclusa*.

## Walks around Maladeta

If you don't want to stay at the *Renclusa* shelter, or if it's full, wilderness **camping** at the Plan dels Aigualluts is highly recommended. You've reached the 2000-metre camping limit, though if you stay more than one night you're supposed to take down your tent during the day. The *plan* is your destination coming west from the Noguera Ribagorçana over either the Coll de Salenques or the Coret de Molières – approaches detailed in "West to Maladeta" on p.281. Using **Plan dels Aigualluts (de Aig. allut)** as a base, you're also well positioned for a few days of rewarding and not too strenuous **day-hikes**; there are four relatively gentle passes on crests to the northeast, and the paths through them can be combined into circuits. Otherwise, starting **from Benasque**, two other day-hike targets are slightly beyond the scope of the local PR excursions in length and effort.

### Itineraries around Plan dels Aigualluts
The way up from Plan dels Aigualluts towards the Coret de Molières along the **Valleta de la Escaleta** brings you to the **Còth deth Hòro/Coll de Tòro** (2236m) and, shortly after, the **Còth deth Aranesi/Coll dels Aranesos** (2446m). Both passes overlook lakes and have sharp but scenic descents – largely cross-country – to the Pla de l'Artiga in the Val d'Aran. You can return to the Aragonese side of the crest via a well-trodden trail up the Pomèro valley, leading to the **Pòrt dera Picada** (Puerto de la Picada; 2477m), where the boundaries of Aragón, Catalunya and France meet.

The **Portillón de Benás/Port de Vénasque** (2445m), the age-old route to Luchon in France, is the next pass west of Picada, an easy two-and-a-half hours' walk by well-trodden paths from either *Refugio de la Renclusa* or Plan dels Aigualluts. Even if you're not bound for France, this notch in the ridge is a worthwhile goal for the opportunity to visit **Tuca de Salbaguarda/Pic de Sauvegarde** (2738m), 45 minutes' climb west of the pass. The views in every direction from the summit are among the best in the Pyrenees, especially south over Maladeta, a giant reef of dark rock striped by patches of snow and ice. Less than an hour north, on the shore of a large lake, is the friendly *Refuge de Vénasque*, well placed for a lunch stop (see p.333).

### Itineraries from Benasque
The first, longer hike from Benasque is the steep trek up to **Lago de Cregüeña** (2657m), the third largest body of water in the Pyrenees, trapped in a deep cirque southwest of Maladeta. To reach the lake, turn off the PR-4 at the fountain and waterfall of **San Ferrer** (San Farré), about ninety minutes' walk above Benasque (limited parking at trailhead). The path up the Ball de Cregüeña is

distinct and cairned; allow at least six hours return (the sign says three-and-a-half hours uphill). Optimistically shown on some tourist office handouts, the route over the 2930-metre pass to the southeast into the Ball de Coronas is a tough exercise only for the properly equipped and experienced. The route north from below the northwest tip of the lake over the 2646-metre Brecha d'Alba into the Ball d'Alba is much more feasible for casual hikers, depending on snowpack, and makes possible a day-loop taking in both lake basins.

About half an hour before San Ferrer, at the **Puente de Ballhibierna** by the Paso Nuevo reservoir, you can also leave the PR-4 to explore the **Ball de Ballibierna** (Valle de Vallhiverna), an idyllic tributary forested in black pine, fir and birch, by following the eastbound GR11 – unfortunately forced onto 4WD track here. There's little traffic when access is limited, but still you're best off saving your stamina for higher altitudes by using the seasonal shuttle-bus service as far as **Puente de Coronas**. Whichever way you arrive, you'll find a permanently open, ten-person **refuge** for use if you're traversing rather than day-hiking; camping is theoretically forbidden, as Coronas lies just under the 2000-metre legal limit.

From Puente de Coronas, you can either tackle Aneto via the valley and glacier of Coronas – final approach of the 1842 pioneers – or, more likely, continue east **along the GR11** into the Anglòs (Angliós) valley on the Noguera Ribagorçana side, via the lakes and **Coll de Ballibierna** (2728m). Even with help from the shuttle bus, it's a long (8hr) day to the *Refugi Sant Nicolau* at the Vielha tunnel mouth; camping is unlikely to cause problems given that the country is so rugged and remote.

# Posets climbs and walks

Seen from Aneto, the magnificent dark granite mass of **Posets** (3375m), topped by an almost complete circle of low schist ridges, looks like a giant's fort. From the west it seems even more formidable, rising as a huge freestanding lump, deeply etched by gullies and false trails. An ascent requires ice-axe, crampons and rope, and perhaps a helmet to shield from falling rocks.

For both day-hikers and long-haul trekkers, Posets is more user-friendly than Maladeta, with three well-sited, staffed refuges, a host of places to camp – though you shouldn't really need to – and options for circuits and traverses of varying length. From Benasque there are two main approaches for climbs and traverses. You're likely to exit the region via the Valle de Chistau to the west, well poised for hikes further into Aragón. The relevant **map** is Editorial Alpina 1:25,000 "Posets"; if you intend walking in or out via the *Viadós* refuge and the Valle de Chistau, take the 1:25,000 "Bachimala/Bal de Chistau" sheet too. Rando Editions Mapa Excursionista no. 23 "Aneto-Posets" is also useful.

## The approach from Estós

More pastorally attractive and unspoilt than the Ésera, the **Estós valley** curls around Posets to the northeast. Although the track's lower reaches can be driven, private cars are banned except for the 4WD belonging to the warden of the modern three-storey *Refugio de Estós* (1890m; ☏974 551 483; 115 places; self-catering kitchen). It's manned all year, though the staff can be curt and unhelpful, so you may prefer to omit the refuge from your overnight plans.

To reach valley and refuge, follow the PR-5 path from Benasque, then a bit of the PR-4, to the medieval **Cuera (San Jaime) bridge** 45 minutes above town, then switch to the GR11 going northwest over the bridge. After another hour or so, the PR-6 peels off from the GR11 and adopts the opposite bank of the valley stream, rejoining it shortly before the *Estós* refuge – though the GR11 track is by no means objectionable. Whichever route you take, count on four hours total from Benasque to the shelter.

### The ascent of the peak

The *Estós* refuge marks the start of the easiest and most popular six-hour hiking **ascent of Posets**. Drop down to cross the bridge and follow the path along the stream's right (south) bank. After a couple of kilometres leave the main valley on the path climbing into the Coma de la Paúl, leading to the **Glaciar de la Paúl**, beyond which you reach the **Collado de la Paúl** (3062m). Once on its south side, cross the **Glaciar de Posets** – normally by a clearly trodden path in the ice – to the east face of the summit. A scramble up a narrow gully brings you to the top, known locally as **Llardana**.

## The approach from Eriste

The much less frequented **Eriste valley** forges into the alpine heart of Posets from the southeast. Near the top stands the *Refugio Ángel Orús (Forcau)*, the alternative base camp for a Posets climb (2095m; ☎974 344 044; 98 places; staffed all year). To get there, follow the PR-7 path from Benasque to Eriste village, then the PR-11 up the narrow wild canyon, cloaked in foothill vegetation thanks to a mild microclimate. After two hours, mostly on track, you come to the bridge and waterfalls of **Espiantosa**, where there's a fair-sized car park – the five-kilometre track up from Eriste is passable to ordinary cars (or alpine taxis). From here it's ninety minutes' walk on the PR-11 to the refuge, nearly four-and-a-half hours in total from Benasque. If *Refugio Ángel Orús* is full, you can **camp** an hour to the north, in or around the simple Cabaña de Llardaneta.

From Espiantosa you could also take a signposted path northeast to the run-down *cabaña* at **Clot de Chil**, well placed for climbing the pointy-headed **Tucas de Ixeia** (2837m), star of many a Benasque postcard, and a favourite launch platform for *parapentistas*.

From the *Ángel Orús* refuge, the best approach to the summit is along the **Ball de Llardaneta**, up the **Canal Fonda** between the outcrops of Tuca Alta and Diente de Llardana at the end of the *canal*, then straight up to the summit – a total of five hours one-way (nine hours return).

## Traverses and circuits

The following **traverses and partial circuits** – except for the day-loop out of Viadós – can be combined into a giant loop around the massif, so that with three or four days at your disposal you trek through the best of Posets. Outside peak season – when space is hard to come by and a tent is mandatory equipment – you can rely on the well-spaced refuges.

### Traverse via Batisielles

A superb traverse from the vicinity of the *Ángel Orús* refuge to the Estós valley, mostly relying on the variant GR11.2, enters the **Ball d'es Ibóns** northeast of Llardaneta and then, just below the Lago de les Alforches, ascends east to the **Collado de la Plana** (formerly Piana; 2702m). On the other side, a marked but non-GR and essentially cross-country route descends more sharply into the **Ball de Perramó**, with the *ibón* of the same name huddled at the base of the Tucas d'Ixeia. The route swings north again to the Escarpinosa lake, where a clearly trodden path leads down to the meadows of **Batisielles** (1900m). The GR11.2 veers northeast from the pass, taking in the Ibón de l'Aigüeta de Batisielles and the Ibón Grán de Batisielles (camping possible) before dropping to the meadows – a wonderful (if somewhat insect-plagued) place to camp, which you may have to do since the trek from *Ángel Orús* is six to seven hours. Without a tent, you might use the little *cabaña* here, or press on for another ninety minutes along the GR11.2 through meadow and woods to the *Estós* refuge.

## The Posets half-circuit

The most popular Posets activity for non-climbers is the **half-circuit** of the massif which follows the main GR11 west, skirting the mountain's north and west flanks. From the *Estós* refuge you continue along the valley, climbing to the **Puerto de Chistau** (2577m; 2hr 15min), before descending the other side to the head of the **Zinqueta de Añes Cruzes**. As you amble down this progressively more hospitable valley, you're treated to impressive views of the mountain's forbidding west flank before arriving at **Granjas de Biadós** (Viadós), a dozen or so scattered barns amongst summer hayfields, and one of the most beautiful spots in the Spanish Pyrenees. You can do the entire walk in five to six hours, with plenty of daylight left for the worthwhile hop up to **Señal de Biadós** (2600m), which has the best possible view east to Posets and west over the Zinqueta valley.

## Biadós – and back to Benasque

At Granjas de Biadós, the welcoming **Refugio de Biadós** (ex-Viadós; 1740m; ☏974 506 163 or 974 506 082; 70 places; open Easter and weekends to June 25, thereafter daily to Sept 25) is privately run by Joaquín Cazcarra and family. Señor Cazcarra is partly responsible for the "Bachimala/Bal de Chistau" Editorial Alpina map, providing regular cartographic updates to the publishers. The refuge is accessible by road, meaning that its meals and bunks are cheaper than the Pyrenean norm. The Cazcarra family also run a **campsite**, *El Forcallo* (same phone numbers; open Easter, July & Aug), fifteen minutes' walk below at 1580m elevation. Free camping in the meadow beside the refuge, at the *parque natural* boundary, is no longer permitted.

It's possible, and highly recommended, to loop **back to Benasque** by one of two demanding but nontechnical routes, which cut through the much-admired Posets crest. You'll need extra water, crampons and an axe after a severe winter. From the *Refugio de Biadós*, follow the instructions for the start of the day-loop given next section, climbing up the Bal de Millars to just below and north from the eponymous lake. Here the GR11.2 guides you steeply up a stable slope to a false pass, and then after a slight dip to the true **Collado de Eriste** (2860m), flanked by the peaks La Forqueta (3007m) and Diente Royo (3010m), three hours from the refuge. Great striated bands of tawny orange and purplish serpentine loom above this pedestrian pass over the Posets flank, where you'll have company on a summer's day. From Collado de Eriste, descend east to the vicinity of the Ibón de Llardaneta, then down its valley to the *Ángel Orús* hut (5hr 30min–6hr from Biadós).

Alternatively, you can continue up to the Ibón d'es Millars for a more challenging route. There's no path up from this lake, with only a few cairns guiding you over the rock-girt **Collado de Millares** (2831m), three and a half hours along. The descent southeast calls for more cross-country work through a moonscape of tortured granite before you reach the upper **Bagüeña lake**. Then simply follow the **Vall de Bagüeña** down to Sahún or Eriste, with a

Granjas de Biadós △

good path (local Camino no. 9, see p.300) once you're below the lower Ibón de Bagüeña (allow eight hours plus).

## Lake circuit from Biadós

Of the various day-hikes out of Granjas de Biadós that Joaquín Cazcarra recommends, the loop taking in a chaplet of lakes and tarns tucked into Posets' southwest flank is the most beautiful, but (in its trail-less stages) the most arduous. Follow the main GR11 back towards the Puerto de Chistau, then turn right downhill just past the last *granja* or barn towards a plank bridge. A *parque natural* sign points the way, with estimated time-courses to the most popular destinations: "Ibón d'es Millars, 2hr", "Ibón d'es Lerners, 2hr 30min", and so forth. Red-and-white waymarks painted over older lime-green-and-turquoise ones should be visible, as this is now officially the GR11.2 variant. From here, you face a steady climb along the northeast (true right) bank of the *barranco* through pines. At about 2300m, or some 1hr 45min with a daypack, the official GR11.2 goes up left towards the Collado de Eriste. Following the older waymarks, it's just over two hours to the **Ibón d'es Millars** (or Millás; 2350m) augmented by a rock dam, with a few turfy patches for a picnic, and where you might want to join the frogs for a swim in August. Continue another half-hour, the path only cairned now, to the **Ibón d'es Leners** (or Lenés; 2530m), wedged into even more severe terrain beneath the hulking Bagüeñola peaks.

Beyond here there's no more trail, but cairns help you up the 2600-metre ridge dividing Leners from the **Ibón d'es Luceros** (aka Ibón de la Solana), your next goal. As ever, some of the cairns are misleading; don't veer south, but

309

rather north to overlook Luceros, with an enormous barrel-cairn at the lowest point of the descending ridge. There are magnificent views of the frontier peaks before you begin the only safe way down to the lake, using turfy patches in the slope below the barrel cairn. Without getting lost, allow an hour from lake to lake; circle anticlockwise around Luceros to its western shore to find the stream gully feeding the **Ibón del Pixón** (just visible). Descend the right bank of this ravine, keeping to the grassy bits or stable granite, avoiding the cavities created by the alpenrose; it's another hour's attentive downhill trekking "door to door", and at scenic del Pixón there's just enough flat ground at the upstream end for an emergency bivouac.

Exit the lake basin, where forest resumes, via the north bank to a tiny pass – the start of another hour's nasty descent along the right bank of the Barranco Pixón. There's still no real path, only cairns and hacked-out blazes on pine trees to guide you. At one point you'll have to briefly slither over forested hillside at a forty-five-degree angle. Your target is a vast sloping meadow, the high side of it at about 1850m, which takes half an hour to cross. At the far end, pick up the resumption of the trail (red paint dots mark it) and broach a little saddle on the shoulder of El Castellazo hill (1728m). It's another twenty minutes, or just under 2hr from Ibón del Pixón, to the junction with the GR19 and a cheerful sign (appropriately disparaged by irate walkers' graffiti) predicting 1hr 30min uphill to the first lake. Follow the GR19 north another 25min to the refuge, making the **total time** nearly seven hours. A reverse itinerary is inadvisable – it would be too difficult to find your way uphill to Ibón del Pixón.

## Onwards from Posets

From Posets your trekking options are to head north **into France** via several passes of varying difficulty in the border ridge, or continue west and south deeper **into Aragón**.

### Into France

If you're walking north from Posets into France, two fairly difficult but spectacular routes lead to the popular **Lac d'Oô** on the GR10 (see p.335). From the *Estós* refuge, ascend north up the **Ball de Gías**, past three tarns and into France via the **Puerto d'Oô** (pronounced "oh"; 2909m). It's an exhausting four-hour climb, much of it through a forbidding boulder field with no real path in the screes for some distance either side of the pass. From here it's another ninety minutes' (easier) trek down to the *Refuge du Portillon* (see p.335), via the **Lac du Port d'Oô** (shown on many French maps as the *Lac Glacé* after its permanent ice floes).

Alternatively, bear east from the Gías trail about a third of the way up, through the **Collada de Molseret** (2520m), to the frontier pass of **Portillón d'Oô** (2913m; 4hr 30min). The *portillón* is guarded by permanent ice and might require crampons, but the seasonally staffed refuge at **Lac du Portillon** (on the HRP) is just an hour away. The next refuge, *Espingo*, is two hours down-valley via the **Lac Saussat**. An hour below *Espingo* is the Lac de Oô, a favourite picnic spot, not far above the roadhead at **Granges d'Astau**. All these areas are covered in detail under "Walks from Luchon", at the end of this chapter.

Two easier ways into France depart from the *Refugio de Biadós*: up the Zinqueta de la Pez to the **Puerto de la Pez** (2458m), opening onto the Louron valley; or through the even easier **Puerto de Urdizeto** (2405m) north of its lake, where a variant of the HRP leads down to the roadhead and hospice in the Rioumajou valley. But neither route can compare to the Oô itin-

eraries; slightly more exciting is a third itinerary (an HRP variant), again starting along Zinqueta de la Pez, then veering west up to the **Puerto d'a Madera**
(2555m). On its far side you descend along the Couarère stream to the main
Rioumajou drainage. All these routes require a full day's walk to reach the next
permanent habitation or suitable camping spot.

### Into Aragón

From the *Refugio de Biadós*, the main treks west and south into Aragón follow
the GR11 or the GR19 Spanish long-distance trails; both begin with a sharp
descent to the valley of the **Zinqueta** stream.

The GR11 stays with the vehicle track until turning right onto another track
at **La Sargueta**, which shortly reaches a junction. Heading up and right puts
you on the main GR11 branch to **Lago Urdizeto** (Ordiceto; 2377m) – popular with picnickers despite its unsightly dam – from where another 4WD track
descends 11km to the main road at Parzán (see p.426), 5km north of Bielsa. It's
best to come here only as a day-walk from *Biadós*, or to enter the French
Rioumajou valley. The track in from La Sargueta has been extended up to the
1900-metre contour, further reducing the appeal of this section of the GR11.

From the ruined **Espital de Chistau**, fifteen minutes southwest of La
Sargueta, another 4WD track leads ninety minutes up to the shallow **Collada
de Pardinas** (2263m). From there you should contour southwest to intercept
the old *camino* from Gistaín and the Collada de la Cruz de Guardia to Bielsa in
the Zinca (Cinca) valley, now waymarked as the GR19.1. Part of the old, mid-
altitude shepherd's route west from Biadós, this follows the Barranco de
Montillo down to Bielsa within three hours.

The GR19 forest *camino* spares you about an hour of trudging down the
main track along the Zinqueta, but it's not brilliant walking so arrange a lift if
you can along the main road, either 11km down to the turning for Gistaín or
the full 14km to Plan, "capital" of the valley described below.

# The Valle de Chistau

Renowned throughout Spain as a repository of medieval Aragonese folk culture, the **Valle de Chistau** (alias Gistau or Xistau) makes a worthwhile rest-
stop if you're trekking between Posets and the Ordesa region. Tourism came
late to the area, but facilities are improving and remain excellent value as (so
far) there's no local ski industry to drive prices up.

The valley was the focus of national attention in 1985 when many of its
bachelors placed a lonely-hearts ad in the press, one of the consequences of
Aragonese rural depopulation. Mountain women were (and still are) unwilling
to marry those not inclined to relocate to more prosperous towns. The bachelors threw a magnificent three-day *fiesta* to welcome the **caravana de
mujeres/"women's caravan"** (as it was dubbed), and a surprising number
of the visitors ended up marrying and settling down here.

**By car**, the valley can be reached during snow-free months from the east,
starting at **Chía** (4km off the A139) in the Ésera valley, via a 26-kilometre,
signposted, forest track over the 1999-metre Puerto de Saunc/Collado de
Sahún. The dirt surface (except for a kilometre of cement either side of the
pass) requires first- or second-gear driving most of the way, but the countryside's superb, with views northwest to numerous frontier peaks. The usual
approach from the west is along the paved side road beginning at **Salinas de**

**Sin**, home to a well-stocked **Turismo** booth which serves most of the valley (mid-June to mid-Sept daily except Thurs 10am–1.30pm & 4.30–7pm; ☎974 504 089). The road threads past the turn-offs for Saravillo and Sin (see below), and then through a series of dramatic tunnels downstream from the local dam on the Río Zinqueta. Before the tunnels were built, the valley's isolation was instrumental in preserving its culture; buses remain few and far between (see "Travel Details").

# Plan, San Juan and Gistaín

A trio of villages, linked by a mesh of PR (plus a few GR) trails on the Benasque model, nestles at the head of the valley, and together they offer most of the area's tourist facilities. With no ski centre nearby, their outskirts were long free of the *urbanizaciones* disfiguring so many Spanish Pyrenean communities – though since 2001 some have appeared around Plan and San Juan.

## H5/Plan

Boasting a couple of hundred inhabitants, broad streets on a grid plan and imposing architectural detail such as carved lintels and window frames, **PLAN** is the de facto valley "capital". Its main attraction is an eighth-to-eleventh-century **church** (usually open), harmoniously blending Visigothic and Romanesque elements. Two side aisles are set off from the main one by arcaded colonnades, all with vaulted ceilings. The nave is slightly asymmetrical to the rear, a consequence of the existing church being built around an older tower.

Plan's top **accommodation** is the recently renovated *Hotel Mediodía* (☎974 506 006, ⓦwww.hotelmediodia.com; ❸), with easy parking and balconied, 2001-renovated rooms (Júlio Iglesias has stayed here). Local *casas rurales* include rooms without baths at *Casa Ruché* on the bypass (☎974 506 072; ❶), and similarly basic rooms at *Casa Ignacio* on Plaza Mayor (☎974 506 051; ❶). The best places to **eat** are the *comedores* of the *Mediodía*, or the *Casa Ruché*, where around €11 will get decent vegetable *platos primeros*, a grilled main course and house wine; it's a popular local hangout, where the forestry wardens lunch. Local amenities include shops, an **ATM** and the Guías del Ball de Chistau (☎974 506 178), offering the usual range of caving, climbing, canyoning and trekking activities.

## San Juan de Plan

**SAN JUAN DE PLAN** (San Chuan de Plan), 2km upstream, is smaller still, but architecturally more interesting, and is also famous for its lively Lenten *Carnaval*. Visitors can enjoy some of the best-value **accommodation** and **food** in the valley, at the welcoming, dead-central *Hostal Casa la Plaza* (☎974 506 052; ❸), with tasteful, wood-decor en-suite rooms, and an excellent, mountain-style *menú* (€10) featuring *chireta* (like a haggis made with rice and *morcilla*) and a range of sweets. *Casa Sanches* nearby on the same plaza, also with a *comedor*, is a worthy fallback (☎974 506 050; ❷), though the rooms aren't en suite; if this is full, ask around about the other comparable *casas rurales* in the village.

## Gistaín

Well perched on the north flank of the valley, with superb views south to the Cotiella massif, **GISTAÍN** (Chistén) has three prominent **medieval towers** visible from afar. One rises from the church, while the other two were built by feuding families during the seventeenth century. Close up, the village is a little disappointing, with a hotchpotch of half-timbered and modern brick walls, and roofs fashioned from asbestos or tin sheet as often as traditional slate. That said, it's a self-sufficient mountain settlement where rural pursuits remain dominant over tourism – no imported fertilizer is used, as there's plenty of animal manure about.

The most central **accommodation** is by the church at *Pension Casa Elvira* (☎974 506 078; ❷), with cheap but sustaining *potajes*, grills and beer by the stein in its ground-floor bar. Gistaín has the biggest concentration of *casas rurales* in the valley, nearly a dozen in all; the best can be taken up for the entire weekend (or a week) by Spaniards, so it's wise to reserve in advance. Most basic are *Casa Cañau*, on the top edge of the village (☎974 506 070; ❶) – also an informal folklore museum – and the volubly friendly Carolina Bruned's *Casa Zueras* (☎974 506 038; ❶), in an old-fashioned but salubrious half-timbered house near the village entrance, with huge breakfasts extra. In the centre, en-suite facilities are available at adjacent, two-hundred-year-old *Casa Guillén* (☎974 506 067; ❷) and *Casa Palacín* (☎974 506 295; ❷).

## West to the Zinca valley

Sparse (3 weekly) bus services to and from the Valle de Chistau are not that useful. Heading west, instead of hitching 12km to the main road at Salinas de Sin, it's better to take either the **GR19** track-and-trail from Gistaín via Serveto and Sin, the **GR19.1** to Bielsa from Serveto, or the wilder **GR15** along the valley's south slope, easily picked up from Plan.

The GR19 leads high along the north flank of the valley through the quiet village of **SERVETO** (Serbeto; 1hr 30min from Gistain), from where a scenic PR curls around Peña San Martín back to Plan. After passing the side track to Señes hamlet and the actual start of the GR19.1, it reaches **SIN** (2hr), with a sixteenth-century grain mill and a municipal *albergue* (☎974 506 212) that's usually filled with school groups. Two hours west from Sin, the GR19 leads through dense forest to **SALINAS DE SIN** in the Zinca valley, where you'll find the *Caserio San Marcial* (☎974 504 010, ⓦwww.lospirineos.com/caseriosanmarcial), a manor-house built around a twelfth-century *ermita*. Open all year, it offers *table d'hôte* meals (€10), basic rooms (❶), a four-person apartment (❸), and a grassy, tent-friendly if basic **campsite** (April–Oct). You'll find it uphill on the west side of the highway, just south of the road junction, conveniently below the onward GR19 into the southeasterly sector of the Ordesa national park (see p.431–434). Avoid the road-walk to either Bielsa (7km north; see p.425) or Lafortunada (5km south; see p.431) by arranging a ride.

From Sin you can descend south by road to **SARAVILLO** (Sarabillo), near the mouth of the valley. There is a large **campsite**, *Los Vivés* (☎974 506 171; Easter & June–Sept), slightly west in the valley floor. One kilometre up the south slope in the village itself there's **accommodation** and **meals** at *Casa Pallaruelo* (☎974 506 273; ❸) and a **horse-riding** centre, Entremon (☎974 506 218). Saravillo sits on the **GR15** trail, which heads west then south to Lafortunada in just over two pleasant hours, the quality of the route improving after an initial stretch of track.

## The Sierra de Cotiella

Saravillo is also a popular starting point for excursions southeast to the two celebrated lakes and *refugio* (oldest in the Spanish Pyrenees) of the evocatively shaped **Sierra de Cotiella**, once among the least visited corners of the Spanish Pyrenees but now well frequented; Editorial Alpina's 1:25,000 "Cotiella" map-pamphlet is the most useful aid.

**Drivers** should follow the dirt track heading out of Saravillo and, 2km along, take the left fork towards "Lavasar", then make another left 1.5km further on. The track expires 13.5km from Saravillo at the Collado del Ibón (1928m) parking area and the locked refuge at **Lavasar**. Here you pick up the GR15, which has toiled uphill from Saravillo, and follow it twenty minutes southeast to the picturesque **Ibón de Plan** in its own conifer-flecked cirque at 1910m. Its alias, *Basa de la Mora*, stems from a charming local legend: if you rise at dawn on Midsummer's Day (June 24) and wash your face in the waters, you'll see a long-lost Moorish princess (*mora* in Castilian) dancing on the surface of the lake. *Basa*, however, means "seasonal pond": this one's not more than 4m deep at best, shrinking after June to a reedy frog-pool ringed by muddy flats.

Southeast from Ibón de Plan, the GR15 effects another two-hour traverse via two moderate passes to the unstaffed but well-equipped *Refugio de Armeña* (1860m; 20 places; open year-round) at the entrance to the Circo de Armeña and half an hour from the **Ibón de Armeña**, the massif's other natural lake. The onward path, then a track, emerges at Barbaruéns village (no facilities), high up the western flank of the Ésera valley, between Castejón de Sos and Campo.

# The Couserans and the Comminges

North of the Val d'Aran sprawls a neglected, isolated corner of France, slashed by eighteen large and small valleys tilting in every direction. Outside its southeastern corner, where the old spa of **Aulus-les-Bains** sees some entrepreneurial activity, the **Couserans** is an eerily remote landscape of unkempt pastures, abandoned terraces and ruined barns. Most of the local mines – principally for iron – have been worked out, and the small farms bankrupted by competition from mechanized plains agriculture. The population has halved since the 1890s, yet unemployment remains high. Traditionally marginal livelihoods included gold-panning, itinerant peddling, bear-training and acting as wet-nurses for city families. Nowadays the main rural products are hay, cheese and honey, the latter two on sale everywhere.

**Saint-Girons**, 44km west of Foix and capital of the Couserans, is not particularly interesting, but you'll come here to visit the adjacent charming old town of **Saint-Lizier**, and for bus services which make it the hub for all local exploration. Heading south into the "Empty Quarter" extending towards the border and the Val d'Aran, one has bus connections to Aulus-les-Bains via **Seix**, an important canoeing centre on the River Salat. Buses also run via **Castillon-en-Couserans** to **Sentein**, near the roadhead for the local stretch of the GR10. The **Vallée de Bethmale**, between Seix and Castillon, is an icon of Pyrenean folklore, its distinctive costume (now rarely displayed) popularized by a number of writers. Here you'll see *Toulousains* based in their holiday homes, and walkers bound for **Mont Valier** – an easy, beautiful and popular ascent.

Just west, straddling the Garonne, is the slightly more prosperous **Comminges** region. Since 1790, it has belonged to a different administrative *département* (Haute-Garonne), yet the Couserans have always had a deeper connection to it – both areas being Catholic and Gascon-speaking – than with historically Protestant and Occitan-speaking Ariège, now in the same *département*. There are relatively few tourist facilities or man-made "sights" in the southern Couserans and the easterly Comminges, the most mountainous part of Haute-Garonne. This changes as soon as you reach the busy road and rail line between **Saint-Gaudens**, functional capital of the Comminges, and **Luchon**, an old-fashioned spa now revelling in its new role as a ski resort and hikers' centre. Southwest of Saint-Gaudens, the magnificent cathedral at **Saint-Bertrand-de-Comminges** is a highlight, along with the **Grotte de Gargas** and its tracings of truncated prehistoric hands.

# Saint-Girons and Saint-Lizier

Well-connected, though relatively sleepy, **SAINT-GIRONS**, known for its local cigarette-paper industry, will possibly be your first taste of the Couserans. It's a pleasant enough town by the River Salat, with two sets of rapids by the old bridge, reddish-pink marble paving stones, but little else of note other than nearby Saint-Lizier.

**Buses** arrive at the **place des Capots** on the left (west) bank; facing east on the sixteenth-century **Pont-Vieux** over the River Salat, you cross onto the right bank and the old commercial centre, with some wonderfully antiquated shops, their fronts and fittings unchanged for generations. To the right (south), past the little cathedral and also by the river, the **place des Poilus** is ringed by elegantly faded period-pieces – including the *Grand Café de l'Union* (see below). Between the square and along the river, a gravelled promenade of plane trees, the **Champ de Mars**, hosts a general market on the second and fourth Mondays of the month, and a produce market every Saturday morning.

### Practicalities

On right-bank place Alphonse-Sentein, a few paces downstream from the Pont-Vieux, there's a well-stocked **tourist office** inside the **Maison de Couserans** (July & Aug Mon–Sat 9am–7pm, Sun 10am–1pm; Sept–June Mon–Sat 9am–noon & 2–6pm; ☎05.61.96.26.60, ⓦ ww.ville-st-girons.fr); there's also **Internet** access at the St-Girons post office. **Bikes** can be rented at Horizon Vertical (☎05.61.96.08.22; they also do caving trips) in St-Girons and at Cycles Carbonne (☎05.34.13.31.31) in St-Lizier (see below).

If you want **to stay**, best value is the two-star *Hôtel Mirouze* on the west bank, 300m southwest of Pont-Vieux (☎05.61.66.12.77, ⓕ05.61.04.81.59; ❷), with rear rooms facing a garden, off-street parking and a full range of menus. Otherwise, the modern and comfortable two-star *La Clairière*, at the edge of town on the road to Seix (☎05.61.66.66.66, ⓦwww.ariege.com/la-clairiere; ❸), has a pool and the best gourmet fare in Saint-Girons (closed Sun eve & Mon Dec–April; *menus* from €14).

The local **campsite**, *Parc de Paletès* (☎05.61.66.06.79; March–Sept), 2km out along av des Évadés, has an excellent terrace **restaurant**, *La Table de l'Ours*, while in town *Chez Alain et Dominique* at 8 place Jean-Jaurès (closed Sun; from €14) is worth a try. For vegetarians, *La Végé'table* at 13 rue Joseph Pujol (menus from €8; closed Sun & Mon out of season) features the local *croustade aux cèpes* – mushroom pie.

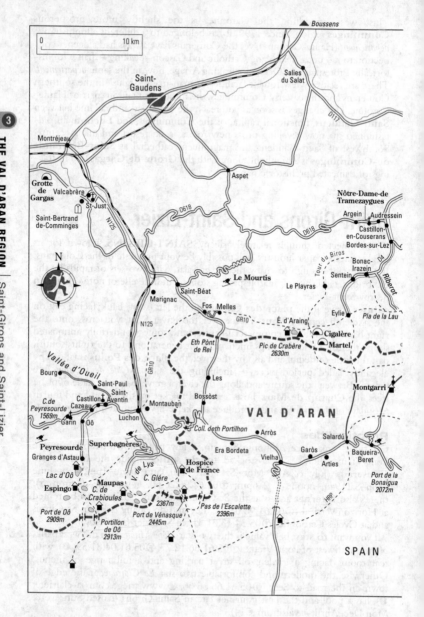

## Saint-Lizier

**SAINT-LIZIER** is just five minutes north of Saint-Girons by bus from the defunct train station on the D117. If you're without transport you may as well stroll the 2km and return via the walled medieval village of Montjoie (3km by

▲ Pamiers    ▲ Toulouse

Mas d'Azil

La-Bastide-de-Serou

Ségalas

D119

D15

D117

Foix

Lescure

Montjoie

La Baure

Saint-Lizier

Saint-Girons

D618

D618

D618

Col du Port

Biert

Massat

Vallée d'Arac

Tarascon-sur-Ariège

FRANCE

Tournac

Aret

Ayet

V. de Bethmale

D17

Col de la Core

Lac de Bethmale

E. de Ayès

Aunac

Seix

D3

Pont de la Taule

Oust

D32

Ercé

Garbet

V. d'Ustou

C. de La Trape

(Shut Dec–April)

Aulus-les-Bains

Capoulet-et-Jounac

Miglos

Vicdessos

Lercoul

Siguer

Montréal de Sos

Auzate

Goulier

Trein d'Ustou

Saint-Lizier d'Ustou

Couflens

Rouze

Cascade d'Ars

Port de Saleix

Estagnous

Mt Valier 2838m

Coll de la Pala

Salau

É. d'Alet

C. de Cagateille

É. de Guzet

Guzet-Neige

É. de la Hillette

Bassiès

Marc

Mounicou

HRP

Port de Salau

Mont Roig 2858m

Bonabé

Noarre

Pic de-Certescan 2853m

P. de Colatx

L'Artigue

Pinet

Montcalm 3077m

Soulcem Reservoir

HRP

Alòs de Isil

Pleta de Prat

Port de l'Artigue 2484m

Estats 3143m

El Serrat

Isil

Vall d'Isil

Sorpe

València d'Aneu

Son del Pi

Esterri d'Aneu

La Guingueta d'Aneu

GR11

Tavascan

Lladorre

Boldis

Arròs

Àreu

GR11

Arinsal

Ordino

ANDORRA

Tor

Espot

Estaon

Ribera de Cardós

Vall de Cardós

Alins

Vall Ferrera

Andorra la Vella

**THE COUSERANS, THE COMMINGES AND MONTCALM/ESTATS**

a minor road), with its fortified church. From there, it's a 45-minute walk back to Saint-Girons.

An important centre of Christianity since the sixth century, when it traded the Latin *Austria* for the name of its first proselytizing bishop, Saint-Lizier is impressive from a distance with its turreted **episcopal Palace** at the top of the hill and red-tiled roofs cascading down to the river. Once inside the stone walls – built on fourth-century Gallo-Roman foundations – you'll wander the atmospheric cobbled streets and tiny arcaded alleys flanked by half-timbered houses. As a showcase specimen, Saint-Lizier lacks many conventional tourist facilities, which gives it a curiously lifeless air, especially outside the summer season.

The main **Cathédrale de Saint-Lizier** (May–Oct daily 9am–noon & 2–7pm; Nov–April Mon–Sat 10am–noon & 2–6pm; free) has an octagonal keep-like tower and severely faded twelfth-century frescoes. The highlight is the Romanesque **cloister**, dating from the same period as the frescoes, with its array of unique sculpted capitals, though these have suffered in recent years compared to those at Ripoll (see p.168) and San Juan de la Peña (see p.454). The church's **treasury** (May–Sept Mon–Sat 10am–12.30pm & 2–7pm & Sun 2–7pm; Oct–April Mon–Sat 10am–noon & 2–6pm; free) is host to a stunning sixteenth-century reliquary bust of St Lizier, as well as other pieces dating back to the eleventh century. A second cathedral, **Notre-Dame-de-Sède**, in the grounds of the bishop's palace, is closed for renovation, though the palace proper houses a **Musée Départementale de l'Ariège** (April–May & Oct, Tues–Fri & Sun 2–6pm; June daily 10am–noon & 2–6pm; July & Aug daily 10am–7pm; €4) which is a permanent ethnographic collection devoted to the Vallée du Bethmale but doesn't really merit the admission fee. On rue des Nobles a **cultural centre** hosts expositions and musical events, while the lower cathedral is also used as a venue during the summer **music festival** from early to mid-August.

Saint-Lizier is a minor stop on the Santiago de Compostela route, and the helpful **tourist office** by the lower cathedral (same hours as in Saint-Girons; ☎05.61.96.77.77, ⓔsaintlizier@wanadoo.fr) will direct bona fide pilgrims to a **hostel**. For non-pilgrims, excellent **accommodation** is available at *Hotel de la Tour* (☎05.61.66.38.02, ⓦwww.hotel-restaurant.net /hoteldelatour; ❷), a restored old building by the river on rue du Pont. The pricier rooms (all with bath) have balconies overlooking the water, and its gourmet yet affordable **restaurant** also takes in the rapids. Best value is the unlimited €18 menu (wine extra), which includes *gésiers* salad, salmon in sauce and pear *croustade*.

# South of Saint-Girons: the "Empty Quarter"

Every day except Sunday, a few buses head **south from Saint-Girons** into the so-called "Empty Quarter" between the town and the Spanish border: some services go southeast to Oust, Seix, Couflens and Aulus-les-Bains (daily during the ski season), others southwest to Castillon-en-Couserans and Sentein. These routes can be used to access the **GR10**, which passes through Aulus, Couflens, Seix and Eylie, south of Sentein. The latter two villages are close to the **Tour du Biros**, which skims the flanks of **Mont Valier**, much loved by climbers and served by both the GR10 and the HRP, as well as a staffed refuge. Between Seix and Aulus, you can detour south at Trein d'Ustou to take in the **Cirque de Cagateille**, second largest in the range after the Cirque de Gavarnie (see p.388), but with a fraction of the crowds. Routes east from Oust towards **Massat** and (eventually) Tarascon are not served by public transport, but under your own steam make an effective corridor between the

Ariège and the Couserans. All these places, if a bit depressed and depopulated, have tourist facilities and some interest in the form of ancient churches or rickety houses. Many houses are up for sale at any given moment, though demand from *Toulousains* has ensured that properties are no longer cheap.

## Seix, Oust and Massat

**SEIX**, the county town of the lower Salat valley, forms a congenial jumble of old, galleried houses strewn by the river, culminating in a vine-draped fifteenth-century castle, now closed up and decrepit. The seventeenth-century riverside church has an elaborate *clocher-mur*, illuminated by night, while the old market hall a few paces north sees lively use on the second and fourth Wednesday of the month. Amongst the shops, cafés and bakeries on the west bank are two retailers for hiking maps and outdoor gear. This is also the region's main **canoeing and kayaking** centre, with Passeur de Vagues (℡05.61.66.84.88), 2km south upriver at Base de Moulin, the principal operator on both the Salat and its numerous tributaries.

All **buses** to and from Saint-Girons stop virtually adjacent to the **tourist office** in a small booth on the Place Champ de Mars on the east bank (summer daily 9am–1pm & 3–7pm; winter Mon–Sat 9am–1pm; ℡05.61.96.52.90, @www.haut-couserans.com), which sells hiking guides and maps, and has bus timetables. At present both the town-centre hotels are closed, and the only **accommodation** in the municipality lies 4km southwest (and 300m above) in the hamlet of **AUNAC**, where the *gîte Pyrénées Anes* (℡05.61.66.82.15, @pyrenees-anes@free.fr), has both dorms and quads as well as serving copious gourmet **meals** with locally sourced ingredients. Alternatively, in **OUST**, 2km north of Seix, the *Hostellerie de la Poste* (℡05.61.66.86.33; @05.61.66.77.08; ❸; closed Nov–Easter) is among the best this side of Aulus, in the same family for five generations, with a pool garden and a well-regarded restaurant. Despite its position at the junction of roads and the rivers Salat and Garbet, the village itself is dead compared to Seix, and turns its back on the Garbet bounding it to the north. Two local **campsites** do take advantage of the riverbanks: *Les Quatre Saisons* (℡05.61.96.55.55), on the D32 towards Aulus, and *La Côte* (℡05.61.96.50.53; mid-May to Sept) between Oust and Seix.

### Massat and Biert

Some 21km north, then east of Oust along the Arac valley and the D618, **MASSAT** does not exactly hum with activity. Its former role as a major market town left a legacy of a large, draughty fifteenth-century church and a **museum-mill** on the river (July & Aug Sat & Sun 5–7pm; otherwise by arrangement on ℡05.61.96.96.66). Massat is among the doziest places in a generally sleepy region, a hangout for alternative types and those after subalpine pursuits such as **horse-riding** (available on the outskirts and in neighbouring Biert). That said, you'll find shops and services, plus a **market** held on the second and fourth Thursdays of every month. Of two surviving **hotels**, the more congenial is the *Hostellerie des Trois Seigneurs* on the Saint-Girons road (℡05.61.04.90.52; closed Nov–Easter; ❷), with modern en-suites in an annexe and an excellent **restaurant** (€14 for four generous courses). Otherwise, *Auberge du Gypaète Barbu*, 3km west in pretty **BIERT**, right opposite the church (℡05.61.04.89.92; ❷; closed mid-Dec to mid-Jan & Mon), has simple rooms with *lavabo* and a trio of gourmet menus at €13–29, serving goat's cheese, duck, *foie gras*, and the like.

# The Vallée de Bethmale

Seix is also the eastern entry, via the D17 over the Col de la Core or the GR10, to the **Vallée de Bethmale**, celebrated in folklore for its vivid, almost Balkan female costumes, and gold-nailed wooden *sabots* (clogs) for both sexes. These have long vanished except for their appearance on a few feast days, for example August 15. What remains is an exceptionally beautiful valley, and exceptionally high depopulation, even by Couserans standards. On the heights there's little specifically to see other than a number of abandoned *granges* or **barns**, traditionally used to store hay but increasingly restored as summer quarters by lowlanders. A little west of the Col de la Core, on both D17 and GR10, the tranquil green **Lac de Bethmale**, ringed by beech trees, is a popular picnic or fishing spot.

In the valley floor, which drains west-northwest from the *col* towards Bordes-sur-Lez in the Vallée du Biros, huddle six half-empty hamlets. The highest, graced by eighteenth-century architecture, **AYET** offers a friendly, twelve-bunk *gîte d'étape* (☎05.61.02.30.80; open all year), where places must be reserved in summer. If you're without a vehicle, you can take a marked, non-GR trail up to the lake from here. Just downhill on the same road, **TOURNAC** has another *gîte*, La Bouche (☎05.61.04.72.12; 20 places). Adjacent **ARET** has the last **sabot-making workshop** in the valley, open all year for purchases. The curvy-pointed clogs were traditionally exchanged as tokens of betrothal between the newly engaged.

## Excursion to the Étang d'Ayès

The Lac de Bethmale marks the start of the most popular excursion from the valley, to the **Étang d'Ayès**, an ideal sampler of the mountains hereabouts if you're not committed to full-pack treks. Without a car, you'll have to hike the whole distance along the GR10 (2hr 30min one way). With a car, you can avoid much of the climb by driving fifteen minutes along the *piste forestière* marked "Mont Ner/Noir" up to a barred gate and car park. Here a yellow-marked path, the old GR10, toils for forty minutes up to the Col d'Auédole and junction with the new GR10. Turn right here (southeast), and continue another twenty minutes on the GR10 to the sizeable glacial tarn, just above treeline at 1694m, and hemmed in by crags to the south but marvellously open to the north. With such easy access, Étang d'Ayès is understandably a popular picnic and camping spot, just about swimmable on a hot day. The return route is the same, and takes as long owing to a steep grade just above the parking area.

## The upper Salat

Upstream and south from Seix, the D3 follows the Salat almost to its source, passing a few hamlets that make tranquil bases and start-points for forays on the GR10 or HRP. **PONT DE LA TAULE**, where the D8 veers up the Vallée d'Ustou (see opposite) 4km south of Seix, is the last spot on the Salat with public transport, and offers the Dutch-run **hotel-restaurant** Auberge des Deux Rivières (☎ & ℱ05.61.66.83.57; closed mid-Nov to early Jan, plus Sun & Mon in low season), where for €19 you can enjoy regional treats at its river-terrace restaurant. Of the rooms, the modern en-suite dormer units (❸) are preferable to the creaky first-floor ones (❷), though some of the latter have showers.

**COUFLENS**, 6km up the still-paved but narrowed D3, is a deceptively substantial village along the river, hemmed in by shaggy hillsides. There's no shop here and all the tourist facilities are slightly out of town: *Camping Les Bouriès,* with six shady sites, lies 1.5km west, while the 14-place **gîte d'étape** (℡05.61.66.95.45), run by the Assémat family and doubling as a cheese farm, is 1km east at Rouze.

The highest village and end of the line for most traffic, **SALAU** is even bigger, with various amenities (but no shop) on the single high street. Like Couflens, the place once lived off nearby, long-abandoned tungsten mines. The Knights Hospitallers formerly had a hospice overhead, now crumbled, though the large village church clearly shows their influence. Salau's single **hotel-restaurant** is the jolly, Dutch-run *Auberge des Myrtilles* (℡ & ℻05.61.66.82.58; ❶; closed Nov to mid-Dec, restaurant closed Tues), whose pricier dormered rooms all have showers. The standard breakfasts (€5) are excellent with eggs and yoghurt (€7.50 gets you *charcuterie* as well). Other meals are à la carte (around €22 with house wine), including the delicious filleted *aiguillettes de canard* and homemade gateaux. If it's full, there's also *La Fourque* (℡05.61.66.96.74, ⓦwww.ariege.com/couflens), a municipally-run *gîte* a few paces downhill.

The HRP skims just above Salau, heading west to the ruined frontier hospice at **Port de Salau**, site of a big solidarity festival (*La Pujada*) between Occitans and Catalans on the first Sunday in August. If you're not interested in a long-haul traverse, the HRP is the partial basis for the **Tour des Montagnes de Salau**, shown on the Carte de Randonnées no. 6 and best spread over two days as it takes in the border peak of Mont Rouch/Roig (2858m).

## The Vallée d'Ustou and the Cirque de Cagateille

From Pont de la Taule, the D8 heads southeast up the sunnier and more generously proportioned **Vallé d'Ustou**, gateway to the Cirque de Cagateille. The main places en route are **TREIN D'USTOU**, home to the comfortable *Auberge des Ormeaux* (℡05.61.96.53.22, ⓔormeaux.ustou@libertysurf.fr; ❸), with the most reliable **restaurant** in the valley (*menus* €12–14.50; closed Weds lunch), and **SAINT-LIZIER D'USTOU** 1km south, astride the GR10. Saint-Lizier has a café/restaurant and shop, plus a sixty-place *camping municipal* with a pool. The closest indoor accommodation is 2km south by road or along the GR10 in **BIDOUS**, where the 30-place *Gîte L'Escolan* (℡ & ℻05.61.96.58.72) also has a handful of doubles (❷).

The road ends above the last farms, 7.5km above Trein d'Ustou, at a car park (1000m) with trailheads for the **Étang d'Alet** (3hr one-way, 1900m) and the underrated, forest-girt **Cirque de Cagateille** (35min to its base at 1250m), where several cascades garland the wall during springtime snowmelt. The Cagateille path, sporadically blazed in yellow and red but often faint and rough, continues to **Étang de la Hillette** (2hr 30min, 1800m), tucked into a hanging glacial valley above the cirque. Rather than crossing the frontier to Certascan at the 2416-metre **Port de Couillac**, you can make a satisfying circuit by continuing west to Alet, then down to the car park, on sporadically maintained paths. It's a seven-to-eight-hour walking day, harder and less travelled than the nearby Cascade d'Ars loop (see p.322): a placard at the car park details all walks.

## Aulus-les-Bains

Thirty minutes southeast by bus from Seix along the Vallée d'Ustou and over the Col de Latrape, the spa of **AULUS-LES-BAINS** has on a clear day one of the most stunning locations in the Pyrenees. Here at the top of the narrow Vallée de Garbet, dense forests and dramatic peaks rise steeply on either side, while rock walls channel water into numerous lakes and into the River Ars with its waterfalls. If you're driving or cycling, it's much easier to arrive on the D32 threading the Vallée de Garbet, via Ercé.

Once famous for its bear-trainers, Aulus is now a sleepy, faded place with little to do other than enjoy the scenery, though new apartment blocks indicate that bigger plans are afoot. The ornate glass-and-wood, centrally placed **thermal baths** are just the thing to soothe trekkers' aches and pains (early May to early Oct Mon–Sat 8.30am–noon & 3–7pm, Sun 9am–noon & 3–7pm), and it also offers a variety of fitness, yoga and massage programmes. For more energetic activities, the **tourist office**, in allées des Thermes (daily: July & Aug 10am–1pm & 2–7pm; Sept–June 10am–noon & 2–6pm; ☏05.61.96.01.79, ✉tourisme@haut-couserans.com), rents out bikes between June and September, and also provides information on canoeing, parapente and horse-riding.

**Accommodation** tends to be on the pricey side; the least expensive places are two *gîtes d'étape*: *Le Presbytère*, 150m downhill from the church (☏05.61.96.02.21; 23 places; open all year), with four- or eight-bunk dorms and secure bike parking, and *La Goulue*, on the grounds of the old casino (☏05.61.66.53.01), with modern four-bunk dorms, good suppers and bike storage. Otherwise, try the one-star *Hôtel de France*, downstream on the main street past the baths (☏05.61.96.00.90, ☏05.61.96.03.29; ❷; closed mid-Oct to mid-Dec). Its old-fashioned **restaurant** epitomizes a dying breed, with various *menus* (€10.50–25) served amidst wooden pillars, live dogs and a stuffed bestiary. After four hearty courses of duck, offal or trout, they'll have to wheel you out in a barrow. The more comfortable, antique-furnished *Hostellerie de la Terrasse*, just upstream from the baths (☏05.61.96.00.98, ☏05.61.96.01.42; closed Oct–May; ❸), has a fancier gourmet restaurant (allow €25), with a river-view terrace, while the two-star *Hotel Les Oussaillès* on the main commercial street (☏05.61.96.03.68, ✉jcharrue@free.fr; open all year; ❸) has modern rooms with TV and phones: the friendly proprietors speak English, and keep a binder documenting local walks. Food at the restaurant (all year, by arrangement on winter weekends), may not be as elaborate as elsewhere but is still good value (*hors d'oeuvres*, trout with carrots and eggplant, *gateaux* for €12), with a wider choice of *ariégoise* specialities and vegetarian plates in peak season. **Camping** is at *Le Couledous* (☏05.61.96.02.26), 500m west between the road to Ercé and the river.

### The Cascade d'Ars and Étang de Guzet

South of Aulus-les-Bains, the famous Cascade d'Ars and the Étang de Guzet are favourite walking destinations, and can easily be combined in a five-hour loop. You are less likely to get lost on an anticlockwise circuit, described as follows: start from the road curve above town, where a sign indicates a non-GR trail for Plan de Souliou and the Étang de Guzet. Climb for one hour through beeches to the junction with the GR10, just past the bracken-covered *plan*, a clearing with great views of the ridges surrounding Aulus. It's another half-hour, with firs now on par with the beeches, to the **Étang de Guzet** (1425m), an idyllic clear pool just west below the GR10 via side trails. Most of the climbing is over; the trail proceeds another hour as a corniche route along the hillside to a meadow and bridge – the **Passerelle d'Ars** (1485m), just above the falls. During the next half an hour the path curls around and under the famous **Cascade d'Ars**, with the best views just before the trail disappears into forest again. The cascades plunge 110m in three stages, though during spring melt it is often just one long drop. From the falls it's another ninety minutes back to Aulus, following the river, mostly by path on the left bank, which gets muddy near the bottom. Cross the **Pont de la Mouline** over the Garbet, turn left, then left again when you meet the asphalt, and you're at the edge of town.

## Guzet-Neige

A half-hour road journey from Aulus-les-Bains to **GUZET-NEIGE** during winter is worthwhile for the view alone. Located on a high shoulder 13km from Aulus, it looks northwest along the Vallée d'Ustou and (from higher points) south to frontier peaks. Ski-season **buses** climb first into the **Col de la Trape** (1111m), then up to the resort itself at 1380m.

The 34 shortish **runs** are fairly evenly divided as to green, blue and red ratings, and well linked by twenty (mostly drag) **lifts**, making Guzet a fair beginners' or intermediates' resort. However, with a top point of just 2050m on the Pic de Freychet, and the westerly orientation of the pistes, Guzet typically operates only from mid-December to mid-March, despite the efforts of numerous snow canons. **Accommodation** at Point 1380 comprises two hotels, and a collection of four-person, wood-and-stone chalets, *Le Hameau du Pas du Loup*, rather attractive by the standard of ski resort architecture. Chalets can be reserved on ☏05.61.96.03.21, with weekly rates typically better value than weekend rates.

# Mont Valier and around

Pyramidal **Mont Valier** (2838m), the most famous mountain of the Couserans, was long mistaken as the highest Pyrenean peak. It's named after a fifth-century bishop, Valerius, who crucifix in hand supposedly made the first ascent. Lying entirely in France, this beacon and mascot of the valleys conceals five lakes in its folds and even a tiny glacier on the north face.

The mines in Mont Valier's foothills may be long defunct, but timber is still a viable enterprise – if you're driving the narrow roads, beware of slow-moving **lumber trucks**. Another potential "local" industry, far less welcome judging from graffiti, is a superhighway of high-voltage power lines proposed to be installed by EDF (Electricité de France).

### Approaches: Castillon and Audressein

Mont Valier is accessible from both the GR10 and the HRP, the former skirting it to the east, north and west, the latter to the south. If you're not following either trail, take a bus or drive from Saint-Girons towards Sentein, along the Vallée du Biros and its River Lez. Some 12km along you'll pass through the old village of **CASTILLON-EN-COUSERANS**, its houses topped by the fortified chapel which is all that Cardinal Richelieu left standing of the château. A regional **tourist office** occupies Castillon's disused train station (summer Mon–Sat 9.30am–12.30pm & 2.30–6.30pm, Sun 9.30am–12.30pm; spring & autumn Mon–Sat 10am–noon & 3–6pm, Sun 10am–noon; ☏05.61.96.72.64); the village also hosts a Tuesday **market**. The only **accommodation** is Jonathan and Myriam Peat's 2003-built five-room inn (☏ & ℱ05.61.04.64.47, ⊛www.jonathanstours.com; ❸ B&B), occupying a restored old house at 58 rue Noël Peyrevidal, by the Crédit Agricole.

The pride of **AUDRESSEIN**, 1km north, is the engaging medieval **church of Notre-Dame de Tramezaygues**, built at the confluence of the rivers Lez and the Bourgane, and venue for a September 8 festival. At other times, its highlight is an unrivalled collection of well-restored fourteenth-century **fres-coes**, adorning the arcade of the west porch (always open; full explanation posted in French). Two pairs of angels in noble period dress play the flute and rebec, and harp and lute; there are ex-voto cartoons of a penitent murderer, a freed prisoner, a recovered invalid, and a curiously bare-arsed youth (presum-ably saved from harm) falling from a tree. A panel of Saint Jacques du Compstelle confirms this as a minor halt on the pilgrim route to Spain, while another of Saint Jean Baptiste shows him dressed in a bearskin (complete with head), so appropriate for the Ariège.

In the village itself, the best accommodation is at *Les Relay des Deux Rivières* (☎05.61.04.76.32; ❸), with modern en-suite rooms. Alternatively, head 4km west to **ARGEIN**, where the *Hostellerie de la Terrasse* (☎05.61.96.70.11; closed mid-Nov to March; ❸) has a decent restaurant specializing in trout.

## Around the Refuge des Estagnous

Most passengers will continue by bus another 4km or so from Castillon to the **Riberot valley** turning on the left. There's a good chance of a lift along the 7km up the Riberot (6km paved) to the parking area and trailhead for the GR10 at **Pla de la Lau** (927m). From here it's four hours' hiking, past the famous **Cascade de Nérech** halfway along, to the **Refuge des Estagnous** (2240m; ☎05.61.96.76.22, 🅕05.61.69.50.07; 70 places; staffed June to mid-Oct, weekends only in May & mid-Oct to early Nov).

From Estagnous, Mont Valier's summit is just a couple of hours away next morning, so leave most of your gear at the refuge. You walk southeast on the clear path to **Col du Faustin** (2643m), then northeast by path to the **summit**. The views facing south are terrific – Montcalm and Estats on your left, the Val d'Aran and Aigüestortes in the middle, the Maladeta massif to your right. Other standard day-walks from the refuge are to the lakes **Étang Rond** and **Étang Long**, just southwest of Mont Valier, or north over the Col de Pécouch on the shoulder of Valier to follow the longer *Circuit de Trois Lacs*, which takes in the lakes of **Cruzous**, **Arauech** and **Milouga**.

## The Tour du Biros

The popular **Tour du Biros** will occupy four to five days and is clearly marked on the Carte de Randonnées 1:50,000 no. 6 "Couserans–Cap d'Aran" map.

From the *Estagnous* refuge, you can pick up the Tour by going back down towards Pla de la Lau in the Riberot valley, and taking the GR10 west. After three hours' steep climbing, followed by an equally severe one-hour descent into the Besset forest, you're on the Tour, waymarked in red-and-yellow stripes and for a time accompanying the GR10. There's a well-sited twenty-bunk *gîte d'étape* (☎05.61.96.14.00) at the former mining hamlet of **EYLIE** another four to five hours ahead, at the top of the Vallée de Biros. If you've reached Eylie by car, you'll finally feel you're in the mountains, with barns and rivulets clinging to the steep slopes all around. As a major trailhead, it has ample sign-posting to various points of hiking interest.

Next day the joint Tour/GR10 climbs past the old lead and zinc mines at Bentaillou, and close by the caves of **Gouffre Martel** and **Cigalère**, the latter discovered by Norbert Casteret (see box on p.326). Four hours from Eylie you reach **Étang d'Araing**, with the **Pic de Crabère** (2629m) reflected in its waters and the *Refuge de l'Étang d'Araing* beside it (1965m; ☎05.61.96.73.73; 52 places; staffed mid-June to Sept, weekends only May to mid-June & Oct). The remainder of the day can be spent scaling Crabère, a three-hour round-trip.

The Tour now diverges from the GR10, swinging back northeast on a relatively easy half-day through beech forests to the abandoned hamlet of **Le Playras**, whose *gîte d'étape* has closed down. So you must carry on from there, along the north flank of the valley, to **BONAC-IRAZEIN** (aka Bonac-sur-Lez) on the valley floor. From here it's a further 2km east to Sentein, where you can overnight (see below). The final, less frequented leg of the *Tour* heads south from Bonac-Irazein along the east flank of the Orle valley to meet the GR10 again at Besset (unstaffed refuge sleeping five) within six hours.

The main village in these parts, just off the Tour and end of the bus line from Saint-Girons, lies 2km west of Bonac at **SENTEIN**, which features in its central square a curious fortified fifteenth-century church with three towers (originally there were four) and some surviving interior frescoes. It also has a shop, a **tourist office** (summer only Mon–Sat 10am–noon & 3–7pm, Sun 11am–1pm & 5–7pm; ☎05.61.96.10.90), a **campsite**, *La Grange*, and the unprepossessing but inexpensive modern **hotel**, *Le Crabère* (☎05.61.96.04.22; ❶), on the through road, with a ground-floor restaurant.

### West to Fos and Melles

Following the **GR10 west** from the Étang d'Araing requires six hours, the last third on asphalt, to **FOS**, a moribund village on the main road between Vielha (in Spain) and Saint-Béat. There's a *gîte d'étape* on place du Sarramoulin (☎05.61.79.87.85; 17 places), a municipal campsite, and a shop, but no reliable restaurant, nor public transport in any direction.

You're better off stopping 40min east of Fos at **MELLES**, a surprisingly substantial, once-wealthy village with excellent-value **accommodation** and **meals** at the *Auberge du Crabère* (☎05.61.79.21.99, ✉patrick.beauchet @wanadoo.fr; ❹ HB only; closed Tues eve & Wed from Sept–June). Chef Patrick's food – duck breast in green-peppercorn sauce, crayfish hotpot, patisserie – is very good, and the €23 *menu* gives you the run of most specialities, though the wine list is pricey; reservations are needed in season.

### Skiing: Le Mourtis

About 11km east of Saint-Béat, just above the Col du Menté on the slopes of Tuc de l'Étang (1816m), the little ski station of **LE MOURTIS** struggles to operate most winters. Its 22 short downhill pistes – nearly half green-rated, and without snow canons – are probably doomed; 45km of cross-country skiing routes through the forest appear to have a brighter future.

# Along the Garonne: into the Comminges

The **Comminges** is an ancient feudal county which, having never had the prestige or power of neighbouring Foix or Bigorre, was absorbed into a unifying France in 1454. Haute-Garonne, the modern successor *département* that approximates the traditional boundaries, is drained by the **Garonne** and its tributary the Pique. The quickest way from the Couserans into the valley of the Garonne is by bus from Saint-Girons to **Boussens**, from where more than a dozen daily trains run fifteen minutes west along the river to **Saint-Gaudens**, the first town of any size. This is chiefly of note as a transport hub for visiting the adjacent great attractions, **Saint-Bertrand-de-Comminges** and the **Grotte de Gargas**.

# Saint-Gaudens to Valcabrère

Although capital of the Comminges, **SAINT-GAUDENS** is essentially a way-station rather than a place to linger, its character epitomized by a lively Thursday **market** – and a cellulose plant across the river, spewing thick white smoke. A small, part-pedestrianized old quarter huddles on an escarpment looking southeast over the Garonne; two *brasseries* on place Napoléon exploit the view. The only sights are the massive church of **Saint-Pierre**, originally eleventh-to-sixteenth-century but more recently over-restored, and a **Musée Municipal**, in the place Mas-St-Pierre east of the church and the main place National Jean Jaurès (Mon–Sat 9am–noon & 2–6pm; €3.50), displaying pre-historic finds and Gallo-Roman ceramics.

The **tourist office** is at 2 rue Thiers (Mon–Sat 9am–noon & 1.30–6pm; ☎05.61.94.77.61), and the town's most pleasant **hotel**, the *Esplanade* (☎05.61.89.15.90; ❸), with some south-facing rooms, stands by the museum. The *Pedussaut*, 9 avenue de Boulogne north of the through road (☎05.61.89.15.70; ❷), is a cheaper option, but forgoes the view. For food, head to the **restaurant** attached to the *Pedussaut* (menus €15–31), *Les Commings*

## Norbert Casteret

Norbert Casteret (1897–1987), who was born and lived at Saint-Martory, 4km out-side Saint-Gaudens, was on of the first professional speleologists, earning his liv-ing from his books and from survey work for hydroelectric companies. His first big coup came in 1922 with the penetration of Montespan, a cave on the south bank of the Garonne halfway between Saint-Gaudens and Salies. Casteret's account captures the moment of discovery:

"We entered a gallery which I had neglected to explore on the former occasion, and stopped in amazement before the statue of a bear modelled in clay. Further on lay more of these figures: two felines walking in file, and some horses. The fol-lowing day we came upon some curious tracks; the cave had undoubtedly been used as a shelter or hiding-place by prehistoric people. We were the first men to enter that chamber since the cave-folk dwelt there several thousand years ago. On the muddy floor there were imprints of their naked feet, and also some stone weapons. The walls had been ornamented with the aid of sharpened flints, and we gazed in wonder upon the fauna of far distant ages: mammoth, reindeer, horses, bison, chamois . . .The clay figures of Montespan . . . date from the beginning of the Magdalenian era, say about 20,000 years ago, and are therefore the oldest known statues in the world."

In 1926, with his wife Elisabeth, Casteret discovered the Grotte Casteret on Mont Perdu/Monte Perdido, the highest known ice cave in the world. Four years later came the discovery of animal engravings at Labastide, west of Saint-Gaudens in the Baronnies. The following year Castaret's dye test – described on p.272 – proved that the Garonne sprang in part from the Aneto glacier, and he also explored the Grotte de la Cigalère, south of Saint-Gaudens. In 1952, as part of a team plumbing the depths of Gouffre Pierre Saint-Martin in the Western Pyrenees, Casteret broke his own cavern-descent mark set two decades previously, at the 303-metre-deep Gouffre Martel near Cigalère. This record of cave exploration in the Pyrenees has no equal, and it's unlikely that anyone will ever surpass his tally of "firsts" in these mountains.

Note: Montespan, Labastide, Cigalère and Pierre Saint-Martin are accessible only to experienced speleologists. For an account of the Grotte Casteret, see p.391.

next to the *Esplanade* (€20 *menu*), or *Restaurant de l'Abattoir*, 2km away on boulevard Leconte-de-Lisle, beyond the *gare* opposite the livestock market (lunch only, plus evenings Thurs–Sat; €11.50–20) with impeccably fresh cuts of meat.

## Valcabrère

En route to Luchon, you pass the village of **VALCABRÈRE**, with its rough stone barns and open lofts for hay-drying. To get there, take the train from Saint-Gaudens to Montréjeau, transfer to the SNCF bus service south to Luchon and get off after 6km at Labroquère, 500m northeast of Valcabrère, just before the road crosses the Garonne. Standing among cypresses and the village graveyard to the south of Valcabrère, you'll find the jewel-box-like twelfth-century Romanesque church of **Saint-Just** (March–June & Oct–Dec daily 9am–noon & 2–7pm; July–Sept daily 9am–7pm; €2). Saint-Just was built largely of stone from the Roman city Lugdunum Conventarum (see below), founded by Pompey in 72 BC. Beyond the elegantly sculpted north portal, showing Christ borne heavenward by angels, flanked by the four Evangelists clutching their symbols, there's ample evidence of recycled masonry: marble in the altar floor, an inscription dated 347 AD on the wall of the nave and several columns augmenting the six massive stone piers upholding the nave. Between the altar and the triple apse with its blind arches looms a carved Gothic freestanding shrine, and a sarcophagus which presumably once contained the saint's relics. The soaring vaulted ceiling creates splendid acoustics, and Saint-Just is a major music venue for the summer *Festival du Comminges*.

A little further on, protruding from grass at each side of the crossroads, are the foundations of **Lugdunum Conventarum** (closed for excavations), a former town of 60,000 and one of the most important in Roman Aquitaine. According to the first-century Jewish historian Josephus, the town was the place of exile for Herod Antipas – who'd executed John the Baptist and received Christ from Pontius Pilate – and his wife Herodias around 39 AD. At its height during the first and second centuries AD, the town survived well into the Christian era despite destructive raids by Vandals and Burgundians in the fifth and sixth centuries.

Taking inspiration from the Romans, Valcabrère supports a posh **restaurant**, *Le Lugdunum* (open Thurs–Sun noon, also Tues & Weds in summer), southeast of the village, just off the N125. Here, from €29 (dessert and drinks extra), you can sample recipes claimed to be favoured by the Caesars themselves, featuring local game and fish (but no tomatoes or lemons, foods unknown in Roman times).

## Saint-Bertrand-de-Comminges

This part of the French Pyrenees harbours few monuments, but one of the finest stands at **SAINT-BERTRAND-DE-COMMINGES** – a magnificent cathedral reflecting three distinct eras of architecture. To reach the village from Saint-Gaudens, follow directions for Valcabrère outlined above as far as Labroquère, then take the turning west for Saint-Bertrand. It's then a pleasant half-hour walk between fields of grain and hay, with the poplar-lined river to your right and the grey, fortress-like cathedral of Saint-Bertrand commanding the plain ahead. Cars are not allowed in the village at peak season between 10am and 7pm, but a minibus shuttle operates from the parking area below, sparing you a ten-minute walk up. At other times, you can drive to the higher car park by the walls.

The Roman city stretched up the hill to where Saint-Bertrand now stands. The lower part was destroyed by the Vandals in 409 AD, and the more protected walled upper part – where a Christian church had since been built – was wrecked in 585 by King Gontran of Burgundy. For five centuries the site lay deserted, until the Gascon aristocrat Bertrand de l'Isle – made bishop of Comminges in 1073 and canonized in 1218 – began to rebuild.

## The village and cathedral

The handsome walled and gated village of Saint-Bertrand-de-Comminges, its half-timbered-and-brick houses dating from the fifteenth and sixteenth centuries, clusters tightly around the **Cathedral** (May–Sept Mon–Sat 9am–7pm, Sun 2–7pm; Oct & Feb–April Mon–Sat 10am–noon & 2–6pm, Sun 2–6pm; Nov–Jan Mon–Sat 10am–noon & 2–5pm, Sun 2–5pm; admission to cloister and choir €4). Dedicated to the Virgin Mary, not to St Bertrand as you'd expect, its white-veined facade and ponderous buttressing seem rather menacing at first. A Romanesque **cloister** with engagingly carved capitals looks south towards the foothills, while the aisleless **interior** forms a showcase of decorative art from three periods. Bertrand's Romanesque church was enlarged during the late thirteenth century in Gothic style by the future Clement V (first of the Avignon popes), and the interior was finally remodelled during Renaissance times by another bishop, Jean de Mauléon. In the ambulatory, a fifteenth-century shrine depicts scenes from Bertrand's life, with the church and village visible in the background of the top right panel; the saint's marble tomb, still venerated by pilgrims, is here too. The small area reserved for the laity at the west end has a richly carved oak organ, a pulpit and a spiral stair, but the cathedral's real treasure is the central **choir**, built by *toulousain* journeymen and installed during the decade or so after 1523.

The 66 elaborately carved choir **stalls** are a feast of virtuosity, mingling piety, irony and malicious satire, each the work of a different journeyman. In the misericords and partitions that separate them, the ingenuity and humour of their creators is best seen; each gangway dividing the misericords displays a representation of a cardinal sin. By the middle gangway on the south side, for example, Envy is represented by two angry monks, faces contorted, engaged in a furious tug-of-war over the abbot's baton of office. The armrest on the left of the rood-screen entrance depicts the abbot birching a monk, while the bishop's throne has a lovely back panel in marquetry depicting St Bertrand and St John.

## Practicalities

**Staying** in Saint-Bertrand is an attractive proposition, at least outside peak season. Across the small square from the cathedral, the *Hôtel du Comminges* (☎05.61.88.31.43, ℉05.61.94.98.22; ❷–❸) makes a fine, old-fashioned overnight stay (assorted rooms). Otherwise, at the modern *Hôtel L'Oppidum* (☎05.61.88.33.50, ✆oppidum@wannado.fr; ❸; closed mid-Nov to mid-Dec & Mon out of season), behind the cathedral on rue de la Poste, the en-suite rooms vary engagingly: the first-floor ones are clean, whitewashed and almost cave-like, the cheaper top-floor ones mansarded and traditional. The ground floor restaurant is excellent, and doubles as a "tea salon" with a profusion of varieties. Menus (€14–31) may feature spicy *salade de volaille*, roasted lamb shank with braised vegetables, and apple tart (drinks extra). The only unaffiliated **restaurant** of note in the village is *Chez Simone*, downhill from the *Hôtel du Comminges*, serving simple fare on its terrace (€13 on weekdays, €16 hols; closed Nov–Dec & supper except July & Aug). The nearest **campsite** – shady, well laid out and with a few chalets to rent – is *Es Pibous* (☎05.61.94.98.20; May–Sept), north of the road to Saint-Just. In July and August the cathedral and Saint-Just in Valcabrère play host to the musical **Festival du Comminges** (information from festival office in the cathedral square: daily 10.30am–12.30pm & 3–7pm; ☎05.61.95.44.44 or 05.61.88.32.00 in summer, ☎05.61.95.81.25 the rest of the year).

## Grotte de Gargas

Easily accessible from Saint-Bertrand, the **Grotte de Gargas** (50-min guided tours; max 25 people; daily 10am–noon & 2–6pm; €5; ☎05.62.39.72.39, ⓦhttp://grottesdegargas.free.fr) deserves a visit for its mysterious hand prints, which make the presence of their prehistoric creators seem almost immediate.

If you want to walk from Saint-Bertrand (inadvisable, as the road is narrow and heavily travelled), drop down from the upper village onto the road again, turn left (northwest) and keep going for another 6km. You can also walk direct from the station at Montréjeau, heading about 4km southwest via Mazères de Neste.

Although it also has engravings and finger tracings of mammoths, horses, bison and deer, what makes the Gargas cave really special are its **hand outlines**, many of them with half-severed fingers. Castillo in Spanish Cantabria is the only other place where hand images have been found in large numbers; the Castillo cavern has 50 against 231 here, though only a fraction are available for viewing.

It's uncertain whether the hand images are genuine outlines – perhaps created by spraying red and black pigment from a reed – or free drawings. If they are true outlines, the hands placed on the cave walls some 27,000 years ago may have been ritually mutilated, or damaged by leprosy or frostbite. But another theory from French prehistorian André Leroi-Gourhan proposes that the hands are deliberately stylized, representing a code such as that used by South African Bushmen for silent communication when hunting.

# The upper Comminges

Upstream from Valcabrère and Saint-Bertrand extends the highest portion of the Comminges. **Luchon** – formerly known as Bagnères-de-Luchon – is a versatile spa resort at the end of all public transport lines, a staging post for numerous classic walking itineraries and slightly less rewarding ski runs. There's also a notable collection of Romanesque churches in the vicinity.

## Luchon

Along with Gavarnie, **LUCHON** – at the junction of the rivers One and Pique – has long been one of the lodestars for Pyrenean explorers. The spa re-entered history in the eighteenth century, when Jacques Barrau and Baron Antoine d'Étigny revived the thermal baths built by the Roman emperor Tiberius. Showing a flair for advertising well ahead of their time, they persuaded Louis Richelieu, governor of Gascony and great-nephew of Cardinal Richelieu, to endorse the *thermes* – and the fashionable set from Paris duly descended for the waters and salons. After the peak-climbing expeditions of Ramond de Carbonnières in the late eighteenth and early nineteenth century, Luchon became a base of choice for serious climbers and also attracted numerous Romantic literati.

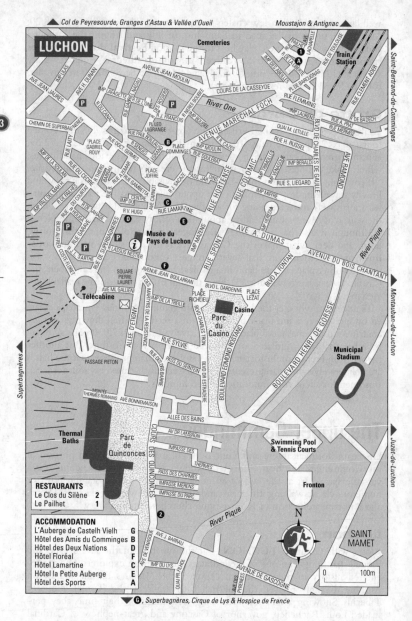

**LUCHON**

Col de Peyresourde, Granges d'Astau & Vallée d'Oueil

Moustajon & Antignac

Cemeteries

Train Station

Saint-Bertrand-de-Comminges

River One

Montauban-de-Luchon

River Pique

Musée du Pays de Luchon

Télécabine

Juzet-de-Luchon

Casino

Parc du Casino

Municipal Stadium

Square Pierre Lauret

Thermal Baths

Parc de Quinconces

Swimming Pool & Tennis Courts

Fronton

**RESTAURANTS**
Le Clos du Silène       2
Le Pailhet              1

**ACCOMMODATION**
L'Auberge de Castelh Vielh   G
Hôtel des Amis du Comminges  B
Hôtel des Deux Nations       D
Hôtel Floréal                F
Hôtel Lamartine              C
Hôtel la Petite Auberge      E
Hôtel des Sports             A

SAINT MAMET

N

0        100m

Superbagnères, Cirque de Lys & Hospice de France

East of **allées d'Etigny**, the main thoroughfare, Luchon's glory days have left a huge neighbourhood of sumptuous villas, which in some way justify the town's name for itself as "Queen of the Pyrenees". If you venture west of the commercial district, the narrow lanes off the place Rouy with vernacular houses suggest the mountain village Luchon once was. Halfway along the French side of the range, it's the largest and arguably most sophisticated Pyrenean resort, much the most elegant place this side of Biarritz. There's little of the usual spa-town fustiness, since Luchon has successfully reinvented itself as a versatile resort, attracting all social classes and age groups, and the nineteenth-century **thermal baths** (daily 4–7pm; dip and massage €35) are once again fashionable, augmented by the **Vaporium**, a natural cave sauna. Because of the peculiar local topography, the valley is also one of the major French centres for parapente and light aviation. Late in the day everyone gathers at the boisterous pavement cafés under the linden trees along allées d'Étigny, looking up from newspapers, drinks and heated debate to watch aeroplanes and parapentes floating high in the still of sundown.

Nineteenth-century statues add a few grace notes to the town's streets and squares: there's a concentration in the **Parc de Quinconces** (around the baths), particularly one of Baron d'Étigny, and in the **Parc du Casino**, where Coutheilai's Rodinesque *Baiser à la Source* provides the town's most pleasing image. On allées d'Étigny, next to the tourist office, the marvellously eclectic **Musée du Pays de Luchon** (Mon–Sat 9am–noon & 2–6pm; €1.60) covers all the bases: nineteenth-century engravings, early twentieth-century travel posters and ancient climbing and skiing gear on the first floor, plus prehistoric bear skeleton and rural impedimenta such as a giant forge bellows and a dog-house-like shepherd's shelter in the attic.

## Arrival and information

From the **train station** on avenue de Toulouse (where **buses** also stop), the way south into town is across the River On and down avenue Maréchal-Foch, which leads into allées d'Étigny, with the **tourist office** at no. 18 (mid-March to June & Nov to mid-Dec Mon–Sat 8.30am–12.30pm & 1.30–7pm, Sun 8.30am–12.30pm & 2.30–6pm; July & Aug daily 9am–7pm; Sept & Oct daily 9am–12.30pm & 1.30–7pm; mid-Dec to early March daily 8.30am–7pm; ℡05.61.79.21.21, ⓦwww.luchon.com). Several **banks** have ATMs, and there's a **laundry** on rue Lamartine.

## Accommodation

There's plenty of **accommodation** in Luchon, though you should avoid the obvious establishments on the allées d'Étigny in favour of quieter side streets, or the countryside immediately around. For stays of a week or more, the tourist office has a noticeboard of apartments and rooms to rent. There's no *gîte* or hostel in town, but there are eight **campsites** in the vicinity, including two adjacent ones on avenue de Vénasque, the continuation of cours de Quinconces. The least cramped and best-equipped is *Camping La Lanette* (℡05.61.79.00.38), 1.5km east over the Pique (down rue Lamartine) near the village of Montauban-de-Luchon.

**Hôtel des Amis du Comminges** 10 place du Comminges ℡05.61.79.00.31. Basic rooms, some en-suite, but furnished with hypoallergenic beds and phones; small garden, restaurant, private parking. Closed Nov & Dec. ❶

**L'Auberge de Castelh Vielh** 2.5km south on the D125, en route to Superbagnères ℡ & ℱ05.61.79.36.79. Just three wooden-trim, en-suite rooms (2 with balcony), in a lovely forested setting at this fine country restaurant (see below). The *castelh vielh* in question is a nearby hilltop

signal tower, originally Celto-Roman and last used during World War II. Open daily April–Oct, weekends only in winter. ❸

**Hôtel des Deux Nations** 5 rue Victor-Hugo ℡05.61.79.01.71, ℱ05.61.79.27.89. Popular well-kept one-star with a busy ground-floor restaurant (closed Sun eve & Mon) and a range of rooms: two lower floors are modernized and en-suite (❷–❸), while the top-storey rooms (❶) are pokey and *lavabo*-only. Limited nearby parking, lift, small garden opposite. Open all year.

**Hôtel Floréal** 11 av Jean Boularan
T05.61.79.01.48, F05.61.79.75.33 Thoroughly modernized, quiet rooms in three grades: basin-only, shower/WC, and "*grand confort*". Pleasant common areas, including a "world cuisine" restaurant. Street parking feasible. Open all year. ❶–❷

**Hôtel Le Jardin des Cascades** above the church in Montauban-de-Luchon, 2km east
T05.61.79.83.09, F05.61.79.79.16. Six peaceful, non-musty, wood-decor rooms (some en suite) in a lovely spot backed by a wild, hilly garden nurtured by the falls. Well-regarded restaurant (see below); both open early April to mid-Oct. ❷

**Hôtel Lamartine** 48 rue Lamartine
T05.61.79.02.68, F05.61.79.60.26. An unassuming façade conceals clean, quiet, pink-decor rooms at this well-priced two-star, with bathrooms recently modernized to include hair-dryers. Ground-floor restaurant. Open all year. ❷

**Hôtel la Petite Auberge** 15 rue Lamartine
T05.61.79.02.88, F05.61.79.30.03. Installed in a fine Belle Époque manse set well back from the street, this is the best value amongst the one-stars, often full with a repeat French clientele. Ample parking, all rooms en suite, decent restaurant doing five-course meals; closed Nov–Dec. ❷

**Hôtel des Sports** 12 av Maréchal Foch
T05.61.79.97.80, Wwww.hotel-des-sports.net. A bit remote, but quiet and with easy parking; all rooms en-suite and (unusually) non-smoking. Ground floor restaurant and a secure bike garage. Open all year. ❷

## Eating

Owing to the enduring spa paradigm of dining at your hotel, independent **restaurants** are limited; these are the best candidates.

**L'Auberge de Castel-Vielh** see above. Converted country house, strong on game and regional dishes including snails and trout, with a reasonable wine list. À la carte will cost at least €30, but *menus* at €15.25, €24.40 and €34.40 (drink extra) offer better value; the mid-priced one features an enormous *pétéram* (sheep tripe stew), hot and cold appetizers, and creative desserts like *pastéras*, a buckwheat biscuit topped with fruit.

**Le Clos du Silène** 19 cours des Quinconces, reserve on T05.61.79.12.00. Occupying a grand villa just beyond the baths, this welcoming outfit seats diners in sumptuous interior salons or in the garden during the day. The wine list is pricey, and à la carte for a light but elegant meal emphasizing seafood will work out at over €30, but the *menus* at €15 and €25 are interesting enough.

**Le Jardin des Cascades** see above. Shaded terrace restaurant, with creative gourmet food, valley views and good service; there are cheaper mid-week lunch *menus*, but normally count on €30–35 per person. Reservations mandatory.

**Le Pailhet** 12 av du Maréchal-Foch, towards the train station. Emphatically non-vegetarian (though vegetarian platters on request) revolving around game and regional specialities such as *pétéram* and *pistache* (a particularly rich *cassoulet*) in portions fit to fell an ox. The €21 menu gives you the run of regional specialties such as frog-legs and magret de canard in ginger-orange sauce, drink (from a good wine list) extra. Allow two-plus hours for a meal on a busy night. Closed Mon off-season.

## Activities

At the Bureau des Guides by the tourist office, you can sign on for organized walks or climbs. Across the Pique, which flows through the heart of town, you'll find the **swimming pool** (daily July & Aug 11am–6.30pm; €2.50) and **tennis courts** (approx €6 per head, racket rental too). The Centre Équestre (T05.61.95.55.34) on the north side of the River One provides **horse-riding**, while **kayaks** can be rented at Base d'Eau Vive (T05.61.79.19.20; April–Nov), 3km north at Antignac, which also gives lessons and organizes **rafting** expeditions. You can get **airborne** in a biplane (€70 for 30min; 2pax) or a glider (€55 for 30min) at Aéroclub de Luchon (T05.61.79.00.48, closed Weds & Thurs) or learn to **parapente** (flights start at €60) from certified instructors at Freddy Sutra (T06.87.34.20.54) or Soaring, 29 rue Sylvie (T05.61.79.29.23). If you're not sure what you want to do, Arapaho at 4 place du Comminges, off avenue du Maréchal Foch, offers a bit of everything, including **mountain-bike rental** and **expeditions** (from €28/day). For the more sedentary, the **télécabine** is the easy way up the 2666-metre distance to Superbagnères (see p.336), with some superb views en route (April daily 1.30–5pm; May to mid-June & Sept to mid-Oct Sat & Sun 1.30–5pm; mid-June to Aug daily 9.45am–12.15pm & 1.30–6pm; €4.60 one-way, €7 return). It's frequently used by parapentists heading up to a launch-pad, and is also a popular way for trekkers to cut out a 1200-metre climb on the westbound GR10. In winter, the ascent is included in the general ski pass. Finally, Luchon has two **cinemas**, the only ones for some distance around, showing first-runs and Hollywood productions.

## Walks from Luchon

There's enough walking **around Luchon** to keep you occupied for a week or so, mostly amongst the frontier peaks and over the border in the Maladeta and Posets massifs. The tourist office sells a booklet of recommended short walks (*Sentiers Balisés du Pays de Luchon*; €7.50), which is fine as far as it goes – but since waymarking sometimes leaves a bit to be desired, a good IGN map is essential.

### Southeast towards Maladeta from Hospice de France

Even if you're not up for the classic approach from Luchon to **Maladeta**, try to do the bit between **Hospice de France** (1386m) and the **Port de Vénasque** (2445m) on the frontier. The roadhead for Port de Vénasque is 11km south of Luchon – if you're car-less, walk or book an excursion at the Bureau des Guides in Luchon (see above). The narrow road is restricted in summer: cars go uphill only until 11.30am and from 2–4.30pm; downhill from noon–1.30pm and after 5pm. There's ample parking beside the abandoned hospice, built into a wooded hollow by the Knights of St John in the fourteenth century.

The way up to the pass – appearing U-shaped against the sky at first but culminating in a narrow passage when you actually get to it – lies initially through a steep stream valley, the grade not deterring a steady procession of dogs and five-year-olds en route. Some two hours along (2hr 30min with a full pack), you reach the four clear, turquoise tarns known as the **Boums du Port** or **Lacs de Boum**, brimming with trout and the occasional hardy swimmer. Beside the highest and largest lake stands the CAF *Refuge de Vénasque* (2249m; ☎05.61.79.26.46; June–Sept; 15 places) whose genial wardens serve excellent four-course lunches (including homemade dessert) until late afternoon, as well as supper to overnighters. Suitably fortified, you can now tackle the thirty-to-forty-minute trail-climb to the Port de Vénasque (3hr total from Hospice de France), where the entire crestline of Maladeta is literally in your face. If you're continuing south, the just-visible *Renclusa* refuge is another two and a half hours along well-trodden paths, while the *Llanos del Hospital* refuge-restaurant is just over half as far, on the floor of the Ésera valley (see p.303).

Otherwise, complete a satisfying circuit by taking the distinct trail labelled as "23" to the left and east, just beyond the Port de Vénasque, leading in 45 minutes to the **Pòrt dera Picada** (2477m) in Spain. Beyond this you descend gradually for about twenty minutes to the peak and pass of Espelette, with half-wild horses grazing nearby. You can slip north through the frontier again via the "23" trail through the **Pas d'Escalette** (2398m; *Còth de Lunfèrn* on some Spanish maps), but staying close to the border until drawing even with the **Pas de Montjoie**, from where you descend through open country and then the woods of the Frêche valley back to the Hospice de France, completing a seven-hour walking circuit.

Alternatively, you can shorten the day to six hours by plunging down to the **Étangs de Fréche**, the higher one visible from the cement cairn on the frontier ridge a few moments west of the Pas d'Escalette. This route is cairned, though initially there's no path; it's half an hour down to the top tarn at 2200m, and another twenty minutes to the lower, banana-shaped lake (2100m). Here the maintained "24" trail kicks in, taking you back to the Hospice de France after ninety minutes, passing riotous growths of wildflowers on bare slopes near the lakes, with the final stretch through beech and fir.

## South of Luchon: the Vallée du Lys and lake circuit

The **Vallée du Lys**, south of Luchon, provides another corridor to serious walking. The D46, then D46a, road up is initially more impressive than the route to Hospice de France, with the broad glacial valley dominated by the **Cirque de Crabioules** overhead, and the lower slopes dotted with holiday chalets. The asphalt ends after 10km at a giant car-park (1132m) and the **Cascade d'Enfer**, a spectacular waterfall dropping 40m in two stages through a cleft in the cliff, though the effect is spoilt a bit by EDF's adjacent dynamo building and disused *téléphérique*.

A large sign details local **day-hikes** on marked and numbered paths. The best can be combined into the suggested seven-hour loop itinerary below, taking in the most spectacular low-alpine lakes and a staffed refuge. First you have a forty-minute stiff climb through fir and beech along trail "40", following a stream up to a slopy meadow at the treeline and the junction right (ignore it) for trail "42" to the Gouffre d'Enfer. At the next junction, 1hr 15min from the car park, turn left towards Lac Vert ("1hr, 2000m") rather than right on "41" to the Refuge de Maupas and Lac Bleu. It's a further 1hr 15min (2hr 30min from the car park) to this lake (ignore a left towards the Col de Pinata and Cirque de la Glère), via a glacial basin where springs well up vigorously beyond the Lac des Grauès, really just a tiny tarn. **Lac Vert**, multi-lobed and green, is a popular family destination and just about warm enough for swimming.

You can continue fairly easily to Lac Bleu just overhead, but the following route is the only safe one. Proceed along the north shore of Lac Vert, forsaking trail "40" for the ridge at the far end; there's no path, but cross-country progress is initially easy over turf, with no scree. Then you face a sharper climb to link up with the path to **Lac Bleu** just west of its dam, conveniently in sight much of the way (allow 3hr 15min to here). The dam is ugly, but the cirque and bare crags overhead, with streamers of water feeding the lake, are magnificent.

From Lac Bleu, the path goes east around the shoulder of the Pic de Grauès, with modest altitude changes, to visit **Lac Charles** and **Lac Célinda** (allow 3hr extra return). In the opposite direction there's a half-hour descent to the junction with the main trail "41", and then fifteen minutes' climb back up to the rather elderly **Refuge Maupas** (2430m; ☎05.61.79.16.07; 27 places; staffed mid-June to mid-Sept), at the top of the *téléphérique*; if you time it right you can have lunch here. Incidentally, *Maupas* is a bit of a trekkers' cul-de-sac; traverses exist in theory to the Portillon hut (see below) and the Ball de Remuñe in Spain, but they're advanced undertakings, with axe and crampons required to cross the glacier at the top of the Cirque de Crabioules and the Col de Crabioules (3012m).

From *Maupas*, descend again on the EDF-engineered path, following the rusty funicular pylons, to **Prat Long** (1940m; 1hr below), where neither rough camping in the hummocky terrain nor a crude, Nissen-type hut is likely to appeal. Another 40min along path "41" returns you to trail "40"; when you reach the meadow at the treeline, vary your return by taking the scenic path "42", which passes above the Cascade d'Enfer, then loops around the far side of the valley before dropping to the car park (2hr 45min from *Maupas*).

The Vallée du Lys and the Hospice de France areas are linked by a good, half-day path, veering off from trail "40" below Lac des Graués. This threads the Col de Pinata (2152m) and the Col de Sacroux (2034m) en route to the lakeless **Cirque de la Glère** before descending sharply towards the hospice. From the cirque, another path climbs southwest to the easy **Port de la Glère/Puerto de la Glera** (2367m), giving access to Spain at the Ibón de Gorgutes (see p.303).

## Southwest to Posets

For **Posets**, take the GR10 steeply south from Luchon up through the Sahage woods to Superbagnères (3hr), then west five hours to the *Refuge Espingo*, situated just south of the GR10, above its namesake lake (see below).

As an alternative you could drive, or take one of the regular daily shuttles (early July to early Sept, 3 daily), to **Granges d'Astau** (1139m), essentially the parking area for **Lac d'Oô**. Here also you'll find the *Auberge d'Astau* (☎05.61.79.35.63, ⓦwww.astau-pyrenees.com; May–Sept), which offers a *gîte d'étape* (16 places), inn (❷) and restaurant. From the roadhead, a crowded section of GR10, initially on broad track, climbs for an hour to the dammed lake (1504m), where the privately run *Refuge Auberge du Lac* (☎05.61.79.12.29; 24 places; May–Oct) perches beyond the west end of the dam, its shoreline tables enjoying views of the superb 300-metre waterfall opposite. The onward path skims the east shore as it mounts to the Col d'Espingo, where the GR10 bears northeast towards Luchon, but most hikers press on to the *Espingo* refuge just below the pass, exactly an hour above Oô. The hut here (1967m; ☎05.61.79.20.01; 60 places; staffed late May–early Oct) overlooks the beautiful, undammed **Lac d'Espingo**, and the frontier ridge; limited snacks and drinks are served to passers-by.

Power lines, and most day-trippers with their toddlers and poodles in tow, stop here; beyond lies serious high-mountain country. The path continues south from the refuge past **Lac Saussat**, on whose shores tents sprout in summer. A short way above, there are two possible routes into Spain, both partly visible from Saussat: directly via the **Port d'Oô** (*Puerto de Oô*), or by an easterly route via the **Lac du Portillon**. The path for the latter, like much of the Oô–Espingo section, is paved with stone slabs, relics of the construction of the Portillon dam in the 1930s.

The *Refuge du Portillon*, an ex-construction workers' hut at the foot of the dam (2571m; ☎05.61.79.38.15; 25 places; staffed mid-June to mid-Sept), lies on the HRP, two hours from Espingo. On a sunny summer's day the lake appears cobalt blue against the surrounding grey rock and scree, its occasional patches of shoreline grass dotted with saxifrage and gentian. Onward routes into Spain are tricky and require proper equipment and experience on glaciers. The *Llanos del Hospital* hospice or the *Refugio de la Renclusa* on Maladeta lies a full day's trekking east through the **Col de Litérole/Collado de Lliterola** (3049m), while the most direct route to the *Estós* refuge in the Ésera valley slips south through the **Portillon d'Oô**, high above the lake, and then southwest – at first over permanent ice – to join the alternative path descending from the Port d'Oô/Puerto d'Oô. Count on four to five hard-slogging hours via either pass to *Estós*.

# Skiing around Luchon

Despite its proximity to the highest peaks in the Pyrenees, Luchon's own ski resort of **SUPERBAGNÈRES** (15km away by D125/D46; regular ski-season bus, plus the *télécabine*) is low and exposed to the sun on an east-facing shoulder at 1800m. Most of the green and blue runs (about half of the 24 pistes) descend from here – bad news that snow canons can't really ameliorate. It's still a good beginner-to-intermediate resort, whose main appeal is 360° views, including 10km of watershed ridge – and on clear winter days, a few *parapentistes*. The *télécabine* drops you just below the main car park and nineteenth-century *Grand Hotel*; there's equipment rental here, but more choice in Luchon. The only full service restaurant is *La Plete*, not too overpriced, though it struggles to cope at weekends. The longest, most challenging and wildest runs are in the north-facing Céciré sector (2260m), served by the two-stage Hount chairlift from the Lac d'Arbesquens (1450m).

When snow cover at Superbagnères is thin and mushy, keen skiers find better conditions at **LES AGUDES** and **PEYRESOURDE** (*"Peyragudes"* in tourist-board-speak; ⓦ www.peyragudes.com), overlooking each approach to the Col de Peyresourde 15km west of Luchon. Although the top is still only 2400m, the east-, west- and north-facing slopes on each side of the ridge from the *col* act as snow-traps. The development is fairly ugly but the skiing is serious, with 16 lifts and 36 pistes, the latter descending to the two low points at 1600m. With a preponderance of blue and red runs, and a somewhat idiosyncratic lift plan, it's best considered an intermediate-to-advanced centre.

# West to the Col de Peyresourde

Along the road west from Luchon over the **Col de Peyresourde** (1569m) you can only hitch or drive – there's no bus beyond the turning to Granges d'Astau. Along the way, three **churches** are worth more than a cursory look. The most famous is twelfth-century **Saint-Aventin**, perched in the namesake village on a very steep slope some 5km from Luchon. Its two Romanesque towers were immaculately renovated in the nineteenth century, and a good deal of **relief decoration** remains on the exterior. Above the south door, the carved tympanum shows Christ in Majesty, borne heavenward in his mandorla by angels, and flanked by the symbols of the Evangelists; on the right is an excellent *Virgin and Child*. The column capitals flanking the door are finely worked as well, depicting the *Washing of the Feet* (left), as well as a bear. The hermit Aventin was the local patron of bears, who would approach him to have thorns removed from their paws. To the right, Aventin is beheaded by the Moors (in 813), and further along on the wall a bullock paws at the ground to reveal the saint's buried body. Inside (key-keeper in the house with a grey gate 100m west; otherwise open Thurs July & Aug), there are more carvings near his tomb showing Aventin helping a bear, and carrying his detached head around, as well as some twelfth-century frescoes.

Two kilometres further on, just above the highway, the parish **church** (usually open daylight hours in July & Aug) of **CAZEAUX-DE-LARBOUST** has a superb, well-preserved series of late fifteenth-century **frescoes** in sombre shades of ochre and red, discovered in the nineteenth century. Opposite the door, a particularly lurid Last Judgement confronts you; also in the vaulting left of the nave are rarely seen panels of St John the Baptist preaching, and (below this) being led to prison. In the apse, just above the altar, angels just to the right of the Nativity give the glad tidings to the shepherds, one of whom plays bagpipes. Just above this in the conch of the apse, Christ reigns in Glory, while the Virgin, on a crescent-shaped throne, is borne heavenward by more angels. In the vaulting to the right of the nave are Old Testament scenes, including Adam sleeping through the Creation of Eve. After another 2km, the squat, barn-like **Saint-Pé-de-la-Moraine** just west of the village of Garin is a rarity, a pre-Romanesque edifice from the ninth century, cobbled together from Roman masonry.

If you'd like to **stay** locally, try the stone-and-wood-built *Hôtel L'Esquérade* just south of the D618 in **CASTILLON-DE-LARBOUST**, between Cazeaux and Saint-Aventin (☎05.61.79.19.64, ⓦwww.esquerade.com; closed mid-Nov to mid-Dec; ❸), where half-board is recommended at the excellent restaurant (closed Mon & Tues lunch except July & Aug; *menus* €15–29). The budget-minded can carry on 2km southwest to the appealing riverside village of **OÔ** and its simple but en-suite *Hotel des Spijeoles* (☎05.61.79.06.05; all year; ❷), with a basic restaurant; the same minor road continues 4km further to Granges d'Astau (see p.310).

### The Vallée d'Oueil

Just before Saint-Aventin, a minor road heads northwest for 10km along the little-visited **Vallée d'Oueil** and its unspoilt villages, most with noteworthy medieval churches. Development has been nipped in the bud by the closure of the ski centre at the top of the valley; the best summer activity is the day-hike loop from Bourg taking in the Lac de Bareilles and Mont Né (2147m). There are two places to stay and eat in the valley. At road's end in **BOURG**, 15km from Luchon, *Le Sapin Fleuri* (☎05.61.79.21.90, ⓔcontact@hotel-sapin-fleuri.com; closed mid-March to May and mid-Oct to Christmas, plus Mon & Tues in low season; ❸) is a chalet-style hotel with views of a forested slope. At the entrance to **SAINT-PAUL D'OUEIL**, 3km up from the D618, *Auberge L'Antenac* (☎05.61.79.85.22; ❷) operates more consistently, with three rooms looking south to the high summits, and serves plainly presented food (*menus* at €14 and €20) in smallish portions.

# Travel details

## Trains

**Luchon** to: Montréjeau (Mon–Sat 2–3 daily, Sun 1–2 daily; 40min).
**Montréjeau** to: Boussens (11–14 daily Mon–Sat, 9 on Sun; 25min); Lourdes (10 daily Mon–Sat, 6 Sun; 1hr); Pau (6 daily Mon–Sat, 5 Sun; 1hr 30min); Saint-Gaudens (12–15 daily Mon–Sat, 10 Sun; 10min); Tarbes (10 daily Mon–Sat, 6 daily Sun; 45min); Toulouse (12–15 daily Mon–Sat, 10 Sun; 1hr 15min).
**La Pobla de Segur** to: Lleida (3 daily; 2hr 10min).

## Spanish buses

**Benasque** to: Barbastro (daily 3pm, also Mon–Sat 6.45pm; uphill 11am, plus Mon–Sat 5.30pm; 2hr).

**Plan** to: Aínsa (Mon, Wed, Fri at 5.45am, returns 8.45pm).
**La Pobla de Segur** to: Barcelona (2 daily; 4hr); Capdella (daily Mon–Fri Oct–May at 5.15pm; 1hr; June–Sept Mon, Wed, Fri only at 5.15pm; returns next day at 8am); Lleida (Mon–Sat 1 daily, at 6.30am; 2hr); El Pont de Suert (1 daily, at 9.30am; 1hr); València de Àneu (Mon–Sat 2 daily, at 11.40am & 2.20pm; 1hr 10min); Vielha via Bonaigua (1 daily early June to mid-Nov, at 11.40am; 3hr).
**El Pont de Suert** to: Boí (summer 1 daily, at 11.15am, returns 2pm; 30min).
**Roda de Isábena** to: El Pont de Suert (1 daily Mon–Fri at 4.37pm, returns next day at 6.15 am; 1 hr); Graus (1 daily at 7.18am, returns at 4pm; 40min).

**Sort** to: La Seu d'Urgell (2 daily by minibus, 7.45am & 5.30pm; returns 10.15am & 7.30pm; 1hr 15min; reserve day before on ☏973 620 733 (am) or ☏973 620 802 (pm).

**Vielha** to: French border (Mon–Fri term-time 7 daily, 3 Sat & Sun; holidays Mon–Sat 4 daily, 2 Sat & Sun; 45min); Lleida via Túnel de Vielha (2 daily at 5.30am & 1.30pm; 3hr); La Pobla de Segur via Salardú and Bonaigua (1 daily, early June to mid-Nov, at 11.40am; 3hr 10min); El Pont de Suert (2 daily, same times at 5.30am & 1.30pm; 1hr); Tredòs (Mon–Fri term-time 7 daily, 3 Sat & Sun; holidays Mon–Sat 4 daily, 2 Sat & Sun; 20min).

## French buses

**Auzat** to: Tarascon-sur-Ariège (1 daily; 30min).
**Luchon** to: Montréjeau (5 SNCF buses daily Mon–Sat, 4 Sun; 50min); Saint-Gaudens (1 daily; 1hr 15min); Toulouse (1 daily; 3hr 30min).
**Saint-Girons** to: Aulus-les-Bains (Mon–Sat 1–2 daily; 1hr 15min); Boussens (Mon–Sat 8 rail coaches daily, 6 on Sun; 45min); Foix (4 daily; 1hr); Massat (4 weekly; 35min); Seix (Mon–Sat 3 daily between noon & 7pm; 20min); Sentein (1–2 daily Mon–Sat term-time, 2–3 daily Tues, Thurs, Sat otherwise; 45min).

# Around the
# national parks

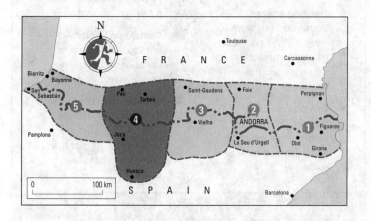

# CHAPTER FOUR

# Highlights

* **Skiing at La Mongie-Barèges** The joint domaine of La Mongie-Barèges is the largest (and often snowiest) in the range. See p.365 and p.368

* **Cirque de Gavarnie** Don crampons and ice axe for the ascent of the Cirque de Gavarnie to the evocative Brèche de Roland. See p.388

* **Trekking around Cauterets** Trek between refuges in the lake-spangled wilderness between Cauterets and Spain. See p.395

* **Spa pool at Eaux-Bonnes** Drown your post-skiing sorrows in this lovely spa pool. See p.409

* **Pau** Take advantage of Pau's cosmopolitan atmosphere between stints in the mountains. See p.399

* **Gorges** Trace the gorges and *fajas* of the Ordesa limestone country. See p.435

* **Pirineos Sur festival** Rock until late with the world musicians at the Pirineos Sur festival. See p.449

* **Castillo de Loarre** Act out your king-of-the-hill fantasies at this story-book castle. See p.459

* **Canyoning in the Sierra de Guara** Get wet and wild as you plumb the yawning canyons of the Sierra de Guara. See p.464

# 4

# Around the national parks

The allure of the Pyrenees' two largest national parks – the French **Parc National des Pyrénées** and the Spanish **Parque Nacional de Ordesa y Monte Perdido** – remains unmatched by any other part of the range. These contain the landscapes that inspired the gentleman-explorers who pioneered numerous Pyrenean ascents from the late eighteenth century, and it was here that many Romantic poets and painters came to brood. While the exaltation that Ramond de Carbonnières felt standing on the summit of Monte Perdido in 1802 was partly due to his mistaken belief that this was the highest point of the range, he had already explored Aneto – the true high point – without feeling the same delight. So great was the devotion of the eccentric Count Henry Russell that he had caves cut near the summit of Vignemale, highest point of the French Pyrenees, from which he and his guests could watch the changing colours on the frontier peaks. Nobody can walk through the Brèche de Roland, the natural gateway through the wall-like Cirque de Gavarnie, without being profoundly impressed: in one direction you look down over the mighty rock faces of Gavarnie, in the other you gaze out towards the thousand-metre-high walls of the Ordesa canyon.

In the two adjoining high-altitude parks, you will almost certainly see Europe's rarest bird of prey, the **lammergeier**, while **griffon vultures**, **golden eagles**, **isards** and **marmots**, reintroduced in 1948, are also fairly easy to spot. A few lynx and brown bear still survive, but the chances of encountering them are very slim.

The standard approaches to the Gavarnie area **from the north** are along the **Gave de Pau**, the river valley named after **Pau**, the elegant, relatively cosmopolitan capital of the *département* of Pyrénées-Atlantiques. Every summer day, tour buses tear along the narrow roads to the cirque, many of them carrying pilgrims from the Marian cult centre of **Lourdes**, upstream from Pau. Less immediately stunning areas such as the **Baronnies**, in the foothills to the north of the high peaks, are spared this seasonal influx, with depopulation and unemployment typical of the whole region.

On the other side of the border, in Alto Aragón, this trend is even more pronounced, depopulation having been accelerated by the effects of the Spanish Civil War and subsequent Falangist policies. **From the south**, heading up

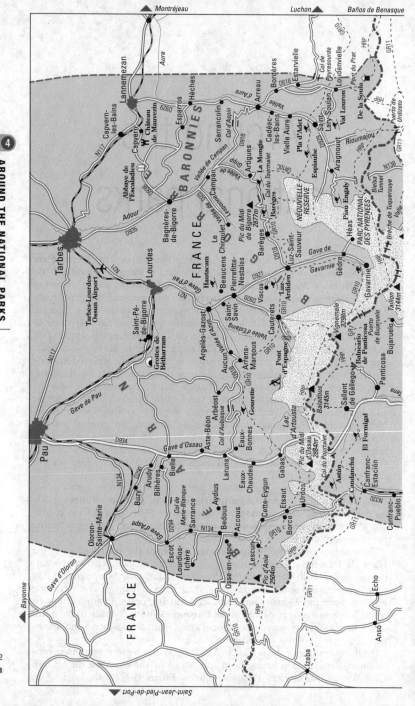

Lannemezan

Capvern-les-Bains
Capvern

N117

Château de Mauvezin

Esparros

Héches

Sarrancolin

Col d'Aspin

Arreau

Bordères

Estarvielle

Col de Peyresourde
Loudenvielle

Pont du Prat

De la Sonia

Puerto de Urdiceto

D929

Aure

D618

Vallée d'Aure

Val Louron

Saint-Lary-Soulan

Cadéac-les-Bains

Vielle Aure

Pla d'Adet

Rioumajou

GR10

GR11

HRP

Abbaye de l'Escaladieu

D938

Aragnouet

Espiaube

N138

Bielsa Tunnel

Brèche de Tuquerouye

Capvern

Adour

D935

Bagnères-de-Bigorre

Vallée de Campan

Vallée de Lesponne

Artigues

La Mongie

Col du Tourmalet

Barèges

NÉOUVIELLE RESERVE

Piau-Engaly

Héas

PARC NATIONAL DES PYRÉNÉES

Vallée de Campan

Le Chiquet

Pic du Midi de Bigorre 2877m

Barèges

D918

Luz-Saint-Sauveur

Gavarnie

Taillon 3114m

FRANCE

Tarbes

Lourdes

Beaucens

Pierrefitte-Nestalas

Viscos

Luz-Ardiden

Luz-Saint-Sauveur

Gave de

Gèdre

Gavarnie

HRP

GR10

Tarbes-Lourdes-Ossun Airport

N21

Gave de Pau

Hautacam

D921

D920

GR10C

GR10

Vignemale 3298m

Puerto de Bujaruelo

Bujaruelo

Saint-Pé-de-Bigorre

Argelès-Gazost

Saint-Savin

Cauterets

Pont d'Espagne

Puerto de

Balneario de Panticosa

Panticosa

Grottes de Bétharram

Aucun

Vallée d'Azun

Arrens-Marsous

HRP

Batanous 3145m

Sallent de Gállego

N21

N117

Aste-Béon

Arbéost

Col d'Aubisque

Gourette

Lac d'Artouste

Pic du Midi d'Ossau 2884m

Astún

El Formigal

Tena

Panticosa

Pau

D934

Gave d'Ossau

Eaux-Bonnes

Laruns

Eaux-Chaudes

Gabas

Col du Pourtalet

Canfranc-Estación

N330

N134

Buzy

Arudy

Bielle

Bilhères

Aydius

Gave de Pau

Urdos

Borce

Canfranc-Pueblo

Oloron-Sainte-Marie

Escot

Lourdios-Ichère

Col de Marie-Blanque

Sarrance

Bedous

Accous

Cette-Eygun

Etsaut

GR10

D294

N134

Osse-en-Aspe

Lescun

Pic d'Anie 2504m

Gave d'Aspe

FRANCE

Echo

Gave d'Oloron

HRP

GR11

GR10

Ansó

Izaba

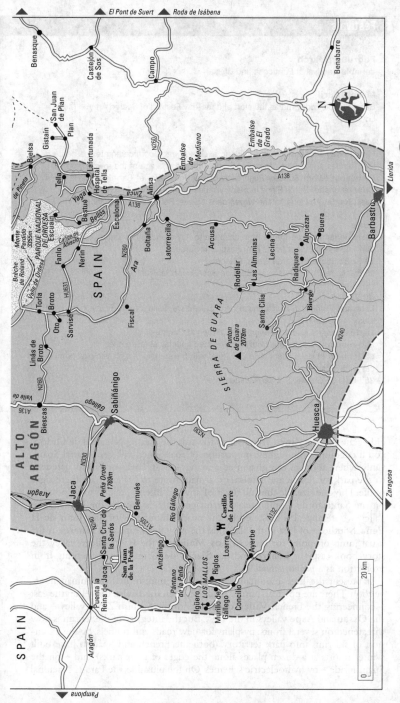

**February/March**
**Variable** Carnival at Panticosa and Bielsa.

**March/April**
**Easter** Good Friday marks the start of a ten-day Festival of Sacred Art and Music in Lourdes.

**May**
**First Friday** Processions and folkloric events in Jaca commemorate the battle of Las Tiendas against the Moors, and celebrate the courage of the town's women.
**Pentecost (Whit) Sunday** Pilgrimage of San Indalecio, at San Juan de la Peña. Celebrations for Santa Elena in many villages of the Valle de Tena.
**Last Sunday** *Romería* for the *Virgen de la Cueva*, Peña Oroel (near Jaca).

**June**
**Early** Regatta of tree-trunks from Laspuña to Ainsa on the Río Zinca.
**Variable** International Travel Film Festival in Tarbes.
**13** Celebrations for Santa Elena, Biescas.
**25** *Fiesta de Santa Orosía*, at Yebra de Basa, near Sabiñánigo.

**July**
**Last half** *Pirineos Sur* at Lanuza near Sallent de Gállego, one of the best world music festivals in Europe.
**15–18** *Fiesta de Nuestra Señora del Carmen* at Canfranc.
**Mid-month, 1 week** *Equestria*: horse-related spectacles at Tarbes.
**Latter half, 11 days** *Festival de Gavarnie*, with the staging of a classic play or musical extravaganza.
**25** *Fiesta de Santiago* at Sabiñánigo.

either the **Ara** or **Zinca** river valleys towards the Parque Nacional de Ordesa, you'll encounter the highest proportion of abandoned villages in rural Spain. Only where tourism can guarantee a living – as at **Torla** or **Fiscal**, gateways to the park, or **Aínsa** and **Bielsa**, on a main route to France – are there signs of life. The one sizeable foothill town of any real interest, thanks to its position on the Santiago de Compostela pilgrimage route, is **Jaca** in the Río Aragón valley, whose appeal is bolstered by the nearby monastery of **San Juan de la Peña**. Southeast of Jaca in the flatlands, the provincial capital of **Huesca** is the usual jump-off point for visits to **Los Mallos** in the Río Gállego valley, the story-book castle at **Loarre**, and the **Sierra de Guara**, also benefiting from protection as a *parque natural*.

At present the high mountains are relatively undisturbed by human intervention. There are no cross-border roads between the **Bielsa** tunnel on the east – connecting the French **Vallée d'Aure** with the Spanish Zinca valley – and the **Ossau** and **Aspe** valleys in the west. But the integrity of the terrain is now threatened on several fronts: by plans for new roads and tunnels, by the extension of ski runs into park territory (both the French and Spanish have built winter resorts at a dozen places along the edges of their parks), and – on the Spanish side – by hydroelectric schemes. On the plus side, the Parque Nacional

**Last two weeks to late August** *L'Été à Pau*: sport, music and theatre events at various Pau venues.
**Late July to early August** Music festival at Oloron-Sainte-Marie.

### August
**Early August** World music festival at Aínsa.
**4** *Virgen Blanca* observances at Candanchú.
**First weekend** *Festival de la Montagne*, Luz-Saint-Sauveur.
**Early August** International Folklore Festival of the Pyrenees in Jaca (odd-numbered years) or Oloron (even-numbered years).
**5** Fiesta at Sallent de Gállego.
**14–15** *Fiestas del Barrio* in Jaca; street markets and parties.
**15 and around** Celebrations for the Assumption of the Virgin at Panticosa, Oto, Bielsa, Héas and Laruns.
**14–17** *Fiesta de San Roque y la Virgen* at Biescas, with a "Big Heads" parade.
**Mid-August to mid-September** Music festival at Bagnères-de-Bigorre.
**31** *Fiesta de San Ramón* at Buesa.

### September
**First Sunday** Procession at Sarrance.
**8** Observance of the Birth of the Virgin at Héas and Sarvisé.
**14** *Fiesta de la Santa Cruz* at Sallent de Gállego and Ainsa; also *La Morisma*, a mock Moors-and-Christians battle, held every odd-numbered year in Ainsa's Plaza Mayor.
**Third Saturday** Pastoral activities festival in Arrens-Marsous.

### October
**First Sunday** *Nuestra Señora del Rosario* in Broto.
**12** *Fiesta de la Virgen del Pilar*, at Sabiñánigo and Torla.
**20** *Fiesta* at Santa Cruz de la Serós.

de Ordesa was expanded in the early 1990s to include the equally spectacular **Cañon de Añisclo** and the head of the glacial **Valle de Pineta**.

# The northern approaches

The French **Parc National des Pyrénées** (PNP) was a long time coming, meeting such strong local resistance to its establishment in 1967 that it was limited to a thin ribbon of territory along the border. It has real girth only around **Pic du Midi d'Ossau**, between **Cauterets** and **Vignemale**, and where it adjoins the older **Réserve Naturelle de Néouvielle**; in places – for example, near the Col du Somport – it measures barely 1500m across.

The traditional independence of and competition between 87 different mountain *communes* in the Central Pyrenees is the reason why the park isn't as

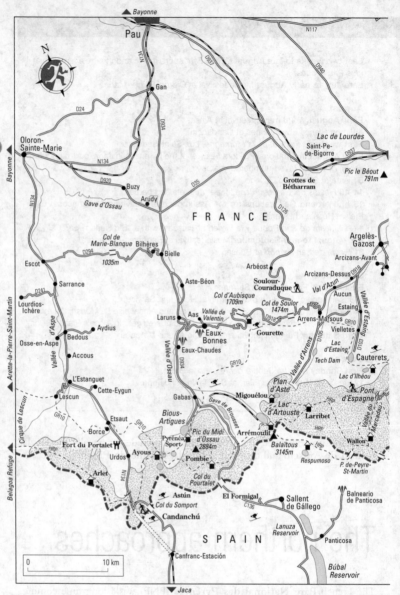

extensive as it should be. Already by medieval times the mountains were carved up between local families, the Catholic Church and a few autonomous valley communities, all grouped together into two huge feudal counties: **Béarn**, created in 820 and not absorbed by the French Crown until 1589, and **Bigorre**,

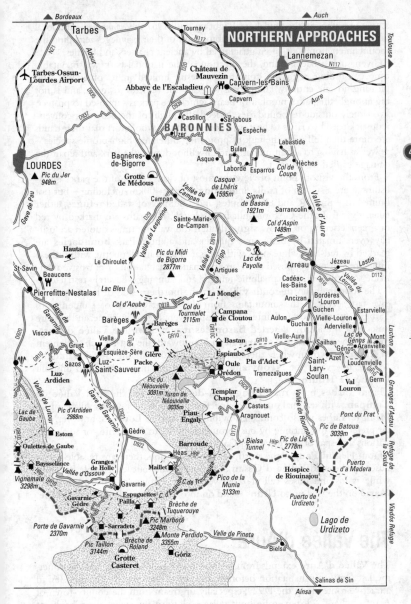

which kept out of Parisian clutches until 1607. Following the unification of France, and the subsequent French Revolution, territory was administratively rearranged into *commissions syndicales*, *syndicats de communes* and *copropriétaires*. However, rivalry between these bodies created a situation nearly as complicated as that prevailing in the feudal era. Right up until 1967 the *communes* – and local hunting clubs – fiercely resisted any abrogation of their privileges regarding the mountain environment, often guaranteed by ancient charters and treaties.

Given such a background, the creation of the national park was inevitably time-consuming, with the compromise result limited in its objectives, and pleasing no one entirely. The park is too easy for vehicles to reach, and is not big enough; the paltry number of bears, which the park is supposed to protect, live largely outside its boundaries. Indeed, the plight of the bears is a convenient stick used by critics to beat park administrators, who retort that their hands are more than full with the task of protecting other, less high-profile species – as well as having to accommodate rural livelihoods near the park and repair the damage caused by tourism.

From the visitor's point of view, the most obvious effects of the park's establishment are a system of **trails** amounting to over 400km, including – but not limited to – the GR and HRP routes, and a number of staffed **refuges**, either taken over from the CAF or built from scratch. The paths are marked by red or green lettering on yellow **signs**, though the walking times quoted are usually overestimated by between a quarter and a third. Park **boundaries** are marked by red-and-white signs with an isard's head in silhouette; within these limits there is not supposed to be any permanent habitation or obtrusive man-made structures other than alpine refuges, and camping is severely restricted.

The four main north–south valleys on the northern side of the watershed give fast access to the mountains from the major centres of Lannemezan, Tarbes, Pau and Oloron-Sainte-Marie respectively. From Lannemezan there are buses past the almost deserted **Baronnies** region down the **Vallée d'Aure**, through the valley capital of **Arreau** and on towards the last French settlement of **Aragnouet**, from where there is spectacular, if demanding, trekking into the wildlife reserve of the **Néouvielle Massif** and the magnificent and unspoilt **Cirque de Troumouse**.

From **Tarbes**, buses run to **Bagnères-de-Bigorre** and the rural **Vallée de Campan**, with seasonal onward connections to the winter-sports village of **La Mongie**. Tarbes is also connected by bus and train to **Lourdes**; however, it is far preferable to continue by bus through Lourdes to **Gavarnie**, or to the ski stations and spas of **Barèges** and **Cauterets**.

From elegant **Pau**, in the northwest of this region, there are reliable direct buses up the wild **Vallée d'Ossau** as far as **Laruns** (but less reliable beyond), while trains and buses call at the river-junction town of **Oloron-Sainte-Marie** on the way up to **Urdos** – and on into Spain – via the **Vallée d'Aspe**.

# The Vallée d'Aure

The **Vallée d'Aure** extends from just south of Lannemezan up to Aragnouet, the last significant habitation before the Bielsa tunnel and the frontier. It's an attractive route along the D929, especially upstream from the county-town of Arreau, where a dozen stone-built villages cling to the steep, green banks of the valley.

Two of the premier ski resorts in the French Pyrenees – **Espiaube** and **Piau-Engaly** – are found southwest of Arreau. The **Réserve Naturelle de Néouvielle**, immediately above the ski stations and south of Pic du Midi du Bigorre and the Col du Tourmalet, offers superb hiking around (or over) the celebrated **Pic de Néouvielle** (3092m) and up one of the easiest three-thousanders, **Turon de Néouvielle** (3035m). The eastern end of the PNP, up against the border, is a tougher proposition but with its own rewards, including a high-mountain approach to the **Cirque de Troumouse**, numbered among the most beautiful spots in the range.

The bus ride along the Vallée d'Aure towards the PNP begins at Lannemezan train station, a major stop on the Pau–Tarbes–Toulouse line. Although the journey provides a geography lesson on glaciation and mountain agriculture – grazing on denuded south-facing slopes, firs on the north-facing hillsides – there's little to justify leaving the bus or your car until the village of **SARRANCOLIN**, 19km from Lannemezan, known for its Romanesque **church of Saint-Ebons**, built to a Greek-cross plan. If you gain admission (it's usually locked), you can see the gilded and enamelled copper casket for the saint's relics, and carved choir stalls with typically grotesque faces. For **eating**, Sarrancolin offers the roadside *Café Bar Restaurant de France* (*Chez Bruno*), with an excellent €10 lunch *menu* and two others under €20; it's a lively spot favoured by local youth and passing tradesmen, and open off-season when most establishments in the valley above are shut.

## Arreau

**ARREAU**, 27km from Lannemezan, sits at the confluence of the Louron, Lastie and Aure rivers, a strategic position that first made it capital of the ancient Comté d'Aure under the kings of Aragón. Later it formed the heart of the Pays de Quatre Vallées, finally absorbed by France in 1475. Arreau enjoys an almost rainless microclimate, lying as it does in the shadow of Pic l'Arbizon to the southwest. A small, neat village, its tone is set by the medieval **market** (Thurs am) building, the half-timbered houses with their *fleur-de-lys* motifs and flower-boxes (especially the Maison des Lys opposite the market), and shops selling the local speciality *gâteau à la broche*, a spit-cooked cake. On the opposite side of the river from the market, the **Chapelle Saint-Exupère** by the post office merits a look for its flamboyant Gothic nave and eroded Romanesque portal. The town's tenth-century **Château des Nestes** now houses both the **tourist office** (summer Mon–Sat 9.30am–12.30pm & 1.30–7pm, Sun 9.30am–12.30pm; winter Mon–Fri 9am–noon & 2–6pm; ☏05.62.98.63.15) and a **museum** devoted mostly to the Cagots (see p.363; same hours; €1.50). If your appetite is whetted for more of the same, the small village of Jézeau, 3km east, can also offer a similarly ancient church surrounded by fine vernacular houses.

Arreau makes an agreeable touring base; places to **stay** include the somewhat noisy *Hôtel de France* on the square by the central crossroads (☏05.62.98.61.12; closed May & Oct 15–Dec 15; ❸); the central *Hôtel de l'Arbizon* behind the riverside park (☏05.62.98.64.35, ✉hotel.larbizon@wanadoo.fr; closed Sun eve & Mon low season; ❺ HB only), simple but clean and en-suite, with some of its six rooms having river views; and the fancier, quieter Logis de France member *Hôtel d'Angleterre* (☏05.62.98.63.30, ☏05.62.98.69.66; open weekends only on B&B basis, restaurant closed Oct–May; ❹), off the south end of the main street, with a peaceful rear garden and private parking. The latter two hotels have good **restaurants**, the *De l'Arbizon*'s offering two decent *menus* (€10 at lunch, or €17.50) and river-esplanade seating; the *D'Angleterre* is pricier (€13–35) with a corresponding bump up in quality. The municipal **campsite** (☏05.62.98.65.56; closed Oct) lies just south of the village on the Cadéac road, or there's the *Camping Le Refuge* (☏05.62.98.63.34) just north of Arreau.

## Southeast of Arreau: the Vallée du Louron

The main excursion from Arreau leads into the **Vallée du Louron**, which can also be reached by road from the Col de Peyresourde, or on foot along the GR10 (see below). There's no bus up this valley, which means making your own way along the D618 road towards Bagnères-de-Luchon, or picking up the footpath at the hamlet of Lançon, 2km above Arreau on the D618.

The local **tourist office** (Mon–Sat 9am–noon & 2–6pm, also Sun 9am–noon peak season; ☎05.62.99.92.00), which runs tours to most of the **painted churches** further up the valley, is at Bordères-Louron, another 2km above Lançon, but there's not much there aside from a Sunday morning riverside market (July & Aug only). The notable concentration of frescoed churches locally is owed to the discovery of the New World, burgeoning Spanish prosperity and consequent new markets for the wool-weavers of the valley; this wealth funded a widespread sixteenth-century mural campaign inside far older churches, part and parcel of the Counter-Reformation.

The first – and one of the best – of the churches is **Saint-Mercurial** at the village of **VIELLE-LOURON**, containing the saint's tomb and an extraordinary Last Supper with Judas bearing the head of Luther; opening hours, especially off-season, are unpredictable. The other notable church is **Saint-Barthélemy**, well up the valley at **MONT**, with secular-historical as well as sacred frescoes in the interior, but you can only rely on it to be open selected late afternoons during August – and even then there's no guarantee; otherwise console yourself with the excellent frescoes in the cemetery chapel. Here Saint Catherine appears in period dress, and a Last Judgement has some vivid demons, with the Saved beneath the Virgin, Christ and John the Baptist. There's another Last Judgement on the church's exterior south wall, with a classically hairy, horned and clawed Devil seen to the right.

The most convenient **hotel** locally, a good choice if you're driving, with a car park on the slope opposite, is *Hôtel Les Cimes* (☎ & ℱ05.62.99.67.21; ❸, also some non-en-suite ❷) above **ESTARVIELLE** on the D618, roughly halfway between Mont and Vielle-Louron. This has several balconied, en-suite rooms with valley views and a decent, inexpensive restaurant with some of the heartiest *garbure* around. Otherwise there's just a youth-oriented *gîte,* the *Centre de Montagne* (☎05.62.99.64.12; dorm plus a few rooms ❷), down by the central church in Estarvielle.

### Approach from the east: the GR10

A popular strategy involves walking west from **Granges d'Astau** to the **Vallée de Louron** via the GR10. Initially the way lies west along the **Val d'Esquierry**, south of the ski development of Les Agudes-Peyresourde, over the **Couret (Col) d'Esquierry** (2131m; 2hr 30min) and then briefly along the **Val d'Aube** into the Louron valley before turning north to the hamlet of **GERM**, high up on the east flank of the valley (1339m; 2hr 30min from the pass). Most people will call it a day here after five hours of trekking, especially with the incentive to **stay** at one of two quality lodgings: the *Auberge de Germ* (☎5.62.99.90.86; ❷), one of the first buildings you encounter in the village, and the *Centre de Montagne Accueil sans Frontière* (☎05.62.99.65.27, ℱ05.62.99.63.22; *gîte* plus chalets ❷), with a restaurant, pool and full sports programmes summer and winter; as of late 2003 they're under new management, so the former calendar of cultural activities may be suspended.

Otherwise, walkers will have to press on downhill to one of two pleasant villages on the southeast shore of the artificial Lac de Génos Loudenvielle (watersports on offer). **LOUDENVIELLE**, 45 minutes by foot from Germ, is a pleasant village with two central **hotels**, the more reliably open being *Les Galets de la Neste* (℡05.62.99.61.10, ✉galets-neste@wanadoo.fr; ❸), with off-street parking and **meals** (*menu* €14–36) served in the summer garden). There's also a campsite, *Pène Blanche* (℡05.62.99.68.85), and a bank ATM. **ARANVIELLE**, the neighbouring hamlet, is graced by the municipally owned, lake-view *Auberge des Isclôts* (℡05.62.99.66.21, ℻05.62.99.66.31; all year; dorm plus rooms ❸, HB urged at ❺), a restored medieval mountain house with a *table d'hôte* restaurant. En-suite doubles are on the small side but fine for couples; the efficient, long-standing management here is now installed at the *Centre de Montagne* in Germ. **GÉNOS**, on the northwest shore, has the only local "sight": a small, thirteenth-century **castle** (locked). Come up for the view over the lake to the snowcapped peaks, not for the stubby fortifications themselves.

From the vicinity of the reservoir, it's two and a half hours further west on foot, mostly on track parallel to the paved, two-lane D25, to the next indoor accommodation. From Loudenvielle the GR10 climbs towards the Col d'Azet (1580m) before dropping to the wonderfully set village of **AZET**. You can **stay** at either the official *gîte d'étape* (℡05.62.39.41.44) or the *Auberge du Col* (℡05.62.39.43.97; ❷), by the church, also offering meals. From here you've less than an hour's walk down to the main N129 road at Vielle-Aure, with the comforts and bus connections of Saint-Lary-Soulan (see p.353) 2km to the south.

### Walking in the Vallée du Louron

At the top of the Vallée du Louron lie a number of eminently scenic lakes and secluded tributary valleys which get a mere fraction of the **hiking** traffic visiting the landscape above neighbouring Luchon. But in some cases the trails up are not nearly as good, so scrambling skills are required. Equip yourself if possible with the excellent, French-only **booklet**, *Randonnées et Ascensions dans la Vallée du Louron* by Jean-François Rouys, published and sold by the tourist office in Bordères-du-Louron, detailing thirty itineraries and designed to be used in conjunction with the IGN **map** TOP 25 1848OT. Most of the recommended routes start from the car park at **Pont du Prat**, at road's end 8km south of Loudenvielle, or from **Pont des Chèvres**, halfway down the young Neste du Louron towards the reservoir. The only facility in the area, designed to serve the HRP, is the *Refuge de la Soula* (1690m; ℡05.62.99.68.40; June–Sept), 1hr 30min above Pont du Prat via the Gorges de Clarabide; you'll need to overnight here, or camp out elsewhere, as the remotest goals are too distant to reach and return from in a single day out of Pont du Prat – though all times given below are logged with a day-pack.

From *Soula*, one branch of the **HRP** goes to dammed **Lac Caillauas** (2171m, 3hr 15min from Pont du Prat), and then into the **Vallée des Gourgs Blancs** (ca. 2550m), under the eponymous border peak (3129m), with half a dozen natural lakes (4hr 30min from Pont du Prat); properly equipped climbers can reach the Lac du Portillon from here. Another, parallel *variante* from the refuge visits **Lac de Pouchergues** (2111m, 3hr 15min from Pont du Prat), continuing another hour to often frozen-over **Lac de Clarabide** (2648m), in turn nestled under its namesake frontier summit (3020m). A final, third *variante* leads initially southeast up the Neste de Clarabide before swinging west at the ruined Cabane de Clarabide to the Lacs et Vallon d'Aygues Tortes (2280m, 3hr 45min from Pont du Prat).

Popular walks from the Pont des Chèvres initially use the **GR10** east along the Val d'Aube to the vicinity of the Couret d'Esquierry, then turn south on a spur path to the **Lacs de Nère**, in the shadow of Pic de Hourgade (2984m). The pair of lakes (2430m, 4hr from Pont des Chèvres) are in much higher, wilder terrain than Oô and Espingo to the east.

### Skiing and parapente: Val Louron

The local ski station of **VAL LOURON** perches southwest of, and high above, the Lac de Génos-Loudenvielle. Although it's across the valley from the ski complexes at Peyresourde (see p.336), Val Louron is not nearly so rigorous, with a top point of only 2150m (descending to 1450m) and just three chair lifts – all in all a tiny centre, which despite a northerly orientation is apt to lose its snowpack quickly to wind and the low average altitude. In summer, it's a popular site for **parapente**, with schools based nearby at Génos, Adervielle and Loudenvielle.

## South of Arreau: the upper Aure

Continuing up the Aure from Arreau along the D929, after 2km vehicles pass under the rock arch that is the porch of Notre-Dame-de-Pène Taillade at **CADÉAC-LES-BAINS**, another possible base. Here two-star Logis de France affiliate *Hôtel Restaurant du Val d'Aure* (☎05.62.98.60.63, ⓦwww.hotel-valdaure.com; closed April & mid-Sept to Christmas, weekdays all winter; restaurant open May–Sept; ❸, ❺ HB only July & Aug) is nicely set in its own park on the riverbank with a pool and tennis courts. The proprietor speaks perfect English and is a certified mountain guide. In the vaulted, ground-floor billiards rooms is a cold sulphur spring, what remains of a spa established here in Roman times. Their three *menus* (€12–23) feature own-raised trout and meat, but if you intend to lunch here, phone ahead. If you're on a budget you might prefer *Le Relais de la Neste*, a self-catering *gîte* with en-suite, two-to-six-person rooms (☎05.62.98.62.51) beyond the old bridge east of the through road.

Alternatively, 8km southwest of Cadéac along the D30 side road from Guchen lies **AULON** (1230m), a strikingly handsome old village in the middle of nowhere at the base of L'Arbizon and Bastan d'Aulon peaks. Since the closure of most facilities serving the **GR10** in Vielle-Aure, Aulon – just 25 minutes off the trail – makes a good goal, and you can **stay** at the excellent *Hôtellerie de Montagne Le Pic Noir* (☎05.62.39.94.83, ⓔlepicnoir@wanadoo.fr; closed Nov; 6-bunk dorms, plus six doubles ❷, HB ❹), with good *table d'hôte* suppers. You can also **eat** well at *Auberge des Aryelets* (closed Sun pm to Tues low season, also Nov 15–Dec 15; reserve on ☎05.62.39.95.59), rumoured to be up for a Michelin star for its hearty cuisine featuring duck, foie-gras, snails and the like; there are *menus* at €17–27, but allow €70 for two if you dip into the wine list.

**VIELLE-AURE**, 9km south of Arreau on the D929 and just before Saint-Lary (see below) – of which it is effectively a suburb – is the last traditional village before the ski-related developments, its older quarter scattered mostly along the west bank. The central **tourist office** (Mon–Sat 10am–12.30pm & 2.30–7.30pm, also Sun school hols; ☎05.62.39.50.00) sells *topo-guides* for local walks and can help with **accommodation**, mostly *chambres d'hôte* since the two local *gîtes* closed down. However, a single, friendly hotel survives, the two-star Logis de France member *Aurelia*, 400m south of town on the old road to Saint-Lary-Soulan (☎05.62.39.56.90, ⓦwww.hotel-aurelia.com; closed Oct–Dec; ❸), with a restaurant and small pool. The closest **campsite**, 1.5km downstream in Agos suburb on the west bank of the Neste d'Aure, is large, grassy *Le Lustou* (℡05.62.39.40.64), next to the local horse-riding centre, Mille'S Abords (℡05.62.39.90.61). **Restaurant** options are similarly limited to *Les Gazaous*, on the campsite road, with four *menus* (€11–26).

## Saint-Lary-Soulan

**SAINT-LARY-SOULAN**, 12km south of Arreau, was one of the first Pyrenean resorts to be featured by foreign package-tour operators, its rustic core now enveloped by highly forgettable modern development. The **tourist office** opposite the fountain-*rond-point* (daily 9am–7pm, closed lunch low season; ℡05.62.39.50.81) can help with accommodation in *résidences* (apartments by the week). Saint-Lary also has a **Maison du Parc National** (June–Sept & Dec–April Mon–Sat 9am–noon & 2–6.30pm, also Sun July & Aug; variable hours otherwise), providing guides and general information on the local flora and fauna. Saint-Lary also has the last **bank** ATMs before the Spanish frontier.

There are nearly a dozen hotels in Saint-Lary, with more at the pair of ski centres overhead, but they're usually pre-booked for ski packages. **Accommodation** worth trying on spec includes two-star *Pons Le Dahu* on rue de Coudères, a quiet street east of the centre (℡05.62.39.43.66; ❸); and the two-star *La Pergola* at rue Principale 25 (℡05.62.39.40.46, ⓔjean-pierre.mir@wanadoo.fr; ❹), set back from the street, with a well-regarded **restaurant**. Choices for eating outside the hotels aren't brilliant, though the *Crêperie La Flambée Auroise* at 20 bis rue des Fougères, behind the Maison du Parc, has wholegrain bread and a good range of beers and juices offsetting rather small portions. If you have transport, it's best to head up to the village of **SAILHAN**, 2km northeast, where *Chez Lulu* (℡05.62.39.40.89; closed Mon) offers filling **meals** (*menus* €9–20) at outdoor tables, with *garbure* evenings and fireplace-grilled meat. There's a high-quality *gîte* here, *Le Relais du Chemin de l'Empereur* (℡05.62.39.45.83; closed Nov; some doubles ❷), plus another, cheaper *gîte*, in Saint-Lary proper: *Le Refuge* (℡05.62.39.46.81; all year; 46 places, some doubles ❷), as well as a **camping municipal**, *La Lanne* (℡05.62.39.41.58). Summertime outdoor activities on offer include **parapente** (℡05.62.39.58.75), **rafting** with Adrenaline (℡05.62.40.04.04) and **climbing** with the Bureau des Guides (℡05.62.40.02.58).

## The Saint-Lary ski stations

The adjacent complexes of **PLA D'ADET** and **ESPIAUBE**, just west of Saint-Lary, have a reasonably linked piste system, with the highest of the thirty lifts (nearly half of them chair or *télécabine*) reaching 2450m, and 43 runs, facing various directions, divided into eight green, twelve blue, thirteen red and three black. The Espiaube sector starts at 1590m, an unobjectionable development of rental shops, eateries and chalets; there's still a hamlet of old barns below – plus a small **hotel**, *La Sapinière* (℡05.62.98.44.04; ❹), often full in ski season. The shuttle bus from Saint-Lary passes Espiaube on its way to Pla d'Adet (1700m), its development by contrast a monstrosity; this also receives the direct *téléphérique* up from Saint-Lary. Piste plans confusingly dub Pla d'Adet as "Saint-Lary 1700", and Espiaube as "Saint-Lary 1900", though they're essentially the same altitude (ca. 1600m); "Saint-Lary 2400" encompasses the entire La Soumaye-La Tourette-Point 2450 area.

The nursery slopes, and a preponderance of drag lifts, are at and above Pla d'Adet; other skiers should instead take the Portet *télécabine* from Espiaube over the Col du Portet (2215m) to La Tourette summit (2320m), or the Mousades and Soumaye chairlifts to Pic La Somaye (2370m), focuses of most serious skiing. The 2450-metre top point is served by the tough Corneblanque drag lift, but Arrouyes adjacent is accessible to most skiers, and allows superb vantages south descending from the edges of the Néouvielle country; in recent winters snow here has been thicker than at much-vaunted Piau-Engaly (see below). At **lunch** time, those who know make for the *Refuge de l'Oule* (meals noon–3pm), where you eat well indeed for under €20; it's accessible either via a red-piste descent or the bi-directional Lac chair-lift. Similarly, at day's end you can take the bubble-lift down to Espiaube or descend 3km of twisty and narrow blue run – it's the Col du Portet-bound road in summer. The two *domaines* are linked by the Lita and Tortes chair lifts and their associated blue pistes.

## Piau-Engaly

**PIAU-ENGALY** (Ⓦ www.piau-engaly.com), the last stop on the valley bus route (in winter anyway), 20km above Saint-Lary, is arguably the most futuristic ski resort in Europe, and the newest in the Pyrenees. Some love the avant-garde architecture while others hate it, but Piau-Engaly has three undeniable advantages: illuminated night-skiing (7–10pm), a reasonable snow record owing to a 2500-metre top height and – for those who hate drag-lifts – 9 chairlifts among 21 lifts in total. The ring-shaped accommodation units are at 1850m, allowing doorstep access to 37 north-facing pistes, which include eight black, eight red and fourteen blue – in short a good intermediate-to-advanced centre.

## The Vallée du Rioumajou

Above Saint-Lary, the main river drainage begins to curl west and fray into half a dozen tributaries. The most scenic of these is the **Vallée du Rioumajou**, which joins the Aure just over 3km upstream from Saint-Lary. The hamlet of **TRAMEZAÏGUES** (meaning "between both waters") stands dramatically at the river confluence, overlooked by the ruins of an eleventh-century **castle-with-church** and by steep rock walls that exclude the sun most of the winter. Bears used to live in the dense surrounding forest – thus the local motto, *En Tramezaïgues que cridé: Qu'aouen aoucitet l'ous!* (In Tramezaïgues one shouts: We have killed a bear!). But only after the bears became locally extinct did the Rioumajou valley become a *site classé* (protected area).

A narrow twelve-kilometre road snakes up the valley; about halfway along, the *Auberge de l'Escalette*, overlooking a tiny reservoir, does lunch and supper. The pavement ends at "Km8", where the enormous, and enormously popular, **Fredançon** riverside picnic meadows under the firs seem to attract half of the tourists in the Vallée d'Aure on any given summer weekend. The other half continue along the final 4km of very rough track to the renovated **Hospice de Rioumajou** (1560m; aka *Rieumajou*), a traditional halt on one branch of the Santiago pilgrimage trail, and before that a stage of a Roman trade route. It's open early July to early September for drinks and light snacks from 11am to 5pm, but owing to lack of electricity there's no supper or accommodation. Tenting down in the vast green meadows all around will go unremarked upon, however, and towards dusk you might see shepherds feeding rock salt to their charges.

The environs of the hospice are a major crossroads of the **HRP** and its variants: you can continue south across the frontier via the **Port d'Ourdissetou/Puerto de Urdizeto** (2403m; 2hr 30min–3hr) for access to Bielsa in Spain; hike east over the **Port de Madère/Puerto d'a Madera** (2560m) to the refuge at Biadós, or go west via **Pic de Lia** (2778m) and continue along the frontier, eventually reaching the *Refuge de Barroude* (see below) within a day.

## Into the Parc National des Pyrénées

The approach to the **Parc National des Pyrénées** from the Vallée d'Aure is a classic alpine walk enlivened at the end by the superb Cirque de Troumouse. Get off the valley bus 13km from Saint-Lary at the stop nearest the Templar chapel (see below), where the side road for Piau-Engaly goes off to the right. From here you take the footpath up the **Vallon de la Géla**, crossing the boundary of the park almost immediately before joining the **HRP** just north of the *Refuge de Barroude* (2377m; 20 places; staffed July–Sept), perched magnificently in a namesake cirque, between two lakes.

It's only a half-day hike up from the chapel, but it's best to spend the night at the refuge, retracing your steps for half an hour next morning to the main HRP. This continues northwest on a path around the base of Pic de la Géla (2851m), via the two passes of **Hourquette de Chermentas** (2439m) and the **Hourquette d'Héas** (2608m). Descending from the second *hourquette*, often snowed up early in the summer, you find yourself in the upper reaches of the **Cirque de Troumouse**; follow the Aguila stream steeply down into the Héas valley, reached some five and a half hours out of the *Refuge de Barroude*. From the valley floor the cirque reveals itself in all its glory; for a description see "The Gavarnie region", p.384.

## A Templar chapel and the Túnel de Bielsa

Beyond several hamlets that comprise the *commune* of **ARAGNOUET**, just north of the D118, stands an intriguing twelfth-century Templar chapel (usually locked). Its almost windowless and plain exterior gives nothing away, though the jagged perpendicular edge of its tall *clocher-mur* suggests that there was once a large hospice here, at the base of the pedestrian route over 2429-metre Port de Bielsa.

Today most people **cross the frontier** by car, via the three-kilometre **Túnel de Bielsa** (daily: April–Sept 24hr; Oct–March 8am–midnight). Such are climate and geography here that a five-minute trip through the tunnel might take you from a damp, misty day on the northern slopes into bright Spanish sunshine, with an attendant change in vegetation from deep green to bare, scorched brown.

# The Réserve Naturelle de Néouvielle

France's first protected area, created in 1935, the **Réserve Naturelle de Néouvielle**, forms a lake-rich "annexe" at the very eastern tip of the far larger Parc National des Pyrénées. It encloses some of Europe's highest forests of mountain pine, with substantial stands reaching 2400m and isolated specimens even growing at 2600m. This is due to a predominantly southern exposure, unusual for the French Pyrenees, which also encourages a riot of smaller flora. Unfortunately, *réserve* status did nothing for the region's isards, which were hunted out and had to be reintroduced in 1987. However, you should see **marmots** and possibly **golden eagles**; there's also a slight chance of spotting **lammergeier**.

Néouvielle – *Neoubieh* or *Neu Bielha* in local languages – means "old snow", perhaps a reference to the vestigial glaciers on certain peaks here. It feels similar to the Aigüestortes-Sant Maurici park in Catalunya: day-trippers and dams at the lower elevations, granite walls, tarns and trekkers' passes higher up. And similar rules apply: no camping except in designated areas, no overnighting in caravans, no mountain-biking and a ban from July 1 to Sept 10 (9.30am–6.30pm) on private car passage along the single road into the *réserve*.

Between these hours a **navette** operates from the fee car-park (€4 per day) at Lac d'Orédon on the south side of the *réserve* up to another car park at Lac d'Aubert. During restricted hours, drivers can get as far as Lac d'Orédon by means of the "**Route des Lacs**", which climbs 14km up from Fabian in the Aure valley, lowest of the Aragnouet hamlets, but as ever in the Pyrenees it's more rewarding to do most of your exploration on foot. **Trails** through the *réserve*, often the GR10 or a variant, are accordingly well signposted. However you arrive, the 1:50,000 Carte de Randonnées no. 4 "Bigorre" **map** is invaluable.

### Lac d'Orédon loop hike

If you're not keen on a full-pack traverse, the following popular three-hour loop, using a small portion of the GR10, gives a good sample of the *réserve*. The starting point is the Touring Club de France-owned *Chalet-Hôtel d'Orédon* (1900m; ☏05.62.39.63.33; 60 places plus 6 in doubles; open & staffed June–Sept; rooms ❷) just above the Orédon dam, with obliging management and excellent food, though sleeping facilities are basic. A bit of road-walking is unavoidable; head 1km up towards Lac d'Aubert, and then bear left onto the trail marked "**Les Laquettes**", three natural, photogenic tarns below the Aubert dam. Also just below Aubert is one of the few legal camping sites in Néouvielle. Next the route swings east past the car park and a defunct refuge overlooking the natural **Lac d'Aumar**. You then pick up the GR10 along a crest, affording fine views over the three southerly reservoirs of Cap de Long, Orédon and Oule, before descending back to the *Chalet-Hôtel d'Orédon* from the **Col d'Estoudou** (2260m) on an unnumbered trail.

### Vielle-Aure to Artigues

Without your own transport, the best way to begin a traverse of the Néouvielle country is to take the **GR10** west from Vielle-Aure, climbing past and through the Saint-Lary pistes and then over the Col de Portet (2215m). After about six hours you reach the rustic, unstaffed Cabane de Bastan, where you have the choice of the variant **GR10C** towards Artigues or the main Barèges route.

For **Artigues**, hike north from the *cabane* and spend your first night at the lakeside *Refuge du Bastan(et)* (2250m; ☏05.62.98.48.80; 24 places; staffed June–Sept), one hour further, beyond a series of small lakes. Next day, you first climb the scree slopes up to the **Col de Bastanet** (2507m), then descend between several lakes for lunch at the *Refuge de Campana de Cloutou* (2200m; ☏05.62.91.87.47; 27 places; staffed June–Sept), before tackling a three-hour afternoon stage to Artigues through the wide Garet valley, which culminates in some waterfalls. Minuscule Artigues, on the D918 some 10km northwest of the scenic Col du Tourmalet, has limited facilities (described on p.364).

### Bastan to Barèges

For **Barèges**, follow the generally westward trail from the Cabane de Bastan, which skims along the eastern, then southern boundaries of the *réserve*, and spend the night at the *Refuge l'Oule* (1820m; ☏05.62.98.48.62, ℻05.62.39.55.38; 28 places; open & staffed early June to mid-Sept; dorms, or doubles ❷), 45 minutes away at the dammed south end of Lac de l'Oule, or at the *Chalet-Hôtel d'Orédon* (see above), just under two hours further. The only problem is that both are easily accessible by the road up from Fabian – the Lac de l'Oule hut in the final instance via a short path from the **Artigousse** parking area, 6km along – and therefore highly popular. After a night at one of these refuges, follow the GR10 or the "Les Laquettes" trail (see above) into the heart of the *réserve* as far as the adjacent lakes of **Aumar** and **Aubert**, where there's a choice of two onward routes north.

For the first route, you climb along the GR10 to the **Col de Madamète** (2509m), where you leave *réserve* territory, drop to the basic Cabane d'Aygues-Cluses, and then follow the idyllic Aygues-Cluses valley to join the D918 road at the Pont de la Gaubie, seven hours after leaving Orédon.

Alternatively, you can use an equally distinct, signposted but unnumbered trail departing northwest from the Lac d'Aubert, which negotiates the **Horquette d'Aubert** (2498m) before descending past half a dozen medium-sized lakes – the largest, **Dets Coubous** – before rejoining the GR10 half an hour before the Pont de la Gaubie. The time course is the same as for the all-GR10 itinerary. Once here, you're almost exactly halfway between Barèges and the Col du Tourmalet, about 5km from either. Barèges is discussed in detail on pp.381–384.

## A Néouvielle circuit

If you have a car to leave at a trailhead, it's recommended that you make a two- or three-day **circuit**, starting from the Lac d'Aubert or the Pont de la Gaubie. Walking instructions for the sectors between the southerly lakes and the D918 are identical to those previously described; what makes a loop feasible is a minor trail heading east from the Cabane d'Aygues-Cluses, over the **Horquette Nère** (2465m), and then southeast to the *Refuge du Bastan* (see above) – it's seven to eight hours from Pont de la Gaubie to the refuge.

## Traverse via Pic du Néouvielle

It's possible to make a more advanced traverse to Barèges via the summit of **Pic du Néouvielle** (3091m), at the western limit of the *réserve naturelle*. Although the ascent of the peak requires no technical climbing skills, it's long and tough, with crampons and ice-axe mandatory. Allowing for stops, plan on twelve hours to the first attended refuge on the far side, from where Barèges is another three hours further on track.

Follow the clearly marked path from the car park at Lac d'Aubert westwards towards the summit, then swing north to cross the bottom of the ridge known as the Crête de Barris d'Aubert. Once over, the path peters out; ascend west again, keeping the ridge to the left, then gradually bear away northeast towards the **Brèche de Chausenque** (2790m). Before you get to the *brèche*, you swing back southwards into a wide, snow-filled valley, making your way among huge boulders until a simple chimney takes you onto the final ridge, from which the **summit** is a short walk south (4hr from Lac d'Aubert).

To continue to Barèges, retrace your steps towards the *brèche*, climb through it this time and descend the steep slope on the other side west to the tiny **Lacs Verts**. Swing north along the shelf and gradually descend towards **Lac det Mail**, one of a succession of other lakes below to the left. Pass around its northeast shore then follow the stream down towards **Lac de la Glère** where you reach the *Refuge de la Glère* (2140m; ☎05.62.92.69.47, ⊕05.62.92.65.17; 70 places; open & staffed weekends & hols March–early June, daily early June–Sept) in about six hours from the summit. From the refuge, Barèges is 10km along a track to the north; the hut warden, Philippe Trey, co-runs the *Gîte d'Étape l'Oasis* in Barèges (see p.382) and can probably arrange transport down to spare you track-walking. He and his British wife Andrea will also be happy to reserve places in the other five staffed refuges in the area if contacted in advance.

# The Baronnies

One of the emptiest areas of the Pyrenees, the **Baronnies** – itself drained by the River Arros – lies between the lower valleys of the Adour and Aure, bounded to the north by the D938 Capvern–Bagnères-de-Bigorre road, and to the south by the D918 linking Sainte-Marie-de-Campan with Arreau. The landscape's too undulating for large-scale agriculture (though you do see the odd tractor or mechanized harrow), too low for skiing and too rounded for technical climbing. For the casual walker and naturalist, however, the Baronnies are excellent: dense forests of beech and pine, lush, little-used pastures and a range of wildlife. Monumental interest, besides lovely old crumbling farms, is lent by the château at Mauvezin and the abbey of Escaladieu, within a few kilometres of each other on the D938.

**Public transport** into this region is inevitably sparse. From the heart of the Baronnies, it's around 20km to the train station at Capvern, with Lannemezan and Bagnères-de-Bigorre slightly further. The Minibus des Baronnies company operates out of Lannemezan on Wednesdays and out of Bagnères on Saturdays, while André Pene runs a taxi service (℡05.62.39.01.14) from Esparros, a village near the centre of the region.

Otherwise you'll have to walk, hitch or drive yourself. You can enter the Baronnies from the south by travelling the 13km along the D918 from Arreau to the **Col d'Aspin** (1489m) and then hiking north from the *col*, but the route **from the east** is more straightforward. Take a bus from Lannemezan to just north of Hèches in the Aure valley (13km); from the bus stop, stroll 4km uphill along the D26 to the **Col de Coupe** (720m), from where the view west into the Baronnies is all-encompassing: emerald pasture, forest and rolling hills. You can continue on the road to Esparros, but it's better to cut off at the pass along the clear and direct horse trail, which takes half an hour.

## Esparros and around

**ESPARROS** was the seat of an ancient *baronnie* of four parishes – hence the name of the region. Like all the villages of the Baronnies, its population has fallen dramatically since the nineteenth century: 844 inhabitants in 1851, under two hundred, mostly elderly, today. Hilltop Laborde, just west, is currently more of a going concern. Norbert Casteret discovered the local **Gouffre d'Esparros** in 1938, describing it as a "vast cavern of indescribable magnificence", thanks to walls gleaming with a "hoar-frost" of white aragonite flowers. You can view these crystal formations, as well as a bat colony, on one-hour guided visits (10am–noon & 1.30–8pm: daily June–Sept; rest of year weekends & hols, by appointment only weekdays Oct–May; €5.50; reserve on ℡05.62.39.11.80).

The Baronnies has two official information points: a **tourist office** in Laborde (℡05.62.39.03.42), 3km west of Esparros, and **La Maison des Baronnies** at Sarlabous, 8km north (summer 9am–noon & 2–5.30pm; ℡05.62.39.05.14). The most central **gîtes** are *Jean Colomes* at Esparros (℡05.62.39.05.96; all year) and the *Moulin des Baronnies* on the River Arros just below Sarlabous (℡ & ℻05.62.39.05.14; all year), also with tenting space. There are also a few simple **inns** hereabouts, specializing in regional food: tiny *Le Relais d'Esparros* (℡05.62.39.02.43; closed Wed except July & Aug; ❷) at Esparros; *La Ferme de Mamette* (℡05.62.39.18.59; open all year; ❹) at Laborde; and the magnificently landscaped *Le Petit Château* (℡05.62.40.90.16, ℻05.62.40.90.18; all year; ❹), at the edge of Laborde. The only **campsite** apart from *Moulin des Baronnies* is *Le Randonneur* at Esparros (☎05.62.39.19.34; mid-June to mid-Sept), well laid out and with a pool.

## Walking: the Tour des Baronnies

Although walking in the Baronnies is not technically difficult, it can present tricky situations. Rainfall is high and mists often dense (some of the valley bottoms are essentially temperate rainforest), and there are vistas devoid of any sign of human habitation, except for the occasional herd of livestock tended by a solitary shepherd and his mangy dog. So you'll need a compass and map, as well as rain gear and possibly waterproof boots.

The **Tour des Baronnies**, marked on the Carte de Randonnées 1:50,000 "Luchon" map, is a lopsided figure-of-eight itinerary with its centre at **ASQUE**, 7km west of Laborde: it takes about four days, generally along tracks. The longer loop leaves Asque – where there's a self-catering *gîte d'étape* (☎05.62.39.18.77; 33 places all year) – towards the flat-topped mountain of Casque de Lhéris, then sweeps around towards Uzer, Castillon and Sarlabous; the shorter arc links Asque with Espèche, Esparros and the **Col de Couradabat**. From the *col* it is possible to walk out southwards towards **Col d'Aspin**, via **Signal de Bassia** (1921m) and the **Col de Beyrède**, but this route is unmarked, requiring some navigational skills.

## Mauvezin and Escaladieu

The two great historical sites of this region, the château of Mauvezin and the abbey of Escaladieu, are situated conveniently close enough to each other to be seen in a single visit. If you're reliant on public transport you'll have to take the train to Capvern, from where it's a five-kilometre walk to Mauvezin, and thence a further three-kilometre walk to the abbey.

### Mauvezin

The **château** (daily: May–Oct 15 10am–7pm; Oct 16–April 1.30–5.30pm; €4) stands on the edge of **MAUVEZIN**, atop a 567-metre-high hill that was first fortified by the Romans. Between the thirteenth and fifteenth centuries it changed hands several times in the wake of protracted hostilities between the English and the French, finally passing after 1373 to Gaston Fébus (see box on p.241).

Built of grey stone, and with a crenellated tower, the square castle is particularly appealing from the outside. Inside, you're left to wander as you please, with the aid of an informative brochure. The now-grassy courtyard was once lined with buildings, the roofs of which funnelled rainwater into the giant cistern, built as an emergency reserve; only once was it drunk dry – during the siege of 1373. On the inside of the cistern it's possible to read the graffito *Dieu seul sera adoré et l'Antéchrist de Rome abisme* ("God alone will be adored and the Antichrist in Rome cast into the abyss"), carved by an imprisoned Huguenot in the sixteenth century.

The current tenant is the Escòla Gaston Fébus, a cultural conservation group that promotes Gascon and Occitan poetry, literature and art, including formal, medieval-themed events in August. The fully restored tower has been turned into a museum, mostly dedicated to the works of the Société Félibrée, a literary organization pledged to revive and preserve the ancient Provençal language. However, the museum is also crammed with various intriguing exhibits: sculptures, paintings, photos and bits of armour.

## The Abbaye de l'Escaladieu

Three kilometres southwest and downhill from Mauvezin in the valley bottom, towards Bagnères-de-Bigorre, you'll find the **Abbaye de l'Escaladieu** (May–Sept daily 10am–1pm & 2–7pm; rest of year daily except Tues 10am–noon & 2–7pm; free), the first Cistercian monastery in the southwest of France. Founded in the middle of the twelfth century, Escaladieu flourished for just a couple of centuries, the monks earning a living by cultivating the Baronnies, a fertile and profitable region before mechanization favoured flat fields. The monastery was burned and plundered by Protestant forces during the Wars of Religion, and early conservationists began restoring the buildings in the seventeenth and eighteenth centuries.

Escaladieu was badly mismanaged and neglected by a private foundation between 1986 and 1993; following litigation, the *départemental* authorities assumed control of the place in 1997 – plus responsibility for a hugely expensive restoration. The place now hosts cinema, seminars, theatre and most accessibly, **concerts**: performances are held sporadically (usually Sun 5pm) from June to September, generally of Baroque music, for which the abbey makes a wonderful setting.

The showpiece of the ongoing restoration is the twelfth-to-thirteenth-century vaulted **chapter house**, opening onto a leafy inner courtyard through the sparse remnants of a cloister, all but two columns of which was shipped to California during the nineteenth century. The rest, by contrast, is typically Cistercian in its plainness, the long, white eastern facade devoid of decoration, and the enormous, echoing abbey church as bare as possible.

There's an unstarred but perfectly tolerable **hotel-restaurant** in **ESCALADIEU** village at the junction with the D14 south, the *Auberge de l'Arros* (☎05.62.39.05.05; all year; ❷), with three inexpensive *menus* – the only reliable facility at either Escaladieu or Mauvezin.

# Bagnères-de-Bigorre

The revival of thermal resorts was something of a 1980s French fad: Luz-Saint-Sauveur did it, Ax-les-Thermes managed it, and **BAGNÈRES-DE-BIGORRE**, 21km southeast of Tarbes along the D935 in the Adour valley, invested tens of millions of francs in its **spa** with its large, well-kept *piscine* (open to hikers and skiers 5–7pm). Descended from the Roman settlement of Vicus Aquensis, Bagnères reached its apogee with the opening of the Grands Thermes in 1823, becoming the "in" place for the likes of George Sand, Gioacchino Rossini and Gustave Flaubert; the Roman connection is echoed in a new thermal complex, Aquensis – behind the facade of the now-defunct casino. In winter, however, the spa district becomes a ghost town, with most of its hotels shuttered and only the sound of water in runnels and fountains to break the silence.

From the 1830s, Bagnères' British community was second in size only to Pau's, many having stayed on after the Peninsular War. So foreign-dominated was Pyrenean exploration at this time that of the four founders of the Société Ramond – the mountaineering club established here in 1864 and predating even the Club Alpin Français – two were British: the barrister-explorer Charles Packe and the photographer-inventor Maxwell Lyte. The third was Henry Russell, whose father was Irish, and only Emilien Frossard was entirely French.

## The Town

Beside the long, grey *thermes* building stands the ornate **Musée Salies** (July & Aug daily 3–7pm; May, June, Sept–Nov Tues–Sun 3–6pm; €4). An elegant collection, mostly landscapes, hangs on its pink walls, but there are some more surprising artists represented, including John Jongkind, a Dutch precursor of Impressionism, and Francis Picabia, a major figure of the Dada movement. Free exhibitions are often held in the downstairs gallery (same hours). The ticket for the Musée Salies also covers the **Musée du Vieux Moulin** (Tues–Fri 10am–noon & 3–6pm), about ten minutes' walk away across the Adour in rue Hount-Blanque, just over rue Général-de-Gaulle; it's a typical folk museum, with exhibits of local furniture, agricultural tools and *Bigourdan* crafts, but attractively laid out and well explained.

The area's main tourist attraction is the **Grottes de Médous** (daily: April–June & Sept–Oct 15 8.30–11.30am & 2–5.30pm; July & Aug 9am–noon & 2–6pm; €5.50; ☎05.62.91.78.46 for off-season tours), 2km south of the centre on the main road. The twelve-people-minimum-per-tour rule can mean hanging about on a slow day, but it's worth waiting to see the wall known as the *Salle d'Orchidée* (Orchid House), rated by Norbert Casteret as one of the great limestone formations of the Pyrenees. The caves were only discovered in 1948, and thus escaped the vandalism suffered by others during the early part of the century.

## Practicalities

The heart of the town lies a five-minute walk south along rue de la République from the train station on avenue de Belgique where only SNCF **buses** from Tarbes stop – though actual resumption of train service is mooted for summer 2004, and coaches continue into the centre for a final halt by the fifteenth-century church of Saint-Vincent, within sight of place Lafayette. Other buses up the Vallée de Campan as far as Payolle (see below) depart from next to the **tourist office** at 3 allée Tournefort (July & Aug Mon–Sat 9am–12.30pm & 2–7pm, Sun 9am–noon & 2–6pm; rest of year Mon–Sat 9am–noon & 2–6pm; ☎05.62.95.50.71, ⓦwww.hautebigorre.com), south of the *place*. From the tourist office it's a short walk northwest to the leafy **allée des Coustous**, the main café street and also home to the post office, west of which is pedestrianized **place de Strasbourg** and the covered market occupying **place Ramond**. Drivers should beware the fairly comprehensive pay-and-display **parking** scheme (in effect Mon–Sat 9am–noon & 2–7pm).

**Hotels** facing the spa tend to be overpriced and musty, catering for an elderly, rather sedentary clientele. Fans of time warps shouldn't miss *Chambres Les Petites Vosges* at 17 boulevard Carnot near Aquensis (☎05.62.95.28.31; ❶–❷), essentially unchanged since World War II, but with showers in the pricier rooms. Otherwise, the quietest area for accommodation lies just north of the *halles* on rue de l'Horloge, named after the clock in the Tour du Jacobins, the last remnant of a convent destroyed during the Revolution. Here you'll find the old-fashioned but comfortable *Hôtel d'Albret* (☎05.62.95.00.90; Feb–Oct; ❷) at no. 26, overlooking quiet place d'Albret. Another good budget choice, central but set back from the busy street at 24 place André-Fourcade, is the well-kept *Hôtel Commerce* (☎05.62.95.07.33; closed mid-Nov to Dec; ❷) north of Saint-Vincent church. Clean and comfortable, with most rooms away from the noisy avenue, is the two-star *Hôtel de la Paix* at 9 rue de la République (☎05.62.95.20.60, ⓦwww.hotel-delapaix.com; closed early Dec to early Jan;

❷–❹), with a decent attached restaurant (*menus* €13–23). A good year-round option is *Hôtel Tivoli*, a rambling structure in its own grounds southwest of the centre on avenue du Salut (℡05.62.91.07.13, ℻05.62.91.15.20; ❷–❸); variable rooms are a bit ramshackle, but the en-suite ones have modern bathrooms, and rear units have small balconies.

**Restaurants** – in hotels or otherwise – aren't Bagnères' strong point; among the few independent ones are *Nhu-Y*, a Chinese on place Lafayette, and *La Fontaine Saint-Blaise*, on rue Saint-Blaise, on the corner of rue du Pont d'Arras, near Aquensis (closed Mon eve summer, Wed eve winter), a cosy place where you can't go wrong with the €21 *menu*. The town's top choice, *Le Bigourdan* (closed Mon) occupies two upper storeys at 14 rue Victor-Hugo, on the corner of rue de l'Horloge; here €21 (drink extra) nets you *cèpe* ravioli, grilled monkfish with relish and a long dessert list – though portions are on the small side. Next door at no. 12, the *Crêperie de l'Horloge* (closed Nov & Sun–Tues low season) also does a range of *plats du jour*, plus of course crêpes to eat in or take away.

Bagnères has a **music festival** every year, normally from mid-August to mid-September, but a more original musical tradition is the male choir, Chanteurs Montagnards, founded in the 1840s and still performing at most civic functions.

With four to six daily SNCF **buses** from Tarbes, and two to three private ones from Lourdes, Bagnères is easy to get to, but it's harder to move on from – only two buses daily (Transportes Cariane) go south past the Grottes de Médous to Sainte-Marie-de-Campan (see p.364). From July to September this service covers the extra 15km southeast along the D918 to Lac de Payolle (see below); during summer buses go southwest on the D918 only as far as Gripp hamlet, though in winter this line extends all the way to La Mongie.

# Upstream from Bagnères

South of Bagnères-de-Bigorre, the valley sides of the Haute-Adour rise steeply into the Baronnies and the **Casque du Lhéris** on the northeast, and towards **Pic du Midi de Bigorre** to the southwest, with the Néouvielle Massif rising ahead to the south. Subsidies, high rainfall and fertile soil keep the thatched farmhouses in business, three crops a year being common, much as they were in the eighteenth century when Tarbes-born politician Bertrand Barère described Haute-Adour as: "The object of admiration by all French people ... the eye being drawn towards the majestic Pic du Midi which forms the centrepiece of a sublime tableau." Another writer of the time noted "the excellence of its butter and the beauty of its marble".

Away from the main Aure valley and its extension, the **Vallée de Campan**, two tributaries can be explored: the lush **Vallée de Lesponne**, with the much-visited Lac Bleu at its head; and the **Vallée de Gripp**, at the top of which is La Mongie, one of the best Pyrenean ski resorts, and the strategically perched observatory on **Pic du Midi de Bigorre**.

## The Vallée de Lesponne

The countryside just north of Barèges, at the head of the **Vallée de Lesponne**, is well worth a day or two. You can take a bus as far as Beaudéan, 5km along the D935, but after that you're dependent on your own resources for the 10.5km along the D29 side road to its end at **LE CHIROULET**

## The Cagots

Numerous towns in the western half of the Pyrenees – Saint-Savin, Luz-Saint-Sauveur, Cauterets and Saint-Jean-Pied-de-Port to name just four – once had sizeable populations of a mysterious people known as **Cagots**, of whom little is known for certain other than that they were persecuted. First mentioned in thirteenth-century manuscripts, Cagots were forbidden to live in the centre of towns, to kiss the Cross, to walk barefoot, to have sexual relations outside the Cagot community or to enter a mill (in case they contaminated the grain). They had to wear a distinguishing symbol on their clothes, variously described as a crow's or a duck's foot, and live in a separate ghetto at the edge of villages. Cagots had their own baptismal fonts – sometimes even their own churches – and were buried in separate graveyards.

There were compensations. Cagots were exempt from feudal duties and taxes, were subject only to ecclesiastical courts and were not expected to bear arms, except for work. Prohibited also from owning land, many therefore became skilled woodworkers in particular, and Gaston Fébus apparently insisted on Cagot carpenters for his fortress at Montaner. But Cagots were excluded from all normal social life, and despite appeals to the pope and the secular authorities, discrimination continued for centuries. The Cagots themselves began agitating for equal rights as early as 1479, but social consciousness lagged behind legal rulings in their favour. It was not until 1789 and the Revolution that their second-class status was officially, and definitely, ended. The measures taken against them sound like those taken against lepers, and indeed one of the many alternative names for the Cagots – *crestianas* – is almost certainly derived from *cristianaria*, the places reserved for "white" lepers – that is, those considered infected but not contagious, and whom modern medicine would probably recognize as afflicted by some minor skin disease.

So the Cagots may have been lepers or the descendants of lepers, but it also seems plausible that they were racially distinct. Some linguists derive the word Cagot from *can goth* or "dog of the Visigoths", implying a descent from the Visigoths who fled into this area after their defeat by Clovis in 507. Furthermore, the architecture of many Basque country churches – with their low "Cagot windows" through which services could be watched, and proportionally low "Cagot doors" – suggests to some commentators that Cagots were a race of less-than-average stature. It's not even certain that these features had anything to do with the Cagots. The mystery will probably never be solved; the subject was already steeped in confusion by the fourteenth century, when in contemporaneous accounts Cagots were variously described as tall, fair and blue-eyed, or short, dark and Moorish-looking.

(1062m). This tiny hamlet supports two **hôtel-restaurants**, the more reliably open being *La Vieille Auberge* (T05.62.91.71.70; ❷). If both are full (just 7 rooms between them), a plush alternative is *Domaine de Ramonjuan* (T05.62.91.75.75, Wwww.ramonjuan.com; open most of year; ❸–❹, HB ❻), 5.5km down-valley at **LESPONNE** hamlet, with a good restaurant, apartments available (4-day minimum stay) and such luxuries as tennis courts, sauna and Jacuzzi.

From Le Chiroulet a popular path rises steeply for nearly three hours to **Lac Bleu** (1950m), set in a peak-ringed cirque, or to **Lac d'Ourrec** in about two hours; a loop walk, shown clearly on the "Bigorre" Carte des Randonnées, takes in both. The Col du Tourmalet (see p.365) can be reached by climbing around the eastern side of the 120-metre-deep lake – the path in places cut into the rock – and then heading due east to the **Col d'Aoube** (2389m), from where a faint path continues down to the D918 a short distance from Tourmalet, four hours beyond Lac Bleu.

# The Vallée de Campan

Upstream from Beaudéan, the Adour is known locally as the **Vallée de Campan**, whose east flank edges into the Baronnies. Below woods of spruce, pine and beech, the gentle valley's meadows are speckled with farms arrayed in south-facing ranks. The individual architecture is unique: house and barn are built as a unit, with the balconied living quarters always to the right as you face the sun. The valley is also known for the local craft tradition of **mounaques** or giant rag dolls; of both genders and variously costumed, these are often propped up on pavements, windowsills or even house gables for summer-long display.

It's indicative of the tenuous nature of tolerance early in the Age of the Enlightenment that when the church of **Saint-Jean-Baptiste** at **CAMPAN** (6km from Bagnères, 1km upstream from the Lesponne turning) was rebuilt after a fire in 1694, a separate Cagot door (see box on p.363) was inserted at the west end; the Cagot ghetto here was on the right bank of the Adour, in the part known as the *Quartier Charpentier* after their habitual trade. The church's personality is now defined by the ornate white-and-gilt *retable* by the local brothers, the Ferrérers of Asté; the fifteenth-century wooden image of Christ, originally at L'Escaladieu, is a cruder but more moving statement of faith. The village itself, with its slate-roofed houses, is attractive; for **accommodation**, the one-star *Hôtel Beauséjour* (℡05.62.91.75.30; closed March; ②), opposite the colonnaded, sixteenth-century market hall, represents fair value. There's also the *Camping de Layris*, on the northwest side of town, and the main **tourist office** for the valley (Mon–Sat 9am–noon & 2.30–6/7pm, also Sun 9am–noon peak season; ℡05.62.91.70.36).

At **SAINTE-MARIE-DE-CAMPAN**, another 6km southeast, there's more **accommodation** at either the *Gîte L'Ardoisière* (℡05.62.91.88.88, ©ardoisiere@wanadoo.fr; closed Nov–Christmas; dorms, or doubles ②, HB ④), or the more conventional *Hôtel Les Deux Cols* (℡05.62.91.85.60, ℻05.62.91.85.31; closed Oct 15–Dec 31; ②), with *menus* at €15–21, a small private car park and rear rooms overlooking the valley. Both cater to cyclists, and are on the main through road (as is the entire town), which as it divides is designated the D918 in either direction.

To the right, this climbs southwest to La Mongie (see below), via Gripp and Artigues. The southeasterly (leftward) fork attains the **Col d'Aspin** – where half-tame horses and cows gambol, causing traffic jams – before dropping into the Vallée d'Aure at Arreau. Just the Campan side of this pass (not open in winter), 25km shy of Arreau, the environs of **Lac de Payolle** offer a respectable 50km of marked cross-country skiing pistes between 1100 and 1450m; during summer, picnickers throng the lakeshore.

# Up the Vallée de Gripp: La Mongie, Tourmalet and Pic du Midi

The D918 road to La Mongie from Sainte-Marie-de-Campan rises steadily along the **Gripp valley** to **ARTIGUES**, where there's a reasonable hotel – the *Relais d'Arizes* (℡05.62.91.90.41; ②) – a campsite and not much else. Nevertheless it's a good start- or end-point for hiking in the Réserve Naturelle de Néouvielle (see p.355) and there are short walks to the nearby Cascades de l'Arises and Cascade du Garet.

## La Mongie

The ski centre of **LA MONGIE**, 6km above Artigues – together with Barèges on the opposite side of the Col du Tourmalet – constitutes the largest skiing area in the Pyrenees, with 34 pistes totalling 60km on the La Mongie side alone. Once you're away from the unsightly high-rise resort at 1800m it's beautiful, with a combination of open bowls, runs through trees and some simple but exciting off-piste itineraries. There are only three short black runs, but it's an eminently suitable place for beginners to intermediates. By taking the Porteilh *télécabine* and then the Quatre Termes chair-lift, you access the top point of 2500m and a reddish blue run descending 3km, with eyefuls of the Pic du Midi the whole way; the easy and intermediate runs dropping east from the Espade and Béarnais chairlifts are even longer, those these tend to get mushy in the afternoon.

## The Col du Tourmalet and the Pic du Midi de Bigorre

The **Col du Tourmalet** (2115m), 4km beyond La Mongie, ranks as the highest driveable pass in the French Pyrenees, often playing a tormenting role in the Tour de France and almost always closed between late October and the end of April. The name literally means "the bad detour", a title perhaps bestowed by the carriers of the sedan chairs that used to taxi the wealthy between the spas of Bagnères and Barèges by this long, cold road. Wheeled transport first used the *col* in 1788, when the road along the Luz valley was blocked by floods; from the La Mongie side of the pass you can still see the faint trace of the old route. The perennially windy pass itself is dominated by an anatomically correct, lumpy statue of a nude cyclist, **"Le Géant du Tourmalet"**, which commemorates the Tour de France's first passage here in 1910. Opposite stands a stone-clad restaurant which is by far the best of several high-altitude eateries for skiers, and may also operate in summer.

From the *col*, a **toll road** (closed to vehicles) leads up towards the summit of **Pic du Midi de Bigorre**, stopping at 2720m, a fifteen-minute walk short of the observatory just below the summit (2877m). Bristling with antennae and radio masts, it's a fairly unsightly place, but has the virtue of being an easily accessible high-altitude look-out. On foot it's about two hours from Tourmalet to the top, from where you can see west as far as Balaïtous, south into the Néouvielle country and east as far as Andorra.

Opened in 1880, the **observatory** has been continuously staffed since, even when cut off for months at a time by snow, with all provisions and equipment carted up on the back of man or mule for the first 66 years. Despite the observatory's successful history of lunar observation and its current studies of Mars, Saturn and Jupiter, the future of the establishment hangs in the balance. Although major television and radio antennae have been built here, and a contract to monitor pollution and the ozone layer was awarded late in the 1980s, serious French investment has been switched to even larger installations in Hawaii, Chile and Tenerife.

For years the observatory's resident scientists and technicians resisted plans to develop it as a tourist attraction, maintaining that casual visitors would cramp their style. But in 2000 they bowed to the inevitable, with the opening of an initially mediocre astronomical museum and restaurant in the grounds, subsequently revamped into a more worthwhile **visitor centre**. This is accessible only by means of a two-stage **téléphérique** from La Mongie (daily: June–Sept & school hols 9am–4.30pm, last descent 7pm; Oct–May 10am–3.30pm, last descent 5.30pm; closed Nov and 1 week early April; €23, or €60 for a family

Every year in July the **Tour de France** passes through the Pyrenees, on its way either to or from the Alps, and most years the riders tackle the savage haul up to the Col du Tourmalet. First incorporated into the route in 1910, it has now been included in almost fifty contests, forming a particularly gruelling (and often wet and freezing) episode in what is invariably one of the toughest days of the three-week race. In 1988, for example, the riders had to cycle through Tourmalet in the course of a 180-kilometre stage that had already climbed the Col de Peyresourde and Col d'Aspin; by 2000 the Pyrenean stage exceeded 200km, and included the the twin *cols* of Aubisque and Soulor.

The Tour brings with it an enormous entourage of back-up teams, advertising people, television crews and journalists, who occupy every hotel room in the vicinity of each day's finishing line. **Accommodation** is not the only problem – actually **seeing the riders** at the crucial points can be tricky, as the race attracts vast crowds even on the mountain-tops. If you want to see the action at any of the major passes, take up your position at least three hours before the bikes are due – when the leaders come over the pass, the crowds will be twenty deep. The most ardent devotees of the Tour position themselves under the banner marking the crest of the *col*, armed with sheafs of **newspapers** – not to fill in the wait reading, but to help the cyclists. As the riders appear, the newspapers are held out for the cyclists, who tuck them under their shirts to provide added insulation for the freezing descent, on which the bikes reach speeds of up to 100km per hour.

Although nearly two hundred riders start each Tour de France, only a dozen or so have the all-round ability needed to win. In the early stages these star riders generally take it easy, checking out the form of chief rivals and letting themselves be nursed along by their team-mates – the so-called *domestiques*. When they reach the mountains, however, the race changes completely. Any rider with pretensions to be wearing the leader's yellow jersey when the Tour finally swings into Paris has to finish each mountain stage near the front, and that requires relentless effort – even a top-class rider can lose fifteen minutes on a bad day in the Pyrenees, and this is a race where the overall winning margin has sometimes been measured in seconds. By the time the Tour moves out of the Pyrenees the leader board will have resolved itself into a chart of the race favourites.

Within the main race, there's another contest going on in the Pyrenees (and the Alps) – the one for the title **"King of the Mountains"**, awarded to the rider who records the best results in the alpine stages. Winning this competition – whose leader wears a white shirt with red polka dots – secures a reputation only marginally less illustrious than the overall winner's. Any rider who takes the polka-dot shirt more than once is assured of quasi-mythical status – the Spanish rider Federico Bahamontes, who won it six times in the 1950s and 1960s, earned himself the reverential nickname "The Eagle of Toledo" for his high-altitude prowess, and Luxembourg's Charly Gaul, winner in 1955 and 1956, became known as "The Angel of the Mountains". The favourites for the yellow jersey of course feature strongly in the "King of the Mountains" tussle, but most teams also have a specialist climber who comes to the fore in this part of the race.

A good illustration of this was the reticent Spaniard **Miguel Indurain** ("The Colossus of Roads" or "The Sphinx"), the first rider to win five Tours in a row from

of 4, includes admission to astronomical museum; ⓦ www.picdumidi.com).

The *pic* was also opened to recreational **ski descents** in winter 2002–03, a great half-day out. Groups of up to six need to be of strong intermediate competence or superior, and must be accompanied by a winter mountaineering

1991 to 1995 (though since the 1960s others had won a total of five contests non-consecutively). Yet his mountain stages didn't always show him at his best, and from 1994 to 1997 Frenchman **Richard Virenque** rode off with the "King of the Mountains" jersey. However, scoring is cumulative over the numerous stages, including the important flatlands time-trials, which Indurain usually dominated. After finishing a disappointing eleventh behind Danish winner Bjarne Riis in the 1996 Tour, Indurain announced his retirement in January 1997; it was the end of an era, with no one cyclist then looking set to dominate competition, despite the German **Jan Ullrich** powering his way to the title in 1997. Except for Virenque, individual French riders – who haven't won an overall Tour since 1985 – have been almost totally eclipsed since then, while entrants from countries as diverse as Colombia, Poland and Uzbekistan have captured stages since 1990.

Tainted by lurid **drug scandals**, the "Tour de Farce" (as some newspapers dubbed it) of **1998** cast a long shadow over the sport. France's Festina Watches team, with Virenque as captain, was disqualified when a huge stock of prohibited doping substances was found in their trainer's car. The police and courts were quickly involved, with arrests and prosecutions of various team managers and trainers. After initial protestations of innocence, and allegations that Festina was being made a scapegoat, scores of riders admitted using drugs since at least the 1980s. Eventually seven of the 21 teams were banned, and by the end of the Tour hardly anyone noticed that Marco Patani had triumphed, the first Italian victor in 33 years. Besides the potential skewing of results, doctors warned that the most popular doping materials were highly dangerous, implicated in blood clots, heart disease and strokes among racers.

At this nadir of the race's fortunes, the Tour needed a wholesome, against-the-odds saga to restore its image – and got it. American **Lance Armstrong**, favoured to do well in both the 1996 Tour and the Atlanta Olympics, had bombed mysteriously in both. A few weeks later, he began coughing up blood and was diagnosed with a cancer that had spread from his testicles to his lungs. Few expected him to live, much less to ever cycle again. But 1999 saw him power through the mountain stages en route to overall victory as head of the US Post Office team. In 2000 he repeated this feat, defying gravity in a miserably cold, sodden Pyrenean stage to overtake Patani, Ullrich and Virenque, finishing just a few seconds behind Javier Otxoa, on his way to a second yellow jersey. When Armstrong got his third title in 2001, commentators openly speculated about a possible successor to Indurain, and the public's faith in the romance of the Tour de France was to some extent restored. In 2002, Armstrong recovered from a crash in the seventh daily stage which lost him 27 seconds and made him trail eventual second-place finisher Joseba Beloki for some time. 2003 saw Armstrong suffer dehydration through infernally hot initial stages (and Beloki end up in hospital after a crash), and then crash himself, his right brake lever catching on the drawstring of a spectator's plastic bag. Armstrong ultimately outduelled Ullrich in a rainy finale, with the latter skidding out of contention on a wet road near Nantes. It was the sloppiest, most accident-prone Tour ever, but Lance had matched Indurain's five back-to-back triumphs, and intends to try for an unprecedented sixth win in 2004, before (probably) retiring honourably.

guide or an ESF instructor. The route down depends on conditions; there are several along the south and north faces. If you end up way to the east, towards Artigues, you may have to trudge 4km up to La Mongie (though institution of a *navette* for such instances is foreseen).

# Tarbes

If you're heading towards the Central Pyrenees from the northeast you'll almost certainly pass through **TARBES**, capital of medieval Bigorre and the contemporary, far larger *département* of Hautes-Pyrénées. A medium-sized, unobjectionable if dull place, it will mainly appeal if you have an interest in things military. Destroyed by the Normans, then ruined by the protagonists from both sides in the Wars of Religion, Tarbes retains little evidence of any past prior to the eighteenth century. An overall view of the city with its suburbs gives a general impression of functional and graceless white apartment and office blocks. More inspiring and exceptional architectural efforts include the futuristic National Music School and the Parvis Cultural Centre. Arms manufacture has long been Tarbes' primary industry, but it now employs just a few hundred people compared to sixteen thousand at the end of World War I, with most of the remaining jobs threatened by automation.

## The Town

Tarbes' few specific attractions lie within walking distance of each other. Off rue Massey sprawls the tranquil, peacock-patrolled **Jardin Massey** (daily dawn to dusk; free), designed by Tarbes-born Placide Massey (1777–1853), who also managed the Parc du Trianon at Versailles. This carefully landscaped botanical collection has its specimens – some local, some as exotic as California sequoias – informatively labelled and discussed in French. Architectural interest is sup-

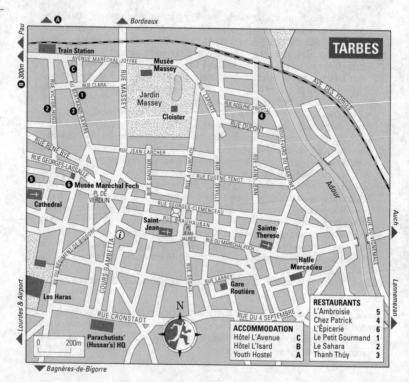

plied by the partially reconstructed Gothic cloister from the abbey of Saint-Sever-de-Rustan, with vivid, if slightly eroded column capitals: swans attacking a bear, and a sword-brandishing angel expelling Adam and Eve from Eden.

The **Musée Massey** (prospective hours March–Nov Mon–Sat 10am–noon & 2–6pm; Dec–Feb Mon–Sat 2–5.30pm; €3.50), housed in a rather eclectic nineteenth-century building in the middle of the *jardin*, will be closed until late 2004 while its section on the military hardware and extravagant uniforms of the Hussars regiment, from its fifteenth-century Hungarian origins to today's parachutists, based in Tarbes, is rehoused in a new purpose-built museum in the Foix-Lescun quarter. When the older gallery reopens, it should more generously highlight its other two themes: fine arts and archeology. The arts section groups a miscellany of pleasant pieces spanning the fifteenth to nineteenth centuries, the most attention-grabbing being a Dutch-school *Wild Boar Hunt*. Archeological exhibits include a bronze death mask of unknown date and a Roman votive altar, discovered during excavations at the train station.

Some 300m southwest of the Jardin Massey, at 2 rue de la Victoire, is the **birthplace of Maréchal Foch** (guided tours only Thurs–Mon: May–Sept 9am–noon & 2–6.30pm; Oct–April 9am–noon & 2–5pm; €3.50), supreme Allied commander on the western front during World War I. A traditional pitched-roof *Bigourdan* town house, it contains two floors of photos, medals and other memorabilia from the field marshal's life – including, a little morbidly, the armchair in which he died.

Tarbes' renowned stud farm, **Les Haras**, lies a couple more blocks south on rue Mauhourat (ⓦwww.haras-nationaux.fr; 1hr guided visits only by reservation, tours depart July & Aug Mon–Fri half-hourly 10–11am & 2–5pm, rest of year Mon–Fri 10am, 11am, 2pm, 3pm, 4pm; also last Sun of each month half-hourly 2.30–4pm; ⓣ05.62.56.30.80; €5). Despite its relatively central location, the farm is set in acres of beautiful grounds that seem an extension of the botanical gardens. The immaculately groomed horses have impeccable manners, displayed at exercise drill, usually held at about 3pm (except Feb–July when most of the horses are out to stud). Founded in 1806 by Napoleon, Les Haras is best known for its *cheval Tarbais*, a cavalry breed produced by crossing English, Basque and Arabian stock.

## Practicalities

From the SNCF **train station** on avenue Maréchal-Joffre there are connections with Toulouse, Lourdes and Pau. In terms of **car rental**, Budget has premises right opposite the station (ⓣ05.62.93.61.15), while Hertz is a few steps west. The **gare routière**, on the south side of Tarbes on place au Bois, off rue Larrey, has services to Bagnères-de-Bigorre, Lannemezan (with onward connections to Saint-Lary) and Pau via Soumoulou. **Tarbes-Ossun-Lourdes airport**, 9km southwest of town, has daily scheduled flights to and from Paris only; the airport bus serves these flights, and the airport has its own train station, with occasional services into the town's station. **Drivers** will find a certain amount of free, relatively abundant, **parking** around the Jardin Massey; elsewhere it is metred or otherwise controlled. The **tourist office** is just off the central place de Verdun at 3 cours Gambetta (Mon–Sat 9am–12.30pm & 2–7pm; ⓣ05.62.51.30.31).

Tarbes has a few reasonable **hotels** in the vicinity of the train station, including the friendly, helpful *Hôtel de l'Avenue*, 80 avenue Bertrand-Barère (ⓣ05.62.93.06.36; ❷), and the remoter, more comfortable *Hôtel L'Isard*, 70 avenue Maréchal Joffre (ⓣ05.62.93.06.69, ⓕ05.62.93.99.55; ❷), as well as a **youth hostel** at 88 avenue Alsace-Lorraine (ⓣ05.62.38.91.20).

In terms of **restaurants**, that attached to *L'Isard* offers *menus* ranging from subsistence (€9.50 *formule*) to a more interesting gourmet *menu* of the month (€31). At 62 rue Bertrand-Barère, *Le Petit Gourmand* is a popular lunch spot, while if you're craving something exotic, *Thanh Thúy* across the street at no. 53 does very passable Vietnamese dishes for under €15 a head. Other independent eateries include the Moroccan diner *Le Sahara* at 21 rue Victor Hugo, and old favourite *Chez Patrick*, 6 rue Adolphe-d'Eichtal, on the corner of rue Saint-Jean, a cheery working-class institution that fills by 12.30pm with a regular clientele who dine on a nine-euro *menu* of *potage*, charcuterie, steak and *frites*, a choice of dessert, house wine and coffee. For more sophisticated cuisine, head for 48 rue Abbé Torné near the Préfecture, where Christine and Daniel Labarrère's *L'Ambroisie* (☎05.62.93.09.34) is the *département's* only Michelin-starred restaurant, with seating in the rooms of an old house or out the back in the orchard on fine days. There's an affordable €25 lunch *menu*, but you'll easily spend €80 for supper. Opposite the Maréchal Foch museum, *L'Épicerie* is pricey for grills, but pleasant, with contemporary decor and tables outside on the cobbles during warmer months.

# Lourdes and around

**LOURDES**, just 20km south of Tarbes on the N21, is difficult to avoid if you're touring the French side of the Central Pyrenees, as it sits squarely astride the direct route up to Argelès-Gazost, Cauterets and Luz-Saint-Sauveur. And even if it weren't so pivotal, the town would be an unmissable detour. East of the main street, Lourdes seems like many other small, French foothill communities. But the western part, around the *cité religieuse* on the banks of the Gave (River) de Pau, is another world – shut down in winter, and in summer seething with the pilgrims who constitute its sole reason for existence. The huge crowds attending the Masses and the grotto make an overwhelming spectacle: over six million people come each year to this town of fewer than eighteen thousand inhabitants. Lourdes' nod to high culture comes each April, when various local churches host an **International Festival of Sacred Music**.

## The cult of Lourdes

The unwitting instigator of the cult of Lourdes was **Bernadette Soubirous**, the fourteen-year-old daughter of a poor local miller. On February 11, 1858 she was collecting firewood near the Grotte de Massabielle when she had a vision of the Virgin Mary, who spoke to her in *Bigourdan* dialect, asking her to return regularly to the cave. At the penultimate of seventeen subsequent visitations, the Virgin revealed her identity (as the "Immaculate Conception") to Bernadette, and commanded the girl to dig at the ground with her hands, thus releasing a spring whose water would supposedly prove to have curative powers. Bernadette's apparition also demanded that she notify the local priests, have a chapel built and organize devotional processions to the spot.

These visions were authenticated by the Church authorities in 1862, and eleven years later the first nationwide pilgrimage took place, organized by the **Assomptionistes**. This was an ultra-conservative Catholic movement founded in 1845 in response to the reigning positivism, republicanism and atheism of the era. Its ranks swelled by press agitation following the short-lived Paris Commune of 1871, the *Assomptionistes* effectively took over the town of Lourdes, dismissing the local clergy and running the pilgrimages as a going concern. Not coincidentally, from its coup dates the proliferation of hotels in Lourdes (more than 350, second most in France after Paris), and shops devoted to the sale of unbelievable (in all senses) religious kitsch: Bernadette and/or the Virgin emblazoned on key rings, candles, candy-bars, thermometers and illuminated plastic grottoes.

With each miraculous cure – of which there were a number, as witnessed by the discarded crutches hanging at the grotto – the pilgrimage to Lourdes gained momentum. Among early rich and famous visitors were Napoléon III and the Empress Eugénie, making the trip on behalf of their sick son. Ironically, the emperor had ordered the closure of the grotto a few years earlier, fearing public disorder. Bernadette herself had been hustled into a convent in 1866, ostensibly for her own safety, where she died of a degenerative bone disease thirteen years later.

No matter how cynical you may be about the motives of some who manage the pilgrim business, you cannot fail to be moved by the thousands of pilgrims, many crippled or quite obviously ill, who converge here to give their faith a chance to cure them. You see them everywhere, being wheeled about by *brancardières* – young volunteers, many foreign and not even Catholic, who are each assigned a sick or handicapped pilgrim to push along for the duration of their stay. They're interspersed with legions of nuns, priests and a surprisingly heavy police presence (not least to dispense citations to those parked illegally). What impresses next is the international mix of the crowds: Madagascans and *Réunionais*, Africans, Spanish, Italians, Poles, Germans, Dutch and quite a few Anglophones.

The flamboyant, gargantuan double **Basilique du Rosaire et de l'Immaculée Conception**, built between 1871 and 1883 in "Romano-Byzantine" and Gothic styles, was no longer large enough by the centenary of the apparitions; hence the construction of the underground **Basilique Saint-Pie X** dominating the Esplanade des Processions, which can hold a further twenty thousand, with overflow capacity of forty thousand more. But the heart of this Catholic Disney World is the **Grotte de Massabielle**, site of Bernadette's visions, for unbelievers merely a small, dark cavity beneath a rock overhang beside the river, below the Basilique du Rosaire. Inside stands a statue of the holy apparition, which Bernadette herself denounced as a mockery of her precise description to the sculptor. Neither the shoddy likeness nor the modest dimensions of the grotto concern the pilgrims who, queuing beside signs demanding silence (in the main obeyed), circumambulate the cave clockwise, stroking the wall with their left hand. To the right of the grotto stand enormous **votive candles** (700 tonnes of wax consumed annually) left to prolong one's prayer, and bathhouses for immersing the sick. On the left, right under the basilica, is a row of taps channelled from the **spring**, for the collection of holy water in containers of every shape, size and material, sold in the souvenir shops and embossed with medallions depicting the Virgin and Bernadette.

## The rest of the town

The Bernadette story is not the only one about Lourdes. Another tells how, during a siege of the Muslim-occupied city by Charlemagne, an eagle let drop an enormous trout into the famine-stricken town. Mirat, the Muslim chief, threw it over the walls, tricking Charlemagne into believing that the Muslims still had plenty to eat, and duly lifting the siege. As with all good Christian moral parables, this one ends with Mirat being converted from his

Mohammedan ways; he took the name Lorus, which in turn, subtly modified, was given to the city that now bears a giant trout on its coat-of-arms.

Lourdes' only secular attraction is its **château**, poised on a rocky bluff on the east bank of the Gave de Pau and entered from rue du Bourg. Briefly an English stronghold in the late fourteenth century, it later became a French state prison, detaining among others Lord Elgin (he of the Parthenon marbles) on his troubled way back to Britain from Ottoman territory. The main reason for the climb up is to visit the worthwhile, if unevenly labelled, **Musée Pyrénéen** (1hr guided visits only, last departure an hour before closure: Easter–Oct daily 9–noon & 1.30–6pm; Nov–Easter daily 9am–noon & 2–6pm; €5). For the dedicated climber or walker, some of the equipment displays are intriguing, particularly the primitive axes, crampons, ropes and other expedition necessities of the pioneer *Pyrénéistes*. On show, too, are some magnificently detailed maps by Franz Schrader, who first came to the Pyrenees in 1873 on a cartographic mission; he also left paintings and drawings of the high peaks (one now named in his honour), among them an evocative view of Monte Perdido. Other exhibits include costumes and everyday items of Pyrenean life during recent centuries, plus local flora and fauna, mostly presented in tableau form. The museum has an excellent library (which you can use with permission), containing early edition books such as Charles Packe's *Guide to the Pyrenees*, original documents such as the 99-year lease of Vignemale granted to Henry Russell (see feature on p.392), and hundreds of rare photographs.

## Practicalities

The **train station** lies on the far north side of Lourdes, about ten minutes' walk from the centre; there are very frequent services to Tarbes (15min) and Pau (30min). The **gare routière** is in the central place Capdevielle, behind the Palais des Congrès, and there's a not particularly helpful, if well-stocked, **tourist office** in a futuristic glass building on place Peyramale (Easter to mid-Oct Mon–Sat 9am–7pm, Sun 11am–6pm; mid-Oct to Easter Mon–Sat 9am–noon & 2–6pm; ☎05.62.42.77.40). **Parking** is strictly controlled everywhere, and having a car here is a distinct liability. **Tarbes-Ossun-Lourdes International Airport**, some 10km north, has only one regular daily bus service, timed to coincide with the domestic flight from Paris, but there are services to Tarbes roughly every hour along the main N21, which pass within a kilometre or so of the airport.

There's an abundance of fairly indistinguishable **accommodation** in Lourdes – some two hundred two- and three-star hotels (mostly ❸), concentrated in the small central streets close to the castle. Establishment names like *Christ Roi*, *Golgotha* and *Calvaire* give a clue as to the usual clientele; for a slightly upmarket hotel choice, in a "normal" part of town opposite the food *halles* at 21 place du Champs-Commun, try the two-star, Logis de France affiliate *Hôtel d'Albret* (☎05.62.94.75.00, ✉albret.taverne.lourdes@libertysurf.fr; ❸), with the co-managed *Taverne de Bigorre* on the ground floor offering a range of *menus* (€15 for 3 hearty courses; €23, 4 courses). Most hotels require half-board, so there are few decent independent eateries in town. A good budget choice is *Hôtel Relais des Crêtes*, at 72 avenue Alexandre-Marqui on the Tarbes side of town (☎05.62.42.18.56; closed Nov to late March; ❷), more of a guesthouse with simple rooms overlooking a courtyard. **Hostel** accommodation is provided by the *Centre Pax Christi* (☎05.62.94.00.66, ☎05.62.42.94.44; April to mid-Oct), route de la Forêt, on the western edge of town. The most central **campsite** is the *Poste* (☎05.62.94.40.35; April to mid-Oct) in rue de Langelle, just south of the train station, though it's cramped and has had hot-water problems in the past.

## Excursions around Lourdes

If you want to stay in Lourdes briefly before heading into the mountains, there are a number of **excursions** to be made around the town, albeit expensive and overcrowded ones. For good views with minimum effort, take the *téléphérique* up the 791-metre-high **Pic le Béout** (Easter to mid-Oct daily 9am–noon & 2–6pm), reached from avenue Francis Lagardère, at the southern end of town. While there, you may like to visit **Gouffre Béout** (same hours), an 82-metre-deep cave discovered, with a number of prehistoric tools inside, by Norbert Casteret in 1938; there's not a lot to see now, and it gets very busy. The other transport-assisted "climb" is up 948-metre **Pic du Jer** (Easter–Oct daily 10am–6pm; €7.50 return, €5.50 one-way), a funicular ride to another panoramic view; you can easily walk down, following a well-marked trail.

For a short trip out of town, head 4km west to **Lac de Lourdes**, a pretty though somewhat oversubscribed picnic spot; there are local buses along the main D937 to Pau. Twelve kilometres further you come to the **Grottes de Bétharram** (March 25–Oct 25 daily 9am–noon & 1.30–5.30pm; Feb 1–March 25 Mon–Fri tours 2.30 & 4pm only; ℡05.62.41.80.04 or Ⓦ www.grottes-de-betharram.com; €8), where barges and trains provide rides through 5km of underground galleries. The name of the caves derives from the Bigourdan phrase *Bét Arram*, meaning "beautiful branch": legend has it that the Virgin Mary saved a young girl from drowning here in the Gave de Pau by throwing a branch to her.

Close to the caves are two **accommodation** choices superior to anything available in Lourdes – and they could just about serve as a base for visiting Pau. The ridgetop *Ferme Campseissillou* (℡05.62.41.80.92, Ⓔmarie-luce.arramonde@wanadoo.fr; reservations mandatory; ❷), 4km by a narrow mountain lane north of **SAINT-PÉ-DE-BIGORRE**, offers five modernized, en-suite rooms in a converted barn with sweeping views, a warm welcome, and good breakfasts. In the centre of Saint-Pé, *Le Grand Cèdre*, 6 rue du Barry (℡05.62.41.82.04, Ⓕ05.62.41.85.89; ❹), is a bit more sumptuous: a seventeenth-century mansion combining original floors and furnishings with modern bathrooms in its large suites. There's a garden, with the monumental cedar of the name, and *table d'hôte* suppers (€20). Saint-Pé itself is sleepy, with an aptly named central place des Arcades, though the parish church is of little interest.

# The upper Gave de Pau

The upper **Gave de Pau**, paralleled by the N21, offers a number of potential stops, such as Argelès-Gazost, the abbey-village of Saint-Savin and an aviary of raptors at Beaucens. Both road and river split in the vicinity of these attractions; the most rewarding side trip is from Argelès itself, up the joint **Vallées d'Azun, d'Arrens** and **d'Étaing**.

## Argelès-Gazost and around

**ARGELÈS-GAZOST**, 13km south of Lourdes, is an innocuously dull if rather congested spa that makes a possible base for the lower Gave de Pau. The town itself extends from the valley floor, quite broad here, up to the busy medieval core on a terrace to the west. The **tourist office** (July & Aug Mon–Sat 9am–12.30pm & 2–7pm, Sun 9am–noon; spring & autumn Mon–Sat 9am–noon & 2–6.30pm; Nov–April Mon–Sat 9am–noon & 2–6pm; ℡05.62.97.00.25) is in the principal place de la République (aka Grande-Terrasse), three minutes south of the church. There are a number of old-fashioned but en-suite **hotels** in and around Argelès, most with attached (and good-value) restaurants. The best-value and quietest is Logis de France affiliate *Beau Site* (℡05.62.97.08.63, ℱ05.62.97.06.01; closed Nov; ❷), at 10 rue Capitaine-Digoy near the tourist office, a classic French country inn with the privileged rooms (and restaurant) overlooking an immense, tumbling garden. A bit out of town opposite the spa at 44 avenue des Pyrénées, Art Deco *Hôtel Le Miramont* (℡05.62.97.01.26, ℠www.hotelmiramont.com; ❹) offers the top standard here, set in spacious grounds, with a respected, more affordable restaurant (*menus* €15 and €18.50). For eating, *Hôtel des Pyrénées* on central place du Foiral, which doubles as the main **car park**, doesn't look like much, but its restaurant doles out massive portions of cheap and savoury food. Finally, *Restaurant Panoramique l'Asie* (closed Mon), just below the square at 3 rue Général-Leclerc, purveys good, clean and cheap generic Thai, Vietnamese and Chinese fare.

Nearby **ARCIZANS-AVANT**, 2km southwest by a minor road, can offer the privately run, rather bogus **Château of the Black Prince** (10am–noon & 2.30–7pm: mid-June to mid-Sept daily; April to mid-June & mid-Sept to Oct Sun & public holidays only), most of it rather later than Edward's time; the château functions mainly as a restaurant, with good-value meals, and has a few **rooms** (℡05.62.97.02.79; ❸). Below the church is another hotel, the *Auberge Le Cabaliros* (℡05.62.97.04.31, ℱ05.62.97.91.48; closed mid-Oct to mid-Dec, & Jan; ❸), with views south over the valley to high peaks from the outdoor seats of the restaurant (closed Tues pm & Wed, *menus* €15–24); the best rooms are under the mansard roof.

## Saint-Savin

The twelfth-century **Romanesque abbey** at **SAINT-SAVIN**, 4km south of Argelès-Gazost, is worth visiting partly for its unusual fortifications – the roof was raised in the fourteenth century to accommodate gun slits, the octagonal tower added simultaneously – and for its connection with the persecuted Cagots.

Monastic fortifications in this part of the Pyrenees generally served a double function: aiding enforcement of the *Trèves de Dieu*, the church-imposed truce days between rival *seigneurs*; and acting as a defence against Aragonese raiders. At Saint-Savin defence from irate locals may have become paramount, the abbey having grown rich, unpopular and embroiled in lawsuits stemming from ventures such as the spa at Cauterets. A monastic community existed as far back as the eighth century, and the monks quickly established a virtual mini-state here and in adjacent valleys, along with a reputation for luxury and ungodliness. The contemporary feel of the main church – perhaps the least numinous in the entire range, with little evidence of continued sacred use – seems to reflect this.

There was once a large local Cagot community, and the low opening, now blocked, to the left of the multi-lobed west portal is possibly where they listened to Mass from outside; scholars have concluded that the two granite figures supporting the water stoup in the south transept are Cagots. The organ cabinet (1557) is carved with grotesque faces whose eyes and tongues were

Notre-Dame-de-Piétat chapel, Saint-Savin △

designed to move when the instrument was played, said to be the grimacing visages of damned souls unable to endure the sound of heavenly music. Saint Savin himself, an obscure local seventh-century hermit, is supposedly entombed in the choir. The vaulted chapterhouse north of the church now serves as the entry to a **treasury** (June–Oct daily 10am–noon & 3.30–6.30pm; €2) whose main highlights are various twelfth-century statuettes of the Virgin.

Many visitors prefer the little **chapel of Notre-Dame-de-Piétat** (daily June–Sept, unpredictable hours; free), which adorns a hill amongst hay meadows 1km south of the village. Its glory is an elaborately painted ceiling, where birds perch on floral motifs covering every available space of the simple vault; you can examine them at close range from the wooden gallery.

Saint-Savin village has three **hôtel-restaurants**, two of them on the square leading up to the church from the south: the functional *Panoramic* (☏05.62.97.08.22; closed Oct–March; ❷), and the somewhat clumsily remodelled *Le Viscos* (☏05.62.97.02.28, ⓦwww.hotel.leviscos.com; closed part Dec & Sun pm/Mon low season; ❹), whose *menus* (€20–48) feature game, duck and fish; *à la carte* will run to at least €55 per person. At the top of the village, peacefully set in its own garden, is the remoter, friendly Logis de France member *Les Rochers* (☏05.62.97.09.52, ⓔhotel.lesrochers@wanadoo.fr; April–Oct; ❸), with easy parking, a rather average restaurant but very high-standard, en-suite rooms (half-board encouraged).

## Beaucens and around

On the opposite side of the valley to Saint-Savin, there's a chance to see birds of prey in captivity at **Le Donjon des Aigles**, the ruined twelfth-century keep of the château at **BEAUCENS** (Easter–Sept 10am–noon & 2.30–7pm; flying displays July 3.30pm & 5pm, Aug 3pm, 4.30pm & 6pm; €6). You might feel these magnificent raptors shouldn't be kept penned for tourists' entertainment, but seeing them close up – a trained griffon vulture actually "buzzes" the audience – should at least teach people to appreciate them.

To reach the *donjon* by public transport, alight at **PIERREFITTE-NESTA-LAS**, where SNCF buses veer off for Cauterets (5–7 daily); cross the bridge and walk the well-signposted 2km. Pierrefitte-Nestalas itself, with its belching chemical plant, has little to detain you, except for a small aquarium, **Le Marinarium** (July & Aug only 9.30am–noon & 2–6pm, closed Sun am/Mon am; €6), 50m from the bus stop, incongruously dedicated to tropical fish.

East of Pierrefitte – though the most direct road access is from Argelès – the dinky beginners' ski station of **HAUTACAM** makes an attractive target for a sixteen-kilometre drive, the uplands being a congenial place for red and black kites, sparrowhawks and other birds of prey. The summertime hike east from the nearby Col de Moulata to Lac Bleu (see p.363) is recommended for lovers of solitude, but the downhill skiing in winter isn't particularly – the top point for fourteen pistes is only 1800m, so the resort's open for a month or two at best most winters, though the 22km of marked cross-country routes could be more worthwhile.

# Vallée d'Estaing, Val d'Azun and Vallée d'Arrens

The D918 southwest from Argelès initially follows the Val d'Azun, with a turn-off after 4km south up the D103, which serves the silky-green and gentle-sided **Vallée d'Estaing**. There are some good places to **stay** and **eat** along this valley, many aimed at GR10 trekkers: the well-signed *Chez Begué*

(℡05.62.96.44.83; ❷), just off the road in **ESTAING** village, various **camp-sites** including *Le Vieux Moulin* (℡05.62.97.43.23) with a pool or the more basic *La Pose* (℡05.62.97.43.10), and a *gîte d'étape* (℡05.62.97.14.37, ✉viel-lettes@free.fr; 22 places; all year) at **VIELLETTES** hamlet, with four-to-ten-bed dorms. Last but not least, just below the Lac d'Estaing, the nouvelle-cuisine at *Hôtel Restaurant du Lac* (℡05.62.97.06.25; open May–Oct 15; ❷) draws customers from far afield. Unusually for a rural eatery, lunch is provided until 2.30pm; skip the humdrum *menus* (€15–26) in favour of the *carte* (€29), which features crayfish in various guises, goose, duck, decent bread and elaborate desserts, most defying translation. The hotel rooms are old-fashioned, with toilets down the hall, but tasteful. At road's end, the natural **Lac d'Estaing** is rather too popular for its own good with weekenders who rent pedaloes, patronize a pony-ride outfit and pack out a **campsite** at the southerly corner. The lake is also an important **trailhead** for the GR10 (which sticks mostly to road and track on its way over from Arrens-Marsous), leading southeast to the Ilhéou refuge (4hr), and for an unnumbered path going south to the numerous tarns around Pene d'Estradère (2593m) and beyond to the Col de Portet and its lake.

## Val d'Azun

The main **Val d'Azun** has two fair-sized villages with facilities and points of interest. At **AUCUN**, 9km above Argelès-Gazost (2 buses daily Mon–Sat), the **Musée Montagnard du Lavédan** (daily during school holidays 5pm tour only; otherwise by appointment on ℡05.62.97.12.03; €3) has a private collection of traditional Bigourdan agricultural and household items. The uncluttered village church of **Saint-Pierre** is also worth a glance for its apsidal south transept (the oldest, eleventh-century bit), a baptismal font with musicians and hunters carved in relief, the two-level gallery and sixteenth-century *retable*. Aucun is also home to the valley's main **parapente** school, Comme un Oiseau (℡05.62.97.47.63 or 06.82.54.82.26), whose introductory tandem flights run at €48.

The closest places to stay are 3km up-valley at **ARRENS–MARSOUS**, where the excellent **gîte d'étape**, *Auberge Camélat* (℡05.62.97.40.94, ✉gite-camelat@wanadoo.fr), occupies a fine, rambling old house just off the central *place*, with a few doubles (❷) in the attic and saunas laid on some evenings. Off-season, the cheerful restaurant is the only one in the area offering lunch (€12; noon–1.15pm) None of the more conventional **accommodation** options in and around town is as appealing, with the exception of *Chambres d'Hôte Lucie & Jo Batan*, at the east edge of Arrens (℡05.62.97.12.93; 🖷05.62.97.43.88; ❸ B&B). In the same area is the better of two local **campsites**, *La Station* (℡05.62.97.00.56; June–Sept). There are just two independent **restaurants**: the somewhat secluded *Le Balaitous*, with relatively ambitious *menus* at €10–12, and the cheap-and-cheerful *La Renaissance*, with terrace dining on the main through road. The **Maison du Val d'Azun et du Parc National** (summer daily 9am–noon & 2–7pm; ℡05.62.97.49.49) sells farm products and doubles as the tourist office.

From Arrens the D918 snakes west over the beautiful *cols* de Soulor and d'Aubisque (both closed winter) into the Ossau valley at Eaux-Bonnes (see p.409); a very minor road also links the village with Estaing in the Vallée d'Estaing, via the Col des Bordères, a route also followed by the GR10. The only facility en route is *La Grange du Pic de Pan* at Col des Bordères, a working Angora goat ranch doubling as a **restaurant**.

## Skiing – and the Tour du Val d'Azun

The environs of the Col du Soulor (1474m) are home to the **Soulor-Couraduque** cross-country skiing network, largest in the Pyrenees with 110km of marked trails extending northeast to the Col du Couraduque, at 1350–1600m elevation. For drivers, Soulor marks the start of the D126 north, an attractive if initially slow shortcut down to the main road between Saint-Pé-de-Bigorre and Pau. After 9km, you intersect the walkers' **Tour du Val d'Azun** at **ARBÉOST**, clinging prettily to the flanks of the Val d'Ouzoum; there's a *gîte d'étape, Petite Jeanne* (✆05.59.71.42.50), by the church. Other *gîtes*, well spaced to the east on the same Tour, are the *Haugarou*, near the Col de Couraduque (✆05.62.97.25.04; 16 places), and *La Ribère* (✆05.62.97.09.11; 15 places), at **ARCIZANS-DESSUS**, 3km east of Aucun. The full Tour, which requires at least three days, taking in a mix of open ridge and secluded canyon, is clearly shown on Carte de Randonnées no. 3, "Béarn".

## Vallée d'Arrens: into the PNP

The most popular excursions, however, involve the **Vallée d'Arrens**, which extends southwest of Arrens-Marsous, threaded by the D105. Some 10km upstream along the road, you reach the Tech dam, with only a primitive camping area as a facility. Neither is there any public transport up the D105, though occasionally the local PNP office arranges shuttles for guided groups. The road ends a few kilometres further at **Plan d'Aste** (1470m), right at the PNP boundary, with limited parking for several trailheads serving the park. The paths link up with the nearby HRP, or go to a trio of refuges, and can be enjoyably combined into short trekking loops of a few days' duration. Trails from either the Tech dam or Plan d'Aste converge on the privately run *Refuge de Migouélou* to the west on its lakeshore (2278m; ✆05.62.97.44.92; 40 places; April 15–Oct); it's indicated "2hr 45min" up from Plan d'Aste, though as ever the PNP signboards are pessimistic, and especially with a daypack you'll shave 20min off that. Another path heads south past little Lac de Suyen (20min) to the *Refuge Ledormeur* (1917m; 12 places; unstaffed), "2hr 15min" distant, and to the staffed *Refuge de Larribet* (2065m; ✆05.62.97.25.39; 62 places; June–Sept & weekends April/May), "2hr 45min" away to the southwest. At either hut you're on the HRP as it threads along between the Lac d'Artouste and the Vallée du Marcadau (see p.413 & p.395); the easiest and most obvious hike circuit, using the HRP and link trails, is Plan d'Aste – Migouélou – Artouste – Larribet – Plan d'Aste, which would enjoyably occupy two very long days (best allow three).

# Luz-Saint-Sauveur and around

The double spa-village of **LUZ-SAINT-SAUVEUR**, with two distinct quarters straddling the confluence of the Gavarnie and Bastan rivers, lies 12km south of Pierrefitte-Nestalas. It makes a practical base if you have a car or are content to make day-trips by public transport – though with your own transport, the handsome settlement of **Viscos** is the most congenial rural headquarters, while various other villages either side of Luz, such as **Sazos**, **Grust** and **Viella**, have facilities suited for **GR10** trekkers. For the serious walker, however, Luz is still a bit too distant from the Gavarnie cirque – the goal of any expedition up this valley – to be ideal, despite a notional situation on the northerly *variante* of the GR10. **Skiing** is more promising, with the small resort of Luz-Ardidens just to the west, and much better ones at Barèges further east. The Gave de Gavarnie, upstream from here as far as Gèdre, also provides some exciting **kayaking**.

## The Town

The oldest, most attractive part of Luz is its upper quarter, whose narrow lanes, hosting a Monday market, radiate from the fortified twelfth-century church of **Saint-André**. Surrounding houses make it difficult to get a good look at the church, a classic of medieval military architecture with its crenellated outer wall, stout, machicolated towers and gun slits just below the roof. These were provided in the twelfth century by the Knights Templar and further modified in the fourteenth by the Knights of St John, who appropriated all of the Templars' strongholds after their suppression. A fine carved Christ in Majesty, flanked by the symbols of the Evangelists, floats on the tympanum over the north portal, and a *clocher-mur* dominates the roofline. The church interior proves disappointing and rather cluttered with three huge confessionals, but in the creaky side chapel there's a **museum** of sacred artefacts (Tues, Thurs & Sat 3–6.15pm school hols, otherwise only Wed 3–6pm; €2) dating back to the twelfth century, including a manuscript on procedures for exorcisms.

The **Saint-Sauveur** quarter to the west consists of the startlingly elegant line of *thermes* buildings and slightly pretentious hotels on the left bank of the Gave de Gavarnie. The 21-year-old George Sand visited and was repelled, writing: "The beautiful people strut and preen and talk amongst themselves about their ailments." The spa itself was immaculately redone in 2000, with a kidney-shaped pool and huge windows overlooking the gorge; there's a range of one-day *forfaits* from €16 to €34 depending on the services used. According to local legend, Napoléon III authorized the superfluous **Pont Napoléon** (built 1861), spanning the canyon, to commemorate his illicit conception at nearby Gavarnie; today, with its 90-metre height, it's a favourite venue for bungy-jumping (*saut à l'élastique* in French). He also paid for the Chapelle Solférino, south of the fortified church in the main part of the village.

You can cross the river bridge to visit the prominent, thirteenth-to-fourteenth-century **Château Sainte-Marie** (unenclosed, free), just 1km northeast in the adjoining village of Esquièze-Sère. Although the surviving pair of round and square towers don't fulfil their promise as glimpsed from afar, the château provides unrivalled views over the town; it's a popular picnic spot, with a spring, and an occasional venue for concerts.

## Practicalities

**SNCF buses** from Lourdes drop you in place du Huit-Mai, hub of the lower part of the village, beside the helpful **tourist office** (summer Mon–Sat 9am–7.30pm, Sun 9am–12.30pm; also Sun 4.30–7.30pm peak season; ☎05.62.92.30.30, ⓦwww.luz.org), which can provide lists of long-term apartments for rent. Off place St-Clément, hub of the Monday market, there's a **Maison du Vallée** (summer Mon–Fri 9am–noon & 2–7pm, Sat & Sun 4–7pm; ☎05.62.92.38.38), which organizes outdoor activities, keeps an exhibition of local flora and fauna, hosts films and live musical events on certain evenings and also provides Internet access. Other outfitters include Luz Aventure/Elastic Pacific, for all extreme and not-so-extreme sports (☎05.62.92.33.47), and the town has several well-stocked equipment shops if you're missing an essential piece of gear.

Among **hotels**, atmospheric two-star *Les Templiers*, right opposite the fortified church (℡05.62.92.81.52, ℻05.62.92.93.05; closed May & Oct; ❸), is an excellent, quiet choice with some antique furnishings and a *crêperie* on the ground floor. Alternatives include one-star *Les Cimes* (℡05.62.92.83.03; ❷), 80m downhill from the *Templiers*, and the imposing *Londres* (℡05.62.92.80.09, ℻05.62.92.96.85; closed May & Oct; ❸–❹), officially in Esquièze-Sère, on the riverbank, with private car park and fine as long as you don't get a room facing the road. If you want to savour the spa atmosphere, and don't mind a short walk into town, stay at two-star *Ardiden* in Saint-Sauveur (℡05.62.92.81.80, ℰardiden@wanadoo.fr; ❷–❸), with gorge views from many rooms. The well-run **youth hostel** (℡05.62.92.94.14; open all year), with a few doubles (❷) and a good restaurant, and *Les Cascades* **campsite** above it (℡05.62.92.85.85; closed Oct–Nov) are in the southern neighbourhood, opposite *Gîte d'Étape Le Piolet* (℡05.62.92.92.67). There's another campsite, *Le Toy* (℡05.62.92.86.85; Jan–April & June–Sept), right by place du Huit-Mai, though several campsites lining the highway along the 3km to the Viscos turning may appeal more. Aside from the hotel restaurants, of which the best by far is the *Londres*, independent **eateries** are limited in quality and quantity. One bright spot is Ghanaian-co-managed *Resto Taxi-Brousse* (supper only; reserve on ℡05.62.92.99.08) at the start of the Barèges road, where stews (eg *porc togolaise*) and curries form the heart of good-value *menus* at €13; *à la carte* is by contrast not really worth the extra expense. As for **nightlife**, *Le Central* is probably the friendliest bar.

## Along the GR10 – and Viscos

If none of this appeals, you might retreat to the hamlet of **VIELLA**, 2km east astride the GR10 and above the D918, where you can **stay** at *La Grange au Bois* (℡05.62.92.82.76; ℻05.62.92.95.93; all year; 33 places in 5/6-bed dorms plus triples/quads), a *gîte* run by a mountain guide and ski instructor, and **eat** either there or at the *Auberge de Viella*, strong on lamb dishes, duck and *garbure* (*menus* at €11.50 & €17).

In the opposite direction out of Luz, initially northwest along a northerly variant of the **GR10**, it's a moderate, six-and-a-half-hour day to Cauterets via the ski resort of Luz-Ardiden and the Col de Riou (1949m). The first four hours, confined initially to paved road surface and then dodging ski paraphernalia, is less than inspiring, but especially coming the other way from Cauterets there are some halts to consider en route. **SAZOS**, half an hour above Saint-Sauveur, can offer a pleasant, grassy **campsite**, *Pyrénévasion* (℡05.62.92.91.54), while **GRUST**, forty minutes beyond, supports a *gîte d'étape*, *Soume de l'Ase* (℡05.62.92.34.79; 15 places, 2 doubles at ❷), just opposite the rambling *Auberge les Bruyères* (℡05.62.92.83.03; ❷, ❹ HB).

But far and away the best rural facilities around Luz-Saint-Sauveur are at quiet, stone-built **VISCOS**, 6.5km northwest up the mountainside; the turning's 4km along the D921. Though somewhat out of the way, locals and visitors alike make a special detour for the sake of *La Grange aux Marmottes*, much the best **restaurant** in the valley; the €24 *menu* (drink extra) usually offered, gives you access to much of the *carte*, though certain weeknights there are €17 theme *menus* (*soirée fondues*, *menu gascon*, etc). Reservations in season are generally needed (℡05.62.92.91.13, ℻05.62.92.93.75), as they always are for the two excellent co-managed **hotels**: *La Grange aux Marmottes* (❹) and *Les Campanules* (❸), both offering fully modernized facilities in restored buildings, and sharing a terrace-pool.

## Skiing: Luz-Ardiden

The associated ski development of **LUZ-ARDIDEN**, nearly 1000m higher than Luz itself, is reached by 12km of hairpins on the D12 heading northwest; there are two or three daily *navettes* from the main bus stop in Luz-Saint-Sauveur. Essentially a small, east-facing bowl, the resort musters 14 lifts (including 6 well-placed chairs) – to a high point of 2450m – and 33 pistes, almost half of them red-rated; the paltry number and length of the blues and greens mean this isn't a good beginners' resort, and the predominantly easterly orientation means the snow is usually ruined after noon. The ski *randonnée* is the best thing about the place, with fine ascents of **Pic d'Ardiden** (2988m), and a possible descent to the Cauterets valley.

# Barèges and around

The two-street village of **BARÈGES**, 8km northeast of Luz-Saint-Sauveur about halfway along the **Vallée de Bastan** towards the Col du Tourmalet, is the most congenial base around the Gave de Pau, if you're willing to forgo instant access to the Cirque de Gavarnie. It pitches itself as an all-in-one sports centre, with opportunities for bike rental (touring and mountain), riding, rafting, squash, walking, snowshoeing, skiing – and, above all, **parapente**. Although this sport is far safer than in the early days of rigid hang-gliders, proper tuition is still a must.

Should you be so unlucky as to break a bone parapenting or skiing, Barèges is not a bad place to do it. It became a fashionable health resort after visits in 1677

---

### Parapente around Barèges

There are five permitted **launch sites** for parapente around Barèges, with four more around Luz-Saint-Sauveur; when the weather is bad this side of the Gave de Pau, local outfitters take to the Val d'Auzun. Most of the Barèges sites cluster around the car-park at **Tournaboup meadows** (1450m; 3km east of Barèges), with launchings from the Capet ridge just north (1900–2000m), the Caoubère ridge just east (1900–2000m) and even the Col du Tourmalet itself. One of the busiest **parapente schools** in France operates most days from Tournaboup: Christian and Christophe's Air Aventure Pyrénées (℡05.62.92.91.60 or 06.08.93.62.02; open all year, weather and demand allowing), with English-speaking instructors; alternative schools are run by Didier Theil (℡06.80.65.85.00) and Henri Nogué (℡05.62.92.91.60 & 06.80.73.07.00). Beginners' *biplace* (tandem) **introductory flights** – *baptêmes de l'air* – typically last about twenty minutes before landing at Tournaboup, though competition-level experts can stay airborne for at least 45 minutes. On a two-seater flight, the instructor sits behind you, and controls the rig, exploiting passive (thermal) lift and creating dynamic lift by changing the air-foil's shape through tugging skilfully on various cord-pulls. Your main task is to run like hell at takeoff when the glider begins to fill, offsetting its tendency to drag you backwards; then you just sit back and enjoy, if you can – some folk never get beyond the guaranteed initial minute of sheer terror. Thermal lift conditions are invariably better later in the day, so higher **rates** are charged for afternoon flights; be warned that it's an expensive sport if you get hooked. Introductory tandem *baptêmes* run €40–48 from Capet or Caoubère, €60 from Tourmalet or for a "long duration" flight. Pupils typically need two-and-a-half days of intensive instruction, both practical and theoretical, before their **initial solo flight**.

by the Duc de Maine, the sickly son of Louis XIV, and the waters were considered particularly efficacious for gunshot wounds – a military hospital was established in 1744, and Napoleon made it one of five military *thermes*. The **military** connection still endures: there's an army R&R facility in the village centre, with a mountain-warfare school for the Armée de Terre just opposite – the Vallée de Bastan's strong similarity to conditions in Bosnia-Herzegovina made it a major training venue for the French contingent during the 1991–95 Yugoslav wars.

Perhaps the spa's most significant guest was the 32-year-old **Ramond de Carbonnières**, whose passion for these mountains can be traced to Barèges, where he came in 1787 as the confidant of the disgraced Cardinal de Rohan. Today the **baths** (May–Oct Mon–Sat unpredictable am hours, & 4–7pm; Christmas–Easter daily 4–8pm) themselves occupy a lovely Palladian building in the centre of Barèges, and have been enthusiastically incorporated into both *après*-trek and après-ski routines. There's little fustiness or Fellini-esque grotesqueness to the place, though you do have to cover or swop your streetshoes and don white bathrobes prior to an attendant shepherding you through. The waters, 38°C and sulphurous, are delivered three ways: a communal pool plunge, a private *hydroxeur* tub (basically a Jacuzzi), and a combination jet-dousing and massage.

## Practicalities

The central **tourist office** (July & Aug Mon–Sat 9am–12.30pm & 2–7pm, Sun 10am–noon & 4–6pm; rest of year 9am–noon & 2–6.30pm; ℡05.62.92.16.00, ⓦwww.bareges.com) can supply all conceivable accommodation lists and ski-lift plans. Year round, Barèges is the end of the line for five to seven daily SNCF **buses** from Lourdes train station; private car **parking** at designated lots is thus far free, but in short supply at peak times. There are a handful of **bank** ATMs – the last you'll see heading east until the Vallée de Campan – and a **post office**. Recreational facilities include an open-air **swimming pool** (daily July & Aug 10am–7pm; €2.50), **squash courts** (daily 9am–8pm; €4 for 40min) and tennis (daily 9am–8pm; €5.50 per hour) at the municipally run Hélios recreation centre. A half-dozen well-stocked outdoor-goods stores can supply most needs if you've forgotten or lost an article of gear.

Especially if you're traversing the GR10, or are interested in sampling Barèges' sporting opportunities, a top choice for **accommodation** would be the welcoming, Anglo-French-run *Gîte d'Étape l'Oasis*, in a handsome old building just behind the spa (℡05.62.92.69.47, ⓦwww.gite-oasis.com; 45 places, mostly in quads), with showers in the rooms, and sinks in the dorm; it's co-managed with the *Refuge de la Glère* (see opposite). Alternatively, there's *L'Hospitalet* (℡05.62.92.68.08, ⓔhospitalet.bareges@wanadoo.fr; dorms, family quads, doubles), another high-quality *gîte* at the south upper edge of town, a vast, somewhat institutional structure owing to its past as a military hospital, with original art on the walls and a ping-pong table in the old chapel. Both offer evening meals and reasonable half-board rates, and tend to close Oct 15–Nov 30 and April 15–May 15. Also worth contacting are British expats Peter and Jude at their small inn *Les Sorbiers* on the main street (℡05.62.92.68.95, ⓦwww.borderlinehols.com; closed Sept 25–Dec 25 & April 1–May 15; ❸); all rooms have shower, some fully en-suite. Half-board rates (❺) are encouraged for excellent gourmet suppers (vegetarian on request) nightly except Wednesday. They're mostly geared to one-week, pre-booked summer hiking and winter skiing holidays, but are happy to take walk-ins space permitting, including them in all activities.

The main through road is lined with a half-dozen gracefully ageing **hotels**, all fairly similar in standard and opening season (May–Oct & mid-Dec to early April). The most modest are no-star but en-suite *Castets d'Ayré* (℡05.62.92.68.17, ✉jean-claude.cueff@wanadoo.fr; all year; ❷), near the lower end of town, and the more central *De la Poste* (℡05.62.92.68.37, ℻05.62.92.69.58; ❷); among the others, *La Montagne Fleurie* (℡05.62.92.68.50, ℻05.62.92.17.53; ❸) was thoroughly renovated in 2002 without losing most of its repeat clientele. Barèges has just one **campsite**, the high-standard *La Ribère* (℡05.62.92.69.01; closed Oct 15–Dec 15), at the downhill end of town.

Independent **restaurants** in the town itself are limited; the best of these by far is friendly *La Rozell*, opposite the lift-pass vendors: pricey (€23 *menu*) but well-presented *crêpes, galettes*, meat and fish dishes, with booking recommended (℡05.62.92.67.61). The closest "out-of-town" choices are *Auberge la Couquelle*, by the roadside just below Tournaboup, with fairly pricey *à la carte* grills but a good-value, four-course €19 *menu*, or friendly *Auberge du Lienz* (aka *Chez Louisette*; closed early May & Nov), a venerable institution serving hearty *menus* from €22, typically four courses with *garbure*; duck, pigeon, boar or fish as mains; a cheese platter and a tart. Weather permitting, they set outdoor tables year-round near the end of various ski runs; Wednesday night, it's the starting point of a post-prandial torchlight descent monitored by the local ski school. To get there in summer, head first 2.5km northeast towards Tourmalet, then 1.5km southwest on the paved road up to the wooded Plateau du Lienz; as from winter 2004–05, it should be accessible during ski season via a new-bubble lift. Local **nightlife** is modest, comprising the occasional cinema showing and a few bars along Barèges' high street, of which the cosiest is Basque-run *La Bodeguita* next to Les Sorbiers, with *pintxos*.

Beyond Barèges the D918 snakes up to the **Col du Tourmalet**, before dropping to La Mongie, Campan and Bagnères-de-Bigorre. At Pont de la Gaubie, 4km from town, is the **Jardin Botanique du Tourmalet** (May–Sept daily 9am–6pm; €4), which has assembled most of the wild flora of the Pyrenees in a single two-hectare site. You can **eat** buckwheat crêpes and light snacks nearby at *Auberge de la Gaubie* (lunch June–Sept only), which flanks the onward trailhead for the GR10.

## Walking and snowshoeing from Barèges

The **GR10** passes through Barèges, heading southeast on an interesting traverse through the Réserve Naturelle de Néouvielle to Vielle-Aure, which is described in reverse sense on p.356. The ascents of **Turon de Néouvielle** and **Pic du Néouvielle** are both challenging expeditions out of Barèges, beginning in earnest at the *Refuge de la Glère*, 10km south of Barèges by track. In winter, the valley terrain lends itself to circuits on *raquettes* or **snowshoes**; the best two begin from beside the *Gîte L'Hospitalet*, and the intermediate station of the now-defunct Funiculaire de l'Ayré; you may end up doing both routes from the bottom as a figure-eight.

## Skiing around Barèges

In a snowy year Barèges has some of the best skiing in the Pyrenees, owing to its affiliation with La Mongie (joint pass the rule) and some enjoyable off-piste itineraries; recent winters have seen it with a better snow record than many spots in the Alps. It is in fact the second oldest ski resort in France after Chamonix, and hosted the 1926 Winter Olympics. Barèges had a military-run ski school as early as 1922 and a famous civilian ski club, Société L'Avalanche, whose members have included French slalom champion François Vignole (1929–1935) and Annie Famose (1968 Olympic multiple medallist). The combined resort (ⓦ www.tourmalet.fr, check snowpack on 2 webcams) has 125km of pistes; on its own, Barèges has about 60km distributed over 32 runs – 11 green runs, 10 blue, 10 red and 1 black.

Since 2001 considerable investment has brought much of the ski *domaine* up to date: four new high-speed, high-capacity chair-lifts on both sides of Tourmalet, many more snow canons, redesigned pistes and a revamped beginners' area at Tournaboup. Hopefully as of winter 2004–05, the derelict Funiculaire de l'Ayré and equally defunct La Laquette *télécabine* will be replaced by a new bubble-lift from behind the tourist office to the Plateau de Lienz, with a high-speed chair lift thence to La Laquette. Failing that, you'll have to use the half-hourly shuttle bus (included in lift passes) up to Tournaboup and (usually) Tourmalet-West, also known as "the bunker" after the architecture of its much-improved restaurant.

Beginning from **Tournaboup** (1450m; parking), the eponymous chair-lift gets you up to the Laquette sector, with higher intermediate runs accessed by drag lifts and blue/green-piste descents through the trees. The link with the Tourmalet-West sector is effected by the high-speed six-seater up to Caoubère (2106m) and the blue Bastan run down from there to the "bunker" (1750m; more parking). When the snow level is low enough, it's even possible for strong beginners to ski all the way back down to the village over two consecutive, monstrously long blue-green runs. Otherwise, at **Tourmalet-West** another high-speed lift gets you to the pass proper, and the link with La Mongie's **Tourmalet-East** sector, which – being sheltered from frequent warm southwest winds – holds snow better. The other main highlights of La Mongie are profiled on p.365.

# The Gavarnie region

South of Luz-Saint-Sauveur, the D921 follows the Gave de Gavarnie 20km upstream to its source – the superlative-laden **Cirque de Gavarnie**, a glacial bowl which first sparked tourist interest in the Pyrenees. Its heyday began in the late nineteenth century, after enraptured Romantics like Victor Hugo lauded it in almost self-parodying prose – "It's the most mysterious of buildings, by the most mysterious of architects; it's Nature's Colosseum, it's Gavarnie!" – and hyperbole, estimating its height as "ten miles" and length as "ten leagues". Such publicity drew increasing crowds to the area, reaching a record two million visitors during 1958. Since then, the annual number of visitors has fallen by 75 percent, thanks perhaps to the boom in overseas travel; the cirque and its environs have thus gained a bit of breathing space, while the creation of the national park has been the occasion for tidying up and a proclaimed, though not always effected, improvement of services in **Gavarnie village**.

It's also possible to stay 9km below Gavarnie, in somewhat calmer **Gèdre**. From there you have easy road access to two other cirques: wide and ethereal **Troumouse** and lonely **Estaubé**. Most people head straight for Gavarnie (45min by bus from Luz), but anyone with a couple of days to spare can traverse all three cirques, one of the most extraordinary hiking experiences in the Pyrenees. Alternatively, two of the cirques provide access to the Ordesa region in Spain – via the **Brèche de Roland** from Gavarnie, and the **Brèche de**

Tuquerouye from Estaubé. Gavarnie village is also the base camp for approaches to Vignemale peak on the more-used, higher, southerly variant of the GR10, which then curves north towards Cauterets. For any such explorations you'll want the 1:50,000 Carte de Randonnées map no. 4, "Bigorre".

## Gèdre and its cirques

Purists can walk south from Luz to Gavarnie in a day along the GR10, but since it's mostly within sight of the D921 road you may as well take the bus at least as far as **GÈDRE** (12km). Almost entirely dependent on nearby electricity-generating installations, Gèdre has no great attraction other than convenience as a base for visiting the nearby Troumouse and Estaubé cirques, but it does hold a place in Pyrenean history as the home of Henri Cazaux and Bernard Guillembet, the guides who in 1837 became the first to climb Vignemale. One of the dynamos, the **Central de Pragnères**, 4km downstream, is home to a worthwhile **museum** (Mon–Fri 7.30am–8pm; free). However, your preferred strategy should be to visit the **turbine hall** itself, the largest in these mountains (July & Aug 2–6pm, small group tours; Sept–June by arrangement on ☎05.62.92.46.66).

Gèdre has a **tourist office** (summer Mon–Sat 9am–noon & 3–7pm, Sun 9am–noon; winter 8.30am–12.30pm & 2.30–6.30pm, Sun 8.30am–1pm; ☎05.62.92.48.05). If you want to **stay**, choose between the two Logis de France members: *Hôtel Les Pyrénées* (☎05.62.92.48.51, ℱ05.62.92.49.64; closed mid-Nov to mid-Dec; ❹) in what passes for the village centre; and the characterful, walnut-wood-furnished *Hôtel La Brèche de Roland* (☎05.62.92.48.54, ℱ05.62.92.46.05; closed late April & mid-Oct to Christmas; ❸), also on the through road, with a good, affordable restaurant (*menus* from €15.50). There are a half-dozen campsites of varying standards above and below the village, plus a pair of highly rated **gîtes d'étape** on the outskirts: *Le Saugué* (☎05.62.92.48.73; closed Nov–April), also with camping space, and *L'Escapade* (☎05.69.92.49.37, ✉hlasserre@wanadoo.fr; all year; 28 places in 3 dorms). As for independent **restaurants**, *La Grotte* at a bend in the road just above *Hôtel La Brèche de Roland* might look and feel like a tourist trap, but it offers an excellent buffet lunch for €14, serves until 3pm and has outdoor seating with a view of the cascade and grotto of the name in the river just below.

### Héas and the Cirque de Troumouse

For the **Cirque de Troumouse**, 15km from Gèdre, take the minor D922 to the east, which starts just south of the village. After 8km you reach the hamlet of **HÉAS**, a collection of farmsteads around a pilgrimage chapel. Until the road was opened in the 1950s – and a branch of the HRP was routed through here from Barroude and Gavarnie (see below) – this must have been a lonely spot indeed; it's still one of the highest (1500m) permanently inhabited places in the Pyrenees.

*Chambres d'hôte*, camping space and simple meals are available at *La Chaumière*, just below the hamlet (☎05.62.92.48.72; May–Oct; ❷), or at the en-suite *Auberge de la Munia*, in Héas proper by the church (☎05.62.92.48.39; April–Nov; ❷). Beyond the toll post (€4 per car; staffed 9am–5pm), the road climbs steeply in hairpins 4km to the *Auberge de Maillet* (☎05.62.92.48.97; June to mid-Oct; dorm plus doubles ❷), ending 3km later at an enormous car park, still not big enough to accommodate all visitors on a summer's day. Walkers avoid both toll and tarmac by using a clear path up the easterly Touyères ravine starting near the *Snack Bar Le Refuge*, by the toll booth.

All around the car park, the desolate, wild cirque stretches 10km from end to end, not as high-walled but much bigger than Gavarnie's and, in bad weather, rather intimidating. In better conditions it's a magical spot early or late in the day, when the day-trippers have gone – and even more so in late winter, when you can get in on snowshoes or skis and have it all to yourself.

Beneath the eastern walls of the cirque are scattered a half-dozen glacial tarns, the **Lacs des Aires**; a marked path describes a circuit of them from Héas (2hr up) or the top car park (30min away), snaking through the pastures spangled with wildflowers (ranunculus, gentian and colchicum the most prominent) and divided by rivulets. The air is full of small alpine birds, and the turf, despite national-park status, is grazed by hundreds of cows and sheep as in centuries past. A 2138-metre knoll topped by a nineteenth-century statue of the Virgin, some fifteen minutes' walk northeast of the parking lot, affords the best view possible of the place.

### The Cirque d'Estaubé – and hiking to Gavarnie

The relatively small **Cirque d'Estaubé** lies at the head of the next valley west of Troumouse. You can walk there within two hours from the *Auberge de Maillet*, but the easiest way of reaching it involves backtracking 2km from Héas to the mouth of the Estaubé valley, and then climbing the D176 side road up to the **Barrage des Gloriettes**. From there, the cirque is 4km further south along a narrow, cliff-lined glen, remote and little visited except by hikers on the HRP which goes through here, linking Gavarnie and Héas. An ice-choked gulley – approached by an easier side trail from the HRP – leads finally to the **Brèche de Tuquerouye/Brecha de Tucarroya**, at the top of the cirque at its western end (see below for detailed instructions on getting through it).

Continuing west, the **HRP** – just below the cirque and marked by a few cairns – climbs sharply in zigzags to the notch-like **Hourquette d'Alans** (2430m), from where the *Refuge des Espuguettes* can be glimpsed below (see "The Cirque de Gavarnie"); to reach it (under an hour), the path first descends slowly north, then steeply westwards in more zigzags, completing a relatively easy trekking day.

## Gavarnie

At first glance **GAVARNIE**, 8km upstream from Gèdre, is nothing but a tacky collection of ramshackle souvenir kiosks and snack bars, besieged in summer by hordes scarcely less numerous than at Lourdes. A huge, earth-surface, high-season car park (€3) at the entrance to the village is a reflection of the prevailing commercialization. Once the trippers have departed in their cars or swarms of tour coaches, Gavarnie's pavements roll up promptly at 8pm, having been first cleared of the huge piles of ordure from the horses, donkeys and mules used to carry tourists up for a quick look at the cirque.

Yet almost every house and hotel here has some connection with two centuries of Pyrenean exploration, which goes some way towards justifying the village's nickname, "Chamonix of the Pyrenees". Beside the Romanesque church, last prayer stop for pilgrims along this minor branch of the Santiago route before crossing into Spain, are buried great early climbers such as Jean Arlaud and the Passet family of guides.

### Practicalities

Gavarnie's *Hôtel des Voyageurs* counted among its guests the mountaineers Henry Russell, Charles Packe and Francis Swan, as well as George Sand,

Gustave Flaubert, Victor Hugo and his mistress Juliette Drouet. Rumour has it that Hortense de Beauharnais conceived the future Napoléon III in one of its bedrooms on the night of August 24, 1807 – the father a Gavarnie shepherd. Alas, this illustrious history failed to save the hotel from hard times and subsequent conversion into apartments in 2003. Currently the best value among six survivors here is offered by Logis de France affiliate *Hôtel Le Marboré* (T05.62.92.40.40, W www.lemarbore.com; ❸–❹) on the main street, and the small but well-placed *Hôtel Compostelle* by the church (T05.62.92.49.43, W www.compostellehotel.com; closed Oct–Christmas; ❷), where most rooms face the cirque, with skylights in the top-floor ones. The modern, less characterful *Hôtel Le Taillon* (T05.62.92.48.20, W www.letaillon.com; closed Nov 1–Dec 15; ❷–❸) offers easy parking and hearty breakfasts.

**Chambres d'hôte** include *La Chaumière*, 500m from the village centre on the way to the cirque (T05.62.92.48.08; closed Nov–Christmas; ❷), with an attractive breakfast bar overlooking the river; and *Jeanine Fernandes*, on the opposite (northern) outskirts, situated up on a knoll (T05.62.92.47.41; April–Nov; ❷). **Hostel**-type arrangements are provided by *Le Gypaète* (T05.62.92.40.61; all year; 45 places in 7 dorms), a fancy *gîte d'étape* near the tourist office, and the CAF refuge *Les Granges de Holle* (T05.62.92.48.77, E josephthirant@wanadoo.fr; closed Nov), 2km out on the road towards the ski station. This is also a convivial and reasonable place to eat or just share a fireside glass of *eau de vie*. As of writing the only surviving independent **restaurant** in Gavarnie village is *Le P'tit Toy* (closed Nov 15–Dec 15) on rue de l'Église just behind *Hôtel Taillon*, with panoramic upstairs seating, quick service and two appetizing *menus* below €19.

The closest **campsite** is *La Bergerie* (T05.62.92.48.41; mid-May to Oct 1) on the east bank of the river 600m above the village; facilities are exceedingly basic, and the ground sloping, but there are unbeatable views up into the cirque, and a breakfast bar. The other local site, *Le Pain de Sucre* (T05.62.92.47.55; June–Sept & Christmas–Easter), is marginally more comfortable (hot water, charged extra) but inconvenient, 3.5km north of the village en route for Gèdre.

The **tourist office** has premises at the entrance to the village (Mon–Fri 9am–noon & 1.30–6.30pm, Sat & Sun 9am–12.30pm & 1.30–6.30pm; T05.62.92.49.10, W www.gavarnie.com); the central **Maison du Parc** (during term time Tues–Sat 9.30am–noon & 1.30–6pm; school hols Mon–Sat 10am–noon & 2–6pm; T05.62.92.42.48), in addition to hiking and wildlife information, plus weather reports, occasionally organizes guided walks. For **snow conditions**, ask the CRS mountain rescue unit opposite *La Bergerie*. There's a Crédit Agricole **ATM** beside the Maison du Parc, and a **post office** nearby.

## Skiing: Gavarnie-Gèdre

Although it doesn't compare in size with Barèges-La Mongie, **Gavarnie-Gèdre** rates as one of the great ski *domaines* of the Pyrenees on account of its snow record and wonderful situation. The resort gets its weather from the south, so has plenty of snow when the rest of the French Pyrenees has little or none (though the reverse is also true). Owing to its exposure, it is an especially cold spot, with high winds often stopping the lifts. When you get off the top lift and ski out from behind the concealing summit of 2400-metre Pic des Tentes, you have spellbinding views towards the cirque; from this lift you can also set off on some of the best *ski-randonnées* in the range, including a tour through the Brèche de Roland (see p.389) into the Parque Nacional de Ordesa in Spain.

Otherwise, Gavarnie-Gèdre is a good beginners' and intermediates' downhill resort; three of the seven green runs are longish and descend from the high slopes, though the five surviving blue runs are less satisfactory. Seven red and two black pistes, out of a total of 22, plus 11 lifts (3 high-speed) round out the tally of facilities (there's no ski hire, so you'll need to come prepared).

## The Cirque de Gavarnie

Approaching from the north along the D921, your first, unforgettable sight of the **Cirque de Gavarnie** comes on the road just above Gèdre, from where the Brèche de Roland – the famous gap at the west side – is clearly visible. Close up, the cirque is revealed as one of Europe's most stupendous natural spectacles, scoured by glaciation into an almost perfect semicircle, 1400m from top to bottom and 890m in diameter. Despite appearances, the palisades are neither completely vertical nor uniform, actually rising in three stages – a layer of granite sandwiched between two limestone beds – separated by sloping terraces, banked by snow and ice. A main **waterfall** – a straight drop during spring, two separate cataracts later in the year – plus numerous smaller ones embellish the great wall. It has now been classified by UNESCO has a World Heritage Site, which should ensure that the meadows between Gavarnie and the cirque (a distance of 4km) should remain unspoiled.

### Visiting the cirque

Ever since Charles Packe wrote in 1867 of "travellers to the cirque who have the indolence and bad taste" to take horses, there has been a tendency to scorn the *muletiers*. But if you do mount up you'll at least be supporting a traditional source of employment, important to most families in a village where lack of work is driving young people away. The *muletiers* jog alongside you for safety, making up to five trips a day. If, as a hiker, you'd rather not share the trail with them – both the crowds and the manure can be overpowering between 9am and 5pm – you can use another, calmer trail along the west bank of the *gave*, below the pilgrim route to the pass.

Either way, on foot it takes nearly an hour to enter the confines of the cirque. The broad, well-trodden "dung trail" climbs first to the *jardin botanique*, where there are more graves of *Pyrénéistes* – Louis Le Bondider and Franz Schrader – and then to the **Plateau de la Prade**, a beautiful area of streams and forest – and now the setting for an open-air summer theatre, used during the annual late-July festival. Beyond the plateau, another short, steepish climb brings you to the *Hôtel du Cirque et de la Cascade* (1580m; 1hr from Gavarnie) – in the last century a famous meeting place for mountaineers, nowadays a heavily subscribed restaurant with reasonable meals and drinks. It's situated well within the bowl of the cirque, and should you be there during an electric storm (quite probable on summer afternoons) you're unlikely ever to forget the echoes of the thunderclaps.

From the *hôtel*, where the mule service stops and most clients just mill around, you can hike half an hour up the Oule valley to the **Grande Cascade**, the source of the Gave de Gavarnie (and ultimately the Gave de Pau) and, at 423m, the longest falls in Europe. Above you, the three-banded walls rise to a summit-ridge of nine 3000-metre-plus peaks, curving over 5km between **Astazou** (3017m) in the east and **Le Casque/El Casco** (3006m) in the west. The ridge – the border between Spain and France – is festooned by the shrunken remnants of the glaciers that formed the amphitheatre, some of the last six square kilometres of glacier remaining in the entire Pyrenees.

Inaccessible though it may seem, the cirque is traced by **climbing routes**, and with modern rope technique, more climbers are overcome by heatstroke than are injured in falls. In winter, the ice routes attract daredevils who jab and stab their way up the frozen waterfalls on twelve-point crampons.

## Alternative return route

Rather than retrace your steps, the most pleasant way back to Gavarnie, starting just behind and above the *Hôtel du Cirque*, is via the marked path up to the meadow-set *Refuge de Pailla* (1760m; ☎05.62.92.48.48; 16 places; open & staffed July 1–Oct 15), the way up a 45-minute corniche route through fir and black pine, with dripping rock overhangs, grotto-springs and fine views.

Just beyond the Pailla meadow, there's a fork in the path. Left and down leads in sharp zigzags, initially beside a stream, within 45 minutes more to Gavarnie, but most prefer to head right and east a similar time uphill to the popular *Refuge des Espuguettes*, 1hr 30min–2hr from the cirque (2030m; ☎05.62.92.40.63; 60 places; weekends Easter–May & Oct, daily June–Sept), huge, grey and isolated above the tree line. Lupins and crocus are abundant on the way up, and the detour is amply rewarded by sweeping views west along the frontier crest from Marboré to Vignemale and beyond. With a day-pack, allow an hour and a half for the total return to Gavarnie from the refuge; with full kit you should add a third to all the times given in this section. From *Espuguettes* you can also continue east in less than a full day to Héas, via the Barrage des Gloriettes (see p.386).

# The Brèche de Roland

Every walker in Gavarnie wants to get to, and through, the **Brèche de Roland/Brecha de Roldán** – a curious, nearly vertical gap at the top of the cirque. Tackle it in summer and you'll have company of all ages, nationalities and walking abilities. Such popularity might detract from the experience, but it does have a big advantage – a lone traveller can risk the climb knowing there's no chance of a mishap going unaided. The glaciers guarding the final approach are especially dangerous when there is no snow to cover the treacherous ice, and an ice-axe and crampons will be a big help at any time. If you're able to stay at the *Refuge de la Brèche de Roland* just below the *brèche*, you'll have the opportunity to ascend some peaks flanking it, or visit some famous ice caves just over on the Spanish side. If you do the trip as a day expedition from Gavarnie, count on a minimum of ten hours there and back.

According to legend, the 100m-by-60m gap was hacked out by the dying Roland, nephew of Charlemagne, as he attempted to smash his magic sword Durandal to prevent it falling into the hands of the Muslims. The eleventh-century *Chanson de Roland* describes how:

> *Count Roland smites upon the marble stone;*
> *I cannot tell you how he hewed and smote;*
> *Yet neither does it break nor splinter,*
> *Though groans the sword,*
> *And rebounds heavenwards.*

The battle in which Roland died actually took place nearly 100km to the west near Roncesvalles (see p.506), so the tale is pretty thin, and the startling views from the top need no legend to augment them.

## Approaches to the Brèche

There are three **approaches** to the *brèche*, all converging on the *Refuge de la Brèche de Roland*. The lazy way involves driving up to the **Port de Gavarnie/Puerto de Bujaruelo** (Port de Boucharo on some maps), at the end of the road to the ski station (13km); from there a clear path climbs east under the north face of **Taillon/Tallón**, rising gradually until a gully just over an hour along, where it joins a footpath coming directly up from Gavarnie. This trail, which is the next easiest way to the *brèche*, begins by the village's Romanesque church, climbs steadily but manageably on the western flank of the valley, turns into the small plateau of Pouey d'Aspé and, after a time, climbs steeply again in zigzags to join the footpath from the Port de Gavarnie (2hr 45min).

Following either of these approaches, you continue on up through the Col des Sarradets to the **Refuge de la Brèche de Roland** (aka *Refuge des Sarradets*; 2587m; ☎05.62.92.40.41 or 06.83.38.13.24; 57 places; staffed daily May–Oct), reached in under an hour from the junction of the paths. Situated in full view of the *brèche* and just 220m below it, the refuge is understandably packed in summer, when an average of ninety walkers a night fight for places.

The third and most challenging route, the **Échelle des Sarradets**, takes between four and five hours from Gavarnie. Having reached the *Hôtel du Cirque* you carry on south a short distance, cross a bridge, then bear southwest on a well-trodden path to the west wall of the lower cirque, below which flourish great banks of Pyrenean irises in midsummer. For the non-climber the next hundred-metre section requires a lot of teeth-gritting and not too much looking down – it's not technically difficult (steps have been cut in places), but it is rather exposed, and you wouldn't want to do it downhill. The final section follows the steep Sarradets valley to the refuge.

From its namesake refuge, the **Brèche de Roland** is about forty minutes' stiff climb away, ending with the glacier crossing. Quite often, on an apparently windless day, you'll be almost bowled over as you step through the rock "doorway" and be sent rushing for something to hold onto, while flocks of calling choughs circle easily and endlessly in the gale. Looking into Spain, a high-altitude scree desert forms the summer foreground, followed by the top of the Ordesa canyon walls and then, receding into the distance, wave after wave of dense blue-green forest, turning pink, red, then purple at sunset. Looking back towards France, you'll find the summits barer and more jagged, the light more yellow.

## Climbs from the Brèche

To the west of the Brèche de Roland, towards Taillon, the rock rampart is known as **Pic Bazillac** (2975m), which ends at the so-called **Fausse Brèche** with its menhir-like finger of rock. For the ascent of **Taillon** (3144m) continue on the path beyond the Fausse Brèche and climb along the east ridge. This is considered to be one of the easiest three-thousanders in the Pyrenees but the views are no less exciting for that – and proficient climbers can opt for the almost vertical north face.

The **Casque/Casco** (3006m) forms the eastern part of the *brèche* and is climbed with only a little more difficulty than Taillon, by passing through to the Spanish side and following the path that runs hard left, keeping close to the rock wall. A steel cable gives moral and physical support over a difficult section, beyond which you bear left to the slopes that separate Le Casque and **Tour/Torre** (3009m) – next peak of the cirque – and then left again to scramble up to the summit.

## The Grotte Casteret

Standing in the *brèche* and looking southeast into Spanish territory, you can see a curious dome-shaped rock about a kilometre away. This is the entrance to **Grotte Casteret**, the most spectacular of a group of 32 ice caves of the Marboré/Monte Perdido Massif, the highest such caverns known in the world. Discovered by Norbert Casteret in 1926, the outer chamber requires no special equipment just to look in. But for the magnificent lower chamber, with the column of ice known as the *Niagara de glace*, you'll need crampons, rope and head lamp. Remember that the formations are delicate and you should do nothing that could break ice off.

It takes a good hour to get to the entrance by one of two routes: either begin as for the Casque/Casco (see above) but then, rather than bearing away left, continue around the boulder- and scree-strewn bowl; or descend into the bowl below the *brèche*, picking your way towards the domed rock and then climbing up again.

## South of the Brèche: into Ordesa

Once through the *brèche* you're in the Spanish **Parque Nacional de Ordesa** (see pp.440–441). If you want to explore further – and perhaps make an ascent of **Monte Perdido** – you should head for the *Refugio de Góriz*, two to three hours away to the east-southeast. The terrain is bleak and exposed karst, with no potable water sources, but anyone who can reach the Brèche de Roland can easily get to this shelter. Keeping the bare **Pico del Descargador** (2627m) to your right and the back of the Gavarnie cirque on the left, cross the **Plana de San Ferlús** and follow the valley draining from the **Cuello de Millaris** (2457m). The only difficulty is at the **Circo de Góriz**, just before the refuge, easily negotiated by a path on the north side; if you miss it you'll be confronted by an impassable succession of vertical descents. For outings from the *Refugio de Góriz*, see p.440.

### Via the Brèche de Tuquerouye

An alternative access from Gavarnie to Ordesa lies via the tougher and much less frequented **Brèche de Tuquerouye/Brecha de Tucarroya** (2660m). The first part of the approach partially reverses the itinerary from the **Cirque d'Estaubé** to Gavarnie (described on p.386), climbing from Gavarnie village to the *Refuge des Espuguettes* and the Hourquette d'Alans. Once through the pass, the route drops eastwards in zigzags towards the floor of Estaubé, then – about halfway down – veers south-southeast, more or less along the 2200-metre contour, to the foot of the gully that leads up to the *brèche*. It's a steep ascent – 400m at an eighty-percent grade – for which crampons and axe are invariably essential. Right in the pass itself, sandwiched between the rock walls and looking like a twinned Nissen hut, stands the oldest hut in the Pyrenees, the unstaffed *Refuge de Tuquerouye* (2660m; 12 places), opened – with a lavish banquet – by the Club Alpin Français in 1890. The Gavarnie guide François Bernat-Salles carried a 75-kilo statue of the Virgin up on his back to watch over it. Thoroughly overhauled in 1999 and fitted with a heating stove, kitchen and solar-powered emergency phone, the hut further justifies an overnight stay by its setting and views south to glacier-hung Monte Perdido. If you have a tent or bivvy sac, you could descend on the other side to the camping area around the **Lago de Marboré**, 80m lower in elevation and the first reliable water since the base of the gully.

It's no exaggeration to say that Comte Henri Patrick Marie Russell-Killough – known usually as **Henry Russell** (1834–1909) – was the most original mountaineer of all time. You'll hear or read his name all over the Central Pyrenees, wherever there are mountains worth climbing: there are original photographs and letters of his at the museum in Luchon, and at the Musée Pyrénéen in Lourdes. God, wrote Russell, is a *présence palpable* in the Pyrenees, and he went to extraordinary lengths to achieve a communion with the spirit of the mountains. One August night in 1880, for instance, he had two guides cover him with scree on the summit of Vignemale, with only his head protruding above the blanket of stone.

Russell was an elegant eccentric who threw great parties and did the full social season in Pau most winters, yet who spoke of Vignemale as his wife and enjoyed nothing more than a seventy-kilometre stroll between Luchon and Bagnères-de-Bigorre. Despite a period of far-flung travel in America, Siberia, Australia and New Zealand, he seemed more than content to come home to Toulouse and explore the nearer wildernesses of the Pyrenees. In 1863, aged 29, he bagged the highest peak of the range, Aneto. In the years that followed he made sixteen first ascents, including a climb of Vignemale in 1869 that was the first winter ascent of a major European summit. The bravery and the flamboyance of the man comes through in his fascinating *Souvenirs d'un Montagnard/Recuerdos de un Montañero*: completely impressionist and untechnical, it contrasts strongly with the writings of his friend and fellow *Pyrénéiste*, Charles Packe, who made precise observations on everything from geology to botany.

Vignemale was Russell's greatest obsession. He climbed it 33 times – his last ascent aged 70 – and his passion led him to dig several cave-homes on the peak. In 1882 work began on a set of three caves close to the head of the Ossoue glacier, which soon were joined by two others; a huge party marked their completion, with fine wines and dishes set on damask tablecloths. Within five years the caves had been made uninhabitable by the shifting glacier, so Russell moved lower, carving out the Grottes Bellevue in 1888. The position didn't satisfy him, and in 1893 his seventh and final cave, Paradis, was hollowed out by explosives only 18m below the peak. By this time the commune of Barèges had granted him a 99-year lease on the summit.

Russell spent much time in his mountain homes, sometimes entertaining lavishly – he insisted on guests getting up at dawn in order to witness sunrise, rewarding them with punch at 11am. He tempted people away from the comfort of the established resorts and into the mountains themselves, a relatively new experience for the time. His activities also boosted local commerce, especially for the hotels and guides of Gavarnie, then a poor, pastoral village. It is therefore surprising that, despite his commemorative statue in the village, the caves that Russell constructed are now completely neglected.

# West of Gavarnie: Vignemale and Russell's caves

Any visit to the **Grottes Russell** and **Vignemale** should begin at the statue of Henry Russell in Gavarnie. The statue – a replacement for one melted down by the Nazis – is beside the main bridge, gazing west up the Ossoue valley towards his beloved Vignemale.

The problem with visiting Vignemale from the east (or any direction, for that matter) is that the approach is long. With a car you can drive on road and track along the Gave d'Ossoue as far as the **Barrage d'Ossoue**, but on foot the

GR10 from Gavarnie takes over three hours. It's a wonderful hike, though, first under spectacular cliffs where lammergeier have been nesting since the 1980s, and then across pasture where marmots whistle and isards are a frequent sight. From the simple hut at the dam, the path runs along the eastern shore to a concrete bridge over the Ossoue stream. Beyond the bridge the landscape gets even more interesting, the path zigzagging across a short section of permanent ice at one point in the climb.

About three hours above the lake you reach the dilapidated but aptly named **Grottes Bellevue**, where Russell spent some summers (see box opposite), with fine views south. Another half-hour's walk brings you to the 2003-renovated *Refuge Baysselance* (2651m; ☎05.62.92.40.25; staffed mid-June to Sept), traditional base camp for the **ascent of Vignemale**.

Make an early start next morning, dropping back down the path towards the Grottes Bellevue, then cutting off west-southwest just above them to the moraine at the foot of the **Ossoue glacier**, the largest remaining one in the Pyrenees. This is grubby-looking in summer, with huge and thankfully obvious crevasses; the trodden path runs a little right of the centre. You'll need crampons and ice-axe, and you should rope up as a precaution. At the top end of the glacier is another of Russell's summer homes, the **Grotte du Paradis**: just 18m below the summit of **Pique Longue** (3289m), an easy final scramble (4hr in total from the refuge). There are several loftier peaks in Spain, but this is the highest Pyrenean point actually on the frontier.

From the *Refuge Baysselance* you can continue on the GR10 over the **Hourquette d'Ossoue** (2734m) to the *Refuge des Oulettes de Gaube* (2hr 30min further; see p.397) and thence to Cauterets.

# Cauterets and around

Contrasting sharply with the settlements along the *gaves* de Pau and de Gavarnie, the elegant spa and mountain-sports playground of **CAUTERETS** – 30km south of Lourdes and 10km up the D920 from Pierrefitte-Nestalas – features colonnaded and iron-balconied Neoclassical buildings in its western quarter, especially on boulevard Latapie-Flurin, facing the more traditional part on the east bank of the Gave de Cauterets. A long and narrow village, its surprisingly tall buildings prompted by the lack of flat ground, Cauterets wears a general air of elegance gone to seed; Belle Époque follies lie abandoned or fitted with cinemas, slot machines, bowling alleys and the like, while hotels now superfluous to requirements are being converted to studios or *résidences* at a rate of knots. Dozens of these, plus a few pensions, are only available by the week or the month, some with a seemingly permanent contingent of OAPs, though the place in fact attracts all ages and classes, intent on having a good time. This contrasts markedly with the idyllic alpine setting, and "endorsements" by numerous notables in centuries past.

The town owes its existence to Count Raymond de Bigorre, who in 945 gave a tidy sum to the monks of Saint-Savin, enabling them to establish the baths. National fame came in the sixteenth century when Marguerite d'Angoulême (see Pau, p.399) became a regular, contented client, reputedly penning her *Heptameron*, the French equivalent of the *Decameron*, while here. In 1807 Louis Napoléon and his wife Hortense stayed for several months after the death of their first son; subsequently George Sand, Gustave Flaubert and Victor Hugo spent time in Cauterets, as did Alfred Tennyson, who with Arthur

Hallam arrived in 1830 carrying dispatches for a revolutionary group plotting against the king of Spain. It was at Cauterets, too, that Châteaubriand finally met Léontine de Villeneuve, with whom he had been carrying on a torrid two-year correspondence; when she set eyes on the elderly poet, however, the affair came to an abrupt end. Later, Baudelaire, Debussy and Edward VII of England added their names to the illustrious guest list.

The lush countryside around Cauterets positively haemorrhages with water-falls and no fewer than eleven **hot springs**, with a million and a half litres of sulphur-laden water claimed to course daily through the two surviving *thermes* of César (daily 7/8am–noon & 4–8pm) and Rocher (Mon–Sat 7am–noon).

Cauterets' reputation as a winter sports resort is equally well deserved, with nightly discos and all the trappings of *après-ski*. As a summer resort it's peren-nially popular, too, offering ample opportunities for climbing, hiking and ten-nis. Most of the best walks depart from the massive *parc national* gatehouse at Pont d'Espagne, 6km southwest of the resort: you can explore the valley of the Marcadau further in the same direction all the way to the border and beyond, or fashion an enjoyable loop through the valleys of Gaube and Latour. The same routes are used in winter for cross-country skiing, for which the Cauterets area is perhaps a better bet than downhill activities.

### Practicalities

The town is small enough that you should have no trouble finding your way around. **SNCF buses** from Lourdes (4–5 daily) arrive at the *fin-de-siècle* wood-en train station at the north edge of the centre; the adjacent **Maison du Parc** (summer daily 9.30am–noon & 3.30–7pm; winter 9.30am–noon & 3–6.30pm; closed Sun & Wed; ☎05.62.92.52.56) has a small wildlife exhibition, film shows on Wednesday and Saturday evenings in season and some enthusiastic wardens. The **tourist office** on place Maréchal-Foch (July & Aug daily 9am–12.30pm & 1.30–7pm; rest of year Mon–Fri 9am–noon & 2–6pm, Sat 9am–noon & 2–5pm, Sun 9am–noon; ☎05.62.92.50.27, ⓦwww.cauterets .com), sells a useful guide to local short walks; at the adjacent Bureau des Guides, at 5 place Clémenceau (mid-June to mid-Sept daily 10.30am –12.30pm & 4.30–7.30pm; ☎05.62.92.62.02), you can obtain current infor-mation on the condition of mountain paths and climbs, as well as the weather report; in winter it's the ski-school headquarters. Cauterets is also an excellent place to stock up if you're on a long-haul trek; there's a fruit-and-vegetable market, several supermarkets and bakeries, a laundry at rue Richelieu 19, plus a half-dozen outdoor-gear shops.

Though many of its twenty-odd **hotels** belong to an era when people took half-board by the month, Cauterets has various affordable short-term places, all pinpointed on a placard at the north end of town. Budget options include *Le Centre et Poste*, 11 rue de Belfort (☎05.62.92.52.69; ❷), and the *Gram* at 4 rue Victor-Hugo, off rue de la Raillère (☎05.62.92.53.01; ❷); half-board is encouraged at both. For something more upmarket, all rated two-star, try *De Paris*, 1 place du Maréchal-Foch (☎05.62.92.53.85, ℱ05.62.92.02.23; closed Nov-Dec & late April; ❸), well decorated, clean and run by friendly staff; the old-fashioned but well-kept *Lion d'Or* at 12 rue Richelieu (☎05.62.92.52.87, ℱ05.62.92.03.67; closed Oct–Christmas; ❸–❹;); the en-suite *César* (☎05.62.92.52.57, ℱ05.62.92.08.19; closed May & Oct; ❸) at 3 rue César on the way up to the namesake baths, offering TVs and phones in all rooms; or the *Welcome* at 3 rue Victor-Hugo (☎05.62.92.50.22, ℱ05.62.92.02.90; ❹). Much the best in this category, however, is *Le Sacca* at 11 boulevard Latapie-Flurin (☎05.62.92.50.02, ℮hotel.le.sacca@wanadoo.fr; ❸), at the end of a Belle-

Époque terrace, with a few balconied rooms and far and away the best restaurant in Cauterets (*menus* €13–28).

There are two fairly comparable **gîtes d'étape**: the hillside *Beau Soleil* at 25 rue Maréchal-Joffre (℡05.62.92.53.52, ⓔgite.beau.soleil@wanadoo.fr; closed Nov; 29 places), with en-suite, one-to-five-bunk rooms, and the less regimented *Le Pas de L'Ours,* 21 rue de la Raillère (℡05.62.92.58.07, ⓦwww.lepasdelours.com; 20 places), with a "hotel" annexe (❸) offering basic but en-suite rooms and saunas some nights. On the way into Cauterets from the north, there are several **campsites**: *Les Glères* (℡05.62.92.55.34); *Les Bergeronnettes* (℡05.62.92.50.69; June–Sept), quietest by virtue of its position, across the river from *Les Glères*; *Le Peguère* (℡05.62.92.52.28) and *La Prairie* (℡05.62.92.54.28; June–Sept), fairly close to town and shaded.

For **eating out**, there's historically been very little choice outside of the hotel diners, though the profile is improving, with some new candidates on rue Richelieu. Latin flavours include *Pizzeria Giovanni* at 5 rue de la Raillère, *Casa Bodega Manolo* at no. 11 of the same street, with Spanish-style seafood and a set menu, and the Spanish-attended *Bodega El Julio*, a theme bar-restaurant at the south end of rue Latapie-Flurin. It's well worth driving up to *La Ferme Basque* (closed unpredictable periods low season; ℡05.62.92.54.32), 3km west of town on the road to the ski station; managing couple Léon and Chantal feature hearty country fare (black pudding, wild-spinach *garbure*, lamb dishes, home-made desserts) in their €15–18 *menus*, though it's fine to just have a coffee and admire the sweeping view – or pick up a jar of their own-made foie-gras, pork pâté or lamb-based concoctions. They're also the closest decent restaurant to the Lys-Courbet skiing *domaine* (see p.398).

## Walking around Cauterets

There is magnificent walking around Cauterets, which lies just at the edge of PNP territory extending immediately southwest. The most useful **map** for local treks is the 1:50,000 Carte de Randonnées no. 4, "Bigorre", though if you're not interested in linking up with the Gavarnie area, no. 3, "Béarn", will do. Most worthwhile itineraries depart from the **Pont d'Espagne**, a scenic old stone bridge high over the confluence of the foaming *gaves* du Marcadau and du Gaube (downstream towards Cauterets is some great kayaking), and an important landmark on the historic route across the mountains to Spain. For those with their own car, there are 1500 spaces (€4 summer, free for winter skiers) in the **Puntas** car park at the end of the D920, 7km above Cauterets, in front of the giant PNP visitors' centre, straddling the way to the bridge. Except for vans servicing the various refuges beyond, vehicles of any sort are not allowed beyond this point. Otherwise *navettes* from Cauterets, up the Val de Jéret (summer 6 daily 8am–6pm uphill, 9am–7pm downhill; winter 2–3 daily, 9am–noon up, 2–5pm down; €3.65 one way, €6 return), leave you at the centre. Purists can walk there from **La Raillère**, a disused satellite spa building 3km south of Cauterets, along a fine streamside section of the GR10, pressed into double service as a park trail; it's about ninety minutes uphill along this Sentier des Cascades, under fine woods of beech and pine.

Next to the bridge itself, just five minutes from the Puntas car park, stands the *Hôtellerie du Pont d'Espagne* (℡05.62.92.54.10, ⓕ05.62.92.51.72; closed mid-Oct to Jan; ❷), with functional rooms, and meals served; some fifteen minutes above here, past the base of the *télésiège* to Gaube (see below), the privately run, youth-oriented *Chalet du Clot* (1581m; 43 places; open Dec–Easter & May–Oct; ℡05.62.92.61.27, ⓔchaletduclot@wanadoo.fr) on the broad

**Plateau du Clot** offers simple meals and overnighting, as well as cross-country skiing on 37km of pistes.

### Refuge Wallon and the Pont du Cayan loop walk

From the plateau, signs for the **Vallée du Marcadau** and the *Refuge Wallon* point southwest along the valley, all sparkling streams, meadows and tall pines. At the **Pont du Cayan**, some forty minutes beyond via either bank of the main stream at the far end of the widest part of the valley, the path climbs left through forest to the **Pont d'Estalaunque**, and then rises more steeply to the rambling, old-fashioned **Refuge Wallon** (1866m; ☏05.62.92.64.28 or 05.61.85.93.43; 112 places; staffed daily early April to early May, June–Oct & winter holidays, plus March weekends), which offers a full meal service as well. Although it's barely two hours from the Puntas car park, you gain a real sense of the surrounding mountains, which are ideal for walks and light scrambles of all sorts, rather than technical climbing. Owing to the mild climate, Scots and black pines, some several hundred years old, flourish up to 2000m elevation hereabouts.

If you're returning to Cauterets, rather than retrace your steps you can loop back to **Pont du Cayan** along the alternative marked footpath that heads initially northwest. After an hour, you reach rock-girt **Lac Nère** (2320m), and after twenty minutes further through a chaos of boulders, you arrive at the even more lunar **Lac du Pourtet** (2420m), a sawtooth ridge bounding it on the north. At a small notch on the lake's east shore you turn down and eastwards, passing the three smaller, turf-fringed tarns called the **Lacs de l'Embarrat** (as well as a marked side trail for the Lac d'Ilhéou – see p.398), and just over an hour an a half from the highest lake you should be back at the Pont du Cayan. This circuit does involve a stiff climb, and you should count on six hours' walking time return from the Puntas car park – as opposd to four if you backtrack entirely along the Vallée du Marcadau from *Wallon*. This is, it must be said, one of the more representative – and deservedly popular – day walks you can do around Cauterets; the lakes are all dissimilar, and wildlife surprisingly conspicuous for such a relatively accessible route.

### Treks above Refuge Wallon

Above and beyond *Refuge Wallon*, there's a choice of routes in several directions, the most exciting of them along the HRP or its *variante sud*. You can follow the **HRP** west towards the important frontier peak of Balaïtous, using the Lac Nère approach for about 25min, then veering away west-northwest up the Gave de Cambalès, through bare terrain strewn with a dozen lakes, to the **Col de Cambalès** (2706m; 3hr from the refuge). The HRP drops southwest on the other side to the very easy **Port de la Peyre-Saint-Martin/Cuello d'a Piedra de San Martín** (2295m) on the border, then goes north down the Arrens valley to the *Refuge Ledormeur* (see p.378 for details), a six-hour day from the *Refuge Wallon*.

If you have the time and energy, press on for an hour or so to the more comfortable *Refuge de Larribet* (see p.378) – to reach it drop northwards to the junctions of the Arrens and Larribet valleys, then curl back south along the latter. From either refuge you can descend if need be to the village of Arrens-Marsous (see p.377 for details).

The **HRP variante sud** skirts Balaïtous (3146m) to the south on a generally westward course to the next staffed French alpine hut at Arrémoulit – a minimum eight-hour trekking day. It runs initially southwest from the *Refuge Wallon* along the Port du Marcadau stream, then climbs westwards to **Col de** la Fache/Cuello da Facha (2664m); once through this you're in Spain, dropping down to the north shore of the huge **Respumoso** reservoir. There's a staffed refuge (see p.447) on its north shore, built to serve the Spanish **GR11**, which runs briefly in tandem with the HRP variant here. From Respumoso you head back into France via the **Arriel** lakes and the **Col du Palas/Cuello de Pallas** (2517m) to the *Refuge d'Arrémoulit* (℡05.59.05.31.79; 2305m; 30 places; staffed July–Sept) between the lakes of the same name, just beyond the southern end of Lac d'Artouste. (For more on Lac d'Artouste and Balaïtous, see p.413.)

To go **south** or **east** from *Refuge Wallon*, take the marked southeasterly HRP trail beginning five minutes below the shelter at a bridge, up the Vallée d'Arratille to the **Col d'Arratille** (2528m; 3–4hr from the refuge). From there you could either continue into the Spanish Ara valley, which drains towards the Ordesa region, or head east for a couple of hours – dropping briefly into the top of the Ara valley and then over the **Col des Mulets/Puerto de los Mulos** (2591m), always on the **HRP** – to the *Refuge des Oulettes de Gaube* in the head of the Vallée de Gaube. This is a fairly strenuous, but short, traverse of five hours, with the route well marked.

### Loop via the Gaube and Lutour valleys

The head of the **Vallée du Gaube** is more usually approached directly from the Pont d'Espagne, as part of the deservedly popular, two-to-three-day **loop** back to Cauterets which also takes in the **Vallée de Lutour**. To accomplish it anticlockwise, you first head up the Gave du Gaube for an hour as far as the popular **Lac de Gaube**, with the snack bar *Hôtellerie du Lac de Gaube* at the north end of the lake. If you're heavily laden, a small *télésiège* (daily summer 8.30am–6.30pm up, 9am–7.30pm down; €4.50 one way, €6.50 return) spares you about half the climb. Done as a day-trip, the lake is another "poodle walk" target for the French, though dogs must be kept on a lead and are banned beyond the *hôtellerie*.

From the top of the lift you continue south two hours to the *Refuge des Oulettes de Gaube* (2151m; ℡05.62.92.62.97; 120 places; staffed daily May 15–Oct, according to weather in winter), where an overnight stay is recommended so that you may contemplate the gaunt, breathtaking north face of Vignemale at leisure. You'd need an extra day to tackle the peak from here; most casual walkers will continue east steeply over the **Col d'Arraillé** (2583m), which permits passage to the far less crowded Vallée de Lutour, which here forms the boundary of PNP territory.

The next suggested overnight stop is at *Refuge d'Estom* (1804m; ℡05.62.92.74.86; 30 places; staffed June–Sept), perched by its lake; were you to stay here an extra night, you could explore the half-dozen sizeable **Soubiran lakes** hiding under the crags defining the head of Lutour. The main itinerary carries on north along the valley for a very easy half-day back towards Cauterets, joining the Val de Jéret at La Raillère; about an hour before the latter you meet the end of the narrow but paved road in at *La Fruitière*, a popular **hôtel-restaurant** (℡ 05.62.92.52.04, 🖷05.62.92.06.12; closed Dec & April; ❷) renowned for its game, trout and *garbure*. The restaurant's prices are reasonable – two *menus* for under €20– though quality can vary, and reservations are suggested at weekends.

### Traverse to Lac d'Estaing via the GR10

One exception to the pattern of walks arrayed around the Pont d'Espagne is the day-long traverse from Cauterets to **Lac d'Estaing** in the eponymous valley via the Lac d'Ilhéou, following the main **GR10**. Taking the **Téléphérique du Lys** from just above bd B. Dulau in Cauterets up to an intermediate station (mid-June to mid-Sept every 30min 9am–12.45pm & 1.45–5.45pm; €5 one-way) spares you the sharp initial climb, while continuing on the ski area's Grand Barbat chair-lift (same schedule; €7 for a combined one-way ticket with the Téléphérique du Lys) brings you to the Crêtes du Lys, actually 500m higher than the Lac d'Ilhéou, with an hour on foot separating you from the refuge there (p.396). For a bit extra you can haul a parapente or mountain bike up too. Without any assistance from mechanical lifts, it will take you the better part of three hours, heading up the Vallée du Cambasque, to draw even with the **Lac d'Ilhéou**, best seen in June when ice floes drift on its calm surface and the surrounding peaks such as Grand Barbat (2813m) are still frosted with snow. The modern, PNP-built *Refuge d'Ilhéou* (1988m; ☎05.62.92.52.38; 50 places) at the northeast end of the lake is staffed all summer and also offers pricey meals and drinks on its outdoor terrace. From here the GR10 bears northwest out of the *parc national*, over the grassy **Col d'Ilhéou** (2242m), dropping down to Lac d'Estaing, with its hotel and campsite, after four more hours.

## Skiing around Cauterets

With a selection of circuits from 1300m to 7500m in length, the **Pont d'Espagne** makes an excellent place to hone cross-country skiing skills, and following the route from the bridge into the Marcadau valley constitutes an easy yet spectacular introduction to **ski touring**. The climb to the *Refuge Wallon* (sporadically staffed in winter) totals 369m over a distance of 7km, which should take around three to four hours for beginners; count on half that to descend.

Beyond the refuge, there are possible itineraries into Spain via the **Col de la Fache/Cuello da Faxa** and the **Port du Marcadau/Puerto de Panticosa** into the Panticosa region, or the **Col d'Arraille** into the Ara valley, but these are for experts only, despite their relative ease as summer walking passes. The same goes for the winter ascent of **Vignemale** from the *Refuge des Oulettes de Gaube*, subject to severe avalanche risk.

### Downhill skiing: Lys-Courbet

Cauterets' reputation for **downhill skiing** is perhaps inflated, but by Pyrenean standards it has a good snow record, and conditions aren't too bad even given the sunny, easterly exposure at the principal area of **Lys-Courbet** at the top of the Vallée de Cambasque. It's accessible either by 6km of road from Cauterets, or the *téléphérique* described above (included in the lift *forfait*). There's no ski rental at the **Courbet** car-park (1350m), and often no *navette* from Cauterets, so non-drivers should take the shoe-box Téléphérique du Lys all the way up from town; drivers use the "egg-shell" Télécabine Courbet to the base of the **Cirque du Lys** (1850m; rental, snack bar). From there, four chair lifts (top point 2500m) climb to strategic points on the ridge leading off 2657-metre Soum de Grum – the long, aptly named "Crêtes" run yields great views, though "Gentiane" and "Dryade" are more challenging – but the piste network isn't extensive, and most of the eighteen runs descend to Point 1850. Nonetheless, it's a good place to hone intermediate skills, with mostly blue and red runs, though they're often poorly marked, so it's easy to stray onto the wrong piste – or off piste, for which there's plenty of (intentional) scope.

# Pau

Once capital of the medieval viscounty of Béarn, and now of the modern *département* of Pyrénées-Atlantiques, the pleasant, surprisingly cosmopolitan city of **PAU** lies an hour or less by road or rail west of Tarbes. From this major stop on the main east–west rail line along the base of the French Pyrenees, you can move on to Bayonne and the Basque country, or directly south to the *parc national* through the Vallée d'Ossau. You may well prefer to use Pau, rather than Lourdes, as a base for heading into the mountains: transport is no problem and Pau is a far more amenable place.

The city first rose to prominence in 1464, when it became capital of Béarn (and Navarre) under Jean d'Albret and his wife Catherine of Navarre. In 1567, their descendant Henri d'Albret married the sister of the French king François I, Marguerite d'Angoulême, a writer of some gifts who turned the local court into a focus of the arts. Her daughter, Jeanne d'Albret, was by contrast a Protestant philistine, bringing ruin to Pau and its environs during the Wars of Religion, when her armies and those of Charles IX competed in the commission of various atrocities. Peace of a sort was restored only upon the accession of her son Henri IV to the French throne in 1589, but Béarn itself was not formally annexed by Paris until 1620 by Henri IV's son Louis XIII.

Pau entered the historical spotlight once more with the arrival of Wellington and his troops in 1814, following their defeat of Marshal Soult at nearby Orthez. So taken were they by the setting and mild climate that many of the officers returned for their retirement, inaugurating an English colony that would endure for nearly a century. By the early 1860s fifteen percent of the city's population was English, numbers swelled through the tireless (and ultimately wrong-headed) promotion of Pau as especially salubrious for tuberculosis patients, by a certain Dr Alexander Taylor. Enduring legacies of the English include the continuing pursuit of horse-racing, fox-hunting, polo, cricket, golf (the first eighteen-hole course in Europe was here), rugby and a few surviving tearooms. The English weren't the only ones attracted here. When the train line reached Pau in 1866, the French intelligentsia followed, among them Victor Hugo, Stendhal and Lamartine, who bestowed an epigram on the place: "*Pau est la plus belle vue de ter, comme Naple est la plus belle vue de mer.*"

Although the city has an altitude of just a couple of hundred metres, it's the only sizeable place on this side of the Pyrenees with any palpable mountain identity. From the **boulevard des Pyrénées** which bounds downtown Pau on the south, you can see a hundred-kilometre stretch of peaks, including Pic du Midi de Bigorre and Pic d'Anie, all identified on a handy *table d'orientation*. In the time of Henry Russell – buried in Pau – the boulevard provided the finest vantage point for the north face of the Pyrenees, overlooking eighty peaks including Vignemale. Now the view is diminished by new construction and a nearly constant veil of pollution, but on a clear day it's still an evocative introduction to the mountains.

Pau's atmosphere (in all senses) changed substantially in the 1950s when a huge natural gas field opened just northwest at Lacq, creating new jobs, suburbs and spin-off industries – plus massive sulphur-dioxide air pollution, subsequently reduced ninety percent by filtration, but still problematic. Gas production and related employment is now down, and the field is set to run out within a decade or so. Accordingly, Pau is having to assume new identities – most obviously as a student town, courtesy of the 1972-opened University of Pau, strong on sciences and general research. An almost non-stop calendar of

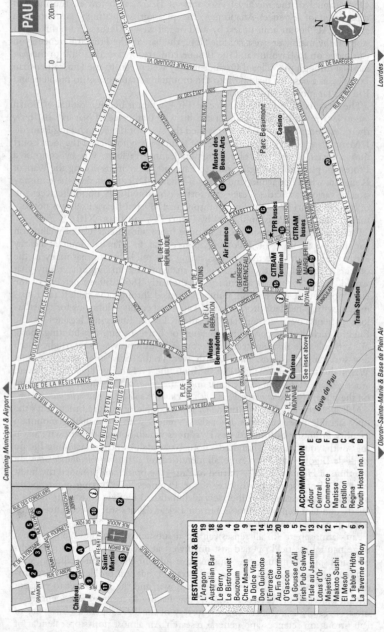

▲ Tarbes

PAU

0    200m

N

◀ Camping Municipal & Airport

Lourdes ▶

Parc Beaumont

Casino

Musée des
Beaux-Arts

Air France

TPR buses

CITRAM
Terminal

CITRAM
buses

Train Station

Musée
Bernadotte

Château

See inset above

Gave de Pau

◀ Oloron-Sainte-Marie & Base de Plein Air

Château

Saint-
Martin

**RESTAURANTS & BARS**

| | |
|---|---|
| L'Aragon | 19 |
| Australian Bar | 18 |
| Le Berry | 16 |
| Le Bistroquet | 4 |
| Bouzoum | 10 |
| Chez Maman | 9 |
| la Dolce Vita | 11 |
| Don Quichote | 14 |
| L'Entracte | 15 |
| Au Fin Gourmet | 20 |
| O'Gascon | 8 |
| La Gousse d'Ail | 5 |
| Irish Pub Galway | 17 |
| L'Isle au Jasmin | 13 |
| Lotus d'Or | 2 |
| Majestic | 12 |
| Makoto Sushi | 1 |
| El Mesón | 7 |
| La Table d'Hôte | 6 |
| La Taverne du Roy | 3 |

**ACCOMMODATION**

| | |
|---|---|
| Adour | E |
| Central | G |
| Commerce | F |
| Matisse | D |
| Postillon | C |
| Regina | A |
| Youth Hostel no.1 | B |

evening concerts and films caters to the student population, while in the centre there are plenty of high-rent designer shops – a marked contrast with the large African and Asian immigrant communities in the north of town, generally as marginalized as they are elsewhere in France.

## Arrival and information

The **train station** (and terminal for SNCF buses) lies at the southern edge of the centre, on the bank of the Gave de Pau. Other buses – such as the SALT service to and from Lourdes – use the **gare routière** on rue Michel-Hounau, north of the centre, except for CITRAM and TPR to Tarbes or Lourdes, which have their own shared terminal near place Georges-Clemenceau. Train services are plentiful along the Bayonne–Pau–Toulouse line, as are SNCF buses to Oloron-Sainte-Marie, from where buses up the Ossau and Aspe valleys are less regular. The **airport**, well to the northeast of town (information on ☎05.59.33.33.00), has daily flights to and from London Stansted; there's a regular shuttle bus to the town centre (☎05.59.02.45.45). Air France, for domestic flights to Paris, has a town office at 10 rue du Maréchal-Foch. Drivers will find **parking** predictably nightmarish (except at lunch or after 6.30pm), though there are often a few unmetred spaces going unclaimed at the far west end of the boulevard des Pyrénées, below the château, and in the streets north of rue Castetnau.

From the train station, a free **funicular** carries you to the boulevard des Pyrénées on its escarpment, opposite place Royale, at the north end of which is the helpful **tourist office** (July & Aug Mon–Sat 9am–6.30pm, Sun 9am–1pm & 2–6.30pm; Sept–June Mon–Sat 9am–noon & 2–6pm; ☎05.59.27.27.08, ⓦwww.pau.fr). Other sources of information include CyberSeventys, 7 rue Léon-Daran, and Cyber Dreams, 9–11 rue Emil Guichenné, the only central **Internet** cafés, and Librairie des Pyrénées at 14 rue St-Louis, a **bookstore** with a good stock of maps and general literature on the mountains but a narrower range of travel guides. Also worth knowing about is a **launderette** at 6 rue Gambetta (daily 7am–10pm), near the post office.

## Accommodation

Following a number of closures, reasonably priced, salubrious **accommodation** is not as plentiful as it was; recommended choices are scattered pretty evenly around the centre of town. The **youth hostel**, *Logis Michel-Hounau*, is at 30 rue Michel-Hounau (☎05.59.30.45.77), convenient for the bus terminal, well run and with a canteen. Of two **campsites**, the *Base de Plein Air* at Gelos (☎05.59.06.57.37; June–Sept), just over the river from the train station, is better equipped and more convenient than the municipal one (☎05.59.02.30.49; June–Sept) on boulevard du Cami-Salié, off avenue Sallenave towards the autoroute, on the northern edge of town – take bus #4, "Palais des Sports", to cover the 5km.

**Hôtel Adour** 10 rue Valéry-Meunier ☎05.59.27.47.41, ☏05.59.83.86.49. On a little-travelled street off place Clemenceau, this has some en-suites, with TV, and parking is just possible at night outside. ❷

**Hôtel Central** 15 rue Léon-Daran ☎05.59.27.72.75, ☏05.59.27.33.28. Soundproofed rooms in two grades ("économie"

and "confort") on an already quiet street, though parking nearby is difficult. ❷–❸

**Hôtel Commerce** 9 rue Maréchal-Joffre ☎05.59.27.24.40, ☏05.59.83.81.74. With all amenities (bar, restaurant, etc), facing a long, narrow courtyard, this kervansaray-like place again has two grades of comfortable, double-glazed rooms. ❸

Hôtel Matisse 17 rue Mathieu-Lalanne, opposite Musée des Beaux-Arts ☎05.59.27.73.80. Rooms here are smart enough, some with shower, others with shower and toilet. ❷

Hôtel Postillon 10 cours Camou ☎05.59.72.83.00, ℉05.59.72.83.13. Another pricier two-star just behind the place de Verdun car park; there's adequate unmetred street parking

too, making this the best solution for drivers. All rooms are fully en suite, and there's a central courtyard garden with fountain. ❸

Hôtel Regina rue Gassion corner rue Maréchal-Joffre ☎05.59.27.29.19, ℉05.59.27.04.62. An even mix of rooms with full bath and just shower at this centrally located, slightly faded no-star; lift to the upper floors. ❷

## The Town

Pau possesses no absolutely unmissable sights or museums, so if you choose you can merely stroll about, soaking up the city's relaxed atmosphere without feeling too guilty. The east end of boulevard des Pyrénées is marked by the twin-towered **Palais Beaumont**, now a convention centre, surrounded by the English-influenced **Parc Beaumont**, with its lake and waterfall. At the opposite end of the boulevard, the landmark **Château** (exterior grounds free and unenclosed) overlooks the crossing of the Gave de Pau on the vital Bordeaux–Zaragoza route. The first castle here was built by Gaston Fébus as part of his grand strategy to create a unified kingdom of the Pyrenees. More importantly for France as a whole, Henri III of Foix-Béarn, king of Navarre and later **Henri IV of France**, was born in the castle in 1553.

Pau was an important theatre of the Wars of Religion, provoked here by the virulent Protestantism of Jeanne d'Albret – Henri's mother – whose activities led to equally ruthless reprisals by the Catholic King Charles IX. Later, when Henri became the French king, switching faiths in the process, he found it necessary to accommodate the sensibilities of his Béarnais subjects by announcing that he was giving France to Béarn rather than Béarn to France. Like other Pyrenean regions that became counties and viscounties in feudal times, it retained separatist leanings even after incorporation into France, and today many of the *Béarnais* still speak their dialect of Gascon along with French – and Gascon-language street signs are making their appearance here.

At the time of Henri's birth the castle was somewhat neglected, only Gaston Fébus's original brick keep remaining in an otherwise grey monolith. The d'Albrets added some sophisticated touches, like the Renaissance windows and doorways, but the most substantial alterations – including the addition of an arcade and tower close to the entrance – were carried out during the nineteenth century, first by Louis-Philippe and then by Napoléon III and Eugénie.

Inside the castle, the **Musée National** (daily: April–June 15 & Sept 15–Oct 9.30am–11.45am & 2–5pm; June 15–Sept 15 9.30am–12.15pm & 1.30–5.45pm; Nov–March 9.30am–11.45am & 2–4.15pm; €7) consists essentially of Napoléon III's and Eugénie's apartments, with their stellar vaulting, coffered ceilings hung with chandeliers, statuary, huge fireplaces and marble-relief lintels. These are expatiated on in minute detail during the skull-thumpingly boring, one-hour guided visit (French only but summary sheet provided), but this is the only way to also take in the vivid eighteenth-century tapestries in the dining hall, with their wonderfully observed scenes of hunting, sheep-shearing, card-playing, harvesting and picnicking. The career of Henri IV is followed in portraits executed at various stages of his life, plus you can see the legendary giant tortoise shell that allegedly served as his cradle.

Just northwest of the castle, centred on the ravine-bottom chemin du Hédas, is the **quartier du Hédas**, what remains of medieval Pau. At the base of the descending **rue Réné-Fournets** is a small square with an ancient fountain and laundry – the only source of water before the Revolution. Today the nearby streets are crammed with numerous places to eat and drink, many of them listed below.

Immediately north of here, at 6 rue Tran, you'll find the mildly interesting **Musée Bernadotte** (Tues–Sun 10am–noon & 2–6pm; €2), birthplace of the man who, having served as a commander under Napoleon, went on to become Charles XIV of Sweden in 1818. As well as pieces of fine traditional Béarnaise furniture, the house contains some valuable works of art collected over his lifetime. At the west end of rue Tran, the arcaded **place Gramont** with its four active fountains is more compelling for most, despite its use as a parking lot.

Pau's final museum, the **Musée des Beaux Arts** (daily except Tues 10am–noon & 2–6pm; €2), lies 500m due east of the quartier du Hédas, on rue Mathieu-Lalanne. This houses an eclectic collection of (sometimes deservedly) little-known works from various European schools spanning the fourteenth to twentieth centuries, arranged thematically and chronologically. It's strong on locally born painters such as Eugène Devéria or Victor Galos – two of the few artists to have discovered the Pyrenean landscape – and Alfred de Richemont, with his intimate *The Sacrifice* (two women burning love letters). But the only really world-class items are Rubens' *The Last Judgement* (ground floor) and Degas' famous *The Cotton Exchange* (upstairs), a slice of finely observed Belle Époque New Orleans.

## Eating, drinking and nightlife

Not surprisingly for a university town, Pau has a fair quantity of affordable, varied places to eat and drink, concentrated in the pleasant pedestrian lanes around the château (slightly touristy) and the quartier du Hédas (less so). If you've such cravings, this is a relatively good place for Moroccan, Indian, Chinese or even Japanese cuisine. The bars and cafés on boulevard de Pyrénées are at their liveliest during the hours either side of sunset; later in the evening, the crowds tend to go to the student pubs or pricey discos near the Hédas multiplex cinema, near the *Hôtel Commerce*. In terms of formal entertainment, the municipal theatre on rue Saint-Louis and the church of Saint-Martin around the corner between them host various events.

### Restaurants and brasseries

**L'Aragon** 18 bd des Pyrénées. An excellent, classic if somewhat pricey *brasserie*, serving from noon until 3pm, and again from 7 till 11pm; outdoor tables are very popular at lunchtime. Seafood choices (including oysters) are particularly good, but also meat dishes.
**Le Berry** south end rue Gachet, near corner rue Louis-Barthou. Popular with a young crowd, who come for the reasonable *brasserie* grub and enclosed terrace shielding from traffic. Arrive early to avoid queuing, though their demi-Chateaubriand with *sauce béarnaise* is worth a wait.
**Chez Maman** 6 rue du Château. A simple but palatable *crêperie/cidrerie*, often with a wait for the outdoor tables facing the castle. A good option for vegetarians, with big salads; for three courses and a bit of cider you'll have change from a twenty-euro note. Open daily 11am–midnight.

**La Dolce Vita** rue du Moulin 13. Salads, good pizzas and pasta dishes, a few grills and Italian wines at €18–20 (*menu* or à la carte) make this the most popular pizzeria in this area, yet service doesn't suffer.
**Don Quichote** 30 & 38 rue Castetnau (two premises a few doors apart). Convenient for the youth hostel, this has Spanish-flavoured fare (*paella, chorizo, zarzuela*) at budget prices – eat and drink for little more than €10 each. Closed Sat & Mon noon, all Sun.
**L'Entracte** rue Saint-Louis, opposite the municipal theatre. Offers a range of original salads and other vegetarian plates at indoor/outdoor tables. Closed Mon.
**Au Fin Gourmet** 24 av Gaston-Lacoste, near the SNCF train station. Several game-oriented *menus* – foie gras terrine, pigeon, rabbit – from €16 weekday lunch, but better to allow €30-plus. Closed Sun pm & Mon.

O'Gascon 13 rue du Château. Currently the most popular and reasonable of the four non-pizzerias on this little *place*; their €25 *menu tradition* – big salad, stuffed quail, free dessert choice – is excellent. Closed Tues.

La Gousse d'Ail 12 rue du Hédas. Well-prepared traditional French cuisine, pricey aside from two affordable *menus* under €35. Closed Wed noon, & all Tues; otherwise daily until 10pm.

Lotus d'Or 1–3 place Gramont. Considered the best Chinese/Vietnamese restaurant in town, with dishes including glazed duck *à l'orange*. Also *menus* €10.50–24. Closed Tues & lunchtime Wed; serves until 11pm.

Majestic 9 place Royal. Cutting-edge cuisine (pigeon with cèpes, monkfish with chorizo and mushroom sauce, *confit* cannelloni) at affordable prices: *menus* €15 (weekday lunch) to €31. Lovely outdoor seating on the place in fine weather. Closed Sun eve & all Mon.

Makoto Sushi rue Tran, corner place Gramont. No more and no less; allow €22. Closed all Sun, & Mon lunch.

El Mesón 40 rue du Maréchal-Joffre. Basque-style *tapas* diner open Mon–Sat from 6pm until late. Closed Sun & all of Aug.

La Table d'Hôte 1 rue du Hédas. An elegant restaurant in a bare-brick former warehouse, spot-lighting lamb, duck, pork, foie-gras and other standard French treats. Affordable gourmet *menus* at €19 and €25, but expect long waits between courses. Closed Sun & Mon.

La Taverne du Roy 7 rue de la Fontaine, quartier du Hédas. Spanish-influenced cuisine, emphasizing salads and seafood; fair-value *menus* €15 & €22, though à la carte a bit overpriced. Serves until 10.30pm; closed all Sun & Mon.

## Bars, cafés and tea rooms

Australian Bar 20 bd des Pyrénées. Pretty much as it says, with decor and TV fare to match.

Le Bistroquet 20 rue du Hédas. Straight-ahead, no-frills drinks bar with outdoor tables in summer.

Bouzoum 6 rue Henri IV. Wide-ranging patisserie and tea room; indoor seating only.

Irish Pub Galway 22 bd des Pyrénées. No comment on authenticity, but it is packed from dusk onwards.

L'Isle au Jasmin 28 bd des Pyrénées. Tea (dozens of varieties) and muffins served outside on chaises longues facing the view. Daily except Wed 10am–7pm.

# The Ossau and Aspe valleys

The parallel north–south valleys of the **Ossau** and **Aspe**, both beginning about 20km south-southwest of Pau, are the French Pyrenees at their most *sauvage*, and the region in which the **brown bears** most tenaciously resist extinction: about a half-dozen survive wild on the slopes of the main valleys, in the **Cirque de Lescun**, and possibly in the adjoining Ansó, Echo and Roncal valleys of Spain. Tourism is less developed here because of unreliable snow for skiing, but what havoc tourism has failed to wreak, a major road-widening scheme in the Vallée d'Aspe (see pp.416–417) may accomplish. Even before this, both valleys were major arteries into Spain. Along these main roads – the D934 through Ossau, the N134 along the Aspe – the steep, densely forested sides obscure everything other than the valley-bottom rivers and the villages directly on their banks. To see the best of the region, you should get out your large-scale map and walk.

Currently the French train service ceases at **Oloron-Sainte-Marie**, though funds have been committed in principle to reopen a trans-border service. Coming from Pau you bypass Oloron completely en route to the Vallée d'Ossau, which has most to offer near the border: surprisingly good skiing at **Gourette**, the touristic train ride up to **Lac d'Artouste**, tough climbing on **Balaïtous** peak, and easier, classic rambles around the **Pic du Midi d'Ossau**. The highlight of the Vallée d'Aspe, and likely to remain relatively undisturbed by the road-widening project, is the **Cirque de Lescun**: not so grand as Gavarnie's, but infinitely satisfying by virtue of its unexpectedness in a much gentler landscape.

# Oloron-Sainte-Marie

The Ossau and the Aspe valleys join at **OLORON-SAINTE-MARIE**, a small town reverberating with the roar of the mingling rivers – and even more so, the roar of traffic converging from three directions. It's the traditional centre for the manufacture of the Béarn woollen **beret**, still considered an archetypal item of French male dress. Nowadays, the single surviving factory mixes imported with local wool, and has diversified into fashion hats for both sexes, though they still make berets for most armed forces worldwide. In the town itself, dignified old commercial properties find themselves sandwiched between modern shops and offices. Overall it's a tolerable, if rather sprawling place, older Oloron poised opposite board-flat Sainte-Marie.

Oloron grew from the Celto-Iberian and Roman *Iluro*, founded on a hill just south of the river confluence, where today's Sainte-Croix quarter is located. When barbarian hordes threatened to take the settlement, the inhabitants crossed the Gave d'Ossau to found the Sainte-Marie district, which in later centuries became the episcopal seat, while Sainte-Croix evolved into a commercial and military centre.

The town's two churches are the sole points of interest for the visitor. Hilltop **Sainte-Croix**, one of the oldest Romanesque structures in Béarn, has unusual interior vaulting, created by thirteenth-century Spanish stonemasons in imitation of the Great Mosque at Córdoba; together with six massive piers, it dominates the two-aisled interior, austere in the extreme except for a few ornate capitals near the apse.

Twelfth-century cathedral portal, Oloron-Sainte-Marie △

## The Pyrenean brown bear

Unlike the American grizzly or the bears of Siberia, the native Pyrenean brown bear – *Ursos arctos* – is **small and timid**, its diet largely herbivorous, which means it prefers to stick to forested terrain below 1800m. (A full-grown male can attain 300kg and females 200kg, but average much less.) The **decline of the bear population** in the Pyrenees has been startlingly rapid. By 1937, when bears had been hunted out of every other corner of France, there were still an estimated 150–200 in the French Pyrenees. In 1954 numbers were down to about 70; by 1960 they had declined to 40, and today there are just 5 or 6 native bears, concentrated in the Béarn region, almost completely outside of the Parc National de Pyrénées. In early 2000 a wild cub was born, the first in the Ossau and Aspe valleys since the late 1980s.

Such facts seem incontrovertible; what sparks heated debate is just why the bears have disappeared. Majority opinion credits the age-old hostility of pastoral communities to the animals, who do occasionally bag a stray sheep or cow, an act which in the past would lead to instant **bounty-hunting** funded by the aggrieved villagers. (This has been illegal since 1962, and the animal absolutely protected since 1981; today the government pays prompt, ample compensation for such losses.)

Rural activities such as wood-cutting, berry-picking, bee-keeping and grazing are also blamed for disturbing the animals. In many parts of the Ossau and Aspe valleys such endeavours are severely restricted or banned, much to the villagers' annoyance, though there has been some cooperation; in the 1980s the villagers of Laruns were allotted a large sum to feed the bears by helicopter and refrained from felling certain groves. Until 1993, national policy goals envisioned the setting aside of over a thousand square kilometres of "tranquillity" – meaning off-limits to humans – enabling the bears to survive into this century. RDP governments backed off from this restrictive approach, and tried to provide incentives for local protection ordinances with grants for local economic development.

This conventional wisdom has been challenged by certain naturalists, who assert that bears actually thrive in proximity to humans. Their habitat is also not quite as restricted as previously thought – paw-prints have recently been sighted as low as 400m, and a den was detected near a roadworks site at Sarrance (350m), proving tolerance of machinery and human activity. These experts consider **depopulation of the Pyrenees** to be the main culprit in the decline of bear numbers, citing as an example the nearby Ariège, abandoned simultaneously by people and bears alike.

The Romanesque-Gothic cathedral of **Sainte-Marie** across the Gave d'Aspe boasts an ornately sculpted portal that has escaped damage by religious vandals – even during the Revolution – thanks to the extremely durable Pyrenean marble from which it is constructed. In the upper arch, the elders of the Apocalypse play violins and rebecs, while in the second arch scenes from medieval life – hunting wild boar and fishing for salmon – are represented. Above the left-hand door, the *Persecution of the Church* is balanced by the *Triumph of the Church* over the opposite door; the two guards above recall Byzantine emperor Constantine's edict of protection for Christians. The gallant knight on horseback over the outer column on the right is Gaston IV, count of Béarn, who commissioned the portal on his return from the first Crusade at the beginning of the twelfth century – hence the inclusion of Saracens in chains amongst the sculptures supporting the portal. Inside the church, well away from the main area of worship, stands a Cagot stoup, a stark reminder of the centuries-long persecution and segregation of this mysterious group (see p.363).

Such revisionists maintain that bears and the country-dwellers should be left to sort themselves out by whatever means, barring shotgun massacres – preferably by fencing rogue individuals away from berry-patches and beehives, rather than banning humans from traditional mountain livelihoods. Unfortunately the truth of competing arguments may not be established before the native bears, for whatever reason, disappear.

"**Restocking**" programmes with "immigrants" have had mixed results. Three Slovenian bears released during 1996–98 at Melles, near the borders of Aran, Haute-Garonne and the Ariège promptly sired seven offspring who all left the area, shunning prepared feeding sites in favour of sheep-bagging. Nearly eighty dead animals resulted before local shepherds shot the main offender, leaving her two cubs orphaned (they died in unrelated accidents in 2001). Though the Slovenian bears are less afraid of humans and more aggressive, the *ariégois* practice of leaving sheep unsupervised to mature into mutton does not help. In Aspe-Ossau, where sheep are milked regularly and closely looked after by shepherds and dogs, just 27 sheep were killed by bears during 2000; throughout the Pyrenees in 2001, only 330 sheep were lost to bears, far below the number that died from accidents or attacks by stray dogs. In fact, a minority of shepherds – in particular the dedicated ones who actually guard their sheep, rather than turning them loose all summer and collecting subsidies – has espoused the view that a coexistence of wild bears and pastoralism is a price worth paying in terms of an enhanced "wild" public image of the Pyrenees with positive impacts on the tourist – and sheep-raising – trade.

The bear has been exploited as a symbol by various factions in the Vallée d'Aspe. Environmental lobbies opposed to the Tunnel de Somport scheme (see pp.416–417) used the presumed fate of the bear as vital ammunition to slow, though ultimately not stop, the project. Tourist brochures for the Vallée d'Aspe have depicted a cute cub clutching a flower, giving the misleading impression that the beasts are as common and locally loved as in North America's Yellowstone Park. And the same farmers and shepherds who execrate wild bears went dewy-eyed over Jojo, retrieved as an orphaned cub in 1974 and long a tame resident in Borce. In 1993, Jojo died, subsequently replaced by two Slovenian bears rescued from a circus and displayed in Borce's "Clos d'Ors" as a paying tourist attraction; the time has long passed since two suitable Pyrenean bears could be found for such a purpose.

## Practicalities

The **train station** lies 200m west of the river confluence; CITRAM **buses** from Pau arrive in place de la Gare out front. The **tourist office** (most of year Mon–Sat 9am–12.30pm & 2–6.30pm; ☎05.59.39.98.00) is on the west bank of the Aspe, housed in the Villa Bourdeu, surrounded by vast car parks.

It's unlikely that you'll need, or want, to stay the night in Oloron, and in any case most accommodation is noisily situated. That said, there are a few reasonable **hotels**: the two-star *Hôtel de la Paix*, 24 avenue Sadi-Carnot, between the train station and the river (☎05.59.39.02.63; ❷); Logis de France affiliate *Hôtel Bristol*, 9 rue Carrérot, downhill from the tourist office (☎05.59.39.43.78; closed Christmas–New Years'; ❸); and another, better-value LDF property opposite, *Hôtel Brun* (☎05.59.39.64.90, ℱ05.59.39.12.28; all year; ❸), at 5 place de Jaca. Of higher standard than any of these is the *Château d'Agnos* (☎05.59.36.12.52; ❻ B&B), 2km south of town via Bidos, a genuine medieval manor with most period features intact, run by a British couple. You can **camp** at the tree-shaded *Camping du Stade* on the D919 heading southwest towards

Arette (☎05.59.39.11.26). Choices of **restaurants** are limited to *Le Biscondau* (closed Sun eve, Mon) on rue de la Filature, overlooking the Ossau, with three *menus*; *La Cour des Miracles* at 13 place de la Cathédrale, cheap and cheerful, with a view of the Romanesque facade; and a late-serving Moroccan, *Samia*, on the Oloron side of the river on place Amédée Gabe.

## Transport up the valleys

Since the closure (in 1973) of the international rail link through the Aspe valley to Canfranc-Estación in Spain, Oloron-Sainte-Marie has been the end of the line for **trains** from Pau. Connecting SNCF **buses** run daily south up the Vallée d'Aspe to Urdos (most of them going on to Canfranc in Spain), and several daily SNCF services, beginning as a Pau–Buzy train, head from the latter up the Vallée d'Ossau to Laruns, supplemented by three through CITRAM buses from Pau to Gourette, east of Laruns. In July and August only, Monday to Friday, Pic Bus offers a twice-daily service all the way up to the frontier at Col du Pourtalet, via Gabas and the Fabrèges dam, with occasional diversions to the campsite below the Lac de Bious.

# Along the lower Ossau

Along the **lower Ossau** between Oloron and Laruns, there are really only two places worth stopping. At **ARUDY**, the **Maison d'Ossau** (July & Aug daily 10am–noon & 3–6pm; Sept–June Mon 10am–noon, Tues, Thurs & Sat 2.30–5pm, Sun 3–6pm; €2.50), housed in the village church, offers a comprehensive account of the prehistoric Pyrenees and an exhibition of the flora and fauna of the *parc national*. **ASTE-BÉON**, a few kilometres further up-valley, is home to **La Falaise aux Vautours** (daily: June–Aug 10am–1pm & 2–7pm; May, Sept & Oct 2.30–6.30pm; April 10am–1pm & 2–7pm; €6), a highly worthwhile griffon vulture breeding and viewing centre, where images of vulture families going about their business are transmitted to a giant viewing screen by cameras trained on nests. Telescopes and binoculars are also available for more low-tech viewing, and staff lead walking safaris to pastures where the vultures feed.

If you have your own transport, a more alluring route into the Ossau starts in the Aspe valley at Escot, from where you cut across over the **Col de Marie-Blanque** (1035m) – through thick beech forests and uplands where more vultures wheel overhead – before descending again through pines to the Ossau valley at Bielle, some 7km north of Laruns. Here, and all along the lower Ossau, the influence of the Atlantic is strong, the fields an Irish green and the forests deciduous. Although it's still some way from the Basque country, many of the villages have a *frontón*, the court used for the Basque game of *pelote*.

## Laruns

The best day of the year in **LARUNS**, 15km upstream from Arudy and 4km from Aste-Béon, is unquestionably August 15, the main festival when young people kitted in traditional red and black – the women wearing multicoloured scarves and the men the local beret – dance to a one-man band of three-holed flute and tambourine. Otherwise it's pretty dull, best kept in mind as the last place to buy provisions before heading up to the PNP. If you need to **stay**, try the dead-central *Hôtel d'Ossau*, place de la Mairie (☎05.59.05.30.14; ❸); the basic *Hôtel de l'Union* adjacent (☎05.59.05.32.35; ❷); or characterful, clean *Hôtel de France* (☎05.59.05.33.71; ❷), with a lively bar, at the end of rue de la Gare, the street leading east from the *place* to the disused train station. There's also a 28-bunk hostel, the *Chalet-Refuge l'Embarcadère*, across the street at 13 avenue de la Gare (☎05.59.05.41.88; 28 places; closed Mon–Tues low season), also offering cheap meals until late. Among half a dozen local **campsites**, the two closest are down in the Quartier Pon, near the old rail station: *Pont Lauguère* (☎05.59.05.35.99) and *Ayguebère* (☎05.59.05.38.55). One of the few independent **restaurants** in town is *L'Arrégalet*, 37 rue du Bourguet, 250m north of the main *place* (closed Sun & Thurs eve, Mon; most of May & Dec), with several *menus* (€11–25) and specialities such as *poule au pot* and the name-sake dish – garlic-bread crumbs sautéed in goose grease – washed down with a strictly local wine list. Another, at no. 55 on the same street – near the edge of town – is the *Auberge Bellevue* (closed Tues eve), with five *menus* taking in both meat and fish. The **tourist office** (Mon–Sat 9am–noon & 2–6pm, Sun 9am–noon; ☎05.59.05.31.41), well stocked with literature on the Ossau valley in general, flanks the main place de la Mairie, sharing a building with the local **Bureau des Guides** (daily 2–7pm; ☎05.59.05.33.04).

## Eaux-Bonnes and the Vallée du Valentin

East of Laruns, the D918 heads up the tributary **Vallée du Valentin** to the spa of Eaux-Bonnes (4km) and the ski station of Gourette (10km), the last stop (after Laruns) for most CITRAM buses out of Pau, from July to mid-September and again during ski season. **EAUX-BONNES**, yet another Second Empire watering-hole, has been spruced up of late, though its Neoclassical central square remains a traffic hippodrome. A seasonal **tourist office** occupies a gazebo on the Jardin Darralde, the landscaped, inclined grounds of the "race track", while the casino doubles as the local cinema. The best of three **hotels** is Logis de France member *La Poste* (☎05.59.05.33.06, Ⓦwww.hotel-dela-poste.com; ❸) in the centre, with well-appointed if old-style rooms arrayed around a four-storey atrium; it's well worth taking half-board (❺), as the four-course *table d'hôte* supper is excellent value. Like many spas near ski resorts, the **thermal baths** at Eaux-Bonnes stay open in ski season (daily 5–7pm), with one of the nicer group pools in the Pyrenees (€6.50 for a plunge or a sauna).

### Gourette

**GOURETTE** is where the *Palois* ski, and the crush at peak times is such that cars are required to use a lower parking area 1.5km before the resort, and their passengers shuttled up in a free *navette*. The development at 1350m is dense and ugly – a dozen or so high-rises below the aptly named Crêtes Blanches – and the altitude means that the half-dozen lowest of 28 runs are often unusable, and the bottom of the Rhododendrons run, where everyone finishes, is always a chewed-up mess. The good news is that most runs face north, so the higher slopes are usually in good shape; moreover Gourette's predominantly red runs are definitely of the blue-ish persuasion, making the entire *domaine* accessible to any reasonably competent skier, with eight well-placed chairs or *télécabines* among 19 lifts in total. Serious skiing begins from Point 2124m (served by the Cotch and Fontaines de Cotch chairs), and Point 2400m, accessed by two successive bubble-lifts. The Pène Blanque run from Point 2400 feels wild and alpine as it threads through a slightly spooky mixed forest; continuing onto the L'Amoulat and Les Bosses runs yields a nice long descent to the base of the Fontaines chair, and thence back into the marginally less difficult Cotch sector. When it comes to **eating**, there's a better than usual range of restaurants overlooking the upper car park at 1350m, but far more aesthetic and perfectly acceptable are two on-piste restaurants.

Among several **ski-season hotels**, the two least obtrusive and most economical, just below the upper car park, are *Face Nord* (℡05.59.05.12.62, ℻05.59.05.14.59; ❹) and *Le Glacier* (℡05.59.05.10.18, ⓦwww.leglacier.fr.st; ❸). In **summer**, Gourette's position on the GR10 and the Tour de la Vallée d'Ossau hiking routes attracts a walking clientele, who stay in one of two **refuges**: either the *Club Pyrénéa Sport* (staffed July–Sept & Dec 15–April 30; ℡05.59.05.12.42; 60 places in dorms or quads), on the main through road, or the CAF-run *Chalet de Gourette* (staffed July 15–Sept 15; ℡ 05.59.05.10.56; 40 places, some quads).

## The Col d'Aubisque and beyond

East of Gourette, the D918 toils up to the **Col d'Aubisque** (1709m, 17km from Laruns), guarded by the Pic de Ger; so does one daily CITRAM bus, dropping you by the summertime café, from where you must find your own way another 18km via the Cirque du Litor and the Col de Soulor to Arrens-Marsous. The only other facility en route, 2km above Gourette, is the no-star *Hôtel Les Crêtes Blanches* (℡5.59.05.10.03; ❷), with shared bathrooms and a *table d'hôte* restaurant, which would be more appealing to trekkers if it weren't slightly off the GR10.

The **GR10** east from Gourette actually shortcuts most of the road on its six-hour way to Arrens, but there's still too much narrow, dangerous tarmac for it to be a really popular stretch of the "trail". East of the pass, the road becomes a dramatic, one-lane corniche route, threading a succession of drippy tunnels; on the bleak moorland outside, shepherds sell ewe cheese amongst the roadside heather. It's best to enjoy the views along the way from your own car, or join the ranks of Tour de France wannabes who make it a point of honour to find the breath for a *bonjour* as they pedal up to the pass.

# The upper Ossau

South of busy Laruns, the Gave d'Ossau narrows drastically as the D934 enters its upper reaches at **EAUX-CHAUDES**, an exceptionally gloomy nineteenth-century spa that makes Eaux-Bonnes seem lively and cheerful by comparison. The lone *curiste* hotel here (May–Oct) struggles to stay in business, with only some excellent **kayaking** in the Gave d'Ossau (subject to EDF water-level manipulations) to prompt a stop.

## Gabas

**GABAS**, 13km south of Laruns, is a one-street hamlet whose farming livelihood has long since been outstripped by its role as an important gateway to the PNP – accordingly here's yet another **Maison du Parc** (summer daily 10am–12.30pm & 1.30–7pm; ℡05.59.05.32.13), with abundant walkers' information.

The best place to **stay and eat** is the *Hôtel Restaurant Chez Vignau* (℡05.59.05.34.06; ❷) at the north entrance to the hamlet, east of the road; most rooms have showers or baths, and the restaurant across the street, with such delicacies as frog's legs *persillade* and prune pie, is outstanding value, though their service is limited even by French standards (noon–1.30pm & 7–8.30pm). Honourable runner-up is the cheap and very cheerful *Restaurant du Pic du Midi*, where you get trout dinners and other local specialities for under €14, watched over by enormous but docile Pyrenean sheepdogs. The slightly overpriced *Hôtel Restaurant Le Biscau* (℡05.59.05.31.37; ❸–❹) is a definite second choice in both categories, though most rooms are of a good standard, with full baths. Cramped dormitory accommodation is provided by the CAF **refuge** above the hamlet, serving the GR10 (1035m; 46 places in 5 dorms; staffed & open June–Sept & weekends in winter, apart from Nov 25–Dec 15; ℡05.59.05.33.14); no cooking is allowed, but good meals are available.

## Around the Pic du Midi d'Ossau

An undisputed Pyrenean classic despite its modest height (2884m), the handsome, double-tipped **Pic du Midi d'Ossau** rears up in magnificent isolation above the Vallée d'Ossau, its distinctive mitten shape recognizable from a great distance. This is one of those summits, like Canigou and Pedraforca in Catalonia, that inspire an affection bordering on reverence; nicknamed "Jean-Pierre" by the locals, it's essentially the logo of high Béarn.

The first recorded ascent of Pic du Midi was by an anonymous shepherd in 1787, who erected a summit cairn confirming his success. Today the peak remains a tough scramble at the very least, and is more of a mecca for rock-climbers, but the celebrated Tour du Pic du Midi, designed for walkers to enjoy from all angles, can be completed in a single summer's day. If you want a **map** more detailed than the 1:50,000 Carte de Randonnées no. 3, get hold of the TOP 1:25,000 1547OT, or the PNP 1:25,000 map no. 1 "Aspe Ossau".

### Bases

Gabas can be used as a base of activities around the Pic du Midi, but you'll get more immediately to grips with the mountain by heading 4km southwest up the very minor D231 to the dammed **Lac de Bious-Artigues**, a seasonally crowded picnic spot with desperately inadequate parking. Just beyond there's the cheerful *Cantine de Bious*, excellent for a pre-hike breakfast or post-trek celebration, and the adjacent *Refuge Pyrénéa Sport*, almost due north of the summit (1430m; 45 places; staffed & open daily mid-June to mid-Sept & weekends May to mid-June & early Oct; ℡05.59.05.45.85). If both Gabas' accommodation and this refuge are full – likely in summer if you haven't phoned ahead – your only fallback is the *Camping Bious-Oumettes* (℡05.59.05.38.76; mid-June to mid-Sept), set 1.5km below the dam on grassy terraces, with a shop; this is as high as the occasional bus goes.

A remoter alternative as a local base – though still hugely popular – is the CAF-run *Refuge de Pombie* on the southeastern flank of the mountain (2031m; ℡05.59.05.31.78; 2031m; 50 places; staffed June 1–Oct 3 & weekends May & Oct), by the Pombie tarn. A well-signposted path, part of the Tour du Pic du Midi (see below) takes you there in about three hours from Bious-Artigues: first head east over the **Col Long de Magnabaigt** (1655m), then south through the **Col de Moundelhs** and **Col de Suzon** (2127m).

### The ascent – and the Tour du Pic du Midi

The standard **ascent** begins from the Col de Suzon, a fairly easy climb, but busy in summer and plagued by loose, falling rocks – helmets are recommended. At the *col* you turn west onto a route that leads directly to the mountain; things soon start to get more serious, with movable iron pegs in one section to make the summit more accessible to inexperienced climbers. The proper course is indicated by occasional cairns, and you'll reach the wide summit in about four hours.

You can make the classic, anticlockwise **Tour du Pic du Midi** in seven hours from Lac de Bious-Artigues, beginning by following the **GR10** along the eastern shore. About 1000m beyond the southern tip of the lake, or roughly an hour from *Refuge Pyrénéa Sport*, the trails divide; take the left-hand path, crossing the **Pont de Bious** and entering the *parc national*. Continue upstream on the true right bank, across flat, wet terrain – similar to the *artigues* (meadows) flooded by the Bious-Artigues dam lower down – until a sign reading "Pombie par Peyreget" directs you left (south). It's a steepish, zigzagging climb along a section of the HRP to the tiny **Lac de Peyreget**, reached just under three hours into the day. Next, slip over the **Col de Peyreget** (2322m), between Pic Peyreget (2487m) and the southern spur of Pic du Midi, and then down past the **Lac de Pombie** to the *Refuge de Pombie* just east of it, well placed for a lunch stop some four hours along. From this refuge you return to Bious-Artigues via the good trail through the **Col de Suzon** and **Col de Moundelhs**, reversing the direct *Pombie* access walk described above.

### West to the Vallée d'Aspe

To traverse **west** from the Pic du Midi d'Ossau region to the Vallée d'Aspe, start out on the **GR10** as described for the Tour, but don't cross the Pont de Bious; instead, keep right at the fork, following a sign reading "Lac d'Ayous 1.30", and continue climbing westwards, initially through forest, to three successive lakes, each larger than the preceding. You arrive at the PNP-managed *Refuge d'Ayous* (1960m; ☎05.59.05.37.00; 30 places; staffed June 15–Sept 15) after well under two hours' walking from Bious-Artigues. Staying the night here – you'll likely camp by the Lac Gentau below, as the refuge is perennially full – is rewarded by the best available vantage point for experiencing spectacular sunrises over the Pic du Midi, reflected in Lac Gentau.

The GR10 heads west through the **Col d'Ayous**, then curves away northwards through the **Col de la Hourquette de Larry** and then down through the Pacq woods and along the spectacular Chemin de la Mâture to Etsaut in the Aspe valley (3hr; see p.418).

### The Tour des Lacs

If you're not confident about tackling the all-day Tour du Pic du Midi, the **Tour des Lacs**, a circuit of about four hours from the Bious-Artigues car park, makes a fine alternative; many contend that it gives better views of "Jean-Pierre". It uses the *Refuge d'Ayous* as a fulcrum and probable lunch halt, and can be combined with the best of the Tour du Pic to make a fine two-day loop, with the Pombie and Ayous refuges (or their environs) as overnight spots.

Begin as for the Tour du Pic at the Pont de Bious, where a sign "Lacs d'Ayous 2.30" hints at what you're about to do, but as the Houn de Peyreget veer southwest, following signs, towards the **Lac Casterau**, then continue northwest over a small pass to the much bigger **Lac Bersau**, and finally north to the refuge, which you should reach two and a half hours along. The downhill return to the car park will take an hour and a half maximum. You should get to the refuge in good time for lunch, as they often run out of dishes in season, and the menu is fairly sparse to begin with.

### East or south from Refuge de Pombie

You can trek to or from the *Refuge de Pombie* towards the east or south, without having to return to Gabas or the Lac de Bious-Artigues. Heading **east**, you descend by path along the Pombie stream, changing banks as necessary, until arriving after two hours at **Caillou de Soques** in the Gave de Brousset, on the D934 road 9km north of the frontier, or 7km south of Gabas. From here you can easily continue northeast on the clear **HRP** trail to the Lac d'Artouste (see below), a steep but scenic four-hour climb via the Col d'Arrious, or directly to the *Refuge d'Arrémoulit* from the *col* via the Lac d'Arrious and the somewhat exposed ledge-path called the Passage d'Orteig.

Leaving Pombie towards the **south**, you shun the Col de Peyreget route in favour of another marked trail leading in one hour to the **Col de Soum** (ca. 2100m), from where it's as long again via a heavily used path to a car-parking area 1500m north of the border at **Col du Pourtalet/Puerto de Portalet** (1794m). The trans-border road is now kept snowploughed all winter, to facilitate French patronage of the Spanish ski resort of El Formigal, 8km southeast. If you get stuck here, there's a small, simple **hotel**, the *Col du Pourtalet* (☏05.59.05.32.00; June–Sept; ❸), opposite a cluster of *ventas* and *supermercados* on the Spanish side, still exploiting what price difference there is between the two countries.

## Around Balaïtous and Lac d'Artouste

**Balaïtous**, almost directly east of Pic du Midi d'Ossau across the Gave de Brousset, is, at 3145m, the westernmost Pyrenean summit to surpass the magic figure of 3000m, and one of the remotest. It was first climbed in 1825 by the military surveyors Peytier and Hossard, but they seem not to have divulged their route. Charles Packe, nearly forty years later, had to find his own way up. Balaïtous, he wrote:

> . . . *lies so completely away from the route of the ordinary traveller that the Eaux-Bonnes guides seem quite at a loss as to its exact whereabouts, as a friend who started from Eaux-Bonnes under their guidance found to his cost; for after passing two wretched nights in the mountain cabanes of the shepherds (a lodging which few Englishmen would prefer to the open air) he failed to attain even the foot of the Pic Balaïtous, the object of his search.*

After a failed attempt in 1862, Packe made a second in 1864 with the guide Jean-Pierre Gaspard, and after a week of searching discovered a route to the summit.

### The miniature train – and skiing

In Packe's day, of course, there was no *téléphérique* from the giant car park and ski station at the north end of the **Lac de Fabrèges**, 7km southeast of Gabas by a roundabout road (regular summer buses). Neither was there the miniature **tourist train** of bright-red, open carriages running the 10km southeast from the top of the lift on Pic de la Sagette (2031m) to just shy of **Lac d'Artouste**. Built in 1924 to serve a hydroelectric project that raised the lake level 25m, the train was later converted for tourist purposes. Weather permitting, the train normally operates daily from late May until late September; the first daily departure from the top of the *téléphérique* is between 9 and 10am depending on the season, but allow a half-hour for the *télécabine* (first departure 8.30am July & Aug, 9.30am May–June & Sept; last departure 2.30pm May–June & Sept, 4.30pm July & Aug). Reservations are suggested (☏05.59.05.36.99), and such is the crush at peak season that you may have a fixed return time stipulated on your ticket. The fare for the combined lift and subsequent train ride is €11–16 depending on season and time of day; walkers may be able to negotiate one-ways. It's a fifty-minute trip along the sonorously named Gave de Soussouéou to the end of the line, where the train waits for ninety minutes while passengers walk down to and around the lake before heading back. Some 45 minutes above the south end of Lac d'Artouste, nearly twice that far from the dam, sits the walkers' base camp of *Refuge d'Arrémoulit* (see p.397).

In **winter** the same *télécabine* gives access to the small beginner-to-intermediate downhill **ski centre** – thirteen runs and nine lifts – on the northeast side of Col de la Sagette. The resort is about half the size of nearby Gourette, and with a top point of barely 2100m isn't reckoned very serious; there's one ski-bus daily, in the morning, from Laruns.

### The ascent of Balaïtous

The **ascent of Balaïtous** from *Refuge d'Arrémoulit* takes almost nine hours (return), and as this is very tough country indeed, you should have the TOP 25 1:25,000 1647OT map, or the PNP 1:25,000 map no. 2 "Balaïtous". Ascend east an hour to the **Col du Palas/Cuello de Pallàs** (2517m) on the frontier, descending southeast on the Spanish side to skirt the **Arriel** lakes and the tarn of **Gourg Glacé/Gorg Helada** (a likely lunch stop). Next follow a line of cairns to the primitive Abri Michaud shelter (2698m); the gully above it – full of loose, dangerous rock – leads to the western ridge and then, via more gullies, to the **summit** (3146m). From the top you can appreciate how opposite in character Balaïtous is from Pic du Midi d'Ossau: the latter showcased by a virtual parkland of lakes and grassy turf, your present vantage concealed by savage, lunar crags in every direction, with nothing to soften the landscape.

### Traverse east to Refuge de Larribet

The HRP also continues **eastwards** from *Refuge d'Arrémoulit* to *Refuge de Larribet*; this is a short (4–5hr) but strenuous outing, intended for lightly laden trekkers experienced in traversing such terrain cross-country, and assuming passes relatively free of snow. From the Col du Palas, cross the head of the Spanish Arriel valley to the **Port du/Puerto de Lavedan** (2615m), dropping down on the far side to the tiny **Micoulaou** lakes; from there go northeast with a clearer path past the **Batcrabère** lakes, and finally through the **Brèche de la Garénère** (2189m) to descend on *Refuge de Larribet* (described on p.378). If you've been hiking westwards from Gavarnie or Cauterets, simply reverse all of the foregoing directions to move on from the Balaïtous area to the Vallée d'Ossau.

## Along the Aspe

The **Vallée d'Aspe** between Oloron-Sainte-Marie and the Col du Somport has long been an important corridor between France and Spain; the Romans had a road through it, the Saracens conducted raids along it, and lately the valley has again become embroiled in controversy over its role in north–south travel (see box on pp.416–417). In 1659, during the Wars of Religion, all the local villages but one suffered the misfortune of being burnt to the ground by Protestant forces; early the next century these settlements were reconstructed simultaneously, and – never having been altered since – now present a pleasingly homogeneous spectacle.

### Escot to Cette-Eygun

The upper valley can be said to begin in earnest just south of Escot, 15km from Oloron, where a narrow namesake defile closes in on the road and river. Upstream from the gorge, along the N134, the attractive village of **SARRANCE** has strangely unexploited associations with Marguerite d'Angoulême, who stayed and wrote here when the weather in Cauterets turned bad. The village surrounds the ancient monastic church of **Notre-Dame-de-la-Pierre**, with a fine organ perched in the gallery and a wonderfully rustic cloister. This now houses the **Ecomusée de la Vallée d'Aspe** (daily July–Sept 15 10am–noon & 2–7pm; rest of year Sat, Sun or hols 2–6pm; €4), devoted to valley history, natural and otherwise. The only other tourist amenity is the humble *Restaurant Labay* on the old through road, now traffic-restricted.

For a base, you could do far worse than **LOURDIOS-ICHÈRE**, 10km west along the minor D241 over the Col d'Ichère (or by path, part of the Tour de la Vallée d'Aspe, from Sarrance), scattered appealingly east of the Lourdios River. Unlike Lescun (see p.418), this is still (just) a working pastoral village, with sheep cheese providing the main livelihood. At the east end of the village, by the *mairie, Chez Lamothe* (☎05.59.34.41.53) does excellent family-style meals and has a few **rooms** (multi-day stays only; ❺ HB).

Back in the main valley and 7km south of Sarrance, the first place of any consequence – though still resolutely rural as reflected in its traditional Thursday morning market – is **BEDOUS**. Here you'll find a fine church, an arcaded *mairie* and the miniature, eighteenth-century **Château Lassalle** on the quiet place de l'Église east of the through road. Also on the *place* is a *crêperie* (May–Sept) and the less institutional of two **gîtes d'étape**, *Le Mandragot* (☎05.59.34.59.33); the other, English-speaking *Le Choucas Blanc* (☎05.59.34.53.71, ✉choucas.blanc@wanadoo.fr; 26 places, some doubles ❷), is on the through road opposite the main car park, and thus noisier. If you're driving, note that Bedous has the highest petrol pump in the valley – there's nothing else until Canfranc-Pueblo in Spain. Several **bars** on the through road, including *Chez Michel*, do snacks and Spanish-style *tapas*.

Villages around Bedous offer further amenities. There's a *gîte* 1500m southwest in **OSSE-EN-ASPE**, *Les Amis de Chaneu* (☎05.59.34.73.23; 28 places), though the campsite is small and noisy. About 7km east along the D237, **AYDIUS** offers *La Curette* (☎05.59.34.78.18, ⑤05.59.34.50.42; ❸), with rooms and *table d'hôte* in an isolated farmhouse, while on the road between here and Bedous, the **Moulin d'Orcun**, the last stone-grinding flour mill in the valley, functions as a museum (July & Aug daily tours at 11am, 3pm, 4–6pm; otherwise by arrangement on ☎05.59.34.51.70). **ACCOUS**, the valley capital 3km south, has a **tourist office** (☎05.59.34.71.48), the highest supermarket in the valley and the two-star *Hôtel Le Permayou* (☎05.59.34.72.15, ⑤05.59.34.72.68; closed Oct; ❸), between the main road and village centre, with clean, fully en-suite rooms and an affordable restaurant.

Some 3km beyond Accous at **L'ESTANGUET** hamlet, the *Auberge Cavalière* (☎05.59.34.72.30, ⓦwww.auberge-cavaliere.com; April–Oct), perched high above the main road, specializes in horse-riding and walking packages (though walk-ins welcome); the stables are on the premises, near the well-regarded in-house restaurant. Accommodation is either at the *auberge*'s attached hotel (❸) or at its *Refuge des Ecuyers Montagnards* further up the hill, accessible by 4WD track.

About 4km southeast from the *Auberge Cavalière* turning, another side road snakes 2km east up the slope to unspoilt **CETTE** village (part of Cette-Eygun), where a fortified twelfth-century manor was sympathetically converted during 2002 to the valley's most distinctive **accommodation**, the municipally run *Au Château d'Arance* (☎05.59.34.75.50, ⓦwww.auchateaudarance.com; ❸). The eight modern, wood-floored, pastel-tinted rooms are excellent value, with TV, Internet access and amazing sunsets; most have full baths, except for the tower unit. The restaurant operates principally for guests.

Since 1990 the **Vallée d'Aspe** has been the focus of a bitter battle between advocates and opponents of a road-widening scheme from Oloron-Sainte-Mairie to the Col du Somport, with the supplementary boring of an 8600-metre-long tunnel under the *col*. Such proposals had been debated for years, but received additional impetus upon Spain's accession to the EU in 1986 – and ETA's continuing terrorist campaign, which made a high-speed route to central Spain bypassing Basque lands that much more attractive. The Spanish region of Aragón in particular, smarting over the closure of the rail line between Oloron and Canfranc, embraced the proposal as a remedy for its perceived isolation. In June 1990, the EU granted the first 98 million francs (of an eventual 210 million) towards the project, with a Franco-Spanish agreement, signed the following year, to share more or less equally the remaining 790-million-franc cost.

As originally envisaged, the plan was to facilitate the passage of one thousand heavy trucks daily, by upgrading the N134 between Oloron and the new tunnel to expressway status as part of the trans-European E7. This meant concreting the banks of the Gave d'Aspe, blasting away sections of mountainside and farmland, and placing the tunnel mouth in *parc national* territory. Only token provision for any rail link was made, and there was no consideration of the effects on the various local animal species: eagle owl, capercaillie and lammergeier, not to mention the famous brown bear.

Besides the Parisian technocrats, the vast majority of local villagers and politicians favoured the scheme, including the then-mayor of Lourdios-Ichère, **Jean Lassalle**. In his simultaneous capacity as president of the Parc National des Pyrénées, he had already gained some notoriety for promoting a cross-country ski resort at the Col du Somport, a notion initially quashed by the Paris-based Council of State as illegal and incompatible with the goals of the park – but now reality. Valley residents, meanwhile, saw the project, with its promise of improved communications north and south, as their last chance of rescuing the Aspe from complete stagnation, in particular halting the drift of young people to the cities.

Opposition to the plans crystallized quickly in the form of the **Coordination pour la Sauvegarde Active de la Vallée d'Aspe (CSAVA)**, based at the *gîte d'étape* in Cette-Eygun and headed by **Eric Pétetin**, who came eventually to be loathed, dismissed as a misguided idealist, or respected – in equal measure – by the inhabitants of the valley. Almost single-handedly, he managed to delay the project for three years.

Already by August 1991, CSAVA and its allies had appealed successfully to the EU to halt funding temporarily, claiming that the Canfranc–Oloron rail line could be reopened to carry both passengers and trucks at a **cost** ten times less than the eventual projected total (one billion francs) for the road works. Next, the anti-development faction raised the spectre of massive **environmental degradation** in the wake of a projected four thousand vehicles in total per day (not just a thousand trucks) through the tunnel by 2010, and also seized on the detail of the tunnel's siting within the PNP.

The French Environment Minister, caught between the ecologists and the numerous *département* officials supporting the tunnel, attempted to placate the former by moving the tunnel mouth slightly out of the PNP, for a total length of over 8km. In August 1992 the prefect of Pau signed the *déclaration d'utilité publique* (**DUP**), or go-ahead decree. But CSAVA had not yet exhausted its legal recourses; in December 1992 an administrative tribunal in Pau found that environmental impact statements had been deficient, nullifying the previous DUP. Rather than appeal against this decision, the government elected to apply for a new DUP, paying careful attention to all the points raised by the ecologists. The government succeeded in July 1993, and the final plan included provisions for bear-crossings and rehabilitation of the abandoned rail line, with work beginning over the winter of 1993–1994. With far less opposition, the Spanish had completed the boring from their side, and their approach road – beginning in Zaragoza, bound for Huesca and Jaca – was already of the necessary standard.

CSAVA and its allies hadn't limited themselves to the courts. Throughout 1991 and 1992 they organized escalating campaigns of **civil disobedience**: graffiti, demonstrations, "Sioux" war dances in full tribal regalia around gendarmes designated as "palefaces" (a strategy which earned Pétetin the nickname "l'Indien du Somport"), road obstructions, and – ultimately – extensive vandalism to surveyors' stakes and the tunnel work site. Their ranks were swelled by large numbers of foreign activists, particularly from Belgium and Holland, where the Pyrenees have many avid aficionados. For his pains Pétetin was arrested and detained no fewer than 35 times, on the final occasion being sentenced to two years' imprisonment.

In the eyes of many *Aspois*, the eco-activists were merely carpetbaggers – as evidenced by the influx of out-of-town agitators during 1992 – who would decamp to the next fashionable cause were the issue decided in their favour, leaving the locals with the consequences. Pétetin was granted a presidential pardon and early release in July 1993 just as the DUP was issued – reflecting the authorities' confidence that work could proceed no matter what new strategies CSAVA devised. Civil disobedience in the Vallée de Aspe took on a new twist: organized by Greenpeace and the WWF, thousands of activists (including soon-to-be French Environment Minister, Green Party member Dominique Voynet) bought tiny plots of land near Bedous, along the proposed course of the approach highway, to spin out for as long as possible the zoning and compulsory land-purchase process. In any event, the highway won't be finished before 2007 at the earliest, owing in part to the Portalet narrows and difficult rocks at Urdos.

In March 1998, municipalities and interested individuals in France and Spain drew up and signed the **Pacte de Somport**, which endorsed a strategy of accepting the tunnel, but pressing for a dual right of way: a reopened rail line to take passengers and heavy freight, with the roadway (of reduced width) reserved for local traffic and light vehicles. Since the Mont Blanc tunnel disaster, in which juggernaut lorries were implicated, the French government may slowly come round to backing a ban on monster vehicles in the Tunnel du Somport – which would undermine much of the justification for a multi-lane highway. EU funding for the rehabilitation of the railway has been approved "in principle", possibly including a Chunnel-type truck shuttle – though an identical proposal for the Bielsa tunnel, involving a new-from-scratch rail line between Arreau and Monzón in Aragón, has been abandoned as unfeasible. The French SNCF and CSAVA dropped mutual lawsuits in 1999, with *La Goutte d'Eau* (the CSAVA activists' *gîte*, now moribund) confirmed in its tenancy of the Cette-Eygun station until the rail line is rehabilitated. Eric Pétetin half-jokingly applied in advance for the job of stationmaster, saying he was best qualified; as of writing, following health problems, he's not active in CSAVA. His colleagues carry on the fight against the widened highway, however, most visibly in ubiquitous SAUVE NOTRE VALLÉE and NON AU BÉTON graffiti.

The tunnel finally opened two years late in January 2003, with more of a whimper than a bang; the *Aspois* mayors boycotted the ceremony, miffed that (except at Etsaut) no bypass road for their villages had yet been furnished, to keep the trucks at bay. In the end the massive engineering and their true impact will probably prove anticlimactic, bringing neither the degree of revitalization to the area that its advocates envision nor quite the environmental damage feared by opponents. However, one enduring legacy of the long campaign against the expressway and tunnel has been to open up decision-making processes to public scrutiny in what has historically been an overly secretive and centralized nation.

## Lescun and its cirque

Certainly the highlight of a trip along the Aspe valley is the grey limestone **Cirque de Lescun**, more intimate than Gavarnie's, contrasting sharply with the pastures and dense forest at its foot. Pyramidal, and often marbled with streaks of snow, the toothy peaks forming the cirque – such as the two Billare summits, the Aigulles de Ansabère and storm-lashed Pic d'Anie (2504m) – rise as a semicircular screen from the quiltwork of fields ingeniously laid out by generations of farmers.

The substantial stone houses of **LESCUN** village, wonderfully placed amidst trickling fountains on a sunny south-facing slope, lend photogenic balance in the foreground. Six steep kilometres along the minor D239 above and west of the valley floor, the village is no longer a going concern; two-thirds of its houses are holiday homes or abandoned altogether, and winter desolation is the rule. This acknowledged, in summer you can buy cheese and milk from one of the few remaining shepherds behind the **post office**, and use Lescun as an excellent base for a walking tour of the cirque. The best **accommodation** is the comfortable, antique-furnished *Hôtel du Pic d'Anie* (☎05.59.34.71.54, ℻05.59.34.53.22; April–Sept; ❸), which has the village's only **restaurant** with decent, hearty fare, and a basic grocery store on the ground floor. Lescun also has two *gîtes d'étape*: a 16-place one run by the hotel, just opposite, and the rival *Maison de la Montagne* a bit north (☎05.59.34.79.14; 22 places in 4- or 5-bed rooms), with drinks on the lawn served to anyone. There's a medium-sized, grassy, well-equipped and incomparably sited **campsite**, *Le Lauzart* (☎05.59.34.51.77; May–Sept), south of and below the village.

## South of Lescun: the head of the Aspe

After the Lescun turning the N134 carries on through Etsaut and passes just below the attractive village of Borce. In the disused train station of **ETSAUT** (signposted in Gascon as "Eth Saut") you'll find the most westerly **Maison du Parc** (May to mid-Sept daily 10am–noon & 1–6pm; ☎05.59.34.88.30), featuring exhibits on the Pyrenean bear. You can **stay** at Logis de France member *Hôtel des Pyrénées* (☎05.59.34.88.62, ℻05.59.34.86.96; closed mid-Dec to mid-Jan; ❷), quite the heart of the village with the only **restaurant**; across the road at *La Maison de l'Ours*, a *gîte d'étape* with three-to-six-bed rooms (☎05.59.34.86.38); or at the quieter, larger *Auberge La Garbure* (☎05.59.34.88.98, ✉pyrenees.aspe@wanadoo.fr; 52 places, some doubles /quads), at the end of the church lane.

**BORCE**, poised above the valley floor on the west bank, is a medieval showcase, the one place to escape the warfare of 1659 and still graced by sumptuous fifteenth-century mansions identified by plaques. There are three *gîte*-style **accommodations** here: *La Communal*, upstairs from the central bar-*épicerie* (☎05.59.34.86.40 or 05.59.34.88.76; 18 places); the cosier *Gîte Saint-Jacques-de-Compostelle* (☎05.59.34.89.25 or 06.81.32.58.32) at the north outskirts, intended for bona fide pilgrims, with just six beds; and *Camping-Gîte du Poey* (☎05.59.34.87.29), with an 18-place *gîte*, just above the village, offering great views and meals.

Both villages lie on the **GR10**, which, en route southeast to Lac d'Ayous, negotiates the spectacular **Chemin de la Mâture**, some 3km south. Hacked out of the sheer flank of a ravine, this path is broad enough, but the edge is not for the vertigo-prone; watch out also for ropes across the trail fastened by avid climbers abseiling down the rock face. If you're not up for a point-to-point traverse, you can still experience the *chemin* as a five-hour day loop. At **Pont de**

Cebers, 1.5km south, take the GR10 through the ravine, then return to Etsaut via the **Col d'Arras** on local trail no. 34. More ambitiously, over two days, you could vary a return from *Refuge d'Ayous* by using a non-GR trail heading via the **Col d'Ayous** and the unattended *Refuge de Larry*, but this path brings you down to Urdos, not Etsaut.

The grim **Fort du Portalet** (privately owned, no visits) appears atop a sheer cliff west of the N134, directly opposite the Chemin de la Mâture gorge. It acquired some notoriety as a political prison during and after World War II, when the Vichy government here detained Léon Blum, Socialist French premier of the 1930s; later Marshal Pétain himself was held here by the Allies.

Shortly after, **URDOS** is the last village on the French side of the Col du Somport, and arguably worth a special trip for the co-managed *Hôtel des Voyageurs Le Somport* (℡05.59.34.88.05, ℻05.59.34.86.74; ❷–❸), a former post house that's been in the same family for seven generations; eulogized fulsomely by Hilaire Belloc in 1909, it still deserves that praise, its rooms managing to retain character without being musty – try for those in the *Somport* annexe facing west over the river, at least until the bypass road gets built. The *Voyageurs'* **restaurant** is superb, offering the best value in the valley – the sort of place where the local *gendarmerie* and firemen hold their Saturday-evening do next to bemused skiers and *voyageurs*; the €16 *menu* gets you vegetarian *garbure*, a fish plate such as *lotte* in squid sauce, a meat/game dish (boned duck breast or shank in green peppercorn sauce) and dessert. There are no longer any shops, petrol pumps or banks in Urdos, though the lanes west of the high street provide a pleasant amble.

Beyond Urdos several daily well-spaced SNCF buses continue on through the beech forests and the PNP through the new tunnel under the 1632-metre **Col du Somport**, and beyond to Canfranc, the terminus for trains from Jaca in Aragón. The twisty old road, recommended for the views, still climbs over the pass itself, accessing the cross-country ski centre of **Somport-Candanchú**, 34km of marked trails (9km on the Spanish side), presumably dodging the numerous ventilation silos for the tunnel; that said, it's one of the best such centres in the Pyrenees, and at this altitude one of the last to close in spring. At the frontier there are a few snack bars, a snowplough station and the abandoned customs post; just below, you turn left for Astún, right for the main onward road and Candanchú (see p.457).

## Walks from Lescun

There any number of walks for all levels of commitment in the fantastic limestone scenery south and west of Lescun, ranging from day-trips and brief circuits of the upper Aspe to long-haul traverses. Hiking is much the best way to tour the heights of the cirque, since public transport on either side of the border – which these peaks form – is almost nonexistent. Water can be a problem in these rock strata, so top up bottles wherever possible; the best **maps** for the area are the IGN 1:25,000 1547 OT TOP 25, or the PNP 1:25,000 map no. 1, "Aspe Ossau".

### West: the GR10, HRP and Pic d'Anie

The **GR10** to Arette-la-Pierre-Saint-Martin is the northernmost route, an easy day's walking of under six hours. It follows a six-kilometre road – no shortcuts possible – for ninety minutes northwest of Lescun as far as the *Refuge de L'Abérouat* (1442m; ℡05.59.34.50.43), eye-to-eye with 2300-metre Billare peak; the refuge specializes exclusively in boisterous children's holidays, but offers meals to all comers. This is as far as cars can go; there's a huge car park for those who've forgone the boring road-tramp up. Next, the route – briefly track, then path and cross-country – enters beech forest under the striking organ-pipe formations of **Orgues de Camplong** before emerging above treeline at the basic, five-person *Cabane d'Ardinet* hut. From here the GR10 climbs to another shepherd's *cabane* – your last reliable water source for the day and sometimes selling cheese – at Cap de la Baigt, and then steeply northwards into the **Pas d'Azuns** (1873m; 3hr from Lescun). After dropping into a slight bowl the path climbs again to the **Pas de l'Osque** (1922m), after which the GR10 crosses karst desert en route to Arette-la-Pierre-Saint-Martin (see p.489), two hours due west.

For an **ascent of Pic d'Anie** (**Auñamendi** in Euskera; 2504m), the most westerly summit over 2000m on the French side, head south from Cap de la Baigt, curving under Pic du Soum Couy and up into the **Col des Anies** (2030m). The main HRP carries on westwards from here to Arette-la-Pierre-Saint-Martin; for Pic d'Anie, follow the easy marked path southwards. From the summit (2hr from the *col*; 4hr 30min from Lescun) you can return to Lescun in rather less than four and a half hours, making this a popular day outing from the village.

The best traverse route, though, is the **HRP variante**, which passes by the *Refugio Belagoa* in Spain. From Lescun you head west on track towards the toe of Petit Billare, reaching an obvious plateau at about 1100m. From here a good trail climbs steeply past a waterfall (fill up) to the **Col d'Anaye** (2052m; 3hr), on the south flank of Pic d'Anie. On the other side of this pass you enter the twisted karst dells of Spain's *Parque Natural Pirenaico*; Belagoa lies two and a half hours further west.

### Tour of the border peaks

Using Lescun or Borce as a starting point, you can make a very worthwhile three-day **tour of the border peaks** which satisfactorily covers the terrain south of the preceding itineraries. Beginning in Lescun, head southwest through the Bois de Landrosque, up the *gave* draining from the **Aiguilles d'Ansabère**. At the base of the lesser pinnacle (2271m) are some shepherds' huts, near which are some all-important springs and camping spots. But since you're only about three hours out of Lescun, you may wish to continue due south up to the frontier. Cross this via a nameless saddle (2030m) above the tiny **Lac d'Ansabère**, where you're poised to tackle the slight descent to **Ibón de Acherito** (1870m; 5hr from Lescun; see p.483 for full description), just inside Spain and another scenic possibility for water and camping.

From here the topography dictates a wide skirting of the border ridge on its southeast face before crossing back into France via the **Col de Pau/Puerto de Palo** (2017m; 90min from Acherito), just northwest of the similarly low **Pic de Burcq/Pic de Burco**. (From Acherito or the Puerto de Pau it's simple to link up with the Spanish GR11, down in the main valley to the south – see p.483 for a reverse itinerary.)

Back on the French side, now within the final westerly extension of the Parc National des Pyrénées, an increasingly good path, as the HRP, hugs the ridge – except for a diversion north over the **Col de Saoubathou** to avoid **Pic Rouge/Pico Rojo** – to deposit you within five hours from the Ibón de Acherito at the PNP-administered *Refuge d'Arlet* (☎05.59.36.00.99, ℱ05.59.34.76.88; 2000m; 30 places; staffed July 1–Sept 15), beside the **Lac d'Arlet**.

The most scenic way of returning to the Aspe valley involves heading east along the HRP to the small **La Banasse** cirque with its spring, and then descending north, initially via the **Baralet** valley, and then over the Col de Lagréou to change to the **Belonce** drainage, which leads out of PNP territory on a good, if steep, path into Borce (5hr from Arlet). If necessary, you can continue northwest along the GR10 to Lescun.

# The southern approaches

South of the Spanish **Parque Nacional de Ordesa y Monte Perdido**, in the region of **Alto Aragón**, depopulation is even more pronounced than in the French Pyrenees, as a glance at the map with its isolated villages will confirm. Of the area's towns, only Jaca and the provincial capital Huesca muster over ten thousand inhabitants, while more than four hundred mountain villages languish all but abandoned – the highest such concentration in Spain – occupied only in summer by older people with flocks to graze, plus a few city-dwellers restoring ruins as holiday homes or "alternative" enterprises. This desolation is owed largely to the late General Franco and his policies. Determined to punish the *Alto Aragoneses* for their staunch support of the Republican cause, his regime withheld vital services, ignored the ravages wrought by natural disasters and dammed numerous arable valleys, leaving the villagers little alternative but to migrate to the cities. In the seven thousand square kilometres of Alto Aragón there are now fewer than fifty thousand inhabitants, an average density of seven per square kilometre.

The salient geographical features in the east of this region are impressive valleys and strange, wedding-cake-like mountains, both eroded from the same banded limestone. The **Valle de Ordesa** – heart of the *parque nacional* and the most popular approach for an ascent of **Monte Perdido**, linchpin of the canyons – was first publicized by the French journalist and adventurer Lucien Briet, who for eight consecutive summers after 1904 traced a route from Gavarnie to Torla. (Some of his photographs can be seen at the Lourdes museum, and a Torla inn has been named in his honour.) Nowadays this landscape needs no advertisement; during holiday periods, the gentle riverside paths of Ordesa and all approach roads from the west or south are packed to the gills, while the gateway villages become increasingly commercialized with each successive year.

Other canyons east or southeast of the Valle de Ordesa, wholly or partly within the park, are no less impressive in their own way but receive far fewer visitors. The absence of public transport to trailheads and limited accommodation here could be both cause and consequence of this neglect, but the extra effort required to visit is amply rewarded. Despite having a road through it, the forbiddingly steep and snow-fringed walls of the **Valle de Pineta**, draining east from Monte Perdido, discourage casual acquaintance with its heights. The **Garganta de Escuaín**, in the **Valle de Tella** south of Pineta, can only be properly appreciated on foot or as part of a canyoning expedition. Continuing clockwise southeast brings you to the bottom of the **Valle de Añisclo**, which gets almost as crowded as Ordesa in high season, but once clear of its lower

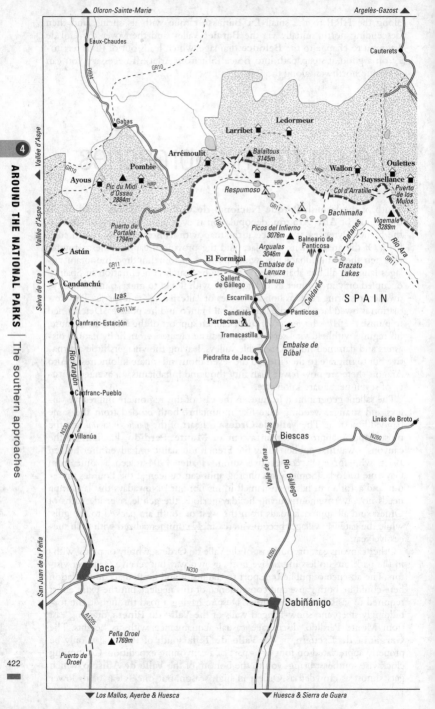

▲ Argelès-Gazost     ▲ Barèges

N

Luz Saint-Sauveur

D929

▶ Arreau

Piau Engaly

**PARC NATIONAL
DES PYRENEES**

FRANCE     Gèdre

Héas

Bielsa Tunnel     HRP

**Barroude**
*Cirque de
Troumouse*

Gavarnie     *Cirque
d'Estarbé*

Lagos de la Munia

Chisagüés

Puerto de
Bujaruelo
2270m     **Espuguettes**

HRP GR10

*Cirque de
Gavarnie*     *Lago de Marboré*     Parzán

**San
Nicolás**     **Sarradets**     Marboré
3253m     Cilindro
3328m     **Balcón
de Pineta**     *Valle de Pineta*     GR11

Bujaruelo     Taillon
3144m     *Brecha de
Roldán*     Monte
Perdido
3355m     *Cinca*     Bielsa

**PARQUE NACIONAL DE
ORDESA Y MONTE PERDIDO**     **Góriz**     *Collado de
Añisclo
2470m*     Salinas
de Sin

*C. de
Soaso*     *Collado
S. de Góriz
2343m*     *Cuello Viceto
2002m*     GR19     ▶ Valle de Gistau

*Valle de Ordesa*     Revilla     GR15

Arazas     *Faja de Pelay*     **San
Vicenda**     Escuaín     Arinzué

C. de
Diazas     Estaronillo     Tella     GR15/19

Torla     *Desfiladero
de las Gloces*     *Castillo
Mayor
2014m*     Lafortunada

Broto     Famlo     *Valle de*     Nerín     Bestué     Badaín

Oto     Buisán     *Vió*     Sercué     Puértolas     **Hospital
de Tella**

Buesa     **San Úrbez**     GR15

Sarvisé     HU631     Vió     *Desfiladero
de las Cambras*     Bellós     Laspuña

Buerba     Puyarruego     *Peña
Montañesa
2291m*

Yeba     Escalona     **San
Victorian**

*Río Yesa*     Los
Molinos

*Ribera de Fiscal*     *Río Zinca*

Lardiés     N260     Ainsa

Fiscal     Jánovas     *Río Ara*     Boltaña

0          10 km     **SOUTHERN APPROACHES**

Barbastro & Sierra de Guara ▼

reaches you'll have only a few long-distance walkers for company.

The main bases for exploring these canyons are **Bielsa**, at the mouth of the Valle de Pineta; **Aínsa**, terminus of public transport and within striking distance of the Añisclo and Tella canyons; and **Torla**, the enduringly popular western gateway to the Ordesa country. All of these villages have an ample range of facilities for both trekkers and those more solicitous of their own comfort. Southwest of the park, **Jaca**, capital of the ancient kingdom of Aragón, the nearby monastery of **San Juan de la Peña** and the **Castillo de Loarre** represent the only man-made attractions rivalling the mountains. **Huesca** and the wine town of **Barbastro** are ignored by most in favour of the range above them, the **Sierra de Guara**, protected as a *parque natural* and Spain's prime venue for canyoning.

Like almost everywhere south of the Pyrenean watershed, the landscape of Alto Aragón is predominantly drier and less vegetated than that of French Bigorre, but towards the west, in the **Tena** and **Canfranc** valleys, the climate becomes more humid. Lakes reappear in large numbers above **Panticosa**, and in winter the nearby skiing centres of **El Formigal**, **Candanchú** and **Astún** do a thriving business.

### Transport and accommodation

Twice as remote as the French approaches in terms of distances from major cities, and twice as deserted, the Spanish side consequently has relatively deficient **public transport**. Of the foothill villages described in this section, only those on the Sabiñánigo–Biescas–Torla–Sarvisé axis see more than one daily summertime bus service, and many have none; careful planning is vital if you're to make the necessary connections. You'll gain considerable advantages by renting a car, or bringing your own, or by trekking along the GR paths that run perpendicular to most of the north–south roads.

**Accommodation** can be a serious problem in peak summer or winter seasons if you haven't reserved well in advance – even the campsites tend to fill – but with a vehicle you can simply drive until you happen upon a vacancy. Once you get settled, you'll find the **prices** of rooms and meals still reasonable despite the recent onslaught of tourism.

# The eastern valleys

Heading west from Posets and the Valle de Gistau on foot, you're perfectly poised to tackle any of the three major easterly valleys draining out of the national park. The GR11 or its variant leads from Biadós to **Bielsa** and the **Valle de Pineta**, while the GR19 or GR15 link the Valle de Gistau with **Lafortunada**, closest base for the **Valle de Tella**, with its tiny, photogenic villages perched on either side of the **Garganta de Escuaín**. The **Valle de Añisclo** (or Cañon de Añisclo) is easiest visited by car from **Aínsa**, but can also be reached by trail from Pineta or Escuaín. If you're moving from south to north, however, remember that there is only infrequent public transport north of Aínsa to Bielsa, although there is a regular service west up the Ribera de Fiscal.

## Aínsa

Sited above the confluence of the Ara and Zinca rivers, **AÍNSA** (*L'Aínsa* in Aragonése) is the natural gateway to the region, with an exceedingly attractive hilltop **old quarter**, focused on a vast, arcaded **Plaza Mayor**. The old town has been prettified with boutiques and stone walkways to cash in on some of the cross-border trade pouring down from the Bielsa tunnel, but it's all in fairly good taste, with nothing like the tackiness associated with Torla; much of the year, traffic is banned and cars directed to a car park on the west (€1.50 in summer). Just off the plaza stands the exceptional Romanesque church of **Santa María**, with a unique triangular cloister dictated by the sloping topography, and an ancient crypt with a forest of magnificently capitalled columns under the apse. For €0.80 you can climb the belfry for splendid views over the river valley, the town, *plaza* and fifteen-to-sixteenth-century **Castillo** to the west. Slowly being restored, this is the venue for the early-August Festival Internacional de Música, attracting big names such as Tarika, Clannad and the Afro-Cuban All Stars, as well as lesser-known Spanish acts. If you've time to fill, the **Museo de Oficios y Artes Tradicionales/Museum of Trades and Traditional Arts** (daily: July 1–Sept 15 10am–2pm & 4.30–9.30pm; spring & autumn 10am–2pm & 5–8pm; €2.50) is worth a few minutes. It resembles a well-lit antique shop, labelled in Spanish only, highlighting ironwork, carpentry, basketry and so forth.

### Practicalities

**Accommodation** in the old quarter includes *Casa del Hospital* (☎974 500 750; ❷), a *turisme rural* by the church, or for a splurge the two-star, slightly kitsch *Hotel Posada Royal* at Plaza Mayor 6 (☎974 500 977, ⓦwww.posadareal.com; ❹), or *Los Arcos* (☎974 500 016; ❹) at no. 23, restored in 2003. There's ample choice for **eating** and **drinking** on or near Plaza Mayor: *Bodegas del Sobrarbe* (closed Nov–March), at no. 2, is the most renowned (€28 *a la carta*, €19 for dull *menús*), while at *Bodegón de Mallacán*, at no. 6, you can just have coffee under the arches. East of the square, local hangout *Bar Restaurante Fes* at c/Mayor 22 offers affordable *menús* (€10) featuring grilled meat and a much more interesting *carta* (allow €18); no-frills cuisine comes in fair-sized portions, and the cavernous, stone-walled interior is bigger than it looks from outside. *Bar Bodega L'Alfil*, c/Travesera s/n, near the church, is the place for *tapas* and cider.

The unsightly, traffic-plagued **new quarter** below has the **tourist office** (summer daily 9am–2pm & 4.30–8.30pm; ☎974 500 767), as well as six *hoteles* and *hostales*. Of these, *Hotel Mesón de l'Aínsa* (☎974 500 028, ⓔmmeson@pirineo.com; ❺) is marginally the quietest, with private parking out front. The local **campsite**, *Camping Aínsa* (☎974 500 260; April–Sept), lies 1km east along the C140 towards Campo. There are four sports-equipment shops along Aínsa's single high street and an equal number of outdoor-activity outfitters running canyoning, rafting and kayaking expeditions. Aínsa is also the last stop for the **bus** line plying the C138 road southeast from Torla, overlapping partly with the Barbastro-Boltaña line.

## Bielsa and Parzán

The surprisingly large town of **BIELSA**, at the entrance to the Pineta valley, hung on as a Republican stronghold long after much of Alto Aragón had been overrun by the Nationalists; when the place finally fell in June 1938, most of it had been bombarded by Franco and then burnt by the defeated, which explains its current appearance. Today it's a prime, if slightly tacky, summertime target for more pacific armies of French (and Spanish) day-trippers, and could experience another identity change if plans for a nearby downhill ski resort come to fruition. Nonetheless, traces of its past as a traditional mountain county-town still persist in its old river bridge and porticoed town hall, with magnificently framed first-floor window, on the Plaza Mayor. Walkers heading towards the Valle de Pineta from the Posets Massif are pretty much obliged to stop off here, since it's the only place close to the valley with supplies and accommodation. Bielsa is also renowned for its lively **carnival celebrations**; you can take in some of the rather outrageous costumes, plus the local civil-war history, from the displays in the **Museo de Bielsa** (July–Sept Tues–Sun 5–9pm; €3), housed in the town hall. There's also a central **information office** for the *parque nacional* (summer daily 9am–1.30pm & 3–6pm).

### Practicalities

Bielsa gets sporadic **bus** services **from Aínsa**, three evenings weekly; if driving, you have to use the free car parks on the southern outskirts and walk in the short distance. Coming **from the north**, the Vallée d'Aure bus only reaches Aragnouet-le-Plan; rather than attempting to hitch through the tunnel (no pedestrians allowed in it), a better plan would be to trek southeast from the *Refuge de Barroude* (see p.355) on an HRP variant to **PARZÁN** village, 4km north of Bielsa, also on the GR11. Sleepy Parzán has a small shop on the main highway, near the friendly *Hostal la Fuen* (☎974 501 047; ❷), which offers decent en-suite rooms and an adequate *menú* (€11 plus drink) in the pleasant Castilian ground-floor *comedor*. Of two local **turismos rurales**, the more welcoming is non-en-suite *Casa Marión* in an older building (☎974 501 190; ❶).

However, Bielsa, with its **banks** and shops, is a better supply point for trekkers than Parzán. Central **accommodation** here includes the welcoming, spotless *Hostal Vidaller* (☎974 501 004; ❶–❸), just west of the *plaza* (info in ground-floor shop), with three grades of affordable rooms from basic to parquet-floored "lux"; the *Hostal Marboré* just north of the *plaza* (☎974/501 111; ❸); the old-fashioned but en-suite *Hostal Pirineos Méliz* (☎974 501 015; ❸), quietly set uphill from the *plaza*, with a ground-floor *comedor*, and the comfortable *Hotel Valle de Pineta* (☎974 501 010, ✉hotelvalledepineta@monteperdido.com; ❹) nearby, with rooms overlooking the Zinca valley. For a proper **meal**, try the local-patronized *comedor* of the welcoming *Hostal Pañart*, out on the A138 highway (☎ & ℻974 501 116; ❹), also endorsed as a lodging, or the well-attended *Pineta* on Plaza Mayor, with a wide-ranging €17 *menú*. Characterful, unassuming *Bar El Chinchecle*, very near the *Marboré*, organizes occasional Aragonese folk-music nights but otherwise urges drinkers on with a versatile taped soundtrack that has even extended to Jimmy Shand's Scottish dance band.

## The Valle de Pineta

A glacial trough scoured into sheer, stepped rock walls, the **Valle de Pineta** extends 15km west-northwest of Bielsa, terminating in the majestic **Circo de Pineta**; just above the *circo* looms **Monte Perdido** (3355m), one of the more celebrated summits in the Pyrenees. The idyllic floor of the valley, where reeds and birches fringe the white, boulder-flecked Río Zinca, broadened in the valley's lower reaches by a dam, contrasts drastically with the awesome cliffs of the Sierra de Espierba to the north and the even more fantastic **Sierra de las Tucas** to the south. At first glance you'll doubt that ascents of either the Circo de Pineta or the Sierra de las Tucas are possible; however, they are attainable, the rewards commensurate with the effort.

The valley's flanking palisades attract legions of technical climbers, but there are a few steep, strenuous **walks** here, too. The classic hikes – up to the Balcón de Pineta, a shelf 1200m higher than the valley floor at the top of the Circo de Pineta, and the GR11 route climbing a similar height over the Collado de Añisclo – both lead into the northeast corner of the *parque nacional*. For all outings, you'll need the Editorial Alpina 1:40,000 "Ordesa Vignemale Monte Perdido" map.

Valley **accommodation** is limited to two **campsites** – the reasonably priced and well-equipped *Pineta* at "Km 8" of the valley road (☏ & ⓕ974 501 089; April to early Oct), and the basic, inexpensive *Acampada Libre Canguro* (☏974 501 041; Easter & June–Aug) in a meadow at "Km 14" – plus the comfortable *Parador Nacional de Monte Perdido* (☏974 501 011, ⓔbielsa@parador.es; ⓦ) at the base of the Circo de Pineta. The *parador* has a bar and lounge from which more sedentary tourists scan the mountains through a telescope. Hikers might use the *Refugio de Pineta*, prosaically set nearby on the left bank of the river (1220m; ☏974 501 203; 71 places), generally overrun with school groups, but serving sustaining meals to all comers.

## Balcón de Pineta and beyond

For the **Balcón de Pineta**, take the path going left (west) just opposite the Ermita de Nuestra Señora de Pineta by the *parador*, which brings you shortly to a bridge at El Felqueral (1400m) and the foot of the cliffs. A subsequent series of tight zigzags gives progressively more unnerving views, as you climb through loose rock to the *balcón* (2530m; 3hr 45min from *parador*). The ascent is particularly steep in the final stages and shouldn't be attempted early in summer without crampons and ice-axe.

Twenty minutes to the northwest, a one-night tent stay is permitted at **Lago de Marboré** (2595m), which on a sunny day is a welcoming blue against the hard grey rock. But most eyes will be on the mass of Monte Perdido to the south, its savage northeast wall aproned by its huge glacier. Just north of the lake, the frontier pass of **Brecha de Tucarroya/Brèche de Tuquerouye** (2660m), with its historic hut, gives access to the Estaubé cirque and the HRP down to Gavarnie (see p.386). West of the lake, it's a ninety-minute climb through snow fields and across scree to the **Cuello de Astazú/Col d'Astazou** for a magnificent view over the Cirque de Gavarnie.

Finally, you can head south from the lake over the **Cuello del Cilindro** (3074m; 3hr); this is rather more difficult than the three-hundred-metre-lower Brèche de Roland, requiring year-round full snow-climbing gear including rope and, preferably, some prior experience in this sort of terrain. From this pass it takes around three hours more to descend to the *Refugio de Góriz* (see p.440); in theory you could get there in one long July day from the Valle de Pineta, but it's highly advisable to break the journey with an overnight at Lago de Marboré.

## The GR11: Parzán to Añisclo

The **GR11** west from Parzán is initially not very exciting: first on a narrow paved road for 3.6km to **Chisagües** hamlet, then 6.6km more up the valley of the **Río Real** as far as the spring of **Petramula** (1940m), just north of the eponymous peak. With care, an ordinary car can make it this far – if not, leave it by the pastoral hut and broad parking area 2km before – and there are usually knots of them parked here below a sharp hairpin curve, as this is also the trailhead for visiting the Munia lakes (see below). If you don't have a car, try and arrange a lift to spare you three hours of fairly dull tramping. A proper GR11 path resumes at the bend, and from the obvious saddle (ca. 2160m) west of Petramula peak you've fine views of the Valle de Pineta before a steady but not gruelling descent (except in the final moments) to an *ermita* by the *parador* (2hr 30min more).

From the vicinity of the *parador* (ca. 1300m), the GR11 then climbs south-west up what appear to be the impossibly sheer palisades of **Las Fayetas**, through the **Collado de Añisclo** (2453m) and beyond. This is a tough walk, like the Balcón route impossible without crampons and ice-axe until late June, and completely out of bounds in spring because of the danger of avalanches, which have gradually killed most of the trees on these slopes. But during summer it offers marvellous scenery close to hand and a bird's-eye view over the valley.

The start of this gruelling four-hour climb is signposted near the *ermita*, and again from the track serving the upper *Canguro* campsite. This is the most reliable river crossing; if you try from the refuge downstream, you're in for a mud-wallow and impenetrable riverbank thickets at the very least. Once over on the far side there are no further trail ambiguities until you're up on the *collado*. Beyond this saddle, the main GR11 was rerouted during 1989 in response to walkers' complaints. If inexperienced, or laden with a heavy pack, you should *not* use the *variante* heading northwest, since this inches perilously for 400m along the sheer face of **Pico de Añisclo** at the 2500m contour, with only a short cable to help you over a particularly nasty stretch always slippery with snowmelt. Instead, descend south for 1hr 45min along the main GR11 to a crude, unattended shelter at the head of the **Añisclo canyon**; there is plenty of turf and water nearby if you prefer or need to camp.

Otherwise, continue west-northwest along the GR11 up the Barranco Arablo (Fon Blanca) – the last reliable water being the vigorous waterfall of **Fon (Fuén) Blanca** at its mouth – where the occasionally scree-laden trail worms its way up along grassy terraces to the **Collado Superior de Góriz** (aka Arrablo; 2343m; 2hr 20min from Fon Blanca). Here you're treated to great views of Monte Perdido, Pico de Añisclo and Sum de Ramond; beyond the *collado* the *Refugio de Góriz* is 40min away, for a total of eight and a half hours' walking from the Valle de Pineta.

### Lagos de la Munia

One of the best half-day outings in the Pineta region is the hike from the Petramula road track-bend to the border-hugging **Lagos de la Munia**, some-times known as the Lagos de la Larri, nestled in the Circo de la Munia. The cairned path there takes off from the high side of the hairpin, *not* from the onward, initially descending GR11; it's well grooved into the landscape the whole way, keeping to the hillside west of Barranco del Clot. Within an hour you attain the Collado de las Puertas (2533m), and a few moments later you have your first glimpse of the lower lake; it's another twenty minutes to the shore of the upper lake (2526m), with surprisingly warm water for the altitude and a few campable, turfy spots on the far shore (though the lakes lie within the national park's peripheral zone). Pale, bald pyramidal **Peña Blanca/Pène Blanque** (2906m) on the northwest is the most striking of frontier peaks here, while 2787-metre Chinipro dominates to the south.

The descent (just over an hour from the upper lake to the track-bend) is enlivened by eyefuls of the Valle de Pineta's south ramparts and the more dis-tant Cotiella massif. It's not possible to continue into France from the upper lake; the only trekkers' route is west, down the Barranco de Fuensanta drain-ing the lower lake, then south along the Río de la Larri, joining up with the GR11 shortly before reaching the Pineta *parador* – allow two-and-a-half hours going downhill.

# The Ribera de Fiscal: the lower Ara valley

The Río Ara is the major tributary of the Zinca from the west, but the lower reaches of its valley are known as the **Ribera de Fiscal** after its most important village. By Aragonese standards the valley bottom is wide and relatively fertile, yet strangely deserted; nearly a dozen ghost villages between Fiscal and Aínsa, within sight of the road, are sporadically squatted by Spanish anarchists and alternative types. There's a roadside placard above the site of a half-built dam, which would disrupt the flow of the last undammed river in the Spanish Pyrenees, detailing its whole sorry history (see box p.430). Although it's now unlikely the dam will ever be built, plans are afoot to bulldoze a mega-highway direct from Fiscal to Sabiñánigo through virgin mountainside.

## Boltaña

**BOLTAÑA**, 8km west of Aínsa along the N260, divides like its near-neighbour into two parts: the ugly roadside development on the through highway, and the atmospheric hill quarter. Here the *plaza* is virtually filled by the sixteenth-century **Colegiata de San Pedro Apostol**, with its rib-vaulted ceiling, sturdy piers and carved choir stalls at the rear. Just downhill in a cul-de-sac, *Casa Coronel* does just two things in its *bar-restaurante*, but it does them well: chef's salad and garnished grills, served indoors or with mountain views in the courtyard. They also keep a few *turismo rural* **rooms** (℡974 502 154; ❶–❷), some en-suite.

## Fiscal

**FISCAL**, 20km upriver from Boltaña, is the next inhabited place, with a genuine country feel: tended kitchen gardens, hay in barns, ambling livestock. Despite falling some distance short of Ordesa it's well worth considering as a base, owing to the tranquillity and high standard of its tourist facilities (including shops and two **banks**, the only ones hereabouts). Up a lane ("Avenida" de Jesús) 200m before the church, with very jolly, slightly loopy but down-to-earth management by Rony and Ana, *Casa del Arco* (℡ & ℻974 503 042; ❷) offers lovely antique- (and textile-) furnished, en-suite rooms in a slate-floored, eighteenth-century mansion. Even higher standard is offered by luxurious *Hostal Casa Cadena*, another restored 1780s farmhouse near the top of the village (℡ & ℻974 503 077; ❹); rooms are modern, but each is different, with central heating. Downstairs is an equally posh **restaurant**, currently the best in Fiscal; the gourmet *carta* (allow €30), strong on fish, meat and Somontano wines, may break budgets, but a *menú* (€12) of chard with clams, grilled *sepia*, dessert and house wine, is eminently affordable, as are *raciones* at the bar. Fiscal also has an **albergue** in a Belle Époque mansion opposite the church, *Saltamontes* (℡974 503 113; 52 places), as well as two all-year **campsites** just upriver: smallish *El Jabalí Blanco* (℡ & ℻974 503 074) with its own pool and a few bungalows, and the giant, slightly cheaper *Ribera del Ara* (℡974 503 035), by the municipal pool.

## The Valle de Tella

The **Valle de Tella**, through which flows the Río Yaga, opens northwest roughly halfway between Aínsa and Bielsa. Though its praises are little sung in conventional tourist annals, it has long been one of the favourite **canyoning** venues on the flanks of Monte Perdido. At the head of the valley, just inside *parque nacional* territory, plunges the **Garganta de Escuaín**, a series of waterfalls,

## Dams in Alto Aragón

The reason behind the lower Ara valley's desolation is a long-mooted **dam at Jánovas**, at a critical set of narrows 6km west of Boltaña. The process of compulsory expropriation of land and houses to be inundated began in 1959, particularly targeting the residents of Jánovas, Lacort and Lavelilla villages. By today's standards, risible sums were offered as compensation; by 1964 most stubborn holdouts had been evicted by the combined threats of Franco's Guardia Civil and privately hired thugs. Those who sold up had their houses dynamited (thus accounting for the ruinous appearance of the three named villages, while "subtler" methods of persuasion such as blocking all water supplies and staving in the door of the Jánovas school with the children still inside were employed *pour encourager les autres*. Just one brave couple – **Emilio and Francisca Garcés** – insisted on staying in Jánovas, holding out in primitive conditions until 1984, when they too gave up and moved to nearby Campodarbe.

Yet this dam **never materialized**, beyond an earthen dyke half-obstructing the riverbed, where earth-movers occasionally appeared to push mud around. Two binding **deadlines** for interim accomplishment came and went, while **Iberduero**, the dam contractor, went bankrupt and re-formed, insisting that it would complete the project in the face of sustained opposition. The dam promoters' legalistic position was that the valley residents were paid full and **final settlement** in 1960, and having departed (or rather, been made to) should stay out. The displaced and their partisans argued that this took place under conditions of dictatorship, with scarcely realistic compensation; furthermore, that by failing to complete the project by stipulated deadlines, Iberduero and its successor **voided the original contract** and, upon repurchase of their property (at the original rates, of course), the villagers have a clear case to return unhindered.

The prevailing uncertainty also caused a wave of abandonment in adjacent Javierre, Santa Oloria and Ligüerre de Ara, eventually affecting seven hundred persons in a total of 17 villages. But despite the hydro-honchos' bluster, an actual dam became less likely with each passing year. It would have to have been substantially **enlarged** to make it economically viable, and the upstream villages affected wised up, demanding hefty sums for their land. Finally, on February 10, 2001, the proposed dam was officially **pronounced dead**, "inappropriate for reasons of adverse environmental impact."

Another dam anecdote serves to further illustrate the ruthlessness and collusion of all the establishment organs in Franco's state. One valley west, in the Río Tena basin, **Lanuza** village was forcibly evacuated and token payouts made when most of its lands, and some houses, were submerged by the namesake dam in 1975. Since then, half the original owners – those 5m or more above the mean water line – have **bought back** their old homes and rehabilitated them. But when they went looking for their beloved 700-kilo bronze **church bells** "Elena" and "Quiteria" (patron saints of Lanuza), they had considerable difficulty finding them. The local bishop, wanting no nostalgic rearguard action, had removed them from the belfry and filed the names off. One was eventually recovered in Torla, but the other is still missing.

smooth chutes and pools where, equipped with ropes and wet suits, devotees abseil, slide and swim.

This is great walking country too, especially when the terrain closer to Monte Perdido is snowed up. The **GR15** and **GR19** overlap near Tella village, on the valley's east flank, and a PR itinerary completes a tour of most highlights; the best single base for walkers is **Lafortunada**, out on the main road below Tella. Scenically, the eight local villages are overshadowed, in all senses, by a landscape dappled by the interaction of soothing vegetation and dazzlingly bare rock. Green, lush scrub – much of it *boj* (box), made into souvenir utensils – blends into low alpine forest, with two-thousand-metre **Castillo Mayor** presiding on the west, and remoter **Peña Montañesa** (2301m) dominating the skyline to the southeast.

## Car access – and canyoning

The top of the valley is easily accessible by ordinary car: paved roads lead to Revilla on the east bank and to the village of Escuaín on the west. The **Revilla turning** leaves the main road at Hospital de Tella, from where it's 8km in total to the end. As the road climbs to the hamlet of Cortalaviña there are wonderful views east to the distinctively tilted lump of Peña Montañesa; then, 2km beyond Cortalaviña, the road divides. The right-hand option climbs to Tella (see below), while the left-hand road continues along a ridge to Revilla, where it ends.

To get into the **Barranco de Consusa** just below Revilla, one of the six main canyoning courses of the area, follow an onward path towards a *mirador* inside the *parque nacional* for ten minutes. The Consusa's course includes a three-hundred-metre-long "staircase" with four thirty-metre chutes and countless smaller drops. It'll take four to six hours to cover the full length of the stream, and at the bottom it's about 45 minutes' walk back to either Revilla or Escuaín.

The **turning for Escuaín** is closer to Aínsa, 9km north on the main A138 to just beyond Escalona, then west along the HU631 towards Añisclo. After 1km on this road, take the paved road on the right (north) signposted to Escuaín (via Belsierre and Puértolas), 15km in total from the A138. Some maps (including the Firestone) mistakenly indicate a nonexistent access road from Hospital de Tella. From Escuaín a track to the northwest (barred to vehicles at the park boundary) affords access to the main canyoning area in the *garganta*.

## Lafortunada and Badaín

**LAFORTUNADA**, on the A138, 17km north of Aínsa and 15km south of Bielsa, isn't the most prepossessing of villages, but it does make the most convenient overnight base for walkers, with a choice of **accommodation**. There's a *turismo rural*, *Casa Tomas* (☎974 504 019; ❶), and the nearby, superior *Hotel Badain* (☎974 504 006, ⓦwww.staragon.com/hbadain; ❸ B&B, ❺ HB), with comfortable, tasteful rooms and one of the best **restaurants** in these valleys. Meals (*menú* only at €12.50) comprise a broad choice of fish or vegetarian dishes, such as lentils with carrots or shark steak grilled to perfection; plum-and-armagnac sorbet and quince liqueur add finishing touches. The hotel is named after the hamlet of **BADAÍN**, 500m southeast, graced by a severe eleventh-century church with a round staircase tacked onto its square belfry, which now houses an **albergue** (☎974 504 000; minimum 2-night stay; all year) intended for groups. The church nave's a bit over-restored, but retains its Gothic stellar vaulting and a finely carved gallery. Both the GR19 and GR15 pass the church: the former on its rather humdrum way along the Río Zinca to Laspuña, the GR15 more excitingly east through the mountains towards Saravillo and the Valle de Chistau (see p.311).

## Walking in the Valle de Tella

If you don't have transport, the quickest way into canyon country is along the joint **GR15/19** trail, well signposted 200m north of the church in

Lafortunada. This climbs initially northwest within two hours to the pictur-esque village of **TELLA**, bigger than it looks from afar and restored for sea-sonal use. There's a park **information office** (July–Oct daily 9am–2pm & 3–9pm) dispensing glossy brochures, but no other facilities except for an all-important fountain. As well as the imposing Romanesque parish church, there is a clutch of *ermitas* (isolated rural chapels) to which you can detour: the old-est are the eleventh-century **Virgen de Fajanillas**, an easy and obvious ten-minute walk west of the village, and **Juanipablo**, fifteen minutes further northwest on an intriguing pinnacle.

Just north of Tella, the GR19 and GR15 part company: the former heads northeast to Salinas, while the GR15 descends to a picnic area and **dolmen**, threads through the hamlet of **ARINZUÉ** and drops to the river at **ESTA-RONILLO** hamlet (4 summer inhabitants; 1hr 15min from Tella). The final track approach to Estaronillo is often jammed with cars belonging to French rafters, who delight in running the **Garganta de Marval** of the Yaga just downstream.

From Estaronillo you and the GR15 climb another hour and a quarter through thick woods to **ESCUAÍN**, a mostly abandoned settlement taken over in summer by strolling cows and rough campers, usually technically equipped enthusiasts exploring the **Garganta de Escuaín**, which lies just upstream. You might pause at the park **information office** (same hours as Tella's) before continuing along paths into the water-sculpted ravine.

From Escuaín a very steep trail drops in twenty minutes to the Río Yaga, then continues on the far bank past a derelict mill, crosses the outflow of the Barranco de Consusa and climbs from the river. Ninety minutes out of Escuaín, five minutes shy of the road up from Tella, be extra observant: here you can veer south on the fairly clear, marked **PR39** trail down to Estaronillo – mistakenly shown on some maps as taking off from the road itself – or north along an overgrown twenty-minute path to **REVILLA**. Even more desolate than Escuaín, with just a few houses modernized as vacation retreats, the ham-let is well camouflaged by the orange and grey cliff immediately behind.

If you opt instead for the PR39 south, you continue past Estaronillo and then along a shelf of land wedged between the Garganta de Marval and Castillo Mayor, finishing after two and a half hours in total at **Hospital de Tella**, 3km west of Lafortunada. It's possible to complete the entire figure-of-eight itiner-ary of Lafortunada–Tella–Escuaín–Revilla–Estaronillo–Hospital in a single, long summer's day, taking in the best this limestone region has to offer.

### Escuaín to Añisclo

Escuaín itself is a good jumping-off point for walking further **into the par-que nacional**, specifically the **Valle de Añisclo**. Head northwest, high up on the right (southwest) bank of the Yaga, at first on track (signposted as "Surgencia del Yaga") and then on path, until you reach the **Cuello Viceto** (2002m; 3hr). From here a wide path curves south down into Añisclo, pausing at a shelf on which are the spring and unstaffed refuge of **San Vicenda** (4hr 30min along), adjacent to one of the park's few permitted camping areas.

From San Vicenda the best trail drops north into the bottom of the canyon past **Fuente de Foradiello**, and then crosses the main Añisclo watercourse just downstream from the mouth of the Capradizas ravine. Once on the far bank, you can head north to Fon Blanca and the GR11 (see above), or follow the main Añisclo canyon trail south for three and a half hours to the **Ermita de San Úrbez**, at the very entrance to the Añisclo canyon (see the following section).

More simply, you can also follow the **GR15 southwest** from Escuaín to the *ermita* in about six hours, leaving you enough daylight to reach accommodation in Nerín or Buerba. The trail initially heads west over the **Cuello Ratón** on the shoulder of Castillo Mayor, and then veers south, mostly on track, to the village of **BESTUÉ**. This has one of the best views southeast in Alto Aragón, with the banded Sestrales ridge on the west separating you from Añisclo; there's also, in theory, an *albergue* in the centre, but this was closed in 2003 and may not reopen – if it isn't open, allow four to five more hours to reach accommodation in Nerín or Buerba. If you manage to stay overnight, find time for the half-day trip **up Castillo Mayor** (2014m) on non-GR paths, worth it for guaranteed sightings of lammergeiers and other vultures. Beyond Bestué on the GR15, you're on scenic path again for three hours to San Úrbez, involving a roller-coaster course over the Sestrales, rewarded by views into Añisclo from the top.

## The Valle de Añisclo

The uninhabited **Valle (Cañon) de Añisclo**, forging due south from the Collado de Añisclo and roughly equidistant from Aínsa or Lafortunada, is on a far grander scale than the Valle de Tella and accordingly more visited. It's a beguiling spot, more intimate and wild than its other rival Ordesa; neither is the path running through it, parallel to the Río Vellos (Bellós), a pram-pushing stroll, given its often sharp grades and vertiginous drops from unguarded edges.

If you have transport, you can reach Añisclo on the minor but paved HU631 road heading west from just north of Escalona on the A138. Once past an initially unpromising landscape – where, 2km along, a large **campsite**, *Valle de Añisclo* (☎974 505 096; Easter–Oct 15), below Puyarruego village, is noteworthy only for a last chance to swim in the Río Vellos, forbidden further upstream – you enter the *parque nacional* at the dramatic **Desfiladero de las Cambras**, appetizers for the Añisclo canyon. Here the road is confined to a shelf blasted out of the rock wall, too narrow for excursion buses, and is designated one-way westbound (eastbound traffic heads to Escalona along a purpose-built detour via Buerba – see overleaf). At the west end of the gorge, 12km from the main highway, knots of parked cars announce the mouth of Añisclo just to the north. It has been proposed to ban private vehicles entirely from the *desfiladero*, and in future a shuttle bus may operate from Puyarruego.

### The canyon walk

From the parking areas, two broad paths – equally valid, as they form a loop around the confluence of the Vellos and Aso rivers – lead north into the canyon. The right-hand path crosses a bridge high above the joint streams, then follows a ledge where a cave has been converted into the **Ermita de San Úrbez**. Some fifteen minutes past the *ermita* you change to the west bank and climb to meet the GR15 trail coming east from Nerín on its way to Bestué. Soon you're passing through box thickets and beech woods, with the occasional conifer or yew, the locality all cool, damp and shady except at midday, thanks to the constant misting from the river. Its flashing cascades and tempting green pools glimmer far below you on the right, tantalizingly out of reach, and perhaps just as well, since you're not allowed to bathe. High, sheer walls amplifying the roar of the torrent culminate in the **Sestrales crest** to the east, here interrupted by an uncanny keyhole-shaped cleft.

By now you'll have noticed that progress upstream is not steady – the path roller-coasters constantly, with a particularly notable climb and hairpins away from the river about two hours along, at the top of which you have the best views possible into the lower canyon. The most spectacular section finishes at the grassy expanse of **La Ripareta** (1400m), only about 500m higher than San Úrbez but because of the nature of the trail nearly three hours distant. Here, you're level with the river once more, but camping is not permitted; otherwise it's a good spot for a picnic, or watching the sky for birds of prey.

From La Ripareta there's a choice of onward routes, and whichever you choose you'll have more solitude, since the gradient stiffens and the trails become fainter. About 2km (40min) north you can cross the main river and follow a path up to the authorized bivouac area and shelter at **San Vicenda**. Continuing on the west bank from La Ripareta for about ninety minutes, you'll reach the Fon Blanca cascade at the Barranco Arrablo (see p.428), which funnels the **GR11** west to the *Refugio de Góriz*. In the opposite direction the GR11 leads over the Collado de Añisclo to the Valle de Pineta; you'll want a fairly early start from San Úrbez to finish either of these traverses in a single day (the *Refugio de Góriz* is a more reasonable goal).

## West from Añisclo: the Valle de Vió

West from the mouth of the Añisclo canyon, the road follows the **Valle de Vió**, a deserted district particularly hard hit by the exodus to the lowland towns; the half-dozen or so local villages have just a handful of residents, and one place is completely abandoned. But in a reversal of the situation prevailing at the Valle de Tella, the villages with their eleventh-to-thirteenth-century churches are far more interesting than the valley itself, which is sun-scorched and overgrazed to barrenness on the north, though still heavily wooded on its south slope.

### Buerba and around

The namesake village of **VIÓ**, 5km south of the Añisclo gorge car parks, is the one village hereabouts where (in summer at least) there are still more tractors than tourists, trundling through the surrounding hayfields, though it's deserted in winter. Not so at **BUERBA**, 2km further and the end of the paved road, always packed with canyoners plumbing the secrets of the **Río Yesa** to the south. For non-canyoners, the best outing from here is the two-hour **walk** on an unmarked path to very attractive Yeba village (no facilities), crossing the river. The GR15.1, a short *variante* path, links Buerba via Vió with the GR15 at San Úrbez, while another leg of the GR15.1 goes to Fanlo via Buisán, making a good day-loop possible.

In terms of **food** and **accommodation**, relaxed en-suite *Casa Marina* (☎608 714 450, ⓦwww.valledevio.com/casamarina.htm; open Easter–6 Jan; ❷), the first building on the right as you enter Buerba, with young, English-speaking management and home-cooked meals (vegetarian on request), is homier than the slick and somewhat sterile *Casa Lisa* (☎974 337 215; ❷), with variable rooms and meals for guests only (bar open to all).

### Nerín

If you're without transport and only committed to day-walks in Añisclo, you'll have to stay either at Buerba or **NERÍN**, an hour's walk west of the canyon on the GR15, via the forlorn, utterly deserted hamlet of Sercué. By road from San Úrbez (not recommended for pedestrians) it's 5km away. Nerín is blessed with an incomparable setting, gazing east to Peña Montañesa, plus a reliable spring and an exceptionally fine Romanesque church. What's locally billed as the "Fanlo" cross-country skiing area is actually accessed from Nerín – but the track in is awful, requiring a 4WD vehicle.

Short-stay tourism and the renovation and selling off of a dozen or so buildings as holiday homes have somewhat revived what was once another dying hamlet. The *Añisclo Albergue* (℡974 489 010, all year; 36 places), with its front garden and ravishing view, sells maps and guides to all-comers, but serves meals to guests only, and requires reservations, as does the more comfortable *Pensión El Turista* (℡974 489 016; ❷) with its panoramic *comedor*. Top standard for some distance around is offered by the much-needed if rather brash 2001-built *Hotel Palazio* (℡974 489 002, ℮ hotelpalazio@ordesa.com; ❸), three floors' worth of plush, loft-style rooms, and a popular ground-floor restaurant.

## Fanlo

The GR15 carries on west to Fanlo, curling through virtually abandoned, though beautifully sited Buisán (population 4), whose hilltop houses have also been restored for seasonal use. **FANLO**, 6km beyond Nerín by the more direct paved road, and again engagingly sited, is the biggest place hereabouts, with a unique turreted manor house and an equally photogenic communal laundry just south of it juxtaposed uneasily with a huge unfinished hotel just downhill. For the moment, there's no short-stay accommodation, just a sandwich-bar (*Las Eras*), unimprovably perched amongst the hilltop grain barns and threshing grounds west of the village.

Just northwest of Fanlo yawns the **Desfiladero de las Gloces**, a good place for a first experience of canyoning, a fact not lost on the French who throng the place. From the high point of the road, west of Las Eras, a path runs north for half an hour through abandoned fields, woods and scrub to the stony riverbed. The first obstacle, a ten-metre chute, presents no problems if you've ever been to a water park, and subsequent drops are easy by comparison. Two to three hours later you emerge a little southwest of Fanlo, though well below the road.

## Moving on

West of Fanlo, 12km of steep, potholed, lightly travelled road bring you down to Sarvisé on the N260 road, 4km south of Broto and 6km south of Torla (see below for descriptions of all of these places). The **GR15** also emerges on the asphalt an hour out of Fanlo, but following a much-needed rerouteing, soon leaves it to approximately adopt the 1300-metre contour west on its way to Buesa village, via the **Ermita de la Virgen de Bun**. Alternatively, you can use a track, a bit higher than the Desfiladero de las Gloces path, heading northwest within three hours to the **Cuello de Diazas** (2133m), which overlooks the Valle de Ordesa. Once there you've a choice of paths and tracks, either north into the valley or west to Torla, the latter easily reached after another two and a half hours.

# The Valle de Ordesa and around

Carved out first by glaciers and later enlarged by the fast-flowing Río Arazas, the eight-hundred-metre-deep trough of the superlative-laden **Valle de Ordesa**, in the north of Alto Aragón, deservedly draws hundreds of thousands of visitors a year. It forms the core of the **Parque Nacional de Ordesa y Monte Perdido**, which takes the second part of its name from the imposing limestone massif lying at the centre of park territory.

The two usual road approaches to the *parque nacional*, both served by **public transport**, are via either Sabiñánigo and Biescas (see p.444) to the west, or from Aínsa (p.424) to the southeast, along the N260 following the Río Ara, which has headwaters close to Vignemale and merges with the Zinca some 60km later at Aínsa. Along the first half of its course, before curling east, the Ara flows south through the **Valle de Broto**, where villages like **Sarvisé**, **Oto** and **Broto** have been rescued by tourism from the desolation that has befallen those further downstream. **Torla**, 45km upstream from Aínsa and 39km northeast of Sabiñánigo, is by far the busiest of these settlements, since it's the closest to the Valle de Ordesa, though surprisingly lifeless in winter as there's no ski centre nearby.

North of Torla, beyond the confluence of the Ara and the Arazas, there are just the campsites and refuge at **Bujaruelo**, beyond which lies a wilderness not included in the park. Coming from the strategic *Refugio de Góriz* below Monte Perdido, the **GR11** threads through the Ordesa canyon, follows the Ara north almost to its source, then crosses west to Panticosa. Alternatively you can hike **into France** through a number of passes: the Brecha de Roldán (Brèche de Roland) towards Gavarnie, or two others at the top of the Ara into the Cauterets basin.

## The Valle de Broto

Travelling upstream from Fiscal (see p.429), the N260 turns north past gradually more forested slopes to reach **SARVISÉ**, the lowest village of the **Valle de Broto**, 38km from Aínsa. In high season you could be compelled to stay in Sarvisé, rather than further north, but in consolation **accommodation** here is of a high standard. Best by some way is the *Hotel Casa Frauca* (☎974 486 353, ⓕ974 486 789; closed Jan 6–early March; reservations mandatory; ❸) on the main highway, its varied wood- or tile-floored rooms, some with balcony, offering unique decor. Otherwise, in descending order of preference, go for the stone-built, quiet *Casa Puyuelo* (☎974 486 140, ⓔ casapuyuelo@staragon.com; ❷), with small but sweet, pastel-toned rooms, an attic lounge and broad front lawn; the *Hotel Viña Olivan*, by itself at the edge of town on the Fanlo road (☎ & ⓕ974 486 358; ❷); or *Hostal Casa Gallán* behind Casa Puyuelo (☎974 486 056, ⓦwww.casagallan.com; ❷), with courtyard parking and a wing of apartments too. *Casa Frauca*'s famous ground-floor **restaurant** (closed Sun & Mon eve low season, except for guests) deservedly draws crowds from near and far; their three-course *menú* (€13, drink extra) of leek mousse, sea bass with roast potatoes and cheesecake represents great value, or allow €23 *a la carta*.

Perched 4.5km away by road on the hillside northeast of Sarvisé (or reached more directly from a PR trail starting from the north edge of Sarvisé), beautiful, secluded **BUESA** consists of two *barrios* flanking a wooded vale – this is rustic Aragón as it was until the 1980s. Grilled suppers are available at *Bar Merendero Balcón del Pirineo*, and rather basic rooms with self-catering kitchen at *Casa Pleto* up by the church (☎974 486 175; ❶–❷) – no palace, but a potential lifesaver in August. Incidentally, between July 1 and August 31, both **buses** from Sabiñánigo call at Sarvisé: the morning one (daily) en route to Aínsa, the evening one (Mon–Sat) turning around here just before 8pm, passing through Broto and Torla before returning to Sabiñánigo.

### Broto, Oto and Linás de Broto

By the time **BROTO** itself is reached, 4km north of Sarvisé, you're in the thick of things; a **Turismo booth** (summer only Tues–Sun 10am–2pm & 4.30–8.30pm; ☎974 486 002) advises on **accommodation** vacancies in high season. The valley's capital is a noisy, teeming place in summer, its old quarter hemmed by traffic and a massive *urbanización*, a plight symbolized by the collapsed Romanesque bridge just upriver, destroyed during the Civil War. Beside this is the quietest place to stay, and usually one of the last to fill: *Taberna O Puente* (T974 486 072; ❷ B&B). Breakfast is served outdoors under what's left of the bridge arch, but other meals here aren't up to much and indeed none of the restaurants in the village is worth singling out. Other accommodation, all on the through road, includes en-suite *Hostal Español* (T974 486 007, Ehsespanol@terra.es; ❷), west of the modern bridge, the more comfortable one-star *Hotel Gabarre* at no. 6 (T974 486 052; ❸), whose en-suite rooms have balconies, and the less pricey *Hotel Latre* (T974 486 053; ❷) at the west end of town, with parking. Grupo Explora (T974 486 432, Wwww.grupoexplora .com), at c/Santa Cruz 18 downhill from the *Gabarre*, is the most active local guides' bureau, specializing in canyoning, caving and especially **rafting** – the stretch of the Río Ara from Puente de los Navarros (see p.443) and Broto is particularly appropriate. Broto also has two **banks** (with ATMs) and the only **auto fuel** between Aínsa, Biescas and Torla.

Alternatively, head for the more attractive village of **OTO**, 1.5km south, which features homogeneous architecture and two notable medieval towers: one on the church, the other on a fifteenth-century baronial mansion. More or less opposite each other in the centre are two surprisingly modern, sterile but spotless **turismos rurales** – *Casa Herrero* (T974 486 093; ❷), above the bar, and *Casa Pueyo* (T974 486 075; ❷), which also manages the large campsite, *Oto* (April 1–Oct 15), 500m beyond the village.

**LINÁS DE BROTO**, a tiny, stone-built hamlet 10km west of Broto on the N260 towards Biescas and Sabiñánigo, would also be a reasonable spot to fetch up, as long as you have a car, with its fine position and clutch of **places to stay** along the through road. These include the en-suite *Hostal Jal* (T974 486 106, Ehostaljal@wanadoo.es; ❷) and the co-managed *Hotel Las Nieves* (T974 486 109, Wwww.hotellasnieves.com; ❸) and *Hostal Cazcarro* (❷). Without a car, you may prefer to trust to luck in Torla; a well-trodden *camino*, part of the **GR15.2**, leads there in 45 minutes from Broto's ruined bridge.

## Torla

The brazenly commercialized village of **TORLA** is the obvious gateway to the park, just over 8km away by road, and besides Broto or Sarvisé is the only feasible base if you don't have any transport. Until the mid-1980s, the village was the sort of place where espadrilles were inadvisable because of the amount of cow dung on the streets. But a mushrooming of concrete construction on the outskirts since then has obscured the village's profile, though the medieval core remains intact and attractive, despite the conversion of every second building for tourist purposes.

Except in July or August – when even the nearby campsites fill and you must book rooms three weeks in advance – and weekdays from October to Easter, when most hotels (and their restaurants) close, **accommodation** is easy to come by. The reasonable, friendly *Hostal Alto Aragón* (T & F974 486 172; ❷) and the co-managed *Hotel Ballarín* (T & F974 486 155; ❸), adjacent at c/Capuvita 11, were both remodelled in 1997 and, especially off-season, are a bargain, with views of the village rooftops; the home-style food served at the *Ballarín*'s *comedor* is filling and good value (*menú* €13). Among four fancier hotels, the most professionally run is the *Villa de Torla* on the main square (T974 486 156, F974 486 365; ❹), which though not exactly cosy understands what foreigners want; try for the superior top-floor rooms. It has a pool in the terrace garden, and a restaurant that will outrage animal-lovers with such dishes as *sarrio* (isard) stew. Also worth considering if you have a car is the three-star *Abetos* (☎974 486 448; ⓔhotelabetos@torla.com; ❺), 2km out towards the national park, with comfortable rooms and generous breakfast offsetting the slightly kitsch common areas. For budget lodgings, choose between two partly en-suite **turismos rurales** on c/Fatás, next to the Turismo: *Casa Laly* (☎974 486 168; ❷) and *Casa Borruel* (☎974 486 067, ❷). There are also two **albergues**: the cramped *L'Atalaya* (☎974 486 022; 21 places in 3 dorms; April–Dec) with a downstairs restaurant, or the friendlier, higher-standard *Lucien Briet* (☎974 486 221; 43 places; 3-to-6-bunk dorms, a few doubles ❷), managed by the *Bar Brecha*, which serves good meals (*menú* €11) in its upstairs *comedor*. Among **bars**, the *bodega* under *L'Atalaya* vies with the more traditionally Spanish ambience of the bars *La Brecha* and *A'Borda Samper* around the corner, the latter with a good selection of *tapas* as well as a proper *comedor*.

Finally, three **campsites** (all April–Oct) line the road to Ordesa. Choose from the *Río Ara* by the river (☎974 486 248), 2km from Torla on the east bank; the fancier, gigantic *Ordesa* (☎974 486 146), 3km along the road, intended mainly for cars and caravans; and the smaller, more basic *San Antón* (☎974 486 063) 3.5km out of town on a terrace above the road.

Rounding off the list of amenities, Torla has both a **bank** (with ATM) and a **post office**, plus a **Turismo** just off central Plaza Nueva (☎974 229 804; Easter & late June to mid-Sept Mon–Fri 10am–1pm & 6–8pm, Sat & Sun 9.30am–1.30pm & 5–8.30pm). Three stores sell a limited range of trekking provisions, while La Tienda on the main through lane doubles as the Compañia de Ordesa mountain guides office (☎974 486 417, ⓔguiasordesa@pirineo .com, especially good for rafting excursions) and supplier of maps and mountaineering gear.

The year-round **bus** to Sabiñánigo, run by La Oscense, leaves Aínsa at 2.30pm, passes Sarvisé and Broto and reaches Torla at around 3.30pm, stopping near the giant car park for the park shuttle bus (see box p.441). During July and August there is also the additional evening service from Sarvisé (Mon–Sat), passing Torla at about 8.15pm on its way to Sabiñánigo.

## Into the park from Torla

From Torla the **shuttle-bus** service rolls 4km northwest by the paved A135 road to the boundary of the **Parque Nacional de Ordesa y Monte Perdido**, at the Puente de los Navarros, at which point the road swings east for just over another 4km, where the bus leaves you at the car-parking area (open winter only to private vehicles), well inside the **Valle de Ordesa**. The closest **drivers** can get in summer is a small car park about 1.5km before Puente de los Navarros; from here a marked PR path goes down to Puente de la Ereta and thence into the park.

If you're **on foot**, you should definitely shun the tarmac in favour of the *camino* marked as part of the GR15.2. This begins in Torla next to the *Hostal Bella Vista* (marked as "Ordesa por Senda Peatonal"), crosses the Río Ara on a cement-and-masonry bridge, then turns sharply left (north) to join the Camino de Turieto at the posted park boundary, 45 minutes from Torla. After that, it's an easy and beautiful hike, two hours in total from the village, signposted all the way and taking you high above the river past some voluminous waterfalls. The path, like the road, eventually leads to the car park at **Pradera de Ordesa**, where there are toilets and a restaurant, predictably world-weary but offering a reasonable midday menu. There is no shop, so come prepared with provisions if you're intent on trekking or picnicking.

# Walks in the Valle de Ordesa

Most of the walks in the valley begin from the vicinity of **Pradera de Ordesa**, specifically at the **Puente de los Cazadores** a little way upstream. There are dozens of possibilities, encompassing all levels of enthusiasm and expertise: the following examples are just a selection. Be aware that some of the "paths" marked on maps are actually technical climbing routes, and don't underestimate the time and difficulty of the more conventional pedestrian itineraries. Once you're out of the shady valley floor, the sun can be taxing, and drinking water is usually unavailable en route – take plenty with you, as the various waterfalls are contaminated.

The most accurate **map** of the Valle de Ordesa is the 1:50,000 Mapa Excursionista/Carte de Randonnées no. 24 "Gavarnie-Ordesa" sheet, which also covers a fair chunk of the French side, though cheaper ones such as the Editorial Alpina 1:40,000 "Ordesa y Monte Perdido" are perfectly adequate if you're going to stick to the popular, signed paths.

## Valley traverse to the Circo de Soaso

This is one of the most popular – certainly in July or August – and rewarding of the short-distance treks. It's not especially difficult: a steep, 7.5-kilometre, three-hour traverse of the entire Valle de Ordesa, along a signposted path from Puente de los Cazadores, to the **Circo de Soaso**, which is also the beginning of the route to the *Refugio de Góriz* (see below). From wonderful beech forest the trail climbs past the *mirador* for the **Cascada del Abanico**, 3000m from Pradera de Ordesa, to emerge into the upper valley pasture, with the *circo* at its head and to your left – fanning out over a cliff – the famous **Cola de Caballo** (Horse's Tail) waterfall.

## Return via Faja de Pelay

Looking back from the *circo*, you have a clear view of one of the artificial-looking but entirely natural ledges known as *fajas*: a standard feature of banded-limestone terrain, they are formed where a layer of softer calcareous rock has been exploded loose by repeated cycles of freezing and thawing. The ledge running along the south side of the canyon – the **Faja de Pelay** – is negotiated along its entire length by an easy path that can be followed back to the car park. Along the way you get more solitude than is possible in the valley bottom, and an aerial view of the canyon; opposite looms a succession of remote peaks and features – most conspicuously the Brecha de Roldán, and the peaks of Cilindro and Monte Perdido.

The route is almost level at first, then drops gently to the *mirador* and stone shelter at **Calcilarruego**. From there, you descend fiercely along the **Senda de los Cazadores** (the Hunters' Path) by a long series of tight zigzags, finally crossing the Puente de Cazadores to return to the bus stop. The total walk back from the Circo de Soaso is four and a half hours; there's no reliable water source until just before Calcilarruego, so you must carry your own supply the whole way. A good case could be made for doing this loop in reverse: fewer crowds on the way back, and the stiff climb up the Senda de los Cazadores (2hr 30min) in morning shade.

## Onward to the Refugio de Góriz

To ascend from the Circo de Soaso to the *Refugio de Góriz*, you have the choice of a gently zigzagging path to the right, or the direct assault up the cliff aided by *clavijas* (pegs and chains). The *clavijas* aren't as bad as they look, but if you've got

The **Parque Nacional de Ordesa y Monte Perdido** was Spain's first protected area, established in 1918 as a reserve of 21 square kilometres to protect the showcase Valle de Ordesa, which lies immediately south of France's Cirque de Gavarnie. In 1982 the *parque nacional* was extended to 156 square kilometres, incorporating half a dozen "three-thousander" summits and the entire Valle de Añisclo, plus the head-waters of the Tella and the Circo de Pineta. This made the Spanish park contiguous with France's *Parc National des Pyrénées*; in the late 1980s the two park administrations signed an agreement for joint policy formulation and management – a sensible strategy given the huge numbers of mountaineers who surge back and forth between the two parks via the Brecha de Roldán (Brèche de Roland; see p.389).

### Geomorphology
From the Ara river valley in the west to well past the Zinca drainage in the east, the Pyrenees incorporate a great mass of **karstic limestone**, heaved up from the sea floor about fifty million years ago, its beds first tilted and folded, then diligently sculpted by glaciers into a startling backdrop of peaks, cliffs and gorges. The process continues today on a smaller scale as dozens of seasonal waterfalls pour off the *circos* of the Ordesa and Pineta valleys in particular.

  **Monte Perdido**, roughly in the centre of the park, ranks as the highest limestone peak in Europe, and the third highest summit in the Pyrenees. This mountain fills the heads of the four major valleys – **Ordesa**, **Pineta**, **Añisclo** and **Tella** – which drain away from it; a glacier still survives on its forbidding northeast face. Invisible to most visitors' eyes, but no less dramatic on acquaintance, are the hundreds of sinkholes and caves riddling the rock strata here, especially in the karst dells between the French frontier and the *Refugio de Góriz*. Bleak uplands surrounding the Valle de Ordesa on all sides, though parched and cheerless in midsummer, delight alpine skiers during wintertime.

### Flora and fauna
Owing to the 2600-metre difference between the highest and lowest points in the park, and the consequent variation in climate, there's a broad spectrum of **flora**. Beech, birch and poplar forests thrive in the moist Valle de Ordesa; in the drier Valle de Pineta pine predominates; while at the mouths of the lower, warmer Añisclo and Tella valleys, an almost Mediterranean vegetation of oaks, yew, box ash and maple prevails, coexisting at slightly higher elevations with fir and black pine. Above the treeline sprawl vast moors of specially adapted pincushion-type plants, with the genus *Festuca* well represented, but tucked among all of this are nearly 1500 species of small flowering plants, scores of them endemics marooned here by the glaciers and found nowhere else.

  **Fauna** around the *parque nacional* – including golden eagles, lammergeiers, griffon and Egyptian vultures, and isards (*sarrios* in Aragonese) – is much the same as

a heavy pack, or the rocks are wet, the path is much better. Once past this point, follow the marked trail north to the **Refugio de Góriz**, 90min from the *circo* (2200m; ☎974 341 201; 72 places; all year; reservations advisable), sometimes known as *Delgado Úbeda*, where you can stay cheaply and eat expensively. The refuge, despite its regimentation and famously abrupt staff, is extremely popular and at peak times floor-space, and even food, might run out. When this happens camping is allowed nearby, but often the immediately adjacent area becomes revoltingly unsavoury – budget for extra daylight time to reach some better sites further east, towards the Collado Superior de Góriz (Arrablo).

on the French side, with the isards so prolific that at times hunters are allowed to cull the surplus. By contrast the last native **ibex** died in January 2000; introduced specimens failed to survive.

## Climate and seasons
**Weather** in the park is notoriously fickle: during some summers there's not a cloud in the sky for days on end, but at other times there's thunder and hail every afternoon. When venturing out of the valley bottoms, always go prepared. In winter the park lies under one to two metres of snow, which persists in the popular Valle de Ordesa – not to mention higher elevations – until early June. Autumn features the spectacle of turning leaves on the beech and poplar trees, yet the weather remains relatively stable, if cool, and the park is far less crowded. Unless you're equipped with snow gear, the ideal visiting season is June to October.

## Rules and regulations
Given ever-increasing tourist numbers, the park seems in real danger of being loved to death, so a few of the **rules** are worth elaborating. **Camping is prohibited** within the confines of the park except for a few specified areas, namely the Balcón de Pineta; at San Vicenda and Fon Blanca in the Valle de Añisclo; beside Escuaín village; and around the *Refugio de Góriz* when it's full. Even at these places, you must dismount tents and leave them lying flat during the day – if you don't, park employees or the hut warden may do it in your absence. The small **stone huts** marked on most maps are intended for daytime use only, as shelter from storms; the sole staffed **refuge** is the *Refugio de Góriz*, roughly at the centre of park territory. In addition to the expected bans on disturbing plant or animal life, no **fires** are allowed anywhere, even in the emergency hut hearths, and **no washing or swimming** is permitted in the rivers (most of them are too cold to get in anyway except on blazing August afternoons). As at Aigüestortes in Catalunya, there's a **peripheral zone** of varying width to the south and east of the main *parque nacional* where development is controlled but few of the above prohibitions apply – you are allowed to swim, for instance, between Torla and the park boundary.

**Motorized vehicles** are not admitted beyond the chained gates at various points on the park periphery, and private-car approach from Torla along the paved access road is banned completely during Easter week and from June 1 to October 15 (winter mountaineers, take note). The Pradera de Ordesa car park is closed during those weeks; the only vehicles allowed now are the **shuttle buses** (departs 6, 7, 7.30 & 8am, then 15-minute intervals to 7pm June–Aug, 8am–5pm only Sept & Oct; €2.50 return fare only) from the fee car park (€6/day) at the southern outskirts of Torla. A control booth has been erected at the road fork near Puente de los Navarros to make sure that all private traffic goes north towards Bujaruelo during the restricted periods.

## Ascent of Monte Perdido
The standard expedition from the refuge is the **ascent of Monte Perdido**, which you do more for the views than anything else, since the southwest flank of the mountain – facing the top of the Valle de Ordesa – is the least impressive. It's more of a walk and scramble than a climb, but Monte Perdido can kill, so take advice from the refuge wardens, who have done the trip countless times. First and foremost get an early start, since thunderstorms can break in the afternoon. Follow the path climbing steeply north up the east bank of the **Barranco de Góriz**, where cairns show the way through alternating tracts of

grass and boulders. After two tough hours you reach the 3000-metre contour and the small frozen **Lago Helado**, in the shadow of **Cilindro**, Perdido's sister summit.

At the lake you almost double back for the final approach, climbing steeply southeast, often over snow and ice, the grade slackening only a little just before the summit (5hr from the refuge). From the top you can gaze down the Pineta valley to the east; over the Tella and Añisclo canyons to the south; across Lago de Marboré to the Brecha de Tucarroya to the north; and towards distant Vignemale to the west.

Once back down at Lago Helado, you don't have to return to the *Refugio de Góriz*, but can execute a traverse. This implies an extra early start, as you'll not only be climbing Monte Perdido, but negotiating the Cuello del Cilindro, dropping along the snowfields on the far side to Lago Marboré and – if you don't camp there – descending to the Valle de Pineta via the steep *balcón* trail. To move on **west** from the *Refugio de Góriz*, trace the north side of the valley past the **Circo de Góriz** to the Brèche de Roland, the Cirque de Gavarnie and the *Refuge de la Brèche de Roland* (see p.390).

### To the Cascada de Cotatuero and beyond

A popular side-trip from the valley bottom goes up to the impressive **Cascada de Cotatuero**. Starting from the wayside shrine of Virgen de Ordesa several hundred metres beyond the Puente de los Cazadores, the Cotatuero route takes you steeply but easily through the woods to a vantage point below the waterfall within an hour.

If you have a head for heights, you can continue on from here into France. With the help of more *clavijas*, you climb above the falls (2hr 30min) to reach the Gruta de Casteret and the Brecha de Roldán (4hr from the Puente de los Cazadores), for access to Gavarnie.

Alternatively, you can ford the stream beside the collapsed bridge here and adopt the un-signposted **Senda Canarrellos**, which roller-coasters up to about the 1800-metre contour on its way southeast, across the lips of hanging valleys and under rock overhangs, to a junction (3hr 30min into the day) with the main valley-bottom track at **Bosque de Haya**. This is just above the **Cascada de la Cueva**, from where the Puente de Cazadores is about an hour downhill. However, the Senda Canarrellos is now unmaintained, with lots of tree-fall and boulder slides, though the path isn't formally closed and shouldn't present problems to experienced hikers. It's certainly the wildest and, after the Faja de Pelay route, the most impressive of the trails in the canyon, and it's a bit easier and quicker if done in reverse from the Bosque de Haya junction (which is still signposted); coming anticlockwise around the flank of Monte Arruebo, you get impressive views of the falls. Going clockwise, allow four and a half hours for this loop; anticlockwise, slightly less.

### To the Cascada de Carriata and the Faja de las Flores

Another route signposted from the former car park leads to the **Cascada de Carriata**, pouring out of the **Circo de Salarons**. You head north into the trees, fork left, and begin a steep zigzag up to the falls, which are most impressive in late spring when melted snow keeps them flowing.

If you want to continue into the *circo*, the left-hand route (at a fork on the open mountainside ninety minutes above the visitors' centre) ascends via a series of thirteen *clavijas*, not nearly as intimidating as those on the Cotatuero route and feasible for any reasonably fit walker; once up top you can carry on to the Brecha de Roldán.

The right-hand fork quickly becomes a nail-biting corniche trail along the **Faja de las Flores**. Nowhere wider than a mere 7m, this terrace runs for about 3000m horizontally along the 2100-metre contour of the valley's north wall, with an immense drop to the south. If you haven't got a head for heights you'll either have acquired one by the end, or be whimpering on your hands and knees. If you cover the entire distance, you meet up with the ascending path for the Circo de Cotatuero in about ninety minutes; reckon on an hour to descend to the Puente de los Cazadores.

## Walks from the upper Ara valley

To reach the **upper Ara valley** on foot from Torla, head up the GR15.2 for just under an hour, as far as the junction with the Camino de Turieto and then instead of continuing east into Ordesa take the **GR11** northwest. This crosses the Arazas at the **Puente de la Ereta**, an anticlimactic concrete aqueduct with some icy pools beneath it (swimming permitted if you don't fear heart stoppage). Half an hour later the GR11 meets the access road for the *parque nacional* at the **Puente de los Navarros**, and then runs north along the Río Ara: first along the very rough dirt road, and then after the Puente de Santa Elena, as an east-bank trail. About 1km above that bridge, on the road, you'll find *Camping Valle de Bujaruelo* (T974 486 348; April–Oct 15), where there's a shop for supplies – the highest one in the valley – and a restaurant (reservations suggested): maybe not worth a detour, but great if you're on trek, where the €10 *menú* might consist of lentil soup, lamb chops and apple mousse.

Staying instead with the east-bank trail, you'll arrive (1hr 30min or 7km from Puente de los Navarros) at the wide riverside meadow of **San Nicolás de Bujaruelo**, graced with the ruined eleventh-to-twelfth-century **church** of that name – and some originally medieval hospice buildings. After a long refurbishment, these again operate as an **albergue**, the *Mesón de Bujaruelo* (T974 486 412, Wwww.mesondebujaruelo.com; mix of dorms, quads, doubles at ❷). Though clients of an affiliated activity centre seem to get first crack at the pastel-coloured rooms, the *albergue* offers lunch (€12 *menú*) to all comers, and also manages the adjacent **campsite**. From the church, there are a number of possible trekking routes out of the Ara basin, all traced on the Editorial Alpina 1:30,000 "Vignemale Bujaruelo" map. You can, incidentally, proceed no further up-valley by vehicle – there's a locked barrier just past the hospice buildings.

### Trekking into France

For the **Gavarnie** basin, take the path that crosses the Ara over a beautiful Romanesque **bridge** (currently scaffolded) and then zigzags quite steeply east to the frontier at **Puerto de Bujaruelo/Port de Gavarnie** (2270m); at the pass you pick up the HRP trail to the *Refuge de la Brèche de Roland*. Work on the dirt road which the Spanish were slowly bulldozing up to the pass appears to have been halted, the project deemed incompatible with the aims of the two national parks.

For the **Cauterets** area, hike northwest upstream beside the Ara along the **GR11**, but at the point – four hours beyond San Nicolás – where the GR climbs west towards Panticosa, continue instead to the head of the valley, where you pick up the **HRP** west through the **Col d'Arratille**, reaching the *Refuge Wallon* (see p.396) after ten hours. You can also use the **HRP** east through the **Puerto de los Mulos** (2591m) to arrive at the *Refuge des Oulettes* in somewhat less time.

For **Balneario de Panticosa**, start out as for Cauterets but stay on the GR11. From the Ara valley floor, the route veers west-southwest up the **Barranco de Batanes** to the **Cuello de Brazato** (2578m; 6hr from San Nicolás) before dropping quite sharply to Balneario de Panticosa (see below) – a spectacular if full trekking day of seven and a half hours. The small tarns in the Batanes valley, plus the larger Brazato lakes, make this route a choice strategy for moving west; as part of a day-hike out of Panticosa, it's covered in detail on pp.446–447. In any event don't make the mistake of following the **old GR11** up the Valle de Otal, still marked as a *variante*. This might appear to be easier – the Collado de Tendeñera at the top of Otal is only 2327m – but it's longer and, as the GR marking committee apparently agreed, pretty tedious.

# The Valle de Tena and around

The next major north–south valley west of the Ordesa region, the **Valle de Tena**, wins few beauty prizes in the judgement of many travellers. The **Río Gállego** which waters it, starting near the Puerto de Portalet/Col du Pourtalet and the ski complex of **El Formigal**, has been extensively dammed, with the usual pipelines and high-tension lines in attendance. At **Lanuza** reservoir, many houses in the namesake village stand poignantly half-submerged, as they have since 1975. Recently, though, owners have had some success in reclaiming their properties (see box p.430), and – complete with offshore floating stage – Lanuza now co-hosts a summer music festival (see p.449), with an excellent, informal atmosphere (patrons and musicians alike have been known to swim from the stage after the show).

Arriving in the crossroads village of Biescas from either Torla or the transport hub of Sabiñánigo (see below), you'll want a sound pretext to head upstream along the A136 road. This is furnished by the westernmost concentration of three-thousand-metre **peaks** and **glacial lakes** in the Spanish Pyrenees, northeast of the Valle de Tena, reached either from **Sallent de Gállego**, near El Formigal, or the side valley of the Río Caldarés, which flows past **Panticosa** village from the agreeable spa of **Balneario de Panticosa**.

## Biescas

Some 26km west of Torla, by the intersection of the N260 and A136, the small town of **BIESCAS** dominates the lower end of the Valle de Tena, with a Templar-built church gracing the medieval upper quarter on the east bank of the Gállego. Biescas comes to life from August 14 to 17, when consecutive festivities in honour of San Roque and La Virgen de la Asunción feature a procession of giant papier-mâché effigies.

At other times of the year, especially if travelling under your own steam, you might schedule a lunch stop at the **hotel-restaurant** *Casa Ruba*, at c/Esperanza 18 (T & F 974 485 001; closed Oct–Nov; ❸) on the east bank of the river. This has been in the same family for three generations, with a lively, authentic bar laying on arguably the best range of *tapas* in the mountains, plus breakfasts. The *comedor* offers only *a la carta* supper, featuring lots of game and fish, though lunch *menús* are a bit dull. Otherwise, in the west-bank quarter, there's *Hostal la Rambla*, Rambla San Pedro 7 (T & F 974 485 177; ❸), with a good restaurant (€11 *menú*), and the en-suite *Pensión Las Heras*, an old stone house at Agustina de Aragón 35 (T 974 485 027; ❷), a quiet cul-de-sac near the Guardia Civil barracks. If you take the evening bus service up from Sabiñánigo to Biescas and fail to get a lift onwards, one of these establishments will certainly come in handy – and Biescas is certainly a more appealing place to spend the night than Sabiñánigo. There's also a **tourist office** by the southerly bridge (most of year: daily 10am–1.30pm & 5–8.30pm; ☎974 485 002).

Biescas has become most famous – or notorious – for one of the worst natural disasters ever to befall the Spanish Pyrenees. On August 7, 1996, a flash flood swept through the *Las Nieves* campsite south of town, causing 87 deaths. An inquest concluded that *Las Nieves* was fundamentally unsafe, lying within the original, pre-"engineered" course of a tributary of the Tena, at the mouth of a ravine. The new, more central **campsite**, *Edelweiss* (☎974 485 084; June 15–Sept 15), is hopefully better placed out of the flood plain.

## Sabiñánigo – and its museum

Unabashedly industrial **SABIÑÁNIGO**, 14km south of Biescas on the A136 and 18km east of Jaca, persuades few to linger, but almost everybody passes through at some point on their way to or from Ordesa, if only because there's an inevitable change here of buses, or from train to bus. The **train station** lies at the northwest edge of town on the Jaca road, right next to the **bus terminal**.

If you've your own transport, do make an effort to visit the **Museo Ángel Orensanz y Artes de Serrablo** (July & Aug daily 10.30am–1.30pm & 5–9pm; April–June & Sept Tues–Sun 10.30am–1.30pm & 4–7pm; Oct–March Tues–Sat 10.30am–1.30pm & 3.30–6.30pm, Sun 10.30am–1.30pm & 4–7pm; €1.50), installed in an eighteenth-century farmhouse (plus a modern annexe) at the extreme southern edge of town by Puente Sardás. Justly reckoned the best ethnological museum in Alto Aragón, its displays are themed by room (musical instruments, religious art, wooden tools, etc). There are also fascinating archival photos and the original kitchen, axis of winter life, with its cooking implements and massive chimney hood. What little English labelling there is is eccentric, but two interrelated truths are worth translating. Until the early twentieth century, the eldest son inherited the entire estate in rural Aragón, and alone would marry; his bachelor brothers, the *tiones*, became the family handymen or even itinerant craftsmen, and to them are owed the wealth of displays here. The items on show have been gathered from the 46 deserted villages of the Serrablo, the zone around Sabiñánigo, which in 1910 had a population of 77; its growth during the 1950–70 industrialization depopulated three-quarters of the Serrablo, and by giving them homes in town finally allowed younger brothers to marry.

Should you need to **stay** overnight, Sabiñánigo has a dozen generally overpriced *hostales* and *hoteles*, mostly on the through road, Avenida de Serrablo. A reasonable choice, near the transport terminals, is *Hostal Laguarta* (☎974 480 004; ❷) at no. 21, above the *Bar Lara*.

## Panticosa: skiing, village, spa

Fifteen kilometres upstream from Biescas, buses detour briefly at the far end of the **Embalse de Búbal** for the three-kilometre run northeast to **PANTICOSA** (Pandicosa) village, before continuing towards Sallent de Gállego. With its stucco exteriors and ornate windows on some of the remaining older buildings, Panticosa makes a tolerable, if pricey, base (though hikers might prefer Balneario de Panticosa). The small local **ski complex** has prompted a mushrooming of chalet growth at the village outskirts; former patronage by Brits has left a legacy of English-language signage. With antiquated equipment and a poor natural snow record, the station nearly closed during the early 1990s, but has been rescued (for now) by massive investment in snow canons, new lifts and a new resort building at 1900m. A state-of-the-art, eight-seater *telecabina* ferries clients from a vast car park at the bottom of the village (1150m) up to Petrosos (1900m), and from there the Sabocos chairlift – one of six – continues to Valle de Sabocos, focus of the meatier runs, with access to the top point of 2200m. Of 38 pistes, 14 are blue and 15 red, making this a good beginner-intermediate resort (Ⓦ www.panticosa-loslagos.com), but a half-dozen runs below Petrosos are seldom usable. In **summer**, the *telecabina* and Sabocos lift take mountain-bikers and walkers to two lakes around the **Valle de Sabocos** (daily 10am–6pm; €10 return).

**Accommodation** in the village centre is heavily subscribed at peak times; top-value choices are the one-star *Vicente* up on the road to Balneario de Panticosa (Ⓣ974 487 022, Ⓕ974 487 529; ❹), offering sweeping views across the valley and private parking, or the two-star *Escalar* at the village entrance (Ⓣ974 487 098, Ⓕ974 487 003; ❹), with plusher rooms, a pool and again off-street parking. The central *Hotel Navarro* (Ⓣ974 487 181, Ⓦ www.hotelnavarro.com; ❸) on Plaza de la Iglesia has variable rooms – the best up to *Vicente* standards – but eccentric management, noise from poor insulation and feeble hot water; its *comedor* is similarly basic, with a restrictive *menú* (€15). Central *Mesón Sampietro* on c/La Parra is the better of just two independent **restaurants**, and where the locals go. You can buy trekking provisions in Panticosa, and there are three **banks**, all with ATMs.

### Balneario de Panticosa

In July and August a noon **bus** from Biescas forges upstream along the Río Caldarés through the **Garganta del Escalar**, whose walls are so close together that sun seldom penetrates and waterfalls spray the road. **BALNEARIO DE PANTICOSA**, 10km beyond the village, is another one of those places claiming to be the highest (1636m) permanently inhabited spot in the Pyrenees. This attractive and traditional **spa** is fed by six mineral springs, each sampled for different complaints. The emperor Tiberius supposedly visited Panticosa – the main baths are named in his honour – and there are, in fact, traces of Roman occupation in the vicinity, as well as an imposing Belle Époque casino, more restrained in appearance than its opposite numbers on the French side of the range. The most affordable of two surviving **hotels** – others have been converted to apartments – are the co-managed one-star *Continental* (Ⓣ974 487 161, Ⓦ www.panticosa.com; ❸) and the more characterful three-star *Mediodía* (❺). The FAM refuge in the northwest corner of the spa, *Casa de Piedra* (Ⓣ974 487 571; 98 places; all year), sited to serve the GR11 which passes through here, is rather unwelcoming and run for the maximum convenience of the wardens; **meals** must be ordered in advance. The sole independent place to eat at Balneario is the summertime **bar** *Casa Belio*, which does *raciones*. The summer-only bus back to Biescas departs at 5.30pm.

## Walking from Balneario de Panticosa

You're well poised at Balneario de Panticosa for treks and climbs of all durations and difficulties: either day-hikes up scarcely trodden nearby peaks, the very long day-traverse to Sallent de Gállego along the GR11 (best broken with an overnight en route), or the equally extended loop east using a GR11 variant. If you're going to attempt any of these routes, the appropriate Editorial

Alpina map is the 1:25,000 "Panticosa Formigal", plus the 1:30,000 "Vignemale Bujaruelo" for the easterly loop.

## Peak ascents

If you want to polish off an easy three-thousander, try **Pico d'o Argualas** (3046m), the summit immediately to the west – count on eight to nine hours there and back from the spa. Starting from a path marked for the Argualas Reservoir, close to the spa's natural lake, you head northwest first for the **Cuello de Pondiellos** (2809m; 3hr 30min), then for the **Collado de Argualas** (2860m), gaining height by following the crest southwest towards the base of **Pico d'Algas** (3021m) and finally tackling a poor footpath to complete the ascent via the west face. From here you have a wonderful view south towards the *sierras* of Telera and Tendeñera, as well as east over Balneario, Pico d'o Brazato and Vignemale.

To tackle the three summits of the **Picos del Infierno** – all of them close to 3100m – repeat the route to Cuello de Pondiellos but then head north towards the saddle that separates the central and eastern peaks, steering a middle course over the easiest terrain. From Pondiellos none of the Infierno peaks is more than ninety minutes away.

## Traverse west via the GR11

Access to the **GR11** in Balneario is poorly signposted; from in front of the *Hotel Mediodía*, ascend the broad staircase just east and turn left at the top onto a wide lane, where a few red-and-white double-bars provide confirmation. Some fifteen minutes along, there's a T-junction just above an avalanche weir: right for Brazato ("2 oras"), left for Bachimaña ("1.15"). These timings are brisk – even with a daypack, it's 80 minutes from here to the lower Bachimaña dam, and 35 minutes more to reach another T-junction at the water-meadows by the inflow of the upper **Ibón Bachimaña** (2hr 15 minimum from Balneario). Here you've the option of going north through the Puerto de Panticosa/Port du Marcadau for the *Refuge Wallon*, a short trekking day of about six hours (see p.396). To continue on the GR11 you swing west over gently rising ground to the upper **Ibón Azul** (3hr from Balneario), where there's good camping.

Next you climb steeply to the double pass of **Cuello d'o Infierno** (2721m) and **Collado de Piedrafita** (2782m), problematic after snowy winters; once through this it's all downhill past the **Ibón de Llena Cantal** (another wonderful campsite) to the **Respumoso (Respomoso) reservoir** (2150m; 3hr from Ibón Azul). This is about as far as you'd comfortably get with a full pack in one day from Balneario; on the north shore stands the *Refugio Respomoso* (☎974 490 203; 2200m; 105 places; open all year). If they're full, or the brusque wardens put you off, there's ample grass for camping on the south shore (the antiquated, unstaffed Alfonso XIII hut, still shown on all maps, is now kept locked). The view north to **Balaitus/Balaïtous** and east to the triple pyramids of **Cambales** (2968m), **Petite Fache** (2947m) and **Grande Fache/Gran Facha** (3005m) more than compensates for the ugly concrete dam and construction debris at the western end of Respumoso. (If you want to climb Balaïtous or head into France on the HRP, see "Around Balaïtous and Lac d'Artouste", p.413.)

To continue on the GR11, drop down the skilfully engineered path west from the lake, following the curving Aguas Limpias stream to Sallent de Gállego village (2hr 30min), the last half hour or so beyond the **Embalse de la Sarra** on asphalt road. If you've made an early start after staying at

Respumoso, it's possible and recommended to lengthen this final stage with a side trip north, on a cairned minor trail, to the **Arriel lakes** just below the HRP.

### Loop east via Circo de Bramatuero

For this scenic circuit – with none of the potential shuttling problems of arriving in Sallent, if you've left a car at Balneario – begin as for the westerly GR11 traverse. But when you reach the junction at the water-meadows by the upper Bachimaña reservoir, turn right instead of left, following a sign to the lower **Bramatuero dam** ("35" – really 40min), bearing right and slightly down at the next fork to avoid going up to the Puerto de Panticosa and *Wallon*. From the lower to the upper Bramatuero lake (2500m) it's 1hr 15min (4hr 15min from Balneario), on a fair trail through more water-meadows and past natural tarns. Gentians are out in profusion during early summer, with a few black-and-white bar-blazes mixed with cairns as waymarks. At the upper dam, the path fizzles out; cairned isard-traces lead above the north shore to natural **Ibón Letrero** (2540m; 5hr) at the top of the **Circo de Bramatuero**, a fine lunch spot where snow lingers into July.

From Letrero, it's a deceptively easy twenty minutes more up to the **Collado de Letrero** (2680m), with magic views of the Ordesa *fajas* and Vignemale. The 45-minute descent to the upper **Ibón de los Batanes** (2380m) is along a nasty couloir, with a scree slope to negotiate towards the bottom. You've another hour, via the equally scenic lower lake, to the junction with the main GR11 (6hr 45min), avoiding unnecessary altitude loss. Looking north, you glimpse frontier pinnacles comprising the **Circo de Ara**, and probably wisps of cloud in the late afternoon, while at the trail junction (turn west) there's the sound of three mingling streams in spate.

You've 45 minutes up the confusingly named Barranco de Batanes to the first tarn (2350m); marmots shriek all around from boulder piles, and a broad meadow just below is popular with campers. The Alpina map tracing is not precise – the good trail spends as much time on the true right bank as the left. Within 35 minutes more, you attain the **Cuello de Brazato** (2578m), where herds of isards are often seen. If you're overtaken by nightfall, camping is congenial at the natural lake just below the pass, but it's only an hour and three quarters more (almost 10hr for the day) to the Balneario. You need stamina and a long June/July day to accomplish this without spending a night out.

## The upper Tena valley

To proceed along the **upper Tena valley** from Panticosa village you can use the once-or-twice-daily onward bus service between Sabiñánigo and Sallent de Gállego. With your own transport, you can easily explore a handful of villages clinging to the slopes just west of the Bubal dam. The southernmost, **PIEDRAFITA DE JACA**, is an attractive place, with both an *albergue* (☎974 487 627; 20 places in two dorms) and the *Refugio Telera* (☎974 487 061; 14 places in 4-to-6-bunk rooms) catering to patrons of the nearby cross-country ski centre at **Partacua**. Claiming to be the largest in Alto Aragón with 40km of prepared routes, Partacua is actually between the villages of of Tramacastilla – largely overrun by *urbanizaciones* – and more unspoilt **SANDINIÉS**, which offers an excellent **hotel–restaurant**, *Casa Pelentos* (☎974 487 500; ❸), with award-winning fare and an €18 *menú*. From Sandiniés you can descend briefly to **ESCARRILLA**, 500m north of the side road to Panticosa, much marred by tower-blocks of holiday flats, though with ample facilities. **Accommodation** is available at the *Hotel Sarao* (℡974 487 065, Ⓦwww.hotelsarao.com; ❸), with a popular restaurant, and at the more luxurious *Hotel Ibón Azul* (℡974 487 211, Ⓕ974 487 242; ❺), both on the main through road.

## Sallent de Gállego

Once past the **Embalse de Lanuza**, a right turn and another bridge over the Gállego takes you into **SALLENT DE GÁLLEGO** (Sallén de Galligo), a sizeable old village 21km from Biescas, at the confluence of the Gállego and the Aguas Limpias, with a fine bridge across the Gállego and a fortified hilltop church – though the nearby ski resort is spurring steady expansion west and northeast along the riverbanks. Sallent plays a dual role as winter sports and summer mountaineering centre, as well as co-hosting (with Lanuza) the *Pirineos Sur* **festival** the last two weeks in July; this is one of the best world music bashes in Europe, attracting the likes of Manu Dibango, Khaled, Alpha Blondy and Youssou N'Dour in years past, and devoting each week to a different theme (eg, Islam, Cuba) within the main festival.

**Accommodation** is fairly abundant and cheaper than in Escarrilla, pitched largely at French trippers. Working your way west from east to west along the single high street of c/de Francia, you encounter *Hostal El Centro* (℡974 488 019, Ⓦwww.valledetena.com/centro; ❸), whose rear rooms face the stream and the peaks, and a decent if simple €12 *menú* with wine served in the tiny *comedor*; the less inspiring *Hostal Mediodía* (℡974 488 071; ❷); *Hotel Familiar Maximina*, tucked away on a side street at c/La Iglesia 3 (℡ & Ⓕ974/48 84 36, Ⓦwww.valledetena.com/maximina; ❹), with family suites for the price; *Hostal Faure* (℡974 488 007; ❷), in a courtyard off the main road, the best budget choice with €10 *menú* at the *comedor*; and last but not least the atmospheric, creaky-floored, originally eighteenth-century *Hotel Balaitus* (℡ & Ⓕ974 488 059, Ⓦwww.hotelbalaitus.com; ❹), with private parking and smallish but well-equipped rooms. For the truly impecunious, there's the friendly *Albergue Foratata* near the west end of c/de Francia (℡974 488 112, Ⓦwww.foratata.com; 100 places), with a few doubles and an inexpensive canteen on the ground floor.

You've a good range of independent **restaurants** around the plaza, with bilingual French/Castilian *menús*; *El Rincón de Mariano* is a reliable and popular locals' choice, with *menús* at €14 but much pricier *a la carta*, while *Casa Martón* is pleasant, though with a dull *menú* so splurge on *a la carta*. *Granja Casa Bernet* has a range of imported beers and homemade pastries, becoming a lively nocturnal **bar**. On c/del Vico, going uphill from the *Faure* & *Maximina*, there's the inexpensive but pleasant *Restaurante El Sarrio* (*menús* from €9) at no. 3 and the much plusher *Casa Socotor* at no. 9, part of a two-star hotel. Sallent also has two **banks** (ATMs) and three shops for trekking supplies. Except for one daily winter service originating in El Formigal (3.45pm, passes Sallent 4.15pm), Sallent is the usual start-point for downhill **bus** departures (Mon–Fri 7am).

## El Formigal

The uphill road from Sallent, with views of striking Peña Foratata on the north, weaves for almost 5km to **EL FORMIGAL**. Neither twee nor chic, it's a more serious ski resort than Panticosa, expanded several times between 1987 and 1997, with further (and controversial) growth planned in the Valle de Izas. Mostly north-facing runs are scattered across a vast, treeless slope across the valley from the chalets, between 1500m and 2200m; as at Panticosa, a *telecabina* gets you up to the hub of the action at 1800m. In total, 22 other lifts (one-third chairs) serve 34 pistes, mostly red-rated – this isn't a great beginners' resort.

Except for the pleasant, small two-star *Hotel Tirol* at the edge of the *urbanización* (☎974 490 377, ⓦwww.valledetena.com/tirol; ❻) with good views, **accommodation** in El Formigal can be extremely expensive for what you get; in ski season beds are hard to find anyway, in which case you'll appreciate Sallent and Escarrilla as useful fallbacks.

# Jaca and around

**JACA** (Chaca), 18km west of Sabiñánigo on the N330, is approached through modern, traffic-choked suburbs – an unpromising introduction to this early capital and stronghold of Aragón, and the base from which the kingdom was recaptured from the Muslims. The old centre, however, is a lot more characterful, overlooked by a huge star-shaped citadel and endowed with a **cathedral**

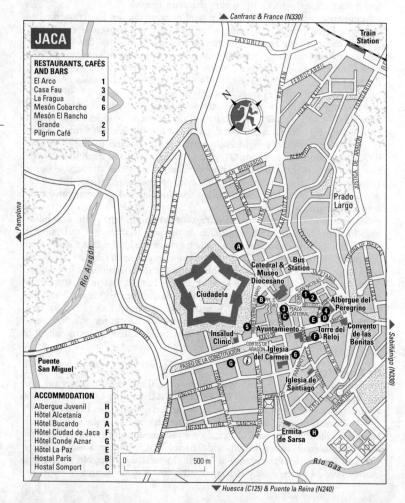

▲ *Canfranc & France (N330)*

**JACA**

**RESTAURANTS, CAFÉS AND BARS**

| | |
|---|---|
| El Arco | 1 |
| Casa Fau | 3 |
| La Fragua | 4 |
| Mesón Cobarcho | 6 |
| Mesón El Rancho Grande | 2 |
| Pilgrim Café | 5 |

**Train Station**

Prado Largo

**Ciudadela**

Ⓐ

Catedral & Museo Diocesano
Bus Station

Ⓑ

Ⓒ

Ⓓ

Ⓔ Albergue del Peregrino

Insalud Clinic

Ⓕ Torre del Reloj

Convento de las Benitas

Ⓖ Ⓘ
Ayuntamiento

Iglesia del Carmen Ⓖ

Iglesia de Santiago

**Puente San Miguel**

Ermita de Sarsa Ⓗ

▼ *Huesca (C125) & Puente la Reina (N240)*

▲ *Pamplona*

▶ *Sabiñánigo (N330)*

Rio Aragón

Rio Gas

**ACCOMMODATION**

| | |
|---|---|
| Albergue Juvenil | H |
| Hôtel Alcetania | D |
| Hôtel Bucardo | A |
| Hôtel Ciudad de Jaca | F |
| Hôtel Conde Aznar | G |
| Hôtel La Paz | E |
| Hostal París | B |
| Hostal Somport | C |

0        500 m

that is one of the finest Spanish examples of Romanesque architecture. This, and the monastery of **San Juan de la Peña** 20km southeast, are the major local sights, while in winter the proximity of **Candanchu** and **Astún**, the westernmost ski resorts in the Spanish Pyrenees, provides an added bonus. Rail enthusiasts may be tempted by the train-trip to **Canfranc**, almost at the French border, and a good place to pick up the GR11 trail.

After a spell in the mountains, Jaca's (relatively) "big town" feel and facilities may well be an equal attraction. It's enlivened by conscripts at the large military academy and students attending a summer English-language university, while boisterous festivals punctuate the spring and summer months.

## Arrival and information

The central **old town**, where you'll spend most of your time, divides into a somewhat frowzy northeastern side – home to all of the budget accommodation, the noisier bars and most of the reasonable restaurants – and the smarter southwestern quarter, abutting Avenida Regimiento Galicia, with its sidewalk cafés, posher restaurants and banks.

The **train station** (ticket office open 10am–noon & 5–7pm) is a fair walk from the centre, so look out for the shuttle bus (€0.50) which plies to and from the **bus station** on Avenida Jacetania, around the back of the cathedral. Useful bus services include those for Pamplona, Biescas via Sabiñánigo, and Echo/Anso, as well as even more frequent services to Zaragoza and Huesca. Although timetables don't explicitly say so, hardly any buses run on Sundays. **Drivers** will find parking easiest in the less congested southwestern quarter, though beware of pay-and-display zones.

It's worth stopping in at the helpful **Turismo**, Avenida Regimiento Galicia (summer Mon–Fri 9am–2pm & 4.30–8pm, Sat 9am–1.30pm & 5–8pm, Sun 10am–1.30pm; winter Mon–Fri 9am–1.30pm & 4.30–7pm, Sat 10am–1pm & 5–7pm; ☎974 360 098, ⓦ www.aytojaca.es), which stocks a range of leaflets on trekking, skiing, mountain-biking, horse-riding and festival programmes.

## Accommodation

Although at an elevation of only 820m, Jaca counts as a Pyrenean resort; as such its accommodation fills up in August or during peak ski season, so advance booking is prudent.

### Hotels and Hostales

**Hotel Alcetania** c/Mayor 45 ☎974 356 100, ⓕ974 356 200. Former *hostal* refurbished as a hotel in 1995; avoid the slightly sleazy ground-floor bar by using the alternate entry from c/Conde Aznar. ❸

**Hotel Bucardo** Avda de Francia 13☎974 362 485, ⓕ974 362 828. Plain, functional en-suite rooms with twin beds only and TV; most face a quieter side street, where there's free parking. ❸

**Hotel Ciudad de Jaca** c/Siete de Febrero 8 ☎974 364 311, ⓕ974 364 395. Centrally located but quiet place with good en-suite rooms. ❸

**Hotel Conde Aznar** Paseo de la Constitución 3 ☎974 361 050, ⓕ974 360 797. An attractive old family-run hotel, with well-renovated rooms and fairly abundant (if metered) street parking. ❺

**Hotel La Paz** c/Mayor 41 ☎974 360 700, ⓕ974 360 400. Large, winter-heated if somewhat airless en-suite rooms. ❸

**Hostal París** Plaza de San Pedro 5 ☎974 361 020. Best budget *hostal* in town, across from the cathedral – clean, spacious rooms with washbasin, currently overlooking an archeological dig. ❷

**Hostal Somport** c/Echegaray 11 ☎ & ⓕ 974 363 410. Jaca's most affordable en-suite digs, in another renovated old building; salubrious ground-floor bar-restaurant. ❷

### Youth hostel and camping

**AlbergueJuvenil** Avda Perimetral s/n ☎974 360 536. This YHA-affiliated youth hostel, in the south of town by the ice rink, has doubles, triples and five-bedded rooms.

**Camping Peña Oroel** 3km east on the Sabiñánigo road ☎974 360 215. An attractive campsite, set amid woods, with excellent facilities. Open Easter week and mid-June to mid-Sept.

**Camping Victoria** 1500m out of town on the Pamplona road ☎974 360 323. An equally shady if cheaper and rather basic site, near the Río Aragón.

## The Town

Sited at the foot of Peña Oroel, on a broad plain where the Río Aragón suddenly twists westwards into the Canal de Berdún, Jaca is a venerable place, called *Iacca* by the Romans after the Iaccitani tribe who dwelt here. The Muslims occupied Jaca briefly from 715 to 760, when the Christians reconquered the town and held it, save for a brief spell, from then on. The battle of **Las Tiendas** (4km west of Jaca), in 795, in which a Moorish army was repulsed mostly by the local women, is still commemorated on the first Friday in May by a mock all-female battle between Christians and Moors.

Within two centuries an embryonic democracy of sorts had emerged among the Aragonese nobility, who stipulated comprehensive customary rights (*fueros*) – confirmed by King **Sancho Ramírez** in 1077 – limiting the power of the king to issue edicts and levy taxes. Jaca itself reached its zenith during the decades after 1035, when **Ramiro I**, Sancho's father, established the Aragonese court here and began work on the present cathedral.

### The Cathedral

The **Cathedral** (daily 8am–2pm & 4–8pm; free) is the main legacy of Jaca's years as the seat of the young Aragonese kingdom, and ranks as one of the Pyrenees' most architecturally important monuments. Rebuilt on old foundations part way through the eleventh century, it was the first cathedral in Spain to adopt the French Romanesque architecture, and, as such, exerted considerable stylistic influence on other churches along the Camino de Santiago.

Ramiro's endowment of the cathedral was undoubtedly intended to confirm Jaca's role as a Christian capital in what was still almost exclusively a Muslim Iberian peninsula. Its design saw the introduction of the classic three-aisled basilica, though unhappily the original Romanesque simplicity has been much obscured by florid decoration in the intervening centuries. It retains some of the original sculpture, however, including realistic carving on the capitals and doorway – a sixteenth-century statue of Santiago looks down from the portal. Inside, the main treasure is the silver shrine of Santa Orosía, Jaca's patron saint; a Czech noble, married into the Aragonese royal family, she was martyred by Muslims for refusing to renounce her faith.

Installed in the dark cathedral cloisters is an unusually good **Museo Diocesano** (June–Sept daily 10am–2pm & 4–8pm; Easter–May daily 10am–1.30pm & 4–7pm; winter Tues–Sun 11am–1.30pm & 4–7pm; may close for works 2004; €2), featuring a superb collection of Romanesque-to-Gothic religious art, mostly frescoes and wooden religious sculpture, gathered from village churches in the area and from higher up in the Pyrenees. Highlights include an eerily modern Pantocrator fresco from a church in Ruesta, a crucified Christ in walnut wood, and the *Flight into Egypt* and *Adoration of the Magi* from Navasa, all twelfth century. The Renaissance work is more variable, but features some splendid *retablos*.

### The Ciudadela and Puente San Miguel

The **Ciudadela**, a redoubtable sixteenth-century fort built to the French star-shaped ground-plan then prevalent, is still partly occupied by the Spanish army.

You can visit parts of the interior (daily: April–June, Sept & Oct 11am–noon & 5–6pm; July & Aug 11am–noon & 6–8pm; Nov–March 11am–noon & 4–5pm; €4) on a guided tour only – though interest is mostly confined to good views of the surrounding peaks and wooded countryside from the walls.

Below the citadel, reached along a track from the end of the Paseo de la Constitución, lies a remarkable medieval bridge, the **Puente de San Miguel**. It was across this bridge over the Río Aragón that pilgrims on Camino Aragonés – a branch of the **Camino de Santiago** – entered Jaca. It must have been a welcome sight, marking the end of the arduous Pyrenean stage for pilgrims following this route from Provence into Spain over the Puerto de Somport. From Jaca, the pilgrims headed on westwards, through Puente la Reina de Jaca, towards Navarra, where they joined up with the more popular route from Roncesvalles. This Aragón section of the Camino de Santiago – like other branches of the route – has experienced quite a revival since the early 1990s and is marked as the **GR65.3**, though it's constantly threatened with either inundation by dams or covering over by building projects. Jaca is now consciously pitched as a way-station: there's an **Albergue de Peregrino** (pilgrims' hostel) in the medieval hospital on c/Conde Aznar (64 bunks; ☎974 355 758; reception open daily 9–10am & 3–10pm), while route maps and pilgrimage-related souvenirs are widely available.

## Eating and drinking

Jaca has a lively and inviting selection of **restaurants** and **bars**, with good choices concentrated in the old town. The entire length of c/Gil Berges, as well as contiguous c/del Barco and c/de la Puerta Nueva, is home to most of the rowdier student bars. More sedate pubs and *tapas* bars for an older crowd concentrate on c/Ramiro Primero, Avenida Primer Viernes de Mayo and Avenida Regimiento Galicia.

**El Arco** c/San Nicolás 4. That rare Spanish breed: a vegetarian, no-smoking restaurant. Fresh, filling, international dishes and inexpensive *menús* at €10–12. Closed Sun in winter.

**Casa Fau** Plaza de la Catedral 4. Jaca's classic *tapas* bar, with a few tables under the arches, a few more inside, and reliably rude staff. All the usual platters, plus *ciervo* (venison) sausage, *boletus* (wild mushrooms) and quiche; €4–6 for three *tapas* and a small *caña*.

**El Conde Aznar** Paseo de la Constitución 3. The *comedor* of the eponymous hotel is reckoned to be one of the best eateries in town. There's a choice of unusually interesting *menús* for about €13, while *a la carta* won't much exceed €18 (booze extra in either case).

**La Fragua** c/Gil Berges 4. Generous, reasonably priced grills without any airs or graces; no *menú*,

budget €20 *a la carta*. Closed Wed.

**Mesón Cobarcho** c/Ramiro Primero 2. Don't let the decor – part Gaudí, part Flintstones – distract you from the excellent cooking and linen-nappery service; the interesting €12 *menú*, inclusive of drink, might feature *alubias con chorizo*, *sepia a la plancha* and a fancy dessert, though *a la carta* is pricey at €25–30.

**Mesón El Rancho Grande** c/del Arco 2. Impressive Aragonese cooking, which uses fish, meat and vegetables equally well; skip the dull €11.50 *menú* in favour of the *carta* (allow €25).

**Pilgrim Café** Avda Primer Viernes de Mayo 7. Inevitably a bit touristy but occupies a fine old triangular, industrial-brick, wood-floored building with outdoor tables facing the Ciudadela's lawn, and serves a variety of breakfasts (including bacon and eggs), as well as snacks.

## Listings

**Adventure activities** Activity expeditions are organized by Jaca Aventura, Avda Francia 1 ☎974 363 521, Mountain Travel on Avda Regimiento Galicia ☎974 355 770, and Alcorce-

Adventura, opposite the Turismo at Avda Regimiento Galicia 1 ☎974 356 781.

**Hospital** Besides the main one on c/Rapitan, off the map beyond the train station, there's the very central, public Insalud clinic on Paseo de la Constitución, good for minor ailments.

**Laundry** There's a self-service *lavandería* next to the supermarket, Superpirineos, on c/Astún.

**Outdoor gear** In the centre, Charli at Avda Regimiento de Galicia 3, and Intersport-Piedrafita, at Avda de Francia 4, have a limited stock; for much the widest selection, go to Sportland, in a

shopping mall at the far northeast edge of town. It's a bit tricky to reach; you have to go under the N330 via two tunnels near the RENFE station.

**Trekking literature** Maps and guides are available from La Unión at c/Mayor 34 (also the central Aragonese outlet for Pirineos magazine), or El Siglo at c/Mayor 17.

# Southwest of Jaca: San Juan de la Peña and Santa Cruz de la Serós

**San Juan de la Peña**, high in the Sierra de la Peña southwest of Jaca, is the best-known monastery in Aragón. In medieval times an important *variante* of the pilgrim route from Jaca to Pamplona detoured here, as San Juan reputedly held the Holy Grail – actually a Roman chalice which later found its way to Valencia cathedral. These days, most tourists (and there are many – including school parties) visit for the views and Romanesque cloister.

The most direct **route to the monastery** begins from the Jaca–Pamplona N240 highway. A side road, 11km west of Jaca, leads south 4km to the village of **Santa Cruz de la Serós** with its massive Romanesque church, and from here it's a further 7km by road up to San Juan. There is no public transport, although you could take the afternoon Puente la Reina/Pamplona-bound bus from Jaca and walk from there – assuming an overnight in Santa Cruz. Getting there **by mountain bike** would be easier: reckon on an hour's cycling from Jaca to Santa Cruz, then a further hour up the very steep road to San Juan. Returning to Jaca, you can make an enjoyable circuit rather than retracing your tyre-treads: a gradual twelve-kilometre descent east to Bernués, a slight climb to Puerto de Oroel, then a fierce drop to Jaca, 17km from Bernués. This is a very scenic – and car-free – itinerary, but not something to do in reverse.

## Santa Cruz de la Serós

The picturesque village of **SANTA CRUZ DE LA SERÓS**, which comes to life in summer, is dominated by its thick-set but nonetheless stylish Romanesque **church** (daily 10am–2pm & 4–7pm; €1); inside, the remarkable stoup incorporates a massive central pillar holding up the vault. The sanctuary was once part of a large Benedictine convent which flourished between the eleventh and sixteenth centuries; indeed *serós* appears to be a corruption of *sorores*, after the nuns who once dwelt here, including (in their old age) the three sisters of King Sancho. There are a couple of places to **eat** and **drink** in the village. The *Casa d'Ojalatero* in the centre serves salubrious if plain fare, such as *trigueros con gambas* and grills (*menú* €9.50, or €16–20 *a la carta*), plus good house wine, while the *Hostal Santa Cruz* (same prices) houses the village bar and also has high-standard, 2002-built **rooms** (☎974 361 975, ⓦwww.san-tacruzdelaseros.com; ❸), four with balconies.

From Santa Cruz, walkers can take the **old path** up to San Juan in about an hour. The path is waymarked as the GR65.3.2 and is signposted from near the church (where there is also a map-placard). The road takes a more circuitous route around the mountainside, giving wonderful views of the Pyrenean peaks to the north and the distinctive Peña de Oroel to the east.

## San Juan de la Peña

**SAN JUAN DE LA PEÑA** actually comprises two monasteries, 2km apart.

Approaching from Santa Cruz, you reach the lower (and older) one first. Built into a hollow under a cliff from which various springs seep, the **lower monastery** (summer Tues–Sun 10am–2pm & 3.30–8pm; spring & autumn Tues–Sun 10am–2pm & 4–7pm; winter Wed–Sun 11am–2pm; €3) is an unusual and evocative complex, even in its partial state of survival. Entering, you pass first into the **Sala de Concilios** – once the refectory – and the adjacent, double-naved, ninth-century **Mozarabic chapel**. Both retain fragments of Romanesque frescoes and were jointly adapted as the crypt of the main Romanesque **church**, built two centuries later. There, in 1071, Cluniac monks replaced the Mozarabic Mass with the Roman rite – the first such substitution in the Iberian peninsula, made possible by the re-establishment of contact with Rome after centuries of isolation.

Upstairs, alongside the main church, is a **pantheon** of Aragonese and Navarrese nobles; reliefs on the nobles' Gothic tombs show events from the early history of Aragón. Another adjacent pantheon for the kings of Aragón was remodelled in a cold, Neoclassical style during the eighteenth century and later sacked by Napoleon's troops.

All these are appetizers, however, for the twelfth-century Romanesque **cloisters**, at the far end of the complex where the rock overhang has been left open to the sky rather than being completely walled off. Only two of the bays are complete – another is in a fragmentary state – but the surviving capitals are among the greatest examples of Romanesque carving anywhere. All depict scenes from the Gospels: *Christ's Entry into Jerusalem*, *Meeting Mary Magdalene*, the *Raising of Lazarus*, and the *Deposition* are the most obvious. They were the artistry of an anonymous, idiosyncratic craftsman who left his mark on a number of churches in the region. He is now known as the Master of San Juan de la Peña, his work easily recognizable by the figures' unnaturally large eyes.

The surrounding cliffs are the nesting grounds of assorted **birds of prey**, and you'll be very unlucky not to see griffon vultures, or the summer-visiting Egyptian vultures. Bonelli's eagles (all year) and short-toed eagles (summer only), identifiable by their habit of soaring with dangling feet, are less frequent sights.

The late-seventeenth-century **upper monastery**, a sizeable complex with a flamboyant Baroque facade, can be seen from the outside only – it now houses a private study centre – but it merits the climb east from the older monastery, if only for the views of the Pyrenees from a nearby *mirador*. Facing the monastery is a popular picnic-ground in a huge, forest-enclosed meadow; if you arrive by car, this is where you must **park** most of the year – a regular shuttle bus takes you down to the older monastery.

## North of Jaca: Canfranc, Candanchú and Astún

Although it is the Río Aragón that drains south from the Puerto de Somport, its valley – extending directly **north of Jaca** – is known as the **Canfranc**. This is also the name of two settlements along the way: **Canfranc-Pueblo**, 19km out of Jaca on the N330, devastated by fire in 1944 and now mustering just forty inhabitants, and **Canfranc-Estación**, 4km further and (currently) the final stop for northbound trains, as well as being near the south end of the **Somport tunnel** which now leads under the watershed into France. A crag-top fortress 2km up the valley, plus the bizarre, round Torre de Fusileros south of the tunnel mouth, attest to the age-old importance of this corridor; just shy of the frontier, 9km beyond Canfranc-Estación along the old road, the ski resorts of **Candanchú** and **Astún** flank the approaches to the Puerto de Somport.

## Canfranc: Pueblo and Estación

Consistent with its depopulation, short-term tourist facilities in the one-street village of **CANFRANC-PUEBLO** are limited, though ski apartments are making their appearance. For somewhere to stay choose from among the *Refugio de Canfranc* (1045m; ☎974 373 217, ⓦwww.sargantana.org; 100 places; all year), an **albergue** for pilgrims on the Camino de Santiago, and two adjacent **bars** for meals and drink, one of which (*La Cabaña*) has **rooms** in a *turismo rural* (☎974 372 119; ❷). **VILLANÚA**, just 4km south in a wider part of the valley, is more attractive, but has only a clutch of overpriced hotels and another **albergue**, *Refugio Bar Triton* on Plaza Mediodía (☎ & Ⓕ974 378 281, ⓦwww.alberguetriton.com; 54 places in 4- or 8-bunk dorms), also offering regional cooking at €18.

Since the French discontinued their part of the local trans-Pyrenean line, most of the enormous train station at **CANFRANC-ESTACIÓN** – equipped with the second-longest platforms in Europe – has become a badly vandalized white elephant where tall weeds grow through the tracks. It's a sad fate for an elegant spot which saw heads of state attend its inauguration in 1928, and which later served as a location for the film *Doctor Zhivago*. Spanish undercutting of French ski-resort rates (ironically, the Spanish slopes are now pricier) prompted the closure of the line in 1973 after 45 years in operation, though the last straw was the collapse of a bridge on the French side, left unrepaired (along with two others later collapsed at Urdos and Estaut) to this day. However, following the opening of the Somport car tunnel in early 2002, EU funding for the rehabilitation of the rail line between Oloron-Ste-Marie and Canfranc has been approved.

The surrounding village, such as it is, was founded to house those made homeless by the 1944 disaster, and now exists primarily to lodge skiers and catch the passing motorist trade (mostly French), with a few gift shops and lodgings. **Accommodation**, all on or just off the through highway, includes the high-quality *Albergue Pepito Grillo* (☎974 373 123, ⓦwww.pepitogrillo .com; 36 places in 4- or 5-bunk dorms; all year), serving the GR11 as well as the Camino Aragonés, and the friendly, quiet, wood-and-stone-built *Hotel Villa Anayet*, towards the north end of "town" at Plaza de Aragón 8 (☎974 373 146; closed mid-April to mid-June & mid-Sept to mid-Dec; ❸). There are also two adjacent, somewhat overpriced *casas rurales* on Plaza Aragón: *Casa Marieta* (☎974 373 365; ❸) and *La Tuca* (☎974 373 104; ❸), as well as a **campsite** (☎608 731 604; April to mid-Sept), 5km north on the road towards Candanchú. For **meals**, the *comedor* at the *Hotel Villa Anayet* offers by far the best value.

Though there's no train service (yet), you can travel on **into France** (5 times Mon–Sat, 3 times Sun), on **SNCF buses**. Coming **from France**, these buses arrive in Canfranc from Oloron with equal frequencies on the days indicated, with awkward **train** connections for Jaca just twice daily; you're more likely to continue south by a much more frequent **municipal bus**, which originates at the ski resorts (see below). Consult Canfranc's **Turismo** (July–Sept Mon–Sat 9am–1.30pm & 4.30–8pm; Oct–June Tues–Sat 9am-1.30pm & 3.30–7pm, closed Nov 1–15; ☎974 373 141, ⓦwww.canfranc.com), opposite the station, for current schedules.

### Walking from Canfranc: the GR11 east and west

The **main GR11** runs **northeast** from between Canfranc and Candanchú via the **Canal Roya** valley, then curls southeast to the attractive, upper **Ibóns de Anayet** (4hr), from where you've fine views of Pic du Midi d'Ossau. From here it's another two hours plus, mostly on 4WD track through the slopes of El Formigal, to Sallent de Gállego, for an easy, six-hour hiking day. For the record, a variant goes east directly from Canfranc along the **Valle de Izas**, the two routes converging at El Formigal, but this is less scenic, and will become even less so if Formigal's expansion into this valley happens.

Heading west from Candanchú itself involves a longer and tougher day's trek hugging the border, enlivened by the **Ibón de Estanés** (2hr), the largest natural lake in these parts. If the campsite at **Selva de Oza**, near the top of the **Valle de Echo,** hasn't reopened as planned in 2005, you'd do better to take the variant via the low Collado de Riguelo and Collado d'o Boxo to the *Refugio de Lizara*, from where Echo is an easy stage away (see p.482).

## Skiing: Candanchú and Astún

Two of the best Aragonese ski resorts – certainly among the more advanced – are **CANDANCHÚ** (Ⓦwww.candanchu.com) and **ASTÚN** (Ⓦwww.astun .com), respectively 8km and 11km north of Canfranc (served by several well-spaced daily buses in winter from Jaca); a bypass on the east side of the valley takes you directly to Astún. These unaesthetic, functional twinned complexes – recently expanded Astún dating from 1975, Candanchú the first established in these mountains – are just 4km apart, though there's no shared lift pass or physical link. Jaca's failed bid to host the 2010 Winter Olympics has, however, left a legacy of pretty decent facilities. Both resorts have extensive north-facing runs in treeless valleys just southeast of the frontier ridge; given the Atlantic-influenced climate, their top points of 2300–2400m should ensure good snow.

The fifty pistes at treeless **Astún**, mostly blue- and red-rated, are served by six chairlifts, though these are prone to closure from high winds, and only two are high-speed; one, "Truchas", operates in summer, shuttling hikers up to one of several lakes either side of the border. From the top point at La Raca, you've fantastic views northeast to the Pic du Midi and west beyond Candanchú, though runs from here can be hard and icy. Also, liaisons between the sectors can be obscure, and you really need to be of intermediate ability to enjoy this resort. Rank beginners are probably better off at **Candanchú**, which has a half-dozen nursery slopes among its 51 runs, 29 of them red or black; though only a quarter of 24 lifts here are chair-type, they're well-placed to serve most of the meatier runs. Off-piste possibilities at both resorts are considerable, with a half-dozen routes recognized and minimally maintained.

Budget **accommodation** in Candanchú is restricted to two *albergues*, the highly rated *El Águila* (Ⓣ974 373 291, Ⓦwww.infovide.com/elaguila; 58 places in 4-bed en-suites or 6-bed dorms; open ski season plus July & Aug), and *Valle del Aragón* (Ⓣ974 373 222), with half-board encouraged at both. Of three surviving **hotels**, marginally the most economical is wood-chalet, two-star *Hotel Candanchú* (Ⓣ974 373 025, Ⓦwww.candanchu.com; ❺). In terms of **eating** out, skiers – and in summer, GR11 trekkers – congregate for lunch or supper at friendly *Cafeteria Cristiania*, which despite the name does full meals (€13–26). Astún has just a single, three-star hotel, the box-like *Europa* (Ⓣ974 373 312; ❾), by the car park.

Beyond Urdos several daily well-spaced SNCF buses continue on through the beech forests and the PNP through the new tunnel under the 1632-metre **Col du Somport/Puerto de Somport**, and beyond to Canfranc, the terminus for trains from Jaca in Aragón. The Romans built the first road through the pass, and the Muslims made grateful use of this handiwork during their northward invasion in 732. This twisty old road, recommended for the views, still climbs over the pass itself, accessing the cross-country ski centre of

Somport-Candanchú, 34km of marked trails (9km on the Spanish side), pre-sumably dodging the numerous ventilation silos for the tunnel; that said, it's one of the best such centres in the Pyrenees, and at this altitude one of the last to close in spring. At the frontier there are a few snack bars, a snowplough sta-tion and the abandoned customs post; just below, you turn left for Astún, right for the main onward road and Candanchú.

# Huesca, Barbastro and the Sierra de Guara

**Huesca**, one of Aragón's three provincial capitals, lies 56km due south of Sabiñánigo on the broad, fast N330/E7 – or more circuitously, and enjoyably, 76km from Jaca via the A1205 southwest through the Puerto de Oroel, and then onto the N240 southeast past the natural wonder of **Los Mallos** and the imposing **Castillo de Loarre**. The rail line out of Sabiñánigo also approxi-mately traces this journey, along the Río Gállego. The next major town east of Huesca is **Barbastro**, smack in the middle of Aragón's most esteemed wine-producing district, just east of the Río Zinca valley, which provides a corridor for the A138 and occasional bus service up to Aínsa or beyond. North of the Huesca-Barbastro road, occupying a huge rectangular territory of roughly 800 square kilometres, looms the low-altitude **Sierra de Guara**, an ever-popular target especially when the higher Pyrenean ranges are still under snow.

## Huesca and around

Despite a big-city feel, with appreciable African, Muslim and gypsy communi-ties, **HUESCA** is perhaps the least memorable of Aragonese foothill towns, and if you're heading for the mountains you might bypass it altogether, or stay on the train to Jaca. However, to the northeast lies the **Sierra de Guara** with its canyonlands, while northwest of Huesca the striking **Los Mallos** pinnacles and the **Castillo de Loarre** provide worthy pretexts for breaking a journey towards Jaca.

Calling Huesca unmemorable is perhaps unfair, since there's a reasonably well-preserved **old quarter** (if a bit over-modernized with contemporary brickwork) tucked into a loop of *paseos* and the Río Isuela. Dead centre stands a late Gothic **Catedral**, whose unusual facade combines the thirteenth-centu-ry portal of an earlier church with a brick Mudéjar gallery, and a pinnacled, Isabelline top section. The great treasure inside is the *retablo* by Damián Forment, a Renaissance masterpiece depicting the Crucifixion and the Deposition. Next door, the **Museo Diocesano** (Mon–Sat 10am–1.30pm & 4–6/7.30pm; closed Sat pm & Sun; €2) contains a rather mixed collection, gathered from churches in the countryside. The liveliest time to visit is during Huesca's big **fiesta** in honour of San Lorenzo, held the second week of August, centred on the 10th.

### Practicalities

Finding your way around Huesca shouldn't be a problem. The **train** station is at the south end of c/Zaragoza, a main thoroughfare, with the **bus station** just in front. The **Turismo** (daily 9am–2pm & 4–8pm; ☎974 292 100, Ⓦwww.huescaturismo.com) is opposite the cathedral inside the Renaissance *ayuntamiento*, stocking various pamphlets on the Aragonese mountains.

**Accommodation** can be hard to find during summer, when trekkers from all over are passing through, so it's worth booking ahead. In the budget range, there's *Pensión Augusto*, c/Aínsa 16 (☎974 220 079; ❶), offering tidy rooms with washbasin above a bar; en-suite *Hostal San Marcos*, c/San Orencio 10 (☎974 222 931; ❸), handy for nightlife; and the en-suite *Hostal El Centro*, c/Sancho Ramírez 3 (☎974 226 823, ℻974 225 112; ❷), in a grand old building housing large, well-renovated rooms, many with balcony. More comfortable choices on Plaza Lizana, just downhill from the cathedral, include *Hostal Lizana/Lizana 2* (☎974 220 776; ❷–❸), and adjacent three-star *Hotel Sancho Abarca* at no. 13 (☎974 220 650, ℻974 225 169; ❻), where most rooms have balconies or air conditioning. The **campsite**, *San Jorge* (☎974 227 416), is at the end of c/Ricardo del Arco.

*Restaurante Marisquería Navas*, c/Vicente Campo Palacio 3 (closed Sun pm & Mon, late June & late Oct), is considered Huesca's top **restaurant** by virtue of delicious fish, game dishes and *artesanal* desserts. The chef's full works will run you €32, with the pricey wine list extra, all delivered by efficient, liveried waiters shuttling between the front bar and the family *comedor* in the back. But there's also an excellent-value *menú* (€18) – typically seafood appetizer, sourdough rolls, grilled asparagus, *chicharro* fish with spinach and cream sauce, plus dessert. Its only serious rival is *Restaurante Las Torres* at c/María Auxiliadora 3 (closed Sun & Aug 20–Sept 3), a fancy place purveying *nouvelle* Aragonese cuisine (try the *menú gastronómico* at €40). For excellent **tapas bars** and **nightlife** head for the *zona* around c/San Lorenzo and c/Padre Huesca, between the Coso Bajo and the Plaza de Santa Clara, while for *horchata* and real *gelato*, make for *Los Italianos* at Coso Bajo 18.

## Castillo de Loarre

The **Castillo de Loarre** (April–Sept 10.30am–1.30pm & 4–7pm; Oct–March 11am–2pm & 4–5.30pm; closed Mon to individuals except Aug, but often possible to tag along with school groups; free) is Aragón's most spectacular and best-maintained fortress. As you approach across a plain carpeted with almond groves, the castle seems to blend into the hillside but up close assumes a breathtaking grandeur: compact but intricate, its south ramparts rooted in a sheer palisade at 1100m elevation, commanding the landscape for miles around.

Its builder was Sancho Ramírez, king of Navarra (1000–35), who used it as a base for his resistance to the Moorish occupation. Once you're inside the curtain walls, the first structure encountered is the **Capilla Real**, consisting of the delicately proportioned Romanesque Iglesia de San Pedro, with fourteen capitalled columns adorning blind arches in the apse, and a beehive-domed and vaulted crypt accessed by either a pair of narrow, claustrophobic stairs from the altar or a conventional door. Elsewhere, the labyrinthine ground plan conforms well to most fantasies of what a castle should be with its dungeons, ruined palace, lancet windows and turrets; accordingly it was used as a location for Ridley Scott's 2003 revisionist-Crusader film *Kingdom of Heaven*. Of a pair of towers, the **Torre de la Reina** has ornate Gothic windows, while the taller **Torre del Homenaje**, climbable to the penultimate storey, is dominated by a massive hooded fireplace.

The castle stands some 30km northwest of Huesca by the most direct back-road through Bolea, and 4km beyond the village of Loarre, itself graced by a fifteenth-century parish church with an ornate spire. By **public transport**, it's an awkward journey, as bus timetables conspire against a day-trip. Loarre has morning bus service only from Jaca, while Ayerbe gets at most three a day in the afternoon and evening. Fortunately there's adequate **accommodation** in both sleepy **LOARRE** and equally provincial **AYERBE**, which has the nearest train station and, judging from the ornate fifteenth-century **Palacio de los Urries** on the central plaza, must once have been a place of some importance. Closest to the castle is the three-star *Hospedaria de Loarre*, a restored seventeenth-century mansion on Loarre's central plaza (℡974 382 706, ℻974 382 713; ❹); its bland, non-air-con rooms are rated one star too many, not really worth the price asked in high season, though the **restaurant** (closed Sun) is well respected (€15 *menú* or about €25 *a la carta*). Failing this, Loarre has one *casa rural*, *Casa Tolta* (℡974 382 605; ❷) – as well as another restaurant, *Casa O Caminero*, from whose terrace you can admire the church – and Ayerbe a further four, the most characterful being the *Antigua Posada del Pilar* at Plaza Aragón 38 (℡974 380 052; ❷), with good suppers offered – though the proprietress will sit and watch you eat every bite. There's also a quiet **campsite** 1500m out of Ayerbe on the road to Loarre, *La Banera* (℡974 380 242). Ayerbe's tried and true **restaurant** options include sustaining, deceptively humble-looking *Floresta*, at the start of the Loarre road (*menús* including drink €9 Mon–Fri/€12 Sat & Sun), and the fancier *Rincón del Palacio* next to the Renaissance palace on the square, where the €19 *menú* lets you sample most of the *carta*.

## Los Mallos

The train line from Huesca to Jaca and the N240 road from Huesca to Puente la Reina de Jaca give views not only of Loarre but of the fantastic, pink-tinged, cylindrical rock formations known as **Los Mallos** – "the ninepins", divided into two separate clusters at Riglos and Agüero. Their majesty, however, may not serve to protect them from partial inundation by a proposed new dam at Biscarrués on the Río Gallego, augmenting the Pántano de la Peña already existing just upstream. Ubiquitous roadside graffiti by the river partisans – RÍO = VIDA (River=Life), PÁNTANO BISCUARRÉS JAMÁS (Biscarrués Dam Never), SOS RÍO – leaves you in little doubt as to prevailing local sentiment. For the moment, the pinnacles remain popular with climbers and parapentists, while the river between the existing reservoir and Santa Eulalia swarms with rafters from April to early summer.

If you're travelling by train and want a closer look, get off at **Concilio** station (you have to ask the conductor to stop) and walk 2.5km along the road to **RIGLOS** village, tucked high up underneath the most impressive stretch of the peaks. At Riglos there's another (unstaffed) station, below the village, from where you can resume your journey. Alternatively, **stay** the night above the *Bar Restaurante El Puro* (aka *Casa Toño*; ℡974 383 176; ❷); Toño himself is a mine of information on climbing routes up the *mallos*. Failing that, there's an en-suite **turismo rural** in the heart of the village, *Casa Escalaretas* (℡974 383 096; ❷). If you're not a technical climber, you can still enjoy a cool-season loop-walk along the marked **PR98 trail** from Riglos, which takes in the villages of Escaleta la Peña and Carcavilla, as well as the base of the cliffs, in under four hours.

Otherwise, an alternative local base is **MURILLO DE GÁLLEGO**, another stunning village above the main A132 highway, pretty much taken over by river enthusiasts in season. No less than four outfitters offering rafting, kayak and hydrospeed are based here along the busy highway; canoeing starts from €25, rafting from €30, depending on group size and rapids rating. **Accommodation** includes the roadside *Hostal Los Mallos* (℡974 383 026; ❸), which also runs an *albergue*; there's another more comfortable *albergue* up in the village at c/La Manga, *Casa Chancabez* (℡974 383 018; 47 places;

March–Nov), as well as a partly shaded, olive-grove **campsite** towards the river, *Armalygal* (☎74 383 005; Easter, July & Aug). Top standard locally is provided by partly en-suite *Casa Leandrón* (☎974 383 275, ⓦwww.casaleandron.com; ❷), also in the village centre. The rafting fraternity **eats, drinks** and listens to music into the small hours at *Bar-Restaurante El Embudo*, between the highway and village-church bluff.

More *mallos* loom behind **AGÜERO**, a completely isolated village 5km off the main N240 road from Murillo de Gállego, or a seven-kilometre walk from Concilio station. Agüero itself is characterful and unspoiled, graced by two Romanesque **churches**: the central, eleventh-century San Salvador and the isolated twelfth-century Santiago 700m east, both with superb portal carvings by the Master of San Juan de la Peña (see p.455). **San Salvador's** north tympanum shows *Christ in Majesty*, attended by the four personifications of the Evangelists; the door itself is flanked by column capitals carved with imaginary beasts. Triple-apsed **Santiago**, accessed by good dirt track, has a blank western wall and sole entry on the south (supposedly the church is unfinished); carvings above the door here show the visit of the Three Kings, with one stooping to kiss the infant Jesus's foot, while Joseph on the right, leaning on his staff and with his right fist dug into his cheek, seems visibly wearied by the august visitors. On the adjacent column capitals, monsters devour a ram, men play rebec and psaltery serenade a lady, and knights engage in combat. If you're intent on admission to Santiago, ask for the key at Panadería San Roque, but it's well worth the trip out just to admire the exterior.

In Agüero, you may **stay** either at *Hostal La Costera* at the very top of the village (☎974 380 330; ❷), reached via the cemetery ring road, with basic, prefab rooms but lovely grounds, a pool and restaurant, or at a *casa rural* in the lane north of the church, *Casa Camilo* (☎974 380 121; ❷), providing evening meals. There's also a grassy if not very shady municipal **campsite** at the lowest margins of the village, *Peña Sola* (☎974 380 533), with a small pool.

## Barbastro

**BARBASTRO**, 51km east-southeast of Huesca and straddling the Río Vero before it joins the Zinca, has considerable historic importance. The union of Aragón and Catalunya was declared here in 1137, sealed by the marriage of the daughter of Ramiro of Aragón to Ramón Berenguer IV, count of Barcelona. Although it's now just a slightly shabby provincial market town, Barbastro retains a significant old quarter. Topping a rise just south of the river, the Gothic **Catedral** (Mon–Sat 10am–1.30pm & 4–7.30pm, Sun 10am–noon; €2), on a site once occupied by a mosque, has a high altar whose construction began under the supervision of Damián Forment: when he died in 1540 only part of the alabaster relief had been completed, so the rest was finished by his pupils. Just northeast, on the Plaza de la Constitución, the facade of the restored fifteenth-century **Ayuntamiento**, designed by the Moorish chief architect to Fernando el Católico, is also worth a look. Elsewhere, narrow, pedestrianized shopping streets are lined by faded-pastel dwellings piled up with their backs towards the river, while the central, tree-lined **Paseo del Coso** at the southwest edge of the old quarter is occupied by outdoor tables for many of the town's bars and cafés.

But the foregoing is incidental to the town's sole present and future prospects: **wine**, wine and more wine. Barbastro lies at the centre of the **Somontano**, the most important *denominación de origen* vintage district in Aragón, and one of the most prominent in Spain. This may seem peculiar for a place dominated by the abstemious, militant Catholic movement, Opus Dei, whose power-base is the nearby monastery of Torreciudad, but Opus Dei members are prominent in Spanish industry – including wine-making – raising money to further the faith. Visits can be organized to three of the biggest local wineries – Bodega Pirineos, Viñas del Vero and Enate (details from the Turismo, see below). Both Hemingway and Orwell tippled in Barbastro during the 1920s and 1930s; their favourite watering-hole, at one corner of the *paseo*, was the ground-floor bar of the Fonda San Ramón. Alas, this closed down in early 2000 when its lease was revoked – and a bit of history died with it (though the sign's still visible outside). There are still, of course, well-stocked bottle shops in Barbastro, one of the best and biggest inside the Turismo.

### Practicalities

The **bus station** is at the southwest end of the *paseo*, with regular daily departures for Huesca and (Mon–Sat) to Benasque. The helpful English-speaking **Turismo** (July & Aug daily 10am–2pm & 4.30–8pm; Sept–June Tues–Sat 10am–2pm & 4.30–8pm; ☎974 308 350, ⓦwww.barbastro-ayto.es) is 200m uphill and south from the station, in the **Conjunto de San Julián y Santa Lucía**, a restored thirteenth-century hospice.

Appealing budget **accommodation** is scarce; about as basic as you'd want is en-suite *Hostal Goya* (☎974 311 747; ❶) at c/Argensola 13, a slightly seedy street just south of the river. More comfort is available at two establishments on c/Corona de Aragón, running parallel to the river at the northeast edge of the old town: *Hostal Roxi* (☎974 311 064; ❷), at no. 21, and the *Hotel Clemente* at no. 5 (☎974 310 186; ❸).

Several decent **restaurants** have sprung up to take advantage of all that wine sloshing about. The most central is *Cenador de San Julián* (closed Sun pm & Mon), just beside the Turismo in a round, brick-walled *comedor*, considered one of the town's best, though its €18 *menú* includes suprisingly average wine. Further afield in the new quarter, within walking distance of the centre via the Avenida Pirineos bridge, are two more possibilities: *Flor* at c/Goya 3 and *Cocina Vasca* (closed Sun) adjacent at no. 5 – *menús* at either run at about €13. Finally, the *Hospedería El Pueyo*, 5km west, has a worthwhile *comedor* (menú €10; Easter–Sept daily except Mon, Oct–Easter daily Sat & Sun, lunch only Tues–Fri) next to the nondescript namesake hilltop monastery dedicated to Barbastro's patroness, La Virgen del Pueyo.

## Sierra de Guara

North of the N240 road linking Huesca and Barbastro sprawls the **Sierra de Guara**, a thinly inhabited region protected as a *parque natural* since 1990. The sierra is definitely Pyrenean foothills – the highest point is 2078-metre Puntón de Guara – with no dramatic peaks to draw the eye to the horizon, and often distinctly scrubby low-altitude vegetation, enlivened by olive and almond groves. The Guara's allure lies lower down, in its unrivalled array of sculpted gorges, painted prehistoric caves and appealing villages. This is the main venue for **canyoning** in all of Spain, and arguably Europe; it's been known to the French for decades, such that French (and Belgian) cars match or outnumber Spanish ones in the popular centres. They retrace the steps of Belle Époque *pyreneistes* who had first discovered and publicized the canyonlands between 1870 and 1900. French-run, too, are many of the adventure outfitters – there's at least one in every village – though the Spanish are having a go at clawing back some of the trade. **Walking** opportunities are relatively limited, owing to

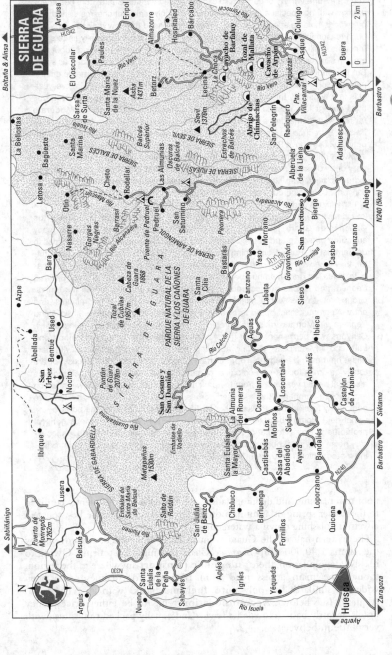

## Canyoning in the Sierra de Guara

There's a **huge variety** of canyons to explore in the Sierra de Guara, from beginners' outings with no special equipment needed, to highly technical chasms visited only by experts holding special permits. Generally you need to know how to swim, and be in reasonable physical condition, since every body part – especially fingers and forearms – will get a workout. Judging from the number of folk hobbling about with arms in slings and bandaged abrasions, canyoning is a moderately dangerous sport. But you shouldn't feel intimidated or excluded: hundreds of people emerge daily in peak season without a scratch, and you frequently see whole families with five-year-olds in tow happily threading the **easier** canyons, such as the Vero near Alquézar, the Peonera just upstream from Bierge and the Barrasil at Rodellar. **Moderate** ravines, with some drops requiring rope or prolonged swims, include Oscuros de Balcés, Estrechos de Balcés and Gorgonchón, all close to Bierge, while **experts-only** abysses above Rodellar include Gorgas Negras, Otín and Mascún Superior, all involving thirty-metre abseilings and strenuous clambering. Organized outings, run daily or by demand from April to October, typically **cost** €36–42 per person, including equipment, with little price difference between the simplest and most difficult canyons. Local *albergues* also offer advantageous "packages", such as three days of expeditions and full board for €200.

Since all the most popular canyons lie within the **Parque de la Sierra y los Cañones de Guara**, park authorities have stipulated **conditions** of access; many are common sense and spelled out in their leaflet "Normativa Sobre el Descenso de Barrancos" (Rules Concerning the Descent of Ravines). If you go with an outfitter, they'll be well aware of the rules, but for those going solo, an English summary follows. The maximum number of persons per group is ten in the Vero, Barrasil, Peonera and Balcés ravines; four in the Gorgonchón and eight in all the others. Groups must enter with a minimum **spacing** between them of ten minutes, and entry in summer must be **no later** than 4pm (though Gorgas Negras, Mascún and Peonera via Morrano must be entered by noon, 1pm and 2.30pm respectively). Canyons with permanent water (most of them) require the wearing of a **neoprene suit**, and any descent involving abseiling means mandatory provision with **harness**, **helmet** and adequate **rope**. Certain canyons have restricted access, or are totally off-limits for safety, ecological or archeological reasons. La Choca requires a special permit year-round from the park authorities, as does Otín between March and June; a number of the less used gorges, in particular the Vadiello system, are completely forbidden from December to May. You're not to enter the pools of the Canal del Palomo (to protect its rare species). Finally, there are various **general prohibitions** similar to that of the Ordesa park: no fires, rough camping, unnecessary noise, leaving rubbish, molesting flora and fauna, defacing rocks, or introducing motor vehicles onto the many 4WD tracks.

poor trail marking and documentation, and hiking is most prudently confined to the cooler spring or autumn months. July or August days are best spent in a wetsuit, splashing down a watercourse.

The eastern half of the Guara is much more frequented, and covered by the Alpina 1:40,000 **map** *Sierra de Guara II*, a must for touring. Owing to massive depopulation, there's **no public transport** anywhere in the region, though the main access road from Barbastro to Adahuesca has been widened; similarly, the only **auto fuel** and **bank** (with an ATM) is at Alquézar (see below). **Accommodation** tends to be either pricey, fancy hotels or fairly basic (crowded *albergues* and equally packed campsites), with very little in between.

## Alquézar and around

At the far southeastern corner of the range and *parque*, 22km from Barbastro, **ALQUÉZAR** ("Alquezra" in Aragonese) is the Guara's gateway and most developed tourist mecca. Perched on the west bank of the Río Vero, it's a supremely atmospheric village, but packed to the gills most weekends and all summer. Arcaded lanes culminate in the eighth-century Moorish **citadel** on a pinnacle dropping to the river; the Christians took it in 1064, and by the start of the following century the **Colegiata de Santa Maria la Mayor** (guided visits summer daily 11am–1pm & 4.30–7.30pm; winter daily except Tues 11am–1pm & 4–6pm; €2) already existed within the fortifications. Only the cloister, its column capitals carved with biblical scenes, remains from the Romanesque era; the Gothic-Renaissance church itself dates from the sixteenth and seventeenth centuries. It's crammed with a miscellany of Baroque art, mostly polychrome wood except for an unpainted pine organ, and a masterly thirteenth-century wooden Crucifixion in the side chapel. The only other specific cultural diversion is the **Museo Etnológico Casa Fabián** at c/Baja 16 (daily except Mon & Wed am 11am–2pm & 4–8pm; €1.50), with a working olive press in the cellar.

From the north end of Plaza Mayor begins the path towards the Río Vero and its **Puente de Villacantal**, one of several ancient bridges in the *sierra*. Just northeast of the village, you ignore a forking northwest towards the Balsas de Basacol, instead continuing over a slight saddle and then sharply down to the river. The double-arched bridge is beautiful and worth the trip, though you'll have to retrace your steps (1hr 15min return) or engage in some river wading to reach another trail back to the citadel going up the Barranco de la Fuente. The bridge itself carries the path onward to Asque hamlet and then Colungo, though much of the hour-plus approach to Asque from Villacantal is along bulldozed track.

There's a **Turismo** at the southwest edge of town on c/Arrabal (Easter & July–Sept Tues–Sun 10.30am–1.30pm & 4–9pm; Oct–June weekends only, same hours), which sells the recommended Alpina map. **Accommodation** is fairly abundant but still needs advance booking at busy times. Among several *albergues*, two worth noting are *Tintorero* (☎974 318 354; April–Sept) in the heart of town at c/San Gregório 18, and *Marmita de Guara* up by the car park and municipal pool (☎974 318 956; March–Oct). There are also two **campsites** close by: *Alquézar* (☎974 318 300, ⓦwww.alquezar.com), 1km downhill by the petrol pump, also with four-person bungalows and generally of a slightly higher standard than *Río Vero* (☎974 318 350; Easter–Sept), down by the river. Among eight **casas rurales**, two renting individual rooms are the friendly, partly en-suite *Casa Jabonero* on c/Pedro Arnal 8 (☎974 318 908; ❷), and the en-suite *Casa Espartero* on Plaza Mayor (☎974 318 071; ❷). The more professional, helpful and reliably open of the two fully fledged **hotels** is *Villa de Alquézar* on c/Pedro Arnal 12 (☎ & ⓕ974 318 416; 3), whose large doubles have castle-view balconies; rates include a generous breakfast with yoghurt and charcuterie, and covered parking.

The **bars and restaurants** crowding Plaza Nueva at the southwest edge of Alquézar, their tables poised to exploit the view, are generally mediocre, pricey and surly to boot; the best independent restaurant is *Casa Gervasio* on the main old-quarter street, with huge portions, though the *comedor* of *Marmita de Guara* also gets good marks. With transport, head 5.5km southwest to **ADAHUESCA**, where *El Puntillo* at c/de la Iglesia 4 offers slightly precious but nonetheless imaginative nouvelle Spanish cuisine (€24 *menú*, sky-high wine list extra), which might include stewed cardoon stems or *callos de bacalao* in saffron sauce. They also have popular rooms and six-person apartments upstairs (☎974 318 168, ✉puntillo@teleline.es; ❸), or alternatively you can stay nearby at *Casa Labata* (☎974 318 019; ❷), a *turismo rural* above a bar at c/Nueva 3. Finally, the village of **BUERA**, 6km southeast across the river, has the best small lodgings of the Guara region in *Hotel Posada de Lalola* at c/la Fuente 14 (☎974 318 347; ❺), with six exquisite designer rooms opening onto a garden and respectable *table d'hôte* fare by appointment for non-guests (€24) in its diminutive bar-*comedor*.

## North: the road to Lecina

The HU340 district road from below Alquézar heads northeast 5km to **COLUNGO**, attractive in a low-key way with its arched doorways and massive buttressed church. You can **dine** and sample the locally made *aguardiente de anís* at *Restaurante A'Olla*, opposite the *Hostal Mesón de Colungo* (☎974 318 195; ❷), your sole option for **staying**, fortunately run by helpful and knowledgeable staff.

The road continues, in and out of the minor Fornocal gorge, passing two of the four **painted caves** of the Vero valley, which can only be visited on escorted tours (Easter week & mid-July to mid-Sept daily; Easter to mid-July & mid-Sept to early Oct Sat & Sun only; otherwise make arrangements with the Barbastro Turismo). During peak season, just show up at the signed turn-outs for the **Covacho de Arpán** (10am & 6pm) and **Tozal de Mallata** (12.15 & 4.30pm); for the **Covacho de Barfaluy**, assemble at the Turismo in Lecina (see below) at 10am or 5pm, while 4.30pm visits to the remote **Abrigo de Chimiachas** must always be booked through the Alquézar Turismo, as a long 4WD transfer is involved. The art in Chimiachas and Arpán is classified as *Levantino* or conventional-figural, while that of Mallata and Barfaluy as *esquemático* (stick-figures).

**LECINA** itself, some 16km from Colungo, has some imposing houses – it was one of the wealthier Guara villages – an enormous oak (thus the name, from *La Encina*) and a sense of height, looking northeast as it does to the main Pyrenean peaks. Moreover, there's a superb place to **stay** and **eat** here: *La Choca* (☎974 343 070 or 659 633 636, ℻974 318 466; ❸), a restored mansion opposite the church with some of the best food in the Guara (*table d'hôte* for about €12; supper only except weekends, Easter, July & Aug). There's also a **campsite** down by the river, *Lecina* (☎974 318 386; May–Sept), which doubles as the closest canyoning outfitter, but this is one of the few Guaran areas where **walkers** are actively catered to.

The local municipality has waymarked sixteen **PR trails**, indicated on a sketch map available from the tiny Turismo in Lecina or from *La Choca*. A particularly good outing is the three-hour loop Lecina–Almazorre–Betorz –Lecina, combining three of the most unspoilt paths (#5, #9, #6). It's an hour on #5 from Lecina (760m), mostly through shaded woods on a walled *camino* (but also a bit of dreary track), to the bed of the Río Vero (670m) and an old, combined **grain mill and olive press**, used until recently; all the workings are still intact. Allow fifteen minutes one-way for the detour up to **Almazorre** village (750m; no facilities), or proceed directly onto trail #9 up a side canyon, first on the left bank, then on the right, through low pines, box and oak to **Betorz** (under 1hr, 970m). This is an attractive, though almost empty, village with a marvellous setting. The descent to Lecina begins with the *camino* starting on the right road verge just past the lowest houses; there's even some cobbling (plus a stretch of track) along the 20 minutes to a **spring**, your only reliable water en route, feeding a round livestock pool in a shady glen. It's an hour in total (not "40min" as posted) along a gentle grade through baby oaks back to Lecina.

## Northwest: the road to Rodellar

West from Alquézar and Adahuesca, the next significant village is **BIERGE**, its *ermita* of **San Fructuoso** adorned with frescoes. **Accommodation** is limited to a single *casa rural* in the centre, *Casa Rufas* at c/La Cruz 2 (T974 318 373; ❷), and a welcoming *albergue* at the southwest outskirts, *Casa Barbara* (T974 318 060, Wwww.casabarbara.net; 24 places; Easter–Oct), aimed at canyoners who don't mind being packed eight to a dorm, but the food – including own-baked breads and turnovers – is excellent, and served out in the garden; half-board is encouraged.

North along the ridge-top HU341, the scenery gets grander after some 5km, with canyons yawning either side. After 11km you descend through woods to *Expediciones* (T974 343 008, Wwww.expediciones.sc.es; June–Sept), the most pleasant **campsite** of three in the Alcanadre river valley; they're also about the most switched-on canyoning operator. **LAS ALMUNIAS**, 2km further, is the first proper village, offering the *Hostal Casa Tejedor* (T974 318 686, F974 343 015; March–Oct; ❷) with a restaurant, plus the *Albergue Las Almunias* across the road (T974 318 602; 42 places; Easter, July & Aug).

**RODELLAR**, some 4km further and 18km from Bierge at the end of the road, looks achingly photogenic draped along a ridge above the Río Mascún, but the reality close up in peak season is likely to be cars parked nose-to-tail for a kilometre before the village, and overstretched **accommodation**. This comprises *Casa Arilla* (T974 318 343; ❷; April–Oct) and *Casa Ortas* (T974 318 364; ❶), while the *Bar-Restaurante Florentino* opposite *Casa Arilla* is the only spot to eat or drink. Two **campsites** – *Mascún* at the edge of the village (T974 318 367, Wwww.guara-mascun.com; April–Sept), and *El Puente* (T974 318 312, Wwww.guara.net/elpuente; April–Oct), 1500m south by the river and the medieval Pedruel bridge, both act as canyoning guide centres. If you're not interested in plumbing the deep gorges, the most popular activity is the two-and-a-half-hour (one-way) **hike** north to the abandoned hamlet of **Otín**, though path-marking is terrible. It's sobering to reflect that before the current canyoning boom, just two families lived in Rodellar (down from 40 in 1900), plus a few pioneering French canyon-explorers like Pierre Minvielle and Christian Abadie who bought houses here during the 1960s.

# Travel details

## French trains

**Pau** to: Lourdes (almost hourly 7am–12.30pm; 30min); Oloron-Sainte-Marie (6–9 daily; 35min); Tarbes (almost hourly 7am–12.30am; 45min).
**Tarbes** to: Capvern (2 daily (1 may be SNCF bus); 30min); Lannemezan (8 daily Mon–Sat, 6 Sun; 25min); Lourdes (almost hourly 4.45am–9.30pm; 20min).

## Spanish trains

**Jaca** to: Canfranc-Estación (2 daily; 35min);

Huesca (2 daily; 2hr 10min); Sabiñánigo (2 daily; 20min); Zaragoza (2 daily; 3hr).

## French buses

**Bagnères-de-Bigorre** to: Campan (3 daily July–Sept, 1 daily in term time; 20min); Lac de Payolle (3 daily July–Sept, 1 daily in term time; 45min); Sainte-Marie-de-Campan (3 daily July–Sept, 1 daily in term time; 35min).
**Lannemezan** to: Arreau (SNCF or Brunet buses; 7 daily year-round; 25min); Bagnères-de-Bigorre (2 weekly during school term; 50min); St-Lary-Soulan

(SNCF buses only; 5 daily year-round; 45min).

**Laruns** to (all except Pau with Canonge-Pic Bus, July & Aug Mon–Fri only): Bious-Oumette campsite (1 daily; 35min); Col du Pourtalet (2 daily, 1hr 20min); Gabas (2 daily; 25min); Lac de Fabrèges (2 daily Mon–Fri with Canonge-Pic Bus; 55min; 1 daily with SNCF bus, 40min); Pau (2–3 daily on SNCF bus, change to train at Buzy; 1hr 10min).

**Lourdes** to: Bagnères-de-Bigorre (2 daily during school term, 3 daily in summer; 45min); Barèges (SNCF bus; 6 daily July & Aug, 5 daily Sept–June; 1hr 5min); Cauterets (SNCF bus; 6 daily July & Aug, 5 daily Sept–June; 1hr); Luz-Saint-Sauveur (SNCF bus; 6 daily July & Aug, 5 daily Sept–June; 45min); Pau (4 daily; 1hr 15min); Tarbes (hourly; 30min).

**Luz-Saint-Sauveur** to: Gavarnie (July & Aug 2 daily with Cars Dubie, 9am & 5.30pm, return 11.40am & 6.30pm; winter 3 weekly, Mon, Thurs & Sat; 40min).

**Oloron-Sainte-Marie** to (all SNCF buses): Bedous (8 daily Mon–Sat, 4 on Sun; 30min); Cette-Eygun/Lescun junction (8 daily Mon–Sat, 4 on Sun; 45min); Urdos (8 daily Mon–Sat, 4 on Sun; 1hr).

**Pau** to: Bayonne (run by TPR; 3–4 daily Mon–Sat, 2 on Sun; 2hr); Col d'Aubisque (CITRAM; July to mid-Sept 1 daily; 2hr); Gourette (CITRAM; 3 daily; 1hr 30min); Laruns (CITRAM; 3 daily; 1hr); Lourdes (4 daily; 1hr 15min); Oloron-Sainte-Marie (Mon–Sat 2–3 daily; 1hr); Tarbes (6 daily; 1hr).

**Tarbes** to: Argelès-Gazost (6 daily; 50min); Arrens-Marsous (Mon–Sat 1 daily; 1hr 20min); Bagnères-de-Bigorre (Mon–Sat 8–9 daily, 3 on Sun; 40min); Pierrefitte-Nestalas (6 daily; 1hr); Tarbes-Ossun/Lourdes Airport (1–2 daily; 30–45min).

## Spanish buses

**Aínsa** to: Bielsa (Mon, Wed, Fri only at 8.45pm, returns 6.15am next day; 40min); Sabiñánigo via Torla (1 daily at 2.30pm; 2hr).

**Barbastro** to: Boltaña via Aínsa (Mon–Sat year-round at 7.45pm, returns next day 6.45am; July 15–Aug 31 also 11am, returning 3pm; Huesca-

Barbastro 10am/6.45pm services link with this); Benasque (daily 11am, plus Mon–Sat 5.20pm; 2hr); Lleida (6 daily Mon–Sat, 4 Sun; 1hr 15min).

**Huesca** to: Ayerbe (3 daily Mon–Fri, 1 daily Sat; 45min); Barbastro (4–6 daily; 50min); Jaca (5 daily via Sabiñánigo, 1 daily Mon–Fri via Ayerbe; 1hr 10min–1hr 35min); Lleida (5 daily Mon–Sat, 4 Sun; 2hr); Pamplona (2 daily July & Aug, otherwise 1 daily; 2hr 35min–2hr 55min); Sabiñánigo (5 daily; 50min).

**Jaca** to: Ansó via Echo (1 daily except Sun at 6.30pm; 1hr 40min); Astún/Candanchú (4–5 daily; 45min); Ayerbe (1 daily, 7.15am; 1hr); Biescas (1–2 daily; 50min); Canfranc-Estación (4–5 daily; 30min); El Formigal (1 daily ski season at 10.15am, returns 3.45–4.15pm; 2hr); Huesca (4–5 daily; 1hr); Loarre (1 daily at 7.15am; 1hr 10min); Pamplona (2 daily July & Aug, 1 daily otherwise; 1hr 40min); Sabiñánigo (4–5 daily 8.15am–7.15pm; 20min); Sallent de Gállego (1 daily Mon–Fri at 6.15pm; 1hr 15min).

**Sabiñánigo** to: Aínsa via Torla (Mon–Sat 1 daily at 11am; 2hr 15min); Biescas (Mon–Sat 1 daily at 11am, plus 1 daily July & Aug at 6.30pm; rest of year Fri & Sun 5pm; 25 min); Jaca (4–5 daily; 20min); Panticosa village (1 daily at 10.45am, also 1 daily Mon–Sat at 6.30pm; July & Aug am service ends at Balneario; 50min); Sarvisé (1 daily at 11am, plus additional service in July & Aug Mon–Sat at 6.30pm; rest of year Fri & Sun at 5.30pm; 1hr 5min); Torla (1 daily at 11am, plus additional service in July & Aug Mon–Sat at 6.30pm rest of year Fri & Sun at 5.30pm; 55min).

**Sallent de Gállego** to: El Formigal (regular ski shuttles in winter; 20min); Sabiñánigo (1 daily Mon–Fri at 7am; 1hr).

## International buses

**Jaca** to: Lourdes via Canfranc, Pau, Tarbes (Sat at 9.45am, Sun at 5.45pm; 4hr 15min for the entire trip).

**Oloron-Sainte-Marie** to (SNCF buses): Canfranc via Urdos (Mon–Sat 5 daily, 3 on Sun; 1hr 20min).

# The Western Pyrenees

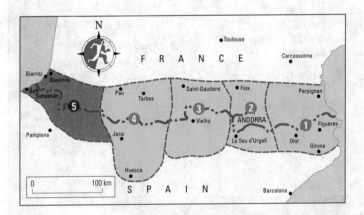

# CHAPTER FIVE

# Highlights

✷ **Monasterio de San Salvador de Leyre** Attend a mass sung in Gregorian chant at this massive monastery. See p.500.

✷ **Biarritz** Catch a wave at elegant Biarritz, France's surfing capital. See p.524

✷ **GR65** Retrace the retreat of the legendary Roland and his army along the GR65 across the border. See p.504

✷ **Haute-Soule gorges** Explore the yawning limestone gorges of the Haute-Soule, on the GR10 or local paths. See p.490

✷ **Pintxos** Sample seafood-rich *pintxos* in the bars of San Sebastián's lively *parte vieja*. See p.543

✷ **Crête d'Iparla** Follow the majestic, airy Crête d'Iparla between Baïgorri and Bidarraï, the Pyrenees' best ridge-walk. See p.513

✷ **Ansó and Echo** Marvel at the substantial stone-built architecture of Ansó and Echo, in Aragón's westernmost valleys. See p.479

# The Western Pyrenees

The widespread notion that the Pyrenees begin or end at Pic d'Anie, 80km from the Atlantic coast, ignores the part of the range containing the densest forests, a seductively green landscape and the most tenaciously retained ethnicity – that of the Basques. The Western Pyrenees lack only lakes and extreme altitude: there's nothing higher than Pic d'Anie's neighbour Tres Reyes (2444m) between it and the sea, and beyond Pic d'Orhy/Pico de Ori (2017m) the summits diminish markedly.

The **Western Pyrenees** cover an area more extensive than **Euskal Herri**, the Basques' name for their homeland on both sides of the frontier. They also include a small pocket of Alto Aragón in the paired **Echo** and **Ansó** valleys, drainages of the same karst country as the **Haute-Soule** in France and **Valle de Belagoa** in Navarra. Geographically the difference between the French and Spanish sides is greater here than anywhere else in the range. In Spain the hills, often alpine in climate and densely tree-clad, extend far from the frontier; the **Irati forest**, for example, while extensive in Spain, has been severely reduced by exploitation on its French slopes (where it's also known as "Iraty"). Much of the French Basque country is strongly reminiscent of rural Scotland, especially near **Saint-Jean-Pied-de-Port**, its chief inland tourist attraction.

This western region also has a high concentration of small gateway cities for the mountains. **Bayonne** and **San Sebastián**, near the Atlantic coast below the foothills, gracefully combine roles as commercial *entrepôts*, resorts and administrative centres, and both – along with the dedicated playground of **Biarritz** – prove livelier and more exciting than anything along the Mediterranean coast of the Pyrenees.

**Public transport** is fairly good on the Spanish side of the Pyrenees, but very poor in France except on the coast and along the Nive valley, so it's easiest to tackle the area from the south. Coming from Jaca, you can take a bus up into the Echo and Ansó valleys, hike west to the Valle de Roncal valley and then over its head to French attractions, such as the Kakouetta gorges. Returning to Roncal or the Valle de Salazar enables you to catch a bus towards Pamplona, from where you could head straight out to the coast of Gipuzkoa, or inland via Auritze towards Saint-Jean-Pied-de-Port, served by French trains.

## The Basques

Nothing is conclusively proved about the **origin of the Basques**. Some consider them to be direct descendants of Europe's **aboriginal** population, a theory supported by archeological finds in the early twentieth century. Skull fragments of late Cro-Magnon man believed to date from around 9000 BC have been shown to be nearly identical to present-day Basque cranial formation.

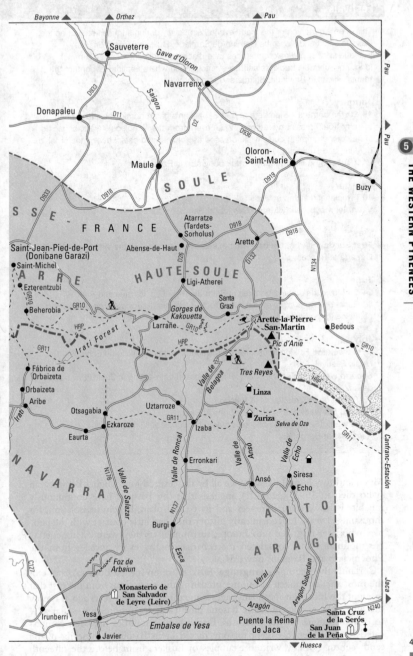

Bayonne ▲   ▲ Orthez   ▲ Pau

Sauveterre

Gave d'Oloron

Saigon

Navarrenx

Pau

Donapaleu

D11

D2

D536

Maule

Oloron-
Saint-Marie

D918

Buzy

Pau

SOULE

SSE-

FRANCE

Atarratze
(Tardets-
Sorholus)

D918

Arette

D132

N134

Saint-Jean-Pied-de-Port
(Donibane Garazi)

Abense-de-Haut

D26

HAUTE-SOULE

D918

Saint-Michel

Ezterentzubi

Ligi-Atherei

Santa
Grazi

Arette-la-Pierre-
San-Martin

Bedous

Beherobia

GR10

Gorges de
Kakouetta

Pic d'Anie

GR10

HRP

Larrañe

GR10

HRP

GR11

Irati Forest

Tres Reyes

GR10

Valle de
Belagoa

Fábrica de
Orbaizeta

Linza

Orbaizeta

Aribe

Otsagabia

Uztarroze

GR11

Zuriza

Selva de Oza

Camfranc-Estación

Ezkaroze

Izaba

Eaurta

Valle de
Ansó

Valle de
Echo

GR11

NAVARRA

Valle de Roncal

Erronkari

Valle de
Salazar

Ansó

Siresa

Echo

N78

ALTO

N137

Burgi

ARAGÓN

Jaca

ESCA

Veral

Aragón Subordán

Foz de
Arbaiun

C127

Aragón

Santa Cruz
de la Serós

N240

Monasterio de
San Salvador
de Leyre (Leire)

Irunberri

Yesa

Puente la Reina
de Jaca

San Juan
de la Peña

Javier

Embalse de Yesa

▼ Huesca

This is only a fraction of the many events, especially during summer, staged on the Basque coast and along the Camino de Santiago. Bullfights, *force Basque* (Basque sports) and *pelota* matches take place at regular intervals all summer long. For schedule booklets and ticket information where applicable, contact the tourist offices in Bayonne, Biarritz and San Sebastián.

### January
**19–20** *Tamborrada* – Members of San Sebastián's gastronomic societies honour the city's patron saint by re-enacting an event from the Napoleonic wars, engaging in raucous drumming duels while dressed as soldiers and chefs; heavy nocturnal drinking and street parties.
**Last Tuesday & Wednesday** *Pottok* pony sale in Ezpeleta.

### February
**10** Traditional dancing at Luzaïde.
**Variable, maybe early March** *Carnival* in San Sebastián.

### May
**First Sunday** Start of the three-month season of *romerías* to the Virgen de Orreaga at Roncesvalles.

### June
**24–26** Music, *pelota* and bonfires at Saint-Jean-de-Luz, Larrañe and Auritze.
**30** *Fiesta de San Marcial* at Irún, with the five-thousand-strong *Alarde* parade and canoeing in the Bidasoa.

### July
**First weekend** Folklore/music festivals, various villages of Valle de Echo; *Pir* Music Festival, Ansó.
**Second weekend** *Fête du Thon*, with music and tuna-eating in Ziburu/Saint-Jean-de-Luz.
**13** *Tributo de las Tres Vacas* at Belagoa.
**Second full week** Surfing competitions at Biarritz.
**Third week (Sat–Thurs)** Folklore, parade, fireworks, bullfights and *Jazz aux Remparts* at Bayonne.

Much anthropological work, above all by the revered Joxe Miguel Barandiaran (who died in 1991, aged 101), suggests that the Basques have continuously inhabited the Western Pyrenees and its coastal plain, largely in isolation, for thousands of years. Indeed, in early history they had little contact with the peoples who later migrated into Europe, surrounded as they were by impenetrable mountains and considered mere barbarians by every invader from the Phoenicians and Romans onwards.

Certainly their complex **language**, Euskera (often spelled Euskara), is one of the most ancient spoken in Europe, predating the migrations from the east that brought the Indo-European languages some three thousand years ago. It is now thought to be as ancient as the Basque race itself, distantly related – if at all – to certain tongues of the Caucasus. Establishing certainties has been complicated by the absence, except for one mixed Latin-Basque manuscript of the tenth century, of any written examples of Euskera from before the fifteenth century. The language has largely been maintained through the oral traditions

**24–28** Prolonged *Fiesta de Santiago* at Izaba and Elizondo.
**25** *Fiesta de Santiago* at Luzaïde; also one including an *encierro* at Puente la Reina de Jaca.
**Variable, last two weeks** Six-day International Jazz Festival at San Sebastián.

### August
**First week** *Fêtes de Bayonne*, five days of heavy drinking and concerts, plus bull-fights, at Bayonne.
**Second week (Sun–Thurs)** *Pelota*, street parties, music, dancing and Basque sports at Cambo-les-Bains (Bas Cambo) and at Baïgorri (Saint-Étienne-de-Baïgorry).
**12–19** *Semana Grande* (*Aste Nagusia* in Euskera) – folk and music festival for *Asunción* at San Sebastián, with fireworks.
**13–15** *Pelota*, folklore and dancing at Saint-Jean-Pied-de-Port.
**15** *Romería* to the Ermita de Nuestra Señora de las Nieves, near Otsagabia; mock Basque wedding at Baïgorri.
**Third weekend** *Fêtes de Petit Bayonne*.

### September
**First ten days** *Pelota* championships at Bayonne.
**First and second weekends** *Trainera* regatta in San Sebastián.
**8** *Fiesta de la Virgen de Guadalupe* at Hondarribia; *romería* to the *colegiata* at Roncesvalles; *Fiestas del Bobo* – masqued dancers at Otsagabia.
**Second Sunday** Start of three-day festival at Sara, with Basque sports, singing and dancing.
**Last two weeks** International Film Festivals at San Sebastián and Biarritz.

### October
**Third week** *Festival du Théâtre* in Bayonne.
**Last weekend** Party, then Mass, in honour of red peppers at Ezpeleta.

### December
**17** *Fiesta de Santo Tomás* – folkloric fun in San Sebastián.
**26–27** *Fiesta de San Estéban* at Yesa.

of *bertsolariak*, or popular poets, specializing in improvised verse, an evolving tradition still alive today. The vocabulary implies a way of life and belief long predating the Christian era, as reflected in terms referring to ancient sites such as dolmens and cromlechs. Further evidence is an extensive mythology relating to *gentilak*, legendary giants supposedly responsible for building these sites, as well as ancient roads and bridges. Yet crucial though it has been for defining Basque identity, Euskera is nowadays a minority language in the region, spoken – mostly along the coastal strip – by about 500,000 people, roughly twenty percent of the total Basque population in France and Spain.

There are strong dialectal differences in usage, spelling and pronunciation throughout the **seven Basque regions** (four in Spain, three in France). It's worth learning to recognize the Basques' term for themselves – Euskaldunak, sometimes Euskualdunak – and their homeland, referred to as Euskadi or Euzkadi in Spain but more generally as Euskal Herri(a). In Spain, the more or less homogeneous autonomous regions of Gipuzkoa and Bizkaia on the coast

## Basque place-names and street-names

Almost everywhere **in Gipuzkoa**, street and road signs appear in both Basque and Castilian, but the latter is often painted over or "edited" by nationalist graffiti artists. Recently, many municipalities have officially chosen to prefer the Basque names and this is reflected in new tourist brochures and maps. **In Navarra** – Nafarroa in Euskera – the process is nearly as advanced, to the considerable annoyance of Castilian-speakers, since only about twenty percent of the population here, mostly in the far northwest on the hilly border with Gipuzkoa, speak Euskera; in the centre and south of Navarra, there's been a backlash against the process, with some place-names reverting officially to Castilian. In the three **French Basque regions** of Labourd (Lapurdi), Basse-Navarre (Behea Nafarroa) and Soule (Zuberoa), Basque nationalists have, since the late 1990s, succeeded in implementing bilingual signage for every town and village (see photo on p.viii), though not yet for every street.

This Guide has treated Basque **place-names** variously, according to their international currency and cartographic conventions. Some places, like Hondarribia, Irún, Ainhoa or Lesaka, have no French or Spanish form in current use, and are cited in **Euskera only**. Others, like Biarritz, Saint-Jean-Pied-de-Port, Roncesvalles and San Sebastián, are increasingly known by Euskera names, but, given their long-established international reputation, are cited in **French or Spanish first**, with **Euskera in brackets following**. Many smaller villages are losing their Spanish/French versions on road or town-limit signage, and these are cited in the text as **Euskera first, Spanish/French variants in brackets following**. International maps have yet to switch over to strictly Euskera tags, except for cases such as Hondarribia and Pasaia (and sometimes Donostia for San Sebastián).

Sometimes the town plans given out by tourist offices are pretty out of date and won't reflect the recent massive campaign of street renaming, especially in **San Sebastián**. Sometimes the difference is slight (Narrika versus Narrica), but just as often the Euskera name is utterly different (c/Nagusia versus c/Mayor). *Kalea*, incidentally, is Euskera for "Street" and follows the proper name. Other common terms you'll see are *jatetxea* (restaurant) and *ostatua* (bar).

It is also worth noting a couple of key **letter changes** that may help to decipher initially confusing words on menus and signs. The Castilian *ch* becomes *tx* (*txipirones* as opposed to *chipirones*) or *ts* (Otsagabia rather than Ochagavía), *v* becomes *b* and *y* becomes *i* (*Bizkaia* as opposed to *Vizcaya*). Above all, Euskera features a proliferation of *k*s, as this letter replaces the Castilian *c* and *qu* (*Gipuzkoa* instead of *Guipúzcoa; Okendo*, not *Oquendo*), and as *-ak* forms the plural. In France, Euskera names are often disguised with the French *ç* and final *y*; thus Esterençuby rather than Ezterentzubi, Baïgorry rather than Baïgorri, Iraty instead of Irati.

account for the bulk of Euskera-speakers; Alaba (Araba) and Navarra (Nafarroa), with long histories of adherence to a unitary Spanish state, experienced – until a recent, conscious revival – a steady decrease in the proportion of Euskera-speakers, to as little as ten percent. The weakening of Euskera's hold was accelerated following the rapid industrialization of Bizkaia and Gipuzkoa during the nineteenth century and the resultant immigration of labour from the rest of Spain, a process deliberately encouraged under Franco (see feature on pp.547–549 for more on Franco's regime and Basque nationalism). By 1975 more than fifty percent of the working class of the coastal Spanish Basque regions came from other parts of the country, whereas in Navarra the proportion of people from elsewhere in Spain was just eighteen percent. During the 1990s labour agitation in Gipuzkoa and Bizkaia, an impulse to protect both a rapidly decreasing number of jobs from outsiders and linguistic purity, neatly coincided.

**Architecturally**, there's a marked difference between the French and Spanish Basque areas. The genuine Basque dwelling – a solid stone structure that often incorporated overhanging upper storeys – is now rare, though some can be seen around Santa Grazi in Haute-Soule, and in a few other settlements. Today the popular image of the Basque house is of a white building with colourful shutters and half-timbering, but this type of building, originally particular to the Labourd region on the French coast, has spread inland comparatively recently, and has been adopted in Spain only along parts of the frontier.

The extended **family** – the word for which, *etxe*, is the same as that for "house" – has always been the basic social unit of Basque life, rather than the village. A farmstead or *baserri* was a multifunctional building housing up to four generations, plopped in the middle of its fields or pastures. A yearning for such a rural idyll probably accounts for the linear, straggled appearance of the smaller Basque hamlets on either side of the border. Property was handed down intact, traditionally from one's paternal aunts, to the oldest son, compelling younger sons to seek their fortunes elsewhere, usually as seamen or emigrants to the Americas.

**Basque food** is recognized as Spain's finest, and certainly garners respect even in France; the people here are prodigious eaters and you'll encounter them seated before enormous spreads in reasonably priced roadside eateries on the outskirts of towns throughout the region. You'll also come across traditional Basque food in the form of *pintxos* in virtually every bar, freshly cooked and always excellent. The tradition of **gastronomic societies**, unique to the Basque regions, deserves special mention: first founded in the mid-nineteenth century, they came about originally as places where craftsmen could socialize. Controversy has surrounded them because women have traditionally not been allowed to enter (although this is changing); all the cooking is done by men who pay a token subscription for the facilities. Members prepare elaborate dishes to perfection as a hobby, and true Basque cookery has largely retreated to these societies. The so-called *Nueva Cocina Vasca* (New Basque Cookery), heavily influenced by French cuisine, is becoming increasingly evident on menus.

# The Karst country and around

Few Pyrenean landscapes have quite the impact as the terrain west of Pic d'Anie. Other parts of the range may have more photogenic glaciers, lakes and wildflowers, but nothing so surreal as the **karst** country around **Tres Reyes**, the highest border mountain of the Basque Pyrenees, and along the Atlantic

THE KARST COUNTRY AND THE VALLE DE SALAZAR

flank of **Pic d'Anie**, the westernmost peak of Béarn. Their upper slopes have been rain-carved into fantastic shapes and sluiced clean of every particle of soil; yet the heights are waterless, the Atlantic precipitation vanishing instantly through waist-deep fissures and bowl-shaped *dolines*, eroding the limestone underneath into a Swiss cheese of potholes and horizontal caverns. Between the two summits lies a zone of shattered boulders, where occasional stunted black pines erupt.

Yet the lower elevations where water reappears – sometimes weeks later, courtesy of the numerous subterranean rivers – are of an almost tropical lushness, with dense forest and pastures of brilliant green, a marked contrast to scattered red-tiled barns and light-grey, stone-built villages. These comprise the valleys of **Echo** and **Ansó** in westernmost Alto Aragón, **Roncal** in Navarra,

Sainte-Engrâce in Haute-Soule and the gorges of **Kakouetta** and **Ehujarré** which open onto the Saint-Engrâce valley.

So far this magnificent landscape is little protected. The French **Parc National des Pyrénées** ends at the border peak of Laraille/Arraya de las Foyas, while the less stringently administered forestry protection zone beyond only guarantees partial preservation of Pic d'Anie and none at all for the Sainte-Engrâce valley. Navarra has conferred *parque natural* status on the **Larra-Belagoa** area at the head of the Valle de Roncal, but it deserves more – not just to protect the dwindling fauna but to reduce wear and tear on the actual terrain, increasingly popular with Spanish city-dwellers. Just to the west, the limestone strata nurture the splendid trans-border **Forêt d'Iraty/Selva de Irati**, though it, too, is much diminished from its former extent and devoid of any formal protection regimen.

# The Echo and Ansó valleys

The **Valle de Echo** and **Valle de Ansó**, northwest of Jaca, are the western-most valleys of Alto Aragón and, in their upper reaches, among the most beautiful, watered respectively by the Aragón Subordán and Veral rivers. They inter-communicate over shallow passes between karst summits, with the Haute-Soule region in France to the north and the Spanish Valle de Roncal to the west.

The principal villages – Echo (833m) and Ansó (860m) – once lived (and grew wealthy) from sheep-raising. In modern times, timber-cutting (in turn suspended) has supplanted livestock, but despite a modest altitude on the valley floor, good roads in and their manifest beauty, seasonal or weekend habitation is now the rule for both villages. Echo and Ansó are lonely places in winter, as it's considered too arduous to commute to jobs in the provincial centres. Until quite recently, both villages felt extremely remote all year round, and Echo preserves an Aragonese dialect known as *Cheso*, widely spoken and taught in the school. Another holdover is the presence of the *espantabrujas*, little hoodoo figures perched atop the domed chimneys or over windows; also found in other parts of Alto Aragón, these were believed to repel witches who were in the habit of entering houses through such openings.

These days, Echo and Ansó find themselves squarely on the tourist map, a favourite target for Spanish weekenders. However, in each case the local country shows its best side and offers the only worthwhile walks some distance upstream from the villages, though the Valle de Echo makes a more dramatic impression within sight of its village. Developers and planners also have their eyes on the valleys. The big local environmental issue is the proposed enlargement of the Yesa reservoir downstream on the Río Aragon – you'll see (rather bizarrely for English-readers) "YESA NO" graffiti everywhere. In spring 2000 the scheme was given provisional approval by the PP government, much to the dismay of local inhabitants (see p.595, in "The Environment"), though the PSOE says that under their government the size increase will be much smaller.

## Access

There is only one daily **bus service** (Mon–Sat), calling first at Echo, then Siresa, and finally Ansó. This departs **from Jaca** at 6.30pm in summer (may be 1hr earlier winter), reaching Echo at 8.10pm and Ansó 45 minutes later, departing at 6am to return the next day.

A **bicycle** is a good means of exploring either valley; reckon on around two and a half hours from Jaca to Echo village, turning off the C134/N240 at Puente la Reina de Jaca, or much the same to Ansó village, turning off at Berdún, 7km west of Puente la Reina de Jaca. The latter side road, not served by bus, is particularly spectacular, passing a privately owned castle at Biniés before threading an unnervingly narrow course through the Foz de Biniés, carved out by the Río Veral.

The **GR65.3.3** – a very minor variant of the Santiago pilgrimage route – also links Berdún and Biniés with Echo, threading over the hills on a variety of surfaces. Trans-Pyrenean trekkers can use the **GR11** to hike into and out of the area, although the trail intersects both valleys a considerable way above the two villages.

## Echo and Siresa

**ECHO** (formerly "Hecho", which may still appear on old maps), the larger of the two villages, is a splendid old place, though historically less wealthy than Ansó. Arcades ring the main double-plaza, which host the outdoor tables of its two bars, while whitewash outlines the windows and doors on some of the massive houses, the more sumptuous of these built around pebble-mosaic fore-courts. Although seemingly ancient, Echo in its present form is less than two centuries old; it – and Ansó – were burnt to the ground during the Napoleonic wars. Echo can otherwise lay modest claim to fame as the seat of an embryonic Aragonese feudal state under Conde Aznar Galíndez in the ninth century, and as the birthplace of the "warrior king" Alfonso I.

An art festival, the Simposio de Escultura y Pintura Moderna, held every summer between 1975 and 1984, left the permanent legacy of an **open-air sculpture gallery** on the hillside west of the village. Created by a group of artists led by Pedro Tramullas, the 46 stone or metal pieces are not terribly stunning individually, but their total effect is riveting. The Simposio was initially resisted by most locals, who eventually came to terms with it – but now there are insufficient funds for the festival's resumption.

Near the enormous central church, there's a more conventional museum, the **Museo Etnológico** (Easter, July & Aug 11am–2pm & 6–9pm; otherwise contact the *Ayuntamiento*; €1), with interesting collections on Pyrenean rural life and folklore.

### Practicalities

The **Turismo** is located in the *Ayuntamiento* (daily June–Sept 10am–2pm & 5–7pm; ☎974 375 329); if it's closed ask upstairs and they may open it for you. In summer or at weekends reservations for Echo's **accommodation** are all but mandatory (the closest alternatives are in Siresa – see below). The clear first choices are *Casa Blasquico*, discreetly marked at Plaza Palacio de la Fuente 1 (☎974 375 007; ❸), next door to the *Bar Subordan*, its five tastefully converted rooms (including one suite) offering all comforts; and the *Danubio-Casa Chuanet* on the hillside opposite (☎974 375 033; ❷), with appealing, 2002-redone en-suite rooms above a bar. Definite fallbacks, both at the north end of the village, are the en-suite *Hostal de la Val* (☎974 375 028; ❸), whose front rooms overlook the village, and *Lo Foratón* (☎974 375 247), comprising a somewhat shabby *hostal* (❷) and a slightly better en-suite hotel (❸). The campsite, *Valle de Echo* (☎974 375 361), lies just south of the village.

By far the most notable **restaurant** in Echo is *Restaurante Gaby* (closed part Sept, reservations essential), on the ground floor of *Casa Blasquico*. Owner-chef

Gaby Coarasa was among the first stars of Pyrenean nouvelle cuisine, and the walls of the tiny, six-table *comedor* (seatings at 1.30 & 8.30pm) are lined with awards to prove it. *A la carta* offers ample choice for vegetarians and fish-eaters – the mushroom crêpe is ace – though these tend to be starters. Game, meat or duck main dishes, any specials, or improbable desserts like fig mousse or wild berry sorbets will bump the bill up, with Denominación de Origen wine, to well over €30 per person. If money's tight, ask about their cheaper *menú* and stick to the adequate house wine. If you can't get in, the *Restaurante Canteré* nearby is nearly as good, doing creative if slightly *minceur* platters such as *hojaldre de espinacas*, game and duck (allow €23 each for three courses; *menú* available). Last but not least, the friendly *Bar Subordán* next door to *Restaurante Gaby* purveys superb, inexpensive *raciones* of *pimientos de piquillo, longaniza* and *chipirones*.

Best of several **bars** is the nocturnal *Coco's* (no sign), the closest thing to a Madrid-style nightspot; *Acher, Danubio* and *Batimala* are more conventional village hangouts, while local families and visitors alike drink at all hours outside the *Bar Subordán*.

Echo has three **banks** (one with an ATM), the only petrol station in these hills, and an **adventure outfitter**: the local Compañía de Guías (☏ 974 375 387 or 676 850 843), offering canyoning, rock-climbing, kayaking, snowshoeing and cross-country skiing depending on the season. Also worth contacting is Alto Aragón (☏ 974 371 281), which offers both summertime treks and winter activities with English-speaking guides. Oddly, Echo has no pool; people just swim in a scooped-out area of the river east of town.

### Siresa

Less than 2km north of Echo stands another beautiful little village, **SIRESA**. Keeping watch over the riverside pastures is a remarkable ninth-century church, **San Pedro** (daily 11am–1pm & 5–8pm; €1.50). A massive structure built to a cruciform, single-apse plan, austerely plain inside, it was once the core of a monastery and is claimed to be the oldest church in Aragón.

The single **hotel**, the *Castillo d'Acher* (☏ 974 375 313; ❸), has decent rooms (attic ones are newest) with large beds, full bathtubs and tiny balconies; they also operate an annexe *pensión* (❷), above the village bar, and a reasonable restaurant. Cheaper still is the YHA-affiliated *Albergue Siresa* (☏ 974 375 385, ✉ albsiresa@arrakis.es), with predictably institutional dorms (4–7 bunks) – it was the old school – but a reliable sales-point for local maps and PR guides.

If you desire more solitude, the *Hotel Usón* (☏ & ☏ 974 375 358; ❺ HB only), 5km north of Siresa, has enthusiastic young management, environment-friendly design, plus good Basque-style food (for guests only), accompanied by a superb wine cellar and served in a conservatory. Rooms are tasteful and colourfully done up, but often fill with UK-based trekking groups, so reservations are mandatory. Immediately across the valley, 3km up the side road to the *Gabardito* refuge, *Camping Borda Bisáltico* (☏ 974 375 098; late June to late Sept & Easter) offers clean facilities, including an *albergue* and simple rooms (❶), plus another restaurant.

## Walks in the Valle de Echo

Above Siresa, the **Valle de Echo** constitutes a tapestry of pasture and beech forest against a backdrop of towering limestone cliffs and summits, harbingers of the karst country at the border. The most popular **day-walks** east of the valley are the ascents of Bisaurín (2669m), Agüerri (2449m) and Castillo de Acher (2390m), of which the finest is the climb up Agüerri, the summit of the huge bluff that forms the easternmost side of the Boca del Infierno gorge, beginning 7km north of Siresa.

The usual starting point lies 12km north of Siresa at **Selva de Oza**, where there's just a pleasant rustic bar and a no-longer functioning campsite. For any outing the best **map** is the Editorial Alpina 1:40,000 "Ansó-Echo", applicable also to all walks discussed up to and including "The Valle de Roncal and the Parque Natural Pirenaico" section, p.486. Beginning from Echo, you can avoid dreary road-trudging by taking the GR65.3.3, well signposted as the **Via Romana** some 3km north of Siresa. This "Roman road", unlike many so called in the Pyrenees, actually was built in the time of Augustus, and threads through the Boca del Infierno gorge, and continues beyond Selva de Oza to the Puerto de Palo/Col de Pau on the frontier.

### Bisaurín and the Osia valley

For **Bisaurín**, make an early start along the variant GR11.1 that climbs east on the southern slopes of the Agüerri valley – it leaves the main valley 6km north of Echo, across the Puente de Santa Ana, and shortcuts the twisty, narrow paved road past *Camping Borda Bisáltico* to run high above the Agüerri stream. About an hour from the valley road, you reach the *Refugio de Gabardito*, 8km in by road (1360m; 50 places; open all year), with a range of en-suite rooms, set on a beautiful grassy clearing near treeline. It's managed by Echo's Compañía de Guías (see p.481), who run the popular cross-country skiing centre at the doorstep here, and who are the contacts for reservations year-round. From Gabardito the path climbs east to the **Collado del Foratón** (2032m), 2hr 30min from the refuge; then it's a stiff two-hour climb further to the summit, rising steeply to the northeast.

You can also use the approach via the Collado del Foratón as a full-pack traverse, finishing 45 minutes southeast of the pass near the top of the **valley of the Río Osia** at the *Refugio Lizara* (1540m; ☎974 371 473), rebuilt in 2003 after a devastating fire. This sits in the middle of another major cross-country ski area; in summer you can trek northeast via the Valle de los Sarrios and over **Los Puertos** pass to link up with the main GR11 route at Ibón de Estanes. The GR11.1 continues east from *Refugio Lizara* in under a day to Canfranc.

Otherwise, the closest indoor facility lies 12km down-valley in the attractively sleepy village of **ARAGÜÉS DEL PUERTO**, where the vast *Albergue Lizara* occupies a 1970s built ex-*hostal* (☎974 371 519). You've a choice between en-suite doubles (❶) or a place in a nine-bunk dorm; half-board is encouraged, supping at the giant basement *comedor*.

### Castillo de Acher and Agüerri

Castillo de Acher and Agüerri can be tackled singly or together in one gruelling day; take plenty of water. Begin along the track that climbs east-south-east from close to the ex-campsite at Selva de Oza; this curves back southwest after crossing the Espata stream and climbs steeply to a simple forest hut (1740m; 2hr), just beyond which the ways divide. The summit of **Castillo de Acher** – from a distance looking exactly like a castle – now lies a little north of east, along a fairly easy path (4–5hr from Selva de Oza).

For **Agüerri**, take the right-hand path just beyond the refuge, climbing east along the **Borreguil de Acher** stream and crossing after about half an hour onto a newer path that doubles back on the other side, rising west to a small saddle. Beyond this, the path swings east again, along the **Jardín** stream; at the head of the valley defined by the Collado de Costatiza, climb south for the summit (5hr 30min from Selva de Oza).

## Frontier peaks and Ibón de Acherito

North of Selva de Oza, the frontier peaks of **Punta Cristian/Pic Lariste** (2168m) and **Arraya de las Foyas/Pic Laraille** (2147m) make classic targets, with near-identical approaches. Continue on the asphalt road north of the closed campsite, through dense forest, with the Río Aragón Subordán to the left; some 2km above Selva de Oza, before the end of the pavement, you veer left to cross a bridge onto a side track, beyond which the main track follows the eastward curve of the valley. Once over the Barranco Acherito side-stream via another bridge, the track ends at the locale known as **La Mina** (1230m). Here there's just a large signboard-map beside a small car park; cows graze all around, with scattered buildings for the use of the herders, plus a derelict refuge. This is the junction with the GR11, descending from the west and continuing up the main valley; it's also the trailhead for the popular day-outing to both the peaks and the **Ibón de Acherito**, second westernmost lake in the Spanish Pyrenees.

Take the path north along the left (east) bank of the Barranco Las Foyas, switching over to the right bank sooner than indicated on the Editorial Alpina map. In July wild irises abound, and the occasional Egyptian vulture wheels overhead. After 45 minutes' climbing, guided by red-and-white or single-yellow waymarks, you reach the T-junction with the HRP variant.

Bear right on this, and leave it soon after to head north into the cirque (ca. 1800m; 1hr 30min) under the frontier summits. The routes divide here: Punta Cristian is the summit immediately north, climbed directly in another hour; Arraya looms to the west, reached by a route of similar duration curving to a point just southeast of the summit, then swinging back for the top. From both summits you look north across the idyllic pine forests and fields of the Lescun valley (see p.419) and westwards over the barren karst – an arresting contrast.

To visit **the lake**, bear left along the well-trodden HRP; some ninety minutes out of La Mina, the path grade slackens on a grassy hillside at the base of Arraya, and you get your first eyeful of the limestone cirque to the west. Fifteen minutes further, you round a corner in the landscape and suddenly the Ibón de Acherito is there: one of the most striking in Aragón, with the crests of the frontier peaks as a backdrop and tadpoles in its shallows. Arraya can be climbed equally easily from the lakeshore; allow 45 minutes each way. Camping, while tempting, is more difficult – there's a flat meadow, with a spring, just ten minutes east along the HRP.

To vary the return to La Mina, and include some ridge-walking with views into France, follow the HRP west from the lake along a hogback to a grassy point on the frontier crest at just over 2000m. From here you can glimpse the stagnant pond of **Ibón de Ansabère** at your feet, or gaze over the **Cirque de Lescun**, and to the shattered peaks closing it off on the west. Now descend gently for twenty minutes or so to a rectangular shepherd's shelter, used more from the French side. The obvious continuation along the border ridge would be to the strategic Puerto de Acherito at the top of the cirque, but there is no non-technical way around or over Pic d'Chourique (2084m), which blocks progress. So you must descend, more or less as traced on the Alpina map, steeply cross-country for twenty minutes to the proper trail in the valley bottom, called the **Barranco de Ferrerías**. From the vicinity of an unstaffed, stone-built shelter here, it's about 1hr 20min down to La Mina; the path is unmarked but obvious and gradual.

## East or west: the GR11

The GR11 arrives at La Mina from Candanchú to the **east** in a full day's trek along the headwaters of the Río Aragón Subordán, a route enlivened by the large **Ibón de Estanés/Lac d'Estaëns** (2hr out), and the squelchy water-meadow of Aguas Tuertas (4hr from Candanchú). Unfortunately, camping is not allowed at La Mina – and plans to restore and staff the refuge here have never passed the talk stage – though you can have a pleasant river-dip just downstream by the end of the asphalt. Even if plans to reopen the derelict campsite at Selva de Oza come to fruition in 2005, civilization and its comforts are far away, and you must provision accordingly.

A much easier traverse continues **west** along the same path to Zuriza in the Valle de Ansó (see overleaf). From the upper bridge over the Barranco Acherito described above, the GR11 climbs steeply west into the Collado de Petraficha (1958m; 2hr uphill from Selva de Oza), from where it's all downhill along the Petraficha stream, the last forty minutes of the four-hour hiking day on track.

### On to Ansó by road or trail

The daily evening bus from Jaca to Echo continues west to Ansó along 12km of narrow, twisting road, climbing over the Sierra de Vedao before dropping into the Valle de Ansó. Final approaches to the valley from the east are guarded by two strangely shaped rocks known locally as "the Monk and the Nun", just above a tunnel.

If you wish to walk there, shun the dangerous road in favour of the very enjoyable **PR18 trail from Siresa to Ansó**, indicated by a sign reading "Fuen d'a Cruz" by the cemetery and stream below Siresa. This, also doubling hereabouts as the **GR15**, is probably the most useful of the area's dozen PR trails; a descriptive booklet, published by Prames Ediciones, is sold locally.

Starting on the south side of the bridge, the path is initially waymarked by red arrows and purple paint splodges as well as newer PR blazes. Gaining height quickly, you collide with an unmaintained track at a saddle about 45 minutes along; turning onto this, fifteen minutes later you top out at a T-junction in the track system (1180m), where you bear right (north). After another half-hour along the serpentine track, you'll emerge at a pass affording a first view of Ansó village; the track continues north, but you should plunge down left (southwest) on the resurgence of the old *camino*. Passing a ruined farm, continue dropping steeply into the valley running west to the village, zigzagging to meet the stream bed, on whose right bank you should arrive some two hours out of Siresa. You'll reach a fountain at the eastern outskirts of Ansó about half an hour later. With the exception of the initial climb from Siresa, the route is shown more or less correctly on the Editorial Alpina map.

## Ansó

Once a more prosperous village than Echo, **ANSÓ** fell upon hard times during the 1950s and 1960s depopulation of rural Aragón. Today, however, there are signs of a small but definite revival, with Jacan and Pamplonan professionals keeping second homes here, plus a growing stream of tourists sampling the village's attractions. It's certainly a congenial weekend base, with a little river beach below for splashing around in the Río Veral. Without having many specific landmarks, the village outshines its setting, whose scrubby pine cover gives no hint of the splendours waiting up-valley. The ancient church is extraordinarily rich inside and houses an interesting **Museo Etnológico** (daily summer only 10.30am–1.30pm & 3.30–8pm; €1.50). In lieu of labelling you're given a plastic-laminated sheet to guide you around the exhibits, which include a video and photographic exhibition of Pyrenean wildlife and rural trades.

## Practicalities

Ansó's popularity is reflected in several places to **stay**, somewhat less expensive than in Echo but filling equally quickly in summer. Best is the *Posada Magoria* (☎974 370 049; ❸), installed in a 1920s mansion by the church at c/Milagros, with en-suite rooms, views and a garden. The four dormer rooms have double beds, and they serve excellent communal vegetarian meals (preference given to guests). A worthy alternative, at the north end of town 200m towards Zuriza on the bypass road, is modern, comfortable *Hostal Kimboa* (☎974 370 184, ℗974 370 130; open all year, winter by arrangement; ❸ B&B). A less likely option is the nearby *Hostal Estanés* (☎974 370 146; summer only; ❸). A summer-only **campsite** (☎974 370 003) operates beside the municipal swimming pool, at the south end of the village.

Among the very few **restaurants**, *Kimboa*'s is easily the best, their cousin's own-raised meat featuring in €12 *menús*, served under the terrace canopy in summer (lunch only, by the fireplace-grill, off-season). Of the many **bars**, liveliest and friendliest is the spit-and-sawdust *Zuriza* on the main street. One of Ansó's two **banks** has an ATM.

To **leave Ansó** by public transport you catch the 6am bus back through Echo towards Jaca. Going west from Ansó, an eighteen-kilometre minor road (the NA176) past the village of Garde, with a campsite and two restaurants, eventually joins the NA137, which threads through the Valle de Roncal, in Navarra. There's no bus service in this direction, and it's 21km in total to Erronkari village.

# Walking in the Valle de Ansó

Other than the path in from Siresa, the lower Ansó valley has little serious trekking potential; to start walking you really must go to Zuriza, 14km north. There's no bus service, and the paved road up-valley makes for tedious trudging, so try to arrange a lift if you don't have transport. The scenery improves as you head upstream, with the Río Veral beside the road, and the steep valley sides covered with pine, later giving way to beech. Dotted around are small stone-built farmhouses, their owners sometimes wearing cloaks of cured but otherwise untreated animal skins. One of these huts has become the *Restaurante Borda Chiquín*, locally popular and the only amenity en route. The mass of **Peña Ezkaurre** (2049m) rises in front, and after 9km you enter the narrow gorge between it and **Espelunga**; there's a chance of seeing rare black vultures here, a species resembling the griffon vulture in outline, but far darker and more solitary.

Eventually the gorge widens onto the luxuriantly green basin of **Zuriza** (1227m), less forested than the Selva de Oza area in Echo. The most obvious amenity is an enormous, somewhat regimented campsite, *Camping Zuriza* (mid-June to early Sept), with an attached *albergue* (☎974 370 196; all year; dorms plus some rooms at ❸), a general store and a decent restaurant. If these are full – a distinct possibility during peak seasons – you'll find another staffed refuge at **Linza** (Plano de la Casa on many maps), 5km north along the track parallel to the Petrechema stream. Here the friendly, well-run *Refugio de Linza* (1320m; ☎ & ℗974 370 112; 100 places; all year) rents out cross-country skis for use on nearby prepared trails.

## Tres Reyes ascent

From Plano de la Casa you can make a day-walk to **Mesa de los Tres Reyes** (*Hiru Erregeen Mahaia* in Euskera), the karst plateau astride the border with France; carry plenty of water, as there's none above the 1900-metre contour.

Start by heading a little north of east along the path to the **Collado de Linza** (1906m; 2hr); from this pass the path heads north a short way then resumes its former trajectory, dropping into the shallow Hoya la Solana and then climbing out to the **Collado de Esqueste/Col d'Escoueste** (2114m; 3hr). You're now on the frontier – dramatically delineated by the sharp drop to the French side – amidst unbelievably barren terrain.

Follow the top of the cliffs north, at a suitably respectful distance, into a small *col* that leads to **Tres Reyes summit** (2444m; 4hr); this meeting point of France, Navarra and Aragón is adorned with a bronze statue of St Francis Xavier, the Jesuit evangelist of the Indies. Again there's an amazing contrast between the lush Lescun valley beyond the tarn of Lhurs to the east, and the lunar rock and summits to the north and west, notably the pyramid of Pic d'Anie.

### West to Belagoa

Rather than return to Zuriza to adopt the GR11, you can partly duplicate the above directions in a mid-altitude traverse to the refuge at Belagoa (see p.488). Instead of going east from the Hoya La Solana, veer north through the Hoya del Portillo de Larra, over the eponymous pass (1829m), and then west through the Larra karst formations and beech forest; allow six hours.

### West to Izaba on the GR11

Zuriza straddles the **GR11**, with Selva de Oza an easy day away to the east (see p.482); heading west towards **Izaba** in the Roncal valley (14km by narrow, paved road), the GR11 was rerouted in the early 1990s. The new itinerary starts from the Puerto Navarra, 700m west of Zuriza, at the border between Aragón and Navarra – where the difference in public-works funding between the two autonomous regions is made graphically apparent by the respective states of the asphalt.

The **new path** heads spectacularly, if strenuously, southwest up the flanks of **Peña Ezkaurre/Ezcaurri** (2049m; 2hr 30min), which, though not especially high, impresses with its profile. Just the other side lies its namesake *ibón*, the westernmost natural tarn in the Spanish Pyrenees. Thereafter, the GR11, now in Navarra, descends west into the **Berroeta valley**, soon becoming a track along the right bank leading to the confluence of the Berroeta and Belabarze streams. From here another track leads west to Izaba, for a six-hour walking day.

# The Valle de Roncal and Parque Natural Pirenaico Larra-Belagoa

The **Parque Natural Pirenaico Larra-Belagoa**, which straddles the road connecting Roncal and Arette-la-Pierre-Saint-Martin in France, occupies the head of the **Valle de Belagoa** and harbours landscapes ranging from karst desert to dense forest, by way of lush pastures. Further downstream, the **Valle de Roncal** – next valley west of Ansó – is famous for the delicious, hard, cylindrical *roncalés* cheese, made from sheep's milk and widely available in the two main valley villages of **Erronkari** and **Izaba**.

If you're coming by public transport, the easiest way into the area is the daily **bus**, run by La Tafallesa, which originates at 5pm in Pamplona via the Foz de Arbaiun and Burgui and follows the course of the Río Esca up the Valle de

Roncal as far as Izaba. Foresters used to float logs down the Esca by lacing them together into a raft, with three or four such rafts linked and controlled by a pair of huge oars; nowadays the rafts are constructed only for fun.

## Erronkari and Izaba

Once beyond the low-altitude villages of Lumbier and Burgui, the road climbs slowly to **ERRONKARI** (Roncal), capital of the valley. Here you cross to the west bank of the river, where the old quarter (including the arcaded town hall) sits, though much of the east bank is spoilt by blocks of modern flats. The churchyard (follow signs to "Mausoleo") is worth visiting for the flamboyant tomb of the great opera tenor **Julián Gayarre** (1844–90), whose sarcophagus is surmounted by four sculpted-bronze nymphs, plus an angel, bearing a mock coffin heavenwards. Born into a Roncal shepherd family, Gayarre was regarded by international audiences as the equal of the later Caruso; he died – eerily, from cancer of the vocal cords – just a bit too soon to be captured by the new technology of the gramophone.

Erronkari supports the regional, helpful **Turismo** (Mon–Sat 10am–2pm & 4.30–7.30pm, Sun 10am–2pm; ☎948 475 136). **Accommodation** includes en-suite *Hostal Zaltua* on the through road (☎948 475 008; ❷), as well as several *casas rurales*, best of which is *Casa Villa Pepita* (☎948 475 133; ❷) opposite the *Zaltua* on the west bank, which also provides *table d'hôte* meals at very reasonable cost (and en-suite rooms), but you'll have more choice in Izaba.

### Izaba

**IZABA** (Isaba), 7km north of Roncal, is larger and busier; a small, modern district at the south end of the village (with a small **Turismo**, and **bank** with ATM) is easily ignored in favour of its old quarter. This sprawls appealingly around a fortified hilltop church, a massive structure with a rib-vaulted nave and ornate *retablo* and organ inside. Unlike Roncal it's a major year-round touring centre for the Western Pyrenees, regularly descended upon by weekend trippers from nearby cities. Accordingly there's a fair amount of conventional **accommodation**; pick of this, east of the busy through road on narrow c/Mendigatxa, is the sleek and clean *Hostal Lola* (☎ & ☎948 893 012, ❸hostal-lola@jet.es; ❸), with limited parking (hopeless elsewhere in Izaba) and the best restaurant in town (allow €24 *a la carta*). At the junction of c/Mendigatxa and the high street, the en-suite *Pensión Txiki* (☎948 893 118; ❷) perches above the simple, namesake *bar-restaurante*, which does a €10 *menú* and good fish soup. *Pensión Txabalkua* (☎948 893 083; peak season only; ❷), west of the through road at c/Izarjentea 16, is the quietest, if not the most characterful, option. Izaba has eight *casas rurales* (all ❷), though expect to try several places at busy times. The *Albergue Oxanea* (☎948 893 153) on c/Bormapéa, west of the main street, is an unusually salubrious private **youth hostel** that offers meals, too. The **campsite**, *Asolaze* (☎948 893 034; closed Nov & Dec), also with bungalows to rent, lies 6km upstream towards the border, at the edge of the *parque natural*.

## The Valle de Belagoa

There's no longer a bus service beyond Izaba, so without your own transport you'll have to arrange a lift from there (easily done) up the valley into the **Parque Natural Pirenaico Larra–Belagoa**. The road enters the park along the Río Belagoa, flanked by forests of beech and silver fir, until the terrain

## The Tributo de las Tres Vacas

Beyond Belagoa the road climbs to the border, crossing close to the frontier cairn which has replaced the original marker of La Pedra de San Martin/Pierre-Saint-Martin. Here, every July 13, the people of the Spanish Valle de Roncal and the French Vallée de Barétous gather to enact the **Tributo de las Tres Vacas**, a ceremony stemming from a 1326 treaty on grazing rights, the oldest of several such agreements or *faceries* still extant. Four representatives of Roncal, dressed in white shirts, black capes and black hats, join hands with four representatives of Barétous *commune*, whose only concession to folklore is sashes in the French national colours. With their hands linked on modern frontier cairn number 262, they chant "Pas aban, pas aban, pas aban" ("Peace above all" in local dialect) while three identical blonde heifers (*las tres vacas*) are handed over to the Roncalese as tribute, securing the right of the French herdsmen to graze cattle in the Spanish valley for another year. Originally such *faceries* and tributes served to prevent violent altercations provoked by illegal bovine immigrants; these days, though, the cows are discreetly returned to the French afterwards. A huge and disparate crowd (up to three thousand strong) of itinerant food-and-drink vendors, French gendarmes, Spanish forestry wardens, journalists, tourists and locals always turn up, even if it's raining, mainly to take part in the *fiesta* afterwards. If you want to coincide with the ceremony, be sure to arrive by 11am; shortly after noon it's all over, save for the feasting.

opens out into flat fields and you begin to climb in tight hairpins to the **Refugio Ángel Olorón de Belagoa** (1460m; ☎ & ℱ948 394 002; 140 places; s/c kitchen), almost at the border but just inside the park. It stands in grand isolation 19km from Izaba, overlooking pastures and the high limestone peaks to the east, with the river gleaming between forested slopes below to the south. The refuge is long overdue refurbishment and service is variable, but it does enjoy a prime location. It's near a meaty section of the HRP and also offers a complete programme of summer and winter sports, including 14km of cross-country skiing routes for all ability levels at 1350–1720m altitude. Its bar-restaurant provides economical, if not terribly exciting, **meals** (€7 *menú*). Otherwise, at the base of the switchbacks leading up to the refuge, the *Venta de Juan Pito* (May–Oct daily; 1–2pm & 7–8pm outside July & Aug) is a **traditional inn** serving hearty meals – including locally concocted milk-based desserts – for under €20.

## Walking in the Parque Natural

The best way of seeing the eastern side of the park – where all the karst formations are – involves taking the **HRP variant** which links the Belagoa refuge with Lescun in France via the Collado de Insolo, also known as the Portillo de Lescun or Col d'Anaye. Don't confuse this pass with the Col des Anies, which is on the north side of Pic d'Anie, well inside French territory (Insolo/d'Anaye is on the frontier, to the south), but you can return via the Col des Anies to make a **circuit**. Take ample water with you, and in deteriorating weather, turn back. Navigating through karst badlands, which form natural mazes, is hopeless when visibility is bad – not to mention the possibility of disappearing down one of the dozens of caves and extremely deep sinkholes that pepper the terrain. Even in the finest weather you should have a compass, the recommended Editorial Alpina map and an update on conditions from the Belagoa refuge wardens.

From the refuge, the path tends slightly south of east, first across pasture and then through beech forest, before arriving in the eerily beautiful Larra region, distinguished by bone-white rock and trees stunted by altitude and lack of soil. Yellow paint splodges then guide you through the boulders, until the **Collado de Insolo** (2052m) is reached in about another two and a half hours.

An ascent of Tres Reyes fills another memorable day out from the refuge. The route lies a little south of the HRP, initially close to the cliff-edge of the shelf on which the refuge stands. After climbing over **Lapazarra** (1777m; 1hr 20min), the path heads east through the Collado Larrería. This is again typical Larra scenery, littered with boulders and dotted with bonsai-sized trees in patterns so repetitious that it's easy to get lost. In autumn the landscape is brightened somewhat by the turning foliage of scattered deciduous specimens.

From Larra you continue up to the frontier ridge at the Col d'Ourtets (2182m), next turning south-southeast along it for the **Tres Reyes summit** (3hr 20min). At this altitude the karst seems more like the landscape of Sinai than the Pyrenees, but the views from the top emphasize the paradoxes of the area, where high-mountain desert is fringed by lower pasture and forest – so lush precisely because all the available water percolates down through fissures in the karst, emerging in quantity below the 1500-metre contour.

## Gouffre de la Pierre-Saint-Martin

Just on the Spanish side of the frontier despite the French name, close to the NA137 road, yawns the entrance – now grilled over – of the **Gouffre de la Pierre-Saint-Martin**, among the largest underground caverns in the world. It was discovered by chance in 1950, when, on the last, disconsolate night of an apparently unsuccessful expedition led by Norbert Casteret (see p.326), a stone was thrown into an opening and clattered audibly down into an abyss. In 1953, the year that Everest was conquered, speleologists reached the bottom of this cavern, at 734m the deepest anyone had ever been in a cave system.

The vertical entrance shaft of 346m remains the longest known, and its largest chamber, the Sala de la Verna (now desecrated by an EDF tunnel), is an incredible 270m by 230m by 180m. Using higher entrances, subsequent expeditions during 1982 measured a total depth of 1342m and explored an overall length of interconnecting passages exceeding 50km – the second largest cave system in the world after the Jean Bernad cavern of the French Alps.

## Arette-la-Pierre-Saint-Martin

Some 10km beyond the *Refugio de Belagoa* and 3km into French territory from the border by road, **ARETTE-LA-PIERRE-SAINT-MARTIN** is a modern **downhill-ski resort**, the westernmost in the entire Pyrenees. Atlantic weather influences generally mean good snow conditions, even in spring, despite a modest top point of only 2153m (descending to 1527m or 1650m). The Basques, both French and Spanish, are well aware of this and at weekends the antiquated lift system (five two-seater chairs, lots of drags) can barely cope. Of the eighteen pistes in this small centre, most are green- or blue-rated – and red runs are blueish, the blues greenish – so Arette-la-Pierre is essentially a beginner-to-intermediate resort, with handicapped access to several lifts. That said, the easterly runs are routed through gnarled trees, and reasonably long – there's a three-kilometre red run from the top, two even longer blue "boulevards", Pyrénées and Myrtilles, plus a 1900-metre black piste; the setting is lovely, with views to the ocean on good days. **Cross-country skiing** is offered in token fashion at **Boucle de Braca**, 1km northeast, and much more substantially at **Issarbe**, 5km northwest. The bleak development at the downhill centre consists of a concentration of Brutalist-style chalets and *résidences* at 1650m.

In **summer** the main thing that counts in Arette-la-Pierre's favour for anyone following the **GR10** between Lescun and Santa Grazi is the *Refuge Gîte d'Étape Jeandel* (☎ & ℱ 05.59.66.14.46; 25 places; May–Oct 15), on a rise at the west edge of the ski pistes. It's a high-quality outfit with one dorm, three-or four-bed rooms mostly pitched at families, hot showers, a fireplace and meal service provided by jolly proprietor Jean Hourticq. There's also a self-catering kitchen, and a small stock of trekking groceries for sale, as the *épicerie* in the ski "village" is unreliable – though a single restaurant operates fitfully there in summer. You might schedule an extra night here and use the intervening day to bag Pic d'Anie (Auñamendi in Euskera) – a six-hour round trip on sections of the HRP and GR10, making this the easiest French "base camp" for the 2504-metre summit. You're just inside Béarn at Arette-la-Pierre, on the border with the Pays-Basque county of Soule.

# Gorges of the Haute-Soule

Four gorges, south of the D113/D26 route linking Arette-la-Pierre-Saint-Martin in the east and Larrañe in the west, are the principal reason outsiders visit the district of **Haute-Soule** (Zuberoa), easternmost and remotest corner of the French Pays Basque. Here, vast green pastures and beech groves stretch under an open, vulture-haunted sky; there are far more sheep than people, few tourist facilities and no villages to speak of except Larrañe, Ligi-Atherei, Abense-de-Haut and (stretching the definition) Santa Grazi.

The superlative-laden **Gorges de Kakouetta** are the best of the managed gorges in the Pyrenees, but if you prefer a completely uncommercialized chasm, the adjacent **Gorges d'Ehujarré** constitute a milder alternative. Both are somewhat difficult to reach without your own vehicle, as there's no public transport on the French side, and the scattered "village" of Santa Grazi – at the mouth of Ehujarré – lies four hours' walk northwest of Arette-la-Pierre-Saint-Martin, along the GR10 or its variants. The best way of visiting both on foot is from Belagoa, trekking down the Ehujarré to Santa Grazi and then up alongside the Kakouetta.

The other pair of great gorges, 18km west of Kakouetta by road, are the interconnecting **Holzarté** and **Olhadybia** (Olhadubi), crossed at their junction by a long, terrifying and absolutely unmissable – though very touristed – suspension footbridge. By the serpentining GR10, these lie seven hours west of Santa Grazi, with Larrañe another half hour or so beyond.

## A walking tour of the gorges

Head up the NA137 road from the refuge at Belagoa for a couple of kilometres until the ridge from the summit of Lakhoura – the 1877-metre peak immediately north of the refuge – subsides at the **Collado de Eraiz**. An HRP variant goes north through this pass onto the Errayzé-Sentolha plateau above

5

the end of the **Gorges d'Ehujarré**, where you quit the HRP and drop into the canyon on another path (see p.492). Palisades rise as high as 400m above you, but it's not a difficult walk, and this route has been used for decades for the movement of sheep from the Sainte-Engrâce valley onto the pastures around Pic Lakhoura.

Three to four hours from the refuge you emerge at the hamlet of Senta, one of three comprising the *commune* of **SANTA GRAZI** (Sainte-Engrâce, Urdaite). Until 1987 this was locally characterized as *le bout du monde*, "the end of the world", approachable by road only from the west and arguably the remotest spot in the French Basque country. The extension of the D113 east to Arette-la-Pierre-Saint-Martin was supposed to change that, but despite increasing traffic the Santa Grazi valley has managed to retain its rural somnolence, still surrounded by hay meadows and losing its young to the big cities.

### The Santa Grazi hamlets, Ligi-Atherei and Abense-de-Haut

**SENTA** has a combination **inn/gîte d'étape**, the *Auberge Elichalt* (℡05.59.28.61.63; 30 places in dorms), which serves light meals, and has space for a few tents on the rear lawn. If it's shut, the *Auberge Chez Berriex* above the village serves sandwiches and drinks on its lawn, and may do hot snacks in the evening. The *Elichalt* overlooks the **church**, a strikingly original example of eleventh-century Romanesque architecture, effectively the logo of the Western Pyrenees. It's an engagingly asymmetrical structure, with a sloping-roofed belfry, a lean-to style nave and a graveyard containing some typically Basque disc-crowned headstones, much in evidence as you move further west. The interior offers graphically carved column capitals near the altar, some gaudily painted in the 1880s; look carefully and you'll find the *Adoration of the Magi*, lions devouring Christians, plus Solomon and the Queen of Sheba apparently copulating. Below this stands a rather Hindu-looking statuette of St Catherine, while grimacing owls peer from the base of some columns. Beside the church, a map placard outlines a loop hike – up the east bank of the Ehujarré gorge, then down its bed – for the benefit of day-trippers based here; full details below.

The middle hamlet of **Calla** (alias "Bourg") lies about 1500m downstream from Senta, but has little to offer passers-by. The northwesternmost settlement is **CASERNES**, 4km beyond Calla, where there's a friendly, well-placed

## Transhumant shepherds

Like other shepherds in south European or Mediterranean climes, the Basques have always been obliged to take their flocks to the high **mountain pastures** in summer in search of better grazing. They live out on the bare slopes in stone-hut sheepfolds called *cayolars*, with a couple of dogs, milking the ewes twice a day and making cheese, the *fromage de brebis*, whose soft and hard versions are a speciality throughout the pastoral Pyrenees. Trekkers are usually welcome to buy small quantities when passing by such huts. Most of the pastures today are accessible by car, at least at the gentler Basque end of the Pyrenees, so the shepherd's life is not as harsh and isolated as it used to be – though there are still areas in the higher mountains accessible only by mule or *pottok* pony. A measure of the traditional pre-eminence of sheep in the local economy is the Basque word for "rich", *aberats* – whose literal meaning is "he who owns large flocks".

**campsite**, *Camping Ibarra* (☎05.59.28.73.59; Easter–Oct), on the riverbank and the only **food shop** in the valley, opposite the *mairie*. The closest proper **hotel** is at **LIGI-ATHEREI** (Licq-Athéry), 4km north on the D26, where *Des Touristes-Chez Bouchet* (☎05.59.28.61.01, ℱ05.59.28.64.80; closed Nov–Feb; ❸) has a decent restaurant, a swimming pool and tenting space on the lawn. The village also has a genuine **brasserie**, *Akerbeltz*, dispensing its own beer. If Ligi-Atherei doesn't suit for some reason, the next facilities are 8km north at **ABENSE-DE-HAUT**, just upstream from Atarratze (Tardets-Sorholus). Here the excellent-value *Hôtel du Pont d'Abense* (☎05.59.28.54.60, ℮uhaltia@wanadoo.fr; closed Sun pm & Mon; ❷–❸ room only, ❺ HB required in summer) overlooks the River Saison, and features a restaurant with weekly-changing menus of wild mushrooms, game, duck and fish (*menus* €15–25).

## Gorges de Ehujarré loop

This suggested itinerary is indicated schematically on a **map** placard by the church in Senta, with an estimated time-course of six hours, but is also traced with reasonable accuracy on the Carte de Randonnées no. 2, "Pays Basque Est". It's suggested you do the loop clockwise, with the climb tackled when fresh, getting you safely down into the gorge by afternoon, when mists tend to obscure the heights. If you have a car, save yourself another half-hour by parking down at the end of the pavement, in the stream valley by the bridge.

The path begins there, marked with green-and-white paint splodges. The initial grade is sharp, and you tangle repeatedly with 4WD tracks, but you've dense shade (and some deerflies) in the **Bois d'Utzia** beech-forest, and trail shortcuts are effective. About 1hr 45min along, the worst climbing is over as you emerge from the forest at the single, tin-roofed hut of **Cayolars d'Utzipia** (1450m). The waymarked route continues up and right (southwest), curling over the brow of the ridge for great views of the Sainte-Engrâce valley, and allowing a glimpse of the Pic d'Anie hovering above the trees to the southeast. The elevation high point of the day (1600m) is reached about 2hr 45min out, as you cross high moorland with heather and sheep; the frontier appears ahead, while the gorge yawns down on the right.

Some 3hr along, you arrive at the **Cayolars d'Utzigagna**, at the edge of the beech/fir woods; there's no reliable water here, despite what the IGN map says. When you meet a dirt track serving an isolated sheep-farm to the left, turn right (west-southwest); some fifteen minutes later, use a ravine-path shortcut to descend right to the **pastures of Errayze**, where herds of *pottok* or Basque ponies often graze. Another quarter hour across the turf should see you to the **Fontaine d'Errayze**, a strong spring at the very top of the gorge – and the only drinkable water en route. A distinct trail appears, initially on the left bank, the torrent disappears into the ravine bed, and beech woods resume. About an hour downhill from the spring, the path crosses to the right bank, where it stays for most of the final hour down to the higher of two tin-roofed barns where you rejoin your uphill route, a few minutes above the end of the asphalt. In many ways this is the most low-key of the four gorges – the dense tree cover and sloping scree means you rarely get an eyeful of the canyon walls – but even in summer you won't pass more than half a dozen people all day.

## The Gorges de Kakouetta

The entrance to the **Gorges de Kakouetta** (daily March 15–Nov 15 8am–dusk; €3.80) yawns between Calla and Casernes. Though Kakouetta lies

Waterfall, Gorges de Kakouetta△

squarely on the tourist trail, don't be put off – the gorge is genuinely dramatic and, outside high summer, not too crowded; allow ninety minutes to two hours for a visit. Again except for July, little light penetrates the gorge except at midday, so the chilly interior is essentially temperate rainforest; the air hangs heavy with mist produced by dozens of seeps and tiny waterfalls, pampering tenacious ferns, moss and other greenery, all of which festoons vertical walls rising up to 300m high and seldom split more than 5m apart. For an organized attraction the going is often hard – sometimes along a narrow metal catwalk with a safety cable, sometimes on a narrow, slippery path right in the gorge bottom, with the stream almost lapping over your feet – so come with good boots. Helmets against rockfalls are offered to the nervous, with emergency phones at strategic spots; the gorge is also prone to flash-flooding after storms, with an alarm system for warning hikers to exit immediately.

Just under an hour along you reach a picnic area, near which pours a twenty-metre waterfall, the accumulated percolation of a winter's precipitation through the karst strata overhead; if you don't mind a spray-bath, you can walk right behind the cascade. About 200m past here, the path ends by a cave (signed as "La Grotte 2km" at the car park), with formations beginning to appear inside. Unfortunately for trekkers, the gorge is a dead end – you'll have to retrace your steps and adopt one or other of the local GR10 variants to get anywhere else.

## Gorges d'Olhadybia, Gorges d'Holzarté and Larrañe village

From the entrance of the Kakouetta to the entrance of the Holzarté is about four hours' walk using the newer GR10, traced when the Pont d'Olhadybia (see below) was temporarily washed out. But if possible it's really preferable to make a full day of it along the original **GR10**, now rated a *variante*, which leaves the D113 just west of the Kakouetta entrance. From there it climbs gradually southwest into the **Col d'Anhaou** (3hr), and shortly after begins to curve north, almost level, towards the **Gorges d'Olhadybia** (Olhadubi).

Owing to the steepness of the terrain, the GR handles the final approach in a giant S-bend which drops to the head of the gorge at the **Pont d'Olhadybia** (5hr). It then continues above the west bank for another hour to the intimidating Himalayan-style suspension bridge **Passerelle d'Olhadybia**, which crosses the mouth of the Olhadybia to meet the **Gorges d'Holzarté**, swinging over a drop of 180m. Rebuilt in 1920, the bridge was originally constructed before World War I by an Italian miner to facilitate getting out of the woods for lunch hour at Logibarrea. Penetrating the Holzarté is for experts only – it was first achieved in 1933 and has only been done about twenty times since.

Once over the bridge, continue north on the corniche path along the cliff forming the east bank of the joint gorges; it's very sharply graded towards the end, with a safety cable, but within an hour you'll reach the gorge car park at **LOGIBARREA** (Logibar), where there's a good *gîte d'étape* (☎ & ℱ05.59.28.61.14; closed Dec–Feb; 30 places in dorms or quads) with reasonable meal service.

If there's no room here, leave the GR and follow the D26 west for 2.5km to the village of **LARRAÑE** (Larrau, Larraiñe) where the stucco walls and steeply pitched grey-slate roofs of the houses contrast with the green, north-facing shoulder of land on which they stand, slashed by little rivulets and nestled in gardens. The church is nearly as impressive as Santa Grazi's, and despite the modest altitude (630m) there's heavy winter snow here – thus the steep roofs and distinctly *béarnais* architecture.

Though Larrañe is quiet – almost dead – out of season, its two friendly, simple **hotels** are usually busy, for good reason. The rambling, old-fashioned *Hôtel Despouey* (℡05.59.28.60.82; closed Nov 15–Easter; ❷), the embodiment of *la vieille douce France*, has rooms with shower, the local **shop** on the ground floor, and a bar/breakfast salon but no restaurant. Open all year are the *chambres d'hôte* next to the bakery run by Jeannette Etchero (℡05.59.28.63.22; ❸), with €13 suppers available four nights weekly. For superb meals, head across "town" to the much fancier *Hôtel Restaurant Etchémaïté* (℡05.59.28.61.45, ⓦwww.hotel-etchemaite.fr; ❸; closed Jan & late Nov), whose unusually polished restaurant (closed Sun pm & Mon low season) goes from strength to strength, serving assorted creative *terrines*, guinea-fowl roulade with braised bacon and cabbage, stuffed artichokes and decadent desserts. Given quality and price (*menus* €16 & €22, but wine is expensive), and diners coming up specially from the coast, reservations are usually required. The rooms are state-of-the-art, with powerful heating, proper shower stalls and dimmers even on the bedside lamps. There's also a small **campsite**, *Ixtila* (℡05.59.28.63.09; April to mid-Nov), at the lower, east end of town.

South of Larrañe, the D26 climbs to the frontier at the **Port/Puerto de Larrau** (1573m; closed in winter), just under **Orhy/Orhi**, the first peak above 2000m as you head east from the Atlantic; on the other side the Spanish NA127 drops down to Otsagabia, 33km away (see p.499).

# Forêt d'Iraty/Selva de Irati

Straddling the frontier between the Port de Larrau on the east and the Puero de Ibañeta on the west, the **Forêt d'Iraty/Selva de Irati** (Iratiko Oihana) is claimed by some to be the largest broadleaf forest on the continent – even if they're mistaken, it's certainly the most extensive in the Pyrenees. The legions of trees, principally beech but interspersed with oak, fir and ancient yew, have long been exploited in boatyards on the nearby Atlantic, as beech-wood especially makes excellent oars. Overcutting was a concern as long as three centuries ago, but only recently has systematic reforestation and controlled logging been implemented – thus, much of what you see is actually second-growth forest, if none the less appealing for that.

From the north, the forest can be reached conveniently from the **Col d'Organbidexka** (1284m), 10km west of Larrañe along a minor but paved road. During September and October the *col* is the site of amazing bird migrations, well attended by hunters and bird-watchers alike. On the pass itself row upon row of watchers stand by tripod-mounted telescopes, while in the surrounding uplands square hunting hides bristle with shotguns. During this period, millions of woodpigeons, thousands of honey buzzards, kites and cranes, and hundreds of white storks pass over the Pyrenees, the majority over the low western part of the range, mostly through the Organbidexka pass.

The hunters, more often well-heeled city-dwellers in full "battle dress" than locals, are particularly interested in the tasty *palombes* or pigeons, but recent years have seen a drastic reduction in their numbers for reasons not directly linked to the slaughter, such that few days during late October see more than a dozen birds bagged. Occasionally there are altercations between hunters and conservationists, which look set to continue since the EU is not yet disposed to promulgate uniform regulations against the mass slaughter of migratory birds.

## Access and practicalities

Without your own transport, the easiest way of reaching the *cols* of Organbidexka and Bagargiak (see below) is along the **old GR10** from Larrañe, now a *variante*, taking three and a half hours, mostly tangled with the road. The **new routeing** from Logibarrea is more attractive but longer at nearly six hours, a ridge-walk which curls northwest, just above the one-thousand-metre contour, then climbs to 1472m before dropping slightly to the Col de Bagargiak.

Just under 1km west of 1327-metre **Col de Bagargiak** (aka Col d'Irati; ploughed in winter), itself 500m northwest of the shooting-and-watching grounds, you'll find a collection of nine wooden chalets, mostly four-bedded, intended primarily for users of the 44km of cross-country skiing pistes. The **information office** (☎05.59.28.51.29 & 05.59.28.55.86, ⊛www.chaletsdiraty .com) at the *col* handles bookings, while across the car park there's a small shop and popular, inexpensive view-restaurant (open most of year) which serves forest mushrooms when in season. Some 2km west along the D19, through some of the densest forest, you pass a **campsite** (same phone as above) well hidden in the trees near a pond, before emerging temporarily into the open at the **Plateau d'Iraty**, aka the **Plateau des Lacs**. Here there's a small dammed lake, a pair of snack bars and a "free" camping meadow crammed to capacity with caravans in season. It's better to continue 1km south on the D18 to the more elegant and well-signposted *Chalet Pedro* (☎05.59.28.55.98; closed Nov 15 to Christmas, Tues Easter–June; open Sat & Sun only in winter), a local streamside institution offering such delicacies as wild trout, roast pigeon, cèpe omelette and eel (*à la carte* €28, 4 *menus* €13.50–25).

## Walking in the forest

There's enough walking here to occupy a few days, in particular the **day-hikes** which the information booth at Bagargiak recommends up Pic d'Orhy (5hr return) or the semi-loop ascending Pic des Escaliers to the north (2hr return), both using well-marked sections of the GR10 or HRP.

But if you're in a hurry, one way to sample all the landscapes of the region is to **traverse** the forest north to south, a two-day itinerary involving a stay at the Casas de Irati on the **GR11**, finishing in Otsagabia at the head of the Spanish Valle de Salazar (see opposite). With an early start, and plenty of stamina, you could make it to Otsagabia in one long day.

From Col Bagargiak follow the GR10 west, shortcutting the D18, as far as the Plateau d'Iraty. Bear south here onto the D18 and keep going for about twenty minutes – ignoring a right turn to Ezterentzubi – to *Chalet Pedro*. If you have time to spare, the summit of **Occabé/Okabe** (1456m) is an easy ascent due west along the wide, briefly conjoined GR10/HRP (75min from the plateau). The bare, flat top is decorated by an Iron Age cromlech, possibly linked with contemporary graves discovered adjacent, and gives views all over the forest and the Sierra de Abodi to the south.

Back at *Chalet Pedro*, the paved road continues south for 2.5km and then becomes track. Another diversion is offered by a path to the east, which crosses the **Pont d'Orgaté** and climbs via the Ourdanitzarreta shepherds' shelters to the summit of **Bizkarzé** (1656m; 2hr 30min from the plateau), an even prettier excursion than up Occabé.

Otherwise, keep on the track along the Iratiko Erreka (which later becomes the Spanish Río Irati), crossing the frontier after 1km. An hour after that, you reach the tiny white-painted **Ermita de Nuestra Señora de las Nieves** (where there's a religious procession on the Sunday before Aug 15) and the nearby derelict huts of **Casas de Irati** (880m). The only "facility" here is an informal camping area serving the GR11.

If you spend the night, you'll have sufficient daylight left to stroll a couple of kilometres west along the GR11 to the Irabia reservoir; despite the power dynamo at the far end, the arrangement of water, mountain and dense forest right down to the shore is eminently satisfying. The main disappointment of the forest is that you see little wildlife, though when the mist licks around the tree-trunks you might mistake it for a *lamin*, the Basque leprechaun that is always blamed when something goes inexplicably wrong.

From Casas de Irati, Otsagabia lies more or less due south. The GR11 climbs steeply over the **Sierra de Abodi** via Harrizabla summit (1496m), with fantastic views over the forest and peaks, then drops more gradually to the village – a minimum four-and-a-half-hour march not to be attempted from the French side without an early start. Moreover, waymarking for the first hour is ambiguous – as on much of the GR11 west of Izaba – so you will certainly lose some time in getting lost. Casas de Irati is also served by a 23-kilometre paved road from Otsagabia, and since the *ermita* is a favourite picnic area there's a slight chance of a lift in peak season.

# The Navarran valleys

From the lowland Navarran capital Pamplona (outside the scope of this book) roads radiate in all directions; towards the Pyrenees, they follow various river valleys, all served by public transport to varying degrees. Attractive **Otsagabia** dominates the head of the **Valle de Salazar** in Spain, just below the Selva de Irati; highlights of the lower reaches are the **Foz de Arbaiun** natural reserve and – just south under a ridge overlooking the Río Aragón – the imposing **Monasterio de San Salvador de Leyre**. The traditional pilgrims' route via Auritze and Roncesvalles is described in the next section, while the quiet Arga valley sees few visitors. The main road due north from Pamplona crosses the Cantabrian watershed at the Puerto de Belate (Velate), beyond which all rivers flow into the Atlantic rather than the Mediterranean. A subsequent major junction gives respective access to the **Valle de Baztán** and the **Valle de Bidasoa**; the latter is busy indeed, being the traditional corridor to the Basque coast in the days before the direct Pamplona–San Sebastián motorway was built.

## The Valle de Salazar

The **Valle de Salazar** (Zaraitzu) isn't particularly spectacular, but it does possess a gentle beauty not entirely compromised by its 2002-widened NA178 trunk road. The main attractions are at either end: handsome **Otsagabia** village near the top, the **Foz de Arbaiun** and the **Monasterio de San Salvador de Leyre** at the bottom. Of particular interest for anyone emerging

NAVARRAN VALLEYS, CAMINO DE SANTIAGO AND BASQUE COAST

from the Selva de Irati is the valley's daily bus service, the quickest way south towards Pamplona.

# Otsagabia

With its white plastered walls, stone-framed windows, wrought-iron balconies and pebble-mosaic entry-ways for the grander houses, **OTSAGABIA** (Ochagavía, Otsagi) forms one of the showcases of Pyrenean Navarra. Like Echo and Ansó, it was largely rebuilt after being sacked and burnt by the French in 1794. The river dividing the town is crossed by a series of low bridges, and cobbled streets meander from the streamside esplanades; to the west, on a slight rise, stands a church nearly as massive – but more graceful – than that at Izaba.

On a low hill 5km to the north, the stone-built **Ermita de Muskilda** has a multi-lobed entrance and a curious square half-timbered tower topped by an overhanging circular roof; every September 8 the festival of the Birth of the Virgin is celebrated by a well-attended *romería* (procession) and followed by dancing in traditional costume.

For conventional **accommodation** on the east bank, go for the riverside *Hostal Urialde* (☎948 890 027; ❸), with wood and antique decor and an in-house restaurant, better value in all respects than the *Hostal Auñamendi* on Plaza Gúrpide (☎948 890 189; ❹). Seven **casas rurales** (❶) offer mostly non-en-suite rooms in traditional stone houses; two worth singling out are the en-suite *Casa Ñabarro* (☎948 890 355; ❷) and *Casa Osaba* (☎948 890 011; ❷) on the west bank, one of the few buildings to predate the French attack. Three **banks** have ATMs, the first you'll have seen for some time if you're coming from France.

At Otsagabia the minor road from Casas de Irati meets the more important

---

## Griffon vultures

**Griffon vultures** (in Castilian *buitres*, in French *vautours fauves*) are found in several other areas of Spain, but their sole French habitat aside from the Massif Central is the Central and Western Pyrenees, in particular the Basque country. In the sky they're fairly unmistakeable, with a span of over 2.5m and fawn leading edges to the wings but almost black trailing edges. Exceeding 1m in length, they seem almost headless in flight, as the long, pale neck is tucked back.

Griffons live and hunt in colonies of between four and twelve pairs, covering a territory radiating up to 60km from the nest, which is rarely built at over 1100m altitude. Nesting time is generally March to May; when they reach maturity the young birds move on to establish a new territory, perhaps within kilometres but possibly as far away as North Africa.

The vultures eat carrion only, especially dead sheep, which are plentiful in the Western Pyrenees. When one of the troupe spots food it descends in spirals, thus attracting the others. The troupe seldom lands immediately but is more likely to keep the carrion under surveillance for one or two days – if the meat is too fresh it will be difficult to penetrate the skin. Once feeding starts a pecking order literally prevails, the dominant bird keeping the others back with menacing extensions of the neck, wings and claws. Only when satisfied does it yield to a subordinate, who in turn gives way to a bird of lower rank.

Besides the Foz de Arabaiun, other reliable places to see griffon vultures include the **Foz de Burgui** in the Roncal valley, **Cumbre de Arangoiti** near the Puerto de Ibañeta and the **Crête d'Iparla** near Baïgorri.

one coming from the Port de Larrau and Izaba. The **GR11** also connects Otsagabia with Izaba via the Sierra de Atuzkarratz, on a mixture of old *camino* and forest track; the grade (except for the final drop to Izaba) is gentle, and the traverse takes under six hours in either direction, but there's no reliable water en route.

The Pamplona-based **bus**, run by La Salacenca, arrives at about 7pm, leaving the village next day at 7am (Mon–Sat); the journey takes 80 minutes. Midpoint of the downhill journey is the Foz de Arbaiun.

## Foz de Arbaiun

The only really remarkable portion of the Valle de Salazar comes near its bottom end at the **Foz de Arbaiun** (Arbayún), a six-kilometre limestone gorge carved out by the Río Salazar. Dense vegetation thrives in the shade at the base of four-hundred-metre-high cliffs; higher up, raptor nests are concealed between clumps of bushes. This is the finest place in the entire Pyrenees to see **griffon vultures**, the largest colony of Navarra's several hundred specimens being protected here by a *reserva natural* of 1200 hectares. You can see the gorge from the viewing platform just to the north of the hamlet of Iso; for the intrepid, very steep trails snake down to the river bed.

## The Monasterio de San Salvador de Leyre

From the Foz de Arbaiun, it's 17km to the N240 highway at Venta de Lumbier, where you turn east and proceed another 13km to Yesa and the paved, four-kilometre side-road up to the **Monasterio de San Salvador de Leyre** (Leire). Yesa is a dull village with a couple of *hostales* and *habitaciones*, but much the best local accommodation is at the monastery itself. Do not be deceived by an apparent shortcut beginning just east of the *foz* from Bigüézal hamlet – this proceeds 4km up, on a single lane, to a radio mast at 1353m in the Sierra de Leyre, and expires at the edge of a precipitous drop.

The monastery contrasts vividly with the hermitages back in the mountains, its massive size underlining its former position as both a political and pilgrimage focus of Navarra – it is still mobbed by locals on Sundays and major holidays. After languishing in ruins for over a century, it was restored and reoccupied by Benedictine monks in 1954 and now basks in an immaculate condition. Although the resolutely institutional monastic buildings are sixteenth to eighteenth century, the **church** is largely Romanesque with thirteenth-century Gothic additions, its tall, severe apses and asymmetrical belfry being particularly impressive. The **west portal**, the Puerta Speciosa, is carved with images of Christ, the Virgin, St Peter, St John and assorted monsters; the **crypt**, with its sturdy little waist-high columns, no two alike, is only visible on a guided tour (Mon–Fri 10.15am–2pm & 3.30–7pm, Sat, Sun & hols 10.15am–2pm & 4–7pm; Spanish-only narration, minimum 15 people, every 45min, €1.80). Otherwise, you can access the church alone by coinciding with mass (5 daily 6am–9.10pm all year). This is well worth doing, since the twenty or so white-habited, purple-suppliced monks employ (except for matins) **Gregorian chant** – albeit in Spanish, not Latin.

The former hospice now operates as a two-star **hotel**, the *Hospedería de Leyre* (℡948 884 100, 𝔽948 884 137, 🌐www.monasteriodeleyre.com; ❹), which, however, actively caters to solo pilgrims of either gender with very advantageous single rates. Even if you don't stay, the restaurant deserves patronizing for the sake of its carefully prepared if limited-choice three-course *menús* (€16); allow €28–36 for *a la carta*). Though nominally still an important halt on the

Aragonese variant of the Camino de Santiago, today codified as the GR65.3, budget-conscious pilgrims are warned by a large sign at the base of the access road that the closest pilgrims' hostel per se is in Sangüesa.

# The Valle de Baztán

Due north of Pamplona, the heavily travelled N121a climbs over the watershed **Puerto de Belate** (Velate) before descending to **ORONOZ-MUGAIRI**, home to the **Parque Señorío de Bértiz** (daily 10am–2pm & 4–7pm; €1.50), a former private estate now combining the functions of botanical gardens and managed recreational forest. At Oieregi, you fork right onto the N121 for the **Valle de Baztán** (meaning "Rat's Tail" in Euskera) with its succession of villages, beautiful countryside and cave formations.

## Elizondo

The "capital" of this most strongly Basque of Navarran valleys is **ELIZONDO**, seat of a municipality composed of fifteen villages. What's visible from the through road leaves a poor impression, but once away from it the town is full of typical Basque Pyrenean architecture, especially along the river with its bridge and weir.

With its several **accommodation** options, Elizondo makes a good base for the valley. One good, inexpensive place is the central, en-suite *Pensión Eskisaroi*, c/Jaime Urrutia 40 (☏948 580 013; ❶), above a recommended restaurant (see below); *Casa Rural Jaén* (☏948 580 487; ❶), with two rooms, makes a good second choice. There are also two considerably more expensive places: the three-star *Hotel Baztán* (☏948 580 050, ℉948 452 323; ❺), on the Pamplona road south of town, an incongruously modern pile complete with garden and huge pool, and in the town itself, *Hostal Saskaitz*, a mock-traditional structure quietly placed 200m east of the through road at c/María Azpilikueta 10 (☏948 580 488, ℉948 580 615; ❹).

**Restaurants** are more reasonable, with again a handful to choose from. In the same family for three generations, the *Txokoto* at c/Braulio Iriarte 25 (west end of the river bridge; closed Wed) has a cosy, water-view *comedor* and a good line in eminently reasonable seafood and meat. The nearby *Eskisaroi* (address as above) can feed you with creative bean dishes, fish fillets, pear tart and assorted drinks (*a la carta* €19, *menú* €9); it's justly popular, with long waits for tables after 2.30pm. Finally, the *Galarza*, at the very northern town limits by the Río Baztan, is strong on seafood (budget €19 for three courses), though you could just have a drink under the trees outside.

Three **buses** arrive daily from both Pamplona and San Sebastián, but there is no public transport to the smaller villages beyond. Elizondo also lies astride the **GR11**, which heads west out of Auritze (see p.505), then turns north along the border (about 10hr). It's worth getting a dawn start from Auritze and trying to polish off this stretch in a day, as there are no facilities in between. If you have to break the journey, **Puerto de Urkiaga** (912m), about halfway, offers water and the possibility of camping.

## Arizkun, Erratzu and Amaiur-Maia

In nearby **ARIZKUN**, beside the minor road to the Izepegi pass on the French border (and beyond to Baïgorri), the seventeenth-century convent of

Nuestra Señora de los Angeles flaunts its striking Baroque facade; just beyond the village, there's a typical example of a fortified house (very common in the valley) where Pedro de Ursua, the leader of the Marañones expedition up the Amazon in 1560 in search of El Dorado, was born. You can **stay** in Arizkun at the friendly and well-run (if non-en-suite) *Pensión Etxeberría*, near the west edge of town and the *frontón* at c/Txuputo 43 (℡948 453 013; ❶), which also functions as a bar, grocery and reasonable if basic restaurant. For slightly more comfort try *Casa Gontxea* (℡948 453 433; ❷).

Some 4km northeast and the last Spanish village before France on this road, **ERRATZU** is another gem, with a few well-preserved **casas rurales**. *Casa Etxebeltzea* (℡948 453 157; ❸) is a fourteenth-century seigneurial manor at the south edge of the medieval core, near a mechanic's. The more isolated *Casa Juanillo* (℡948 453 356; ❷) is a well-converted farmhouse, which also offers evening meals.

**AMAIUR-MAIA**, 6km north of Arizkun but just off the N121, where the last unsuccessful battle to preserve the independence of Navarra took place, is another unspoilt village worth a stop. The gateway to its single street displays the village shield depicting a red bell – most houses still proudly emblazon their door lintels with this coat-of-arms. There are several **casas rurales** here too, including *Casa Goiz-Argi* (℡948 453 234; ❷) and the *Casa Miguelenea* (℡948 453 224; ❷), both with en-suite rooms.

## Urdazubi and Zugarramurdi

Northwest of Amaiur-Maia, the N121 climbs over the **Puerto de Otxondo** at the top of the Valle de Baztán to the villages of Urdazubi and – reached by side road – Zugarramurdi, both potential stopovers between Pamplona and the French Basque coastal towns of Biarritz and Bayonne.

**URDAZUBI** (Urdax), ringed by hills and guarded by a tiny castle, has three *hostales* and *pensiones*, the most upmarket and central of which is *Hostal Irigoiena* (℡948 599 267, ℻948 599 243, ✉hoirigoienea@jet.es; ❹), in a renovated farmhouse. If your budget won't stretch to that, try the more modest *Pensión Beotxea* on the Zugarramurdi road (℡948 599 114; ❷), with en-suite rooms, or the only *casa rural* here not let by the week, *Dutaria* (℡948 599 237; ❷). For **eating**, the *Bar Restaurante Indianoa-Baita* opposite the church has reasonable *menús*.

**ZUGARRAMURDI**, 4km southwest of the border, off the N121, is famous for its **Cueva de las Brujas** (allow 45 minutes for a walking visit), whose highlight is the giant natural arch through which the *regata de infierno* (Hell's stream) flows. The cavern was a major centre for witchcraft in the Middle Ages and consequently the area bore the brunt of persecution at the time of the Inquisition. Underneath the arch, *akelarre*s or witches' sabbaths allegedly took place as recently as the seventeenth century; these seem to have survived, in a tame derivative, as the *zikiroyate* rite every August 18, which features a "love-feast" of roast meat held in the grotto. The appealing village makes a good base for excursions into surrounding countryside; one possibility is to walk 3km along the track beyond the caves into France to another set of caves, the **Grottes de Sare** (see p.533). The actual frontier divides the village of Dantxarinea/Dantxaria (the latter just inside France) – a fairly shabby place offering little other than cheap Spanish booze and petrol, best seen from your rear-view mirror.

Zugarramurdi has three **casas rurales** letting rooms short-term, heavily sub-scribed at weekends: *Casa Iparrea Bajo* (℡948 599 225; ❶), *Casa Sueldeguía*

(T948 599 088; **②**) and *Casa Teltxeguia* (T948 599 167; **①**), all in the village centre.

# The Valle de Bidasoa

If at Oieregi you instead bear left to stay with the N121a, you exit Navarra along the scenic **Valle de Bidasoa** towards Irún, Hendaye and Hondarribia. There's a direct bus service between Pamplona and San Sebastián, as well as a considerable amount of other traffic, especially long-distance lorries – so a restful country road it isn't. But en route are a series of well-preserved villages worth a stop or even an overnight. Where the river meets the sea at Cabo Higuer beyond Hondarribia, so too does the **GR11**, finishing its 700-plus-kilometre course from the Catalan Costa Brava.

## Etxalar

**ETXALAR** is a small, bucolic place, 4km off the main road on the way up to a minor border crossing at the Lizarrieta pass, but is perhaps the best-preserved village of the valley, famous for the impressive array of Basque funerary steles in the churchyard. Among numerous **casas rurales** here, mostly houses or apartments rentable only by the week, are two good ones doing en-suite rooms for a short **stay**: the central *Casa Domekenea* (T948 635 031; **②**), and another, *Casa Herri-Gain* (T948 635 208; **②**), perched on a steep hill, with fantastic views of the surrounding area. There are also a couple of restaurants and bars near the giant church, so you won't starve or go thirsty.

## Lesaka

Slightly down-valley but up a short side road on the opposite side lies **LESAKA**. Despite the large, eyesore factory and lumber depots on the outskirts of town, it's an attractive place dominated by the hill-top parish church in which the pews bear family names of the local farms and mansions. On the banks of the irrigation channel that flows through town is one of the best remaining examples of a *casa torre* (fortified private house) of a design peculiar to the Basque country, dating back to the days when northwestern Navarra was in the hands of a few powerful and constantly feuding families.

Places to **stay** include the helpful *Hostal Ekaitza* at central Plaza Berria 13 (T948 627 547; **③**), in a converted ancestral home flanking the central car park, or the more upmarket *Hotel Bereau* (T948 627 509, F948 627 647; **④**), somewhat more noisily set by the main highway, 2km east of Lesaka proper, but with its own **restaurant** – options in Lesaka proper, other than the Ekaitza's snack bar, are few. The most noteworthy local **casa rural** is *Agiña*, 9km west on the road to Oiartzun (T948 387 057; **③**), a spectacularly set hillside inn with non-smoking rooms and evening meals provided.

## Bera

The last substantial place before the Navarra/Gipuzkoa border, **BERA** (Vera de Bidasoa) offers some of the finest examples of old wood-beamed and traditional stone houses in the region; the brightly painted buildings on c/Altzarte and the main plaza are particularly attractive. About a hundred metres off the square, just past the old customs house, is the former dwelling (no. 24) of the

Basque writer Pío Baroja; at the time of writing this museum is closed indefinitely. From Bera, border-straddling Larrun (la Rhune), see p.532, is an easy climb.

Options for **staying** include the comfortable *Hostal Euskalduna* at the noisy central junction (℡948 630 392; ❸); the *Hostal Zalain* (℡948 631 106; ❶), beyond the industrial-warehouse district in the remote Barrio de Zalain; and a large *casa rural*, *Casa Alkeberea* (℡948 630 540; ❷), 2km out on the Lizuniago road, with secure parking and ample common areas.

## Walking: the end of the GR11

Heading northwest from Elizondo, the **GR11** finishes its course passing through or very near many of the places above. The tough, penultimate day of a trans-Pyrenean traverse from **Elizondo to Bera** crosses deserted country to skim the frontier between Etxalar and Sara; count on seven hours to reach Bera. The final half-day is more perfunctory, skirting rather than climbing the **Peñas de Haya**, and then unrelentingly urban in character once you enter Irún and Hondarribia. Only at the end is there a bit of drama, as you emerge beyond the beach of Hondarribia onto **Cabo Higuer**, the promontory marking the terminus of both the GR route and the Spanish Pyrenees.

# Along the Camino de Santiago

Despite the attractions of the other Navarran valleys, the most popular itinerary from Pamplona entails moving northeast along the principal branch of the **Camino de Santiago** into France, via the fabled **Puerto de Ibañeta**. It's a route easily covered by bus, car, mountain bike or – for purists or pilgrims – on foot along the **GR65** long-distance trail.

**Auritze**, a village on a wide plain at the foot of the frontier peaks, is an obvious and comfortable staging-point. A short distance north, the abbey of **Roncesvalles** has long been a hallowed stop on the pilgrim route to Santiago de Compostela, and occupies a central location in the legend of **Roland**. The famous ambush of Charlemagne's rearguard, supposedly under Roland's command, took place close by – possibly after the Franks emerged from the thick, gloomy beech forest onto the barren expanse of the Puerto de Ibañeta.

This pass notches the main Pyrenean watershed, but an anomalous finger of Spanish territory encompassing **Luzaïde** protrudes north and down halfway to **Saint-Jean-Pied-de-Port**, touristic mecca of the French Pays Basque since its days as a pilgrimage way-station. The main Chemin de Saint-Jacques arrived here from Ostabat to the northeast; a minor branch of the *chemin* – now paralleled by the modern road and rail line – heads northwest along the valley of the River Nive to the attractive cathedral city of Bayonne, with relatively little to compel a stop before then. In doing so this pilgrim route transects the two westerly historic divisions of the French Basque country, **Basse-Navarre** and **Labourd**.

# Auritze

**AURITZE** (Burguete) is a typically pleasant, one-street Basque Pyrenean set-tlement, surrounded by fields, cattle barns and wooded ridges on the horizon. The place appears to be not much bigger than in Ernest Hemingway's time – he (and his fictional characters Jake and Bill) used to come trout fishing near-by, before or after Pamplona's San Fermín festival.

The GR65 and GR11 both pass through here on the same right-of-way just outside Burguete to the west, a fact somewhat confused by lingering, faded waymarks for the old GR11 to the east. The new GR11 traces a very circuitous route north, then east towards Otsagabia for two walking days, with little in the way of facilities or habitation in between. For short day-strolls along streams and through the woods, with Auritze as a base, the rolling countryside imme-diately east of the village is still your best bet. The relevant Editorial Alpina **map** is "Roncesvalles-Irati".

## Practicalities

The best of three conventional **hotels** is the *Hostal Burguete* at the north end of the main street (☎948 760 005; Easter–Oct; ❸), the oldest establishment here: three echoing storeys of huge, spotless, squeaky-wood-floored, en-suite rooms, with literary cachet to boot. Hemingway stayed here during the early 1920s and immortalized it in his first novel *Fiesta*; the room he occupied, now #25 (formerly 18), is still preserved much as he described it, save for discreet-ly placed photos of the great man (including one with his second wife, Martha Gellhorn). The four washbasin-only rooms of the *Hostal Juandeaburre* (☎948 760 078; May–Oct; ❶) at the south end of the high street are rather more basic, while directly opposite stands the three-star *Hotel Loizu* (☎948 760 008; Ⓕ948 790 444; ❹), whose somewhat overpriced, double-glazed rooms have all the charm of an airport Hilton. Failing these, try one of the *casas rurales* for a more traditional feel: en-suite *Casa Pedroarena* (☎948 760 164; ❷), *Casa Loperena* (☎948 760 068; ❶), above the **bank** (next-to-last one before the frontier), or en-suite *Casa Vergara* ☎948 760 044; ❷). A **campsite**, *Urrobi* (☎948 760 200; April–Oct), lies 3km south of the village at Auritzberri (Espinal). When it comes to **eating** out, the *Loizu* has the best restaurant in town, with *menús* for about €13 (though game and regional specialties only cost €22 *a la carta*); oth-erwise there's little to distinguish the cheaper, sustaining fare at the *Burguete*'s *comedor* from the *Txikipolit* across the way.

## East of Auritze

The afternoon bus from Pamplona first calls at Roncesvalles (see below) and then continues 10km east past attractive Garralda to **ARIBE** (Arive), an equal-ly appealing little village on the banks of the Río Irati, with a lovely stone bridge and **rooms** at *Casa Txikirrin* (☎948 764 074; ❷). The bus carries on eastwards from Aribe, terminating 18km later at **EAURTA** (Jaurrieta), anoth-er attractive village with a good deal of half-timbering, several *casas rurales* and a reasonable **inn-restaurant** in the centre, the *Sario* (☎948 890 187; ❸). With your own vehicle, you're just 6km shy of the Valle de Salazar at Ezkaroze (Escaroz), 2km below Otsagabia, but road-walking there is not suggested – the grade to Ezkaroze is stiff and the right of way narrow.

# Roncesvalles

It would indeed be surprising if contemporary **RONCESVALLES** (Orreaga in Euskera, Roncevaux in French), a hamlet 2.5km north of Burguete on the N135, matched the expectations prompted by its semi-legendary history. As you approach from Auritze the impact of its **Colegiata**, an Augustinian abbey founded by Sancho VII el Fuerte (the Strong) of Navarra in 1219, is considerably diminished by the ramshackle associated buildings, topped with sheets of oxidized zinc roofing and overawed by swivelling tower cranes engaged in renovations (due to finish in 2005).

Sancho was one of the heroes of the battle of Las Navas de Tolosa (1212), a decisive defeat for the Almohadan Moors symbolized by the broken chain – which had guarded the Muslim chieftain's tent – in the Navarran coat-of-arms. Sancho's **tomb** lies in the Sala Capitular of the cloister, topped by a massive 2.25-metre-long effigy of the man, said to be life-size; nearby, safe behind an iron grille, a purported bit of the chain is displayed.

The best of the architecture is the echoing **church** (free), with a thirteenth-century crypt (€1 fee) and a Gothic **cloister**, rebuilt after a fire in 1400. The cloister is visited with the same ticket for a separate, small **museum** (April–Oct daily 10am–2pm & 3.30–7pm; Nov–March daily 10am–2pm & 3.30–5.30pm; Jan daily except Wed 1.30–2.30pm; €2) at the southwest corner of the monastery building, which contains the expected ecclesiastical reliquaries (one

## The legend of Roland

In 778 the Frankish emperor Charlemagne besieged and demolished the fortifications of Pamplona on his way out of Spain, which he had invaded – the only time he ever crossed the Pyrenees – to assist one faction during an outbreak of inter-Moorish strife. He was continuing homeward, laden with booty from various other raids in the Ebro valley, when on August 15, 778, the rear of his army was ambushed somewhere in the area of the Puerto de Ibañeta, by Basques determined to avenge the attack on Pamplona.

The episode hasn't much historical significance, but it achieved international prominence through the myth of Roland, supposedly the greatest of Charlemagne's paladins, who is said to have commanded the rearguard and been killed in the battle. The precise source of the Roland tale is impossible to determine, but its distant origins lie in knightly ballads that were popular at the time of the battle. By the ninth century, *cantilènes* (chanted stories) were being told throughout the Ariège and Andorra about this valiant companion of Charlemagne. He was held up as an example of bravery to the Norman battalions at the Battle of Hastings, and the tale worked its way around Europe to Germany and Italy. But it was during the twelfth century that the legend really took off, with the appearance of the mysterious epic called **La Chanson de Roland** (The Song of Roland).

In 1130 the archbishop of Pamplona, Sancho de Rosa, relived the ambush in a dream that pinpointed its location at the Puerto de Ibañeta. The vision was well publicized, and elaborated in 1170 by an anonymous clerk who wrote the *Chanson de Roland*, the ultimate medieval heroic epic. The Catholic Church eagerly exploited the story, not just as a propaganda device against the Infidel – ignoring the minor detail that Roland's final, Basque adversaries were also Christians – but also to promote the sales of souvenirs and relics along the *camino*. Although the geographical and historical accuracy of the poem is open to question, its evocation of chivalric valour adds poignancy to a visit to Roncesvalles; the Penguin edition in English fits easily into a backpack.

showcasing the mummified fingers of Saint Marina), processional crucifixes, mitres, croziers and chalices, as well as an exquisite eighteenth-century gold cigarette box from Paris, embossed with a swan confronting a fox – possibly a pilgrim's donation.

Roland's purported martyrdom notwithstanding (see opposite), the original role of the abbey was as a way-station on the Camino de Santiago; after all, its founding – centuries after the battle – was motivated by the need for a strategically placed pilgrims' hospice a day's journey south of Saint-Jean-Pied-de-Port. Had it really been intended as a memorial to Roland, the *colegiata* would have been sited (rather impractically) up on the Puerto de Ibañeta. The tale of the attack merely provided a general endorsement for exemplary defenders of Christianity.

In the years immediately following its establishment, the abbey enjoyed a meteoric success, ranking among the wealthiest and most powerful of the thirteenth century; it was said that a pilgrim of the era could travel from London to Roncesvalles entirely on lands belonging to the *colegiata*. Today the place is more commonly the destination of numerous local *romerías*, from both the French and Spanish valleys, by virtue of its thirteenth-century image of the *Virgen de Orreaga*, honoured with special fervour on September 8.

### Practicalities

**Accommodation** is fairly abundant, considering that there's no real village here. Non-pilgrims should head for the small *Hostal Casa Sabina*, right next to the monastery (☎948 760 012; ❷), or the much larger *La Posada* (☎948 760 225; ❸), run by the monastery; both serve **meals**. Bona fide **pilgrims** following the Camino de Santiago can use either the **YHA hostel** (☎948 760 302) or the more spartan **pilgrims' hostel** at the monastery (token donation requested). All this seems a mere echo of the medieval hospice here, which for seven centuries listed its services for the (predominantly male) pilgrims as follows: a bath, haircut, shave and mending of shoes or clothes, performed – as various manuscripts attested – "by women solicitous and far from ugly".

# The Transpyrenean Camino de Santiago

A better way to get a sense of the Roland legend is to take the half-hour hike up through the beech woods from the back of the abbey to the **Puerto de Ibañeta** (1057m). According to many scholars, you'll be walking through the site where Roland's defeat occurred. On a misty day – and there are many – the pass can seem suitably melancholy. An ugly modern chapel stands on the saddle, on the site of the ancient chapel of San Salvador, whose bell used to guide pilgrims in foggy weather. There are also a couple of small medieval stone monuments to Roland and the vestiges of another built by a doctor from Pamplona in 1934.

Thirty-two years after Charlemagne followed approximately this route, his son, Louis le Débonnaire, avoided a repeat performance of the Basque ambush by forcing the wives and children of local villagers to accompany his troops through the pass. It was also the route taken by Edward the Black Prince to the battleground of Navarrate in 1367; Napoleon's troops retreated this way after the Peninsular War; and the defeated Republicans fled in thousands through the sombre scenery here as the Spanish Civil War drew to a close.

The **Camino de Santiago**, officially marked as the GR65, no longer goes via the Puerto de Ibañeta, but on a more northeasterly bearing from Roncesvalles, avoiding most major roads. It's seven to eight hours to Saint-Jean-Pied-de-Port, much of it on narrow country lanes but occasionally on medieval cobbles, through beautiful countryside.

From the *colegiata*, it's nearly ninety minutes by path through thick beech woods to the **Collada Lepoeder** (1445m), flanked by the rounded summit of Astobizkar (1506m). You descend slightly, past the ruins of the Elizacharre chapel, to cross the border at the **Col de Bentarte/Collado de Betartea pass** (1340m) – which many insist was the more likely place for the ambush (and an extra justification, perhaps, for rerouteing the *camino*). The joint GR11/12 heads east here, parting company with the GR65, which heads north to meet the paved D428 for Saint-Jean after about half an hour, just below **Pic Urdanarré** (1240m). Alternatively, you can walk eastwards on the marked path to the **Urkulu burial tower** (dating from about 1500 BC), and join the same road there, a diversion which cost you an extra hour round-trip.

From the base of Pic Urdanarré, Saint-Jean is about 16km or 4hr away, with the GR65 providing just a few shortcuts across woods and farmland. Much the best place to break the trek if it looks like you'll be overtaken by darkness – or if you don't fancy the idea of busy Saint-Jean-Pied-de-Port, ninety minutes further – is the tiny French hamlet of **HONTO**, which offers excellent *chambres d'hôte* and hearty evening meals at *Ferme Ithurburia* (☎05.59.37.11.17; ❷) – it's a big hit with pilgrims following the Camino de Santiago in summer, so phone in advance if possible.

## Luzaïde

Alternatively, you can drive from Roncesvalles – beyond which there's no public transport – along the main road into France down the Luzaïde valley, a narrow salient of Spanish territory jutting north from the usual frontier ridge. **LUZAÏDE** (Valcarlos), 16km below the Ibañeta pass, is a typical border town full of tatty souvenirs and booze – though the views are better than usual. There are a number of **accommodation** options, so you shouldn't be stuck if you need to stay, except perhaps in August. Conveniently situated on the main road is *Hostal Maitena* (☎948 790 210; ❸). On the Frenchward side of the village, the excellent *Casa Etxezuria* (☎948 790 011; ❶) has just two beautifully furnished rooms offering comfort at a bargain price. Other **casas rurales** include the remoter but en-suite *Casa Navarlaz* (☎948 790 042; ❷), in a thirteenth-century house. Arnegi (Arnéguy), 3km on, is the first French village, right against the border; again it has no public transport links north.

# Saint-Jean-Pied-de-Port

**SAINT-JEAN-PIED-DE-PORT** (Donibane Garazi), 8km from the border on the young River Nive, is a seasonally overrun tourist attraction, its highly photogenic old quarter enveloped in pink sandstone walls and watched over by an imposing fortress. Once capital of Basse-Navarre, Saint-Jean thrived until the sixteenth century on the pilgrimage traffic to Santiago de Compostela, and all over town you'll see the tell-tale, scallop-shell emblem. The three main pilgrim routes across France converge some 20km northeast at Ostabat, from where caravans of travellers used to descend on Saint-Jean, singing in reply to the church bells that would ring when a group was spotted on the horizon. From the north, they entered by **Porte de Saint-Jacques** in the town walls and left by **Porte d'Espagne**, heading up to the Puerto de Ibañeta – hence the suffixed Pied-de-Port, meaning "Foot-of-the-Pass".

The oldest neighbourhood lies on the right bank of the River Nive, behind the medieval fortifications, and consists essentially of a single street. This begins as the rue d'Espagne, heading north from Porte d'Espagne, and lined on both sides with souvenir shops and pastel-painted houses, some with carved lintels dating them to the sixteenth century. Crossing the **Vieux-Pont**, which offers the best photo opportunities in town – balconied houses, decked in washing and flowers, handsomely reflected in the placid, trout-filled waters of the Nive – you pass through the well-preserved **Porte Nôtre-Dame** to reach the four-teenth-century, largely Gothic **Nôtre-Dame-du-Bout-du-Pont** on the right. Here the street becomes the cobbled rue de la Citadelle, climbing steeply past the long and narrow **Prison des Evêques** (Bishops' Prison; open daily Easter–Oct mornings and late afternoons; €2.50), separated by a garden from the episcopal residence. The pilgrimage to Santiago inevitably attracted a few shady characters who preyed on the occasionally gullible genuine pilgrims; when discovered, the con-men were arrested by guards employed by the Church and flung into dungeons such as this. Accordingly you are shown, in addition to a small gallery of knick-knacks, a subterranean earth-floored chamber still complete with chains for restraining the prisoners.

At the top of the rise, above the Porte de Saint-Jacques, looms the classical **citadel**, built in 1628 on the orders of Cardinal Richelieu, and redesigned by Vauban in 1685. It's now a college, but the lower, grassy ramparts have unrestricted access, and are worth the climb up for the sweeping views west and north. You can also walk around part of the town's lower walls, though you see little other than people's back gardens.

## Practicalities

The **tourist office** (Sept–June Mon–Sat 9.30am–noon & 2–6.30pm; July & Aug daily 10.30am–12.30pm & 3–6pm; ℡05.59.37.03.57, Ⓦwww.terre-basque.com) is at 14 place du Général-de-Gaulle, a tile-roofed kiosk opposite the *mairie*. The **train station** is ten minutes' walk away at the end of avenue Renaud, on the northern edge of the centre.

For **pilgrims' and trekkers' accommodation** there are various possibilities. The basic *Accueil Saint-Jacques* at 39 rue de Citadelle (℡05.59.37.05.09; Easter–Sept; donation) is for bona fide pilgrims only, while Dutch-run *L'Esprit du Chemin* opposite at no. 40 (℡05.59.37.24.68; April–Sept) is less fussy, welcoming *randonneurs* as well. *Chambres d'hôte* on the same street include *E. Bernat* at no. 20 (℡05.59.31.23.10, Ⓦwww.ebernat.com; ❸), with a small restaurant. The helpful *Gîte d'Étape Etchegoin* is at 9 route d'Uhart, on the Bayonne road (℡05.59.37.12.08; 12 bunks). There's a **camping municipal**, the *Plaza Berri* (℡05.59.37.11.19; April–Oct), on the south bank of the Nive, beside the *frontón*, as well as the site *Arradoy* (℡05.59.37.11.75; March–Sept), north of town on the far side of the rail line.

Less expensive **hotels** include *Les Remparts*, 16 place Floquet (℡05.59.37.13.79, Ⓔremparts.hotel@wanadoo.fr; closed Nov–Dec; ❸), just before you cross the Nive coming into town on the Bayonne road, not too noisy and with parking spaces nearby (a problem here), or the 1997-renovated *Hôtel Itzalpea*, 5 place du Trinquet (℡05.59.37.03.66, Ⓕ05.59.37.33.18; ❸), whose restaurant offers a wide choice of *menus* (average €20). More expensive and comfortable are the Logis de France affiliate *Ramuntcho*, just inside the city walls at 1 rue de France (℡05.59.37.03.91, Ⓕ05.59.37.35.17; closed mid-Nov to mid-Dec & Tues pm & Wed all year; ❹), with a good and reasonably priced restaurant, and the *Hôtel Central* on place du Général-de-Gaulle (℡05.59.37.00.22, ℻05.59.37.27.79; closed mid-Dec to March; ❹), with some marginally quieter river-view rooms and free parking, plus hearty meals at €18–40 per head in its restaurant. With a car to park, you're probably best off staying at the friendly *Hôtel Camou* (℡05.59.37.02.78, ℻05.59.37.12.23; closed Dec & Jan; ❸), 600m west of the centre in Uhart-Cize suburb, and walking to the action.

**Eating out**, there's no better place for a splurge than *Chez Arrambide*, the restaurant of the luxury *Hôtel des Pyrénées* at 19 place du Général-de-Gaulle (closed Jan & mid-Nov to mid-Dec, also Mon pm & Tues low season), reckoned one of the best in the Pyrenees: count on €40–90 for the works, which often include dishes like baby rabbit, duck breast in fruit and spice sauce, roast pigeon with mushroom ravioli and decadent desserts. Inside the old town, choose between the very Basque *Restaurant Cidrerie Hurrup Eta Klik* at 3 bis rue de la Citadelle, serving huge portions of cod omelette, almost-rare beefsteak in rock salt and brebis cheese with cherry conserve, accompanied by equally generous measures of cider; and the cheap but sometimes not very cheerful *Chez Arbillaga* (closed Tues pm, also Wed low season; June & Oct), at 8 rue de l'Église just inside the walls (*menus* €13, €19.50 on Sat), with a pleasant dining area. Otherwise, there are a dozen rather slapdash, fairly indistinguishable pavement *brasseries* and *crêperies* aimed at the not-too-demanding day-tripper, packed to the gills in season.

The only ways of moving on by public transport are the **train** west to Bayonne or the **bus** west to Baïgorri. You can enquire about **bike rental** at Steunou (℡05.59.37.25.45), next to the tourist office, or at Garazy (℡05.59.37.21.79) for mountain bikes.

# Southeast: the upper Nive valley

Heading southeast of Saint-Jean, the D301 road provides access to the upper reaches of the **Nive valley**, with its attractive villages and small red- or green-shuttered farmhouses. The GR10 stays well northeast of the river, first paved, then on track and trail along Handiamendi ridge, running roughly parallel to the D301. The road continues almost all the way to the river's source, with a short final approach on foot.

## The villages

Sleepy **SAINT-MICHEL** (Eiheralarre), 4km along the D301, may prompt a halt for its excellent *Hôtel Xoko-Goxoa* (℡05.59.37.06.34, ℻05.59.37.34.63; closed mid-Jan to early March; ❷) on the main through road. Best are the rear, balconied rooms overlooking hayfields and a stream valley; the restaurant, equally panoramic, purveys simple but savoury and reasonable fare (*menus* €11–25).

Proceeding 4km further – or three and a half hours' walk from Saint-Jean along the meandering GR10 – brings you to tiny **EZTERENTZUBI** (Esterençuby) with its medieval galleried church and ample **accommodation**. Choose between the *Auberge Carricaburu* (℡05.59.37.09.77; closed Feb; ❷) by the *trinquet*, with a streamside restaurant (*à la carte* €24) and the lively village bar, and the more institutional *Hôtel Restaurant Larramendy-Andreinia* (℡05.59.37.09.70, ℻05.59.37.36.05; closed mid-Nov to mid-Dec; ❸), which also keeps a *gîte d'étape* on a nearby knoll.

The valley-floor road continues alongside the Nive, now no more than a mountain stream; there's little cultivation in the progressively deepening valley other than vast hay meadows, scythed and raked in early summer, and equally extensive tracts of bracken fern, prized as animal bedding. Some 4km from Ezterentzubi the road reaches tiny Beherobia before climbing to the border and then looping back to Saint-Jean-Pied-de-Port. At **BEHEROBIA** (Béhérobie), in the valley bottom beside the infant Nive, one of just a few buildings is the *Hôtel des Sources de la Nive* (☎05.59.37.10.57, ℱ05.59.37.39.06; ❷; closed Jan & Tues Nov–March); its restaurant offers game-and-fish-dominated *menus* for €12–27. The hotel is invariably booked out in October – like most of the valley's lodgings – for the wood-pigeon shooting season, but otherwise makes a relaxing hideaway; all rooms are en-suite, but ask for the quieter, eight-room annexe with larger bathtubs.

### The Sources de la Nive

Just before the bridge at Beherobia, a lane keeps up to the left, signposted for the **Sources de la Nive**. With a car, you can drive to the end of the road by another bridge and a few farmhouses, then continue on foot by the dirt track heading left, not the one over the bridge (which carried the old, now-abandoned GR10 from St-Jean – you'll see waymarks covered over with grey paint). The track soon dwindles to trail along the fifteen-minute walk to the springs; water percolates a thousand metres down through karstic hillside to well up as a surging pool feeding rapids. Lost in dense beech woods, it's a magic spot in any weather, with a faint mist often rising from the surface of the water.

## East: walking the GR10 or driving

There are just a few other **walking** possibilities in the immediate area, most of them utilizing the **old GR10**; with the waymarks painted over and systematic maintenance suspended, you should probably not attempt them without a 1:25,000 IGN map and an altimeter or GPS device. The old trail follows a tributary of the Nive southeast, high up the side of the valley to emerge into lush grasslands about an hour out. Another hour should see you at the Col d'Errozaté (1076m), just north of which is Errozaté peak (1345m); if you're traversing rather than day-hiking, it's possible to continue east, via Occabé (see p.496), to the vicinity of *Chalet Pedro* in the Forêt d'Iraty – six to seven hours from Beherobia.

The **new GR10** has been re-routed to head from Ezterentzubi to the Forêt d'Iraty via Phagalcette hamlet and Iraukotuturru peak, meeting up with the old route at Occabé. It's nearly six hours to *Chalet Pedro* (see p.496), the first two hours a rather dull, stiff climb on paved, one-lane road. But once you're off this onto farm track and path, the scenery is enlivened by wandering herds of healthy-looking horses and ponies, masses of sheep and big, sleek, caramel cows with bells at their throats on wooden collars marked with their owners' names. There are superb places to camp if you've started late, with views west to the orange and crimson striations of the sunset and the revolving beacon of the Biarritz lighthouse visible in the dark.

**Drivers** should follow the D301 east out of the Nive valley from the junction 3km south of Ezterentzubi, signposted for the Forêt d'Iraty. This is very steep, narrow and full of tight hairpins, frequent oncoming traffic and the ambling livestock noted above; it's to be avoided at night or in misty conditions, is not kept snowploughed in winter, and needs an hour in low gear at the best of times to the junction with the D18 at the Plateau d'Iraty. But there is ample compensation: as you climb higher up the steep spurs and round the heads of labyrinthine gullies, ever more spectacular views open beneath you. You can see way back over the valley of the Nive, St-Jean and the hills beyond. Stands of beech fill the gullies, shadowing the lighter grass whose green is so intense it seems almost theatrical – an effect produced, apparently, by the juxtaposition of outcrops of rock whose purplish hue brings out the cadmium yellow in the grass.

# Baïgorri and the Vallée des Aldudes

Although **BAÏGORRI** (Saint-Étienne-de-Baïgorry) lies only 11km west of Saint-Jean-Pied-de-Port along the D15, it's a different world, where agriculture rather than tourism is the prime focus of life. Like most other foothill Basque settlements, Baïgorri is divided into quite distinct quarters, more like separate hamlets than a unified village. Market centre of the **Vallée des Aldudes**, it's a prosperous, rather sleek place, its highly profitable farming co-operatives presenting their public face through several sales outlets in town. The strong local **Irouléguy (Irulegi) wines**, the only *appellation* red, white and rosé produced in the Pays Basque, are worth stocking up on; you can taste them at the vintner's outlet 5km east on the D15 (daily 9am–noon & 2–6pm; not Sun in winter). Other local specialities include ham, sheep's-milk cheese and preserved mushrooms.

There are few great sights here: just a hump-backed medieval bridge juxtaposed with the small castle of the Etxauz (Etchaux) quarter, and a seventeenth-century church with an extravagantly gilded Baroque *retable*. The town's Euskera name translates as "beautiful view" and from the outlying quarters, which clamber up pastured and vine-clad hills, you do indeed get a marvellous panorama of the gentle lower slopes of the Pyrenees.

## Practicalities

The **tourist office** (Mon–Sat 9am–noon & 2–6pm; July & Aug also Sun 10am–noon & 3–6pm; ☎05.59.37.47.28) is opposite the church and can help with longer stays in local *chambres d'hôte*. The only budget **accommodation** is the *Gîte d'Étape Mendi* (☎05.59.37.42.39; 30 places), in the northerly Lespars quarter. Otherwise, the least expensive central hotel is *Juantorena* on the through road (☎05.59.37.40.78, ℻05.59.37.42.43; ❷). For more comfort at essentially the same rates, there's *Hôtel Restaurant Maechenea*, 4km north in the hamlet of **Urdos** (☎05.59.37.41.68, ✉hotel-manechenea@wanadoo.fr; ❸; closed Dec–Feb), tranquilly set on a stream bank. Back in central Baïgorri, just over the bridge by the church, the professionally run *Hôtel-Restaurant Arcé* (☎05.59.37.40.14, ⓦwww.hotel-arce.com; ❼) lives up to its three stars with a pool, tennis courts and enormous, wood-floored, antique-furnished rooms with modern, well-equipped baths (best are the river-view balcony units); the more reasonable restaurant is open to all, with *menus* at €18 and €28. At the opposite end of the spectrum, the *Mendi* has lawn space for **tents**, while the riverside *Camping Irouléguy* (☎05.59.37.40.80) is more central and has better amenities. About the only independent **eateries** in town are the friendly *Bar Chez Oronos*, in Bourg district, where a three-course, daily-changing menu won't top €12 with drink, and *L'Etape Gourmande* (aka *Chez Petricorena*) near the swimming pool, considerably more upmarket fare for considerably more outlay.

Regular SNCF **rail-bus** services connect Baïgorri with the train station at Ossès-Saint-Martin-d'Arrossa, 8km northeast along the D948.

## The upper Vallée des Aldudes

The villages of the upper **Vallée des Aldudes** are quiet rural spots, beyond the reach of public transport, major hiking routes and most tourism. Although it lies on a fairly major corridor to Pamplona, accommodation and food here are simple and reasonably priced, though there seem to be fewer lodgings with each passing year.

The first village, about 8km south of Baïgorri, is **BANKA** (Banca), shoehorned into the steep narrows carved out by the river here. It used to live from mining lead and copper – you can see the ruined works – but now depends on hosting trout fishermen. They stay mostly at the one-star, en-suite *Hôtel-Restaurant Erreguina* above the church (☎ & 🖷05.59.37.40.37; ❷; hotel April–Oct, restaurant all year), offering much the highest standard food or lodging in the valley – though the front garden's been ruined by a car park. There are three *menus* under €17 served in the cave-like, beam-ceilinged dining room, though going *à la carte* for scarcely more gives a better selection of pigeon, venison and fish both ocean and local. The HRP passes high above Banka, though the link route down from the Col d'Ehunzaroy is poorly marked and unshaded; best to follow tracks if in doubt.

Some 7km further upstream, the valley opens out considerably, with **ALDUDE** (Les Aldudes) plopped in the middle of the fields. The dead-central, somewhat scuffed *Hôtel Restaurant Baïllea* (☎05.59.37.57.02; closed Nov 15–March 1; ❶), with equally basic food, is the only facility. For more comfort, follow the main road 1500m towards Spain to **ESNASU** (Esnazu), where just one hotel survives, the Logis de France affiliate *Saint Sylvestre* (☎05.59.37.58.13, 🖷05.59.37.93.96; closed mid-Nov to March; ❷), though the *Auberge Mentea* still does meals.

## Walking around Baïgorri: the Crête d'Iparla

The **GR10** arrives circuitously in Baïgorri from Saint-Jean in about six hours, curling southwest via 1021-metre Monhoa hill, then northeast. It's a rather dull stretch of the route, with a lot of track sectors.

Not so the continuation west towards Bidarraï, by far the more popular and rewarding outing, which begins near the *gîte* in Lespars district. A sharp, two-and-a-half-hour climb, first through woods and then along a bare ridge, emerges at the **Col de Buztanzelhay** (843m), at the southern end of the **Crête d'Iparla**, which here forms the border. Iparla offers the classic ridge-walk of the French Pays Basque, and indeed one of the best in the entire Pyrenees.

Once up, it's hard to get lost: you simply follow the ridge due north, as close to the eastern face as is prudent. You're virtually guaranteed close-range sightings of griffon vultures and the occasional rare black vulture, though they tend to go to ground after midday when the thermal qualities of the air change. Although the highest point, **Pic d'Iparla** (under 3hr from Buztanzelhay), is only 1044m, it's as impressive a walk as you could hope for, with France precipitously below to the east, and a gentler decline towards a much less developed, almost secret corner of Spain on the west.

You'll need a full eight hours (an hour less with a daypack) to traverse the length of the entire crest to Bidarraï village. You should only attempt it in settled conditions; otherwise you won't get its views or vulture sightings, and every year hikers are struck by lighting or fall off the sheer precipice in mist. It's possible to return to your start-point the same day by public transport, a somewhat easier undertaking if you begin the walk from Bidarraï, a common strategy. Consult current SNCF schedule placards before setting out so that you coincide with one of the afternoon rail-buses back from Baïgorri to the proper train station of Ossès-St-Martin-d'Arrossa, one stop above Pont-Noblia (Bidarraï).

Starting the walk from Bidarraï, begin following the GR10 markers at the *gîte d'étape* and then bear right at each of two subsequent track junctions. The climb is brutal for the first ninety minutes, then slackens at a jagged crag where your spirits will be further lifted by your first glimpse of the vultures – who seem to have lost most fear of humans. Once around the Pic d'Iparla – about 2hr 45min out of Bidarraï with a daypack at a good pace – you descend to the important **Col de Harrieta** (808m) within another hour.

Immediately to the left (east), a communally maintained path, then tractor track, marked with single yellow paint-dashes, descends within ninety minutes to **Urdos** hamlet, your safety bail-out if the weather has turned nasty. From Urdos it's two-and-a-half hours back to Bidarraï, mostly on track and road. Diagonally off to the right or southwest from the *col*, a clear trail leads within five minutes to the **only spring** on Iparla, though even this may run low or dry by August. Straight south along the GR10 should get you to Baïgorri, and the late afternoon rail-bus, within three-and-a-half more hours.

## Bidarraï

If you've come by train, **BIDARRAÏ** (Bidarray) on first sight seems to be restricted to a few scattered houses on the riverbank near its medieval, hump-backed Pont-Noblia, also the name of the SNCF station on schedules. Hikers arriving on the GR10, whether from Ainhoa on the west or Baïgorri to the south, get a truer picture of the upper village, scattered appealingly on a ridge with superb views; the first building encountered coming from either direction, at the extreme south edge of the village, is *Gîte d'Étape Auñamendi* (℡05.59.37.71.34; 50 places plus 30 in annexe). Further along, the central place de l'Église is flanked by the 1999-refurbished *Hôtel Restaurant Barberaenea* (℡05.59.37.74.86, Ⓦwww.hotel-barberaenea.fr; closed mid-Nov to mid-Dec), with three grades of rooms: old-style with sinks (❷), en-suite (❸) and a less appealing modern annexe (❸). It's worth enduring often "leisurely" service at the restaurant for the tasty four-course €21.50 *menu du terroir* (drink extra), typically including *garbure* and cod-stuffed red peppers, served under the plane trees. Down in the riverbank quarter, the better choice of two is the welcoming *Hôtel Restaurant du Pont d'Enfer* (℡05.59.37.70.88, Ⓕ05.59.37.76.60; closed Dec & Jan; ❶–❷) better known as *Chez Anny* after the proprietor, again with three grades of large, non-musty rooms in the main building and annexe opposite, plus a restaurant serving on a river-view terrace in summer – among several *menus*, the €20 one is best value. A bit east, equidistant from upper and riverside quarters, lies the *Camping Errekaldia* (℡05.59.37.72.36).

# Through Labourd to the coast

Beyond Baïgorri and Bidarraï, travelling along the Nive by road or train, you enter **Labourd** (Lapurdi), the westernmost of the three traditional French Basque regions which are now gathered into the *département* of Pyrénées-

Atlantiques. The Basque farm- and town houses get more and more sumptuous as you approach the coast, and the soft, rolling hills maintain their electric-
green livery even in the summer.

The spa of **Cambo-les-Bains** is the biggest place between Saint-Jean-Pied-
de-Port and Bayonne; here also, with your own vehicle, you can forsake the
Bayonne-bound artery for the westerly D918, which passes through or near
such tourist-friendly villages as **Ezpeleta** and **Ainhoa** on its way to Saint-
Jean-de-Luz. A bus based in the latter town serves Ezpeleta several times daily
in summer.

## Itsasu and Laxia

The small, spread-out village of **ITSASU** (Itxassou), 11km northwest of
Bidarraï in a bowl of wooded hills, makes a good introduction to the region
and a great place to hide away (though only one daily train stops here). The
seventeenth-century **church of Saint Fructueux** (open daylight hours), 1km
south of the centre on the minor D349, retains a minority of ancient, keyhole-
shaped tombstones in its graveyard. Inside you'll find the typical French Basque
three-tiered galleries, constructed to deny the Devil mischievous opportunities
arising from the mingling of the sexes during Mass: the men sat upstairs, the
women down in the nave. With a two-euro coin, you can illuminate the sumptuous *retable*. Another kilometre southeast along this road, which runs parallel
to the rail line, the River Nive loops through a narrow defile at the **Pas de
Roland**, yet another element in the Roland legend. Merely a hole in a boulder above the river, it's claimed to have been punched out by the hooves of the
great knight's horse.

In terms of local **accommodation** and **eating**, don't bother with any of the
obvious central establishments – the best choices are either on the outskirts, or
in bucolic **LAXIA** hamlet a bit further down the road past the Pas de Roland
(Laxia can also be reached via a spur trail off the GR10 and Artzamendi peak
with its naval-air installation). The *Hôtel du Chêne* (☎05.59.29.75.01,
Ⓕ05.59.29.27.39; closed Jan, Feb & Mon, also Tues low season; ❷), opposite
Saint Fructueux, represents excellent value with its large, bright, well-kept
rooms with full baths; the restaurant is equally creditable, the €22 *menu* getting
you piperade, salad, rabbit and a simple dessert (decent own-cuvée wine extra).
At Laxia, the *Hôtel-Restaurant Teillerie* (☎05.59.29.75.39, Ⓕ05.59.29.254.99;
closed Nov 15–Jan & Mon; ❷) enjoys an amazing situation within sight and
sound of the river gorge, where meals (*menus* €12–23 include parsleyed eel or
cèpe omelette) can be taken on a wisteria-festooned terrace. Just about the
only other building in the hamlet is rival *Hôtel Pas de Roland* down the hill
(☎05.59.29.75.23; ❷), with a more basic restaurant and a *gîte* (❶) for hikers.

## Cambo-les-Bains

Ten minutes downstream by train from Itsasu, the spa of **CAMBO-LES-BAINS**
(Kambo) ranks as one of the largest towns in the Labourd region. An attractive
mixture of town and country, with plentiful shops, bars and hotels encircled by
richly rural landscape, it makes an appealing (if somewhat stuffy) place to break
the journey. Long a magnet for sufferers of respiratory ailments – though Isaac
Albéniz (p.171) came to live out his last years before dying of kidney failure
– the thermal establishment here is the focal point of the ornate houses and hotels
that radiate out along the heights above the Nive. The original town of **Bas
Cambo**, typically Basque with its square, whitewashed houses and galleried
church, lies down in the valley, right beside the river and train station.

The most famous resident was Edmond Rostand, author of *Cyrano de Bergerac*, who from 1903 to 1918 lived in the huge **Villa Arnaga**, a couple of kilometres west of Bas Cambo on the Bayonne road. Today the house is a museum (guided visits April–Sept daily 10am–12.30pm & 2.30–6.30pm; Oct 1–Nov 15 daily 2.30–6.30pm; Feb–March Sat & Sun only 2.30–6.30pm; €4.60), surrounded by a bizarre formal garden defined by reflecting pools, with patches of lawn punctuated by blobs, cubes and cones of topiary hedges, and the boundaries lined by limes and blue cedars. Inside, it's very kitsch, with a minstrels' gallery, fake pilasters, allegorical frescoes, chandeliers, numerous portraits and various memorabilia.

The **tourist office** is in a purpose-built structure next to the *mairie* (mid-July to Aug Mon–Sat 8.30am–noon & 2–6.30pm, Sun 10am–12.30pm; rest of year Mon–Sat till 5.30pm, closed Sun; ℡05.59.29.70.25, ℮Cambo.les.bains.tourisme@wanadoo.fr). For an overnight **stay**, try the *Auberge de Tante Ursule* (℡05.59.29.78.23, ℱ05.59.29.28.57; closed Feb 15–March 15 & Tues; ❷–❸), in Bas Cambo by the *pelota* court and almost the lone "non-*curiste*" establishment, but convenient only to the rail station. The rooms are in a modern annexe with parking, while the excellent **restaurant** in the red-and-white older building offers rich *menus* from €14, featuring sweetbreads, black pudding and the like. The nearest **campsite** is *Urhegia* on route des Sept-Chênes (℡05.59.29.72.03; March to mid-Dec), also in Bas Cambo; *Camping Bixta Eder* is on the other side of town on avenue d'Espagne (℡05.59.29.94.23; mid-April to mid-Oct).

## Ezpeleta

From Cambo it's a five-kilometre trip southwest on the D918 (occasional buses) to **EZPELETA** (Espelette), a substantial village of wide-eaved houses, with a church notable for its heavy, square tower, carved doors and painted ceiling. A new southerly bypass road has substantially quieted traffic on the main street. Large red pimentos are the principal crop here, and during summer and autumn the streets are garlanded with strings of colourful peppers, hanging in the sun to dry; on the last Sunday in October a special Mass is preceded by a Saturday-night party celebrating the various Basque culinary uses of the pepper. Ezpeleta is primarily an agricultural town, holding a regular Wednesday livestock and general market, and the major event of its social calendar is the annual January fair for trading **pottok** (pronounced *potiok*) ponies. An ancient, stocky breed of Paleolithic origin, apparently little changed from the horses depicted in prehistoric Pyrenean cave paintings, *pottoks* were once exported to work in British mines, but are now reared locally for both riding and meat.

The *Hôtel Euzkadi*, on the high street at the northeast edge of the village (℡05.59.93.91.88, ℱ05.59.93.90.19; ❸), with calmer rear rooms and tennis courts, also has what is reckoned among the best traditional **restaurants** in Labourd – reservations mandatory – and very reasonable for what you get, with *menus* at €17–28 (closed Mon all year, Tues in low season & Nov–Dec). The nearby *Hôtel Chilar* (℡05.59.93.90.01, ℱ05.59.93.93.25; ❷), set back slightly from the same road, has cheaper rooms, but its restaurant can't compare.

## West to Saint-Jean-de-Luz

The D918 curls west from Ezpeleta via Saint-Pée-sur-Nivelle (Senpere) en route to Saint-Jean, a 25-kilometre distance served occasionally by bus. You might, however, veer south along the D20 to Ainhoa, 8km from Ezpeleta and just 3km shy of the frontier at Dantxarinea.

## Ainhoa – and the end of the GR10

Yet another showcase village in a region not lacking in them, **AINHOA** gets understandably busy in season, when tourists fill its single street lined with substantial, mainly seventeenth-century houses, whose lintel plaques offer mini-genealogies as well as foundation dates. Take a look at the bulky-towered, two-galleried church with its extravagant Baroque altarpiece of prophets and apostles in niches, framed by Corinthian columns made of the same gilded wood.

There's no longer any budget **accommodation** per se, but Logis de France two-star *Hôtel Oppoca* (℡05.59.29.90.72, ℻05.59.29.81.03; closed Nov 15–Dec 15; ❷–❸) remains affordable, its restaurant (closed Sun pm & Mon) offering four *menus* (€15–35). *Hôtel Ohantzea* (℡05.59.29.90.50; ❸), also on the main street, offers less good value, though it too has an attractive back garden. If money's no object, then plump for the three-star *Hôtel Ithurria* (℡05.59.29.92.11, ⊛www.ithurria.com; ❼), a former coaching inn on the pilgrim route, with sauna, pool and gourmet restaurant. **Campers** should head for the basic *Camping Harazpy* (℡05.59.29.89.38; June–Sept) near the village centre. Alternatively, up on the frontier at otherwise dismal **Dantaxarinea** (Dantxaria) you'll find the small, shady, well-run *Camping Xokoan* (℡05.59.29.90.26).

Just over the frontier from the campsite stand several little **ventas**, relics of pre-EU times when these rough-and-ready Spanish-run inns, essentially the retail outlets of smugglers, did a roaring trade in the many items – mainly alcohol and canned goods – that were far cheaper in Spain than in France. Today, with price parity nearly attained for many items, they face an uncertain future.

If you've hiked west six hours from Bidarraï on the **GR10**, Ainhoa is a logical stop. From here towards the Atlantic, the GR meanders over to Sara within three-and-a-half hours, next brings you to the base of La Rhune (see p.532 for both) and finally reaches civilization again at Biriatu, an impossible walking day of nearly eleven hours. Thus it's best to halt six hours from Ainhoa at the isolated *gîte d'étape* at **Olhette** hamlet, *Manttu Baïta* (℡05.59.54.00.98; 14 places). Only purists do the final, urbanized stretch through to Hendaye; for detailed reverse walking directions to La Rhune, see p.536.

# The Basque coast

For a region with such a long maritime tradition, the **Basque coast** – *Côte Basque* in French, *Costa Vasca* in Castilian – is surprisingly short and devoid of good natural harbours. It's scarcely more than 120km from the mouth of the River Adour, separating Bayonne and Biarritz from the dunes of the Landes on the north, to the Cantabrian border just past Bilbao in the west. Of that just 50km – between Bayonne and San Sebastián – can be considered to be Pyrenean shoreline, and only at the mouths of the rivers Nivelle, Bidasoa and Oiartzun is there evidence of past Basque prowess in whaling, navigating and piracy.

The all-enveloping carpet of green vegetation, so unlike the Mediterranean coast, reflects a damp, often misty climate, without sharp differences between winter and summer temperatures. Yet the sun does shine, just enough in season

## Basque sports

The Basque sport of **pelota** (*pelote* in France) is played – and keenly wagered on – all over Spanish Euskadi and the French Pays Basque. Even the smallest village has a *frontón* or *trinquet* (court), and indeed these are found well east into Aragón and Béarn where the sport has also caught on. Over twenty different versions of the game are known throughout the Basque country, including the most famous and spectacular, *cesta punta*, played in a covered court called *jaï alaï* (now widely confused with the name of the game itself). In essence it resembles a high-risk version of squash, the players smashing the ball against the *frontón* either with bare hands or encased in the merest of leather gloves (the *pasaka*), and with a wooden bat (*pala*) or a *chistera*, a narrow wicker-work "claw" that extends the player's forearm. The largest *chisteras* launch the ball at speeds of around 200km an hour, making *pelota* one of the most dangerous games in the world. The *pelotas* themselves are balls of fibre wound tightly around a rubber core, encased in two layers of leather; tedious to make and thus only made to order, they are phenomenally expensive and sensitive to extremes of temperature and humidity.

Other unique Basque sports include *palankaris* (tossing an iron bar), *aizkolaritza* (log-chopping), *harri-jasotzea* (stone-lifting), *soka-tira* (tug-of-war) and *segalaritza* (grass-cutting). The finest exponents of the first three are popular local, sometimes international, heroes. The world champion stone-lifter Iñaki Perurena's visit to Japan resulted in the sport being introduced there – he remains the only lifter to surpass the legendary 315-kilo barrier. All form an important part of the many local *fiestas*.

to attract hordes of holidaymakers, and if you've been up in the hills for any length of time, the sea comes as a very welcome sight. Unfortunately it is often just for looking: frequently dangerous and wave-lashed – to the delight of wet-suited surfers, and ensuring steady employment for lifeguards – and sometimes murky.

This last detail is regrettable, since otherwise the Basque coast has all the ingredients for a perfect vacation: excellent food and drink, seductive scenery, characterful architecture and a handful of not-too-demanding inland side-trips to **Azkaine**, **La Rhune** and **Sara**. The two defining cities of **Bayonne** and **San Sebastián** are the biggest attractions, though the small ports of **Pasaia** and **Saint-Jean-de-Luz**, the historic border town of **Hondarribia** and the period-piece resort of **Biarritz** also have considerable appeal.

# Bayonne

Although contiguous with the fashionable resort of Biarritz (see p.524), the inland, beachless position of **BAYONNE** (Baïona) protected it until the mid-1990s from significant touristic exploitation – which for many makes it a more interesting place to visit. Built astride the confluence of the rivers Adour (navigable) and Nive (less so), 6km from the sea and roughly 60km down the Nive from Saint-Jean, the city has long served as an important commercial port, its future guaranteed by some determined engineering works in 1578 to fix the wandering mouth of the Adour. This followed on from Grand Bayonne's substantial fortification in 1523, to ward off the Spanish. Bayonne is both a Gascon city and the capital of the Pays Basque, and street signage is now trilingual – the third language being Gascon. However, tall, white older houses, their shutters and beams picked out in the distinctive brownish-reds and greens of the Basques, betray the major influence.

The place was founded by the Romans as the garrison town of Lapurdum. The name, corrupted to Lapurdi (Euskera) and Labourd (French), was later extended to signify the entire westernmost French Basque province; the current Euskera-derived name – Bayonne/Baïona – means "good river". For three centuries until 1451, it enjoyed prosperity and relative peace under English domination, until falling to the French in the course of the Hundred Years' War. Some fifty years later, Sephardic Jews fleeing the Iberian Inquisitions arrived, bringing their knowledge of chocolate manufacturing. The city's heyday came during the eighteenth century, based on the dubious underpinnings of armaments manufacture (the word *bayonet* derives from the place) and a judicious amount of piracy. After the French Revolution, it lost considerable prestige when centralizing zealots in the Parisian regime merged the three traditional French Basque regions into the single modern *département* of Pyrénées-Atlantiques, governed from Pau.

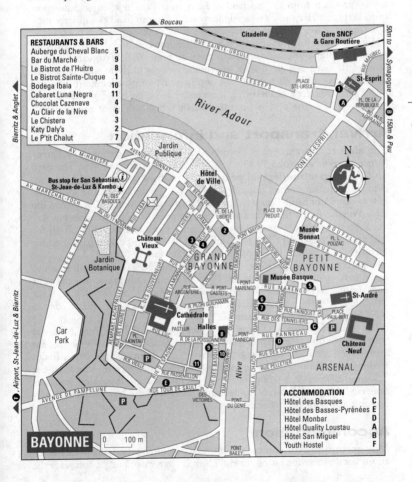

RESTAURANTS & BARS
| | |
|---|---|
| Auberge du Cheval Blanc | 5 |
| Bar du Marché | 9 |
| Le Bistrot de l'Huitre | 8 |
| Le Bistrot Sainte-Cluque | 1 |
| Bodega Ibaia | 10 |
| Cabaret Luna Negra | 11 |
| Chocolat Cazenave | 4 |
| Au Clair de la Nive | 6 |
| Le Chistera | 3 |
| Katy Daly's | 2 |
| Le P'tit Chalut | 7 |

ACCOMMODATION
| | |
|---|---|
| Hôtel des Basques | C |
| Hôtel des Basses-Pyrénées | E |
| Hôtel Monbar | D |
| Hôtel Quality Loustau | A |
| Hôtel San Miguel | B |
| Youth Hostel | F |

BAYONNE

0    100 m

Just as Perpignan became a refuge for Catalans who opposed Franco, so did Bayonne for the Spanish Basques, seeking refuge among their own. For decades the Petit Bayonne quarter was a haven for Basque nationalists (especially ETA fugitives), until a late 1980s clampdown by Parisian authorities. Wall posters and murals in the neighbourhood still demand freedom for imprisoned ETA members, or failing that, confinement within the Basque country – an accounting by the powers that be of those supposedly "disappeared" – and urge *insumisoa* (disobedience) in the face of new repressive measures by the French or Spanish governments.

Economically there are also parallels between Bayonne and Perpignan, as both hope to gain from the single European market, sitting as they do beside increasingly busy truck and train routes between Portugal, northern Spain and Western Europe. Bayonne needs the business, for although the aerospace industry is a big employer and electronics companies are growing in number, this area still has unemployment above the French average. Traditional footwear and clothing industries have declined severely, as have the chemical plants processing by-products from the gas field at Lacq, near Pau. In a major distinction from Perpignan, Bayonne's riverside harbour at Boucau handles a quarter-million tonnes of freight annually, making it the ninth busiest French port.

None of this is likely to affect you as a visitor, however, and despite a growing amount of tourist-oriented tattiness in the shop fronts, initial favourable impressions of Bayonne as a small-scale, easy-going city are likely to stick. Wherever you're headed you're likely to at least stop in, as it's a major transport hub; you might even consider it as a relatively inexpensive and quiet base for a seaside holiday, except of course during the festival season when beds are at a premium.

## Arrival, transport and information

The **airport**, Biarritz-Anglet-Bayonne/BAB, lies 6km southwest at Parme (general airport info ☎05.59.43.83.83; #6 or 'C' bus from/to town). The **gare SNCF** and **gare routière** for points in Béarn, Basse-Navarre and Soule are next door to each other, just off place de la République in the somewhat frowzy district of Saint-Esprit on the north bank of the Adour, 700m across the wide Pont St-Esprit from the city centre. There is, however, another bus terminal on the place des Basques on the Adour's south bank, used by STAB for Biarritz and Anglet, ATCRB to Cambo and Saint-Jean-de-Luz (changing for Hendaye) and Spanish PESA coaches to San Sebastián.

If you arrive by car, **parking** – either free or metred – is easiest just south of town, around rue Tour-du-Salt and Pont du Genie. Otherwise, you can **rent cars** from several booths at the airport, or from Continental Car Rent (☎05.59.50.09.09, ✉bayonne@continentalrent.com), 20 place de la République, a small French chain.

The **tourist office** is also in place des Basques (July & Aug Mon–Sat 9am–7pm, Sun 10am–1pm; rest of year Mon–Fri 9am–6.30pm, Sat 10am–6pm; ☎05.59.46.01.46, ⓦwww.bayonne-tourisme.com), with a booth at the train station and the airport in summer only (July & Aug Mon–Sat 9.30am–12.30pm & 2–6.30pm). They're useful for accommodation information, city plans and details of guided tours, such as to the Izarra liqueur distillery on Quai Bergeret in Saint-Esprit.

## Accommodation

Most **accommodation** lies south of the Adour, often with wide price fluctuations within the same establishment. The most agreeable budget hotels are the spartan but adequate *Hôtel des Basques*, on the corner of place Paul-Bert and rue des Lisses (℡05.59.59.08.02 or 06.88.54.40.29; ❶); the en-suite, well-run *Hôtel Monbar*, at 24 rue Pannecau in Petit Bayonne (℡05.59.59.26.80; ❷), its rooms all furnished with large beds, though a few with windows opening onto a stairwell; and the *Hôtel San Miguel* at 8 rue Sainte-Catherine in Saint-Esprit (℡05.59.55.17.82; ❷), handy for the train station and with a ground-floor restaurant. More comfortable alternatives include the slightly overpriced, not wildly welcoming *Hôtel des Basses-Pyrénées* at 14 rue Tour-de-Sault (℡05.59.59.00.29, ✉hotel.basses.pyrenees@wanadoo.fr; ❷–❸; closed Jan), a well-converted medieval building (quieter rooms overlook the rear place des Victoires) with nearby street parking just possible; and the top-end, sound-proofed, river-view *Hôtel Quality Loustau*, on place de la République (℡05.59.55.08.08, ℻05.59.55.69.36; ❺ but frequent weekend/businessmen's specials), overlooking the river beside Pont St-Esprit; both these have afford-able attached restaurants (*menus* from under €16).

Another possibility is the **youth hostel** at 19 route des Vignes in Anglet (see p.529), between Bayonne and Biarritz; take STAB bus #4 from the Hôtel de Ville, direction "Biarritz-Mairie", which stops right outside. The only **camp-site** nearby is relatively luxurious *Airotel la Chêneraie* (℡05.59.55.01.31; April–Sept), off the N117 Pau road close to the Bayonne-Nord exit from the autoroute, and also on the #4 bus route; take direction "Sainsontan" and get off at Navarre, from where the campsite is a 500-metre walk.

## The City

Bayonne is more a *flâneur's* town than one offering great sights, though it does have a handful of diversions scattered throughout the three central quarters. You'll spend most of your time south of the Adour, in the quarters of **Grand Bayonne** (in turn on the west bank of the Nive tributary) or **Petit Bayonne** (on the east bank), both still encircled by Vauban's defences. The less monu-mentally compelling neighbourhood of **Saint-Esprit** spreads out on the Adour's north bank, long home to immigrants of every description.

### Grand Bayonne

The twin-towered **Cathédrale Sainte-Marie** (Mon–Sat 10–11.45am & 3–5.45pm, Sun 3.30–5.45pm) on magnolia-shaded place Pasteur at the sum-mit of **Grand Bayonne**, looks best from a distance, with its steeple rising with airy grace above the houses. Up close, the yellowish stone reveals bad weath-ering, with most of the decorative detail lost to post-Revolutionary vandalism as well. The interior is more impressive, thanks to the height of the nave and some sixteenth-century glass (restored in 2002) set off by the prevailing gloom. Like other southern French Gothic cathedrals of the period (about 1260) it was based on more famous northern models, in this case Soissons and Reims. On the south side is a fourteenth-century **cloister** (daily: May–Sept 9am–12.30pm & 2–6pm; Oct–April 9.30am–12.30pm & 2–5pm; free) with a lawn in the middle: a quiet, secretive spot affording a rather flattering view of the church.

From place Pasteur, rue de la Monnaie and its continuation rue du Port-Neuf lead downhill to the main **place de la Liberté**, where historic *Café du Théâtre* is the last survivor of many *pâtisseries* and *confiseries* which have vanished from the now traffic-plagued, uncongenial square. Chocolate is *the* Bayonne special-ity, on a par with its famous air-cured hams; most of it is still made in the Saint-Esprit quarter, but the prestigious retail outlets are Cazenave and Daranatz, arcade shops at nos. 19 and 15 respectively in **rue du Port-Neuf**. South and west of the cathedral, along rue des Faures and the streets above the old walls, and **rue d'Espagne**, the old commercial centre, there's a distinctly Spanish feel, with washing strung at the windows and strains of music drifting from dark interiors.

The **Jardin Botanique** (daily April 15–Oct 15 9am–noon & 2–6; free) lies just west of the Château Vieux, near the end of the sixteenth-century ramparts – a well-designed, enormous garden with plants labelled in French, Euskera and Latin.

## The Nive Quais and Petit Bayonne

East of the cathedral, the **Nive Quais** are a lively, picturesque and authentic part of town; the *halles* on the Grand Bayonne side host a comprehensive market on Tuesdays, Wednesdays and Saturdays. On the right bank, tall, sixteenth-century houses are reflected appealingly in the placid Nive; one of these, near the end of Pont Marengo, contains the excellent Basque ethnographic museum, the **Musée Basque** (ⓦwww.musee-basque.com; May–Oct Tues–Sun 10am–6.30pm; Nov–April Tues–Sun 10am–12.30pm & 2–6pm; €5.50, or €9 joint ticket with Musée Bonnat), finally reopened in 2002 after a thirteen-year "restoration" (really an arcane political dispute). Several floors of ethnographic and historical exhibits on Basque life through the ages are exhausting as much as exhaustive, with labelling in French, Castilian and Euskera only. Highlights include (on the second floor) collections of eighteenth-century faience pottery and medlar wood *makilak* – innocent-looking walking sticks, often elaborately carved from medlar wood, but with a concealed steel spear tip at one end, used by pilgrims and shepherds for self-protection. Agricultural artefacts include a solid-wheeled oxcart, wooden ploughs plus a roller to tamp down the field afterwards, and wine presses. The seafaring room features a superb rudder-handle carved as a sea-monster, a wooden-hulled fishing boat, plus a model of Bayonne's naval shipyards ca. 1805; Columbus's skipper was Basque, and another Basque, Juan Sebastián de Elkano, completed the first circumnavigation of the world in 1522.

The painting collection of Bayonne's second museum, the **Musée Bonnat**, at 5 rue Jacques-Laffitte (ⓦwww.musee-bonnat.com; daily except Tues & hols: May–Oct 10am–6.30pm; Nov–April 10am–12.30pm & 2–6pm; €5.50, or €9 joint ticket with Musée Basque), provides welcome variation from the usual dross of provincial galleries. Thirteenth- and fourteenth-century Italian art is well represented, as are most periods up to (but not including) Impressionism; highlights include Goya's *Self-Portrait* and *Portrait of Don Francisco de Borja*, Rubens' powerful *Apollo and Daphne* and *The Triumph of Venus*, plus works by Murillo, El Greco and Ingres. A whole gallery is devoted to high-society portraits by Léon Bonnat (1833–1922), whose personal collection formed the original core of the museum. There are also frequent temporary exhibits of the work of prominent artists in an annexe at 9 rue Frédéric-Bastiat (same days, 2–6pm), well worth catching.

## North of the river: Saint-Esprit

Apart from savouring the wide river skies, there is little reason to venture onto the north bank of the Adour. A deliberately inconspicuous, early nineteenth-century **synagogue** at 33 rue Maubec serves as a reminder that Bayonne's Jewish community first settled here in France on arrival from Spain and Portugal during the sixteenth century. Saint-Esprit in effect became their ghetto, since Grand Bayonne was consecrated to the Virgin and off-limits for residence by nonbelievers. The **church of Saint-Esprit**, opposite the train station, is all that remains of a hostel that once ministered to the sore feet and other ailments of pilgrims on the Chemin de Saint-Jacques – worth a peek inside for a fifteenth-century wood sculpture of *The Flight into Egypt*, showing Nôtre-Dame-des-Voyageurs (appropriately, given the nearby train station) seated in voluminous robes on a donkey, holding the Child. Just above the station is Vauban's massive **citadelle**; built in 1680 to defend the town against Spanish attack, it actually saw little action until the Napoleonic wars, when its garrison resisted a siege by Wellington for four months in 1813 (though it fell the next year).

## Eating, drinking and entertainment

The best area for **eating and drinking** is along the right-bank (Petit Bayonne) quay of the Nive and in the back streets to either side of the river. Besides the listings below, you'll find other possibilities of varying quality in Petit Bayonne, especially along rue Pannecau, rue des Cordeliers and rue des Tonneliers. For non-European food such as South American, Turkish, Indian, Tunisian or Chinese, try rue d'Espagne and rue Gosse in Grand Bayonne, or rue Sainte-Catherine in Saint Esprit.

As far as **festivals** go, Bayonne's biggest bash of the year is the *Fêtes de Bayonne*, which starts on either the last Wednesday of July or the first Wednesday in August, encompassing five days and nights of continuous, boozy street parties and entertainment. This finishes with a *corrida* on the following Sunday, and there are three or four more days of bullfighting beginning on August 15. The *Jazz aux Remparts* festival held in mid-July (typically five days of the third week) has run consistently since 1990, and every October there is a Franco-Spanish theatre festival.

If you hear Spanish, French or Basque sounds you'd like to take home, Bayonne has several sizeable **record shops**, including a Virgin Megastore off rue Port-Castets, and Harmonia Mundi at 5 rue du Port-Neuf. There are two **cinemas**: Le Vauban on the corner of allées Paulmy and rue Vauban, and L'Atalante at 7 rue Denis Etcheverry, with "art" fare and v.o. screenings.

Besides *pelota*, **rugby** is the sport that commands the greatest loyalty in Bayonne, and the town's top-class rugby team has produced many members of the national squad. You might catch a view of them in action by following the Vauban fortifications to the Parc des Sports south of Grand Bayonne, where the solid walls act as grandstands.

### Restaurants

**Auberge du Cheval Blanc** 68 rue Bourg-Neuf, Petit Bayonne ☏05.59.59.01.33. Decadent desserts a speciality at this durable gourmets' mecca (it's had Michelin stars in the past); for all that, affordable €23 and €32 weekday lunch *menus*, though you can easily spend €70 and up. Reservations suggested. Closed Mon except Aug, Sun eve all year round, Feb school hols, variable weeks in July & Aug.

**Le Bistrot de l'Huître** corner of *halles* building, facing Pont Pannecau. Mainly Quiberon and Marrennes oysters, washed down with Jurançon or Irouléguy wine. Closed Sun pm & all Mon.

**Le Bistrot Sainte-Cluque** 9 rue Hughes, St-Esprit ☏05.59.55.82.43. Very upmarket for a slightly shabby area, and the one culinary bright spot

across the Adour. Thus both indoors and terrace are perennially packed for the sake of very creative Franco-international cuisine, excellent value whether as three-course *menu* (€10 at lunch or more wide-ranging €15 one at supper, plus drink) or *à la carte* (€27 for the works). Reservations for more than two required. Open daily except Mon Oct–July.

**Le Chistera** 42 rue Port-Neuf. *Pelota* decor, as you'd expect with the proprietor, a player in his own right, being the son of a *cesta-punta* champion and trainer. Hearty *bayonnais* specialties based on fish, pork and tripe best ordered off the daily-specials board; budget €14 for the *menu* or €17–22 *à la carte*. Closed Mon, 2 weeks in May & Tues/Wed eves in winter.

**Au Clair de la Nive** 28 quai Galuperie, Petit

Bayonne. Indoor or outdoor seating on a riverside terrace; €16 *menu*, or more interestingly choose two or three courses *à la carte* (€19–31, pricey drink extra). *Cuisine* – roast anchovies, steamed cod in pepper sauce, delicate desserts – is *minceur* but tasty. Closed Mon noon & Sun.

**Le P'tit Chalut** 24 quai Galuperie. Not as upmarket as its neighbour across the street, but a decent venue for seafood under the arcades; two lunch *menus* for under €16.

### Bars and cafés

**Bar du Marché** 39 rue des Basques. This begins purveying food and drink at 5am to a mix of market sellers and bar-flies on their way home to bed, continuing with economical *plats du jour* at lunchtime. You can eat very well for €17, plus drink, though there's not much seafood. Closed Sat pm & Sun.

**Bodega Ibaia** 49 quai Jauréguiberry. Lively, well-loved bar, reputedly Bayonne's favourite, with a mixed crowd and *plats du jour* for under €8 at midday. One of several similar here, if you can't squeeze in.

**Cabaret Luna Negra** 7 rue des Augustins, but main entrance on rue Gosse ⊛lunanegra.free.fr. More venue than bar, really, with musical events, cabaret, mime, theatre. Open Wed–Sat 7pm–2am, closed Aug.

**Chocolat Cazenave** 19 rue du Port-Neuf. Drink a hot cup of local cocoa under the arcades, or inside in the back; also every conceivable chocolate goodie to take home.

**Katy Daly's** 3 place de la Liberté. Passably authentic Irish theme pub, with live music Tues, Fri & Sat, Guinness on tap, major sporting matches on a wide screen. Open nightly.

# Biarritz

**BIARRITZ** (Miarritze), 8km west of Bayonne, makes no secret of its identity as an Atlantic answer to Monte Carlo, and thus a resort that expects a little refinement from its guests. Much of this hotch-potch of giant ocean-liner-style hotels and mock-Gothic châteaux wears a bygone air that appeals to more traditional middle-class visitors, while the town's newer neighbourhoods attract a younger, variably prosperous market.

Biarritz burst into prominence during the mid-nineteenth century when the Spanish-born Empress Eugénie, wife of Napoléon III – whom she met here – brought the entire entourage of the Second Empire to what had been the favourite seaside watering-hole of her childhood. Others soon followed, including Edward VII, who virtually held a second court here, nominating Asquith as prime minister in Biarritz in 1908. After World War I had destroyed the existing European social order, high fashion moguls like Hermès and Lanvin, film stars like Douglas Fairbanks and Gloria Swanson and various other glitterati replaced the crowned heads and nobility.

Following the next global convulsion, and the rise of the Côte d'Azur during the 1960s, Biarritz went into seemingly terminal decline not unlike that of certain resorts on England's Kent or Devon coast. But since the late 1980s, events have conspired to divert the place from crash-landing on the dust-heap of touristic history. Initially the recovery was slow, spurred by the town's embrace of less elitist pursuits like golf, conferences and even a small cinema festival – but the biggest shot in the arm was Biarritz's transformation into **Europe's biggest surfing mecca**. That began in 1957, when American screenwriter Pieter Viertel, here for the filming of *The Sun Also Rises*, took to the waves with a board and inspired a group of locals to join him. You still can see many of these white-haired old-timers – *Les Tontons Surfeurs* or "Surf Uncles" as they call themselves – bobbing in the waves with kids their grandsons' age. This international surf-bum fraternity, and more sedentary Parisian yuppies, together fuel a respectable nightlife, existing fairly harmoniously with a population that's one-third retirees. Against all the odds, Biarritz is undeniably chic and trendy once more, new money (or no money) rubbing shoulders with old, and without any Côte d'Azur pretensions.

## Arrival, information and transport

The **tourist office** occupies a Belle Époque structure abutting the square d'Ixelles (daily: July & Aug 8am–8pm; rest of year Mon–Sat 9am–6.45pm, Sun 10am–5pm; ☎05.59.22.37.00, ⓦwww.biarritz.fr).This has information in particular about the various festivals, as well as Internet access.The **gare SNCF** (☎05.59.23.15.69) lies an inconvenient 3km southeast at the end of avenue Foch/avenue Kennedy in the *quartier* known as La Négresse (STAB bus #2 or #9 from square d'Ixelles). Other STAB **buses** from Bayonne and Anglet also stop on the square, near the tourist office, while TPR (from/to Pau) and ATCRB (from/to Saint-Jean-de-Luz and Hendaye) use stops on the south side of the square, as do PESA trans-border services. **Scooters** can be rented from Sobilo (☎05.59.24.94.47). Arriving with your own car, you'll find **parking** mayhem year-round.The best strategies are to opt for a €9, one-week ticket (valid near the Port-Vieux), strike out into the uncontrolled streets just south of the centre (eg avenue Carnot) or resign yourself to forking out for the *parkings couverts*.

## Accommodation

Contrary to expectations, there are a handful of affordable **hotels** in town, though for July or August advance reservations are mandatory. **Campers** should try *Biarritz Camping*, at 28 route d'Harcet, the inland continuation of avenue de la Plage (☎05.59.23.00.12; mid-May to mid-Oct), behind Plage de la Milady, to the south of town. The nearest official **youth hostel** (☎05.59.41.76.00; 96 places; closed Christmas–New Year's Day) is 2km southwest of the centre at 8 rue Chiquito de Cambo, on the shore of Lac Mouriscot, just walkable from the gare SNCF; otherwise get #2 bus from the centre and look out for the "Bois de Boulogne" stop.

**Hôtel Atalaye** 6 rue des Goëlands ☎05.59.24.06.76, ⓕ05.59.22.33.51. A bit funky but serviceable and all en-suite, this is better value and quieter than most of its nearby rivals on rue Port–Vieux. The best rooms (including a few tiny singles) have equally small balconies and face the place and sea obliquely. Some parking available on said square, though the management could be jollier. ❸

**Hôtel Le Baron de Biarritz** 13 av Maréchal-Joffre ☎05.59.22.08.22, ⓕ05.59.22.14.65. One-star, Vietnamese-family-run outfit, offering gracious service and all rooms with at least a shower; street parking conceivable. Attached to a Chinese-Vietnamese restaurant (closed Mon) which can get lively at weekends with seemingly the entire Vietnamese population of this coast. ❷

**Hôtel Beaulieu** 3 esplanade du Port Vieux ☎05.59.24.23.59, ⓕ05.59.24.93.69. Unbeatable location, with about half the modern, en-suite rooms overlooking said *port*. Closed Christmas–Feb. ❸

**Hôtel Gardénia** 19 av Carnot ☎05.59.24.10.46, ⓦwww.hotel-gardenia.com. Mix of rooms, some with plumbing down the hall, in this old-fashioned but quiet and well-cared-for two-star. Free street parking. Closed mid-Nov & mid Jan. ❸

**Hôtel Maïtagaria** 34 av Carnot ☎05.59.24.26.65, ⓦwww.hotel-maitagaria.com. Rooms, being updated in stages, are already mostly smart and non-fusty; quiet location near a landscaped square, pleasant back garden and indoor lounges, fair bit of metered and free parking nearby. ❸–❹

**Hôtel Palym** 7 rue du Port-Vieux ☎05.59.24.16.56, ⓕ05.59.24.96.12. A welcoming place offering a variety of rooms, with not a right angle remaining in the building. The hot water sometimes runs out on summer evenings, though. Ground-floor bar-restaurant. ❷–❸

**Hôtel Rocher de la Vierge** 13 rue du Port-Vieux ☎05.59.24.11.74. Salubrious budget digs, as close to the sea as you'll find in this category. ❷–❸

**Hôtel Restaurant au St-James** 15 rue Gambetta

**CENTRAL BIARRITZ**

| ACCOMMODATION | |
|---|---|
| Atalaye | C |
| Le Baron de Biarritz | I |
| Beaulieu | E |
| Gardénia | G |
| Maïtagaria | H |
| Palym | B |
| Rocher de la Vierge | D |
| St-James | F |
| Victoria | A |
| Youth Hostel | J |

| RESTAURANTS | |
|---|---|
| Bains du Minuit | 3 |
| Bar Jean | 7 |
| Bistrot des Halles | 9 |
| Blue Cargo | 12 |
| Cayo Coco | 5 |
| Le Clos Basque | 1 |
| Le Saint Amour | 8 |
| Saon de Thé Orangerie | 2 |
| Santa Maria | 6 |
| Le Surfing | 11 |
| Ventilo Café | 4 |
| Vivier des Halles | 10 |

ATLANTIC OCEAN

Plage Miramar

Grande Plage

Villa Eugénie

Casino Municipal

Casino Bellevue

STAB

ATCRB

Hôtel de Ville

Musée de la Mer

Port dês Pecheurs

Plage du Port-Vieux

Musée du Vieux Biarritz

Les Halles

Musée d'Art Oriental

Plage de la Côte de Basque

N

0    100m

Airport

THE WESTERN PYRENEES | Biarritz

---

℡05.59.24.06.36, ℻05.59.24.87.25. Dead central if potentially noisy, well appointed and with a good restaurant. ❸–❹

**Hostellerie Victoria** 12 av de la Reine Victoria ℡05.59.24.08.21. Worth a mild splurge for the unbeatable location two blocks in from the Grande Plage, private parking and often huge rooms in this Neo-Gothic mansion, with comfortable beds, iron bathtubs and the odd chandelier. ❹–❻

## The Town

Most specific attractions are strung out along the landscaped, clifftop terraces just inland from the promontories and coves around which Biarritz grew. The focus of town is the Art Deco **Casino Municipal**, just behind the Grande Plage, now restored as an exhibit and conference venue. Inland, the town forms a suprisingly ordinary and workaday sprawl, with the sole points of interest being the **Musée d'Art Oriental/Asiatica** on 1 rue Guy-Petit (Mon–Sat 10.30am–6.30pm, Sun 2–7pm; €7), exhibiting the collection of Indian and

Tibetan art specialist Michel Postel, and the **Musée du Vieux Biarritz**, installed in a disused Anglican church on rue Broquedis (Tues–Sat 10am–noon & 2.30–6pm; €3), displaying knick-knacks and documents relating to Belle Époque royalty.

Like several spots on the coast hereabouts, Biarritz started life as a whaling centre, a local industry which collapsed late in the eighteenth century, and whose only remnants are a whale-spotting tower near place de l'Atalaye and some memorabilia in the **Musée de la Mer** (daily: July & Aug 9.30am–midnight; rest of year 9.30am–12.30pm & 2–6pm; €7), which sits atop the claw-shaped promontory west of town. Along with exhibitions on local fishing and wildlife, this offers a small aquarium and seal-frolicking section as well, making it – if not exactly a must – at least a good place to take the kids. The promontory ends in the **Rocher de la Vierge**, an offshore rock adorned with a white statue of the Virgin, and linked to the mainland by an iron catwalk built by Eiffel, he of the tower. Around it are scattered other rocky islets where the swell heaves and combs; the scenery figured largely in Eric Rohmer's wonderful film *Le Rayon Vert*. This spot seems irresistible to lovers, the seaward view always obscured by pairs of backs and interlocking arms apparently in thrall to the ocean. Just below is the picturesque **Port des Pêcheurs**, easiest approached by pedestrian lanes zigzagging down through banks of pink and blue hydrangeas. The professional fishermen have now gone, replaced by pleasure boats, but there's a scuba outfitter here and a clutch of pricey seafood restaurants.

The only inland **streets and squares** really conducive to relaxed strolling are those between the Musée de la Mer and the place Sainte-Eugénie. Both that square and the place de l'Atalaye, high above the Port des Pêcheurs, can muster a number of whimsically **turreted and balconied hotels and villas**. In recent years, any number of these have fallen to the wrecker's ball, but in 1997, under threat of a fifty-acre development proposed to replace the Casino Municipal by Gaullist councillors, the rest of the council stood down, forcing the resignation of the mayor. He was replaced by a centrist acceptable to conservationists, who immediately slapped a preservation order on the town's surviving 230 follies, not coincidentally guaranteeing work for restoration architects and maintenance men over the next generation.

Downhill and south from place Atalaye, you can stroll the length of the characterful if now touristified **rue du Port-Vieux**, which links its namesake beach (see below) with rue Mazagran. At the junction of the latter with the far west end of **place Clemenceau**, one of several central squares, you can nibble a cake or sip a lemon tea at *Miremont's Salon de Thé* – a prissy and frightfully superior place epitomizing old-money Biarritz.

## The beaches

The wave-pounded **beaches** either side of the promontory are generously sandy and, according to the fickle weather, either carpeted with a mix of beautiful people and middle-class families tanning themselves cheek by jowl, or abandoned to wet-suited surf fanatics of all descriptions. Served by STAB buses #4, #6 or #9 from Biarritz centre, the strands extend about 5km from the southernmost **Plage de la Milady** to **Pointe Saint-Martin** in the north. The southerly sections, set apart from one another by smaller headlands, are **Plage Marbella**; **Côte des Basques**, focus of the annual surf championships; and **Plage du Port-Vieux**, the most sheltered and intimate of the beaches, tucked in the lee of the Rocher de la Vierge.

But most of the action takes place along the contiguous Grande Plage and

Plage Miramar, sweeping northeast from the Port des Pêcheurs. An immaculate sweep of sand, the **Grande Plage** was originally dubbed the "Plage des Fous" after the 1850s practice of taking lunatics to bathe here as a primitive form of thalassotherapy. Picasso later used it as the setting for his *Les Baigneuses*; today it's a highly regimented playground, with separate sections for surfers and bathers, and lifeguards tweeting their whistles or paddling out into the water to shoo people out of several danger zones. The **Plage Miramar** just beyond is shadowed by the domes of a Russian Orthodox church dating from 1908, and also overlooked by the former **Villa Eugénie**, a present of Napoléon III to his wife in 1855. Now the luxury *Hôtel du Palais*, it was gutted by fire in 1881 and 1905, so that little remains of the original fabric. Beyond Pointe Saint-Martin and its landmark **lighthouse** (April 15–June Sat & Sun 3–7pm; July & Aug Tues–Sat 10am–noon & 2–7pm; €1.50), built in 1834, begin the even wilder, broader beaches of Anglet (see below).

## Eating and drinking

Finding a reasonable place to **eat** is trickier than finding somewhere to stay, but there are some possibilities near the market *halles*, and it's easy to eat well for a price, away from the touristy snack bars on rue du Port-Vieux – and for once in France, until 11pm or so in summer.

**Les Bains du Minuit** Plage du Port-Vieux ☏05.59.24.21.22. Art Deco beach pavilion under energetic new management since 2002; the fare's a mix of nouvelle seafood and heartier French classics. Other than a €21 lunch *menu*, it's pricey, but you are paying for one of the most spectacular views in town.

**Bistrot des Halles** 1 rue du Centre ☏05.59.24.21.22. Within sight of the *halles*, this is strong on generously portioned, tasty fish dishes, but count on €31 a head plus service, and a stiffly priced wine list. Reservations essential.

**Blue Cargo** With transport, there's currently no hotter (summer-only) spot, just south of the city limits on the Plage d'Ilbarritz ☏05.59.23.54.87. Here the beau monde downs mostly fish and salads on the terrace by an old villa, while the lower tent-bar gets going as a jam-packed dance club after midnight. Count on €28 à la carte, plus drink. Reserve in advance.

**Cayo Coco** 5 rue Jaulerry. Cuban theme bar with free salsa dance lessons.

**Le Clos Basque** 12 rue Louis-Barthou ☏05.59.24.24.96. A genuine bistrot tucked back slightly from the street, this does three meaty, hearty traditional French courses for €22.50 – and is accordingly packed out at supper (less so at lunch). Reservations suggested. Closed Sun eve & Mon.

**Bar Jean** 5 rue des Halles. Popular, long-running bullfighting-theme spot with tapas at the bar from €10, full sit-down meals €25–30 à la carte.

**Le Saint Amour** 26 rue Gambetta ☏05.59.24.19.64. Lyonnais-style bistrot where a pleasant environment offsets rather startling à la carte prices (€33) for three average courses; beer on tap, or a *pot* of wine also helps, plus there are cheaper lunch *menus*. Large parties should book the quieter room in back. Closed Sun & Mon low season.

**Salon de Thé L'Orangerie** 1 rue Gambetta. Whether you've slept the night before or not, this makes the best start for the day, serving all sorts of hot drinks (including 34 kinds of tea, novelty coffees) and a great variety of breakfasts.

**Santa Maria** You can tipple from the afternoon into the small hours at this little beach bar overlooking the Plage du Port-Vieux. Summer only.

**Le Surfing** California-style diner-cum-pilgrimage-site for surfers, behind Plage de Côte des Basques, and run by Robert Rabagny, organizer of the annual Surf Festival. As much shrine-museum, festooned with antique boards, as purveyor of grills and *frites*; more seafood in winter, €23 *menu*.

**Ventilo Caffe** rue du Port-Vieux. Nothing special to look at, but the haunt of Parisian thirtysomethings for the district. Open all year.

**Le Vivier des Halles** 8 rue du Centre. The *vivier* is the fish-tank in the middle with your potential dinner in it – seafood and nothing but. À la carte will run to €28–31, but the €24.50 *menu de la mer* (pricey drink extra) gives you a good sampling, including half a grilled lobster with Ezpeleta pepper sprinkles. Supper until 11pm.

# Anglet

Sprawling north and east from Biarritz, amorphous **ANGLET** (pronounced *Anglett*, Angelu in Euskera) occupies most of the triangular territory between the Pointe Saint-Martin, the mouth of the Adour and Bayonne. There is nothing here of note except half a dozen excellent beaches – the most famous being **Chambre d'Amour**, so named after two lovers who were trapped and drowned in their trysting place by the rising tide, and the surfers' mecca of **Sables d'Or**, with boards for rent. As the pair's fate indicates, swimming here is generally dangerous owing to treacherous currents and you should heed the warning signs and lifeguards.

You can catch a #9 bus here from the central stop in Biarritz, or walk the distance in about thirty minutes, along avenues de l'Impératrice and its continuation Général-MacCroskey, then second left down to the seaside boulevard des Plages. Anglet is a good place to stay if you're hostelling, with a spacious, friendly and well-run **youth hostel** in quartier Chiberta at the north end of route des Vignes (℡05.59.58.70.00; 96 places; closed mid-Nov to mid-Feb), which offers a full programme of sporting activities – including, of course, surfing. For **eating and drinking**, the most notable seaside establishment is the *Havana Café* overlooking the parking lot (and ocean) at Chambre d'Amour, a permanently crowded bar (midday only Oct–April) that does *plats du jour* at lunch for under €8. Inland, choose between old warhorse *Udala* at 165 avenue de l'Adour, uninspiringly located on a busy road halfway to Bayonne, but esteemed for its fish, grilled meat, game and cider (allow €32 à la carte), or *La Fleur de Sel* (closed Sun pm, Mon & Tues–Thurs lunch; open nightly July & Aug), off avenue des Plages at 5 avenue de la Forêt in the Chiberta pine forest near the youth hostel, more *nouvelle Basquaise* but popular (€24.50 *menu*).

# Saint-Jean-de-Luz and around

Just fifteen minutes and 20km south of Biarritz by one of the many fast trains, **SAINT-JEAN-DE-LUZ** (Donibane Loitzun – "Saint John of the Marshes" – in Euskera) rates as one of the most popular, though still attractive, resorts on the Basque coast, its broad beach studded with striped beach tents all summer long. Saint-Jean has long been an active fishing port, whose tuna, sardine and anchovy catches still find their way onto the menus of countless restaurants around town.

Previously the fishermen were mainly preoccupied with whales and cod; local sailors travelled as far as Newfoundland, which the Basques claim to have discovered one hundred years before Columbus reached America. In the seventeenth century, Dutch and English whalers drove them from their habitual ports in Arctic waters, so the enterprising Basques devised a method of boiling down the blubber on board, enabling the ships – essentially the first factory whalers – to stay at sea much longer. Later, by the provisions of the eighteenth-century Treaty of Utrecht, the local skippers lost their cod-fishing grounds off Newfoundland and only saved themselves from ruin by becoming pirates. The more respectable pursuit of anchovies, tuna and sardines only resumed during the nineteenth century.

## The Town

Wrecked in a fire set by invading Spanish in 1558, Saint-Jean has since developed into a solid and pleasant place, its seafaring wealth transmuted into the seventeenth- and eighteenth-century homes of merchants and shipowners. Apart from wandering the partly pedestrianized streets of the old quarter, you can visit one of these dwellings, the so-called **Maison Louis XIV** (guided visits Mon–Sat: June–Sept 10.30am–noon & 2.30–5.30pm; July & Aug 10.30am–noon & 2.30–6.30pm; €5). Today beside the Hôtel de Ville, it was actually built for the shipowning Lohobiague family in 1635 but became the temporary residence of the Sun King in 1660 when he came to Saint-Jean for his marriage of political convenience to Maria-Teresa, the Infanta of Castile. (Oddly perhaps, the couple managed to fall in love, and the widowed king years later remarked that her death was "the only annoyance she ever caused me".) The stately interior is authentically Basque, with heavyweight wooden fixtures, some more delicate pieces of furniture and fine examples of tableware and glass. Maria-Teresa lodged in the equally impressive pink Italianate villa known as the **Maison de l'Infante** (June–Sept Tues–Sat 11am–12.30pm & 2.30–6.30pm, Sun & Mon 2.30–6.30pm; €2.50) overlooking the harbour on the quay of the same name. The corner house on rue Mazarin, nearby, was the Duke of Wellington's HQ during the 1813–14 winter campaign against Marshal Soult.

The royal couple's sumptuous, not to say extravagant, wedding took place in the church of **Saint-Jean-Baptiste** on pedestrianized rue Gambetta. Cardinal Mazarin alone presented the queen with twelve thousand pounds of pearls and diamonds, a gold dinner service and a pair of sumptuous carriages drawn by teams of six horses – all paid for by money made in the service of France. The door through which Louis and Maria-Teresa left the church was permanently sealed immediately afterwards (it's on the right as you enter the existing door). Even without this curiosity, the church deserves a look inside: the largest French Basque church, it has a barn-like nave roofed in wood, lined on three sides with tiers of dark oak galleries reached by wrought-iron staircases. Hanging from the ceiling is an ex-voto model of the Empress Eugénie's paddle-steamer, the *Eagle*, which narrowly escaped running aground near Saint-Jean in 1867.

## Practicalities

The **gare SNCF** is on the southern edge of the centre, 500m from the beach, while **buses** arrive at the outdoor terminal at place du Maréchal-Foch, also home to the somewhat harried **tourist office**, behind the Hôtel de Ville (July & Aug Mon–Sat 9am–8pm, Sun 10.30am–1pm & 3–7pm; rest of year Mon–Sat 9am–12.30pm & 2–7pm, Sun 10am–1pm; ℡05.59.26.03.16, Ⓦ www.saint-jean-de-luz.com). On Tuesday and Friday there's a **market** in the adjacent boulevard Victor-Hugo. **Bikes** can be rented at Luz Evasion on place Maurice-Ravel or ADO on avenue Labrouche, as well as at the gare SNCF; **parking** in the centre is a non-starter – leave cars in the suburbs and walk in. **Pelote** matches take place throughout the summer in both St-Jean and Ciboure; ask in the tourist office for details.

### Accommodation

Opposite the train station, on and around avenue Verdun, are a few inexpensive (for St-Jean anyway) if uninspiringly located **hotels** – for example the *Hôtel de Verdun*, 13 avenue de Verdun (℡05.59.26.02.55; ❸), with a decent attached restaurant, the *Relais de St-Jacques* (closed Sat pm & Sun), or the totally en-suite, 1999-redone *Hôtel de Paris*, 1 boulevard du Comandant-Passicot, on the corner of avenue Labrouche (T05.59.85.20.20, W www.hoteldeparis-stjeandeluz.fr; May–Dec; ❷). If you want a quieter old-town or sea-view location, you pay accordingly. About the cheapest of these, though getting some noise from nearby restaurants, is the *Lafayette* at pedestrianized 18–20 rue de la République (T05.59.26.17.74, F05.59.51.11.78; ❸–❹), bigger than it looks from the font, the best two rooms with balconies. Next notches up are the *Hôtel Bolivar* at 18 rue Sopite (T05.59.26.02.00; May–Sept; ❸–❹), a dull modern pile but with an excellent location, or the fully en-suite *Hôtel Ohartzia* (T05.59.26.00.06, W wwww.hotel-ohartzia.com; ❺), just inland from the beach, with rear rooms overlooking the lovely garden, and front ones with balcony. A three-star choice overlooking the Grande Plage, the obviously named *Hôtel de la Plage* (T05.59.51.03.44, W www.hoteldelaplage.com; closed Jan–March; ❻), overhauled in 2003, has its own (fee) car park and ground-floor brasserie. With or without a car, the most practical and best-value three-star choice is *Hôtel Les Goelands* at 4–6 avenue Etcheverry (T05.59.26.10.05, W www.hotel-lesgoelands.com; all year; ❹–❻, good single rates), two co-managed buildings occupying tranquil gardens in a hillside residential district east of the Grande Plage. There's on- and off-street parking, an atmospheric dining room and well-kept units with the baths being redone in stages. Numerous **campsites** are all grouped in the *zone des campings* to the left of the N10 between St-Jean and Guéthary.

### Eating and drinking

Leading off **place Louis-XIV** – with its cafés, sidewalk artists and free summertime concerts in the bandstand (Tues–Sun 10pm) – rue de la République has numerous, variably touristy **restaurants**. *Le Kaiku*, in a handsome old house at no. 17, has an excellent reputation for fish and seafood but costs upwards of €34 without drink (though there's a cheaper lunch *menu*). Less expensive alternatives on the same street include, at no. 19, popular *La Ruelle* (closed Mon, also Tues low season), with three seafood *menus* (€16–27) strong on *marmitako*, *ttoro* and *marmite du pecheur*, though service is "relaxed" and drinks stiffly priced; and *L'Alcalde* at no. 22, with mixed platters and seafood specials from €16. The next street east, rue Tourasse, also has a fair selection, notably *La Vieille Auberge* (closed Weds & Tues lunch), offering six *menus* (€10–23), and *Le Tourasse*, another classic for seafood and dessert (*menus* at €15 and €26).

There's ample scope elsewhere in Saint-Jean for good-value eating, especially for seafood. In summer only, *La Grillerie du Port* sets up on the quayside near the tourist office; a sardine- or tuna-based meal will cost €16–17, though portions are somewhat small. No such problem at the *Buvette de la Halle* (lunch only to 3pm, closed Mon off season) on the corner of the market hall on boulevard Victor-Hugo, where abundant meals of impeccably fresh crab, oysters and sardines, plus *piperade*, drink and dessert, won't dent the wallet more than €19 each. Around the corner at 3 rue Sallagoïty, fresh hake and cod reign supreme at *Pil-Pil Enea* (*menu* €22), where the chef is supplied daily by his wife, in command of an all-female boat at the port.

## Across the river: Ziburu, Zokoa, Urruña

Saint-Jean shares the Nivelle estuary with **ZIBURU** (Ciboure) on its south bank, both *communes* taking maximum advantage of one of the very few sheltered anchorages along the Atlantic coast south of Bordeaux. The harbour is closed off by the village of **ZOKOA** (Socoa) with its little fortress, today home to the local sailing and windsurfing club, plus a scuba school; in summer, a navette-boat (€2 each leg) shuttles regularly on a triangular route between the Digue au Chevaux jetty on the Grand Plage, Zokoa and Saint-Jean's port.

From the Pont Charles de Gaulle linking Saint-Jean and Ciboure, you look over the dock stacked with nets, blackened lobster traps and other fishing paraphernalia towards the extremely narrow harbour entrance clogged with grubby tuna boats. In the opposite direction the view inland over small craft beached in the river mud at low tide is dominated by the 900-metre landmark peak of La Rhune (see below).

By comparison to Saint-Jean, Ziburu is calm and untouristy, with two beautiful streets opposite the end of the bridge over from Saint-Jean: the waterfront **quai Maurice-Ravel** (a plaque commemorates the composer's birth at no. 12), and the parallel **rue Pocolette** behind. The latter forms an exquisite terrace of wide-fronted, half-timbered and balconied town houses, many built by seventeenth-century traders who did business with the West Indies and the Orient. Near the south end of rue Pocolette protrudes the octagonal tower of the sixteenth-century church of **Saint-Vincent**, inside which are particularly good examples of a Pays Basque altarpiece and three-tiered gallery, and yet another model-ship ex-voto suspended in the middle.

If Saint-Jean-de-Luz is full, Ziburu makes a possible fallback with its two **hotels**: *Bakea* on place Camille Julian, opposite Pont Charles de Gaulle (℡05.59.47.34.40, ⓦwww.hotel-bakea.fr.st; ❸), including a moderately priced seafood **restaurant**, and the hillside *Agur Deneri* at 14 chemin de Muskoa (℡05.59.47.02.83, ⓔhotel-agur.deneri@wanadoo.fr; ❸), with a garden and parking.

The area's only formal attraction is the **Château d'Urtubie** (daily March 15–Oct, 1hr tours only 2–6pm & 11am except Tues & Thurs; €5.50) at **URRUÑA** (Urrugne), 1500m southwest of Ziburu, which has belonged to the same family since its construction as a fortified château in 1341. It was enlarged and gentrified during the sixteenth and eighteenth centuries, and provided hospitality for the French King Louis XI, as well as for Maréchal Soult and later the Duke of Wellington during the Napoleonic Wars. If you fancy following in their footsteps, it is also a very upmarket restaurant taking groups only by advance arrangement (℡05.59.54.31.15, ⓕ05.59.54.62.51); otherwise you can pay an extra €4.50 to take tea in the salon.

## Inland from Saint-Jean: Azkaine, La Rhune and Sara

Heading southwest from Saint-Jean, perhaps on one of the two or three summer weekday buses (on Le Basque Bondissant) towards Sara from the train station, you reach **AZKAINE** (Ascain) after 7km along the D918. Like so many *labourdan* foothill villages, it's doll's-house cute and thus inevitably a target of the overspill from Saint-Jean in season. There are several moderately affordable **hotels** here, in one of which – *De la Rhune* (℡05.59.54.00.04, ⓕ05.59.54.41.67; ❹) – Pierre Loti stayed while writing *Ramuntcho* (see p.534).

### La Rhune

Conical **La Rhune** (Larrun), straddling the frontier with Spain, is the last skyward thrust of the Pyrenees before they decline into the Atlantic. *The* landmark of Labourd, in spite of its unsightly TV/radio/mobile phone masts, it is predictably popular as a vantage point, offering fine vistas way up the Basque coast and east to the rising Pyrenees. Like nearby Zugarramurdi (see p.502), it was a haunt of witches during medieval times, and the local authorities used to pay a religious hermit to live on top and keep the shady ladies at bay with his sanctity.

To reach La Rhune, you could walk directly from Azkaine in about two and a half hours, or stay on the minor D4 road for 4km more until the **Col de Saint-Ignace**, from where you can ride up on the tourist **rack-and-pinion railway** (daily: July–Sept about every 35min 8.30am–5pm; mid-March to June & Oct to mid-Nov 9am–3pm, according to weather conditions; €6.50 one-way, €8 return; book on ☎08.92.39.14.25). The 4200-metre journey to the top takes just half an hour, but allow two hours round-trip because of the queues – it's a massively popular outing in high season, with long waits and two snack bars near the base station taking advantage of a captive clientele. Even with a meal to work off, it's a fairly easy, two-hour climb to the top from the *col*.

### Sara and its caves

With or without the bus or your own transport, it's worth going on to **SARA** (Sare), a hilltop village ringed by satellite hamlets in the shadow of La Rhune. This proves to be another perfectly proportioned Basque village, where a summertime ban on central parking enhances enjoyment of the galleried church, *frontón* and tree-shaded streets. Pierre Loti used it, disguised as "Etchezar", for the setting of his 1897 romance *Ramuntcho*. Animal-lovers might avoid the place in autumn, when Sara earns its nickname of *l'enfer des palombes* – "woodpigeon hell" – as thousands of the creatures are both shot and trapped in nets strung between trees.

You can either walk on the **GR10** from the intermediate station below the summit of La Rhune in about an hour and a quarter, or drive the 3km of road from Saint-Ignace in rather less time. If you plan to continue further east, you can make an overnight stop at one of the area's **hotels**: The 2003-redone *Pikassaria*, 1.5km south in Lehenbizkai hamlet (☎05.59.54.21.51, Ⓕ05.59.54.27.40; ❸, but ❻ HB only summer; closed late Nov & Jan–March), has a decent restaurant (*menus* €16–28), as does the *Baratchartea* (☎05.59.54.24.48, Ⓕ05.59.47.50.84; ❸; closed Jan 1–March 15), 1.5km east in Ihalar hamlet, serving big-portioned meals (€15–21) and offering various rooms, some with balconies. There's also the three-star, antique-furnished *Arraya* on the village square (☎05.59.54.20.46, Ⓦwww.arraya.com; ❺; closed Nov–late March), a former hospice on the St-Jacques pilgrimage route. Even if you only plan to take the bus back to Saint-Jean, it's worth stopping in for a (normally priced) drink at their bar, or better yet patronize *Lastiry* (closed Tues, also Mon low season) across the way, the area's only independent **restaurant**, rendering the Basque classics with a *nouvelle* twist. There are two **campsites** just south of Sara: *La Petite Rhune* (☎05.59.54.23.97; May–Sept), opposite the *Hôtel Pikassaria*, and the more basic *Telletchea* (☎05.59.54.26.01; July & Aug).

These lie on the D306 road to the **Grottes de Sare** (Ⓦwww.sare.fr; daily except Jan: typically spring & autumn 10am–6pm; July & Aug 10am–7pm; €6), occasionally served by the Saint-Jean-based bus. These were inhabited as long as 47,000 years ago, with a small gallery on site displaying finds from the caves.

# Hendaye

Running parallel, the D912 road and the **Chemin Piétonnier Littoral** footpath follow the cliffs of the remarkably unspoilt "Corniche Basque" 15km southwest from Saint-Jean-de-Luz to **HENDAYE** (Hendaïa), the road cutting inland a little only at the Pointe Sainte-Anne. The path goes through the Domaine d'Abbadia, a vast nature reserve around the **Château d'Abbadia** of the nineteenth-century Dublin-born explorer **Antoine d'Abbadie**, on the headland overlooking Hendaye-Plage (June–Sept guided visits Mon–Fri 10am–6pm every 30min, Sat unescorted visit 10am–12.30pm & 2–5.30pm, Sun unescorted 2–5.30pm; Feb–May & Oct to mid-December Mon–Fri guided visit at 10am & 11am, unescorted visit 2–4.30pm; €5.30 unescorted, €6.40 guided). After expeditions in Ethiopia and Egypt, d'Abbadie had the château built between 1860 and 1870; the architect was Eugène Viollet-le-Duc, and the result is a bizarrre Scottish Gothic folly, with Arabian boudoirs, Ethiopian frescoes, and inscriptions over the doors and lintels inside in Irish, Basque, Arabic and Ethiopian. It is also filled with objects collected by d'Abbadie on his travels. He became president of the Académie des Sciences in 1891, to which he donated the château on his death in 1897.

Arrival in town may prove anticlimactic; neither **Hendaye-Ville** nor the coastal annexe of **Hendaye-Plage** have much intrinsic interest despite a significant past. This includes the long-time residence (and death in 1923) of **Pierre Loti**, author of the locally set *Ramuntcho* as well as assorted orientalist romances. Loti was popular in his time for syrupy, exotic novels, their settings – including Istanbul and Tahiti as well as the Pays Basque – gleaned from a lifetime of far-flung postings in the service of the French navy. You can see his house (no visits, privately owned) in rue des Pêcheurs, on the waterfront below boulevard de Gaulle.

The best **beach**, at Hendaye-Plage, is just west of the promontory. The N10 inland road and rail line continue a couple more kilometres to dull Hendaye-Ville, set where the Bidassoa widens into the Txingudy estuary. Hendaye–Plage, unlike Saint-Jean-de-Luz, is a major yachting centre, and again unlike the latter is pretty much a ghost town from October to Easter.

Hendaye-Ville, served by both the Paris–Bordeaux–Irún and Toulouse–Irún rail lines, lies on the estuary of the River Bidassoa (the French spelling of Bidasoa), with the border running down the middle for about 8km at this point. Just upstream from the town, the tiny wooded island known as **Île des Faisans** or Île de la Conférence is administered jointly by the two countries. It looks insignificant now, but was once used for meetings between their respective monarchs. François I, taken prisoner at the battle of Pavia in 1525, was ransomed here; in 1659 it was the scene of the signature of the **Treaty of the Pyrenees**. The following year it again became the centre of attention when the marriage contracts between Louis XIV and the Spanish Infanta Maria-Teresa were signed here. The great painter Velázquez reputedly died of a chill caught while painting the interior of the negotiations room.

Hendaye almost made history once more on October 23, 1940, when Spanish General Franco met Hitler in the Hendaye train station. The version promulgated by Franco and his publicists, long believed even by his opponents, has it that "El Caudillo" preserved Spanish neutrality by refusing the Führer's invitation to join the war on the Axis side; in reality, Franco, dazzled by Hitler's early victories and the prospect of a greatly enlarged Spanish Morocco at the expense of France, begged to be allowed to fight alongside Germany. But Hitler – mindful of how much assistance the Nationalists had needed to win the Civil War, and aware of Spain's dire economic state at the time – considered the proposed alliance a liability and was having none of it. Everyone agrees that Hitler was later overheard saying to Mussolini that he would rather have three teeth pulled than meet his potential ally again.

## Practicalities

The area's **tourist office** is at 12 rue des Aubépines in Hendaye-Plage (July & Aug Mon–Sat 9am–8pm, Sun 10am–1pm; rest of year Mon–Fri 9am–noon & 2–6pm, Sat 9am–noon; ☎05.59.20.00.34, ⓦwww.hendaye.com). As for **parking**, only the beachfront is metered; elsewhere it's unregimented. Hendaye-Ville **hotels** are generally grim and moribund; almost everyone stays down at more pleasant Hendaye-Plage. Attractive, affordable choices here include the *Hôtel Valencia* near the southeast end of beachfront boulevard de la Mer (☎05.59.20.01.62, ⓦwww.hotelvalencia.net; ❸), its near neighbour *Hôtel Lafon* at no. 99 (☎05.5920.04.67, ⓕ05.59.48.06.85; ❹) or, in the centre of Hendaye-Plage, the well-run *Hôtel Bergeret-Sport* at 4 rue des Clématites (☎05.59.20.00.78, ⓔmariecarmen.bergeret@wanadoo.fr; ❸, ❺ HB only July & Aug), with an excellent patio restaurant (*menus* €14–21). Among no less than ten local **campsites**, almost all southeast of town and inland from the D912, *Deux Jumeaux* (☎05.59.20.01.65; April–Sept) is small, inexpensive and fairly close to the beach, but backs onto the rail line; *Ametza* (☎05.59.20.07.05; April–Oct) slightly further along route de la Corniche towards the Château d'Abbadia, is much bigger and with better amenities, including a pool. **Restaurant** fare is, unsurprisingly, overwhelmingly fishy; two reasonable inland choices, both with €16 *menus*, are *La Petite Marée* at 2 avenue des Mimosas, one block back from the beach, and *Battela* around the corner at 5 rue d'Irun, rond-point du Palmier. Oyster fiends should head for *Le Parc à Huîtres* at 4 rue des Orangers opposite the yacht drydock (€6.50–10 the half-dozen, to eat in or take away; closed Tues, also Wed low season), while if you crave a sea view with your meal, *La Cabane du Pêcheur* (closed Sun eve, Mon, Tues eve, Wed eve Oct–May), opposite the fishing anchorage on quai de la Floride, does good grilled or stewed fish (*menus* €14–25).

## Walking from Hendaye

The **GR10** and **HRP** both start their trans-Pyrenean course beside the former casino at Hendaye-Plage. The first, two-hour stage to Biriatu is dull and gives no sense of the glories that lie ahead: along avenue Général-Leclerc to Hendaye-Ville, under the rail line via a pedestrian tunnel, across the N10 and finally to the A63 highway. A cattle track passes underneath this and continues to the tiny hilltop village of **BIRIATU** (Biriatou), where the walking starts to get interesting. (If you have your own transport, or means for a taxi, you should start from Biriatu.)

A short, steep section leads to a Basque church with a collection of weather-worn tombstones, next door to the *frontón* and the fifteenth-century *Auberge Hirribarren*, a temporary haven for many Allied soldiers during World War II and now an excellent **restaurant**, with meals at €15–26 a head (until 9pm; closed Jan, & Mon low season). It's also possible to overnight near the village, as there are two isolated **hotels**: *Bakea* (☎05.59.20.76.36, ⓦwww.bakea.fr.st; ❸; closed Feb), spread over two premises, with another excellent restaurant (closed Sun pm & Mon Oct–March, Mon & Tues lunch April–Sept), and *Larretcheko Borda* (☎05.59.20.20.32; ❷; closed Christmas–New Year's Day), out at the Col de Courlecou. Beyond Biriatu the main footpaths and a number of local variations rise rapidly above the coast to semi-isolation, with only the buzzing power lines (which you soon leave behind) and the occasional long-distance walker or local jogger to disturb the peace. From Biriatu to the *gîte d'étape* at Olhette (see p.517) it's nearly five hours' trek, and from there to Sare via the base of La Rhune, another 2hr 45min – a tent could be handy.

A couple of day-hike circuits are possible: looping west of the main path at the **Col des Joncs** (500m) and descending along the frontier to follow the Bidassoa back to Biriatu, or circling east by cutting away shortly after the *col*, at frontier stone 11. Both alternatives are well waymarked, and shown clearly on the Randonnées Pyrénéennes 1:50,000 map no. 1, "Pays Basque Ouest-Labourd".

# Eastern Gipuzkoa

The Spanish Basque coastal province of **Gipuzkoa** adjoins the French frontier, and its border town, **Irún**, is one of the major road and rail entry points into Spain. The tiny village of Behobia (Béhobie) – an unsightly collection of truck stops, bottle shops and pumps full of cheap petrol – straddles the frontier. There are fast public transport connections to San Sebastián, although if you're travelling more leisurely or with a car, the fishing ports of **Hondarribia** and **Pasaia** are worth a stop. Foot passengers coming from France can bypass Irún altogether by using the *navette*-launch plying between Hendaye-Plage's yacht port and Hondarribia (€1.50 each way).

## Irún

Like most border towns, sprawling, graceless and largely modern **IRÚN**'s chief concern is how to make a quick buck from passing travellers. The main point in its favour is the ease with which you can leave; there are trains to Hendaye in France and to San Sebastián throughout the day, with regular long-distance and international connections. If you're arriving by train from Paris (or elsewhere in France) at Hendaye, the quickest way across the border involves taking the *topo* (mole train, so called because of all the tunnels it goes through) from the separate platform on the right outside Hendaye's main station; it runs every thirty minutes to Irún station, at Avenida de Colón 52, then on to San Sebastián. Of the town's few attractions, the **Ermita de Ama Xantalen** (alias de Santa Elena; open Tues & Thurs 3–5pm, Sat & Sun 10am–noon; free), an eleventh-century chapel serving as a museum containing Roman remains discovered here in 1969, is worth a visit. To get there, head up c/Prudéncia Arbide next to the *Ayuntamiento*, bear left at the first major intersection, and then right at c/Santa Elena.

### Practicalities

In the vicinity of Irún's main train station are several small, reasonably priced **hostales** and **restaurants** specializing in good local food, with prices markedly lower than in France, Hondarribia or San Sebastián. *Pensión Bidasoa*, c/Estación 14 (☎943 619 913; ❷), and *Bar Pensión los Fronterizos*, c/Estación 7 (☎943 619 205; ❷–❸), have some of the least expensive rooms; for more comfort try the nearby *Hostal Matxinbenta*, Paseo Colón 21 (☎943 621 384; ❸). There is also one reasonable **casa rural** nearby: the *Mendiola*, Barrio Ventas (☎943 629 763; ❷), 2km west of town on the N1 road. For a modest outlay, the *Asador Baserri* at c/Berrotarán 5 (closed Sun evening and Mon) serves Basque, farm-style meat dishes (allow €15).

# Hondarribia

The fishing port and fortified stronghold of **HONDARRIBIA**, 6km north of Irún and looking over the Río Bidasoa to Hendaye, is a far more attractive prospect, though the waterfront itself is disappointingly modern, enlivened with just a few cafés. The town's real appeal lies in main streets running parallel to the front, and the cobbled backstreets further inland, where traditional, wood-beamed Basque houses are interspersed with bars offering some of the best seafood and *pintxos* around. During summer, the fine **beaches** immediately north of the town are an alternative to ultra-crowded Playa de la Concha in San Sebastián.

Hondarribia has a picturesque, walled old town entered via the fifteenth-century **Puerta de Santa María**, carved with the town coat-of-arms and angels paying homage to Our Lady of Guadalupe, who is said to have saved the town during a two-month French siege in 1638. Calle Mayor, leading up to the Plaza de Armas, has further fine examples of wood-beamed houses adorned with wrought-iron balconies and studded doors, some displaying the family coats-of-arms above the entrance. At the end of c/Mayor stands the church of **Santa María**, predominantly Gothic, though extensively and misguidedly renovated in the seventeenth century. The proxy wedding between Louis XIV and Maria-Teresa which confirmed the 1659 Treaty of the Pyrenees took place here in 1660, six days before the official signing ceremony on the Île des Faisans. The Plaza de Armas itself is dominated by the **Palacio de Carlos Quinto** (now the *parador*), started originally in the tenth century by Sancho el Fuerte of Navarra and subsequently extended by Carlos V in the sixteenth. Slightly uphill and southwest, the smaller, arcaded Plaza Gipuzkoa with more wrought-iron railings is also worth seeking out.

## Practicalities

The helpful **Turismo** is on Javier Ugarte 6, at the base of the road up the old town (July & Aug Mon–Sat 9am–8pm, Sun 10am–2pm; Sept–June Mon–Fri 9am–1.30pm & 4–6.30pm, Sat 10am–2pm; ☎943 645 458). There's no train service; buses for San Sebastián leave frequently from a stop on c/San Pedro.

There's a fair amount of characterful, if rather pricey, **accommodation** in Hondarribia. On the budget side, try the en-suite if somewhat bland *Hotel San Nikolas* on Plaza de Armas 6 (☎943 644 278; ❹), or the *Txoko-Goxo*a on c/Marrua 22 near the Puerta de Santa María (no phone; ❷). Pick of the plusher establishments is the two-star *Hotel Obispo*, offering modern rooms with balconies in an old stone manor on Plaza del Obispo, birthplace of Ricardo de Sandoval, later bishop of Seville and chaplain to Charles V (☎943 645 400, Ⓕ943 642 386; ❼), or the *Parador Nacional El Emperador Carlos V*, in the fortified *palacio* at Plaza de Armas 14 (☎943 645 500, Ⓔhondarribia@parador.es; sometimes closed Nov–Feb; ❼).

If you have your own transport, some excellent **casas rurales** just outside town offer better value, though they're very popular and need to be reserved well in advance. The closest, uphill from the airport in Barrio Arkoll-Santiago, is *Iketxe* (☎ & Ⓕ943 644 391; ❸), meticulously built in 1988 in traditional style, offering a variety of huge, wood-ceilinged, tile-floored rooms with balconies and good views. Alternatively, 3km from town in Jaizubia hamlet, friendly *Arotz-Enea* (☎ & Ⓕ943 642 319; ❸), in a half-timbered medieval farmhouse at the end of a lane, offers particularly good breakfasts. Two others are found on the Jaizkibel uplands, accessed from the roundabout outside the old town walls: the over-modernized *Postigu* (☎943 643 270; ❸), 3km from the centre near the shrine of Guadalupe, and the remoter (2km more) *Artzu* (☎943 640 530; ➋), a converted farmhouse (mostly non-en-suite) near the top of a sea-cliff at the end of the road.

The barracks-like **youth hostel**, *Juan Sebastián Elkano*, is at Higer Bidea 7, the shore road north of town (☎943 641 550; all year), though it's often packed out in summer with school groups. The closest **campsite**, *Camping Jaizkibel* (☎943 641 679), is 2km west of town along Carretera Guadalupe towards Pasaia Donibane (Pasajes San Juan) – but there's no public transport to it.

A dozen or so **restaurants** and **bars** along parallel c/Santiago and c/San Pedro, three to four short blocks in from the water, are the best hunting ground for **food** and **drink**, though despite Hondarribia's still-active fishing fleet, seafood isn't particularly cheap. Among the bars, *Itxaropena* at c/San Pedro 67 is typically among the liveliest. For something special, try the *Hermandad de Pescadores* (Confraternity of Fishermen) at c/Zuloaga 12 (reservations on ☎943 642 738; closed Sun pm & Mon), one of the parallels to the waterfront, once strictly the fishermen's clubhouse but now open to all. Every July 25, preceded by a brass band and dressed in holiday finest, the confraternity parades into the place, oars aloft, for a ceremonial meal. Inside, nautical decor includes *trainera* photos, and you eat at suitably institutional, long tables. The cooking's deceptively simple, in ample portions; rapid turnover (you'll be in and out within an hour) guarantees freshness, but that said the €13 *menú* is rather dull, and you'll do better choosing from the *a la carta* menu (allow €30 with abstemious drinking). In the upper town, tucked away in a narrow, cobbled alley two streets behind c/Mayor, the *Mamutzar* (closed Tues) serves a good-value *menú*, as does the *Danontzat* at c/Las Tiendas 6, near the church (*menú* €15, *a la carta* 29).

## Mount Jaizkibel

The stretch of coastline from here as far as the port of Pasaia is particularly rugged and has long been a haven for smugglers; it's the sea-washed flank of the sandstone **Jaizkibel** massif, whose vast uplands, a mix of pasture and parkland, are criss-crossed by trails and tracks beloved of joggers, ramblers and other solitude-seeking locals. With your own transport you should forsake the busy highway inland in favour of the initially winding minor road G13440, which starts at the roundabout just west of Hondarribia's old town, towards the chapel of **Nuestra Señora de Guadalupe** (5km), target of a September 8 festival. The road continues climbing more gradually through pine forests to a pass (9km, 455m) just below the 545-metre peak, with wonderful views along the Basque coastline – if the mist hasn't descended to the 200-metre contour, an all-too-common occurrence. You then descend to Pasai Donibane (see below), a total of 18km.

## Pasaia

The other place you might consider stopping at for any length of time en route between Hondarribia and San Sebastián is the port of **PASAIA**, the collective name for three separate settlements built around the sheltered mouth of the Río Oiartzun. Pasai Antxo and Pasai Senpere on the south bank are modern, industrial ports, where cranes steadily pick through heaps of scrap metal. Considered the least problematic anchorage on a stretch of coast known for its difficult swells, it was from here that the Marquis de Lafayette, general and statesman, sailed to America to fight for the colonists in the War of Independence.

Well-preserved **PASAI DONIBANE** on the north bank, however, retains its charm, especially since vehicles must be left at a car park on the outskirts. From the patron saint's church, a restrained Baroque edifice of the seventeenth century, narrow cobbled c/San Juan (now officially Donibane Kalea; Victor Hugo once lived at no. 65) leads past Plaza de Santiago with its colourful houses, ending almost a kilometre later at the river channel. En route you pass Ontziola, a traditional **boat-building workshop** and educational exhibit (Easter–Sept Tues–Sun 11am–2pm & 4–7pm; Oct–Easter Mon–Sat 10am–2pm & 3–5pm). The village is famous for its waterside **fish restaurants**, which work out rather less expensive than those in San Sebastián's old quarter. Three to try are *Casa Camara*, c/San Juan 79, for shellfish (closed Sun pm & Mon low season; €27 *menú, a la carta* €35); *Ziaboga*, at no. 91, with more of an emphasis on fish (from €30); and cheapest of all, *Txulotxo* (lunch *menú* €16, *carta* €24). A **launch** (*txalupa*) runs throughout the day and evening across the harbour to Pasai Senpere, from where frequent buses depart to San Sebastián.

# San Sebastián (Donostia)

Capital of Gipuzkoa autonomous region, and the undisputed queen of the Basque resorts, **SAN SEBASTIÁN** (increasingly known as **DONOSTIA**) is a picturesque – and expensive – seaside town with good beaches. It has always been among Spain's most fashionable places to escape the heat of the southern summers, and in July and August it's packed. Although San Sebastián tries hard to be chic, it's still too much of a family resort to compete in those terms with the Catalan Mediterranean spots like Collioure or Cadaqués. Set around the deep, still bay of La Concha and enclosed by rolling low hills, the town is beautifully situated; the old quarter sits on a promontory between the bay and the Río Urumea which divides the town, its back to the wooded slopes of Monte Urgull, while newer development has spread along the banks of the Urumea, around the edge of the bay to the foot of Monte Igeldo and onto the hills overlooking the bay.

## Arrival and information

Most **buses** arrive at Plaza Pío XII, fifteen minutes' walk along the river from the centre of town (the ticket office for these companies is around the corner next to the river on Paseo de Bizkaia). Buses from Pasaia arrive on the Alameda del Boulevard, and from Hondarribia on Plaza de Gipuzkoa. RENFE's mainline **Estación del Norte**, for arrivals from Pamplona, lies across the Río Urumea on Paseo de Francia, although local lines of the *Eusko Tren* from Hendaye, or Bilbao (Bilbo) via Zarautz and Zumaia (neither line accepts InterRail passes), have their terminus on Plaza Easo at the **Estación de Amara**. The small (domestic flights from Madrid only) **airport** is 22km from the city centre, just outside Hondarribia; an airport bus plies back and forth as necessary.

San Sebastián's helpful **Turismo** is on c/Regina Regente (June–Sept Mon–Sat 8am–8pm, Sun 10am–2pm; Oct–May Mon–Sat 9am–1.30pm & 3.30–7pm, Sun 10am–2pm; ☎943 481 166, ⓦwww.sansebastianturismo.com), and produces *Donostiaisia*, a very useful free monthly guide to what's on.

## Accommodation

Places to **stay**, though plentiful, can be pricey and hard to come by in season; if you arrive between mid-July and the end of August, or during the film festival

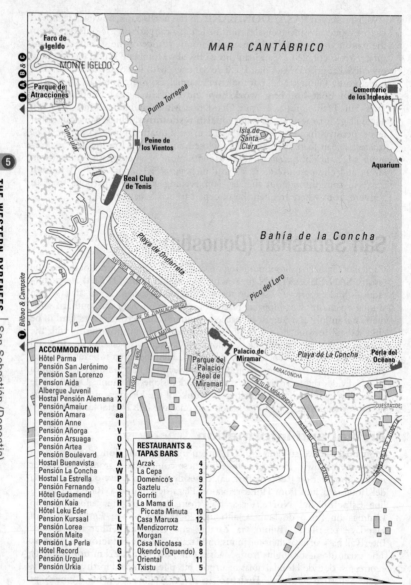

MAR CANTÁBRICO

Faro de Igeldo

MONTE IGELDO

Parque de Atracciones

Funicular

Punta Torrepea

Peine de los Vientos

Real Club de Tenis

Isla de Santa Clara

Aquarium

Cementerio de los Ingleses

Bahía de la Concha

Playa de Ondarreta

AVENIDA DE SATRUSTEGUI

AV. DE ZUMALACARREGUI

CALLE MATIA

PASEO DE HERU

Pico del Loro

Parque del Palacio Real de Miramar

Palacio de Miramar

Playa de La Concha

Perla del Océano

MIRACONCHA

ALTO DE MIRACONCHA

PASEO DE EGUIA

CUESTA DE

| ACCOMMODATION | |
| --- | --- |
| Hôtel Parma | E |
| Pensión San Jerónimo | F |
| Pensión San Lorenzo | K |
| Pension Aida | R |
| Albergue Juvenil | T |
| Hostal Pensión Alemana | X |
| Pensión Amaiur | D |
| Pensión Amara | aa |
| Pensión Anne | I |
| Pensión Añorga | V |
| Pensión Arsuaga | O |
| Pensión Artea | Y |
| Pensión Boulevard | M |
| Hostal Buenavista | A |
| Pensión La Concha | W |
| Hostal La Estrella | P |
| Pensión Fernando | Q |
| Hôtel Gudamendi | B |
| Pensión Kaia | H |
| Hôtel Leku Eder | C |
| Pension Kursaal | L |
| Pensión Lorea | N |
| Pensión Maite | Z |
| Pensión La Perla | U |
| Hôtel Record | G |
| Pensión Urgull | J |
| Pensión Urkia | S |

| RESTAURANTS & TAPAS BARS | |
| --- | --- |
| Arzak | 4 |
| La Cepa | 3 |
| Domenico's | 9 |
| Gaztelu | 2 |
| Gorriti | K |
| La Mama di Piccata Minuta | 10 |
| Casa Maruxa | 12 |
| Mendizorrotz | 1 |
| Morgan | 7 |
| Casa Nicolasa | 6 |
| Okendo (Oquendo) | 8 |
| Oriental | 11 |
| Txistu | 5 |

Bilbao & Campsite

T

in September, you'll have to start looking early in the day if you haven't booked ahead. There's scant difference in rates between the cheapest places in the *parte vieja* (old quarter) and elsewhere, although *hostales* along the Alameda del Boulevard tend to be slightly pricier. There is often more chance of finding

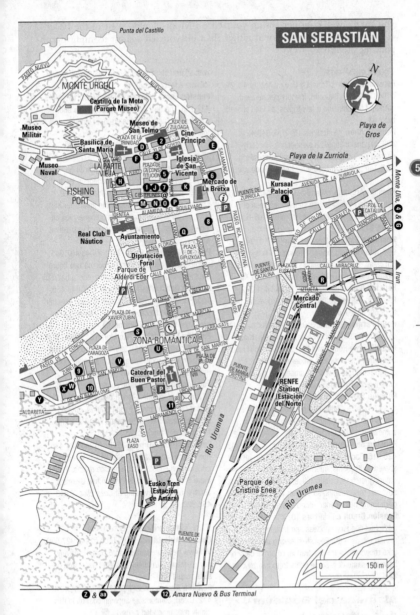

space in the *zona romántica* district around c/Easo, c/San Martín, c/Hondarribia and c/San Bartolomé, or on one or other bank of the river, either in Gros (east of the *zona romántica*) or in the new part of town, Amara Nuevo, on the way to the Anoeta sports complex. If you're driving and have a bit of cash to spare, you might well consider basing yourself on Monte Igeldo west of the beaches, and taking a bus into town rather than pit yourself against its nightmarish parking situation.

## Parte Vieja

**Pensión Amaiur** c/Treinta y Uno de Agosto 44, 2° ☎943 429 654. Pleasant, friendly *pensión* with carpeted doubles and a few triples, all with shared bath. **②**

**Pensión Anne** c/Esterlines 15, 2° ☎943 421 438, **ⓔ**pensionanne@euskalnet.net. Recently-opened *pensión* with friendly, English-speaking staff. Ten percent discount for Rough Guide users. **③**

**Pensión Arsuaga** c/Narrika 3, 3° ☎943 420 681. Very friendly *pensión* with simple, spacious doubles. Has its own restaurant and offers full-board deals. **③**

**Hostal La Estrella** Plaza de Sarriegi 1 ☎943 420 997. Attractive old *hostal*, offering old-fashioned but clean rooms – some en suite – either overlooking the plaza or Alameda del Boulevard. **③**

**Pensión Kaia** c/Puerto 12, 2° ☎943 431 342. Pleasant, modern rooms with bath. Prices fall by a third out of season. **④**

**Hotel Parma** c/General Jauregi Gudalburuaren 11 ☎943 428 893, **ⓦ**www.hotelparma.com. Nicely located between the *parte vieja* and Paseo Nuevo, this rather characterless modern building offers comfortable rooms with all amenities, the best ones overlooking the sea. **⑥**

**Pensión San Jerónimo** c/San Jerónimo 25, 2° ☎943 420 830. Adequate *pensión*, though the rooms are spartan and the hallway and stairs somewhat the worse for wear. **②**

**Pensión San Lorenzo** c/San Lorenzo 2, 1° ☎943 425 516. Backpackers' cheapo haven with just six shared-bath rooms, Internet access and a self-catering kitchen; usually full, and does not accept advance reservations, so contact them the evening or morning before your intended stay. **②**

**Pensión Urgull** c/Esterlines 10, 3° ☎943 430 047. Just five airy, spotless and tastefully furnished rooms – the English-speaking owner won't take reservations far in advance, so arrive early or book the same day. Some noise from nearby bars. **③**

## Alameda del Boulevard and around

**Pensión Boulevard** Alameda del Boulevard 24 1° ☎943 429 405. Comfortable, modernized rooms in an older building, but only one en-suite room. **②**

**Pensión Fernando** Plaza de Gipuzkoa 2, 1° ☎943 425 575. Fair-sized, relatively quiet rooms with shared showers at this friendly *pensión* overlooking a leafy square. **③**

**Pensión Lorea** Alameda del Boulevard 16 ☎943 427 258. The best en-suite option at this address, with heating and TV in the en-suite (shower and toilet) rooms. **④**

## Zona Romántica

**Hostal Pensión Alemana** c/San Martín 53, 1° ☎943 462 544, **ⓔ**halemana@adegi.es. Perfectly located just behind La Concha, this fine Belle Époque two-star offers affordable splendour in its large en-suite rooms with all mod cons, plus off-street parking. Reservations required year-round. **⑤**

**Pensión Añorga** c/Easo 12, 1° ☎943 467 945. Large, fairly plain one-star *pensión* on two floors, but the rooms are clean and some have a bath. **③**

**Pensión Artea** c/San Bartolomé 33 ☎943 455 100. Recently renovated pension offering en-suite rooms in a good location near La Concha; rates drop by a third out of season. **④**

**Pensión La Concha** c/San Martín 51 ☎943 450 389, **ⓔ**hostallaconcha@telefonica.net. Excellent value en-suite rooms in a salubrious neighbourhood just a few steps from La Concha. **③**

**Pensión La Perla** c/Inazio Loiola 10 ☎943 428 123. Another excellent-value *pensión*, near Buen Pastor cathedral and the food market, offering spotless heated en-suite rooms with TV; a firm favourite with readers. **③**

**Pensión Urkia** c/Urbieta 12, 3° ☎943 424 436. Run by the sister of the owner of *La Perla*, this *pensión* has equally good en-suite rooms, though there is some street noise. When full, there's another relative in waiting at *Casa Elisa* ☎943 453 950. **③**

## On the river banks

**Pensión Aida** Iztueta 9, 1°, Gros ☎943 327 800, **Wⓦ**ww.pensionesconencanto.com. Relatively new *pensión* with cheerful, pastel decor and en-suite rooms. **④**

**Pensión Amara** Isabel II 2, 1°, Amara ☎943 468 472. Clean, comfortable accommodation in this highly recommended *pensión*. **③**

**Pension Kursaal** c/Peña y Goñi 2, 1°, Gros ☎943 292 666, wⓦww.pensionesconencanto.com. Co-managed with the similar *Aida*, this enjoys a superb location just a few steps from Zurriola and the Kursaal itself. Great value and even better out of season when prices dip. **④**

**Pensión Maite** Avda de Madrid 19, 1° B, Amara ☎943 470 715, ℱ943 454 826. Good-value rooms with shower and TV; handy for the bus station, Astoria cinema and Anoeta football stadium. The owners also run the *Bar Maite* opposite. ❸

**Hotel Record** Calzada Vieja de Ategorrieta 35, Gros ☎943 271 255, ℱ943 278 521. At the east end of this district and a pleasant alternative to the bustle of the *parte vieja* and *zona romántica*; well connected by bus, or a fifteen-minute walk from the centre, with plenty of parking. All rooms with shower or bath (though the cheapest lack toilet); the larger ones have terraces. ❹–❺

## Monte Igeldo

**Hostal Buenavista** Barrio de Igeldo ☎943 210 600. Stone-clad, mock-trad Basque chalet on the main road to Monte Igeldo, featuring sweeping sea views and a good restaurant. Good value for the area. ❹

**Hotel Gudamendi** Paseo de Gudamendi, Monte Igeldo ☎943 214 000, ℱ943 215 108. In a peaceful, park-like cul-de-sac near the top of the mountain, this rambling, converted hunting lodge

scores for its pleasant pool and common areas. There are usually vacancies even in summer because it's somewhat overpriced. Rooms were completely rebuilt in 2003 so expect rates to inch up in the future. ❼

**Hotel Leku Eder** Barrio de Igeldo ☎943 210 964, ℱ943 210 107. Just a few hundred metres below the *Buenavista*, this is a rather sterile concrete block, but many rooms have great views towards the lighthouse. ❹

## Youth hostel and camping

**Albergue Juvenil** Paseo de Igeldo ☎943 310 268, ℱ943 214 090. San Sebastián's youth hostel, known as *La Sirena*, is just a few minutes' walk from the end of Ondarreta beach (or take bus #5 or #16). En-suite 6-bunk rooms; open all year.

**Igeldo** Paseo Padre Orkolaga 69, Barrio de Igeldo ☎943 214 502, ℱ943 280 411. San Sebastián's campsite is excellent, but it's 5km from the centre on the landward side of Monte Igeldo (up a steep hill), reached by bus #16 from the Alameda del Boulevard. Open all year.

# The Town

The **parte vieja** (old quarter) at the base of Monte Urgull is the town's highlight – cramped and lively streets where the crowds congregate in the evenings to wander among the many small bars and shops or sample the shellfish from the street traders down by the fishing port. Much of it was destroyed by a fire in 1813, though buildings lining the narrow thoroughfares were renovated so expertly that you'd never suspect their comparative modernity. The quarter's medieval wall was swept away to allow expansion later the same century; the Alameda del Boulevard marks its former course.

The *parte vieja* contains San Sebastián's chief sights: the elaborate Baroque facade of the eighteenth-century church of **Santa María**, and the more elegantly restrained sixteenth-century Gothic church of **San Vicente** (or Bizente, somewhat confusingly on Plaza de la Trinidad). The centre of the old quarter is **La Plaza de la Constitución** (known by the locals simply as *La Consti*) – the numbers on the balconies around the square date from the days when it was used as a bullring. Situated just off c/Treinta y Uno de Agosto (the only street to survive the great fire of August 31, 1813), behind San Vicente, is the excellent **Museo de San Telmo** (July & Aug Tues–Sat 10.30am–8.30pm, Sun 10.30am–2pm; rest of year Tues–Sat 10.30am–1.30pm & 4–7.30pm, Sun 10.30am–2pm). Its displays – around the cloisters of a former convent – include a fine Basque ethnographic exhibition and the largest collection of keyhole-shaped funerary steles in the País Vasco. The convent chapel is decorated with a series of frescoes depicting scenes from Basque life by José Sert.

A stairway off the plaza flanking the museum rises to **Monte Urgull**, its parkland crisscrossed by winding paths. From the mammoth figure of Christ and dilapidated ruined castle on its summit, a 45-minute climb, there are great views out to sea and back across the bay to the town. On the way down you can stop at the **Aquarium** (mid-June to mid-Sept daily 10am–9pm; mid-Sept to mid-June Mon–Fri 10am–7pm, Sat & Sun 11am–8pm; €9) on the harbour; it contains the skeleton of a whale caught in the nineteenth century and an extensive history of Basque navigation. Although there's not a greal deal of fish, you can walk through the middle of a giant aquarium in a Perspex tube. Close by, at Paseo de Muelle 24, is the **Museo Naval** (Tues–Sat 10am–1.30pm & 4–7.30pm, Sun 11am–2pm; €1.50), with video facilities and exhibits tracing the tradition and history of Basque fishing.

Still better views across the bay can be had from the top of **Monte Igeldo**: take the #16 bus marked *Igeldo* from the Boulevard or walk around the bay to its base near the Real Club de Tennis, from where a **funicular** (daily: summer 10am–8pm; winter 11am–6pm; every 15min; €1 round trip) will carry you to the summit. Continuing along the *paseo* past the tennis club you end up at Eduardo Chillida's striking iron **sculpture**, *El Peine de los Vientos* (The Comb of the Winds), looking as if it is trying to grasp the waves in its powerful rusting arms.

## Beaches

There are **four beaches** in San Sebastián: Playa de la Concha, Playa de Ondarreta, Playa de la Zurriola and Playa de Gros. **La Concha** is the most central and the most celebrated, a wide crescent of yellow sand stretching around the bay from the town. Despite the almost impenetrable mass of flesh here during much of the summer, this is the best (if most regimented) of the beaches, enlivened by sellers of peeled prawns and cold drinks, and with great swimming out to the diving platforms moored in the bay. Further out sits the small **Isla de Santa Clara**, which makes a good spot for picnics; a boat leaves from the port every half-hour in the summer (daily 10am–8pm; €1.50 round trip).

**La Concha** and **Ondarreta** are the best beaches for swimming – the latter is a continuation of the same strand beyond the rocky outcrop which supports the **Palacio de Miramar**, once a summer home of Spain's royal family. Set back from Ondarreta beach are large villas, some of the most expensive properties in Spain, and mostly owned by wealthy families from Madrid who holiday here – the area used to be known as La Diplomática for this reason and has a reputation for being rather more staid than the central area, although the lively district of **El Antiguo** with its many bars is only a few minutes' walk beyond.

Far less crowded, and popular with surfers, **Playa de la Zurriola** and the adjacent **Playa de Gros** were regraded during the 1990s and breakwaters added to shield them from dangerous currents and river pollution. A recent addition to the elegant promenade is the giant beached glass blocks of Rafael Moneo's **Kursaal**. In addition to an auditorium and art gallery, the building houses a pleasant café-restaurant with an outside terrace in summer. One of the best views of the whole town and bay may be had by climbing up the steps to the *sidrería* (see box p.546) on the side of **Monte Ulia** from the far end of the beach. This walk can easily be extended for about 5km along the coast to the lighthouse overlooking the entrance to Pasaia harbour.

## Eating and drinking

San Sebastián is a great place for a gastronomic treat, with some of the best **restaurants** in Spain, as well as plenty of lively **bars**. Most are in the *parte vieja* but there are also a few in the *zona romántica*; the majority close for some of Sunday and all of Monday. Prices tend to reflect the popularity of the old quarter, but lunchtime *menús del día* are generally good value, and the *pintxos* and *raciones* set out in all but the fanciest bars are a great way to eat reasonably. For those on a budget, there are a few worthy Italian and Asian eateries, while the **Mercado de la Bretxa**, a former *pescadería*, is a 2001-refurbished mall housing some affordable snack bars. One of the best establishments here, in the Zinekale section, is *Padang*, a fruit-juice bar serving every conceivable variety of fresh-whipped *zumos* and *batidos*.

**Arzak** Alto de Miracruz 21, Monte Ulia ☎943 278 465. A shrine of Basque cuisine, with three Michelin rosettes and a superb *menú* for around €50.

**La Cepa** c/Treinta y Uno de Agosto 7, Parte Vieja. Inexpensive *raciones* served amidst decor of bullfighting kitsch and dangling hams; also a pricier *comedor*. Closed Wed.

**Domenico's** c/Zubieta 3, Zona Romántica ☎943 471 537. Smart but affordable Italian restaurant with an emphasis on pasta; budget for €18–24 or choose the €10 weekday *menú*. Very popular, so reservations essential.

**Gaztelu** c/Treinta y uno de Agosto 22, Parte Vieja. Bland decor in the rear *comedor*, where sustaining fare with no airs or graces forms the cheapest (€7.50) *menú* in the *parte vieja*; more exciting *a la carta* runs to €18, or good *raciones* available in the front bar. Closed Wed.

**Gorriti** c/San Juan, corner c/Lorenzio, Parte Vieja. One of the town's best counter-top collections of fresh, seafood-strong *bocadillos* and *pintxos* to be found at this hole-in-the-wall with no seats or *comedor*.

**La Mama di Piccata Minuta** c/San Bartolomé 18, corner c/Triunfo, Zona Romántica. Good, relatively inexpensive Italian restaurant serving vegetarian dishes and pizzas. Allow about €18, without drink.

**Casa Maruxa** Paseo de Bizkaia 14, Amara. Specializes in food from Galicia and attracts the crowd on their way to the Astoria cinema complex just around the corner.

**Mendizorrotz** Barrio Igeldo, at the central plaza two stops before end of #16 bus line ☎943 212 023. Brief but superbly executed choice of dishes

with specialities like *pimientos de padrón* (grilled green peppers) and *pudding de txangurro* (spider-crab mousse). Reckon on €22–30 including local cider and dessert in the tiny *comedor* or have the cheap *menú* (Mon–Fri) at the bar tables. Usually closes one week in March.

**Morgan** c/Narrika 7. Bohemian clientele and a jazz soundtrack set the tone for this spot specializing in the "new Basque" school of cookery, emphasizing lighter, first courses – stuffed eggplant, venison carpaccio – and creative desserts, rather than the tradional hearty main courses. The bill can quickly mount to €30 *a la carta*, though there is a €12 lunch *menú*.

**Casa Nicolasa** c/Aldamar 4, 1° ☎943 421 762. Classic – and expensive – Basque cookery featuring seafood, game and meat; there's a €46 *menú*, but otherwise the bill can climb to €75. Closed Sun & Mon eve.

**Okendo (Oquendo)** c/Okendo 8. A decor of cinema-festival posters and delicacies such as crab cannelloni, venison and pigeon help justify the *menú's* €30 price tag; *a la carta* isn't much more.

**Oriental** c/Reyes Católicos 6. Extremely friendly Chinese restaurant that's the best in terms of quality of food and value – allow €16 *a la carta*; eat in or take away. Open daily.

**Txistu** Plaza de la Constitución 14. Vast range of *pintxos* inside, plus much-sought-after table service outside; the usual Basque suspects including mushrooms, kidneys, cuttlefish on skewers. Closed Tues.

**Warrechena** c/Nagusia (ex-Mayor), corner c/Puerto. Busy place serving up basic if sustaining fare (menús from €9) to *Donostiara* shoppers in tarted-up greasy caff surroundings.

# Entertainment

In the evenings, you'll find no shortage of action, with clubs and bars everywhere. The two main areas are the *parte vieja*, especially along Fermín Calbetón, Puerto and Juan de Bilbao and in the *Zona Romántica* around the intersection of c/Reyes Católicos and c/Larramendi, where a large number of the city's more expensive music pubs and cafés are located. For **jazz**, try *Altxerri* at c/Reina Regente 2 (closed Mon), or *Etxekalte* (no sign) at c/Mari 11 on the fishing port. Once the pubs close around 2am, the action moves on to various **clubs** until dawn: try the handful along Fermín Calbetón. **Film** venues include the ten-plex Cine Principe, on the Plaza de Zuloaga by San Telmo, and

## Sidrerías

If you're in San Sebastián between late January and early May, a visit to one of the many **sidrerías** (*sagardotegiak* in Basque, or cider houses) in the area around **Astigarraga**, about 6km from town, is a must – take the red Hernani-bound bus from the Alameda del Boulevard or a taxi for about €6.

**Cider** production is one of the oldest traditions in the Basque country – until the Civil War and the subsequent move towards industrialization, practically every farmhouse in Gipuzkoa and to a lesser extent the other provinces produced cider, which was a valuable commodity used for barter. Barter remained the main form of exchange in rural communities here until comparatively recently, and the farms were practically open houses where local people drank cider and socialized – the *bertsolariak* tradition of oral poetry originated in these places.

Since the 1980s, cider houses have been flourishing again, and for €9–18 you can feast on delicious food, drink unlimited quantities of cider and in general enjoy the raucous atmosphere. Of the seventy or so sidrerías, some of the most accessible include *Petritegi* and *Gartziategi*, just a few kilometres out of town in Astigarraga, while many of the more rustic and authentic ones, such as *Sarasola* and *Oiarbide*, are on the *ruta de las sidrerías* (cider trail) just beyond Astigarraga. Check in the *Turismo* for a full, current list with phone numbers.

the Cine Trueba at Secundino Esnaola 2, across the Santa Catalina bridge in Gros, which often shows art and *versión original* movies.

### Festivals

Throughout the summer there are constant **fiestas**, many involving Basque sports including the annual rowing (*trainera*) races between the villages along the coast, which culminate in a final regatta on September 9. The **Jazz Festival** (℡943 440 034, Ⓦwww.jazzaldia.com), held at different locations throughout the town for six days during the latter half of July, invariably attracts top performers as well as hordes of people on their way home from the fiesta in Pamplona. The week around August 15 – known as **Semana Grande** or Aste Nagusia (Ⓦwww.paisvasco.com/donostia/ingles/index.htm) – sees numerous concerts, special events and fireworks laid on. There is also the **Film Festival** (Ⓦwww.sansebastianfestival.ya.com) during the second half of September and frequent theatrical and musical performances throughout the year at the Auditorio del Kursaal or the Teatro Principal.

## Listings

**Bike rental** You can rent mountain bikes from Comet, Avda de la Libertad 6 ℡943 426 637.
**Books and maps** Graphos on the corner of Alameda del Boulevard and c/Nagusia has all conceivable documentation of the Pyrenees and Basque country; Bilintx, c/Fermín Calbetón 21, has more books, plus CDs of local music.
**Car rental** Atesa, Amezketa 7 ℡943 463 013; Avis, c/Triunfo 2 ℡943 461 527; Hertz, c/Zubieta 5 ℡943 461 084; and Europcar, RENFE station, Paseo de Francia ℡943 322 304; Sixt, c/Amezketa 4 ℡943 444 329.

**Laundry** Wash'n'Dry, Aussie-run laundromat at c/Iparragirre 6 in Gros (open daily 8am–10pm).
**Internet café** Most central is *Donosti-NET*, with two premises at c/Embeltrán 2 and c/San Jerónimo 8 (daily 9am–11pm).
**Swimming pools** The sports centre in Anoeta, Polideportivo de Anoeta (℡943 458 797), has an open-air pool, track, tennis courts and a gym. There's another pool, Termas La Perla, at Paseo de la Concha (℡943 458 856), which also has a gym and sauna.

## Basque nationalism

Despite the high-profile activities of **ETA** (*Euskadi ta Askatasuna* – "Freedom for the Basques"), **Basque nationalism** is not an especially recent phenomenon. Richard Ford wrote in 1845 that "these highlanders, bred on metal-pregnant mountains, and nursed amid storms in a cradle indomitable as themselves, have always known how to forge their iron into arms, and to wield them in defence of their own independence". The Visigoths perceived the *Vascones* as a "dangerous rural population emerging from the mountains to threaten the settled inhabitants of the valleys". Visigoth king Recared, unable to completely subdue the region, used to send his troops there just to keep them fit.

For much of the history of both France and Spain, the Basques jealously defended their *fors* or *fueros* – ancient customary privileges guaranteeing them effective autonomy – against constant pressure from Paris and Madrid, and guarded the wealth brought by seafaring skills, mineral riches and industrial enterprise. After the Revolution, in 1790, the French Basques' millennium-old *fors* were abolished as part of the general centralizing strategy of the Jacobins, and the three traditional French Basque regions were amalgamated with Béarn in a new administrative *département*. In Spain, 1876 and the second, final defeat of the Carlists, whom the Basques supported as upholding their own traditionalist values, saw the victorious Liberals finally abolish the *fueros* altogether to punish the rebellious Basques.

Although the conservative, traditionalist **Basque National Party** (PNV) emerged in Spain towards the end of the nineteenth century, under the leadership of the frankly racist, Catholic extremist **Sabino Arana**, it was only during the 1930s that Basque nationalism became associated with the political Left, mostly in reaction to Franco's regime. Cut off from their Republican allies by predominantly rural Navarra and Alava, whose conservative landowners sided with the Nationalists, the urbanized Basque coastal provinces of Gipuzkoa and Vizkaia were conquered in a vicious campaign that included the infamous German bombing of **Gernika** (Guernica) in April 1937. Franco's vengeful boot went in hard, and up to 21,000 people died in his post-war attempts to crush the Basques. Public use of Euskera was forbidden, and central control was asserted by force – plus covert activities overseas, including the kidnapping from the US, torture and murder of Jesus Galíndez, member of the last pre-war regional Basque government.

But Spanish state violence failed signally, merely nurturing new resistance focused on ETA, which scored its first kill in 1968. Their activities have included scores of bombings and shootings, with nearly nine hundred victims to date; their most spectacular success was the 1973 assassination of Franco's right-hand man and probable successor, Admiral Carrero Blanco. Even today Spanish military and police personnel are regarded – and behave – as an army of occupation, and more radically minded Basques continue to support ETA's aims, if not their every tactic.

Since the **return to democracy**, however, things have changed substantially. The Spanish Basque parliament exercises considerable independence in home affairs (it's the only autonomous community allowed to collect its own taxes), plus there's a Basque police force, the *ertzaintza* (distinguished by its red berets). The Basque **language** is flourishing again, taught in over half the primary schools of the coastal areas. The Basque **flag** (the *ikurriña*, designed by Arana and not particularly ancient) flies everywhere, and street as well as town names are signposted preferentially in Euskera across the region.

Since securing autonomy, Spanish Euskadi has been controlled by the political Centre-Right. When the conservative Partido Popular (PP) failed to gain an outright parliamentary majority in the March 1996 national elections, they were forced into a coalition pact with Catalan and Basque conservative parties. Among the concessions made was the transfer of 32 convicted ETA terrorists (out of more than 600)

*(box continues overleaf)*

*(box continued)*

to jails in or close to the Basque country, a persistent demand of **Herri Batasuna** (Popular Unity), ETA's political wing. Otherwise, Herri Batasuna had little influence in a Basque parliament dominated by the PNV and the Socialists; their electoral support rarely topped ten percent except in parts of Gipuzkoa and Bizkaia. Polls showed that, while wanting increased autonomy, most Basques opposed forming a breakaway state.

Local economic woes had much to do with this – the former industrial glories of Bizkaia in particular have, since the 1930s, been reduced to rusty, outdated factories and idle steel foundries and shipyards. Terrorism discourages needed new investment, and unemployment remains high. In January 1988 a historic pact by all the Basque parties, except Herri Batasuna, condemned ETA's methods while upholding their goals. HB's claim to act independently of the terrorists was further undermined in 1997 by its street marches in support of ETA; in subsequent all-party rallies and statements against ETA, HB always conspicuously abstained.

The Spanish government periodically offered **amnesties** to activists who publicly renounced ETA's methods – though the few who did so risked (and in many cases suffered) assassination by their former comrades – and until 1989 engaged in secret negotiations with ETA leaders. But Madrid wielded a big stick while apparently granting concessions. A death squad known by the acronym **GAL**, which liquidated over twenty ETA fellow-travellers during a 1983–88 clandestine "dirty war", was first thought to consist mainly of off-duty Guardia Civil members. Their operations were even carried out in the French Basque regions, while an extradition treaty with France denied ETA operatives their former safe refuges across the border. But a series of **spectacular trials** in Spain, culminating in 1999, resulted in the exposure of GAL's civilian control – and the convictions of former PSOE interior minister José Barrionuevo, his deputy, the governor of Gipuzkoa, and a Guardia Civil general.

ETA has a French counterpart, **Iparreterrak**, based largely in Lapourd. But despite this, there is no real desire among ordinary French Basques for an independent, trans-border homeland, and any French sympathy for ETA has evaporated since Franco's death and the institution of home rule across the frontier. That said, top ETA members still seek refuge in France, while periodically the French authorities arrest and either try or extradite figures always identified as the core leadership of what's clearly a hydra-headed organization.

GAL or not, ETA terror continued, a strategy seen by many as a desperate attempt to force a government return to negotiation; since 1994 younger hardliners, including many firebrand women, have seized control from the historic leadership, now mostly in exile in Latin America. The **youth** of Euskadi apparently have few other compelling role models, and most recent ETA recruits are under 25. At the same time, ETA forged sensationally publicized operational links with the IRA, Columbia's FARC and assorted Palestinian groups.

# Travel details

## Spanish trains

**San Sebastián to:** Bilbao (9 daily; 2hr 30min–3hr); Hendaye, France (every 30min 7am–10pm; 35min); Irún (every 30min 5am–11pm; 30min).

## French trains

**Bayonne to:** Biarritz (14 daily; 10min); Hendaye

Ex-premier Aznar himself narrowly escaped death from a 1996 car bomb detonated by ETA in Madrid, and summer of that year saw numerous small devices – designed more to scare than kill – set off in coastal resorts popular with Britons. Almost annually since, ETA has warned foreign **tourists** – as "legitimate targets" – to avoid Spain, and has exploded bombs in various **resorts**. Other tactics, such as extorting **"revolutionary taxes"** from Basque-run businesses and kidnapping VIPs for ransom, emerged during the mid-1990s to fund the estimated $8 million annual ETA "budget". Money is laundered in a vast network of front businesses, including Basque hotels and restaurants not just in France and Spain, but also in the expatriate communities of Mexico, Venezuela and Uruguay.

But each outrage generated increasing revulsion, especially when PP municipal councillor **Miguel Ángel Blanco** was kidnapped in July 1997 and soon found mortally wounded when ransom demands were ignored. The kidnapping, and funeral, prompted street demonstrations a million strong in the Basque country and across Spain. It was, unfortunately, the first in what became almost monthly **assassinations** by ETA (and counter-demonstrations) until 2001, with the exception of a fourteen-month truce which ended in late 1999, having failed to induce Madrid to return to negotiations. Since Ángel Blanco's killing, numerous military personnel, two judges, many more municipal councillors, MPs and an ex-governor of Gipuzkoa have died at ETA hands, mostly PP members, but PNV and PSOE personalities as well. The hit-men consider fair game anyone of any political stripe who disagrees with their agenda, as well as convenient symbolic targets in the judiciary and armed forces. Civilian bystanders – including foreigners – are also seen as acceptable **"collateral damage"** by ETA.

With a clear majority in the March 2000 elections, the PP did not have to make concessions to any nationalist coalition partners, and Aznar's government stepped up efforts to eradicate ETA. They were indirectly aided by the results of regional Basque elections in May 2001, which saw the PNV and a moderate coalition partner get 43 percent of the vote, and HB much reduced – prior to its mandatory **closure** by Madrid judges and MPs in August 2002, along with various "cultural" groups deemed to be ETA fronts. In February 2003, *Egunkaria*, the only all-Euskera newspaper, was shut down forcibly for being an ETA mouthpiece, and hundreds of candidates deemed to be crypto-HB were disqualified from the May 2003 Basque elections. The **police** were also busy throughout 2003 in this official war of attrition, with the arrest of twenty top ETA-ites, the seizure of several explosive caches, and consequent annual reduction in ETA-caused deaths to just three. As heavy-handed as some of these measures may seem, they wouldn't have been tenable without the effective social marginalization of both HB and ETA on its home turf; even confronted by the PP's belligerently intransigent "no talks" stance, an overwhelming majority of the Basque population feels that more will be achieved through available democratic channels than by violence.

(14 daily; 35min); Irún (10 daily; 40min); Lourdes (4–8 daily; 1hr 45min); Pau (7–8 daily; 1hr 15min); Saint-Jean-de-Luz (14 daily; 25min); Tarbes (7–8 daily; 2hr).
**Saint-Jean-Pied-de-Port** to: Bayonne (4–5 daily; 1hr); Bidarraï (Pont-Noblia, 4–5 daily; 20min); Cambo-les-Bains (4–5 daily; 45min); Itsasu (1 daily; 30min).

## Spanish buses

**Ansó/Echo** to: Jaca (Mon–Sat 1 daily at 6am; 1hr 40min).
**Pamplona** to: Auritze (Mon–Sat 1 daily; 1hr 30min); Elizondo (Mon–Fri 3 daily, Sat & Sun 1 daily; 2hr); Eaurta (Mon–Sat 1 daily; 2hr 30min); Irún (3 daily; 2hr); Izaba (Mon–Fri 1 daily; 2hr);

Jaca (July & Aug 2 daily, rest of year 1 except Fri & Sun 2; 1hr 45min); Irún (3 daily; 2hr); Otsagabia (Mon–Sat 1 daily; 2hr); Roncesvalles (Mon–Sat 1 daily; 1hr 35min); Yesa (July & Aug 2 daily, rest of year 1 except Fri & Sun 2; 1hr).

**San Sebastián** to: Bera de Bidasoa (2 daily; 1hr); Elizondo (3 daily; 2hr); Hondarribia (every 20 min; 30min); Lesaka (2 daily; 1hr 15min); Pamplona (6 daily; by *autovía* 1hr, others 3hr).

## French buses (including SNCF coaches)

**Bayonne** to: Biarritz (every 10–20min on STAB urban buses; 15–20min); Cambo-les-Bains (several daily; 40min); Hendaye-Ville & -Plage (3–7 daily by inland route; 70–90min); San Sebastián (2 daily Mon–Sat on PESA; 1hr 45min); St-Jean-de-Luz (6–14 daily summer, 4–6 winter, on ATCRB; 40min).

**Baïgorri** to: Ossès-St-Martin-d'Arossa rail junction (3–6 daily; 10min).

**Biarritz** to: Hendaye-Plage & -Ville (5–7 daily by coastal corniche road; 30min).

**Saint-Jean-de-Luz** to: Cambo-les-Bains (2–3 daily in summer; 45min); Ezpeleta (2–3 daily in summer; 35min); Hendaye (9–16 Mon–Sat, 5 Sun in summer by coast or inland route, reduced winter frequency; 30min); Sara (2–3 daily in summer; 25min).

# Contexts

# Contexts

# History

The history of the Pyrenees inevitably draws on that of both France and Spain, although through the ages the border region has often found itself well out of the social and political mainstream. The following summary highlights the salient events and trends which directly impinged on the mountains and their people.

## Prehistoric habitation

Pyrenean history begins with a man who died aged 20 some 455,000 years ago near the present-day village of Tautavel in the Fenouillèdes foothills. Excavated from the floor of a limestone cave in 1971, the bones of "Tautavel Man" rank as some of the earliest human remains found anywhere in Europe. However, the trail then grows cold until late Paleolithic times (35,000–10,000 BC), the era of the cave-paintings left by hunter-gatherers in various parts of the Pyrenees. The most spectacular discoveries date from the end of the Paleolithic era – known as the Magdalenian period – at Niaux and Bédeilhac in France. In around 5000 BC **dolmens** appear, either stone burial chambers or – as recently conjectured – seasonal shelters for shepherds, found throughout most of the Pyrenees. No habitations from this period have been discovered, but it can be assumed that perishable huts of some sort were erected, and farming had certainly begun by this time.

## Early invasions

Before the start of the **Bronze Age** (around 2000 BC), Pyrenean people – as elsewhere in Europe – began to move into fortified villages, and from then until the thirteenth century AD, when the Muslims were effectively driven out of Spain, the area experienced a succession of **invasions**. First, around 1000 BC, came a mix of Celtic and Germanic peoples. The **Celtic** "urnfield people" settled in Catalonia, and later mingled with the Iberians from the south to become the **Celto-Iberians**. The mysterious **Vascones**, whose origins remain unclear, had probably already occupied what is now the Basque country long before this time.

Later, by 550 BC, the **Greeks** established a trading post at Roses, on the Catalan coast. During the third century BC the ~~Car~~thaginians occupied Catalonia, principally in the Spanish part, from where then most famous commander, Hannibal, crossed the Pyrenees in 214 BC on his way to Italy. But after the Second Punic War (218–201 BC) the Carthaginians were expelled from the peninsula by the **Romans**, who despite strong resistance from the Celto-Iberian tribes – and never-complete dominance of the Vascones – succeeded in making the Pyrenees, as well as Iberia and Gaul to either side, an integral part of their empire. Although a political backwater, the Pyrenean foothills were endowed by the Romans with a network of roads, bridges, villas and garrison towns; most of the modern highways in the area follow Roman thoroughfares.

Roman rule soon began to be eclipsed – a process not completed for several centuries – with raids by **Franks** and **Suevi** (Swabians), who overran the Pyrenees between 262 and 276 AD. Two centuries later followed new invasions of **Alans** and **Vandals**, eventually superseded by the fifth-century incursions of the **Visigoths** from Gaul, former Romanized allies of Rome who had been pushed out of France by the Franks under King Clovis. The Visigoths established a capital first at Toulouse and then another at Barcelona in 531 AD. By the end of the sixth century, the Visigothic kingdom extended from the Pyrenees to include most of modern Spain and half of modern France, although the Basque region retained its independence. Apparent strength and unity were spurious, however: the Visigothic monarchy was elected, leading to constant factional strife; adherence by many to the Arian heresy forfeited the kingdom support from the Byzantines; and the bulk of the population lived in a state of virtual serfdom.

# The "Moors" and the reconquest

With the Visigothic state in terminal decline, the **Moorish** (or more properly, Muslim North African) **conquest of Spain** was – in contrast to Rome's protracted campaigns – startlingly rapid. In 711, less than a century after Mohammed had left Mecca, governor of Tangier Tariq the Berber led a force of seven thousand across the Strait of Gibraltar and defeated the Visigothic army of King Roderic. Little effective resistance was mounted elsewhere, and within ten years these Berber clans controlled most of the peninsula, including the foothills of the Pyrenees. By the standards of its time, Muslim administration was remarkably tolerant: effective autonomy was conceded to remoter communities in return for regular payment of tribute, while Jews and Christians were allowed to continue in their faith, those who did not convert being called **Mozarabs**.

The Muslims called the area they controlled **al-Andalus**, whose borders expanded and contracted over the next eight centuries. Their authority soon stretched beyond the Pyrenees, a progress only halted in 732 by the Frank, **Charles Martel** – so named because he crushed the invaders like a *marteau* (hammer). A scion of the Merovingian dynasty which then dominated what is now modern France, he drove the Muslims south out of Aquitaine, a fight continued by his son Pepin, and his more famous grandson **Charlemagne** (768–814), whose empire at its height effectively included the southern slopes of the Pyrenees as well as the northern, most of modern Catalonia and much of Navarra. But Charlemagne endured setbacks, most notably the massacre of his rearguard near Navarran **Roncesvalles** in 778. No reliable account of this event exists, but it seems he had crossed the Pyrenees to assist a Catalan Muslim faction opposed to the Umayyad emir of Córdoba. His putative ally defeated, Charlemagne contented himself with raiding and sacking most of the important towns of the Ebro valley, slighting their fortifications for good measure. By demolishing the walls of Pamplona as well, he antagonized its Basque inhabitants; as his army retreated over the Pyrenees, the Pamplonans retaliated by wiping out part of his army.

After Roncesvalles, Charlemagne switched his attention to the Mediterranean side of the Pyrenees in an attempt to defend his empire against the Moors. He took Girona in 785, and his son Louis le Débonnaire directed the successful siege of Barcelona in 801. Continued Frankish military success meant that any influence the Muslims had wielded in the Pyrenees waned long before the turning point for the whole peninsula, the battle of **Las Navas de Tolosa** in 1212, won by the united Christian kings of León, Castile, Aragón and Navarra.

To secure recaptured territory, castles were built in strategic places south of the Pyrenean crest from Barcelona to the hills of western Aragón. A vassal who held a castle in fief for his lord was variously known as a *castellanus*, *castlá* or *catlá*, from which is possibly derived the name **Catalonia** – or, in Catalan, Catalunya. To the west, the Navarran capital of Pamplona and the Aragonese early-medieval capital of Jaca remained important strategic towns, and from the ninth century onwards lay astride, or just to one side, of the two main pilgrim routes to the shrine of Santiago de Compostela in Galicia. Protected by the castles and made wealthy by the patronage of kings and pilgrims, **monasteries** flourished throughout the Pyrenees. Benedictine monks established themselves in Roussillon, Catalunya, Aragón and the Comminges, beginning in the tenth century and taking advantage of lands and funds granted by local Pyrenean leaders to build on a grand scale. Thus there are numerous surviving **Romanesque churches** across the range, the cathedral at Jaca being one of the finest examples.

Although Islamic influence lingered in Spain until as late as the sixteenth century, when the last **mudéjars** – Moors living under Christian rule – were expelled from Andalucía, it's hotly debated whether or not any remained on the north side of the Pyrenees. Partisans in favour point to apparent versions of the word "Moor" in the names of mountains and places – Moreau, Serre Mourène and Pouey-Morou, for example. But these are more easily explained as variations on the old French word *moreau*, meaning brown. If they colonized any of the high ground, it could only have been briefly: by 920 Jaca was out of Muslim hands for the last time, Huesca was reconquered in 1096, and Barbastro returned to Christian rule in 1100.

# Early nation-building

Charlemagne's grandsons divided his empire between themselves after 843, and it was only a matter of time before the Frankish empire fell apart. In the face of destabilizing attacks by Normans and Norsemen during the ninth century, the **Carolingian kings** were forced to delegate more power and autonomy to provincial governors, whose lands already had acquired strong identities of their own. With the death of the last Carolingian in 987, **Hugues Capet** was elected king of what was left of the empire, founding a dynasty of Paris-based rulers that lasted until 1328.

The **Capetians** were initially no more than first among (un)equals, surrounded by nominal vassals who were often more powerful than the king. In feudal France, such provincial *seigneurs* spent their time fighting each other, occasionally besieging each other's castles but more usually destroying crops, stealing cattle and burning villages. Things got so out of hand that the bishops introduced *La Trève de Dieu* (God's Truce), which banned fighting from Wednesday evening until Monday morning – but they fortified their own monastic churches as a precaution, examples being at Saint-Savin and Luz near Lourdes.

The situation began to change when **Eleanor**, daughter of the powerful William VIII, duke of Aquitaine, married the future Louis VII, thus bringing that duchy under Parisian control. But Eleanor divorced him and immediately – in 1152 – remarried Henry of Normandy, who shortly became Henry II of England. Thus the English gained control of a huge chunk of what would become modern France, with the vast **Angevin empire** stretching from the Channel to the Pyrenees. The most notorious British personality was **Edward the Black Prince**, whose harsh tactics – thus the epithet – provoked revolts in Bigorre late in the fourteenth century.

At the same time, Catalunya and Aragón were also active in "French" territory. In 1137 the betrothal of Count Ramon Berenguer IV of Catalunya to Petronella, the two-year-old daughter of King Ramiro II of Aragón, united the two kingdoms. His son Alfonso I added Roussillon and much of southern France to his territories, and fancied himself as the "Emperor of the Pyrenees".

**Philippe Auguste** (1180–1223) began to reverse the Angevin gains, undermining English rule by exploiting the bitter relations between Henry II and his sons, one of whom was Richard the Lionheart. By the end of his reign, the Capetian royal lands were for the first time greater than those of any other French lord, a process assisted by the support given to the pope's crusade against the **Cathars**, which began in 1209. The Cathars – also known as the Albigensians – were a heretical religious group who had rapidly gained support in Languedoc and the Eastern Pyrenees. By convention, the lands and other property of defeated heretics went to the victors, which explains the enthusiasm of Paris for the venture.

First Béziers fell to the papal crusade, then Carcassonne. In 1213 Pedro (Pere) II, son of Alfonso I and king of Aragón and Catalonia, intervened on the Cathar side, but was killed besieging the papal general Simon de Montfort at Muret. His defeat signalled the end of Catalan aspirations north of the Pyrenees: had he won, Languedoc might be Spanish today. The outcome of the crusade was the virtual extinction of Catharism and the strengthening of French influence in the Pyrenean foothills. Much of the property of Raymond VII, defeated count of Toulouse, was forfeited to the Crown, and the walls of Toulouse and many other fortified places were razed. Indirectly, the success of the crusade also spelt the end of patronage for the **troubadour poets**, with whom the local nobility had been associated, and consequently the decline of the *langue d'oc*, the southern French language that they had championed. From this period also date the first **bastides**, some three hundred fortified new towns scattered across the Pyrenean foothills by the victors, built to a grid plan around well-proportioned central squares.

With the death of Pedro, **Jaume I of Aragón**, nicknamed "the Conqueror" (1208–76), succeeded to the throne at the age of five. The 63 years of his reign were a period of concerted expansion for the joint kingdom of Aragón and Catalunya: he drove the Muslims from Mallorca in 1229, took Menorca in 1231 and Ibiza in 1235, and reached Valencia in 1238. Realizing that the Catalan future lay to the south and east, he was less determined north of the Pyrenees and in 1258 signed the **Treaty of Corbeil**, by which he renounced all territorial rights in France (except Montpellier, the Cerdagne and Roussillon), in return for King Louis of France's renunciation of claims on Catalunya.

# From the Hundred Years' War to the Wars of Religion

The northern part of the Angevin empire was lost by King John in 1204, and from then on the Capetians steadily chipped away at English rule in Aquitaine. When the Capetian male line expired in 1328, the French throne went to Philippe VI of Valois, nephew of Philippe the Fair, but this succession was quickly disputed by Edward III of England, Philippe the Fair's grandson. Thus began the **Hundred Years' War** (1338–1453), with Paris aiming to take Aquitaine and Gascony – which included much of the western Pyrenees – and the English attempting to recover what John had lost.

Against this background **Gaston Fébus**, count of Foix, contended with the powerful house of Armagnac for the part of Gascony known as Bigorre. Fébus' defeat of the Armagnacs at the **Battle of Launac** in 1362 was the first step towards the creation of a small **kingdom of the Pyrenees**, and at its zenith the area ruled by Fébus included Foix, Bigorre, Béarn and Soule. However, he died without an heir in 1391, and the chance of an independent northern Pyrenees went with him.

**Roussillon** was taken from an increasingly united Spain by Louis XI of France in 1463, but Perpignan revolted against the French a decade later. Although the city was recaptured in 1474 after a harsh siege followed by brutal repression, Charles VIII – who succeeded Louis in 1483 – decided there were richer pickings to be had in Italy and handed Roussillon back to Spain in 1493.

Despite coming out on top in the Hundred Years' War, France was eventually forced by the Spanish to relinquish most of its interest in the Pyrenean-straddling kingdom of **Navarra/ Navarre**, which it had held since the early thirteenth-century election of Theobald (Thibaut), count of Champagne, as king of Navarre. Later Navarre passed first to the Fébus clan of Foix, and then early in the sixteenth century to the French house of Albret, which was shortly to embrace Protestantism. All of Navarra was conquered by Fernando of Aragón in 1512, though the region of Basse-Navarre north of the watershed was returned to the French in the person of Henri II d'Albret in 1530, who ruled – as did his descendants – from Pau.

His daughter, the militantly Calvinist **Jeanne d'Albret**, created an important secondary theatre in the **Wars of Religion** racking France at this time, defeating the Catholic troops of Charles IX at nearby Navarrenx. Like the Cathars before them, the Protestants were especially strong in the south of France, but also claimed a considerable number of adherents in the west. Jeanne's more easy-going son, Henri III of Béarn and Navarre, put himself in line for the French Crown by marrying Marguerite of Valois in 1572. Accordingly when he acceded to the throne of France in 1589 as **Henri IV**, his inheritance of Foix-Béarn and Basse-Navarre was incorporated into France, and the Pyrenean boundary of southwestern France was thus finalized. But as a Protestant, Henri was unacceptable in the Catholic north, and it was only after four years of fighting against the ultra-Catholic league led by the Guise family, and his own eventual conversion to Catholicism ("Paris is worth a Mass", he is reputed to have said) that he could truly claim to be king of all France.

Henri set about reconstructing the country and attempting to accommodate the religious factions that had been at war since 1562. By the 1598 **Edict of**

## Pyrenean life in the Middle Ages

Before the Black Death struck the Pyrenees in the mid-fourteenth century, the **population** in the mountains was greater than it is today, with a well-developed social structure. Each village had its minor aristocracy acting as military agents for the local count, plus a bailiff to collect rents and dues, and settle small disputes. However, there was little of the rigid class distinction of major towns in Spain and France, and aristocrats, clergy and villagers met on fairly equal terms.

There were no taverns, so socializing was limited to the fireside, the village square and Sunday Mass. Though knowledge of religious teaching was rudimentary, the **Church** was an enormously significant force for social cohesion, and all people were highly God-fearing. The local priest was accepted as one of the villagers, but the distant bishop was despised as the one who imposed unjust tithes – though outright opposition to these was a recipe for trouble with the **Inquisition**. The poorest houses, and even the shepherds' summer huts, were repositories of ancestral superstition, maintained through years of continuous habitation by the same families, who would keep fingernail clippings and locks of hair as household talismans.

It was an introverted society. Most people married within the village and spent their entire lives there, except for visits to the nearest **market** town to buy or sell produce. Money was little used: villagers survived on their own farm produce and craft, by bartering and swapping favours. Only the shepherds moved freely, sometimes over surprisingly long distances: it was not uncommon to winter the flock in the very south of Catalonia, but to spend the summers in the lush upland pastures of the Ariège.

Little is known about the general **health** of people in the Pyrenees in the late Middle Ages, but all social classes were certainly infested with parasites such as lice. Bathing was unheard of, except for medical reasons at one of the spas. The lot of **women** was correspondingly harsh. Treated as chattel, they were married off to enhance a family's status and could expect frequent beatings. Apart from the inevitability of regular childbearing, a woman's duties included fetching water and kindling, tending the fire and the garden, cooking, weeding the fields and harvesting.

**Nantes** the Huguenots – as the Protestants were also called – were accorded freedom of worship in specified places, the right to education and public office on the same basis as Catholics, their own courts and the retention of certain fortresses as a guarantee against renewed attack. But Henri's assassination in 1610 ended royal protection for the growing numbers of Protestants in the French Pyrenees. The new King Louis XIII's agent **Cardinal Richelieu**, having crushed the Protestant strongholds of La Rochelle and Montpellier, then set about razing various Pyrenean fortresses such as Miglos in the Ariège.

# Franco-Spanish war and the Treaty of the Pyrenees

In 1635 an ascendant France and a greatly weakened Spain were again at war, and by 1640 the Catalans had taken advantage of this state of affairs to declare themselves an **independent republic**, under the presumed protection of Louis XIII. Their marching song, "Els Segadors" (The Reapers), was later to become the Catalan national anthem. Louis annexed Roussillon from the Spanish Crown and came personally to supervise the siege of Perpignan, which fell on September 9, 1642. The inhabitants were grateful, and looked forward to an independent Catalonia, but this was never to be: Barcelona fell to Spanish forces in 1652 and Catalonia was effectively split in two. In July 1654, the French besieged Villefranche-de-Conflent, which capitulated after eight days, and in October the key Cerdanyan town of Puigcerdà also fell to France. The French razed the walls of Villefranche in 1656 fearing that the Spanish might retake the city, which was somewhat rash, since the town soon became theirs by the **Treaty of the Pyrenees**. This, negotiated by the respective foreign ministers of France and Spain on a neutral island in the River Bidasoa near Bayonne in 1659, provided for permanent French control of Roussillon and part of the Cerdagne. The Spanish paid a heavy price when the details were thrashed out the following year at Llívia, ancient capital of the Cerdanya/Cerdagne. They lost Perpignan – then one of the most important towns in Europe – and the fortified port of Collioure. Puigcerdà and Llívia remained Spanish, but the surrounding territory became French, leaving Llívia as an enclave. As for the Catalans, they forever lost the prospect of a united, independent country.

With **Louis XIV,** the *Roi Soleil* or "Sun King", reigning alone after the death of Cardinal Mazarin in 1661, **Sébastien le Prestre de Vauban** began fortifying dozens of towns for the king along the north slopes of the Pyrenees, his most famous work being **Mont-Louis** in the Cerdagne. Even Vauban, however, was to fall out of favour for his criticism of Louis' war-mongering and wealth-amassing, financed by taxation from which aristocrats and clergy were exempt.

Although the boundary envisioned by the treaty was not formally delineated until the mid-nineteenth century, it has long been one of the most stable and peaceful in Europe. For the Pyrenean population, especially in the upland of Cerdanya/Cerdagne, the treaty's terms conferred dubious benefits: age-old local customs were superseded by centralizing states; the power of the Church – whose dioceses frequently overlapped the new boundaries – was severely challenged; and smuggling was an inevitable consequence of the zealously re-energized customs services. For the first time many Pyreneans, especially on the French side, became liable to conscription and thus saw parts of the wider world, often settling far away in the lowlands – the beginning of the massive mountain depopulation that continues to this day. Not only the Catalans but the Basques at the opposite end of the range suffered progressive erosion of the *fors/fueros*, ancient charters which had guaranteed some degree of home rule.

# War of the Spanish Succession

With the death of the Habsburg King Charles II of Spain in 1700, the throne was offered to the grandson of Louis XIV, Philippe d'Anjou, provided he renounce his rights to the throne of France. Louis XIV's acceptance of the deal, which put a Bourbon on the throne of Spain and gave him indirect control there, guaranteed war with Habsburg Austria, whose Archduke Charles had already been named as successor. England too was drawn into the conflict, fearing a combined French-Spanish power. The **War of the Spanish Succession** lasted thirteen years from 1701, with Holland, Portugal and Denmark on the side of Austria and England, arrayed against France, Spain and Bavaria. Peace was eventually achieved by the treaties of **Utrecht** (1713) and **Rastatt** (1714), with Philippe remaining as **King Felipe V** of Spain, but his realm was divested of all territory in Belgium, Luxembourg, Italy and Sardinia, with Gibraltar and Menorca being ceded to England. In revenge for its support of the Austrian claimant, Felipe V suppressed what little remained of Catalunya's autonomy. The war effort had effectively bankrupted the French, and Louis XIV, his sun well and truly set, died in 1715.

# The French Revolution and the Peninsular War

On the evening of July 28, 1789, a group of strangers arrived in the *Roussillonnais* town of Prades, sounded the alarm bell and forced the doors of the salt store, instrument of the hated *gabelle* (salt tax). The **French Revolution** had reached the eastern Pyrenees, and within a few days all the crown agents and tax-gatherers had been beaten up and ejected from Roussillon. But the euphoria was short-lived. After the solidarity of the anti-tax riots, the Revolution degenerated into a settling of old personal scores, of village against village; peasants went armed just to tend their vines. People soon realized that they had swapped a despised but distant monarchy for a system of government that would far more effectively pervade every aspect of their lives, not least in the suppression of the traditional regions such as Bigorre and Béarn and their replacement with new, gerrymandered *départements* designed to sever all old loyalties.

**Land reform**, with its abolition of feudal dues and tithes, was popular on the plains but less significant in the mountains where there was already a complex system of communal grazing rights. There was no support for the war with the royalist empires of Prussia and Austria who were determined to crush the Revolution, and men became fugitives rather than be conscripted, turning instead to smuggling. The **Terror** of 1792–95 claimed few Pyrenean lives, but when it did peasants suffered disproportionately. In Tarbes, for example, six people who had been overheard to criticize the new regime were guillotined: one naval officer, one priest and four peasants.

## The Peninsular War

Soon after becoming emperor of France in 1804, **Napoleon** saw an opportunity to take over Spain. The Spanish fleet was defeated at the Battle of Trafalgar in 1805, precipitating the abdication of Carlos IV. In April 1808 Napoleon summoned the disgraced Spanish royal family to Bayonne, deported Carlos IV and his wife to Italy and imprisoned their sons Fernando and Carlos in France. Napoleon then installed his own brother, Joseph Bonaparte, as king of Spain. Among Spanish intellectuals, opposition was initially muted by the hope that French rule would serve as a liberalizing force, but optimism quickly evaporated, and Britain and Portugal joined Spain against France in the **Peninsular War** (1808–14). Napoleon organized hospitals for his troops at Bagnères-de-Bigorre, Cauterets, Barèges and Capvern, a move that led to the revitalization of these spa towns. The emperor also planned various civil engineering projects in the Pyrenees to support his troops in Spain, including roads across passes above Marcadau and Gavarnie, but his army was forced back before anything came of them. His men retreated along the famous pilgrim route via Roncesvalles and were pursued eastwards along the Pyrenees by **Wellington**. Welling-

ton's armies were rapturously received by a people sick of Napoleonic belli-
cosity – scoring extra points by paying for supplies rather than just requisition-
ing them – and many of his officers returned after the war to settle at Pau.

# Seeds of the Spanish Civil War

Between 1810 and 1813 a *Cortes* or Spanish parliament attempted to found a
liberal regime, envisioning ministers answerable to it in the framework of a
constitutional monarchy. But Fernando VII, upon being restored to the throne
in 1814, immediately abolished this embryonic parliament and remained an
implacable opponent of any liberalization, presiding at the same time over the
loss of most of Spain's colonies in South America. Upon his death in 1833 the
crown was claimed both by his daughter Isabella II (a child under the regency
of her mother), and by his brother Carlos, backed by the Church, the conser-
vatives and the Basques. The **First Carlist War** (1833–39) ended with victory
for the (relatively speaking) liberals supporting Isabella, who came of age in
1843. Her reign was a long record of scandal, political crisis and constitutional
compromise, until liberal army generals forced Isabella to abdicate in 1868. The
experimental **First Republic** (1873–75) failed, and following the **Second
Carlist War** the throne went to Isabella's son Alfonso XII.

Thereafter, attempts to balance monarchism with parliamentary government
were only partly successful. Working-class **political movements** such as the
Socialist Workers' Party were developing rapidly: the socialist trade union, the
UGT, formed in 1888, took hold in the industrialized Basque country, while
the anarchists' rival union, the CNT, was especially well represented in
Catalunya. The loss of Cuba, Puerto Rico and the Philippines to the USA in
1898, and the "Tragic Week" of rioting in Barcelona in 1909 – following a call-
up of army reserves to fight in Morocco – represented significant blows to
national morale.

During World War I Spain was neutral but inward turbulence continued, and
in 1923 **General Primo de Rivera** overthrew the government to establish a
dictatorship. After his death in 1930, the success of antimonarchist parties in the
municipal elections of 1931 led to the abdication of the king and the foundation of the **Second Republic**.

**Catalunya** declared itself an independent republic two days after the municipal elections on April 14, 1931, but had to settle for a statute of limited autonomy granted by Madrid the following year. A relatively dynamic region, it had
long felt itself exploited by the rest of Spain. Meanwhile the Madrid government was too paralysed by the expectations of left-wingers and the potential
of right-wing reaction to accomplish anything substantial in the way of agrar-
ian or tax reform. Additionally, all the various brews of extreme political ideology that had been fermenting in Spain over the course of the previous century were ready to explode. Anarchism, communism and socialism all derived
some impetus from the Russian Revolution, while at the other end of the
spectrum was the **Falange** – a black-shirted fascist youth group founded in
1923 by José Antonio Primo de Rivera, son of the dictator.

The **army** was divided between the anti-monarchists, monarchists who supported the Bourbon dynasty and monarchists who supported the Carlist line –
whose power base was conservative Navarra. But they were sufficiently united
in their opposition to left-wing government, and though General José

Sanjurjo's 1934 coup attempt failed, it spawned the infamous **Spanish Military Union**, whose members included General Manuel Goded, General Emilio Mola and **General Francisco Franco**, all openly talking of another rebellion should the Catholic right fail to win the coming election. When the left-wing Frente Popular (Popular Front) won the election of February 1936 by a tiny majority, the stage was set.

# Events in France 1810–1938

Following the end of Napoleonic rule, France endured over half a century of turbulence despite nominal restoration of the monarchy in 1815. There were reversals of revolutionary tenets under a series of reactionary kings or self-styled emperors, alternating with growing popular discontent and periods of liberal retrenchment, all taking place against a backdrop of growth in industrial and economic power.

The trauma of defeat in the 1870 Franco-Prussian War resulted in the definitive declaration of a **republic**, and indirectly in the growing influence of the political Left; the Spanish UGT had a near-exact counterpart in the French CGT, which eschewed political organization in favour of "direct action". As in Spain, the various socialist and communist parties found it difficult to cooperate, even amidst the opportunity presented by the aftermath of World War I, whose 25 percent casualty rate among the French ranks and massive devastation on French soil had dealt the old social order a huge blow. The scale of the demographic decimation can be gauged by the memorial cenotaphs in every French Pyrenean village, with their long lists of the dead – often far more numerous than the current local male population.

The Catholic right, whose **Action Française** shock troops dated from the early years of the century, mirrored the analogous groupings in Spain. Faced by the growing threat of both Nazism across the Rhine and homegrown fascist activism, the French Left papered over its internal differences and – in the same year as the Spanish Popular Front victory – won a rather more convincing mandate in the Parisian Chamber of Deputies. "Encouraged" by a wave of spontaneous sit-ins and wildcat strikes celebrating the poll triumph, the first **Front Populaire** government of 1936–37, headed by **Léon Blum**, nearly succeeded in ratifying the sorts of reforms – nationalization of key industries, forty-hour week, collective bargaining – which the Spaniards were only able to contemplate. But within a year these measures had been stymied by a corollary proposal on currency exchange control. Similarly blunted by "reasons of state" (for which read "fear of the English and the Germans") were Blum's ineffectual attempts, despite his evident personal sympathy with the Spanish Frente Popular, to intervene openly in the Civil War – or even just supply armaments to the Republicans – until the fall of his second government in 1938.

# The Spanish Civil War

On July 17, 1936, the military garrison in Morocco rebelled under the leadership of Franco, the agreed signal for revolt throughout Spain. Sanjurjo, by now in exile in Portugal, was the Military Union's choice for provisional head of state but was killed when his plane crashed between Portugal and Burgos. Another Franco rival, Goded, was captured by Republican loyalists in Barcelona and shot, leaving the way open for Franco to be proclaimed commander of the rebels – and "Head of State" – in October 1936.

The Nationalists, as the rebels styled themselves, had expected a short campaign but the **Spanish Civil War** (1936–39) turned out to be long and bloody. In the Pyrenees, only Navarra immediately came out in favour of the Nationalists, who had convinced the heirs of the Carlists to allow themselves to be absorbed into Franco's Falange. Gipuzkoa and Bizkaia, which had recently benefited from a home-rule statute similar to Catalunya's, remained devoutly Republican as did Catalunya and Aragón, where the mountain villages were particularly attracted by anarchism, an ideology that shared their traditional values of equality and personal liberty. Whatever their precise stripe, Republicans were overwhelmingly secular and virulently anticlerical, and the opening months of the war saw numerous instances of churches or monasteries sacked, with priests and nuns murdered or raped.

Although the Nationalists initially had little popular support, they gradually swept across the country by a mixture of audacity and deliberate terror, backed by a flood of arms and men from Nazi Germany and Italy. The Republicans were far less effectively supplied by Russia, Mexico and very sporadically by France, and reinforced by the socialist International Brigade. An international arms embargo and declaration of nonintervention was universally and selectively winked at by interested parties. Nominally a civil war, the Spanish conflict was really the opening act of World War II, and the first "modern" campaign: Italian and German airmen demonstrated the efficacy of terror bombings on civilian targets, and radio saw service as a propaganda weapon.

In the north, their foothold in Navarra allowed the Nationalists to attack both east and west. The Basque country was overwhelmed by the end of 1937, paving the way for a major Nationalist offensive into Aragón during March 1938. As the Nationalists advanced eastwards, **Republican** soldiers, marooned in the valleys of Alto Aragón and Catalunya, fled north across the high passes into France, joined or preceded by their families, and others fearful of a Falangist victory. Many Republicans believed, or perhaps deluded themselves, that theirs was a tactical withdrawal, and hoped to be saved by a pan-European war in the wake of Hitler's provocations in Czechoslovakia. But by the beginning of 1939 it was all over, and the majority of refugees now arrived quite openly at ordinary road frontier crossings like Le Perthus, sometimes in columns of thousands. The Republican parliament held its last meeting at Figueres on February 1, 1939.

# World War II

Ironically, the outbreak of **World War II** soon led to a refugee movement in the opposite direction. With the capitulation of France in spring 1940, small numbers began making their way over the Pyrenees, intent on reaching England via neutral Spain or Portugal, in response to de Gaulle's June 1940 radio appeal to join the Free French forces. There was also a weekly movement from France into Spain of Swiss gold ingots, two truckloads at a minimum, as payment for humanitarian food aid to occupied Europe from America.

The Germans were initially content to leave the south of France, including the Pyrenees up to Saint-Jean-Pied-de-Port, under the control of the collaborationist **Vichy** government, but the Allied landings in North Africa in November 1942, only briefly opposed by Vichy troops in Morocco and Algeria, left them vulnerable to attack from across the Mediterranean. Hitler immediately ordered the formal occupation of the south, prompting a new wave of escapes over Pyrenean passes.

## Escapees and escape routes

These later refugees fell into four categories: **Allied personnel**, mainly airmen who had been shot down; **évadé(e)s**, who had escaped prison or internment in France (though the word *évadé(e)s* tends to be applied to all escapees); **réfractaires**, French people who were in trouble with the Vichy or German authorities for falling foul of Occupation rules; and, of course, **Jews.**

Their guides were known as **passeurs** in French, **pasadores** in Castilian. Some of these knew the old contraband trails from lengthy experience, but the majority were ordinary people, working in hotels and cafés and perhaps smuggling occasionally for a little extra money. Another contingent was made up of Spanish Republicans who, having fled from the frying pan into the fire, lived in hiding along the border, especially around the Cerdanya/Cerdagne. Some clergy were involved, as well as a few shepherds, a handful of mountaineering guides, and even a scattering of officials such as mayors and customs officers. Altogether, about three thousand French (including two hundred women) were active in the Pyrenean escape routes, and five hundred Spaniards.

Until the **German occupation** of the French Pyrenees on November 11, 1942, it was left to the French themselves to patrol the frontier, a task entrusted to no more than eight hundred customs officers, policemen and support staff, and these were easily circumvented by well-established methods. Fugitives and their guides, for example, could take the Sunday afternoon train to Latour-de-Carol, stroll up to the frontier to mingle with the local Spanish and French who by custom gathered there to chat, and then just drift away onto the Spanish side. In Vichy Marseille, the American and Mexican consulates simply provided escapees with visas and put them on the train to Spain via Cerbère and Portbou.

However, from the end of 1942 the frontier was patrolled by over a thousand military police, backed by mobile units that doubled their number. In addition, there were about a hundred Nazi agents working covertly in the region, assisted by French volunteer forces and informers motivated by money, anti-Semitism or both. Though the Germans were mostly older men considered unsuitable for the rigours of a combat front, these frontier guards were nevertheless formidable – tough Bavarian or Austrian mountaineers, well trained and well equipped, using reconnaissance aircraft to track their quarry. The Spanish had about eight hundred border guards and police on their side, and additionally 30,000 troops were also stationed not more than 30km south of the frontier.

The **escape organization** that developed to counter this intensified border security was run like a business, and an occasionally ruthless one. Known by the codename **MAURICE**, it had an annual income of more than 16,000,000 francs for transport, false documents, food, the hiring of guides and other expenses. Much of the money was raised by loans from sympathizers, for whom coded messages were broadcast on the BBC to acknowledge the receipt of funds and confirm later repayment. The cost of each crossing depended on the negotiating skill of the organizer and the difficulties of the route involved: if transport had to be arranged to the start of a crossing, the cost shot up astronomically as fuel was difficult to obtain. As particularly "hot" items, Jews had to pay – or be paid for – at many times the normal going rate to be guided out of the country, whether individually or in a group. Those who demurred, and attempted to flee via the normal daily rail link between Oloron and Canfranc, were liable to be returned by the Spanish authorities or sent to an internment camp (see below).

In the early days of the war the consequences of arrest on the French side were not too harsh: imprisonment, a fine or perhaps "volunteering" for the Vichy Foreign Legion. Later, the penalties became more severe: about a thousand escapees died in concentration camps in France or elsewhere, as did 150 of the five hundred *passeurs* who were caught. Arrival in Spain did not mean the end of danger; Spain might have been neutral but it was a pro-fascist country, and no official could be trusted. Anyone captured on the Spanish side would be sent to one of the local **internment camps**, where conditions were so bad as sometimes to be fatal – and approximately one out of seven escapees ended up in internment. Despite these hazards, about 35,000 civilians succeeded in escaping into Spain, including approximately 5000 Jews, 2000 Belgians, 500 Dutch, 800 Poles and around 1000 members of the Resistance. Moreover, some 700 highly trained British, American and Canadian airmen had been spirited across the border and returned to combat.

## Spain: abortive invasion

Although the Spanish Civil War had left more than half a million dead, destroyed a quarter of a million houses and sent a third of a million Spaniards into exile in France and Latin America, Franco was in no mood for reconciliation. He set up **war tribunals** which sentenced thousands of Republicans to death and interned nearly two million others in concentration camps until "order" had been restored. The Falange was the only permitted political organization, and censorship was rigidly enforced.

As World War II ground towards its conclusion, exiled **Spanish Republicans** distinguished themselves fighting for the Allies, especially among the ranks of the French Resistance, with many units active in the French Pyrenees from 1942 on. Implacable foes of Franco and fascists in general, the Basques even formed their own Gernika Batallion, which in April 1945 was instrumental in crushing a large German force in southwest France, still being supplied by Spain.

Some months before this, about 15,000 Spanish Republicans, logically concluding that total Allied victory would encompass the overthrow of Franco's pro-Nazi regime, had attempted to occupy the Spanish Pyrenean valleys as a prelude to anti-Falangist uprisings across Spain. With minimal, half-hearted support from the French Resistance and the British SOE, they invaded on **October 19, 1944** along the entire length of the Pyrenees, principally at the Val d'Aran, but also at Luzaide, Urdizeto, Benasque and the *valles* of Roncal and Pineta. Although they arrived fully supplied to avoid relying on the locals and thus provoking reprisals against them, the Republican guerrillas in any case found many villages already forcibly depopulated, and the wells poisoned. After some initial success in Aran, "**Reconquista de España**" (as the operation was called) failed to take Vielha or seal off the Bonaigua pass and the half-built tunnel, and was forced to withdraw after a week. In the wake of this debacle, Franco's regime strongly reinforced its border defences (so that there would be no further significant incursions), and vicious reprisals (especially in Aran) were exacted anyway.

**Surviving Spanish Resistance members** resident in France, for the most part ardent communists, were for many years shabbily treated by the French government in respect of (belated) decorations and pensions, and still tend to segregate themselves from locally born fighters at commemorative ceremonies. On the Spanish side, only in spring 2001 were official references to the combatants of 1944 – and a few guerrilla cells who battled on in Spain until the early 1960s – as "bandits" and "brigands" struck from the official record, though the survivors failed to gain the right to military pensions.

# The Pyrenees after the wars

By the end of World War II, during which Spain was neutral if actively pro-Nazi, Franco ranked as the last remaining fascist head of state in Europe, and had in fact sanctioned more judicial deaths than any other ruler in Spanish history. Spain remained politically and economically isolated into the early 1950s, home to thousands of Nazi war criminals beyond the reach of extradition, despite diplomatic recognition of Franco's regime by most of Europe. With the economy at a standstill, Pyrenean villagers began to drift down to the towns in a usually fruitless search for work, accelerating the **depopulation** of the mountains. Mismanagement of the economy was so blatant that by 1953 the country was exporting less than it had twenty years earlier. The traditional livelihood of **smuggling** across the Pyrenees mushroomed into a major enterprise, but even this was dwarfed by the corruption of army officers and customs officials who imported luxury goods on false documents, an illicit trade that was equal to half the official imports.

Franco's otherwise probable overthrow was only averted in 1953 by the acceptance of **American aid**, on condition that he provided land for American air bases; Spain's pariah status finally ended the same year in a concordat with the Vatican, establishing Catholicism as the state religion, and subsequently in 1955 with its belated admission to the UN, with American sponsorship. The economy was revitalized not only by US loans, but remittances from tourism and Spaniards working in northern Europe, resulting in a growth rate during most of the 1960s second only to Japan's. Such investment, however, merely brought forward the death of traditional Pyrenean agriculture, as the **mechanization of farming** on the plains marginalized mountain life even further. A Spain of increasing urbanization and lowland agriculture required massive amounts of water and power, supplied by a burgeoning number of dams in Catalunya and Aragón; their flooding of Pyrenean pastoral valleys, combined with the punitive neglect of Madrid in failing to provide the most basic services to the overwhelmingly pro-Republican mountaineers, pretty well finished off any hope of subsistence in various parts of the Pyrenees.

Meanwhile in **France**, with **Charles de Gaulle** emerging as the undisputed leader of the Free French government-in-exile, the Allies had little choice but to cooperate with him; as of D-Day and the subsequent liberation, an uneasy coalition of Right and Left, the Conseil National de la Résistance, emerged as the basis of a provisional government for the demoralized, bankrupt nation. By 1947, thanks to the Cold War and the Marshall Plan, the Left – as well as (temporarily) de Gaulle – had been excluded from what became the Fourth Republic, though not before a new constitution had been agreed upon, providing for women's suffrage, the nationalization of key industries, trade union rights and the rudiments of a welfare state.

In the French Pyrenees themselves, hundreds of communities had been destroyed by the German burning of villages in reprisal for supporting the Resistance. Thousands of villagers who had been driven out decided to remain in the valley towns after the war, and even today villages are still abandoned entirely or in part – though this changed somewhat after 1968 (see below).

If thoroughgoing political reform had been thwarted, France during the 1950s transformed itself from a primarily agricultural country to a modern industrial giant, its growth rate often rivalling that of West Germany, with whom it established in 1957 the European Coal and Steel Community, predecessor to the Common Market/EC/EU. Although the country, like Spain, was a member of NATO, much of France's military resources soon became embroiled in the **Algerian colonial rebellion**, which coming on the heels of the 1954 catastrophic defeat at Dien Bien Phu in Indochina proved to be an eight-year experience nearly as traumatic as the German occupation. By 1958, hard-line rightists among the army and the so-called **pieds noirs** – a million civilian settlers in Algeria virulently opposed to its possible independence – threatened to take on both loyal army units and the native rebels. De Gaulle returned from political limbo, dissolving the Fourth Republic and demanding extraordinary powers to settle the Algerian mess. For his pains, as president of the Fifth Republic, de Gaulle provoked an even more serious military revolt in 1961, with the **OAS** – a rogue army faction intent on preventing any settlement – mounting several attempts on his life. But Algerian independence was finally granted in 1962, prompting a flood of refugees – mostly Jews, *pieds noirs* and Arabs who had fought for the central government – into France. The *pieds noirs* in particular, many of them settling in the south of France, would later lend considerable support to a resurgence in assorted racist and fascist activities, including the Front National of the 1990s.

# Cracks in the old order

De Gaulle's style in diplomacy was idiosyncratic, to put it mildly; by the mid-Sixties he had ruffled numerous feathers abroad by blocking British entry to the Common Market, rebuking the US for its policy in Vietnam, calling for a "free Québec", withdrawing from the central command structure of NATO and refusing to sign any nuclear test-ban treaties. Even at home he was far from universally popular, and not just among the rightist fringe; a young challenger on the Left, **François Mitterrand**, nearly upset him in the 1965 presidential elections.

Yet despite these rumblings of discontent, the events of **May 1968** took everyone by surprise. What started as a provincial student protest against the paternalistic education system quickly escalated into a broad spectrum of agitation by both blue-collar and white-collar workers as well as academics, culminating in a protracted general strike. *Autogestion* – workers' self-management – was the dominant slogan; rather than specific demands for reform, there was general sentiment that all French institutions were too hierarchical and elitist. De Gaulle dropped out of sight for two weeks, consulting with army commanders; upon his return, he dissolved parliament and, to quell the "revolution", demanded a fresh electoral mandate from the frightened silent majority – who complied.

Although the protesters could point to few specific gains except in education, the events of 1968 changed French society in subtler ways over the next two decades; there was a perceptible lessening in formality and authoritarianism, and various domestic alternative movements (such as the Green Party) can trace their start to the "days of May". Numerous self-employed professionals who felt themselves thwarted by the return to normality in the main power centres **fled south**, as had generations of dissidents before them, to the shelter of the Cévennes and the Pyrenees, forming the advance guard of the **nouveaux ruraux** (new rurals) who would slowly repopulate the abandoned villages and eventually set up tourism-related enterprises.

**Spain's increasing prosperity** as the 1960s proceeded merely underlined the intellectual and financial bankruptcy of Franco's regime, and its inability to cope with popular demands. Higher incomes, the need for contemporary education and skills, plus a creeping invasion of outside culture, made the anachronism of the Falange starkly clear. Franco's only reaction was an attempt to withdraw what few traces of increased liberalism had emerged, and his last years mirrored the repression of the early 1940s. Basque nationalists, whose 1973 assassination of Admiral Carrero Blanco effectively destroyed Franco's last hope of a like-minded successor, were singled out for particularly harsh treatment. When Franco finally died in November of that year, few expected much of his second-choice heir as head of state, the Bourbon prince **Juan Carlos**, cynically nicknamed El Breve (The Brief) for the anticipated duration of his reign.

In the event, and much to his credit, over the next seven years the new Spanish king oversaw a cautious, gradual but steady progress towards "democracy without adjectives", the demand of street activists in the late 1970s. The first **free elections of 1977** returned a coalition government, with the extreme Left and Right marginalized. Recognizing that his own future depended on the maintenance of the fledgling democracy, Juan Carlos declined to support the **attempted coup** of February 1981 by disaffected elements of the Guardia Civil and the army; its collapse, and attendant further discreditation of those nostalgic for the old order, set the stage for the landmark elections of October 1982.

Meanwhile, **in France**, the 1970s had been dominated by the two presidential terms of the centre-rightist **Valéry Giscard d'Estaing**, who defeated Mitterrand in 1974 and 1978. Despite a series of embarrassing scandals and the defection of Giscard's prime minister Jacques Chirac to form his own party, the Left seemed incapable of presenting a united front for the 1978 polls in particular. As in Spain of the late 1970s, few would have predicted the decisive result of the French elections of May 1981.

# The first post-war Socialist governments

In May 1981, Parisians gathered spontaneously at the Place de la Bastille to celebrate the victory of Mitterrand's Socialists, the first left-of-centre triumph in France since the 1930s. Just over a year later, Felipe González's PSOE – the Spanish Socialists – also came to power with massive support, an even more dramatic reversal considering the nearness of the Falangist past. Despite enjoying substantial goodwill at the outset, both movements subsequently foundered on domestic and international realities, amidst increasingly acrimonious accusations of unprincipled betrayals of campaign promises and party manifestos. As a result, the French Socialists lost power between 1986 and 1989, and again between 1993 and 1996, while their Spanish counterparts only just squeaked back into office in 1993 before being eased out in 1997, not to return until 2004.

The presence of four Communist ministers in the first post-1981 French cabinet reflected the initial commitment to an aggressively leftist agenda; by 1984, in the face of capital flight and bureaucratic foot-dragging, Mitterrand was compelled to backpeddle to a centrist cabinet under Prime Minister **Laurent Fabius**. 1986 saw the return of the Right under **Jacques Chirac**'s Gaullists, an uneasy arrangement under a sitting Socialist president – because parliamentary and presidential elections were then out of sync in France – referred to as **cohabitation**. Chirac's monetarist fumblings and flirtations with **Jean-Marie Le Pen**'s overtly racist Front National resulted in a centre-left parliamentary coalition returning by a bare margin in 1989, under Social-Democrat prime minister **Michel Rocard**. Though some of Chirac's privatization programmes were stalled, the unpopularity of Rocard's own austerity measures resulted in **Édith Cresson** replacing him in 1991. Her abrasiveness and numerous gaffes prompted her sacking in 1992 in favour of **Pierre Bérégovoy**, a confidant of Mitterrand. All these comings and goings virtually guaranteed a landslide coalition victory of the RPR and the UDF, the two conservative parties, in 1993; two months later, Bérégovoy – accused of accepting a private loan from a dubious character – shot himself, leaving no explanatory note.

This thumbnail summary of French elections and regimes to the early 1990s gives just a hint of the malaise which gripped the French scene. Scandal had been a near-constant feature of public life since 1981; equally disappointing was the Socialists' failure to change traditional militarism, all-pervasive secrecy, and environmental-unfriendliness in one of the most centralized states in the world. In the Pyrenees especially, despite lip service to ecological considerations, mega-projects such as the Somport tunnel were usually only slowed or modified rather than halted.

**Spain** by contrast enjoyed a certain amount of stability throughout the 1980s; the PSOE was convincingly re-elected in 1986, and only began to falter visibly in 1989 as the recession started to bite. Yet there was a similar pattern of compromise on core issues, which often made the PSOE government seem indistinguishable from Britain's contemporaneous Conservative government or from Germany under Chancellor Kohl. **Felipe González** had entered office in 1982 partly on an anti-NATO platform, but campaigned for continued membership in the hard-fought 1986 referendum on the issue, which went narrowly in favour. Control of inflation, supposedly in deference to EC-stipulated goals, had a higher priority than employment, and loss-making state-owned industries were drastically overhauled, and many privatized. **Anti-labour measures** such as cuts in already meagre unemployment benefits, a pay freeze for civil servants and a differential minimum-wage law for under-25s resulted in general strikes coordinated by the PSOE's own trade union, the powerful UGT (resurrected after the Franco years).

By the early 1990s, it became increasingly obvious that prolonged time in office had made the PSOE not just corrupt but complacent, with only the lack of compelling alternatives to "Felipe" (as the prime minister was universally called) and the enduring suspicion of the Right combining to maintain the status quo. The PSOE barely survived a strong 1993 challenge by the centre-right Partido Popular (PP) under its uncharismatic chief **José María Aznar**, and continued to govern only by dint of support from the Catalan nationalist party, having fallen short of an outright majority. As in France, spectacular scandals regularly punctuated the news, eroding the PSOE's position still further. Most damaging of these was the discovery of **GAL** (Grupo Antiterrorista de Liberación), a semi-autonomous antiterrorist unit which had been waging a "dirty war" throughout the 1980s, kidnapping and/or assassinating suspected ETA members and fellow-travellers. The press and an independent judiciary – both interfered with repeatedly by the PSOE government – exposed police participation in these acts and a clear chain of command extending up to the highest echelons of the PSOE.

# France: the Right in power – and out again

The first major crisis for Prime Minister **Edouard Balladur**'s centre-right government in early 1994 was the violent reaction to his proposal of reduced wages for young people. A similar response by Air France workers, farmers and fishermen to further monetarist measures caused Balladur to back down, losing him the respect of his natural constituency. Political violence in the south of France and corruption scandals continued unabated, adding – along with stubbornly high unemployment – to the support for fringe parties on the Left and Right (especially the racist Front National).

Meanwhile **Mitterrand**, terminally ill with prostate cancer, clung to office until mid-1995 despite various assaults on his reputation – specifically revelations about his war record as an official in the Vichy regime before he belatedly joined the Resistance. Yet when he **died** in January 1996, after fourteen years as head of state, he was mourned as a man of culture and vision, a tenacious political operator and a committed European.

The **May 1995 presidential elections** saw the Socialist Lionel Jospin pitted against a rightist field split between Balladur, Chirac, Le Pen (who scored 15.5 percent) and the anti-European Philippe de Villiers, a French equivalent to James Goldsmith. In a run-off, **Jacques Chirac** narrowly edged Jospin by mouthing comforting noises about unemployment and social exclusion.

One of Chirac's first decisions was the **abolition of conscription**, in favour of supposedly more efficient professional armed forces. The decree – not actually implemented until 2001 – provoked impassioned response from left-wing parties, for whom conscription represented social levelling and the revolutionary spirit expressed in the words of the national anthem: "Aux Armes, Citoyens . . .". Another Chirac move was to delay signing the Nuclear Non-Proliferation Treaty until France had carried out a new series of **nuclear tests** in the South Pacific. These provoked almost universal condemnation, boycotts of French goods, attacks on French embassy buildings in Australia and New Zealand, plus full-scale riots in Tahiti. The French navy captured Greenpeace's *Rainbow Warrior II*, almost ten years to the day after French secret service agents had sunk *Rainbow Warrior* in Auckland harbour.

On the domestic front, Chirac's new prime minister was **Alain Juppé**, a clever but clinical technocrat. It was left to him to fulfil election pledges of job creation and maintenance of pensions or welfare benefits with promised tax cuts, a continued strong franc and a reduction of the budget deficit with an eye to European monetary union. Juppé also promised to clean up corruption but ironically became immediately involved in an uproar concerning his own subsidized luxury flat in Paris. This and other scandals irritated voters, who had previously accepted nest-feathering as a perk of power but now, hard-pressed by austerity programmes, took a dim view of double standards.

The last straw came in autumn 1995, when Chirac announced that fiscal rectitude would have to take precedence over social comfort, and Juppé proposed changes in social security and "downsizing" of the rail network. The response was an all-but-general **strike** in November and December, when five million public-sector workers took to the streets with considerable support from becalmed private-sector commuters – the strongest show of protest in France since May 1968. Amazingly, Juppé survived this storm, abandoning some proposals and postponing others. A new tax to pay off the social security deficit was imposed, and cuts in the health service proceeded; the economically depressed Pyrenean regions, always net beneficiaries of every sort of public welfare programme from crèches to SNCF buses, were starkly affected by every policy wobble.

The UDF-RPR coalition stumbled through 1996, fulfilling predictions by Mitterrand and Giscard d'Estaing that Chirac's opportunism and impetuousness would make him and his government a laughing stock within months of assuming power. Although Chirac and Juppé enjoyed a huge parliamentary majority, valid until spring 1998, hanging on to the bitter end was not Chirac's cup of tea. Incredibly, in April 1997 he called **snap elections** for late May, perhaps hoping for a smaller but less fractious majority – and an end to future potential *cohabitation* by making the start of the next parliamentary and presidential terms coincide in 2002.

In the event Chirac totally miscalculated the public mood and the Socialists' ability to attract potential coalition partners, while his arrogant ploy to strengthen the presidency backfired spectacularly over two rounds of voting. **Jospin** and his allies, the Communists, the Greens and the anti-Maastricht Citizens' Movement, swept back to power in June on a programme featuring a proposed 35-hour week, minimum wage hikes, an emergency youth employment programme and a more humane policy on immigration and naturalization. Thirty-eight Communists, seven Greens and more than a hundred women took seats. The *cohabitation* Chirac had gone to such lengths to avoid had come to pass a year earlier than it otherwise probably would have.

# Spain: the Right finally back in power – and out again

Despite the ongoing woes of the PSOE, the Spanish **elections of March 1996** yielded yet another **hung parliament**, though this time Aznar's PP had a bare plurality of fifteen seats over the PSOE. Denied the "absolute majority" he had believed to be his throughout the campaign, Aznar had to do a **coalition** deal with the Catalan, Basque and Canary Island nationalist parties (whom he had previously described as "greedy parasites") to get a parliamentary majority. In return for their support, these regional parties – including those in the Pyrenees – expected continued, often disproportionate benefits to their regions.

González, for his part, seemed not to have drawn the proper conclusion from the result: "A couple more weeks of campaigning and we would have won" was his off-the-cuff reaction, as he dismissed the idea of retirement. The close finish initially denied the PSOE a period of urgently needed self-reflection that a crushing defeat and a quick change of leadership would have permitted. But early in 1998, languishing in public opinion and with the PSOE still in turmoil, **"Felipe"** finally **resigned** the leadership of the party he had dominated for 23 years.

The reasons for Aznar's failure to win an outright majority in 1996 were equally significant. At the last moment, memories of the long and repressive Franco era unnerved many voters wary of losing hard-won decentralization and the PSOE-established social benefits system – a vital lifeline in many poorer regions, including the Pyrenees. The electoral weight of Andalucía, González's power base, fulfilled its traditional role of offsetting the conservative North by supplying many of the discredited PSOE's surviving MPs.

During his first term as prime minister, Aznar gradually moved his party towards the "reforming centre", sidelining PP hardliners in the hope of gaining the electorate's confidence and a working majority not dependent on alliances with the regional nationalists. He frequently declared his admiration for the ideas of British Prime Minister Tony Blair; apparently, one of the notions to be emulated was keeping a **tight rein on the news media**. Economically, the PP seemed intent on continuing as the PSOE had begun: withdrawing subsidies from ailing industries such as shipbuilding, accelerating privatization of former state-owned industries, reducing corporate taxes and "liberalizing" labour laws.

The PSOE replaced González with **José Borrell**, a former transport minister in González's government, but not his preferred choice of successor. González hovered constantly in the background, making it impossible for Borrell to stamp his own mark on the party. In 1999, when a financial scandal erupted, involving Borrell's performance as minister, he resigned and was replaced by the party hierarchy's – and González's – original nominee, **Joaquín Almunia**. With a general election now on the horizon and the PSOE still trailing in the polls, Almunia fashioned an electoral pact with the ex-Communist Izquierda Unida (United Left), thinking that their combined votes could overturn a likely Aznar victory.

The outcome of the March 2000 **general election** was a stunning **triumph for Aznar** and the PP, who took 183 of the 350 parliamentary seats with a ten-percent plurality; for the first time since the death of Franco the Right were in power with a clear majority.

The electorate had apparently been unconvinced by the "shotgun marriage" between the PSOE and the IU (bitter enemies since the Civil War), which smacked more of an opportunistic patchwork than a government-in-waiting, as well as by warnings from the Left during the campaign that, once in power with an overall majority, the PP's social-democratic mask would come off and wholesale dismantling of the social welfare systems would follow, together with attacks on the trade unions. Moreover, large numbers of voters seemed unwilling to risk the indisputable economic gains of Aznar's period in office – Aznar had kept the economy on course with a **growth rate** among the best in Europe, with unemployment below twenty percent for the first time since 1988 – while many of the Left's traditional supporters didn't bother to vote at all. On election night, when the scale of the PSOE/IU defeat became clear, Joaquín Almunia **resigned** from the leadership of the PSOE, which clung to just 125 seats. At the party convention which followed, the old guard and its candidates were swept aside when delegates elected a young, (born 1961), relatively unknown, **José Luis Rodríguez Zapatero**, a member of the moderate-socialist "Nueva Vía" (New Way) faction with PSOE.

Early in his second term, the always-enigmatic Aznar announced that he would not lead the PP into the next general election, and by late 2003 had anointed as his designated successor the deputy prime minister **Mariano Rajoy**. Why Aznar, styled *el pequeño bigotudo* ("the little guy with the mustache") by self and others, chose to effectively resign (he was only 52 when Rajoy's appointment was rubber-stamped by the PP ruling council) remains a mystery; presumably Aznar's ambitions were of a grander order, and perhaps he was hankering after a Europe-wide, NATO or UN post as a reward for being at the forefront of Donald Rumsfeld's "New Europe". More likely, he opted to exit on a roll before all the gloss had rubbed off the PP's accomplishments: unemployment remained the highest in the EU, the **economy** overall was slowing (owing probably to lack of investment in education and training), while labour law and social-security benefit "reforms" had prompted an acrimonious general strike in June 2002. After years in opposition spent rooting out sleaze in the PSOE government, the PP was also becoming vulnerable to charges of cronyism and corruption.

But far worse was to come from the standpoint of the incumbent government. In mid-November 2002, the single-hulled oil-tanker **Prestige** encountered difficulties off the coast of Galicia, and within a week had broken up, releasing hundreds of thousands of tonnes of crude oil over the next few months. The effects of lack of preparedness and the studied indifference of various PP officials (including the head of the Galician *autonomía* and Madrid's Minister of the Environment) were ameliorated only by strenuous clean-up work by thousands of volunteers and soldiers; though the EU subsequently banned single-hulled vessels, the damage from the worst environmental disaster ever in Spain was and is ongoing, with invisible, carcinogenic pollutants contaminating the Galician fisheries for the foreseeable future. Normally placid, pro-PP Galicia rose up in protest at the perceived incompetence of the government, and when Aznar proposed to visit the stricken area in December, he was advised to stay away as his safety could not be guaranteed.

Aznar procured another hostage to fortune with his enthusiastic support of the inexorable American and British **march to war** over the winter of 2002–03, despite the opposition of ninety percent of the Spanish electorate to the Iraq adventure. Madrid's relations with the Basque country (see pp.547–549) remained tense, as were those with Catalunya following the December 2003 formation of a left-wing, pro-separatist regional government. Yet the PSOE had done much worse than expected in the municipal elections of May, and all indicators pointed to a third term for the PP after the parliamentary **elections** set for **March 14, 2004**.

However, the events of March 11 threw everything off course: during morning rush hour, ten terrorist **bombs** planted on four crowded Madrid commuter trains killed nearly two hundred and injured more than 1400. Aznar and his ministers rather crassly tried to reap immediate electoral benefit from the tragedy by pinning the blame, from the very first hours of the aftermath, on ETA, the PP's favourite bugbear, despite ETA's immediate denial of responsibility. Over the next three days, however, as the police and fire brigades did their job, it emerged – despite the government's best efforts to hide the fact – that a local, Moroccan-dominated "franchise" of Al-Qaeda, not the Basques, were responsible. In their fury at being manipulated and lied to by the Aznar government, and at being put in harm's way by its eager support of the Iraq war, the Spanish electorate turned out in force, both at street demos and at the polling booths, and handed the **PSOE a plurality** of nearly 43 percent of the vote and 164 seats; the PP plunged to just under 38 percent and 148 seats. No other single party won more than ten seats, but among these minor victors were the Catalan Republican Left with eight seats – one of the separatist entities much maligned by the PP, and on whom the PSOE – though it intends not to form a coalition – will have to rely on for an absolute parliamentary majority.

Prime Minister-elect Zapatero immediately announced his intention to **withdraw** the 1300 Spanish troops serving in **Iraq** by June 30, 2004, and delivered a stinging rebuke to Spain's erstwhile mentors: "You can't organize a war with lies. Mr Blair and Mr Bush must do some reflection and self-criticism." Some observers noted, with alarm, that it was the first European election in decades to be swung, albeit indirectly, by terrorist action. On April 3, police cornered four terrorists in a Madrid suburban apartment, presumed members of the "**Moroccan Islamic Combatant Group**" and key actors in the March 11 atrocity, who proceeded to blow themselves (and a policeman) up. Zapatero came under intense pressure not to pull Spanish troops out of Afghanistan as well as Iraq, but the country's decision-making process was hampered by the weird, one-month twilight zone between the PP government's **resignation** on March 15 and the PSOE's assumption of power nearly a month later; as of writing the composition of Zapatero's cabinet was uncertain. In the heightened security climate of the region, police also made a number of serendipitous arrests and confiscations of ETA members and explosives caches.

# France: the second cohabitation – and the end of Jospin

Jospin's victory inevitably raised unrealistic expectations of how much a left-of-centre government could accomplish, with its room for manoeuvring severely limited by Brussels and economic globalization. But to its credit, the new government quickly adopted a consensual style of government, with decisions reached only after debate and monitoring of public opinion, markedly in contrast to Juppé's high-handed, from-the-top-down style. By so doing it was able to propose a 15-billion franc **increase in taxation** for social programmes, borne equally by corporations and individuals, without seriously denting its popularity.

Jospin's **poll ratings** remained high through 1999, despite increased friction with Chirac, dissension in the Left coalition's own ranks and some predictable back-pedalling on campaign stances. By spring 1999, despite his execrating the practice on the hustings, Jospin had surpassed all former French prime minsters in **privatizations** of major state enterprises, selling off over $20 billion worth; unlike in other countries, though, it was made sure that small shareholders would benefit. In the March 1999 **Euro-elections**, the Greens did surprisingly well, temporarily surpassing the Communists as France's second party of the "Left". Accordingly, at the Greens' party conference in September 1999 there were murmurings that, with their strong position, they should press for more action from Jospin on such issues as the future of nuclear power, a 35-hour work-week, GM foods and regional languages, or consider pulling out of the government (where their member **Dominique Voynet** was minister of environment). By year's end, universal health cover to include the unemployed had been introduced, as well as a measure to ensure equal representation for women on all parties' candidacy lists in national and regional elections, plus municipal contests in towns of more than three thousand inhabitants.

The long-promised **35-hour work-week**, designed to reduce the still-stubborn unemployment rate, was finally implemented in February 2000, and initially pleased nobody. Public unions threatened to strike, freelancers demanded the right to work as much as they liked, and owners warned that it would make French industry uncompetitive. In April, Jospin carried out a radical cabinet reshuffle, replacing old friends and non-Socialist personalities with a "traditional" Socialist line-up. In August the cabinet became still less diverse when Interior Minister **Jean-Pierre Chevènement**, sole representative in the government of the pro-sovereignty Citizens' Movement, resigned, supposedly because he disagreed with Jospin's handling of negotiations with Corsican separatists (but in actuality to prepare his 2002 run for the presidency).

Despite Jospin's government having pulled France out of a long recession and spurred renewed economic growth, and despite the 35-hour work-week proving wildly popular and effective with almost everyone by late 2000, its re-election in 2002 was by no means certain. However, the UDF and RPR were still each beset by sleaze, and French patience with the arrogance and corruption of the traditional elite, most of them schooled at the École Nationale d'Administration, had worn thin to the point of transparency. Chirac himself stood under threat of indictment for various financial fiddles, and France's highest court ruled that he would enjoy immunity from prosecution only as long as he stayed in office. Future *cohabitations*, at least, seemed far less likely: by the terms of a September 2000 referendum, France's presidential term, formerly seven years, would be brought into step with the five-year parliamentary term as of the 2002 elections.

Even by French standards, the year 2001 was rich in **high-profile scandals**. Former Gaullist foreign minister Roland Dumas was imprisoned for embezzling funds from state-owned Elf Aquitaine petroleum company; Chirac narrowly escaped impeachment for involvement in criminal corruption in the matter of non-official perks for himself and his family while he was mayor of Paris between 1992 and 1995; and the late Mitterrand's son Jean-Christophe was tried for his part in illegal arms trafficking to Angola.

## The "earthquake" – and after

Against a backdrop of ongoing sleaze and voter apathy, the presidential elections of spring 2002 promised at first to be a poorly attended yawn. Once again Jospin was squaring off against Chirac and Le Pen – as well as thirteen other splinter-party candidates. At the outset of the campaign season, Jospin seemed to stand a good chance; he'd performed well on the economy, remained personally scandal-free, and had been further boosted by the election of gay Socialist Bertrand Delanoë as Mayor of Paris in March 2001, the first time any stripe of the Left had won control of the capital since the Commune of 1871 (though they did badly elsewhere). However, his authority had taken a big denting by his energetic sponsorship, in the teeth of Gaullist opposition, of an autonomy statute for Corsica, only to have it declared unconstitutional in January 2002. Moreover, Jospin had never overcome his charisma shortfall, being described by one journalist as akin to that of a retired Swedish professor of religious studies. The glad-handing, high-living Chirac, despite his scandal-splattered history and non-existent accomplishments during the previous seven years, had lost little of his ability to charm.

## Basque and Catalan nationalism: a comparison

Although the **Basque and Catalan separatist movements** share certain concerns – resistance to exploitation from central governments, and the preservation of a distinctive language and culture – they also differ markedly. In Catalunya, demands for autonomy haven't acquired the same dimension as in much of the Basque country; the notion of an independent Catalan nation has few adherents aside from extremists of the Terra Lliure group, and some members of the more recent Republican Left party. Whereas the Catalan complaint is of a relatively successful province milked by the rest of Spain, and therefore draws support from all social classes, the Basque protest remains fundamentally motivated by fears over non-Basque immigrant labour and is predominantly lower-middle-class and working-class in character. Finally, there are sharp political differences within the Basque provinces: urbanized, industrialized Bizkaia and Gipuzkoa are Basque-nationalist, but more rural Navarra and Araba are conservative and Spanish-loyalist, while the French Basque areas see themselves as separate from both their Spanish counterparts and the rest of France.

Tension between Madrid and the Spanish Basques first arose in the eighteenth century, with the abrogation of the region's *fueros*, the age-old charters guaranteeing a measure of self-government. The situation worsened considerably after Franco's victory in the Civil War, when the October 1936 statute of autonomy granted by the Republicans to Gipuzkoa and Bizkaia was rescinded, the Basque language banned outside the home and "politically unreliable" teachers dismissed. The Catholic Church's opposition to supposedly atheistic socialism had made it pro-Falangist during the war, but the reality of Franco's victory prompted a gradual change. From the 1950s onwards, the Church encouraged part-time Basque schools or *Ikastolas*, and by the end of the Franco era there were 33,000 pupils enrolled in them.

The nature and prevalence of Euskera is an index of the distinctness – and precariousness – of Basque culture. While a Catalan-speaker stands a chance of being understood in the rest of Spain and even in France, someone speaking only the archaic Basque language cannot communicate with outsiders. A poll in 1970 (before Franco died) highlighted the relative strengths between the two principal minority languages of the Pyrenees: 90 percent of Catalan housewives were found to understand Catalan, 77 percent to speak it, 62 percent to read it and 38 percent to write it; for the Basque country the figures were 50 percent, 46 percent, 25 percent and 11 percent respectively. By 1996, moreover, a survey of all Catalans aged 2 and up showed that 95 percent understood, 80 percent spoke, 84 percent read and 53 percent wrote the language – a testimony to almost-universal schooling in Catalan since the 1980s.

The failure of the **Basque National Party** (PNV or Partido Nacionalista Vasco), founded in 1895, to gain lasting political autonomy for the coastal Basque provinces, followed by the Francoist repression, led to the emergence by the early 1950s of ETA (*Euskad Ta Azkatasurra* – "Basque Homeland and Freedom"). Originally a middle-class student movement whose methods included – and still embrace – bank robberies, kidnappings for ransom, protection rackets and assassinations, it eventually split into two factions: the violent ETA-Militar and the ETA-Politico-Militar, the latter being socialists first and Basque nationalists second. Although full-time ETA membership has never exceeded one thousand, its methods provoked widespread reprisals, including mass arrests, torture and show trials as at Burgos in 1970, which backfired internationally, and closer to home caused Catalan intellectuals to stage a sympathy sit-in at the monastery of Montserrat. Meanwhile, there was little violence in Catalunya itself and no counterpart of ETA: a 1963 petition against language restrictions, or a pointed rendition of the traditional anthem "Els Segadors" in Franco's presence, was more typical of the Catalan approach.

Following the restoration of unfettered democracy in 1976, the free elections of the following year gave **Pacte Democratico per Catalunya** – an alliance of pro-Catalan parties – ten seats in the lower house of the Spanish parliament; among the Basques, the reconstituted PNV won eight seats and a new left-wing nationalist party, **Euskadi Eskerra**, won one. The PNV and Euskadi Eskerra remained theoretically committed to independence but sought change by constitutional means – in contrast to **Herri Batasuna** (United People), linked to ETA-Militar. In the 1980 elections, HB won eleven seats in the Basque regional parliament, in 1984 eleven again and in 1986 thirteen, but in all cases the deputies refused to take up their seats, leaving the PNV in control. Subsequently, the PNV divided: Carlos Garaikoetxea, the first Basque premier, decamped with half his regional deputies to form the centralist **Eusko Alkartasuna** (EA), leaving the PNV to the decentralist José Antonio Ardanza. Herri Batasuna, prior to its 2002 banning, was also beginning to fracture into various non-violent, leftist or centrist, nationalist groups such as Aralar, Navarra-based Batzarre and Zutik.

Although Catalunya's experiences earlier last century paralleled those of the Basque country – the granting of a statute of autonomy by the Republicans, followed by severe cultural repression after 1939 – relations with Madrid are currently more cordial. Catalunya is now effectively run day-to-day by its **Generalitat**, the regional government, which controls education, health, social security, tourism, commerce, agriculture and cultural matters. Curiously, in light of the Republican past, centre-right regional parliaments were consistently returned by Catalunyan voters from 1978 until late 2003; they were apparently seen as better able to look after Catalan business interests, and – by participating in the coalition governments of 1993 and 1996 – to extract fiscal concessions from Madrid. Late 2002 saw Artur Mas, successor to long-ruling Jordi Pujol at the head of the Catalan government, call for greater local autonomy and re-negotiation of the 1978 constitutional agreements, sparking a predictably gruff reaction from the obsessively centralizing PP regime. In December 2003, local Socialist leader and ex-mayor of Barcelona Pasqual Maragall, now President of the Generalitat, formed a coalition government with the pro-independence Republican Left Party and a Green-Communist alliance, thus excluding Jordi Pujol's long-ruling Convergence and Union party.

For many Basques the wounds of large-scale immigration, exploitation by a non-Basque elite and denial of significant independence still fester. Yet alone thus far among Spain's autonomous regions, the Basque provinces have the right to collect and disburse all of their own revenues, and the Guardia Civil has been replaced by a home guard, the *Ertzainza*.

Continuing **ETA outrages**, apparently designed to provoke centralist repression which will convince waverers to support the extreme solution of independence, garner less and less approval, and would seem to be a desperate rearguard action by a fringe group that perceives its support to be waning (see p.549). Nonviolent Basque local parties have moved to oust HB mayors in certain ETA strongholds, in conjunction with Madrid's efforts to break up the front-business networks (often hotels and restaurants) which finance ETA. But PP-inspired calls during 1997 to "socially isolate" HB in the Basque country, for example by boycotting its supporters' shops, have been denounced, somewhat hyperbolically, as reminiscent of early Nazism. Eventually, the PP opted for a juridical solution, having **HB banned** for three years from August 2002 on charges of supporting terrorism, seizing its assets and closing down its offices and websites; HB supporters protested by casting spoilt ballots – their typical ten percent of the total – in the following year's regional elections. Over the next year or so, Basque premier Juan José Ibarretxe repeatedly tabled rather nebulous **proposals** for a "free association" of Araba, Gipuzkoa and Bizkaia with Spain, essentially a state within a state, with the right of representation

## Basque and Catalan nationalism: a comparison (continued)

in the European Union and the plan to be put to referendum in the Basque country – similar to the contemporaneous proposals in Catalunya.

ETA never took much root in the overwhelmingly rural **French Basque regions**, where – except in Bayonne – an urban proletariat is almost nonexistent. Grievances here have more to do with a perceived Parisian policy of relegating the Pays Basque to "Third World" status, promoting only tourist-related industries at the expense of others. As for cultural identity, the 61 teachers in the *ikastolak* or Basque-language primary schools around Bayonne were finally recognized as state employees in November 1989. Since signing the European Charter on Regional and Minority Languages in May 1999, Paris must acknowledge the existence of **regional languages** such as Euskera (and Catalan, Gascon, or Occitan), and allow them to be read, spoken, taught and broadcast. But according to a French Supreme Court decision the same year, the government is not obliged to accord them any official status for legal or administrative procedures – ie, no title deeds, weddings or trial transcripts in minority languages – and formal ratification is pending. The chances of a separate Pays-Basque *département*, with its capital at Bayonne, being hived off from Pyrénées-Atlantiques any time soon would appear to be similarly remote, though such a proposal is now in the public arena, much to the dismay of prominent figures who balefully predict the "balkanization of France" and "the dislocation of French identity".

In early 2004, the Catalan and Basque sagas coincided rather bizarrely. **Josep Lluis Carod-Rovira**, head of the Republican Left party and (since December 2003) Prime Minister of the Generalitat of Catalunya, was obliged to resign after admitting that reports in right-wing newspaper *ABC* that he'd held a secret meeting with top ETA members in Perpignan were true. At the same time ETA announced a "partial truce" whereby Catalunya was declared an off-limits zone for terrorist activity. In the run-up to the March elections, the PP attempted to make a meal of this "coincidence", but this demonization strategy backfired, with Carod-Rovira's party actually increasing its representation in the Madrid parliament.

---

The shock-horror announcement on the eve of April 21 and the first round of the presidential poll was that, at 16 percent, Jospin had been eliminated by none other than Le Pen at 16.9 percent; Chirac had a plurality of 19.9 percent. This result, characterized as an "earthquake" by the press, sent ripples across the country and abroad as it emerged that nearly thirty percent of voters had abstained, while others had voted for fringe candidates in protest against the mainstream parties. The leftist tally had been dissipated amongst several hopefuls (even Trotskyite perennial Arlette Laguiller polled 5.7 percent), thus dooming Jospin's bid. Jospin (temporarily) resigned from the Socialist Party, handed over the reins to party secretary François Hollande and lapsed into a nine-month public silence: a sad end to a fundamentally decent and (by French standards) honest politician.

This result acted as a wake-up call for those who had abstained or voted frivolously in the first round, as nearly a million took to the Parisian streets on May 1 to protest the ascendancy of Le Pen – who'd run a shrewd campaign, playing on voter alienation and fear of crime, while downplaying his core racist message. The Socialists and Communists were reduced to endorsing Chirac to keep Le Pen out, and Chirac duly romped home with 82 percent of the vote in the May 5 second round.

With the **parliamentary elections** set for June 9–16, Chirac's supporters cobbled together an umbrella group of right-wing parties, the Union for Presidential Majority, to scotch any chance of another *cohabitation*. The

Socialists, still shaken by Jospin's defeat, were in no shape to put up much of a fight, and the Right took 369 of 577 seats in the National Assembly; the Greens, with just three seats, nearly disappeared from the electoral map, while the Communists fared scarcely better.

Chirac named an all-but-unknown, **Jean-Pierre Raffarin**, as prime minister, and (surprisingly for the centralizing Right) promulgated a bill devolving considerable power to the 26 regional assemblies, ending the absolute domination of Paris for the first time since 1789. Chirac also survived a Bastille-Day assassination attempt by a young rifle-toting neo-Nazi, widely diagnosed as an indirect consequence of the loony right being denied any parliamentary representation despite polling its typical thirteen percent of the vote nationwide. New interior minister **Nicolas Sarkozy** presided over a well-publicized, controversial drive against TV porn and prostitution, and earmarked funds for extra police and coordination between the police forces and gendarmerie in a general crackdown on crime. In November 2002, the UPM was formally renamed the Union pour un Mouvement Populaire, incorporating Démocratie Libérale as well as the RPR and UDF.

Much of early 2003 saw France, and its articulate, telegenic foreign minister **Dominique de Villepin**, lead "old Europe" in its fight against the US and UK's slide towards war in Iraq. During the latter half of 2003, however, Raffarin's government ran into a domestic ditch. Large-scale unemployment was back with a vengeance, while pension reforms (including a proposal for retirement at 70) were vigorously resisted by a wave of strikes. The French regional elections of March 2004 saw the Left **storm back** to take control of over three-fourths of the local assemblies; this does not necessarily translate into future parliamentary success, but Raffarin is clearly seen as a spent force, and few expect him to continue in office after an anticipated bruising round of reform to the social security system in autumn 2004. **Alain Juppé**, once seen as a probable candidate for president in 2007, has been convicted on corruption charges and stripped of his civic rights pending a likely appeal, leaving the field clear for Sarkozy, as Chirac is unlikely to run again.

# The contemporary outlook

Despite ongoing political turmoil **in France** since the 1980s and frequent (often self-inflicted) damage to the country's international reputation, the **French economy** remains sounder, with lower unemployment and a higher standard of living than in Spain.

The overriding contemporary issues in France are the interrelated, xenophobic ones of **racism**, relations with the **Muslim and African world**, remorse (or lack thereof) for the fate of its **Jews** during World War II and **immigration control**. The main exploiter of these concerns has been the quasi-fascist **Front National** under its foot-in-mouth leader **Jean-Marie Le Pen**, which, although it has long since lost its parliamentary seats through some creative gerrymandering, has captured four municipalities in Provence since 1995 and (of course) scored its embarrassing second-place finish in the 2002 presidential elections. Until the 2002 elections it consistently polled about fifteen percent nationwide (on one occasion thirty percent around Perpignan). Personal rivalry between Le Pen and his protégé **Bruno Mégret** led to the FN splitting into two separate parties on January 24, 1999.

Other politicians of various stripes have seen fit to jump on the nativist bandwagon at critical times, for example in the wake of the Algerian terrorist incidents which punctuated 1996. Charles Pasqua, Balladur's minister of the interior, considerably tightened up procedures for granting right of residence, let alone citizenship, to immigrants or their descendants, and introduced random street identity checks. Under Juppé, matters worsened when police evicted hundreds of unsuccessful Malian asylum-seekers from the Paris church where they had sought refuge. In a welcome gesture which reduced tension, Jospin's government almost immediately regularized the position of the Malian church-occupiers, and in a one-off amnesty granted residence to thousands of other illegals who had been working and paying taxes in France for years. While the extreme Right considers Jews, in particular those of North African descent, no better than Muslims, in September 1997 French Catholic bishops formally apologized for the Church's complicity in the 1942 rounding-up of local Jews.

But no single event improved the racial climate in France, if only temporarily, as much as the French football team's unexpected **triumph in the 1998 World Cup**, which France hosted. Of the 22 squad members, half of them were of foreign descent, including two born overseas, despite Le Pen's calls for immigrants to be excluded from the team. Hero of the hour was **Zinedine "Zizou" Zidane**, from Marseille but the grandson of settlers from Algeria, who scored two of the goals in the team's 3-0 win over favoured Brazil. The wild celebrations across France, with blacks, whites and *beurs* (French-born of North African descent) embracing in the streets just two days before Bastille Day, were a revelation in a country which had just published a survey showing its populace to have among the most racist attitudes in Europe. For once, the odious Le Pen had nothing to say other than mumbling he'd always meant that France could be "composed of different races and colours", provided they were patriotic. President Chirac had early on come out as a high-profile supporter of the team and its composition, praising the "tricolour and multicolour" victory and warning the conventional Right to cease its extended flirtation with National Front policies. But as the warm glow of the victory faded, glaring details re-emerged, such as the absence of any MPs of North African descent, the lack of Arabs or Africans in high-visibility media positions, or the fact that the official racism phone hotline (opened May 2000) receives about five hundred substantiated cases of discrimination daily.

Much of 2003 was spent in an acrimonious debate, brokered by Chirac, on whether to ban the wearing of conspicuous religious symbols, such as the **Islamic headscarf**, in state schools; the ban went into effect in early 2004 amid dire warnings that it would aggravate, not ameliorate, sectarian tensions.

**Spain's** voice is now listened to with respect in international circles, and its cities are conceded to be some of the art and entertainment beacons of Europe. But too often there has been lavish spending on high-profile, prestige projects – such as high-speed rail links and the Sevilla Expo – while sustained, incremental investment in the country's infrastructure and human resources is neglected. For example, following France's lead, conscription in Spain was phased out by 2002, leaving a professional army – and a 125,000-man annual shortfall in staffing for the numerous charities which used to rely on a steady stream of conscientious-objector volunteers, in the absence of funds for salaried positions.

Nearly seven decades after the putative **end of the Civil War**, a new generation with no memory of Franco has begun to question the "don't ask, don't tell, don't blame" coping strategy which accompanied the return to democracy of the mid-1970s – and which contributed substantially to the often-perceived vacuousness and amorality of public life. Seemingly not a month goes by in Spain without the uncovering of yet another mass grave, almost always of civilians shot by the Falange during the opening months of the war, as witnesses who always literally knew where the bodies were buried finally feel able to speak out, and volunteer diggers are recruited. Accompanying this has been a veritable avalanche of published and recorded memoirs by veterans of the conflict, and the formation of "historical memory" groups across the country, as the main post-Franco taboo is definitively breached in a process not unlike the torrent of Holocaust-survivor testimonies of the last two decades.

In accordance with the constitution of 1978, there has been an appreciable **devolution of powers** to the seventeen autonomous regions or **autonomías** into which Spain is divided. Each has its own president, parliament and civil service – an enormously expensive duplication of functions. Variable statutes of autonomy have been granted to Catalunya, Aragón, Navarra and Gipuzkoa, which between them include the entire Spanish Pyrenees. However, Madrid has reserved too many powers – most notably tax collection, followed by proportional disbursement – for the system to have yet approached true federalism, though Catalunya's Generalitat has extracted from the central government the concession of collecting, and spending, thirty percent of its own budget. Elsewhere, especially in Aragón where the regionalist Partido Aragonés (and ample graffiti in the local language) are much in evidence, the political authority has been present for local Pyrenean initiatives, but funds have often proved to be insufficient. Another obvious downside to decentralization is the tendency of *autonomías*, when they do get cash, to subsidize one-off payments to buy votes, rather than fund economic development. Balancing peripheral self-determination with fiscal responsibility is the task confronting Madrid governments of any complexion, and one that goes against the grain of the national impulse to live for the moment and let tomorrow take care of itself.

The stubbornly high Spanish **unemployment** rate – still into double figures even in the most prosperous regions – means that petty crime is a constant feature of life, even in isolated areas. Catalunya, especially Girona province, is markedly better off for work; many of the young people you'll see in seasonal jobs at Catalan Pyrenean resorts are **migrants** from distant provinces (and distant countries ranging from Latin America to Poland), working with little in the way of employment contracts or security. North Africans tend to settle in Andalucía and Catalunya rather than the mountains proper, but estimates of Spain's overall **Muslim** numbers approach half a million (in a total population of forty million), and in the wake of the March 2004 Madrid bombings, anti-Muslim (and anti-immigrant) feeling is bound to increase.

**Mountain agriculture** has long since ceased to be profitable on either slope of the Pyrenees, so the ancient terraces are crumbling back into wilderness. Repopulation is therefore left to the *nouveaux ruraux/neo-rurales* in search of alternative lifestyles, and to people renovating second homes. France in particular offers a range of grants for permanent mountain-dwellers, but **full-time Pyrenean residence** remains a precarious undertaking. The advent of solar-power panels (especially on the Spanish side), fixed telephony capable of supporting Internet processes and mobile phones does mean that self-employment and residence are now feasible in previously abandoned, non-viable spots, which conventional state utilities have historically refused to supply.

While Spain is no longer as starry-eyed about the **EU** as it was during the 1990s, a significant majority of Spaniards still strongly back European integration and see their participation in the first wave of euro-using countries as a landmark in Spain's move into the European mainstream. Most citizens are also acutely aware of the benefits accruing to the country from huge EU "convergence" grants for important infrastructure projects, as well as subsidies to the pivotal farming sector under the Common Agricultural Policy. The **single European market** has had a discernible impact on towns like Perpignan and Bayonne (as well as Jaca and Girona), which handle or service much of the freight and transit personnel moving north and south. The effect of EU money is highly visible in the Pyrenees, where it funds civil engineering projects otherwise beyond the means of the autonomous regions. Much of this development is highly unsympathetic to the environment, with the mountains at risk of transformation into a cluster of tame theme parks linked by motorways, where genuine indigenous culture and wildlife have been destroyed. That said, commercial exploitation is still far below the level prevailing in the Alps, even as the Pyrenees have "arrived" as a popular tourist destination from overseas since the mid-1990s.

# Wildlife

There is plenty of wildlife to observe in the Pyrenees, despite the effects of hunting and environmental damage (see "The Environment", p.591). The range is especially rewarding for bird-spotters, with a variety of magnificent resident indigenous species, and enormous numbers of migrating birds to be seen flying over the western Col d'Organbidexka and, in the east near Canigou, the Col d'Eyne.

The round-up below picks out the major animal species that you might encounter (as well as the declining species that you probably won't), and details some of the more interesting types of Pyrenean flora. However, it is only a general guide to occurrence and habitat. For something more specific, see the list of recommended wildlife titles on p.604.

# Birds

The **lammergeier** or bearded vulture (*gypaète barbu* in French; *quebrantahuesos* in Castilian) was persecuted almost out of existence by herdsmen fearing for their livestock, but since the 1970s has made a slight recovery. It is easily identified by the wonderful pinkish-gold breast of the adult, a long wedge-shaped tail, narrow wings and enormous size – weighing up to 6kg, with a wingspan of almost 3m. Lammergeiers can most reliably be seen in several places: at Gavarnie, in the Aspe/Ossau region, in the Valle de Ordesa and in their principal strongholds of the Echo, Ansó and Roncal valleys northwest of Jaca.

The lammergeier's diet consists mainly of bone marrow, which it exposes by dropping bones onto a rocky surface from a height of 30–50m (hence the Castilian name, meaning "breaks-bones"). To locate its meal, the solitary lammergeier often works in conjunction with a flock of **griffon vultures** (*vautour fauve* in French; *buitre común* in Castilian), which are similar in size, but lack the wedge-shaped tail and streamlining, and have a distinctive white head and neck, as well as black wing-tips. Only when the griffons have finished stripping the flesh from the carcass does the lammergeier move in. Flocks of griffon vultures patrol much of the Pyrenees, especially in the Basque country and the Aspe/Ossau valleys.

Occasionally, the rare **black vulture** is seen in the Western Pyrenees, particularly in the Valle de Echo or over the Iparla ridge, either with griffons or on its own. This bird can be distinguished from the griffon by its longer and more rounded tail, its much darker plumage and a black area around the eye.

Unlike the above species, the **Egyptian vulture** (*percnoptère* in French; *acantilados alimoche* in Castilian) is found in the Pyrenees only during the breeding season, when it can be seen in the Aspe, Ossau and Soule valleys or around the Ordesa region. The smallest of the vultures – with a wingspan of about 150cm – the Egyptian has white plumage and black wingtips. Nicknamed *Marie-Blanque* or *La Dame Blanche* in the French valleys, its arrival in the April skies announces the start of spring.

The **golden eagle** (*aigle royal* in French; *aguila real* in Castilian) is glimpsed everywhere in the high mountains, each breeding pair having a territory of between 90 and 130 square kilometres. You can identify juveniles by the white patches on the wing underside, but for adult birds over five years old, identification is more by size (around 80cm from beak to tail, with a wingspan of 3m) and the open V-shape of its upturned wings as it soars. Whereas the golden eagle and the scarcer Bonelli's eagle – dark on top, paler underneath, with a dark, striped tail – are seen all year round, the **booted eagle** and the **short-toed eagle** settle here only during the summer breeding season. The booted eagle is the smallest of the European eagles, with a wingspan of up to 120cm. It has a long, narrow tail and is either pale with an almost white front and white-flecked head, or uniformly mahogany-coloured with slender white stripes along the front of the wings. The short-toed eagle is often almost pure white with darker banding all round the wings, and has a head that seems disproportionately large. A unique characteristic is its habit of hovering motionless over its intended prey, commonly snakes, with its legs dangling freely.

The acrobatic kites are perhaps the most entertaining birds to watch. The **red kite** (*milan royal* in French; *milano* in Castilian) has a deeply forked tail, and continuously twists in the air as it manoeuvres over carrion. The **black kite** (*milan noir* in French; *milano negro* in Castilian) is darker than the red kite, its tail shorter and straighter-edged, and its wingspan smaller at around 115cm. It is most often seen circling over municipal rubbish dumps, unconcerned by the comings and goings of the trucks. The autumn migration to the Pyrenees greatly supplements the summertime population.

Since it is seldom seen in flight, except when flushed out of hiding, the **ptarmigan** (*lagopède alpin* in French; *perdiz blanca* in Castilian) is also difficult to spot. It's found in pairs around the central Pyrenees during summer, and in winter in flocks, when the birds are almost totally snow-camouflage white, except for a black tail and red "eyebrows".

**Ptarmigan** (*lagopède alpin* in French; *perdiz blanca* in Castilian), difficult to spot, since they're seldom seen in flight, are found in pairs around the central Pyrenees during summer, and in winter in flocks, when the birds are almost totally snow-camouflage white, except for a black tail and red "eyebrows".

Several smaller but distinctive birds of high altitude are the playful and acrobatic **alpine chough**, a slim crow with a curved yellow beak, sometimes seen with its red-beaked cousin, the **common chough**; the **snow finch**, like a large sparrow, but noticeably black and white in flight; and the **wall-creeper**, red, grey and black, with a thin curved beak and usually found on or near cliffs. Lower down, the **white-backed woodpecker** has its only Western European home among the broad-leaved trees of the Pyrenees, while the much larger but elusive, red-crested **black woodpecker** prefers pine woodland.

# Mammals

The most agile and conspicuous wild mammal of the high mountains is the **isard** or **Pyrenean chamois** (*rebeco* or *camuza* in Castilian; *sarrio* in Aragonese), a member of the antelope family and a close relative of the larger Alpine chamois. Living among the peaks in summer and descending in the winter, they are numerous in the Parc National des Pyrénées and the contiguous Parque Nacional de Ordesa y Monte Perdido. Individuals around Port d'Espagne, near Cauterets, as well as in Ordesa are uncharacteristically tame because of their contact with tourists. Gavarnie, the Sierra del Cadí, Canigou and Aigüestortes are other good places to see them. A few individuals do manage to survive at high altitudes during the snowy months, so you should brace yourself for the surprise value of isards darting across ski runs, or the path of your lift.

The **mouflon** (*muflón* in Castilian), which resembles a very large and sturdy sheep with curling black horns, is a recently reintroduced species. Bones found near Perpignan show that they inhabited the region thousands of years ago, but Corsica, Sardinia and Cyprus were this sheep's only modern natural strongholds. Mouflon are now doing well in the Carlit massif and on Pic Pibeste, near Lourdes, where the arid, Mediterranean-like microclimate allows them to thrive.

The dark-bristled **wild boar** (*sanglier* in French; *jabalí* in Castilian) is nocturnal, and nomadic when under hunting-season pressure, covering up to 40km between dusk and dawn. You may see it at its mud-bath, to which the beast returns regularly, but are more likely to notice signs of its presence than the animal itself. Large areas of disturbed earth are often indicative that a wild boar has been rooting around with its tusks, especially in woodland where it forages for beech-nuts and acorns. Boar are much disliked locally, owing to their habit of damaging fields; they have become a prolific pest since the 1990s owing to mild winters and overzealous reintroduction programmes by hunting clubs.

**Red deer** and the much smaller, slim-horned **roe deer** live in the central Pyrenees, both favouring calcareous zones where open pasture meets forest and the necessary combination of food and cover is provided. Dawn and dusk are the best times to view deer, when feeding activity is most intense; they are elusive animals, though, and local advice will usually be needed to find them. On the Spanish side, however, hunting reserves set aside for them have proven too small for exploding populations; hungry animals have wandered out of the limited areas, resulting in numerous traffic accidents and demands from hunters to be allowed to cull the surplus. Numerous deer migrating south from central France have attracted a following of **wolves** – animals not known in the Pyrenees in living memory – to within 70km of the range, and they should arrive within the next few years.

The **marmot** (*marmotte* in French; *marmota* in Castilian) is effectively the mascot of the range; once so endangered they had to be reintroduced, they're now so numerous that culling is being considered. For the full story on this creature, see the box on p.iv.

The **Pyrenean wildcat** (*chat sauvage* in French; *gato montés* in Castilian) is genetically much the same as that found in other parts of Europe; it looks like a domestic tabby, only much larger, with a distinctively thick tail. Pyrenean wildcats prefer south-facing forests well below alpine habitats, where their preferred prey of field-mice and voles is abundant; they dislike snow, and descend as necessary in winter. Protected on both sides of the Pyrenees, wildcats are actually increasing in numbers and expanding their range, but are shy and seldom seen.

Wildcats shouldn't be confused with the **genet**, which inhabits lower altitudes up to about 1000m. Neither a feline nor a member of the weasel family, these curious creatures have a cat-like head, a leopard-spotted body and an outsize ringed tail. They're an introduced species, having been brought as pets from North Africa by the Moors – and subsequently escaping into the wild. Opportunist carnivores, they will eat anything from frogs to rabbits.

**Stoats** are another small, sinuous carnivore, of the weasel family, which prey on small rodents and rabbits. In their reddish-brown summer fur with a black-tipped tail and cream-coloured belly they are fairly conspicuous, but towards winter they gradually change to white over a period of weeks to camouflage themselves in the snow, at which time they are called **ermines** (*armiños* in Castilian). A larger relative is the **pine marten** (*martre* in French; *marta garduña* in Castilian), which remains a warm brown colour all year round, and is found up to the tree line in the Pyrenees in coniferous and mixed woodland. The **red squirrel** (*écureuil rouge* in French; *ardilla roja* in Castilian) favours much the same habitat and – not subject to competition from greys as in Britain – remains relatively abundant, though prone to the disturbing habit of dashing across the road – and under one's car wheels. **Rabbits** and **hares** are both present; among these, the snowy hare (*lièvre variable* in French) changes like the ermine from tawny to white in winter, and thrives at high elevations where its splayed paws, covered with coarse fur, enable it to sprint across the snow. **Bats** also frequent the Pyrenees up to 2000m altitude, the most striking of several species being *Plecotus auritus* with its outsized ears.

# Endangered species

The **Pyrenean ibex** (*bouquetin* in French; *cabra montés* in Castilian, *bucardo* in Aragonese), a stocky species of wild goat, is effectively extinct. Until 1999 the slopes of the Valle de Ordesa supported the range's single troupe, but conservation-programme blunders, a harsh winter or two, inbreeding and bad luck doomed it; the last individual died in January 2000, struck by a falling tree. However, cells from the fresh corpse were quickly rescued, and it's now planned to clone new specimens, with the less hardy Gredos ibex serving as surrogate mothers. Some five thousand of the latter survive, though they are a distinct subspecies of those formerly native in the Pyrenees. Hunting has been the principal cause of the Pyrenean ibex's demise, their distinctive ribbed horns a much-esteemed trophy during the nineteenth century.

The small, unaggressive Pyrenean subspecies of **brown bear** (*ours brun* in French; *oso pardo* in Castilian) is nearly as close to extinction. No one knows precisely how many native bears remain in the Pyrenees but the top figure is less than ten. Bears are most likely to survive in an area straddling the border around the Aspe, Ossau and Roncal valleys; there may still be some in the border area between Luchon and Benasque, plus another definitely existing group in the Couserans. Experience with other species shows that so small a population seldom retains sufficient genetic diversity to reproduce successfully. Effectively, the Pyrenean brown bear is therefore finished as a distinct subspecies, though there might still be time to cross the remaining specimens with stock from other European brown bear populations; Slovenia was the source of a few individuals introduced into the Couserans in 1997. For a lengthier discussion of bears, see the box on p.406–407.

The only other large carnivore of the area is the rare **lynx** (same in French; *pardelo* in Castilian), which like the bear has been widely persecuted. Out of a total French/Spanish population of some six hundred, just a few dozen remain in the western French Pyrenees, but these are vulnerable to loss of habitat through deforestation. Wildcats (see above) are sometimes mistaken for them.

Few have heard of the **desman** (same in French; *almizclera* or *desmán* in Castilian), yet this trunk-nosed, aquatic, mole-like mammal is one of the great curiosities of the Pyrenees, with its only living relatives in south Russia. Most attempts to study the creature have failed, since in captivity specimens die almost immediately, and it is extremely scarce in the wild. Needing undisturbed and unpolluted streams to survive, the desman has been sighted (on the French side) in the Baronnies, in the Aspe and the streams of the Eastern Pyrenees, which are among the cleanest in the range; the parks and reserves south of the watershed are promising too, especially Aigüestortes, the headwaters of the Ara, and Roncal's Parque Natural Pirenaico. Not exceeding 25cm in length (including tail), it dives for small crustaceans, insects and other invertebrates, consuming daily up to two-thirds its own weight in food.

Another, slightly less endangered aquatic mammal is the **otter** (*loutre* in French; *nutria* in Castilian). It nests among the roots of riverside trees, but is a famously strong swimmer, capable of up to six minutes of submersion; preferred otter prey are amphibians and **trout**, including the rare native species now restricted to the headwaters of the Río Ara on the Spanish side. A successful protection regimen at the Parc Natural dels Aiguamolls de l'Empordà has resulted in the release and tagging of adolescent individuals across the range, but progress in restocking areas that were depopulated of otters several decades ago is under threat by the various dams proposed for Alto Aragón (see p.430).

The turkey-like **capercaillie** (*grand tétras* in French; *urogallo* in Castilian), hunted and harassed to extinction in the French Alps, survives in small numbers in the Pyrenees, protected – albeit ineffectively – in the national parks and in Andorra. Although evolved to survive in extreme winter conditions and with a near-starvation diet, it cannot tolerate human interference, and a campaign – only made feasible by the long life span (avg. 15 years) of the surviving adults – has been launched on the Spanish side. Despite its size the capercaillie is a very elusive bird, but you might see one breaking noisily from cover, or witness the late-winter mating display of the cock, when it throws back its green-ringed neck and dances and sings. The hen is duller, mostly brown flecked with white, and with smaller bright red "eyebrows" than the male.

# Amphibians, reptiles and butterflies

The slow-moving **fire salamander** (*salamandre jaune et noire* in French; *salamandra común* in Castilian) is like a soft-skinned lizard, with brilliant yellow-and-black markings that warn potential predators of its toxic skin secretions. They are primarily nocturnal, and usually only seen by day in damp weather, when heavy rain can lure them out onto paths and roads, especially in the Val d'Aran. The smaller, camouflaged **Pyrenean brook salamander** (*tritón pirenaico* in Castilian) is endemic to the mountains between 1500m and 2200, and found in cold lakes and streams; oddly, they fall into a stupor when the water temperature *exceeds* 15° C, at which time they're easy prey for the local trout (see above). Salamanders are only active during the four warmest months of the year, hibernating on land otherwise. The most spectacular local **frog**, known as *ranita de San Antón* in Castilian, has almost harlequin-pattern markings in red, green and black.

A true reptile, the **Iberian rock lizard** can be found, unlike most of its sun-loving relatives, at surprisingly high altitudes in the Pyrenees. Several snakes occur in the area, none of them poisonous except the **asp viper**. Like most snakes, this species, with a dark wavy or zigzag pattern along the spine, only bites if under threat of attack and needs merely to be left alone. The only snake capable of enduring really low temperatures, it may even interrupt its November-to-February hibernation to take advantage of a sunny winter day.

Numerous **butterflies** (French *papillon*; Castilian *mariposa*) make a home in the Pyrenees, even to quite high altitudes, with July and August being the best months; the Val d'Aran is one of the prime locales for them. Apollo butterflies are white, with distinctive red or yellow eyespots on the wings, whereas the humbler clouded apollo could be mistaken for a small cabbage white. The endemic Gavarnie blue is a rather disappointing shade of grey, but the slightly more widespread Alcon and Eros blues can equal the colour of the gentians it feeds among. Ringlets are a group of medium-sized brown butterflies, with wings marked by black eyespots. They are difficult to distinguish, even for experts, but two species and seven subspecies are endemic to the Pyrenees.

# Flora

Pyrenean high-altitude flora resembles that of the Alps in many ways, but with the warmer average temperatures, the treeline of the Pyrenees can be much higher in a few favoured positions, reaching 2600m on southern slopes of the Néouvielle massif, or 2100m in the Marcadau valley. The highest-altitude **trees** are Pyrenean mountain pines (either *Pinus uncinata* or *Pinus mugo*, and hybrids), with distinctive hooked tips to the cone scales – thus the French name of *pin crochet*. **Black pines** (*Pinus nigra*, ssp *salzmanii*) are the next most tolerant of alpine conditions, occurring up to about 2100m; lower down, in roughly descending order of occurrence, Scots pine, beech, silver fir, birch and poplar form dense forests, with some of the finest being in the Ordesa National Park. Lower still (below about 1000m) grow maple, hornbeam, sweet chestnut and various deciduous oaks. To the east, near the Mediterranean coast, appear groves of umbrella-shaped stone pine, whose edible seeds are gathered as pine nuts (*pignon* in French, *piñon* in Castilian).

Because of the rainfall disparity between some of the dry Spanish slopes and the much wetter French slopes, particularly in the Eastern Pyrenees, the vegetation in one country is often very different to that at a similar altitude on the opposite side of the border. The underlying igneous and metamorphic rocks are hard and slow-weathering, but often overlaid with more plant-friendly limestone. The range's altitude has made the mountains an effective barrier, preventing the spread of many lower-altitude Spanish species northwards into France, and vice versa. June and July are the best months for finding the medium- and high-altitude wildflowers in bloom, but a few species begin as early as May, while others carry on into August, with a few exceptional autumn flowers. A good selection can be seen labelled in the botanical gardens at Tourmalet (see p.383).

More than 3300 species of **plants** are recorded for the Pyrenees, about 180 of them endemic (found growing wild nowhere else). The two unspectacular and very similar species of **Pyrenean yam**, with tiny green flowers, a swollen starchy root and tropical relatives, are ancient relicts of a warmer climate. Both are confined to the Pyrenees, with the rarer one growing only in the Noguera Ribagorçana gorge. **Xatardia** is a stocky, green-flowered, celery-like plant restricted to a few high screes in the east of the range. A much more attractive relict from the Tertiary period is the **ramonda**, named after Ramond de Carbonnières, the doyen of Pyrenean exploration in the late eighteenth century. Although not rare, it is endemic to limestone slopes in northeastern Spain and the Pyrenees. Resembling its distant relative, the African violet, it has fleshy, wrinkled leaves and, in summer, small purple flowers with a central yellow cone of stamens.

Other endemics are more flamboyant. The long-leaved **butterwort**, clinging spectacularly to the cliffs at Gavarnie, has "flypaper" leaves that trap and digest insects. The large purple **storksbill** sports bright, almost garish flowers, while the ashy and western **cranesbills** have far more subtle shades of soft pink on their trumpet-shaped flowers. More delicate still are the little **horned pansies**, with fragrant violet blooms. The rare **silvery vetch** has spikes of pea flowers that are white with thread-like violet veining. The Pyrenean and Aragonese **columbines** have long-spurred flowers of a wonderful blue, while their relative, the Pyrenean **adonis** or pheasant's eye, produces huge golden bowl-shaped flowers over feathery foliage in early summer. The higher areas of the Pyrenees are home to tussocky **fescue** grasses (*genus Festuca*), many species of which are endemic to these mountains. South-facing slopes in Alto Aragón turn yellow with **broom** during early summer.

Several **primroses** in subtle shades of lilac to red can be found in rocky or marshy places, but their small, compact and more delicate relatives, the **rock jasmines**, are mostly restricted to high-altitude cliffs and screes; *Androsace ciliata* and *A. cylindrica* are two of the rarest, confined to the central areas around Gavarnie and Monte Perdido. The **Pyrenean snowbell** has deeply fringed violet flowers and favours damp, shady conditions in the west of the range.

Growing mostly above the treeline, though sometimes in shady woodland, are many species of **saxifrage**, five of them endemic to the Pyrenees. Their flowers are usually small, numerous and starry, coloured white or pinkish in loose sprays. The endemic **water saxifrage** grows in mountain bogs and along streams up to about 2500m, its white flowers appearing in midsummer; the cliff-dwelling **Pyrenean saxifrage** has a large rosette of lime-encrusted leaves, which eventually produces a tall red-stemmed spike of flowers before dying. The **paniculate** (or livelong) **saxifrage** is similar to the Pyrenean but has a smaller, more ragged rosette, with yellow and white flowers only at the top. The most spectacular of this group, the **purple saxifrage**, has large, stemless flowers over carpets of tiny leaves, and grows on the highest peaks.

Succulent **stonecrops** (*Sedum* spp), with yellow, white or pink flowers, and frequently red leaves, grow in dry, open places, often where there is little soil. The equally fleshy, but neatly rosetted, **houseleeks** produce occasional spikes of reddish flowers, and are capable of growing at altitudes of nearly 3000m. A smaller, pale pink flowered species of houseleek is endemic to the Sierra del Cadí.

**Globularias** are dwarf shrubs, with spherical tufted heads of blue or purple flowers and a long flowering period of May to August. There are numerous types of **daisy**, some with large flowers, like the endemic purple **Pyrenean aster**, and the even larger shasta daisy – the latter now widely cultivated elsewhere as a garden plant. The huge **cardoon knapweed** brandishes spectacular purple thistle heads, up to 7cm across, in late-summer meadows; parts of this plant, a close relative of the artichoke, are edible and sometimes appear stewed in restaurants.

Members of the heather family cover large areas, and add colour to the slopes all through the summer. **Bilberries** (April–July), **bearberries** (June–Sept) and **cowberries** all have greenish-white or pinkish, often bell-shaped flowers, followed by edible berries. The prostrate, mat-forming creeping **azalea** (May–July) produces tiny pink flowers, but its bigger cousin the **wild rhododendron** (May–Aug) or alpenrose has clusters of conspicuous red flowers. Various species of heather itself provide colour from May to October.

The higher alpine meadows are home to some gorgeous members of the lily family, such as the chocolate or deep purple bells of the **Pyrenean fritillary**;

the large white trumpets of **Saint Bruno's lily**; the yellow **Turk's-cap lily**, which prefers cliffs or rockpiles; the **dogstooth violet**, which takes its name from the pointed white oval bulb, not the magenta blossom; and *Brimeura*, a small amethyst **hyacinth**. Belonging to the same family, but crocus-like in shades of pink and white, are *Bulbocodium*, *Colchicum* and pink-purple *Merendera*, most of these autumn-blooming. The **true crocuses** appear both in early summer amongst receding snow-patches, and in autumn as the season cools. During spring, half a dozen small members of the **daffodil** family appear, usually in damp meadows and often in great quantity; the rush-leaved narcissus, rock narcissus and lesser wild daffodil are among the more common. **Buttercups** are also well represented, for example the glacier crowfoot (*Ranunculus glacialis*), conspicuous as shiny white or pink flowers on high-altitude glacial moraines or screes, to 3000m and beyond. They are followed, in summer, by the deep, purplish-blue, so-called "English" **iris** (*Iris latifolia*, *ex-xiphioides*), which despite its name is more or less confined in the wild to the Pyrenees, forming spectacular, early-summer clusters on treeless slopes between 1600m and 2000m elevation. This species is the parent of many cultivated forms in northern Europe, and shouldn't be confused with the more widespread, lower-altitude Spanish iris (*Iris xiphium*).

Thirteen types of **gentian** are recorded for the Pyrenees, at elevations over 1500m, but they can sometimes be tricky to identify. Most species are small and delicate, with starry or trumpet-shaped flowers of a piercing blue that can mirror the sky or mountain tarns, but the more robust yellow gentians can attain a metre in height. The most common are the large, deep-blue trumpet gentians, *Gentiana acaulis* (*ex-kochiana*) and closely related species. Another legendary alpine dweller which may grow with them is the **edelweiss**, though the fuzzy whitish flowers can be disappointing up close and lack the gentian's charisma.

Numerous blue **bellflowers** occur, including a number endemic to the Pyrenees. The taller ones grow in open or woodland areas, but the real gems grow nestled into crevices of the limestone, or running delicate stems through the debris of scree slopes. With them, but in contrasting shades of purplish-red through to pale pink, are **wild carnations** and **pinks** (*Dianthus* spp), which often have powerful fragrances according to the kind of soil or rock rooted in; the fringed pink, thriving up to 2000m, is one of the most attractive.

A number of alpine or central European **orchids** grow in woodland and meadows on the French side, while lower areas on the Spanish side and at the hotter eastern and western ends of the range are home to more Mediterranean species. *Epipactis parviflora* and *Dactylorhiza caramulensis* are two specialities of the area, but the endangered **lady's slipper** still survives in a few places in the east.

Local people harvest the abundant **wild fungi** during seasons that vary from spring to late autumn depending on the region. Robust ceps, crinkly yellow chanterelles and saffron milk-caps are favourites, but most in demand are the brown honeycombed morels of springtime, scarce but almost worth their weight in gold when gathered and dried. You will see favourite picking grounds jealously signposted against non-residents on the Spanish side (*Cota de Setas – Prohibido Coger Hongos sín Autorización*/Mushroom Reserve – Forbidden to Pick Fungi without a Permit).

**Marc Dubin and Lance Chilton**

# The environment

Human populations may be lower in most of the Pyrenees than they were during the nineteenth century, but the landscape is nonetheless threatened, and since the early 1980s French and Spanish conservationists have turned considerable attention to the region. Concerns are numerous: the potential extinction of endangered species, massacres of migrating birds, the death from pollution of thousands of hectares of trees, and (most pressing) obstruction of waterways and inundation of valleys by hydroelectric schemes. Their arguments might not be changing developmental priorities yet, but environmental protests get a hearing these days, and occasionally succeed in stopping or at least altering destructive projects. At ground level, the standard of rural tidiness has improved, especially on the Spanish side of the range: dumpster or recycling bins are ubiquitous and well used, and public education campaigns on environmental matters seem slowly to be having an effect.

However, there are still formidable obstacles to be overcome, not least the mind-set of governmental officials in Spain, from regional levels all the way to the top. During its eight-year tenure, the PP government of Spain established unenviable credentials as perhaps the most environmentally unfriendly one in Western Europe; vice-president Álvarez Cascos set the tone in 1997 when he proclaimed, more or less verbatim, that environmental considerations were the concern of a few smelly hippies, and that any opposition to developmental projects should be ignored or brushed aside. Rubbish collection and many local, issue-specific pressure groups notwithstanding, there is no powerful country-wide Spanish Green party as in France, and environmental awareness remains embryonic in Spain, which like many other recently developed countries remains in thrall to high-prestige projects such as high-speed trains, dams and motorways. It remains to be seen whether the PSOE government elected in March 2004 will pay more than just lip service to environmental concerns.

# Natural reserves

Among the qualifications for national park status, as defined by the International Union for the Conservation of Nature and Natural Resources (IUCN), are that there should be no hunting and no exploitation other than that consistent with the "natural" way of life of mountain people, such as grazing or wild-food gathering. So far there are just three **national parks in the Pyrenees**, and only two of those – the Parc National des Pyrénées in France and the adjoining Parque Nacional de Ordesa y Monte Perdido in Spain – actually meet the IUCN criteria. The Parc Nacional d'Aigüestortes i Sant Maurici in Catalunya is not officially recognized by the IUCN because of its numerous hydroelectric installations, a source of constant friction with conservationists.

Other areas of the Pyrenees are administered under less stringent conservation schemes. In Spain there are the *parques naturales* of Cadí-Moixeró, Maladeta-Posets, the Sierra y Cañones de Guara, the Garrotxa and Larra-Belagoa; France has various *réserves naturelles*, including that of Néouvielle – but these do not entirely protect wildlife from hunting.

# Hunting

Hunting in the Pyrenees is **controlled** in a number of ways besides the out-right ban in the national parks. Various private reserves keep the numbers of hunters down by charging high fees; permits are limited by auction or the drawing of lots; certain animals are designated as protected species; the number of hunting days is restricted; and voluntary management plans have been implemented by (French more than Spanish) hunting associations.

In some instances these restraints have been effective. There are around fifteen thousand **isards** on the French side of the range and probably a similar number on the Spanish, a reasonably healthy situation that leads hunters to insist that further kill limits are unnecessary. However, permitted hunting has taken a heavy toll of this species in places: the Néouvielle region's population, for example, had to be restocked after being depleted. Herds have territories of just a few square kilometres, so those within the protected areas are fairly safe; the animals at risk – solitary old males, youngsters rejected by their mothers and mature males driven off by rivals – are those that stray outside the protected reserves.

But the hunters' main interest is in **smaller game animals**, and for these species the situation is far from satisfactory. For instance, there is no explicit protection for capercaillie in the management plans of many hunting associations, even where it is on the verge of local extinction.

Even if an animal is classified as a protected species, it isn't necessarily safe. The 25,000 annual pigeon-hunters often illegally kill other species, such as vultures and kestrels, in the same barrages of shot. Since the late 1990s the migratory pigeon population has crashed dramatically owing to conditions in the species' summer or winter quarters, but their previous slaughter at strategic Pyrenean passes certainly didn't help. The one avian bright spot is a steady increase in lammergeier populations in the Western Pyrenees, thanks to EU-funded conservation projects and growing awareness amongst country people that these raptors feed only on already-dead livestock.

In any event, the power of the hunting lobby – at least in France – cannot be underestimated. Their **political party**, Hunting, Fishing, Nature and Traditions (CPNT in French), caused a major upset in the March 1999 Euro-elections by equalling the 6.8 percent tally of the Communists – in some *départements* they got over a quarter of the vote – and sending several Euro MPs to Brussels.

# Ski development

Given the relatively poor snow record of the Pyrenees, **ski development** here has lagged far behind that of the Alps, especially on the Spanish side of the range. A recent EU report has advised, in light of **global warming** being a confirmed phenomenon, that no new downhill developments should plan to have a base point of under 2000m elevation; an even more current study, carried out in late 2003 by the UN Environment Programme, warned that any resort worldwide (except for Scandanavia) with a base station of under 1500m would be non-viable by 2030, and predicted the demise of many Alpine (let alone Pyrenean) resorts by that date. At present, most Pyrenean ski centre base stations lie at 1600–1850m, and many French stations have a top lift point of under 2000m. Already on the Spanish side, the 1990s saw Llessui and La Tuca close down owing to various combinations of financial mismanagement and uncooperative climate, and others such as Panticosa and Cerler narrowly escaped **bankruptcy** through massive investment in snow-canons and new lifts. However, all the snow-canons in the world will not make a difference if average winter temperatures remain too high. While many French Pyrenean winter-sports centres have hitherto got away with lower siting owing to severe Atlantic weather, a half-dozen minor resorts – including Hautacam, Le Mourtis, Mijanès-Donezan and Guzet-Neige – now spend most of each winter inoperative, and are clearly on the way out (indeed Goulier-Neige and Bourg d'Oeuil closed permanently in 1999). In France, most ski stations are publicly owned and run at a loss, kept going as the major local employer and spur to the mountain economy. Despite the worsening climatic situation, more downhill ski resorts are planned, with a similar justification, on the Spanish side, ie to keep young people in the high mountain valleys employed year-round; they simply cannot live on the proceeds of a three-month summer season.

Expanding the network of **cross-country** ski destinations has not yet proven sufficiently attractive to planners or investors. Though a lower-profit game, it's also lower-risk and lower-impact – if warm winters force them to fold, there's no hardware left littering the slopes and no scarred mountainsides where pistes used to be.

Existing downhill stations frantic over recent poor winters are, in accordance with the above-cited reports, looking to the **highest slopes** of the range to alleviate their problems – one rejected expansion plan at Candanchú actually hoped to blast away part of the Pico d'Aspe to lengthen its ski runs. Worse, other resorts propose to drain natural lakes to feed new snow-canons. An as-yet unapproved French scheme – to link the *domaine* of La Mongie with that of Saint-Lary-Soulan – demands exemption from the ban on development in the Parc National des Pyrénées and the Réserve Naturelle de Néouvielle. On the Spanish side, Formigal and Astún are to be united into one "macro"-station via the Valle de Izas, notwithstanding opposition from Ecologistas en Acción de Aragón and the region's failed bids to host the 1998 and 2010 **Winter Olympics**. Further east, Cerler has submitted plans to expand by fifty percent, up to the boundaries of the Parque Natural Posets-Maladeta; Baqueira-Beret wishes to expand into the Val d'Arreu, a move vigorously opposed by the group Ipcena, who have pointed out that the EU must approve this now that the particular valley has been included in the "Nature Net" of high-value natural sites. In Andorra, the Pal-Alins joint station is set to grow further, as is Grau Roig, with only Associació per la Defensa de la Natura and P3M de Andorra speaking against this.

However, despite global warming making any further investment in downhill ski infrastructure extremely risky, and local surveys showing that the number of skiers is not set to grow significantly, funds continue to pour in. The main potential beneficiaries of such plans are developers who have constructed hundreds of apartments around Jaca since the 1980s; the cheapest interest rates ever in Spain mean a continued orgy of building despite the uncertainties of climate and Olympic hosting. In fact, proposals for new ski centres are a means, not an end, for speculators wishing to justify yet more of the **urbanizaciones** (chalet complexes) that blight nearly every alpine village on the Spanish side not falling within the protection zone of a national park; the Cerdanya and the Val d'Aran in particular have been almost completely disfigured. Once the blocks of flats are up and sold, developers couldn't care less whether the adjacent ski resort is viable in the long term.

Such projects have repercussions beyond the obvious visual disturbance, sewage pollution, increase in traffic densities and disruption of natural habitats. There is growing awareness, for example, that the clearance of forests for the construction of pistes and resorts can lead to a higher incidence of **avalanches**, with devastating effects on hitherto protected settlements.

# Forests

In 1989, research institutes at Toulouse and Lannemezan in France and Vitoria in Spain reported that 21 percent of Pyrenean trees were sick, with the worst-affected forest being the silver firs of the Luchon valley. Several causes have been identified, including repeated dry periods, late frosts and errors of forestry management, but **acid rain** emerges as a major culprit, with the gas field at Lacq, near Pau, particularly singled out. A filtration system at Lacq has drastically cut the release of sulphur into the air, but emissions remain high here and in the industrial conglomerations of Catalunya, Aragón and the Basque country – as well as Andorra, where the main power station launches 324 tonnes of sulphur into the air each day. On the north flank of the Pyrenees 79 percent of forest environments register a pH factor of between 4 and 5 (pH7 is neutral), which ranks with the level in the Vosges, long considered the worst-affected area of France.

Forest **fires** have so far had less impact in the Pyrenees than in Provence, but throughout the range, fires have begun to break out progressively earlier in the year, yet another symptom of global warming. Many are deliberately set by shepherds attempting to clear fresh grazing land, or are the result of burning field-stubble in early spring, with flames escaping into adjacent woodland (and doing nothing, incidentally, for ambient air quality). In one incident during February 2000, four Spanish mountaineers were burnt to death while hiking the French GR10 near Ezterentzubi when such a blaze was driven into their path by sudden winds. In the Albères, on the Mediterranean side of the range, there has been talk of planting more cork oak, a species highly resistant to fire. Improved husbandry of vineyards and olive groves through the clearance of undergrowth and the construction of firebreaks has given some protection to vegetation in the vulnerable Alt Empordà region, behind Catalunya's Mediterranean coast, but the nearby Cap de Creus promontory in Catalunya seems to burn with depressing regularity every few years, especially in the Spanish Valle de Ansó.

# Hydroelectric power – and new dams

Although **hydroelectric power** is in principle more acceptable than fossil-fuelled or nuclear alternatives, and can be almost benign environmentally, neither Spain nor France has devoted much effort to make it so in the Pyrenees. Valleys have been scoured and flooded in an entirely unaesthetic way, with almost no money spent on landscaping or tidying up. Construction has often occurred with no thought given to the impact on wildlife – the Laparan dam project near Ax-les-Thermes, for example, helped hasten the local extinction of the bear. Tunnel-sized feed pipes have been routed through once-wooded areas, and substations send out their rhythmic roar day and night even in the remotest locations. High-tension pylons are strung across otherwise empty sky, while leftover construction and maintenance materials, including rusty, aerial cable cars, deface the most unexpected places. In 1999 it was officially agreed by assorted power companies and Alto Aragón municipalities that €200,000 was to be budgeted for hauling away the rubbish from a dozen badly affected lakes near the frontier; to date nothing has been done. Virtually no major river is untouched, and multilingual warning notices advise you to keep away from the banks downstream from dams in case the power company instigates sudden changes in water level.

The pace of hydroelectric development on the French side, which hit its stride between the world wars, has now slowed down considerably as France enjoys a kilowatt surplus (often sold abroad). The latest north-to-south scheme envisions a 400,000 volt line – the high-tension **autopiste/autopista** – through the Couserans to Graus in Aragón. The route is as yet undecided – it's distinctly unpopular on both sides of the border, if graffiti is any indication – but it may cross over the already-sullied Parc Nacional de Aigüestortes, or even skim the boundaries of the Ordesa park.

The Spaniards were latecomers to the hydro-game: while the very first dams appeared in the hills of Catalunya at the beginning of the last century, most Spanish projects were commissioned after World War II, and proposals for **new dams** are still on the drawing boards for depopulated Alto Aragón and Navarra – with the bulk of accumulated water to be sent, in all cases, down to farms and towns in the flatlands, or even as far away as the giant plantations of southern Spain, by means of giant **trasvases** or pipelines. Under Franco, dams served a dual purpose: as prestige projects proving that the country was "developing", and as a convenient way to clear the hills of potentially independent-minded folk. While paying token homage to rural-dwellers as the repositories of ur-folkloric values, authoritarian regimes have always distrusted them as unlikely to fit in well with their social engineering schemes. In democratic Spain, there has been a subtle shift: projects approved under Franco (mostly) remain valid, and Pyrenean dwellers are expected to sacrifice their homes and livelihoods for the benefit of the millions in the thirsty cities and fields of Valencia, Almería and Murcia in the south. But they are not going quietly – those affected are considerably more sophisticated than the villagers who were terrorized into leaving Jánovas in 1960 (see box on p.430). Encouraged by the success of anti-dam movements in India and Turkey, locals have mounted vigorous, if not always successful, **campaigns against hydro-projects** in their own country.

Besides dams on the Noguera Pallaresa near Rialp, the Río Ésera at Santaliestra and the Río Gállego at Biscarrués (see p.460), the most controversial projects at present are the enlargement of the existing Embalse de Yesa on the Río Aragón, and the completion of an extremely high dam at Itoiz on the Río Irati. Together, they form part of the twenty-billion-euro National Water Plan, designed in the late 1990s ostensibly to alleviate the natural imbalance in water resources between northern and southern Spain, but effectively to benefit the then-ruling PP's major sponsors in the agricultural and construction sectors. Even after their March 2004 defeat, the PP continued handing out contracts for *traverse*-related work during the month interregnum before the POSE assumed power.

The original **Yesa reservoir**, built in 1960, caused the abandonment of three villages with 1500 people and inundated 2500 hectares of arable land – with token or no compensation. The dam's enlargement to triple the reservoir's capacity will destroy three more villages, displace 400 inhabitants, and inundate a large number of Roman and early Christian monuments in the Canal de Berdún (including 22km of the original Camino de Santiago). The extra water will go to irrigate fields near Bardenas, and address an alleged shortfall of drinking water for Zaragoza. Opponents of enlargement charge that Zaragoza loses nearly half its mains water to leaks at present, doesn't bill for roughly the same fraction and hasn't adequately explored the option of obtaining potable water from the Ebro, its own river. Moreover, the Bardenas irrigation zone is apparently not authorized to expand more than eight percent anyway, and the current water-delivery systems are obsolete and inefficient. Following months of street demos in major Aragonese towns, the "anti" faction saw the government approve the new Yesa project in spring 2000; their best recourse, should opponents choose to pursue it, is to appeal the matter to the European Court in Strasbourg. Prior to its surprise victory in the March 2004 elections, the PSOE promised that, were it to gain power, the new Yesa dam would be "only" 25m higher than the existing one; it remains to be seen if Zapatero and Co can walk the walk as well as talk the talk.

The **Itoiz dam** has had an even stormier history. The project, which foresaw the construction of a 135-metre-high dam on the Río Irati downstream from Auritze and Aribe, was first conceived in Franco's last years as a way of irrigating farms on the plains near Pamplona. In 1985, when plans were revived, locals first mobilized to oppose the reservoir, citing among other issues the inundation of three villages upstream, and the ecological value of the Itoiz valley with its two nature reserves and bird protection zone, sheltering rare bearded vultures. By 1992, the Navarran government had dismissed these arguments and began to build. The environmental activists went to the Spanish supreme court – and won. The judges ruled that nature reserves could not be flooded, and ordered a reduction in dam height from 135m to 25m – which would completely undermine the project's economic viability. The Navarran parliament responded in 1995 by dissolving the nature reserves and ordering that construction resume. At this point, faced with the limits of the local justice system, a direct-action group called **Solidarios con Itoiz** (ScI) formed. With members of the press invited to watch, in spring 1996 eight members of ScI overpowered a security guard at the dam site and severed critical cables with power-grinders, delaying further construction for a year. For their pains, the eco-saboteurs got a thorough beating from the Guardia Civil who came to arrest them, and a draconian five-year sentence at their subsequent trial. The ScI 8 served their time, but before going inside they conducted a tour of Europe during late 1999 to publicize their cause, beginning with a press conference at the European Parliament and culminating in attention-getting stunts such as scaling London's Millennium Wheel, Berlin's Brandenburg Gate and even the Dome of St Peter's at the Vatican. In early 2000 the last Spanish legal obstacle to the high dam was removed by its proponents, and construction is proceeding. The ScI 8 subsequently failed to turn themselves in, are in hiding and officially "wanted", though the authorities are making no particular effort to hand them in, to avoid further hassles and embarrassment.

# Books

This list is a sample of general and specific books that will enrich a visit to the range. Not all are concerned exclusively with the Pyrenees, but certain titles that deal with the whole of France and Spain have been included because they contain much that is relevant to the mountains and their cultures. New, in-print books, whose publishers tend to change frequently, can be found on any book retailing website such as ⓦwww.amazon .com/.co.uk or ⓦwww.barnesandnoble.com; out-of-print (o/p) books are usually easily available on the excellent used-book sites ⓦwww.abe .co.uk/com or ⓦwww.bookfinder.com, or at a library. Books below marked with the symbol ★ are especially recommended.

## Travel and memoirs

★ **Rosemary Bailey** *Life in a Postcard: Escape to the French Pyrenees.* In which the author buys a minor Romanesque monastery on the outskirts of Mosset (see Chapter One) and proceeds to restore, and then live in, it for some years. Part cautionary tale, part chronicle of expat/local-born interactions in a *Roussillonnais* village, and rather more engaging than the current glut of "a new life in the sun" programmes on British TV.

★ **Hilaire Belloc** *The Pyrenees.* Originally written in 1909, this is inevitably dated but still fascinating to dip into and covers a wealth of topics (eg, why the Somport and Portalet passes have always been militarily strategic). His tips on Pyrenean high-altitude navigation remain valid, Spanish *botas* (goat-hairy insides and all) are extolled, and even back then maps on the Spanish side lagged behind their French counterparts. Easily findable on the recommended antiquarian websites (see above); later editions (1916, 1923) are much cheaper.

★ **Alastair Boyd** *The Essence of Catalonia* (o/p). Part history, part guide, this is strong on the art and architecture of the obvious towns and monuments, but weaker on the Pyrenean mountain side of things.

**Norbert Casteret** *The Descent of Pierre Saint-Martin* (o/p). English translation of Casteret's *Trente Ans sous Terre*, dealing with the exploration of what was then the world's deepest known cave system. Other translations of books by Casteret, the greatest of Pyrenean speleologists, include *Ten Years Under the Earth* (o/p but easy to find), *Cave Men New and Old* (o/p) and *The Darkness Under the Earth* (o/p).

**Eleanor Elsner** *Romance of the Basque Country and the Pyrenees* (o/p). Published in 1927, but still a treasure for its old photographs and anecdotes.

**Nina Epton** *The Valley of Pyrene* (o/p). Record of a tour through the Ariège in the 1950s, with copious anecdotes and reflections. Encounters with luminaries – including Dalí – give added depth to the account.

★ **Mark Kurlansky** *The Basque History of the World.* Eminently readable, unconventional chronicle of this mysterious people, from prehistory to the ETA era; black-and-white illustrations, maps and even recipes illuminate Basque contributions to European cuisine, economic growth, Catholicism and international relations (thus the title).

★ **Norman Lewis** *Voices of the Old Sea.* Set between 1948 and

1950, this blend of novel and social record movingly charts the lives of two remote Costa Brava villages and the breakdown of the old ways with the arrival of tourism.

**Rose Macaulay** *The Fabled Shore* (o/p). The Spanish coast as it was in 1949 (read it and weep), travelled and described from Catalunya to the Portuguese Algarve.

**Edwin Mullins** *The Pilgrimage to Santiago*. While just a brief section of the medieval pilgrims' route from Paris to the shrine of St James (Santiago) passes through the Pyrenees, this gives a good overview of the Santiago legend and the pilgrimage it sparked. Mullins, an amiable if somewhat sedentary cicerone, who never walks when he can ride a vintage car or a spirited horse, points

out churches along the way, giving incisive accounts of their social and architectural background.

**Henry Myhill** *The Spanish Pyrenees* (o/p). The Spanish side as it was in the early Sixties; excellent for its historical speculation and human anecdotes, less commendable for an obvious pro-Francoist bias.

**Paul Richardson** *Our Lady of the Sewers*. An articulate and kaleidoscopic series of insights into rural Spain's customs and cultures, fast disappearing.

**John Sturrock** *The French Pyrenees* (o/p). Another detailed historical travelogue, but one in which the author rarely gets out of his car. Sturrock starts at the west coast and works east, stopping abruptly at the border with the exception of a detour to Roncesvalles.

# History, society and politics

★ **Raymond Carr** *Modern Spain, 1875–1980* and *The Spanish Tragedy: The Civil War in Perspective*. Two of the best concise narratives on the modern era.

**Alfred Cobban** *A History of Modern France* (3 vols: 1715–99, 1799–1871 & 1871–1962). A complete and very readable account of the main political, economic and social strands in French history from Louis XIV's death to the middle of the de Gaulle era.

**Roger Collins** *The Arab Conquest of Spain, 710–797*. Controversial study which documents the "Moorish" invasion and the significant influence that the conquered Visigoths had on early Muslim rule. His *Early Medieval Spain, 400–1000* takes a broader overview of the same subject.

**John A. Crow** *Spain: The Root and the Flower*. Cultural and social history from Roman Spain to the present.

★ **Natalie Zemon Davis** *The Return of Martin Guerre*. A man presents himself as a woman's long-

lost husband, and persuades many doubters, despite his extremely tenuous resemblance to the missing spouse. A perplexing and titillating hoax which actually occurred in the Pyrenean village of Artigat during the sixteenth century; even better than the movie or the musical.

★ **J.H. Elliot** *Imperial Spain 1469–1716*. Best introduction to the centuries immediately after unification – academically respected and a gripping tale.

**Jonathan Fenby** *France on the Brink*. Somewhat alarmist diagnosis of France's current woes, putting the blame squarely on its complacent, greedy ruling class.

**L.P. Harvey** *Islamic Spain 1250–1500*. Comprehensive account of this period, encompassing both the Islamic kingdoms and the Muslims living beyond their protection.

**Christopher Hibbert** *The French Revolution*. Good, concise popular history of the period and salient events.

**John Hooper** *The New Spaniards* (Penguin). A 1995 update of a perceptive 1987 portrait of post-Franco Spain and the new generation by the *Guardian's* long-time Madrid correspondent. Though the revision in turn is due for rewriting, still the best one-volume introduction to contemporary Spain.

**Peter Sahlins** *Boundaries: The Making of France and Spain in the Pyrenees*. Using the partition of the Cerdanya/Cerdagne as a model, this explores the process of instilling French and Spanish national identi-

ties in a formerly unified area of the Catalan Pyrenees; academic and groaning with charts and tables, but has its readable moments.

**Alexander Werth** *France 1940–1955* (o/p). Excellent and emotionally engaging portrayal of the most taboo period in French history: the Occupation, followed by the early Cold War and colonial-struggle years in which the same political tensions and heart-searchings were at work; that said, written with perhaps too little hindsight, in 1956.

## The Cathars

In its anti-centralist, anticlerical essentials, the Cathar issue still fascinates the French. The publication of material on the Cathar era is something of a major industry in the Pyrenean provinces in particular, with two Toulouse publishers – Éditions Privat and Éditions Loubatières – specializing in it. The following are just some of the titles currently available in French and English.

**Catherine Bibollet and Michel Roquebert** *Ombre et Lumière en Pays Cathare* (Éditions Privat). Attractive coffee-table effort, available also in an English edition.

**Anne Brenon** *Petit précis de catharisme* (Éditions Loubatières). Short summary of the sect's beliefs, drawn from a course given at the University of Montpellier. Her *Le vrai visage du catharisme* (Éditions Loubatières) discusses its flourishing in the Occitan-speaking areas and the details of its suppression.

**Jean Duvernoy** *Histoire et Religion des Cathars* (2 vols, Éditions Privat). Over forty years, Duvernoy completed the original translation from Latin of the Inquisition's records, which made Le Roy Ladurie's work possible; this is his own history. Vol. 1 analyses the records; Vol. 2, more interestingly, tallies all the medieval sects, from Asia Minor to Britain, allied with Catharism.

**Emmanuel Le Roy Ladurie** *Montaillou*. Life in a last-ditch Cathar village in the Pays de Sault, as recorded by the Inquisition early in the fourteenth century, and stored

away until the 1970s in the Vatican archives. Hard going in places but a fascinating insight.

**Zoé Oldenbourg** *Massacre at Montségur*. English translation of the standard (1961) history of the Cathar crusades. Vivid and partisan (as in extremely sympathetic to the Cathars), stressing the connection between the suppression of the heresy and that of Languedoc separatism. Good appendices give some insight into Cathar beliefs – and the Church's horror of them.

**Stephen O'Shea** *The Perfect Heresy: The Life and Death of the Cathars*. If time is limited, this is an excellent one-stop overview of the sect and the crusade against them, clear-eyed and without pandering to any of the New-Agey speculation which has grown up around the Cathars.

**Michel Roquebert** *L'Épopée Cathare* (4 vols, Éditions Privat). Exhaustive but readable history, 31 years in the making, drawing on nearly everything known about the sect. His more focused *Montségur, Les Cendres de la Liberté* (Éditions Privat) may be more accessible.

**Steven Runciman** *The Medieval Manichee*. Classic account of the evolution of the dualist heresy from the Bogomils and Paulicians up to the Cathars.

★ **Jonathan Sumption** *The Albigensian Crusade*. Lively, somewhat revisionist history of the crusade in which the Cathars are made out to be nearly as contemptible as their adversaries, who are given more depth than usual. Good on the cultural clash between the dour Normans, who largely staffed and directed the campaign, and the anarchistic Languedocians – as well as the extensive Aragonese involvement in the wars.

★ **René Weis** *The Yellow Cross: The Story of the Last Cathars, 1290–1329*. Catharism had a final resurgence in the Pays de Sault during the cited period. Weis, better than almost anyone thus far, has drawn on primary archival sources and his own extensive travels in the area to (albeit novelistically) re-create events of the time, with fully rounded characters, useful sketch maps and photos of the locales as they are now.

## The Spanish Civil War

★ **Gerald Brenan** *The Spanish Labyrinth: An Account of the Social and Political Background of the Spanish Civil War*. As the subtitle says: not a straight history of the war, but one of the best nonacademic studies on Spanish rural society of the time.

**Ronald Fraser** *Blood of Spain*. Subtitled *The Experience of Civil War*, this oral history of 1936–39 gives a voice to the people who fought in and lived through the war. As a record of ordinary lives in extraordinary times, more immediately accessible than conventional histories.

★ **George Orwell** *Homage to Catalonia*. Journalist Orwell cut his teeth on this – if not his most celebrated book, certainly his best reportage. A forthright account of battles on the Aragón front, followed by Orwell's injury and disillusionment with the factional fighting among the Republican forces.

★ **Paul Preston** *Franco* is a penetrating, monumental biography of Franco and his regime, demonstrating how he won the Civil War, how he survived in power so long, and what his ultimate significance was. Preston's more recent *Concise History of the Spanish Civil War* is a compelling introduction to the subject, and more digestible than Hugh Thomas' tome.

★ **Hugh Thomas** *The Spanish Civil War*. Massive, exhaustive political study of the period, and still the best single telling of the convoluted story.

## World War II: French occupation and resistance

**Marc Bloch** *Strange Defeat*. Moving personal study of the reasons for France's defeat and subsequent caving-in to Nazism. Found among the papers of this Sorbonne historian and Resistance member after his death at the hands of the Gestapo in 1942.

**Philippe Burin** *Living with Defeat*. Excellent French account of the Occupation, focusing in particular on the experiences of ordinary people.

**Emilienne Eychenne** *Les Pyrénées de la Liberté, 1939–1945* (Éditions Émpire, France). History of World War II escapes over the Pyrenees into Spain, by a historian who has made this her special subject. She has also written other titles dealing with specific segments of the range.

**H.R. Kedward** *In Search of the Maquis: Rural Resistance in South*

France 1942–44 (available on print-on-demand basis). Slightly dry, but full of fascinating detail about the brave and often mortal struggle of the countless ordinary people in the region who fought to drive the Germans from their country.

★ **Ian Ousby** *Occupation: The Ordeal of France 1940–1944.* Somewhat revisionist 1997 account which shows how relatively late resistance was, how widespread col-

laboration was, and why. Good mix of salient events and how it felt to live through these times.

**Paul Webster** *Pétain's Crime: The Full Story of French Collaboration in the Holocaust.* The fascinating and alarming story of the Vichy regime's more than willing collaboration with the deportations of Jews and the bravery of those, especially the communist resistance in occupied France, who attempted to prevent it.

## Ethnography, nationalism and folklore

**Claude Bailhé** *Autrefois les Pyrénées* (Éditions Milan, Toulouse, France). The French Pyrenees as they were from the latter half of the nineteenth century until World War I, in early photos. Organized by topic (mountaineering, family life, local industries) with intelligent text.

**Daniele Conversi** *The Basques, the Catalans and Spain: Alternative Routes to Nationalist Mobilisation.* Scholarly exploration of the differing evolutions of Basque and Catalan nationalism.

**Antoine Lebègue** *Lieux Insolites et*

*Secrets des Pyrénées* (Éditions Sud Ouest, France). Inexpensive miscellany of legends, odd rites and semi-mythic personalities, organized by region. Sketchy (quite literally, with reproductions of old engravings) but fun.

**Severino Pallaruelo** *Pastores del Pireneo* (Spanish Ministry of Culture; o/p). A thorough – though rather specialist – research into the arts and popular traditions of Pyrenean mountain people, with good photographs.

## Art and architecture

**Jean Clottes and David Lewis-Williams** *Les Chamanes de la Préhistoire* (Éditions Seuil, France). Revisionist view of the Ariège cave paintings, declaring that designated shamans rendered the art from their visions; see box on p.239.

**Kenneth J. Conant** *Carolingian and Romanesque Architecture, 800–1200.* Fastidious, scholarly treatment of the subject, with excellent material on the French side of the Saint-Jacques (Santiago) pilgrim route.

**John Golding** *Cubism: A History and an Analysis 1907–14* (o/p). The standard work on the years of purist Cubism – essential reading to get the most out of a trip to Céret.

**Michael Jacobs** *The Road to Santiago de Compostela.* A good architectural guide to the Spanish section

of the pilgrimage route, but only about one-fourth of the book's coverage falls within this Rough Guide.

**Bertrand Lorquin** *Aristide Maillol.* Short and surprisingly reticent monograph on the sculptor by the curator of the Paris Maillol museum – and son of Maillol's last model, Dina Vierny.

**Meyer Schapiro** *Romanesque Art.* An excellent illustrated survey of Spanish Romanesque art and architecture – and its Visigothic and Mozarabic predecessors.

**Ann Sieveking** *The Cave Artists* (o/p). Comprehensive introduction to late-Paleolithic cave painting, with explanations of the theories on meaning and layout; two chapters devoted to the Pyrenees.

**Sarah Whitfield** *Fauvism.* Although

its reproductions can't do justice to the vibrant colours of Matisse and the artists in his circle, this serves well as an introduction to the preoccupations of the Fauves.

## The Pyrenees in literature

**Victor Català** (pseudonym of Caterina Albert i Paradis) *Solitude*. This tragic 1905 tale of sex, death and greed in and around a Pyrenean *ermita* is regarded as the most important pre-Civil War Catalan novel.

**Pierre Loti** *Ramuntcho* (in French). Cloyingly tragic romance, a sort of early, high-class Mills & Boon-type affair, set in the French Basque country.

**The Song of Roland.** The most famous French epic, translated by Glyn Burgess. Written around the end of the eleventh century, this mini-saga conjures up the whole legend of Roland and the famous ambush near Roncesvalles in the Basque Pyrenees.

**Colm Tóibín** *The South*. Tóibín's wonderful first novel follows a woman fleeing her boring, middle-class family in Ireland for a lover and new life in the Spanish Pyrenees.

## Specific guides

**The Confraternity of Saint James** publishes two *Pilgrim Guides to the Roads through France to Santiago de Compostela*, which are more useful and current than the Cicerone guide. Volume 1, *The Camino Francés*, despite the name, covers the stretch from Saint-Jean to Pamplona; volume 4, *Arles to Puenta la Reina*, goes via Jaca. Both have good route and facilities details, but no maps. In case of difficulty purchasing, contact them directly at 1 Talbot Yard, Borough High Street, London SE1 1YP (☏020/7404 4500).

**GR11, Senderos de Gran Recorrido/Senda Pirenaica** (PRAMES, Zaragoza, Spain). In Castilian. Comes in three packagings: the complete range, covered in a two-ring binder – you extract sections and carry them about in the provided case; paperbound in three separate volumes: *Andorra/Catalunya*, *Aragón*, *Navarra/Gipuzkoa*; or (most recently) as one volume, with 47 route maps at 1:40,000. Invaluable, and updated regularly (current pages available for the binder edition), though as ever for things Spanish some of the timings are way out.

**Paul Lucia** *Through the Spanish Pyrenees, GR11: A Long-Distance Footpath*. Now in its second edition, with accurate time-courses, altitude profiles and lists of available facilities, but poor maps and coverage of variants.

**Pierre Merlin** *Guide des Raids à Skis* (Denoël, France). Guide, in French only, to the Pyrenean traverse on skis.

**Pierre Minvielle** *Randonnées en Aragon* (Diffusion Randonnées Pyrénéennes, France). A well-illustrated pocket-sized walking guide devoted to one of the most spectacular walking areas of the Pyrenees.

**Jean-Paul Pontroué and Fernando Biargue** *Au coeur des Sierras du Haut Aragón* (Éditions J-C Bihet, Pau, France). French-language guide to the canyons, best on Ordesa area walks and canyoning but also with sketchy summaries of the Valle de Gistau, Echo/Ansó and Panticosa/Sallent. Also by the same authors, *Canyons et Barrancos du Haut Aragón* and *Parc National d'Ordesa et du Mont Perdu* (Randonnées Pyrénéennes, France), though currently out of print, are much better than Biargue's later solo effort *Senderos del Parque Nacional de Ordesa* *y Monte Perdido, 100 Itinerarios* (self-published).

**Por los Valles de Ansó, Echo y Aragües** (PRAMES, Zaragoza, Spain). Everything you would want to know (in Castilian) about the valleys and their settlements, plus tips for walking, rock-climbing and canyoning.

**Les Guides Rando** (Rando Éditions, France). Compact, definitive, region-by-region guides for the French side, designed to be used in conjunction with the same company's *cartes des randonnées*; the one for the Néovielle in particular is indispensable.

**Alison Raju** *The Way of St James: Pyrenees–Santiago–Finisterre*. Covers the pilgrim route from Saint-Jean-Pied-de-Port to Pamplona and beyond; some useful route maps, self-contained latter half of Cicerone's previous one-volume guide from Le Puy (France) to the sea beyond Santiago de Compostela.

★ **Kev Reynolds** *Walks and Climbs in the Pyrenees*. Now in its fourth edition, this is the standard English-language guide for trekkers and scramblers by the foreigner who knows these mountains best, covering the most spectacular parts of the range. Reynolds' *Classic Walks in the Pyrenees* (o/p) is a bit more clearly presented for route-planning, if rather purple in the prose; his 2004-issued *The Pyrenees* may be easier to get, for the same purpose.

**Patrick Santal** *White Water Pyrenees* (Rivers Publishing/Menasha Ridge Press). All you could possibly need to know about every worthwhile (and a few not so worthwhile – they tell you) rafting and kayaking river in the range, in this English translation of a year-2000 French guide. Meticulous ratings, diagrams, instruc-

tions and outfitter contacts in what's clearly a labour of love.

**Douglas Streatfield-James** *Trekking in the Pyrenees*. The best and most current (2001, revision due out 2005) English-language guide to the GR10 and its variants, also including choice sections of the Camino de Santiago, the Parque de Ordesa and the Aigüestortes/Sant Maurici area. Easy-to-use sketch maps, but some complaints about inconsistent time courses.

**Sua Edizioak** is a Bilbao-based mountaineering publisher with several guides (unfortunately in Castilian and Euskera only) pertaining to the Pyrenees. These include *GR11, Pirineo Vasco*, a *topoguía* describing the trail from Zuriza to Hondarribia; *La Alta Ruta de los Pirineos en Bici*, for mountain-biking close to the HRP; *El Camino de Santiago en Bici*, rather less strenuous touring-bike itineraries along the pilgrim route; and *Rutas y Paseos por Belagoa*, selected excursions in the *parque natural* at the head of the Roncal valley.

**Georges Véron** *Pyrenees High Level Route* (o/p). English translation of the standard mountaineer's traverse of the Pyrenees (original published by Gastons).

**Rafael Vidáller Tricas** *Guía del Valle de Benasque* (Editorial Pirineos, Huesca, Spain). More rigorous than the Aragonese government's and mountain club's co-published PR booklet (see p.301); this one grades the progressively more difficult walks.

**Derek Walker** *Rock Climbs in the Pyrenees*. The first English guide for climbers; serious stuff, including Pic du Midi d'Ossau and the palisades of the Valle de Ordesa.

## Wildlife field guides

Most of the following titles are best mail-ordered through specialist dealers; a good one in the UK is Summerfield Books, Main Street, Brough, near Kirkby Stephen, Cumbria CA17 4AX (☎017683/41577, ⊛www.summerfield-books.com). They not only have new botanical titles, but also rare or out-of-print natural history books on all topics. Postage is extra for smaller orders, but they often have special offers on select products. The shop is open Mon–Sat 9.30am–4.30pm.

Note that the system of Linnaean classification is in a constant state of flux in the case of small flora, where entire families have been suppressed in recent decades, and various species have been renamed or even assigned to a different genus. So while you may find photos of the live specimens in front of you, you can't always expect to have a currently correct identification.

**Marjorie Blamey and Christopher Grey-Wilson** *The Alpine Flowers of Britain and Europe*. Comprehensive field guide, with coloured drawings; recent and taxonomically fairly current.

**John A. Burton** *Field Guide to the Mammals of Britain and Europe*. A bargain: well illustrated and thorough.

**John A. Burton, E. N. Arnold and D. W. Ovenden** *Field Guide to the Reptiles and Amphibians of Britain and Europe* (o/p). For all those alpine newts, lizards and frogs.

**Lance Chilton** *Plant List for the Pyrenees* (Marengo Publications, UK). Slim but dense pamphlet, cataloguing every tree and plant known to occur in the range, whether as a native or introduced species. Order direct from Marengo at ☎01485/532710 or ⊛www.marengowalks.com.

**Corbet and Ovenden** *Collins Guide to the Mammals of Europe*. The best of several field guides to warm furries.

**Jacquie Crozier** *A Birdwatching Guide to the Pyrenees*. Illustrated and mapped guidelet, detailing 18 regions in Spain, France and Andorra; includes practical directions and checklist.

**Pierre Delforge** *Orchids of Britain and Europe* (HarperCollins, UK). The best and most up-to-date guide, though beware small inaccuracies in the translation from the French. An updated version is available in French.

**Heinzel, Fitter and Parslow** *Collins Guide to the Birds of Britain and Europe*. One of the best general guides to the subject.

**Lionel Higgins and Norman Riley** *Field Guide to the Butterflies of Britain and Europe*. Not specific to the Pyrenees, but an excellent start.

**Oleg Polunin and B. E. Smythies** *Flowers of South-West Europe*. Covers all of Spain, Portugal and southwest France, including the Pyrenees; taxonomy is old despite relatively recent (1997) printing, but still unsurpassed for its introductions, plates, line drawings and keys.

**A. W. Taylor** *Wild Flowers of the Pyrenees* (o/p). This rare, slim volume is the only guide specifically dedicated to the range. Easy to use, but somewhat elderly (1971) and far from comprehensive.

# Language

# Language

# Language

One of the characteristics of the Pyrenees is the number of regional languages – linguists recognize Catalan, Aranés, Aragonese, Occitan, Gascon and Euskera – and the strong dialects which seemingly exist in every French valley. There will be little opportunity to learn any of these on a short visit, though a smattering of French and Castilian Spanish should serve you adequately for most purposes.

## French

**French** is far from an easy language, despite the number of words and structures it shares with English, but the bare essentials are not difficult to master, and they make all the difference. Even just saying "Bonjour, Monsieur/ Madame" when you enter a shop will usually get you a smile and helpful service. People working in tourist offices, hotels and so forth almost always speak better English than you do French, and so tend to reply in it when you're struggling to stammer out something in French – be grateful, not insulted.

Differentiating words is the initial problem in understanding spoken French, as it's very hard to get people to slow down – if all else fails, get them to write what they've said, as you are bound to recognize more words that way. Even outside the Basque and Catalan areas, there are districts where the language of daily life is a strong dialect of French or, in places, something more like a different species. Don't be dismayed – though you'll probably never understand an overheard conversation, any attempt to make yourself understood in school-book French will meet with a sympathetic response and a fairly comprehensible reply.

---

### French learning materials

**Rough Guide French Phrasebook** (Rough Guides). Mini dictionary-style phrasebook with both English–French and French–English sections, along with cultural tips for tricky situations, and a comprehensive menu-master.

**French and English Slang Dictionary** (Harrap/Prentice Hall); **Dictionary of Modern Colloquial French** (Routledge). Both volumes will be a bit bulky to carry in the mountains, but they're the key to all you ever wanted to understand about street-level vernacular. The **Collins Gem** (HarperCollins, UK) is a far more compact dictionary, cheap and adequate for beginner's needs.

**Breakthrough French** (Pan; book and 2 cassettes). Excellent teach-yourself course.

**Verbaid** (Verbaid, Hawk House, Heath Lane, Farnham, Surrey GU9 0PR). CD-size laminated paper "verb wheel" giving you the tense and conjugation endings for the regular verbs.

**A Vous La France; France Extra; France-Parler** (BBC Publications/EMC Publishing; each course a book and 2 cassettes). BBC radio courses, running from beginners' to fairly advanced levels.

# A brief guide to speaking French

## Pronunciation

One easy rule to remember is that **consonants** at the ends of words are usually silent. *Pas plus tard* (not later) is thus pronounced "pa-plu-tarr". But when the following word begins with a vowel, you run the two together: *pas après* (not after) becomes "pazapray".

**Vowels** are the hardest sounds to get right. Approximately:

| | |
|---|---|
| a | as in **ta**r |
| e | as in g**e**t |
| é | between g**e**t and g**a**te |
| è | between g**e**t and g**u**t |
| eu | like the **u** in h**u**rt |
| i | as in m**a**chine |
| o | as in h**o**t |
| ô, au | as in **o**ver |
| ou | as in f**oo**d |
| u | as in a pursed-lip version of **u**se |

More awkward are the **combinations** in/im, en/em, an/am, on/om, un/um at the ends of words, or followed by consonants other than n or m. Again, roughly:

| | |
|---|---|
| in/im | like the **an** in **an**xious |
| an/am, en/em | like the **don** in **Don**caster when said with a nasal accent |
| on/om | like the **don** in **Don**caster said by someone with a heavy cold |
| un/um | like the **u** in **u**nderstand |

**Consonants** are much as in English, except that: ch is always "sh", ç is "s", c is "s" before i or e only, but always hard at the end of a word, h is silent, th is the same as t, w is "v", and r is growled (or rolled).

## Gender

French nouns are divided into masculine and feminine. This causes difficulties with adjectives, whose endings generally have to change to agree with the gender of the nouns they qualify. If you know some grammar, you will know what to do. If not, stick to the masculine form, which is the simplest – it's what we have done in the glossary, except for adjectives of nationality which have the feminine final 'e' or 'ne' in brackets.

## Basics

| | | | |
|---|---|---|---|
| today | aujourd'hui | woman | une femme |
| yesterday | hier | here | ici |
| tomorrow | demain | there | là |
| in the morning | le matin | this one | ceci |
| in the afternoon | l'après-midi | that one | celà |
| in the evening | le soir | open | ouvert |
| now | maintenant | closed | fermé |
| later | plus tard | big | grand |
| at one o'clock | à une heure | small | petit |
| at three o'clock | à trois heures | more | plus |
| at ten-thirty | à dix heures et demie | less | moins |
| | | a little | un peu |
| at midday | à midi | a lot | beaucoup |
| man | un homme | cheap | bon marché |

| expensive | cher | cold | froid |
| good | bon | with | avec |
| bad | mauvais | without | sans |
| hot | chaud | | |

## Question words

| where? | où? | why? | pourquoi? |
| how? | comment? | at what time? | à quelle heure? |
| when? | quand? | what is.../ which is...? | quel est...? |
| how many /how much? | combien? | | |

## Talking to people

When addressing people, plain *bonjour* by itself is not enough; you should always use *Monsieur* for a man, *Madame* for a woman, *Mademoiselle* for a younger woman or a girl..This isn't as formal as it seems, and it has its uses when you've forgotten someone's name or want to attract someone's attention.

| Excuse me | Pardon | Please speak slower | S'il vous plaît, parlez moins vite |
| Do you speak English? | Parlez-vous anglais? | | |
| How do you say it in French? | Comment ça se dit en français? | OK/agreed | d'accord |
| | | please | s'il vous plaît |
| What's your name? | Comment vous appelez-vous? | thank you | merci |
| | | hello | bonjour |
| My name is . . . | Je m'appelle . . . | goodbye | au revoir |
| I'm | Je suis | good morning /afternoon | bonjour |
| ...English | ...anglais[e] | | |
| ...Irish | ...irlandais[e] | good evening | bonsoir |
| ...Scottish | ...écossais[e] | good night | bonne nuit |
| ...Welsh | ...gallois[e] | How are you? | Comment allez-vous?/Ça va? |
| ...American | ...américain[e] | | |
| ...Australian | ...australien[ne] | Fine, thanks | Très bien, merci |
| ...Canadian | ...canadien[ne] | I don't know | Je ne sais pas |
| ...New Zealander | ...néo-zélandais[e] | Let's go | Allons-y |
| yes | oui | See you tomorrow | À demain |
| no | non | See you soon | À bientôt |
| I understand | Je comprends | Leave me alone (aggressive) | Fichez-moi la paix! |
| I don't understand | Je ne comprends pas | | |
| (I'm) sorry | (Je suis) désolé[e] | Please help me | Aidez-moi, s'il vous plaît |
| Sorry | Pardon/Je m'excuse | | |
| I'll be right with you | J'arrive | | |

## Getting around

| bus (long-haul) | autobus, bus, car | What time does it arrive? | À quelle heure arrive-t-il? |
| bus (shuttle) | navette | | |
| bus station | gare (routière) | a ticket to . . . | un billet pour . . . |
| bus stop | arrêt | single ticket | aller simple |
| car | voiture | return ticket | aller retour |
| train/taxi/ferry | train/taxi/ferry | Validate/cancel your ticket | Compostez votre billet |
| boat | bâteau | | |
| plane | avion | valid for . . . | valable pour . . . |
| railway station | gare (SNCF) | ticket office | vente de billets |
| platform | quai | How many kilometres? | Combien de kilomètres? |
| What time does it leave? | À quelle heure part-il? | | |
| | | How many hours? | Combien d'heures? |

| | | | |
|---|---|---|---|
| hitchhiking | autostop | right | à droite |
| on foot | à pied | straight on | tout droit |
| Where are you going? | Où allez-vouz? | on the other side of | à l'autre côté de |
| I'm going to . . . | Je vais à . . . | on the corner of | à l'angle de |
| I want to get off at . . . | Je voudrais descendre à... | next to | à côté de |
| | | behind | derrière |
| the road to . . . | la route pour . . . | in front of | devant |
| the path to . . . | le sentier pour . . . | before | avant |
| Beware! Field set with animal traps | Attention! Piégé | after | après |
| | | under | sous |
| near | près/pas loin | to cross | traverser |
| far | loin | bridge | pont |
| left | à gauche | old town | vieille ville |

## Cars

| | | | |
|---|---|---|---|
| to park the car | garer la voiture | petrol can | bidon |
| car park | un parking | inflate the tyres | gonfler les pneus |
| no parking | défense de station ner/stationnement interdit | oil | huile |
| | | battery | batterie |
| | | The battery is dead | La batterie est morte |
| service station | garage | spark plugs | bougies |
| petrol station | poste d'essence | to break down | tomber en panne |
| fuel | essence | traffic lights | feux |
| (to) fill it up | faire le plein | insurance | assurance |

## Accommodation

| | | | |
|---|---|---|---|
| a room for one/two people | une chambre pour une/deux personnes | sheets | draps |
| | | blankets | couvertures |
| a double bed | un lit double | quiet | calme |
| a room with a shower | une chambre avec douche | noisy | bruyant |
| | | hot water | eau chaude |
| A room with a (full) bath | une chambre avec salle de bain | cold water | eau froide |
| | | Is breakfast included? | Est-ce que le petit déjeuner est compris? |
| for one/two/three nights | pour une/deux/trois nuits | | |
| | | I would like breakfast | Je voudrais prendre le petit déjeuner |
| Can I see it? | Puis-je la voir? | | |
| a room on the courtyard | une chambre sur la cour | I don't want breakfast | Je ne veux pas le petit déjeuner |
| a room over the street | une chambre sur la rue | Can we camp here? | Est-ce q'on peut camper ici? |
| first floor | premier étage | campsite | un camping/terrain de camping/aire de camping |
| second floor | deuxième étage | | |
| with a view | avec vue | | |
| key | clef | tent | une tente |
| to iron | repasser | tent space | un emplacement |
| do laundry | faire la lessive | youth hostel | auberge de jeunesse |

## Numbers

| | | | |
|---|---|---|---|
| 1 | un | 6 | six |
| 2 | deux | 7 | sept |
| 3 | trois | 8 | huit |
| 4 | quatre | 9 | neuf |
| 5 | cinq | 10 | dix |

| 11 | onze | 70 | soixante-dix |
| 12 | douze | 75 | soixante-quinze |
| 13 | treize | 80 | quatre-vingts |
| 14 | quatorze | 90 | quatre-vingt-dix |
| 15 | quinze | 95 | quatre-vingt-quinze |
| 16 | seize | 100 | cent |
| 17 | dix-sept | 101 | cent-et-un |
| 18 | dix-huit | 200 | deux cent |
| 19 | dix-neuf | 300 | trois cent |
| 20 | vingt | 500 | cinq cent |
| 21 | vingt-et-un | 1000 | mille |
| 22 | vingt-deux | 2000 | deux mille |
| 30 | trente | 5000 | cinq mille |
| 40 | quarante | first | première |
| 50 | cinquante | second | deuxième |
| 60 | soixante | third | troisième |

## Days and dates

| January | janvier | Sunday | dimanche |
| February | février | Monday | lundi |
| March | mars | Tuesday | mardi |
| April | avril | Wednesday | mercredi |
| May | mai | Thursday | jeudi |
| June | juin | Friday | vendredi |
| July | juillet | Saturday | samedi |
| August | août | August 1 | Le premier août |
| September | septembre | March 2 | Le deux mars |
| October | octobre | July 14 | Le quatorze juillet |
| November | novembre | November 23 | Le vingt-trois novembre |
| December | décembre | 2004 | deux mille quatre |

# French menu reader

## Basic terms

| pain | bread | vinaigre | vinegar |
| beurre | butter | bouteille | bottle |
| oeufs | eggs | verre | glass |
| lait | milk | fourchette | fork |
| huile | oil | couteau | knife |
| poivre | pepper | cuillère | spoon |
| sel | salt | table | table |
| sucre | sugar | l'addition | the bill |

## Typical French snacks

| un sandwich/une baguette au . . . | a sandwich with . . . | pâté (de campagne) | with pâté (country-style) |
| jambon | ham | croque-monsieur | Grilled cheese and ham sandwich |
| fromage | cheese | | |
| saucisson | salami | croque-madame | Grilled cheese and ham sandwich, with an egg |
| à l'ail | garlic | | |
| poivre | pepper | | |

| oeufs | eggs | concombres | cucumber |
|---|---|---|---|
| au plat | fried | carottes rapées | grated carrots |
| à la coque | boiled | crêpe | pancake |
| durs | hard-boiled | au sucre | with sugar |
| brouillés | scrambled | au citron | with lemon |
| omelette . . . | omelette . . . | au miel | with honey |
| nature | plain | à la confiture | with jam |
| aux fines herbes | with herbs | aux oeufs | with eggs |
| au fromage | with cheese | à la crème de marrons | with chestnut purée |
| salade de . . . | salad of . . . | | |
| tomates | tomatoes | | |

## Other fillings/salads

| anchois | anchovy | hareng | herring |
|---|---|---|---|
| boudin | black pudding | langue | tongue |
| coeurs de palmiers | hearts of palm | poulet | chicken |
| fonds d'artichauts | artichoke hearts | thon | tuna |

## Some terms

| chauffé | heated | mi-cuit | part cooked, blanched |
|---|---|---|---|
| cuit | cooked | | |
| cru | raw, uncooked | pané | breaded |
| emballé | wrapped | salé | salted/spicy |
| À emporter | to take away | sucré | sweetened |
| fumé | smoked | | |

## Soups (soupes)

| bisque | shellfish soup | potage | thick soup, usually vegetable |
|---|---|---|---|
| bouillabaisse | fish soup | | |
| bouillon | broth or stock | rouille | red pepper, garlic and saffron served with fish soup |
| bourride | thick fish soup | | |
| consommé | clear soup | | |
| pistou | parmesan, basil and garlic paste, sometimes added to soup | velouté | thick soup, usually fish or poultry |

## Starters (hors d'oeuvres)

| assiette anglaise or assiette de charcuterie | plate of cold meats | crudités | raw vegetables with dressings |
|---|---|---|---|
| assiette or salade composée | mixed salad, with cold meat and pickled vegetables | hors d'oeuvres variés | combination of the previous two plus smoked or marinated fish |

## Fish (poisson), Seafood (fruits de mer) and shellfish (crustacés or coquillages)

| anchois | anchovies | cabillaud | cod, unsalted |
|---|---|---|---|
| anguilles | eels | calmar | squid |
| baudroie | monkfish, anglerfish | carrelet | plaice |
| brème | bream | claire | type of oyster |
| bulot | whelk | colin | hake |

612

| | | | |
|---|---|---|---|
| congre | conger eel | loup de mer | sea bass |
| coques | cockles | louvine | similar to sea bass |
| coquilles | scallops Saint-Jacques | maquereau | mackerel |
| | | merlan | whiting |
| crabe | crab | morue | salt cod |
| crevettes grises | shrimps | moules (marinière) | mussels (with shallots in white wine sauce) |
| crevettes roses | prawns | | |
| dorade, daurade | sea bream | | |
| ecrevisse | freshwater crayfish | palourdes | clams |
| éperlan | smelt or whitebait | poulpe | octopus |
| escargots | snails | praires | small clams |
| espadon | swordfish | raie | skate |
| favou(ille) | tiny crab | rouget | red mullet |
| flétan | halibut | sandre | zander (pike-like fish) |
| gambas | king prawns | | |
| grenouilles (cuisses de) | frogs (legs) | saumon | salmon |
| | | Saint-Pierre | John Dory |
| homard | lobster | sole | sole |
| huîtres | oysters | thon | tuna |
| langouste | spiny lobster | tortue | turtle (sea) |
| langoustines | saltwater crayfish | truite | trout |
| limande | lemon sole | turbot | turbot |
| lotte de mer | monkfish | violet, figue de mer | sea-squirt |

## Terms (fish)

| | | | |
|---|---|---|---|
| aïoli | garlic mayonnaise served with salt cod and other fish | fumé | smoked |
| | | fumet | fish stock |
| | | gigot de mer | large fish baked whole |
| anchoïoade | anchovy paste or sauce | | |
| | | grillé | grilled |
| béarnaise | sauce made with egg yolks, white wine, shallots and vinegar | hollandaise | butter and vinegar sauce |
| | | à la meunière | in butter, lemon and parsley sauce |
| | | mousse/mousseline | mousse |
| colbert | fried in egg and breadcrumbs | raito | red wine, olive, caper, garlic and shallot sauce |
| darne | fillet or steak | | |
| la douzaine | a dozen (ie oysters) | | |
| frit | fried | yourte | tart or pie |
| friture | assorted deep-fried small fish | | |

## Meat (viande) and poultry (volaille)

| | | | |
|---|---|---|---|
| agneau | lamb | caneton | duckling |
| andouille, andouillette | tripe sausage | cervelle | brains |
| bavette d'échalote | cheap steak fried with shallots | châteaubriand | porterhouse steak |
| | | cheval | horse meat |
| boeuf | beef | chevreau | kid goat |
| bifteck | steak | contrefilet | sirloin roast |
| boudin blanc | sausage of white meats | coquelet | cockerel |
| | | coeur | heart (esp. of duck) |
| boudin noir | black pudding | dinde, dindon, dindonneau | turkey of different ages and genders |
| caille | quail | | |
| canard | duck | entrecôte | ribsteak |

| | | | |
|---|---|---|---|
| faux filet | sirloin steak | porc, pieds de porc | pork, pig's trotters |
| foie | liver | poulet | chicken |
| foie gras | fattened liver of duck or goose | poulette | young chicken |
| | | poussin | baby chicken |
| fraises de veau | veal testicles | ris | sweetbreads |
| fricadelles | meatballs | rognons | kidneys |
| gibier | game | rognons blancs | testicles |
| gigot d'agneau | leg of lamb | sanglier | wild boar |
| langue | tongue | steak | steak |
| lapin, lapereau | rabbit, young rabbit | toro | bull meat |
| lard, lardons | bacon, diced bacon | tournedos | thick slices of fillet |
| lièvre | hare | travers de porc | spare ribs |
| marcassin | young wild boar | tripes | tripe |
| merguez | spicy North African sausage | truie | sow |
| | | veau | veal |
| mouton | mutton | venaison | venison |
| oie | goose | | |

## Dishes and terms (meat and poultry)

| | | | |
|---|---|---|---|
| aile | wing | au feu de bois | cooked over wood fire |
| blanc | breast or white meat | | |
| blanquette, daube, estouffade, hochepôt, navarin, ragoût | regional types of stews | au four | baked |
| | | galantine | cold dish of meat in aspic |
| boeuf bourguignon | beef stew with burgundy, onions and mushrooms | garni | garnished (with vegetables) |
| | | gésier | gizzard |
| à la broche | spit-roasted | gigot de . . . | leg of any meat |
| canard à l'orange | roast duck with an orange-and-wine sauce | graisse | fat |
| | | grillade | grilled meat |
| | | grillé | grilled |
| carré | best end of neck, chop or cutlet | hâchis | chopped meat or hamburger |
| cassoulet | casserole of beans, carrots and meat, usually sausage | jambonneau | joint, shank |
| | | jarret | knuckle |
| choucroute | pickled cabbage with peppercorns, sausages, bacon and salami | magret de canard | cured duck breast slices |
| | | marmite | casserole |
| | | médaillon | round piece |
| | | mijoté | stewed |
| civet | game stew | museau | muzzle |
| confit | meat preserve, often served baked or roasted | os | bone |
| | | pavé | thick slice |
| | | persillade | cooked in parsley and oil |
| coq au vin | chicken cooked until it falls off the bone, with wine, onions and mushrooms | poêlée | pan-fried |
| | | rillade | coarse pork-and-goose paté |
| côte | chop, cutlet or rib | rôti | roast |
| cou | neck | sauté | lightly cooked in butter |
| croustillant | in a pastry crust | | |
| en croûte | in pastry | steak au poivre (vert/rouge) | steak in a black peppercorn sauce (green/red) |
| cuisse | thigh-and-leg portion | | |
| épaule | shoulder | | |
| farci | stuffed | steak tartare | raw chopped beef |

|  | usually accompanied by a raw egg yolk | terrine | solid loaf of finely puréed substance (duck liver, raspberry, etc) |
|  |  | tête de veau | calf's head in jelly |

## Terms for steaks

| bleu | almost raw | bien cuit | well done |
| saignant | rare | très bien cuit | very well cooked |
| à point | medium rare | brochette | kebab |

## Garnishes and sauces

| beurre blanc | sauce of white wine and shallots, with butter | diable | strong mustard seasoning |
| bordelaise | in a red wine, shallots and bone marrow sauce | forestière | with bacon and mushroom |
|  |  | fricassée | rich, creamy sauce |
|  |  | mornay | cheese sauce |
| à la boulangère | baked with potatoes and onions | Pays d'Auge | cream and cider |
| à la bourgeoise | with carrots, onions, celery, bacon and braised lettuce | à la périgordine | in a truffle and foie gras sauce |
|  |  | piquante | gherkins or capers, vinegar and shallots |
| chasseur | white wine, mushrooms and shallots | provençale | tomatoes, garlic, olive oil and herbs |

## Vegetables (légumes)

| algue | seaweed | fenouil | fennel |
| artichaut | artichoke | fèves | broad beans |
| asperges | asparagus | flageolet | white beans |
| avocat | avocado | haricots (verts/ rouges/ blancs/beurres) | beans (string or French/kidney/ white/butter) |
| betterave | beetroot |  |  |
| carotte | carrot |  |  |
| céleri | celery | laitue | lettuce |
| champignons | mushrooms; types include: de bois, de Paris, cèpes, chanterelles, girolles, grisets, mousserons | lentilles | lentils |
|  |  | maïs | corn |
|  |  | navet | turnip |
|  |  | oignon | onion |
|  |  | oseille | sorrel |
|  |  | panais | parsnip |
| chicorée frisée | curly chicory | pâte | pasta or pastry |
| chou (rouge) | (red) cabbage | petits pois | peas |
| choufleur | cauliflower | pignons | pine nuts |
| citrouille | pumpkin | pissenlits | dandelion leaves |
| cogollos | lettuce hearts | poireau | leek |
| concombre | cucumber | pois chiche | chickpeas |
| cornichon | gherkin | pois mange-tout | snow peas |
| cresson | watercress | poivron (vert, rouge) | sweet pepper (green, red) |
| échalotes | shallots |  |  |
| endive | chicory | pommes (de terre) | potatoes |
| épinards | spinach | primeurs | spring greens |
| épi de maïs | corn on the cob | radis | radishes |

| riz | rice | seigle | rye |
| salade verte | green salad | tomates | tomatoes |
| sarrasin/ | buckwheat | truffes | truffles |
| sarrazin | | | |

## Herbs (herbes) and spices (épices)

| ail | garlic | menthe | mint |
| anis | aniseed | moutarde | mustard |
| basilic | basil | persil | parsley |
| cannelle | cinnamon | piment | pimento |
| ciboulettes | chives | pistou | ground basil, olive oil |
| estragon | tarragon | | and garlic |
| genièvre | juniper (berry) | raifort | horseradish |
| gingembre | ginger | romarin | rosemary |
| girofle | clove | safran | saffron |
| laurier | bay leaf | serpolet | wild thyme |
| marjolaine | marjoram | | |

## Some vegetable dishes and terms

| allumettes | very thin-sliced chips | ratatouille | mixture of aubergine, |
| biologique | organic | | courgette, |
| farci | stuffed | | tomatoes and |
| gratin dauphinois | potatoes baked in | | garlic |
| | cream and garlic | rémoulade | mustard mayonnaise |
| gratiné | browned with cheese | | and herb dressing |
| | or butter | salade niçoise | salad of tomatoes, |
| jardinière | with mixed diced | | radishes, cucumber, |
| | vegetables | | hard-boiled eggs, |
| à la parisienne | sautéed in butter | | anchovies, onion, |
| | (potatoes); with | | artichokes, green |
| | white wine sauce, | | peppers, beans, |
| | and shallots | | basil and garlic |
| parmentier | with potatoes | sauté | lightly fried in butter |
| pommes château | quartered potatoes | à la vapeur | steamed |
| fondantes | sautéed in butter | Je suis végétarien(ne) | I'm a vegetarian. |
| pommes | fried onions and | Est-ce qu'il y a | Are there any non- |
| lyonnaise | potatoes | quelques plats sans | meat dishes? |
| râpée | grated or shredded | viande? | |

## Fruits (fruits) and nuts (noix)

| abricot | apricot | dattes | dates |
| amandes | almonds | figues | figs |
| ananas | pineapple | fraises | strawberries |
| banane | banana | fraises de bois | wild strawberries |
| brugnon, | nectarine | framboises | raspberries |
| nectarine | | grenade | pomegranate |
| cacahouètes | peanuts | groseilles | red currants or |
| cassis | blackcurrants | | gooseberries |
| cérises | cherries | marrons | chestnuts |
| citron | lemon | melon | melon |
| citron vert | lime | mirabelles | small yellow plums |
| coing | quince | myrtilles | blueberries |

| | | | |
|---|---|---|---|
| noisette | hazelnut | raisins | grapes |
| noix | nut(s) | rhubarbe | rhubarb |
| orange | orange | | |
| pamplemousse | grapefruit | **Terms** | |
| pastèque | watermelon | | |
| pêche (blanche) | (white) peach | beignet | fritter |
| pistache | pistachio | compôte de . . . | stewed . . . |
| poire | pear | coulis | sauce of puréed fruit |
| pomme | apple | flambé | set aflame |
| prune | plum | | in alcohol |
| pruneau | prune | frappé | iced |

## Desserts (desserts or entremets) and pastries (pâtisserie)

| | | | |
|---|---|---|---|
| bombe | an ice cream dessert made in a round or conical mould | | sponge cake |
| | | palmiers | caramelized puff pastries |
| brioche | sweet, yeasty breakfast roll | parfait | frozen mousse, sometimes ice cream |
| charlotte | custard and fruit in lining of almond fingers | petit-suisse | a smooth mixture of cream and curds |
| clafoutis | fruit tart, usually with berries | petits fours | bite-sized cakes or pastries |
| crème Chantilly | vanilla-flavoured and sweetened whipped cream | poires belle Hélène | pears and ice cream in chocolate sauce |
| | | religieuse | coffee or chocolate -coated pastry puffs, supposedly in the shape of a nun |
| crème fraîche | sour cream | | |
| crème pâtissière | thick pastry-filling made with eggs | | |
| crêpes | filled pancakes | | |
| crêpes suzettes | thin pancakes with orange juice and liqueur | sablé | shortbread biscuit |
| | | savarin | a filled, ring-shaped cake |
| flan caramel | caramelized pudding | tarte | tart |
| fromage blanc | cream cheese, more like strained yoghurt | tartelette | small tart |
| | | tarte tatin | upside-down apple tart |
| gâteaux | fruit pies, usually apple, peach or pear | tiramisu | mascarpone cheese, chocolate and cream |
| gaufre | waffle | truffes | truffles, the chocolate or liqueur-filled variety |
| gênoise | rich sponge cake | | |
| glace | ice cream | | |
| Îles flottantes/ oeufs à la neige | soft meringues floating on custard | yaourt, yogourt | yoghurt |
| lait caillé | cream-based dessert, like Italian panna cotta | **Terms** | |
| | | barquette | small boat-shaped flan |
| macaron | macaroon | | |
| madeleine | small, scalloped-edge sponge cake | bavarois | refers to the mould, could be a mousse or custard |
| marrons Mont Blanc | chestnut purée and cream on a rum-soaked | | |
| | | coupe | a serving of ice cream |

## Cheese (fromage)

There are over four hundred types of French cheese, most of them named after their place of origin. *Chèvre* is goat's cheese, *brebis* is ewe's cheese. *Le plateau de fromages* is the cheeseboard, and bread, but not butter, is served with it. Some useful phrases: *une petite tranche de celui-ci* (a small piece of this one); *puis-je le goûter?* (may I taste it?)

## Regional food

### Catalonia

| | |
|---|---|
| bouillinade | Fish stew flavoured with dry Banyuls wine |
| perdreau à la Català | Partridge cooked with bitter oranges |
| cargolade | Small grilled snails |
| palombe | Pigeon |
| bolet | Wood mushroom, often fried in olive oil, to accompany game dishes |
| bouillade | A stew of mixed vegetables and charcuterie, a popular winter dish in the Cerdagne |
| bunyetes | Custard doughnuts |
| rosquillas | Almond cake |

### Béarn

| | |
|---|---|
| tourin | Onion, garlic and tomato soup |
| cousinette | Mixed soup that often includes beet, sorrel or chicory |
| garbure | A very thick soup using carrots, turnips, cabbage, parsley and beans in poultry, lamb or pork stock |
| poule au pot | Boiled chicken with vegetables |
| tourtière | Puff pastry flavoured with rum or plums soaked in Armagnac |

### Pays Basque

| | |
|---|---|
| axoa | veal-based dish, typical of Ezpeleta |
| bar | sea bass |
| gasna, (ardi) gazna | type of hard sheep's cheese, often served with Itsasu cherry jam |
| piperade | omelette with peppers and tomatoes, served as a main dish but often just the vegetables served as an accompaniment |
| ttoro | fish stew |
| chipirones, txiporomes | small squid, either casseroled or stuffed and baked |
| piballes | baby eels |
| tripotcha | veal tripe cooked with spices |
| loukinkas | small garlic sausages |
| jambon de Bayonne | ham from Bayonne, eaten cold and thinly sliced |
| gâteau Basque | almond-custardy pie in a crumb crust, usually topped with cherry conserve |
| touron | marzipan garnished with pistachio nuts |
| macarons | macaroons, especially good from Saint-Jean-de-Luz |
| mamia | Same as cuajada (see Spanish sweets, p.626) |
| marmite | grilled cod in a spicy mussel-and-scallop sauce |

# Castilian Spanish

Although Spain, like France, has its regional dialects and six recognized written languages, **Castilian** Spanish – the language of the central *meseta* – is understood over most of the peninsula. Once you get into it, Castilian is – as John Hooper memorably put it – the easiest language to speak badly, and you'll be helped everywhere by people who are eager to try and understand even the most faltering attempt. English is spoken, but only in the main tourist areas to any extent, and wherever you are you'll get a far better reception if you at least try communicating with Spaniards in their own tongue. Being understood, of course, is only half the problem – and getting the gist of the reply, often rattled out at a furious pace, may prove more difficult.

The following pages contain lists of a few useful words and phrases that will enable you generally to get what you want. Anyone travelling for any length of time, however, would be well advised to invest in a decent dictionary or phrasebook. A cursory glance at a Spanish **dictionary** might be perplexing – bear in mind that until 1994 CH, LL and Ñ counted as separate letters, and in older dictionaries will still be found after the C, L and N words respectively.

## Euskera and Catalan

After French and Castilian, the two most prevalent languages of the Pyrenees are Euskera and Catalan. There are no written records of **Euskera**, the Basque tongue, before the Middle Ages, even though it had been spoken for at least a thousand years by then. Its origins are contentious: some scholars propose that it can be traced to a language spoken on the Iberian peninsula before the Roman occupation, while others maintain that it bears a familial resemblance to certain Caucasian languages, such as Georgian. There are currently about half a million Euskera-speakers in Spain and France, at the western end of the Pyrenees.

**Gascon**, the native tongue of Béarn and several valleys all the way to Bayonne, is the westernmost variant of Occitan, and continued in official use until the eve of the Revolution. Long of merely folkloric value, it's making a

---

### Castilian and Catalan learning materials

**Spanish Rough Guide Phrasebook** (Rough Guides). Mini dictionary-style phrasebook, with Castilian–English and English–Castilian sections, cultural tips and menumasters.

**España Viva and Dígame** (BBC). Decent tape-only series to get you started in a hurry.

**Breakthrough Spanish** (Pan). The best teach-yourself course comprising a book and two cassettes.

**Collins Gem Spanish Dictionary** (HarperCollins). Compact, cheap and good enough for most beginners' queries.

**Teach Yourself Catalan** (Hodder & Stoughton/David Mackay). A not very ambitious primer, presented in English.

**Catalan Grammar** (Dolphin Book Company). Exactly as it says.

**Parla Català** (Pia, Spain). The only available English–Catalan phrasebook.

**Digui Digui** (Generalitat de Catalunya). The best total-immersion course if you're serious about learning Catalan, comprising a series of books and tapes. In Britain, it's most easily available at Grant & Cutler, 55 Great Marlborough St, London W1 (☎020/7734 2012).

modest comeback in the media (Ràdio Pais, 89.8 FM) and in a chain of optional primary schools, les Calandretas.

**Catalan**, a Romance language evolved from medieval Provençal, survived centralising campaigns either favouring Castilian or actively suppressing *Català* (as it calls itself), from the fifteenth to the twentieth century. Although the teaching, printing and broadcasting of Catalan was prohibited under Franco, it is again a flourishing language, spoken by between three and four million people around the eastern part of the range. Since the early 1990s, all signposting in Catalunya (as well as rural restaurant menus) has been solely in Catalan, the official language.

To the outsider, **written** Catalan is a far easier language to comprehend than Euskera – with a knowledge of both high-school Castilian and French you can get the gist of most tourist pamphlets or trekking booklets in *Català*. **Spoken** *Català*, with its harsh sound and strong dialects, is much harder to follow. The **sounds of letters** in Catalan are often completely different from those of Castilian; the most important points of divergence are summarized below, enabling you to at least pronounce place-names accurately. Though the Catalans in particular are always delighted if you make some attempt to use their language, all Basques and Catalans understand and speak Castilian or French as the case may be, if sometimes grudgingly. Thus the basic French and Spanish vocabularies given in this section should be sufficient to make yourself understood as you travel through either end of the Pyrenees.

However, a few **local terms** can be useful for interpreting maps and signs in the Basque and Catalan regions (as well as those French valleys with strong dialects), so a comprehensive "Mountain Terminology" section appears on p.628. Be aware, also, when travelling with internationally published maps that these usually lag well behind nationalistically motivated **name-changing campaigns** in every region of the Pyrenees, but particularly in Aragón, Gascony and the Basque country. Often the local-vernacular name is proudly displayed on an official highways-division sign, but equally often Castilian or French signs have been suitably "edited" with spray paint.

## Catalan pronunciation

| | |
|---|---|
| **IG** or **TG** | sound like "tch" in scratch; thus *Contraig* is pronounced "con traytch", *Mitg* sounds like "meetch" |
| **Ç** | is like S; *plaça* is pronounced "plassa" |
| **C** | followed by E or I is a soft S-sound, not a TH as in Castilian |
| **G** | followed by E or I is like the "zh" in Zhivago; otherwise hard |
| **J** | is soft as in French, unlike the Castilian *jota* |
| **LL** | strong L, except when medial: thus "Ripoll" sounds like "ripole", "llac" like "lak", but "Mulleres" sounds like "muyeres" |
| **L.L** | pronounced as two separate "l"s |
| **L-L** | pronounced as two separate "l"s |
| **NY** | replaces the Castilian Ñ |
| **T** | can sound like D, as in the words *viatge* (pronounced "veeadzheh") or *dotze* (pronounced "dodzeh"). Almost silent when final: thus "Pont de Suert" sounds like "Pon de Swear" |
| **UI** | is same as U – the I is silent; thus "maduixa" sounds like "madusha", "puig" like "pootch" |
| **X** | is like CH when initial, SH when medial, but as in English for certain loan-words like *excursionista* |
| **Y** | in the final syllable is all but silent: thus "Morunys" sounds like *morunsh*, "Montgrony" like *montgron'* |

# A brief guide to speaking Castilian Spanish

## Pronunciation

The rules of **pronunciation** are pretty straightforward and, once you get to know them, strictly observed. Unless there's an accent, words ending in d, l, r and z are **stressed** on the last syllable, all others on the second to last. All **vowels** are pure and short; combinations of letters have predictable, regular results.

| | |
|---|---|
| A | as in f**a**ther |
| E | as in g**e**t |
| I | as in pol**i**ce |
| O | as in r**o**le |
| U | as in r**u**le |
| C | is a theta (lisped) before E and I, hard otherwise: *cerca* is pronounced "thairka" |
| G | varies similarly: a guttural "H" sound (like the *ch* in loch) before E or I, a hard G elsewhere – *gigante* becomes "higante" |
| H | always silent |
| J | the same sound as a guttural G: *jamón* is pronounced "hamon" |
| LL | sounds like an English Y: *tortilla* is pronounced "torteeya" |
| N | is as in English unless it has a tilde (accent) over it (**Ñ**), when it becomes NY: *mañana* sounds like "manyana" |
| QU | is pronounced like an English K |
| R | is rolled, **RR** doubly so |
| V | sounds like B, *vino* becoming "beano" |
| X | has an S sound before consonants, normal X before vowels. More common in Basque, Gallego or Catalan words, where it's "sh" or "zh" |
| Z | is the same as a soft C, so *cerveza* becomes "thervaytha". Catalan does not lisp c or z before i or e |

## Gender

Spanish nouns are divided into masculine and feminine. This causes difficulties with adjectives, whose endings generally have to change to agree with the gender of the nouns they qualify. If you know some grammar, you will know what to do. If not, stick to the masculine form, which is the simplest – it's what we have done in the glossary.

## Basics

| | | | |
|---|---|---|---|
| yes | sí | with | con |
| no | no | without | sin |
| OK | vale | good | buen(o) |
| please | por favor | bad | mal(o) |
| thank you | gracias | big | gran(de) |
| here | aquí | small | pequeño |
| there | allí | more | más |
| this | este | less | menos |
| that | eso | a lot | mucho |
| now | ahora | a little bit | un poco |
| later | más tarde | today | hoy |
| open | abierto | tomorrow | mañana |
| closed | cerrado | yesterday | ayer |

## Talking to people

| | |
|---|---|
| hello | hola |
| goodbye | adiós |
| good morning | buenos días |
| good afternoon/ evening | buenas tardes |
| good night | buenas noches |
| see you later | hasta luego |
| sorry | lo siento/disculpeme |
| excuse me | con permiso/perdón |
| How are you? | ¿Cómo está (usted)? |
| You're welcome | De nada |
| I (don't) understand | (No) entiendo |
| Do you speak English? | ¿Habla (usted) inglés? |
| I don't speak Spanish | No hablo castellano |
| My name is . . . | Me llamo . . . |
| What's your name? | ¿Cómo se llama usted? |
| I'm ... | Soy ... |
| ...English | ... inglés(a) |
| ...Scots | ...escosés(a) |

| | |
|---|---|
| ...Irish | ...irlandés(a) |
| ...American | ...estadunidense |
| ...Canadian | ...canadiense |
| I want . . . | Quiero ... |
| I'd like . . . | Querría ... |
| Do you know . . . ? | ¿Sabe . . . ? |
| I don't know | No sé |
| There is (is there)? | (¿)Hay (?) |
| Give me . . . (one like that) | Deme . . . (un tal) |
| How much? | ¿Cuánto? |
| Do you have . . . ? | ¿Tiene . . . ? |
| . . . the time . . . | la hora |
| What is there to eat? | ¿Qué hay para comer? |
| What's that? | ¿Qué es eso? |
| What's this called in Spanish? | ¿Cómo se llama este en español? |
| When? | ¿Cuando? |
| Where? | ¿Donde? |

## Getting around

| | |
|---|---|
| How do I get to . . . ? | ¿Cómo se va a . . . ? |
| left, right, straight ahead | izquierda, derecha, derecho |
| old inter-village track | camino |
| trail | sendero, senda |
| forest road | pista forestal |
| bus | autobús |
| train | tren |
| shuttle bus | naveta |
| Where is . . . ? | ¿Dónde esta . . . ? |
| . . . the bus station . . . | la estación de autobuses |
| . . . the train station . . . | la estación de ferrocarriles |

| | |
|---|---|
| . . . the nearest bank . . . | el banco mas cercano |
| . . . the post office . . . | el correo (la oficina de correos) |
| . . . the toilet . . . | los aseos/servicios |
| Where does the bus to . . . leave from? | ¿De dónde sale el autobús para . . .? |
| Is this the train for Jaca? | ¿Es este el tren para Jaca? |
| I'd like a (single/ return) ticket to . . . | Querría un billete (sencillo/de ida y vuelta) para . . . |
| What time does it leave (arrive at . . . )? | ¿A qué hora sale (llega en . . . )? |

## Accommodation

| | |
|---|---|
| Do you have . . . ? | ¿Tiene . . . ? |
| . . . a room . . . | una habitación |
| . . . with two beds/ double bed . . . | con dos camas/ cama matrimonial |
| It's for one person (two people) | Es para una persona (dos personas) |
| . . . for one night (one week) | . . . para una noche (una semana) |
| It's fine, how much is it? | Está bien, ¿cuanto es? |

| | |
|---|---|
| It's too expensive | Es demasiado (caro) |
| Don't you have anything cheaper? | ¿No tiene algo más barato? |
| Can one . . . ? camp (near) here? | ¿Se puede . . . ? acampar aquí (cerca)? |
| Is there a hostel/ fonda/hostal nearby? | ¿Hay una albergue/ fonda/hostal aquí cerca? |

## Numbers

| | | | |
|---|---|---|---|
| 1 | un/uno/una | 19 | diez y nueve or |
| 2 | dos | | diecinueve |
| 3 | tres | 20 | veinte |
| 4 | cuatro | 21 | veintiuno |
| 5 | cinco | 30 | treinta |
| 6 | seis | 40 | cuarenta |
| 7 | siete | 50 | cincuenta |
| 8 | ocho | 60 | sesenta |
| 9 | nueve | 70 | setenta |
| 10 | diez | 80 | ochenta |
| 11 | once | 90 | noventa |
| 12 | doce | 100 | cien(to) |
| 13 | trece | 101 | ciento uno |
| 14 | catorce | 200 | doscient(os)/(as) |
| 15 | quince | 500 | quinient(os)/(as) |
| 16 | diez y seis or | 700 | setecient(os)/(as) |
| | dieciséis | 1000 | mil |
| 17 | diez y siete or | 2000 | dos mil |
| | diecisiete | first | primer(o)/(a) |
| 18 | diez y ocho or | second | segund(o)/(a) |
| | dieciocho | third | tercer(o)/(a) |

## Days and dates

| | | | |
|---|---|---|---|
| January | enero | November | noviembre |
| February | febrero | December | diciembre |
| March | marzo | Monday | lunes |
| April | abril | Tuesday | martes |
| May | mayo | Wednesday | miércoles |
| June | junio | Thursday | jueves |
| July | julio | Friday | viernes |
| August | agosto | Saturday | sábado |
| September | se(p)tiembre | Sunday | domingo |
| October | octubre | 2004 | dos mil cuatro |

## Spanish menu reader

### Basics

| | | | |
|---|---|---|---|
| pan | bread | miel | honey |
| mantequilla | butter | botella | bottle |
| huevos | eggs | vaso | glass |
| ajo | garlic | tenedor | fork |
| aceite | oil | cuchillo | knife |
| pimienta | pepper (black) | cuchara | spoon |
| sal | salt | mesa | table |
| azúcar | sugar | desayuno | breakfast |
| vinagre | vinegar | la cuenta | the bill |

### Typical Spanish snacks

The most usual **fillings for bocadillos** are *lomo* (loin of pork), *tortilla* and *calamares* (all of which may be served hot), *jamón* (*york* or, much better, *serrano*), *chorizo*, *salchichón* (and various other regional sausages – like the small, spicy Catalan *botifarras*), *queso* (cheese) and *atún* (probably canned).

## Standard tapas and raciones

| | | | |
|---|---|---|---|
| aceitunas | olives | huevo cocido | hard-boiled egg |
| albondigas | meatballs | jamón serrano | cured ham |
| arroz a la cubana | rice topped with fried egg and red sauce | jamón york | ordinary ham |
| | | longaniza | spicy sausage |
| berberechos | cockles | morcilla | blood pudding |
| boquerones | anchovies (marinated) | navajas | razor clams |
| calamares | squid | patatas alli olli | potatoes in mayonnaise-garlic sauce |
| callos | tripe | | |
| caracoles | snails | patatas bravas | spicy potatoes |
| carne en salsa | meat in tomato sauce | patatas riojanas | potato stew with flecks of vegetable and chorizo |
| champiñones | mushrooms | | |
| chorizo | spicy sausage | pimientos | peppers |
| cocido | stew | pincho (pintxo) moruno | kebab |
| empanadilla | fish/meat turnover | | |
| ensaladilla | russian salad | pulpo | octopus |
| escalibada | aubergine/egg plant and pepper salad | riñones al Jerez | kidneys in sherry |
| | | salchichon | salami |
| gambas | shrimps | sepia | cuttlefish |
| habas | beans | tortilla española | potato omelette |
| habas con jamón hígado | beans with ham liver | tortilla francesa | plain omelette |

## Soups (sopas)

| | | | |
|---|---|---|---|
| sopa de mariscos | seafood soup | gazpacho | cold tomato and cucumber soup with garlic and other spices |
| caldo de gallina | chicken soup | | |
| sopa de pescado | fish soup | | |
| caldo verde/gallego | thick cabbage-based broth | | |
| | | sopa de cocido | meat soup |
| caldillo | clear fish soup | sopa de pasta (fideos) | noodle soup |

## Seafood (mariscos)

| | | | |
|---|---|---|---|
| almejas | clams | arroz con mariscos | rice topped with assorted seafood |
| calamares | squid | | |
| centolla | spider-crab | arroz a la banda | similar to paella but with no chicken |
| cigalas | king prawns | | |
| conchas finas | large scallops | chipirones en su tinta | squid in ink |
| gambas | shrimps | merluza/calamares a la romana | hake/squid (or just about anything else) fried in batter |
| langosta | lobster | | |
| langostinos | crayfish | | |
| mejillones | mussels | | |
| nécora | sea-crab | paella | classic Valencian dish with saffron rice, chicken, seafood etc |
| ostras | oysters | | |
| percebes | goose-barnacles | | |
| pulpo | octopus | | |
| sepia | cuttlefish | zarzuela de mariscos | seafood casserole |
| vieiras | scallops | | |

## Fish (pescados)

| | | | |
|---|---|---|---|
| anchoas | anchovies (fresh) | lubina | sea bass |
| anguila | eel | merluza | hake |
| angulas | elvers (baby eel) | mero | perch |
| atún | tuna | pez espada | swordfish |
| bacalao | cod (often salt) | rape, sapito | monkfish |
| bonito | another type tuna | raya | ray, skate |
| callos de bacalao | filleted rings from | rodaballo | turbot |
| | choice cod-jaw meat | salmonete | red mullet |
| chanquetes | whitebait | sardinas | sardines |
| jurelas | similar to anchovies | tiburón | shark |
| lenguado | sole | trucha | trout |

## Meat (carne) and poultry (aves)

| | | | |
|---|---|---|---|
| butifarra | bratwurst | habas con jamón | ham and beans |
| callos | tripe | hígado | liver |
| carne de buey | beef | jabalí | wild boar |
| cerdo | pork | lengua | tongue |
| chuletas | chops | lomo | loin (of pork) |
| ciervo | venison | manitas de cerdo | pig's knuckles |
| cochinillo | suckling pig | pato | duck |
| codorniz | quail | pavo | turkey |
| conejo | rabbit | perdiz | partridge |
| cordero | lamb | pintada | guinea fowl |
| criadillas | testicles | pollo | chicken |
| escalope or milanesa | breaded schnitzel | rebeco | chamois |
| fabada asturiana | hotpot with butter | riñones | kidneys |
| | beans, black | solomillo | pork flank steak |
| | pudding, etc | ternera | veal |

## Vegetables (verduras y legumes)

| | | | |
|---|---|---|---|
| ac(i)elga | chard | lechuga | lettuce |
| alcachofas | artichokes | lentejas | lentils |
| alubias | beans | patatas (fritas) | potatoes (fried) |
| arroz | rice | pepino | cucumber |
| berenjena | aubergine | pimientos | peppers |
| boletus | ceps | pimientos de padrón | medium-hot small |
| calabacín | courgette/zucchini | | green peppers |
| cardo, cardón | cardoon thistle | puerros | leeks |
| | stems | repollo | cabbage |
| cebollas | onions | tomate | tomatoes |
| champiñones, setas | mushrooms | trigueros | green asparagus |
| cogollos | lettuce hearts | zanahorias | carrots |
| coliflor | cauliflower | ajo blanco | purée of garlic, bread |
| endivia | endive | | crumbs, almonds, oil |
| espinacas | spinach | ensalada | salad |
| garbanzos | chickpeas | (mixta/verde) | (mixed/green) |
| grelos | turnips | menestra/panacha | vegetable medley |
| guisantes | peas | de verduras | |
| habas | broad beans | pimientos rellenos | stuffed peppers |
| judías blancas | haricot beans | pisto manchego | ratatouille |
| judías verdes, | green, red, | verduras con patatas | boiled potatoes with |
| rojas, negras | black beans | | greens |

## Fruits (frutas)

| | | | |
|---|---|---|---|
| albaricoques | apricots | melocotónes | peaches |
| arándanos | blueberries | melón | melon |
| chirimoyas | custard apples | naranjas | oranges |
| cerezas | cherries | pavías | nectarines |
| ciruelas | plums, prunes | peras | pears |
| datiles | dates | piña | pineapple |
| frambuesas | raspberries | plátanos | bananas |
| fresas | strawberries | sandía | watermelon |
| higos | figs | toronja/pomelo | grapefruit |
| limón | lemons | uvas | grapes |
| manzanas | apples | | |

## Sweets (postres)

| | | | |
|---|---|---|---|
| arroz con leche | rice pudding | nata | whipped cream |
| cuajada | sheep-milk-based dessert, like Italian panna cotta, served with honey | natillas | custard |
| | | pasta/tarta de queso | cheesecake |
| | | pastel ruso | thin-crust "sandwich" filled with nut paste |
| flan (de huevo) | crème caramel (egg-based) | | |
| | | requesón | whipped or beaten sweet-whey dessert, served with honey |
| helados | ice cream | | |
| macedonia | fresh fruit salad | | |
| melocotón en almíbar | peaches in syrup | | |
| membrillo | quince paste | yogur | yogurt |

## Cheese

Cheeses (*quesos*; *formatges* in Catalan) are on the whole local, though you'll get the hard, slightly salty, sheep-based *queso manchego* everywhere. The best variety is *roncalés*, a sheep-milk product from the Valle de Roncal.

## Some common terms

| | | | |
|---|---|---|---|
| al ajillo | in garlic | chilindrón | tomato, olive-oil and pepper sauce served on poultry and meat |
| asado | roast | | |
| a la Navarra | stuffed with ham | | |
| a la parilla/plancha | grilled | | |
| a la romana/rebozado | fried in egg batter | en salsa | in (usually tomato) sauce |
| al horno | baked | | |
| ali olli | with garlic mayonnaise | frito | fried |
| | | guisado | casserole |
| ¡Bon Profit! (Catalan) /¡Buen provecho! or ¡Aproveche! (Castilian) | bon appétit | hojaldre | in puff pastry |
| | | jarrete | joint (of meat) |
| | | rehogado | baked |
| cazuela, cocido | stew | salteado | stir-fried |

## Regional food

### Catalunya: recipes and dishes

| | | | |
|---|---|---|---|
| | | | *a l'all cremat* (creamed garlic) |
| amanida (catalana) | salad (with salami) | cabrit | goat, kid |
| arròs negre | rice cooked in squid ink | calçots | grilled baby spring onions |
| bacallá | salt cod, served *a l'all* (with garlic) or | carn d'olla | thick meat soup |

| | |
|---|---|
| escalivada | baked or fried mixture of aubergines, tomatoes and peppers, often on toasted bread |
| escudella | thick soup based on ham or veal stock |
| espinacs a la catalana | spinach, pine nuts and raisins |
| esqueixada | salt-cod and tomato salad |
| faves a la catalana | Catalan version of fabada asturiana |
| faves estofades | pork and broad beans |
| fideuà | paella made with noodles, not rice |
| galtes de porc | roast pig cheek |
| mongets (amb ventresca) | white beans (with pancetta) |
| pa amb tomaquet | tomato-ed and garlic-ed bread, usually taken as a late breakfast, though available all day |
| peus de porc | pigs' feet |
| rap | monkfish |
| samfaina | ratatouille |
| suquet de peix | Fish soup |
| trinxat | Cerdanyan hot-pot made from bacon, winter cabbage, and potatoes or turnips |

## Catalunya: desserts

| | |
|---|---|
| crema catalana | scorched-top custard |
| flan | flan as elsewhere, but often flavoured |
| gelat | ice cream |
| mel i mató, recuit | same as Castilian requesón |
| menjar blanc | almond pastry |
| pijama | medley of various flans and gelats |
| profiterols | as in English |
| sorbet | as in English |
| trufes | truffles (frozen) |

## Catalunya: meat, game, fowl

| | |
|---|---|
| ànec | duck |
| botifarra | bratwurst-like sausage |

| | |
|---|---|
| cansalada | bacon |
| carn | meat |
| conill | rabbit |
| guatlles | quails |
| llebre | hare |
| pernil | ham |
| pollastre | chicken |
| senglar | boar |
| vedella | veal |
| xai | lamb |

## Catalunya: seafood

| | |
|---|---|
| anxoves | anchovies |
| llobarro | sea bass |
| musclos | mussels |
| sèpia | cuttlefish |
| ruita | trout, or omelette |
| xipirons | baby squid |

## Catalunya: fruit and vegetables

| | |
|---|---|
| albergenia | eggplant/aubergine |
| cigrons | garbanzos |
| codony | quince |
| llentics | lentils |
| maduixas | strawberries |
| pebrot | peppers |
| pèsols | peas |

## Catalunya: miscellaneous

| | |
|---|---|
| a la brasa | grilled |
| barrejat | mixed, assortment |
| civet | any game stew |
| confit | tender roast poultry thigh-leg, usually de ànec |
| esmorzar de forquilla | savoury breakfast of meats, cheese, omelette and perhaps wine |
| farcit | stuffed |
| graellada | barbecued |
| pastis | tureen, pâté |
| pastisso | cake, torte |
| suc | fruit juice |

## Aragón

| | |
|---|---|
| boliches | bean and sausage hot-pot |
| chireta | haggis made with rice and blood pudding |
| guirlache | almond-and-toffee dessert |
| guiso | bony pork stewed in |

|  | a sweet sauce |  | national dish of |
| --- | --- | --- | --- |
| migas | fry-up of bread crumbs, bacon and spices |  | Gipuzkoa |
|  |  | ajoarriero | salted cod, served with potatoes, red peppers, tomatoes, garlic |
| magras | wind-dried raw ham, served thinly sliced |  |  |
| menestra de Tudela | vegetable stew, using artichokes, beans, asparagus and anything else in season | angulas | baby eels, now rare, sautéed with garlic and hot peppers |
|  |  | calderete | potato stew with sausage |
| salmorej | egg concoction like a potato and rice omelette, eaten with lots of garlic or an unusual poached-egg stew | gulas | fake angulas, made from compressed Pacific pollack |
|  |  | Idiazábal | a smoked cheese, identifiable by its yellow rind |
| sopa de cana | Christmas mix of milk, bread, cinnamon and turkey fat | marmitako | fish, potato, pepper and tomato stew |
|  |  | merluza a la vasca | hake in sauce |
| ternasco | lamb back, stewed or baked; quality varies; also in Catalunya | pimientos de piquillo | red, sweet-hot peppers stuffed with cod |
|  |  | pochas | greenish-white autumn beans |
|  |  | salmí | pigeon prepared in wine and herbs |

### Basque Country

|  |  | ttoro | mixed fish stew |
| --- | --- | --- | --- |
| alubia de Tolosa | reddish-black beans stewed with cabbage, green peppers and blood sausage: the | txangurro | spider crab |
|  |  | txipirones en su tinto | tiny squid cooked in their own ink |
|  |  | txistorra | a spicy sausage |

# Mountain terminology

## Eastern and Central Pyrenees

| Agua/aigue/aygue | Water | Cap | Highest point on a ridge; also means coastal cape, or the rear/back side of something |
| --- | --- | --- | --- |
| Aigüeta | Small stream |  |  |
| Artigue/artiga | Pasture, meadow |  |  |
| Bal/ball/bat/batch/ val/vall | Valley |  |  |
| Barrage/presa | Dam | Cirque/circ/cirro | Alpine amphitheatre |
| Borde/borda | Isolated cottage | Clot | A depression or narrow valley |
| Boum | Deep lake |  |  |
| Brèche | Gap in a ridge-line | Col/coll/collado/ | A pass or saddle |
| Caillaouas | Rocky | coret/cuello |  |
| Camí | Inter-village drovers' track | Corral mals | Enclosure for ani- |
| Campana | Pointed rock | Cortal | Shepherd's hut |
| Can, cal | Isolated lowland farmhouse | Coma/Coume | Bare incline between trees |

| | | | |
|---|---|---|---|
| Desfiladero/garganta /congost(o)/foz | Gorge | Oule/oulette | Small "bowl" in terrain |
| Embalse | Reservoir | Pántano/Pantà | Reservoir |
| Eras/Eres | rain barns, usually by a threshing cirque | Passerelle/passarella | Suspension bridge, catwalk |
| Estanyet/estanyol | Small lake, pond | Peña/Peyre | Prominent rock outcrop |
| Estibe/estive | High pasture | | |
| Étang/estany/llac | Lake | Port/porteille/puerto | Pass (implies long use as a trade or pilgrimage route) |
| Faja/faxa/feixa | Natural terrace in limestone | | |
| Farge/fragua | Forge | Prat/prado/pradère | Meadow |
| Font/fount/fuente | Source of a river | Pic/puig | Peak |
| Gave | River (Béarn) | Pujol/puy/puyo/pouey | High point |
| Gorg | Tarn | Raillère/ralhère | Avalanche gallery |
| Grange/granja /grangera | Barn | Ribera/ribèra | Riverbank or river valley |
| Grau | Pass | Río/riu | River |
| Hont/hount | Source of a river | Salhèt | Riverbank |
| Hourquette/forqueta /horcado | Steep pass | Salto/sault | Waterfall, cascade |
| | | Seilh | Glacier |
| Ibón | Tarn, small lake | Serre/serra | Serrated, tooth-like ridge |
| Mas/masia | Farmstead (Catalunya/ Roussillon) | Soula/solana/soulane | South-facing slope |
| | | Soum/turon/turoun | Rounded summit |
| Né/ner/nère | Black | Tartera/tartère | Scree slope |
| Neste | River (Bigorre) | Tozal/tuc/tuca | Peak |
| Noguera | River (Catalunya) | Veinat | District, neighbourhood |
| Obaga/ubago/ umbría | North-facing slope | | |

## Basque Pyrenees

| | | | |
|---|---|---|---|
| Aran | Valley | Goyen/gora | High |
| Ardi | Sheep | Handi | Big |
| Arri | Stone | Harri | Stone |
| Artz | Bear | Hegi | Hill |
| Artzain | Shepherd | Ibar | Valley |
| Beltz | Black | Ichouri/itxurri | Slope |
| Bide | Route | Ithourri | River source |
| Celhay/selhai | Plateau | Kayolar/cayolar | Pastoral hut |
| Chara | Wood | Larra/larria | Moor, pasture |
| Chipi | Small | Lepo | Pass |
| Churi/chouri/txuri | White | Orri/orry | Pastoral hut |
| Çuby/(t)zubi | Bridge | Mendi | Mountain |
| Erreka | River | Oyhan | Forest |
| Etche/etxe | House | Portilloua | Pass |
| Etchola/etxda | Hut | Tchipi/txipi/ttipi tiki | Small |
| Gain/gagna | Summit | Ur | Water |
| Gorri | Red | | |

# Glossary

**ABBATIALE** (French) Abbey church.

**ABONO** (Castilian) A daily or multi-day ski-resort pass.

**APLEC** (Catalan) A pilgrimage to a rural shrine.

**APSE** Often multiple, semicircular or polygonal terminations at the east end of a church.

**AYUNTAMIENTO** In Spain, the town hall; **AJUNTAMENT** in Catalan.

**BAROQUE** Late-Renaissance period of art and architecture, distinguished by extreme ornateness.

**BARRIO** (Castilian) Suburb or quarter.

**BASTIDE** One of the grid-plan fortified towns established in southern France during the thirteenth century.

**CAMINO DE SANTIAGO/CHEMIN DE SAINT-JACQUES** The medieval pilgrim's route to the shrine of Saint James at Santiago de Compostela in northwest Spain, with several branches crossing the Pyrenees west of Luchon.

**CARRER** Catalan for "street".

**CATALONIA** The geographical and cultural homeland of the Catalan people, disregarding the frontier established between France and Spain in 1659.

**CATALUNYA** The autonomous region of Spain comprising the provinces of (from northwest to southeast) Lleida, Girona, Barcelona and Tarragona.

**CATHARISM** Heretical religion of the thirteenth century, with strongholds in the Ariège and Pays de Sault.

**CESTA PUNTA** The most spectacular, high-speed version of pelota/pelote, played by teams of two; sometimes called jaï alaï.

**CLAVIJAS** A fixed peg-and-chain for hauling yourself up rock faces.

**CLOCHER-MUR** A triangular bell wall, either freestanding or at one end of the church, often topped with decorative detail and often attributed to the Knights Templar.

**CLOISTER** Colonnaded walled courtyard, usually Romanesque and square, adjoining a monastic church on its south side.

**COLEGIATA** (Castilian) Large parish church, not quite ranking with a cathedral.

**COMARCA/COMARQUE** (Castilian/Catalan). Equivalent to an English county.

**COMEDOR** Formal dining room of a hotel, or at the rear of a bar/restaurante.

**COMMUNE** Smallest administrative division of the French Pyrenees.

**CORREOS/CORREUS** (Castilian/Catalan) Post office.

**DÉPARTEMENT** One of the French administrative provinces created after the Revolution of 1789, replacing the traditional feudal duchies.

**DOLMEN** Neolithic stone monument, consisting of two or more upright slabs and a capping stone, thought to be either tombs or – from their frequent position on ridgelines – shepherds' shelters.

**ERMITA/ERMITAGE** (Spain/France). A wayside chapel, usually (but not always) out in the country.

**FORFAIT/FORFET** (French/Catalan) A daily or multi-day ski-resort pass.

**FRESCO** A wall painting made more durable by being applied to wet plaster.

**FRONTÓN** The playing court for pelota/pelote, found in most villages of the Basque country.

**GENERALITAT** The governing authority of Spanish Catalunya.

**GOTHIC** Architectural style prevalent from the twelfth until the sixteenth century, distinguished by pointed arches and rib-vaulting.

**HALLE(S)** In France, a covered produce market.

**HOSPICE/HOSPITAL/HÔPITAU** Medieval travellers' hostel built by religious or chivalric orders, often at the foot of strategic passes.

**HÔTEL DE VILLE** The town hall of a larger town in France.

**ISARD** French or Catalan for the Pyrenean chamois or izard, ubiquitous at higher elevations; known as rebeco in Castilian, sarrio in Aragonese.

**MAIRIE** The municipal office of a village in France.

**MAJESTAT** Carved medieval wooden image of a fully dressed Christ, formerly common in Catalunya; most examples were destroyed during the Republican church-sackings of 1936.

**MAQUISARD** A French resistance fighter of World War II; derived from maquis, the dense Mediterranean scrub-forest where they preferred to hide.

**MAS, MASIA** A Catalan farmstead, usually isolated; precedes the proper name of the farm, which may be a family surname or some nearby natural feature.

**MENJADOR** Catalan for comedor.

**MIRADOR** A viewing point or platform intended for trekkers or motorists in the mountains.

**MODERNISME/MODERNISTA** (noun/adjective) Catalan version of Art Nouveau, prevalent between 1890 and 1920, relying heavily on stylized or grotesque curved forms from the natural world.

**MOZARABIC** Pertaining to the religion, art/architecture or culture of Mozarabs, medieval Spanish Christians living under Muslim rule.

**MUDÉJAR** Pertaining to the religion, art/architecture or culture of medieval Spanish Muslims living under Christian rule.

**NAVE** Main body of a church.

**PARADOR** Luxury hotel in Spain, often installed in a minor historical monument.

**PASADOR/PASSEUR** (Castilian/French) Person who during World War II guided refugees and Allied servicemen over the Pyrenees from occupied France into neutral Spain.

**PELOTA/PELOTE** (Castilian/French) A court ballgame similar to fives/handball, originating in the Basque country, and played in several versions.

**PETANCA/PÉTANQUE** (Catalan/French). A game, similar to English bowls, where two teams of one to three persons each compete to pitch heavy balls as close as possible to a cochonnet or wooden marker jack 6–10m distant. From the Provençal pied tanqués or "feet together", after the small circle within which bowlers must stand as

they pitch.

**PLAÇA** Catalan spelling of plaza.

**(LA) POSTE** (French) The post office.

**RAMBLA** Elongated rectangular promenade in a Catalan town, usually tree-shaded, pedestrianized and equipped with café tables.

**RETABLE/RETABLO** (French/Castilian). Intricately carved altarpiece.

**ROMANESQUE** Unadorned, squat architectural style prevalent from the eighth to the thirteenth century; characterized by rounded arches and naively sculpted column capitals.

**ROMERÍA** In Spain, a religious procession to a rural shrine, often with a venerated image in tow.

**SALLE CAPITULAIRE** (French) Chapterhouse off a Romanesque cloister, often with fine rib-vaulting.

**SANTUARI(O)** (Catalan/Castilian) Remote religious shrine, larger and more exalted than an ermita – may have permanent staff.

**TEMPLE** Protestant church in France.

**TRANSEPT** Transverse arms of a church, at right angles to the nave.

**TRINQUET** Smaller version of a frontón.

**TYMPANUM** The vertical, half-circular space above a Romanesque church portal, often decorated with a relief of Christ in Majesty.

**URBANIZACIÓ(N)** (Catalan/Castilian) Can be any new apartment development, but in this guide refers to a ski-chalet complex surrounding certain Spanish Pyrenean villages.

**VARIANT(E)** An alternate routeing of the long-distance trails GR10, GR11 and HRP.

## Acronyms

**ARP** Alto Ruta Pirenaico in Castilian; see HRP below.

**CAF** Club Alpin Français, the French Alpine Club, administering many staffed refuges.

**CEC** Centre Excursionista de Catalunya, rival to the **FEEC** (see below).

**CIMES** Centre d'Information Montagne et Sentiers; French entity administering a number of refuges in the Ariège.

**EDF** Électricité de France; national power corporation responsible for all dams and dynamos in the Pyrenees.

**ENHER** Spanish power company active across the Pyrenees.

**FAM** Federación Aragonesa de Montañismo, the Aragonese alpine club and refuge-managing entity.

**FECSA** Catalan power company restricted to the Catalan Pyrenees.

**FEEC** Federació de Entitats Excursionistes de Catalunya, important alpine club and refuge operator in Catalunya.

**FNM** Federación Navarra de Montaña.

**GR** Gran recorrido (Castilian), grande randonnée (French), long-distance trekking trails for which you must have overnighting/mountaineering gear.

**HRP** Haute Randonnée Pyrénéenne, strenuous, longitudinal traverse of the range, sticking close to the watershed.

ICONA Instituto Nacional Para la Conservación de la Naturaleza, the Spanish natural resources administrator, responsible for certain picnic grounds, unattended campsites and unstaffed shelters.

PNP Parc National des Pyrénées, administering most staffed mountain refuges within its area.

PR Pequeño recorrido (Castilian), petite randonnée (French), resort-based walking itineraries which take a day or less, without special experience or equipment.

RENFE Red Nacional de Ferrocarriles, the Spanish state rail corporation.

SNCF Société Nationale des Chemins de Fer, the French state rail corporation.

# Rough Guides

## advertiser

# Rough Guides travel...

**UK & Ireland**
Britain
Devon & Cornwall
Dublin
Edinburgh
England
Ireland
Lake District
London
London mini guide
London Restaurants
London & SE England,
 Walks in
Scotland
Scottish Highlands &
 Islands
Wales

**Europe**
Algarve
Amsterdam
Andalucía
Austria
Baltic States
Barcelona
Belgium & Luxembourg
Berlin
Brittany & Normandy
Bruges & Ghent
Brussels
Budapest
Bulgaria
Copenhagen
Corfu
Corsica
Costa Brava
Crete
Croatia
Cyprus
Czech & Slovak
 Republics
Dodecanese & East
 Aegean
Dordogne & The Lot
Europe
First-Time Europe
Florence
France

Germany
Greece
Greek Islands
Hungary
Ibiza & Formentera
Iceland
Ionian Islands
Italy
Languedoc & Roussillon
Lisbon
The Loire
Madeira
Madrid
Mallorca
Malta & Gozo
Menorca
Moscow
Netherlands
Norway
Paris
Paris Mini Guide
Poland
Portugal
Prague
Provence & the Côte
 d'Azur
Pyrenees
Romania
Rome
Sardinia
Scandinavia
Sicily
Slovenia
Spain
St Petersburg
Sweden
Switzerland
Tenerife & La Gomera
Turkey
Tuscany & Umbria
Venice & The Veneto
Vienna

**Asia**
Bali & Lombok
Bangkok
Beijing

Cambodia
China
First-Time Asia
Goa
Hong Kong & Macau
India
Indonesia
Japan
Laos
Malaysia, Singapore &
 Brunei
Nepal
Philippines
Singapore
South India
Southeast Asia
Thailand
Thailand Beaches &
 Islands
Tokyo
Vietnam

**Australasia**
Australia
Gay & Lesbian Australia
Melbourne
New Zealand
Sydney

**North America**
Alaska
Baltic States
Big Island of Hawaii
Boston
California
Canada
Chicago
Florida
Grand Canyon
Hawaii
Honolulu
Las Vegas
Los Angeles
Maui
Miami & the Florida
 Keys
Montréal

New England
New Orleans
New York City
New York City Mini
 Guide
New York Restaurants
Pacific Northwest
Rocky Mountains
San Francisco
San Francisco
 Restaurants
Seattle
Skiing & Snowboarding
 in North America
Southwest USA
Toronto
USA
Vancouver
Washington DC
Yosemite

**Caribbean
& Latin America**
Antigua & Barbuda
Argentina
Bahamas
Barbados
Belize
Bolivia
Brazil
Caribbean
Central America
Chile
Costa Rica
Cuba
Dominican Republic
Ecuador
First-Time Latin
 America
Guatemala
Jamaica
Maya World
Mexico
Peru
St Lucia
South America
Trinidad & Tobago

# ...music & reference

Also! More than 120 Rough Guide music CDs are available from all
good book and record stores. Listen in at www.worldmusic.net